CONSUMER BEHAVIOR

Fourth Edition

John C. Mowen

Oklahoma State University

Prentice-Hall International, Inc.

A Division of Simon & Schuster
Englewood Cliffs, NJ 07632

Printed in the United States of America

10 9 8 7 6 5 4 3 2 1

ISBN 0-13-320987-3

Prentice-Hall International (UK) Limited, *London*
Prentice-Hall of Australia Pty. Limited, *Sydney*
Prentice-Hall Canada Inc., *Toronto*
Prentice-Hall Hispanoamericana, S.A., *Mexico*
Prentice-Hall of India Private Limited, *New Delhi*
Prentice-Hall of Japan, Inc., *Tokyo*
Simon & Schuster Asia Pte. Ltd., *Singapore*
Editora Prentice-Hall do Brasil, Ltda., *Rio de Janeiro*
Prentice-Hall, Inc., *Englewood Cliffs, New Jersey*

Preface

From the naturalistic study of body piercing to the probing of the human brain with electronic devices, researchers in the field of consumer behavior tackle a broad array of fascinating topics. In doing the revisions for the fourth edition of *Consumer Behavior*, I had three goals. First, write a book that provides a current, balanced, and comprehensive treatment of the field: readers will discover within the chapters the latest research in the field of consumer behavior, whether it pertains to the dramaturgical analysis of white-water rafting and sky-diving, to the investigation of customer relationships, or to the dimensions of brand knowledge. Second, dramatically improve the visual quality of the book by employing a four-color format and by employing an outstanding and relevant set of illustrative print advertisements. Third, increase the managerial relevance of the book by relating the consumer behavior concepts to the problems faced by marketers, nonprofit organizations, and public policy makers. As such, *Consumer Behavior* is positioned to possess

- High knowledge content
- High experiential content
- High managerial content

I began the process of writing the fourth edition of *Consumer Behavior* by asking our newly formed editorial board to identify the current trends having the most impact on the consumer behavior field. Four important areas emerged: the study of consumer and marketing relationships, cross-cultural issues, business-to-business marketing, and social-ethical consumer issues. These ideas became the nucleus around which the revisions were made in the fourth edition.

The fourth edition of *Consumer Behavior* continues the evolutionary process of adapting the text to the changing nature of the field. In addition to thoroughly updating the book with the latest research findings, the following substantive changes were made in the fourth edition:

1. *A Four-Color Format.* To increase the excitement and experiential elements of the book for students, a four-color format is used throughout. Care was taken to select color ads that illustrate important consumer behavior concepts.
2. *Relationships and Consumer Exchange.* The role of relationships and exchange processes have been integrated throughout the text. In particular, Chapter 2 (Consumer Exchange Processes) and Chapter 16 (Household and Organizational Buying Processes) focus on these topics.

3. *Cross-cultural Consumer Issues.* The analysis of cross-cultural forces and the international environment has been increased dramatically in the text. A new chapter has been written on cross-cultural processes (Chapter 19). In addition, the consumer vignettes frequently focus on how the topics under discussion apply to cross-cultural issues. Finally, cross-cultural research studies that illustrate consumer behavior concepts are included in many of the chapters.
4. *Social, Public Policy, and Ethical Issues.* The role of consumer research in public policy formulation has been a central area of study in each of the editions of *Consumer Behavior*. In the fourth edition I have placed even greater emphasis on the social impact of marketing activities. Such information is found in Chapter 20 on public policy, in Chapter 2 on consumer exchange, in numerous consumer vignettes. In addition, public policy implications of consumer concepts are integrated within the chapters.
5. *Business-to-Business Marketing.* Organizations, as well as consumers, make purchases. A major section on organizational buying behavior has been incorporated into Chapter 16. In addition, a substantial proportion of the consumer vignettes focus on business-to-business issues. Finally, business-to-business buying examples have been inserted throughout the text.
6. *Services Marketing.* Examples of services marketing have been integrated throughout the textbook.
7. *Consumer Satisfaction and Perceived Quality.* These concepts are at the forefront of business today. They are covered extensively in Chapter 13. In addition, the related concepts of total quality management and just-in-time purchasing are covered in the new organizational buying section of Chapter 16.
8. *Popular Culture.* A major section has been added to Chapter 17 that discusses the impact of social trends on consumer buying behavior.
9. *Marketing Research.* Greater emphasis has been placed on showing the relationship of consumer behavior to marketing research. Such applications have been placed in the consumer vignettes and integrated into the chapters.
10. *Expanded Supplements.* A one-hour video tape has been produced specifically for *Consumer Behavior* and is available to adopters of the text. The video tape features John Mowen as the narrator and uses advertisements and other video materials to create four high-impact, fast-paced video lecturettes. Fully discussed in the Teacher's Manual, these lecturettes can be incorporated into classes. Fifty four-color transparencies of key advertisements and figures have been produced to enhance the teaching of the class. In addition, the Teacher's Manual and test bank have been thoroughly expanded and updated.

Readers will find two additional substantial changes in the fourth edition. While retaining the managerial applications analyses at the end of each chapter, the matrices that summarized the relationship between the consumer and managerial concepts have been replaced by tables. The tables more clearly identify the relationship between the consumer concepts and their managerial implications. The second major change in the fourth edition was eliminating the chapter on the economics of consumption. With the addition of so much new material, some material had to be sacrificed.

I believe that instructors and students will find the fourth edition of *Consumer Behavior* to be exciting to read, balanced, and managerially relevant. With *Consumer Behavior*, instructors do not have to sacrifice content to obtain a fascinating and managerially relevant text that is at the cutting edge of the field.

Of course, without the support of numerous individuals the fourth edition would not have been possible. Many individuals at Macmillan Publishing Company deserve recognition. I would like to thank my editor, David Borkowsky, for his able guidance and attention to the details of the process. Margaret Comaskey did a superb job in producing an eye-catching book. Lauren Rosen is recognized for her excellent work in obtaining advertisements and permissions for the fourth edition.
Thanks also go to the Editorial Board and reviewers for the 4th edition. The Editorial Board is composed of

Richard P. Bagazzi, University of Michigan

Meryl Gardner, University of Delaware

James Gentry, University of Nebraska, Lincoln

Cathy Goodwin, University of Manitoba, Canada

David Hartman, University of Virginia

Vaughan Judd, Auburn University at Montgomery

Harold Kassarjian, UCLA

Michael Minor, University of Texas, Pan American

William Rodgers, St. Cloud State University

Linda Showers, Illinois State University

Appreciation also goes to the following individuals for their reviews of various portions of the fourth edition of the text: David Hartman, University of Virginia, Vaughan Judd, Auburn University at Montgomery, William Rodgers, St. Cloud State University, and Linda Showers, Illinois State University. I would also like to express my continuing regard to Gary Gaeth (University of Iowa). A consulting editor on the third edition, Gary has been a continuing source of excellent ideas. The outstanding efforts of Jane Licata, Robert Jeffries, and the folks at Multi-Media Cable Vision in Stillwater, Oklahoma, are especially acknowledged for their assistance in developing the video-tape lecturettes. In addition, Jane Licata is recognized for her excellent work in revising the Teacher's Manual.

Special thanks are extended to Michael Minor (Pan American University) for creating Chapter 19 (Cross-cultural Consumer Processes) and doing the revisions on Chapter 20 (Public Policy and the Regulatory Environment). With his strong background in international relations and excellent writing style, Michael developed two extremely strong chapters.

Finally, my deep gratitude goes to my family—Maryanne, Katie, and Cara—for their support of this project. They are truly special people.

JCM

Contents

PART 1
INTRODUCTION 1

PART 2

INDIVIDUAL CONSUMER PROCESSES 67

PART 3
THE CONSUMER ENVIRONMENT

Part 1

INTRODUCTION

Chapter 1

An Introduction to Consumer Behavior

CONSUMER VIGNETTE

The Piercing, Cutting Field of Consumer Behavior

Michael Jordan has one. But Queen Elizabeth has two. Women in India and the Congo wear them. But so do Phil Collins and Mick Jagger. All these people wear earrings. They have pierced their bodies in order to attach decorated rings for the purpose of enhancing their beauty. Indeed, an entire, multifaceted, $1-billion-plus industry has developed to create products and services that improve the perceived physical appearance of people. At one extreme, companies sell innocuous lotions and potions to soften and protect skin and hair. At the other extreme, consumers permanently change their bodies through such means as tattooing, body piercing, and cosmetic surgery.

Body piercing goes far beyond the simple insertion of a ring through the lobe of one's ear. Listen to the magazine writer L. A. Kauffman as she describes having her tragus pierced:

> Painful? That's putting it mildly. First, I felt the pinch of clamps and then the slow burn of a very thick needle and finally the bone-chilling insertion of the earring itself—sans anesthetic. It was excruciating. . . . I didn't get a sound night's sleep for weeks. Months later an affectionate caress from my lover anywhere on the left side of my face could still make me wince. But I never regretted it.[1]

Now, you may ask, "Where in the heck is the tragus?" The tragus is the little sliver of cartilage at the opening to the ear. But why would an intelligent person possibly want an earring in that location? As described by Ms. Kauffman, she did it not only for decoration, but also as a symbolic act soon after she left a dreary marriage. Other reasons for body piercing include marking an important event (e.g., a birth), eroticism, and symbolically taking charge of yourself and your life.

The tragus, however, is one of the more innocuous places in which to insert a ring. For example, there are the "three n's"—nipples, navels, and nostrils. In addition, in the lore of the piercing world, urban legends abound of interesting problems that body rings create. For example, there is the story of the fellow who had a sensitive place in his groin area pierced. Shortly thereafter, he set off a metal detector in an airport. Other passengers became entranced as they watched the guard's magnetic wand slowly circle until it homed in on the area that contained the offending piece of metal.

The behavior, however, of those who have their bodies pierced pales in comparison to that of people who become addicted to cosmetic surgery. Egged on by the physical transformation of rock and movie stars (e.g., Michael Jackson and Cher) and by a pursuit of a physical ideal, otherwise normal people have mangled themselves in the pursuit of beauty. For example, one woman had the following procedures done: nose job, brow lift, upper and lower eye lifts, breast reduction, and liposuction of chin and body. Total cost—only $35,000.[2] In another case, a woman seeking facial perfection had a series of face lifts. The only problem was that after the fifth operation her sideburns were behind her ears.

Figure 1-1

Wearing jewelery is a type of consumer behavior that has symbolic meaning. What does the lip ring worn by this attractive young woman symbolize?

Perhaps the most difficult dilemma in cosmetic surgery involves the doctor–patient relationship. Most people have trust in their physicians, and for common medical problems, the procedures are relatively clear cut. Patients assume that doctors know what is good for them and when to stop. For example, when a bone is broken, it needs to be set. Because of its elective nature, however, plastic surgery creates ethical dilemmas for physicians. One person's deformity can become another's most prized possession (e.g., model Cindy Crawford's mole or Barbara Streisand's nose). As one surgeon said, "I'm not the one telling the person she has flat cheekbones—that's her decision. I know how to fix them." But what are the ethical implications of such an attitude?

INTRODUCTION

Why do women, and men, risk pain and possible physical deformity to enhance their physical appearance? For that matter, what motivates anyone to purchase a particular brand of athletic shoes or to go to a specific restaurant? Why do teenagers enjoy going to horror movies and being scared half to death? Why would the popular country singer Garth Brooks promise to purchase his tee-shirts for his concerts from a small businessman in Stillwater, Oklahoma? Why are automobile companies hooked on giving rebates to consumers to sell their cars? Why do tribes in Amazonian jungles enjoy dining on giant water bugs? These are examples of the types of questions that consumer researchers address. (See note 27 at the end of this chapter for a brief answer to the question about Garth Brooks.)

Consumer behavior is an exciting and dynamic field of study. A wonderful aspect of taking a course in consumer behavior is the wealth of examples available for study. Because all of us are consumers, we can draw on our everyday experiences in the marketplace to understand consumer behavior concepts and theories. One of the major goals of this book is to provide copious illustrations of the use of consumer behavior concepts by corporations, public policy makers, and nonprofit organizations.

The chapter-opening consumer vignette reveals how closely connected consumer behavior is to our everyday lives. While not all of us wear earrings or body rings, or have had cosmetic surgery, everyone knows someone who has done one or more of these things. Most of us have had the queasy feeling that occurs when we see someone breaking social norms, such as noticing a person who has had his or her nose or tragus pierced. On the other hand, all of us have made a purchase of clothing or jewelry for the purpose of enhancing our physical attractiveness. Similarly, we may be interested in developing an understanding of the factors that influence consumers' response to the marketing of beauty through the selling of cosmetics, clothing, body rings, and plastic surgery. Finally, we may share concerns about the ethical and social responsibility issues in the marketplace, such as that occurring between physicians and patients.

WHAT IS CONSUMER BEHAVIOR?

Consumer behavior is a young discipline: the first textbooks were written in the 1960s. Its intellectual forefathers, however, are much older. For example, Thorstein Veblen talked about conspicuous consumption in 1899. Similarly, in the early 1900s writers began to discuss how psychological principles could be used by advertisers.[3] In the 1950s ideas from Freudian psychology were popularized by motivation researchers and used by advertisers. It was not until the enunciation of the marketing concept in the 1950s, though, that the need to study consumer behavior was recognized. As stated by Theodore Levitt, the marketing concept embodies "the view that an industry is a customer-satisfying process, not a goods-producing process. An industry begins with the customer and his needs, not with a patent, a raw material, or a selling skill."[4] The general acceptance of the concept that businesses function to fulfill consumer needs and wants by thoroughly understanding their exchange partners (i.e., customers) makes the study of the consumer essential.[5]

Consumer behavior is defined as the study of the buying units and the exchange processes involved in acquiring, consuming, and disposing of goods, services, experiences, and ideas. Within this simple definition, a number of important concepts are introduced. First, included in the definition is the word "exchange." A consumer is inevitably at one end of an **exchange process** in which resources are transferred between two parties. For example, an exchange takes place between a doctor and patient. The physician trades medical services for money. In addition, however, other resources, such as feelings, information, and status, may also be exchanged between the parties.

When exchanges occur, the possibility exists that ethical improprieties can occur. As the next chapter will discuss, both marketers and consumers can violate ethical norms. Because of the importance of ethics to the field of consumer behavior, boxed highlights on ethical issues will be found throughout the book. Highlight 1-1 discusses some ethical issues in the exchange relationship between plastic surgeons and consumers.

This textbook views the exchange process as a fundamental element of consumer behavior. Exchanges occur between consumers and firms. Exchanges also occur

HIGHLIGHT 1-1

Ethics—Dilemmas in Cosmetic Surgery

Ethics is the study of the normative judgments concerned with what is morally right and wrong, good and bad. By their very nature, ethical dilemmas occur in contexts that involve an exchange process. In particular, the doctor–patient exchange relationship is rife with the possibility of ethical misconduct because of the great trust that consumers must place in the hands of their physicians.

The consumer vignette in this chapter ended with a physician stating, "I'm not the one telling the person she has flat cheekbones—that's her decision. I know how to fix them." This comment indicates a relationship in which the physician takes a neutral stance and merely responds to the desires of the client. However, one merely has to look at the advertising by plastic surgeons to realize that they actively solicit customers. For example, the headline of one advertisement read, "New Nose . . . New Outlook." The copy began, "Straighten it, shorten it. Thinner . . . Wider. Lose the bump . . . The procedure usually takes about two hours, and the results can last a lifetime."

Another advertisement featured the photo of an attractive woman. The copy read, "The most important decision I ever made was choosing my spouse. The second, my plastic surgeon. Since plastic surgery lasts as long, if not longer than marriage, it is imperative that you choose the right surgeon." While some may view the ad as somewhat humorous, it presents several ethical problems. First, the copy is misleading. Marriages are supposed to last for a lifetime, but many types of plastic surgery, such as face lifts, are measured in much shorter intervals. Even worse, by playing on susceptible consumers' fears and anxieties, the advertisement may cause them irrevocable harm.

As will be discussed more fully in Chapter 2, ethical issues come into play when serious human injuries or benefits may occur and when self-interest may overwhelm impartial considerations. Each of these conditions is present in the relationship between the plastic surgeon and the consumer of his or her services.

between firms, such as in industrial buying situations. Finally, exchanges occur between consumers themselves, such as when a neighbor borrows a cup of sugar or a lawn mower.

Consider again the definition of consumer behavior. Notice that the term "buying units" is used rather than "consumers." Purchases may be made by either individuals or groups. An important area of study for consumer researchers is that of organizational buying behavior. Particularly in business-to-business marketing, the purchase decision maker may be a group of individuals in a buying center rather than a single decision maker. Fortunately, the same basic principles apply to organizational buying behavior as to consumer behavior. While the focus of this text is on consumer buying, specific applications to organizational buying and business-to-business marketing will be identified in the "Highlights" throughout the text.

The definition of consumer behavior also reveals that the exchange process involves a series of steps, beginning with the acquisition phase, moving to consumption, and ending with the disposition of the product or service. When investigating the **acquisition phase**, researchers analyze the factors that influence the product and service choices of consumers.

Much of the research in consumer behavior has focused on the acquisition phase. One factor associated with the search for and selection of goods and services is product symbolism. That is, people may acquire a product to express to others certain ideas and meanings about themselves. For example, some men wear earrings to make a symbolic statement to others about who and what they are.

The consumption and disposition phases have received much less attention by consumer researchers than the acquisition phase. When investigating the **consumption phase**, the researcher analyzes how consumers actually use a product or service and the experiences that the consumer obtains from such use. The investigation of the consumption process is particularly important for service industries. In some industries, such as restaurants, amusement parks, and rock concert promotions, the consumption experience is the reason for the purchase. Elements of consumption and usage processes are also found in the chapter-opening vignette. Where a body ring is worn represents an aspect of how a product is used.

The **disposition phase** refers to what consumers do with a product once they have completed their use of it. In addition, it addresses the level of satisfaction that consumers experience after the purchase of a good or service. In the vignette, for example, one critical problem faced by physicians and patients concerns the level of satisfaction with the results of the medical procedure. If consumers have unrealistic expectations, the anticipated outcomes are not likely to occur, and dissatisfaction will result. From the surgeon's perspective, such customer dissatisfaction is likely to increase the likelihood that lawsuits will be filed. For the patient, unfulfilled expectations may result in a loss of self-esteem and possibly even more cosmetic surgery. For example, the woman described in the vignette, who after five face lifts had her sideburns behind her ears, was still searching for a plastic surgeon to correct the problem.

The student of consumer behavior will be struck by the diversity of the field. It incorporates theories and concepts from all the behavioral sciences. When studying the acquisition, consumption, and disposition of products, services, and ideas, one also explores the disciplines of psychology, social psychology, sociology, anthropology, demography, and economics.

WHY STUDY CONSUMER BEHAVIOR?

Possessing an understanding of consumers and the consumption process provides a number of benefits. These benefits include assisting managers in their decision making, providing marketing researchers with a knowledge base from which to analyze consumers, helping legislators and regulators create laws and regulations concerning the purchase and sale of goods and services, and assisting the average consumer in making better purchase decisions. In addition, the study of consumers can help us to understand more about the psychological, sociological, and economic factors that influence human behavior.

Consumer Analysis as a Foundation of Marketing Management

The importance of understanding the consumer is found in the definition of **marketing** as a "human activity directed at satisfying needs and wants through human exchange processes."[6] From this definition emerge two key marketing activities. First, **marketers** attempt to satisfy the needs and wants of their target market. Second, marketing involves the study of the exchange process in which two parties transfer resources between each other. In the exchange process, firms receive monetary and other resources from consumers. In return, consumers receive products, services, and other resources of value. For marketers to create a successful exchange, they must have an understanding of the factors that influence the needs and wants of consumers.*

Indeed, one can argue that the principle of **consumer primacy** represents the central point on which marketing is based.[7] The concept states that the consumer should be at the center of the marketing effort. As Peter Drucker, the well-known management scholar, stated, "Marketing is the whole business seen from the point of view of its final result, that is, from the customer's point of view."[8] Similarly, in his critique of General Motors Corporation, Ross Perot proclaimed that for the company to turn around, managers must perceive that ". . . the consumer is king!"[9]

Public Policy and Consumer Behavior

A knowledge of consumer behavior can also assist in the development of public policy. As it pertains to consumer behavior, **public policy** involves the development of the laws and regulations that have an impact on consumers in the marketplace. In its

*In 1985 the American Marketing Association developed the following definition of marketing: "Marketing is the process of planning and executing the conception, pricing, promotion, and distribution of ideas, goods, and services to create exchanges that satisfy individual and organizational objectives." Although this definition emphasizes the importance of the exchange concept, it neglects the concept that marketing functions to fulfill the needs and wants of consumers. In the author's view, downplaying a consumer focus is a setback for marketing. The field of consumer behavior can assist the marketer in obtaining this information.

legislative, regulatory, and judicial roles, the federal government often deals with issues involving consumers. For example, proposals have periodically surfaced to limit, or even cut off entirely, commercials accompanying television programming aimed at young children. Work done by consumer researchers concerning the impact of advertising on children has figured prominently in the formulation of the regulations.

Consumer Behavior and Social Marketing

The ideas and concepts of marketing may also be applied to nontraditional business areas. For example, various nonprofit groups, such as political parties, religious organizations, and charitable groups, all engage in consumer research; however, rather than marketing tangible products, these organizations tend to market intangible ideas. Another example of the nontraditional use of consumer behavior concepts is found in efforts of the AMC Cancer Research Center to influence women's actions in order to lower the high incidence of breast cancer. One element of the strategy has been to use high-profile celebrity endorsers. Figure 1-2 presents an advertisement whose message is delivered by Cher.

The Personal Value of Consumer Behavior

A general knowledge of consumer behavior also has considerable **personal value**. It can help people become better consumers by informing them of the way in which they and others go about their consumption activities. In addition, it can assist consumers in the buying process by informing them of some of the strategies used by companies to market their products. Knowledge of the factors influencing consumption also has intrinsic value for many people. It is simply fun to know why product rumors start, why subliminal advertising messages are unlikely to influence buying, and why some product endorsers (e.g., the ex-basketball player Michael Jordan) are so much more effective than others (e.g., the basketball player Patrick Ewing). Finally, being able to understand one's own personal consumption motivations as well as those of others is satisfying and is part of being a well-rounded, educated person.

As an overall statement, the study of consumer behavior provides three types of information: (1) an orientation, (2) facts, and (3) theories. The study of the consumer helps to orient managers and public policy makers so they consider the impact of their actions on consumers. The field also provides facts, such as the size of various demographic groups. In addition, the study of consumer behavior provides theories. "Theory" tends to be ridiculed with statements such as: "That's only theory; it has nothing to do with what really happens." In fact, nothing is more practical than a theory. Detectives develop theories for why a crime was committed. Medical doctors develop theories for why a person gets sick, and managers develop theories for why a product fails to sell.

A **theory** is a set of interrelated statements defining the causal relationships among a group of ideas. Theories may be big or small, but all should have research support. A major practical reason for studying consumer behavior is that the field has a variety of theories that do have research support and that can be used to understand and solve managerial and public policy problems. Table 1-1 summarizes the reasons for studying the field of consumer behavior.

Figure 1-2 Cher acts as a high-profile spokeswoman to influence women's attitudes and behaviors about performing breast examination to prevent cancer. (Courtesy of AMC Cancer Research Center and Adolph Coors, Inc.)

TABLE 1-1

Reasons for Studying Consumer Behavior

1. Consumer analysis should be the foundation of marketing management. It assists managers in
   a. Designing the marketing mix
   b. Segmenting the marketplace
   c. Positioning and differentiating products
   d. Performing environmental analysis, and
   e. Developing market research studies
2. Consumer behavior should play an important role in the development of public policy.
3. The study of consumer behavior will enhance one's own ability to be a more effective consumer.
4. Consumer analysis provides knowledge of human behavior.
5. The study of consumer behavior provides three types of information:
   a. A consumer orientation
   b. Facts about human behavior
   c. Theories to guide the thinking process

AN ORGANIZING MODEL OF CONSUMER BEHAVIOR

To provide an overview of the broad field of consumer behavior, an organizing model is developed. Shown in Figure 1-3, the consumer behavior model has five primary components that form the field's core areas of study: the buying unit, the exchange process, the marketer's strategy, the individual influencers, and the environmental influencers. In the model, buying units are connected to the marketer's strategy via an exchange relationship. Buying units may consist of either an individual, a family, or a group that makes a purchase decision. The term "marketer" is used extremely broadly in the model; a marketer could be a firm selling a good or service, a nonprofit organization, a governmental agency, a political candidate, or another consumer who wishes to borrow or trade something. The marketer seeks to create an exchange with consumers by implementing a marketing strategy through which it attempts to reach its long-term customer and profit goals. A **marketing strategy** is implemented by creating segmentation and positioning objectives. A **marketing mix**, consisting of product, price, promotion, and distribution factors, is then developed to execute the overall strategy.

A major focus of the text will involve identifying how an understanding of the exchange process, the individual influencers, and the environmental influencers can be used to develop marketing strategy. In the development of strategy, the marketer employs environmental analysis to anticipate the likely effects of the environmental influencers. Market research is used to obtain information on individual consumers. Based upon the environmental analysis and market research, managers develop posi-

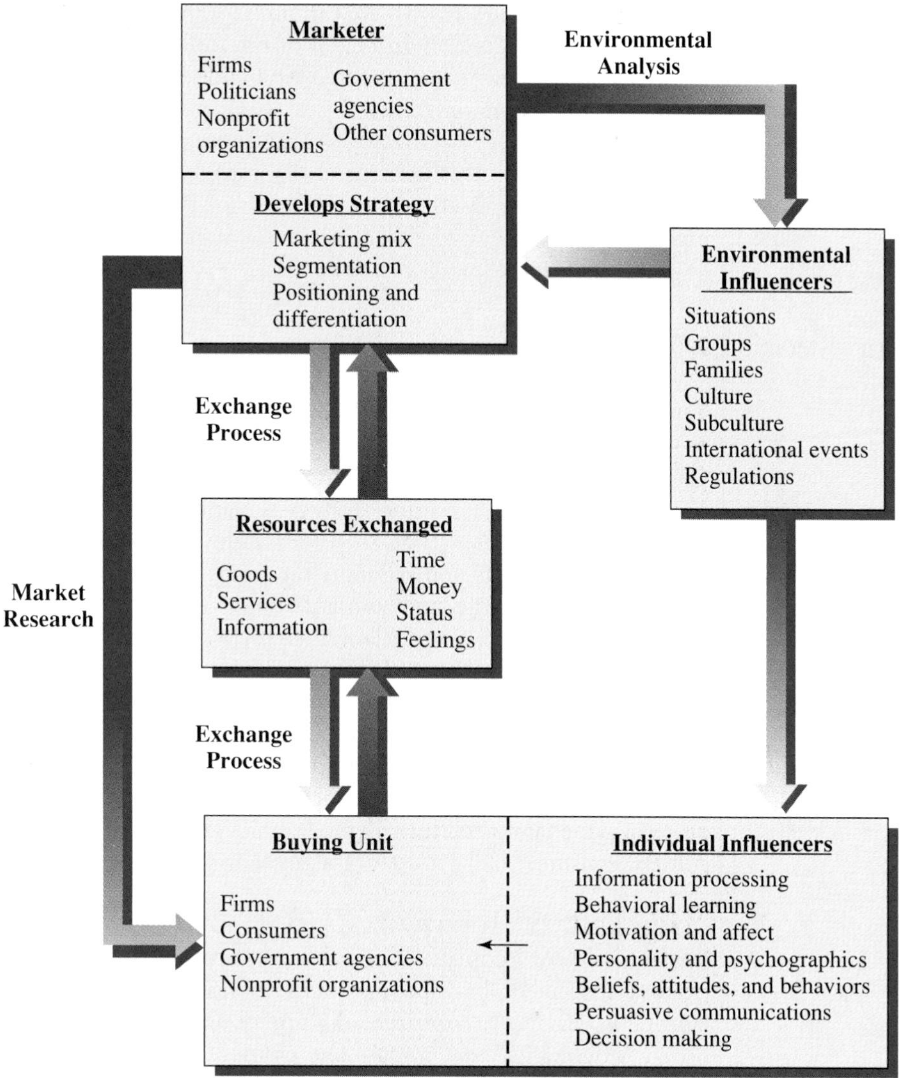

Figure 1-3 An organizing model of consumer behavior.

tioning and segmentation strategies, which are implemented through the marketing mix.

The model of consumer behavior connects the buying unit to both the individual influence factors and the environmental influencers. The **individual influence factors** represent the psychological processes that affect individuals engaged in acquiring, consuming, and disposing of goods, services, and experiences. The **environmental influencers** represent those factors outside of the individual that affect individual consumers, decision-making units, and marketers.

For pedagogical purposes, the individual influencers and the environmental influencers have been divided into two distinct groups. However, a more accurate statement is that they lie on a continuum that moves from a narrow micro to a broad macro focus. The continuum begins at the individual level with the most basic psychological processes involving perception and learning. As one moves along the continuum, the analysis moves to the study of personality, attitudes, persuasion, and finally consumer decision making. At this point, the emphasis changes from the study of the individual to investigations of the impact of situations and groups of people on consumer behavior. At the broadest levels of the continuum, consumer researchers examine how people in different nations and cultures acquire, consume, and dispose of goods, services, experiences, and ideas.

The Book's Organization

The major sections of the textbook are organized around the consumer behavior model. Part I acts as an overview of the field and is composed of two chapters. Chapter 1 defines the field and identifies how a knowledge of consumer behavior can be used to develop marketing strategy. Chapter 2 focuses on the exchange process. The chapter proposes that an understanding of how resources are exchanged between buying units and sellers is the fundamental link between the study of consumer behavior and the study of marketing.

Part II presents a set of chapters that cover factors that influence individual consumers. As shown in Figure 1-3, individual consumer processes include information processing, behavioral learning, motivation, personality and psychographics, attitudes, persuasive communications, and decision making.

Part III considers the environmental influencers that affect buyers and sellers. Figure 1-3 also portrays these concepts, which include consumer situations, group processes, the family, culture, demographics and subcultures, international and cross-cultural consumer behavior, and the regulatory environment.

"Highlighted" Topics

Within the broad domain of consumer behavior, four topics have been identified as needing special emphasis because of their importance: social and ethical issues, cross-cultural issues, market research, and organizational buying. Each chapter will include boxed "Highlights" that discuss one or more of these important areas. In addition, miscellaneous Highlights will be found that present unusual and fun aspects of consumer topics. Highlight 1-2 discusses a specific case in which consumer behavior concepts apply to both consumer marketing and business-to-business marketing.

THREE RESEARCH PERSPECTIVES ON CONSUMER ACQUISITION BEHAVIOR

Although only about 30 years old, the field of consumer behavior has produced a number of research orientations. One way of summarizing the behavioral science foundations of the field is to organize them according to three research perspectives on what factors influence consumer acquisition behavior: the decision-making perspective, the experiential perspective, and the behavioral influence perspective.[10]

HIGHLIGHT 1-2

Consumer Behavior in Business-to-Business Marketing

IBM's OS/2: Will It Meet Business's Needs? International Business Machines' OS/2 is a computer operating system, like Microsoft Corporation's DOS or AT&T's Unix system. The OS/2.1 is a successor to an earlier version developed by IBM that bombed in the marketplace. One IBM manager succinctly identified the reasons for the problems of the earlier version. He said:

> You want to know how to screw up a product launch? Announce the product 20 minutes after you finish development, price it aggressively but then don't send it to the stores right away, sell it directly to customers and tick off your dealers, and have no business applications for it.

The IBM manager had pinpointed a series of problems that turned off the business users at whom the company had targeted the product. First, the product was released with bugs that took time to correct. Second, the company priced it appropriately, but then did not have enough copies in stock to meet initial demand. Third, by selling the product directly to business customers, the company bypassed retailers, who would account for the vast majority of sales. Not surprisingly, retailers were unhappy about the strategy.

Consumer behavior concepts apply to business-to-business marketing as well as to consumer marketing. Products must have high quality standards for businesses as well as consumers. Stock outages irritate both parties. In addition, developing long-term exchange relationships is important to both businesses and consumers. The initial strategy of bypassing retailers broke a trust bond in the exchange relationship. Later, when IBM wanted the support of retailers, the trust was difficult to regain. As a result, this past behavior threatens the success of a new operating system that many experts in the field consider to be technically superior to competing products.

Based upon Peter H. Lewis, "A Strong New OS/2, With an Uncertain Future," *The New York Times*, June 20, 1993, p. F8.

The Decision-Making Perspective

During the 1970s and early 1980s, researchers tended to view the consumer as a decision maker. From this perspective, buying results from consumers first perceiving that a problem exists and then moving through a rational problem-solving process. The **decision-making perspective** portrays consumers as moving through a series of steps when making a purchase. These steps include problem recognition, search, alternative evaluation, choice, and postacquisition evaluation. The roots of this approach are in cognitive and experimental psychology and some areas of economics.

Thinking back to the cosmetic surgery vignette, the decision-making perspective would focus on the steps through which consumers move when deciding which physician to hire to do cosmetic surgery. For example, in analyzing the choice process, researchers would attempt to identify the characteristics sought by consumers in their physician, such as his or her qualifications, bedside manner, explanation of risks, and price charged.

Researchers taking a decision-making approach to consumer behavior tend to approach problems via a particular scientific philosophy, labeled logical empiricism. Those employing **logical empiricist research methods** focus on using the scientific method to collect data, attempt to eliminate sources of error in collecting data, and seek to predict the choices of consumers.

The Experiential Perspective

The **experiential perspective** on consumer buying proposes that in some instances consumers do not make their purchases according to a strictly rational decision-making process. Instead, people sometimes buy products and services in order to have fun, create fantasies, and obtain emotions and feelings.[11] Classified within the experiential perspective would be purchases made from impulse and purchases made to seek variety. Variety seeking occurs when consumers switch brands to lower boredom levels and obtain stimulation.[12] Many consumer services and products bought for leisure purposes have a strong experiential component to them, including such activities as going to rock concerts, symphonies, amusement parks, and movies. The goal of these leisure products is largely to create feelings among consumers.

A researcher analyzing the introductory vignette from the experiential perspective would focus on identifying the feelings, emotions, and symbols that accompany the purchase of body rings or cosmetic surgery. The roots of the experiential perspective are in motivational psychology and in areas of sociology and anthropology. In particular, researchers who take an experiential perspective will frequently use **interpretive research methods** that differ from the logical empiricist methods employed by those who take a decision-making approach. Interpretivists believe that researchers inevitably influence the data collection effort. They focus on understanding rather than prediction and believe that reality is socially constructed. Interpretivists frequently employ naturalistic research methods in which the investigator directly observes and records the activities of interest or even actively participates in the activities.[13] Interpretivists can even be found recording the folklore and traditions of society in order to obtain an understanding of their consumption process.[14] Table 1-2 compares logical empiricist research methods to interpretivist research methods.

Advertisers frequently use emotional appeals to influence consumers. Figure 1-4 shows an advertisement that successfully creates positive feelings in many people. Note that the ad also reveals the increasing importance to companies of the international dimensions of consumer behavior.

The Behavioral Influence Perspective

Behavioral influence occurs when strong environmental forces propel consumers to make purchases without necessarily first developing strong feelings or beliefs about the product. In this instance the consumer does not necessarily go through a rational decision-making process or rely on feelings to purchase a product or service. Instead, the action results from the direct influence on behavior of environmental forces, such as sales promotion devices (e.g., contests), cultural norms, the physical environment, or economic pressures.[15]

Researchers analyzing the consumer vignette from the behavioral influence per-

TABLE 1-2

Logical Empiricist Versus Interpretivist Research Methods

Topic Area	*Logical Empiricists*	*Interpretivists*
What is reality?	One reality exists with multiple interpretations.	Multiple realities exist but all are not equally valid.
Research goal	Description and explanation Seeks to determine causes even if only probabilistic.	Seeks to understand meaning through "thick" descriptions.
Role of context	Context interacts with personality and product type to influence behavior.	Behavior is relatively context bound.
Role of value	While inquiry is affected by values, attempt to eliminate to the extent possible.	Inquiry is value bound.
Role of researcher	Researcher and phenomenon interact but attempt to make independent.	Researcher and phenomenon interact and that must be recognized.
Research methods	Focus on employing quantitative methods.	Focus on employing qualitative methods.
View of data	Seek to obtain valid, reliable, unbiased data.	Seek dependable data that can be confirmed but generally believe that data are biased.
Type of sample	Seek random, stratified, and other probability sampling methods.	Convenience and purposive samples are okay.
Role of theory	Goal is to test theory deductively.	Induction and emergent designs used to interpret behavior.

SOURCE: Based in part on ideas of Timothy B. Heath, "The Reconciliation of Humanism and Positivism in the Practice of Consumer Research: A View from the Trenches," *Journal of the Academy of Marketing Sciences*, Vol. 20 (Spring 1992), pp. 107–118.

spective would look to determine if exceedingly strong group or social pressures might propel an individual to have his or her body pierced. In such instances, the person may actually have a strong distaste for the procedure but still engage in the act because of the force of the situation. The roots of the behavioral influence perspective are found in behavioral learning theory, which will be discussed in Chapter 5. In addition, researchers who employ a behavioral influence approach are strong proponents of logical empiricist research methods.

Readers should note that most purchases will have some elements of each of the three perspectives. For example, the purchase of the services of a plastic surgeon will involve some level of decision making, such as when a consumer searches for information, evaluates alternatives, and makes a rational choice. However, it is also likely that an experiential process operates in which strong emotional elements drive the consumer to engage in actions that have a high level of symbolic meaning, such as having a face lift to create a youthful image. Finally, as noted previously, strong pressures found in a social situation may also impact the behavior. In sum, it is useful to

Figure 1-4 For many consumers, this AT&T ad strongly influences feelings and emotions. (Courtesy of AT&T, 1991.)

examine consumer behavior from each perspective to fully appreciate the impact of logical decision making, of feelings and emotions, and of environmental influencers.

THE MANAGERIAL IMPLICATIONS OF THE STUDY OF CONSUMER BEHAVIOR

As noted, consumer behavior concepts can be used to develop marketing strategy in five areas: the marketing mix, segmentation, positioning and differentiation, environmental analysis, and market research. In this section each managerial area is discussed. Then, a technique is explained for using consumer concepts to develop marketing strategy. The approach involves doing a managerial applications analysis. The chapter concludes with a case that uses the introduction of "New Coke" into the marketplace to illustrate how consumer behavior principles can be used to develop managerial strategy and solve marketing problems.

Developing Marketing Mix Strategy

The development of a marketing mix strategy involves the coordination of activities in four areas—the product, promotion, pricing, and distribution. The term "product" is a generic concept that can denote a good, service, idea, or even a person, such as a political candidate. A variety of consumer behavior concepts have importance for product development. For example, the study of the choice component of consumer decision making is vital for the determination of what features to build into a product. Consumers choose among alternatives in part based upon those product characteristics most desired. Thus one target group may focus on price and ease of operation in selecting a camera, whereas another may emphasize picture quality and camera durability. As a result, understanding the choice process and the features desired is critical to the physical development of most products.

Promotional strategy is a broad area that deals with advertising, personal selling, sales promotions, and public relations. Consumer behavior concepts apply to each of these managerial areas. For example, researchers have found that attitudes toward advertisements strongly affect consumer reactions to brands. The topic of attitudes will be discussed in Chapters 8 and 9. In the personal-selling area, the marketer must be adaptable in his or her approach to making the sale. Adaptive selling depends upon recognizing that individual differences in personality and decision making cause diverse reactions to sales messages. These issues are discussed in Chapter 7 on personality and psychographics and Chapters 11 through 13 on decision making.

Consumer behavior topics can also guide pricing strategy. For instance, one component of the individual consumer analysis is information processing. Particularly when changing prices, the manager must consider whether the change will be meaningful to consumers. An example of whether a price change is perceptually meaningful is found in the rebates so frequently used by automobile companies. A key issue concerns how large the rebate on a car must be before it influences consumer demand. If the rebate is too small, it may have little influence, and the net result would be a lowering of profit margins. (The lower margins would occur because no more cars would be sold as a result of the rebate, and for those that were sold, a lower price would be received.) The issue of how large to make a rebate depends upon having an understanding of the perceptual processes discussed in Chapter 3.

Finally, consumer behavior concepts influence distribution strategy. For example, retail stores are a vital element of the distribution channel for many types of goods and services. The physical environment within the retail store has a large impact on consumers. Within a grocery store, for example, the arrangement of aisles can guide consumers in desired ways so that they encounter high-margin goods. In a department store or restaurant, the use of appropriate music, lighting effects, and materials can create desired images and mood states. Chapter 14 on situational influences discusses how the physical environment affects consumers.

Segmentation

Segmentation refers to the division of the marketplace into relatively homogeneous subsets of consumers having similar needs and wants. A segment can become a target market that is reached via a distinct marketing mix. Markets can be segmented in terms of demographic, personality, and life-style characteristics. They also can be segmented in terms of behavior, such as whether a consumer is a light, moderate, or heavy user of a product. Another means of segmentation is to categorize the situations in which consumers use a product. For example, people may be grouped according to the situations in which they use a watch, such as for athletics, formal wear, or everyday wear. By targeting specific segments of consumers who possess distinct sets of needs and wants, marketers can potentially expand total market share, increase their own market share, and more readily build and retain brand loyalty.

One of the most important uses of consumer behavior concepts is to help managers identify lucrative market segments. Areas of study useful for performing segmentation analysis include motivation, personality and psychographics, attitudes, decision making, situations, cultural values, subcultures, demographics, and economics. Table 1-3 identifies the various consumer behavior areas that are important for performing segmentation analyses.

Product Positioning and Differentiation

Product positioning involves influencing how consumers perceive a brand's characteristics relative to those of competitive offerings. For example, automobiles have been positioned based upon their cost and their expressiveness (i.e., conservative versus outgoing). In the automotive industry Mercedes-Benz is positioned as expensive and conservative. In contrast, Porsche is positioned as expensive and highly expressive. A Chevrolet Caprice is positioned as inexpensive and conservative. (Figure 1-5 portrays the positions of a number of automobile brands.)

To the extent that a particular brand fails to share a position with any competitor, it can be said to be differentiated. **Product differentiation** is the process of positioning the product by manipulating the marketing mix so that consumers can perceive meaningful differences between a brand and competing brands. A highly differentiated brand may have a strong competitive advantage because it is easily recognizable as being different from competitors.

Figure 1-5 illustrates the problems of product differentiation faced by General Motors in the late 1980s. Its Cadillac, Buick, and Oldsmobile divisions occupied the same niche: each was perceived to be high cost and conservative. Pontiac was the

TABLE 1-3

Bases for Segmenting the Consumer Market

I. Characteristics of the person
- **A.** Demographics
  - **1.** Age
  - **2.** Sex
  - **3.** Income
  - **4.** Religion
  - **5.** Marital status
  - **6.** Nationality
  - **7.** Education
  - **8.** Family size
  - **9.** Occupation
  - **10.** Ethnicity
- **B.** Consumption behavior
  - **1.** Benefits sought
  - **2.** Demand elasticity
  - **3.** Brand loyalty
  - **4.** Usage rate
  - **5.** Other—media usage, marketing factor sensitivity

II. Situation
- **A.** Task definition
- **B.** Time
- **C.** Physical surroundings
- **D.** Social surroundings
- **E.** Antecedent states

III. Geography
- **A.** National boundaries
- **B.** Regions
- **C.** State boundaries
- **D.** Urban/rural
- **E.** Census block

only division that was distinctively positioned, occupying a space completely different from the others: expressive and slightly below average in cost. Not surprisingly, Pontiac had the best sales performance of the five divisions in the 1980s.[16]

Consumer behavior areas of analysis that are particularly important for successfully developing, positioning, and differentiation strategies are information processing, attitude formation and change, decision making, and communications.

Environmental Analysis

Environmental analysis consists of the assessment of the various external forces that act upon the firm and its markets. Through environmental analysis, managers identify potential marketing opportunities and liabilities. Of course, the forces that result in opportunities and liabilities are the very ones that make up the consumer environment examined in Part 3 of the text. Thus environmental analysis is concerned with

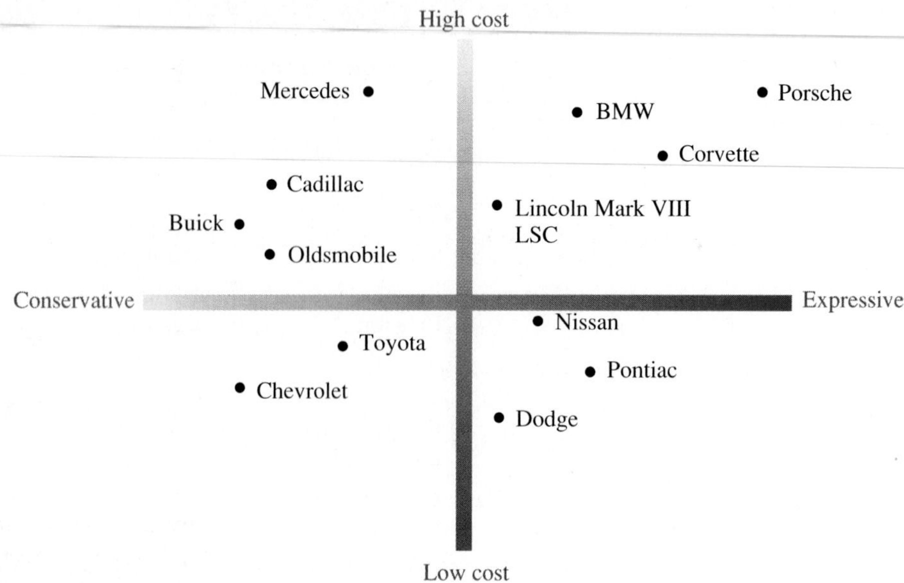

Figure 1-5 Positioning of autos.

identifying the environmental factors that may have an impact on consumers and on the firm.

Market Research

Market research may be thought of as applied consumer research. The market researcher attempts to analyze consumers and markets in order to provide information to managers. The analysis of consumers and markets should be based upon knowledge of consumer behavior principles. The problem is analogous to attempting to forecast the economy. One presumes that a knowledge of economics is necessary to predict economic movements. Similarly, to predict the behavior of buyers, one should have a knowledge of the field of consumer behavior.

Consider the use of market surveys of consumers. To know what kinds of questions to ask in the survey, the researcher needs to have an understanding of the factors that influence buying behavior. One cannot develop questions in a vacuum. A knowledge of consumer behavior can even help the market researcher to identify which methodology to use. For example, if the researcher believes that the problem involves how consumers process information, controlled psychological experiments are most appropriate. However, if the researcher believes that the problem involves experiential processes and symbolic behavior, it may be best to use an anthropological approach, such as participant observation, to investigate the problem area.

Factors associated with the individual consumer discussed in Part 2 of the text are particularly important for market researchers to understand. In addition, market researchers should have a good understanding of many of the environmental forces that influence consumers, such as groups, situations, culture, and subcultures.

CONSUMER BEHAVIOR AND SOLVING MANAGERIAL PROBLEMS

To develop managerial plans to solve problems, the analyst needs to have an understanding of consumer behavior concepts, of the managerial strategy elements, and of how to combine the two types of information to develop managerial plans. A three-step **managerial applications analysis** is advocated:

1. Gather information and identify the problem/opportunity.
2. Identify the relevant consumer behavior concepts and determine how they apply to the problem.
3. Develop a managerial strategy by identifying the managerial implications of each applicable consumer behavior concept.

In step 1 the analyst gathers as much information as possible about the case and carefully sifts through the information to identify the fundamental question(s) that need to be answered. This step is important because the remainder of the analysis will flounder if inadequate information is gathered or if the problem is not adequately identified.

In step 2 the analyst systematically examines the problem by identifying the consumer concepts relevant to it. Each of the topic areas from the **individual level of analysis** and from the **environmental level of analysis** are evaluated for potential application to the problem. Table 1-4 identifies the areas that should be appraised. As the reader will note, these are in the chapters that compose Parts II and III of the text. Thus, within the individual level of analysis, the analyst begins with the information processing area. Based upon his or her knowledge of the area, the analyst asks whether the problem involves concepts of information processing. If the answer is "yes" or "maybe," the analyst then examines the extent to which specific information processing concepts have relevance to the problem. The process is continued for each area discussed in the textbook. Within each chapter, the consumer concepts that should be considered are printed in bold letters and summarized at the end.

Step 3 involves identifying the managerial implications of the consumer behavior concepts. In all cases, the managerial implications will involve one of more of the five managerial strategy elements discussed earlier: the marketing mix, segmentation, positioning/differentiation, environmental analysis, and market research. The analyst examines the extent to which the various consumer concepts affect each of the five managerial areas and develops managerial strategies from the concepts.

A MANAGERIAL APPLICATIONS EXAMPLE

In 1985 Coca-Cola changed the taste of Coke. Responding to a long, slow decline in market share and to the "Pepsi Challenge," corporate officers announced with much fanfare that a new and better soft drink had been developed: A "new" Coke was introduced. The decision to change Coke's taste was made after long and careful

TABLE 1-4

Consumer Areas to Consider When Developing the Managerial Applications Analysis

A. Consumer exchange concepts
B. Individual level of analysis areas
 1. Information processing
 2. Behavioral learning
 3. Motivation
 4. Personality and psychographics
 5. Beliefs, attitudes, and behaviors
 6. Changing beliefs, attitudes, and behaviors
 7. Persuasive communications
 8. Decision making
C. Environmental level of analysis
 1. Situational factors
 2. Group/organization/family factors
 3. Cultural and international factors
 4. Demographic and subcultural factors
 5. Economic environment
 6. Regulatory environment

study. Perhaps the single factor most responsible for the strategy was the success of the Pepsi Challenge, in which person after person would select Pepsi over Coke in taste tests. The rational executives at Coke decided that if taste was the problem, a change in the taste of the beverage would solve the problem. After extensive research and testing, a new drink was created. Market research on hundreds of consumers confirmed that the new formulation tasted better than Pepsi in blind taste tests.

After the announcement and the distribution of the new product into the marketplace, public response was swift. Within a few days a mass revolt was underway. Lawsuits were filed. Over 40,000 letters poured into corporate headquarters in Atlanta, Georgia, complaining about the bold change. One writer fumed, "I don't think I would be more upset if you were to burn the flag in the front yard."[17] After receiving the negative publicity, Coca-Cola hired Bill Cosby to endorse "new" Coke. The strategy appeared to have little impact and was quickly discontinued. Of course, Coca-Cola finally capitulated, and six weeks after the original announcement, it brought back the old flavor in the form of Coke Classic. In an attempt to explain the marketing failure, one Coca-Cola executive stated, "It didn't matter how 'New Coke' tasted: what these people resented was the audacity of Coca-Cola in changing the old taste."[18]

What happened when the executives at Coca-Cola relented and brought back "Coke Classic"? On the day of the announcement, the consumer affairs department received 18,000 calls of thanks. Consumers seemed to feel as though the public had beaten the corporation. Even the company's image improved, and at the end of 1985, the image ratings of Coke had moved from a position lower than Pepsi's to a level substantially higher than Pepsi's.[19]

Two years later, during the summer of 1987, both Pepsi and Coca-Cola launched advertisements in which Pepsi challenged "Coke Classic" and "New Coke" challenged Pepsi. *The Wall Street Journal* commissioned a taste test of "Coke Classic," Pepsi, and "New Coke." It revealed that 70% of the 100 tasters confused the three colas. When confronted with their confusion of brands, the consumers became defensive and accused the testers of shaking the bottles. Others blamed the results on the use of plastic cups rather than glass.[20] In the interviews, consumers were asked why they preferred the various brands. When asked why he wouldn't drink Pepsi, one person said, "It's too preppy. Too yup. The New Generation—it sounds like Nazi breeding. Coke is more laid back." On the other hand, a Pepsi drinker said, "I relate Coke to the status quo. I think Pepsi is a little more rebellious, and I have a little rebellion in me."[21]

Even though "old Coke" was brought back, the company continued marketing the new drink as Coca-Cola. Early in the experiment, "New Coke's" market share varied by region. Nine months after the new brand's introduction, it was outsold by Classic by 9 to 1 in Minneapolis and by 8 to 1 in Dallas. However, in Detroit, New Coke outsold "Classic."[22] Even three years after the introduction of "New Coke," it represented only 2.3% of the market. The low market share occurred despite the company spending twice as much on advertising for the new product as for "Classic."[23]

In the 1990s Coca-Cola Corporation continued to struggle to identify a marketing strategy for New Coke. By 1991 the brand was no longer one of the top ten soft drinks. The corporation even began experimenting with a new name for the drink. In a market test in Spokane, Washington, the brand was called "Coke II." Long a Pepsi stronghold, the bottlers in Spokane responded vigorously to the campaign. A retaliatory ad was created in which four countrified men sit on a porch talking about the colas. One says to another while he sips from a Pepsi, "Shoot. They're changing Coke again. What do you suppose made them do that?" Just then a Pepsi delivery truck drives by and honks its horn at the men. According to one report, Coke II's market share jumped to 4% in Spokane, but then fell back quickly when the market test ended.[24]

By 1994 Coca-Cola still had not developed a coherent strategy for New Coke. It seems that the brand may have been demoted to a backup role. If Pepsi brought back its taste tests, Coke could always counter with its own ads showing that people like "Coke II" better than Pepsi. Will the company introduce "Coke II" nationally? The company continued to do test marketing on the new name in such cities as Chicago. According to some critics, however, the idea is foolish. As one expert said, "It's crazy to squander resources on a brand that everybody knows is dead."[25]

The Managerial Analysis of the Introduction of New Coke

The story of "New Coke" illustrates why having an understanding of the field of consumer behavior is so important to marketing managers. Possibly, had the Coca-Cola executives more carefully considered certain consumer behavior concepts, principles, and theories, the ego-bruising and costly affair could have been avoided.

Recall that managerial applications analysis is a three-step process. First, the problem must be identified. In this instance, the question is: "What factors caused the marketing strategy of Coca-Cola to go wrong?" In addition, information on the problem must be gathered. For this case, the details presented earlier will be used for the task.

The second step in the managerial applications analysis is to identify the consumer concepts that apply to the problem. For example, in the "New Coke" case, one important consideration is the exchange relationship between the marketer and the buyer. One can view Coke customers as having a long-standing relational exchange with the company. Many individuals had consumed Coke all of their lives, and when the firm changed the taste of its flagship brand, it seemed to have forgotten that many of its customers were fiercely loyal to the product. In effect, the company was breaking a bond of trust between it and its customers by changing the taste of a product that many had consumed for years. Understanding the nature of the exchange relationship between a firm and its customers is an important managerial responsibility.

In step 3 of the procedure, the analyst identifies the managerial implications of the consumer concepts identified. In the "New Coke" case the concept of relational exchange would influence two managerial areas: the marketing mix and market research. The basic decision of whether to eliminate the current brand and launch a totally new one involved the "product element" of the marketing mix. Coca-Cola executives should have carefully examined whether eliminating the original beverage would break the bonds of trust established over half a century. If the decision were still made to change the product after the analysis, relational exchange ideas would then be used to develop promotional strategy, another marketing mix element. That is, based upon ideas from relational exchange, a strategy could be developed for how to present the new product to consumers in a way that would lower the perception of exchange inequities.

Several other consumer behavior concept apply to the "New Coke" case—consumer expectations, psychological reactance, the self-concept, and regional subcultures. Within the information processing area, the concept of expectations is discussed. One finding is that expectations influence how people perceive and interpret information, such as that received through the taste sense. Corporate executives and researchers at Coca-Cola failed to consider the effects of **consumer expectations** in their market research. By not allowing respondents to know the brand names, the effects of expectations on taste could not be ascertained. As a result, Coca-Cola could not obtain a meaningful estimate of potential consumer reactions to the change. Clearly, executives should have allowed the researchers to include some test consumers who were given the brand names of the colas being tested.

The area of consumer motivation is also relevant to the "New Coke" problem. To maintain secrecy, the managers decided *not* to inform any of the participants in the research of the possible change in the taste of Coke. As a result, it was difficult to anticipate the staggering negative emotional response that occurred as the result of the effect of an emotional state called **psychological reactance**. Reactance, discussed in Chapter 6 on motivation and affective processes, occurs when people perceive that their freedom of choice has been violated.[26] When psychological reactance occurs, consumers are aroused to take steps to restore their behavioral freedom, and Coke drinkers did so with a vengeance.

The concept of reactance applies to both the market research and the marketing mix areas. In the realm of market research, the implication is that a group of test consumers should have been sworn to secrecy and asked how they would react if regular Coke was withdrawn from the market. In the marketing mix arena, the managerial implication of reactance is the idea that perhaps the company should have kept "old" Coke and introduced and promoted an entirely new brand to compete in taste against Pepsi.

The consumer behavior area that involves the self-concept (see Chapter 7) also applies to the problem. The results of *The Wall Street Journal*'s taste test also revealed that the participants in the survey viewed Coke and Pepsi drinkers as different types of people. Consumers frequently buy a specific brand in order to connect its image to their **self-concept**.

The self-concept has application to four managerial areas. First, market research must be used to identify the images that consumers obtain from Coke and competing brands. Second, this information should be used to identify potential market segments of consumers who wish to portray themselves as possessing a particular self-image. Third, a positioning strategy is created for how to portray the image of Coke. Fourth, a promotional strategy is developed that implements the positioning strategy.

The Coke affair also illustrates the importance of considering the effects of demographics and subculture (see Chapter 18). One important idea found in the chapter is the concept of **regional subcultures**. People in different regions of the United States can have markedly different tastes and preferences. In the Coke case, market research should have been conducted to identify these differences, which if found could have lead to the segmentation of the marketplace by region. Different promotional strategies can then be developed for each region. Finally, environmental analysis should be conducted to analyze how long-term changes in regional population distributions could impact marketing strategy. For example, if urban centers are expected to decrease in size, it could indicate trouble for "New Coke."

Table 1-5 shows the managerial applications analysis developed for the Coke case. Along the left side are the consumer concepts identified as relevant to the development of marketing strategy. To the right of each consumer concept the managerial strategy elements are identified that should be considered as a result of the consumer analysis.

SUMMARY

Consumer behavior is a broad field that studies the exchange process through which individuals and groups acquire, consume, and dispose of goods, services, ideas, and experiences. The principles of consumer behavior are useful to business managers, government regulators, nonprofit organizations, and everyday people. For marketing managers, knowledge of consumer behavior has important implications for environ-

TABLE 1-5

Coke Case: Managerial Applications Analysis

Consumer Concepts	*Managerial Applications Areas*
1. Exchange relations	*Marketing mix*—Determine the impact on exchange relationship if you eliminate product.
	Promotional strategy—Identify messages to deliver to minimize perception of exchange inequities.
2. Consumer expectations	*Market research*—Estimate impact of expectations on taste perception.
3. Psychological reactance	*Marketing mix*—Introduce "New Coke" as a second product to avoid creating reactance by withdrawing "Old Coke" from the market.
	Market research—Assessing potential reactions by swearing test group of consumers to secrecy and telling them of plan to replace "Old Coke."
4. Self-concept	*Market research*—Identify images that consumers attach to Coke and Pepsi.
	Segmentation—Identify through psychographic analysis characteristic segments of consumers who view themselves as similar to the image of Coke. Consider whether the segment is large enough, is reachable, and has spending power.
	Positioning—Identify image that management desires "New Coke" to establish in marketplace.
	Marketing mix—Develop a promotional strategy to communicate the desired image to the identified target market.
5. Regional subcultures	*Market research*—Identify how tastes and preferences differ across regions of the United States.
	Environmental analysis—Analyze changes in population patterns across regions to develop long-term strategy.
	Segmentation—Target specific regions for different degrees of promotional effort if regional differences exist for soft drink preferences.

mental analysis, for product positioning, for the segmentation of the marketplace, for designing market research studies, and for developing the marketing mix.

The high impact of consumer behavior on marketing management should not be surprising. Modern marketing managers believe in the "marketing concept" and the idea that facilitating exchange processes is the basic premise of the marketing discipline. As a result, they view the consumer as the focal point of the marketing effort.

Consumer behavior is an applied discipline. It borrows theories and knowledge from other fields such as anthropology, sociology, demographics, economics, and psychology. It is, however, a discipline in its own right. Consumer researchers are developing their own body of knowledge to supplement that obtained from other fields.

An organizing model of consumer behavior was developed in this chapter. It is composed of five primary elements: the individual influencers, the consumer environment, the exchange process, the buying unit, and the marketer. In addition, three research perspectives on consumer acquisition behavior were identified: the decision-making perspective, the experiential perspective, and the behavioral influence perspective.

This textbook focuses on identifying the factors that influence the exchange process between the consumer and the marketer. It is organized around the two levels of consumer behavior analysis. Part 2 of the text will analyze concepts related to the study of the individual consumer. Areas discussed in those chapters include information processing, behavioral learning, motivation and affect, personality and psychographics, attitudes, attitude change, persuasive communications, and consumer decision processes. Part 3 will present the areas that compose the consumer environment, consisting of those stimuli that influence consumers. Chapters in Part 3 cover such areas as group, organizational, and family processes and the effects of various consumer situations. In addition, Part 3 includes chapters on culture, cross-cultural processes and the international environment, subcultures and demographics, and the regulatory environment.

To provide a coherent approach to applying consumer behavior concepts to managerial and public policy issues, the text introduced the concept of the managerial applications analysis. The analysis employs a three-step procedure in which (1) the problem is defined, (2) applicable consumer concepts are identified, and (3) a managerial strategy is formed based upon the implications of the consumer behavior concepts. The managerial areas to which the consumer concepts apply are the marketing mix, segmentation, positioning and differentiation, environmental analysis, and market research.

KEY TERMS

acquisition phase
behavioral influence perspective
buying units
consumer behavior
consumer expectations
consumer primacy
consumption phase
decision-making perspective
disposition phase
environmental analysis
environmental influence factors
environmental level of analysis
exchange process
experiential perspective
individual influence factors
individual level of analysis
interpretive research methods
logical empiricist research methods
managerial applications analysis
market research
marketer
marketing
marketing mix
marketing strategy
personal value
product differentiation
product positioning
psychological reactance
public policy
regional subcultures
segmentation
self-concept
theory

REVIEW QUESTIONS

1. Define the term "consumer behavior." Why is consumption viewed as a process?
2. Identify the reasons why an understanding of consumer behavior acts as a foundation for the development of marketing strategy and planning.
3. How can the study of consumer behavior assist managers in environmental analysis?
4. How can the study of consumer behavior assist managers in product positioning and product differentiation?
5. How can the study of consumer behavior assist managers in the segmentation of the marketplace?
6. Through what means does consumer behavior assist the market research function?
7. In what ways can the study of consumer behavior provide consumers, managers, and public policy makers with theories, facts, and an orientation?
8. What are the behavioral science fields from which consumer behavior may draw theories and concepts?
9. Draw a diagram of the consumer behavior model presented in the text.
10. Describe the three research perspectives that can be used to analyze the consumer purchase process.
11. Briefly describe the two broad levels of analysis from which consumer behavior may be analyzed—that is, the individual influencers and the environmental influencers.

DISCUSSION QUESTIONS

1. Consider the soft drink industry. Through what means do such companies as Coca-Cola, Pepsi-Cola, and Dr Pepper attempt to differentiate their products from those of other companies? (Think in terms of product characteristics and images.)
2. Define the concept of environmental analysis. What environmental factors may surface in the next ten years to influence soft drink consumption. (*Hint:* Think in terms of changes in the global marketplace and of demographic changes.)
3. Define the concept of market segmentation. From your knowledge of the automobile industry, try to identify different segments of customers that auto manufacturers attempt to reach.
4. Define the concept of consumer primacy. Next, identify several ways in which marketers can demonstrate to customers the concept of consumer primacy. Finally, from your own buying experiences, develop two to three instances in which marketers or retailers failed to follow the principle of consumer primacy.
5. Identify several environmental factors that should be considered by a marketing manager of a national company that builds middle-income houses. What are the managerial implications of these factors?
6. Consumer researchers are highly interested in the study of demographic trends. Identify three major demographic trends that may influence corporate market planning for marketers of golf clubs or of microwave ovens.
7. Identify three types of purchases you have made that were based mostly upon a careful, rational thought process. Briefly explain the nature of your thought process for each purchase.
8. Identify three purchases you have made that were based mostly upon a desire to obtain feelings and experiences. What feelings and experiences were you hoping to obtain from the purchase?
9. Identify three of your purchases that were made principally because of pressures from the environment. What was the nature of the pressure that encouraged each purchase?

10. Identify three of your purchases in which some combination of rational thought, desire for experience, and/or behavioral influence affected your purchase. Have you experienced decisions in which conflicts occurred among the three factors?

11. In the "New Coke" case, do you think that the company should change the name of the drink to "Coke II"?

ENDNOTES

1. Quotations on body piercing are from L. A. Kauffman, "Beauty Knows No Pain," *Elle*, July 1993, pp. 65–66.
2. The quotations on cosmetic surgery are from Kathy Healy, "Plastic Surgery Addicts," *Allure*, April 1993, pp. 80–82.
3. Scott Ward and Thomas Robertson, "Consumer Behavior Research: Promise and Prospects," in *Consumer Behavior: Theoretical Sources*, Scott Ward and Thomas Robertson, eds. (Englewood Cliffs, NJ: Prentice-Hall, 1973), pp. 3–42.
4. Theodore Levitt, "Marketing Myopia," in *Modern Marketing Strategy*, Edward Bursk and John Chapman, eds. (Cambridge, MA: Harvard University Press, 1964).
5. Philip Kotler, *Marketing Management Analysis, Planning, and Control*, 4th ed. (Englewood Cliffs, NJ: Prentice-Hall, 1980), p. 21.
6. Brent Stidsen, "Directions in the Study of Marketing," in *Conceptual and Theoretical Developments in Marketing*, Neil Beckwith et al., eds. (Chicago: American Marketing Association, 1979), pp. 383–398.
7. As cited in Kotler, *Marketing Management*, p. 3.
8. Frank Houston, "The Marketing Concept, What It Is and What It Is Not," *Journal of Marketing*, April 1986, pp. 81–87.
9. Ross Perot, "How I Would Turn Around GM," *Fortune*, February 15, 1988, p. 45.
10. John C. Mowen, "Beyond Consumer Decision Making," *Journal of Consumer Marketing*, Vol. 5 (Winter 1988), pp. 15–25.
11. Morris Holbrook and Elizabeth C. Hirschman, "The Experiential Aspects of Consumption: Consumer Fantasies, Feelings, and Fun," *Journal of Consumer Research*, September 9, 1982, pp. 132–140.
12. For a review of variety seeking, see Leigh McAlister and Edgar E. Pessemier, "Variety Seeking Behavior: An Interdisciplinary Review," *Journal of Consumer Research*, December 9, 1982, pp. 311–322. Also see Werner Kroeber-Riel, "Emotional Product Differentiation by Classical Conditioning," in *Advances in Consumer Research*, Vol. XI, Thomas Kinnear, ed. (Ann Arbor, MI: Association for Consumer Research, 1984), pp. 538–543.
13. Russell Belk, John Sherry, and Melanie Wallendorf, "A Naturalistic Inquiry into Buyer and Seller Behavior at a Swap Meet," *Journal of Consumer Research*, March 14, 1988, pp. 449–469.
14. John Sherry, "Some Implications of Consumer Oral Tradition for Reactive Marketing," in *Advances in Consumer Research*, Vol. XI, Thomas Kinnear, ed. (Ann Arbor, MI: Association for Consumer Research, 1984), pp. 741–747.
15. Michael L. Rothschild and William Gaidis, "Behavioral Learning Theory: Its Relevance to Marketing and Promotions," *Journal of Marketing*, Vol. 45 (Spring 1981), pp. 70–78. Also see Peter H. Reingen and Jerome B. Kernan, "More Evidence on Interpersonal Yielding," *Journal of Marketing Research*, Vol. 16 (November 1979), pp. 588–593.
16. Jesse Snyder, "4 GM Car Divisions Are Repositioned in Effort to Help Sales," *Automotive News*, September 15, 1986, pp. 1, 49.
17. Thomas Oliver, *The Real Coke, The Real Story* (New York: Random House, 1986).

18. Ibid.

19. Ibid.

20. Betsy Morris, "In This Taste Test, the Loser Is the Taste Test," *The Wall Street Journal*, June 3, 1987, p. 31.

21. Betsy Morris, "Coke vs. Pepsi: Cola War Marches On," *The Wall Street Journal*, June 3, 1987, p.

22. Ibid.

23. "Coke 'Family' Sales Fly as the New Coke Stumbles," *Advertising Age*, January 27, 1986, pp. 1, 91.

24. Laura Bird, "Coke II: The Sequel," *Adweek's Marketing Week*, Vol. 31 (July 30, 1990), pp. 4–5.

25. Walicia Konrad, "The Real Thing Is Getting Real Aggressive," *Business Week*, November 26, 1990, pp. 94–96.

26. Mona Clee and Robert Wicklund, "Consumer Behavior and Psychological Reactance," *Journal of Consumer Research*, Vol. 6 (March 1980), pp. 389–405.

27. To answer the question about Garth Brooks in the chapter introduction, Garth Brooks attended Oklahoma State University, where the author of this textbook teaches. He also wrote and sang country songs for local clubs. In addition, he worked in Dupree's Sports Equipment Company for its owner, Eddie Watkins. One of the things that Garth did on his job was silk screen tee-shirts. But even then he was "sure" that he would some day become a country singing star. He told Eddie Watkins that after he became a star, he would let Eddie print some of his tee-shirts for his concerts. Garth Brooks kept that promise, and Eddie Watkins makes thousands of tee-shirts a year because of it. This example illustrates business-to-business marketing and the idea of relationship building, which will be discussed in the next chapter on consumer exchanges.

Chapter 2

Consumer Exchange Processes

CONSUMER VIGNETTE

JCPenney's Exchange Problems

The corporate investor relations specialist turned up her nose when asked if she ever purchased her own clothing at JCPenney. She said, "The few times I've looked, there might be an attractive blouse, but it will be polyester and look hot, like it would smell like New Jersey if you wore it in the summer."[1] Unfortunately, other professional women and the big-name clothing suppliers agree with the executive. JCPenney had an image problem that was impeding its corporate strategy of becoming a fashionable national department store targeting middle- and upper-middle-income customers.

Historically, JCPenney competed against Sears and Montgomery Ward in selling cookie-cutter basics to Middle America. In the three decades after World War II, consumer choices were influenced largely by product price and reliability. Then came the 1970s and 1980s when discounters such as Wal-Mart and Kmart emerged with a cost structure that allowed them to steal away the price conscious. In addition, regional malls began to sprout from the landscape, and they housed trendy department stores and specialty retailers. These stores captured a new, emerging set of customers focusing on fashion and status. Along with Sears and Montgomery Ward, JCPenney was caught in a vicious squeeze play.

To their credit, managers at JCPenney saw the problem coming during the 1970s and ordered a massive reevaluation of their business. After investigating the company, the competition, and the expected changes in the market for "full-line retailers," management concluded that "the company was trying to do too many things in the wrong places." As a result, it began a monumental repositioning effort. In 1983 the company closed out its

Figure 2-1 A photo of the "new" JCPenney.

appliance, lawn and garden, paint, hardware, and automotive lines. In 1988 the home electronics and sporting goods lines were eliminated. Brand names began to be substituted for private labels. Tile floors were replaced with parquet and carpet. Men's and women's fashion departments were expanded. Then during the recession of the early 1990s, the company slashed costs and rewrote product specifications to raise quality. In addition, prices were cut and a "value" theme was emphasized in advertising. The reward was a 47% increase in earnings in 1992.

Despite these improvements, JCPenney remained in a Catch-22 situation. On the one hand, the middle- and upper-middle-income customers that it targeted wanted certain important brand names. On the other hand, the "big-name" suppliers refused to sell to the company because it failed to attract the customers who purchased their brands. For example, the big-name suppliers of apparel and cosmetics such as Elizabeth Arden, Estée Lauder, and Liz Claiborne refused to sell to JCPenney because they feared that the chain would discount their goods and cheapen their images. The chairman of one prestigious women's apparel maker congratulated JCPenney for its efforts at changing its image but also suggested that the price of his clothing was still too high for JCPenney stores. As he said, "Perhaps someday we'll do business with them."

The company has met with some success, however, in luring brand-name suppliers. In 1979 it pleaded with Levi Strauss & Company to allow it to sell its jeans, promising that it would change dramatically in the 1980s. One executive described a meeting where his plea was followed by the room going "very quiet, and that was about the end of the meeting." Some years later, however, Levi Strauss changed its mind, and by 1990 the company was selling $100 million a year of Levi's Dockers brand alone. As of 1993, however, the company still could not attract Liz Claiborne into the fold. In frustration, JCPenney's CEO said, "It's hard for us to understand why somebody would not want Penney's when we would be their largest account."[2]

INTRODUCTION

The consumer vignette illustrates a number of the features of the exchange process, which is the underlying basis of the fields of consumer behavior and marketing. An **exchange** involves "a transfer of something tangible or intangible, actual or symbolic, between two or more social actors."[3] Not only do exchanges occur between consumers and retailers, but also they transpire between retailers and their suppliers. JCPenney is a customer of Levi Strauss just as you and I are customers of JCPenney. Thus a retailer, such as JCPenney, is involved in a complex set of relationships. It must trade resources with its various suppliers as well as with its customers. In a consumer behavior context, a variety of resources are exchanged. They include money and products. In addition, however, other value-laden entities may be transferred, such as information, services, status, and feelings. The JCPenney vignette illustrates the transfer of each of these resources along with the complex nature of consumer exchange processes.

The concept that money, goods, services, and information act as **resources** in the exchange process is intuitive. When a customer purchases a set of towels from JCPenney, a **good** is transferred in return for cash (**money**). Similarly, the idea that **services** can be exchanged also makes sense. When JCPenney personnel wrap a package, provide credit, and give refunds, they add value to the exchange relationship. Even consumers supply services to retailers. For example, some grocery stores charge lower prices to customers in return for the customers bagging their own merchandise. **Information** becomes a resource when clerks give instructions to customers on product characteristics. Similarly, advertising and displays provide information to buyers. Consumers also give information to retailers in the form of their input to market research studies and their comments to the sales force.

Status as a type of resource is harder to fathom but, nonetheless, is a crucial component to many exchanges. The JCPenney vignette well illustrates its role. When customers buy a product, they connect themselves to the brand and to the retailer who sells it. For some types of products, the status of the retailer becomes associated with the brand and ultimately with the customer's self-concept. For middle- and upper-middle-income women, JCPenney's humble status had little impact on their purchase of products—such as towels, window coverings, and their children's and husband's clothing—that are unrelated to their own self-concept. In contrast, the JCPenney name had a major negative impact on their purchase of clothing for themselves. What one wears is closely associated with the self-concept. A significant number of people do act as though clothes make the woman or man.

Feelings are also a resource transferred between two parties. The emotional reactions that emerge from an exchange have a major impact on whether future transfers of resources occur. When salesclerks are courteous and friendly to customers, positive feelings are apt to emerge. These act as rewards that will increase the likelihood of future exchanges. A part of the repositioning of JCPenney involved the upgrading and training of their salesclerks to create a more positive buying experience for customers.

An important concept to be explained in this chapter is the idea that two parties will probably cease their relationship if either fails to profit from the exchange. This idea is clearly demonstrated in the exchange relationship between JCPenney and its suppliers. Some companies, such as Clinique and Liz Claiborne, perceived that they would not profit from the exchange, in part because JCPenney failed to offer sufficient status resources. That is, the lower status of JCPenney acted as a negative input into the potential exchange relationship with the retailer. They also risked monetary resources because large department stores, which represent their main channel to the consumer, might stop buying from them if their goods were placed in JCPenney. The firm is working hard to attract brand names to raise its status level. The agreement with Levi Strauss to sell its jeans was an important accomplishment.

In sum, the analysis of the JCPenney vignette from an exchange perspective underscores the validity of the company's repositioning efforts. It also highlights the role of exchange in business—business marketing as well as consumer marketing. Thus JCPenney had to substantially upgrade its status image to influence brand-name suppliers to sell their merchandise to the company. In addition, the firm's status strongly affected consumer perceptions of the profitability of exchanges with JCPenney. Only by making the necessary investments to change its image could it successfully persuade the targeted suppliers and consumers to enter into an exchange relationship with the firm.

EXCHANGE PROCESSES, CONSUMER BEHAVIOR, AND MARKETING

As described in Chapter 1, an exchange process connects the buyer to marketers. Whenever a consumer makes a decision to purchase a brand from a particular retailer, he or she is also deciding to engage in an exchange. The concept that exchange is fundamental to marketing has been discussed for at least 30 years. In 1957 Wroe Alderson, one of the early founders of the field, said: "Marketing is the exchange which takes place between consuming groups and supplying groups."[4] Similarly, Philip Kotler has defined marketing as "a social process by which individuals and groups obtain what they need and want through creating and exchanging products and value with others."[5] In 1975, Richard Bagozzi proposed that exchange is the most basic element of the marketing function. Finally, in 1985 the American Marketing Association defined marketing as "the process of planning and executing the conception, pricing, promotion, and distribution of ideas, goods, and services to create exchanges that satisfy individual and organizational objectives."[6] In each of these definitions the concept of exchange was central to defining the field of marketing.

Prerequisites for Exchange

For an exchange to take place, a number of conditions must exist. Five of these conditions are:

1. Two or more parties must be present.
2. Each party must have something that is of value to the other party.
3. Each party must be capable of communication and delivery.
4. Each party must be free to reject or accept the other's offer.
5. Each party believes that it is appropriate or desirable to deal with the other.[7]

An important issue when investigating exchange is explaining why one person is willing to give up one thing to receive something else in return. If one person has one collection or assortment of goods and another person has a second collection or assortment of goods, what will make them enter into an exchange? The basic reason for exchanging one good for another is that different people possess divergent tastes and preferences. As described by economists, consumers act to increase the total utility of the assortment of goods possessed by making exchanges. As such, the fundamental principle driving the exchange is that people have different utility functions. Thus, if I have something that has lower value to me than to you, and if you have something that has lower value to you than to me, we have a basis for exchange.[8] In such instances both parties profit from the exchange because each receives something that they value more than what they gave up.

What Are the Elements of Exchange?

Researchers have worked hard to identify what is exchanged between two people or between two social units (e.g., a family and a firm).[9] As discussed earlier in the chapter, good evidence exists that the things or resources exchanged can be placed into six categories. The types of resources exchanged are goods, services, money, status, information, and feelings.[10] Table 2-1 provides examples of each of the six categories. Figure 2-2 presents an ad for Perrier bottled water. In the ad Perrier has selected an exchange context in which not only are a variety of product resources offered but also feelings and information.

Figure 2-3 presents a diagram of the exchange process. It shows that each party to the exchange possesses certain resources. The resources input by one party represent his or her costs and become the outcomes received by the other party. Outcomes are derived not only from the resources exchanged, but also from the experiences obtained from engaging in the exchange act. Thus each party may derive rewards or costs from the exchange process itself in addition to those obtained from the goods, services, or money transferred.

TABLE 2-1

Examples of the Six Categories of Resources

1. *Feelings.* Expressions of affectionate regard, warmth, or comfort.
2. *Status.* Evaluative judgment conveying high or low prestige, regard, or esteem.
3. *Information.* Any advice, opinion, or instructions.
4. *Money.* Any coin or token that has some standard of exchange value.
5. *Goods.* Any product or object having exchange value.
6. *Services.* Any performance of labor performed for someone else.

SOURCE: Based in part on Gregory Donnenworth and Uriel Foa, "Effects of Resource Class on Retaliation to Injustice in Interpersonal Exchange," *Journal of Personality and Social Psychology*, Vol. 29 (1974), pp. 785–793.

Creating positive feelings from the exchange process is becoming increasingly important to marketers in highly competitive industries. For example, J. D. Power & Associates compiles a Customer Satisfaction Index (the CSI) for new automobiles each year. A six-page questionnaire is mailed to 73,000 people who purchased new automobiles. From the responses, an index of satisfaction is created, and the competing brands are ranked. "Customer handling," which in large part measures feelings, accounts for 40% of the final CSI score. In discussing the reason for the heavy weight of customer treatment in the survey, the administrator of the CSI said, "How they're treated at the dealership has become more important to customers and should carry greater weight."[11]

Figure 2-2 What are the resources offered for exchange in this ad for Perrier bottled water?

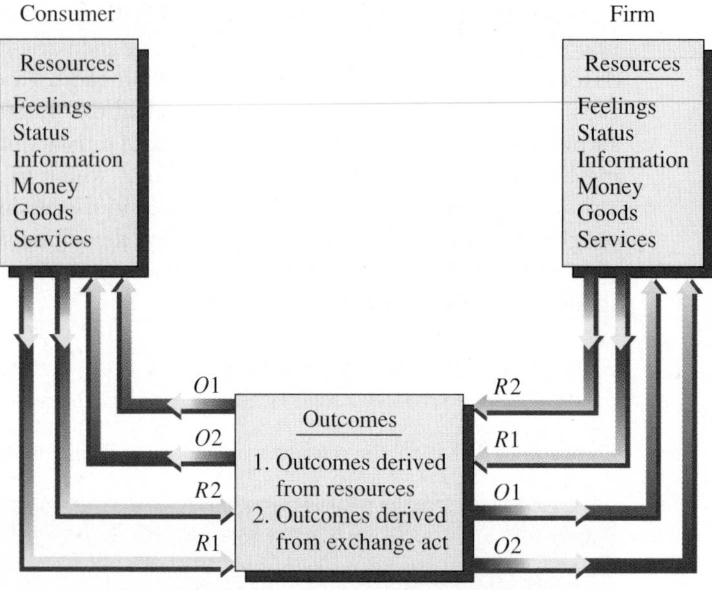

Figure 2-3 Diagram of the exchange process.

DIMENSIONS OF EXCHANGE RELATIONS

A variety of types of consumer exchange relations exist. These are identified and briefly defined in Table 2-2.

Restricted Versus Complex Exchanges

One key dimension concerns the complexity of the exchange relationship.[12] The most **simple type of exchange** involves "two parties in a reciprocal relationship." An example might be a consumer and her stockbroker or a patient and his physician. At the most complicated level, one finds "complex exchanges." **Complex exchanges** involve a set of three or more actors enmeshed in a set of mutual relations. An example would be a channel of distribution in which an automobile goes from a manufacturer (e.g., Ford Motor Company) to a dealer, which then sells it to a customer. Each party depends upon the other to supply resources. For example, even though car buyers and manufacturers are separated by a dealer, the consumer depends upon the manufacturer to build a quality product. Similarly, the manufacturer is dependent upon consumers purchasing its autos.

TABLE 2-2

Types of Exchange Relations

1. Restricted versus complex
   - **A.** *Restricted exchange*—Concerns a two-party relation
   - **B.** *Complex exchange*—Involves a set of three or more actors
2. Internal versus external
   - **A.** *Internal exchange*—Occurs within a group
   - **B.** *External exchange*—Occurs between groups
3. Formal versus informal
   - **A.** *Formal exchange*—Involves explicit written or verbal contracts
   - **B.** *Informal exchange*—Involves unwritten, unspoken, social contracts
4. Relational versus discrete
   - **A.** *Relational exchange*—Creates long-term relations
   - **B.** *Discrete exchange*—Constitutes one-time exchange in which no relations are formed

Internal Versus External Exchanges

A second way to think about exchange relations concerns whether they occur within a group (an internal exchange) or between parties that are in separate groups (an external exchange).[13] An example of an **internal exchange** would be the complex sets of relations that occur within a family. Internal exchanges involve a situation in which the members of the organization or group avoid going into the market to obtain a good or service. The particular need is satisfied within the organization. An example of an **external exchange** would involve transactions between members of a family or firm and retailers. Here members of the group are importing goods or services from an outside source to fulfill a need.

As a general statement, consumer researchers have focused on developing an understanding of external exchanges. However, internal exchanges are also important. For example, consider the decision by family members to make their own Sunday dinner or go out to a restaurant. Engaging in "self-production" to make their own meal involves an internal exchange of services by family members. Owners of restaurants are extremely interested in the factors that impact whether a group decides to fulfill its needs internally or externally. Of course, the same ideas hold in business-to-business marketing as well. For example, should an automobile company produce its own car motors? On the other hand, should it purchase them from another supplier (e.g., Ford purchasing a motor from Yamaha for its Taurus SHO car).

Formal Versus Informal Exchanges

Exchanges can occur either formally or informally. A **formal exchange** involves an explicit, written, or verbal contract. They will frequently occur in external exchanges. Exchanges can also occur informally. In an **informal exchange**, unwritten, social contracts are created between parties. Occurring more frequently in internal exchanges, one finds that social norms and peer pressure replace formal contracts.

One arena in which informal exchanges frequently occur is in dating. From an exchange perspective, people can be viewed as possessing a set of resources that are exchanged. As such, people have a set of characteristics, such as physical beauty, intelligence, money, a high-status occupation, and a good personality. These characteristics are the resources exchanged when individuals become involved in romantic exchanges. Thus the dating process may be argued to consist of men and women exchanging various resources.

In one study, one researcher investigated personal dating advertisements found in *The Washingtonian* magazine and in *New York* magazine.[14] In both magazines males and females publish short descriptions of themselves and of the type of person they would like to meet. An example of a personal dating advertisement follows:

> Very attractive, college-educated, professional female (in science), 28, 5' 8", dark hair, exercise fanatic, active and outgoing, seeks male counterpart: Tall, handsome (blond?), muscular, secure, professional man (Law, MD) under 36, for sports, fun dates, and possibly great relationship. Note and photo appreciated.

The author of the dating study performed a content analysis of the personal advertisements in the two magazines. The resources offered and sought were placed into ten categories: love, physical attractiveness/beauty, money, occupational status, educational status, intellectual status, entertainment services, information-personality, information-ethnic, and information-demographic. The researcher proposed a series of hypotheses concerning what resources are emphasized in the initial stages of dating exchanges.

Table 2-3 depicts the set of resources that men and women were hypothesized to offer and seek. Women were hypothesized to offer (and men were proposed to seek) physical attractiveness, love, entertainment services, and information. In contrast, men were proposed to offer (and women were proposed to seek) money, educational status, intellectual status, and occupational status.

TABLE 2-3

Resource Exchanges Between Men and Women in the Dating Setting

I. Resources hypothesized to be advertised by men and women

- **A.** Women advertise physical attractiveness, love, entertainment services, and information.
- **B.** Men advertise money, educational status, intellectual status, and occupational status.

II. Actual resources found in study to be advertised and sought

- **A.** Women offered physical attractiveness.
  Women sought monetary resources and love.
- **B.** Men offered monetary resources and occupational status.
  Men sought physical attractiveness and love.

SOURCE: Elizabeth Hirschman, "People as Products: Analysis of a Complex Marketing Exchange," *Journal of Marketing*, Vol. 51 (January 1987), pp. 98–108, published by the American Marketing Association.

The results of the study revealed that women more than men tended to offer physical attractiveness resources and to seek monetary resources. Conversely, men tended to offer monetary resources and to seek physical attractiveness resources. Somewhat sadly, both men and women sought love resources much more frequently than they offered them.

Relational Versus Discrete Exchange

An important component of many exchanges is the ongoing relationship between the parties to the exchange (e.g., dating partners or consumer and marketer). An important distinction is that between discrete exchange and relational exchange. A **discrete exchange** is a one-time interaction in which money is paid for an easily measured commodity. Discrete exchanges are short, one-time purchases that do not involve the creation of a relationship. In contrast, a **relational exchange** involves a transaction involving a long-term commitment in which trust and the development of social relations play an important role.[15]

Relational exchanges have been equated to a marriage between buyer and seller. As one author stated, "The sale merely consummates the courtship. Then the marriage begins. How good the marriage is depends on how well the relationship is managed by the seller."[16] Thus, when viewed from a relational exchange perspective, transactions should be analyzed in terms of their history and anticipated future. Such transactions are noted for the social relations that occur as well as the benefits derived from the characteristics of the product or service obtained. Consumers will make long-term commitments with marketers to reduce overall transaction costs (e.g., by minimizing search costs), to lower risk, and to gain the positive feelings that result from interacting with someone who is liked. From an economic perspective, the total utility of a relational exchange depends upon the utility of the acquisition itself (e.g., the product or service) and the utility of the social relations that take place within the exchange. Based upon this formulation, total utility equals acquisition utility plus the exchange utility resulting from the social relations.

Table 2-4 depicts some of the characteristics of the relational exchange. Included are such concepts as long duration, commitment, multiple-party involvement, potential for conflicts of interest, and high levels of interdependence.

Examples of relational exchanges are found in both the industrial and consumer sectors. For instance, a company producing a complex product—such as a jet aircraft, a submarine, or a large building—must contract with other corporations to supply specific components and services. In one survey of banking, high-tech, and manufacturing customers, it was found that respondents considered "the personal touch" to be the most important element of providing good service. Personal touch was defined as "how committed a company representative is to a client and whether he or she remembers a customer's name." The personal touch factor was found to be more important than convenience, speed of delivery, and how well the product worked.[17] Personal touch is simply another term for what happens in relational exchanges. Figure 2-4 presents an ad from Paine Webber that emphasizes the importance of building relationships between broker and client.

The importance of relational factors is evident in a study that examined how wealthy individuals choose an investment firm. These individuals (defined as having common stock portfolios worth over $400,000) valued the discretion of the invest-

TABLE 2-4

Some Characteristics of Relational Exchanges

1. *Timing*—Long term reflects an ongoing process.
2. *Obligations*—Obligations are customized and detailed. Promises are made, and laws and regulations may apply.
3. *Relationship expectations*—Conflicts are anticipated, but they are countered by trust and efforts to create unity.
4. *Rewards*—Rewards are derived from economic and noneconomic means.
5. *Communications*—Communications are extensive through formal and informal means.
6. *Cooperation*—A great deal of cooperation is needed to maintain exchange.
7. *Power*—Increased interdependence increases the importance of judicious application of power in the exchange.
8. *Planning*—There is significant focus on the process of exchange. Detailed planning is required for future exchanges.

ment firm, the manager's investment style, and the reputation of the firm as the most important factors in selecting a firm. Next to last in importance was the investment performance track record of the firm. In a discussion of these findings, *Fortune* magazine described the wealthy investors as "wacky." From an exchange perspective, however, the investors can be viewed as acting quite rationally. They were merely weighing relational factors, such as discretion, reputation, and style, as more important than performance.[18]

Social relations are particularly important in facilitating exchanges at home buying parties. Indeed, the term **market embeddedness** has been used to describe the situation in which the social ties between buyer and seller supplement product value to increase the perceived value of the exchange.[19] The importance of social relations has been recognized by companies such as Tupperware and Mary Kay Cosmetics. These companies frequently employ parties to sell their merchandise. In these parties one finds a hostess, a demonstrator, and the invitees. Usually, close relationships exist within the group of invitees and between the invitees and the hostess. The authors who identified the term market embeddedness performed a study in which they investigated the extent to which purchasing at such parties was influenced by the products offered and by the extent of the social relations. The results revealed that the invitees to the parties had a real demand for the products offered. In addition, they had stronger social ties to the hostess than to the demonstrator. Most important, the results revealed that as the invitees' sense of prior obligation to the hostess increased, so did the likelihood of purchase. Thus the total utility obtained from the purchase resulted in part from the acquisition of the product and in part from the utility of the exchange itself.

Relationship Quality

The concept of **relationship quality** is another important predictor of whether consumers will want to continue buying from a salesperson. Relationship quality is defined as the extent to which consumers trust a salesperson and have satisfaction

Figure 2-4 PaineWebber emphasizes relationship quality in this print ad. (Courtesy of PaineWebber.)

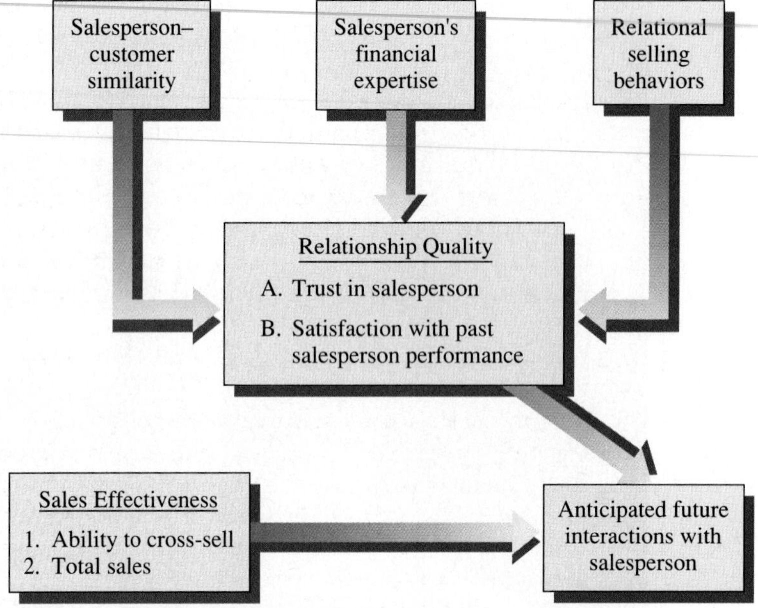

Figure 2-5 A relationship quality model of buyer perceptions of life insurance salespersons. (Adapted from Lawrence Crosby, Kenneth Evans, and Deborah Cowles, "Relationship Quality in Service: An Interpersonal Influence Approach," *Journal of Marketing*, Vol. 54, July 1990, pp. 68-81.)

with the salesperson's past performance. In a study of 151 consumers who had bought whole life insurance, the authors found that relationship quality had a direct effect on customers' expectations of future interactions with the salesperson.[20] Figure 2-5 reveals the model developed by the authors of the study. The model shows that relationship quality is influenced by the similarity between the salesperson and the consumer, the salesperson's financial expertise, and the salesperson's ability to relate to the consumer. Likewise, the extent to which that the consumers anticipated having future interactions with the salesperson was based upon the perception of relationship quality and the perception of sales effectiveness.

Table 2-5 summarizes the important findings concerning relationship exchanges.

TWO MODELS OF EXCHANGE

A number of researchers have proposed theories that attempt to identify the underlying factors at work in an exchange. One influential model was developed by George Homans. Homans viewed the exchange process from the dual perspectives of operant conditioning and economics. Taking an operant conditioning perspective, he argued that if interactions result in satisfying (i.e., reinforcing) outcomes, they will be repeated. Conversely, if an exchange yields dissatisfying (i.e., punishing) outcomes, it will be discontinued.[21] From the operant conditioning perspective, exchanges involve a complex set of reinforcers and punishers to shape the behavior of the other. (Chapter 5 discusses operant conditioning in more detail.)

Homans analyzed whether or not an exchange would be continued from an economic perspective. He proposed that people use a kind of economic cost–benefit analysis to determine if they will stay in an exchange. To the extent that the rewards from the exchange are greater than the costs, it will be profitable for the participants, and the exchange will continue. However, if the costs exceed the rewards for the participants, they will discontinue the exchange or seek to change the nature of the exchange. The **basic exchange equation** developed by Homans is

$$\text{Profit} = \text{Rewards} - \text{Costs}$$

From the exchange perspective, both consumers and firms attempt to profit from the interaction. The firm calculates its profits by subtracting its monetary costs from its monetary benefits. Consumers calculate their profit by subtracting their monetary and psychological costs from the rewards derived from the product or service purchased. If either individual perceives that he or she is not profiting from the exchange, dissatisfaction will result.

The basic exchange equation has direct application to the advertising of expensive products such as automobiles. Figure 2-6 presents an advertisement for the Infiniti G20 automobile from its 1992 campaign. When the Infiniti brand was initially launched, the advertising showed "rocks and trees" rather than the vehicle. About a year after the brand's introduction, the company changed its strategy and began to emphasize the rewards of purchasing the Infiniti. The ad shown in Figure 2-6 is the second page of a two-page layout. The first page shows a red G20 slashing through a rain-drenched road with the copy—"Imagine a Rollerblade with fuel injection." The second page identifies the cost of owning the vehicle ($21,485). In addition, it emphasizes the rewards obtained from owning the brand—140 horsepower, sunroof, sophisticated sound system, leather seats, and so on. Of course, the goal is to persuade consumers that the rewards of owning the brand are greater than the costs.

TABLE 2-5

Summary of Some Key Findings Concerning Relationship Exchanges

1. Relational exchanges become more important when services and products are complex, customized, and delivered over time.
2. Relationships are more important when buyers are more unsophisticated.
3. Relationships are more important when the buying environment is dynamic.
4. Consumers make purchases in part for the product or service and in part for the feelings that result from the exchange.
5. Trust and satisfaction with the past performance of the exchange partner influence perceptions of relationship quality.

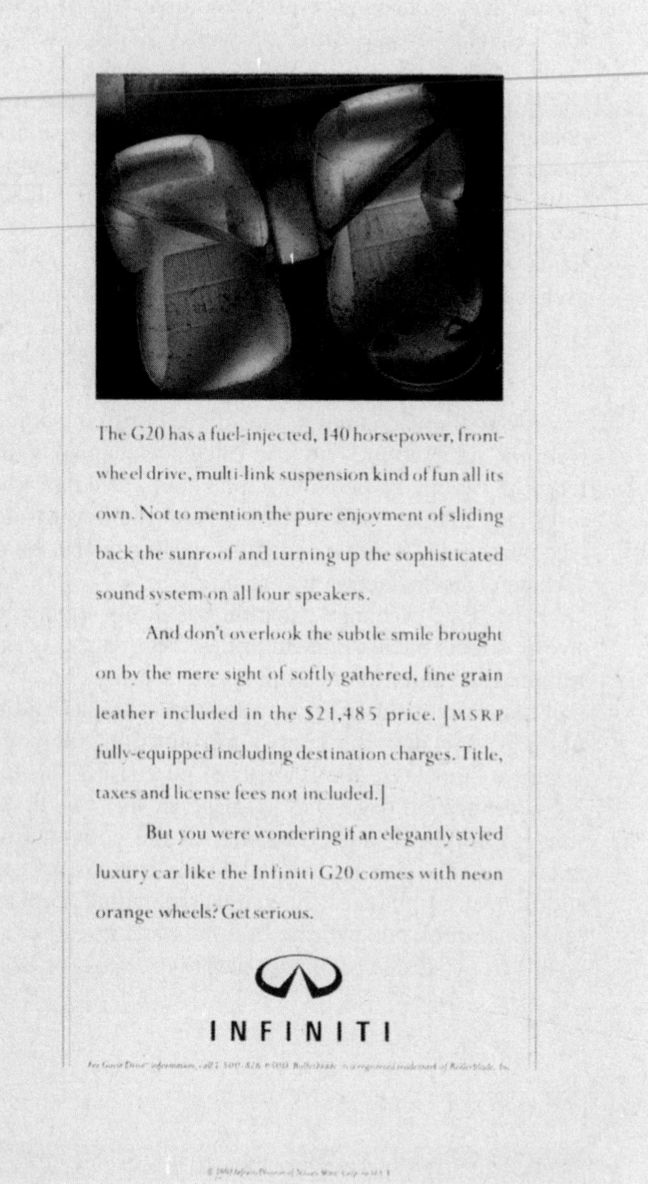

Figure 2-6 In this ad for the G20, Infiniti attempts to persuade buyers that the rewards of owning the car outweigh its costs. (Courtesy of Nissan Motor Corp. USA.)

Equity Theory and Exchange

In a number of situations, consumers habitually believe that they have been treated unfairly. Two of the most common instances are when they sell a house and when they pay their income taxes. An approach to understanding the exchange process, called equity theory, helps to explain this dissatisfaction.[22] **Equity theory** holds that people will analyze the ratio of their outcomes and inputs to the ratio of the outcomes and inputs of the partner in an exchange. If the person perceives that his or her ratio of outcomes to inputs is unfavorable in relation to the other member of the exchange, the individual will tend to have feelings of dissatisfaction. The following equation shows these ratios:

$$\frac{\text{Outcomes of A}}{\text{Inputs of A}} \approx \frac{\text{Outcomes of B}}{\text{Inputs of B}}$$

According to equity theory, the outcomes that person A receives from an exchange divided by the inputs of person A to the exchange should about equal the outcomes of person B from the exchange divided by the inputs of person B to the exchange. The inputs and outcomes are analyzed as perceived by one of the parties. In many instances the two parties may diverge substantially in their perception of the equity of an exchange because they view their inputs and outcomes divergently. If the consumer doing the evaluation finds that the ratio of outcomes to inputs is unfavorable, he or she will express dissatisfaction with the exchange.[23]

The outcomes and inputs consist of the exchange resources identified earlier in the chapter. In general, consumers provide monetary resources as inputs to the exchange and receive in return resources in the form of goods, services, information, status, time, and feelings. In some cases, consumers may also provide inputs to the exchange in the form of services, information, feelings, and even status.

So why do people tend to view their exchange with real estate brokers so negatively? One explanation is that many inputs of the real estate agents go unnoticed. The screening and evaluation of potential buyers, the advertising, and the hidden costs of running a business (e.g., buildings, secretaries, and office equipment) are not readily visible to sellers. Similarly, in the exchange relationship with the IRS, consumers fail to see the inputs of the government. Tax dollars spent for roads, national defense, weather forecasting, social security, and welfare are not readily apparent to most in the middle class. In both the IRS and the real estate examples, consumers will tend to perceive that the exchange relationship is inequitable because the inputs of the other party have low salience, whereas the inputs of the consumer (i.e., taxes and commissions paid) are highly salient.

A number of authors have investigated equity theory in consumer behavior. For example, one team of researchers found that people may consider the outcomes of other consumers in determining their satisfaction with a transaction.[24] In this study respondents role-played that they had purchased an automobile. After the purchase, they found that another person had obtained either a better or worse deal on the auto. The results revealed that when the comparison consumer had received a better deal on the same car, the respondents were less satisfied with the transaction and with the auto dealer than when they had obtained the better buy. This study shows that factors unrelated to their own transaction (in this case the deal obtained by another consumer) may strongly influence feelings of satisfaction with the exchange.

In another research study the perceptions of 415 car buyers were analyzed in terms of the equity of the exchange. Measures were obtained of their perceptions of their inputs and outcomes, as well as those of the car seller. Additional measures were taken of the extent perceived that a fair or equitable exchange occurred for both parties and of the extent perceived that the buyer got the better end of the deal. The results revealed that when buyers perceived their outcomes to be high and the seller's inputs to be greater than their own, they viewed the exchange as fairer. Buyer inputs or seller outcomes, however, did not influence their perceptions of fairness. The authors found that the greater the perceived fairness in the exchange, the greater the satisfaction with the salesperson by the buyer.[25] In sum, buyers in the study revealed a one-sided view of fairness in an exchange. Buyers appeared to view the transaction as fair only if their outcomes were high and the seller's inputs were large. Thus what buyers view as a fair exchange is likely to be viewed as inequitable by the salesperson.

The Impact of Comparison Levels on Exchange

Why did the market share of automobiles sold by GM, Ford, and Chrysler in the United States plunge during the 1980s? Why did this occur when the quality of their products increased substantially? One can answer the question by analyzing the exchange relationship between consumers and automakers in terms of two types of comparisons made by consumers.

Researchers have found that consumers base their evaluation of the adequacy of outcomes based upon two factors: (1) the comparison level for outcomes (CL) and (2) the comparison level for alternatives (CL_{alt}).[26] The **comparison level for outcomes** is the minimum level of positive outcome (profit) that an individual feels he or she deserves from an exchange. The CL is affected by such factors as the principle of equity—that is, the more one puts into an exchange relative to the exchange partner, the more one should get back. The CL is also affected by a person's past history. If a person consistently obtained very high levels of profits in the past, he or she will come to expect high levels of profits in the future. Individuals will find an exchange attractive to the extent that their outcomes exceed the CL. The single factor that probably most influenced the CL of American consumers was the rapid increase in the price of American cars during the 1980s. As prices rapidly increased, the CL would increase, and consumers expected to find substantial increases in the quality of the vehicles. If quality improvements were not made rapidly enough, one would anticipate dissatisfaction with American-made vehicles.

When a person's outcomes are lower than the CL, however, it does not necessarily mean that he or she will leave the exchange relationship. The person must ask what other alternatives are available. The **comparison level for alternatives** is defined as "the lowest level of outcomes a member will accept in light of available alternative opportunities."[27] The concept of CL_{alt} brings into focus the importance of competition in determining whether a person will leave an exchange relationship. If no other satisfactory alternatives are available (i.e., no competition exists), an individual may be forced to stay in an unsatisfactory exchange.

One can see the operation of the CL_{alt} in the American automobile market. Japanese companies entered the market with products that raised the CL_{alt}. Because the quality of American autos was lower than the CL_{alt}, buyers responded by purchasing record numbers of Toyotas, Nissans, and Hondas. The concept of a comparison level for alternatives operates for any good or service. For example, Americans are increasingly expressing dissatisfaction with the health care industry. One reason may be that the industry is being compared to other service providers, such as banks. Because of high levels of competition in the banking industry, consumers receive quick service at relatively low cost. In contrast, in the health care industry consumers receive extremely slow service at a relatively high cost.[28]

THE ROLE OF EXCHANGE IN CONSUMER AND INDUSTRIAL BUYING BEHAVIOR

In the discussion of JCPenney's relationship with its suppliers, it was argued that concepts related to exchange and consumer behavior apply to industrial as well as consumer marketing. In consumer marketing the firm directs its selling efforts to persuade individual consumers, such as you and me, to purchase a good or service. In industrial marketing the target of the selling effort is another firm. It is somewhat controversial to state that the same principles apply to both consumer and industrial marketing. Traditionally, these areas have been separated, and it has been argued that a dichotomy exists between the fields.

Table 2-6 identifies a series of proposed differences between consumer and industrial purchases. The differences are classified as to whether they originate from market characteristics, product differences, organizational setups, or other factors. For example, in the area of market differences, it has been argued that industrial markets tend to be driven by derived demand—that is, the demand for industrial products is created by demand for other products in which the industrial products are used. Other supposed market differences involve the belief that industrial buyers are more rational, more knowledgeable, more geographically concentrated, and so forth.

More recently, however, researchers have begun to believe that there are many more similarities than differences between industrial and consumer marketing.[29] Counterexamples can be given for most situations in which a difference is purported to exist. For example, in many situations consumer demand is derived. Just as in

TABLE 2-6

Differences Between Consumer and Industrial Buying Behavior

Market	*Product*	*Organization of Operational Setup*	*Others*
Derived versus primary demand	Technical complexity	Channel length	Message appeal
Elasticity of demand	Purchase frequency	Promotion mix	Delivery importance
Demand fluctuation	Classification	Reciprocity	Sales force compensation
Number of suppliers	Service requirement	Adequacy of supply	Sales force training
Numbers of buyers	Amount of information search	Degree of integration	Leasing
Number of influencers	Negotiated prices		
Geographic concentration	Dollar volume		
Knowledgeability	Riskiness		
Rationality			

SOURCE: Based on Table 1 in Edward Fern and James Brown, "The Industrial/Consumer Marketing Dichotomy," *Journal of Marketing*, Vol. 48 (Spring 1984), pp. 68–77, published by the American Marketing Association.

industrial buying situations, consumers' purchase of flour, sugar, gifts, lumber, and many other items is made so that these products can be used to make something else. Furthermore, industry buys many products for primary demand purposes, such as typewriters, light bulbs, and so forth. Although it is argued that groups more frequently make industrial buying decisions, one can find instances in which consumers engage in group decision making (e.g., a family) and instances in which a single person controls an industrial purchase. Although the number of buyers of industrial products is often smaller than for consumer products, in some instances the numbers do run into the hundreds of thousands for materials such as racks, heavy-duty carpeting, and so forth. Similarly, one can find cases in which consumers act highly rationally and industrial purchasers act irrationally. Just like industrial buyers, consumers sometimes negotiate on price, such as when buying a car or house. Finally, consumers not only engage in the leasing of products, such as automobiles, but also buy extremely technical products, such as computers.

The relationship between industrial and consumer buying behavior is shown in Figure 2-7. The figure shows the number of products bought by industrial buyers and consumer buyers on the vertical axis and the types of products bought on the horizontal axis. Two circles are drawn—one for consumer buying and one for industrial buying. What the intersecting circles suggest is that the marketing mix is similar for many

Figure 2-7 Industrial consumer goods marketing. (Based on a discussion in Jagdish Sheth, "The Specificity of Industrial Marketing," *P.U. Management Review*, Vol. 2, January-December 1979, pp. 53-56.)

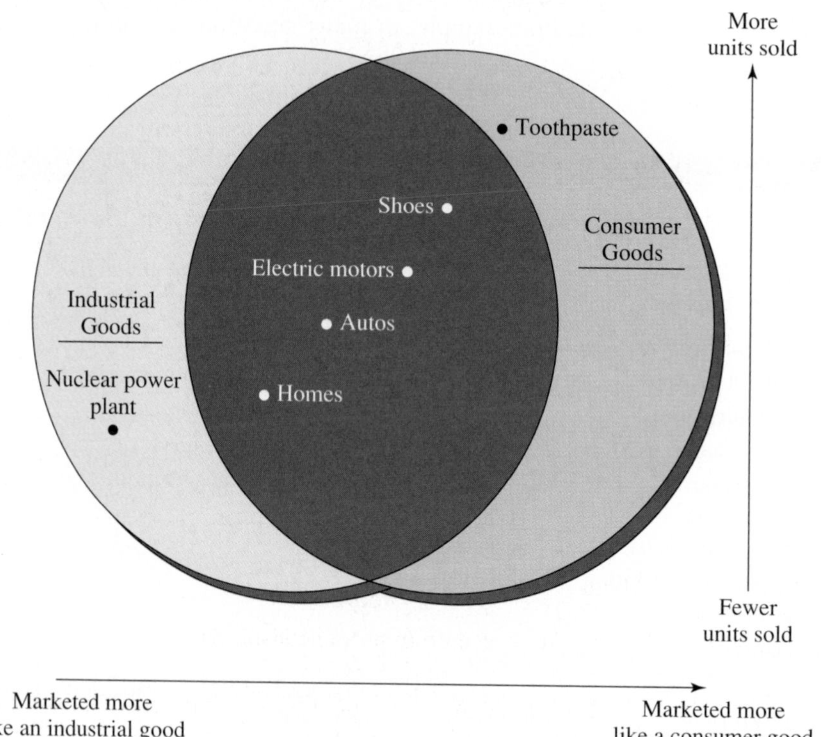

products, such as selling houses and autos to consumers and selling electrical motors to a corporation. Differences are found only at the extremes. The marketing mix for a consumer product, such as toothpaste, will not precisely find an industrial counterpart.

Similarly, the marketing mix for selling an industrial product, such as a nuclear power plant, will not have a consumer counterpart. All in all, however, more similarities than differences exist between consumer and industrial marketing.

In summary, the difference between industrial and consumer purchasing is a matter of degree: it is not a dichotomy. Both involve an exchange process, and the same sociological, economic, anthropological, and psychological principles that you will study here work in both environments. This statement should not be surprising when you recognize that in both instances an exchange process takes place in which people make decisions.

ETHICAL ISSUES IN CONSUMER EXCHANGE RELATIONS

Within relational exchanges, the trust between the buyer and seller is an extremely important element. One factor that influences the bonds of trust is the ethical conduct of the buyer and seller. The issue of ethics has taken on increased prominence in the business and academic communities. The American Association for Colleges and Schools of Business (AACSB) has begun to demand that business colleges include material on ethics in the courses taught. The need for instruction in ethics was vividly demonstrated on October 19, 1987—Black Tuesday. When the stock market plunged further in a single day than ever before, thousands of small investors (i.e., the consumers of financial services) were financially ruined when they could not reach their brokers to sell their stock investments. It seems that many brokers simply turned off their phones when the news became too depressing.

The need for the study of ethics in business colleges was also demonstrated in a survey of 15,000 college students from "prestigious" universities. The survey asked students with seven different majors to give anonymous answers to a series of questions about whether or not they cheated in their classes. The results revealed that 76% of business students reported that they cheated. (This percentage was higher than for any of the six other majors.) Engineering students cheated next most frequently. Education students cheated the least. In addition, more business students than any others were found to be "regulars"—that is, they cheated more than four times while in school.[30]

Ethics is the study of the normative judgments concerned with what is morally right and wrong, good and bad. Judgments of what is morally right or wrong are based upon standards that

1. Deal with serious human injuries and benefits
2. May or may not be laid down by authoritative bodies
3. Override self-interest
4. Are based on impartial considerations

Ethical judgments frequently involve a conflict between one's own self-interest and a standard of conduct. Thus to act ethically sometimes requires people to do things that are against their self-interest. Thus, in the "Crash of '87" example, ethical stockbrokers should have returned calls to clients even though it might have been unpleasant. When making a decision that may have ethical implications, the person must use impartial considerations in reaching the decision. The decision should be based upon moral guidelines and not upon who is helped or hurt by the outcome of the action.

Business managers are likely to face at least one major ethical dilemma during their careers. A classic example occurred in 1992, when Dow-Corning, Inc., had to decide how to handle the negative publicity concerning leaking silicon breast implants. The company had previously acted unethically (and possibly illegally) by hiding information that the artificial breast implants leaked more frequently than expected. In 1992 the company responded by firing its CEO and replacing him with an individual who took a much more pro-consumer stance. The Dow-Corning case illustrates a definition of an **ethical dilemma**: "A decision that involves the trade-off between lowering one's personal values in exchange for increased organizational or personal profits."[31]

A major function of a society's moral standards is the prescription of specific ways in which its members are to cooperate with each other and deal fairly with each other. By following ethical principles, individuals may avoid social conflicts. The principles provide publicly acceptable justification for actions and policies. Another way of saying this is that ethics form an important means for prescribing how the exchange process should take place. Thus, whenever consumers engage in exchange relationships, ethical principles may come into play.

As a general statement, the following components occur in an **ethical exchange**:

1. Both parties will know the full nature of the agreement that they are entering.
2. Neither party to the exchange will intentionally misrepresent or omit relevant information to the other.
3. Neither party to the exchange will unduly influence the other.[32]

Figure 2-8 presents an exchange matrix that examines how marketing resources flow in exchange situations. One can identify the source of the resource (either the business firm or the consumer) and the recipient of the resource (either the business firm or the consumer). When one business extends resources to another business, it is engaging in **industrial marketing**. When a business sends resources to consumers, it is engaging in **consumer marketing**. In these two cases ethical issues should influence the firm's actions. In particular, the firm must fulfill commitments made

Information Sender	Information Receiver: Business	Information Receiver: Consumer
Business	Industrial marketing	Consumer marketing
Consumer	Consumer-induced contact	Personal marketing

Figure 2-8

Consumer exchange matrix. (*Note*: Ethical principles should govern the exchange process in each cell of the matrix.)

concerning its inputs to the exchange. Thus service, product, and informational inputs must be performed as promised or implied.

The exchange matrix also illustrates the idea that consumer ethical dilemmas may occur.[33] An ethical dilemma happens when consumers feel a conflict between doing what is in their interest and doing what is ethically correct. When a consumer inputs resources to a business, a consumer-induced contact occurs. Similarly, when a consumer makes an exchange with another consumer, personal marketing is being undertaken. (An example of personal marketing would be selling a used car to another consumer.) In each instance, consumers may experience ethical conflicts.

Most discussions of ethics deal with industrial or consumer marketing. Such discussions typically focus on the firm's actions in such areas as misleading advertising, selling products that fail to comply with the claims made about them, producing unsafe products, exerting undue influence (e.g., bribery), and failing to disclose important relevant information (e.g., not telling a customer that a product has been used previously). In addition, consumers also have a responsibility to act ethically in their exchanges with firms and other consumers. Thus, if an acquaintance wishes to purchase your old car or lawn mower, you have an ethical duty to warn the person of safety problems, to avoid coercing the person to make the purchase, and to avoid misleading the person in terms of how it will perform.

Consumers should also act ethically in their dealings with business firms. For example, when consumers return products to a firm, they have an ethical duty to return the product in satisfactory condition. They also have a duty not to mislead the firm as to the reasons for the return. For example, is it ethical to purchase a dress, wear it on a single, special occasion, and then return it, claiming that it simply did not fit properly?

Another way in which consumers may act unethically in their dealings with firms is through **free riding**. Free riding occurs when a consumer or organization obtains a resource, such as information, from another entity and then fails to pay back resources in return. For example, consumers will frequently go to full-service retailers as part of the search process to obtain product information and to identify satisfactory alternatives. If the consumer obtains product information from sales personnel and then uses the information to make a purchase from a low-cost discount store (that does not offer personal service), the person is guilty of free riding. The consumer is acting unethically in such an instance because he or she had no intention of making a purchase and did not convey this information to the retailer. Real harm is done to the retailer because the consumer received informational and service resources while having no intention of buying.

A reciprocity exists between consumers and businesses. When sufficient numbers of consumers act unethically, businesses will have to respond in some manner. If sufficient numbers of consumers engage in free riding, real harm results because full-service retail stores will either close their doors or become discount stores. Consumers will then lose an important source of marketplace information. Similarly, if too many consumers abuse return privileges, companies will be forced to install "no-return" policies.

In sum, ethical behavior is a two-way street. Both consumers and firms have a right to expect the other to act ethically. Researchers have identified four rules that managers should follow to ensure that their decisions are ethical.[34] Although originally designed to apply to managers, these four rules for ethical decision making

HIGHLIGHT 2-1

Ethics in Higher Education

Students and faculty at colleges and universities are increasingly having to face tricky ethical issues, caused in part by the corporate invasion of college campuses. For example, corporate raider Asher Edelman taught a finance class at Columbia University. In the class he offered $100,000 to any student who provided information leading to the successful takeover of a firm. Columbia University, where he taught his class, rescinded the offer and stated that cash incentives are inappropriate in a learning environment. Is offering large cash incentives to students in a university ethical?

Increasingly, universities are turning to corporations for financial support and teaching expertise. Many question, however, the prudence of the business–academic linkage. One activist stated, "There's an increasing school of thought that universities should serve the corporation. If the ethics of the corporation become the ethics of the universities, then we're really in trouble." Is this indictment warranted?

One problem is that professors and students are ill prepared to deal with the ethical conflicts that may arise. One recent incident illustrates such conflicts. According to a recent *Wall Street Journal* article, in a graduate-level marketing class at an eastern university students were required to go into the field and work for corporate clients to apply the concepts learned in class. Two groups of students worked for two Caterpillar heavy-equipment dealerships with whom the instructor had a consulting contract. The students developed competitive analyses for the large dealerships. They were given names of key competitors and questions to ask.

The students then went to the competitors and began asking questions. They were able to obtain information on inventory levels, sales volume, advertising expenditures, and new product introductions. The problem, according to the *Wall Street Journal* article, was that they forgot to tell the companies they were working for a competitor. As one marketing manager said, "I thought I was doing them a favor." Another of the interviewees said, "People let their guard down when dealing with students, making them perfect disguises for information-hungry clients. That's not ethical in my mind."

What did the professor have to say about the incident? Two rules were given to the students to guide their conduct—"no invading privacy and no lying." Because the companies never asked whether the students were working for a competitor, the professor felt that none of the students lied. The students had concerns, however. As one said, "We weren't worried about ethical issues. We were worried about getting through the course."

What did the students learn from the experience? As stated by one student, "You learn that the boss has the final say in everything, that you get things done or forget it." Perhaps this attitude is what scares those who criticize industry–academia linkages. As one director of the American Assembly of Collegiate Schools of Business said, university–business programs "walk a lot thinner line regarding ethics than they used to." Industry–academia linkages are crucial for universities. The financial resources of companies and the practical experience of executives are invaluable to educational institutions. However, the ethical problems that arise can be difficult, and must be analyzed carefully.

Based on an article by Clare Ansberry, "For These M.B.A.s, Class Became Exercise in Corporate Espionage," *The Wall Street Journal*, March 22, 1988, p. 33.

apply to consumers as well and have been slightly rewritten to link them to managerial and consumer decision making. The rules are

1. *The golden rule*—Act in a way that you would expect others to act toward you.
2. *The professional ethic*—Take only actions that would be viewed as proper by an objective panel of your business managers and consumers.
3. *Kant's categorical imperative*—Act in a way such that the action taken under the circumstances could be a universal law of behavior for everyone facing those same circumstances.
4. *The TV test*—Always ask, "Would I feel comfortable explaining this action on TV to the general public?"

Highlight 2-1 discusses the ethical behavior of consumers of higher education (i.e., university students).

A MANAGERIAL APPLICATIONS EXAMPLE

Made in Korea, the Hyundai Excel leaped to automotive prominence in 1986 when it set record first-year sales by an import car company. Two years later the company sold 264,282 units in the United States. With prices starting at an unbelievable $4,995, the car's future seemed assured. Then, the bottom fell out, and sales plummeted.

As suggested by Peter Drucker, there was nothing wrong with the basic Excel concept.[35] Just as the Japanese had attacked the undefended low end of the market in the 1970s, the Koreans were striking at the same market position in the late 1980s. The Japanese, however, had learned their lessons well from Henry Ford. Eighty years ago he reputedly said, "We can sell the Model T at such a low price only because it earns such a nice profit." Although pricing their cars below what American companies charged, the Japanese still maintained high profit margins.

In contrast, the Koreans failed to heed Henry Ford's message. They priced the Excel at such a low level that the company had insufficient profits. Although the basic car was adequate in the short term, too little money was left to build a dealer network that could provide outstanding service to customers. The promotion of the brand lagged the competition. Not enough funds were left to improve the car itself and develop new models. Worst of all, by 1990 the company ranked last in consumer surveys on quality.[36] Companies have extreme difficulty overcoming reputations of selling poor-quality products. As a result of all these factors, sales fell by over 40% in 1990, and Hyundai was struggling for existence in the hotly contested American automobile industry.

Problem Identification

The problem faced by Hyundai went beyond the single issue of how to price the Excel. The company had to develop an overall strategy that (1) identified an appropriate market position for its brands and (2) targeted segments of consumers with sufficient size and buying power for the company to make a profit. It then had to create a marketing mix that would accomplish its positioning and segmentation goals.

The Consumer Behavior Analysis

Viewing the Hyundai Excel situation from an exchange perspective offers a number of insights into the problem. The consumer analysis begins by taking each of the key terms in the chapter and asking whether they have relevance to the case. The concept of exchange appropriately begins the list of key terms. The idea of exchange focuses attention on the concept that both parties must profit from their interchange, particularly if it is to become relational and last over time. By pricing the Excel so low, Hyundai jeopardized its long-term survival.

The next key term is the types of resources exchanged. Here the analyst examines what resources consumers and auto manufacturers exchange when an automobile is purchased. Certainly, the manufacturer receives money from consumers. The resources obtained by consumers from firms are more diverse, however. Consumers receive a good in the form of a car, but they also receive a variety of services, information, status, and feelings. Although the good offered by Hyundai (i.e., the Excel in this instance) had a variety of positive qualities, the other types of resources obtained by consumers had problems. In part because of a lack of promotion and in part because of a poor dealer network, the brand lacked status—even within its entry-level market niche. Further, the service received from the dealers was poor. In general, interactions with sales and service personnel created negative, rather than positive, feelings.

Applying the basic exchange equation to the situation, consumers were not profiting from their relationship with Hyundai. Although their monetary costs were low, the lack of adequate product, informational, status, service, and feeling resources caused the equation to result in a loss rather than a profit. Interestingly, when applied to Hyundai, the exchange equation also resulted in a loss. Because of their pricing strategy, Hyundai failed to profit from its exchange with consumers.

Another key term having particular relevance to the Hyundai case is the comparison level for alternatives. This concept suggests that marketers must also examine competitive offerings. If competitors offer a superior set of resources, consumers will buy from them. The Excel had the unenviable task of competing against such cars as the Honda Civic, Nissan Sentra, and the Toyota Tercel. Although not priced as low as the Excel, these entry-level vehicles offered higher status, service, and feelings than the Excel.

The final key term applicable to the Hyundai case is relational exchange. When marketplace interactions are viewed with the expectation that they will last through time, it increases the recognition that what happens after the sale is extremely important. It causes the marketer to analyze carefully the feelings created during the sale as well as when the customer returns to have the vehicle serviced. By failing to attend to such issues, Hyundai doomed itself in the marketplace.

The Managerial Analysis

The final step in the analysis is to identify the managerial implications of the consumer behavior concepts. Table 2-7 summarizes the results. Four consumer concepts are identified as applicable: exchange resources, the exchange equation, comparison level for alternatives, and relational exchange.

TABLE 2-7

Managerial Applications Analysis of Hyundai Excel Case

Consumer Concepts	*Managerial Applications*
1. Exchange resources	*Market research*—Identify the resources (e.g., reliability, status, good service, and positive feelings) that consumers seek in the exchange and their relative importance.
	Segmentation—Identify segments of customers that have similar resource desires that can be fulfilled by company.
	Positioning—Develop strategy that positions car against competitors so that it provides the set of resources desired by the targeted segment of consumers.
	Marketing mix—Develop product and price, promote, and distribute it in a manner that fulfills the positioning strategy.
2. Exchange equation	*Marketing mix*—Price the vehicle so that the company earns sufficient profit to stay in business while at the same time competing effectively against the competition.
3. CL_{alt}	*Environmental analysis*—Analyze product offerings of competitors and the resources offered to consumers.
	Marketing mix—Employ the information gained from the environmental analysis to develop and price the product. In addition, use the information to develop customer service programs through the distribution system.
4. Relational exchange	*Market research*—Employ research to assess customer satisfaction (i.e., customer feelings) regarding the outcomes received. Identify any problems extant in the marketing of the product.
	Marketing mix—Use the marketing mix to "fix" the problems identified. An example would be correcting the problems extant in the service departments at Hyundai dealerships.

The concept of exchange resources has particular implications for market research, segmentation, positioning, and marketing mix. The recognition that Hyundai is in an exchange relationship (in which both parties must profit) forces the firm to focus on learning what consumers seek in an automobile. Market research is used to obtain information on the characteristics desired in the vehicle itself. In addition, market research gauges the importance of other resources exchanged, such as feelings, service, status, and information. Based upon the results of market research, managers identify specific segments of consumers that will become the target market for the firm. A positioning strategy for the brand is then developed that will appeal to the target market. Finally, a marketing mix is created offering the resources desired by consumers.

The basic exchange equation focuses attention on the concept that both sides must profit from the interaction. One implication is that Hyundai must price the Excel at levels high enough for the company to profit and for the firm to offer the other resources demanded by consumers, such as good service and good feelings.

The concept of the comparison level for alternatives has relevance for environmental analysis and the marketing mix. Researchers must carefully analyze the market offerings of competitors who operate within the marketing environment.

What are the resources offered by competing autos, and how does the Excel compare? This information is then used to guide the development of the marketing mix. For example, Toyota follows up every sale with consumer contacts to check for satisfaction with the product and the service. To be successful, Hyundai had to consider carefully whether it should respond to this marketing action by a formidable competitor.

Relational exchange has implications for market research and the marketing mix. To build loyal customers who will continue to purchase its products, the firm must perform market research to determine their satisfaction with the mix of resources offered by the firm. Problems identified through the market research should then be corrected in the marketing mix of the firm. For example, suppose that market research revealed that customers hated dealing with the service department when the car was brought back for maintenance. Action steps should then be taken to improve the service offered and the feelings of the customers.

SUMMARY

The chapter discussed the exchange processes that take place between consumers and marketers. Exchange involves a transfer of something tangible or intangible, actual or symbolic, between two or more social actors. The concept of exchange is fundamental to consumer behavior because to obtain a good, service, or idea, some type of transaction must occur. The study of exchange is also basic to understanding the field of marketing, because marketing is defined in terms of exchange. An important issue concerns the question of what is exchanged. Researchers have proposed that people exchange resources from six categories—status, information, money, goods, feelings, and services.

Four dimensions of exchange relations were identified in the chapter: restricted versus complex exchanges, internal versus external exchanges, formal versus informal exchanges, and relational versus discrete exchanges. The study of relational exchange is extremely important for marketers. In relational exchanges the transaction is viewed in terms of its history and anticipated future. Relational exchanges frequently take place in the industrial sector, where different companies produce major components of a large industrial item, such as an airplane. However, relational exchanges also occur between consumers and firms. Those who market nonprofit organizations, such as charities and universities, frequently attempt to develop relational exchanges. Indeed, one marketing goal of many firms is to build strong relationships with consumers that result in high levels of brand loyalty.

Two models of exchange were identified in the chapter. Homans viewed exchange from the perspective of operant conditioning and economics and proposed that people seek to profit from an exchange. Further, profit is determined by subtracting the costs of the exchange from the rewards.

A second model of exchange is equity theory, which proposes that people will analyze the ratio of their outcomes and inputs to the ratio of the outcomes and inputs of the partner to the exchange. If the ratio of outcomes and inputs is unequal, the individual will be dissatisfied with the exchange. Researchers have found that when consumers examine their own equity relationship with a retailer, they also analyze the inputs and outcomes of other consumers with the retailer to assess the extent of their satisfaction with the exchange. Other researchers have found that consumers' perception of fairness in an exchange is one sided and is likely to be viewed as inequitable by a salesperson.

Likewise important in the study of exchange is the comparison level for outcomes. This concept suggests that people develop a minimum level of positive outcomes (profits) that are expected from an exchange. If the minimum level is not attained, they will not be happy in the exchange relationship. A second concept, the comparison level for alternatives, is more predictive of whether they will leave an unsatisfactory exchange. The comparison level for alternatives is the lowest level of outcomes a member will accept in light of available alternative opportunities. It can be either higher or lower than the comparison level. If the comparison level for alternatives is higher than the consumer's current state, he or she will leave the exchange and move to the comparison other.

A long-standing issue in consumer behavior concerns whether the concepts and theories apply to industrial buying as well as to consumer buying. One can identify instances in which the buying process within an industrial setting differs from that found in a consumer setting. However, when the problem is analyzed, more differences are found to exist within industrial or consumer buying than between industrial and consumer buying. As a general statement, the same principles apply to both consumer and industrial marketing, although some concepts may be emphasized more in one area than another.

An emerging area of study in consumer behavior is ethics—the study of the normative judgments concerned with what is morally right and wrong, good and bad. Such judgments deal with standards that pertain to serious human injuries and benefits, that may or may not be laid down by authority, that override self-interest, and that are based on impartial considerations. In consumer behavior, ethical issues pertain to actions engaged in by both businesses and consumers. Thus consumers can act unethically, just as businesses can.

KEY TERMS

basic exchange equation
comparison level for alternatives
comparison level for outcomes
consumer marketing
discrete versus relational exchange
equity theory
ethical dilemma
ethical exchange characteristics
ethics
exchange
feelings
formal versus informal exchange
free riding
goods
industrial marketing
information
internal versus external exchange
market embeddedness
money
relational exchange
relationship quality
resources
services
simple versus complex exchange
status
types of resources

REVIEW QUESTIONS

1. Why is the concept of exchange fundamental to the understanding of the field of marketing?
2. What is meant by distributive justice?
3. What is the basic exchange equation, as developed by Homans?
4. Identify the basic prerequisites for exchange.

5. Identify the six categories of resources that are exchanged.
6. What does equity theory say about the exchange process?
7. What is meant by relational exchange? Identify the characteristics of relational exchanges.
8. What are four areas in which industrial and consumer markets may differ? Give specific examples of each of these areas.
9. What is meant by the statement that more differences exist within industrial or consumer markets than between industrial and consumer markets?
10. What is the definition of ethics?
11. What are the standards that should be used to judge whether an action is ethical?
12. Draw the consumer ethics matrix. Give an example of an ethical problem in each cell of the matrix.

DISCUSSION QUESTIONS

1. Consider the exchange relationship that you have with your parents. Identify the resources that are exchanged in the relationship. To what extent do you and your parents profit from the exchange?
2. Identify a relational exchange that you have with a retailer or service provider. What are the characteristics of the exchange that allow it to be considered relational?
3. Computers are sold to both businesses and consumers. Go to a local computer store and discuss with the salespeople the differences in how they market their product to businesses as compared to consumers. To what extent do you agree with the statement that the same behavioral principles apply to the marketing of industrial and consumer products?
4. In one of your local newspapers, there is a personal section in which individuals advertise to meet those of the opposite sex. Collect five to ten of these personals and analyze each for the resources offered and received. To what extent do your results match those found in the dating exchange study discussed in the textbook?
5. Students may be thought of as being in an exchange relationship with a university. As a consumer of university life, first discuss the resources exchanged with the university. Then analyze your relationship with the university from an equity theory perspective.
6. Considering the exchange relationship between students and a university, identify instances where ethical problems arise. Identify the moral standards that may be used in judging the ethical nature of these instances. What happened in each case?
7. Consider Highlight 2-1, which discussed ethical problems that can occur when business and academia mix. To what extent was ethical conduct breached by the professor and by the students in the marketing class?
8. Consider the problem of students who cannot take pets with them when they graduate. Is this an ethical dilemma? What are the solutions to the dilemma?

ENDNOTES

1. The JCPenney chapter opening vignette was based upon Karen Blumenthal, "Penney Moves Upscale in Merchandise but Still Has to Convince Public," *The Wall Street Journal*, June 7, 1990, pp. 1–10.
2. Wendy Zellner, "Penney's Rediscovers Its Calling," *Business Week*, April 5, 1993, pp. 51–52.
3. Richard Bagozzi, "Marketing as Exchange," *Journal of Marketing*, Vol. 39 (October 1975), pp. 32–39.

4. Wroe Alderson, *Marketing Behavior and Executive Actions* (Homewood, IL: Richard D. Irwin), 1957.
5. Philip Kotler, *Marketing Essentials* (Englewood Cliffs, NJ: Prentice-Hall, 1984).
6. "AMA Board Approves New Marketing Definition," *Marketing News*, March 1, 1985, p. 1.
7. Philip Kotler, *Marketing Management*, 4th ed. (Englewood Cliffs, NJ: Prentice-Hall, 1980).
8. These ideas are based upon the law of exchange articulated by Wroe Alderson, *Dynamic Marketing Behavior* (Homewood, IL: Richard D. Irwin, 1965).
9. Franklin Houston and Jule Gassenheimer, "Marketing and Exchange," *Journal of Marketing*, Vol. 51 (October 1987), pp. 3–18. This excellent article was the basis for a number of the ideas expressed in the section on exchange processes.
10. Uriel Foa and Edna Foa, *Societal Structures of the Mind* (Springfield, IL: Charles C Thomas, 1974). Please note that Foa and Foa employed love as the sixth resource rather than feelings. The change was made in the text because love is an inappropriate term for the types of feelings engendered in a consumer exchange. In addition, in some contexts negative, rather than positive, feelings may be communicated.
11. Larry Armstrong, "Who's the Most Pampered Motorist of All?" *Business Week*, June 10, 1991, pp. 90–91.
12. Richard P. Bagozzi, "Toward a Formal Theory of Marketing Exchanges," in *Conceptual and Theoretical Developments in Marketing*, O. C. Ferrell, Stephen W. Brown, and Charles W. Lamb, Jr., eds. (Chicago: American Marketing Association, 1979), pp. 32–39.
13. Robert F. Lusch, Stephen W. Brown, and Gary J. Brunswick, "A General Framework for Explaining Internal vs. External Exchange," *Journal of the Academy of Marketing Science*, Vol. 20 (1992), pp. 119–134.
14. Elizabeth C. Hirschman, "People as Products: Analysis of a Complex Marketing Exchange," *Journal of Marketing*, Vol. 51 (January 1987), pp. 98–108.
15. F. Robert Dwyer, Paul Schurr, and Sejo Oh, "Developing Buyer-Seller Relationships," *Journal of Marketing*, Vol. 51 (April 1987), pp. 11–27.
16. Theodore Leavitt, *The Marketing Imagination* (New York: The Free Press, 1983), p. 111.
17. "What Customers Really Want," *Fortune*, June 4, 1990, pp. 58–68.
18. Andrew Evan Serwer, "The Wacky Way the Wealthy Invest—And How to Do It Right," *Fortune*, July 1, 1991, pp. 21–22.
19. Jonathan K. Frenzen and Harry L. Davis, "Purchasing Behavior in Embedded Markets," *Journal of Consumer Research*, Vol. 17 (June 1990), pp. 1–12.
20. Lawrence Crosby, Kenneth Evans, and Deborah Cowles, "Relationship Quality in Services Selling: An Interpersonal Influence Perspective," *Journal of Marketing*, Vol. 54 (July 1990), pp. 68–81.
21. George Homans, *Social Behavior: Its Elementary Forms* (New York: Harcourt, Brace & World, 1961), p. 235. Also, see Marvin Shaw and Philip Costanzo, *Theories of Social Psychology* (New York: McGraw-Hill, 1970). Readers should note that exchange theory has been criticized as focusing too much on the selfish, hedonic aspects of human interactions. See Bergt Abrahamson, "Homans on Exchange: Hedonism Revisited," *American Journal of Sociology*, Vol. 76 (1970), pp. 273–285.
22. J. S. Adams, "Toward an Understanding of Inequity," *Journal of Abnormal and Social Psychology*, Vol. 67 (1963), pp. 422–436.
23. The equity ratio has been criticized and is given primarily for pedagogical purposes. See John C. Alessio, "Another Folly for Equity Theory," *Social Psychological Quarterly*, Vol. 43 (September 1980), pp. 336–340.
24. J. C. Mowen and Stephen Grove, "Search Behavior, Price Paid, and the Comparison Other: An Equity Theory Analysis of Post-Purchase Satisfaction," in *International Fare in Consumer Satisfaction and Complaint Behavior*, Ralph Day and H. Keith Hunt, eds. (Bloomington: Indiana University School of Business, 1983), pp. 57–63. For other studies

of equity in consumer behavior, see J. W. Huppertz, S. J. Arenson, and R. H. Evans, "An Application of Equity Theory to Buyer-Seller Exchange Situations," *Journal of Marketing Research*, Vol. 15 (May 1978), pp. 250–260. Also, see R. P. Fisk and C. E. Young, "Disconfirmation of Equity Expectation: Effects on Consumer Satisfaction with Services," in *Advances in Consumer Research*, Vol. XII, E. C. Hirschman and M. B. Holbrook, eds. (Ann Arbor, MI: Association for Consumer Research, 1985), pp. 340–345.

25. Richard Oliver and John Swan, "Consumer Perceptions of Interpersonal Equity and Satisfaction in Transactions: A Field Survey Approach," *Journal of Marketing*, Vol. 53 (April 1989), pp. 21–35.

26. J. W. Thibaut and H. H. Kelley, *The Social Psychology of Groups* (New York: John Wiley, 1959).

27. Ibid.

28. For another perspective on the study of exchange process, see Russell Belk, John Sherry, Jr., and Melanie Wallendorf, "A Naturalistic Inquiry into Buyer and Seller Behavior at a Swap Meet," *Journal of Consumer Research*, Vol. 15 (March 1988), pp. 449–470.

29. For an excellent discussion of the industrial–consumer dichotomy, see Edward J. Fern and James R. Brown, "The Industrial/Consumer Marketing Dichotomy: A Case of Insufficient Evidence," *Journal of Marketing*, Vol. 48 (Spring 1985), pp. 68–77.

30. Rick Tetzeli, "Business Students Cheat Most," *Fortune*, July 1, 1991, pp. 14–15.

31. Gene R. Laczniak and Patrick E. Murphy, "Fostering Ethical Marketing Decisions," *Journal of Business Ethics*, Vol. 10 (1991), pp. 259–271.

32. Manuel Velasquez, *Business Ethics: Concepts and Cases* (Englewood Cliffs, NJ: Prentice-Hall, 1982).

33. Lawrence Marks and Michael Mayo, "Modeling Consumer Ethical Dilemmas: A Preliminary Investigation," *AMA Educator's Conference Proceedings* (William Bearden et al., eds.), 1990, p. 121.

34. Laczniak and Murphy, "Fostering Ethical Marketing Decisions."

35. Peter F. Drucker, "Marketing 101 for a Fast-Changing Decade," *The Wall Street Journal*, November 20, 1990, p. A20.

36. Laxmi Nakarmi and Larry Armstrong, "Honk If You'd Buy a Hyundai," *Business Week*, September 10, 1991, p. 52.

Wal-Mart, Small Merchants, Customers, and Communities: A Set of Complicated Exchange Relations

In 1991 Wal-Mart Corporation became the largest retailer in the United States. While developing a strategy based upon building discount stores in small communities, the company grew rapidly in the 1970s and 1980s. Using sophisticated buying and distribution techniques, the company has been able to price its vast selection of merchandise lower than its competitors. In addition, every shopper who enters one of its stores is greeted personally by an employee. Wal-Mart even allows customers to return merchandise for full refunds with no explanations. (Prior to being prosecuted, one woman hunted through trash dumps for small appliances that she would clean up and return for cash.)

While Wal-Mart prospered, however, other retailers suffered. Each time the company opened a new store, competitors would liken it to a "merchant of death." *The Wall Street Journal* described what happened in Anamosa, Iowa (population 3,700), when Wal-Mart built its new store in a cornfield. Stores that failed shortly after Wal-Mart opened included two men's clothing shops, a shoe store, a children's clothing store, a drugstore, a hardware store, and a dime store. Even the local JCPenney was closed after a horrible Christmas in which sales dropped 50%.

Recently, some small retailers have awakened to the Wal-Mart challenge. For example, in Viroqua, Wisconsin, the merchants developed a plan for revitalizing the downtown area threatened by the new Wal-Mart being built. Led by the owner of the local agribusiness retailer, groups visited communities with Wal-Marts to gather intelligence on how to cope. They checked prices, product assortments, and talked to competitors to learn their tactics. As a result of investigations, a plan was created that included obtaining a grant from a nonprofit historic preservation organization to help preserve the Main Street in the community.

Individual retailers reshaped their marketing strategy. The agribusiness owner shrank his inventory of toys and housewares and eliminated his health and beauty aid departments. He focused his attention on stocking better brands of tools, clothing, and giftwares. In addition, he stocked a broader range of options than did Wal-Mart. He expanded his repair and parts-ordering business. In addition, he increased his hours of operation and liberalized his return policies. Most important, however, he began to stress service. Customers were greeted by their name. Personal attention was given to each shopper. As a result of the shift in strategy, annual sales of the agribusiness center increased from $6.8 to $8 million while maintaining profit levels.

As sophisticated marketers, Wal-Mart's managers recognize that merchants, city councils, and chambers of commerce in small towns fear the giant corporation. It sends materials to the towns it is about to enter that describe all the positive effects of having a new Wal-Mart store. In particular, it obtained testimonials from 300 chambers of commerce describing some of these positive effects. For example, the firm argues that a new Wal-Mart store creates a retail hub around it because it attracts new businesses from outside the community. In addition, it "plugs" the retail leakage that occurs when shoppers go to larger communities to shop. The manager of the Wal-Mart store in Viroqua, Wisconsin, worked hard to maintain good relations in the community. He avoided directly comparing his prices with those charged by local merchants.

The store has supported local business development and given small grants to the local industrial development board. The manager even suggested the slogan for the 1990 Christmas season—"Feel the Warmth of Viroqua."

QUESTIONS

1. Define the problem faced by small retailers when Wal-Mart builds a new store. Define the problem faced by Wal-Mart when it enters a small community.
2. What exchange concepts apply to the problem faced by small retailers? What exchange concepts apply to the problem faced by Wal-Mart? (Here focus on the resources being exchanged and on the importance of relationships. Make sure that you explain how the concepts apply to the problems.)
3. What managerial strategies did the owner of the agribusiness firm develop to counter the Wal-Mart threat? Can you identify additional options? What managerial strategy did Wal-Mart employ to solve its problem?
4. In analyzing the case, students may wish to visit local retailers in their area to analyze how exchange concepts have relevance to the marketing battles that take place between discount stores and the smaller specialty shops.

The case is based in part upon an article by Barbara Marsh, "Merchants Mobilize to Battle Wal-Mart in a Small Community," *The Wall Street Journal*, June 5, 1991, pp. 1–4.

Part 2

INDIVIDUAL CONSUMER PROCESSES

Chapter 3

Information Processing I: Involvement and Perception

CONSUMER VIGNETTE

Ford Successfully Adapts Its Customers

In the early 1980s Ford Motor Company designers had a terrific idea: build a highly aerodynamic car for the mass market. A car designed to slip through the air with minimal drag would have the utilitarian outcome of improving gas mileage. In addition, the totally new design could attract an untouched segment of customers and improve the company's competitive position.

By 1985 the designs of the Ford Taurus and Mercury Sable were complete, and the company began gearing up for production. However, the marketing group was extremely concerned that the designs would be too radical for the targeted customers. The Sable and Taurus were the "bread and butter" models of the firm and were targeted to middle-class Americans. The teardrop-shaped vehicles were like no others produced in the United States. Would their target market buy something so revolutionary?

The company decided to violate established automotive principles to reduce the problem of visual shock when the cars were launched. Rather than keeping the design secret from the press and the public, the company actively sought to publicize what the new vehicles would look like. Thus, in the spring of 1985, six months prior to the models' launch, photos of the new 1986 Sable and Taurus were released to the press, and auto magazines splashed them all over their front covers. On its cover, *Car and Driver* had to use a photograph of a full-scale fiberglass mock-up of a Sable because the car was not yet in production.

Interestingly, the automotive press knew exactly what Ford was doing and supported the company. As stated in the *Car and Driver* article, "The Ford Motor Company wants the masses to see its provocative new cars now, so that the shock will have worn off by the time they go on sale in the fall." Noting the dramatic change in the design of the vehicles, the magazine added—no wonder Ford is "sweating bullets."[1]

The marketing strategy worked, and the car lines were a massive success. By 1988 Ford had become the most profitable auto company in history. By 1992 the Taurus was the top-selling car in the United States. The success resulted in part from the company recognizing several key principles of consumer information processing—the topic of Chapters 3 and 4.

INTRODUCTION

One of the most frequently reported problems encountered by marketers is getting prospects to receive, comprehend, and remember information about their product or service. The problem is particularly acute for advertisers. Millions of dollars can be spent developing and delivering a national campaign. If consumers fail to be exposed to the information, fail to attend to it, fail to comprehend it, or fail to remember it, the investment will be wasted. The definition of information processing is based upon these ideas. **Consumer information processing** is defined as the process through which consumers are exposed to information, attend to it, comprehend it, place it in memory, and retrieve it for later use.

The introductory vignette to this chapter illustrates a variety of concepts related to the topic of information processing. Two particularly important ideas depicted are those of the orientation reflex and adaptation. When people are first exposed to a stimulus, such as a photo of a new automobile, they will have some initial reaction to it. If the stimulus is highly novel and unexpected, they will reflexively orient to it and become activated in a type of "flight-or-fight" reaction. If the stimulus is too novel, its very "newness" may cause a negative reaction. However, if exposed to the stimulus a number of times (and if nothing negative occurs), the feelings generated will tend to become more positive. The process is called **adaptation**.[2]

Ford Motor Company's strategy of going against tradition and revealing the car prior to its introduction helped consumers adapt to the novel shape of the Taurus. This element of the company's promotional strategy was one of the reasons for the Taurus's phenomenal success. Figure 3-1 shows the Taurus; now that it has been out for a number of years, it looks quite normal because we have adapted to it.

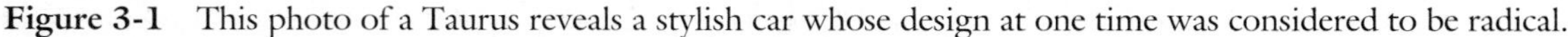

Figure 3-1 This photo of a Taurus reveals a stylish car whose design at one time was considered to be radical.

INDIVIDUAL INFLUENCERS AND THE EXCHANGE PROCESS

This chapter on the perception component of consumer information processing begins Part 2 of the text, which analyzes the psychological factors that influence buying units in the acquisition, consumption, and disposition of products, services, and ideas. The processing of information is the initial step that occurs in any consumer action. Therefore, chapters on information processing are natural starting point for the coverage of individual influence processes.

Prior to beginning the discussion of consumer information processing, however, it is important to show how the various individual influence processes fit together. Looking at Figure 3-2, one sees that the individual influencers are directly connected to the buying unit. The diagram reveals an input–output model in which (1) the marketer inputs exchange resources to the buying unit, (2) individuals within the buying unit process information about the resources, and (3) resources are output by individuals within the buying unit to the marketer. The resources input into the exchange by marketers and buying units carry information. Indeed, whenever resources are exchanged, information flows between the participants in the transaction.

Figure 3-2 identifies the individual influencers that will be discussed in Part 2 of the text. Information on the exchange resources offered by the marketer and information from the environment flow into the information processing component of the "individual influencers." Once attention is directed to the information and it is comprehended, a decision-making process takes place. As a result of the decision-making process, the buying unit may or may not enter into an exchange process with the marketer. Both the information processing and the decision-making stages are affected by the other individual influencers of behavioral learning; motivation; personality and psychographics; attitudes, beliefs, and behaviors; and persuasive communications.

In sum, Part 2 of the text discusses each of the individual influence processes. It begins with a two-chapter sequence on information processing. The first chapter in the sequence discusses the topic of perception, whereas the second focuses on memory and cognitive learning. Next, individual chapters cover the subjects of behavioral learning, motivation and affect, and personality and psychographics. Part 2 then investigates how consumer attitudes, beliefs, and behaviors relate to each other. These topics are covered in a three-chapter sequence that identifies how they are formed and how they are changed, and the impact of persuasive communications on them. Part 2 ends with another three-chapter sequence on consumer decision making.

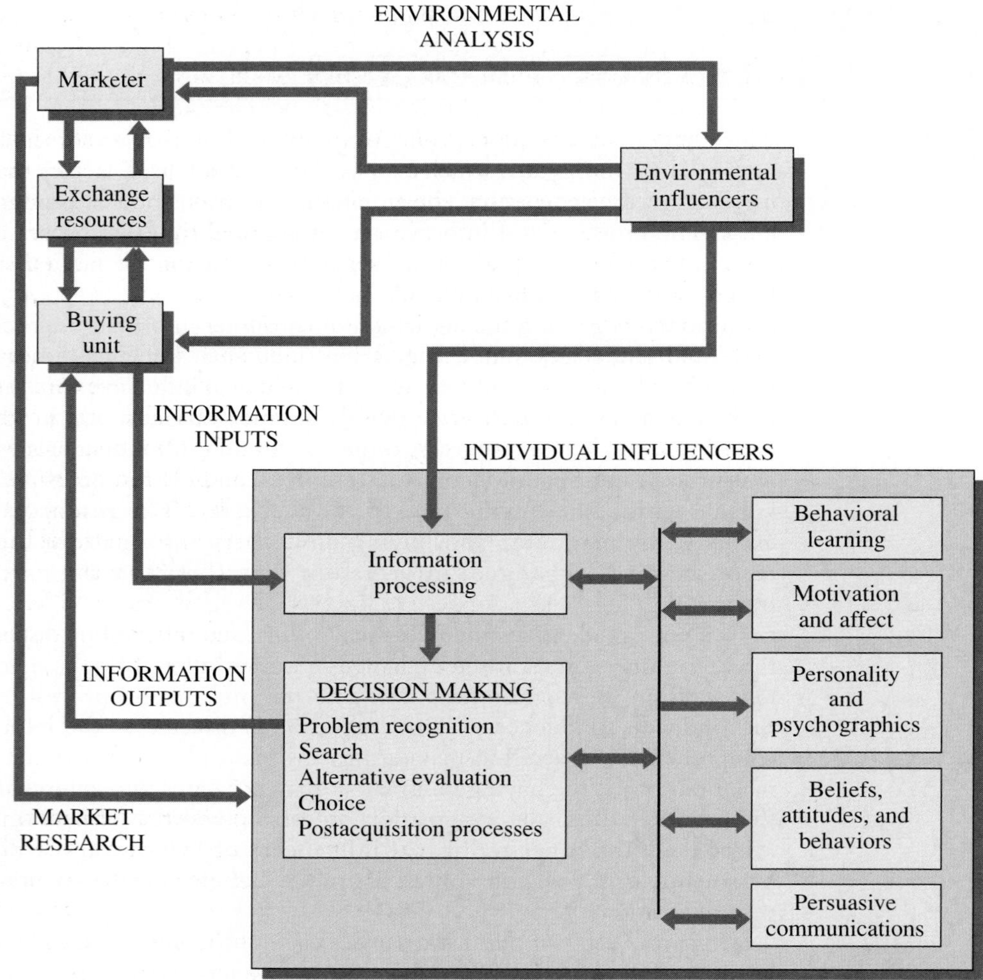

Figure 3-2 Individual influencers and the exchange process.

AN INTRODUCTION TO INFORMATION PROCESSING

What Is Information?

Information may be defined as the content of what is exchanged with the outer world as we adjust to it and make our adjustment felt upon it.[3] By reacting appropriately to information, or by generating information ourselves, we can adapt to and even influence the world around us. For example, the purchase of socially visible products, such as clothing or watches, provides information about a buyer's self-concept to others. Thus a young executive may purchase a highly conservative business suit to communicate meaning about herself (or himself) to business colleagues (perhaps that she is a no-nonsense, aggressive person). Figure 3-3 presents an ad for Rolex watches that communicates meaning by linking the brand to celebrities known for their high levels of competitiveness and achievement.

Consumer information is obtained through the senses of vision, hearing, taste, smell, and touch. Visual images include the various television advertisements we see, the salesclerks we encounter, the words we read, and so forth. Similarly, information in the form of words and various noises is received through our ears. Other types of stimuli are perceived based upon information processed through the sensory organs that register taste, smell, and touch. Through information processing, the raw information is transformed into something meaningful.

An important point is that the raw stimuli and the perception of the stimuli are quite different. The raw stimuli are composed of sound waves, light waves/particles, bits of chemicals, textures, and levels of temperature. The interpretation of and the meanings derived from the stimuli result from information processing. Different people may assign divergent meanings to exactly the same stimulus because its perception is influenced by their expectations and by their general background. One cannot assume that because two people receive exactly the same stimulus, say in a message, they will perceive it and react to it in a similar manner. For example, ask two avid fans of opposing basketball teams how well the game was refereed. Quite likely the two will have very different views of the officiating because of the differences in the way they perceived the game.

What Is Information Processing?

Figure 3-4 presents a simplified diagram of consumer information processing. The diagram shows that in the initial **exposure** stage consumers receive information through their senses. In the **attention** stage consumers allocate processing capacity to a stimulus. In the **comprehension** stage they interpret the information to obtain meaning from it. Comprehension involves the process of making sense of stimuli so that they may be understood. The three stages of exposure, attention, and comprehension form the general area of study called perception. **Perception** is defined as a process through which individuals are exposed to information, attend to the information, and comprehend the information. One goal of this chapter is to reveal the importance of perceptual processes in consumer behavior.

Another extremely important factor that influences information processing is the degree of involvement of the consumer in the task. A consumer's involvement level influences whether he or she moves from the exposure, to the attention, to the comprehension stage of perception. In addition, involvement influences memory functions as well. Because an understanding of involvement is central to the understanding of information processing and perception, the next section discusses this important construct.

As suggested, the final component of the information processing model is the memory function. As can be seen in Figure 3-4, memory plays a role in each of the stages. Memory helps to guide the exposure and attention processes by allowing consumers to anticipate the stimuli with which they may come into contact. It assists in the comprehension process by housing the consumer's knowledge about the environment. This knowledge base may be accessed to assist the person in comprehending

"Some people have a talent for serving or volleying.
I have a talent for competing." *Jim Courier*

Jim Courier has established himself as the most punishing athlete in his sport. Serving or receiving, Courier often seizes control with his first shot, then forces his opponent from corner to corner with his distinctive slap shot ground strokes until the ball stops coming back or he hits an outright winner. "Jim doesn't just beat you," says one top-ranked peer, "he takes you for a ride."

In just two years, Courier won four Grand Slam titles. On his way to his second Australian Open championship, incredibly, he committed only five unforced errors in one match. "He's taking power tennis to a new level," wrote *Tennis Week*.

Yet this fiery young pro retains a gracious perspective on his game. "When someone comes out and plays better than I play, it's not a problem. I'm just determined to improve next time," says Courier.

Whether it's a five setter on the slow red clay in Paris or the blazing hard courts in Melbourne where court temperatures can reach a saunalike 130° F, Courier produces his finest tennis under the most debilitating conditions. For a competitor who seems only to get better as the pressure intensifies, it's not surprising he's chosen a timepiece whose record for performance is unsurpassed. Rolex.

ROLEX

Rolex Oyster Perpetual Thunderbird Datejust Chronometer in stainless steel and 18kt gold with matching Jubilee bracelet. Write for brochure. Rolex Watch U.S.A., Inc., Dept. RLX, Rolex Building, 665 Fifth Avenue, New York, N.Y. 10022-5383. Rolex, ♛, Oyster Perpetual, Thunderbird, Datejust and Jubilee are trademarks.

Figure 3-3 Rolex communicates information concerning the meaning of its watches by linking them to celebrities known for their competitiveness and achievement. (Courtesy of Rolex Watch U.S.A., Inc.)

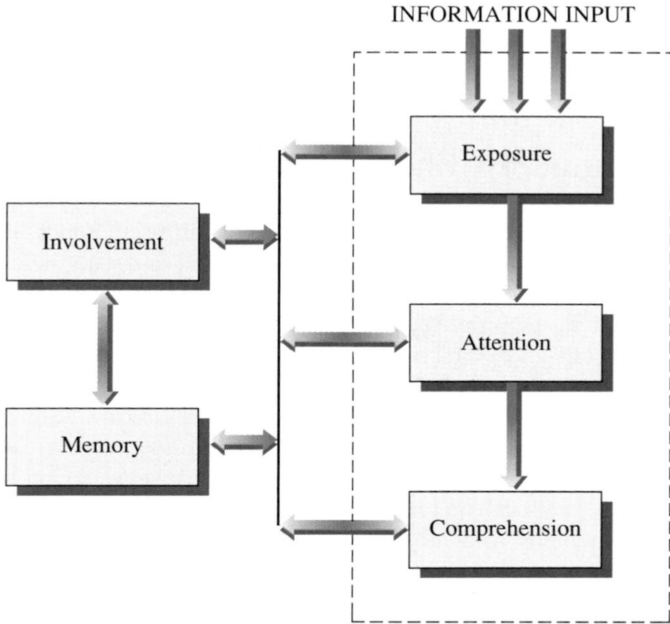

Figure 3-4 An information processing model.

the meaning of a stimulus. Because of the large role of memory in information processing, Chapter 4 deals with it exclusively.

CONSUMER INVOLVEMENT

The level of a consumer's **involvement** in a purchase is influenced by the perceived personal importance and/or interest evoked by a stimulus.[4] Personal importance increases as the expected benefits or losses (i.e., the perceived risk) from a purchase increase. Thus, if the consumer believes that in a particular instance a great deal rides on making a good decision, then his or her involvement level is likely to increase. As involvement increases, consumers have greater motivation to comprehend and elaborate on information salient to the purchase.

Just what are the stimuli that may evoke differential levels of perceived personal importance? Such factors may originate from the product under consideration, from a communication received by the consumer, and from the characteristics of the situation within which the consumer is operating. For example, as the product or service under consideration becomes more expensive, socially visible, and risky to purchase, it is likely that a consumer's involvement in the purchase would increase. Communications can also raise a consumer's involvement by skillfully arousing emotions. The situation can influence involvement by defining the context within which a purchase is made. For example, if the task definition is to buy a gift for an important person, such as a fiancee, the involvement of the purchaser is likely to increase.

In addition, different consumers may react with divergent levels of involvement to various products, situations, and communications. Figure 3-5 diagrams the interrelationships among person, product, communication, and situation.[5]

Types of Consumer Involvement

Researchers have identified several different types of involvement, one of which is the distinction between situational and enduring involvement.[6] **Situational involvement** occurs over a short period of time and is associated with a specific situation, such as a purchase. In contrast, **enduring involvement** represents a longer commitment and concern with a product class. Thus enduring involvement exists when a consumer consistently spends time thinking about the product on a day-to-day basis. Based on the combination of situational and enduring involvement, involvement responses result. **Involvement responses** refer to the level of complexity of information processing and the extent of decision making by a consumer.[7]

What happens when someone with high enduring involvement with a product suddenly finds himself faced with a situation in which a need exists to purchase the product? Recent research indicates that in such circumstances the effects of enduring and situational involvement add together. As a result, a high number of involvement responses occur, because the total level of involvement is equal to the enduring plus situational involvement levels.[8]

In one study situational and enduring involvement were evaluated independently.[9] Two groups of subjects received mail surveys that assessed various behaviors related to automobiles. One group had recently purchased an auto, and the other had not. Respondents were asked how frequently they acquired information about autos from the media and from friends, how frequently they gave information to others about cars, and to what extent they took care of their cars. All respondents completed a scale that measured their enduring involvement with auto purchases on two occasions, before and after purchasing a car. (Table 3-1 gives the enduring involvement scale used in the study.)

The results revealed that enduring involvement was significantly related to various ongoing behaviors, such as reading about cars, talking to friends about cars, and so on. As expected, situational involvement decreased after the purchase of a car. In contrast, no change in enduring involvement occurred for those who had recently

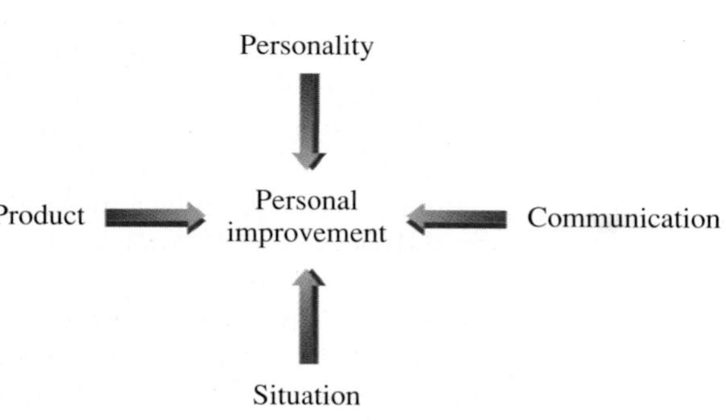

Figure 3-5
The factors influencing consumer purchase involvement. (Based in part on John H. Antil, "Conceptualization and Operationalization of Involvement," in *Advances in Consumer Research*, Vol. 11, Thomas C. Kinnear, ed. (Ann Arbor, MI: Association for Consumer Research, 1984), pp. 203–209.

TABLE 3-1

A Scale Designed to Measure Enduring Involvement with Products

1. I would be interested in reading about this product.
2. I would read a *Consumer Reports* article about this product.
3. I have compared product characteristics among brands.
4. I usually pay attention to ads for this product.
5. I usually talk about this product with other people.
6. I usually seek advice from other people prior to purchasing this product.
7. I usually take many factors into account before purchasing this product.
8. I usually spend a lot of time choosing what kind to buy.

SOURCE: Scale developed by Edward F. McQuarrie and J. Michael Munson, "A Revised Product Involvement Inventory: Improved Usability and Validity, *Diversity in Consumer Behavior: Advances in Consumer Research*, Vol. 19 (Provo, UT: Association for Consumer Research, 1992), pp. 108–115.

purchased a car. These results supported the concept that situational involvement and enduring involvement are two distinct concepts.

Evidence also exists indicating that involvement has multiple dimensions. Researchers have found that the following characteristics, among others, compose the involvement construct:

1. *Self-expressive importance*—Highly involving products may help to express one's self-concept to others.
2. *Hedonic importance*—Highly involving products can be pleasurable, interesting, fun, fascinating, and exciting.
3. *Practical relevance*—Highly involving products may be needed, essential, and beneficial for utilitarian reasons.
4. *Purchase risk*—Highly involving products may create uncertainty of choice, and a poor choice would be extremely annoying to the buyer.[10]

The importance of each of these dimensions will vary depending upon the type of good or service being purchased and upon the characteristics of the individual consumer making the purchase. For example, the purchase of expensive jewelry would have a high degree of self-expressive importance, hedonic importance, and purchase risk. On the other hand, in most cases it would have little practical relevance. In contrast, the purchase of a refrigerator would have high practical relevance and purchase risk but little self-expressive and hedonic importance. In terms of managerial strategy, market research should be conducted to identify the extent and type of involvement that the target market has with the product being sold.

The Effects of High Involvement

What happens when a consumer's involvement level increases? Evidence suggests that under higher levels of involvement, consumers begin to process information in more depth. Along with the increased information processing, one sees a general

TABLE 3-2

Consumer Involvement: Some Important Points

1. *Definition:* Involvement is the level of perceived personal importance and/or interest evoked by a stimulus.
2. The level of involvement is influenced by the characteristics of the product, the situation, the communication, and the consumer's personality.
3. Two types of involvement have been identified: *situational involvement* occurs over a short period of time and is associated with a specific situation; *enduring involvement* represents a longer commitment and concern with a product class.
4. Four dimensions of involvement have been identified: *self-expressive*, *hedonic importance*, *practical relevance*, and *purchase risk*.
5. The effects of high involvement include greater depth of information processing, increased arousal, and more extended decision making.

increase in arousal levels. Consumers are likely to give more diligent consideration to information relevant to the particular decision.[11] This means that consumers are more likely to think hard about a decision when it is made under high-involvement circumstances. In addition, higher levels of involvement are likely to lead consumers to engage in a more extended decision process and move through each of the decision stages in a more thorough manner. Some authors have suggested that the type of decision process diverges sufficiently in high- and low-involvement circumstances to warrant discussion of two categories of decision making—limited decision making in low-involvement circumstances and extended decision making in high-involvement circumstances.[12]

As involvement level increases, consumers will tend to give more diligent consideration to the information that they receive. Consequently, advertisers can develop more complex messages. The advertisement from Saab, shown in Figure 3-6, illustrates this concept. Indeed, the headline of the advertisement ("A Saab Will Surrender Its Own Life to Save Yours") immediately indicates to the reader that the message may be relatively complex. Saab can use such an advertising approach because it is likely that its target market consists of individuals more highly involved in the buying process.

In summary, the involvement concept is critical to understanding consumer behavior. Level of involvement not only influences the amount of information processing, it also has important implications for the decision-making process, attitude formation and change, and word-of-mouth communication.[13] Consumer involvement will be discussed again when these concepts are presented in later chapters in the textbook.[14]

Table 3-2 summarizes the important ideas about consumer involvement.

THE EXPOSURE STAGE

As noted in the model presented in Figure 3-4, exposure to a stimulus is the first step in the processing of information. With information exposure, a consumer's sensory organs are activated by a stimulus. One characteristic of consumer informa-

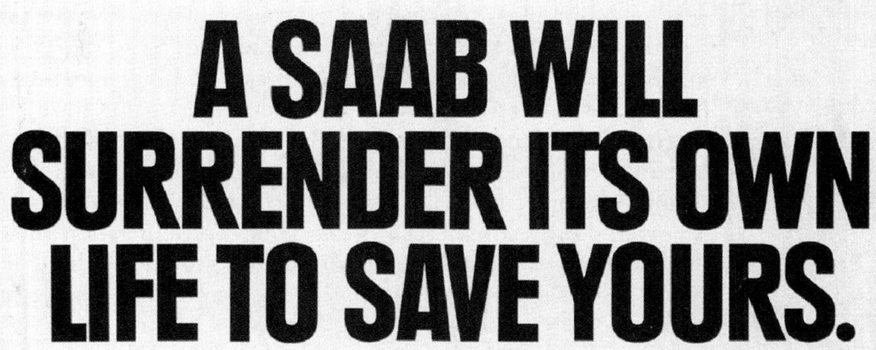

Figure 3-6 Saab uses a detailed message to target buyers involved in extended decision making. (Courtesy of Saab-Scania of America, Inc.)

tion processing in the exposure stage is its selectivity. Through a process of **selective exposure**, consumers actively choose whether or not to expose themselves to information. Importantly, as involvement with a particular type of product increases, consumers are more likely to selectively expose themselves to information about that product.

The concept of selective exposure is of great interest to advertisers. The tendency of consumers to selectively screen information to which they are exposed and to which they attend can dramatically lower the effectiveness of advertising dollars. To minimize the effects of selective exposure, television executives program what have became known as "Big Events." Examples are miniseries (e.g., "Roots"), telecasts of major movies (e.g., *Batman*), or telecasts of huge sporting events (e.g., Olympic Games). Sanitation supervisors at water departments have found that during these events water consumption would fluctuate dramatically. Over a two- or three-minute period, water-holding tanks would be drained, and the system would be strained to capacity. Called the "flush factor," the sudden increase in water usage occurred during commercial breaks when consumers left their televisions to rush to their bathrooms. The flush factor illustrates the point that consumers watching television will selectively avoid exposing themselves to commercials and attend to other matters.[15]

The extent to which consumers engage in selective exposure to advertising has also been influenced by cable television. Remote-control devices on television have proliferated with the influx of cable television systems. With such devices consumers can rapidly and easily change from one channel to another. Called **zapping** in the industry, about 6 to 19 percent of consumers at any one time are zapping commercials by remotely switching channels.[16] One study found that 64% of homes with cable zap advertisements.

A symposium was held by advertisers on the zapping problem and the related issue of audience erosion during commercial messages. The consensus appeared to be that an erosion rate of 59% exists for television commercials. Thus only about four of every ten people watching a television program will actually observe any one commercial. The general response by professionals was that to reduce the audience erosion problem, commercials would have to become more appealing. One executive commented that to prevent people from selectively avoiding commercials, advertisements would have to be made so well that people would want to view them.[17] Table 3-3 presents some other suggestions on how to deal with the problem of audience erosion.

The Study of Sensation

With exposure to a stimulus, a consumer's sensory organs are activated. The study of **sensation** is the investigation of the ways in which people react to the raw sensory information received through their sense organs. The goal is to analyze the raw responses that a person has to a stimulus prior to attending to it, comprehending it, and giving it meaning. Thus a person studying sensation might ask the question, "How loud does a sound have to be before it is detected?" or "How much difference in the level of the hem of a skirt must there be before a consumer can detect the difference?" The topic of sensation has a number of important applications to marketing and in particular to the field of advertising.

Once a consumer is exposed to information, whether or not he or she goes beyond mere exposure to actively attend to and focus on the stimulus is determined by a number of factors. One determinant of whether or not a stimulus is actually detected is its intensity. The lowest level at which a stimulus can be detected 50% of the time is called the **absolute threshold**. As the intensity of a stimulus (such as the loudness of an advertisement) increases, the likelihood that it will be sensed also increases. Advertisers therefore have an incentive to make their commercials as loud

TABLE 3-3

Methods to Reduce Problems of Audience Erosion

1. Format change	Place less important material in the interior of programs. Zapping occurs most at beginning and end of programs.
2. Spread commercials	Since consumers often switch from network shows to cable programming, place more ads on cable channels.
3. Strategic timing	Zapping frequently occurs after five to ten seconds of commercial are completed. Place important material early in commercials. Also, try to obtain first position in a series of commercials.
4. Budget more for print and other media	With audience erosion in television growing, why not place more emphasis on other media? *Reader's Digest* has run ads in trade magazines pointing out the erosion problem on TV.
5. Persuade networks to show fewer ads	Audiences may be reacting to comercial clutter and advertising overload by zapping commercials.

SOURCE: Extracted from Bernie Whalen, "$6 Billion Down the Drain!" *Marketing News*, September 14, 1984, pp. 1, 37, 38.

as possible without offending the consumer. Indeed, a common complaint by consumers is that television advertisements are louder than the programs that they accompany. Although the maximum intensity of sound coming from a commercial is no greater than that coming from a program, advertisers do take steps to create the sensation that the loudness is greater, such as by recording the entire commercial near peak, allowable sound levels.

Subliminal Perception

Closely related to the absolute threshold is the concept of subliminal perception. In 1957 audiences at a movie theater in New Jersey were exposed to briefly presented messages that said, "Drink Coca-Cola" and "Eat popcorn." The messages were superimposed on the movie and presented so quickly that the audience did not consciously realize that the messages had appeared. Although no evidence was presented, the marketing firm that created the messages claimed that sales of the items increased dramatically.

The media and consumers were shocked. *The New Yorker* stated that people's minds had been "broken and entered." However, others saw potential in subliminal messages, and a radio station began broadcasting subaudible messages that "TV's a bore."[18]

The term *subliminal* means "below threshold." That is, a subliminally perceived stimulus cannot be reported because it is below the absolute threshold. Thus **subliminal perception** refers to the idea that stimuli presented below the level of conscious awareness may influence behavior and feelings. Three different types of subliminal stimulation have been identified—briefly presented visual stimuli, accelerated speech in low-volume auditory messages, and embedding or hiding sexual imagery or words in print advertisements.[19] In fact, one author has written two books claiming that advertisers intentionally embed erotic and death symbols in print advertisements.[20]

Does subliminal advertising work? According to one psychologist, the answer is, "No, what you see is what you get."[21] He argues that subliminal stimuli are extremely weak and most certainly overridden by a host of other more powerful messages. In addition, because people are generally in control of their overt responses to stimuli, they will screen out attempts to affect undesired behavior.

More recently, however, evidence is beginning to accumulate that perhaps we should be more concerned about the effects of subliminal advertising. In one study the authors investigated the effects of "subliminal embeds" on the ratings of ads by college students, who acted as simulated consumers. Two actual print ads were used—one for a popular cigarette and the other for a well-known Scotch whiskey. After the stimuli were pointed out by the experimenters, students reported that they could identify the nude body of a woman in the liquor ad and the representation of male genitals in the cigarette ad. A second version of each ad was created by having a professional photographer airbrush out the embedded material. Four other groups of students then evaluated the four ads. The results revealed that the ratings differed between the control (airbrushed ads) and the embedded ads for the liquor advertisement having the female body, but not for the cigarette ad. A second study was run in which measures of autonomic arousal were taken. In this study the students showed evidence of differences in arousal for both advertisements containing the embedded material.[22]

Other research supports the argument that subliminal advertising effects exist. For example, researchers found that presenting the word "Coke" at levels below the absolute threshold increased the thirst ratings of subjects.[23] Similarly, another group of researchers presented slides of a well-known brand of soap for washing wool at a rate of 1/60th of a second during a film about how to wash woolens. This speed of presentation is much too quick for conscious recognition. In comparison to subjects who had not been exposed to the brand, those who received the subliminal information rated the brand significantly higher.[24]

How does one explain the effects, assuming that they are real, of subliminal advertisements? Two theories have been proposed.[25] The incremental effects theory states that over many presentations of a stimulus, a stimulus representation is gradually built in the person's nervous system. At some point the representation reaches a behavioral threshold and causes changes in the actions of the consumer. However, the cause of the changes in actions is never recognized by the consumer. The incremental effects theory assumes that numerous repetitions of the stimulus are needed. Indeed, both the Coke study and the woolen study used multiple repetitions.

The second theoretical approach is the psychodynamic theory of arousal. This theory assumes that unconscious wishes to engage in some behavior may be activated by unconsciously presented stimuli. Thus, in the liquor advertisement, one must assume that the students harbored an unconscious wish for sexual activity that was activated by the nude body embedded in the advertisement. The activation of this unconscious wish presumably influences the actual perception of the advertisement.

The results of recent research on subliminal perception indicate that the idea should not be dismissed.[26] Clearly, additional work is needed on the topic—in part because of the public's intense interest in the area. Consumers are estimated to spend over $50 million a year on audio tapes that contain subliminal messages to help people quit smoking, lose weight, and even improve sexual functioning. Great care must be taken, however, in performing the research to ensure that alternative explanations of the effects are eliminated.[27] Highlight 3-1 discusses the high impact that messages presented above the absolute threshold can have.

The Just Noticeable Difference Threshold

In addition to the absolute threshold, a difference threshold exists. The **just noticeable difference (JND)** is the minimum amount of difference in the intensity of a stimulus that can be detected 50% of the time. The idea that people cannot always distinguish between two stimuli has marketing implications.

HIGHLIGHT 3-1

Attracting Attention with Pro-social Messages

The potato chip package featured drawings of three young, multicultural women. The brand name—HOMEGIRLS. In the slang of the inner city, a homegirl is a young woman from the neighborhood. On the back of the package, a message was printed that read in part: "We should save ourselves for marriage. Why should a man respect us if he can have us before marriage? No ring, no thing."

In the fight to gain attention, not only from consumers, but also from supermarket managers, Homeboys Inc. has taken a new approach in its promotional strategy. The small, upstart company in Philadelphia is using social messages that urge its inner-city youth target market to avoid drugs, to stay in school, and to get married before having sex.

The $4-billion-a-year potato chip industry is highly competitive. For a new company to even get space on supermarket shelves is a major task. As said by one analyst, the use of pro-social messages helped. Distributors reacted by saying, "Why not give them a chance?" The pro-social messages found on the back of each package appeal to them. For example, the antidrug copy says, "Let's make it plain, Homeboys! Tell those drug dealers to "STEP OFF" and "GET A LIFE."

The marketing strategy of HOMEBOYS is effective. The low prices of its chips make them highly competitive. To attract the attention and goodwill of inner-city youths, the company uses their language. For example, the company's first product was called "Chumpies," a slang word meaning "the best of the best." A barbecue-flavored chip is called "Bumpin Barbecue." As said by the company's owner, "bumpin" refers to something hot and good.

Mail pours into the firm from people touched by the messages. One young woman described a situation one night when on her way home, a boy "swept her off her feet." When they stopped at a convenience store to buy some beer, she picked up a package of "Homegirls" and read the message. She said, "I ditched the dud who I thought was a stud. Thanks for helping girls like me."

Meanwhile, the company is making money while helping people. Started in 1991 on a $100,000 investment, by 1993 it had over 100 distributors in Philadelphia and was moving into Washington, D.C. One of Homeboys Inc.'s African-American owners described the company's goal: "For too long, African-Americans have been discouraged from being entrepreneurs. Once we begin to own, we will begin to promote positive images of our people.

Based upon an article by Veronica J. Bush, "Homeboys Inc. Chips In to Help Inner-City Teenagers," *The Wall Street Journal*, May 21, 1993, p. B2.

The study of absolute and difference thresholds has important implications for marketing research. For example, companies in the food industry are interested in producing products that give the optimum taste at the lowest cost.[28] In formulating the recipe for the product, they frequently have a choice between two ingredients that may differ in price. The question is, "Will a change in ingredient create a just noticeable difference in the taste of the product?"[29] Highlight 3-2 discusses the market research implications of taste perception.

Weber's Law and the JND

One important aspect of the just noticeable difference is that it varies with the level of the stimulus. Discovered by a German scientist, E. H. Weber, the relationship between the size of the JND and stimulus intensity has become known as Weber's law. **Weber's law** states that as the intensity of the stimulus increases, the ability to detect a difference between the two levels of the stimulus decreases. Weber identified a formula that expresses these relationships:

$$\text{JND} = I \times K$$

where I is the intensity level of the stimulus and K is a constant that gives the proportionate amount of change in stimulus level required for its detection.

One controversial application of Weber's law is to pricing. A rule that retailers use is that markdowns must be at least 20 percent before consumers recognize them.[30] This 20 percent figure is equivalent to K, the constant in Weber's law. Thus, if a diamond ring is priced at $1,200, it must be marked down by $240 ($1,200 × 0.20 = $240) for the sale to be meaningful. In contrast, if the diamond were priced at $8,000, the markdown must be $1,600 for the sale to be effective. The JND increases in size proportionate to K as the dollar value of a purchase increases. This application is controversial because, strictly speaking, a small difference between two prices (say, $1,000 and $1,001) is clearly noticeable; it just has little meaning to the consumer. More will be said about this issue later in the chapter.

Information on absolute and difference thresholds may influence the packaging strategy of companies as well. Why does Campbell's Soup package its pork and beans in a 20¾-ounce can while its major competitor uses a 21-ounce can? The reason is probably because consumers do not notice the difference. Similarly, Bohemia Beer lowered the quantity of beer in each bottle from 12 to 11 ounces. The cost savings was used to increase the ad budget and develop a fancier container. As a result, sales nearly doubled.[31] On the other hand, the JND principle has been used to increase the size of portions as well as decrease them. After a 12-month test, the candy company M&M/Mars found that increasing the size of its candy bars increased sales by 20 to 30%. As a result, the company changed nearly its entire product line.

Table 3-4 identifies a number of marketing uses of the concept of the JND.

HIGHLIGHT 3-2

Market Research and Taste Perception

How many different flavors can people actually taste? The answer is four—sweet, sour, salty, and bitter. All the other "tastes" that humans experience are actually smells. In fact, here is a surefire way to win a bar bet. Hold out three differently colored jelly beans to your mark, and ask him if he can tell them apart by their taste. When he says, "sure," then tell him to close his eyes and hold his nose—after all we are only doing taste here. With his visual and olfactory senses gone, he will not have a chance.

How can researchers determine if two flavors are distinguishable by consumers? How can managers be sure that the "new and improved" taste of a food product is really "new and improved"? Two methods are employed by researchers to investigate how consumers perceive the taste of food and drink. One employs market research in which actual consumers are given samples of the food. The most effective method for conducting such taste discrimination tests involves asking consumers to compare, two at a time, each of the competing formulations and identify the most preferred. For example, suppose that the researcher wanted to determine if consumers could tell if any of three different formulations of instant coffee was different from or better than the others. Each person would compare formulation *a* with *b*, *b* with *c*, and *a* with *c*. Less effective is a method in which subjects sample each of the three options and then rank their preferences.[1]

A second general approach for conducting taste tests is to employ professional flavor analysts. These individuals make their living tasting and sniffing food, beverages, and even pet products. For example, brewers use 120 standard terms to describe the taste of beer. They employ such terms as "woody," "grassy," "leathery," and "light-struck," which is the code word for "redolent of skunk."[2]

Enology, the sensory evaluation of wine flavor, is another arena within which professional flavor analysts work. One researcher has developed an "aroma wheel" to make the process more scientific. It includes such flavors/aromas as "vanilla," "geranium," "diesel," and the highly appealing "wet dog." The researcher also attempted to adapt the flavor wheel for cultural differences. Because the wine industry tends to be dominated by the French, their culture must be carefully considered. Thus the flavor "green bean" had to be discarded from use. In France "green bean" connotes "fresh abundant flavor." In contrast, in the United States "green bean" implies a "dead, canned smell."[3]

References

1. David Stipp, "A Flavor Analyst Should Never Ask, 'What's for Lunch?'" *The Wall Street Journal*, August 3, 1988, pp. 1–10.
2. Bruce Buchanan, Moshe Givon, and Arieh Goldman, "Measurement of Discrimination Ability in Taste Tests: An Empirical Investigation," *Journal of Marketing Research*, Vol. 24 (May 1987), pp. 154–163.
3. Carrie Dolan, "Chardonnay's Bouquet May Hint of Fido," *The Wall Street Journal*, June 17, 1993, pp. B1–B10.

Although marketers usually do not overtly state that they are going to use Weber's law, they show evidence of implicitly understanding its implications. For example, Procter & Gamble had made no fewer than 19 changes in the wrapper of Ivory Soap between 1898 and 1965.[32] The difference between any two of the

TABLE 3-4

Some Marketing Examples of the JND

Area of Application	*Example of Use*
Pricing	When raising the price, try to move less than a JND.
	When lowering the price for a sale, move more than a JND.
Sales promotion	Make coupons larger than the JND.
Product	Make decreases in size of food product less than JND, e.g., shrinking of candy bars.
	When the word "new" is used, make sure product change is greater than JND.
Packaging	To update package styling and logo, keep within JND.
	To change image, make styling changes greater than JND.

changes was extremely subtle. However, when the 1898 and 1990 wrappers are compared, the differences are astounding. P&G made the changes in the wrapper so gradually that they probably stayed within the consumer's JND with each adaptation of the wrapper.

A potential problem should be noted, however, in applying psychological principles such as Weber's law to consumer behavior problems. In some cases the idea of the principle applies quite well; however, the exact process through which it operates may not match the consumer behavior context. Weber's law describes quite accurately the sensory impact of changes in the intensity of a stimulus. The question is, "Does a change in sales price influence consumers at the sensory level or at a cognitive level where the information is being interpreted?" Strictly speaking, Weber's law would be misused if the change in sales price influenced people at the comprehension stage rather than at the sensory level. Indeed, this author strongly suspects that in most consumer behavior situations the use of the term just noticeable difference is inappropriate. Perhaps a more appropriate term would be just meaningful difference.

Practically speaking, however, it makes little difference to the marketing manager whether or not Weber's law is being applied precisely from a psychological perspective. Weber's law helps the manager to understand the relationship of the level of the stimulus to the amount of change required in the stimulus to make it meaningful—an important phenomenon in consumer behavior and marketing information.

Consumer Adaptation

Closely related to the concepts of the absolute threshold and the JND is that of adaptation. Everyone has experienced the process of adaptation before. When first sitting in a hot bath, the steaming water may seem nearly unbearable. After a few minutes, however, the water will feel quite pleasant. The change in sensation did not occur because the water got colder. It occurred because nerve cells adapted to the water's temperature and no longer fired signals to the brain telling it that the water was too hot. In sum, adaptation is a process in which an individual has repeated experience with a stimulus. The **adaptation level** is the amount or level of the stimulus to which the consumer has become accustomed. It is a reference point to which changes in the level of the stimulus are compared.

The concept that consumers become adapted to stimuli has implications for both product and advertising strategies. Consumers become adapted to a certain look, style, or message over some period of time. To keep product or service communications fresh, marketers should attempt to vary them periodically. Thus Miller Lite Beer bombarded consumers with the same message for years—that is, "it won't fill you up, and it tastes great." The message did not become boring because of the highly creative use of dozens of different advertisements in which various ex-jocks give the message in unusual circumstances. The net result was a long-running advertising campaign that propelled the brand to become the largest-selling light beer.

The Butterfly Curve

In the early 1990s the market share of U.S. airlines began slipping to foreign carriers on transatlantic flights. In seeking to identify reasons why American, TWA, and other airlines were rated lower than competitors, one executive suggested that the problems were not caused by poor service. Rather, he said that service on foreign airlines really isn't better, it's "just different. It seems better because it's not what they normally get."[33] Is there any merit in the conclusion of this executive?

The idea that something slightly different may be perceived more positively is supported by an effect called a butterfly curve. Illustrated in Figure 3-7 on the vertical axis is the degree of liking for a stimulus. On the horizontal axis is the level of the stimulus and the position of the adaptation level. (If you look hard, the humps in the figure could look like the wings of a butterfly.) The **butterfly curve** shows that the preference for a stimulus is at its greatest level at points just higher or lower than the adaptation level. At the adaptation level, preference declines slightly because the person has become habituated to the stimulus. However, as the level of the stimulus moves too far from the adaptation level, the preference steadily decreases.[34]

The simple idea of the butterfly curve nicely explains why fashion trends are constantly changing. Consumers quickly become adapted to a certain look, and its pleasure falls. Designers will then modify the current look in some relatively small

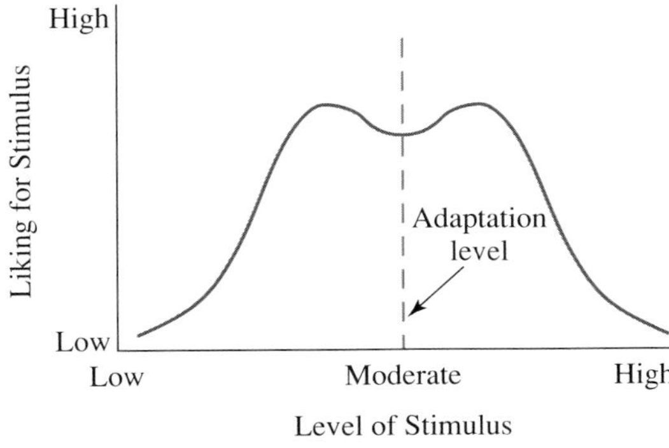

Figure 3-7
Butterfly curve.

way, and it will appear fresh and interesting because the stimulus has diverged from the adaptation level. The up-and-down movement of the hems of skirts over the years well illustrates the principle. Similarly, the width of men's ties and lapels shows the same confounded tendency to change in size.

The butterfly curve also suggests that unusual fashion looks are adopted slowly, because they are at first too far away from the adaptation level. For example, when Madonna first wore a bustier the public was horrified. However, after several years consumers adapted, and bustiers became familiar sights on dance floors and even in that fashion kingdom—the mall.

Another consumer behavior phenomenon that the butterfly curve can potentially account for is **spontaneous brand switching**. Consumers frequently switch brands, even when nothing indicates that they are unhappy with the brand previously used. The phenomenon seems to occur most frequently with low-involvement products in which little difference exists between brands. Applying the concept of the adaptation level, consumers may switch brands because they have adapted to the one most frequently used. Changing to a new brand moves the consumer off the adaptation level, thereby providing some increment in the pleasure received from the product class. Companies seem to implicitly recognize the problem and frequently come out with "new and improved" versions of their products.

THE ATTENTION STAGE

Marketers are vitally concerned with attracting consumers' attention: It is a necessary first step so that consumers comprehend information and place it into long-term memory. **Attention** involves the allocation of cognitive capacity to an object or task. Thus, when a consumer attends to an advertisement, a public relations piece of information, or a personal-selling communication, he or she is allocating mental capacity to the task. The more demanding the task, or the more involved the person is in the task, the greater the amount of attention focused upon it.[35]

Types of Attention

Attention can be activated either voluntarily or involuntarily.[36] When **voluntary attention** occurs, consumers actively search out information that has personal relevance. Voluntary attention is selective. As involvement with a particular product increases, through a process called **selective attention**, consumers will selectively focus attention on relevant information. Thus someone who is interested in buying a car, some furniture, or an expensive camera will actively seek information about the product. When reading newspapers, he or she will be on the lookout to find advertisements and articles that deal with the product sought. Conversely, if the marketing communication is not perceived as matching a goal, the consumer will tend not to focus attention on it. Again, this is a major problem for advertisers on television and radio. Consumers may be exposed to the message but simply decide not to attend to the information contained in the communication because of their low involvement level.

In addition to voluntary attention, attention can be placed upon a stimulus involuntarily. **Involuntary attention** occurs when a consumer is exposed to something surprising, novel, threatening, or unexpected. Such stimuli result in an autonomic response in which the person turns toward and allocates attention to it. This response, which the consumer cannot consciously control, is called an **orientation reflex.**[37] Because most advertisements to which consumers are exposed are unrelated to the immediate goals of the audience, marketers go to some trouble to elicit the orientation reflex. Figure 3-8 portrays an ad from ITT Automotive that attracts attention via a stop sign. Because we are conditioned to respond to stop signs, the ad elicits an orientation reaction.

With both voluntary and involuntary attention, cognitive capacity is allocated to the stimulus. When the individual attends to the information, he or she will reveal physiological arousal. The arousal may result in an increase in blood pressure, a change in brain wave patterns, a quickening of breathing, a slight sweating of the hands, and dilation of the pupils, among other things. One way of assessing the impact of advertisements is to measure the arousal elicited when consumers view the ad. To assess attention levels, market researchers have employed devices that assess blood pressure, pupil dilation, and brain wave patterns; even the temperature of the eardrum has been used.

Capturing Consumers' Attention

Marketers attempt to capture attention by varying the nature of the stimulus received by consumers. The goal is to activate the orientation reflex by adroitly creating stimuli that surprise, threaten, or violate the expectations of consumers. A number of stimulus factors can be used to achieve such a goal. The clever use of surprise, illustrated by the stop sign in the ITT automotive ad, is an example. In television advertising, the "Energizer Bunny" is effective in part because of the use of surprise. In one of the ads, a group of women is seen sitting together discussing the merits of various coffees. Just as the viewer is set to hear what brand is being advertised, out pops a pink bunny, running amok, banging a big drum, knocking things over, and totally destroying the scene. The announcer then intones—"The Energizer just keeps going, and going, and going." (The storyboard for this ad is found in Figure 3-9.) One executive for the ad agency that developed the campaign said, "The key element is surprise: Where will this bunny turn up next?"[38] The ad people have had a field day creating bogus products to parody with the bunny. In another commercial for the bogus "Sit-Again" hemorrhoid preparation, the bunny intrudes just after a stunt actor jumps from a second-story window to land grimacing in the saddle of a horse. The commercials have been highly successful according to managers at Eveready Batteries. One executive claimed that unaided brand awareness increased by 33% because of the campaign.

A variety of strategies can be employed to activate the orientation reflex. For example, movement attracts attention. Thus, on highways and in cities, one finds retailers using neon signs that simulate motion as lights in the series flash on and off. Unusual sounds can also be effective. Television advertisers have recently taken to using distinctive, nonverbal sounds to activate the orientation response. For example, ads for the financial corporation Shearson Lehman Brothers used a buzzing sound that grew louder as the commercial progressed. Executives claimed that ad awareness

Figure 3-8 The stop sign triggers an orienting reflex that increases the likelihood that consumers will pay attention to this ad for ITT Automotive.

Figure 3-9 The Energizer Bunny ads use surprise to capture attention. (Courtesy Eveready Battery Company, Inc.)

increased by 50% with the use of the funny sound in the commercials. The ad agency created the noise to mimic the sound of thinking in the ad campaign, which was called "Minds over Money." General Electric reported similar positive effects from its "beep ads" in which a symphony of peculiar beeps comes from digital kitchen appliances.[39]

Another stimulus factor that may influence attention is the size or magnitude of the stimulus. For example, all else equal, large-print advertisements are more apt to be attended than small ones. A loud television commercial is more likely to be processed than a soft one. Color can attract attention, particularly when amid black-and-white print materials.[40] The principle of contrast is also an important stimulus factor. Contrast occurs when a stimulus diverges substantially from surrounding background stimuli. A loud noise in a quiet room or a print ad with very little copy in a sea of verbose ads illustrates the concept of contrast.

Finally, marketers can gain consumers' attention by placing ads in circumstances in which consumers have little choice but to attend to the information presented. An example is movie theaters playing commercials prior to the beginning of a show. Theater operators, however, are extremely cautious about what kinds of ads to show for fear of aggravating customers. Corporations that own large numbers of theaters screen the ads to make sure that they are appropriate and avoid a hard sell. Thus the commercials shown tend to be highly lavish productions. Although the cost per thousand viewers is higher than that of television advertising, theater advertising is claimed to be recalled three times better.[41] An interesting problem, however, is that many national advertisers are reluctant to use movie advertising for fear of associating their products with violent or sex-laden movies. In addition, Walt Disney Productions forbids theater owners from showing advertisements with any of its movies.

Table 3-5 summarizes the factors that can be used to attract consumers' attention.[42]

THE COMPREHENSION STAGE

As noted earlier in the chapter, comprehension refers to the process through which individuals organize and interpret information. **Perceptual organization** deals with the way people perceive the shapes, forms, figures, and lines in their visual world. In the **interpretation process** people draw upon their experience, memory, and expectations to attach meaning to a stimulus. The study of comprehension is particularly important for advertisers. For example, researchers have found that when people fail to correctly comprehend an advertisement, they are generally less persuaded by it.[43] In one study researchers asked a random sample of 1,347 adults to read a short communication. Immediately afterward, they were given a six-item quiz on its contents. Somewhat surprisingly, they answered only 63% of the questions correctly. When one considers that the respondents were in a high-involvement state and they answered the questions immediately, the low percentage of correct responses indicates that consumer miscomprehension is a major problem for marketers.[44] (Table 3-6 presents the communication and the quiz used in the study.)

Perceptual Organization

What do you see when you look at Figure 3-10? The goal of the ad is to have consumers perceive the light and dark images as various types of light bulbs. Philips, Inc., made excellent use of various principles of perceptual organization to create the ad. Here, the principle of closure is illustrated in that observers automatically fill in the lines to form a coherent image. People have a tendency to see a "whole" figure, even if there are gaps in it. They automatically try to make sense out of incomplete information by organizing it into a meaningful whole.

Much of the work on perceptual organization comes from the work of German psychologists active early in the twentieth century. Called **Gestalt psychologists**,

TABLE 3-5

Stimulus Factors That Attract Consumers' Attention

1. *Surprise:* the Energizer Bunny popping up unexpectedly in a commercial, for example.
2. *Movement:* flashing lights on motel signs.
3. *Unusual sounds:* beeps in television commercials.
4. *Size of stimulus:* loud television commercials, large two-page print ads.
5. *Contrast effects:* use of black-and-white print ads when all others are in color.
6. *Color:* the use of visually colorful stimuli that stand out from background.

TABLE 3-6

Advertisement and Quiz for Comprehension Study

INCREASE YOUR CAR'S
CARGO CAPACITY
By Slaton L. White

When you replace your large car with a smaller, more fuel-efficient one, expect to forfeit a lot of storage space. Many of the newer cars have sacrificed trunk space for less weight—all in the name of fuel economy. Short of jettisoning one of the kids, leaving your luggage behind, or buying a mini pickup instead of a car, what options does the owner of a down-size automobile have when he wants to head out on vacation or carry large, bulky cargo?

Basically, there are two options: tow the gear in a trailer or tote it on the roof. Both choices involve trade-offs, most noticeably a measurable decrease in fuel economy as well as a marked change in the car's handling characteristics. However, many manufacturers offer a broad range of products designed to minimize the trade-offs.

Sample Quiz

The instructions for the quiz were as follows:
Based upon the passage you just read, which of the following statements is True and which is False?
Remember: Base your answers *only* upon what you think the passage said or implied.

1. To increase space for a downsize automobile, there are three main options. (False/Fact)
2. When a trailer is added, a subcompact has all the advantages of a larger car. (False/Inference)
3. Toting gear on a roof will decrease fuel economy. (True/Fact)
4. In general, you should *not* buy a subcompact if you have a family unless you have to. (False/Inference)
5. Manufacturers offer products which are designed to minimize problems with towing. (True/Fact)
6. You should *not* give in to a lack of space if you own a subcompact car. (True/Inference)

these individuals attempted to identify the rules that govern how people take disjointed stimuli and make sense out of the shapes and forms to which they are exposed. Gestalt is the German word for "pattern" or "configuration," which suggests these psychologists' goals of understanding how people perceive patterns in the world.

Figure 3-11 presents a number of the Gestalt rules of perceptual organization. Many of the rules deal with how people decide what things go together. For example, the "rule of common fate" states that elements that move in the same direction are assumed to belong to each other. Other rules applicable to the problem of deciding "what-goes-with-what" are similarity, proximity, and closure. Another area of Gestalt interest involves determining how people distinguish figure and ground. Example 4 in Figure 3-11 illustrates figure–ground principles. At one moment the reversible figure shown in Example 4 resembles two faces looking at each other. The next moment it looks like a vase. The image switches back and forth because our

Figure 3-10

Principles of closure and figure–ground are illustrated in this ad for Philips light bulbs. (Courtesy of Philips Lighting Company.)

brain cannot decipher whether the black or the white portion of the drawing is the figure. In an advertising context, managers want their product to be the figure moving against the background of an ad because the figure attracts more attention than does the background.

From a marketer's point of view, perceptual organization is generally applied to visual communications, such as print advertising, television advertising, and package design. For example, when drawing an ad, the artist may consciously or unconsciously use Gestalt principles to create the desired effect on the consumer. In particular, the artist is attentive to the figure–ground concept. For the product to be noticed, it is important that it stand out from the background of the print ad. Similarly, if the goal is to associate the product with something else desirable—such as a popular celebrity endorser—the principles of proximity, closure, and common fate could be used.

Interpretation

During and after attention to a stimulus, the consumer attempts to gain an understanding of what it is and how he or she should react to it. In this interpretation phase, people retrieve from long-term memory information pertinent to the stimulus. In addition, expectancies regarding what the stimulus "should be like" are retrieved from long-term memory and used to help interpret it. The personal incli-

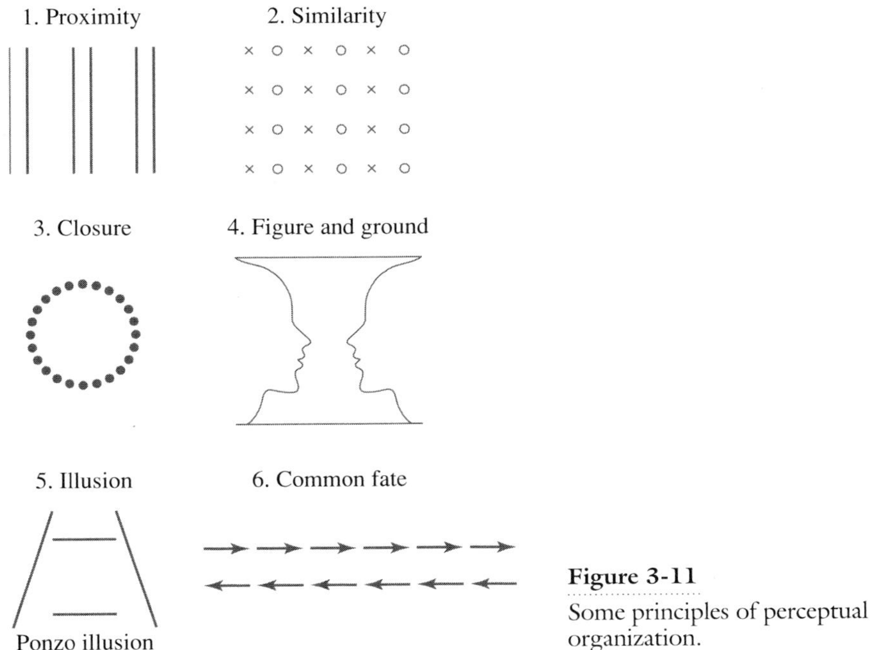

Figure 3-11
Some principles of perceptual organization.

nations and biases of the consumer also influence the interpretation of the stimulus. Through the interpretation process, consumers arrive at an understanding of what the stimulus is.

As noted earlier in the chapter, one problem for marketers is that consumers may interpret the same stimulus differentially. For example, classic examples of differences in interpretation can be found in cross-cultural marketing. Differences in the meaning of colors can be found throughout the world. Yellow flowers are a sign of death in Mexico, whereas in France they denote infidelity.[45]

The Role of Expectations

A consumer's expectations also influence how he or she comprehends and interprets marketing stimuli. **Expectations** are a person's prior beliefs about what should happen in a given situation. The fact that expectations influence the interpretation of information created problems for Adolph Coors, Inc. In 1988 the company decided to change the label on its flagship brand from "Banquet Beer" to "Original Draft." The change was made in response to Miller Brewing Company's successful new entry of "Genuine Draft" into the market. The problem was that many Coors drinkers in the Southwest believed that the taste of the beer had been changed as well. As one Coors executive explained, "We tried to convince them it was the same product, and they'd say, 'Oh, no it isn't.' With a change in the label, the Coors drinkers expected a change in the beverage. As a result of the expectation, they perceived a change in taste. When Coors changed the label back to the old one, a Coors distributor described customers as being elated and saying, 'You brought it back just for me?' His response to each was, 'You bet I did, old buddy.'"[46]

Market researchers must be concerned with assessing the impact of consumer expectations on their evaluations of marketing stimuli. One recently reported study vividly indicates how the perception of taste can be influenced by visual cues that influence taste expectations. In the study, the color of vanilla pudding was made dark brown, medium brown, or light brown by adding a tasteless and odorless food coloring. Respondents then rated the puddings on a variety of scales. About 62% of the respondents rated the dark-colored pudding to have the best chocolate flavor and to be the thickest. The lighter-colored puddings were rated as more creamy than the dark pudding. As the authors of the article stated, "It's the consumer's subjective perception of the product that counts, not the product's objective reality."[47] Other researchers have found that coloring food in unexpected colors (e.g., dyeing potatoes blue) can make people physically ill.[48]

The Price–Quality Relationship

An understanding of consumer expectations can have an important impact on pricing strategies. In general, the greater the price, the less likely a consumer is to buy a particular product item. (Basic microeconomic theory makes this prediction through the idea of the downward-sloping demand curve.) However, in some circumstances consumers develop expectations concerning the **price–quality relationship**. Within certain ranges of price for a product, consumers may expect that higher prices are indicative of greater product quality.[49] The price–quality relationship is probably learned over time through such aphorisms as, "You get what you pay for." One summary of the evidence on the price–quality relationship gave the following occasions when price may be used to indicate the quality of a product:

1. The consumer has some confidence that in the situation price predicts quality.
2. Real or perceived quality variations occur among brands.
3. Actual quality is difficult to judge through objective means or through brand name or store image.
4. Larger differences have a greater impact on perceived quality differences than do smaller price differences.
5. Familiar brands are better able to use price as an indicator of quality.[50]

Semiotics

Within the comprehension stage of information processing, consumers decode the meaning of information received from the environment. An entire field, called **semiotics**, has been developed to analyze how people obtain meaning from signs. **Signs** are the words, gestures, pictures, products, and logos used to communicate information from one person to another. The discipline of semiotics has been studied in one form or another since before the time of Socrates.[51] Indeed, some have argued that what sets the human species apart from others is its ability to adroitly use and manipulate symbols.[52] The field is highly relevant to the entire area of promotional strategy in marketing. It is through the use of various symbols or signs that information about a product or service is communicated to consumers.

The study of semiotics is an important aspect of the experiential perspective on consumer behavior. Thus, to understand how people emotionally react to symbols in the environment, one must gain an understanding of the shared meanings of various signs. For example, Figure 3-12 shows the logo of Eskimo Joe's, a restaurant/bar in Stillwater, Oklahoma. (Stillwater is the home of Oklahoma State University, where the author of this text teaches.) When you look at the logo, what do the grinning Eskimo and drooling dog symbolize to you? When the logo was developed for the restaurant, it was meant to represent a place to have a good time where you could buy the coldest beer in town. The logo was so successful that Eskimo Joe's owner, Stan Clark, started putting it on tee-shirts. By 1992 the Eskimo Joe's tee-shirts were the second largest selling in the world—second only to those of the Hard Rock Cafe. In fact, a new company was spawned—called Joe's Clothes Worldwide. Stan Clark is now a wealthy entrepreneur in large part because of the appealing symbolism of a grinning Eskimo, named Joe, and his dog Buffy.

Semiotics has relevance to a number of consumer behavior areas, including the use of Freudian symbolism in advertising, the utilization of symbols to express one's

Figure 3-12 Eskimo Joe's logo symbolizes cold beer and a good time. (Courtesy Stan Clark Worldwide.)

self-concept, and cross-cultural communications. Researchers doing work on semiotics emphasize that meaning is in part determined by the cultural context within which the sign is embedded. Thus a sign in one culture may have an entirely different meaning from a sign in another culture. For example, associating animals with products is done frequently and effectively in the United States. However, in some Asian cultures, the practice is viewed negatively. Thus advertisements by an optical company showing cute little animals wearing eyeglasses failed miserably in Thailand, because animals symbolize a lower form of life among many people in the Thai culture.

Symbols and signs are used to communicate meaning to others. A paradigm, called *semiosis analysis*, has been proposed that shows how signs function in such a communications role. Shown in Figure 3-13, semiosis analysis involves identifying an object, a sign, and an interpretant. The object is the thing whose meaning is to be communicated (e.g., a product, a person, or an idea). The sign is the symbol or set of symbols used to communicate the meaning of the object. The interpretant is a person's reaction to and meaning derived from the sign.[53]

As shown in Figure 3-13, the object whose meaning is desired to be communicated is a shirt. The sign is the logo on the shirt. It could be a pony (Ralph Lauren), a boot (L. L. Bean), or a bear (Jack Nicklaus) among many possibilities. The logos were developed to impart meaning to the object. Thus the meanings derived from the "pony" logo may include expensive, high quality, sophisticated, "snooty," and stylish. Meanings obtained from the "boot" may include practical, high quality, and outdoor oriented. Finally, meanings obtained from the "bear" may include golf oriented, high quality, and ability to play under pressure—qualities associated with golfer Jack Nicklaus, who is nicknamed "the Golden Bear."

The field of semiotics has particular importance in marketing communications. Marketing and advertising managers must be alert to the use of symbols and how their target market will interpret them. Indeed, advertising has been described as "the modern substitute for myth and ritual, and directly or indirectly, it uses semiotics (the science of signs) to invest products with meaning for a culture whose dominant focus is consumption."[54]

The meaning of signs is learned early in life as a result of the general acculturation of a person. Evidence exists that the ability to recognize the social implications of consumption choices is minimal among preschoolers. However, by the second grade children have developed an ability to make inferences about what it means to

Figure 3-13
Semiosis analysis.

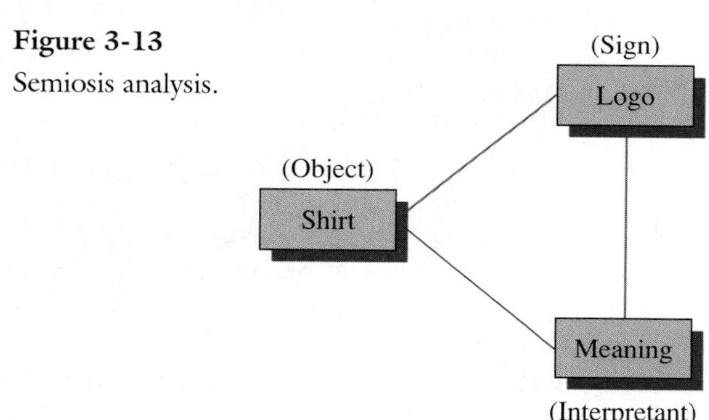

purchase a Camaro versus a Caprice or purchase a new, modern house versus an older, traditional house. By the sixth grade these skills are almost fully developed. Interestingly, some evidence exists that college students show the greatest extent of consumption stereotyping and that the stereotyping then weakens with age.[55]

Semiotics is a fascinating area of study. Students will find that its ideas and concepts will reappear throughout the text.

A MANAGERIAL APPLICATIONS EXAMPLE

The managerial implications of knowing how consumers process information are broad ranging. The introductory vignette at the beginning of this chapter on the Ford Taurus and Sable illustrates how an understanding of perception can influence managerial strategy. The analysis that follows examines the product introductions from the perspective of the mid-1980s when marketers at Ford Motor Company were making decisions about how to introduce the new line of cars.

Problem Identification

The basic problem suggested by the vignette concerned how consumers would perceive the radical designs of the Taurus and Sable models and what, if anything, Ford Motor Company could do to minimize negative reactions.

The Consumer Behavior Analysis

Concepts from the study of perception are relevant to the Taurus case in a number of ways. One issue concerns whether purchasing an automobile is a high- or low-involvement process. For most consumers it is likely that high-involvement decision making occurs. The high-involvement nature of the product should enhance the likelihood that many consumers would attend to promotional materials about the car lines. Those consumers with a high level of enduring involvement would tend to expose themselves to and attend to messages even if not currently in the market for an auto. In addition, those consumers having great situational involvement, due to an immediate need to purchase an auto, also would be likely to attend to product-related messages.

The radical design of the Taurus models suggests that consumers would readily perceive a just noticeable difference between it and other autos in the market. Such readily identifiable differences would have strong implications for the positioning of the models. Figure 3-14 presents a perceptual map of how consumers would likely perceive the models in relation to competing models of roughly the same size. In the figure, the models are positioned as being moderately priced and highly expressive. The competitor closest to this position was the Audi 5000, but it is significantly more expensive. The Audi 5000 is, in addition, German-made and therefore distinguishable from the Taurus/Sable lines based upon country of origin.

As can be seen in Figure 3-14, the positioning of the Taurus should allow Ford to build a strong brand image for the model. The more a brand can specifically

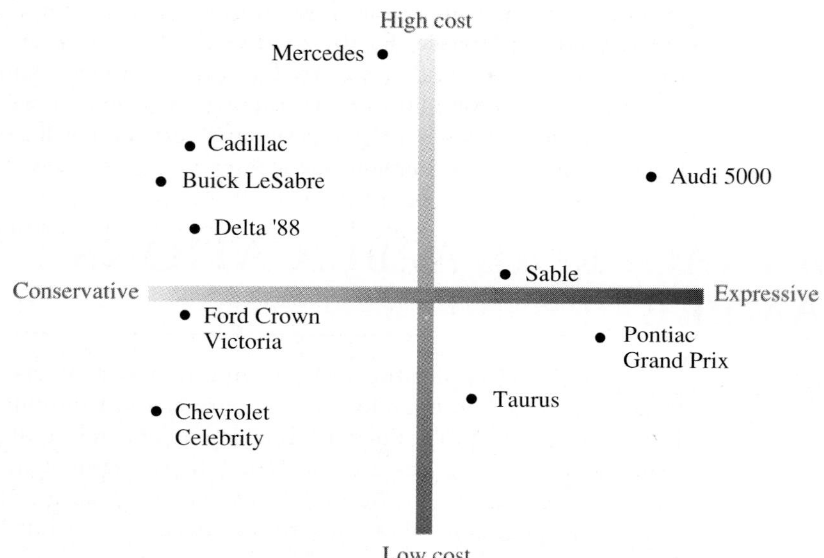

Figure 3-14 Positioning of Taurus/Sable autos.

position itself, the greater its likelihood of developing a strong brand image. **Specific positioning** involves the ability to create strong connections between the product, certain key attributes, and the product's benefits in consumers' minds.[56] In the case of the Taurus/Sable, it would be possible to create an image in which the autos were perceived by consumers as moderately priced, highly expressive, and technologically advanced.

Another positive feature of the brands was the ease with which they could be competitively positioned. **Competitive positioning** relates to the issue of how a brand is positioned relative to its competitors.[57] The goal of competitive positioning is to emphasize the attributes possessed by the product in relation to other leading brands. As Figure 3-14 illustrates, the positioning of the Taurus/Sable models clearly distinguished them from the competitors. Companies frequently engage in comparative advertising when competitively positioning a brand. However, the Taurus/Sable models were positioned so uniquely that comparative advertising would have been unnecessary and undesirable.

Consideration of the butterfly curve may have had implications for the promotional strategy of Ford Motor Company. Because of the radical design of the models, it was possible that consumers' initial reactions would be negative. As discussed in the chapter-opening vignette, Ford used a strategy of publicizing what the cars would look like a full six months prior to their launch date. Of course, the goal was to begin to adapt consumers to the cars' style so that they would not be perceived as radical in design when seen in the showroom.

Because of the highly distinctive appearance of the product, Ford Motor Company was in the enviable position of not having to worry a great deal about capturing the consumers' attention. The radical shape of the models could possibly cause an orientation reaction to occur when customers first encountered the promotional materials released by the company. In sum, the design of the product enhanced the ability of the company to gain the consumer's attention. Accordingly, Ford continues to prominently display design in the models' advertising.

When developing advertising strategy, managers should consider principles of perceptual organization. The distinctive design of the Taurus/Sable models would allow the cars to stand out from the background. Indeed, one strategy would be to simply show photographs of the car in various settings emphasizing use—or in settings that might have symbolic value. Because of their unique design, little danger existed that the models would not act as the figure moving against the background in the advertisement.

The Managerial Implications

Table 3-7 presents the managerial applications of the consumer concepts that were identified as applying to the Taurus case. The first consumer concept that appears in the table is involvement, which relates to the managerial areas of conducting marketing research, doing segmentation analysis, and creating promotional strategy. Market research studies should be conducted to identify market segments composed of consumers having different levels of product involvement. These segments can then be targeted with different messages or reached through different media. (As noted in the chapter, scales have been developed to assess variations in enduring involvement.) For example, it would make sense to

TABLE 3-7

Managerial Implications of Consumer Concepts in the Taurus Case

Consumer Concepts	*Managerial Implications*
1. Involvement	*Market research*—Employ to identify market segments having enduring and/or situational involvement.
	Segmentation—Create different marketing strategies for reaching those with enduring versus situational involvement.
	Promotional strategy—Develop divergent messages and use different media for reaching target markets.
2. Just noticeable difference	*Product design*—Utilize to ensure that the Taurus was different from competitors.
	Promotional strategy—Employ to enhance perception that Taurus was a unique vehicle.
	Environmental analysis—Analyze competition to develop a unique vehicle.
3. Butterfly curve	*Promotional strategy*—Release photos of cars early to encourage the adaptation process.
4. Perceptual organization	*Promotional strategy*—Enable advertisers to focus on showing the unique design of the cars, rather than "trick up" the ads with extraneous visual material (e.g., beautiful models) to create a brand image.

specifically target as a market segment consumers who possess high amounts of enduring involvement with autos. Such individuals could act as opinion leaders. By identifying the characteristics of this group, management would be better able to design advertisements that would reach and influence appropriately the desired target market.

The concept of the just noticeable difference relates to the managerial areas of the marketing mix, positioning/differentiation, and environmental analysis. The distinctive design of the Taurus helped to ensure that consumers could differentiate it from competitors. Promotional strategy was developed to position the Taurus as a distinctive vehicle representing a departure from traditional American cars. As a part of this strategy development, Ford also had to perform environmental analyses to study the competition and to anticipate their countermoves.

The concepts of the butterfly curve and of adaptation can be used together to influence marketing mix strategy. Because the company released photos of the Taurus early to the press, consumers were able to adapt to the highly novel looks of the vehicle. From the perspective of the butterfly curve, this would result in an increase in liking for the model—because exposure to the photos would move consumers closer to the adaptation level.

Concepts from perceptual organization have direct application to developing promotional strategy. Because of the distinctive shape of the model, it would act as a figure that stands out from the background. As a result, managers did not have to "trick up" print advertisements with lots of beautiful models or employ comparisons with competing brands. Instead, they could merely show the auto alone for consumers to comprehend its novelty.

SUMMARY

Information processing may be defined as the process through which consumers are exposed to information, attend to it, comprehend it, place it in memory, and retrieve it for later use. Several areas are closely related to the study of information processing. These include the study of consumer involvement and the processes of exposure, attention, comprehension, and memory. (Because of their importance, Chapter 4 will focus on memory processes.) In addition, the field of semiotics has strong relevance to the study of comprehension processes.

Consumer involvement refers to the level of perceived personal importance and/or interest evoked by a stimulus in a specific situation. Such situational involvement will change as the person, product, situation, and communications change. In contrast, enduring involvement refers to a longer-term commitment and concern with a product class. There are a number of dimensions of involvement, including self-expressive importance, hedonic importance, practical relevance, and purchase risk.

Exposure refers to the process through which consumers initially receive information through their senses. Consumers show a strong tendency to selectively expose themselves to information. Advertisers must be concerned with how they can prevent consumers from selectively exposing themselves to commercials through remote-control channel changing, or "zapping." An important aspect of the exposure process is the study of sensation. Sensations are the immediate impressions left by the firing of nerve fibers in response to the physical stimulation of the senses. For consumer researchers, important aspects of the study of sensation include investigation of absolute and differential thresholds, the adaptation level, the butterfly curve, and subliminal perception.

The study of attention is another important area of information processing. Voluntary attention involves the consumer in actively searching out information to achieve some type of goal. Through selective attention, consumers focus on stimuli that match their goals. Involuntary attention occurs when a consumer is exposed to something surprising, novel, or unexpected. Through the orientation reflex, people will focus attention on such a stimulus to comprehend its nature.

Another important area in information processing is the study of comprehension. Comprehension refers to how consumers organize and interpret information. Marketers must recognize that different people can perceive the same stimulus in quite divergent ways. Such perceptual differences can result from variations in expectancies and the peculiar ways in which different people organize information.

Semiotics is a field devoted to the study of symbols and the meanings that people obtain from signs. Signs are the words, gestures, pictures, products, and logos used to communicate information from one person to another. Semiosis analysis is used to identify how signs function to communicate information and involves identifying an object, a sign, and an interpretant. The interpretant is a person's reaction to and the meaning derived from a sign.

KEY WORDS

absolute threshold
adaptation
adaptation level
attention
attention stage
butterfly curve
competitive positioning
comprehension
comprehension stage
consumer information processing
enduring involvement
expectations
exposure
Gestalt psychologists
information
interpretation process
involvement
involvement responses
just noticeable difference (JND)
orientation reflex
perception
perceptual organization
price–quality relationship
selective attention
selective exposure
semiotics
sensation
signs
situational involvement
specific positioning
spontaneous brand switching
subliminal perception
voluntary versus involuntary attention
Weber's law
zapping

REVIEW QUESTIONS

1. Define the concept of information.
2. Define the concept of information processing.
3. Distinguish the concepts of exposure, attention, and comprehension.
4. What is meant by the term "consumer involvement"?
5. What are the types of consumer involvement? What happens when consumers are in a high-involvement state?
6. Briefly discuss what happens during the exposure stage of information processing.
7. What does the study of sensation involve?

8. Can subliminal perception have an impact on consumers? Why or why not?
9. What are absolute and difference thresholds?
10. Discuss the concepts of selective exposure and attention.
11. Define and give a marketing example of Weber's law. Why is it better to use the term "just meaningful difference" rather than "just noticeable difference"?
12. What is meant by adaptation level? How does it relate to the butterfly curve?
13. Discuss what is meant by attention. What are two types of attention?
14. What happens during the comprehension stage of information processing?
15. What is the relationship between expectations and interpretation?
16. Identify five of the six principles of perceptual organization discussed in the chapter.
17. Briefly discuss the relationship that consumers frequently perceive between price and quality.
18. What is meant by the term "semiotics"? What happens during semiosis analysis?

DISCUSSION QUESTIONS

1. Consumer involvement is influenced by the product, the situation, the communication received, and the person. Give two examples each of high- and low-involvement products, high- and low-involvement situations, and high- and low-involvement communications. Give an example of a case in which you are highly involved with a product and in which a specific acquaintance is not highly involved. How does this affect information processing for the two of you?
2. Select five products with different prices—ranging from less than a dollar to thousands of dollars. For each product, indicate what you would consider to be the JND for a sale price. To what extent do you find that these JNDs exemplify Weber's law?
3. To what extent do you think that clothing designers utilize the concept of the adaptation level? Would it make a difference in their behavior if they understood the concept of the butterfly curve?
4. Select three print advertisements. Identify as many instances as you can of examples of stimulus factors that are used to gain your attention.
5. Using the same three advertisements, identify as many examples as you can of perceptual organization.
6. Look through magazines that contain cigarette and liquor advertisements. Find three possible examples of subliminal messages in the ads. Were these embedded symbols placed there deliberately, in your opinion?
7. Conduct interviews with five of your friends. In these interviews identify cases in which these individuals have used price as an indicator of quality. To what extent do these cases match the occasions discussed in the chapter when price is most frequently used as an indicator of quality?
8. Watch a popular evening soap opera, such as "Melrose Place." Discuss how consumer products/services were used as symbols to help develop the plot of the show.
9. Go through one or more popular magazines and carefully examine the print advertisements. Identify three examples of symbols used in the ads. Conduct a semiosis analysis for each ad to show how the signs communicate meaning about the product or service.

ENDNOTES

1. Rich Ceppos, "The 1986 Mercury Sable," *Car and Driver*, March 1985, pp. 43–46.
2. Charles Osgood, *Method and Theory in Experimental Psychology* (New York: Oxford University Press, 1964).
3. Norbert Wiener, "Cybernetics in History," in *Modern Systems Research for the Behavioral Scientist*, Walter Buckley, ed. (Chicago: Aldine, 1968), pp. 31–36.
4. Richard L. Celsi and Jerry C. Olson, "The Role of Involvement in Attention and Comprehension Processes," *Journal of Consumer Research*, Vol. 15 (September 1988), pp. 210–224. Also, see Anthony Greenwald and Clark Leavitt, "Audience Involvement in Advertising: Four Levels," *Journal of Consumer Research*, Vol. 11 (June 1984), pp. 581–592. For a general review of the strength of involvement effects, see Carolyn Costley, "Meta Analysis of Involvement Research," in *Advances in Consumer Research*, Vol. 15, Michael Houston, ed. (Provo, UT: Association for Consumer Research, 1988), pp. 554–562.
5. See John H. Antil, "Conceptualization and Operationalization of Involvement," in *Advances in Consumer Research*, Vol. XI, Thomas C. Kinnear, ed. (Ann Arbor, MI: Association for Consumer Research, 1984), pp. 203–209.
6. Marsha Richins and Peter H. Bloch, "After the New Wears Off: The Temporal Context of Product Involvement," *Journal of Consumer Research*, Vol. 13 (September 1986), pp. 280–285.
7. Marsha Richins, Peter H. Bloch, and Edward F. McQuarrie, "How Enduring and Situational Involvement Combine to Create Involvement Responses," *Journal of Consumer Psychology*, Vol. 1, no. 2 (1992), pp. 143–153.
8. Richins, Bloch, and McQuarrie, "How Enduring and Situational Involvement Combine."
9. Richins and Bloch, "After the New Wears Off." Other researchers have distinguished cognitive and emotional involvement. See C. Whan Park and S. Mark Young, "Consumer Response to Television Commercials: The Impact of Involvement and Background Music on Brand Attitude Formation," *Journal of Marketing Research*, Vol. 23 (February 1986), pp. 11–24. High cognitive involvement occurs when the message contents of a stimulus have a high degree of personal relevance. In contrast, high affective involvement occurs when the personal relevance is emotionally based, such as when the stimulus has implications for the person's self-concept.
10. The four dimensions identified were obtained from this author's synthesis of several research articles: Kapil Jain and Narasimhan Srinivasan, "An Empirical Assessment of Multiple Operationalizations of Involvement," *Advances in Consumer Research*, Vol. 17 (Provo, UT: Association for Consumer Research, (1990), pp. 594–602; Thomas Jensen, Les Carlson, and Carolyn Tripp, "The Dimensionality of Involvement: An Empirical Test," *Advances in Consumer Research*, Vol. 16 (Provo, UT: Association for Consumer Research, 1989), pp. 680–689; Robin Higie and Lawrence Feick, "Enduring Involvement: Conceptual and Measurement Issues," *Advances in Consumer Research*, Vol. 16 (Provo, UT: Association for Consumer Research, 1989), pp. 690–696.
11. Richard E. Petty, John T. Caccioppo, and David Schumann, "Central and Peripheral Routes to Advertising Effectiveness: The Moderating Role of Involvement," *Journal of Consumer Research*, Vol. 10 (September 1983), pp. 135–146.
12. Herbert Krugman, "The Impact of Television in Advertising: Learning Without Involvement," *Public Opinion Quarterly*, Vol. 30 (1965), pp. 583–596.
13. Costley, "Meta Analysis of Involvement Research."
14. For a discussion of how increased involvement and physiological arousal impacts the processing of information, see David M. Sanbonmatsu and Frank R. Kardes, "The Effects of Physiological Arousal on

Information Processing and Persuasion," *Journal of Consumer Research*, Vol. 15 (December 1988), pp. 379–385.

15. Bernie Whalen, "$6 Billion Down the Drain!" *Marketing News*, September 14, 1984, pp. 1–37.
16. "Background on Zapping," *Marketing News*, September 14, 1984, p. 36.
17. Whalen, "$6 Billion Down the Drain!"
18. Timothy E. Moore, "Subliminal Advertising: What You See Is What You Get," *Journal of Marketing*, Vol. 46 (Spring 1982), pp. 38–47.
19. Ibid.
20. W. Key, *Subliminal Seduction* (Englewood Cliffs, NJ: Prentice-Hall, 1973).
21. Moore, "Subliminal Advertising."
22. William Kilbourne, Scott Painton, and D. Ridley, "The Effect of Sexual Embedding on Responses to Magazine Advertisements," *Journal of Advertising*, Vol. 14, no. 2 (1985), pp. 48–56.
23. Del Hawkins, "The Effects of Subliminal Stimulation on Drive Level and Brand Preference," *Journal of Marketing Research*, Vol. 7, no. 3 (1970), pp. 322–326.
24. R. Cuperfain and T. K. Clarke, "A New Perspective on Subliminal Perception," *Journal of Advertising*, Vol. 14, no. 1 (1985), pp. 36–41.
25. Joel Saegert, "Why Marketing Should Quit Giving Subliminal Advertising the Benefit of the Doubt," *Psychology and Marketing* (Summer 1987), pp. 107–120.
26. Ibid.
27. Philip M. Merikle and Jim Cheesman, "Current Status of Research on Subliminal Perception," in *Advances in Consumer Research*, Vol. 14, Melanie Wallendorf and Paul Anderson, eds. (Provo, UT: Association for Consumer Research, 1987), pp. 298–302.
28. David Stipp, "A Flavor Analyst Should Never Ask, 'What's for Lunch?'" *The Wall Street Journal*, August 3, 1988, pp. 1–10.
29. Bruce Buchanan, Moshe Givon, and Arieh Goldman, "Measurement of Discrimination Ability in Taste Tests: An Empirical Investigation," *Journal of Marketing Research*, Vol. 24 (May 1987), pp. 154–163.
30. Richard Lee Miller, "Dr. Weber and the Consumer," *Journal of Marketing* (January 1962), pp. 57–61.
31. John Koten, "Why Do Hot Dogs Come in Packs of 10 and Buns in 8s or 12s?" *The Wall Street Journal*, September 21, 1984, pp. 1–26.
32. See Leon G. Schiffman and Leslie L. Kanuk, Figure 6-1, in "Sequential Changes in Packaging That Fall Below the J.N.D.," *Consumer Behavior* (Englewood Cliffs, NJ: Prentice-Hall, 1983), p. 140.
33. Jonathan Dahl, "Tracking Travel," *The Wall Street Journal*, May 15, 1990, p. B1.
34. Flemming Hansen, *Consumer Choice Behavior* (New York: Collier Macmillan, 1972).
35. Daniel Kahneman, *Attention and Effort* (Englewood Cliffs, NJ: Prentice-Hall, 1973).
36. Ibid.
37. Ibid.
38. Julie Liesse Erickson, "Energizer Bunny Gets the Jump," *Advertising Age*, October 23, 1989, p. 4.
39. Sana Siwolop, "You Can't (Hum) Ignore (Hum) That Ad," *Business Week*, September 21, 1987, p. 56.
40. Pamela S. Schindler, "Color and Contrast in Magazine Advertising," *Psychology and Marketing*, Vol. 3, no. 2 (1986), pp. 69–78.
41. Ronald Alsop, "Coming Attractions: TV Ads at Movie Houses Everywhere," *The Wall Street Journal*, July 3, 1986, p. 17.
42. The factors that influence attention are closely related to the effects of salience on memory. These issues are discussed in the next chapter. Also see John Lynch and Thomas Srull, "Memory and Attentional Factors in Consumer Choice: Concepts and Research Methods," *Journal of Consumer Research*, Vol. 9 (June 1982), pp. 18–37.
43. David W. Stewart, "The Moderating Role of Recall, Comprehension, and Brand Differentiation on the Persuasiveness of Television Advertising," *Journal of Advertising Research*, Vol. 25 (March–April 1986), pp. 43–47.

44. Jacob Jacoby and Wayne D. Hoyer, "The Comprehension/Miscomprehension of Print Communication: Selected Findings," *Journal of Consumer Research*, Vol. 15 (March 1989), pp. 434–443.

45. E. T. Hall, *The Hidden Dimension* (Garden City, NY: Doubleday, 1966).

46. Marj Charlier, "Beer Drinkers in Texas, California Don't Swallow Change in Coors Label," *The Wall Street Journal*, December 29, 1988, p. B4.

47. Gail Tom, Teresa Barnett, William Lew, and Jodean Selmants, "Cueing the Consumer: The Role of Salient Cues in Consumer Perception," *Journal of Consumer Marketing*, Vol. 4 (Spring 1987), pp. 23–27.

48. M. Tysoe, "What's Wrong with Blue Potatoes?" *Psychology Today*, Vol. 19 (December 1985), pp. 6–8.

49. Kent B. Monroe, "The Influence of Price Differences and Brand Familiarity on Brand Preferences," *Journal of Consumer Research*, Vol. 3 (June 1976), pp. 42–49; and Valarie Zeithaml and Merrie Brucks, "Price as an Indicator of Quality Dimensions," paper presented at the 1987 Association for Consumer Research Annual Conference, October 9–11, Cambridge, Massachusetts. Also, see Chr. Hjorth-Anderson, "The Concept of Quality and the Efficiency of Markets for Consumer Products," *Journal of Consumer Research*, Vol. 11 (September 1984), pp. 708–718.

50. Kent B. Monroe and Akshay R. Rao, "Testing the Relationship Between Price, Perceived Quality and Perceived Value," paper presented at the 1987 Association for Consumer Research Annual Conference, October 9–11, Cambridge, Massachusetts.

51. David Mick, "Consumer Research and Semiotics: Exploring the Morphology of Signs, Symbols, and Significance," *Journal of Consumer Research*, Vol. 13 (September 1986), pp. 196–213.

52. Kenneth Boulding, *The Image* (Ann Arbor: University of Michigan Press, 1956), p. 44.

53. Charles Sanders Peirce, *Collected Papers*, Charles Hartshorne, Paul Weiss, and Arthur W. Burks, eds. (Cambridge, MA.: Harvard University Press, 1931–1958); and David Mick, in "Consumer Research and Semiotics," noted that scholars have had great difficulty determining precisely what Peirce meant by the "interpretant."

54. Richard Zakia and Mihai Nadin, "Semiotics, Advertising, and Marketing," *Journal of Consumer Marketing*, Vol. 4 (Spring 1987), p. 6.

55. Russell Belk, Kenneth Bahn, and Robert Mayer, "Developmental Recognition of Consumption Symbolism, *Journal of Consumer Research*, Vol. 9 (June 1982), pp. 4–17.

56. Philip Kotler, *Marketing Management: Analysis, Planning, and Control*, 4th ed. (Englewood Cliffs, NJ: Prentice-Hall, 1980).

57. Ibid.

CHAPTER 3 CASE STUDY

The Compact Disc Longbox: A Packaging Dilemma

In the early 1980s consumers were introduced to a new form of audio medium that has since revolutionized the music industry—the compact disc (CD). When compact discs began to replace LPs, a problem concerned how to package them. The solution was to put the jewel box (i.e., the hard, clear plastic disc casing) inside a long cardboard box measuring 6 inches by 12 inches. Commonly called the "longbox," this packaging allowed the retailer to replace one LP with two CDs, due to their smaller size. The solution seemed a clever and efficient way to handle the packaging problem without replacing shelves. In addition, it also acted to deter theft of the small jewel box.

The use of longboxes, however, quickly came under criticism. The jewel box measures 5 inches by 5½ inches, which leaves the remainder of the longbox as a wasted use of resources. This increases shipping, storing, and manufacturing costs and adds anywhere from $0.75 to $1.50 to the cost of a CD [1]. Further, in 1989, longboxes accounted for some 20 million pounds of garbage [2].

Some have advocated eliminating longboxes, which would decrease the price of CDs by lowering shipping, storage, and manufacturing costs as well as cut down on wasted natural resources. In rebuttal, retailers claimed that the act could have negative effects on the consumer. Changing CD packaging would require new retail display fixtures and added theft deterrence measures, which would increase the cost of CDs. In addition, two-thirds of the sales of CDs are impulse purchases in which decisions are made within 8 seconds [3]. A decrease in the size of a CD box could result in consumers paying less attention to new artists and albums. Graphics are a key element in attracting attention to CDs for impulse sales. An executive of a major music retail chain said, "We deliver feelings, nothing we sell, people need. . .but it is an integral part of their lives" [4].

Advocates of banning longboxes feel the decrease in size of the package would not influence actual stimulus size because most CD titles in longboxes use only the top 5 square inches to reproduce the cover of the booklet for graphics. Furthermore, in countries that sell CDs in only the jewel boxes, sales have been quite successful, even with the limited amount of graphics space [5].

Some companies have found that eliminating the longbox increased sales of CDs. One alternative is to put the jewel boxes into a special locked cabinet or glass casing. This helps solve security problems and also acts to enhance the product image. Roger Whiteman, vice president of inventory and distribution for a major music store chain, commented, "Psychologically, there's an attraction to browsing, and it allows people to touch the product. The CD in just the jewel box looks more expensive than in a dirty, grubby, old longbox." Whiteman also noted that the longbox displays are a "mishmash to the eye," saying that "When you have a wall of just jewel boxes, in a uniform, colorful display, it can only attract customers" [6]. Further, a uniform package of jewel boxes could decrease the possibility of information overload and consequently lead to better decision quality.

By 1992 several new approaches to the longbox began to appear in the marketplace. Each could be expanded to the full longbox size. In addition, each could be made into a more compact shape, either by folding the package or by sliding the jewel box into a drawer. Only time will tell which design will win over the marketplace.

QUESTIONS

1. What are the major problems facing the music industry concerning the use of longboxes?
2. Which concepts from perception apply to the longbox case, and how do they apply to the problems faced by the music industry?
3. Develop a managerial applications analysis. Using applicable information processing concepts as a foundation for your answer, what managerial strategies should the music industry follow when attempting to deal with the longbox issues?

REFERENCES

1. Robert Simonds, "A Modest Proposal on CD Packaging," *Billboard Magazine*, October 7, 1989.
2. Gerry Wood, "Save Mother Earth: Bag the CD Longbox," *Billboard Magazine*, June 9, 1990, p. 6.
3. Geoff Mayfield, "Dealers Defend Longbox: CD Packaging Argued at NARM Meet," *Billboard Magazine*, October 7, 1989, p. 1.
4. Ed Christman and Nigel Hunter, "NARM '90: National Association of Recording Merchandisers Conference," *Billboard Magazine*, March 17, 1990, p. N3.
5. "Quid Pro Quo Indicated on 6-by-12 Box," *Billboard Magazine*, October 21, 1989, p. 11.
6. Trudi Miller, "Pandora's Longbox Opened in Canada: Retailers Scramble for CD Pack Options," *Billboard Magazine*, June 9, 1990, pp. 6, 45, 50.

Case developed by Cody Roberts and Jeri L. Jones.

Chapter 4

Information Processing II: Memory and Cognitive Learning

CONSUMER VIGNETTE

The Xerox Copier Failure

It was 1980, and industrial buyers were in the process of rejecting Xerox Corporation's new 8200 office copier. Xerox's management was stunned because it was the first time that consumers had balked at one of its products. Meanwhile, the market share of Japanese competitors jumped. What was causing the firm's customers to reject the 8200? A technological masterpiece, the copier had the three most advanced features demanded by businesses—collating, enlarging, and reducing capabilities. In the lab the copier worked perfectly. It was reliable, contained an onboard computer, and produced excellent copies.

A crash program was established to identify the cause of the market failure. The project manager brought in cognitive scientists, anthropologists, and the repair personnel who were the closest to the product's users. Quickly, the problem became apparent—ordinary people could not use the copier. As said by the manager, "no one paid attention to the human interface—to the user. People had to wade through buttons and visual noise and manuals for all features, including the most frequently used one, copying a page or two." The people who used the 8200 copier hated it. As a result of the analysis, the copier was totally redesigned. Clear, graphic displays and touch-screen menus were created that quickly and easily guided users through the machine's operations. By paying attention to the customer, the redesigned copier succeeded in the marketplace.

XEROX

News like this is enough to turn all other color copiers green.

Annual Design Awards

COLOR IT USER-FRIENDLY

DIGITAL COLOR COPIER

DESIGNER: XEROX CORP.

The new Xerox 5775 Digital Color Copier is the product of innovative thinking. So we're pleased that the Industrial Designers Society of America and BusinessWeek thought enough of our ideas to make it the envy of our competition.

We're also pleased because it confirms our belief that the best ideas come from listening to our customers. Before we built the 5775, we asked thousands of people what they really needed in a color copier.

They told us they wanted more than color copies. They said they wanted to be able to add color to the black and white documents they use in business every day; from presentations to forms and bills. They wanted color that was accessible, affordable, and faster.

The article above gives you a fair idea of how well we listened. What it doesn't tell you is that the same kind of thinking goes into the design of every single Xerox product, from our smallest copiers and faxes to our largest laser printers.

To learn more, call us at **1-800-TEAM-XRX, ext. 577A.**

We'll show you all the ways adding Xerox color to your documents can help keep your business in the black. And even turn your competition green.

Xerox
The Document Company

In order to make the processing of information easier for consumers, XEROX designs copiers, such as the model 5775, that are highly user firiendly. (Courtesy of XEROX Corporation.)

INTRODUCTION

Problems, such as those faced by Xerox in the design of the 8200 office copier, have reached epidemic proportions in the marketplace. Many products have become so complicated that even engineers with Ph.D.s cannot figure them out. Comedians joke that unless a teenager lives in the home, VCRs constantly blink 12:00 because adults cannot figure out how to set the time on the complicated devices. The issue was illustrated by the admission of the CEO of Digital Equipment Corporation (a talented engineer) that he could not solve the problem of how to heat a cup of coffee in the company's microwave oven. An article in *Business Week* describes the effect of these overly complex designs: "Manufacturers of consumer products are not only losing the interest of their customers but they're also alienating them." Indeed, the ability to make personal computing simpler was the key factor contributing to the success of Apple Computer's wildly successful Macintosh. As one Apple executive explained, "On the desktop today, 80% of computing power is going toward ease of use, such as menus, windows, and pop-ups. Only 20% is actually going toward doing the job, such as calculating your spreadsheet."[1] Table 4-1 illustrates the problem by presenting the directions for two consumer products. Can you understand what you are supposed to do?

The problem of prohibitively complex consumer products illustrates a number of issues involving the role of memory in consumer information processing. Most significantly, the vignette depicts the concept that customers have a limited capacity to process information. To use the Xerox 8200 office copier effectively, consumers were forced to process large amounts of data quickly. Because of the limitations of "working memory," only limited amounts of information can be processed at a time.

TABLE 4-1

Information Overload and Electronic Directions

Here are two examples of the confusing and maddening directions frequently found on electronic devices. Can you understand what to do?

1. An early model VCR.

   After pretuning, if you wish to change the real channel number to correspond to the actual pretuned station, press the CH NO. SET button after calling up the corresponding channel position number on the display and enter the desired channel number using the READ OUT buttons ("10" and "1"). The "1" button changes the figures of the units digit: numerals 0 and 9 are available. The "10" button changes the figure of the tens digit: blank, numerals 1 to 9, U and C are available.

2. Radio alarm clock.

   Set the alarm time for radio/tape or buzzer:

   Set the radio-tape alarm time with TIME SET H and M while holding down ALARM A RADIO/TAPE.

   Set the buzzer alarm time with TIME SET H and M while holding down ALARM B BUZZER.

If too much information is received at once, the problem-solving process breaks down. This occurred to consumers attempting to use the 8200 copier, and as a result, customers stopped buying the machine.

A second area of study illustrated by the vignette concerns the effects of consumer knowledge on product usage. Different individuals possess divergent amounts of experience with and knowledge of products. With increased consumer knowledge comes the ability to quickly process greater amounts of information. The engineers who designed the copier had extensive knowledge of the 8200 and to them it was quite simple to use. Customers, however, had much less knowledge of the copier, and for them it proved intractable. As a result, they felt frustrated and unhappy. Products must be designed for the eventual user, not for the engineers who develop them.

Finally, the chapter-opening vignette points out the salient role of emotions in information processing. When information overload occurs, arousal levels increase. Negative feelings result from the situation and cause customers to become dissatisfied with the product and to form disapproving attitudes toward it. Emotions strongly influence how information is processed and affect how customers react to the product use experience.

It was not until the 1990s that most companies began to recognize that products had to be designed for ease of use with the customer in mind. Interestingly, the Japanese appeared to be the slowest to catch on to the demand for simplicity. One retailer of stereo equipment said, “I don’t know why the Japanese put so many buttons on their machines. They have given us programming, and programming is not music. Programming means computers.” Particularly at the ultrahigh end of consumer electronics, one finds an extreme focus on simplicity. One upscale retailer said, “We have an audio system that sells for $150,000. It takes me 30 seconds to show a customer how to use it, and he never has to ask me again.” The system has three controls—volume, balance, and a selector button to choose among CD, tape deck, and other sources.[2] It seems that people with $150,000 to burn do not want to clutter their minds with too much information.

In studying the relationship between memory processes and how these processes can affect managerial strategy, a useful starting point is the development of a simplified memory model.

A SIMPLIFIED MEMORY MODEL

In the last chapter on consumer information processing, the focus was on perception (i.e., the exposure, attention, and comprehension stages). In the diagram of information processing, memory was shown to affect each of the stages. Memory allows consumers to anticipate the stimuli they might encounter. As a result, they can selectively expose themselves to desired stimuli. Similarly, memory influences attention processes by guiding a person’s sensory system so as to focus on particular stimuli. Finally, comprehension is affected by the expectations and associations elicited in memory by the stimuli encountered.

Figure 4-1 presents a simplified model of memory. The **multiple-store model** identifies three different types of memory storage systems—sensory memory, short-term memory, and long-term memory.[3] As can be seen in the figure, information is first registered in sensory memory where the preattention stage occurs. Here the stimulus is briefly analyzed in an unconscious manner—to determine if additional processing capacity should be allocated to it. If in the preattention stage the stimulus is perceived to be related to the person's goals, capacity will be allocated to it and the information shifts to short-term memory. In short-term memory, people actively process information. Long-term memory is connected to short-term memory through encoding and retrieval processes. **Encoding** refers to the process of transferring information from short- to long-term memory for permanent storage. **Retrieval** refers to the process of accessing information stored in long-term memory so that it can be utilized in short-term memory. Finally, affective and arousal states are conceptualized as influencing short-term and long-term memory.

Sensory Memory

The perception of a sight, sound, touch, or taste occurs because a stimulus activates nerve fibers in a person's sensory organs. This image becomes a part of the sensory memory. Lasting only a fraction of a second, the **sensory memory** of a stimulus consists of the immediate impression caused by the firing of the nerve cells. Because the nerve fibers fire for only very short lengths of time in response to outside stimulation (in most cases for less than a second), the stimulus information will be quickly lost unless it is processed further.[4] The firing of the nerve cells is monitored in the preattention stage. If the information is relevant to the person or activates an orienting response, it will be actively monitored in short-term memory.

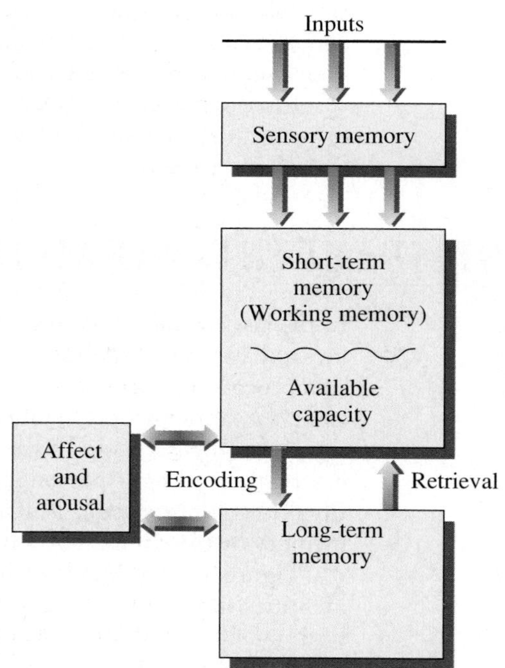

Figure 4-1
A simplified memory model.

Short-Term Memory

Short-term memory is the site where information is temporarily stored while being processed. For example, when a consumer thinks about a television commercial or actively attempts to solve a problem, the cognitive processing may be thought of as occurring in short-term memory. **Working memory**, which is another term for short-term memory, connotes the idea that individuals actively process information in this memory stage.

Evidence indicates that both auditory and visual information can be stored temporarily in short-term memory. However, it is more common to encode the visual information into words or sounds for further processing.[5] This occurs in part because auditory stimuli can be maintained in short-term memory longer than can visual stimuli.[6]

Just as the images contained in sensory memory are lost if not attended to, so is the information contained in short-term memory. The evidence indicates that if information in short-term memory is not rehearsed, it will be lost within about 30 seconds.[7] **Rehearsal** occurs when a person silently repeats information to encode it into long-term memory. One way such information is lost is through its replacement by other information in the limited storage capacity of short-term memory.[8]

The Limited Capacity of Short-Term Memory

Short-term memory has a number of important characteristics. First, it has a limited capacity. Psychologist George Miller has stated that the average person has the ability to process only about seven (plus or minus two) chunks of information at a time.[9] A chunk may be conceptualized as a single meaningful piece of information. A chunk could be a single letter, a syllable, or an entire word. This recognition that people can handle seven (plus or minus two) bits of information at a time has been labeled **Miller's law**. Some researchers have noted that Miller may have been too optimistic about the capacity of short-term memory. Indeed, in consumer contexts five (plus or minus two) bits may be a better estimate.

The limited capacity characteristic of short-term memory means that it acts as a kind of bottleneck. If more information is received than the consumer can handle, some of it will be lost. This limited capacity of working memory is one reason why customers had such difficulty using the Xerox 8200 copier discussed in the introductory vignette. The machine required consumers to process too much information, and as a result, they became highly uncomfortable with it.

The term **information overload** is used to describe the situation in which more information is received than can be processed in short-term memory. In addition to being unable to process all the information, consumers may react to overload by becoming aroused and by more narrowly focusing attention on only certain aspects of the incoming stimuli.[10] The consumer may simply make a random choice, not buy anything, or focus on the wrong product qualities for his or her decision.

Consumer research on information overload has been somewhat controversial.[11] In the information overload controversy, two questions are of importance. First, can consumers become overloaded with information? The answer here is an unequivocal "yes."[12] In the consumer societies of the United States, Western Europe, and many parts of the Far East, so many product choices abound, with so many options and characteristics, that far more information is available than can be processed.

The answer to the second question—Do consumers become overloaded?—is not as clear-cut. On one side of the argument is the knowledge that people actively manage the information they receive in order to avoid becoming overloaded. According to this view, "they stop far short of being overloaded."[13] On the other hand, a highly motivated consumer may attempt to collect so much information that it is impossible to handle all of it. In such instances decision quality may actually decrease.

The author of this text believes that information overload does occur in consumers. For example, information overload can easily occur when a salesperson is explaining the characteristics of a complex product, such as a computer. The uninformed buyer can quite easily be overwhelmed with facts. The consumer is likely to become aroused and nervous and to focus on narrow aspects of the product, which may or may not be appropriate. Such overarousal can lead to poor decisions and is often just the opposite of what the well-intentioned salesperson had in mind. The introductory vignette on the Xerox 8200 copier illustrated the difficulties that result for companies when their products cause information overload. Another occasion in which information overload can occur is when consumers make purchases in a culture in which they must speak a foreign language.[14] Under such circumstances, people become highly aroused and uncomfortable.

Involvement and Short-Term Memory Capacity

The amount of arousal felt by the consumer will influence the capacity of short-term memory.[15] In high-involvement situations the consumer is likely to be more aroused and more attentive, thereby expanding the capacity of short-term memory to its maximal extent. In contrast, under low-involvement conditions the consumer's arousal level is apt to be low, so the consumer focuses relatively little memory capacity on the stimulus. Advertisers generally maintain that the number of copy points that can be transmitted in an ad are limited to about three or four ideas. If copy points are viewed as analogous to chunks of information, this would indicate that in television advertising the cognitive capacity of consumers is quite low. This idea makes perfect sense when viewed from the perspective that most television advertising is done in low-involvement situations in which arousal levels are low and little cognitive capacity is allocated to the task of processing the information in the ad. For companies advertising on television or radio, the implication is direct—keep your messages simple.

Transfer of Information from Short-Term to Long-Term Memory

One of the functions of short-term memory is to assist in the transfer of information to **long-term memory**, where information is permanently stored. As a person allocates more capacity to a stimulus, the likelihood of it being transferred to long-term memory increases. One way to allocate increased capacity to a stimulus is through the process of rehearsal. This process may involve the silent verbal repetition of information or the application of more energy to the task. An example of rehearsal is the silent repetition of a telephone number between the time we look it up and the time when the number is dialed.

One research study investigated the impact of rehearsal on the recall of advertised products by young children.[16] In the study children either rehearsed or did not rehearse the names of the products by saying them aloud. The results revealed that when the children (ages 4 to 9) rehearsed the names of the products, they were better able to recall information about the brands. The implication of the study for advertisers is the possibility that commercials that induce repetition of material (e.g., jingles and slogans) may improve the transfer of information from short-term to long-term memory.

Some debate exists as to how long it takes to transfer a chunk of information into long-term memory. Evidence exists to indicate that it depends upon just how the information is to be recalled from long-term memory. If the goal simply involves recognizing that a stimulus has been seen, it may take only two to five seconds for transfer if the information is processed. In contrast, if the information must be recalled without assistance at a later time, the transfer time is longer—from five to ten seconds for a single chunk.

These differences in transfer times have important implications for marketers. When developing messages for consumers, the marketer should consider whether the consumer will be in a recognition task or a recall task. In a **recognition task**, information is placed in front of a consumer. The goal of the person is to judge whether the information has been seen previously. In a **recall task**, the consumer must retrieve the information from long-term memory. Thus, in recognition tasks, memory recall is said to be aided; in recall tasks the retrieval of memories is unaided.

Grocery shopping frequently involves consumers in a recognition task. For example, if the product is of a low-involvement nature, such as laundry detergent, the shopper may merely scan the shelves for ideas on what to buy. Because the shopper is engaging in a recognition task, the transmission time from short-term to long-term memory will probably be shorter than for recall tasks. As a consequence, the commercials used to advertise the brand may not have to be as long, be repeated as frequently, or attract as much attention from the consumer as when the consumer must recall the information without aid.

Figure 4-2 shows a print ad that may activate recognition memory. The ad for Goodyear tires shows two people water skiing behind a car. It is likely to elicit recognition memory for a popular television commercial that literally showed a man and woman water skiing behind a car driving through shallow water. By eliciting recognition memory, the print ad will have surplus meaning that goes beyond its written and pictorial content.

In other instances, the direct recall of a product name from memory may be required. For example, suppose that a group of friends decide to go out to lunch on the spur of the moment. Each person will name a restaurant choice, and from this list of options a decision is made. If the name of a restaurant is not recalled from memory, it simply will not be selected. This set of restaurants recalled from memory is called the **consideration set**. It is crucial that a company's product be included in the consideration set for it to have a chance for consideration in such circumstances. Because the time required to transfer information from short-term to long-term memory is longer when unaided recall is required, firms may have to go to greater lengths to have consumers exposed to messages about their brand.

Because short-term memory has a limited capacity, information temporarily stored there will be replaced when new information is input into it. As a result, the earlier material may not be transferred to long-term memory. When consumers watch television or read a magazine, they are bombarded by dozens of advertisements competing for attention. The problem of too many ads has been called

Figure 4-2 This print ad for the AQUATRED tire should activate recognition memory for television ads that featured skiers being pulled by a car driving over a thin layer of water.

clutter. For example, the 1993 Super Bowl football extravaganza lasted 3 hours and 25 minutes. During that time viewers saw 68 commercials. A market research study conducted after the game found that less than half of the respondents could remember any ads for PepsiCo, which was the game's biggest sponsor, spending $6.8 million. One researcher said that there was so much clutter that it was ". . .hard for any company to break through."[17] Highlight 4-1 discusses further the market research on the 1993 Super Bowl game.

The research findings on how information is transferred from short-term to long-term memory suggest that clutter could be a major problem for advertisers. Advertising clutter impedes the ability of consumers to move information from tem-

HIGHLIGHT 4-1

Clutter in the 1993 Super Bowl

While the 1993 Super Bowl game was another "blow-out" in which the Dallas Cowboys branded and slaughtered the Buffalo Bills, the advertising hype reached new highs. During "regular" prime-time television, approximately 15% of each television hour is devoted to commercials. In contrast, in the 1993 Super Bowl game commercials took up 30% of broadcast time. Indeed, during one 45-minute period, 44% of the time went to advertisements. Despite this extreme level of clutter, advertisers willingly spent $28,000 a second to promote their products during the game.

One independent research firm contacted by telephone 300 consumers after the game and assessed their top-of-the-mind awareness of the advertisers who promoted their products during the game. The results of the survey proved highly disappointing to advertisers. For example, Frito-Lay sponsored the Michael Jackson half-time show. While 80% of the consumers remembered watching the show, only 7% could identify its sponsor.

Gillette spent $3.4 million to introduce a new line of men's toiletries, but only 2% of the respondents could recall the ads. AT&T fared better. Six percent of the respondents recalled seeing its ads. However, AT&T did not do any advertising during the game. Master Lock company spent its entire yearly advertising budget to do a half-minute spot during the first quarter. Unfortunately, no one mentioned seeing the ad.

The research director of the advertising recall survey said that so much clutter occurred in the 1993 Super Bowl that ". . .it was hard for any company to break through." But companies appeared to be able to rationalize the results of the survey. A Gillette Co. publicist said, "We've come to expect clutter." Then, there was the response of a spokesperson for Seven-Up Co., which had the misfortune to advertise late in the game after 1.2 million people had turned off the game because of the rout. The company spent $2.5 million for a 9% recall rate. The manager said, "We don't know if the audience was still paying attention. But we created brand awareness. You're calling me, aren't you?"

The key problem for marketing researchers, however, is: how do you measure and then assess the impact of brand awareness on consumer buying behavior? When the fortunes of entire companies and thousands of workers' jobs are at stake, such as in the case of Master Lock and Seven-Up, this question is one of the most important in the field of marketing.

Based upon Kevin Goldman, "Barrage of Ads in Super Bowl Blurs Messages," *The Wall Street Journal*, February 3, 1993, p. B6.

porary storage in short-term memory to permanent storage in long-term memory, particularly when unaided recall is required.[18] Table 4-2 summarizes some important points concerning short-term memory.

Long-Term Memory

In contrast to short-term memory, long-term memory has an essentially unlimited capacity to store information permanently.[19] The stored information tends to be either semantic or visual in nature. Semantic concepts are the verbal meanings

TABLE 4-2

Summary of Short-Term Memory (STM) Processes

1. STM has a limited capacity of seven, plus or minus two, chunks of information.
2. STM is the site at which information is processed and temporarily stored.
3. Information overload can occur if more information is received than can be processed in STM.
4. As involvement levels increase, consumers may allocate more capacity to a stimulus.
5. Information is transferred from STM to long-term memory by allocating more capacity to it. One method for allocating more capacity involves the rehearsal of the material to be learned.

attached to words, events, objects, and symbols. Thus long-term memory stores the meanings of words, symbols, and such along with the associations among various semantic concepts. Long-term memory can also store information in terms of its sequence of occurrence (episodic memory), in terms of its modality (e.g., visual, smell, touch senses), and in terms of its affective, or emotional, content.[20]

The permanent nature of long-term memory is illustrated by the enduring quality of brand names. In 1987 General Motors brought back the name Nova in a new car model despite its translation problems. (In Spanish Nova can be interpreted to mean "no go.") The name had not been used since 1980. However, consumers retained an image of the brand as reliable and low cost, so it seemed appropriate for a new car built jointly with Toyota. Herbert Krugman, an important scholar-practitioner in marketing, noted: "Bringing back well-known brand names could be a clever idea because so much of the marketing work is done. People's memory of old advertising campaigns and packaging is remarkably persistent."[21]

Relative Superiority of Picture Versus Word Memory

An important finding from psychology and consumer behavior is that pictures tend to be more memorable than their verbal counterparts, particularly under low-involvement circumstances.[22] In one study consumers received one set of information about a brand from the written copy of the print ad and a different set of information from the pictorial content of the ad. Thus the visual material pertained to one characteristic of the brand (e.g., its durability) and the verbal material talked about another characteristic (e.g., its value for the money). The results of the study revealed that significantly more pictorial information was recalled and recognized than verbally presented information.[23] Thus the aphorism "a picture is worth a thousand words" has some scientific support.

Another study found that if the words in a message have high-imagery content, then the addition of pictures is not as important. (A high-imagery word would be "table"; a low-imagery word would be "future.") In the study, high- and low-imagery versions of advertisements were created. The messages were either accompanied or not accompanied by a photograph. The results revealed that the photograph did not significantly enhance the recall of the message when high-imagery words were used. In contrast, when low-imagery words were used, the picture did significantly enhance recall. Two managerial implications can be drawn from the research. First, advertisers should use high-imagery words whenever possible. Second, the use of photographs can significantly increase recall if the words in the message have relatively low-imagery content.[24]

Researchers have also found that visual material is particularly easily recognized if the objects to be remembered are perceived as interacting in some way. Thus, to associate a product with a famous endorser, the advertiser would want to show the endorser actually using the product in everyday scenes.[25]

One can make the following generalizations about the effects of the verbal and pictorial content of ads on memory:

1. In general, pictorial content is recognized and recalled more readily than verbal content, particularly if the verbal material has low-imagery content.
2. Verbal material is best recalled when it is processed under high-involvement circumstances.
3. If consumers are engaged in high-involvement information processing, greater overall recall may result from giving different information about a product via verbal and pictorial means.
4. Words and pictures can be used to complement each other in ads.[26]

Memory-Control Processes

Although it is important for the consumer researcher to understand how memory is structured, it is equally important to understand how people get information into and out of memory. Called **memory-control processes**, these methods of handling information may operate consciously or unconsciously to influence the encoding, placement, and retrieval of information.[27]

Encoding

Although rehearsal influences whether or not information is transferred from short-term to long-term memory, how the information is coded has a great impact on the speed of transfer and on the placement of the information in memory. During rehearsal, a consumer can simply repeat the stimulus over and over or attempt to link the stimulus to other information already placed into long-term memory. As the consumer grows more adept at coding information by drawing associations between it and information already in memory, the storage process is likely to speed up proportionally.[28]

The development of brand names by marketers should be governed by a recognition that an encoding process occurs. As a product name fits more and more closely with the associations evoked by the product class, there is proportional improvement in recall of the name.[29] In one study the researcher argued that highly concrete names, which could be easily visualized, would be remembered better because they would be coded both visually and verbally. In addition, such names might be better coded with existing knowledge structures. In the study respondents were given either high-imagery or low-imagery brand names. Examples of high-imagery names were ocean, orchestra, frog, and blossom. Examples of low-imagery brand names were history, capacity, truth, and moment. The results revealed that subjects recalled more of the high-imagery names. An example of a product with a high-imagery name is Head & Shoulders shampoo.

Retrieval and Response Generation

The act of remembering something consists of the control processes of retrieval and response generation. As noted earlier, the retrieval process consists of the individual searching through long-term memory to identify within it the information desired to be recalled. In **response generation**, the person develops a response by actively reconstructing the stimulus.[30] The individual or consumer does not access stored replicas of the encoded stimulus information. Instead, traces of stimuli are activated and reconstructed into a recollection of the stimulus. The consumer uses logic, intuition, expectations, and whatever else is available to help reconstruct a memory.

A major problem for advertisers involves the issue of how to improve the consumer's ability to retrieve information from memory. One means is to provide consumers with retrieval cues on the packaging of a product. Such **retrieval cues** may be created by placing the verbal or visual information, originally contained in an ad, on the product or the packaging to assist consumers' memories during decision making.[31] For example, in one advertising campaign for Life cereal, a cute kid, Mikey, was used as a guinea pig to test an unknown cereal because he hated everything. When he actually liked the cereal, the other kids knew it had to be good. Consumers responded well to the commercials. To help them retrieve the memories of the commercials when in the grocery store, managers placed a photo of Mikey on the package of Life cereal. The photo acted as an effective retrieval cue. Another means marketers use to assist retrieval and response generation is employing music in advertisements. Good evidence exists that if messages are sung, people will recall them better. For example, jingles can stay in consumers' heads for years. The maker of Mounds/Almond Joy brought back the "sometimes you feel like a nut" jingle because, even though the company had not played it for years, customers still remembered it. By bringing it back, the firm could capture an entire new generation of consumers with its message.

A recent study tested empirically the impact of attaching a message to music. In the study, a message was either sung or read to consumers. The results revealed that the respondents could recall significantly more words when the three verses of the message were sung. The author argued that music acts as a very powerful retrieval cue that can substantially improve recall.[32]

CONSUMER KNOWLEDGE

Stored in long-term memory is a person's knowledge about the consumption environment. Consumer knowledge has been defined as the amount of experience with and information that a person has about particular products or services.[33] Consumers possessing greater amounts of knowledge can think about a product across a number of dimensions and make finer distinctions among brands. For example, a person with large amounts of knowledge about wine can think in terms of several dimensions, such as a wine's color, bouquet, nose, acidity, and so on. A novice might think in terms of one dimension (e.g., how much he or she likes its taste).

For marketing managers, what are the implications of the study of consumer knowledge? As consumer knowledge increases, consumers become better organized, they are more efficient and accurate in their information processing, and they have better recall of information. The implication of these findings is that managers should consider the extent of consumer knowledge when developing the product. As illustrated in the chapter-opening vignette, Xerox Corporation failed to consider the amount of consumer knowledge when the 8200 copier was developed. The result was extreme dissatisfaction with the machine. The extent of consumer knowledge should also influence promotional strategy. Specifically, a message targeted to a knowledgeable prospect can be much more complex than a message addressed to a novice.

Semantic Memory Networks

One aspect of consumer knowledge involves **semantic memory**, which refers to how people store the meanings of verbal material in long-term memory. Strong evidence exists that information in semantic memory is organized into networks.[34] Figure 4-3 presents an example of what a memory network for automobiles might look like. The network is a series of memory nodes that represent the stored semantic concepts; the lines connecting the nodes indicate the associations that exist. According to one popular theory of semantic memory, information is recalled from the semantic network via spreading activation.[35] Thus, if a stimulus activates a node, activation will spread through the network and activate other nodes. Each node that is activated represents a memory that is recalled. Researchers have argued that five types of information can be stored at the memory nodes:[36]

1. The brand name
2. The brand's characteristics
3. Advertisements about the brand
4. The product category
5. Evaluative reactions to the brand and the ad

Referring to Figure 4-3, suppose that the Corvette node were activated by someone mentioning that he or she plans to buy one. The activation of the node would result in a spreading of activation into the semantic network. As a result a number of additional nodes will be activated. These nodes become the associations that a person will have with the semantic concept of Corvette. Thus various attributes of the car could be elicited as associations (e.g., sports car, fast, expensive, and prestigious). In addition, similar other brands of cars could be activated in memory (e.g., Porsche), as could various evaluative reactions stored in memory. Of course, consumers possess divergent memory structures, and the activation of a semantic concept may result in quite different sets of associations.

As seen in Figure 4-3, which portrays a fictitious memory network for a Corvette, consumers form a set of semantic associations with a brand name. A consumer's **brand knowledge** can be defined as consisting of a ". . .brand node in memory to which a variety of associations have been linked."[37] Thus in Figure 4-3 the brand name Corvette forms a node to which a variety of concepts are associated, such as its characteristics (e.g., goes very fast, is sexy, carries a high cost), brand connections (sports cars, Porsche), and evaluative reactions (e.g., fun). Figure 4-4 presents a diagram that identifies the dimensions of brand knowledge, which form into a memory network.

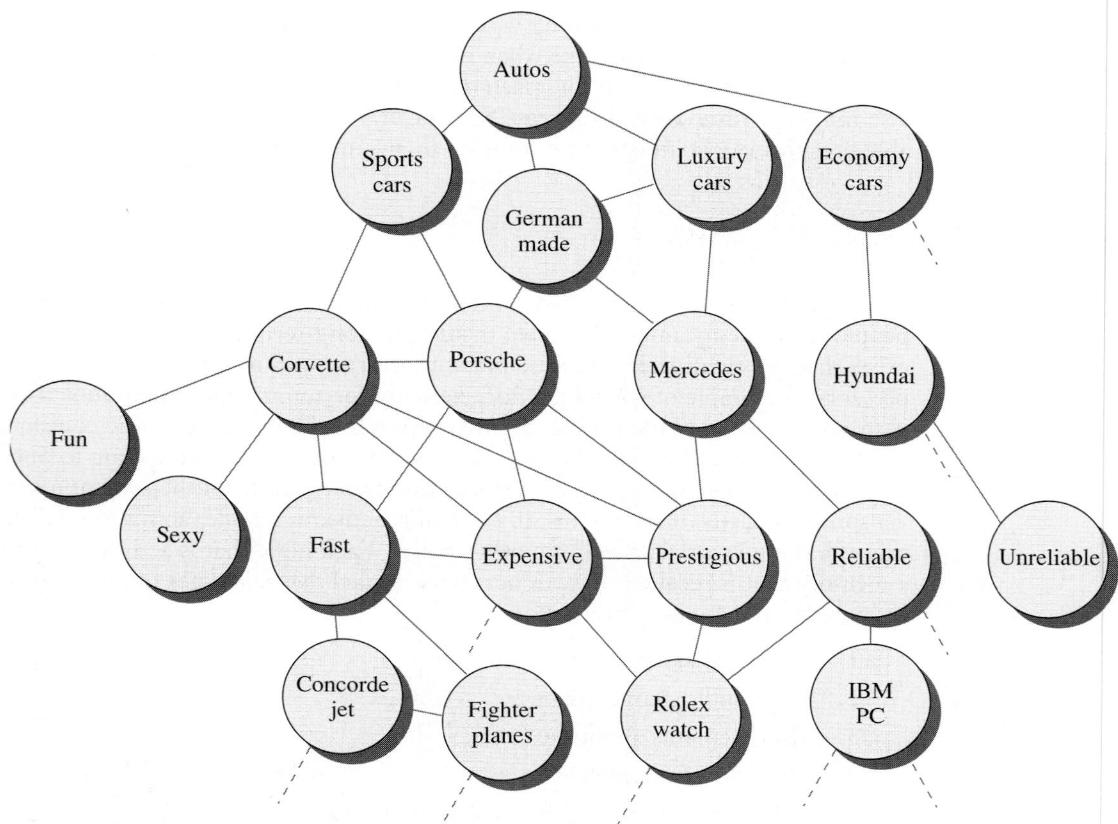

Figure 4-3 A semantic memory network.

Schemas

The total package of associations brought to mind when a node is activated is called a schema. Specifically, a **schema** is an organized set of expectations held by a person about an object. Schemas (also called schemata) are ". . .stored frameworks of knowledge about some object or topic and are represented by nodes in semantic memory."[38] Thus the Corvette schema consists of those associations and expectations that a particular person has about the car.

Researchers have found that when new information is inconsistent with a schema, consumers engage in more diligent processing and, consequently, have improved memory about the stimulus. Thus, when a consumer receives information that deviates from expectation, he or she tends to place more cognitive capacity on the information (i.e., process it in greater depth). In such circumstances it is more likely that the information will be transferred from short-term to long-term memory.[39]

One study tested these ideas in a personal-selling situation.[40] Suppose a customer in a clothing store encounters a salesperson who interacts with the person in a

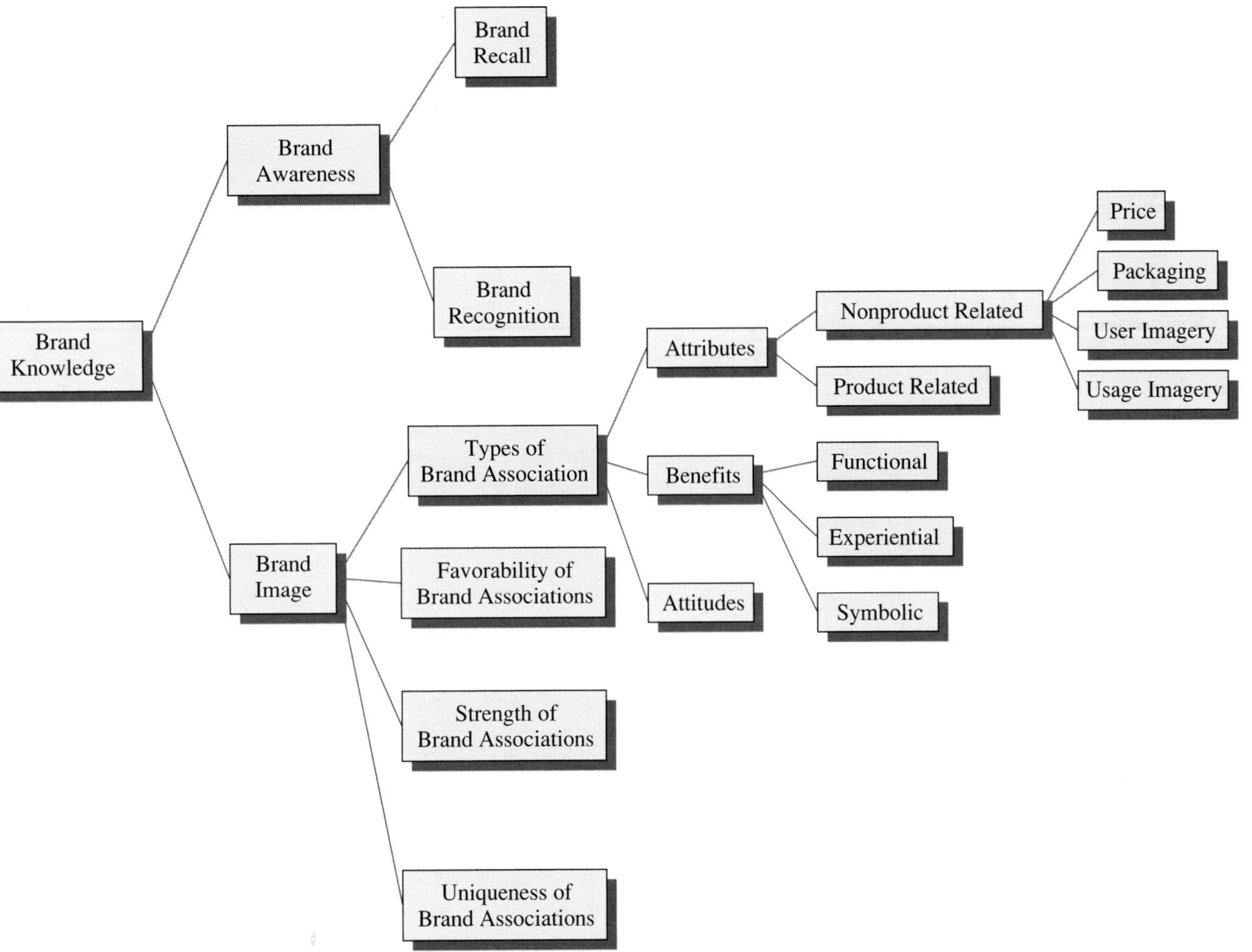

Figure 4-4 Dimensions of brand knowledge. (Source: Reprinted with permission from Kenneth Lane Keller, "Conceptualizing, Measuring, and Managing Customer-Based Brand Equity," *Journal of Marketing*, January 1993, pp. 1–22.)

TABLE 4-3

Summary of Major Implications of Memory Processes for Promotional Strategy

Memory Area	*Implications*
Short-term memory	Develop messages that match the capacity level of consumer's STM.
Long-term memory	Enhance message presentation by using vivid visual information as well as verbal information.
Consumer knowledge	**1.** Construct messages matching target's knowledge.
	2. Messages should match consumer's level of abstraction.
	3. Attempt to develop understanding of target market's schemas and semantic memory networks that include your product/service and create messages that fit into schemas.
Forgetting	**1.** Create promotional material having distinctive and unique characteristics in order to minimize interference in memory caused by competing material.
	2. Creating interruptions in advertisements may enhance their recall.
	3. To maintain memory for ads use a pulsing strategy of showing ads periodically, rather than of spending an entire budget in a short time period.
Cognitive learning	**1.** Recognize that consumers are insightful information processors who perceive products as integrated wholes.
	2. Make use of the law of contiguity by pairing product/service with positive associations.
	3. Avoid having key product information buried in the middle of a commercial.
	4. Avoid having your advertisements buried in the middle of a series of commercials.
Affect and memory	In general, attempt to cause people to be in positive mood states when evaluating your product/service.

different style. If the customer is surprised by the sales approach, he or she might pay more attention to the information and recall it better in the future. The results supported these ideas. When the seller met expectations of the typical salesperson, product evaluations were not affected by the quality of the arguments of the sales speech. However, when the salesperson violated the schema, subjects recalled more about the product from the arguments and had generally more positive attitudes about the product.

Table 4-3 summarizes the major implications of memory processes for promotional strategy.

FORGETTING

One important area of memory research involves the question of why people forget. When information is placed in long-term memory, it tends to stay there. However, it may be extremely difficult to retrieve. In one study over 10,000 people were polled on the advertisements that they could remember. Of these 53% were unable to remember any specific ad that they had seen, heard, or read in the last 30 days.[41] These results are devastating to advertising managers, because the recall of ads is an important measure of advertising effectiveness. Researchers have investigated forgetting for many years, and the discussion that follows relates some of the findings.

Interference Processes

Two factors that can cause problems in retrieval and response generation are proactive interference and retroactive interference. When **retroactive interference** occurs, new material presented after old material has been learned interferes with the recall of the old material. That is, the learning of new material interferes with the retrieval or the response generation of the old material from memory. With **proactive interference**, material learned prior to the new material interferes with the learning of the new material.[42] The possibility of interference causing problems in the recall of advertisements is enormous because of the number of promotional messages to which people in the United States are exposed every day (from 300 to 600 per day). A recent series of studies investigated interference processes in an advertising context.[43] In the studies, respondents were given a series of print advertisements. The results revealed that advertising for competing brands, as well as for other products offered by the same manufacturer, could inhibit the ability to remember brand information. The interference effects were particularly pronounced when the competing material was similar in nature to the target information.

Forgetting that results from retroactive and proactive interference can create problems for marketers. A classic finding is that interference between sets of material to be learned increases as the similarity of their content increases.[44] Based upon these findings in experimental psychology, one can predict that, if consumers receive a series of commercials for products in which similar types of claims are made, confusion will result and learning will be impeded. The work on retroactive and proactive interference suggests that confusion grows proportionally to the degree that the competing commercials involve similar types of products, or that different products use similar adjectives to describe their performance (such as high quality, low cost, low maintenance, etc.).

The von Restorff Effect

A finding of particular importance to advertisers has been called the **von Restorff effect.**[45] Experiments have shown that a unique item in a series of relatively homogeneous items is recalled much more easily, because the effects of proactive and retroactive interference are minimized. The von Restorff effect is illustrated by the unique ads for Infiniti automobiles. In 1989 Nissan Corporation introduced its new flagship line of cars. The company employed an unusual advertising campaign in which "rocks and trees" were shown rather than the cars. While controversial, the ads scored very high on recall tests. Figure 4-5 presents one of the ads. (The end-of-chapter case concerns the Infiniti campaign.

The von Restorff effect illustrates the importance of information salience. **Information salience** refers to the level of activation of a stimulus (e.g., a brand name) in memory.[46] The level of salience is increased if the person has just purchased a product. It can also be increased by making something unique, by using continuously high levels of advertising, and by using cues (e.g., point-of-purchase displays) to remind consumers of a product.[47] In addition, stimulus factors such as novelty, contrast, color, surprise, movement, and size can all act to make a stimulus salient. Generally, the more salient something is, the more likely it will be encoded into memory and later recalled. One of an advertiser's primary goals should be to make an advertisement highly salient to the consumer.

Recent research has revealed another interesting effect of making a brand highly salient. If one brand is highly salient to consumers, the recall of competing brands may be lower.[48] Thus, if a manager can develop the marketing mix so that a brand is highly salient to consumers, recall of competing brands as a part of the **evoked set** may be decreased. The reason for this is that through retroactive interference, the presence of the salient brand in memory inhibits the recall of competitors.

The Zeigarnik Effect

Another factor that influences whether something will be forgotten is the Zeigarnik effect. Named after the German Gestalt scientist who discovered it, the **Zeigarnik effect** occurs when an individual is involved in a task and is interrupted.[49] If the recall of information is compared between a task that has been interrupted and one that has been completed, the findings consistently show that material in the interrupted task is recalled better.

In the late 1980s ads run for Post Grape-Nuts cereal used such a strategy. In the ads an attractive couple is discussing the cereal, and the female indicates that it will stay crunchy for a long time. The male shows disbelief, and she challenges him to wait and see. The ad then ends and a completely new commercial appears and runs for 30 seconds, thereby interrupting the Grape-Nuts ad. After the second commercial is over, the couple again appears after the imaginary passage of the allotted period of time. Sure enough, the cereal is still crunchy. The interruption of the ad may have caused a deeper processing of information resulting in the creation of a stronger memory trace.

An interesting question concerns whether the interrupted story or the inserted material causing the interruption is recalled better. Research indicates that the inserted material may actually be more salient.[50] Additional work is required to analyze the Zeigarnik effect in advertising.

Time and Forgetting

Because of the operation of proactive and retroactive interference, the recall of verbal information decreases over time. Classic work by Ebbinghaus tracked the loss of recall over time.[51] Figure 4-6 shows the results of one of his experiments. After learning a list of nonsense words (e.g., xlp, mqv, etc.), the percentage of words remembered decreased dramatically at first and then leveled off over time.

Figure 4-5 An early ad for Infiniti cars illustrating the von Restorff effect. The prose in the ad read, "In our mind, the balance of three things is essential to making a luxury car luxurious: performance, comfort, styling." The add continued at a later point, ". . . balance . . . it's why walls that were built 200 years ago haven't fallen down, and why designs that are classic in 1990 will still stand up in 2010." Over 80% of those in its target market could remember the ads. (Courtesy Nissan Motor Corporation USA.)

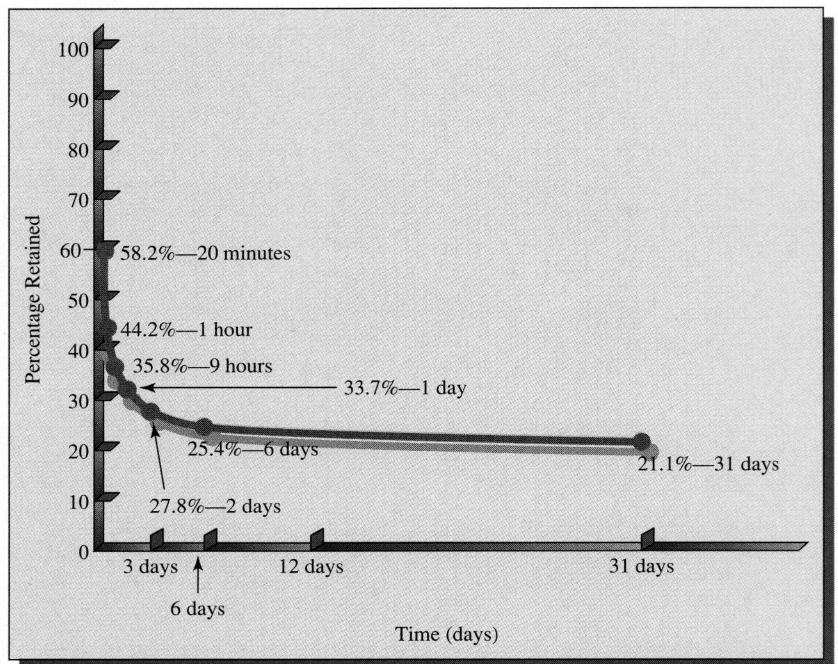

Figure 4-6 Relationship between time and forgetting. (Source: Data from H. Ebbinghaus, *Memory*, H. A. Ruger and C. E. Bussenius, trans., New York: New York Teachers College, 1913.)

The rapid forgetting that occurs immediately after learning has been shown to occur in advertising as well. In a classic experiment, Zielske had advertisements for a product run once a week for 13 weeks.[52] At the end of the 13-week period, 63% of the housewives could recall having seen the ad. After 13 weeks, no more ads were given, and forgetting showed the same pattern as that found 70 years before by Ebbinghaus. That is, forgetting occurred very rapidly at first and then leveled off. After 20 weeks, the recall of the ads had dropped to below 30%; by the time nine months had passed, less than 10% of those surveyed could remember the ads.

In addition to giving one group of housewives one ad a week for 13 weeks, another group was given 13 ads spaced 4 weeks apart. In this case the ability to recall the ads increased slowly, but at the end of the year some 48% could remember the ads. The difference between the group that had the ads bunched together and the group who received the ads spaced over time has important implications for advertisers. If the advertiser wants to obtain rapid awareness of a product, a high frequency of ads over a short period of time will be most effective. However, rapid forgetting occurs after the burst of advertisements. If the goal is to build long-term awareness of the ad, the commercials should be pulsed such that the ads are seen by consumers regularly over a long period of time. Often companies will combine the approaches and use a high-intensity campaign to bring out a product and then pulse regularly after the introduction to maintain awareness.

AFFECT AND MEMORY

One of the major themes of the text is that when investigating consumer behavior, the researcher must be concerned with experiential–affective processes. The term **affect** refers to the feelings, emotions, and moods that consumers may experience. Recently, researchers have begun to develop theories that describe how a person's feelings influence memory and judgment.[53] In the consumer behavior field, researchers have been most concerned with the relationship between the consumers' mood states and memory processes. As noted by one prominent researcher, "Mood is important and its effects need to be accounted for. Mood states pose an important and difficult challenge because information-processing theorists have seldom dealt with the affective system."[54]

A **mood** is a transient feeling state that occurs in a specific situation or time. It is not a personality variable because moods are temporary in nature, whereas personality is longer lasting. Similarly, it is not an emotion, which is more intense and attention getting.[55] Despite their short duration and mild intensity, people's moods have been found to influence the recall of information. Specifically, people are better able to recall information that has the same affective quality as their mood state. Thus, when people are sad, they are more likely to recall information that is sad. Conversely, when people are happy, they are more likely to remember happy information. Indeed, evidence exists that mood states can influence the encoding of information, the retrieval of information, and how information is organized in memory.[56]

In one study, researchers asked consumers to think about happy, sad, or neutral past experiences to induce positive, negative, or neutral moods. They were then shown a single print advertisement for a Mazda RX7 sports car. When the respondents were asked to form an impression of the car while reading the ad, the mood affected their rating of the car 48 hours later. The researchers hypothesized that when the evaluation was made at the time the ad was read, their mood state influenced how the information was encoded. A sad mood caused the evaluation to be lower than when in a neutral mood state. Similarly, the highest ratings occurred when the subjects encoded the information when in a positive mood state.[57]

In another study, subjects saw either a sad television show (e.g., "60 Minutes") or a happy television show ("Real People") and then evaluated a commercial embedded in the show. The results indicated that consumers recalled more information about the ad when it was embedded in the television show that caused a happier mood. One possible explanation of the results is that the positive mood influenced consumers to bring from memory a broader and more integrated set of knowledge categories, resulting in more effective encoding of the information.[58]

The research on the relationship between affect and memory indicates the possibility of strong managerial implications. In general, one can argue that marketers should attempt to place consumers in a positive mood state when they are receiving information on a product or service. A number of devices can be used to create these moods, such as the use of humor in an advertisement or purchasing a nice meal for a client in a personal-selling situation.

OGNITIVE LEARNING

Closely related to information processing and the study of memory is a field of study sometimes called cognitive learning. **Cognitive learning** focuses on such mental activities as thinking, remembering, problem solving, developing insight, forming concepts, and learning ideas. Such learning involves an intuitive hypothesis-generating process in which consumers adapt their beliefs to make sense of new data.[59] Thus cognitive learning is an active process in which consumers seek to control the information obtained.

An important issue concerns how people learn in the consumer environment. In one influential article, it was proposed that consumers learn through education and through experience.[60] **Learning through education** involves obtaining information from companies in the form of advertising, sales personnel, and the consumer's own directed efforts to seek data. In contrast, **learning through experience** involves the process of gaining knowledge through actual contact with products. Overall, learning from experience is a more effective means to gain consumer knowledge. It promotes better retrieval and recall because the consumer is involved in the learning experience and the information obtained is more vivid, concrete, and salient.

Product managers have a large stake in influencing what consumers learn about their products. Through a firm's promotional activities, consumers can learn through education. Such beliefs formed may directly influence consumer attitudes and actions regarding a product. In addition, what consumers have learned through education can also influence the experience with the product. For example, advertisements can influence the expectations of product performance. If the product fails to live up to these expectations, the psychological interpretation of the actual experience is likely to be negative.

The process through which cognitive learning takes place is important for managers to understand so that they may influence what consumers learn about their products. The work on memory and information processing discussed earlier in the chapter explains in part this process. However, other researchers, such as the Gestalt psychologists, have made contributions to the field.

Early Cognitive Theorists—The Gestalt Psychologists

The **Gestalt psychologists** believed that biological and psychological events do not influence behavior in isolation from each other. Instead, people perceive the inputs from the environment as part of a total context. The work of the Gestalt psychologists was in marked contrast to other learning theorists in the first half of the twentieth century. Whereas other psychologists viewed man as a static organism who responded automatically to inputs from the environment, the Gestalt psychologists focused on the active, creative nature of learning and action.[61] As one noted consumer researcher stated,

> When we look at an automobile, we do not see glass and steel and plastic and bolts and paint. We see instead an organized whole, an automobile. And perhaps not even just an automobile but also comfortable transportation, prestige, status, and a symbolic sense of achievement. This is the familiar Gestalt dictum; the whole is different from, if not greater than, the sum of the isolated parts.[62]

The work of the Gestalt psychologists has important implications for marketers. A tendency exists for market researchers to perceive products in terms of their individual characteristics, such as price, color, features, reliability, and so forth. In contrast, consumers tend to perceive the product as an integrated whole. In isolation a particular color or style may be judged as unacceptable. However, when seen in the overall context of a product, the characteristic could be quite satisfactory. Thus, when considered in isolation, using plaid seats in a car might seem silly; however, when placed in a sports car, the multicolor seats might fit quite well.

Another contribution of the Gestalt school is the idea that people do engage in problem-solving activities and have sudden bursts of insight. Although consumer researchers have emphasized low-involvement learning processes in the past few years, many products or situations can activate the consumer so that he or she begins problem-solving activities. For example, advertisements for V-8 cocktail vegetable juice were created to activate the consumer to engage in problem-solving activities rather than to buy out of habit. The advertising campaign was based on actors having the sudden insight that "I could have had a V-8." Of course, the goal was to portray the actor as having the sudden "aha-experience" that, rather than drinking a sweet soft drink, he or she could have had a healthful glass of V-8.

The Associationists

Another approach to cognitive learning is to analyze the associations that consumers form between marketing stimuli. Early experimental work within the **associationist school** was performed by Ebbinghaus in the late eighteenth century. It was Ebbinghaus who discovered what become known as serial learning.

Serial Learning

The study of **serial learning** concerns how people put into memory and recall information that is received in a sequential manner. For example, consider what happens during a commercial break during a television show. Viewers could be exposed to as many as six or more advertisements. An important question concerns whether the position of the ad in the series influences how well it is remembered. A **serial-position effect** occurs when the order of presentation of information in a list influences recall of the information in the list. As shown in Figure 4-7, researchers have found that items at the beginning of the list and items at the end of the list are the most readily learned. In contrast, items in the middle of the list are learned much less rapidly.

A serial-learning effect has been discovered by consumer researchers. In one study, respondents watched a series of three commercials and were then asked to recall information about each of the ads. Significantly less information was recalled about the middle advertisement.[63]

One explanation for the serial-learning effect is that the beginning and end of a list become anchors for learning. Due to limitations of short-term memory, people identify reference points for when to attempt to start or end the learning process. With the ability to store only limited amounts of information in short-term memory at a time, it is only the items right around the beginning and end of the list that are recalled readily. Items in the middle take many more repetitions of the material to be recalled.

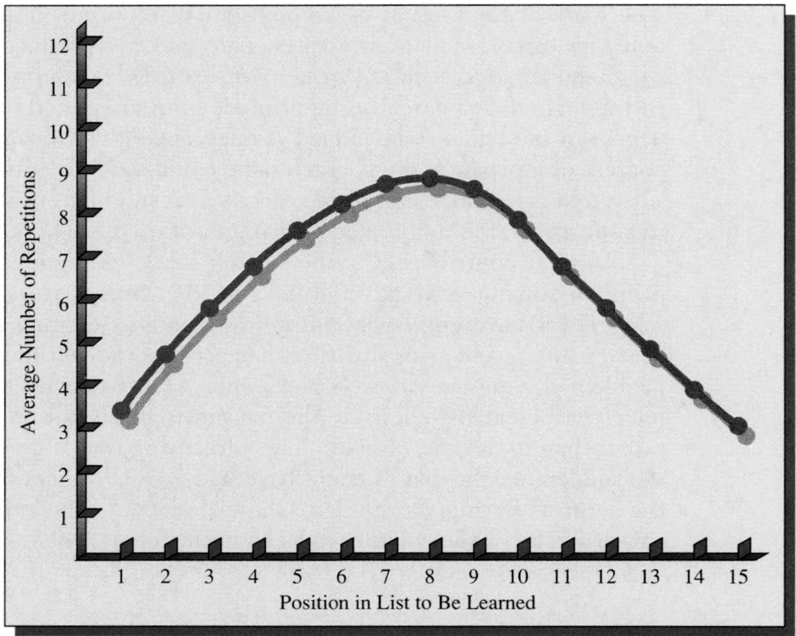

Figure 4-7 Serial-position effect: a hypothetical example. More repetitions are required to learn the material in the middle of the list. (Source: The hypothetical curve shown here is based in part on serial-position curves found in Charles E. Osgood, *Method and Theory in Experimental Psychology*, New York: Oxford University Press, 1964.)

The serial-learning effect has important implications for marketers. Key information in an advertisement should be placed at the beginning or end of the message. If important information is embedded in the middle of the communication, it may take a larger number of repetitions of the advertisement for consumers to learn the information. In addition, advertisers should strive to have their commercials placed either at the beginning or the end of a series of television ads.[64]

In some instances, however, the first information received in a list tends to be recalled better. Research on "pioneering advantage" has found such an effect. A **pioneering advantage** occurs when the first brand to enter a product category has a long-term edge over competitors. Research on the pioneering advantage has found that information on the pioneer is perceived as more interesting and novel than information on later entrants. In particular, for consumers who follow a product category and monitor the entry of brands into it, the benefits of being first to enter the marketplace are most observable.[65]

Paired-Associate Learning

In addition to studying how consumers learn lists of information, the associationists also investigated how consumers remember words that are paired with each other. Called **paired-associate learning**, the task requires people to associate a series of response words to stimulus words. Thus three pairs of stimulus and response words might be Maytag–quality, Toyota–"Oh-what-a-feeling," and peas–Jolly Green Giant. Maytag, Toyota, and peas would be the stimulus words, and subjects would be asked to recall from memory the response words of quality, "Oh what a feeling" and Jolly Green Giant, respectively. An important finding in paired-associate learning is that learning is speeded up if the stimulus and response items can be readily associated with each other and are familiar.[66] In particular, if mental images can be developed between stimulus and response words, learning is more rapid.

The findings of studies in paired-associate learning suggest that, for these associations to be learned most rapidly, the following conditions should be met:

1. The stimulus and response words should be easily pronounceable.
2. The person should be familiar with the stimulus and response words.
3. The stimulus and response words should be meaningful.
4. The stimulus and response words should be easily associated.
5. Visual images should be created to link the stimulus and response words together.

Readers should note that these recommendations are totally consistent with the more recent work cited earlier in the chapter on the effects of visual processing of information and on the encoding of information.

Marketers appear to instinctively use ideas from paired-associate learning to create cooperative advertising campaigns. In such campaigns two distinct products are promoted together. An example occurred during the tax season in 1987. Alka-Seltzer and H&R Block developed a joint campaign in which the product and the service were touted as helping "tax-time upsets." As one Alka-Seltzer manager said, "Alka-Seltzer has a heritage of being caring, empathetic, like Mother Teresa. This touches an underlying emotion at tax time."[67] In the ad in Figure 4-8, the California Raisins were linked with the song "I Heard It Through the Grapevine."

When ads are positioned beside other unflattering ads or news stories, the impact of the promotion may be reduced or may even become negative. Indeed, some of the earliest work in cognitive learning was performed by researchers who developed the concept of the **law of contiguity**, which states that things that are experienced together become associated.[68] Marketing managers reveal a strong intuitive awareness of the law of contiguity. For example, most companies check carefully to ensure that their television advertisements are not shown in conjunction with programs that could be offensive to their target market.

A MANAGERIAL APPLICATIONS EXAMPLE

In 1987 the California Raisin Advisory Board pulled off a gigantic coup. On an advertising budget far less than that of such giants as McDonald's and Coca-Cola, their television ads for the lowly raisin were rated first in consumer awareness. Created by Claymation, Inc., the animated raisin figures were made from clay and shown in "cool" sunglasses and white gloves, struttin' their stuff to Marvin Gaye's classic song, "I

Heard It Through the Grapevine." The appeal of the creatures and the music was immediate, and the ads won the hearts and captured the memories of consumers.

To obtain advertising awareness scores, consumers are asked the following question: "Of all the advertising you have seen, heard, or read in the past thirty days, which ad first comes to mind?" In addition to an overall question, more specific questions are asked about advertising awareness for various product categories. In the first quarter of 1987 the California Raisins ads were mentioned first in comparison to all other ads 3.1% of the time.[69] For four years in a row, the raisins rated at or near the top of ten commercials.[70]

Although the "Raisin" campaign was a huge success, it also created some problems for the company that produced it. Soon after the original commercials went on the air, other companies clamored for Claymation, Inc., to do ads for them. As a result, one found dancing clay burgers and clay chicken nuggets. The creator of the ads, however, soon realized that the fad of using his animated clay figures would end quickly. He said, "The perception is that Claymation equals raisins." One advertising executive said that any new commercial using the technique "is never going to have the power or impact or significance that the raisins did. The raisins are so identified with the technique, they end up owning it. Everything else tends to look like a rip-off."[71] Figure 4-8 contains a photo of the California Raisins.

Problem Definition

The question posed by the California Raisins campaign concerns how an understanding of memory processes can be used to develop managerial strategy. In the consumer analysis, we will consider how information on consumer memory processes

Figure 4-8 The California Raisins earned high audience awareness ratings. (Courtesy of the California Raisin Advisory Board.)

can be used (as in this chapter's consumer vignette) to develop managerial strategy and to understand why this particular execution of a strategy became so successful.

The Consumer Analysis

First, the use of the California Raisins campaign illustrates principles related to forgetting. These unusual characters created for the campaign acted as unique stimuli and were highly salient to consumers. The ads stood out from the clutter of competing commercials and were easily encoded and retrieved from memory. As such, they are excellent examples of the von Restorff effect. The implication of the von Restorff effect is that managers should attempt to develop promotional messages and use message sources that are perceived as unique to enhance the encoding and recall of the information.

The California Raisins ads also illustrate semantic memory processes. For many consumers the semantic network of concepts related to the song "I Heard It Through the Grapevine" could become associated with the product. As a result, the product information would be readily encoded into existing memory structures. As a result, the advertisement would be highly memorable. Concepts from paired-associate learning also have relevance to the recall of the ads. In particular, the unusual visual image of the Raisins effectively linked the brand to the song and extremely strong associations were formed. Indeed, the linkage was so strong that the use of the Claymation characters became inextricably tied to the California Raisins. As a result, Claymation, Inc., has had a difficult time selling its services to other advertisers.

Knowledge of the impact of affect on memory also relates to the case. Through the semantic memory network, the positive feelings associated with the music could also be associated with the product. As a result, the ads could place many consumers in a positive mood state. The positive feelings associated with the brand could then influence purchase behavior at a later time period.

The Managerial Applications Analysis

Table 4-4 presents the managerial areas to which the consumer behavior concepts have application. As shown in the table, four concepts presented in this chapter have relevance to the case: the von Restorff effect, semantic memory networks, paired-associate learning, and affect.

The von Restorff effect applies principally to promotional strategy and the development of novel advertising images. The unusual raisin characters that sang and danced to Marvin Gaye's classic song were highly memorable. The effect has market research implications as well. Prior to rolling out an advertising campaign that employs unusual characters, market research should be conducted to ensure that consumers react positively to them.

The study of semantic memory networks applies to the managerial areas of segmentation, marketing mix, and market research. When developing promotional messages, managers should recognize that divergent segments of consumers may possess strikingly different semantic memory networks. Individuals who were music enthusiasts in the 1960s would have a highly developed semantic memory network for the Marvin Gaye classic. This group would certainly be a target for

TABLE 4-4

Managerial Applications of the California Raisin Case

Consumer Concepts	*Managerial Applications Areas*
von Restorff effect	*Promotional strategy*—Develop ads that are novel so that they are highly salient to consumers.
	Market research—Conduct research on the ad concept to assess whether it will be readily encoded and retrieved from memory.
Semantic memory network	*Segmentation*—Identify segments that will have similar positive associations in memory with the key ad concept.
	Promotional strategy—Develop commercials around key concepts with which the target market has strong positive associations in memory.
	Market research—Test the ad to ensure that the associations with the ad concept are as expected.
Paired-associate learning	*Positioning*—Pair the brand with a song to create a particular image.
	Promotional strategy—Develop ads that pair the product with endorsers, songs, or images that create the desired positioning of the brand.
	Market research—Test the ad to ensure that pairing of the brand with the image creates the desired effects.

the commercials. In contrast, other market segments, such as people now over 60 years of age, may not have knowledge of the song. For these consumers it may have little impact. Market research is needed to assess consumer knowledge and the associative networks between the brand and the images created in the advertisement.

The consumer concept of paired-associate learning has application to the managerial areas of the marketing mix and product differentiation. Claymation's products are its advertisements using the clay figures. Because of the close association of the clay characters with raisins, every time consumers saw an ad using clay characters, they immediately recalled the raisin advertisements. The implication is that the company must change the look of its product (i.e., its advertisements) and take steps to differentiate it from the raisin ads.

The concept that affect influences consumer information processing has importance for market research, marketing mix, and positioning. The linkage among the clay raisins, Marvin Gaye's song, and the brand was extremely strong. It effectively acted to position California Raisins as fun-loving and hip. As a result, the positive feelings associated with "I Heard It Through the Grapevine" would be transferred to the product. One cannot always depend, however, on consumers reacting so positively to such associations. Market research should be conducted to ensure that consumers react emotionally in the desired way to the ads. Steps should also be taken to determine whether the advertisements caused consumers to perceive the position of the brand relative to others in the desired manner.

SUMMARY

In the model of memory presented in the chapter, information is input into sensory memory. If the information relates to the consumer's goals, it will be shifted into short-term memory for further processing. The more elaborate the processing in short-term memory, the greater the likelihood that it will be permanently stored in long-term memory.

Short-term memory is characterized as having a limited processing capacity of seven (plus or minus two) chunks of information (Miller's law). If more information is received than can be processed, the person enters a state of information overload. The capacity of short-term memory is influenced by the involvement of the consumer. As the involvement level increases, capacity tends to increase.

Encoding involves the movement of information from short-term memory into long-term memory. The recall of information from long-term memory back into short-term memory is called retrieval. The likelihood that information is encoded into long-term memory increases as the person places more cognitive effort on the information through rehearsal or through a process of connecting the information with other knowledge stored in memory. Encoding is also enhanced if associations can be drawn between the new information and other knowledge held in memory.

The retrieval process is enhanced if cues are available to assist the consumer in recalling information. Stored in long-term memory are verbal, visual, and other information from the senses. In addition, people can encode sequences of events, or episodes, in memory. Evidence exists that picture memory is superior to verbal memory. An approach to enhancing verbal memory for information, such as people's names, is to use a visual image that depicts the name in some manner.

Also encoded in long-term memory is a consumer's knowledge. Consumer knowledge involves a person's familiarity and expertise with a product or service. It has a number of characteristics, including in how many dimensions a person can think about something. Knowledge is also organized into semantic memory. Semantic memory concerns how people store the meanings of verbal material in long-term memory. In semantic memory, concepts are represented by nodes that are connected together. The activation of a node by a cue may result in a spreading activation, so information related to connected nodes is also recalled.

The study of forgetting is particularly important for advertising managers. One impediment to the recall and recognition of information is information interference. Through the action of retroactive and proactive interference, information may be made more difficult to encode and retrieve from memory.

The memory for information can be enhanced by making use of the von Restorff effect and the Zeigarnik effect. The von Restorff effect shows that a unique item in a series of relatively homogeneous items is recalled more easily. Such a unique item is more salient and avoids some of the effects of interference. The Zeigarnik effect occurs when a task or story is interrupted. Such an interruption appears to cause people to engage in deeper processing and form a stronger memory trace.

As time passes people tend to forget information because of interference processes. As a result, advertisers should consider pulsing information over time, rather than repeating the information in a short amount of time. Similarly, the serial-position effect occurs when interference processes make it harder for people to encode and retrieve information placed in the middle of messages.

The cognitive learning theorists emphasized ideas of importance to consumer researchers. From a Gestalt perspective, consumers may be viewed as active problem solvers who tend to perceive products and services in terms of the total environmental context. The associationists argue for the law of contiguity, which states that things that are experienced together tend to become associated. Therefore, consumer researchers should attempt to analyze the kinds of entities with which a product or service is associated. If a product is paired with something negative, consumers may well make an unfortunate association.

Researchers should also recognize the role of affect in memory processes. Evidence exists that a consumer's mood state may influence the type of thoughts that come to mind. Further, some evidence exists that brand evaluations can be influenced by a consumer's mood state when information is being received. In general, marketers should attempt to create positive consumer mood states to increase the chances of consumers recalling positive information about the product or service.

KEY TERMS

affect
associationist school
brand knowledge
clutter
cognitive learning
consideration set
encoding
evoked set
Gestalt psychologists
information overload
information salience
law of contiguity
learning through education
learning through experience
long-term memory
memory-control processes
Miller's law
mood
multiple-store model
paired-associate learning
pioneering advantage
proactive interference
recall task
recognition task
rehearsal
response generation
retrieval
retrieval cues
retroactive interference
schema
semantic memory
sensory memory
serial learning
serial-position effect
short-term memory
von Restorff effect
working memory
Zeigarnik effect

REVIEW QUESTIONS

1. What are the three types of memory that have been proposed? How do they differ?
2. What happens when information overload occurs?
3. What is the difference between a recognition and a recall task?
4. Compare the effectiveness of picture memory and word memory under high- and low-involvement conditions.
5. What is a memory network?
6. Define and give examples of memory-control processes.
7. Discuss what happens in short-term memory. What is the relationship between involvement and short-term memory?
8. How is information transferred from short-term to long-term memory?
9. Summarize the major findings concerning long-term memory and knowledge processes.
10. Why does forgetting occur?

11. What is the relationship between time and forgetting?
12. What is the serial-position effect?
13. What is the law of contiguity?
14. What is the relationship between affect and memory?
15. What is the difference between learning through education and learning through experience?

DISCUSSION QUESTIONS

1. Listen carefully to three television advertisements. Identify the number of "copy points" (i.e., chunks of information) that can be found in each ad. To what extent do you think consumers will remember these points? What factors might influence the placement into memory of these copy points?
2. Go through a magazine and locate three print advertisements. Identify the number of copy points found in the ads. Compare the number of copy points found in the print ads to the number you observed in the television ads. What factors might account for any differences you found?
3. Describe two instances of consumer recognition tasks and two instances of consumer recall tasks. Do you find any differences in the advertising associated with the products identified in each instance?
4. It has been said that "one picture is worth a thousand words." Relate this aphorism to the capabilities of picture versus word memory. What are the implications for advertisers?
5. Draw a diagram of your memory network for fast-food restaurants.
6. Suppose that you had to develop a name for a new product. The product is a soybean-curd (tofu)–based dessert, which uses real fruit, has no cholesterol, and does not bother people who have trouble eating milk-based products (a sizable portion of the population). Create several names for the product and identify how each utilizes the various memory-control processes.
7. Go to a grocery store and identify as many examples as you can of point-of-purchase (POP) advertising that effectively help the consumer associate national advertising with the brand on the grocery shelves. What are the memory factors that make the POP displays more or less effective?
8. Outline a fictitious ad for any product that makes use of the Zeigarnik effect.
9. Outline a fictitious ad for any product that makes use of the von Restorff effect.

ENDNOTES

1. This quote and the introductory vignette are based upon Bruce Nussbaum and Robert Neff, "I Can't Work This Thing!" *Business Week*, April 29, 1991, pp. 58–66.
2. Bruce Nussbaum, "High-End Stereo: Simplicity for a Price," *Business Week*, April 29, 1991, p. 62.
3. James R. Bettman, "Memory Factors in Consumer Choice: A Review," *Journal of Marketing*, Vol. 43 (Spring 1979), pp. 37–53.

The evidence is mixed as to whether three types of memory exist and, if so, whether memories are stored in three separate locations in the brain. Other approaches to memory have been proposed, such as one suggesting that short- and long-term memories are distinguished only by the depth of processing. Researchers have also identified another type of memory, called "implicit memory." For a discussion of this concept, see Abhijit Sanyal,

"Priming and Implicit Memory: A Review and Synthesis Relevant for Consumer Behavior," in *Diversity in Consumer Behavior: Advances in Consumer Research*, Vol. 19, John F. Sherry, Jr., and Brian Sternthal, eds. (Provo, UT: Association for Consumer Research, 1992), pp. 795–805. However, the multiple-store approach has a strong intuitive appeal, and its predictions are generally consistent with other approaches to memory. Thus it has been chosen for discussion.

4. George Sperling, "The Information Available in Brief Visual Presentations," *Psychological Monographs*, Vol. 74 (1960), p. 498.
5. D. F. Fisher and R. Karsh, "Modality Effects and Storage in Sequential Short-Term Memory," *Journal of Experimental Psychology*, Vol. 87 (1971), pp. 410–414.
6. S. W. Keele, *Attention and Human Performance* (Santa Monica, CA: Goodyear Press, 1973).
7. Herbert Simon, *The Sciences of the Artificial* (Cambridge, MA: MIT Press, 1969).
8. Richard M. Shiffrin and R. C. Atkinson, "Storage and Retrieval Processes in Long-Term Memory," *Psychological Review*, Vol. 76 (1969), pp. 179–193.
9. George A. Miller, "The Magical Number Seven, Plus or Minus Two: Some Limits on Our Capacity to Process Information," *Psychological Review*, Vol. 63 (1956), pp. 81–97. Readers should note that other researchers have argued about the capacity of short-term memory. Some have argued that it is limited to as few as 3 chunks of information. Others have argued that it can be as high as 20 chunks.
10. Daniel Kahneman, *Attention and Effort* (Englewood Cliffs, NJ: Prentice-Hall, 1973).
11. Robert S. Owen, "Clarifying the Simple Assumption of the Information Load Paradigm," in *Diversity in Consumer Behavior: Advances in Consumer Research*, Vol. 19, John F. Sherry, Jr., and Brian Sternthal, eds. (Provo, UT: Association for Consumer Research, 1992), pp. 770–776. Also, see Naresh Malhotra, "Reflections on the Information Overload Paradigm in Consumer Decision Making," *Journal of Consumer Research*, Vol. 10 (March 1984), pp. 436–440.
12. Jacob Jacoby, "Perspectives on Information Overload," *Journal of Consumer Research*, Vol. 10 (March 1984), pp. 432–435.
13. Ibid., p. 435.
14. Claudia Dolinsky and Richard Feinberg, "Linguistic Barriers to Consumer Information Processing: Information Overload in the Hispanic Population," *Psychology and Marketing*, Vol. 3, no. 4 (1986), pp. 261–271.
15. Kahneman, *Attention and Effort*.
16. M. Carole Macklin, "Rehearsal Processes in Children's Recall of Advertised Products," in *Proceedings of the Division of Consumer Psychology*, Wayne Hoyer, ed. (Washington, DC: American Psychological Association, 1986), pp. 21–25.
17. Kevin Goldman, "Barrage of Ads in Super Bowl Blurs Messages," *The Wall Street Journal*, February 3, 1993, p. B6.
18. Tom J. Brown and Michael L. Rothschild, "Reassessing the Impact of Television Advertising Clutter," *Journal of Consumer Research*, Vol. 20 (June 1993), pp. 138–146. This important article found little evidence of the negative effects of clutter on the recognition of advertisements embedded in television programming. Additional research, however, is required before we can conclude that clutter presents few, if any, problems for advertisers.
19. For a more detailed description of memory and memory-control processes, see Bettman, "Memory Factors in Consumer Choice."
20. Benton Underwood, "Attributes of Memory," *Psychological Review*, Vol. 76 (November 1969), pp. 559–573.
21. Ronald Alsop, "Old Chewing-Gum Favorites Find There's Life After Death," *The Wall Street Journal*, September 11, 1986, p. 37.
22. Terry Childers and Michael Houston, "Conditions for a Picture-Superiority Effect on Consumer Memory," *Journal of Consumer Research*, Vol. 11 (September 1984), pp. 643–654.
23. Terry Childers, Susan Heckler, and Michael Houston, "Memory for the Visual and Verbal Components of Print Advertisements," *Psychology and Marketing*, Vol. 3 (Fall 1986), pp. 147–150.

24. H. Rao Unnava and Robert E. Burnkrant, "An Imagery-Processing View of the Role of Pictures in Print Advertising," *Journal of Marketing Research*, Vol. 28 (May 1991), pp. 226–231.

25. For a review of this literature, see Kathy Lutz and Richard Lutz, "Effects of Interactive Imagery on Learning: Applications to Advertising," *Journal of Applied Psychology*, Vol. 62 (August 1977), pp. 493–498.

26. Michael Houston, Terry Childers, and Susan Heckler, "Picture-Word Consistency and the Elaborative Processing of Attributes," *Journal of Marketing Research*, Vol. 24 (November 1987), pp. 359–369. Closely related is the field of mental imagery. For a review of this area, see Laurie A. Babin, Alvin Burns, and Abhijit Biswas, "A Framework Providing Direction for Research on Communications Effects of Mental Imagery-Evoking Advertising Strategies," in *Diversity in Consumer Behavior: Advances in Consumer Research*, Vol. 19, John F. Sherry, Jr., and Brian Sternthal, eds. (Provo, UT: Association for Consumer Research, 1992), pp. 621–628.

27. Bettman, "Memory Factors in Consumer Choice."

28. R. N. Kanungo, "Effects of Fittingness, Meaningfulness, and Product Utility," *Journal of Applied Psychology*, Vol. 52 (August 1968), pp. 290–295.

29. Kim Robertson, "Recall and Recognition Effects of Brand Name Imagery," *Psychology and Marketing*, Vol. 4 (Spring 1987), pp. 3–15.

30. Bettman, "Memory Factors in Consumer Choice."

31. Kevin L. Keller, "Memory Factors in Advertising: The Effect of Advertising Retrieval Cues on Brand Evaluations," *Journal of Consumer Research*, Vol. 14 (December 1987), pp. 316–333.

32. Wanda T. Wallace, "Jingles in Advertising: Can They Improve Recall?" in *Advances in Consumer Research*, Vol. 17, Marvin Goldberg and Gerald Gorn, eds. (Provo, UT: Association for Consumer Research, 1990), pp. 239–242.

33. Joseph Alba and J. Wesley Hutchinson, "Dimensions of Consumer Expertise," *Journal of Consumer Research*, Vol. 13 (March 1987), pp. 411–454.

34. John Lynch and Thomas Srull, "Memory and Attentional Factors in Consumer Choice: Concepts and Research Methods," *Journal of Consumer Research*, Vol. 9 (June 1982), pp. 18–37.

35. Alan Collins and Elizabeth Loftus, "A Spreading Activation Theory of Semantic Processing," *Psychological Review*, Vol. 56 (1975), pp. 54–59.

36. J. Wesley Hutchinson and Daniel Moore, "Issues Surrounding the Examination of Delay Effects of Advertising," in *Advances in Consumer Research*, Vol. 11, Thomas Kinnear, ed. (Provo, UT: Association for Consumer Research, 1984), pp. 650–655.

37. Kevin Lane Keller, "Conceptualizing, Measuring, and Managing Customer-Based Brand Equity," *Journal of Marketing*, Vol. 57 (January 1993), pp. 1–22.

38. Tom J. Brown, "Schemata in Consumer Research: A Connectionist Approach," in *Diversity in Consumer Behavior: Advances in Consumer Research*, Vol. 19, John F. Sherry, Jr., and Brian Sternthal, eds. (Provo, UT: Association for Consumer Research, 1992), pp. 787–794.

39. Houston et al., "Picture-Word Consistency."

40. Mita Sujan, James Bettman, and Harish Sujan, "Effects of Consumer Expectations on Information Processing in Selling Encounters," *Journal of Marketing Research*, Vol. 23 (November 1986), pp. 346–353.

41. Julie Franz, "$95 Billion for What: Ads Remembered as Forgettable in 1985," *Advertising Age*, Vol. 57 (March 3, 1986), p. 4.

42. Ernest Hilgard, Richard Atkinson, and Rita Atkinson, *Introduction to Psychology* (New York: Harcourt Brace Jovanovich, 1975).

43. Raymond Burke and Thomas Srull, "Competitive Interference and Consumer Memory for Advertising," *Journal of Consumer Research*, Vol. 15 (June 1988), pp. 55–68.

44. Charles E. Osgood, *Method and Theory in Experimental Psychology* (New York: Oxford University Press, 1964).

45. Ibid.

46. Joseph Alba and Amitava Chattopadhyay, "Salience Effects in Brand Recall," *Journal of Marketing Research*, Vol. 23 (November 1986), pp. 363–369.

47. John Lynch and Thomas Srull, "Memory and Attentional Factors in Consumer Choice: Concepts and Research Methods," *Journal of Consumer Research*, Vol. 9 (June 1982), pp. 18–37.

48. Ibid.

49. Osgood, *Method and Theory in Experimental Psychology*.

50. Richard Harris, Ruth Sturm, Michael Klassen, and John Bechtold, "Language in Advertising: A Psycholinguistic Approach," *Current Issues and Research in Advertising*, Vol. 9 (1986), pp. 1–26.

51. H. Ebbinghaus, *Memory*, H. A. Ruger and C. E. Bussenius, trans. (New York: Teachers College, 1913).

52. Hubert A. Zielske, "The Remembering and Forgetting of Advertising," *Journal of Marketing*, Vol. 23 (January 1959), pp. 231–243.

53. G. H. Bower, "Mood and Memory," *American Psychologist*, Vol. 36 (1981), pp. 129–148.

54. Thomas Srull, "Memory, Mood, and Consumer Judgment," in *Advances in Consumer Research*, Vol. 14, Melanie Wallendorf and Paul Anderson, eds. (Provo, UT: Association for Consumer Research, 1986), pp. 404–407.

55. Meryl Gardner, "Mood States and Consumer Behavior: A Critical Review," *Journal of Consumer Research*, Vol. 12 (December 1985), pp. 281–300.

56. Patricia A. Knowles, Stephen J. Grove, and W. Jeffrey Burroughs, "An Experimental Examination of Mood Effects on Retrieval and Evaluation of Advertisement and Brand Information," *Journal of Academy of Marketing Science*, Vol. 21 (Spring 1993), pp. 135-142. Also, see Meryl Gardner, "Effects of Mood States on Consumer Information Processing," *Research in Consumer Behavior*, Vol. 2 (1987), pp. 113–135.

57. Srull, "Memory, Mood, and Consumer Judgment."

58. Goldberg and Gorn, "Happy and Sad TV Programs."

59. Stephen J. Hoch and John Deighton, "Managing What Consumers Learn from Experience," *Journal of Marketing*, Vol. 53 (April 1989), pp. 1–20.

60. Hoch and Deighton, "Managing What Consumers Learn from Experience."

61. David Horton and Thomas Turnage, *Human Learning* (Englewood Cliffs, NJ: Prentice-Hall, 1976).

62. Harold H. Kassarjian, "Field Theory in Consumer Behavior," in *Consumer Behavior: Theoretical Sources*, Scott Ward and Thomas Robertson, eds. (Englewood Cliffs, NJ: Prentice-Hall, 1973), p. 120.

63. Marvin Goldberg and Gerald Gorn, "Happy and Sad TV Programs: How They Affect Reactions to Commercials," *Journal of Consumer Research*, Vol. 14 (December 1987), pp. 387–403.

64. Frank R. Kardes and Paul M. Herr, "Order Effects in Consumer Judgment, Choice, and Memory: The Role of Initial Processing Goals," in *Advances in Consumer Research*, Vol. 17, Marvin Goldberg and Gerald Gorn, eds. (Provo, UT: Association for Consumer Research, 1990), pp. 541–546.

65. Frank R. Kardes and Gurumurthy Kalyanaram, "Order-of-Entry Effects on Consumer Memory Judgment: An Information Integration Perspective," *Journal of Marketing Research*, Vol. 29 (August 1992), pp. 343–347.

66. Horton and Turnage, *Human Learning*.

67. Sandra Atchison, "Block, Block, Fizz, Fizz," *Business Week*, March 30, 1987, p. 36.

68. Horton and Turnage, *Human Learning*.

69. Julie Franz, "Raisin Recall," *Advertising Age*, March 30, 1987, p. 71.

70. Joanne Lipman, "Claymation's Creator Faces a Tough Sell," *The Wall Street Journal*, April 26, 1991, p. B3.

71. Scott Hume, "McMan-in-Moon Spots Shine," *Advertising Age*, October 26, 1987, p. 4.

Rocks, Trees, and Infiniti

In September 1989 Nissan Motor Corporation U.S.A. released a revolutionary automobile advertising campaign. The ads featured "rocks and trees" and philosophical musings rather than information about the vehicle's characteristics, such as its handling, performance, and safety features. For example, in various ads viewers were shown a rock wall, hay stacks, a stream flowing, the sky, leaves blowing, and waves pounding a beach. The television ads used minimal dialogue. An announcer talked about the car in terms of nature, not in terms of its characteristics.

One two-page print advertisement was called "Beauty in Balance." On one page the reader saw a close-up photo of the intricate detail of a stone wall layered by a master mason. The second page contained sparse dialogue: "In our minds, the balance of three things is essential to making a luxury car luxurious: performance, comfort, styling. No one idea is more important than the other. Each idea contributes in its way to a personal definition of luxury." After a few more brief comments, the ad continues: "Balance. It's why walls that were built 200 years ago haven't fallen down and why designs that are classic in 1990 will still stand up in 2010."

The goal of the Infiniti ads was to create customer awareness, and it worked. On November 8, 1989, the Infiniti was available for sale, and three weeks before the car officially became available for sale, people began appearing in showrooms across the country [1]. Research revealed that in two areas, the ads were highly effective. First, the advertising brought consumers into showrooms. An overwhelming 80% of the customers said they had seen the commercial. As one Chicago area sales manager said, "The advertising clearly worked. The number of people coming in here has been tremendous. It's been like an auto show" [2]. Information compiled by the company found that 80% of Infiniti's target market, households with an annual income of $60,000 or more, could identify the marque in aided awareness tests. Customers commented that the advertising was unusual, and they had never seen anything like it.

The second benefit of the ads was that they created high brand awareness. Results from a Gallup survey conducted in November 1989 showed that Infiniti ads were rated highest in "top-of-the-mind" awareness by *Adwatch*. And despite the lack of performance information furnished, consumers were well informed about the facts of the car. As a dealer in Van Nuys, California, noticed, "They seemed to have read every article ever written about Infiniti. In fact they knew more about the cars than the salesman" [3].

Infiniti sold 1,723 cars in its first seven weeks ending December 31, 1989, which works out to an annual rate of 12,800 cars. Unfortunately, these figures were far below what Infiniti executives expected. Infiniti had projected sales of 30,000 cars by year-end 1990. In contrast, the sales of Toyota's upscale competitor, the Lexus, were extremely strong. Introduced two months prior to the Infiniti ads, Lexus ads were more conventional. The commercials displayed the car and emphasized its benefits available to their customers. During the same time period Lexus sold over 4,500 cars [4].

Although awareness was high, the response to the Infiniti advertising was mixed. Some dealers were furious. They had never seen anything like it, and with sales of the luxury sedans faltering, their immediate reaction was to blame the problem on the advertising. Comedian Jay Leno captured many people's feelings when he said, "The new Japanese car, Infiniti, isn't selling well. I guess the advertising isn't working, although, I understand the sale of rocks and trees is up 300%."

Although the company had planned on showing the "rocks and trees" ads for a full year after the Infiniti was launched, the poor sales caused a revision in plans. In April 1990 new ads were created that focused on the cars. As one manager said, "The new ads are more traditional in terms of beginning to tell a story; the voice-overs now will reinforce the visual elements of the commercials" [5]. With the new advertising campaign, Infiniti's sales picked up. Interestingly, during the recession of 1990–1991, Infiniti's sales increased 45%, the highest increase for any luxury car [6].

QUESTIONS

1. Define the advertising problem faced by Infiniti's managers when the company was about to launch the vehicle several months after Toyota had introduced the Lexus.
2. What consumer concepts from the chapter apply?
3. Discuss the managerial applications of the consumer behavior concepts to the case.

REFERENCES

1. Cleveland Horton, "Infiniti Ads Pull Traffic," *Advertising Age*, November 27, 1989, pp. 2, 112.
2. Scott Hume, "Infiniti Shoots to Top of Best Recalled Ads," *Advertising Age*, January 8, 1990, p. 10.
3. Ibid.
4. Cleveland Horton, "Infiniti Ads Trigger Auto Debate," *Advertising Age*, January 22, 1990, p. 49.
5. Cleveland Horton, "Infiniti Revises Ads: Snubs Nature Theme," *Advertising Age*, April 9, 1990, p. 2.
6. Mark Landler, "Mercedes Finds Out How Much Is Too Much," *Business Week*, January 20, 1992, pp. 92–96.

Chapter 5

Behavioral Learning

CONSUMER VIGNETTE

Sales Promotions: Savior or Disease?

The general manager of the Oldsmobile dealership had a problem. Despite offering massive discounts, he had been unsuccessful in selling his last five slow-moving Toronados. His solution was to give away a $4,480 Yugo when someone purchased a Toronado at list price. Within a month all five cars were gone, and people drove hundreds of miles to get in on the deal.[1] Why was the deal so successful when the Yugos were worth no more than the discount that the dealer had been offering to potential buyers all along?

In another case, promotions for J&B Scotch offered buyers of the $15 item a free watch, radio, or movie videocassette. Each prize had a retail value of between $20 and $50. To get the gift customers had to soak off the label and send it with proof of purchase to the company.[2] How could the company risk losing more than the value of the product on each sale?

Casinos spend as much as 20% of their revenues on complimentary services, ranging from free transportation to the casino from anywhere in the world to rolls of nickels for players from church groups. Why? The answer is quite simple. By giving away "comps," the casinos attract gamblers who will lose more than the value of the comp. Thus at the Golden Nugget casinos certain guidelines are given on comps. For example, a player betting an average of $25 for 15 minutes will be given free parking. In contrast, a player who bets an average of $1,000 a hand for over two hours will be given free lodging, a limo, and free gourmet meals.[3]

Corporations recognize the impact of sales promotions, and they are increasingly using them. Thus, from the late 1970s to the late 1980s, the percentage of promotion dollars spent on consumer sales promotions increased by over 17%. In contrast, the percentage spent on media advertising decreased by about 17%.[4] Then, during the recession of the early 1990s, the use of sales promotions jumped again. As one contest supervisor for an ad agency said, "Every time there has been a downturn in the economy, contest use goes way up." An executive for a beverage company said, "In bad times, it's more important than ever to get a focused marketing program out there stimulating consumers to action."[5]

INTRODUCTION

When analyzing the topic of learning, consumer researchers typically discuss two types—cognitive learning and behavioral learning. Cognitive-learning theorists focus on relatively complex forms of learning, such as how people retain verbal material (e.g., advertising messages), how people have insights, and how people plan. As such, most cognitively oriented theorists view learning as occurring via information processing; thus Chapter 4 discussed these two areas together.

This chapter focuses on another view of learning. Called behavioral learning, the approach forms the basis of the behavioral influence perspective and holds that behavior is primarily made in response to environmental stimuli. The overall goal of the approach is to solve practical problems effectively rather than to create a science that develops theories of behavior through explanations of internal events within the person.[6]

Behavioral learning may be defined as a process in which experience with the environment leads to a relatively permanent change in behavior or the potential for a change in behavior. As such, all learning results from experience—not from changes in physiology caused by growth, injury, or disease. Thus temporary states, such as those that occur from ingesting drugs, would not be classified as learning. Consumers, however, may experience learning but not reveal it through a change in behavior. For example, a person may have been conditioned to respond to price rebates by purchasing a product. However, if the person moves to an underdeveloped country, where rebates are never offered, the effects of the learning could not be observed.

Researchers have identified three major approaches to behavioral learning—classical conditioning, operant conditioning, and vicarious learning. In **classical conditioning**, behavior is influenced by a stimulus that occurs prior to the behavior and elicits it in a manner that has the appearance of being a reflex. In **operant conditioning**, behavior is influenced by the consequences of the behavior. **Vicarious learning** occurs when individuals observe the actions of others and model or imitate the actions.

Advertisers are particularly interested in the study of classical conditioning. They attempt to identify stimuli (e.g., messages, sights, or sounds) that will elicit positive reactions from consumers. Their goal is to associate their product or service with the positive stimulus, so that the product will elicit a similar positive reaction when the consumer thinks about or encounters it.

The principles of operant conditioning are important in a variety of marketing activities. Strategies in sales promotion and personal selling frequently involve providing consumers with reinforcers and/or punishments that may influence their later behavior. The behavior of customers playing the slot machines at casinos well illustrates the effects of operant conditioning. Their incessant gambling, even in the face of staggering losses, their superstitious behavior, and their high levels of arousal all can be explained to a large extent via operant-conditioning principles. The incredible public participation in the state lotteries that are springing up across the country also illustrates the strong **reinforcement properties** of the chance to win millions of dollars. Indeed, because of the ability of such reinforcers to control behavior, B. F. Skinner, a founder of behaviorism, has questioned the ethics of creating state lotteries.

The chapter-opening vignette illustrated how the use of sales promotion devices can influence the actions of consumers. The effects of sales promotion devices can be explained via operant-conditioning principles. Thus, for consumers to obtain a premium (e.g., a free Yugo), a rebate, or a chance to win a prize in a contest, they must engage in a behavior, usually involving the purchase of a product. One does not have to refer to internal states, such as beliefs or attitudes, to explain the effects of sales promotions from a behavioral-learning perspective. The prior learning history of consumers with such reinforcers has conditioned them to respond by purchasing the product or services.

The effects of sales promotion devices on consumers can be extremely strong. When General Motors offered 2.9% financing to purchasers of its cars in the summer of 1986, buyers lined up. At John Lee Oldsmobile in Ann Arbor, Michigan, more than a month's worth of cars were sold in just a few days. However, a few months later the dealership was in agony. Showroom traffic was gone, caused by the discontinuance of the sales promotion. Just as pigeons learn to respond to changes in a reinforcement schedule of when their food is given, so had consumers learned to respond to the changes in sales promotions. The owner of a Buick dealership noted that customers now buy cars the way they buy shirts. "They wait for a sale: and if they miss it, they aren't worried."[7] Such anecdotes reveal that the use of sales promotional devices, although successful in the short run, can cause serious long-term problems. Their use may cause consumers to buy only for the free gift or contest, which can dramatically decrease the ability to obtain brand loyalty.

Figure 5-1 presents a recent print ad for General Motors announcing a sales promotion in which consumers can save up to $1,000 a year on the purchase of a new GM car if they sign up for the GM Gold Card. This strategy avoids the brand-loyalty problems mentioned earlier. That is, the free gift that is obtained with the Gold Card is a reduction in the cost of the key product offered by the company—a car.

For auto manufacturers the reliance on sales promotion devices has become almost an addiction. Each time one is introduced, consumers tend to respond. When the promotion ends, people stop buying. In effect, the auto companies themselves have been conditioned to use sales promotion devices. The result is that many American auto companies became hooked on the promotional strategy, possibly reducing their overall profits. A company that has avoided sales promotions, however, is Honda. During the depths of the recession of the early 1990s, one auto analyst said of the company, "Honda has never been willing to do car clearance carnivals on the level of its competitors. Even in this market it is still taking the high road of marketing vs. the bargain basement. In the long run this will serve Honda's image of quality well."[8]

Another question brought up in the introductory vignette concerned why managers risked losing money in the promotion of J&B Scotch. Again, the answer lies in the reinforcement structure of the situation. The managers hoped that the offer of expensive premiums (i.e., watches, radios, and videocassettes) would be sufficiently reinforcing to increase the number of purchases of the product. However, the managers also hoped that some "slippage" would occur. **Slippage** is the term used to describe the percentage of customers who purchase a product but fail to redeem a premium offer. Based upon their knowledge of the target market, the managers gambled that few customers would go to the trouble of redeeming the premium. The task of soaking off the label and keeping a proof of purchase would be so punishing that few would engage in the inconvenient task. Thus, in this case, a punisher would keep many from cashing in on the offer.

Figure 5-1 General Motors Corporation uses operant conditioning principles in a highly effective sales promotion campaign to entice consumers to sign up for its new credit card—up to $1,000 off each year on a new GM car.

Having an understanding of vicarious, also called observational-learning, processes are also important for managers. For example, a frequent advertising strategy is to show appealing models using a product and experiencing positive outcomes from its use. The hope is that consumers will imitate the behavior of the model and purchase the product. Figure 5-2 shows an ad from Nike Inc. that effectively employs observational-learning ideas.

CLASSICAL CONDITIONING

Would the background music played during a television commercial influence whether or not you bought the product advertised? An experiment found that the like or dislike for background music may actually influence consumer choice.

Figure 5-2 Nike used principles of observational learning in this effective ad for its cross-training shoes.

Although controversial, the study may well illustrate classical conditioning.[9] In the experiment, college students were shown slides of either a light blue or beige fountain pen. (The pens were exactly the same; only the colors differed.) While the students saw the slides of one of the pens, music that they either liked or disliked was played in the background. (The "liked" music came from the movie *Grease*, and the "disliked" music was a one-minute piece of classical Indian music.) The students were later given a choice of a free pen—either the color of pen with which the music was paired or the color of pen that had not been paired with any music. The results showed that when the popular music was played, 79% chose the pen with which the music was paired. In contrast, when the unpopular music was played, only 30% chose the pen associated with the music. The presence of music influenced the students' preferences, depending upon whether it was liked or disliked.

At the conclusion of the study, the experimenter asked the students the reasons for their choices. Only 2% of the subjects gave the presence of the music as a reason for their choice. The influence of the music on the students in most cases seemed to take place without their awareness. One possible explanation for the effect of the music on the students' choice of ballpoint pens is the process of classical conditioning. First identified by the Russian physiologist Ivan Pavlov in the 1920s, classical conditioning is a primitive form of learning that affects the behavior of all animal species, from worms to dogs to humans.

What Is Classical Conditioning?

Also called **respondent conditioning**, in the process of classical conditioning a neutral stimulus is paired with a stimulus that elicits a response. Through a repetition of the pairing, the neutral stimulus takes on the ability to elicit the response. Pavlov discovered the phenomenon when he was working with dogs. The dogs had the messy propensity to begin salivating profusely (the response) each time meat powder (the stimulus) was presented to them. The stimulus of the meat powder reflexively elicited the response of salivation.

Humans also have a variety of such stimulus–response linkages. For example, puffing air into someone's eye elicits the response of blinking. Playing soothing music may elicit the response of relaxation. The soothing music is called the **unconditioned stimulus** (UCS). The reflexive response elicited by the stimulus is called the **unconditioned response** (UCR).

When classical conditioning occurs, a previously neutral stimulus (called the **conditioned stimulus**, or CS) is repeatedly paired with the eliciting stimulus (the unconditioned stimulus, or UCS). In the pairing the CS needs to occur prior to the UCS, so that it predicts the UCS. After a number of such pairings, the ability to elicit a response is transferred to the CS. The response elicited by the CS is called the **conditioned response** (CR). Current research on classical conditioning emphasizes that mere contiguity (or closeness in time) of the pairing of the CS with the UCS is not enough to achieve classical conditioning.[10]

Conditioning results from the informational relationship of the CS and the UCS. For the CS to provide information about the UCS, it must predict the occurrence of the UCS. Figure 5-3 depicts these relationships. For optimal conditioning to occur, the CS should slightly precede the UCS in time.[11] In the experiments by Pavlov, the presence of the meat powder (the UCS) was preceded in time by the ringing of a bell (the CS). After a number of such pairings, the mere ringing of the bell would elicit the conditioned response of salivation (the CR). One can observe the same phenomenon in household pets. In the movie *Roxanne*, Steve Martin played Charlie, a clever but outrageously long-nosed fire chief. In one scene his volunteer fire department is going crazy attempting to coax a cat from a tree. The inept firemen are falling all over themselves attempting to climb the tree to reach the feline. Charlie arrives at the scene, surveys it, and takes out a can of cat food and a can opener. The familiar popping sound of the can being opened alerts the cat and elicits a salivation response, and the cat begins licking its chops. The cat casually climbs from the tree to consume the food. The sound of the can being opened had become paired with the food. Over time, the sound became a conditioned stimulus that elicited salivation.

In the music experiment described earlier in the section, the unconditioned stimulus was the positively or negatively regarded music heard by the students. The unconditioned response was the positive or negative emotional response to the music. Because the ballpoint pen was paired with the music, it may have became a conditioned stimulus. It, in turn, elicited a conditioned emotional response. Presumably, when the students were making their choice of pens, the emotional response elicited by the pen influenced their behavior. Thus, when the emotional response was negative, the pen was avoided. Conversely, when the emotional response was positive, the pen was actively sought.

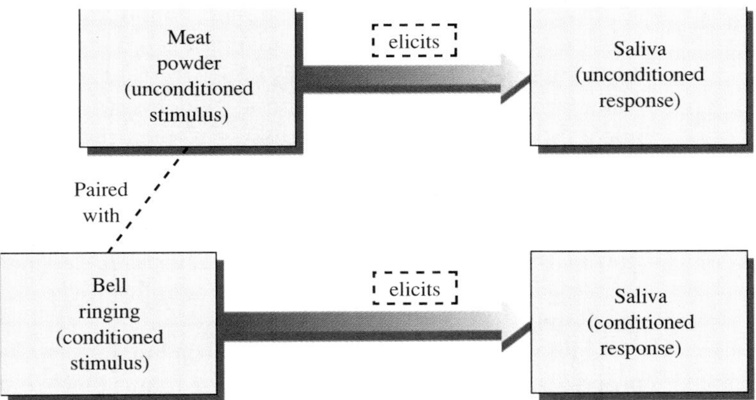

Figure 5-3 The classical-conditioning framework.

Consumer Studies of Classical Conditioning

Researchers have found additional cases in which music may influence consumers via a classical-conditioning process. Suppose that you were the manager of a chain of supermarkets. What would you do if you learned that by playing slow-paced music in your stores you could increase sales? An experiment actually found these results. Over a period of nine weeks, an experiment was conducted in a grocery store in which the tempo of music was varied. At various times, customers heard no music, slow-tempo music, or fast-tempo music. The results of the study revealed significant differences in buying when slow- or fast-tempo music was played. When the pace at which customers moved between two points was measured, it was found that those in fast-tempo conditions moved significantly faster than did those in the slow-tempo conditions.

Interestingly, daily gross sales volume was found to be significantly higher in the slow-tempo conditions. Indeed, sales were 38% higher in the slow-tempo conditions.[12] One cannot make wild generalizations from one study performed in one grocery store over a period of only nine weeks. However, the results seem to show that music can influence consumer behavior. Assuming that the phenomenon is real, what is the mechanism through which the situational variable of music influences behavior? One possibility is that people have been classically conditioned during their lives to respond to music in certain predictable ways. Thus fast-paced music, when played in a grocery store, may elicit a response in which customers move faster. The fast pace, then, impedes buying. In another context, slow-paced, pleasant music may relax patients in the dental office enough to raise their threshold for pain.

Researchers continue to find new evidence of phenomena that act like classical conditioning. For example, the author of the grocery store study has replicated it in a restaurant. In a carefully designed study, either fast-tempo or slow-tempo music was played in a popular restaurant. The results revealed that when slow-tempo music was played, customers tended to stay longer at tables and to purchase more from the bar. The estimated gross margin of the restaurant was significantly higher because of the increased bar sales.[13]

In another recent study researchers conducted four experiments to test for classical-conditioning effects in an advertising–consumer behavior setting.[14] Carefully applying the procedural controls necessary to distinguish classical conditioning from other processes, the authors found evidence of classical-conditioning effects. The unconditioned stimuli in the study were pictures of beautiful landscape scenes. The conditioned stimulus was a fictitious brand of toothpaste. The conditioned response was evaluated by various measures of attitude toward the brand. The results across the four experiments were strongly supportive of a classical-conditioning interpretation of the results. Thus, when the toothpaste was paired with beautiful landscape scenes, the attitude toward the ad was significantly more positive than in the control conditions.

Additional research has provided tantalizing evidence of classical-conditioning processes.[15] In these studies the author found that stimuli associated with spending money (specifically credit card insignias) may actually elicit spending responses. In the carefully controlled series of studies, one group of subjects was placed in a spending situation in which a MasterCard sign was in view. Another group of subjects was placed in the same situation, but the card was not present. The presence of the sign caused respondents to

1. Make buying decisions to spend more quickly.
2. Indicate that more would be spent on a clothing purchase and other consumer goods.
3. Estimate that they would give more to a charity.
4. Actually give more to a charity.

In explaining his results the author proposed that credit cards become paired with the buying act. For many people the buying act takes on the properties of an unconditioned stimulus that elicits the unconditioned response of positive feelings. Through many pairings of the credit card with the buying act, the credit card becomes a conditioned stimulus that elicits a conditioned response of positive feelings. The positive feelings elicited by the credit card in turn make it more likely that a person will spend money when it is present.

Figure 5-4 presents a subset of the credit card placards that are frequently placed in highly salient locations in stores to attract consumers' attention.

In an important recent series of studies, researchers analyzed the extent to which positive attitudes could be conditioned to various unknown and known brands of colas. The unconditioned stimuli were photos of beautiful water scenes, and the conditioned stimuli were the various brands of colas. A slide presentation was used to show the stimuli to the subjects in the study. In the experimental conditions, the beautiful water scenes always preceded the slides showing the colas. In the control conditions, no relationship existed between the presentation of the cola and the beautiful photo slides. (That is, sometimes a cola was shown before the water picture and sometimes after the water picture.) The results provided evidence of classical conditioning occurring: attitudes were changed in the experimental conditions. The researchers obtained two important additional findings. First, attitudes toward the unknown colas changed the most. Second, conditioning occurred only if the subjects had some awareness of a relationship between the conditioned stimulus and the unconditioned stimulus.[16]

Figure 5-4

Retailers often prominently display credit card insignia. Research has indicated that such displays may act as conditioned stimuli that elicit buying behavior. (© Ray Ellis 1986/Photo Researchers, Inc.)

In sum, evidence is accumulating that consumers appear to respond to a variety of stimuli in a manner consistent with a classical-conditioning interpretation. Because early experiments involved conditioning animals to salivate to bells and to reveal other assorted "rudimentary" behaviors, the tendency has been to view classical conditioning as a simple process in which organisms "stupidly" react to stimuli. In contrast, researchers are currently taking a much more sophisticated view of the phenomenon. One internationally recognized researcher in the field has argued that the organism "is better viewed as an information seeker using logical and perceptual relations among events, along with its own preconceptions, to form a sophisticated representation of the world."[17]

Table 5-1 summarizes the key concepts found in classical conditioning as it applies to consumer behavior.

Is It Classical Conditioning?

A warning is necessary, however, in interpreting the results of classical-conditioning studies performed in a consumer context. Despite the evidence of the studies mentioned in the last section, the concept that advertisers can classically condition consumers to respond positively to their products is highly controversial.[18] For example, one study failed to replicate the research reported earlier in the chapter on the effects of pairing music with the color of ballpoint pens to influence preferences.[19]

One argument against classical-conditioning processes working in consumer contexts is that in general the studies have failed to control for the awareness of the subjects used in the studies. Those who argue against classical-conditioning explanations suggest that the effects are generally found only among subjects who were aware of the pairing of neutral stimulus with unconditioned stimulus.[20] If people were aware of the pairing, does one have unambiguous evidence of classical conditioning? Because researchers are increasingly viewing classical conditioning as involving higher-level cognitive processes, the criticism is much less damaging to the idea that consumers can be classically conditioned.[21]

A more important criticism of classical-conditioning studies is that a completely different explanation may exist for the results found in consumer behavior studies.[22] The researchers suggested that the presence of the unconditioned stimulus, such as pleasant music, places people in a better mood. The change in mood state causes the stimulated consumers to retrieve positive thoughts. It is the retrieval of these positive thoughts that accounts for the preference for the classically conditioned brands. (Readers should recall that this proposal of how mood affects information processing is consistent with the discussion of mood in the last chapter.)

For the marketing manager or public policy person, however, the issue concerns whether the behavior of consumers can be influenced—regardless of whether the

TABLE 5-1

Some Key Concepts from Classical Conditioning

1. *Unconditioned stimulus*—The stimulus that elicits a response. For example, soothing music may elicit the responses of relaxation and positive feelings. Other examples of unconditioned stimuli in a consumer context are physically attractive people, beautiful visual scenes, the American flag (for U.S. citizens), religious symbols, etc.
2. *Unconditioned response*—The responses elicited by unconditioned stimulus.
3. *Conditioned stimulus*—A previously neutral stimulus that takes on some of the properties of the unconditioned stimulus when appropriately paired with it.
4. *Conditioned response*—The response elicited by the conditioned stimulus. It is generally a reduced version of the unconditioned response.
5. *Sign tracking*—The attention-drawing ability of unconditioned and conditioned stimuli.
6. *Higher-order conditioning*—The ability of a conditioned stimulus to classically condition another previously neutral stimulus.

change results from classical conditioning or some other process. This author believes that by following the proper conditioning procedures, behavioral change results. Knowledge of whether or not the change results from conditioning or some other phenomenon is only of interest to a manager if it affects his or her marketing strategy.

Additional Classical-Conditioning Concepts

Two additional concepts from classical conditioning are relevant to consumer research—sign tracking and higher-order conditioning. Another important problem concerns identifying the conditions necessary to most effectively obtain classical conditioning.

Sign Tracking

Consumer researchers have shown evidence that, through advertising, products may become conditioned stimuli and elicit a positive emotional response in consumers. In addition, the classical-conditioning process may also result in increased attention being place on the product. This attention-drawing ability of conditioned stimuli results from a phenomenon called **sign tracking**.[23] Organisms have the tendency to attend to, to orient themselves toward, and to approach a conditioned or unconditioned stimulus. Evidence indicates that the ability of the unconditioned stimulus to draw attention to it can be transferred to the conditioned stimulus. Thus, if a product can be paired with an unconditioned stimulus so that it becomes a conditioned stimulus, it may also acquire the ability to draw attention itself. With the increasing commercial clutter found today, the ability of a product to induce people to engage in sign tracking could be a major advantage in getting the message attended to and stored for later use.

Figure 5-5 reveals a photograph that depicts the phenomenon of sign tracking. The photo shows a college student and his dog avidly reading the second edition of *Consumer Behavior* by John Mowen. While some believe that the book is interesting for people to read, how in the world could it capture the dog's attention? The clever photographer had the college student hold a dog biscuit against the book. As a strong reinforcer, the biscuit caused the dog to engage in sign tracking, and as a result, he stared intently at the object of his desire.

Higher-Order Conditioning

Of particular importance to marketers is the concept of **higher-order conditioning**—where a conditioned stimulus can, in and of itself, act to classically condition another previously neutral stimulus. Indeed, most of the stimuli used by marketers to create conditioned stimuli are probably themselves conditioned stimuli. For example, the pairing of a particular sports announcer, such as Curt Gowdy, with exciting sports events may have made his voice a conditioned stimulus for many people. Thus, when one hears Curt Gowdy, a certain degree of excitement is elicited. His voice can then be used as a stimulus to classically condition a product. However, the voice of Curt Gowdy is itself a conditioned stimulus.

One frequently used approach by companies is to associate their products, or even their company, with a country's flag or with patriotic themes. The flag may be

Figure 5-5 This photo illustrates how a dog biscuit held behind a textbook can cause a dog to engage in sign tracking and appear to be interested in the book. (Photo by Jarenwoi L. Parauich.)

conceptualized as a conditioned stimulus that may in turn condition other previously neutral stimuli through a higher-order conditioning process. Highlight 5-1 discusses how companies in the United States have used "Old Glory" to influence the behavior of consumers. This trend reached epic proportions during the Persian Gulf War with Iraq in 1991.

Requirements for Effective Conditioning

To classically condition a response most effectively, a number of requirements should be met.[24] First, to condition a neutral stimulus, it should precede in time the appearance of the unconditioned stimulus. The concept is that the conditioned stimulus needs to predict the occurrence of the unconditioned stimulus. Thus in commercials the product should be shown prior to the appearance of the unconditioned stimulus. By preceding the UCS, the CS provides information to the organism on its occurrence.

A second finding is that classical conditioning is most effective if the product is paired consistently with the unconditioned stimulus. If the product is seen very frequently and the unconditioned stimulus is seen very rarely, conditioning is less likely to occur. This requirement implies that television advertising should be supported by a strong sales promotion effort. For example, if a celebrity endorser is used as the

HIGHLIGHT 5-1

Products and Old Glory

A recent trend among companies has been to promote their products as made in the United States. For example, JCPenney, the nation's third largest retailer, developed a promotional theme, called "American Style," in which products were touted as American made. Sears and Kmart have also started similar campaigns. Indeed, on the cover of one Sears catalog was a picture of the Statue of Liberty and the inscription "Thank you, America."

The highly successful Wal-Mart, which sells most of its goods to blue-collar workers in small towns, has initiated a program in which its buyers actively seek out American manufacturers. The company claims that $400 million has gone to U.S. firms that previously would have been funneled to foreign suppliers. The U.S. textile industry launched a $40 million ad campaign to get consumers to buy American. The campaign used the slogan "Crafted with Pride in the U.S.A."

Some empirical evidence exists that a patriotic theme has benefits. In 1986 Hanover House Industries put out two versions of its catalog. One version showed each domestically produced item with a "Made in the U.S.A." logo, and the other did not. The patriotic versions elicited 10% more responses to their line of moderately priced women's apparel and accessories.

One explanation of the positive effect of "Made in the U.S.A." themes is classical conditioning. Photos of the flag and patriotic themes may act as unconditioned stimuli and elicit positive emotions. If a product is successfully paired with the stimulus, it could become a conditioned stimulus and elicit positive feelings that could influence buying behavior.

Based in part on "Draping Old Glory Around Just About Everything," *Business Week*, October 27, 1986, pp. 66–68.

unconditioned stimulus in television advertising, his or her picture should be shown prominently with the product in point-of-purchase displays. A third finding of importance is that classical conditioning is most effective when both the conditioned stimulus and the unconditioned stimulus are highly salient to the consumer. Particularly in television commercials, the product and the unconditioned stimulus should stand out from the background of the advertisement and from the clutter of competing ads. How many pairings of conditioned stimulus and unconditioned stimulus are necessary to obtain classical conditioning? Recent research indicates that learning can be surprisingly rapid, depending on the organism and the kind of conditioning being investigated. In a number of cases, one pairing of conditioned stimulus and unconditioned stimulus is all that is necessary for conditioning to occur.[25]

Managerial Applications of Classical Conditioning

The problem for managers in using classical conditioning involves attempting to identify strong unconditioned stimuli with which a product or service can be paired. For marketers perhaps the most important effects of classical conditioning involve attempts to condition positive emotional responses to brands via promotional activities. A variety of unconditioned stimuli may elicit positive emotional responses, such as sexy actors or actresses, patriotic music, exciting sporting events, beautiful scenery, and so forth. These positive emotional reactions are the unconditioned responses. By pairing on numerous occasions a product (the conditioned stimulus) with the unconditioned stimulus (e.g., sexy people), the product itself may elicit a positive emotional response.

An excellent example of this process may be seen in television advertisements for various brands of beer and colas in the early 1990s. For example, in ads for Coors Light beer, pictures of the beverage were followed by views of the scantily clad bodies of highly attractive men and women. Hard-driving background music enhanced the overall emotional impact of the advertisements for many people.

Figure 5-6 shows an ad for Levi's 531 jeans, titled "Everything Basic Evolves," that is targeted to men. Although the man is certainly shown in a "loose" pose, the focus of the ad is more upon his athletic body. An interesting question concerns whether the ad may be using a classical conditioning approach. It is likely that positive emotional reactions will be triggered in men by the ad, because it depicts a look that is highly desired.

Classical-conditioning processes may also influence shopping behavior and, therefore, have application to distribution issues. Thus the playing of music has been found to influence the speed with which consumers move in a grocery store or eat in a restaurant. Through a similar process, the appearance of credit cards may actually facilitate spending. These results suggest that the physical design of buildings should be considered in terms of its emotional impact on people.

OPERANT CONDITIONING AND CONSUMER BEHAVIOR

From a cognitive perspective, learning is hypothesized to result from some change within a person's brain. Although not easily observable, the change is assumed to involve the existence of a memory trace, as postulated by the Gestalt psychologists, or the creation of new protein chains, as proposed by recent physiological psychologists. In contrast, the operant-conditioning perspective actively avoids reference to any mental processes. Indeed, the dominant figure and theoretician in the scientific movement, B. F. Skinner, opposed his students' making any reference to such words as "mind," "thoughts," "wants," "needs," "motivations," or "personality" as anything other than behaviors. Although readily admitting that thoughts and feelings occur, Skinner and his followers simply viewed these as covert or hidden behaviors that result from conditioning by their consequences. From this behavioristic view, feelings and thoughts do not cause actions. Rather, they are actions themselves.[26] Skinner was even unhappy with the use of the word "learning" because for many people it implies the operation of some internal mental operation that itself causes behavior.[27]

Just what is operant conditioning and what are operants? **Operants** are the naturally occurring actions of an organism in the environment. Dogs walk, bark, and sniff. Pigeons peck at objects. Human babies crawl, babble incessantly, and love to put disgusting things in their mouths. Managers should be concerned with a variety of consumer operant behaviors, including purchasing a product or service, telling friends or acquaintances about a product's performance, writing or calling the

Figure 5-6 Could this ad for Levi's 531 jeans be using principles of classical conditioning? (Courtesy of Levi Strauss, Inc.)

company about product problems, and searching for the best product or the best price for a product.

The initial cause of operants is the natural tendency of organisms to explore the environment. They are not elicited reflexively by some stimulus.[28] Operants are often called **instrumental responses**—that is, the operants serve as instruments to obtain reinforcements from the environment. Formally, operant conditioning may be defined as a process in which the frequency of occurrence of a bit of behavior is modified by the consequences of the behavior.[29] Thus, when a consumer emits a behavior, such as buying a product, the consequences of the behavior will change the probability of that behavior occurring again. If the behavior is positively reinforced, say, by the product performing well or by friends complimenting the person on his or her purchase, the likelihood of the purchase being made again will increase. If the behavior is punished, say, because the product failed or because friends ridiculed the purchase, the likelihood of making the purchase again will decrease.

The concepts of operant conditioning have wide application to consumer behavior and marketing management. Of extreme importance to marketing managers is the analysis of the **contingencies of reinforcement** being received by consumers when purchasing and using a good or service. This analysis refers to the study of all the reinforcers and punishers that accompany the purchase of a product. The relationship, or contingency, between when the reinforcers and punishers occur and the consumer's behaviors influences the likelihood of that behavior occurring again. For instance, consider a consumer who goes into a fast-food restaurant to make a purchase. A variety of stimuli will act to reinforce or punish the consumer. Such factors as the cleanliness of the restaurant, the speed of the lines, the courtesy of the employees, and the quality and price of the food can act as either reinforcers or punishers. Managers must carefully analyze these contingencies of reinforcement to determine their impact on customers.

Table 5-2 identifies and defines eight key concepts of operant conditioning. A number of these are discussed in the paragraphs that follow.

Reinforcement and Influencing Behavior

As noted previously, a reinforcer is anything that occurs after a behavior and changes the likelihood that it will be emitted again.[30] There are three different types of reinforcers that influence the probability that these various behaviors will reoccur. A **positive reinforcer** involves placing an appropriate reward immediately after a behavior occurs. The reinforcer acts to increase the likelihood that the behavior will be repeated. Giving consumers $25 if they will test drive a car is an example of a positive reinforcer. During the recession in 1980–82, Chrysler found that the $25 did increase the likelihood that consumers would test drive its cars.

A second type of reinforcer is a negative reinforcer. **Negative reinforcers** involve the removal of an aversive stimulus. A behavior that results in the elimination of something negative is reinforced and is more likely to occur again in the future. Examples of negative reinforcers are somewhat hard to find in marketing because their use would involve ethical problems. One humorous example of the use of a negative reinforcer was employed by a nonprofit organization that operated a shelter for teenagers. The fund drive was called "The Great Gerbil Giveaway." People received a letter indicating that their name had been placed in a drawing to receive

TABLE 5-2

Some Basic Operant-Conditioning Principles

Reinforcer—A stimulus that increases the probability of repetition of a behavior that it follows.

Positive reinforcer—A stimulus whose *presence* as a consequence of a behavior increases the probability of the behavior recurring.

Negative reinforcer—A stimulus whose *disappearance* as a consequence of a behavior increases the probability that the behavior will recur.

Secondary reinforcer—A previously neutral stimulus that acquires reinforcing properties through its association with a primary reinforcer.

Punisher—A stimulus whose presence after a response decreases the likelihood of the behavior recurring.

Shaping—A process through which a new operant behavior is created by reinforcing successive approximations of the desired behavior.

Extinction—A gradual reduction in the frequency of occurrence of an operant behavior resulting from a lack of reinforcement of the response.

Schedule of reinforcement—The frequency and timing of reinforcers form a schedule of reinforcement that can dramatically influence the pattern of operant responses.

SOURCE: These definitions are based on material found in G. S. Reynolds, *A Primer of Operant Conditioning* (Glenview, IL: Scott, Foresman, 1968).

two gerbils. However, they could buy insurance against the possibility of winning the gerbils for a $5 or $10 contribution to the shelter. The letter noted that without the insurance, "you just might WIN Gus and Gwendolyn who, we have it on an unimpeachable authority, 'Go for the Gusto,' and have multiplying personalities."[31] In other words, recipients had to engage in the behavior of making a cash contribution to avoid receiving a negative reinforcer in the form of two gerbils. Of course, the premise was that most people would rather pay $5 than receive the gerbils as a gift.

A secondary reinforcer is the third type of reinforcer. Early in one's life all reinforcers are of a primary nature. Such primary reinforcers are stimuli that are necessary for life and basic happiness, such as food, water, salt, and soft touching. Over a period of time, previously neutral stimuli can become **secondary reinforcers**. The process occurs by pairing the neutral stimulus over and over with the primary stimuli. As a result of the pairing, the neutral stimulus will take on reinforcing properties similar to those of the primary stimuli. Thus, if a mother coos softly just prior to softly touching her baby, over a period of time the soft cooing will in itself become reinforcing to the baby. Thus a mother might unconsciously condition a baby to cry to be picked up. If the mother cooed each time she picked up the child, the cooing would become a secondary reinforcer, leading the baby to emit behaviors simply to obtain the cooing.

In the marketing environment, most reinforcers are of a secondary nature. A product performing well, a reduction in price, and a friendly "hello" by a salesperson are all examples of secondary reinforcers. Even though they are secondary reinforcers, they still may have a major impact on consumer behavior.

Another operant-conditioning concept of importance to marketers is that of a punisher. A **punisher** is any stimulus whose presence after a behavior decreases the likelihood of the behavior reoccurring. For a marketer a key goal is to avoid punishing consumers for using their product or service. A great number of punishers exist in the environment to discourage product purchases. Some examples include poor product performance, ridicule of the product by friends, irritating actions or remarks by a salesperson, or stock outages of a product.

Extinction

Once an operant response is conditioned, it will persist as long as it is periodically reinforced. However, if the operant response goes without reinforcement for an extended number of occasions, it will tend to disappear. This disappearance of a response due to lack of reinforcement is called **extinction**. Interestingly, immediately after the reinforcement ceases, the vigor of the response may actually increase. In humans, the reaction would probably be called anger. Suppose that a salesman over the years has reinforced his customer for buying his product by taking him or her out to lunch each time the product was purchased. Suddenly the salesman decides that this is too expensive and stops providing the reinforcer. The initial reaction of the customer may be anger, and the eventual outcome could be the extinction of the buying response.

HIGHLIGHT 5-2

Behavioral Influence and the "Blue Light"

In 1955 an assistant manager at a Kmart store put a police light on a pole and began one of the more peculiar rituals in retailing. The "blue light" specials occur about twice an hour and last from 5 to 15 minutes. The light flashes above inexpensive impulse items on which the store runs a brief special. (By the way, originally the light was red; it was changed to blue because of image problems.)

Used frequently to lure customers to slow parts of the store, the flashing light attracts people like moths to a flame. In the presence of the stimulus, pacifists become aggressive, mothers leave their infants, and salesclerks get out of the way. Once when prices of ironing boards were slashed, people were knocking each other over as they swung the boards around to exit the melée.

The effectiveness of the blue light illustrates the behavioral influence perspective on consumer purchasing. The light acts as a conditioned reinforcer that functions as part of a chain of stimuli and responses. Prior to an experience with Kmart stores, the light has no impact on behavior. With experience, however, consumers learn that the light acts as a discriminative stimulus, which when followed by a buying response leads to a conditioned reinforcer (i.e., the big discount). Over time the blue light itself becomes a conditioned reinforcer, and consumers begin to emit responses in order to be in its presence, such as following it around.

In sum, the effectiveness of the blue light may be viewed as resulting from an operant-conditioning process in which behavior is shaped by the contingencies of the environment. One does not have to resort to discussions of decision-making processes or of feelings and emotion to explain the sometimes weird behavior of Kmart shoppers. Rather, the effectiveness of the blue light results from its influence as a discriminatory stimulus that becomes a secondary reinforcer.

Based in part on Melinda Grenier Guiles, "Attention Shoppers: Stop That Browsing and Get Aggressive," *The Wall Street Journal*, June 16, 1987, Section 1, p. 15.

Schedules of Reinforcement

The way in which reinforcers are applied can have an enormous impact on the behavior of consumers. A reinforcer does not have to be applied each time a particular behavior is emitted to reinforce it. In these intermittent **schedules of reinforcement**, the behavior is reinforced after a certain number of repetitions or after a certain length of time has passed. One outcome of using schedules of reinforcement is that the operant responses become more resistant to extinction. Thus the reinforcer can be omitted for quite a number of cases and the behavior will persist.

Automobile rebates provide an example of consumers being placed on an intermittent schedule of reinforcement. Auto rebates employ what is called a variable interval schedule—that is, the timing of when the rebates go into effect varies. Sometimes a rebate is put in place relatively quickly after the last one is discontinued. In other cases, a considerable length of time passes before a new rebate is initiated. This schedule conditions consumers to wait for rebates; such behavior is resistant to extinction.

Discriminative Stimuli

Discriminative stimuli are those stimuli that occur in the presence of a reinforcer and do not occur in its absence. They are like signals that indicate whether or not a reinforcer will be present if a behavior is emitted. Because the discriminative stimulus is paired with the reinforcer, the likelihood of the operant response occurring increases. The organism learns to emit the operant response when the discriminative stimulus is present and not to emit the response when it is absent. There is nothing special about a discriminative stimulus. For example, the word "sit" has no particular impact on a dog until it is followed by a dog biscuit (if the animal does sit on the floor). If the word is consistently followed by a reward after the behavior has appeared, it will come to gradually elicit the instrumental response of sitting.

Discriminative stimuli act as signals to inform an organism when a particular behavior is likely to result in a reinforcer. Earlier in the chapter, the example of Steve Martin opening a can of cat food to attract a cat from a tree was used to illustrate classical conditioning. However, the popping sound of the can also serves as a discriminative stimulus. The sound is a signal to the cat that if it engages in the behavior of walking toward the familiar sound, it will be fed.

From an operant-conditioning perspective, the messages and information that consumers receive about products and services act as discriminative stimuli.[32] Such information can signal the reinforcements that may result from a purchase. Discriminative stimuli are found in advertisements, on product packaging, and in the brand names, product logos, and other symbols used by marketers. The strategy of using branded products illustrates the managerial use of discriminative stimuli. Companies with broad product lines may identify prominently each product as being a part of the same brand. Thus Campbell's Soup Company clearly displays its name on every one of its soup products to cue consumers that each is produced by the same company. The distinctive cans have become discriminative stimuli that indicate to consumers that their contents will be reinforcing. The use of corporate logos has a similar function. Figure 5-7 diagrams the relationship among the discriminative stimulus, the behavior, and the reinforcer. Highlight 5-2 discusses a discriminative stimulus effectively employed by Kmart.

Figure 5-7 The relationship among discriminative stimulus, behavior, and reinforcer.

Stimulus Discrimination and Generalization

An important goal of companies is to have consumers differentiate their brands from those of competitors. Product differentiation is quite similar in nature to the operant-conditioning idea of stimulus discrimination. **Stimulus discrimination** occurs when an organism behaves differently depending on the presence of one of two stimuli. Thus Procter & Gamble would like consumers to discriminate between Crest toothpaste and its competitor, Colgate toothpaste, by buying Crest when in the grocery store. When a consumer is reinforced for responding to a particular stimulus, the probability of the response occurring in the presence of other similar stimuli increases.

Stimulus generalization occurs when an organism reacts similarly to two or more distinct stimuli. Suppose that a consumer was reinforced for buying a new type of coffee by really enjoying how it tasted. The next time the person is in the grocery store he sees that brand as well as other new brands. He then decides to try one of the other new brands. In this case the buying response is said to have generalized from one brand to another. In general, the greater the similarity between stimuli, the greater the likelihood of stimulus generalization occurring.

Stimulus discrimination and generalization are essentially different sides of the same coin. Thus, when stimulus generalization occurs, one can say that stimulus discrimination has not occurred. The extent of stimulus generalization is influenced by the nature of the discriminative stimulus that signals the presence or absence of a reinforcer or punisher, contingent on a behavior. A major goal of marketers, then, when attempting to differentiate products, is to identify the discriminative stimuli that consumers use to signal whether a product or service will be responded to favorably or unfavorably. Such discriminative stimuli may be the price of the product, its packaging, its advertising, and how it is distributed. Basically, in controlling the elements of the marketing mix, the manager is attempting to make use of discriminative stimuli to differentiate and position a product or service.

A good example of stimulus discrimination and generalization is found in battles fought by companies over the color of pain-relief tablets. Highlight 5-3 discusses how companies use color to sell pain relief.

Shaping Consumer Responses

Have you ever wondered how animal trainers are able to teach assorted animals, such as dogs, killer whales, and elephants, to do such bizarre tricks? Certainly, jumping through a hoop filled with fire is not an instinctive behavior for the average killer whale. The process through which animals are taught such amazing tricks is shaping.

HIGHLIGHT 5-3

Using Color to Sell Pain Relief

What color is the coating of an Advil pain-relief tablet? American Home Products Corporation went to court to protect its product from having generic competitors emulate the "terra cotta" color of its ibuprofen tablets. American Home Products argued that the distinctive color was part of the brand's image and that if competitors could use the color, consumers might be misled into thinking that the generic product was Advil. (The strong defense of its product makes sense. The company had poured over $100 million into advertising the distinctive tablets.) In response, the generic companies stated that they are not trying to mislead. They contended that you cannot convince the public that two brands contain the same chemicals if they are different colors. As the attorney for the generic company said, "The issue is psychological." Recognizing the psychological significance of the color and arguing that generics are different enough to prevent confusion, the judge ruled that some generic ibuprofen tablets can be colored "Advil brown."

The Advil case well illustrates the important psychological concepts of stimulus generalization and stimulus discrimination. Corporations have begun using the color of pain-relief tablets as discriminative stimuli. Companies selling generic pain relievers are using principles of stimulus generalization to sell their products. For generic ibuprofen tablets to be successful, consumers must perceive them to have the same ingredients as Advil. However, if the generic tablets look different, stimulus generalization is unlikely to occur, and consumers will be less likely to purchase the generics.

On the other hand, the strategy of creating a distinctive color for Advil makes use of stimulus discrimination. One of the major messages of the promotional campaign for Advil is that the product is different from aspirin and Tylenol. By creating a tablet that physically looks different, the company is able to help consumers discriminate the products.

Based on Ronald Alsop, "Advil Loses Claim to the Color Brown." *The Wall Street Journal*, April 9, 1987, p. 27.

Through **shaping**, totally new operant behaviors can be created by selectively reinforcing behaviors that successively approximate the desired instrumental response.

A brief example may help to clarify the shaping process. A number of years ago I used the shaping process to teach my dog Troon how to catch a Frisbee. First, Troon was introduced to the Frisbee by playing tug-of-war with it on the lawn. Troon loved to play tug-of-war, and this became the reinforcer that was used to control his behavior. After getting him accustomed to tugging on the Frisbee, I began to hold it out to get him to jump for it. He quickly mastered this behavior and would run and jump for the Frisbee with abandon. Each time that he successfully grasped the Frisbee from my hand without tearing my arm off, I reinforced him by playing tug-of-war with the Frisbee. After Troon learned to jump for the Frisbee, I began to drop it just before he took it from my hand. Each time he successfully caught it in the air, I reinforced him. If he failed to catch it, I did not reinforce him. Over a period of days, Troon became progressively better at adjusting his jump to catch the Frisbee—as I gradually tossed it farther and farther away. After about a month of training, I could throw the Frisbee as far as I wanted and he would speed after it and catch it in midair. Importantly, he would always bring it back to be reinforced with the tug-of-war game.

In the same way, companies may be able to arrange contingencies so as to shape consumers. For instance, a car dealership might use the shaping process to encourage consumers to buy cars. First, they might provide free coffee and doughnuts to anyone who comes into the dealership. Next, the dealership would give $5 to a licensed driver who test drives a car. Third, they would give a $500 rebate to the person for buying the car. Finally, the dealership would provide outstanding service to the customer when the car is brought in for maintenance. The ultimate behavior desired is repeat buying (i.e., loyalty) from the dealership. To obtain the behavior, selective actions of the consumer that were related to the terminal behavior desired must be reinforced.[33]

Similarly, the act of buying a low-involvement product in a grocery store can be shaped by first giving a free sample. The consumer uses the sample and is reinforced by its good performance. The consumer is next given a coupon to shape the behavior of buying the product in the store. Once this behavior is reinforced by the product's good performance, it can be maintained by giving additional coupons of a lesser value. Over a period of time the performance of the product may be the only reinforcer required to maintain the behavior of buying the product.[34]

Similarities of Operant and Classical Conditioning

A number of the characteristics of operant conditioning are similar to those found in classical conditioning. Like classical conditioning, operant conditioning is more likely to occur as the number of pairings between conditional and unconditional stimuli increase. Extinction, discrimination, and stimulus generalization may also occur in a manner similar to classical conditioning.

In some instances operant-conditioning and classical-conditioning processes can overlap. In the credit card study discussed earlier in the chapter, it was noted that both operant- and classical-conditioning processes seemed to be occurring. The "MasterCard" stimulus may be conceptualized as a type of discriminative stimulus—that is, it was paired with the act of buying (i.e., if a person owns a credit card, he or she only needs to pull it out to buy something). Buying something is the instrumental response that is frequently followed by a reinforcer, such as other people lauding the buyer for the purchase. However, the credit card also acts as a conditioned stimulus that precedes the unconditioned stimulus of the possession of a product. (The possession of the product elicits the unconditioned response of good feelings.) Thus the presence of the credit card may elicit a conditioned response of good feelings.

Operant Conditioning and Marketing

Operant conditioning can be applied to most of the managerial strategy areas of marketing. For example, in the promotional mix, operant-conditioning principles have particular application to the personal-selling and sales promotion areas. A salesperson is in close enough contact with his or her clients to successfully reinforce desired behaviors. The skillful use of social reinforcers (i.e., compliments, pats on the back, and smiles) can create a situation in which the salesperson becomes a secondary reinforcer. In such a case, the client may buy from the salesperson as a means of being rewarded by having the salesperson around. The skilled salesperson may also make use of monetary reinforcers through free lunches, Christmas gifts, rebates, and the use of pricing discounts to shape the buying response. However, managers should be aware of potential unethical and even illegal behavior that can occur if the reinforcements turn into real or imagined bribes.

In the sales promotion area the principles of operant conditioning also become important. As noted earlier, discounts, coupons, samples, contests, and so forth may be used to shape the behavior of buying the product. Figure 5-8 shows an ad used by General Motors to announce a sweepstakes and premium offer. Of course, the goal of the ad is to use the sales promotion as a device to bring customers into GM dealerships to service their car. The offering of sweepstakes prizes has become a popular means of bringing customers into fast-food restaurants also. Sweepstakes influence consumers through the application of an intermittent schedule of reinforcement.

Perhaps the most important implication of operant-conditioning principles to managers is in the area of product performance. How a product performs has strong reinforcing qualities. If it performs well and positively, the likelihood of the consumer repurchasing the product increases. Conversely, if the product performs poorly, the consumer is punished and the likelihood of a repurchase of the product diminishes. In the area of segmentation, the manager should attempt to determine if different groups of people respond similarly to various types of reinforcers. For example, are there groups of people who are "deal-prone," that is, do they respond particularly well to sales promotion devices? If such segments can be found, they may be targeted specifically by the firm.

As noted earlier in this section, operant-conditioning principles help position and differentiate a product. Particularly pertinent are the concepts of stimulus discrimination and stimulus generalization. The goals of the marketing manager are (1) to use discriminative stimuli that help to position the product—through stimulus generalization—and (2) to differentiate the product through stimulus discrimination.

Applied Behavior Analysis

A technology has been developed that can be used as a guide in the use of operant-conditioning techniques. Called **applied behavior analysis**, this technology has been shown in numerous cases to be an effective means of altering the behavior of people. Applied behavior analysis may be defined as a process in which environmental variables are manipulated to alter behavior.[35] As such, it focuses on how manufacturers and marketers can vary the contingencies of the environment by structuring reinforcements, discriminative stimuli, and punishers in a manner to modify the behavior of consumers. Indeed, consumers can utilize the techniques to modify their own behavior.

Table 5-3 identifies the steps in developing a behavior modification program. The steps are straightforward and begin with the identification of the behavior that is to be modified. For example, management might want to cause people to enter a store in a mall. A series of steps is followed, measures are developed to determine how often the behavior currently occurs, reinforcers that may influence the behavior are determined, and a behavior modification strategy is developed.

Thus, in an analysis of a retail mall, management may find that only 1 in 20 people enter a particular store. The question then becomes one of identifying what

YOUR NEXT OIL CHANGE COULD BE WORTH $65,000.

MR. GOODWRENCH QUICK LUBE PLUS "FLAG A WINNER" SWEEPSTAKES

How would you like to win the Chevrolet,® Pontiac,® Oldsmobile,® Buick,® Cadillac® or GMC Truck® of your choice? Just come in, scratch a "Flag A Winner" Sweepstakes gamecard, and you could win a GM car or light truck worth as much as $65,000! Or win one of twenty other GM vehicles, a Delco car phone, a Mr. Goodwrench jacket or coupons for your next oil change at a Mr. Goodwrench Quick Lube® Plus dealership. Everyone's a winner because a Mr. Goodwrench® Quick Lube Plus oil change is guaranteed to take 29 minutes or less, or your next one is free. And it costs a lot less than you might expect at a dealership. We're serious about putting service back in the service department...and $65,000 proves it! For the Mr. Goodwrench Quick Lube Plus dealership nearest you, phone 1-800-GM-USE-US.

Guarantee applies to GM cars and light trucks. See your participating dealer for details. No purchase necessary. Void where prohibited. Must be licensed driver 18 years of age or older. Contest ends May 30, 1992.

29 minutes or less. For less than you'd expect.

© 1992 GM Corp. All rights reserved.

Figure 5-8 Sweepstakes employ intermittent schedules of reinforcement to influence consumers.

TABLE 5-3

Steps in Using Applied Behavior Analysis

1. Identify the specific behavior to change.
2. Determine how to measure how frequently the behavior occurs.
3. Identify the environmental reinforcers and punishers that shape behavior.
4. Develop procedure to utilize the reinforcers/punishers to shape behavior.
5. Test the behavior modification strategy.
6. Evaluate the costs and benefits of the strategy.

SOURCE: Based on William Gaidis and James Cross, "Behavior Modification as a Framework for Sales Promotion Management," *Journal of Consumer Marketing*, Vol. 4 (Spring 1987), pp. 65–74.

reinforcers could be used to attract customers into the store. One possibility would be to give a small gift to some proportion of those who enter. Such an intermittent schedule of reinforcement has been found to have only a moderate initial impact, but it remains effective over a long time period.

Remember, however, that problems can occur if reinforcers are relied upon too heavily. If the behavior of purchasing a product or service is influenced largely by external reinforcers (i.e., sales promotion devices) and if the product has few intrinsic reinforcing properties, the behavior will not reoccur when the reinforcer is withdrawn. Thus suppose marketers make use of frequent price discounts to reinforce consumers for buying their brand. The buying behavior may become controlled by the discount rather than by the positive features of the brand. Thus, if the price discounts are discontinued, consumers may shift to other brands.[36]

OBSERVATIONAL LEARNING

Another approach to learning links aspects of cognitive learning to operant conditioning. **Observational learning**, which is also called **social learning**, is the phenomenon whereby people observe actions of others to develop "patterns of behavior."[37] Such patterns of behavior can vary from purchasing a product, to learning a skill (e.g., riding a bicycle), to avoiding the buying of drugs.

Three important ideas have been mentioned as emerging from observational-learning theory.[38] First, observational-learning theorists view people as symbolic beings who foresee the probable consequences of their behavior. People anticipate the future and vary their behavior accordingly. Second, people learn by watching the actions of others and the consequences of these actions (i.e., by vicarious learning). Social-learning theorists particularly emphasize the importance of models in transmitting information through observational learning. A **model** is someone whose behavior a person attempts to emulate. Third, people have the ability to regulate their own behavior. Through this self-regulatory process, people supply their own rewards and punishments internally by feeling either self-critical or self-satisfied.

These three ideas illustrate how social-learning theory forges linkages between cognitive learning and operant conditioning. The concept that people are symbolic and can foresee consequences is fully compatible with principles of cognitive learning. The belief that reinforcers control the behavior of people comes from operant conditioning. Observational-learning theory adds the concept that people can learn by observing how the behaviors of other people are reinforced and punished. Thus, from a social-learning perspective, the reinforcers and punishers do not always have to occur to the person being influenced. People can learn from observing the actions of others.

Further, social-learning theorists argue that people can control their own behavior by creating their own reinforcement structure. As symbolic beings with expectations, people reward themselves for doing something well or properly. Consumers often reward themselves by making a purchase. Similarly, people can punish themselves for doing something of which they disapprove. For example, the author of this book knew a person who enjoyed playing golf. One day, the person borrowed a five-wood from the golf pro to try it out with the intention of purchasing it. During the round, he hit the club well and was ready to make the purchase. However, on the seventeenth hole—in a fit of anger—he accidently broke his driver after hitting a poor shot. Ashamed of himself, the man decided not to purchase the five-wood as a means of punishing himself for doing something so foolish.[39]

Factors Influencing a Model's Effectiveness

The characteristics of the model, of the observer, and of the modeled consequences have all been found to influence the effectiveness of social learning. Interestingly, the characteristics of the model that enhance vicarious learning are highly similar to those found to increase the effectiveness of sources of information. Source effects will be discussed in greater detail in Chapter 10, which deals with communications processes. The effectiveness of a model has been shown to increase in the following instances:

1. The model is physically attractive.
2. The model is credible.
3. The model is successful.
4. The model is similar to the observer.
5. The model is shown overcoming difficulties and then succeeding.[40]

Figure 5-9 shows an ad for Rolex watches. Jim Courier, a top-seeded tennis player, is used as the model in the ad. Note that he exemplifies many of the characteristics of an effective model.

Different people also react divergently to the consequences of the behavior of models. Some evidence exists that people who are dependent and lack self-esteem are particularly prone to model the behavior of successful people. But, in general, any person who places a great deal of value on the consequences of the modeled behavior tends to imitate it.[41]

According to observational-learning theorists, the consequences of the model's behavior influence the likelihood that the actions will be emulated. Evidence indicates that vicarious learning occurs most readily when the consequences of the behavior are very clear and salient to the observer. In addition, the more positively the observer evaluates the consequences, the greater the tendency to imitate the

Figure 5-9 What key ideas from observational learning are illustrated by this ad for Rolex watches?

model's behavior. In a consumer setting it makes a great deal of sense for people to learn from the positive outcomes, as well as from the negative outcomes (i.e., mistakes) that others have experienced. In part, word-of-mouth communication may have a modeling component. If a neighbor describes in detail the positive or negative consequences of purchasing a product, a person will tend to react strongly to the information by engaging in appropriate modeling activity. Albert Bandura, the psychologist who has done much of the work on vicarious learning, has argued that new product adoption may be based in part on vicarious learning. From a social-learning perspective, it is the observation of the actions of others and the consequences of these actions that determine whether people buy new products or services. According to Bandura, "Models not only exemplify and legitimate innovations, they also serve as advocates for products by encouraging others to adopt them."[42]

Marketing Uses of Social-Learning Theory

Vicarious-learning principles can be used for three major purposes. First, a model's actions can be used to create entirely new types of behaviors. Second, a model can be used to decrease the likelihood that an undesired behavior will occur. Third, the model can be used to facilitate the occurrence of a previously learned behavior.[43]

Just as the use of positive reinforcers can cause people to undertake new actions, such as visiting a new retail store, observing the actions of others may result in a consumer engaging in the model's behavior. Advertisers make heavy use of ideas from social-learning theory to create new behaviors. Advertisers frequently use attractive endorsers whom they hope consumers will emulate. In such an advertisement the model's behavior of using the product is positively reinforced, say, by other people congratulating the model on his or her purchase. The advertiser's hope is that consumers obtain vicarious reinforcement so that the probability of their behavior of buying the product will increase.

The ability to cause consumers to engage in new behaviors is particularly important for companies that introduce innovative products. For example, in the early 1980s IBM brought out its new personal computer. The innovative product was unfamiliar to most consumers, and getting them to purchase and use it was a difficult task. In one series of advertisements IBM used principles of observational learning. The ads showed regular people, such as a "good-old-boy" farmer, going into a computer store, purchasing an IBM, and then using it effectively. The farmer was shown being reinforced by the positive consequences of using the computer. In addition, he was shown receiving social reinforcement by the comments of neighbors, who were amazed that he was capable of using such a device.

Modeling processes can also be used to inhibit undesirable behaviors. In these cases a model is shown being punished for engaging in an undesirable behavior. Currently, a great deal of attention is being given to the problem of drugs in the United States. One frequently used approach is to have people who have been harmed by drugs make speeches urging people to "say no." In one campaign ex-football star Mercury Morris urged young people to avoid drugs. In the ad he described how the use of drugs ended his football career and destroyed his life. The goal of these ads was to convince people that the best way to avoid drug abuse is to not even try drugs, as the "ruined" celebrity did.

Corporate advertisers have even used modeling principles in attempts to cause industrial buyers to avoid engaging in undesirable behaviors. Of course, the undesirable behavior would be to purchase a competitor's product. AT&T created an outstanding campaign that is effective because it causes observers to want to avoid the model's action of purchasing a non-AT&T product. In one compelling ad, a manager is shown in a highly uncomfortable situation in which he has learned that the non-AT&T phone system that he authorized for purchase is already outmoded because of software incompatibility. A newly hired manager reacts by indicating that his previous employer didn't have that problem. The two managers' new boss asks whose phone system his company used, and the new manager responds, "AT&T." The boss, who is clearly Japanese, turns to the now fear-struck manager and says, "Why didn't you think of that?"

The AT&T ad was highly effective because of the implication that the manager was in strong danger of losing his job. In an age of corporate takeovers and of hard-nosed Japanese managers running businesses in the United States, the ad seemed all too real.

The third use of vicarious-learning principles in advertising involves the goal of increasing the likelihood that a previously learned behavior will occur. In these cases the behavior of the model acts as a kind of discriminative stimulus that indicates when the behavior is appropriate. Examples of this type of vicarious learning may be found in attempts of companies to reposition a product or service. The Florida Citrus Growers have for years attempted to persuade consumers to drink orange juice at times other than breakfast. The advertisements feature attractive people, who act as models, drinking orange juice after swimming or engaging in an athletic event. In these cases the behavior of drinking orange juice is already in the consumers' repertoire of actions. By using the actions of models as discriminative stimuli, the ads attempt to increase consumers' consumption of orange juice at occasions other than breakfast. If successful, the strategy results in an increase in the total sales of orange juice.

A MANAGERIAL APPLICATIONS EXAMPLE

As an overall summary of the managerial applications of behavioral-learning theories, Table 5-4 summarizes the managerial implications of classical conditioning, operant conditioning, and observational learning.

Ideas from behavioral learning can be applied to governmental and nonprofit programs as well as traditional business problems. Just like business firms, governmental agencies must market their programs to consumers. This was the problem faced by one agency in Miami that sought to provide social services to the poor on a shoestring budget. The question was, "How could you get people to volunteer to perform various services for others, such as doing household chores for a person in the hospital, driving an elderly man to see a doctor, or making repairs on a house for an invalid?"

A possible solution to the problem was suggested by a professor at the District of Columbia School of Law. Why not treat the number of hours that someone works as though it were currency? By working volunteer hours, people could receive credits that would be banked. The credits would then be refunded at a later date when someone else helped them. As the professor said, "We want the economy to give a reward and incentive for decency that is as automatic as the market's reward for selfishness."

The professor's idea was implemented in Miami and quickly caught on at other locations in the United States. In Miami a work force of 700 regular volunteers was established, and social services dramatically increased. For example, the number of meals delivered to the housebound elderly increased from 200 per day to 1,600 per day. Further, the program's volunteer dropout rate was low—under 10%. Indeed, its

TABLE 5-4

Application Examples of Behavioral Learning Principles

I. Operant conditioning
- **A.** Marketing mix
  - **1.** Develop sales promotions based on operant-conditioning principles.
  - **2.** Have sales personnel use operant conditioning to shape customers.
  - **3.** Recognize that the product or service acts as a reinforcer or punisher.
  - **4.** Assess distribution to ensure that punishers that will decrease the likelihood of buying behavior do not exist.
- **B.** Segmentation
  - **1.** Analyze different segments to determine if they respond differentially to reinforcers or punishers.
- **C.** Environmental analysis
  - **1.** Perform an in-depth analysis to identify the reinforcers and punishers that influence the purchase of a product or service.
- **D.** Market research
  - **1.** Use market research to analyze the differential reinforcing or punishing properties of various stimuli on the target market.

II. Classical conditioning
- **A.** Marketing mix
  - **1.** Recognize that ads may be used to create positive emotional responses.
  - **2.** Pay close attention to the in-store environment and how various stimuli, such as lighting and music, may influence consumers.
  - **3.** Recognize that the consumer's attention may be attracted through the sign-tracking process by using unconditioned stimuli.
- **B.** Segmentation
  - **1.** Use market research to identify segments that may respond positively to unconditioned stimuli.
- **C.** Environmental analysis
  - **1.** Identify environmental stimuli that may create positive or negative emotional responses.
- **D.** Market research
  - **1.** Perform studies to identify positive and negative unconditioned stimuli and their impact on consumers.

III. Observational learning
- **A.** Marketing mix
  - **1.** Use models in advertising to:
    - **a.** Facilitate the occurrence of previously learned behavior.
    - **b.** Decrease the likelihood of undesired behaviors.
    - **c.** Create entirely new behaviors.
- **B.** Segmentation
  - **1.** Conduct research to determine if specific target groups are prone to engage in observational learning.
- **C.** Market research
  - **1.** Conduct studies to identify characteristics of the model that is most appealing to the target group.

major problem seems to be that the volunteers have been reluctant to cash in on their credits. After roughly a year of operation only 1.1% of the credits had been redeemed.

But the impact of the program is best illustrated by the individual cases in which someone in need is truly helped. For several months Elsa Martinez worked to help others by driving them on errands and by doing some of their shopping and cleaning. Then the unmarried 64-year-old garment worker learned that she had a brain tumor. In her time of need, the people that she had befriended returned with flowers and visits to her hospital bed. Ms. Martinez whispered gratefully from her bed, "When you're sick, they come."[44]

The Managerial Analysis

Problem Statement

The problem faced by the social service agency involved obtaining volunteers to perform needed tasks without spending large amounts of taxpayer dollars.

Consumer Behavior Analysis

The Miami volunteer program was implemented to obtain volunteers without spending large amounts of taxpayer money. It succeeded, in part, because it employed a variety of behavioral-learning concepts, in particular, ideas from operant conditioning and observational learning. The credits obtained from working volunteer hours acted as positive reinforcers that modified the behavior of the participants in the program. By influencing the participants to join the program, the credits brought people together. The result was that the volunteers obtained another positive reinforcer in the gratitude of those whom they helped. In sum, the contingencies of reinforcement found in the program resulted in the behaviors of the participants being resistant to extinction. As a result, few volunteers dropped out.

Observational-learning concepts also helped to ensure the success of the program. Those volunteers already in the program acted as models for the actions of newcomers. By seeing a person receive personal benefits from his or her participation, others would emulate the behavior.

The Managerial Applications Analysis

Table 5-5 presents a summary of the managerial implications of the case. In the table, three behavioral-learning concepts are identified that have particular relevance to the case—positive reinforcers, contingencies of the environment, and modeling. The work credits, which served as the primary positive reinforcer in the program, played an important role in the program's strategy. (In this case the program itself is the product being sold.) Because work credits were the primary inducement to attract volunteers, the success of the program relied on informing potential participants about them. The use of the credits also acted to position the program as helping people to help themselves, rather than as merely giving handouts. From an operant-conditioning perspective, giving a reward to someone who does nothing to earn it merely reinforces that individual for doing nothing.

Contingencies of the environment are often relevant to environmental analysis and product development. When implementing the program, it was important for the administrators to carefully analyze the contingencies of the environment to

TABLE 5-5

Managerial Applications of Miami Volunteer Program

Consumer Concepts	*Managerial Implications*
Operant conditioning	*Promotional strategy*—Develop sales promotion device in the form of credits to act as reinforcers to influence volunteering behavior.
	Product development—Use credits as a basic component of the program itself. Thus, in addition to acting as sales promotion devices, these reinforcers also acted as a vital part of the volunteer program.
Observational learning	*Product development*—Use volunteers already in program as models for newcomers. By observing volunteers receiving help from the program, newcomers are more likely to join and stay in the program. Thus observational learning is an integral part of the program (i.e., product) itself.

ensure that participants were positively reinforced for desired behaviors and that undesired actions were punished by the withdrawal of rewards. The goal was to design the program by carefully analyzing the contingencies of the environment—to ensure that the desired behaviors were brought about.

Observational learning is particularly relevant to the development of promotional strategy. In the program's promotion, it was important to have volunteers visit various clubs and organizations to describe the program. In effect, the volunteers work as models for others. By using credible and successful volunteers as spokespersons for the program, others may want to emulate them and join the ranks of volunteers.

A Final Word of Warning

Although classical-conditioning, operant-conditioning, and observational-learning principles appear to have major implications for managers and public policy makers, a number of warnings are in order. Much of the basic work in classical and operant conditioning has involved animal learning rather than human learning. Few studies have investigated consumer behavior problems from the perspective of observational learning. Market researchers and managers must be very cautious in assuming that the findings can be generalized to consumer settings. As suggested earlier in the chapter, some authorities have criticized the consumer research that supports the applicability of classical conditioning. Similarly, in many of the consumer behavior examples of operant conditioning, it seems questionable that people can be conditioned with so few pairings of behavior with reinforcer.

For the manager, however, the key issue concerns whether one can influence consumer behavior by following the procedures to implement classical conditioning, operant conditioning, and observational learning. In this case, the answer is a definite "yes." For the manager interested only in obtaining results, the question of exactly what processes account for the behavioral change has little importance.

SUMMARY

Behavioral learning is a process in which experience with the environment leads to a relatively permanent change in behavior or the potential for a change in behavior. The study of behavioral learning is important because it is the foundation for investigating the behavioral influence perspective on consumer buying. Three different types of behavioral learning have been identified—classical conditioning, operant conditioning, and observational learning.

In classical conditioning a stimulus of some type elicits behavior, or an unconditioned response. In consumer behavior contexts, the behaviors of most interest are the positive and negative emotional responses that may be elicited by various stimuli. By pairing a previously neutral stimulus (the conditioned stimulus) with the eliciting stimulus (the unconditioned stimulus), the neutral stimulus gradually comes to elicit the response.

Classical conditioning has particular implications for advertisers who wish to create positive feelings in consumers as they think of a particular product. As shown by several studies, an unconditioned stimulus, such as music, may elicit an unconditioned response of positive feelings. If a product is paired appropriately with the unconditioned stimulus, the product may become a conditioned stimulus. The product then may have the ability to elicit the conditioned response of positive feelings.

Two important concepts in classical conditioning are sign tracking and higher-order conditioning. Sign tracking involves the tendency of organisms to attend to, orient themselves toward, and approach an unconditioned stimulus. In higher-order conditioning, a conditioned stimulus acts to classically condition another previously neutral stimulus. In most instances the stimuli used to influence consumers take on their properties as a result of higher-order conditioning.

Operant conditioning occurs when an organism's behavior changes as a consequence of something happening after the behavior. Operants are the naturally occurring actions of an organism in the environment. In a consumer behavior setting, operants include such activities as purchasing a product or service, engaging in word-of-mouth communication, and complaining about a product to a service manager. From an operant-conditioning perspective, behavior is influenced by the reinforcers and punishers received after engaging in an action.

Reinforcers are stimuli that increase the likelihood that a behavior occurring prior to the reinforcer will reoccur. Punishers are stimuli that decrease the likelihood of a behavior reoccurring. Marketers must be particularly concerned about the rewards and punishments that consumers receive while using their products or services. Important reinforcers-punishers that may influence consumer behavior include the performance of the product, the favorable and unfavorable information and reactions received from other people about products and services, and the positivity of the interactions that consumers have with sales personnel.

For consumer researchers, another important concept in operant conditioning is that of the discriminative stimulus. Discriminative stimuli are the stimuli that occur in the presence of a reinforcer and do not occur in its absence. Discriminative stimuli signal to the consumer that a reinforcer is likely to result when a given behavior is emitted. Through advertisements, brand names, packaging, and other symbols, marketers use discriminative stimuli to indicate to consumers that they will be positively reinforced if a product is purchased.

Marketers frequently attempt to arrange reinforcers and punishers to shape consumers. Shaping may create totally new behaviors. In a consumer setting a salesperson may attempt to shape a person by using various sales promotion devices and social reinforcers (e.g., pats on the back). Of course, the ultimate behavior that the salesperson wants to shape is a buying response. The technology of applied behavior analysis was developed to use operant-conditioning techniques to influence behavior.

The third behavioral-learning theory is observational learning. Also called vicarious learning, the theory proposes that people develop patterns of behavior by modeling the actions of others. Observational-learning theorists view people as symbolic beings who learn by observing others and the outcomes of their actions. Further, these researchers believe that people can act to control their own behavior by providing their own rewards and punishments contingent on their behavior. Advertisers frequently make use of models in attempting to influence the behavior of consumers. Models can be used to (1) teach consumers entirely new behaviors, (2) encourage consumers to learn to avoid engaging in undesirable actions, and (3) facilitate the occurrence of previously learned behavior.

Consumer researchers, managers, and public policy officials should be concerned with whether behavioral-learning principles can be applied directly to consumer behavior. Much of the research has been performed on animal learning. Whether the principles can be applied directly to human learning is still controversial. However, evidence is beginning to accumulate that such behavioral change is possible.

KEY TERMS

applied behavior analysis
behavioral learning
classical conditioning
conditioned response
conditioned stimulus
contingencies of reinforcement
discriminative stimuli
extinction
higher-order conditioning
instrumental responses
model
negative reinforcer
observational learning
operant conditioning
operants
positive reinforcer
punisher
reinforcement
respondent conditioning
schedules of reinforcement
secondary reinforcer
shaping
sign tracking
slippage
social learning
stimulus discrimination
stimulus generalization
unconditioned response
unconditioned stimulus
vicarious learning

REVIEW QUESTIONS

1. Define the concept of behavioral learning. What are the three types of learning that consumer researchers discuss?
2. What is meant by observational learning? What are three important ideas that result from its study?
3. Define operant conditioning and describe its process.
4. Discuss the different effects of positive and negative reinforcers.
5. What is meant by extinction?
6. What is meant by a schedule of reinforcement?
7. How are discriminative stimuli used by marketers?
8. Give an example of how a marketer might be able to shape a consumer response.
9. What are the primary differences between classical and operant conditioning?
10. What are the relationships among conditioned stimuli, unconditioned stimuli, conditioned responses, and unconditioned responses in classical conditioning?
11. Identify two managerial uses for each of the theories of learning discussed in the chapter.

DISCUSSION QUESTIONS

1. Observational learning is an important means of socialization for children, teenagers, and adults. Consider the content of the popular television shows appearing in prime time. What are the patterns of behavior that people may learn as a result of watching prime-time television? Are there public policy implications that result from such an analysis?
2. What would you identify as the five major consumer reinforcers? To what extent can a salesperson use these to influence the behavior of prospective clients?
3. Try to remember the worst experiences you have ever had in a restaurant. What were the various ways in which you were punished for eating there?
4. One problem that many instructors face is how to get students to participate in classroom discussions. Develop a systematic plan in which reinforcers are applied to draw students into frequent classroom discussions.
5. Develop the outline of an advertising campaign for a new line of bath towels to include television commercials and point-of-purchase displays that make use of classical-conditioning ideas. Make sure you identify the conditioned stimulus, the unconditioned stimulus, the conditioned response, and the unconditioned response.
6. Visit a supermarket or a mall in your area. Take along a notebook and record specific examples of how retail stores make use of behavioral-learning principles to influence consumers. In which of the three types of behavioral learning did you find the most examples?

ENDNOTES

1. Timothy Smith, "Buy One Car, Get One Free: Marketers Experiment with Freebies on a Grand Scale," *The Wall Street Journal*, March 16, 1987, p. 21.
2. Richard Edel, "No End in Sight to Promotions' Upward Spiral," *Advertising Age*, March 3, 1987, pp. S1–S8.
3. "How Casino Computers Stretch the House Odds," *Business Week*, July 30, 1984, pp. 112–114.
4. Len Strazewski, "Promotion Carnival Gets Serious," *Advertising Age*, May 2, 1988, pp. S1–S2.
5. Thomas R. King, "Marketers Bet Big with Contests to Trigger Consumer Spending," *The Wall Street Journal*, April 4, 1991, p. B6.
6. J. Paul Peter and Walter Nord, "A Clarification and Extension of Operant Conditioning Principles in Marketing," *Journal of Marketing*, Vol. 46 (Summer 1982), pp. 102–107.
7. Melinda Guiles, "Latest Incentives on Cars Prove Confusing and Fail to Stir Much Showroom Traffic," *The Wall Street Journal*, January 30, 1987, p. 17.
8. Kate Ballen, "Honda's High Road," *Fortune*, April 8, 1991, p. 13.
9. Gerald J. Gorn, "The Effects of Music in Advertising on Choice Behavior: A Classical Conditioning Approach," *Journal of Marketing*, Vol. 46 (Winter 1982), pp. 94–101. This experiment has been severely criticized for inadequately controlling the subjects' awareness of the purpose of the research. However, it has been successfully replicated by Calvin Bierley, Frances McSweeney, and Renee Vannieuwkerk, "Classical Conditioning of Preferences for Stimuli," *Journal of Consumer Research*, Vol. 12 (December 1985), pp. 316–323.
10. Robert Rescorla, "Pavlovian Conditioning: It's Not What You Think It Is," *American Psychologist*, Vol. 43 (March 1988), pp. 151–160. Readers should recognize that a "cognitive revolution" has taken place in the understanding of classical conditioning. The idea that actions follow stimuli in a reflexive manner is no longer held by theorists. See Terrence A. Shimp, "The Role of Subject Awareness in Classical Conditioning: A Case of Opposing Ontologies and Conflicting Evidence," in *Advances in Consumer Research*, Vol. 18, Rebecca Holman and Michael Solomon, eds. (Provo, UT: Association for Consumer Research, 1991), pp. 158–163.
11. An excellent review of applications of classical conditioning and operant conditioning to marketing may be found in Walter R. Nord and J. Paul Peter, "A Behavior Modification Perspective on Marketing," *Journal of Marketing*, Vol. 410 (Spring 1980), pp. 36–47.
12. Ronald E. Milliman, "Using Background Music to Affect the Behavior of Supermarket Shoppers," *Journal of Marketing*, Vol. 42 (Summer 1982), pp. 86–91.
13. Ronald E. Milliman, "The Influence of Background Music on the Behavior of Restaurant Patrons," *Journal of Consumer Research*, Vol. 13 (September 1986), pp. 286-289.
14. Elnora W. Stuart, Terence A. Shimp, and Randall W. Engle, "Classical Conditioning of Consumer Attitudes: Four Experiments in an Advertising Context," *Journal of Consumer Research*, Vol. 14 (December 1987), pp. 334–349.
15. Richard A. Feinberg, "Credit Cards as Spending Facilitating Stimuli: A Conditioning Perspective," *Journal of Consumer Research*, Vol. 13 (December 1986), pp. 348–356.
16. Terence A. Shimp, Elnora W. Stuart, and Randall W. Engle, "A Program of Classical Conditioning Experiments Testing Variations in the Conditioned Stimulus and the Context," *Journal of Consumer Research*, Vol. 18 (June 1991), pp. 1–12.
17. Rescorla, "Pavlovian Conditioning," p. 154.
18. Chris T. Allen and Thomas J. Madden, "A Closer Look at Classical Conditioning," *Journal of Consumer Research*, Vol. 12 (December 1985), pp. 303–315.

19. James J. Kellaris and Anthony D. Cox, "The Effects of Background Music in Advertising: A Reassessment," *Journal of Consumer Research*, Vol. 16 (June 1989), pp. 113–118.

20. Lynn Kahle, Sharon Beatty, and Patricia Kennedy, "Comment on Classically Conditioning Human Consumers," in *Advances in Consumer Research*, Vol. 14, Melanie Wallendorf and Paul Anderson, eds. (Provo, UT: Association for Consumer Research, 1987), pp. 411–413.

21. Shimp, "The Role of Subject Awareness in Classical Conditioning."

22. Chris Allen and Thomas Madden, "A Closer Look at Classical Conditioning," *Journal for Consumer Research*, Vol. 12 (December 1985), pp. 301–315.

23. Francis K. McSweeney and Calvin Bierley, "Recent Developments in Classical Conditioning," *Journal of Consumer Research*, Vol. 11 (September 1984), pp. 619–631.

24. Ibid.

25. Rescorla, "Pavlovian Conditioning."

26. Gordon Foxall, "Radical Behaviorism and Consumer Research: Theoretical Promise and Empirical Problems," *International Journal of Research in Marketing*, Vol. 4 (1987), pp. 111–129.

27. B. F. Skinner, *Contingencies of Reinforcement: A Theoretical Analysis* (New York: Appleton-Century-Crofts, 1969).

28. G. S. Reynolds, *A Primer of Operant Conditioning* (Glenview, IL: Scott, Foresman, 1968).

29. This section on operant conditioning relies heavily on G. S. Reynolds, *A Primer of Operant Conditioning*.

30. William Gaidis and James Cross, "Behavior Modification as a Framework for Sales Promotion Management," *Journal of Consumer Marketing*, Vol. 4 (Spring 1987), pp. 65–74. Gordon Foxall has developed another view on the types of reinforcers in which he distinguishes hedonic from informational reinforcers. See Gordon R. Foxall, "The Behavioral Perspective Model of Purchase and Consumption: From Consumer Theory to Marketing Practice," *Journal of the Academy of Marketing Sciences*, Vol. 20 (Spring 1992), pp. 189–198.

31. Dolores Curran, "Putting the 'Fun' Back in Fundraisers," *Eastern Oklahoma Catholic*, April 21, 1991, p. 21.

32. Foxall, "Radical Behaviorism."

33. This example may be found in Peter and Nord, "A Clarification and Extension of Operant Conditioning Principles."

34. A version of this example may be found in M. L. Rothchild and W. C. Gaidis, "Behavior Learning Theory: Its Relevance to Marketing and Promotions," *Journal of Marketing*, Vol. 45 (Spring 1981), pp. 70–78.

35. Gaidis and Cross, "Behavior Modification as a Framework."

36. Carol A. Scott, "The Effects of Trial and Incentives on Repeat Purchase Behavior," *Journal of Marketing Research*, Vol. 14 (August 1976), pp. 263–269.

37. Albert Bandura, *Social Learning Theory* (Englewood Cliffs, NJ: Prentice-Hall, 1977).

38. Ernest Hilgard, Richard Atkinson, and Rita Atkinson, *Introduction to Psychology* (New York: Harcourt Brace Jovanovich, 1975).

39. John C. Mowen, "Today's Round of Golf and My Expensive Mistake," *Personal Diary*, May 15, 1988, p. 69.

40. Charles C. Manz and Henry P. Sims, "Vicarious Learning: The Influence of Modeling on Organizational Behavior," *Academy of Management Journal*, Vol. 6 (January 1981), pp. 105–113.

41. Bandura, *Social Learning Theory*.

42. Ibid., p. 51.

43. Peter and Nord, "A Behavior Modification Perspective."

44. Steven Waldman, "Credit for Good Deeds," *Newsweek*, January 15, 1990, p. 61.

CHAPTER 5 CASE STUDY

That Great New Pepsi Can

The sleek Lamborghini pulls up to the Halfway Cafe somewhere out in nowhere. Its gull-wing door opens, and the beautiful form of supermodel Cindy Crawford emerges from the cockpit. Writing in *Advertising Age*, columnist Bob Garfield described the scene this way: "Simultaneously smoldering and insouciant, she emerges from the gull-wing door of her Lamborghini Diablo like Venus on the half-shell. We are way out in the country, at the crossroads of astonishing loveliness and transcendent sexuality. Watch her as she ambles sleekly across the dusty parking lot. This is no mere stroll; it is a ballet for the glands—her supple, sinuous, slow-motion feline languor on the surface concealing the coiled, smoldering, feral cat beneath. In other words: what a dish" [1].

Crawford glides to the soda machine, inserts the coins, and a Pepsi emerges. She throws back her head, closes her eyes, and gulps the cold beverage.

But Crawford is not alone. Two young boys, perhaps 10 years old, happen upon the scene. Drawn by curiosity at the sight of the car, they move closer to the vision and hide behind a fence. They are enchanted, their mouths agape.

The scene shifts rapidly between Crawford and the peeping boys. Finally, after having been refreshed, she turns to leave. At that instant, one of the awestruck boys manages to utter a short sentence. He says in astonishment, "Is that a great new Pepsi can, or what?" The camera then cuts back to Crawford, and a voice-over narrator says, "Introducing a whole new look at Pepsi and Diet Pepsi." The camera again moves to the boys, and the second boy declares, "It's beautiful."

In analyzing the ad Bob Garfield raises the question of whether it objectifies women. His answer: "yes" and "no." He said that the ad does objectify Crawford in a "wry and self-conscious way, toying with men's libidos at least partly to make light of them." He continued, "It's not the Old Milwaukee 'Swedish Bikini Team,' which uses a coarse parody of men's adolescent preoccupations as a transparent pretext to trot out a paratroop squad of busty blondes wiggling their pulchritude at the camera." Instead, Garfield suggests that the ad explores the meaning of beauty, whether in the form of the female or of the logo on a can of pop. He says, "Cindy Crawford in slow motion is a goddess, with aesthetic appeal exceeding erotic, sure to transfix women as well as men" [2].

But the critical issue is, "Will the ad have a positive effect on consumers?" This question is answered affirmatively by the last two sentences in Garfield's column: "Not incidentally, every time you see this new logo you will conjure up Cindy Crawford. And that, I believe, is advertising" [3].

QUESTIONS

1. What was the managerial problem that Pepsi executives were attacking in developing the Cindy Crawford commercial?
2. What consumer concepts from behavioral learning apply to the Pepsi commercial? Please explain.
3. Create a managerial applications table that summarizes how the consumer behavior concepts identified relate to managerial strategy.

4. Discuss the ad in terms of the objectification of women. Do you think that women's groups should be upset by the advertisement?

REFERENCES

1. Bob Garfield, "Sultry Cindy Saunters into Pepsi's Portfolio," *Advertising Age*, January 13, 1992, p. 46.
2. Ibid.
3. Ibid.

Chapter

6

Consumer Motivation and Affect

CONSUMER VIGNETTE

Pushing Consumers' Buttons

The 28-year-old systems analyst didn't think he was doing anything crazy when he sampled a little of his colleague's crack (a concentrated form of cocaine). However, the experience was far more pleasurable than he expected, and the executive described himself as "feeling up, really up." Soon thereafter, the rapidly acquired addiction was costing him $300 per month, and his career skidded downhill. He couldn't complete his assignments because he anxiously planned occasions to get to his car—where he kept his cache.[1]

Addictions can take a variety of forms in addition to the illegal varieties. A skydiver from South Carolina described his feelings about the sport: ". . . the skydiving, it just calls you back every time . . . it was my love and lust." Or consider the journalist who described his feelings after a failed attempt to climb Mount Everest. He said, "And, yet, I have climbed a bit of Everest . . . it changes you. It makes you a better person. But it [the feeling] lasts about two weeks. That's why you keep going back."[2]

Taking crack, parachuting, and mountain climbing push people's motivation buttons in part because of the physiological reactions to the experience. People can also become highly motivated because of social interactions. A skydiving photographer described the social elements of his sport in terms of a family. He said, "It's almost like a family out there. There is a certain kind of camaraderie among skydivers that you just don't get anywhere else."

Then, there was Josephine Esther Mentzer. She began her career humbly by traveling from Queens to Manhattan to sell her uncle's skin cream concoctions to upscale beauty salons. Once Josephine had the audacity to admire the blouse of the owner of a salon and ask where she had purchased it. "An irrelevant question," snipped the woman, "since a salesgirl could never afford such a blouse." The scolding burned and fueled her ambition. Some years later, Josephine changed her name to Estée Lauder, and today she is the billionaire baroness of the beauty industry. Remarking on the anecdote, she said, "I wouldn't have become Estée Lauder if it hadn't been for her."[3]

Crack, skydiving, and derisive challenges can have a great motivational influence on people. The impact of each illustrates how people's buttons can be pushed in a way that makes them engage in extreme behaviors from risking their lives to building a great company.

INTRODUCTION

Consumer researchers tend to investigate socially approved forms of behavior. However, consumers can become involved in various deviant forms of buying activities, such as the purchase and use of illegal drugs. How is it that sane, highly educated people can ruin their lives by getting involved in cocaine or other addictive drugs? A glimpse of the addictive process can be seen in the effects of crack. The drug acts by giving users a quick, exhilarating high. However, depression follows shortly afterward, as does a yearning for another hit. In the late 1980s on street corners near Wall Street one could hear offers of "V's" and "E's", code words for Valium and Elavil—two prescription antidepressants used to lessen the depressive plunge after the high.[4]

One theory of motivation discussed in this chapter, called opponent-process theory, gives one explanation of why certain types of drugs can become addictive. The

Figure 6-1

Rock climbing exemplifies consumer behavior motivated by the desire to obtain hedonic experiences.

theory also helps to explain other "legal" addictions. For example, a woman from Miami, on business in New York, grimaced each time she lifted her leg to step onto a curb. She was frantic because she was missing her daily aerobics class. As a result, she had been pacing the streets for hours even though her shinsplints hurt so much that she couldn't put a sheet over her legs at night. Exercise compulsion has become a major problem among many middle- and upper-class professionals. The prolonged exercise seems to bring about the same type of high that drugs create. If they must stop exercising because of injury, such addicts may report withdrawal symptoms of depression, nervousness, and insomnia. One medical writer half-joked that jogging shoes should carry a warning label, just as cigarettes do.[5]

Why is it that some people enjoy such high risk-taking sports as skydiving, mountain climbing, and hang gliding? The answer seems to be that people need to gain feelings through the senses, to capture feelings of achievement and camaraderie, and to obtain emotional arousal.[6] According to actuarial studies, the death rate among skydivers is 1 per 700 participants per year. The riskiest sport appears to be hang gliding, where 1 in 250 participants dies each year.[6] By testing themselves at their limits, they can experience emotional highs. Indeed, many of our leisure pursuits are designed to create hedonic experiences. The study of the motivation to consume leisure is discussed in this chapter. Figure 6-1 shows a photograph of a rock climber practicing his skills on an indoor wall.

Finally, what was it in the comment of the salon owner that motivated Josephine Mentzer to become Estée Lauder? The answer may lie in the reactance theory of motivation. Reactance theory proposes that when a person's behavioral freedom is restricted a strong desire to restore the freedom results. In Josephine's case the comment that a mere salesgirl could never afford such an expensive blouse became a challenge to prove the owner wrong. For Josephine the comment resulted in a strong motivation to achieve. In 1987 the company that she founded, Estée Lauder, Inc., sold $1.3 billion worth of fragrances and cosmetics and commanded a 37% share of department store sales of these goods.[7]

Each of these anecdotes illustrates an approach to understanding the motivational process. However, before discussing these and other theories of motivation in more detail, we must precisely define the concept of motivation.

WHAT IS MOTIVATION?

Within a consumer behavior context, **motivation** refers to an activated state within a person that leads to goal-directed behavior.[8] It consists of the "drives, urges, wishes, or desires that initiate the sequence of events leading to a behavior."[9] Figure 6-2 presents a simple model that depicts the flow of events that occur when an individual enters a motivated state. In the model, five key concepts are identified: need activation, drive state, goal-directed behavior, incentive objects, and affect. These are discussed in the paragraphs that follow.

Motivation begins with the presence of a stimulus that is processed by the individual. Thus, just like any stimulus, it goes through the information-processing stages of exposure, attention, and comprehension. The stimulus could come from inside the consumer (e.g., from physiological changes resulting from a lack of food) or from outside the consumer (e.g., from hearing about or seeing a product). If the

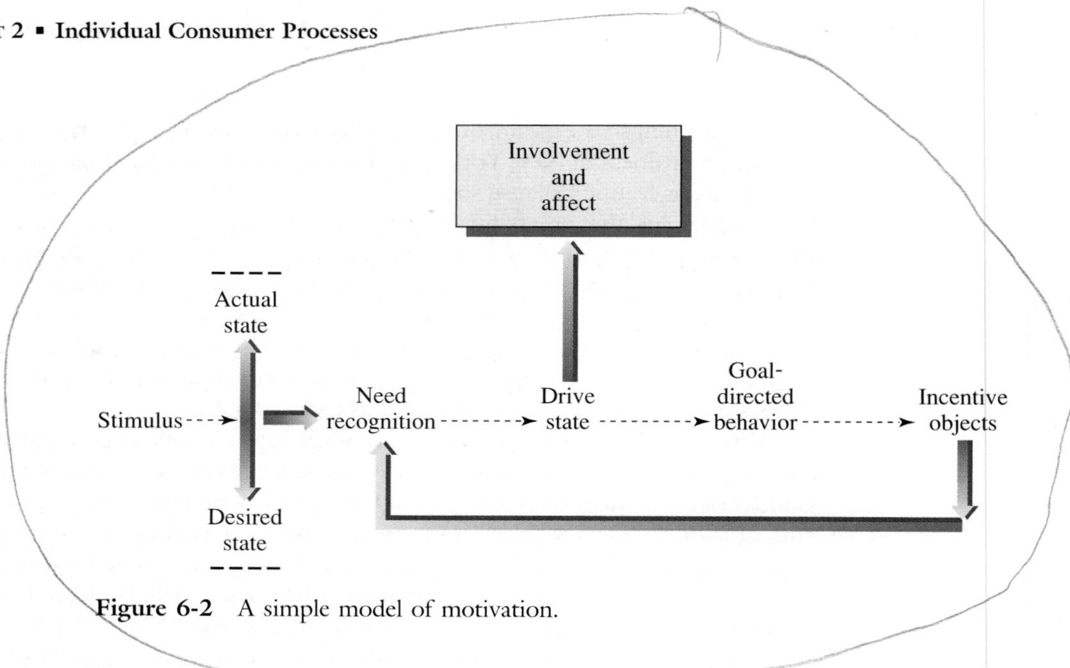

Figure 6-2 A simple model of motivation.

stimulus causes an actual state of being to diverge from a desired state of being, a need results. Thus **needs** occur when a perceived discrepancy exists between an actual and a desired state of being. The nature of the need state is influenced by the interpretation of the stimulus and by the general goals of the consumer. For example, a need for a compact disc player could result from a person disliking the sound that his or her current record player provides (i.e., the actual state) and from the realization that the compact disc would provide a clearer, cleaner sound (the desired state).

Researchers have differentiated between expressive needs and utilitarian needs. **Expressive needs** involve desires by consumers to fulfill social and/or aesthetic requirements. Expressive needs are closely related to the maintenance of the self-concept of consumers. For example, expressive needs may be felt when clothing purchased two years in the past fails to match a person's self-concept of being at the forefront of fashion. **Utilitarian needs** involve desires by consumers to correct basic instrumental problems, such as filling a car's gas tank or removing a spot from a rug.[10]

Various generalizations have been made about the operation of needs. Needs can be either innate or learned. They are never fully satisfied. If one need is fulfilled, another will spring up to take its place. If two needs are in conflict, people will tend to act to fulfill the more basic (i.e., the more physiologically based) need first. Thus, in a consumer setting, needs are ubiquitous. Of course, marketers attempt to fulfill these needs by creating products and services and compete to do a better job satisfying such needs.

When a need is aroused, it produces a drive state. A **drive** is an affective state in which emotions and physiological arousal are experienced. The arousal can be measured through such means as monitoring the heart rate, blood pressure, and pupil size of consumers. The drive state activates the person to engage in goal-directed action to obtain an incentive object. The level of a consumer's drive state influences his or her level of involvement and affective state. As the drive state increases, feelings and emotions intensify, resulting in increased levels of involvement and information processing.

When consumers experience a drive state, they engage in goal-directed behavior. **Goal-directed behavior** consists of the actions taken to relieve the need state, such as searching for information, talking to others, shopping for the best bargain, and purchasing products and services.

Readers should note the similarity between needs and problem recognition and between goal-directed behavior and the search for information. In Chapters 11, 12, and 13, consumer decision making is discussed. Consumer decision making is activated by a person recognizing that a problem exists. Interestingly, problem recognition is defined as occurring when an actual state diverges from a desired state of being. Thus problem recognition and need activation are essentially synonymous concepts. Similarly, goal-directed behavior and the search for information are closely related. In each instance, the consumer engages in a series of behaviors to fulfill a need or solve a problem. In sum, concepts from motivation have importance for understanding the nature of consumer decision making.

Consumer incentives are the products, services, information, and even other people that are perceived to satisfy a need. In Figure 6-2, the incentive objects are connected back to the need recognition stage where they act to narrow the gap between the actual state and the desired state. Incentive objects are similar to reinforcers, and consumers will direct their behavior to obtain them to fulfill needs. Like all reinforcers, consumer incentives can be either positive or negative. An example of a negative consumer incentive might be dirt in a grocery store or a lack of lighting around shopping centers. Consumers react quite negatively to dirt in a grocery store. Similarly, poor lighting within shopping centers may elicit fear in consumers who would like to shop during evening hours. Because people move toward positive incentives and away from negative incentives, the goal of the marketer is to develop products, services, retail stores, packaging, advertising, and so forth that are positively reinforcing to consumers.

THE CONCEPT OF AFFECT

As noted earlier in the chapter, when a need is felt, a drive state occurs that creates affective reactions in consumers. **Affect** may be defined as a "class of mental phenomena uniquely characterized by a consciously experienced, subjective feeling state, commonly accompanying emotions and moods."[11] Thus affect is a broad term that encompasses both emotions and moods. Emotions are distinguished from moods by their greater intensity and their greater psychological urgency.[12] Examples of emotions include feelings of anger, distress, fear, interest, joy, and surprise.[13]

The study of affective processes has recently become an important topic among consumer researchers. Most important, it forms the central concept on which the experiential perspective of consumer behavior is based. For consumer researchers the study of affect has implications for at least seven separate areas. Table 6-1 summarizes these areas. When analyzing a managerial or public policy problem, one should consider the causes and impact of the affective states that consumers experience.

TABLE 6-1

Areas of Application of Affective Processes to Consumer Research

1. *Experiential perspective*—The experiential perspective asks researchers, managers, and individuals to consider the role of affect in motivating consumer behavior. Areas of particular interest include investigating leisure pursuits, the affective impact of advertising, and the role of affect in the purchase of high-involvement products.
2. *Attitude formation*—Affect is one component of an attitude regarding a product, advertisement, or other object. (See Chapter 8.)
3. *Information processing*—Affective states may influence memory, cognitive capacity, and attention. (See Chapters 3 and 4.)
4. *Choice behavior*—A choice may be based upon a rule of selecting the option that makes one feel the best. This is called the "affect referral heuristic." (See Chapter 10.)
5. *Postpurchase processes*—Affect is closely linked to postpurchase satisfaction, brand loyalty, and complaining behavior. (See Chapter 12.)
6. *Communication processes*—Messages can be created that focus on eliciting emotions. (See Chapter 10.)
7. *Situational influences*—Mood states result in part from the consumer situation and represent a mild affective state. (See Chapter 14.)

The Structure of Emotions

A number of different attempts have been made to identify the various emotions that people experience. Table 6-2 presents two attempts to identify the basic feelings that influence people. The taxonomy of affective experience was developed by a psychologist.[14] This approach describes the basic emotions that people feel, and has been used extensively by consumer researchers. For example, in one study the researchers asked new car owners about their feelings regarding the new cars that they had just purchased. Measures were taken of ten emotions: interest, joy, surprise, sadness, anger, disgust, contempt, fear, shame, and guilt. The results revealed that pleasant surprise and interest were associated with satisfied customers. In contrast, those who were dissatisfied revealed a general pattern of anger, disgust, contempt, guilt, and sadness, which combined to create a generally hostile customer.[15]

The second view described in Table 6-2 was developed by two consumer researchers as an initial effort to describe emotional responses that people may experience when viewing advertisements. In their research on emotional responses to advertising, the researchers attempted to identify specific executional cues that advertisers could use to elicit these emotions from consumers. For example, to elicit anger the authors suggested that advertisers often show actors personally insulting each other, deliberately blocking important goals, and treating each other unfairly in various circumstances.[16]

Two questions are important for consumer researchers to answer in the study of affect: (1) in a consumer setting do people really experience emotions with sufficient strength to have any impact on behavior and (2) even if consumers feel emotions, do they experience the full range of feelings identified in Table 6-2?

TABLE 6-2

Two Alternate Views on the Structure of Feelings

A. Izard's Taxonomy of Affective Experience

1. interest	5. distress	8. fear
2. joy	6. disgust	9. shame
3. surprise	7. contempt	10. guilt
4. anger		

B. Emotional Responses in Advertising

1. fascination	9. affectionate love	16. distress/anxiety
2. surprise	10. compassion	17. fear
3. excitement	11. romantic love	18. disgust
4. fun/playfulness	12. gratitude	19. contempt
5. joy	13. sexual desire	20. shame
6. bliss	14. sentimentality	21. anger
7. belonging	15. sadness	22. guilt
8. pride		

SOURCES: (A) Carroll Izard, *Human Emotion* (New York: Plenum Press, 1977); (B) Deborah MacInnis and Robert Westbrook, "The Relationship Between Executional Cues and Emotional Responses to Advertising," Working Paper; Department of Marketing, University of Arizona, October 1987.

Does Advertising Create Affective Responses?

Particularly in an advertising context, the question arises as to whether consumers really experience anger, fear, sexual desire, surprise, and so forth when viewing a television commercial. Certainly, even if these emotions are experienced, they must be at relatively low levels. If a feeling is experienced at a very low level, does it affect behavior? Evidence is beginning to accumulate suggesting that even if the intensity of feelings is low, these feelings still may affect cognition and behavior.[17]

Thus a well-executed advertisement that depicts fear may be able to cause consumers to experience a smaller, but nonetheless detectable, fear response.[18] Figure 6-3 shows an advertisement that uses such a fear appeal to promote the usage of condoms. Wouldn't the ad create some anxiety, particularly if the person viewing it was leading an active sex life with numerous partners and not using condoms?

The relationship of the study of emotions to promotional strategy is clearly shown in Figure 6-3. The ad makes a highly emotional point with the simple words "An ounce of prevention because there is no cure." Indeed, the development of message strategies is based in part on determining what kind of emotion the creative people want to elicit in the target audience. For example, several different types of messages are labeled in terms of the emotions they wish to elicit. Thus communications researchers may speak of fear appeals, guilt appeals, sexual appeals, and of commercials that show people having fun. The development of messages will be discussed in much more detail in Chapter 10.

Figure 6-3 An illustration of a fear approach used to persuade consumers to purchase a product. (Courtesy of Ansell-America.)

Do Consumers Experience the Full Range of Emotions?

A second question of importance to consumer researchers concerns whether consumers experience the full range of emotions and feelings identified in Table 6-2. Early evidence indicates that consumers may experience a subset of these emotions.[19] One consistent finding in the literature is that a consumer's response to advertisements has two emotional dimensions. One dimension consists of positive affective states and the other consists of negative affective states. The implication of this finding is that a single message or event can simultaneously create both good and bad feelings.

When are good and bad feelings simultaneously created? Such combinations may actually occur in many instances. For example, a frequent theme of advertising involves the story of someone achieving a goal through a great deal of effort. The military services often use such an approach in their advertising. Thus, in one memorable scene, a group of young men are shown jumping out the back of a hovering helicopter and rappeling to the ground. The voiceover narrator says, "Rangers never do things the easy way." A combination of emotions may be created by such advertisements. Negative feelings include fear and anxiety. Positive feelings include pride, excitement, fun, and belonging.

When the analysis moves from advertising to consumer responses to products, the range of affective responses increases dramatically. For example, when Coca-Cola withdrew Coke from the market in 1986, many consumers reacted with anger and rage. Likewise, consumers who purchase an automobile that turns out to be a lemon experience anger, disgust, and contempt. People who illegally consume the services of prostitutes experience a range of emotions including sexual desire, fear, and power.

One final question needs to be asked concerning the impact of affect on consumer behavior: What is the mechanism through which feelings influence behavior? This is an extremely difficult question that has received little attention among researchers. Three possibilities, however, seem to be likely candidates. First, emotions and feelings may influence how consumers process information.[20] Second, when classical-conditioning processes are operating, the stimulus that elicits the emotion may become paired with previously neutral stimuli, resulting in the conditioned stimulus eliciting a lessened version of the emotion. Third, the emotion created could activate the consumer and place him or her into a drive state. Thus, by creating fear, an advertisement may activate a person to take steps to lower the fear. An important area of research involves developing explanations of how emotions influence the behavior of consumers.

SOME GENERAL THEORIES OF MOTIVATION

Most textbook discussions of motivation focus on describing certain well-known broad theories, such as Maslow's hierarchy of needs and Murray's social needs. (Figure 6-4 presents a brief review of the needs identified by Maslow and by Murray.) Indeed, by the time students take a consumer behavior course, they have usually had the Maslow hierarchy presented in several other classes. However, very little research has been performed on either of these theories, and in many cases, the research that has been performed has not been supportive of them.[21] In contrast, there is one broad theory of motivation that has received substantial amounts of research support—McClelland's theory of "learned needs."

McClelland's Theory of Learned Needs

David McClelland developed an important stream of research around the idea that three basic learned needs motivate people—the needs for achievement, affiliation, and power. Those with a high **achievement motivation** seek to get ahead, to strive for success, and to take responsibility for solving problems. In one study McClelland found that 83% of students with a high need for achievement entered occupations noted for the ability to take risks, make decisions, and achieve great success, such as in business management.[22]

McClelland seemed to view the **need for affiliation** in a manner similar to Maslow's belongingness need. Such a need motivates people to make friends, to become members of groups, and to associate with others. Those with a high need for affiliation tend to place the desire to be with others ahead of the need to succeed. For example, in

A. Maslow's Hierarchy of Needs

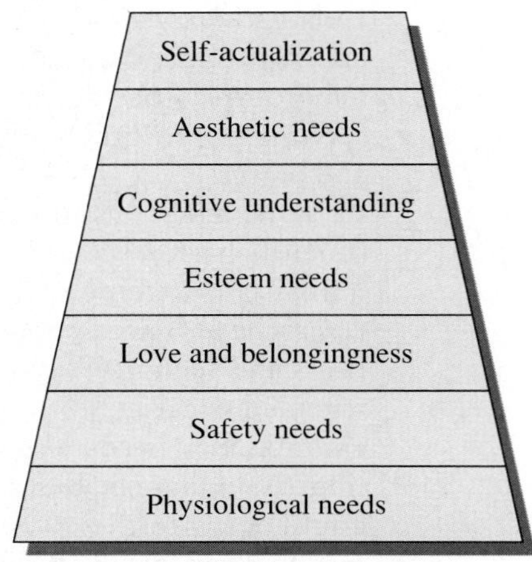

B. Murray's List of Human Needs

Abasement	Harm avoidance
Achievement	Infavoidance
Affiliation	Nurturance
Aggression	Order
Autonomy	Play
Counteraction	Rejection
Defendance	Sentience
Deference	Sex
Dominance	Succorance
Exhibition	Understanding

Figure 6-4

Needs identified by Maslow and Murray. (Source: A. H. Maslow, *Motivation and Personality*, 2nd ed., New York: Harper & Row, 1970; and A. H. Murray, *Exploration in Personality*, New York: Oxford, 1938.)

one study subjects were given the opportunity to choose a partner to assist them on a task. Those with a high need for achievement chose a partner based upon that person's demonstrated competence. In contrast, those with a high need for affiliation were more likely to choose their friends. Apparently, those with a high need for affiliation chose their partner more out of a desire to enjoy the experience than to succeed in the task.[23]

The **need for power** refers to the desire to obtain and exercise control over others. The goal is to influence, direct, and possibly dominate other people. The need for power can take two directions, according to McClelland. It can be positive, resulting in persuasive and inspirational power, or it can be negative, resulting in the desire to dominate and obtain submission from others.

Some research has investigated the relationship between McClelland's ideas and consumer behavior. For example, one study found that those with a high need for achievement tended to buy more outdoor leisure products, such as skis and boating equipment, than did those with a low need for achievement.[24]

A clear prediction from McClelland's work is that products can be advertised with motivational themes derived from the three basic consumer motivations that he identified. The idea would be to analyze the characteristics of the target market of the product to determine its basic motivational structure. Advertising would then be

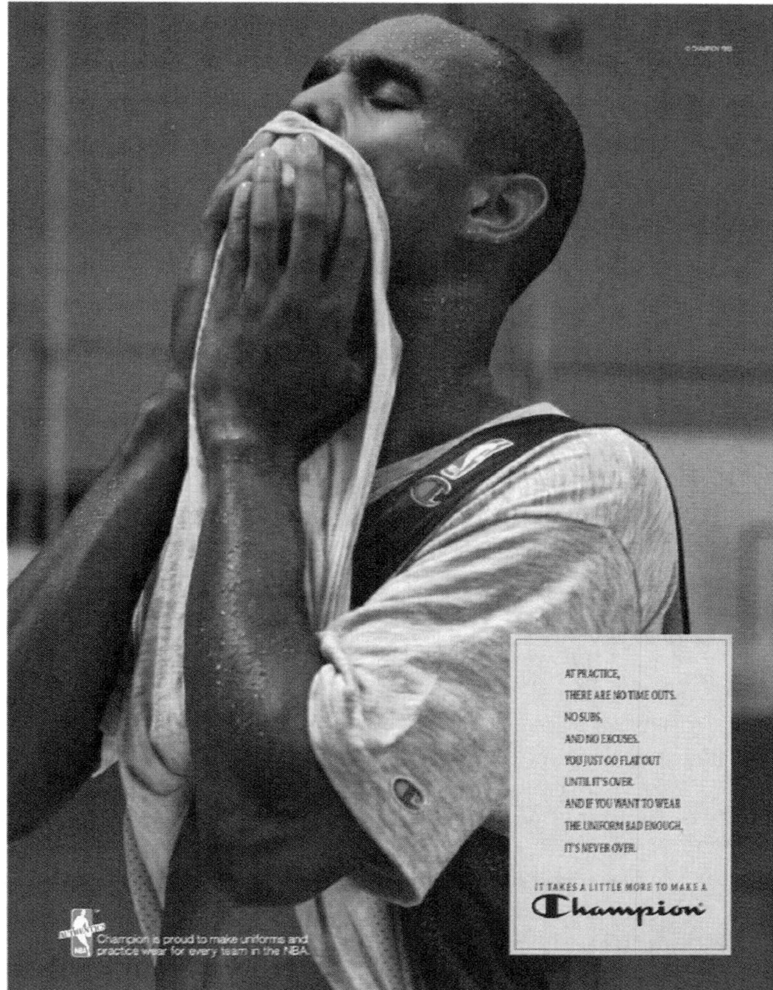

Figure 6-5 Champion uses an achievement motivation theme in this ad. (Courtesy of Champion.)

developed to place the product in such a context. An example of an advertisement that uses an achievement theme is found in Figure 6-5. The ad talks about the effort one must exert in practice in order to achieve when it really counts.

The trend over the past 20 years, however, has been to move away from developing broad theories of motivation, such as McClelland's social needs, to creating more restricted midrange theories. The goal of each of the midrange theories is to explain a narrower facet of human behavior. Each of the midrange theories of motivation discussed in this chapter has been supported through research, and one can be fairly confident of its validity.

MIDRANGE THEORIES OF MOTIVATION

Figure 6-6 lists the midrange theories of motivation that this chapter will discuss. Their order of description moves from the more physiologically based theories (e.g., opponent-process theory) to the more cognitively oriented (e.g., attribution theory). Thus opponent-process theory attempts to explain such phenomena as why people may feel exhilarated after doing something frightening, such as parachute jumping, or bad after doing something exhilarating, such as taking a drug. At the other end of the continuum, attribution theory operates at a more cognitive level and seeks to explain how people go about determining the causes of their actions and the actions of others.

Opponent-Process Theory

A researcher made an interesting observation about the emotional reactions of parachutists. During their first free fall, before the parachute opens, they may experience terror. They yell, their eyes bulge, their bodies go stiff, and they breathe irregularly. Upon landing safely, they at first walk around stunned, with stony-faced expressions. Then they begin smiling, talking, gesticulating, and showing every indication of being elated. Why would someone who was in terror suddenly become elated? The answer seems to lie in a theory of motivation called the opponent-process theory of acquired motivation.[25] According to **opponent-process theory**, when a person receives a stimulus that elicits an immediate positive or negative emotional reaction, two things occur. First, the immediate positive or negative emotional reaction is felt. Next, a second emotional reaction occurs that has a feeling opposite to that initially experienced. The combination of the two emotional reactions results in the overall feeling experienced by the consumer. Because the second emotional reaction is delayed, the overall experience consists of the consumer first experiencing the initial

Figure 6-6 Some midrange theories of motivation.

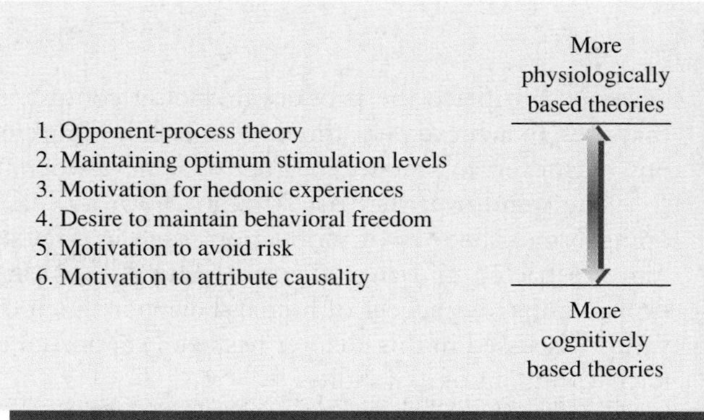

positive or negative feeling. After some time period, however, this feeling gradually declines and the opposite feeling begins to be felt. Likewise, the parachutists first felt extreme fear, but after landing the fear turned to its opposite emotion—elation. Figure 6-7 diagrams these relationships.

The idea that pleasure and pain often go together has been noted for many centuries. One such example is a quote from Plato found in the work Phaedo.

> How strange would appear to be this thing that men call pleasure! And how curiously it is related to what is thought to be its opposite, pain! The two will never be found together in a man, and yet if you seek the one and obtain it, you are almost bound always to get the other as well, just as though they were both attached to one the same head. Wherever the one is found, the other follows up behind.

Although opponent-process theory is quite simple, it has broad explanatory power. It can be used to account for a variety of consumer behaviors, such as drug addiction, cigarette smoking, jogging and marathoning, sauna bathing, and video game playing. For example, why would seemingly sane individuals go through the pain of running a marathon? The answer may be that through the operation of opponent processes the pain that accompanies the endurance run is followed by physiological pleasure. When combined with the positive reinforcement from friends and acquaintances, the overall experience of marathoning may be viewed extremely positively.

Opponent-process theory applies to everyday buying activities, at least superficially. The credit card problems that so many consumers experience may be based on

Figure 6-7 A diagram of the opponent-process theory.

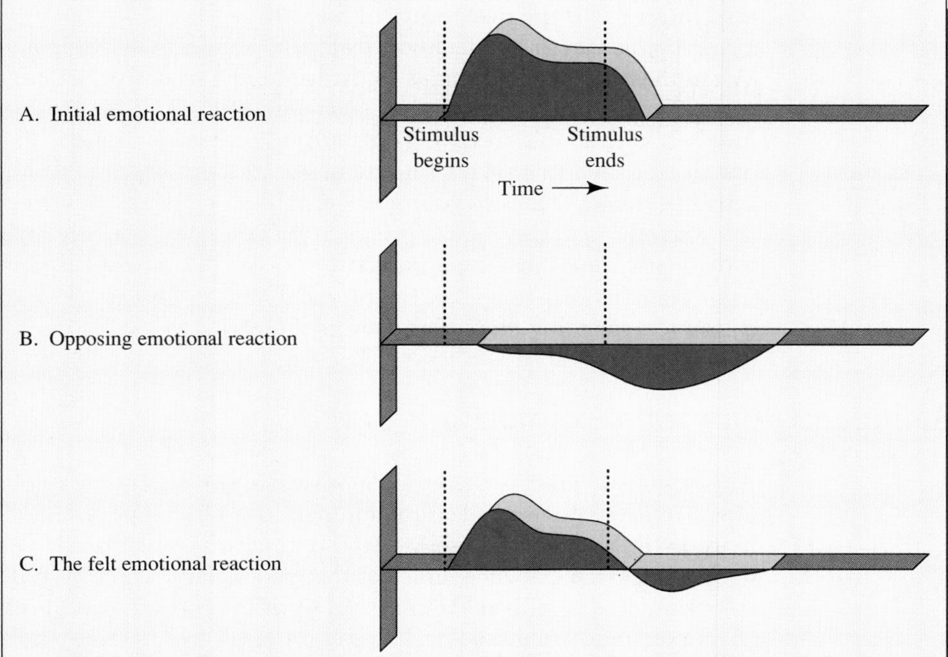

an opponent process. To make themselves feel better, consumers use a charge card to make a purchase. After the purchase, however, they begin to feel bad because of the negative rebound (as predicted by the theory). Further, the bills that will inevitably arrive further exacerbate the negative feelings. To combat the negative feelings, the consumer again visits the local mall or calls a favorite mail-order firm to make another purchase. The vicious circle results in major financial problems.

Priming

Another concept closely related to opponent-process theory is that of priming. **Priming** occurs when a small amount of exposure to a stimulus (e.g., food, playing a video game, or watching television) leads to an increased drive to be in the presence of the stimulus. Examples include the taste cravings consumers may get. After eating one potato chip, it is extremely hard to stop and not consume more. The taste of the first potato chip activates the consumer such that the drive to consume additional chips is greater than the drive prior to eating the first one. The effects of priming may influence consumers in their consumption of drugs (e.g., cocaine and alcohol) and food (e.g., nachos and rich desserts.)

A study was conducted to investigate the effects of priming on video game playing.[26] In the study college students rated their desire to play the video game "Pac-Man" at various points in time. One group made its ratings after playing the game for ten minutes, whereas another group made its ratings after playing for three minutes. The results showed that the interest ratings made after playing the game for only three minutes were significantly higher than were those made after playing for ten minutes. Furthermore, the ratings made after playing for three minutes were significantly higher than ratings made prior to starting the game. People wanted to play the game even more after playing for three minutes than they did before beginning to play the game. Figure 6-8 reveals the ratings of interest in the game after various time intervals for the two groups of subjects.

Priming may be understood from the perspective of opponent-process theory. When the reinforcing stimulus is just beginning to be consumed, the opposite motivation has not had a chance to start building up. The experience then may be intensely pleasurable, resulting in a strong drive to continue. Thus eating that first potato chip creates a strong sensation. Because the opposite feeling has not yet been activated, the tendency to continue consuming the salty snack is extremely strong.

Marketers intuitively use principles of priming on a regular basis. For example, providing samples in a supermarket is a classic example of priming. In one study it was found that providing free samples of donuts to grocery store shoppers resulted in consumers spending more than they had intended.[27]

Maintaining Optimum Stimulation Levels

The opponent-process theory of motivation provides a physiological explanation of how people respond to pleasure and pain. Another approach to motivation that has its roots in human physiology is the optimum stimulation level theory. A growing body of research evidence indicates that people have a strong motivation to maintain an optimum level of stimulation.[28] An **optimum stimulation level** is a person's preferred amount of physiological activation or arousal. Activation may vary from very low levels (a coma) to very high levels (severe panic). Individuals are motivated to

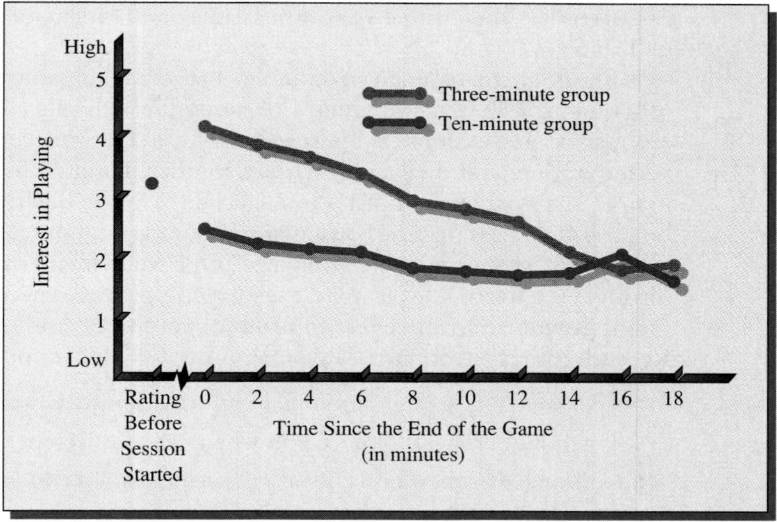

Figure 6-8 The effect of priming on video game playing. (Source: Peter DePaulo, "The Opposite of Satiation: Motivational Priming as an Aftereffect of a Pleasurable Consumption Experience," in *Advances in Consumer Research*, Vol. XIII, Richard Lutz, ed., Ann Arbor, MI: Association for Consumer Research, 1986.)

maintain an optimum level of stimulation and will take action to correct the level when it becomes too high or too low.

Internal and external factors may influence a person's level of stimulation at any given point in time. Internal factors include the individual's age, learning history, and personality characteristics. For example, people who prefer higher levels of stimulation score high on a scale that measures sensation seeking.[29] To maintain the high levels of stimulation required, sensation seekers are more apt to engage in such activities as parachute jumping, mountain climbing, gambling, and such. External factors influencing the stimulation level are those that affect the uncertainty and risk of the environment. Thus, if a person seeks a goal and some doubt exists as to whether the goal can be reached, his or her level of activation tends to rise. People attempt to manage their actions and the environment to maintain an optimum stimulation level. In other words, if the level of arousal is too high, the individual takes steps to lower it. Conversely, if activation is too low, the individual attempts to arrange his or her behavior to raise the stimulation level.

The motive of people to maintain an optimum stimulation level has implications for marketers, because a host of products and services exists that act to arouse or depress a person's activation level. For example, various types of drugs exist to lower arousal levels (e.g., sleep aids) and to raise arousal levels (e.g., stimulants such as caffeine and amphetamines). Many leisure activities strongly influence levels of arousal, such as parachute jumping, white water rafting, and hunting. Indeed, the desire of consumers to attend sporting events is likely to be influenced in part by the need for excitement. Similarly, some rides at amusement parks are built to scare their customers. To determine your arousal-seeking tendencies, complete the scale found in Table 6-3.

The desire to maintain an optimum level of stimulation may account for some cases of spontaneous brand switching. Consumers periodically change brands for no apparent reason. For example, a housewife may use Tide detergent consistently for a long period of time and then suddenly buy another brand. When asked why she switched brands, she might say, "I just wanted a change." The likely cause of such spontaneous brand switching is that the consumer was bored and wanted to vary her everyday life to temporarily change her activation level. One study found that people who have a need for higher activation levels tend to engage in greater amounts of brand switching, to reveal greater innovativeness in product purchases, and to be greater risk takers.[30] Recently, other researchers found that those with higher optimum stimulation levels

- engaged in greater amounts of information seeking,
- felt higher levels of boredom when exposed to repetitive ads,
- revealed higher levels of variety seeking when choosing fast food, and
- exhibited greater tendencies to gamble and seek risk.[31]

The Motivation for Hedonic Experiences

The desire for hedonic experiences is closely related to the need to maintain an optimum stimulation level. For consumer researchers, **hedonic consumption** refers to the needs of consumers to use products and services to create fantasies, to gain feelings through the senses, and to obtain emotional arousal.[32]

TABLE 6-3

A Scale to Measure Arousal-Seeking Tendencies

Directions: Answer each of the questions with a "yes" or "no." The greater the number of "yes" answers you have, the more you tend to seek to be aroused.

1. I frequently change the pictures on my walls.
2. I enjoy seeing people in strange clothing.
3. I continually seek new ideas and experiences.
4. I get bored when I am always around the same people and places.
5. I enjoy doing foolhardy things just for the fun of it.
6. People view me as an unpredictable person.
7. I like surprises.
8. I enjoy having lots of activity going on around me.
9. I like a job that offers change, variety, and travel even if it involves some danger.
10. I enjoy dangerous sports like mountain climbing, airplane flying, and skydiving.
11. I feel restive when I am safe and secure.
12. I would like to try the group-therapy techniques involving strange body sensations.

SOURCE: Adapted from a scale developed by Albert Mehrabian and James Russell, *An Approach to Environmental Psychology* (Cambridge, MA: MIT Press, 1974).

The systematic study of hedonic consumption dates only from the late 1970s; however, it has roots in other areas of study, such as the motivation research that began in the 1950s. Motivation researchers usually adopted a Freudian perspective in their interpretation of consumer behavior. They focused on the emotional reasons for people's consumption patterns and emphasized how products could be used to arouse and fulfill fantasies. (Freudian ideas are discussed in greater detail in Chapter 7, Personality and Psychographics.) In addition, the hedonic consumption approach borrows concepts from sociologists on the symbolic nature of products—that is, products are not simply objective entities but also symbolize much broader concepts to consumers. Thus diamonds are not only carbon crystals but also symbols of love and permanence.

Desires to Experience Emotion

The term **hedonism** usually refers to gaining pleasure through the senses. However, as used in the present context, the feelings that consumers seek to gain may not be uniformly pleasurable. Consumers may seek to experience a variety of emotions, such as love, hate, fear, grief, anger, and disgust. At first thought it seems odd that someone would seek out negative experiences. However, remember that amusement parks are built in part to create fear. In particular, roller coasters exist to fan the flames of fear. Even their names are designed to instill fright, such as "Screamer" and "The Beast." Horror movies are created to frighten and disgust people. Overall, people go to movies and plays to experience secondhand the emotions of love, hate, and anger.

One particularly important point made by hedonic consumption theorists is that emotional desires sometimes dominate utilitarian motives in choosing products.[33] From a utilitarian perspective, why would a sane man give a woman a dozen roses? In 1995 the gesture would have cost him forty-five dollars or so—for a gift that would perish within a couple of days. Sending roses only makes sense in terms of their symbolic value and the emotions created by such symbolism.

The types of products and services that hedonic consumption researchers investigate are different from those traditionally analyzed. Most consumer research has focused on packaged goods (e.g., toothpaste, beer, cigarettes, and laundry detergent). Hedonic consumer research investigates such products as movies, rock concerts, theater, dance, pornography, and sporting events. These products are intrinsically more emotionally involving than using a particular toothpaste or toilet paper. The choice of a hedonically relevant product tends to be based on its symbolic value and on the likely emotion that it is anticipated to elicit in the consumer.

Figure 6-9 presents an ad with a clear hedonic tone.

Desires for Leisure Activities

Another type of hedonic consumption rests on the desire to engage in leisure activities, that is, those activities that occur in "free time" or "nonwork time." In addition, however, leisure is an experience. Thus, what one person defines as leisure, another may define as work.[34] The concept of leisure is multidimensional, and the research evidence indicates that a number of different needs propel people to seek leisure. For example, through leisure activities people can express themselves not only to others but also to themselves. Leisure also provides the opportunity to obtain pleasure and fun. Leisure can also be used to maintain an optimal stimulation level, as described

Figure 6-9 Guess what hedonically based feelings the advertiser is attempting to elicit in this perfume ad.

earlier in the chapter. In addition, people appear to want to engage in nonwork activities for several other reasons. These include

1. *Desire for intrinsic satisfaction.* Here the activity is viewed by the consumer as rewarding in and of itself, such as reading a good book. Thus performing the activity does not have to lead to any other extrinsic rewards—monetary or otherwise. Some argue that the idea of **intrinsic satisfaction** is the key element defining leisure and that all other concepts merely explain how the intrinsic satisfaction is obtained.[35]
2. *Involvement in the activity.* The person is totally absorbed in the activity so that everyday life is forgotten (e.g., playing a pickup game of basketball).

Thus the consumer becomes so intensively engaged in a pleasurable activity that all else is screened from thought.

3. *Perceived freedom.* The person has the **perceived freedom** to engage or not to engage in the activity. No coercion or obligation exists to force the person to engage in the activity (e.g., taking a hot bath). Thus leisure experience can be conceptualized as operating on a continuum of obligation–discretion. Activities that a person is obligated to perform are categorized as nonleisure. In contrast, activities that a person is free to perform or not would be categorized as leisure.[36]
4. *Mastery of the environment or of oneself.* The person attempts to learn something well or to overcome some obstacle (e.g., mountain climbing). The idea is to test oneself or to conquer the environment. One may particularly find mastery operating in leisure activities involving sports and intellectual games such as chess.
5. *Arousal.* The need for arousal has been identified as a motivator of leisure activities. Seeking leisure activities that are novel, complex, and risky can temporarily raise the arousal levels of consumers, which may produce pleasurable feelings.[37] An example might be bungee jumping.

The Motivation to Maintain Behavioral Freedom

One of the motivators of leisure activities mentioned in the last section was the desire to engage in activities without externally imposed restrictions. This motive to maintain behavioral freedom has broad implications for marketers and is an important consumer behavior concept. If the freedom to select a product or service is impeded, consumers respond by reacting against the threat. The motivational state resulting from the response to threats to behavioral freedom has been labeled **psychological reactance**.[38]

The term "reactance" describes the motivational state of the person whose behavioral freedom has been threatened. The reaction of consumers to the withdrawal of "old" Coke from the market illustrates the effects of reactance. A similar reaction occurred among loyal users of Crayola crayons. In 1990 corporate managers of Binney & Smith made a decision to retire eight colors from the popular 64-crayon flip-top box and replace them with more contemporary colors. Thus "boring" colors were eliminated, such as raw umber, maize, and lemon yellow. They were replaced with sexy new hues, including wild strawberry, fuchsia, teal blue, and cerulean. Consumers reacted to the change with a boycott. In one protest march, protestors carried a coffin. One marcher said, "They call it a retirement. I call it a burial." A first grader named Ebony Faison said, "Whenever I draw me, I use raw umber. What color should I color now?"[39] For a year following the change, the company received 334 calls and letters a month protesting the change. One spokesperson said, "We were aware of the loyalty and nostalgia surrounding Crayola crayons, but we didn't know we hit such a nerve." At last report, the company was considering bringing back the old colors as part of a new collection.[40]

Reactance can occur in a variety of consumer settings. Thus sharp restrictions of the supply of products can increase demand because their perceived value increases as a result of reactance. For example, in the early 1970s phosphate detergents were banned in Miami, Florida. Interestingly, researchers found that after the ban, Miami residents had more favorable attitudes toward phosphate detergents than did residents of Tampa, where the products were not banned.[41] Similarly, researchers have found that one-day-only sales increase consumer desires to make purchases in comparison to three-day-only sales. In sum, restricting the ability to obtain a product (e.g., phosphate detergents) or to buy during a sale increases the desire to engage in the action.[42]

The impact of limiting behavioral freedom can be observed among investors of rare art or automobiles. Auto companies, such as Ferrari and Porsche, make use of the effect by turning out exceedingly expensive, limited-production models. For example, in 1990 the sticker price on a 475-horsepower Ferrari F40 was a mere $350,000. However, because only 1,000 were built, the autos grew in demand and asking prices quickly increased to over $1 million. One dealer said, "If you say to a rich man, 'You can't have it,' he'll want it more. That's part of the appeal."[43] On the other hand, reactance can also move against the sale of a product. For example, if a salesperson pushes a product too hard, the consumer may move against the sales pitch and actively avoid buying the product.

Two types of threats can lead to reactance. **Social threats** involve external pressure from other people to induce a consumer to do something. Examples might include pressing the consumer to buy a certain product, to go to a certain play, or to vote for a particular political candidate. If the pressure is too great, the consumer may react against it—resulting in a "boomerang effect." In such instances the consumer moves in the opposite direction intended by the person engaging in the social influence attempt. In the personal-selling area of marketing, the problem of boomerang effects is great. Salespeople must take definite steps to persuade customers to buy their products. However, they cannot push too hard or risk alienating the prospect. A time-tested strategy is to give customers information so that they can persuade themselves that the product is the right one to buy.

A second threat to behavioral freedom comes from impersonal sources. Generally, the **impersonal threats** are barriers that restrict the ability to buy a particular product or service. The barriers may result from a shortage of the product, from the possibility that someone else will buy the product, or even from a rise in its price. In each case something comes between the consumer and the purchase of the product. The consumer's likely reaction is to reevaluate the product and want it even more. Even the decision to buy one product over another can result in the person's reevaluating the unchosen alternatives more positively.[44]

Three basic requirements exist for consumers to experience reactance. First, the consumer must believe that he or she has the freedom to make a choice in a given situation. If the general ability to make a choice is unavailable—perhaps because alternative products are unavailable—reactance will not occur. Second, a threat to the freedom must be experienced. Third, the decision must be one that is of some importance to the consumers.[45]

Interestingly, companies sometimes attempt to create reactance via advertising messages. For example, Avia Athletic Footwear placed the following message in their ads: "For athletic use only. If you're after frilly, faddish shoes, open someone else's catalog." The approach may seem foolish since 80% of all athletic shoes sold in the United States are for street use. However, as discussed in *Advertising Age*, the company is banking on human nature. The Avia vice president for marketing explained:

"People will yearn to buy shoes just because you tell them not to. It's the perfect strategy for our core customer [serious athletes]; and, if executed correctly, it will be very effective with the non-core as well."[46]

The Motivation to Avoid or Seek Risk

Suppose that you were suddenly given the opportunity to ride on the space shuttle on its first commercial trip to an orbiting space station. What would be your thoughts? Certainly, you would consider the hedonic elements of the ride—the excitement, the adrenalin flow, the social approval of your friends. In addition, you might consider the various negative outcomes that could result from the trip—nausea, being away from your job for an extended period of time, or even death. You might also attempt to weigh the likelihood that these various negatives outcomes could occur. When you go through such a process, you are analyzing the perceived risk of the decision.

Although some debate exists as to its definition, consumer researchers view perceived risk as the consumer's perception of the overall negativity of a course of action based upon an assessment of the possible negative outcomes and of the likelihood that those outcomes will occur.[47] As such, perceived risk consists of two major concepts—the negative outcomes of a decision and the probability that these outcomes will occur.

While engaged in their everyday activities, consumers are constantly faced with decisions that involve uncertainty and the possibility of negative outcomes. Examples of such decisions include buying products or services, determining where to go on a vacation, selecting a retailer from which to buy a product, and deciding whether to take an illegal drug (e.g., steroids). As can be seen, almost any decision a consumer makes involves uncertainty. A general rule found by researchers over the past 25 years is that people usually seek to avoid taking risks perceived as being too great. In general, consumers are risk averse in their actions. However, exceptions to the rule do exist. As discussed earlier, some consumers appear to seek risk in part to raise their activation levels to optimum heights.

Highlight 6-1 further explores consumer risk taking and links it to matters of ethics in corporations.

This section on consumer risk taking will first discuss the types of risks that consumers perceive. Next, it will identify a number of factors that influence the perception of risk. The section then presents a number of means through which consumers reduce risk. Finally, it will briefly discuss a number of factors that influence consumers to take risks.

Types of Consumer Risks

The first discussion of the concept of perceived risk appeared in marketing literature in 1960.[48] Since that time, much of the effort of consumer researchers has been placed on identifying the various types of risk about which consumers are concerned. Table 6-4 identifies seven different types of risk to which consumers may respond.[49] These are financial, performance, physical, psychological, social, time, and opportunity loss risks.

The promotional work of marketers is often geared toward lowering the perceived risk of consumers. Advertisements may be used to point out how a particular product or service may lower risk. For example, insurance advertising stresses the

HIGHLIGHT 6-1

Seeking Risk in Leisure Activities: Implications for Corporate Ethics

On August 1, 1987, five prominent advertising executives were killed when their raft capsized in giant rapids in the Chilko River in British Columbia, Canada. Six others in the expedition nearly lost their lives as well. The same year a Houston attorney was killed in Wyoming while rock climbing. His guide had anchored a belay and signaled the attorney to climb. The ex-professional football player began climbing and fell once—his guide catching the fall with the safety ropes. Trying again, he fell a second time. However, this time the guide felt the rope go limp. The attorney had slipped from his harness and fallen 135 feet to his death. On average, 26 people a year die in mountaineering, and 30 die in parachuting accidents in the United States. In one recent year, a minimum of 70 people were killed while exploring caves.

A peculiar combination of factors appears to drive some consumers to engage in leisure activities that are downright dangerous. The high levels of stimulation resulting from placing their lives at risk are a factor. People can compensate for low-arousal jobs by risk seeking on weekends. In addition, successful enthusiasts (i.e., those who are still alive) have to exert control over their bodies and their minds. They must show dedication, organization, and coolness under pressure.

Indeed, one can see all three of McClelland's learned needs operating. The feelings obtained from successfully completing a climb, a dangerous trip through a cave, or a parachute jump illustrate achievement motivation. The concentration and attention required for success are indicative of exerting power and control over one's own body and mind. Positive feelings of affiliation are also felt within the group of people, who for safety reasons climb, jump, or explore caves together. Opponent-process elements are probably also operating. One accounting executive said about climbing, "Maintaining the edge of fear for sustained periods is very intoxicating." "Rock jocks" describe such a feeling as "the jazz." However, those who engage in such dangerous leisure activities probably rate high on scales that assess a need for stimulation. One caver described his brethren as the "weirdest bunch of people I've ever run into."

To write a story about caving, a *Wall Street Journal* reporter joined an expedition. She spent the morning swimming through pools of water and crawling through muddy passages, one of which was so narrow that it was called "the birth canal." After a cold lunch, the group inched along a slick ledge above a crevice too deep to see the bottom. As they approached the end, they had to straddle a three-foot-wide crack, and her legs began to shake from the combination of fear and fatigue. Just then the guide yelled, "Are we having fun yet?" Her only response was a louder "no!" as she thought of being "flat rocked," a process in which a caver asks to have his or her body buried under flat rocks so that companions don't have to risk their lives carrying him or her from the cave.

A key issue concerns asking employees to take risks that could result in the death of employees. Was it ethical to ask members of the advertising firm to go white water rafting? Was it ethical of *The Wall Street Journal* to ask its reporter to risk being "flat rocked?" How do you draw the line in such matters?

Based in part upon Wendy Wall, "The Sport of Caving: It's Dangerous, Dirty, Damp—and Popular," *The Wall Street Journal*, September 1, 1987, pp. 1, 5; and Marilyn Wellemeyer "Away From It All on a Granite Wall," *Fortune*, April 13, 1987, pp. 119–20.

TABLE 6-4

Types of Perceived Risk

1. *Financial*—Risk that the outcome will harm the consumer financially (e.g., will buying a car cause financial hardship?).
2. *Performance*—Risk that the product will not perform as expected (e.g., will the car really accelerate faster than a Porsche 928?).
3. *Physical*—Risk that the product will physically harm the buyer (e.g., will the car protect me in a crash?).
4. *Psychological*—Risk that the product will lower the consumer's self-image (e.g., a swinging single wonders, will I look like a typical housewife if I buy this car?).
5. *Social*—Risk that friends or acquaintances will deride the purchase (e.g., will my best friend think that I am trying to show him up by buying a Porsche?).
6. *Time*—Risk that a decision will cost too much time (e.g., will buying a sports car cost me time because I have to tune it so frequently?).
7. *Opportunity loss*—Risk that by taking one action the consumer will miss out on doing something else he or she would really prefer doing (e.g., by buying a Porsche 928, will I miss out on buying several expensive oil paintings?).

reduction of financial risk. Automobile manufacturers, such as Volvo, mention the reduction of physical risk when touting the safety of their brands. Many personal-use product advertisements use a reduction-of-social-risk theme. Thus products are available to help consumers ward off "ring around the collar," bad breath, and dandruff, all of which can cause social embarrassment. Deodorant ads frequently use a social-risk theme. For example, by using the right deodorant, you can "raise your hand, if you're sure." The advertisement shown in Figure 6-10 cleverly uses such a social-risk theme. Headlined, "Take Control, Never Let Them See You Sweat," the ad for Dry Idea humorously suggests that a person loses social effectiveness if others observe him or her sweating.

For each of the seven types of risk, one can identify the two components of risk—the likelihood of loss and the amount of loss. Thus suppose that the decision involved deciding whether or not to take steroids to build muscles and assist training. The individual would either explicitly or implicitly assess the likelihood of having a negative outcome as well as the severity of the negative outcome. Advertising campaigns to decrease steroid use have been implemented, and these have tended to focus on negative outcomes. Figure 6-11 presents one of the ads, which visually depicts one of the negative outcomes for men—the development of breasts.

Factors Influencing the Perception of Risk

Researchers have found that a number of factors influence the amount of risk consumers perceive in a given situation. First, the characteristics of the individual consumer influence his or her perception of risk. Various researchers have found that personality factors can influence the extent to which a particular person reacts to the risk in a given situation. The following personal characteristics have been found to be associated with a greater willingness to accept risk: higher self-confidence, higher

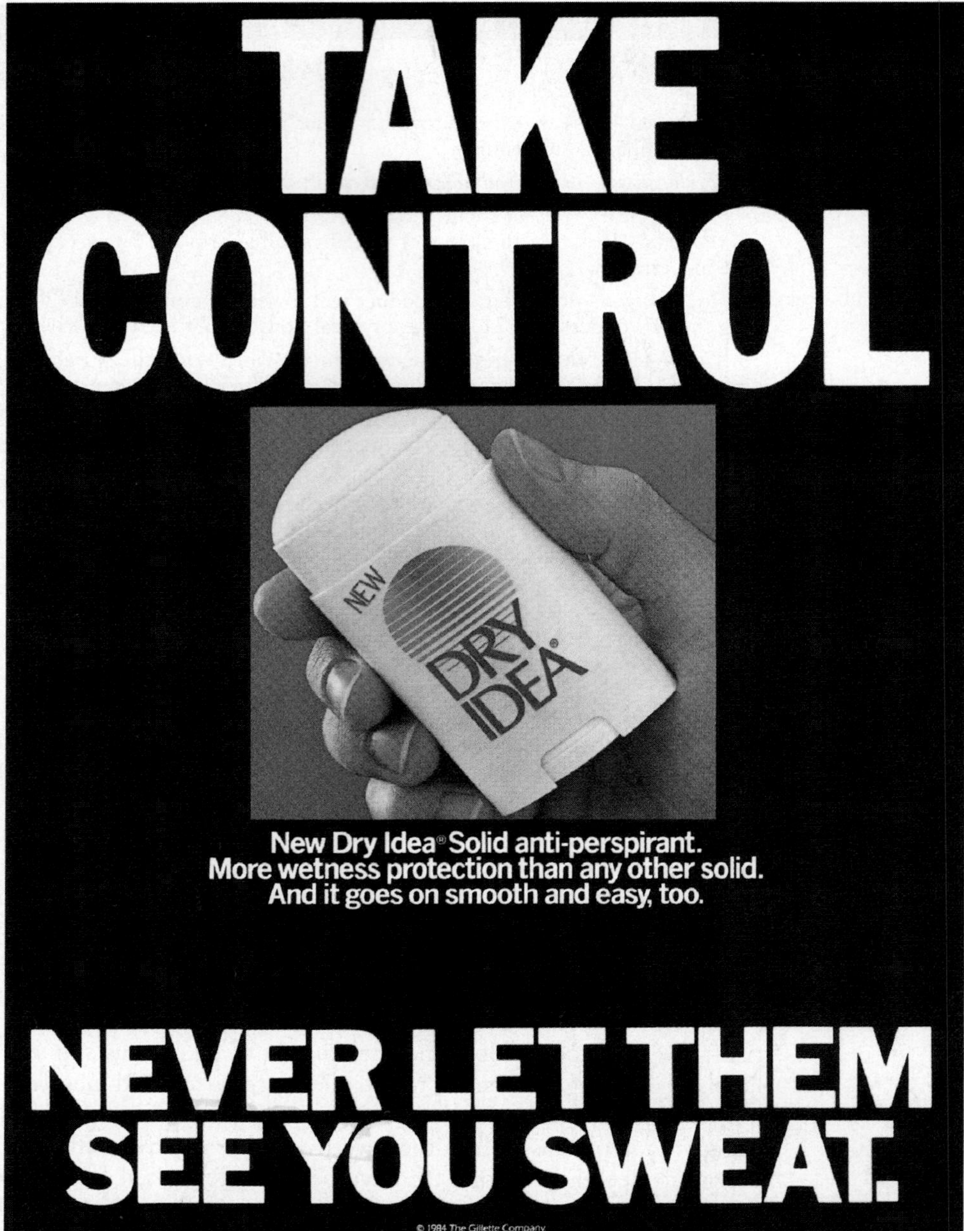

Figure 6-10 Gillette cleverly uses a social-risk theme to promote a deodorant. (Courtesy of The Gillette Company.)

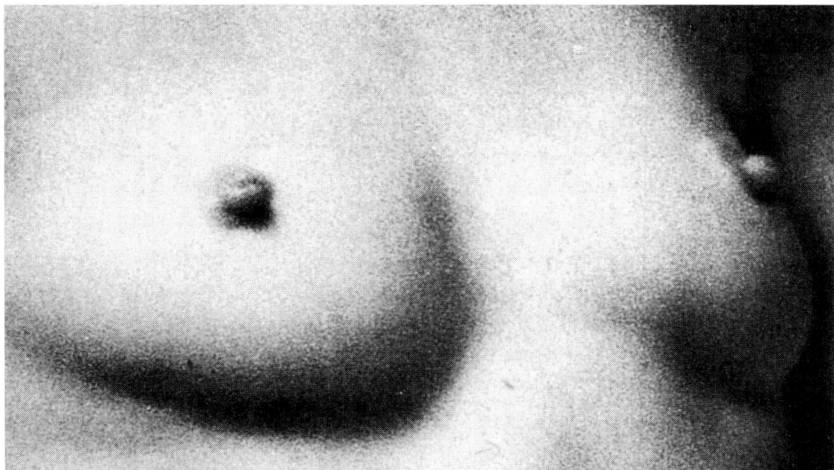

Figure 6-11 This ad was created to visually depict one negative outcome of steroid use among males. (Courtesy of Fallon McEglligott, Minneapolis.)

self-esteem, lower anxiety, and lower familiarity with the problem. Also, individuals who tend to make choices from a wider range of alternatives also tend to see lower risk in a particular selection.[50]

Situational factors may also influence the perception of risk. One type of situational variable concerns the nature of the task. For example, researchers have found that voluntary risks are more acceptable to people than involuntary risks.[51] Voluntary risks include such things as choosing to drive a car on a trip or choosing to go on a ski vacation. Involuntary risks include living in a home near where a nuclear power plant is being built or undergoing surgery for a life-threatening condition. For voluntary activities, consumers perceive systematically less risk than there really is. In contrast, for involuntary ones, consumers perceive more risk than is actually present. Another example of the nature of the task as an influence on risk perception concerns whether consumers make purchases from catalogs or local retailers. Researchers have found that consumers perceive that greater risk is involved in shopping through the mail than in shopping in a retail store.[52]

The characteristics of the product or service can also influence perceived risk. In general, high-involvement products are perceived to have a greater degree of risk attached to them. Thus products or services whose use may result in highly negative outcomes are perceived as riskier. Factors associated with such negative outcomes include the cost, the social visibility, and the potential physical danger in the use of the product or service.

Perception of risk may also be influenced by how consumers process information. When negative outcomes resulting from product or service failures are highly salient, they may be more available in memory, and consumers may erroneously perceive the product or service as riskier than it really is.[53] In 1991 the travel industry scrambled when hundreds of thousands of American tourists suddenly canceled plans to travel to Europe. Airlines canceled flights and European writers branded U.S. tourists as "crybabies." The cause of the sudden downturn in European travel was the Persian Gulf war, and Americans were afraid of potential hijackings and terrorist attacks. Of course, the chance of being killed in an auto accident was still over 1,000 times greater, but information on terrorism was highly available in memory and strongly influenced the risk perception of American consumers.

In sum, the amount of perceived risk in a purchase is likely to increase if

1. The product is expensive in terms of time or money for the target market.
2. Others evaluate the purchaser based upon his or her choice of brand.
3. Consumers get ego satisfaction from owning the product.
4. Consumers perceive that they could be harmed physically, psychologically, or socially by the purchase of the product.
5. Consumers have to give up purchasing other products or services to buy the product.
6. The activity is of an involuntary nature, and the outcome is out of the control of the consumer.

If managers find through market research that consumers perceive significant amounts of risk when purchasing a brand, steps should be taken to lower the perception of risk. Table 6-5 lists a number of these strategies.

It is also possible to develop advertising campaigns that focus on how a particular product or service can reduce consumer risk. General Motors has successfully used

TABLE 6-5

Managerial Strategies to Lower Consumer Perceptions of Risk

1. Price the product higher than average.
2. Give good warranties and guarantees.
3. Distribute through retailers with high-quality image.
4. Use a high-quality sales force composed of people who can give reassurance.
5. Provide prompt service to lower the time risk.
6. Obtain seals of approval (e.g., Underwriters Laboratories Approved).
7. Develop an extensive image-building campaign for the company and product.
8. Provide hot-line numbers so consumers can get information.
9. Give free trials, test drives, etc. (e.g., "test drive an Apple").
10. Give lots of information about one's product through brochures, packaging, instructions, write-ups in magazines, and the sales force.
11. Possibly have trusted endorsers promote one's product or service.
12. Focus on developing good word-of-mouth communications about the product.

such a strategy in a campaign touting the safety of its vehicles. Focusing on the physical risk of driving an automobile, GM has forcefully pointed out the good safety record of many of its cars. Figure 6-12 presents one of the ads.

How Do Consumers Reduce Perceived Risk?

Because some degree of perceived risk is inherent in nearly all consumer decisions, individuals must have methods that help them to make decisions with some confidence. One important idea is that consumers may compare their perception of the amount of risk present to some criterion of how much risk is acceptable. Thus consumers may be conceptualized as comparing the perceived risk to the acceptable risk.[54] If the perceived risk is greater than the acceptable risk, the consumer is then motivated to reduce the risk in some way or forgo making the decision. What actions do consumers take to reduce the amount of risk perceived in a decision? In general, all the risk-reduction strategies involve taking steps to lower the perceived likelihood

Latest HLDI Report on Highway Safety:

GM CARS RATED BEST 8TH YEAR IN A ROW.

1982-1984 passenger cars with "Substantially Better than Average" overall injury claim experience.

	Make	Body	Relative Frequency
✓1.	Oldsmobile Custom Cruiser	SW	54
2.	Volvo 240	SW	56
3.	Mercedes-Benz 380SL Coupe	SS	57
✓4. Tie	Oldsmobile Delta 88	4D	59
✓4. Tie	Buick Electra	SW	59
6.	Mercedes-Benz 300SD/SE	SS	60
✓7. Tie	Buick LeSabre	4D	62
✓7. Tie	Oldsmobile Ninety-Eight	4D	62
✓9. Tie	Chevrolet Corvette	SS	63
9. Tie	Jaguar XJ6	SS	63
9. Tie	Dodge Caravan	SW	63

Source: Highway Loss Data Institute. **Body Styles:** SW=Station Wagon; SS=Specialty. All results are stated in relative frequency of injury claims. A relative injury claim frequency of 100 is average. Relative frequencies of less than 70 are defined by HLDI as "Substantially Better than Average."

The Highway Loss Data Institute (HLDI) is a non-profit public service organization associated with the Insurance Institute for Highway Safety. As it has done for several years, HLDI has summarized and published its findings on the frequency of automotive insurance claims.

This year, HLDI finds that 6 of the top 11 models with overall injury claim experience defined as "substantially better than average," are General Motors cars.

We are pleased that GM cars are rated best again, as they have been ever since HLDI started summarizing its findings eight years ago.

We believe this continued excellence reflects not only our cars—their quality, size, weight, and design—but also how and where they are driven.

The HLDI results show that our cars and our customers go well together. And we trust it will continue that way in the years ahead. Because we are doing our part to see that it does.

That's the GM commitment to excellence.

Chevrolet
Pontiac
Oldsmobile
Buick
Cadillac
GMC Truck

Nobody sweats the details like GM.

Figure 6-12

General Motors points out that its cars may reduce physical risk for drivers and passengers. (Reproduced with permission of General Motors Corporation.)

that negative outcomes will occur. The following list includes six risk-reduction strategies:

1. Be brand loyal.
2. Buy through brand image.
3. Buy through store image.
4. Seek out information.
5. Buy the most expensive brand.
6. Buy the least expensive brand.

Why Do Consumers Sometimes Seek Risk?

As noted earlier in the chapter, consumers sometimes actively seek risk rather than attempt to avoid it. The occasions when this occur appear to center on experiential–hedonic activities, such as going to amusement parks, participating in dramatic sports (e.g., parachuting), and taking addictive and/or illegal drugs. Approaches, such as optimum-stimulation-level theory and opponent-process theory partially explain why consumers seek risk. However, processes in addition to those that occur at a physiological level appear to be needed to explain why people willingly risk their lives pursuing highly dangerous activities.

A group of researchers recently suggested that three fundamental motives exist for engaging in high-risk sporting activities—normative, hedonic, and personal efficacy motives.[55] First, the reasons for parachuting, hang gliding, or bungee jumping appear to revolve around needs to comply with the desires and expectations of others. This motive frequently occurs at the early stages of participating in the sport. The person participates in the activity to become part of the group. A second motive identified is hedonic, in which people seek arousal, pleasure, fun, and "the flow." People experience "the flow" when they become totally absorbed and involved in the experience. People describe such a state as occurring so that "nothing else in the world exists but the moment itself."

The third motive for engaging in high-risk sports is personal efficacy. After overcoming worries about safety and equipment, participants begin to focus on skill development. Feelings of achievement and increased self-confidence lead to the construction of a new identity that is based around the sport and its subculture. The authors argued that a type of transcendence occurs in which a new identity is created.

In sum, in circumstances in which consumers are purchasing goods and basic services (e.g., financial, medical, and food service), they generally seek to minimize risk. However, in areas that involve hedonic consumption, consumers may actively seek risk. Unfortunately, at this point in the research enterprise, researchers have little ability to predict the precise circumstances under which risk is avoided or sought.

The Motivation to Attribute Causality

As consumers move through their everyday life, events happen for which they seek explanations. The performance of a good or service may fall below expectations, a product endorser may strongly tout a brand of soft drink, or a salesperson may flatter a customer's ego. In each case consumers may seek to understand the cause for the action. They will want to identify why the product brought dissatisfaction, why the endorser advocated buying the soft drink, and why the salesperson was so ingratiating.

The explanation of the processes through which people make such determinations of the causality of action has been labeled attribution theory.[56] According to **attribution theory**, people attempt to determine whether the cause for action resulted from something internal or external to the person or object in question. Thus, if the referent is another person (e.g., the endorser), a consumer may ask whether the endorser recommended the product because he or she actually liked the product (an **internal attribution**) or because he or she was paid for endorsing it (an **external attribution**). Similarly, if someone asks the person why he or she bought a particular brand, the consumer then seeks to determine if the cause for action was something internal to the product (e.g., the product's good qualities) or something external to the product (e.g., pressure from a salesperson or a temporary reduction in price).

People are motivated to make attributions as to the cause of actions to determine how to act in the future. This concept is very similar to Maslow's "need for cognitive understanding" identified in Figure 6-4. Thus, if a consumer decided that an endorser advocated a product merely because he or she was paid, the consumer would tend to discount the message—that is, the consumer would not rely on the message as giving the endorser's real opinion. Such an attribution would likely result in the message having little or no impact on the consumer's attitude toward the product. Similarly, if the consumer were asked why he or she bought a product in spite of a high price, the consumer would tend to make the attribution that he or she really liked the product. It is as though the consumer said: "The product must be good, or why would I have bought it?" An internal attribution was made because the product was bought even though it had a high price.

Attribution theory is actually composed of a family of theories, each of which explains how people determine causality in various situations. Insufficient space exists to discuss each of the attribution theories, and only two concepts will be examined here—the augmentation–discounting model of Harold Kelley and the fundamental attribution error.

The Augmentation–Discounting Model

Harold Kelley was one of the first social psychologists to articulate the basic ideas about how people make attributions of causality. Kelley was interested in determining how people decide whether an action represents a person's true beliefs—or whether it has been caused by external forces (so that it says little about what the person really believes). Consumers frequently make such attributions. For example, does the endorsement of Nike basketball shoes by Michael Jordan represent his true beliefs about the shoes (an internal attribution) or did he merely do the endorsements for the money (an external attribution)?

In one classic paper, Kelley developed two important concepts—the augmenting principle and the discounting principle.[57] The augmenting–discounting model is based upon the idea that people examine the environmental pressures that impede or propel a particular action to determine the underlying cause for an action. Discounting occurs if external pressures exist that could provoke someone to act in a particular way—so the actions would be expected given the circumstances. In this case the person making the attribution would tend to believe that the actions of the observed person were caused by the environment rather than by that person's actual beliefs, feelings, and desires. In such circumstances the person making the attribution discounts the action as representing the other's real beliefs. In summary, the **discounting principle** may be stated as follows: the role of a particular cause in producing a given outcome is discounted if other plausible causes are also present.

What happens if a person moves against environmental pressures to do something? In this instance, the action would be unexpected given the circumstances. As a consequence, the observer will tend to believe that the person must have been highly internally motivated. In sum, the **augmenting principle** states that when a person moves against the forces of the environment to do something unexpected, the belief that the action represents the person's actual opinions, feelings, and desires is increased. An example of the augmentation principle would be a computer salesperson telling a prospective customer that a computer made by a competitor was superior to one he sold. In such an instance, the salesperson would be moving against his own best interests. Such an unexpected event would augment the belief that he really believed the statement. It would also increase the customer's trust in the salesperson.

The augmenting–discounting model applies to many consumer behavior problems. Indeed, one of the major difficulties faced by marketers is how to avoid having consumers discount their messages. Consumers recognize that pressures exist to sell products and to make profits. Thus, when they watch advertisements on television or receive promotional messages, they tend to discount the message and make external attributions. In general, consumers are not particularly confident that promotional messages accurately describe the characteristics of products. For example, in the mid-1980s a study found that over 59% of its respondents found "statistical" claims in advertisements to be unbelievable.[58]

As a result of the tendency of consumers to discount messages, marketers frequently attempt to identify ways to create the impression that the message actually goes against the pressures of the environment. A classic example has been the advertisements run by the Lincoln/Mercury division of Ford Corporation. In the ads, owners of Cadillacs evaluate the performance of Lincolns. After driving the Lincoln, a large percentage indicate that they preferred the Lincoln overall. In most cases consumers expect people who own a particular car to like it better than other models. Why else would they have bought it? Thus, when the Cadillac owners show a preference for Lincolns, the message is augmented so that the belief in its veracity is increased.

Figure 6-13 illustrates a case when a message would be augmented. In the ad, R. J. Reynolds Tobacco Company tells young people "You don't have to smoke to express yourself." Coming from a tobacco company, the message is certainly unexpected and seemingly against its best interests. The likely result is an augmentation in the belief of the trustworthiness of the company.

Another way to avoid consumer discounting of messages is to use person-on-the-street interviews. Such interviews leave the impression that no external pressure existed for the seemingly randomly selected person to advocate the product. In this way, advertisers hope that discounting is avoided. Pepsi-Cola has run an effective campaign against Coca-Cola with its "Pepsi Challenge" series, in which people were asked to taste the two colas and give their preferences. More people in the taste test favored Pepsi, and the ads dramatically improved the brand's market share. To respond to the ads, Coke had its endorser, Bill Cosby, suggest that those taking the Pepsi Challenge deliberately chose Pepsi to go on television. The implication was that people didn't really prefer Pepsi; they chose it merely to have the chance to be

Figure 6-13 By implicitly arguing against young people smoking, R. J. Reynolds may augment consumer beliefs—consumers might see Reynolds as a more trustworthy company. (Courtesy of R. J. Reynolds.)

seen on television. The goal of Coke was to give the audience a reason to discount the Pepsi message.

Highlight 6-2 identifies one additional means to avoid discounting—have your product appear in movies.

The Fundamental Attribution Error

One consistent finding is that people are biased to make internal attributions.[59] That is, when an individual engages in an action, people tend to believe that it was caused by that person's true beliefs and preferences. Even when an individual had no choice as to which action to take, people have a bias to attribute it to his or her personality or attitudes. This bias to make internal attributions is called the **fundamental attribution error**.

HIGHLIGHT 6-2

"Grab a Red Stripe Out of the Fridge"

Gene Hackman (playing Avery Tolar) yelled these eight little words to Tom Cruise (Mitch McDeere) in a scene from the movie *The Firm*—one of 1993's hottest movies. Red Stripe is a beer that comes in little brown bottles that vacationers quaff on their Caribbean vacations. Until the scene in *The Firm*, it was almost unknown in the United States. As estimated by the company's U.S. brand manager, on the opening night alone over 7.4 million consumers heard about the brand. But how much did it cost the brewery for the advertisement? It seems that all the company did was supply the film crew with free Red Stripe at a cost of about $5,000.

Of course, it is well known that appearing in a movie can result in a huge boost in sales for a product. The classic case was "Reese's Pieces" in the megahit *E.T.: The Extra-Terrestrial.* Since then, companies have been willing to pay handsome fees of $50,000 plus to have their product featured in a movie.

But the practice of offering cash to include brands in movies has come under fire by consumer activist groups. They charge that it is tantamount to "advertising masquerading as art." They argue that the practice borderlines on being unethical.

As a result of the pressure, movie executives are increasingly hesitant to accept cash for product exposure in their movies. In 1993, several movies featured products for which no money was paid, including Nike products in *Free Willie* and Evian Water and Keds sneakers in *Sleepless in Seattle*. The director of *The Firm* argued that Red Stripe was specifically mentioned in the book on which the movie was based and that the brand is an authentic part of tourist life in the Caribbean.

But despite the pressure by consumer groups, you can expect to see the continued use of branded products in movies. Brand managers recognize that consumers will discount the testimonials of product endorsers. They understand that by exposing consumers to their brands in "nonselling" circumstances the authenticity the product is dramatically increased. These ideas can be directly derived from the work in attribution theory discussed in this chapter.

Based in part on Laura Bird, "A Star Is Brewed as Beer Scores in Hit Film," *The Wall Street Journal*, July 8, 1993, p. B8.

Evidence of the fundamental attribution error was found in a recent study, where respondents received persuasive messages from an automobile salesperson. The participants were either told or not told that the salesperson had received special incentives to sell the car—called the "Austin." Those in the special incentive condition learned that the salesperson would get a bonus for selling the Austin and that the sales manager was pushing him to sell the car. Even under these circumstances, the respondents inferred that the salesperson's attitudes were consistent with the sales message. Somewhat amazingly, the researcher found that "Even when the salesperson clearly had no choice in the views that he or she expressed, subjects inferred that the product was more valuable when the salesperson spoke favorably compared to unfavorably."[60]

In addition to investigating how consumers react to advertising and personal-selling messages, concepts from attribution theory can be applied to several other problem areas in consumer behavior. For example, the attributions made by consumers concerning the factors that caused a product's failure can have strong implications for a corporation. If consumers attribute the cause of a product failure to the company, it could have severely negative long-term implications for the company. Conversely, if the cause of a product problem is attributed to bad luck and chance, the negative repercussions may be minimized. The ability of Johnson & Johnson, Inc., to rapidly rebuild Tylenol's market share after the poisonings that occurred in the early 1980s illustrates the point. Consumers reacted positively to the company's efforts to recall the brand from the market; as a result, they attributed the cause of the poisonings to bad luck and not to the corporation.

Attribution theory also has implications for the sales promotion area. When companies make heavy use of sales promotion devices, they should be concerned with the attributions that consumers make concerning why they bought the product. If consumers attribute the cause of their purchase to the sales promotion device (e.g., a rebate or prize), it may be extremely difficult for the company to build repeat purchase behavior and brand loyalty.[61] The goal of companies should be to encourage consumers to attribute their purchase of a product or service to the brand, not to some situational variable, such as a rebate.

Table 6-6 summarizes the managerial applications of attribution theory.

TABLE 6-6

Managerial Applications of Attribution Theory

A. *Develop believable advertisements*—Use strategies that enhance message augmentation by influencing consumers to perceive that the endorsement was made for internally caused, rather than externally caused, reasons.

Develop messages that give both sides of arguments—Include those that would be unexpected from the organization.

B. *Resolve product problems*—Respond quickly and proactively to product problems to enhance consumer beliefs that the cause involved bad luck rather the intentions or negligence of the firm.

C. *Assess sales promotions*—Use sales promotions cautiously to avoid having consumers attribute the cause of their purchase to the incentive rather than to the qualities of the product.

A MANAGERIAL APPLICATIONS EXAMPLE

The airline industry has been very successful in attracting passengers with their frequent-flier plans. One consumer described his feeling about frequent flying to a *Wall Street Journal* reporter. He said collecting frequent flyer miles is "an obsession, a compulsion. I live, eat, and breathe the United Airlines Mileage Plus Program." On the day of *The Wall Street Journal* interview, he and his wife had gotten up for a 5:24 A.M. flight from San Francisco to Oakland. They took a bus back from Oakland to their hotel in San Francisco and had enough time to go back to bed. The flight was so short that the plane didn't even have to retract its landing flaps, and the couple earned 3,188 frequent flier miles.[62]

In 1987 and 1988 the problem of mileage maniacs grew to epidemic proportions for the airlines. The junkie mentioned earlier earned 214,842 miles in 1988 but flew only 50,551 miles. The mileage maniacs develop great skill in figuring out how to find every loophole in the programs to maximize their return. By going for triple mileage, breaking trips up into lots of short hops, and using certain credit cards, an expert can extract tens of thousands of extra miles in a year. One lawyer and her husband had six credit cards, each of which netted a free mile for each dollar spent. When they applied for another card and were rejected, they still received 2,500 free miles. Her husband described her as addicted. "It's like drugs; you first start small and it gets bigger." Another traveler said, "It's no fun to get on an airplane anymore. These programs have become an outlet for a little excitement. It's like being a Boy Scout and collecting badges."[63]

Some of the frequent-flier junkies cheat. They enlist people to ride airlines under their names. Many sell their frequent-flier awards to coupon brokers. In 1986 frequent fliers sold $75 million in awards to brokers. How to deal with such cheaters, who flaunt the rules and ultimately drive up costs for everyone, is a major problem for airlines.[64] Indeed, an even larger problem concerned how to deal with the potential revenue loss resulting from all the free miles racked up by passengers. In the early 1990s the estimated total cost of the free miles approached $940 million.[65]

Problem Definition

The problem of airline executives can be stated succinctly. How can they gain control over the misuse of frequent flyer programs by consumers?

The Consumer Analysis

Several concepts from motivation apply to the problems of the airline industry, including (1) affective processes, (2) optimum-stimulation-level theory, (3) reactance, and (4) perceived risk. When applying concepts from the study of affect, the analyst should ask what kinds of feelings may be elicited from the experience. Certainly, the frequent-flier junkie may experience feelings of interest, surprise, joy, and occasionally fear. The manager attempting to control those who misuse such programs should ask how the experience for these people can be made less affectively positive. Some companies force their executives to return frequent-flier miles to the company. The airlines are beginning to sue those who cheat. Of course, the problem concerns how to discourage the junkies without turning off regular passengers.

Consumers may participate in the programs in part as a means of increasing their stimulation levels. The excitement and energy obtained from traveling make it difficult to wean people from the program. Further, because of people's commitment, it is likely that if the programs were withdrawn suddenly, consumers would feel their behavioral freedom to be threatened. If airlines decide to end the programs suddenly, strong and angry reactions can be expected.

Certain ideas concerning perceived risk have implications for controlling cheaters. It seems clear that early in the program the airlines should have taken steps to lower the outcomes for cheaters and decrease the probability of successfully cheating. Changing either the outcome or probability element of the perceived risk equation could increase the perception of risk.

The Managerial Applications Analysis

Table 6-7 presents the managerial applications analysis of the frequent-flier case. It is important to recognize that the frequent-flier program is a type of sales promotion technique. Thus each of the consumer concepts applies to promotional strategy

TABLE 6-7

The Managerial Applications Analysis of the Frequent-Flier Case

Consumer Concept	*Managerial Implications*
Affect	*Market research*—Investigate the emotions and feelings that consumers obtain from the program.
	Promotional strategy—Consider how changes in the program will influence consumer feelings.
Reactance theory	*Promotional strategy*—Recognize that eliminating the program will likely threaten consumers' behavioral freedom and lead to strong negative reactions.
Optimum stimulation level	*Market research*—Conduct research to determine the characteristics of consumers who show evidence of accumulating frequent flyer miles through illegitimate means.
	Segmentation—Use market research information to identify segments of consumers for special attention to minimize the chances of cheating on the program.
Perceived risk	*Promotional strategy*—Identify alternative approaches of implementing frequent-flyer programs that increase the likelihood of getting caught or the severity of penalties for being caught if consumers misuse the program.
	Market research—Conduct market research to identify which of the strategies are most likely to be effective without irritating customers.

within the marketing mix. Because consumers obtain a variety of types of affect from the program, marketing researchers should be concerned about measuring the feelings and emotions that consumers obtain from the program.

Managers must be concerned that any changes in the program to reduce cheating do not also create negative reactions to the program as a whole. Indeed, reactance theory suggests that if the program were discontinued, consumers would react strongly to their loss of behavioral freedom. Market research must be employed to identify how changes in the program could be implemented that would result in the least amount of reactance and negative affect among consumers. Perhaps replacing the program with one large sweepstakes would be an alternative. Another alternative might be to slowly make it more difficult for passengers to use their frequent-flier miles. If adopted in small enough increments, the changes might stay within the just noticeable difference of consumers, and negative reactions would be minimized.

Optimum-stimulation-level theory suggests that some segments of consumers participate in the program to increase their arousal to optimum levels. Market research could be performed to identify the characteristics of such individuals. Such information could be used as a screening device to determine which passengers to investigate for possible cheating.

The consumer concept of perceived risk has implications for market research and the marketing mix. To reduce cheating, airlines must increase the perceived risk of cheating. This could be accomplished by changing passengers' perception of the likelihood of getting caught and of the resulting penalties. Market research would be conducted to predict passengers' reactions to changes in the program that would affect the likelihood of being caught and the severity of punishment. Based upon the market research, changes in the program would then be implemented.

In sum, concepts from motivation suggest that the entire frequent-flier sales promotion strategy may have problems. Its potent motivational impact on consumers sometimes drives them to the point of cheating. But because consumers have come to expect frequent-flier premiums, it is a practice that would be difficult to abandon. Further, by its very nature the program influences other elements of the mix, such as pricing. Indeed, to end the frequent-flier program, it may be necessary to replace it with another sales promotion strategy, such as a sweepstakes. A second approach might be to slowly phase out the program in increments so small that consumers would fail to notice the subtle changes.

SUMMARY

Motivation refers to an activated state within a person that leads to goal-directed behavior. In the model of motivation, a stimulus creates a gap between a desired and an actual state. When such a gap exists, a need state is recognized that leads to a drive state and goal-directed behavior. The goal-directed behavior is focused on obtaining incentive objects that are perceived to move the actual state closer to the desired state. In a consumer behavior context, marketers hope to create products that fulfill the needs initiating the goal-directed behavior.

Accompanying a motivated state are various feelings and emotions. These affective states are characterized by consciously experienced internal sensations, which include feelings of anger, distress, fear, interest, joy, and surprise. In consumer settings the various feelings have been found to be represented by a positive dimension and a negative dimension. As a result, the same situation can cause both positive and negative feelings to occur simultaneously.

A number of general theories of motivation exist, such as McClelland's theory of learned needs. McClelland's theory suggests that different people have divergent needs for achievement, affiliation, and power.

The midrange theories of motivation discussed in this chapter include opponent-process theory, optimum-stimulation-level theory, motivation for hedonic experiences, the desire to maintain behavioral freedom, the motivation to avoid risk, and the motivation to attribute causality. The core concept forming the basis of opponent-process theory is that whenever a person receives a positive or negative stimulus, two processes are activated in a sequential manner. First, the process having the same affective content as the stimulus is elicited. Thus, if the stimulus is positive, initial feelings are positive. Shortly after the initiation of the primary response, however, a second opposing response begins to occur. The overall feeling that results is the sum of the two processes. Opponent-process theory can explain a wide variety of consumer actions, ranging from participation in daredevil sports (e.g., hang gliding) to taking drugs.

The research on maintaining optimum stimulation levels has found that people take action to raise or lower their input of stimulation to maintain their desired levels. Thus consumers may seek out amusement parks to raise their level of activation or consume alcohol to lower their activation.

Some researchers argue that consumers have a need to experience fantasies, feelings, and emotional arousal. The study of these needs represents the core of the experiential perspective on consumption. This need for hedonic experiences may well be an extension of the need to maintain an optimum stimulation level. One of the research findings is that consumers will in certain instances allow hedonic or emotional desires to dominate utilitarian motives in choosing products. Researchers tend to focus on different types of products and services when the emphasis is on the experiential side of consumer behavior. Rather than investigating the buying of consumer durables and package goods, the focus tends to be on such services as rock concerts, dancing, sporting events, and symbolic goods, such as automobiles and jewelry.

Another midrange theory of interest to consumer researchers is reactance theory. Reactance theory states that consumers have a need to maintain their behavioral freedom. When this behavioral freedom is threatened, they react in a manner necessary to restore it. Companies can act to threaten a consumer's behavioral freedom in a variety of ways, such as by having salespeople push customers too hard or by suddenly withdrawing a product from the marketplace, as in the case of Coca-Cola. When consumers feel their freedom threatened, they take actions, such as refusing to buy a product from a pushy salesperson or filing lawsuits to have a product placed back on the market.

Although consumers will sometimes engage in high-risk activities, they generally seek to avoid risk. Researchers have identified a variety of consumer risks, such as financial, performance, and social risk. Two components of risk have been identified—the likelihood of a loss occurring and the amount of possible loss. Overall risk is assessed by combining these two perceptions. A number of factors influence the perception of risk, including the situation, the characteristics of the individual, and the nature of the product.

The last midrange theory discussed was attribution theory. According to attribution theory, people attempt to identify why various things occur to have an understanding of the environment and of the actions of themselves and others. The fundamental attribution error states that people have a general tendency to attribute the cause of a person's actions to his or her personality and disposition. Marketers and consumer researchers should be concerned with identifying the attributions that consumers make in various situations. In particular, it is important to identify the attributions consumers make toward the actions of product endorsers and sales personnel. If consumers believe that these corporate representatives are giving information merely to sell the product rather than to help and assist the consumer, it is likely that consumers will place little trust in the statements of such people.

KEY TERMS

achievement motivation
affect
attribution theory
augmenting principle
consumer incentives
discounting principle
drive
expressive needs
external attribution
fundamental attribution error
goal-directed behavior
hedonic consumption
hedonism
impersonal threats
incentives
internal attribution
intrinsic satisfaction
motivation
need for affiliation
need for power
needs
opponent-process theory
optimum stimulation level
perceived freedom
priming
psychological reactance
social threats
utilitarian needs

REVIEW QUESTIONS

1. Define the concept of motivation. Draw the model of motivation presented in Figure 6-1 and indicate how needs, drives, and goal-directed action interrelate.
2. Identify the seven needs identified by Maslow.
3. Identify the three needs identified by McClelland.
4. Discuss how the opponent-process theory of acquired motivation can explain why someone becomes elated after making a parachute jump.
5. Define the concept of priming. How can it be used by retailers to increase sales?
6. Define the concept of optimum stimulation level. How can the desire to maintain optimum stimulation levels lead consumers to purchase products or engage in specific types of leisure activities?
7. What is meant by the term hedonic consumption? What types of products and services tend to fall into the hedonic consumption category?
8. Name four reasons why people engage in nonwork leisure other than the desire to maintain optimum stimulation levels.
9. Define the concept of reactance. What factors can lead consumers to engage in reactance?
10. Define the concept of perceived risk. Identify five of the seven types of risk to which consumers may respond.
11. Identify five of the six ways discussed in the text through which consumers may act to reduce risk.
12. What occurs when a consumer makes an attribution? Why are people motivated to make attributions?

13. Discuss what is meant by the augmenting and discounting principles.
14. A number of managerial strategies have been identified to lower consumer perceptions of risk. Identify six of these possible strategies.
15. Define the concept of affect. Does advertising influence consumers' affective states?

DISCUSSION QUESTIONS

1. Following are a number of slogans that have been used by corporations. Indicate which of the needs identified by motivational theorists each slogan best represents.
   - a. "Be all that you can be" (U.S. Army).
   - b. "Join the Pepsi generation" (Pepsi-Cola).
   - c. "For all you do, this Bud's for you" (Budweiser).
   - d. "Get a piece of the rock" (Prudential).
   - e. "All my men wear English Leather, every one of them" (English Leather).
   - f. "We have one and only one ambition. To be the best. What else is there?" (Lee Iacocca for Chrysler).
2. You are on an advertising team assembled to develop a campaign for a new running shoe. Develop three slogans that could be used in an advertising campaign. Each slogan should illustrate one of the needs identified by McClelland.
3. Priming may be a potent method of encouraging consumers to purchase large amounts of a product. How could the following types of companies make use of priming: a sausage company, a movie distribution company, and an auto dealership?
4. Consider your own leisure activities. Which of your activities do you engage in to increase your level of activation?
5. You are marketing director for a company that makes camping equipment. Develop the copy for a print advertisement for a backpack. In the advertisement, utilize three of the five reasons identified for people's desire to engage in nonwork activities.
6. Reactance can often cause problems for companies in their personal-selling efforts. However, under some circumstances reactance may be beneficial to companies. Try to identify one or more of these instances.
7. Mail-order companies face a major problem because consumers perceive greater risk in purchasing from them. What are some steps that mail-order companies can take to reduce the perceived risk among consumers?
8. What are some steps advertisers can take to convince consumers to attribute internal rather than external motivations to endorsers of products?
9. Make a list of your own leisure activities. What are the reasons you engage in each of these activities? Compare these to the reasons for people engaging in nonwork activities identified in the text.
10. Identify in specific terms two ads that have caused you to experience positive affect and negative affect.

ENDNOTES

1. Peter Kerr, "Crack Addiction Spreads Among the Middle Class," *The New York Times*, June 8, 1986, pp. 1, 42.
2. Richard L. Celsi, "Transcendent Benefits of High-Risk Sports," in *Advances in Consumer Research*, Vol. 19, John F. Sherry, Jr., and Brian Sternthal, eds. (Provo, UT: Association for Consumer Research, 1992), pp. 636–641. Also, see Richard L. Celsi, Randall L. Rose, and Thomas W. Leigh, "An Exploration of

High-Risk Leisure Consumption Through Skydiving," *Journal of Consumer Research*, Vol. 20 (June 1993), pp. 1–23.

3. Jaclyn Fierman, "The Best of Their Class," *Fortune*, October 12, 1987, pp. 144–145.
4. Kerr, "Crack Addiction." For a detailed discussion of the "consciousness of addiction," see "Elizabeth C. Hirschman, "The Consciousness of Addiction: Toward a General Theory of Compulsive Consumption," *Journal of Consumer Research*, Vol. 19 (September 1992), pp. 155–179.
5. Marj Charlier, "In Name of Fitness, Many Americans Grow Addicted to Exercise," *The Wall Street Journal*, October 1, 1987, pp. 1, 20.
6. Celsi, Rose, and Leight, "An Exploration of High-Risk Leisure Consumption Through Skydiving."
7. Fierman, "The Best of Their Class."
8. Ernest Hilgard, Richard Atkinson, and Rita Atkinson, *Introduction to Psychology*, 6th ed. (New York: Harcourt Brace Jovanovich, 1975).
9. James A. Bayton, "Motivation, Cognition, Learning—Basic Factors in Consumer Behavior," *Journal of Marketing*, Vol. 22 (January 1958), pp. 282–289.
10. Robert A. Westbrook,"Product/Consumption-Based Affective Responses and Postpurchase Processes," *Journal of Marketing Research*, Vol. 24 (August 1987), pp. 258–270.
11. Meryl Gardner, "Effects of Mood States on Consumer Information Processing," *Research in Consumer Behavior*, Vol. 2 (1987), pp. 113–135.
12. Deborah J. MacInnis and Bernard J. Jaworski, "Information Processing from Advertisements: Toward an Integrative Framework," *Journal of Marketing*, Vol. 53 (October 1989), pp. 1–23.
13. Carroll E. Izard, *Human Emotion* (New York: Plenum Press, 1977).
14. Ibid.
15. Robert A. Westbrook and Richard L. Oliver, "The Dimensionality of Consumption Emotion Patterns and Consumer Satisfaction," *Journal of Consumer Research*, Vol. 18 (June 1991), pp. 84–91.
16. Deborah MacInnis and Robert Westbrook, "The Relationship Between Executional Cues and Emotional Response to Advertising," Working Paper, Series 27, Department of Marketing, University of Arizona, Tucson, Arizona, October 1987. More recently, researchers have found that consumer emotions are related to consumer values and the self-concept. In particular, emotions are related to what the authors called the "hedonic self," the "private self," and the "public self." See Debra A. Laverie, Robert E. Kleine, and Susan Schultz Kleine, "Linking Emotions and Values in Consumption Experience: An Exploratory Study," in *Advances in Consumer Research*, Vol. 20, Leigh McAlister and Michael L. Rothschild, eds. (Provo, UT: Association for Consumer Research, 1993), pp. 70–75.
17. Chris Allen, Karen Machleit, and Susan Marine, "On Assessing the Emotionality of Advertising via Izard's Differential Emotions Scale," in *Advances in Consumer Research*, Vol. 15, Michael Houston, ed. (Provo, UT: Association for Consumer Research, 1988).
18. For an empirical study on the impact of advertisements on affect and decision making, see Haim Mano, "Emotional States and Decision Making," in *Advances in Consumer Research*, Vol. 17, Marvin Goldberg et al., eds. (Provo, UT: Association for Consumer Research, 1990), pp. 577–584.
19. See Julie Edell and Marian Burke, "The Power of Feelings in Understanding Advertising Effects," *Journal of Consumer Research*, Vol. 14 (December 1987), pp. 421–433. Also see Westbrook, "Product/Consumption-Based Affective Responses."
20. Meryl Gardner, "Effects of Mood States on Consumer Information Processing," *Research in Consumer Behavior*, Vol. 2 (1987), pp. 113–135.
21. Hilgard et al., *Introduction to Psychology*.
22. David McClelland, "Achievement and Entrepreneurship: A Longitudinal Study,"

Journal of Personality and Social Psychology, April 1965, pp. 1, 389–392.

23. E. H. French, "Effects of the Interaction of Motivation and Feedback on Test Performance," in *Motives in Fantasy, Action, and Society*, J. W. Atkinson, ed. (New York: Litton Educational Publishing, 1958).
24. David H. Gardner, "An Exploratory Investigation of Achievement Motivation Effects on Consumer Behavior," Association for Consumer Research, 1972 Proceedings of Third Annual Conference, pp. 20–23.
25. Richard L. Solomon, "The Opponent-Process Theory of Acquired Motivation," *American Psychologist*, Vol. 35 (August 1980), pp. 691–712.
26. Peter DePaulo, "The Opposite of Satiation: Motivational Priming as an Aftereffect of a Pleasurable Consumption Experience," in *Advances in Consumer Research*, Vol. XIII, Richard Lutz, ed. (Ann Arbor, MI: Association for Consumer Research, 1986), pp. 192–197.
27. Sandon A. Steinberg and Richard F. Yalch, "When Eating Begets Buying: The Effects of Food Samples on Obese and Nonobese Shoppers," *Journal of Consumer Research*, Vol. 4 (March 1978), pp. 243–246.
28. Jan-Benedict E. M. Steenkamp and Hans Baumgartner, "The Role of Optimum Stimulation Level in Exploratory Consumer Behavior," *The Journal of Consumer Research*, Vol. 19 (December 1992), pp. 434–448. Also, see Michael Driver and Siegfried Streufert, "The General Incongruity Adaption Level (GIAL) Hypothesis," Paper No. 114, Institute for Research in the Behavioral, Economic, and Managerial Sciences, Krannert Graduate School of Management, Purdue University, West Lafayette, Indiana.
29. Marvin Zuckerman, *Sensation Seeking: Beyond the Optimum Level of Arousal* (Hillsdale, NJ: Lawrence Erlbaum, 1979).
30. P. S. Raju, "Optimum Stimulation Level: Its Relationship to Personality, Demographics, and Exploratory Behavior," *Journal of Consumer Research*, Vol. 7 (December 1980), pp. 272–282.
31. Steenkamp and Baumgartner, "The Role of Optimum Stimulation Level in Exploratory Consumer Behavior."
32. Morris Holbrook and Elizabeth Hirschman, "The Experiential Aspects of Consumption: Consumer Fantasies, Feelings, and Fun," *Journal of Consumer Research*, Vol. 9 (September 1982), pp. 132–140.
33. Elizabeth Hirschman and Morris Holbrook, "Hedonic Consumption: Emerging Concepts, Methods, and Propositions," *Journal of Marketing*, Vol. 46 (Summer 1982), pp. 92–101.
34. Suzana de M. Fontenella and George M. Zinkhan, "Gender Differences in the Perception of Leisure: A Conceptual Model," in *Advances in Consumer Research*, Vol. 20, Leigh McAlister and Michael L. Rothschild, eds. (Provo, UT: Association for Consumer Research, 1992), pp. 534–540. Also, see Lynette S. Unger and Jerome B. Kernan, "On the Meaning of Leisure: An Investigation of Some Determinants of the Subjective Experience," *Journal of Consumer Research*, Vol. 9 (March 1983), pp. 381–392.
35. Seppo Iso-Ahola, *The Social Psychology of Leisure and Recreation* (Dubuque, IA: William C. Brown, 1980).
36. Douglass K. Howes, "Time Budgets and Consumer Leisure-Time Behavior," in *Advances in Consumer Research*, Vol. IV, William Perreault, ed. (Ann Arbor, MI: Association for Consumer Research, 1977), pp. 221–229.
37. Philip Hendrix, Thomas Kinnear, and James Taylor, "The Allocation of Time by Consumers," in *Advances in Consumer Research*, Vol. V, William Wilkie, ed. (Ann Arbor, MI: Association for Consumer Research, 1979), pp. 38–44.
38. Jack W. Brehm, *A Theory of Psychological Reactance* (New York: Academic Press, 1966). For a review of consumer research on reactance, see Greg Lessne and M. Venkatesan, "Reactance Theory in Consumer Research: The Past, Present, and Future," in *Advances in Consumer Research*, Vol. 16, Thomas K. Srull,

ed. (Provo, UT: Association for Consumer Research, 1989), pp. 76–78.

39. Virginia Daut, "Roses Were Reds, Violets Blues, Till They Redid Crayola's Hues," *The Wall Street Journal*, September 11, 1990, p. B1.

40. Suein L. Hwang, "Hue and Cry Over Crayola May Revive Old Colors," *The Wall Street Journal*, June 14, 1991, p. B1.

41. Michael B. Mazis, Robert Settle, and Dennis Lislie, "Elimination of Phosphate Detergents and Psychological Reactance," *Journal of Marketing Research*, Vol. 10 (November 1973), pp. 390–395.

42. Greg J. Lessne, "The Impact of Advertised Sale Duration on Consumer Perceptions," in *Development of Marketing Science*, Vol. 10, J. M. Hawes, ed. (Atlanta: Academy of Marketing Science, 1987), pp. 115–117.

43. Carrie Dolan, "Well, Would You Expect 475 Horses to Sell for Peanuts?" *The Wall Street Journal*, February 15, 1990, p. 1.

44. Darwyn Linder and Katherine Crane, "Reactance Theory Analysis of Predecisional Cognitive Processes," *Journal of Personality and Social Psychology*, Vol. 15 (July 1970), pp. 258–264.

45. Mona Clee and Robert Wicklund, "Consumer Behavior and Psychological Reactance," *Journal of Consumer Research*, Vol. 6 (March 1980), pp. 389–405.

46. Marcy Magiera, "Avia Ads Say Shoo to Non-Athletes," *Advertising Age*, August 22, 1988, p. 4.

47. G. R. Dowling, "Perceived Risk: The Concept and Its Measurement," *Psychology and Marketing*, Vol. 3 (Fall 1986), pp. 193–210. For another discussion of problems in defining the concept, see James Bettman, "Information Integration in Consumer Risk Perception: A Comparison of Two Models of Component Conceptualization," *Journal of Applied Psychology*, Vol. 60 (1975), pp. 381–385.

48. Raymond A. Bauer, "Consumer Behavior as Risk Taking," in *Dynamic Marketing for a Changing World*, Robert S. Hancock, ed. (Chicago: American Marketing Association, 1960), p. 87.

49. The first five risks in Table 6-4 were identified by Jacob Jacoby and Leon Kaplan, "The Components of Perceived Risk," in *Advances in Consumer Research*, Vol. 3, M. Venkatesan, ed. (Chicago: Association for Consumer Research, 1972), pp. 382–383. "Social risk" was identified by J. Paul Peter and Michael Ryan, "An Investigation of Perceived Risk at the Brand Level," *Journal of Marketing Research*, Vol. 13 (May 1976), pp. 184–188. "Opportunity cost" was identified by William Zikmund and Jerome Scott, "A Factor Analysis of the Multi-dimensional Nature of Perceived Risk," Proceedings of the Southern Marketing Association, Houston, Texas, 1973, p. 1036.

50. Thomas Pettigrew, "The Measurement and Correlates of Category Width as a Cognitive Variable," *Journal of Personality*, Vol. 26 (December 1968), p. 532.

51. Baruch Fischhoff, Paul Slovic, and Sarah Lichtenstein, "Which Risks Are Acceptable?" *Environment*, Vol. 21 (January 1979), pp. 17–38.

52. Homer Spence, James Engel, and Roger Blackwell, "Perceived Risk in Mail-Order and Retail Store Buying," *Journal of Marketing Research*, Vol. 7 (August 1970), pp. 364–369.

53. Valerie S. Folkes, "The Availability Heuristic and Perceived Risk," *Journal of Consumer Research*, Vol. 15 (June 1988), pp. 13–23.

54. Donald Popielarz, "An Exploration of Perceived Risk and Willingness to Try New Products," *Journal of Marketing Research* (November 1967), pp. 368–372.

55. Richard L. Celsi, Randall L. Rose, and Thomas W. Leigh, "An Exploration of High-Risk Leisure Consumption Through Skydiving"; this discussion may be found on page 11.

56. For a general review of the attribution process in consumer behavior, see Valerie Folkes, "Recent Attribution Research in Consumer Behavior: A Review and New Directions," *Journal of Consumer Research*, Vol. 14 (March 1988), pp. 548–565.

57. Harold H. Kelley, "The Process of Causal Attribution," *American Psychologist*, Vol. 28 (February 1973), pp. 107–128.

58. Nancy Millman, "Product Claims Not Believable," *Advertising Age*, March 15, 1984, pp. 1, 32.

59. Lee Ross, "The Intuitive Psychologist and His Shortcomings: Distortion in the Attribution Process," in *Advances in Experimental Social Psychology*, Vol. 10 (New York: Academic Press, 1977).

60. Robert Baer, "Overestimating Salesperson Truthfulness: The Fundamental Attribution Error," in *Advances in Consumer Research*, Vol. 17, Marvin Goldberg et al., eds. (Provo, UT: Association for Consumer Research, 1990), pp. 501–507.

61. Carol Scott, "The Effects of Trial Incentives on Repeat Purchase Behavior," *Journal of Marketing Research*, Vol. 4, no. 13 (August 1976), pp. 263–269.

62. Robert Rose, "Frequent-Flier Plans Become Obsessions," *The Wall Street Journal*, September 9, 1988, p. 29.

63. Michael Manges, "Frequent-Flier Awards Tougher to Sell as Airlines Tighten Rules, Press Brokers," *The Wall Street Journal*, September 9, 1988, p. 29.

64. Robert Rose, "There's Still Time to Triple Miles," *The Wall Street Journal*, September 9, 1988, p. 29.

65. Peter Nulty, "Why Do We Travel So *!?*! Much?" *Fortune*, March 28, 1988, pp. 83–88.

CHAPTER 6 CASE STUDY

"In-Your-Face Advertising"

Furious, the clothing saleswoman stated, "It's an invasion of our privacy. It's dangerous. It's annoying. I have made a concentrated effort to boycott any products advertised here." Another woman said, "It's so unnecessary. Anyone who would advertise in doctors' waiting rooms is an immediate turnoff. I resent it" [1].

What raised the anger of these working women? The answer—captive advertising. Found in movie theaters, doctors' offices, airports, health clubs, and a growing number of other locations, captive advertising barrages consumers with advertising messages while they are engaged in another activity, such as waiting or exercising. A marketing professor said, "People are going to become more and more violent in their reactions and in terms of trying to avoid such gimmicks" [2].

Disparagingly called "in-your-face advertising," the use of captive advertising is growing rapidly. One company, called Health Television Network, supplies programming for health clubs. The programming consists of shows on exercising and health but also consists of about 30% advertising. Similarly, Turner Broadcasting has launched the "Airport Channel." Another company has a "checkout channel" for supermarkets.

Members of the Vertical Club, a health club for the well-to-do, launched a petition against the advertising. It was sent to companies that advertised on the Health Television Network. Calling the advertising the equivalent of a "commercial police state," the petitioners also attacked the company through press releases. A spokesperson for Dannon Co., which advertises on the network, said, "Obviously, we aren't reaching someone if they're annoyed by the message" [3]. A manager at Playtex Inc. called a leader of the group to assure him that the company would pull its ads.

Some companies have long had a policy of not associating their company with captive advertising. For example, Walt Disney Productions has a general policy of not allowing movie theaters to show advertisements for products or services prior to its movies.

Meanwhile, executives at Health Club Television played down the petition. One manager said that the petitioners are a bunch of rich malcontents and that they represent a minority at the club. According to this spokesperson, marketing research indicates that over 80% of people like Health Club Television.

QUESTIONS

1. Define the problem from the perspectives of Health Club Television, from the health club itself, and from the advertising company.
2. What consumer behavior concepts from Chapter 5, on motivation and affect, apply?
3. What are the managerial implications of the consumer behavior concepts for each of the entities involved? Draw a managerial applications table to show the relationship between the consumer concepts and the managerial strategy implications.
4. What are the ethical implications, if any, of "in-your-face" advertising?

REFERENCES

1. Joanne Lipman, "Consumers Rebel Against Becoming a Captive Audience," *The Wall Street Journal*, September 13, 1991, pp. B1, B8.
2. Ibid.
3. Ibid.

Chapter 7

Personality and Psychographics

CONSUMER VIGNETTE

Fantasy, Symbols, and the Self-concept

In 1980 slightly over 100 million credit cards were owned by consumers in the United States. Estimates are that by 1995 almost 350 million credit cards will be in the hands of consumers. How can such an increase be explained?[1] One psychologist argued that owning a card enhances a person's self-esteem. "The great modern nightmare is discovering that you're unrecognized, a nobody. With that card you can be surrounded by strangers, but you walk up and say, "Look what I've got in my hand."[2] In its "Do You Know Me" campaign, American Express Corporation used this need to propel the company into a leader in the credit card industry.

Researchers at the McCann–Erickson ad agency were bewildered. Why weren't low-income women from the South responding positively to a new roach killer in a tray, which they believed was more effective and less messy than traditional products? Psychologists at the agency performed depth interviews and asked the women to draw roaches. The women portrayed the roaches as male scavengers. One woman wrote, "A man likes a free meal you cook for him; as long as there is food he will stay." Paula Drillman, the director of strategic planning at the ad agency, said, "Killing the roaches with a bug spray and watching them squirm and die allowed the women to express their hostility toward men and have greater control over the roaches."[3]

Charles Revson described the cosmetics industry as "hope in a bottle." The fantasy of looking younger that is held by millions of consumers has been aided and abetted by a plethora of new products and treatments that claim to cure baldness, remove wrinkles, and eliminate unwanted fat. Indeed, one prescription product, Minoxidil, actually grows vellus, a fine colorless fuzz, on the heads of about one-third of those who use it. Of course, Minoxidil is extremely costly and must be used continuously or the hair will disappear.

In addition to hair restorers and "miracle" skin lotions, consumers can fulfill their fantasies of youth through plastic surgeons. One technique, called liposuction, can be used to suck the fat out of just about any body part—from eyelids to thighs. One woman lamented, "I couldn't even use eyeshadow or wear Guess jeans." The five-foot, five-inch, 126-pound woman had fat sucked from her eyelids, stomach, hips, inner thighs, and knees. Her husband now calls her the $10,000 woman. (By the way, the procedure can be dangerous, and disfigurement or death may occur.)[4]

Code named "Project Virile Female," a new cigarette project was launched by RJR Nabisco, Inc., in early 1990. With cigarette smoking decreasing among the well-to-do and the higher educated, the company decided to target a distinct group of women—called virile females.

The company employed psychographic analysis to identify the characteristics of this target market. One marketing research firm described virile females along the following lines:

> She is a "white 18–24-year-old female. She has only a high school degree and work is a job, not a career. Her free time is spent with her boyfriend, doing whatever he is doing. That includes going to tough-man competitions, tractor pulls, hot rod shows, and cruising. She watches lots of television, entertainment she can afford, in particular—Roseanne. One of her chief aspirations is to have an ongoing relationship with a man."[5]

These brief vignettes illustrate how the enhancement of the self-concept, the interpretation of symbols, the importance of fantasy, and the use of psychographic analysis can be used by marketers. Each of these areas is related to the study of personality and psychographics, the topic of discussion in this chapter.

INTRODUCTION

The study of personality and psychographics involves the analysis of how the patterns of behavior of one individual differ from another. Indeed, when a person is described as having a personality, the connotation is that the person acts in ways that differentiate him or her from others. For consumer researchers the goal is to identify individual difference variables that distinguish large groups of people from each other. Such personality variables apply most directly to the development of promotional strategy. By developing an understanding of the underlying personality and psychographic characteristics of target markets, more effective advertising campaigns can be created.

The consumer vignette introduces several concepts directly related to the study of personality and psychographics. First, central to the understanding of a person's personality is analyzing that individual's self-concept. People have a strong need to act consistently with who and what they think they are.[6] In addition, they purchase products and services to build their self-image and to express themselves to others. The American Express credit card campaign played on these consumer needs by revealing how use of the card leads to feelings of confidence—feelings that result, in part, because people experience through vicarious learning the feelings portrayed by the attractive models in the ads.

Building customers' self-esteem is an important marketing tactic. Figure 7-1 shows a direct mail advertisement that I received from *Advertising Age*. With the certificate, I could save $40 on a subscription to the trade publication. To bolster my ego, and those of thousands of other recipients of the sales promotion, a cartoon was printed on the certificate. In the cartoon, a manager says, "We need someone with vision, creativity, and great marketing instinct someone like John Mowen." Of course, I saw through this blatant attempt to flatter my ego. I know that each recipient of the ad had his or her name printed in the cartoon. I should add, however, that I continue to subscribe to this terrific trade publication.

Figure 7-1 The direct mail sales promotion sought to bolster John Mowen's self-concept. (Courtesy *Advertising Age*.)

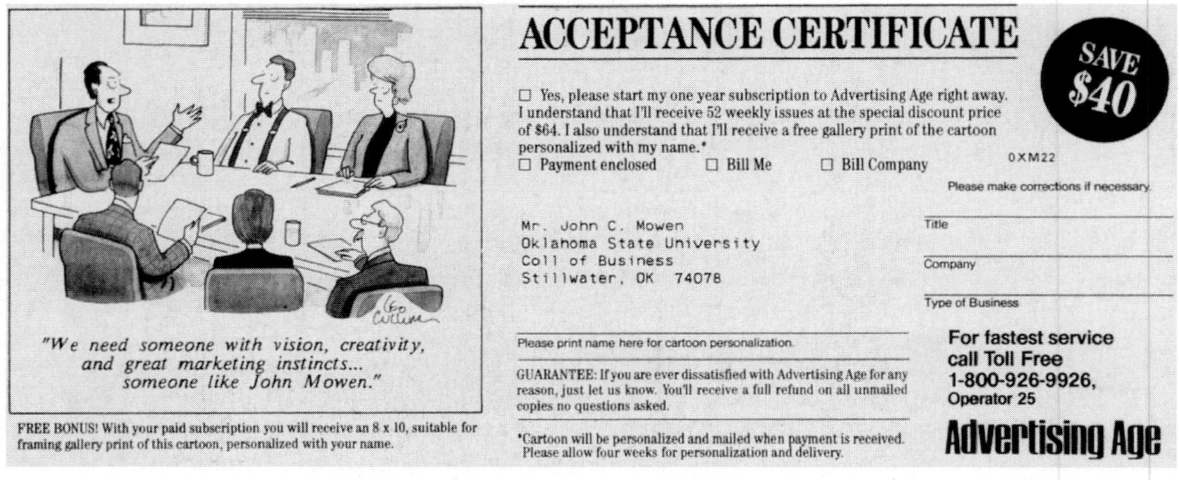

The chapter-opening vignette discussed how the ad agency used depth interviews to analyze consumer reactions to cockroaches. This approach is based upon ideas from psychotherapy. When conducting psychotherapy, psychologists analyze the symbolic content of their client's dreams, drawings, and verbal statements. By using depth interviews and by discovering that the women drew the cockroaches as men, the agency was able to understand better how to design ads that would appeal to its target market.

Also related to personality is the study of fantasy. Practiced predominantly by researchers having psychoanalytic training, the investigation of consumer fantasies may give insights into the reasons behind buying behavior. Thus the fantasy of making a 40-year-old body look like a 20-year-old body may drive women and men to plastic surgeons. By understanding the fantasies, hopes, and wishes of market segments, managers can better design advertising campaigns and product offerings.

Closely related to the study of personality is psychographic analysis. Through psychographic analysis, market researchers attempt to measure the life-styles of consumers. The marketing of Dakota cigarettes was based upon the identification of a psychographic profile of a target market called virile females. The strategy backfired for RJR Nabisco, however, when critics discovered the plan. As stated by one antismoking lobbyist, Dakota advertising "represents an effort through false image-based advertising to lure young, healthy women to smoke."[7]

Figure 7-2 shows a photo of the Eagle Vision, one of Chrysler Corporation's new and successful autos. According to a *New York Times* article, the psychographic

Figure 7-2 Chrysler has targeted the Eagle Vision to a younger, but upscale, psychographic segment of the marketplace.

profile of its target market is a young couple with two children under 10 years old. Highly educated and possessing high incomes, the couple dislikes television but enjoys jazz music, works out twice a week, collects Art Deco objects, and takes three vacations a year.[8]

Managerially, psychographic analysis can be used to develop promotional strategy. That is, by understanding the life-styles of specific target markets, managers can tailor the themes of advertisements and sales messages to appeal to the consumers that compose the targeted groups. In effect, the groupings of consumers who reveal similar psychographic/life-style characteristics become market segments. Thus young women who shared the life-style patterns identified by market researchers at RJR Nabisco (i.e., young, high school–educated females looking for a man) became a market segment that was targeted by the firm for its new brand of cigarettes. The individuals in this group fit all the criteria for a market segment. That is, they can be reached, they have buying power, they exist in large numbers, and they share similar needs and wants.

This chapter begins with an introduction to the study of personality, focusing on the theories most frequently used by consumer researchers. It then discusses the self-concept and how it can influence buying behavior. The chapter then analyzes psychographics—an area that attempts to assess the life-styles of consumers—and concludes with the managerial applications example.

PERSONALITY AND CONSUMER BEHAVIOR

The word "personality" comes from the Latin term *persona*, which means "actor's face mask." In a sense, one's personality is the "mask" worn as a person moves from situation to situation during a lifetime. Over the years many different definitions of personality have been proposed by psychologists. One of the best from the consumer researcher's point of view states that "**Personality** is the distinctive patterns of behavior, including thoughts and emotions, that characterize each individual's adaptation to the situations of his or her life."[9]

At a general level, the concept of personality has a number of characteristics. First, to be called a personality, a person's behavior should show some degree of consistency—that is, the behaviors must show a consistency that distinguishes them from a person's random responses to different stimuli. Personality characteristics are relatively stable across time rather than short-term in nature.

Second, the behaviors should distinguish the person from others. Thus, in the definition of personality just presented, the phrase "distinctive patterns of behavior" connotes the idea that a personality characteristic cannot be shared by all consumers.

A third characteristic of personality is that it interacts with the situation. As will be discussed further in Chapter 14 on situational influences, consumer situations refer to those temporary environmental factors that form context in which a consumer activity occurs. One type of situation is the social context in which purchases occur. Researchers have found that consumers act differently depending upon whether or not other people are observing their purchase behavior. This situational variable may interact with a personality characteristic that distinguishes people on their tendency to conform to social pressures when making purchases. A scale, called the ATSCI (attention to social comparison interaction), has been developed to measure this disposition to conform to others.[10]

Figure 7-3 shows how the situational context may interact with this tendency to conform to others to influence purchase behavior In most circumstances people will go shopping with plans to make certain purchases. Could the social situation interact with the tendency to conform to others so as to impact the extent that the consumer *fails* to make the intended purchases? As shown in Figure 7-3, one can predict that a person who has a *low tendency to conform* will tend to make her desired purchases whether or not she shops alone or with a group In contrast, a person with a *high tendency to conform* will make many more changes in purchase plans when shopping with a group than when shopping alone.

A fourth aspect of the study of personality is that it cannot be expected to accurately predict an individual's behavior on one specific occasion from a single measure of personality.[11] Personality characteristics are not rigidly connected to specific types of behavior. Thus one cannot predict how many cans of peas a person will buy or the type of furniture a person will own by looking at specific personality characteristics. The choice of a particular brand depends upon the interaction of personality, the situation, and the product. Within each of these categories, a variety of interacting forces may operate. Thus the consumer may be under time pressure, may be buying a gift to be given at a social occasion, or may be in a lousy mood. At the same time, the person may be very low in **dogmatism** but also very high in self-confidence.

Figure 7-3 A personality (attention to social comarison information) by situation (whether or not shopping with others) interaction. (Note: The "tendency to conform" is a personality characteristic based upon the Attention to Social Comparison Scale. See William Bearden and Randall Rose, "Attention to Social Comparison Information: An Individual Difference Factor Affecting Conformity." *Journal of Consumer Research*, Vol. 16, March 1990, pp. 461–471.)

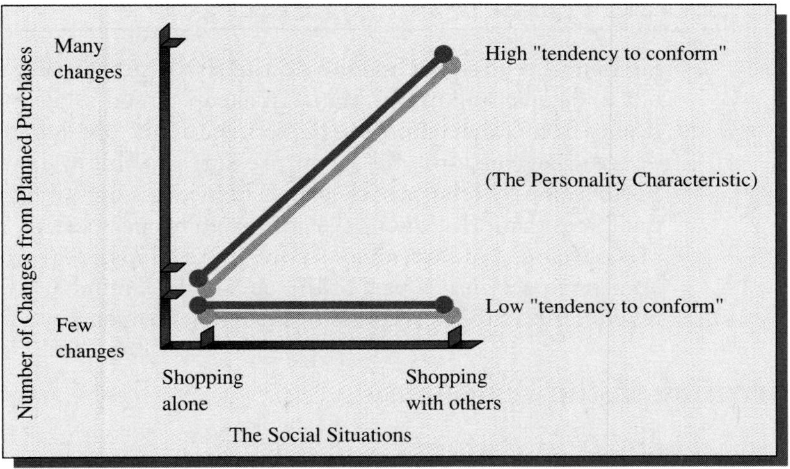

TABLE 7-1

Characteristics of Personality

1. Behavior shows consistency.
2. Behaviors distinguish one person from another.
3. Behaviors interact with the situation.
4. Single measures of personality cannot predict specific behaviors, such as which brand of car a consumer will purchase.

(Dogmatism refers to the extent that people reveal rigid and inflexible behavior.) The complexity resulting from the potential interaction of all of these factors well illustrates the idea that consumers must be viewed as a dynamic whole. Simple stimulus–response connections between personality and purchase are unlikely to be found.

Another factor contributing to low correlations between personality measures and behavior is that single measures of behavior are apt to be highly unreliable.[12] One recent study investigated the relationship between a scale assessing cat owners' and dog owners' emotional attachment to their pets and their tendency to feed them human food. The authors found that the correlation between emotional attachment and feeding human food increased when the number of days assessed was increased. The study indicates that behavior must be measured on multiple occasions to assess personality–behavior relationships. Table 7-1 summarizes the four characteristics of personality relevant to consumer researchers.

For consumer researchers four distinct approaches to personality have had an impact on developing managerial strategy. They are psychoanalytic theory, trait theory, social–psychological and cognitively based personality theories, and self-concept theories. Each of these is discussed in the paragraphs that follow.

PSYCHOANALYTIC THEORY

Sigmund Freud's **psychoanalytic theory of personality** has had a major impact on our understanding of our human makeup. Freud argued that the human personality results from a dynamic struggle between inner physiological drives (such as hunger, sex, and aggression) and social pressures to follow laws, rules, and moral codes. Furthermore, Freud proposed that individuals are aware of only a small portion of the forces that drive their behavior. From his perspective, humans have a conscious, a preconscious, and an unconscious mind. This idea—that much of what propels humans to action is a part of the unconscious mind and not available for scrutiny—revolutionized the perception of the human personality.[13]

The Structure of the Personality

According to Freud, the personality results from the clash of three forces—the id, ego, and superego. Present at birth, the **id** represents the physiological drives that propel a person to action. These drives are completely unconscious and form a chaotic cauldron of seething excitations.[14] The id requires instant gratification of its instincts. As such, it operates on the **pleasure principle**. That is, the id functions to move a person to obtain positive feelings and emotions.

The ego begins to develop as the child grows. The function of the ego is to curb the appetites of the id and help the person to function effectively in the world. As Freud stated, the **ego** stands for "reason and good sense while the id stands for untamed passions."[15] Freud viewed the ego as operating on the **reality principle**. The reality principle helps the person to be practical and to avoid the extremes of behavior to which the id and superego can push an individual.

The **superego** can be understood as the conscience or "voice within" a person that echoes the morals and values of parents and society. Only a small portion of it is available to the conscious mind. It is formed during middle childhood through the process of identification, according to Freud. The superego actively opposes and clashes with the id, and one role of the ego is to resolve these conflicts. The focus on the conflict between the id and superego is what classifies the psychoanalytic view of personality as a conflict theory.

Psychoanalytic Theory and Promotional Strategy

As used by motivation researchers, psychoanalytic thought had a major impact on marketing in the 1950s. Advertising firms hired psychoanalysts to help develop promotional themes and packaging to appeal to the unconscious minds of consumers. Psychoanalytic theory emphasized the use of dreams, of fantasy, and of symbols to identify the unconscious motives behind a person's actions. Marketers hoped that they could turn the tables and use symbols and flights of fantasy to propel people to buy products.

As noted, Freudian theory stresses the importance of fantasy to the human psyche. Advertisers frequently attempt to move consumers to fantasize about using the product or the consequences of using the product. A nice illustration of an advertisement that may invoke fantasies among consumers is portrayed in Figure 7-4. In the ad, General Mills attempts to link drinking its "New Italian Cappuccino" brand of coffee to dancing and romance. The figures rising from the steamy cup and the ad's copy (i.e., "More than just a cup of coffee") are employed to create fantasies.

A number of symbols exist in psychoanalytic theory that could be used by marketers. For example, phallic (male) and ovarian (female) symbols were thought to activate the release of sexual energy or **libido**. Indeed, some writers have sold large numbers of books by sensationalizing the charge that advertising agencies place ovarian and phallic symbols in advertisements to arouse sexual energy and thereby generate sales.[16] Phallic symbols are represented by figures that are long and cylindrical, whereas ovarian symbols are represented by figures that are round and receptive. In some instances it is quite clear that companies make use of such symbols. For example, the concave shape of Jovan perfume and the convex shape of Jovan aftershave appear to be highly symbolic. Figure 7-5 shows an ad for MerCruiser engines from a Freudian symbolism perspective. The erect figure of the skier represents a phallic symbol.

According to psychoanalytic theory, people may also have a death wish, which is symbolized in advertising by death masks. Death masks are facial covers that portray the contorted faces of people in unbearable pain. One author has argued that liquor advertisers place death masks in the ice cubes of liquor advertisements to activate the death wish of heavy drinkers.[17]

Figure 7-4 This ad for Italian Cappuccino coffee employs fantasy images to create feeling and emotions.

Do advertising agencies really engage in such activities? The answer is a qualified no. A college professor conducted a survey that asked advertising people if they ever deliberately embedded a subliminal message—such as a word, symbol, or sexual organ—in advertising artwork for a client. Of those surveyed, 96% said they did not. When asked if they knew of anyone doing it, 91% said they did not.[18] Although the percentage admitting to awareness of the use of embedded symbols in ads was low, it is somewhat surprising that anyone admitted to the practice at all. One has to ask, however, whether portraying the ideas symbolically has any impact on the observer, given the highly open use of sex and violence in television and magazines today.

Psychoanalytic Theory and Consumer Research

The psychoanalytic approach to personality has had the greatest impact on consumer behavior through the research methods developed by Sigmund Freud and his followers. They developed projective techniques to assist psychologists in identifying the

Figure 7-5 From a psychoanalytic perspective, the erect figure of the skier represents a phallic symbol.

unconscious motives that spur people to action. Examples of the projective techniques include word association tasks, sentence completion tasks, and thematic apperception tests (TATs). (TATs are ambiguous drawings about which people are asked to write stories.) Freud's major therapeutic tool was to have people lie on a couch and relax both physically and psychologically. The therapist helped them to bring down their defenses to understand more of their unconscious motivations. Later, psychologists began to bring people together for group therapy. These two approaches have been translated by marketers into the use of depth interviews and focus groups. **Depth interviews** are long, probing, "one-on-one" interviews undertaken to identify hidden reasons for purchasing products and services. **Focus groups** employ long sessions in which five to ten consumers are encouraged to talk freely about their feelings and thoughts concerning a product or service.

TRAIT THEORY

The trait theory approach to personality attempts to classify people according to their dominant characteristics or traits. A **trait** is "any characteristic in which one person differs from another in a relatively permanent and consistent way."[19] Trait theories attempt to describe people in terms of their predispositions on a series of adjectives. As such, a person's personality would be described in terms of a particular combination of traits. Table 7-2 gives a list of 16 traits that could be used to describe a person. Note, however, that many such lists have been developed by various authors. Indeed, one of the problems of trait theories is the huge number of traits that can be used to describe people.

Much of the early empirical work done in the 1960s by consumer researchers on personality involved the use of trait theories. Studies investigated the personality profiles of Ford owners versus Chevrolet owners,[20] of owners of convertibles versus compacts versus standard model cars,[21] and of filter versus nonfilter cigarette smokers.[22] In general, the results of the studies were weak, inconclusive, and, in turn, severely criticized.[23]

The criticism of the trait theories led to the realization that, for the approach to be useful to marketers, the consumer characteristics selected for measurement should be carefully identified in terms of their relevance to the specific buying behavior being investigated. The early studies had selected trait inventories used by psychologists for purposes that had nothing to do with buying behavior. In addition, researchers using a trait approach needed to recognize the importance of situational factors and assess the validity and reliability of their measures.

A recent study used a trait approach to study coupon proneness and value consciousness.[24] The authors proposed that the tendency of consumers to redeem coupons is based in part on their view of coupons and in part on their value consciousness. Value consciousness was defined as the amount of concern the consumer has for the need-satisfying properties of the product in relation to the price paid for the product. In contrast, coupon proneness deals with the tendency of a consumer to buy because the purchase offer includes a coupon, which such people view almost as

TABLE 7-2

Sixteen Personality Traits Identified by Cattel

1. Reserved versus outgoing	**9.** Trusting versus suspicious
2. Dull versus bright	**10.** Practical versus imaginative
3. Unstable versus stable	**11.** Unpretentious versus polished
4. Docile versus aggressive	**12.** Self-assured versus self-reproaching
5. Serious versus happy-go-lucky	**13.** Conservative versus experimenting
6. Expedient versus conscientious	**14.** Group-dependent versus self-sufficient
7. Shy versus uninhibited	**15.** Undisciplined versus controlled
8. Tough-minded versus tender-minded	**16.** Relaxed versus tense

SOURCE: Adapted from R. Cattel, H. Eber, and M. Tatsuoka, *Handbook for the Sixteen Personality Factor Questionnaire* (Champaign, IL. Institute for Personality Ability Testing, 1970).

an end in itself. Table 7-3 presents the scales developed to measure coupon proneness and value consciousness.

In the study 350 adults were surveyed and asked how frequently they redeemed coupons in the past month. They also completed the two scales. The results revealed that the coupon proneness trait was strongly related to coupon redemption behavior. In addition, value consciousness also predicted the use of coupons even after the impact of the coupon proneness trait had been accounted for. In sum, the results revealed that traits of coupon proneness and value consciousness are distinct and that both influence consumer buying behavior. The trait approach to personality can be highly valuable for market researchers, if used properly. The "coupon proneness" scale exemplifies such an approach.

TABLE 7-3

Items Comprising Coupon Proneness and Value Consciousness Scales

All items are seven-point scales ranging from strongly agree to strongly disagree. All scale items were coded/recoded so that higher scores reflect higher levels of the construct.

Coupon Proneness

1. Redeeming coupons makes me feel good.
2. I enjoy clipping coupons out of the newspapers.
3. When I use coupons, I feel that I am getting a good deal.
4. I enjoy using coupons, regardless of the amount I save by doing so.
5. I have favorite brands, but most of the time I buy the brand I have a coupon for.
6. I am more likely to buy brands for which I have a coupon.
7. Coupons have caused me to buy products I normally would not buy.
8. Beyond the money I save, redeeming coupons gives me a sense of joy.

Value Consciousness

1. I am very concerned about low prices, but I am equally concerned about product quality.
2. When grocery shopping, I compare the prices of different brands to be sure I get the best value for the money.
3. When purchasing a product, I always try to maximize the quality I get for the money I spend.
4. When I buy products I like to be sure that I am getting my money's worth.
5. I generally shop around for lower prices on products, but they still must meet certain quality requirements before I will buy them.
6. When I shop, I usually compare the "price per ounce" information for brands I normally buy.
7. I always check prices at the grocery store to be sure I get the best value for the money I spend.

SOURCE: Scales developed by Donald R. Lichtenstein, Richard G. Netemeyer, and Scot Burton, "Distinguishing Coupon Proneness from Value Consciousness: An Acquisition-Transaction Utility Theory Perspective," *Journal of Marketing*, Vol. 54 (July 1990), pp. 54–67.

SOCIAL–PSYCHOLOGICAL AND COGNITIVE PERSONALITY THEORIES

Early personality theorists, such as the psychoanalysts, tended to view personality as resulting from biological factors. Somewhat later, researchers began to view personality as resulting from the social nature of people and/or from the way they processed information. Each of these approaches to personality is discussed in the paragraphs that follow.

Social–Psychological Personality Theory

From a **social–psychological personality theory** perspective, personality describes the consistent patterns of behavior that people show with regard to social situations. A number of these theories have been used by marketers to help explain buyer behavior. For example, the personality concept of dogmatism, mentioned earlier in the chapter, is socially and psychologically based. The construct of dogmatism relates principally to the rigidity with which people approach the social environment. Other social–psychological personality theories used by marketers include gender schema theory,[25] consumer anxiety,[26] consumer ethnocentrism, and the compliance, aggression, detachment model (CAD).[27]

A social–psychological scale of particular importance to consumer researchers is the "attention to social comparison information" scale (called the ATSCI scale, as noted earlier).[28] Presented in Table 7-4, the scale assesses the extent to which consumers tend to conform to social pressures to make purchases. Those consumers who score high on the ATSCI scale reveal an awareness of how others react to their behavior and will tend to change their attitudes to be consistent with the group. More will be said about the ATSCI in Chapter 9 on attitude, belief, and behavior change.

Cognitive Personality Theories

Psychologists have also developed **cognitive personality theories**, which focus on identifying individual differences in how consumers process and react to information. For example, researchers have attempted to assess **consumer cognitive complexity**.[29] The goal is to measure the structural complexity of the organizing schemas used by different groups of consumers to code and store information in memory. Another approach involves investigating the extent to which different people engage in **verbal versus visual information processing**.[30] A third cognitively oriented personality variable is called the **need for cognition**, a scale that assesses differences in the extent that people enjoy thinking and engaging in cognitive work.[31] The need for cognition is particularly relevant to understanding the persuasion process. As a result, it is discussed in Chapter 9.

One cognitively oriented approach receiving attention from consumer researchers concerns the tolerance for ambiguity held by consumers.

TABLE 7-4

A Scale Developed to Measure the Attention to Social Comparison Information (ATSCI)

1. It is my feeling that if everyone else in a group is behaving in a certain manner, this must be the proper way to behave.
2. I actively avoid wearing clothes that are not in style.
3. At parties I usually try to behave in a manner that makes me fit in.
4. When I am uncertain how to act in a social situation, I look to the behavior of others for cues.
5. I try to pay attention to the reactions of others to my behavior in order to avoid being out of place.
6. I find that I tend to pick up slang expressions from others and use them as part of my own vocabulary.
7. I tend to pay attention to what others are wearing.
8. The slightest look of disapproval in the eyes of a person with whom I am interacting is enough to make me change my approach.
9. It's important to me to fit into the group I'm with.
10. My behavior often depends on how I feel others wish me to behave.
11. If I am the least bit uncertain as to how to act in a social situation, I look to the behavior of others for cues.
12. I usually keep up with clothing style changes by watching what others wear.
13. When in a social situation, I tend not to follow the crowd, but instead behave in a manner that suits my particular mood at the time.

Note that each item is scored 0 (always false) to 5 (always true) and that item 13 requires reverse scoring.

SOURCE: Scale developed by William O. Bearden and Randall L. Rose, "Attention to Social Comparison Information; An Individual Difference Factor Affecting Consumer Conformity," *Journal of Consumer Research*, Vol. 16 (March 1990), pp. 461–471.

Tolerance for Ambiguity

The **tolerance for ambiguity** personality construct can predict how a person will react to situations that have varying degrees of ambiguity or inconsistency.[32] Those individuals who are tolerant of ambiguity react to such situational inconsistency in a positive way. In contrast, those identified as intolerant of ambiguity tend to view situational inconsistency as threatening and undesirable.

Three different types of situations have been identified as ambiguous.[33] First, completely new situations about which a person has little information are considered ambiguous. Second, highly complex situations that tend to overwhelm a person with information have a high degree of ambiguity. Finally, situations containing contradictory information are ambiguous. One can characterize these situations as (1) novel, (2) complex, and (3) insoluble.

The personality construct of tolerance for ambiguity may influence people in a number of consumer tasks. For example, one study found that those categorized as tolerant of ambiguity reacted more positively to products perceived as new than those intolerant of ambiguity.[34] Thus, when purchasing a new product, a consumer is encountering a novel situation. Those who are tolerant of ambiguity are more likely to react positively to the new product. When introducing a new product, managers should attempt to identify the level of their target market's tolerance for ambiguity. If the target market has a very low tolerance for ambiguity, it will likely be very difficult to launch the new product successfully.

A second area of application for the tolerance for ambiguity personality variable is in identifying those consumers who are most likely to search for information. One study investigated the factors that influence the extent to which consumers search for information when making a product choice. The results revealed that those consumers who are tolerant of ambiguity were more likely to search for information as the choice task became more complex and as the products became more novel.[35] The implications of these results are quite interesting. Individuals with higher tolerance for ambiguity may actually like to receive information about products. If this were found to be the case, it would have implications for promotional strategy. If the firm's target market consisted of large numbers of individuals who sought information, it would suggest that the company should produce pamphlets and brochures to accompany the product. In contrast, if the target market were composed of those intolerant of ambiguity, the strategy may involve giving relatively little information about the product. Perhaps in such cases more emotional appeals could be used. Of course, these are speculations that require additional research.

Another cognitively oriented personality characteristic is an individual's degree of cognitive moral development, which may be related to the tendency to act ethically in consumer buying situations. Highlight 7-1 presents a research study that investigated cognitive moral development in a marketing setting.

On the Managerial Use of Personality Scales

A key issue for marketing managers and market researchers concerns how to make practical use of personality scales. By using census information, market researchers have a great deal of data on the demographic characteristics of the population in the United States, Canada, and Western Europe. However, no consistent information exists on the personality characteristics of consumers In addition, it is much too expensive for any single firm to collect such data on the population as a whole. Given these limitations, how can managers make use of personality measures?

As a general rule, to employ personality measures, the manager must first identify the demographic characteristics of their target market. For example, consider the demographic characteristics of the target market of the Eagle Vision automobile identified by Chrysler Corporation—25–40 years of age, college educated, two children, high income. Once this description is obtained, market researchers can pay a sample of these individuals to complete a series of personality inventories (e.g., tolerance for ambiguity, attention to social comparison information, and value consciousness). Based upon how the target market responds to these questions, the marketing manager can develop promotional messages that are more likely to appeal to the group.

HIGHLIGHT 7-1

Is There an Ethical Personality Characteristic?

A psychologist named Lawrence Kohlberg developed a scale that measures people's level of cognitive moral development. He argued that advanced moral behavior requires people to have the ability to employ logical reasoning. Kohlberg identified six stages through which people *may* progress in their moral reasoning ability. In the early stages people respond to moral rules based upon whether or not they will be punished for breaking them. In the middle stages people follow societally accepted standards, such as the "golden rule." Such people act to maintain order within a society and to contribute to the society. At the highest levels of moral development, people follow rules of behavior that uphold societal and individual rights regardless of what majority opinion may indicate. They identify universal ethical principles that may supersede those upheld by a society.

Recently, researchers surveyed marketing professionals to assess their level of cognitive moral development. In addition, they sought to identify variables that may be associated with higher levels of moral development. The results revealed that those with higher moral development levels tended to be female, to have more years of schooling, and to possess more socially responsible attitudes. Thus they tended to believe that corporations and managers have social responsibilities that go beyond merely maximizing the profit for a firm.

An interesting issue for researchers involves investigating the cognitive moral development of consumers. A key question concerns whether those consumers with higher levels of cognitive moral development act more ethically in their exchange relations with firms?

Based upon Jerry R. Goolsby and Shelby D. Hunt, "Cognitive Moral Development and Marketing," *Journal of Marketing*, Vol. 56 (January 1992), pp. 55–68.

THE SELF-CONCEPT IN CONSUMER RESEARCH

The **self-concept** represents the "totality of the individual's thoughts and feelings having reference to himself as an object."[36] It is as though an individual "turns around" and evaluates in an objective fashion just who and what he or she is.[37] Because people have a need to behave consistently with their self-concept, this perception of themselves forms part of the basis for the personality. Such self-consistent behavior helps a person to maintain his or her self-esteem and gives the person predictability in interactions with others. Indeed, Russell Belk (a well-known consumer researcher) has suggested that possessions play a major role in establishing a person's identify. As such, possessions become part of ourselves and form an **extended self**. His argument may be summarized in his statement that "we are what we have . . . (which) may be the most basic and powerful fact of consumer behavior."[38]

An important finding is that people have more than one self-concept. Table 7-5 identifies eight types of self-concept. The actual self relates to how a person actually perceives himself or herself The ideal self denotes how a person would like to perceive

TABLE 7-5

Various Types of Self-concept

1. *Actual self*—How a person *actually* perceives himself or herself.
2. *Ideal self*—How a person *would like* to perceive himself or herself.
3. *Social self*—How a person thinks *others* perceive him or her.
4. *Ideal social self*—How a person *would like others* to perceive him or her.
5. *Expected self*—An image of self somewhere in between the actual and ideal selves.
6. *Situational self*—A person's self-image in a specific situation.
7. *Extended self*—A person's self-concept that includes the impact of personal possessions on self-image.
8. *Possible selves*—What a person would like to become, could become, or is afraid of becoming.

himself or herself.[39] The social self concerns how a person believes that others perceive him or her. In contrast, the ideal social self relates to how a person would like others to view him or her. The expected self describes how a person would like to act. The situational self portrays how a person would like to act in various contexts. For example, at a sporting event a person might want to be carefree. In contrast, when conducting a business deal, the person would want to be serious. The extended self denotes the impact of possessions on self-image. Finally, researchers have identified a self-perception called "possible selves." This perspective on the self refers to what a person perceives that he or she would like to become, could become, or is afraid of becoming. Thus the possible selves idea has a more future orientation than the other self-concept types.[40]

Symbolic Interactionism and the Self

Sociologists have argued that the relationships that people form with others play a large role in the development of the self-concept.[41] From this perspective consumers are viewed as living in a symbolic environment, and the way people interpret these symbols determines the meanings derived. Within a society, people develop shared meanings as to what the symbols represent. Further, by linking themselves to these symbols, consumers can depict to others their own self-concept.

The idea of the "looking glass self" plays an important role within the symbolic interactionist perspective.[42] A looking glass is a mirror, and the "looking glass self" metaphor describes the idea that people obtain signals about who they are by looking at the reactions of others to themselves. It is as though we see reflections of ourselves in the faces of others as we interact with them. We define ourselves in part based upon how we imagine that other people view us. As a result, people's self-concept is determined in part depending upon whom they believe is observing them at any particular time. Thus a woman may be shy and retiring as an office worker because that is how she believes that her bosses and co-workers view her. In contrast, on the weekends she may be a party animal as she moves from one bar to another. Again, she is using the reactions of others to determine in part her self-concept, which diverges markedly from that emerging in an office situation.

The Self-concept and Product Symbolism

As noted by the symbolic interactions, products may act as symbols for consumers. Symbols are things that stand for or express something else. (For additional information on symbols, see Chapter 3.) Some writers have argued that the primary reason for buying many products is not for their functional benefits but for their symbolic value.[43] Indeed, consumers' personalities can be defined through the products they use. Finally, many researchers believe that people view their possessions as an extension of themselves. In fact, various studies have found a relationship between the self-image of a person and of certain products that he or she buys. Products for which such self-image/product-image congruence have been found include automobiles, health products, cleaning products, grooming products, leisure products, clothing, retail store patronage, food products, cigarettes, home appliances, magazines, and home furnishings.[44]

Just which products are most likely to be viewed as symbols by consumers? One might argue that the products consumers use to communicate themselves to others act as symbols. Such communicative products have three characteristics.[45] First, they must have visibility in use, such that their purchase, consumption, and disposition are readily apparent to others.

Second, the product must show variability—that is, some consumers must have the resources to own the product, whereas others do not have the time or financial resources to possess it. If everyone owned the product or could use the service and if it were identical for everyone, it could not be a symbol. Third, the product should have personalizability. Personalizability refers to the extent to which a product denotes a stereotypical image of the average user. One can easily see how such symbolic products as automobiles or jewelry possess the characteristics of visibility, variability, and personalizability.

Figure 7-6 shows an ad for Mont Blanc pens that explicitly links their possession to an expression of personality. This expensive writing instrument fulfills the three characteristics of products that communicate the self-concept. It has visibility in use, due to its distinctive shape and color. It has variability, because few can afford to pay hundreds of dollars for a fountain pen. And it has personalizability, because it makes a statement about the type of person who would invest in such a costly writing instrument.

The importance of recognizing the symbolic nature of products is depicted in Figure 7-7. In the figure there are three boxes representing (1) a person's self-concept, (2) an audience or reference group, and (3) a product that acts as a symbol. The consumer may purchase a product that symbolizes a feature of his or her self-concept to the audience. In step 1 the consumer buys a product that may communicate his or her self-concept to the audience. As shown in step 2, the consumer hopes that the audience will have the desired perception of the symbolic nature of the product. In step 3 the consumer hopes that the reference group views him or her as having some of the same symbolic qualities as the product.[46] Thus consumers may be conceptualized as purchasing products to communicate symbolically various aspects of their self-concepts to others. The theory that the consumer selects products and stores that correspond to his or her self-concept has been called the **image congruence hypothesis**.[47]

Figure 7-6 The ad suggests that ownership of a Mont Blanc pen can be used as a means to express one's self-concept to others. (Courtesy of Mont Blanc.)

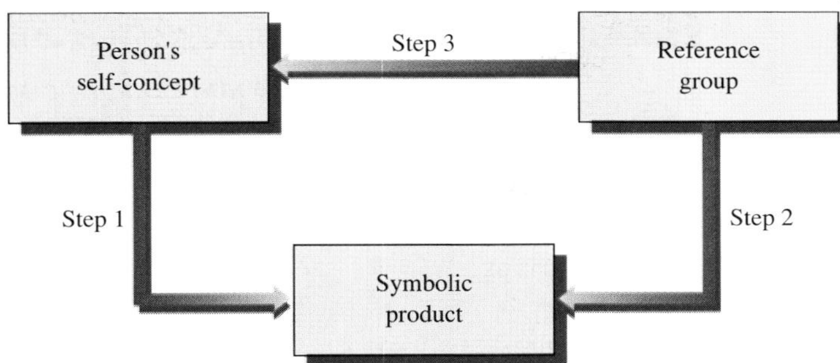

Step 1: Person buys product that is symbolic of self.
Step 2: Reference group associates product with person.
Step 3: Reference gruop attributes to person the symbolic qualities of the product.

Figure 7-7 The communication of self to others via symbolic products.

A Scale to Measure the Self-concept and Product Image

One of the problems for the market researcher is knowing how to assess the self-concept of consumers in a market segment and the image that these consumers have of a brand. Ideally, one scale should be used to assess both product image and self-image, if the researcher is going to match optimally the segment to the product. One researcher developed a scale specifically for this purpose.[48] Shown in Table 7-6, the scale is composed of 15 items that are presented in a semantic differential format to consumers. (A semantic differential scale uses bipolar adjectives, such as light–heavy, on which a person rates something.) Researchers ask members of the target market to rate themselves and various products on the scale. Brands that are rated in a manner similar to how consumers rate themselves are predicted to have an image that corresponds to the self-concept of the consumers. Although additional work needs to be performed to test the scale's reliability and validity, it does offer promise as an approach for assessing product image and consumer self-image congruity.

The advertisement for the Toyota Camry, shown in Figure 7-8, illustrates how manufacturers may directly link the personality of the automobile to that of consumers. In the ad, the copy boldly states, "If you could describe a car by a personality trait, this one would be the strong and silent type." Durability and a quiet ride are two positive attributes in an automobile Similarly, strength and a quiet personality can be highly positive in a person. For those consumers who would like to think of themselves as the strong and silent type, or who appreciate it in others, the ad might be highly appealing.

One's Body and the Self-concept

In the chapter-opening vignette, cosmetic surgery was discussed as a consumer behavior phenomenon related to the self-concept. A recent study examined the relationship of plastic surgery to consumers' self-concept. In-depth interviews were conducted with nine individuals who had undergone plastic surgery for various reasons,

TABLE 7-6

A Scale to Measure Product Images and Self-Images [a]

1. Rugged	1	2	3	4	5	6	7	Delicate
2. Exciting	1	2	3	4	5	6	7	Calm
3. Uncomfortable	1	2	3	4	5	6	7	Comfortable
4. Dominating	1	2	3	4	5	6	7	Submissive
5. Thrifty	1	2	3	4	5	6	7	Indulgent
6. Pleasant	1	2	3	4	5	6	7	Unpleasant
7. Contemporary	1	2	3	4	5	6	7	Uncontemporary
8. Organized	1	2	3	4	5	6	7	Unorganized
9. Rational	1	2	3	4	5	6	7	Emotional
10. Youthful	1	2	3	4	5	6	7	Mature
11. Formal	1	2	3	4	5	6	7	Informal
12. Orthodox	1	2	3	4	5	6	7	Liberal
13. Complex	1	2	3	4	5	6	7	Simple
14. Colorless	1	2	3	4	5	6	7	Colorful
15. Modest	1	2	3	4	5	6	7	Vain

[a] Consumers are asked to rate either their actual, ideal, or social self-concept on the scale. They are then asked to rate one or more brands on the same scale. Brands whose pattern of responses most closely match a consumer's self-concept are expected to be preferred by a consumer.

SOURCE: Adapted from Naresh K, Malhotra "A Scale to Measure Self-concepts, Person Concepts, and Product Concepts," *Journal of Marketing Research*, Vol. 18 (November 1981), pp. 456–464.

such as to have breasts augmented or reduced, to have wrinkles removed, and to have noses or chins fixed.[49] The researcher found that in general the respondents had the plastic surgery performed because of dissatisfaction with their body and that their self-esteem improved greatly after the surgery.

The results of the study revealed that patients sought the surgery during role transitions, such as after a divorce or after changing jobs. In addition, the researcher found that respondents felt much more confident in social–intimate situations after the plastic surgery. As a result, they substantially improved their view of their social self. The author suggested that plastic surgery enables a person to take control of his body and its appearance. Just as a new car or the clothing that a person wears says something about who and what he is, so too does his body. In discussing the actions of one male respondent, named Chuck, the author said, "Just like any other stock or commodity in his portfolio, Chuck could manage his body to increase his overall return from it."[50]

Materialism: You Are What You Own

It has been argued that "What we possess is, in a very real way, part of ourselves."[51] Indeed, William James in 1890 stated that we are the sum total of all our possessions.[52] Four types of possessions help to make up our personal sense of self: (1) body and body parts, (2) objects, (3) places and time periods, and (4) persons and

How else can you describe the all-new Toyota Camry? Try well-built, good-looking and, yes, even intelligent.

Take, for example, our two new engines with more well-appreciated power than ever before. There's an enhanced 185 hp V6 engine. Also available is an energetic 135 hp 4-cylinder engine. Whichever you prefer, both are attached to a more rigid body thanks to the increased use of high-strength tensile steel.

V6 Engine

Now turn the key and what you'll discover is that noise, vibration and harshness have all surprisingly been hushed. That's because our engineers have, once again, done the unexpected. They employed new anti-vibration subframes. They utilized new hydraulic engine mounts. They even smoothed body surfaces to cheat the wind.

All of which you'll find as either a luxury or, quite possibly, a necessity.

Depending on your personality, of course.

IF YOU COULD DESCRIBE A CAR BY A PERSONALITY TRAIT, THIS ONE WOULD BE THE STRONG AND SILENT TYPE.

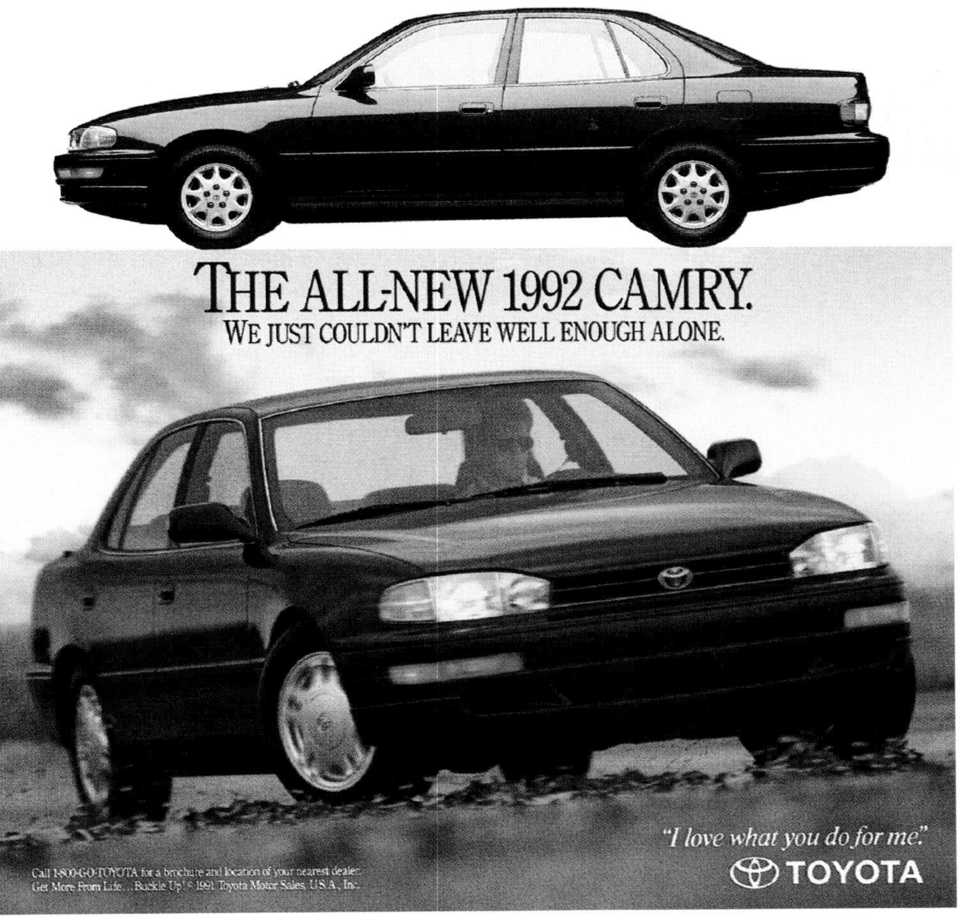

Figure 7-8 Toyota explicitly links the Camry to a particular type of consumer self-image.

pets. Body parts vary in importance to people. Eyes, hair, heart, legs, and genitals have been identified as most essential to the sense of self. In contrast, throat, liver, kidneys, chin, knees, and nose are perceived as less central to the self. The implication is that if one loses a body part central to one's identity, one will feel a loss of part of one's identity. Interestingly, evidence suggests that women perceive their bodies as more central to their identities than men.

The concept that different body parts have different levels of importance to a consumer's self-concept has an important practical element. One major medical problem today is finding sufficient body parts for organ transplants. From a psychological perspective, transplanting important body organs can be extremely traumatic for both the donor and recipient. Furthermore, decisions by next of kin to donate organs of a deceased person are made in part based upon how sacrosanct the organs are perceived to be. Thus organs important to the self-concept, such as the eyes and heart, are most frequently vetoed for donation.[53]

After body parts, objects are the most important possessions of people. Highly important possessions include dwellings, automobiles (particularly for men), and favorite clothing. (Clothing can be seen as a type of second skin that embellishes the self that we present to others.) For some people, collections of objects are extremely important to their sense of self.[54] Collections serve as extensions of the self because they represent the person's judgment and taste. In addition to expressing information about a person's past experiences, collections may be used to express a person's fantasies. Thus the middle-aged male who collects thousands of baseball cards may be seen as keeping alive his boyhood desire to be a major league ball player.

Recently, researchers have begun to investigate consumers' individual differences with regard to how highly they value their possessions. The tendency to seek happiness through ownership of objects has been called materialism. Formally, **materialism** may be defined as

> the importance a consumer attaches to worldly possessions. At the highest levels of materialism, such possessions assume a central place in a person's life and are believed to provide the greatest sources of satisfaction and dissatisfaction.[55]

People rated as having high levels of materialism have been found to have the following characteristics:

1. They are less willing to donate body organs for transplants.
2. They are more approving of spending large amounts of money on cars and houses.
3. They are less likely to want to eat at expensive restaurants.
4. They are more likely to view Christmas as a time for shopping.
5. They are less likely to believe that others will appreciate their help.

Much work remains in exploring the impact of individual differences in materialism on consumption behavior. Potentially, materialism may be found to relate to a variety of important consumer behavior areas, such as consumption innovativeness and brand loyalty. Efforts are under way to develop scales to measure individual differences in materialism. Table 7-7 provides a recently developed scale to measure materialism. Note that the researchers identified three dimensions of materialism, namely, the extent that purchasing and possessing material goods (1) are used to define success by a person, (2) are central to the life-style of a person, and (3) are important

TABLE 7-7

A Scale to Measure Materialism

Success Subscale

I admire people who own expensive homes, cars, and clothes.

Some of the most important achievements in life include acquiring material possessions.

I don't place much emphasis on the amount of material objects that people own as a sign of success.

The things I own say a lot about how well I'm doing in life.

I like to own things that impress people.

I don't pay much attention to the material objects other people own.

Centrality Subscale

I usually buy only the things I need.

I try to keep my life simple as far as possessions are concerned.

The things I own aren't all that important to me.

I enjoy spending money on things that aren't practical.

Buying things gives me a lot of pleasure.

I like a lot of luxury in my life.

I put less emphasis on material things than most people do.

Happiness Subscale

I have all the things I really need to enjoy life.

My life would be better if I owned certain things I don't have.

I wouldn't be any happier if I owned nicer things.

I'd be happier if I could afford to buy more things.

It sometimes bothers me quite a bit that I can't afford to buy all the things I'd like.

for the happiness of the person.[56] Because materialism is also a cultural value, it will be discussed further in Chapter 17, Cultural Processes.

The personality construct of materialism relates directly to the tendency to purchase material goods. However, for some people the buying process can become compulsive, leading to bankruptcy, divorce, and other serious personal consequences. Researchers have begun to investigate compulsive buying as a personality characteristic. Highlight 7-2 discusses this important societal issue.

LIFE-STYLES AND PSYCHOGRAPHICS

The early portion of this chapter focused on measures of personality as a means to identify individual differences among consumers. Marketers, however, do not have the time or resources to analyze the individual consumer's personality as a psychologist would when performing therapy on a client. In addition, marketers, unlike therapists, tend to work at a group level rather than at the individual level.

HIGHLIGHT 7-2

Socially Conscious Consumer Behavior: Compulsive Buying as a Personality Characteristic

Currently, a major societal problem in the United States involves consumers falling into debt and going bankrupt. During the early 1990s, personal bankruptcies were at an all-time high level. While overspending can result from factors beyond a person's control (such as unexpectedly losing a job), poor money management may also result from compulsive buying. Compulsive buying can be described as "chronic, repetitive purchasing that becomes a primary response to negative events or feelings." As such, compulsive buying is a negative component of consumer behavior. Compulsive buyers have been found to have lower self-esteem, to fantasize more frequently than normal, and to reveal higher than average levels of depression and anxiety.

Two consumer researchers (Ronald Faber and Thomas O'Guinn) have developed an instrument to measure the tendency to engage in compulsive buying. The instrument can be used to screen consumers in order to identify those at risk of becoming compulsive buyers and encountering severe financial difficulties. Some of the questions on the instrument that successfully identified compulsive buyers included

- Bought things even though I couldn't afford them.
- Felt others would be horrified if they knew of my spending habits.
- Felt anxious or nervous on days I didn't go shopping.
- Bought something in order to make myself feel better.

Answering "yes" to one or two of the questions on the scale does not indicate potential problems. However, revealing a consistent pattern in which an individual answers "yes" to most of the questions would suggest that the person should seek assistance from a professional. The study is a nice example of how consumer behavior research can be used to enhance society and the individuals who comprise it.

Based upon Ronald J. Faber and Thomas C. O'Guinn, "A Clinical Screener for Compulsive Buying," *Journal of Consumer Research*, Vol. 19 (December 1992), pp. 459–469.

For most consumer products or services to be successful, they must be purchased by thousands or millions of people. Thus the focus of marketers and consumer researchers has generally been on identifying the broad trends that influence how consumers live, work, and play. Such broad trends have been called consumer life-styles. The study of consumer life-styles is called psychographics.

Consumer Life-styles

The concept of consumer life-styles has been defined in a variety of ways. "Life-style" has been defined simply as "how one lives."[57] Or the term life-style can be used to describe different levels of aggregation of people. It has been used to describe an individual, a small group of interacting people, and larger groups of people (e.g., a market segment).[58] Thus the concept of life-style denotes a set of ideas quite distinct from that of personality. **Life-style** relates to how people live, how they spend their money, and how they allocate their time. Life-style concerns the overt actions and behaviors of consumers. In contrast, personality describes the consumer from a more internal perspective.[59] It delineates the consumer's "characteristic pattern of thinking, feeling, and perceiving."[60]

Of course, life-style and personality can be closely related. A consumer who has a personality categorized as low risk will probably not indulge in a life-style that includes an occupation as a speculator in the futures market or activities such as mountain climbing, hang gliding, and jungle exploration. Nonetheless, life-style and personality should be distinguished for two important reasons.

First, they are conceptually distinct: personality refers more to the internal characteristics of a person, whereas, life-style refers more to the external characteristics of how a person lives. Although both concepts describe the person, they describe different aspects of the individual.

A second reason for the distinction between life-style and personality is that the process of distinguishing the two has managerial implications. Some authors have argued that market segments can be too narrowly targeted if the target market is defined by personality too early in the process.[61] They recommend that marketers should sequentially segment the market by first identifying life-style segments and then by analyzing these segments for personality differences. By first identifying life-style segments that show consistent patterns of overt behavior in how they buy products, use their time, and engage in various activities, the marketer is able to identify a large number of people with similar life-style characteristics.

An important question, however, has not yet been addressed in this discussion on life-styles. How are life-styles measured by marketers? That question, discussed in the following section, involves psychographic analysis.

Psychographics

The term "psychographics" means different things to different researchers. The term itself connotes the idea of describing (graph) the psychological (psycho) makeup of consumers. In practice, however, psychographics is employed to assess consumers' activities, interests, and opinions (AIOs). In turn, AIOs are used to measure consumer life-styles. In general, then, researchers tend to equate psychographics with the study of life-styles.

The goals of psychographic research are usually of an applied nature—that is, psychographic research is used by market researchers to describe a consumer segment so as to help an organization better reach and understand its customers. Psychographic studies usually include questions to assess a target market's life-style and the personality characteristics of its members that distinguish them from other groups. In sum, **psychographics** may be defined as the quantitative investigation of consumers' life-styles and personality characteristics. Because psychographics is used to assist marketing decision making, one usually finds it combined with the analysis of the demographic characteristics of the target market.

Psychographics and AIO Statements

One of the features that distinguishes psychographic research from more traditional approaches is the use of questions called **AIO statements**. AIO statements attempt to describe the life-style of the consumer through his or her activities and the personality of the consumer through his or her interests and opinions. Activity questions ask consumers to indicate what they do, what they buy, and how they spend their time. Interest questions focus on what the consumers' preferences and priorities are. Opinion questions ask for consumers' views and feelings on such things as world, local, moral, economic, and social affairs. Table 7-8 lists questions representative of AIO items.

No hard-and-fast rules exist for developing AIO items. One dimension on which they frequently differ is their level of specificity. AIO questions may be highly specific and ask the respondent to provide information on his or her attitudes and preferences regarding a specific product or service. For example, a researcher for General Mills might be interested in consumer perceptions of Post Grape-Nuts. The researcher might ask respondents to agree or disagree with the following highly specific questions:

> I find Grape-Nuts to be too hard to chew.
>
> Grape-Nuts remind me of the outdoors.
>
> When I eat Grape-Nuts, it makes me feel healthful.

TABLE 7-8

Some Typical Questions Found in AIO Inventories

1. Activity questions
   - **a.** What outdoor sports do you participate in at least twice a month?
   - **b.** How many books do you read a year?
   - **c.** How often do you visit shopping malls?
   - **d.** Have you gone outside of the United States for a vacation?
   - **e.** To how many clubs do you belong?
2. Interest questions
   - **a.** In which of the following are you most interested—sports, church,or work?
   - **b.** How important to you is it to try new foods?
   - **c.** How important is it to you to get ahead in life?
   - **d.** Would you rather spend two hours on a Saturday afternoon with your wife or in a boat fishing alone?
3. Opinion questions (ask the respondent to agree or disagree)
   - **a.** The Russian people are just like us.
   - **b.** Women should have free choice regarding abortions.
   - **c.** Educators are paid too much money.
   - **d.** CBS Inc.™ is run by East Coast liberals.
   - **e.** We must be prepared for nuclear war.

On the other hand, AIO questions can be much more general. Some highly general questions researchers might ask consumers to agree or disagree with include the following:

I consider myself an outdoor person.

I believe in world peace.

I think cities are where the action is.

Of course researchers will have different purposes for asking the two types of questions. The highly specific questions give researchers information on what consumers think about the product and how that product relates to themselves. From such information products may be developed or changed and specific messages created. Indeed, unique selling propositions may be formulated. A **unique selling proposition** is a quick, hard-hitting phrase that captures a major feature of a product or service. For example, the makers of Wheaties have used for many years the unique selling proposition "The Breakfast of Champions." By asking people to describe through AIO statements the specific product, such unique selling propositions may be formulated.

The more general types of AIO questions also have a purpose. From these questions profiles of consumers can be developed. Such profiles can be used to obtain an understanding of the general life-style of a consumer segment being targeted. Based upon the profile, advertisers can develop ideas for the general themes of ads and for the setting within which to place an ad. For example, in the "Project Virile Female" discussed in the opening consumer vignette to the chapter, RJR Nabisco found that one of the chief general life-style aspirations of their target market was to have an ongoing relationship with a man. Such knowledge would suggest employing an advertising theme in which an attractive male is highly visible.

The psychographic inventory that receives the most attention among consumer researchers and corporations is **VALS** (Values And Life-styles). More recently, consumer researchers have begun to address a second approach, called LOV. These two inventories are discussed in the following text.

The VALS Psychographic Inventories

Perhaps the best-developed psychographic inventory of consumers is the **VALS life-style classification scheme**. Developed by the Stanford Research Institute (SRI), VALS has been widely used by U.S. corporations to segment the market and to provide guidance for developing advertising and product strategy.[62] SRI has in fact developed two psychographic inventories. The first, called VALS, is based upon motivational and developmental psychological theories—in particular, Maslow's theory on the hierarchy of needs. The second approach, called VALS 2, was developed specifically to measure consumer buying patterns. Both inventories are currently being used by firms.

The Original VALS Inventory

The originators of VALS viewed consumers as moving through a series of stages that have been described as a double hierarchy. Shown in Figure 7-9, the double hierarchy consists of four general categories of people.[63] These are (1) the **need-driven** group, (2) the **outer-directed** group, (3) the **inner-directed** group, and (4) the integrated group. Table 7-9 summarizes the characteristics of the VALS groups.

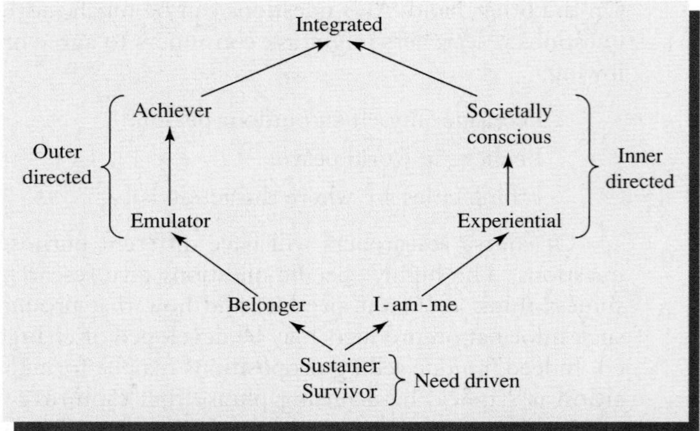

Figure 7-9 The VALS double hierarchy. (Source: Arnold Mitchell, *The Nine American Lifestyles*, New York: Macmillan, 1983.)

Because of the popularity of the VALS inventory, a substantial number of studies are available that describe the consumption and activity differences of the various VALS groups. One organization that has specifically used the VALS inventory to plan its marketing strategy is the Beef Industry Council. The beef industry faced major problems in the 1970s and 1980s because of declining per capita consumption.[64] To understand these ominous trends in beef consumption better, the Beef Industry Council authorized a survey of consumers to classify them into the VALS categories and to analyze their consumption of beef, lamb, fish, and other main course items. Table 7-10 provides an index of consumption of the eight VALS segments of beef, lamb, fresh fish, chicken, and turkey breast. As evident in the table, the survivors and sustainers simply do not consume much meat, probably because of limited financial resources. Achievers and the societally conscious in particular are heavy meat eaters in all categories. Again, it is quite likely that income plays a major role in explaining these results—that is, the achievers and societally conscious groups have high incomes and can afford serving all types of meat, fish, and poultry. However, life-styles also clearly influence the consumption patterns of these groups. In particular, the experiential segment eats very little lamb, whereas the I-am-me's eat much more than average.

Based in part upon the VALS analysis, the advertising agency of the Beef Industry Council recommended that the council's promotional activities should be targeted to active, contemporary adults. In VALS terms this target market would be identified as achievers, I-am-me's, experientials, and the societally conscious. These groups were selected for targeting because they are growing in numbers, because the achievers and the societally conscious are opinion leaders, and because the I-am-me's and the experientials have somewhat negative attitudes regarding beef. An interesting question for the advertising agency is whether "turning its back" on the belongers, who represent by far the largest market for beef, was a proper course of

TABLE 7-9

The VALS Market Segments

1. *The Need-Driven Group*
   a. *Survivors*—Marked by poverty, old age, poor health, and poor education.
   b. *Sustainers*—Also marked by poverty but feel left out of things. Have not given up hope. Younger than survivors, frequently a minority, sustainers are more self-confident, do more planning, and expect more of the future than do survivors.
2. *The Outer-Directed Group.* Focus on what other people think of them and gear their lives to the visible, tangible, and materialistic.
   a. *Belongers*—Middle-class America. Most are white, possess middle incomes, and are middle-aged or older. They cherish the institutions of family, church, and country.
   b. *Emulators*—Intensely striving to get ahead by imitating achievers. Highly ambitious, but spend rather than save.
   c. *Achievers*—Wealthy, high-income, self-employed professionals. Conservative and Republican in political persuasion.
3. *The Inner-Directed Group.* Inner focused, they seek intense involvement tasks.
   a. *I-am-me group*—Young, unmarried, and marked by major shifts in emotions, feelings, and viewpoints. Enthusiastic, daring, and seeking new ideas and possessions.
   b. *Experientials*—Highly involved in activities, such as causes, hedonism, or sports. Independent, self-reliant, and innovative. Moderate incomes and in late twenties.
   c. *Societally conscious*—Small, successful, mature, liberal group concerned with societal issues. The inner-directed equivalent of the achievers.
4. *The Integrated Group.* Composing 2% of the population, they approximate the self-actualized person. Mature, balanced people who have managed to "put together" the best of the characteristics of the inner- and outer-directed personalities. Although the integrated have the highest incomes of any of the VALS groups, their small numbers make them difficult to target successfully.

TABLE 7-10

A VALS Analysis of Meat and Fish Consumption[a]

	Beef	*Lamb*	*Fresh Fish*	*Fresh Chicken*	*Turkey Breast*
Survivors	64	21	62	69	41
Sustainers	77	54	111	93	62
Belongers	98	96	90	97	75
Emulators	102	62	111	107	63
Achievers	115	125	108	107	155
I-am-me	90	174	119	90	110
Experiential	95	36	79	100	85
Societally conscious	109	160	121	108	154

[a]Based on an index in which 100 is average. The respondents were asked to indicate if they had eaten the product in the last seven days.

SOURCE: T. C. Thomas and S. Crocker, *Values and Lifestyles—New Psychographics* (Menlo Park, CA: SRI, 1981).

action. Figure 7-10 presents a storyboard of one of the ads targeted to these groups of individuals.

The VALS 2 Inventory

After VALS 1 began receiving criticism, SRI brought out a second psychographic inventory called VALS 2. The goal of VALS 2 is to identify specific relationships between consumer attitudes and purchase behavior. It divides the American population into eight segments based upon their self-identity and their resources. Three different categories of self-identity orientations were identified by the VALS 2 researchers. Those oriented toward "principle" make consumer choices based upon their beliefs rather than upon feelings, events, or a desire for approval. Consumers oriented toward "status" make choices based upon their perception of whether others will approve of their purchases. Finally, consumers oriented toward "action" make decisions based upon desires for activity, variety, and risk taking.

The second major dimension in the VALS 2 classification scheme is the resources of the consumer. Resources are defined broadly to include not only financial–material resources, but also psychological and physical resources. People with abundant resources are at one end of the spectrum, whereas those with minimal resources occupy the other end. Figure 7-11 shows the VALS 2 network. Table 7-11 describes each of the eight categories of consumers identified by VALS 2.

VALS was used by Transport Canada (the equivalent of the U.S. Department of Transportation) to survey travelers at Canadian airports. The results revealed that most of the travelers were actualizers (37%). Actualizers have high incomes, and they buy products as an expression of their good taste, independence, and character. These characteristics suggested to the researchers that stores like The Sharper Image or the Nature Company could do well in airports. As the researcher explained, "Actualizers are a good market for quality arts and crafts."[65] Table 7-12 identifies activity patterns and product ownership of the eight VALS 2 categories.

Readers should note that a problem with assessing the utility of the VALS and VALS 2 psychographic inventories is that they are proprietary instruments (i.e., not in the public domain). The Stanford Research Institute allows little access to the instruments by outside consumer researchers. Therefore, their reliability and validity are difficult to assess.[66]

The List of Values Approach

A scale that shows promise of correcting some of the problems of VALS is called the **List of Values (LOV) scale**. The goal of the LOV scale is to assesses the dominant values of a person.[67] Although not strictly a psychographic inventory (i.e., it does not use AIO statements), it has been applied to the same types of problems as VALS. Further, because it is available for public scrutiny, its validity and reliability can be assessed. The nine values assessed by LOV are

1. Self-fulfillment
2. Excitement
3. Sense of accomplishment
4. Self-respect
5. Sense of belonging

Figure 7-10 The storyboard for a beef ad targets active, contemporary adults who represent particular psychographic groups. (Courtesy of Beef Industry Council.)

6. Being well respected
7. Security
8. Fun and enjoyment
9. Warm relationships with others

When used in a market research capacity, questions to assess the respondent's demographic profile are added to the questions used to identify the nine values. Evidence indicates that the LOV scale has three dimensions. Questions regarding the first four

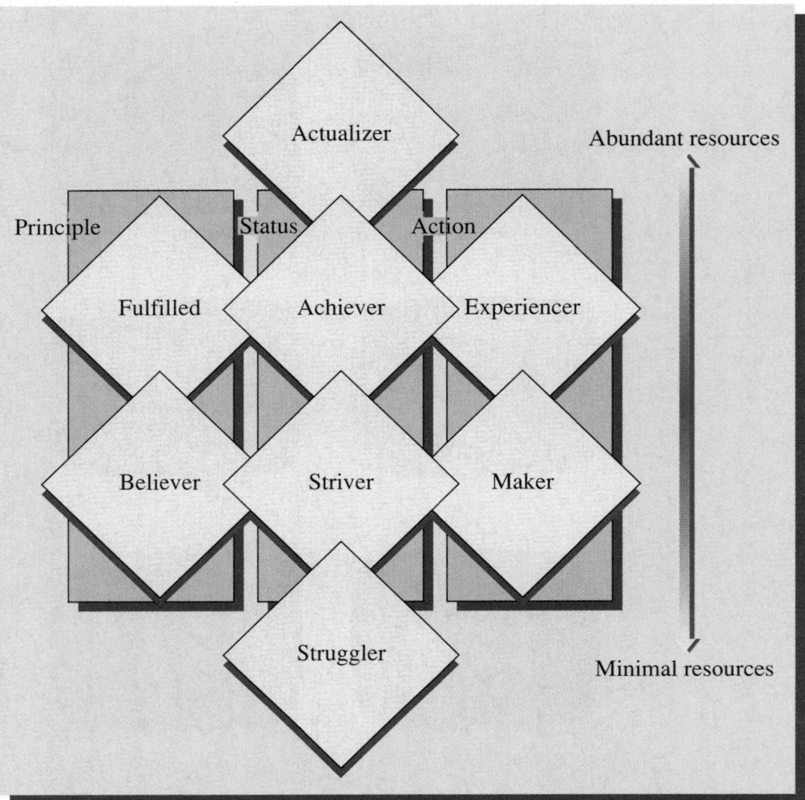

Figure 7-11 The VALS 2 framework. Principle, status, and action are the three dimensions of self-orientation proposed by SRI. (Source: SRI International.)

items (i.e., self-fulfillment, excitement, sense of accomplishment, and self-respect) represent individual values that are of an internal nature. The next three questions (i.e., regarding sense of belonging, being well respected, and security) represent a focus on the external world. Thus a person who worries a lot about crime and unemployment would tend to have a need for security. The third dimension consists of the last two questions (i.e., regarding fun and enjoyment and warm relationships with others) reflects an interpersonal orientation.[68]

The LOV scale has received extensive testing and can be used for differentiating consumers along the three dimensions of internal focus, interpersonal focus, and external focus. One recent study revealed that consumers with an emphasis on internal values seek to control their lives. This desire for control extended to such decisions as where to eat and where to shop, and was expressed by a need to obtain good nutrition and to avoid food additives by purchasing "natural" foods. In contrast, those with an external orientation tended to avoid natural foods, perhaps out of a desire to conform with society at large.[69]

TABLE 7-11

Descriptions of the VALS 2 Consumer Segments

1. *Actualizers*—High resources with focus on principle and action. Active, take-charge expression of taste, independence, and character. College educated, they compose 8% of the population. Median age is 43. Income is $58,000.
2. *Fulfilleds*—High resources with focus on principle. Mature, satisfied, well-informed people for whom image has little importance. Generally married with older children. Composing 11% of population, their median age is 48, they are college educated, and their median income is $38,000.
3. *Believers*—Low resources with focus on principle. Traditional and moralistic, they live predictable lifestyle tied to family and church. Loyal to American products—noninnovative. High school educated, they represent 16% of the population. Median age is 58, with income of $21,000.
4. *Achievers*—High resources with focus on status. Successful, career-oriented individuals. Low risk takers, they respect authority and status quo. Highly image conscious, they buy expensive, expressive autos. College educated, they represent 13% of the population. Aver-age age is 36 and average income is $50,000.
5. *Strivers*—Low resources with focus on status. Impulsive and trend conscious, these individuals seek social approval for actions. Money defines success for them. They frequently have some college education and represent 13% of the population. Median income is $25,000 and median age is 34.
6. *Experiencers*—High resources with focus on action. Young, enthusiastic individuals who like sports and risk taking. Single and impulsive purchasers, they have not yet completed their education. Representing 12% of the population, their average age is 26 and their income is $19,000.
7. *Makers*—Low resources with focus on practical action. Conservative and practical, they focus on family, working with their hands. They represent 13% of the population. Median age is 30 and income is $30,000. High school educated.
8. *Strugglers*—Poor, with little education, they have few resources and must focus on living for the moment. Cautious but loyal shoppers, they represent 14% of the population. Median age is 61 and income is $9,000. High school educated.

A Consumption Life-style Inventory

Recently, researchers developed a new life-style inventory that identified nine "consumption communities."[70] The researchers employed a behavioral segmentation approach in which the actual expenditure patterns of consumers were employed to cluster consumers into groups of people who revealed similar spending patterns. Table 7-13 identifies the nine consumption life-styles found by the researchers.

A MANAGERIAL APPLICATIONS EXAMPLE

The application of concepts from personality and psychographics to managerial issues is illustrated by analyzing the advertising of the U.S. Army.

TABLE 7-12

Buying and Activity Patterns of VALS 2 Segments

Activity Patterns

Item	*Actualizer*	*Fulfilled*	*Believer*	*Achiever*	*Striver*	*Experiencer*	*Maker*	*Struggler*
Buy hand tools	148	65	105	63	59	137	170	57
Barbecue outdoors	125	93	82	118	111	109	123	50
Do gardening	155	129	118	109	68	54	104	80
Do gourmet cooking	217	117	96	103	53	133	86	47
Drink coffee daily	120	119	126	88	87	55	91	116
Drink domestic beer	141	88	73	101	87	157	123	50
Drink herbal tea	171	125	89	117	71	115	81	68
Drink imported beer	238	93	41	130	58	216	88	12
Do activities with kids	155	129	57	141	112	89	116	32
Play team sports	114	73	69	104	110	172	135	34
Do cultural activities	293	63	67	96	45	154	63	14
Exercise	145	114	69	123	94	143	102	39
Do home repairs	161	113	85	82	53	88	171	58
Camp or hike	131	88	68	95	84	156	158	33
Do risky sports	190	48	36	52	59	283	171	7
Socialize weekly	109	64	73	90	96	231	94	62

Buying Patterns

Item	*Actualizer*	*Fulfilled*	*Believer*	*Achiever*	*Striver*	*Experiencer*	*Maker*	*Struggler*
Own SLR camera	163	124	80	138	83	88	115	29
Own bicycle > $150	154	116	90	33	83	120	88	43
Own compact disc player	133	108	119	97	96	94	94	69
Own fishing equipment	87	91	114	87	84	113	142	67
Own backpacking equipment	196	112	64	100	56	129	148	29
Own home computer	229	150	59	136	63	82	109	20
Own < $13K import car	172	128	80	143	68	109	89	44
Own > $13K import car	268	105	70	164	79	119	43	32
Own medium/small car	133	117	89	101	112	92	112	54
Own pickup truck	72	96	115	104	103	91	147	52
Own sports car	330	116	43	88	102	112	90	5

Note: Figures under each segment are the index for each segment (100 = base rate usage).

SOURCE: SRI International.

TABLE 7-13

Nine Consumption Life-styles

1. *Functionalists*—Spend money on essentials. Average education, average income, largely blue collar. Tend to be less than 55 years old and married with children.
2. *Nurturers*—Young. Lower income. Focused on child-rearing, initial household start-up, and family values. Above-average education.
3. *Aspirers*—Focused on enjoying the "high life" by spending above-average amounts on status goods—particularly housing. Highest total expenditures of the nine groups but only fourth highest in income level. Possess classic "Yuppie" characteristics. Highly educated, white collar, and married without children.
4. *Experientials*—Spend above-average amounts on entertainment, hobbies, and convenience goods. Average in education but above-average incomes because they hold white-collar jobs.
5. *Succeeders*—Established households. Middle-aged. Highly educated. Highest incomes of the nine groups. Spend a great deal on education and self-advancement. Spend above average on work-related expenses.
6. *Moral Majority*—High expenditures on educational organizatons, political causes, and church. In empty-nest stage. Second highest incomes. Single wage earner.
7. *The Golden Years*—Frequently retired, but with third highest incomes. Engaged in buying second homes or remodeling. High expenditures on labor-saving products and entertainment.
8. *Sustainers*—Mature, oldest group. Frequently retired. High level of income spent on necessities and alcohol. Lowest education levels, second lowest incomes. Frequently retired.
9. *Subsisters*—Low socioeconomic status. Above-average percentage live on welfare. Many are single-earner families and single parents. Above-average number of minority groups.

SOURCE: Based upon Susan Fournier, David Antes, and Glenn Beaumier, "Nine Consumption Lifestyles," in John F. Sherry, Jr., and Brian Sternthal (eds.), *Advances in Consumer Research*, Vol. 19 (Provo, UT: Association for Consumer Research, 1992), pp. 329–337.

Background

In 1980 the Army was having major recruiting problems. The all-volunteer concept was threatened because each of the previous three years' recruiting had fallen short of the 100,000-person-per-year goal. In addition, the quality of the recruits was poor. A full 45% were high school dropouts, and 75% measured below average on intelligence tests.[71] One cause of the dismal recruiting effort was an unfocused advertising campaign during the 1970s. Campaigns changed at the whim of Army and congressional leaders. Believing that the Army wasn't for sissies, these influential people wanted "blood and guts" ads. For example, in a campaign called "This is the Army," scenes were shown of soldiers trudging through a swamp and of one man suddenly being sucked under the slime. One recruiter observed that promising enlistees had a tendency to walk out after being shown the film. As he said, "Being shot and killed in some foreign country never appealed to recruits."

In 1979 a new commanding officer hired a consultant who recommended that the Army first change the product and then the advertising message. Thus a program was put into place that gave recruits who signed up for two years $15,200 toward their college educations. The "Be All You Can Be" campaign was launched. The writer of the slogan explained, "I wanted a line that could be used in the Army, not just in the ads."

The change in product and promotional strategy succeeded. The proportion of recruits in the bottom 25% in intelligence fell from 56% in 1980 to 19% in 1982. The proportion of recruits who possessed high school diplomas increased from 54% in 1980 to 91% in 1984. Furthermore, recruiting quotas were being met.

Problem Statement

The problem faced by the U.S. Army was how to develop a marketing strategy that would appeal to high-quality young men and women.

The Consumer Behavior Analysis

When the Army's strategy is analyzed from the view of personality and psychographics, several insights result. From psychoanalytic theory, one can identify appeals to the id, ego, and superego. Appeals to the rational ego focused on how joining the Army could help the recruits achieve various goals, such as paying for college and helping them as civilians. Appeals to the primitive id focused on the adventure aspects of the military. Appeals to the superego are also found in the ads. For example, in one ad a young man is shown returning home and talking to his brother about whether his father is still angry with him for joining the Army. The young man walks hesitatingly into the living room in his dress green uniform; his father takes one look and hugs him. Images of patriotism and parental pleasure can be interpreted as appealing to the moralistic id.

Trait theory also has relevance to the campaign. In developing a segmentation strategy, managers could attempt to develop a profile of traits that describes the target market. Thus some of the traits that might be desired in new recruits could include bright (not dull), serious (not happy-go-lucky), conscientious (not expedient), tough-minded (not tender-minded), aggressive (not docile), and controlled (not undisciplined). Such traits could be assessed in the battery of tests given to new candidates. In addition, they could be included as themes in promotional material and in sales presentations by recruiters.

The application of the work on tolerance for ambiguity suggests that the Army's target market of qualified young men and women should be assessed on the scale measuring the construct. Indeed, the individuals sought by the Army should possess moderate to high levels of tolerance for ambiguity. If this were the case, ads should depict soldiers exhibiting flexibility and adaptiveness of behavior.

Ideas involving the self-concept are also relevant to the campaign. The images portrayed in advertisements should probably focus on the potential recruits' ideal self-image. Thus market research should be performed to identify the goals and ambitions of the target market. If these include college, achievement, and self-actualization, then promotional materials should portray individuals using the Army to achieve these ends. Here the use of well-chosen models who depict the ideal self-concept would be an excellent strategy.

An example of the portrayal of the ideal self-concept is an Army ad involving a young man and woman leaving a college class. The man mentions that the woman knew a lot about computers. She responds, "Yeh," that she learned about them in the Army. Amazed, he asks, "You were in the Army, too? What branch?" She replies, as she effortlessly hops over a fence, "Airborne." Totally incredulous, he looks up into the sky and responds, "You mean you jumped out of airplanes?" For young women whose ideal self-image consisted of being adventurous and confident, the ad was great.

Of course, psychographics also has important implications for developing the full description and profile of the target market. Because psychographic analysis is managerially oriented, this application borrows many relevant approaches for use. The psychographic analysis might include materials from trait theory, self-concept scales, and cognitive/social–psychological theory. It would certainly attempt to describe the target market on relevant demographic variables. In addition, it would include AIO questions to develop a profile of the life-style of the target market. Possibly, the VALS psychographic inventory could be used to describe the target market. In particular, the researcher would want to develop promotional materials that would appeal to belongers, who make up the largest segment. The LOV scale could also be used in psychographic analysis. Profiles of the values of the target market could be developed through market research.

The changes in product and promotional strategy illustrate a number of consumer behavior areas besides personality and psychographics. For example, the college tuition incentive is a sales promotion device whose effectiveness could be explained by behavioral learning principles. Similarly, "Be All You Can Be" is a strong appeal to self-actualization and achievement motivations.

The Managerial Applications Analysis

Table 7-14 presents the managerial applications analysis for the U.S. Army ad campaign. A consistent pattern emerges in the table. In each case the consumer concept applies to three managerial areas—market research, segmentation, and marketing mix. This outcome should be expected. Personality and psychographics are used principally to segment the marketplace, whereas market research is used to identify the segments based upon the personality and psychographic variables. Finally, individuals in the segments identified for targeting are reached via the marketing mix. In particular, promotional campaigns are built around the knowledge gained about the personality and psychographic characteristics of the target market.

The U.S. Army advertising campaign case well illustrates these ideas. In the advertisements one finds appeals to the id, the ego, and the superego. To develop the ads, market research was required to determine that such appeals would be effective with the group of young men and women targeted. The ads themselves would have to be developed and then tested to ensure that they had the desired impact. In a similar manner, concepts from trait theory and from tolerance for ambiguity could be used to describe the target market and to develop promotional strategy.

The self-concept is a particularly important idea that managers should consider when doing market research, segmenting the marketplace, and developing promotional campaigns. Market research should be conducted to determine the ideal self-image of potential target groups. Promotional campaigns could then be developed to show how purchasing the product (in this case joining the U.S. Army) would enhance the group's actual self-image.

TABLE 7-14

Managerial Applications Analysis of U.S. Army Ad Campaign

Consumer Concepts	*Managerial Applications Areas*
Psychoanalytic theory	*Segmentation*—Identify themes based upon id, ego, and superego concepts that appeal to the young men and women who fit the demographic profiles of the targeted population.
	Promotional strategy—Develop advertisements based upon psychoanalytic theory that would appeal to the target group.
	Market research—Test the advertisements on a sample from the target group.
Self-concept	*Market research*—Conduct market research to determine the ideal self-concept of various alternative target groups.
	Segmentation—Identify the demographic characteristics of the identified target groups.
	Promotional strategy—Identify advertising themes that appeal to the target groups based upon the ideal self-concept.
Psychographic analysis	*Market research*—Employ psychographic analysis techniques to identify the life-styles of demographically appropriate individuals.
	Segmentation—Identify a number of segments based upon psychographics that can be reached with different messages.
	Promotional strategy—Identify alternative messages and themes for each of the target groups.
	Positioning—Consider developing new positioning strategies for the U.S. Army if a particularly large segment is identified that seeks a particular life-style that the Army can provide.

Information gleaned from the psychographic analysis should also be used to make decisions regarding segmentation, market research, and promotional strategy. In addition, psychographics could be used to help identify appropriate positioning objectives. Based upon knowledge of the psychographic characteristics of the target market, advertisements could be developed that position the U.S. Army in a manner consistent with the desired life-style sought by the group. Such life-style depiction in advertisements can be highly effective. For example, in the advertisements, the U.S. Army positioned itself as exciting, modern, and achievement oriented. In addition, it positioned itself as acting to assist recruits in getting to college and finding a job in the civilian work force. When the military moved away from "blood and guts" appeals to the more sophisticated positioning strategy, its recruitment success improved dramatically.

A final point should be made, however, concerning ethics. The Army has been criticized for conveying a false impression of what life is like in the military. (As a Ranger-qualified member of the U.S. Army many years ago, I can vouch for the fact that it is not all high technology and excitement.) The decision to enlist in the military is one that will have implications for a recruit's entire life. It is far more important than deciding whether to purchase Gleem versus Crest toothpaste. Puffery in military promotional materials must be carefully monitored.

A Final Warning

A focus on life-styles, values, and personality has become extremely popular over the past ten years. Consumer researchers and corporations have invested large amounts of time and financial resources in these areas. A strong risk exists, however, that classifications of consumers into neat pigeonholes can grossly oversimplify the understanding of the buying process. Consumer buying results from the interaction of the person, the product–service offering, and the buying situation. The amount of behavior explained by a single-minded focus on personality or psychographics is apt to be quite small.

The danger of oversimplification arises in part because of the neat and tidy descriptions of people that can be developed from psychographic analysis. For example, consider the fictional person named "Chet." The description is meant to convey the meaning of an emulator in the VALS system.

> Chet seemed personable and dressed stylishly, yet the symbolism of his life always exceeded the reality. He owned a flashy car like the one pictured in his bedroom, but the glamorous model pictured with the car eluded Chet's reality. Chet was clearly trying to prepare for success but lacked the savvy to attain it. Life had been fairly good to Chet, but it was often a bit too big for him to manage with competence.[72]

Because this description is strongly representative of people that all of us have known, we immediately develop a stereotypical view of the people in a market segment that is described as composed of Chets. In reality it is highly doubtful that the description accurately describes the complexity of the people it is meant to portray. Managers should attempt to avoid the fallacy of stereotyping segments based upon psychographic profiles. As a general statement, managers should attempt to combine personality scales, psychographic inventories, and demographic indicators to describe and segment markets.

SUMMARY

Marketing managers are interested in the study of personality and psychographics because its concepts are useful in each of the managerial application areas: segmenting markets, developing market research, creating marketing mix strategy, positioning products, and conducting environmental analysis.

The study of personality is typically conducted by psychologists, and personality is defined as the "distinctive patterns of behavior, including thoughts and emotions, that characterize each individual's adaptation to the situations of his or her life." Although marketers cannot expect to predict from personality profiles the specific brands purchased by a consumer, it is possible to gain an increased understanding of the factors that motivate and guide his or her purchases. Four different approaches to the study of personality were identified in the chapter—the psychoanalytic approach, trait theory, social–psychological and cognitively based personality theories, and self-concept.

Psychoanalytic theory views the personality as resulting from the conflict among the id, the ego, and the superego. It has had a major influence on marketers through its contribution to the motivation researchers. In the trait approach to personality an attempt is made to classify people according to their dominant characteristics. Over the past 10 to 15 years, the trait approach has been used extensively in psychographic studies. The social–psychological approaches to personality investigate the consistent patterns that individuals reveal when interacting with others. An example is the CAD model. The tolerance of ambiguity scale is an example of a cognitive personality approach.

The study of the self-concept is also an area relevant to personality. The self-concept is defined as the totality of a person's thoughts and feelings with reference to himself or herself as the object. Evidence exists that many products are bought in part to reflect the self-concept of the consumer. As such, products become symbols representing the consumer's self to others.

Marketers have moved away from the study of personality to a greater focus on identifying the psychographic characteristics of consumers. One can define psychographics as the quantitative investigation of consumers' life-styles, cognitive styles, and demographics that can be used to assist in marketing decision making. The goal of psychographics is to describe individual consumers in a way that helps managers to segment the marketplace, position products, and develop marketing mix strategy. Because of this highly applied purpose, marketing researchers borrow from any source possible those questions to be included in psychographic inventories.

As a general statement, psychographic inventories contain questions that assess three different aspects of consumers—their life-styles, personalities, and demographic characteristics. The term life-style refers to how people live, how they spend their money, and how they allocate their time. Generally, it is assessed by questions concerning a consumer's various activities, interests, and opinions. It concerns the overt actions and purchases of consumers. In contrast, personality refers to the characteristic patterns of thinking, feeling, and perceiving held by individual consumers. The personality of consumers is generally assessed through questions that focus on identifying consumer traits and consumer attitudes. Demographic questions are also asked in psychographic inventories to further describe the characteristics of individual consumers.

One of the most frequently used psychographic inventories is the VALS life-style classification scheme. In the original VALS approach, consumers are divided into four broad groups of individuals—the need-driven group, the inner-directed group, the outer-directed group, and the integrated group. In VALS 2, eight different consumer segments were identified based upon their self-identify and the amount of resources possessed. Numerous companies and organizations have used VALS to segment the market and to assist in the development of the marketing mix. Another approach relevant to performing psychographic analysis is the List of Values (LOV) scale.

KEY TERMS

AIO statements
cognitive personality theories
consumer cognitive complexity
depth interviews
dogmatism
ego
extended self
focus groups
id
image congruence hypothesis
inner-directed person
libido
life-style
List of Values (LOV) scale
materialism
need-driven person
need for cognition
outer-directed person
personality
pleasure principle
psychoanalytic theory of personality
psychographics
reality principle

self-concept
social–psychological personality theories
superego
symbols
tolerance for ambiguity
trait
unique selling proposition
VALS life-style classification scheme
VALS 2
verbal versus visual information processing

REVIEW QUESTIONS

1. Compare and contrast the concepts of personality and psychographics.
2. Discuss the structure of personality as developed by Freud.
3. In what areas has psychoanalytic theory had an impact on marketing?
4. Describe what is meant by trait theory. What has been the major problem with the use of trait theory by marketers?
5. To what types of consumer tasks might the concept of tolerance of ambiguity be relevant? What types of consumer situations have been identified as ambiguous?
6. Define what is meant by self-concept. Identify five of the six different types of self-concepts.
7. Explain how consumers can communicate themselves to others via symbolic products.
8. A scale has been developed to measure product images and self-images. What are examples of the questions asked on the scale? What procedure must respondents go through in order to assess the relationship between product image and self-image?
9. Define the terms consumer life-style and psychographics.
10. What is meant by the term sequential segmentation?
11. Provide three examples of questions that would be classified as obtaining psychographic information on activities, interests, and opinions.
12. Outline the basics of the VALS psychographic inventory.
13. Compare and contrast the LOV scale to VALS.
14. What are the major managerial uses of personality and psychographics?

DISCUSSION QUESTIONS

1. Think about your own tastes and preferences for food and automobiles. How do your preferences differ from those of your friends? Speculate on what personality differences might explain why your preferences are different from those of other people.
2. Go through a magazine and look carefully at the print advertisements. Identify two ads that possibly use Freudian symbolism. To what extent do you think people are influenced by these symbols?
3. One function of the superego, according to Freudian theory, is to create guilt. To what extent do advertisers attempt to use guilt as a mechanism to promote their products? Try to cite some specific examples.
4. Fantasy is a technique frequently used by marketers of perfumes, autos, and other products with a heavy symbolic emphasis. Develop a draft version of a print advertisement for a new perfume called "Temptation." Develop the ad so that it uses fantasy as a major theme.
5. In developing a trait profile of personality it is important to utilize adjectives that are closely associated with the product or service. Develop a ten-item trait scale that might be used to identify the trait characteristics of people who are heavy consumers of diet foods.

6. Rate yourself on the scale provided in Table 7-6. Next, rate two of your material possessions that are particularly important to you on the scale. To what extent did you rate the material possessions in a manner similar to how you rated yourself?
7. Go through a popular magazine, such as *Newsweek* or *Time*, and identify advertisements that use products as symbols of the self. Describe the relationships you found.
8. Develop a psychographic inventory that might be used to distinguish between heavy and light users of video recorders.

ENDNOTES

1. Charles McCoy and Steve Swartz, "Big Credit-Card War May Be Breaking Out, to Detriment of Banks," *The Wall Street Journal*, March 19, 1987, pp. 1, 24.
2. Ibid., p. 24.
3. Ronald Alsop, "Advertisers Put Consumers on the Couch," *The Wall Street Journal*, May 13, 1988, p. 17.
4. Carrie Dolan, "Fat-Cutting Surgery Gains Wide Popularity But Can Be Dangerous," *The Wall Street Journal*, June 26, 1987, pp. 1, 9.
5. Alix M. Freedman and Michael McCarthy, "New Smoke from RJR Under Fire," *The Wall Street Journal*, February 20, 1990, pp. B1, B4.
6. Darrell Bem, "Self-Perception Theory," in *Advances in Experiential Social Psychology*, Vol. 6, L. Berkowitz, ed. (New York: Springer Press, 1965).
7. Judann Dagnoli, "RJR's Dakota Test Faces Counterattack," *Advertising Age*, March 12, 1990, p. 6.
8. Doron P. Levin, "Chrysler's New L/H, as in Last Hope," *The New York Times*, July 12, 1992, Section 3, p. 1.
9. Walter Mischel, "On the Future of Personality Measurement," *American Psychologist*, Vol. 32 (April 1977), p. 2 (emphasis added). For a general review of personality in consumer behavior, see Harold H. Kassarjian and Mary Jane Sheffet, "Personality and Consumer Behavior: An Update," in *Perspectives in Consumer Behavior*, 4th ed., Harold H. Kassarjian and Thomas S. Robertson, eds. (Englewood Cliffs, NJ: Prentice-Hall, 1991), pp. 81–303.
10. William O. Bearden and Randall L. Rose, "Attention to Social Comparison Information: An Individual Difference Factor Affecting Consumer Conformity," *Journal of Consumer Research*, Vol. 16 (March 1990), pp. 461–471.
11. Harold H. Kassarjian and Mary Jane Sheffet, "Personality and Consumer Behavior: One More Time," American Marketing Association 1975 Combined Proceedings, Series No. 37, 1975, pp. 197–201.
12. John Lastovicka and Erich Joachimsthaler, "Improving the Detection of Personality-Behavior Relationships in Consumer Research," *Journal of Consumer Research*, Vol. 14 (March 1988), pp. 583–587.
13. For an interesting overview of psychoanalytic theory, see Spencer Rathus, *Psychology* (New York: Holt, Rinehart and Winston, 1981).
14. Sigmund Freud, "New Introductory Lectures," in *The Standard Edition of the Complete Works of Freud*, Vol. 22, James Strachey, ed. (London: Hogarth Press, 1964).
15. Ibid.

16. Wilson Bryan Key, *Subliminal Seduction: Ad Media's Manipulation of a Not So Innocent America* (Englewood Cliffs, NJ: Prentice-Hall, 1973).
17. Ibid.
18. Jack Haberstroh, "Can't Ignore Subliminal Ad Charges," *Advertising Age*, September 17, 1984, pp. 42, 44. Also, see John Caccavale, Thomas Wanty, and Julie Edell, "Subliminal Implants in Advertisements: An Experiment," in *Advances in Consumer Research*, Vol. 9, Andrew Mitchell, ed. (Ann Arbor, MI: Association for Consumer Research, 1981), pp. 418–423.
19. Ernest Hilgard, Richard Atkinson, and Rita Atkinson, *Introduction to Psychology*, 6th ed. (New York: Harcourt Brace Jovanovich), 1975.
20. F. B. Evans, "Psychological and Objective Factors in the Prediction of Brand Choice," *Journal of Business*, Vol. 32 (October 1959), pp. 340–369.
21. R. Westfall, "Psychological Factors in Predicting Consumer Choice," *Journal of Marketing*, Vol. 26 (April 1962), pp. 34–40.
22. A. Kaponin, "Personality Characteristics of Purchasers," *Journal of Advertising Research*, Vol. 1 (January 1960), pp. 6–12.
23. Harold Kassarjian, "Personality and Consumer Behavior: A Review," *Journal of Marketing Research*, Vol. 8 (1971), pp. 409–418.
24. Donald R. Lichtenstein, Richard G. Netemeyer, and Scot Burton, "Distinguishing Coupon Proneness from Value Consciousness: An Acquisition-Transaction Utility Theory Perspective," *Journal of Marketing*, Vol. 54 (July 1990), pp. 54–67.
25. See Bernd H. Schmitt, France Leclerc, and Laurette Dube-Rious, "Sex Typing and Consumer Behavior: A Test of Gender Schema Theory," *Journal of Consumer Research*, Vol. 15 (June 1988), pp. 122–128.
26. See Ronald Hill, "The Impact of Interpersonal Anxiety on Consumer Information Processing," *Psychology and Marketing*, Vol. 4 (Summer 1987), pp. 93–105.
27. Terence Shimp and Subhash Sharma, "Consumer Ethnocentrism: Construction and Validation of the CETSCALE," *Journal of Marketing Research*, Vol. 24 (August 1987), pp. 280–289. For information on the CAD scale, see J. Noerager, "An Assessment of CAD," *Journal of Marketing Research*, Vol. 16 (February 1979), pp. 53–59.
28. William O. Bearden and Randall L. Rose, "Attention to Social Comparison Information: An Individual Difference Factor Affecting Consumer Conformity," *Journal of Consumer Research*, Vol. 16 (March 1990), pp. 461–471. The study presented here was but one of four studies discussed by these authors. In this study, the differences between low- and high-ATSCI subjects were not large. The trend over the four studies, however, is strong.
29. George Zinkhan and Abhijit Biswas, "Using the Repertory Grid to Assess the Complexity of Consumers' Cognitive Structures," in *Advances in Consumer Research*, Vol. 15, Michael Houston, ed. (Provo, UT: Association for Consumer Research, 1988), pp. 493–497.
30. Evelyn Gutman, "The Role of Individual Differences and Multiple Senses in Consumer Imagery Processing: Theoretical Perspectives," in *Advances in Consumer Research*, Vol. 15, Michael Houston, ed. (Provo, UT: Association for Consumer Research, 1988), pp. 191–196. Also, see Deborah MacInnis, "Constructs and Measures of Individual Differences in Imagery Processing: A Review," in *Advances in Consumer Research*, Vol. 14, Melanie Wallendorf and Paul Anderson, eds. (Provo, UT: Association for Consumer Research, 1987), pp. 88–92.
31. Curtis P. Haugtvedt, Richard E. Petty, and John T. Cacioppo, "Need for Cognition and Advertising: Understanding the Role of Personality Variables in Consumer Behavior,"

Journal of Consumer Psychology, Vol. 1, no. 3, pp. 239–260.

32. Stanley Budner, "Intolerance for Ambiguity as a Personality Variable," *Journal of Personality*, Vol. 30 (1962), pp. 29–50.

33. Ibid.

34. Brian Blake, Robert Perloff, Robert Zenhausern, and Richard Heslin, "The Effect of Intolerance of Ambiguity Upon Product Perceptions," *Journal of Applied Psychology*, Vol. 58 (1973), pp. 239–243.

35. Charles Schaninger and Donald Sciglimpaglia, "The Influence of Cognitive Personality Traits and Demographics on Consumer Information Acquisition," *Journal of Consumer Research*, Vol. 8 (September 1981), pp. 208–215.

36. Morris Rosenberg, *Conceiving the Self* (New York: Basic Books, 1979).

37. Mehta and Belk, however, note that concepts of self differ cross-culturally. Thus Hindus are less susceptible to the Western view of self as both subject and object. See Raj Mehta and Russell Belk, "Artifacts, Identity, and Transition: Favorite Possessions of Indians and Indian Immigrants to the United States," *Journal of Consumer Research*, Vol. 17 (March 1991), pp. 398–411.

38. Russell W. Belk, "Possessions and the Extended Self," *Journal of Consumer Research*, Vol. 15 (September 1988), pp. 139–168. The quote is found on p. 160.

39. For an excellent review of the self-concept in consumer behavior, see M. Joseph Sirgy, "Self-Concept in Consumer Behavior: A Critical Review," *Journal of Consumer Research*, Vol. 9 (December 1982), pp. 287–300. Also, see Newell D. Wright, C. B. Claiborne, and M. Joseph Sirgy, "The Effects of Product Symbolism on Consumer Self-Concept," in *Diversity in Consumer Behavior, Advances in Consumer Research*, Vol. 19, John F. Sherry, Jr., and Brian Sternthal, eds. (Provo, UT: Association for Consumer Research, 1992), pp. 311–318.

40. Amy J. Morgan, "The Evolving Self in Consumer Behavior: Exploring Possible Selves," *Advances in Consumer Research*, Vol. 20, Leigh McAlister and Michael L. Rothschild, eds. (Provo, UT: Association for Consumer Research, 1993), pp. 429–432.

41. George H Mead, *Mind, Self and Society* (Chicago: University of Chicago Press, 1934).

42. Charles H. Cooley, *Human Nature and the Social Order* (New York: Scribners, 1902).

43. Sidney J. Levy, "Symbols for Sale," *Harvard Business Review*, Vol. 37 (1959), pp. 117–124.

44. Russell W. Belk, Kenneth D. Bahn, Robert N. Mayer, "Developmental Recognition of Consumption Symbolism," *Journal of Consumer Research*, Vol. 9 (June 1982), pp. 4–17.

45. Rebecca H. Holman, "Product as Communication: A Fresh Appraisal of a Venerable Topic," in *Review of Marketing*, Ben M. Enis and Kenneth J. Roering, eds. (Chicago: American Marketing Association, 1981), pp. 106–119.

46. Edward L. Grubb and Harrison Grathwohl, "Consumer Self-Concept, Symbolism, and Market Behavior: A Theoretical Approach," *Journal of Marketing*, Vol. 31 (October 1967), pp. 22–27. However, the author conceived of these relations from the work of Fritz Heider on balance theory. See Fritz Heider, *The Psychology of Interpersonal Relations* (New York: John Wiley, 1958).

47. Sak Onkvisit and John Shaw, "Self-Concept and Image Congruence: Some Research and Managerial Issues," *Journal of Consumer Marketing*, Vol. 4 (Winter 1987), pp. 13–23.

48. Naresh K. Malhotra, "A Scale to Measure Self-Concepts, Person Concepts, and Product Concepts," *Journal of Marketing Research*, Vol. 18 (November 1981), pp. 456–464.

49. John Schouten, "Selves in Transition: Symbolic Consumption in Personal Rites of Passage and Identify Reconstruction," *Journal*

of Consumer Research, Vol. 17 (March 1991), pp. 412–425.

50. Ibid., p. 419.
51. Russell Belk, "My Possessions Myself," *Psychology Today*, July–August 1988, pp. 50–52.
52. William James, *The Principles of Psychology*, Vol. 1 (New York: Henry Holt, 1890).
53. Russell Belk, "Materialism: Trait Aspects of Living in the Material World," *Journal of Consumer Research*, Vol. 12 (December 1985), pp. 265–280.
54. Russell Belk, Melanie Wallendorf, John Sherry, Morris Holbrook, and Scott Roberts, "Collectors and Collecting," in *Advances in Consumer Research*, Vol. 15, Michael Houston, ed. (Provo, UT: Association for Consumer Research, 1987), pp. 548–553.
55. Belk, "Materialism."
56. Marsha L. Richins and Scott Dawson, "A Consumer Values Orientation for Materialism and Its Measurement: Scale Development and Validation," *Journal of Consumer Research*, Vol. 19 (December 1992), pp. 303–316. For another materialism scale, see Russell Belk, "Materialism: Trait Aspects of Living in the Material World, "*Journal of Consumer Research*, Vol. 12 (December 1985, pp. 265–280.
57. Del Hawkins, Roger Best, and Kenneth Coney, *Consumer Behavior: Implications for Marketing Strategy* (Plano, TX: Business Publications, 1983).
58. W. Thomas Anderson and Linda Golden, "Lifestyle and Psychographics: A Critical Review and Recommendation," in *Advances in Consumer Research*, Vol. 11, Thomas Kinnear, ed. (Ann Arbor, MI, Association for Consumer Research, 1984), pp. 405–411.
59. Life-style has been distinguished from "cognitive style" by Anderson and Golden, "Lifestyle and Psychographics."
60. Ron J. Markin, *Consumer Behavior: A Cognitive Orientation* (New York: Macmillan, 1974).
61. Sunil Mehotra and William D. Wells, "Psychographics and Buyer Behavior: Theory and Recent Empirical Findings," in *Consumer and Industrial Buying Behavior*, Arch Woodside, Jagdish N. Sheth, and Peter D. Bennett, eds. (New York: North-Holland, 1979).
62. For an in-depth discussion of VALS, see Arnold Mitchell, *The Nine American Lifestyles* (New York: Macmillan, 1983), p. 57.
63. Ibid., p. 6.
64. 1985 Meat Board Consumer Marketing Plan, National Live Stock and Meat Board, 1985.
65. Rebecca Piirto, "VALS the Second Time," *American Demographics*, July 1991, p. 6.
66. A number of researchers have noted that problems exist with the original VALS inventory. See John L. Lastovicka, John P. Murry, Jr., and Eric Joachimsthaler, "Evaluating the Measurement Validity of ATSCI Typologies with Qualitative Measures and Multiplicative Factoring," *Journal of Marketing Research* (February 1991), pp. 11–23. Also, see Lynn R. Kahle, Sharon Beatty, and Pamela Homer, "Alternative Measurement Approaches to Consumer Values: The List Values (LOV) and Values and Life Style (VALS)," *Journal of Consumer Research*, Vol. 13 (December 1986), pp. 405–409; Sharon E. Beatty, Pamela Homer, and Lynn Kahle, "Problems with VALS in International Marketing Research: An Example from an Application of the Empirical Mirror Technique," in *Advances in Consumer Research*, Vol. 15, Michael Houston, ed. (Provo, UT: Association for Consumer Research, 1988), pp. 375–380.
67. Kahle et al., "Alternative Measurement Approaches to Consumer Values."
68. Pamela Homer and Lynn Kahle, "A Structural Equation Test of the Value-Attitude-Behavior Hierarchy," *Journal of Personality and Social Psychology*, Vol. 54 (April 1988), pp. 638–646.
69. Kahle et al., "Alternative Measurement Approaches to Consumer Values." Also, see Thomas P. Novak and Bruce MacEvoy, "On Comparing Alternative Segmentation Schemes: The List of Values (LOV) and Values and Life Styles (VALS), *Journal of*

Consumer Research, Vol. 17 (June 1990), pp. 105–109. For a recent article that further explores the LOV scale, see Wagner A. Kamakura and Thomas P. Novak, "Value-System Segmentation: Exploring the Meaning of LOV," *Journal of Consumer Research*, Vol. 19 (June 1992), pp. 119–132.

70. Susan Fournier, David Antes, and Glenn Beaumier, "Nine Consumption Lifestyles," *Advances in Consumer Research*, Vol. 19, John F. Sherry, Jr., and Brian Sternthal, eds. (Provo, UT: Association for Consumer Research, 1992), pp. 329–337.

71. Janet Meyers, "Learning to Deploy a Strategic Weapon," *Advertising Age*, November 9, 1988, pp. 94, 96.

72. Ernest Dichter, "Whose ATSCI Is It Anyway?" *Psychology and Marketing*, Vol. 3 (March 1986), pp. 151–163.

Materialism Wanes in a Recessionary World

With the United States in a full-scale recession in 1991 and 1992, companies selling luxury goods had to scramble. It was so sad. Sales of Dom Perignon champagne were flat, and Cartier couldn't move its $10,000 watches. Ferraris selling for $300,000 in 1989 languished at $150,000 in 1991. Poor babies!

Carolyne Roehm, the wealthy fashion designer, commented on the new need to restrain spending. She said, "It's almost looked down upon." The son of billionaire Marvin Davis said that people have stopped talking about "how much money they've just made, what boat they're going to buy or what fancy vacation they've just taken." The chairman of The Sharper Image said that in this environment "People want to live well for less." As a result, during the 1991 Christmas season the company carried so many $25 items "that people will be surprised it's the Sharper Image" [1].

One suffering wine merchant employed an interesting strategy. He invited his best clients to a polo match and served for free French Burgundy and Bordeaux wines costing as much as $100 a bottle. His goal was to show his customers that spending $100 for a bottle of wine for your friends is not the same as conspicuous consumption.

Meanwhile Crystal Brands Inc. was attempting to create a marketing strategy for its troubled Izod Lacoste polo shirts. Its managers decided to bring out a new version of its shirt with a crest to be priced at $30 to $35, a full 20% lower than the shirt with the alligator on the front. (Actually, the crest is really a crocodile.) In the early 1980s the company sold $450 million worth of the Izod shirts. At one time Saks Fifth Avenue devoted an entire wall to the 24 shades of the shirts, but by the late 1980s, most retailers had phased out the brand. Price discounting by retailers and a plethora of cheap "knock-offs" had seriously tarnished the brand.

When discussing Izod's problems, one analyst argued that a consumer rebellion has occurred against visible logos that extends from shirts, to jeans, to cars. He said, "People today are embarrassed to say that they identify with a logo. They want to say, 'I'm a more interesting and individualistic person'" [2].

The strategy of the company is to market its lower-priced, crested shirts under the Izod name to retailers selling moderately priced merchandise. It would then sell the "alligator" shirts to upscale retailers and use the Chemise Lacoste label. The question, however, is whether the cheaper crest shirt will harm the more expensive alligator shirt because the Izod name has become so closely associated with the Chemise Lacoste label. Further, during poor economic times with people avoiding symbols of excess, will consumers go for the "gator"?

QUESTIONS

1. Identify the problems faced by Izod Lacoste.
2. Discuss which consumer behavior concepts from this chapter apply to the case.
3. Discuss the managerial implications of the consumer behavior concepts relevant to the problems faced by Izod Lacoste.

REFERENCES

1. Francine Schwadel and Judith Valente, "With Money Tight and Ostentation Passe, Luxury Goods Suffer," *The Wall Street Journal*, September 3, 1991, pp. 1, 4.
2. Teri Agins, "Izod Lacoste Gets Restyled and Repriced," *The Wall Street Journal*, July 22, 1991, pp. B1, B4.

Chapter

8

Consumer Beliefs, Attitudes, and Behaviors

CONSUMER VIGNETTE

Sales of Ecology, V-8 Engines, Safety, and "Watwheats" Heat Up

In June 1993, Wal-Mart opened its first "eco-store." Billed as being environmentally friendly, the store employs a recycling theme. It is brighter and less cramped, uses wood beams instead of steel girders, employs partially recycled shopping bags, and uses air conditioners that are environmentally safe. Hanging throughout the store is its unique selling proposition, "Together, we're making a difference." In the first week after opening, sales were up 75% from the year before without any advertising being done.[1]

The 65-year-old veterinarian said, "At this stage of my life, I want something that really can move. I got tired of lagging along. I'm tired of the girls passing me." So what did Dr. Carlin do? He purchased a turbo-powered Dodge Lancer, and he says that it makes him feel 15 to 20 years younger. With the cheap gas of the late 1980s, high performance became important to many American consumers. Indeed, GM and Ford had planned to totally eliminate V-8 engines by the late 1980s. However, consumer demand for high-performance autos forced the companies to continue producing the fuel-thirsty vehicles.[2]

Analysts called 1955 the year that "Ford sold safety and Chevrolet sold cars." Ford ads touted the new "lifeguard design," which included stronger doors and padded instrument panels. In contrast, Chevy sold performance and style, and it won the sales contest by a landslide. For over 30 years after Ford's sales debacle, Detroit concluded that safety does not sell cars. By the late 1980s, however, safety features had become important automobile attributes. In 1988 Chrysler Corporation vowed to place air bags in all its U.S.-built cars by 1990.[3] Then, in one television advertisement shown in 1990, Chrysler actually crashed a car going 20 miles per hour, with a real person driving it without padding or helmet. His only protection was a seatbelt and an air bag. This was the first time that a real person had been shown in a crash test. As an executive at the ad agency explained, "We couldn't represent the safety of our air bags if we padded him in any other way."[4] By the mid-1990s auto companies as diverse as Chrysler, Cadillac, Subaru, Volvo, Audi, and Mercedes were touting the safety features on their vehicles.

What makes a dog perfect for a pet? In 1981 Steven M. Brown asked this question. His answer—the perfect dog should be healthy, have a coat that does not shed, and be gentle. The problem was that when he looked for such a dog, it did not exist. Most pedigreed dogs tend to be plagued by genetic diseases and are often aggressive. Others tend to shed excessively. Mr. Brown's solution was to create his own dog—a "watwheat." Over the next decade, he carefully bred Portuguese water dogs with soft-coated wheaten terriers. The results appear to have been a success, and by the 1990s, customers were clamoring for his $800 puppies.[5]

The sales of ecology, turbo-powered cars, safety, and dogs illustrate the relationships among beliefs, attitudes, and behaviors, which will all be explored in this chapter.

INTRODUCTION

The concepts of beliefs, attitudes, and behavior are closely linked together and are highly important to consumer researchers. The generic phrase consumer attitude formation and change is often used to describe the field. In fact, more has been written on consumer attitudes than on any other single topic in the field of consumer behavior.[6] The goal of this chapter is to describe the interrelationships among beliefs, attitudes, and behavior and to discuss how such knowledge can assist marketing managers and public policy makers.

Figure 8-1 For many years Volvo has advertised the safety of its cars, as illustrated by this ad.

The chapter-opening vignette illustrates several important concepts in the study of consumer beliefs, attitudes, and behavior. The success of the Wal-Mart eco-store illustrates how adding a belief about the benefits of a store or a product can influence behavior. Consumers believed that in addition to providing plentiful, low-cost merchandise, the eco-store was environmentally friendly. The change in belief structure influenced the buying behavior of thousands of people.

The story of Dr. Carlin illustrates two important points about beliefs and attitudes. First, it points out the importance of the relationship between attributes and benefits. The Dodge Lancer possessed the attribute (i.e., characteristic) of a turbo-powered engine. Dr. Carlin formed the belief that a turbo-powered engine could provide the benefits of having fun and feeling younger. In addition, the example denotes the importance of the role of feelings and affect in attitude formation. Obtaining a positive feeling from the auto was an important factor for Dr. Carlin. As will be discussed in this chapter, the term attitude refers to the positive or negative feelings/affect that a person has for something, such as an automobile, another person, or a corporation.

The discussion of auto safety and air bags illustrates the concept that the importance of attributes can change over time. In the 1950s and 1960s, auto safety was simply not an important attribute to consumers. By the late 1980s and early 1990s, however, firms were using their vehicles' safety features as a positioning tactic. By performing market research to analyze the importance that consumers attach to product features, researchers were able to gauge changes in consumer evaluations of safety features. Figure 8-1 shows one such advertisement from Volvo.

The creation of the "watwheat" dog illustrates the importance of understanding what are called multiattribute attitude models. Attitudes can be conceptualized as resulting from the combination of the attributes or characteristics that an object possesses. Thus attitudes may result from the multiple attributes that consumers perceive in a product. For Mr. Brown, the perfect dog consisted of the attributes of healthiness, nonshedding tendencies, and gentleness—a combination of characteristics not present in existing canines. Subsequently, he set out to breed his own pet, which resulted in the creation of the watwheat.

In this author's view, possessing an understanding of the factors that influence the formation and change of beliefs, attitudes, and behavior is the most important set of consumer behavior concepts for the marketing manager or public policy maker to know. The next section defines these important ideas.

THE CONCEPTS OF BELIEFS, ATTITUDES, AND BEHAVIORS

The starting point for understanding the relationships between beliefs, attitudes, and behavior is in the study of consumer belief formation.

Consumer Beliefs About Product Attributes

Consumer beliefs represent the knowledge that a consumer has about objects, their attributes, and their benefits provided. But just what are objects, attributes, and benefits? **Objects** are the products, people, companies, and things about which people hold beliefs and attitudes. **Attributes** are the characteristics or features that an object may or may not have. **Benefits** are the positive outcomes that attributes may provide to the consumer.

It is important for managers to remember that beliefs about objects, attributes, and benefits represent consumer perceptions. As a result, beliefs may differ from one consumer to another. In addition, the beliefs that a target market has about a particular brand are likely to be quite different from those of the manager of that brand. Beliefs are formed from the connections linking objects, attributes, and benefits. As shown in Figure 8-2, three types of beliefs are formed:

1. Object–attribute beliefs
2. Attribute–benefit beliefs
3. Object–benefit beliefs

These beliefs result from cognitive learning, and they represent the associations that consumers form among objects, attributes, and benefits.

Object–Attribute Beliefs

The knowledge that an object possesses a particular attribute is called an object–attribute belief. Thus an attribute of the auto engine in the introductory vignette was that it was turbo-powered. Similarly, an attribute of the eco-store is that it recycles and uses biodegradable materials. In sum, object–attribute beliefs link an attribute to an object, such as a person, good, or service.[7] Through object–attribute

Figure 8-2 Forming beliefs among objects, attributes, and benefits.

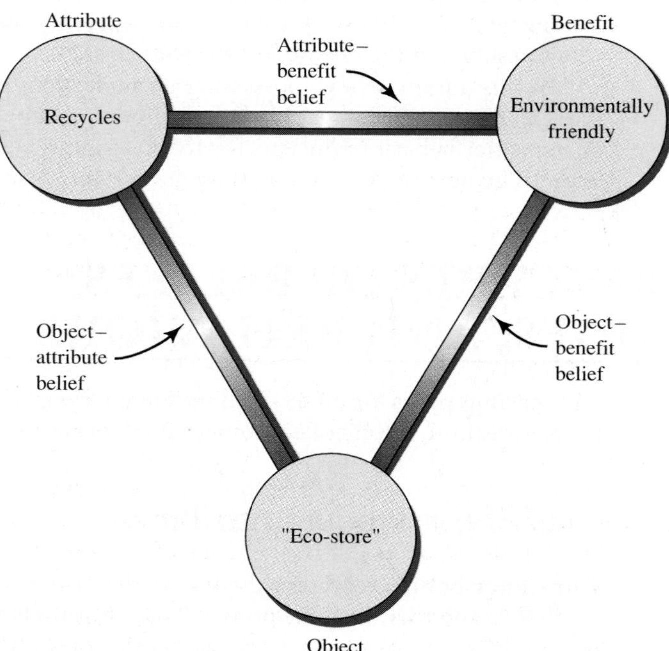

beliefs the consumer defines what he or she knows about something in terms of various attributes.

Attribute–Benefit Beliefs

People seek products and services that solve problems and fulfill needs. Thus the attributes that consumers seek are those that provide recognizable benefits. This link between attributes and benefits represents a second type of belief, which may be called an attribute–benefit belief. An attribute–benefit belief is the consumer's perception of the extent to which a particular attribute will result in or provide a particular benefit. Thus an attribute–benefit belief would be the perception that a store that uses biodegradable materials and recycles provides the benefit of being environmentally friendly. Table 8-1 gives examples of some attributes and their potential benefits in a hypothetical "perfect" sports car.

Object–Benefit Beliefs

The third type of belief is formed by linking an object with a benefit. Thus an object–benefit belief is a consumer's perception of the extent to which a particular product, person, or service will lead to a particular benefit. In the case of ecology, an object–benefit belief would be that by going to Wal-Mart you will be helping the environment.

Consumer Beliefs and Their Managerial Implications

The beliefs that consumers hold about brands, corporations, and other attitudinal objects in the consumer environment have important managerial implications. For example, managers should recognize that the product-attribute beliefs held by consumers may not match reality. For a variety of reasons, consumers may have an inaccurate impression of the extent to which a product possesses a particular attribute. For example, when a brand has a low promotional budget, consumers may simply not be aware of the extent to which the product possesses an attribute. Thus few buyers of personal computers in 1993 were aware that an IBM clone, Gateway Computer, had one of the best quality ratings. With this lack of information, consumers may simply assume that the product ranks poorly on the attribute.

Halo effects are one source of misperceptions about product attributes in the marketplace. A **halo effect** occurs when consumers assume that because a product is good or bad on one product characteristic, it is also good or bad on another product characteristic. Thus a consumer who believes that Crest toothpaste is the best cavity-fighting toothpaste might also think that it also has the lowest abrasive qualities. (In fact, Crest has an above-average tendency to abrade teeth.)

Brands are frequently positioned based upon the attributes that they possess. An example is the positioning of Apple Computer's Macintosh line of personal computers. With the entry of IBM into the personal computer field in the 1980s, a shakeout occurred, and many companies went out of business. Successful brands used the same DOS system as the IBM PC on which software, such as spreadsheets and word processing programs, was run. A major question for Apple was whether to produce an IBM-compatible computer. The company shunned the advice of many analysts and decided to disassociate itself from IBM and position itself as an alternative that

TABLE 8-1

Examples of Attributes and Their Benefits for the "Perfect" Sports Car

Attribute	*Benefit*
Quick acceleration	Creates thrills by snapping head back.
	Allows driver to pass more safely.
	Allows driver to navigate winding roads more quickly.
	Creates feelings of excitement and fun.
Superior handling	Allows driver to navigate winding roads more quickly.
	Heightens arousal when going fast around corners.
	Creates feelings of excitement and fun.
Small size	Helps improve acceleration.
	Improves gas mileage.
Good gas mileage	Lowers expenses.
Low sticker price	Lowers expenses.
Good repair frequency	Saves money and time.
Futuristic styling	Makes owner feel good.
	Turns people's heads.

was highly user-friendly. The positioning was successful, and the company flourished despite the dire warnings of many marketing pundits.

The study of attributes and their benefits also applies to segmentation strategy. Within the marketplace groups of consumers may seek specific product benefits. Such groups may become important segments for a company to target via benefit segmentation. **Benefit segmentation** involves the division of the market into relatively homogeneous groups of consumers based upon a similarity of benefits sought. Within the marketplace, companies can often identify groups of people who seek particular benefits from products that may satisfy specific needs. Thus a consumer who has computer phobia has a need for a user-friendly computer. Apple developed a product that fulfills such a need—the Macintosh. Procter & Gamble has built huge market shares for many of its brands by establishing a strategy of focusing on how a product provides a benefit that fulfills one particular consumer need. For example, Crest toothpaste has built its dominant market share around providing one primary benefit—decay prevention. Similarly, Charmin toilet tissue has built its market share around providing the benefit of softness.

The analysis of attributes and benefits can affect promotional strategy. Within the consumer marketplace, different segments of consumers have various amounts of knowledge about the attributes of products and their benefits. Researchers have found that consumers with a great deal of knowledge (i.e., experts) process information differently from novices. In one research study, information on computers was expressed in the form of attribute information (e.g., large memory capacity expandable to 512K for bank switching) or benefit information (e.g., large memory capacity adequate to handle heavy-duty word processing better than the existing word

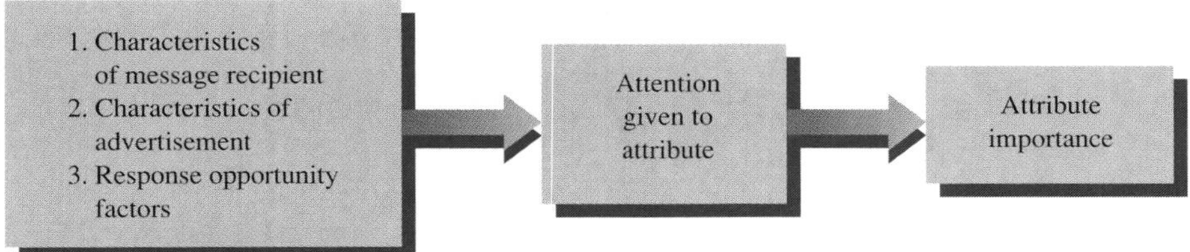

Figure 8-3 Factors influencing attribute importance. (Based on Scott Mackenzie, "The Role of Attention in Measuring the Effect of Advertising on Attribute Importance," *Journal of Consumer Research*, Vol. 13, September 1986, pp. 174–195.)

processors).[8] The results revealed that experts had more positive evaluations when they received the attribute information. In contrast, novices had more positive evaluations when they received the benefit information. These results suggest that managers should carefully determine the expertise of their target market prior to determining whether to advertise a brand by presenting attribute information, benefit information, or a combination of the two.

Attribute Importance

Attributes differ widely in their importance to consumers. **Attribute importance** can be defined as a person's general assessment of the significance of an attribute for products or services of a certain type.[9]

Figure 8-3 presents a diagram that depicts factors proposed to influence attribute importance. The approach takes an information-processing perspective, arguing that attribute importance is directly influenced by the amount of attention directed to a specific attribute. Thus the greater the attention directed to an attribute, the more important that attribute becomes.

Three factors are proposed to influence the amount of attention directed to the attribute: (1) characteristics of the message recipient, (2) characteristics of the advertisement, and (3) factors that influence the response opportunity of the recipient. First, characteristics of the message recipient may influence attention. A person's cultural norms and values may influence how attention is directed. In addition, attention could be influenced by how closely the attributes are tied to a consumer's self-concept. Thus, if a consumer has a self-concept that includes being environmentally friendly, the recycling attribute of Wal-Mart could strongly attract attention.

The second factor that may influence the amount of attention directed to an attribute is advertising. Recent evidence indicates that advertising can influence the importance of attributes. Advertisements that can direct consumers' attention to an attribute and cause them to allocate cognitive capacity to the attribute (i.e., make them think about it) may result in an increase in the perceived importance of the attribute. For example, making the copy in an advertisement that pertains to an attribute highly concrete and vivid may direct attention to the attribute and increase its perceived importance. Figure 8-4 presents an ad that AT&T employed in its massive campaign for "The i plan." The surrealistic ad focuses the viewer's attention on the bald man's ears. The goal was to raise the importance to consumers of the sound quality of telephone calls as a product attribute.

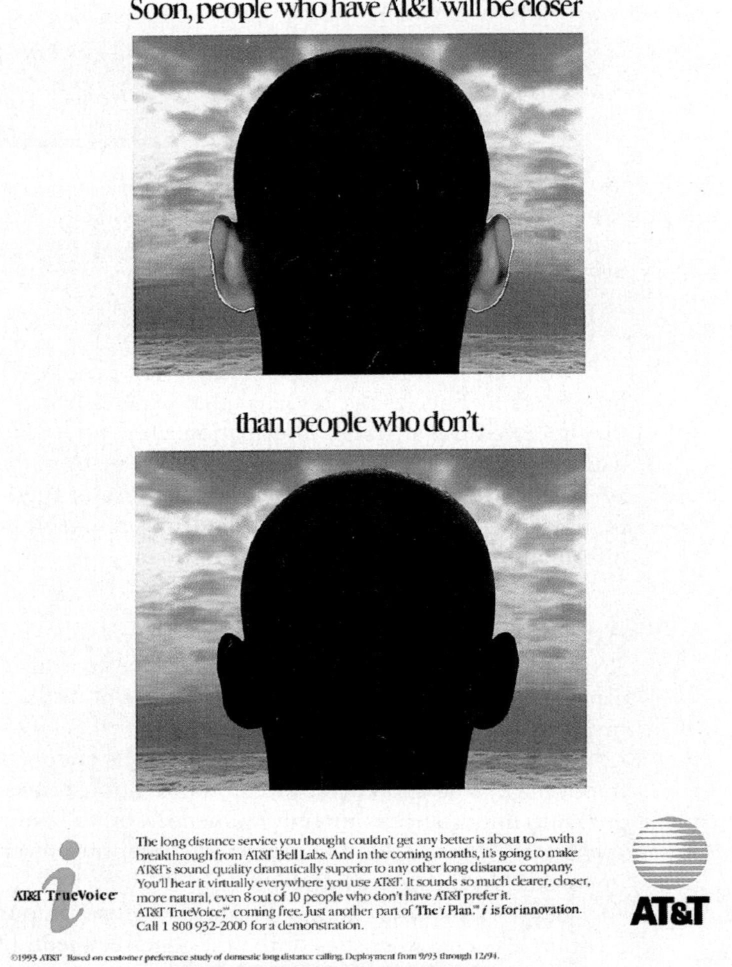

Figure 8-4 AT&T seeks to increase the importance of sound quality to consumers in this surrealistic ad.

The characteristics of the message can impact attribute importance in attempts to "demarket" the use of products. **Demarketing** refers to attempts by regulatory agencies and nonprofit organizations to reduce the frequency of consumer behaviors viewed to have a negative impact on the consumer or society. Efforts to reduce the usage of illegal drugs, the smoking of cigarettes, and the drinking of alcohol illustrate the demarketing of products. One method of demarketing the consumption of alcoholic beverages and cigarettes is to place warning labels on bottles and packages. The goal of the warning labels is to influence attitudes by identifying an attribute that results in a negative outcome (i.e., harm to one's health). The problem, however,

HIGHLIGHT 8-1

Pro-social Consumer Behavior Increasing the Salience of Alcoholic Warning Labels

Since 1989, warnings labels are required to appear on all alcoholic beverage containers sold in the United states. However, simply placing a warning label on a container does not mean that it will have any impact on consumer beliefs, attitudes, or behaviors. The goal of the law that made warning labels mandatory is to demarket the consumption of alcoholic beverages, particularly by susceptible groups, such as pregnant women and youths. Recently, experiments were conducted to assess the impact of different messages and message format strategies on recall of the warning labels. Three of the messages used were as follows:

1. Drinking alcohol during pregnancy may cause the baby to have behavior problems, mental retardation, or deformities.
2. Daily drinking of alcohol increases the risk of throat, stomach, and prostate cancer and diseases of the liver and heart.
3. Drunk driving is the number-one killer of children and young adults. There is an alcohol-related death every 22 minutes.

In the first study, researchers varied the size of the warning labels, which were placed in magazine ads for actual alcoholic beverages. In the second study, warnings were developed for commercials that were embedded in a sports-oriented television show. The results revealed that increasing the size of the warning label did impact recall. Inconspicuous labels were no better than having no label. When used as a television ad, the impact of the message was greater when it was both printed in the ad and also stated verbally in the ad. In sum, the results revealed that increasing the saliency of the warning labels increased their impact. A key question, however, for market researchers is whether increasing the recall of the warning label will impact the beliefs, attitudes, and behaviors of the target market.

Based upon Todd Barlow and Michael S. Wogalter, "Alcoholic Beverage Warnings in Magazine and Television Advertisements," *Journal of Consumer Research*, Vol. 20 (June 1993), pp. 147–156.

concerns how to make the attribute sufficiently salient and important to consumers to influence their behavior. Highlight 8-1 discusses recent research on this issue.

Third, many researchers believe that response opportunity factors influence attention. Response opportunity factors are those factors that determine the extent to which a person must process information about an attribute. Response opportunity is increased if information about the attribute is repeated and if consumers are not distracted from processing information about the attribute.

From a manager's perspective, it is crucial to identify the relative importance that a target market assigns to the attributes of a product. Thus department stores need to be aware of which market segments may value environmental friendliness. For young adults it could be extremely important; however, for some other groups of people it may have little or no importance. In addition, managers should work with advertising personnel to ensure that creative strategy is consistent with developing ads that place consumers' attention on appropriate attributes.

Price as an Attribute

In many cases the product's price is one of the most important attributes evaluated by consumers. Managers should be highly aware of the role of price in the consumer's decision process. In some instances consumers may be highly price sensitive (i.e., demand elastic), so that a high price relative to competitors might eliminate the product from consideration. In other cases price can be used as a surrogate indicator of product quality, resulting in a higher price being viewed positively by certain segments.

An important concept is that product price can act either positively or negatively to influence consumers. Recently, researchers identified seven different dimensions of the price attribute.[10] In its *negative role*, a concern for price has been found to influence people to have

1. *Value consciousness*—the extent to which consumers are concerned with the ratio of product quality to price.
2. *Price consciousness*—the extent to which consumers focus exclusively on paying low prices.
3. *Coupon proneness*—the extent to which consumers respond to a purchase offer that includes a coupon.
4. *Sale proneness*—the extent to which consumers respond to a purchase offer that includes a reduction in price.
5. *Price mavenism*—the extent to which consumers attempt to become sources of information to others about price information in the marketplace.

On the other hand, in some circumstances the price attribute can play a *positive role* in influencing consumer attitudes and behaviors. In its positive role, price has been found to influence consumers in two types of circumstances:

1. *Price–quality relationship*—the extent to which a person tends to use price as an indicator of quality. (See Chapter 3 for a discussion of the price–quality relationship.)
2. *Prestige sensitivity*—the extent to which a consumer forms favorable perceptions of the price attribute based upon a sensitivity to other people's perceptions of the status that higher prices signal.

The researchers found that individual differences exist in the extent to which people tend to respond to each of the seven dimensions of price sensitivity. In addition, these individual differences were related to shopping behavior. For example, consumers who were value conscious tended to read *Consumer Reports* magazine more frequently. Similarly, consumers who were price conscious looked at advertisements for grocery store sales more frequently. Finally, those consumers who were coupon prone revealed a strong tendency to redeem coupons more frequently.

In sum, price is a multifaceted construct. Depending upon the characteristics of the consumer, the situation, and the product, it can take on quite different meanings to consumers.

Consumer Attitudes

The word "attitude" comes from the Latin term *aptus*, which means "fitness" or "adaptedness." By the eighteenth century the expression had come to refer to bodily posture, and to this day the word "attitude" can mean something's general physical orientation with respect to something else. Late in the eighteenth century Charles Darwin used the word in a biological sense as a physical expression of an emotion. Indeed, well into the twentieth century, researchers tended to link attitudes with physiological tendencies to approach or avoid something.[11]

Over the past 30 years the term attitude has been defined in numerous ways. The definition that best captures the ideas developed in this text was put forth by L. L. Thurstone, who was one of the originators of modern attitude measurement theory. Thurstone viewed an **attitude** as "the amount of affect or feeling for or against a stimulus."[12] The idea that attitudes refer to affect or a general evaluative reaction has been expressed by many researchers, and the trend in recent years has been to link the concept to feelings rather than beliefs. Examples of some definitions of attitudes include the following:

> Attitudes are ". . .the categorization of an object on an evaluative continuum."[13]
>
> The "major characteristics that distinguish attitude from other concepts are its evaluative or affective nature."[14]
>
> Attitudes are the core of our likes and dislikes for certain people, groups, situations, objects, and intangible ideas.[15]

Whereas beliefs are the cognitive knowledge that consumers have linking attributes, benefits, and objects, attitudes are the feelings or affective responses that people have about attributes, benefits, and objects.

The Functions of Attitudes

If a market researcher asks consumers how much they like something or how they feel about something, consumers are expressing their attitudes toward the object. Once these attitudes are formed, they can be viewed as being stored in long-term memory. When appropriate occasions arise, the attitude can be retrieved from memory to help the person deal with the issue or problem. In this way, attitudes can be used to help people interact more effectively with the environment. Thus, when one speaks of the functions of attitudes, the goal is to identify the use to which the attitude is put.[16]

Although a number of functional theories of attitudes have been developed, the one that receives the most attention was developed by Daniel Katz. Katz identified four functions of attitudes: the utilitarian function, the ego-defensive function, the knowledge function, and the value-expressive function.[17]

The Utilitarian Function The utilitarian function of attitudes relates to the concept that people express feelings to maximize rewards and minimize punishments received from others. Thus attitudes guide behavior to gain positive reinforcers and avoid punishers. In this sense, the expression of an attitude is like an operantly conditioned response. Indeed, Katz specifically identified an attitude as an operantly conditioned behavior. For example, a salesperson might learn that making positive comments to a client (i.e., expressing favorable attitudes) is more likely to result in a sale (i.e., a positive reinforcer). Similarly, a consumer might express a positive attitude toward a particular rap star (e.g., Hammer) to gain the affection of someone known to love the frenetic dancing performer.

The Ego-Defensive Function Also called the self-esteem maintenance function, attitudes may be held to protect people from basic truths about themselves or from the harsh realities of the external world. The ego-defensive function identified by

Katz is derived from psychoanalytic theory (see Chapter 7 for a discussion of this approach). In this context the attitude acts as a kind of defense mechanism. Thus prejudice against minorities can be viewed as an attitude that serves to defend bigots from basic insecurities about themselves.

In a consumer setting, an example would be people who hold positive attitudes toward smoking to defend themselves against the reality of what they are doing to their bodies. Similarly, consumers may purchase and express positive attitudes toward beauty aids and diet products to defend themselves against underlying feelings of physical inadequacy.

The Knowledge Function Attitudes may also serve as standards that help people to understand their universe. As such, attitudes help a person to give meaning to the unorganized and chaotic world. For example, consumers may develop attitudes toward salespeople in "loud" jackets or toward retail stores with soft music and plush interiors. When such a person or store is encountered, the consumer interprets the information based upon these attitudes. Such a procedure helps to simplify the world for the consumer. Thus, if the consumer views salespeople who wear loud jackets negatively, he or she is likely to resist selling attempts from such people. In such instances the consumer does not have to think about whether to listen to such a person. Instead, the attitude simplifies the encounter, allowing the consumer to focus on more important matters.

Through the knowledge function attitudes form a frame of reference by which the world is interpreted. As such, attitudes can result in selective exposure and attention to marketing communications. The knowledge function also helps to explain some of the effects of brand loyalty. By remaining brand loyal and maintaining a positive attitude toward a product, consumers can simplify and maintain stability in their world. Similarly, having a positive attitude toward a brand may reduce the amount of search time required to find a product to fulfill a need. Thus, if you run out of toothpaste and you have a positive attitude toward the Viadent brand, you will probably purchase it time after time without undergoing an extensive search process for other alternatives.

The Value-Expressive Function The value-expressive function expresses a person's central values to others. Thus it has also been called the social identify function. The expression of attitudes may even serve to help an individual define his or her self-concept to others. In consumer settings the value-expressive function can be seen in instances in which people express positive views about various products, brands, and services to make a statement about themselves.[18] For example, consider the ad for Rolex watches found in Figure 8-5. In the copy of the ad, the naturalist George Schaller expresses an attitude in the statement "If we don't protect the Chang Tang now, the magnificent species found here could soon vanish forever." This attitudinal statement expresses a set of values held by Mr. Schaller, with which Rolex hopes that its target market will identify.

Behaviors and Intentions to Behave

As noted earlier in the text, the primary goal of the marketer is to understand, to predict, and to a certain extent control the behavior of consumers. Thus **consumer behaviors** are everything that consumers do related to acquiring, using, and

Figure 8-5 In this ad for Rolex watches, George Schaller voices an attitude that illustrates the value-expressive function of attitudes.

disposing of products and services. Examples of consumer behaviors include buying a product or service, providing word-of-mouth information about a product or service to another person, disposing of a product, and collecting information for a purchase.

Prior to engaging in an action, people may develop behavioral intentions regarding their likelihood of engaging in the behavior. **Behavioral intentions** may be defined as the intentions of consumers to behave in a particular way with regard to the acquisition, use, and disposition of products and services. Thus a consumer may form the intention to search for information, to tell someone else about an experience with a product, to buy a product or service, and to dispose of a product in a certain way. As discussed in more detail later in this chapter, the formation of behavioral intentions precedes behavior in high-involvement circumstances. Thus predicting behavioral intentions is a frequent goal of consumer researchers.

HOW BELIEFS, ATTITUDES, AND BEHAVIORS ARE FORMED

Beliefs, attitudes, and behaviors may be formed in two distinct ways. The first is through direct formation in which a belief, attitude, or behavior is created without either of the other states occurring first. Thus, as the behavioral influence perspective on consumer behavior suggests, a behavior could be induced to occur without the consumer having formed strong attitudes or beliefs about the object to which the behavior is directed. Similarly, as the experiential perspective suggests, an attitude (i.e., a feeling) may be created without the consumer having specific beliefs about the attitudinal object, such as a product or service, and without the consumer ever having bought the product.

After a belief, attitude, or behavior is formed directly, a tendency exists for the states to build upon each other to create hierarchies. Thus the consumer may first form beliefs about a product, then develop attitudes toward it, and finally purchase it. In a similar manner, the consumer may first engage in the behavior of buying a product and then form beliefs and attitudes. Thus the indirect formation of beliefs, attitudes, and behaviors occurs when the formation of one state (e.g., a belief) results in the creation of another state (e.g., an attitude) to build a hierarchy of effects.

The Direct Formation of Beliefs, Attitudes, and Behaviors

Disparate processes cause the direct formation of beliefs, attitudes, and behaviors. These processes are directly linked to the three research perspectives on consumer behavior. Belief formation corresponds to the decision-making perspective. Thus beliefs are viewed as being formed primarily through cognitive-learning principles. In contrast, the direct formation of attitudes is linked to the experiential perspective, such that attitudes result from sources that directly elicit emotional responses (e.g., mere exposure and classical conditioning). Finally, the direct creation of behavior corresponds to the behavioral influence perspective. Behavior may result from people engaging in behaviors because of environmental or situational factors.

Creating Beliefs Directly

The direct formation of beliefs occurs through the information-processing activities of the consumer. Information about the attributes of a product is received, encoded into memory, and later retrieved from memory for use. Figure 8-6 shows an advertisement for Dr. Scholl's callus removers that attempts to create the following specific attribute–object beliefs about the product—fast, safe, eliminates pain, eliminates corns, and eliminates calluses. The goal of Dr. Scholl's and its ad agency is to influence the reader's beliefs via information processing and cognitive learning.

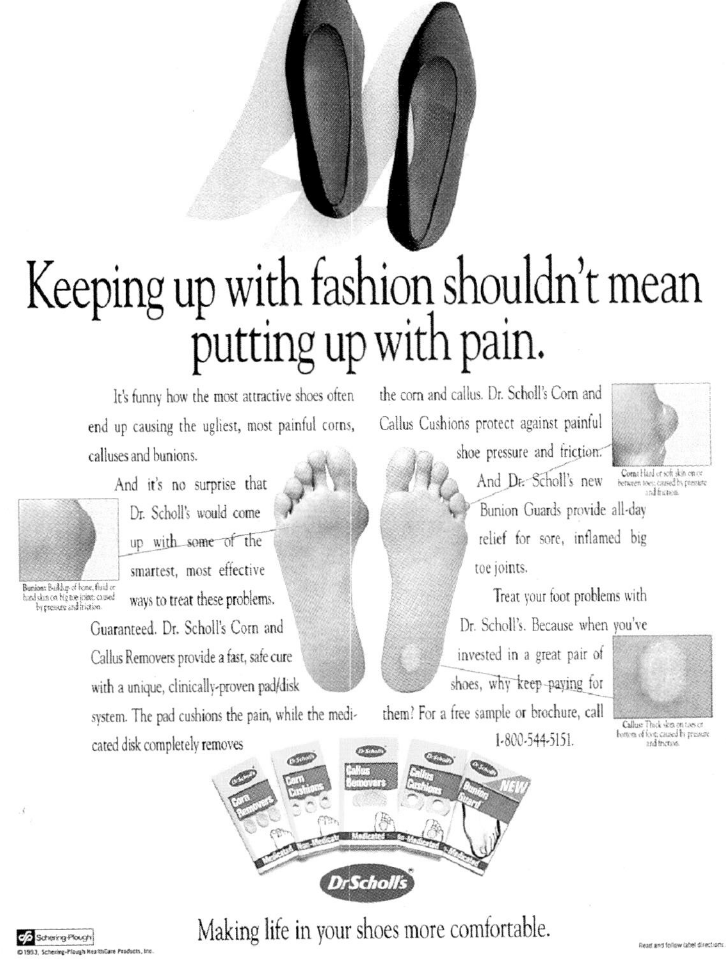

Figure 8-6 The goal of this ad is to influence consumers' attribute-object beliefs.

Forming Attitudes Directly

Earlier in the chapter, an attitude was defined as the amount of affect or feeling for or against a stimulus object, such as a person, product, company, or idea. Two mechanisms explain how attitudes are formed directly. The first is through behavioral-learning processes. The second mechanism of direct attitude formation is through a process called the mere exposure phenomenon.

BEHAVIORAL LEARNING AND ATTITUDE FORMATION Attitudes may be created directly through the behavioral-learning processes of classical conditioning, operant conditioning, and observational learning. (For a detailed description of these processes, see Chapter 5.) From a classical-conditioning perspective, an attitude is a conditioned response that can be elicited by a conditioned stimulus. Researchers have found evidence of the classical conditioning of attitudes in a consumer behavior setting.[19] In one set of four studies, good evidence was found that attitudes toward a brand could be influenced by using the unconditioned stimuli of pleasing pictures, such as a mountain waterfall. The sexy ads for Calvin Klein's products illustrate the attempt to classically condition consumers so that feelings and emotions are elicited by a brand.

Attitudes may also result from operant-conditioning processes. For example, an individual may have a conversation with friends about various cars. During the conversation, the person may make statements about alternative models. The positive and negative responses of the friends may act to reinforce or punish the individual's evaluations. The positively reinforced evaluations are likely to reoccur, whereas the punished evaluations are likely to be suppressed. Thus social reinforcement may be a major factor influencing attitude formation.

The operant conditioning of attitudes is closely related to the utilitarian function discussed earlier in the chapter. As discussed by Katz, the expression of attitudes may be viewed as learned responses resulting from reinforcement and punishment.[20] From this perspective, the affect that makes up the feeling base of the attitude can be viewed as a result of operant conditioning.

Vicarious learning may also lead to the direct formation of attitudes. The observation of important others expressing their feelings and evaluations of products may result in the target audience's modeling these actions. Through such a process, a person may form his or her attitudes in part by taking on the attitudes of opinion leaders. Celebrity endorsers may have such an effect on consumers. Very popular endorsers, such as Bill Cosby or Victoria Principal, may influence the attitudes of their admirers through such a modeling process.

Mere Exposure and Attitude Formation Another method through which positive feelings may be formed is through repeated exposures with a stimulus. All else equal, through the mere exposure phenomenon, people's liking for something may increase simply because they see it over and over again.[21] The all-else-equal caveat is important: if the consumer perceives the stimulus negatively, the repeated exposures could lead to an increase in the dislike for the stimulus.[22]

An interesting aspect of the mere exposure phenomenon is that it does not seem to be cognitively based. The positive feelings created from repeated exposures can occur without the person consciously knowing or perceiving that the object is familiar.[23] Figure 8-7 shows a mundane scene of a Wal-Mart store parking lot. The retailer is having a back-to-school sale. But notice the Coca-Cola logo on the tent. In the consumer environment, images of Coke are ubiquitous. Possibly, part of its appeal results from the mere exposure effect that results from its omnipresence.

The effects of mere exposure have important implications for marketers. By developing a corporate strategy to have a product, its name, or its symbol repeatedly encountered by consumers, the company may be able to subtly influence the feelings that large numbers of people have toward it. The omnipresence of the Coca-Cola name is an example. One sees it repeatedly flashed on television, at baseball parks, in theaters, in restaurants, on buses, and elsewhere. The effects of mere exposure may be one of the factors making Coke the largest-selling soft drink.

Figure 8-7 The Coca-Cola logo can be found everywhere and thus illustrates the mere exposure effect.

Creating Behavior Directly

Traditionally, consumer researchers have viewed the behavior of buying a product or service as occurring after the formation of beliefs and attitudes. However, in certain circumstances behavior may be influenced directly, without consumers first having developed strong beliefs or attitudes about the product. As discussed in Chapter 5, behavior tends to be directly influenced when strong situational or environmental forces propel the consumer to engage in an action. The ecological design of the physical environment is an excellent example of how behaviors can be directly induced.[24] Retailers and restaurateurs must pay particular attention to the physical layout of their building. The appropriate arrangement of aisles in a supermarket can move customers in desired directions past high-margin food and nonfood items. Similarly, the arrangement of seating in a restaurant can either enhance or detract from the ability of customers to interact during their meals, thereby influencing the rate of turnover of patrons during prime eating hours. Sales promotion tactics used by marketers are likewise designed to directly influence behavior.

Operant conditioning can also be used to influence behavior directly. Indeed, its proponents claim that people may not even be aware of conditioning when it occurs. Shaping is an example of the direct influence of behavior through operant conditioning. Shaping occurs when reinforcers are skillfully applied so as to create new behaviors.

Auto dealerships are skillful shapers of behavior. For example, in 1988 Buick attempted to improve sales of its slow-selling Regal by coordinating its sales promotion efforts with the Buick Open golf tournament. The division ran a large contest, called the "Longest Drive Sweepstakes," that gave any person who entered a showroom a chance of winning $126,000. If the person test drove a Regal, he or she was given a sleeve of golf balls. Finally, the customer was given a large discount on the purchase of a Regal.

The direct influence of behavior has not received much attention from consumer researchers. Thus the frequency with which it occurs among consumers is unknown. However, it would not be surprising to find through future research that a large number of consumers' activities result from direct induction without specific attitudes or beliefs occurring first.

Hierarchies of Beliefs, Attitudes, and Behaviors

Although behaviors, attitudes, and beliefs can be formed directly, a tendency exists for them to be formed indirectly. In such instances, they become linked together to form hierarchies of effects. The term **hierarchies of effects** was developed to delineate the order in which beliefs, attitudes, and behavior occur. The factor that most directly controls which hierarchy is implemented appears to be the type of purchase process in which the consumer is engaged. Table 8-2 identifies four different purchase processes in which consumers may be involved and the hierarchy of effects associated with each process. The four hierarchies are the high-involvement hierarchy, the low-involvement hierarchy, the experiential hierarchy, and the behavioral influence hierarchy.

Decision-Making Hierarchies

The early proponents of the hierarchies of effects theory proposed that beliefs about objects occurred first. Next, consumers developed affect (feelings) toward the object. Finally, consumers engaged in some behavior relative to the object, such as purchasing a product. This pattern in which behavior follows affect, which follows beliefs, has been called the **standard learning hierarchy**[25] or the **high-involvement hierarchy**. In high-involvement circumstances, it makes sense that consumers should

TABLE 8-2

Purchase Processes and Their Possible Hierarchies of Effects

Purchase Process	*Hierarchy of Effects*
1. High involvement	Standard learning hierarchy: Beliefs—affect—behavior
2. Low involvement	Low-involvement hierarchy: Beliefs—behavior—affect
3. Experiential/impulse	Experiential hierarchy: Affect—behavior—beliefs
4. Behavioral influence	Behavioral influence hierarchy: Behavior—beliefs—affect

first investigate a product to learn about its characteristics. Based upon this information, they evaluate it and form feelings and attitudes. If attitudes are positive, they may then purchase the product. Beginning in the mid-1960s, however, consumer researchers began to recognize that many, if not most, consumer purchases do not follow the pattern of the standard hierarchy.[26]

Researchers began to believe that in many cases, products were purchased without consumers developing any feelings or affect. In such instances it was proposed that consumers first form beliefs about a product. These beliefs are then followed directly by the product's purchase. Only after the purchase does the consumer develop an attitude regarding the product.[27]

Why does the formation of an attitude sometimes take place after the occurrence of a behavior? The answer appears to lie in the involvement of the consumer with the product and the purchase situation.[28] As defined earlier, involvement is a state of motivation resulting from an act of purchase or consumption having high personal importance or relevance. As the amount of involvement in the decision increases, the consumer tends to engage in increased problem-solving activities. The problem-solving activity involves the consumer in extensively searching for information about alternative products or services that may be bought. As a result, the consumer is likely to form a relatively large number of beliefs about the alternatives. In addition, the consumer is likely to take the time to evaluate the alternatives and compare them. Through such activities, attitudes may be formed. With the formation of beliefs and attitudes, behavioral intentions are likely to result, as is ultimately the action of purchasing the product or service. Thus, when the consumer is highly involved in a particular purchase decision, he or she tends to engage in extended problem-solving activities and move through the standard learning hierarchy—forming beliefs, then attitudes, and then behavior.

The flow of events is quite different when the consumer is involved in a low-involvement decision. In such a case the consumer is not motivated to engage in extensive problem solving. Instead, the consumer moves through a limited decision process in which a few alternatives are considered in a superficial manner. As a result, only a limited number of beliefs are formed about the product alternatives. Furthermore, because the consumer does not evaluate the alternatives closely, he or she may not form any attitudes. In low-involvement situations, attitudes tend to occur only after the product or service is bought and the consumer reflects on how he or she feels about it. It is through product or service use that attitudes are formed in low-involvement situations. When consumers have low involvement in a decision, they tend to engage in limited problem solving and move through what is called a **low-involvement hierarchy** consisting of belief formation, then behavior, and finally attitude formation.[29]

Experiential Hierarchy

From the experiential perspective, consumers may be viewed as engaging in a behavior because of a strong desire to obtain feelings or excitement. In such instances the hierarchy of effects may be conceptualized as initiated by feelings or attitudes. For example, a friend may ask you to go to a rock concert. Your decision will probably be based on the feelings that you have toward the group and the concert. If questioned about the reason for going, you would be able to voice a series of beliefs. However, such beliefs are probably far less influential in your decision than the feelings possessed. Indeed, any belief statements you make may be done to justify the decision.[30]

The **experiential hierarchy** begins with a strong affective response. Behavior follows the strong feelings. Finally, beliefs are developed in part to justify the behavior. Impulse purchases exemplify the experiential hierarchy. In an **impulse purchase** a strong positive feeling is followed by the buying act.[31]

Readers should note, however, that little research has been conducted that directly tests for the existence of the experiential hierarchy. Although the suggestion that affect can occur prior to the formation of strong beliefs is intuitively appealing, it is still a controversial hypothesis. The reason for identifying a distinct experiential hierarchy is to emphasize the point that in some cases affective processes appear to dominate and precede highly dispassionate and rational decision making. Indeed, some researchers have noted that affect may predominate in some of the most highly involving situations. For example, when purchasing a house or a car, the stakes may be so high that information processing stops for some people, and feelings and emotions predominate. Similarly, emotions can have a strong impact on behaviors that provoke fear in some consumers, such as giving blood. A study recently investigated the role of emotion in blood donations. The authors found that for those less experienced in blood donations, emotional responses of sadness, contempt, and joy played a major role in predicting donations. Interestingly, for those most experienced with giving blood, the emotion of fear became strongly negatively associated with donations. That is, those who were least fearful tended to have a greater likelihood of donating blood.[32]

Figure 8-8 portrays a print ad for United Airlines that incorporates many of the ideas that form the basis for the experiential hierarchy. In particular, note the focus on creating affective responses.

Behavioral Influence Hierarchy

The **behavioral influence hierarchy** predicts that strong situational or environmental forces may propel a consumer to engage in buying behavior without the person having formed either feelings or affect about the object of the purchase. For example, research on the effects of music on the pace with which consumers move in retail stores illustrates the direct effects of external stimuli on behavior. In these studies no evidence was found that the consumers were aware of the effects of the music. Yet the tempo of the music influenced buying behavior. Similarly, the increased buying behavior associated with the display of credit card insignias depicts the direct influence of behavior.

When behavior is induced directly through the operation of environmental or situational factors, the hierarchy of effects begins with the behavior. Whether feelings or beliefs follow the behavior in the hierarchy cannot be definitely answered at this time. One researcher has argued that the hierarchy may move from behavior to feelings to beliefs.[33] This has been called the "Do-Feel-Learn" hierarchy. Common experience does seem to support such a view. People can at times feel very good or very bad after a purchase. Postpurchase processes are discussed in greater detail in Chapter 13.

The study of beliefs and attitudes and their relationship to purchase behavior has major implications for promotional strategy. How companies promote a brand depends upon the type of buying process that the brand's target market uses in buying products from its particular category. Table 8-3 summarizes some promotional strategies that companies may use depending upon the buying process involved.

Figure 8-8 United Airlines seeks to create positive affective reactions in this ad.

Additional Comments on Hierarchies of Effects

Twenty-five years ago, consumer behavior researchers had a simplistic, one-dimensional view of the relationship of beliefs, feelings, and behavior. Today the view is highly complex, with various authors proposing different hierarchies of effects operative under various buying circumstances. Indeed, the current view may well be overly complex. For example, does it make sense to say that when a consumer is engaged in a routine decision process absolutely no affect exists prior to purchasing a product? Similarly, is it likely that in impulse purchases the consumer has formed no beliefs about the product? Such reasoning leads to the realization that the various

TABLE 8-3

Some Promotional Strategies Based on the Type of Consumer Purchase Process

Buying Process	*Possible Promotional Strategies*
High involvement	Emphasize developing product–attribute and product–benefit beliefs through cognitive learning procedures. Can emphasize print advertising and personal selling. Help create affect through product demonstrations and advertising using classical-conditioning procedures.
Low involvement	Emphasize developing product–attribute beliefs through repetition of simple messages. Tie point-of-purchase displays to advertising. Place product and displays in high-traffic area.
Experiential/impulse	Emphasize the fun and feelings that can be obtained by experiencing the product or service. Emphasize creating affect through the classical conditioning of positive feelings toward the product.
Behavioral influence	Use sales promotion techniques, such as sweepstakes, rebates, samples, or coupons.

hierarchies of effects are idealized representations of consumer buying behavior. Regardless of the decision process involved, it is likely that consumers have some rudimentary beliefs and some vague attitudinal feelings about a product or service prior to buying it. What the various hierarchies of effects provide is a feel for the relative emphasis of beliefs, attitudes, and behavior within the various purchase processes.

PREDICTING CONSUMER ATTITUDES THROUGH MULTIATTRIBUTE MODELS

As noted earlier in the chapter, the formation of consumer attitudes in high-involvement situations may be best described by what are called **multiattribute models**. These models identify how consumers may combine their beliefs about product attributes to form attitudes about various brand alternatives, corporations, or other objects. As a result, multiattribute models assume that consumers are using the standard hierarchy of effects approach in which beliefs lead to attitude formation. Attitudes, in turn, may lead to purchase behaviors.

Numerous multiattribute models have been developed.[34] In this chapter two will be presented. The first focuses on predicting the attitude that a consumer forms toward a specific attitude object, such as a product, service, person, or idea. The second type of model focuses on predicting the behavioral intentions of consumers to perform some type of action such as buying a product or service. The behavioral intentions model has appeared more recently than the attitude-toward-the-object model and in fact builds upon this earlier approach.

Attitude-Toward-the-Object Model

A number of different multiattribute models have been developed to predict a consumer's attitude toward an object. The model that receives the most attention from consumer and marketing researchers is called the **attitude-toward-the-object model**, or the Fishbein model.[35] The model identifies three major factors that are predictive of attitudes. First, the model identifies the salient beliefs that a person has about an object. (**Salient beliefs** are those attribute–object beliefs activated when a person evaluates an attitudinal object.) From an information-processing perspective, these are the beliefs that are activated in memory when attention is focused upon an object. These beliefs tend to concern the attributes that are important to the consumer.

The second component of the Fishbein attitude-toward-the-object model is the strength of the belief that an object has a particular attribute in question. The strength of the object–attribute linkage is usually assessed by asking a person "How likely is it that object 'x' possesses attribute 'y'?" For example, suppose that a researcher wished to determine the strength of consumers' belief that a 1995 Chevrolet Corvette has great acceleration and great handling. She would ask consumers to answer the following questions:

1. How likely is it that the 1993 Corvette has great acceleration?
   Extremely unlikely 1 2 3 4 5 6 7 8 9 10 Extremely likely
2. How likely is it that the 1993 Corvette has great handling?
   Extremely unlikely 1 2 3 4 5 6 7 8 9 10 Extremely likely

The third component of the Fishbein model is the evaluation of each of the salient attributes. The evaluation ratings provide an assessment of the goodness/badness of the salient attributes. For example, in the Corvette example, some consumers may evaluate having a large V-8 engine positively and some may evaluate it negatively. Researchers obtain evaluation ratings of the attribute by asking consumers how good or bad the attributes are. In the Corvette example the researcher would ask consumers to rate the following two questions:

1. How bad/good is it for a car to have great acceleration?
   Very bad -3 -2 -1 0 +1 +2 +3 Very good
2. How bad/good is it for a car to have great handling?
   Very bad -3 -2 -1 0 +1 +2 +3 Very good

In this example wide variations probably exist in the evaluation of the goodness/badness of the attribute of great acceleration. After all, many consumers want to avoid the temptations that a fast car creates. On this attribute ratings may range widely from -3 to +3. In contrast, for most people the attribute "great handling" is a positive characteristic. Few would want a car to have poor handling. On the other hand, many consumers simply desire a car to handle safely and adequately. The trade-offs of great handling are high costs and a harsh ride, which many seek to avoid. As a result, evaluations of the attribute "great handling" would probably range from 0 to +3.

When attempting to predict a consumer's attitude, information on the evaluation and strength of the salient beliefs is combined via an algebraic formula.

Algebraically the model is expressed as

$$A_o = \sum_{i=1}^{N} b_i e_i$$

where

A_o = the overall attitude towards object o
b_i = the strength of the belief of whether or not object o has some particular attribute i
e_i = the evaluation of the goodness or badness of attribute i
n = the number of beliefs

Table 8-4 presents the results of the evaluation conducted by two hypothetical market segments (the High Fliers and the Charlie Conservatives) of three cars—a Corvette, a Buick Park Avenue, and a Mercedes 300E. Both groups used five salient

TABLE 8-4

Predicting the Attitudes of Two Consumer Segments

Segment A: High Fliers

		Corvette		Buick Park Avenue		Mercedes 300E	
Attribute	e_i	b_i	$b_i \times e_i$	b_i	$b_i \times e_i$	b_i	$b_i \times e_i$
Sporty styling	+3	8	24	5	15	7	21
Good handling/ride	+3	8	24	4	12	7	21
High cost	-1	7	-7	6	-6	8	-8
Great acceleration	+3	7	21	3	9	6	18
Low repair frequency	+1	3	3	2	2	8	8
$A_o = \sum_{i=1}^{N} = b_i e_i$			+65		+32		+60

Segment B: Charlie Conservatives

		Corvette		Buick Park Avenue		Mercedes 300E	
Attribute	e_i	b_i	$b_i \times e_i$	b_i	$b_i \times e_i$	b_i	$b_i \times e_i$
Sporty styling	-1	9	-9	5	-5	7	-7
Good handling/ride	+3	3	+9	9	27	7	21
High cost	-3	8	-24	6	-18	10	-30
Great acceleration	-2	10	-20	2	-4	6	-12
Low repair frequency	+3	2	+6	8	24	9	27
$A_o = \sum_{i=1}^{N} = b_i e_i$			-38		+24		-1

b_i = strength of belief (1 = extremely unlikely; 10 = extemely likely)
e_i = evaluation of goodness/badness (-3 = very bad; +3 = very good)
A_o = overall attitude toward object o

attributes on which to rate the cars—their sporty styling, outstanding handling, high cost, superb acceleration, and low repair frequency.

An inspection of Table 8-4 shows that the High Fliers would prefer the Corvette, followed by the Mercedes and the Park Avenue. For these individuals it was highly desirable to have sporty styling, good handling, and great acceleration. Paying a great deal for a car was not evaluated too negatively. In contrast, the Charlie Conservatives rated the Park Avenue most highly. Members of this group reacted negatively to the Corvette with an overall score of −38. Because the Conservatives valued low repair frequency and good handling, they rated the Mercedes second. Also note that both the Charlie Conservatives' belief ratings and evaluations diverged from those of the High Fliers.

The computed attitude scores have meaning principally for comparison purposes. That is, one does not learn much from knowing that the Corvette had an attitude score of +65 for the High Fliers. It is only when one knows that the High Fliers rated both the Buick and the Mercedes lower that the score provides information. Comparing the ratings of the two segments also reveals that in general the High Flier segment liked cars more than did the Conservatives. The car rated lowest by the High Fliers (i.e., the Buick) had a higher score than the car rated best (also the Buick) by the Conservatives. Figure 8-9 shows an ad for the Buick Park Avenue. Note that the ad seeks to create beliefs about the same types of attributes identified in the Fishbein attitude-toward-the-object model discussed earlier.

From a managerial perspective, the attitude-toward-the-object model suggests that three factors influence attitude formation: (1) the salient attributes, (2) the extent to which consumers believe that the object possesses the attributes, (3) the degree of positivity/negativity on which the attributes are evaluated. One important role of advertisements is to communicate to consumers in a way that causes them to form appropriate beliefs concerning the extent to which an object possesses an attribute.

How does Fishbein's attitude-toward-the-object model deal with differences in the importance of the attributes? Interestingly, the Fishbein model makes no direct attempt at measuring the differential importance of attributes. For example, a High Flier's overall attitude score could change dramatically if acceleration were not at all important to him. As it turns out, evidence indicates that the omission of ratings of importance has little or no effect on the ability of Fishbein's model to predict attitudes—because the importance of an attribute is in part assessed by the evaluation ratings. Researchers have found that as the importance of an attribute increases, the evaluation ratings become more extreme.[36] Thus, if an attribute is not important, the evaluation rating is close to zero on the "goodness–badness" dimension. This is equivalent to rating the attribute as having low importance.

Global Attitudes Versus Attitudes Toward the Object

The measure of attitude obtained from a multiattribute model is an indirect measure of attitude. In other words, the researcher can estimate the level of consumers' attitudes toward an object by measuring the strengths of their beliefs about the attributes possessed by the object and their evaluations of the attributes of the object. In contrast, direct measures of consumers' global attitudes can be taken. Thus a **global attitude measure** is the direct measurement of the overall affect and feelings held by a consumer regarding an object.

To measure global attitudes several questions are asked on semantic differential scales. (Semantic differential scales ask respondents to rate an object on various scales

Figure 8-9 Buick seeks to influence beliefs about attributes of importance to conservative car buyers in this ad for the Park Avenue.

anchored by opposite meaning adjectives.) For example, global attitudes regarding a Chevrolet Corvette might be phrased in the following manner:

Please describe your feelings about Corvettes by circling the appropriate number on the scales.

Good	*1*	*2*	*3*	*4*	*5*	*Bad*
Positive	*1*	*2*	*3*	*4*	*5*	*Negative*
Like	*1*	*2*	*3*	*4*	*5*	*Dislike*

Whenever possible, market researchers collect data on global attitudes as well as sufficient information to predict the attitudes through an attitude-toward-the-object model. The results of the two estimates can then be compared. If global attitudes and predicted attitudes match closely, researchers can conclude that they have a good understanding of the factors influencing consumer attitude formation. In contrast, if predicted and global attitudes fail to correlate, additional research is required to identify what is happening.

When Do Attitudes Predict Behavior?

A classic problem for consumer researchers has involved explaining why the knowledge of consumer attitudes does not allow for a better prediction of actual behavior. In fact, many consumer researchers have been highly pessimistic about the ability of attitudes to predict overt behavior.[37]

Recently, researchers have recognized that the issue is one of knowing when attitudes predict behavior. A variety of factors have been found to influence the extent to which attitudes predict behaviors.[38]

1. *Involvement of the consumer*. In the purchase decision, attitudes are likely to predict behavior only under conditions of high involvement when the standard learning hierarchy operates.
2. *Attitude measurement*. The measurement of the attitude should be reliable and valid. In addition, the measure of attitude should be at the same level of abstraction as the measure of behavior. For example, if the behavior involves consumers contributing to a specific charity, such as the American Cancer Society, the attitude questions cannot deal with less specific (i.e., more abstract) questions about attitudes towards charities in general. A similar point concerns the variable of time. If the behavior involves buying a new Porsche in the next six months, the measure should include a time parameter. The longer the time between attitude measurement and the time of the behavior, the weaker the relationship is.
3. *Effects of other people*. The desires of other people toward the purchase, as well as the consumer's motivation to comply with these desires, influences the extent to which attitudes predict behavior.
4. *Situational factors*. Situational factors, such as holidays, shortage of time, sickness, and so forth may intervene and cause attitudes to not predict behavior well.
5. *Effects of other brands*. Even though the attitude toward a brand is quite high, if one's attitude toward another brand is higher, the second brand is more likely to be purchased. Because the attitude-toward-the-object model fails to include attitudes toward other objects as well, it may have problems predicting behavior.
6. *Attitude strength*. For an attitude to influence behavior, it must be held with sufficient strength and conviction to be activated in memory.[39] The degree of association between an attitude and an object varies on a continuum. At one end of the continuum, one finds nonattitudes in which the consumer has few positive or negative feelings about an object, such as a particular brand. At the

other end of the continuum, a consumer may have extremely strong feelings. The results of a number of research studies indicate that the stronger the attitude, the more likely it is to be retrieved from memory and subsequently influence behavior.

One way of measuring the strength of an attitude is through a procedure called response latency. In this procedure, the researcher asks respondents to press either a "like" or "dislike" key on a computer when a series of products are displayed. The computer then measures how long it takes the respondent to press a button. The longer the response latency, the weaker the attitude held by the consumer. In one study this procedure was followed for 100 products, such as various candy bars, salty snack foods, chewing gums, and canned foods. After completing the rating task, the respondents were given an opportunity to choose, from ten of the products, their five most preferred. The results revealed that the more accessible in memory the attitude (i.e., the more quickly the "like" computer key was pushed for a brand), the more likely the person would be to select the brand.[40]

These ideas are consistent with findings indicating that the expression of an attitude is a constructive process. When asked to state an attitude toward an object, people search through memory to retrieve information concerning their feelings. Because memory is a constructive process in which any information available is used to assist the recall process, the attitude that is recalled is dependent in part on what is current, salient, and available in memory. As a result, situational circumstances and moods may well influence the attitude expressed. Indeed, some researchers have found that merely asking someone to think about his or her attitude can itself change the attitude. That is, the person seeks to justify his or her statements by giving reasons for feelings. The process of giving reasons can make new attributes salient and, thereby, change the view. These ideas have direct implications for conducting market research. Market researchers should seek to take indirect measures whenever possible because the process of thinking can itself influence the attitude expressed.[41]

These six issues limit the ability of attitude-toward-the-object models to predict behavior. Fishbein and his colleagues recognized these deficiencies and developed another model of attitude formation. However, rather than attempting to predict the attitude toward the object, the model focused on predicting a person's intentions to behave in a specific manner, such as purchasing a product. The model recognized that a person may have a positive attitude toward buying a brand, such as a Corvette, but never engage in the behavior of buying it.

The Behavioral Intentions Model

The behavioral intentions model, also called the **theory of reasoned action**, was developed by Martin Fishbein and his colleagues for the purpose of improving on the ability of the attitude-toward-the-object model to predict behavior. It extended the basic attitude-toward-the-object model in several ways.[42] First, it proposed that behavior results from the formation of specific intentions to behave. Thus the model did not attempt to predict behavior per se, but rather the intention to behave.

Second, the behavioral intentions model contained a new construct called the subjective norm. The **subjective norm** (SN) assessed what consumers believe other people think that they should do. In other words, SN introduces into the formulation the powerful effects of reference groups on behavior.

The third change in the model involves the object to which attitudes are directed. Instead of assessing the consumer's attitude toward the brand itself, the model assessed the consumer's attitude toward the overt behavior of purchasing the product. The key difference in assessing attitude toward behavior, rather than attitude toward the object, is that the focus is on the consumer's perception of what the consequences of the purchase would be. When the consequences of the purchase are assessed rather than whether or not the product possesses certain attributes, the researcher has an enhanced ability to take into consideration factors that may act to impede intentions to behave. Considering the purchase of a sports car, some consequences of the purchase might be: (1) buying the car would cause the person not to take a vacation, (2) buying the car would cause the person to have to deal with obnoxious salespeople, and (3) buying the car would involve the person in deciding how to get a loan at a very high interest rate. Models that assess only the attitude toward the object have a difficult time measuring such factors.

Algebraically, the behavioral intentions model is expressed as

$$B \approx \text{BI} = w_1(A_B) + w_2(\text{SN})$$

where

B = behavior
BI = behavioral intention
A_B = attitude toward performing the behavior
SN = the subjective norm
w_1 and w_2 = empirically determined weights

The weights (w_1 and w_2) are determined empirically through regression analysis. A_B and SN are obtained directly from consumers via questionnaires. In fact, A_B and SN are themselves indexes that are obtained from other measures. Specifically, the attitude toward the behavior is obtained from the following equation:

$$\text{A}_B = \sum_{i=1}^{n} b_i e_i$$

where

A_B = attitude towards the behavior
b_i = the person's belief that performing the behavior will result in consequence i
e_i = the person's evaluation of consequence i
n = the number of beliefs

Note that the equation is very similar to that used in other multiattribute models. The major difference is in the belief variable. Rather than assessing the belief that an object has an attribute, the behavioral intentions model assesses the person's belief that performing a particular behavior would result in a particular consequence.

The equation for obtaining the subjective norm is

$$\text{SN} = \sum_{j=1}^{n} \text{NB}_j \text{MC}_j$$

where

SN = subjective norm
NB_j = the normative belief that a reference group or person j thinks that the consumer should or should not perform the behavior
MC_j = the motivation to comply with the influence of referent j
n = number of relevant reference groups of individuals

The subjective norm is calculated similarly to a belief. The normative belief is equivalent to a belief statement, and the motivation to comply is like an importance rating. Thus, for each person or reference group, these ratings are multiplied, and the result is added across all people or reference groups considered.

Researchers have found that beliefs about normative pressures to engage in a behavior can play a dominant role in whether a person behaves in a particular way. For example, one study investigated the use of condoms by adults. The results revealed that perceived normative pressure was by far the best predictor of condom usage. Pressure from socially important people was more important than other variables, such as AIDS knowledge, perceived susceptibility, and condom use outcome expectancies.[43]

A number of researchers have tested the behavioral intentions model against the standard multiattribute models. In general, the results reveal that the behavioral intentions model is superior.[44] However, various authors have suggested that the model as specified may not be completely accurate. In particular, questions have arisen concerning the role of the subjective norm variable. The evidence tends to indicate that purchase behavior is influenced to a much greater extent by the attitudinal component than by the subjective norm component of the model.[45]

Highlight 8-2 discusses an extremely interesting phenomenon that may occur when market researchers measure behavioral intentions. It seems that merely measuring behavioral intentions can actually increase the likelihood that a consumer will make a purchase.

Managerial Applications Summary

Table 8-5 summarizes some of the applications of the concepts to managerial issues found in the chapter.

A MANAGERIAL APPLICATIONS EXAMPLE

An example of how concepts from beliefs, attitudes, and behaviors can be used to analyze managerial issues concerns the recent problems at IBM. Since the late 1980s IBM has encountered difficulties in the marketing of its PS/2 line of personal computers.[46] One of the advantages IBM claims for the PS/2 is the "Micro Channel," the computer's internal data pathway. The company claims that the new computers allow for faster processing, for quicker data storage, and for performing multiple tasks simultaneously. However, as stated by a manager of Businessland, Inc. (a large

HIGHLIGHT 8-2

Market Research Highlight

DOES MEASURING PURCHASE INTENT INFLUENCE BEHAVIOR? A critical question for market researchers concerns how the process of doing research impacts consumers. For example, could merely asking consumers about their purchase intentions actually influence their subsequent purchases? Recently, researchers investigated this question. They asked nearly 5,000 consumers whether they intended to purchase a new car or computer. The researchers employed a six-point scale ranging from "yes, within six months" to "never." Next, they determined whether the consumers actually made a purchase during the next six months. These results were compared to a control group of 5,000 similar consumers who were not asked the purchase intent question. The results revealed that those who received the purchase intent question were significantly more likely to actually make a purchase, regardless of whether they said "yes" or "no." While the overall increase in tendency was slightly less than 1%, it is meaningful. In large consumer goods industries, a 1% change in sales translates into tens of millions of dollars in profits.

Based upon Vicki G. Morwitz, Eric Johnson, and David Schmittlein, "Does Measuring Intent Change Behavior?" *Journal of Consumer Research*, Vol. 20 (June 1993), pp. 46–61.

chain of computer dealers), "IBM has had a hard time getting the message across about why the Micro Channel is better." Few companies have begun developing clones of the model, which leads potential customers to question the touted advantages. In addition, a group of major competitors had promised to have a pathway with similar flexibility within a year. Because complex software that uses the capabilities of the Micro Channel has arrived slowly, the delay has not been a problem.

The Problem Statement

The basic problem faced by IBM involves persuading customers that the Micro Channel offers a superior approach to running personal computers.

The Consumer Behavior Analysis

A number of concepts from this chapter have particular relevance to the problem, including hierarchies of effects, beliefs, multiattribute models, and benefit segmentation. The hierarchy of effects concept makes salient the importance of identifying what type of purchase process customers are likely to use to select an IBM PS/2 computer. Because most of the customers would be corporate users, and because of the high cost of the product, one could expect that the consumer would be highly involved. In such instances beliefs are formed, followed by attitudes and behavior. Thus a focus on belief formation should be crucial to influencing attitudes.

TABLE 8-5

Examples of Managerial Applications of Key Chapter Concepts

I. Beliefs
   A. Market research
      1. Conduct studies to determine the belief structure and needs and wants of consumers concerning your brands and competitive brands.
   B. Marketing mix
      1. Develop products possessing attributes that provide the benefits sought by consumers.
      2. Use promotional strategy to form consumer beliefs and attributes of benefits.
   C. Segmentation
      1. Segment market based upon the similar benefits sought by large numbers of consumers.
   D. Positioning and differentiation
      1. Position and differentiate products based upon the attributes they possess.
   E. Environmental analysis
      1. Conduct studies to determine the belief structure and needs and wants of consumers for competitive brands.

II. Attitudes
   A. Market research
      1. Conduct studies to determine the global attitudes of consumers regarding your brands, sales personnel, retail stores, and corporations and those of your competitors.
   B. Marketing mix
      1. Use advertising to form positive attitudes by associating the product with positively evaluated spokespersons, music, and images.
      2. Train sales force, retail clerks, and other personnel to create positive feelings among customers.
      3. Carefully analyze the distribution system to ensure the minimization of factors, such as stockouts and dirty facilities, that would create negative feelings.

III. Multiattribute models
   A. Market research
      1. Conduct studies to predict attitudes toward the object and intentions to behave, and compare the outcome of these analyses to measures of global attitudes and to actual behavior.
   B. Marketing mix
      1. Use results of multiattribute attitude studies as the basis for making appropriate changes in the product, pricing, promotion, and distribution strategy to create more positive attitudes and to influence behavioral intentions.

IV. Hierarchies of effects
   A. Market research
      1. Conduct market research studies to determine the operative hierarchy of effect.
   B. Marketing mix
      1. Develop strategy based upon the type of hierarchy of effect the target market uses. For example, if it is a high-involvement hierarchy, focus on using promotional strategy to create beliefs. If it is an experiential hierarchy, focus on creating appropriate affective states. For the behavioral influence hierarchy, use sales promotion devices to influence behavior.

Considering beliefs and their formation, the marketer should make a careful analysis of product attributes and product benefits. In the PS/2 example one can see problems in the formation of attribute–benefit beliefs. Although the PS/2 line has the attribute of microchannel architecture, customers have had a hard time understanding the benefits of the attribute. In addition, IBM should carefully consider using multiattribute models to predict customer attitudes toward the PS/2 line. By taking measures of how consumers evaluate each of the computer's attributes and their perception of the likelihood that the computer possesses the attributes, IBM could take appropriate managerial action to influence consumer attitudes.

The concept of benefit segmentation should also be considered by IBM managers. They should actively seek to identify target groups that have a specific need for the benefits offered by the PS/2, such as the ability to perform multiple tasks at the same time.

The Managerial Applications Analysis

Table 8-6 is the managerial applications analysis table for the IBM case. Hierarchies of effects concepts apply directly to market research and the marketing mix. Market research is required to determine the level of involvement of the target market. Because the purchase of a PS/2 would likely require high-involvement decision making, its marketers should focus on using promotional strategy to influence belief formation.

Because of the importance of customer belief formation, market researchers should carefully analyze the object–benefit beliefs formed by potential customers. In the PS/2 case, a major problem exists regarding whether customers believe that the microchannel architecture provides any benefits. This suggests that IBM should conduct an analysis of the product itself to determine exactly what the technology's benefits are. Once the benefits have been identified, these must be communicated to appropriate market segments via the promotional mix. Given the high-involvement nature of the purchase, the sales problem becomes unsolvable if the computer's benefits do not really exist. Customers would evaluate closely the claims made by the firm and would certainly notice if the product failed to provide its advertised benefits. Assuming that the benefits are real, however, the company must determine how to communicate and promote those benefits. In other words, the company must tackle the question of how to develop the attribute–benefit and object–benefit beliefs.

In this case, managers should also consider the importance of concepts related to multiattribute models. IBM should perform market research to identify the salient attributes on which customers evaluate personal computers. Such knowledge is useful in designing new products and in developing promotional strategy that communicates the important features of the PS/2. The multiattribute model can also be used to predict overall customer attitudes toward the PS/2 and toward competitors' offerings. If buyers exhibit a low strength of belief that the PS/2 offers the benefits claimed and a low evaluation of the value of the benefits, researchers could predict that attitudes toward the product are not positive.

Managers should also consider the concept of benefit segmentation. By analyzing the results of the multiattribute analysis, segments of consumers may be identified that seek specific types of benefits. A marketing mix strategy can then be

TABLE 8-6

Managerial Implications of IBM PS/2 Case

Consumer Concepts	*Managerial Implications*
Hierarchies of effects	*Market research*—Identify type of hierarchy employed by buyers of personal computers.
	Promotional strategy—Develop advertising messages that fit the type of hierarchy employed by target market.
Consumer beliefs	*Market research*—Identify the beliefs that target market possesses about product's attributes and benefits.
	Product—Develop product that provides the attributes and benefits sought by target market.
	Promotion—Develop promotional messages that create the desired object–benefit, object–attribute, and attribute–benefit beliefs.
Multiattribute models	*Market research*—Identify the salient attributes employed by target market to evaluate personal computers. Also, employ research to predict overall consumer attitudes toward the brand.
	Promotional strategy—Attempt to influence perceptions of salient attributes via messages in advertising or by sales personnel.
	Product strategy—Develop product that yields high consumer ratings on salient attributes.
Benefit segmentation	*Market research*—Identify particular market segments that seek specific benefits from personal computers.
	Product strategy—Develop products that provide benefits sought by market segments.
	Promotional strategy—Develop messages that influence target market's object–benefit beliefs.

developed to directly target such groups with a product, price, promotional, and distribution strategy tailored to reach the groups.

SUMMARY

The study of the interrelationships among beliefs, attitudes, and behaviors is highly important to the marketing manager, the marketing researcher, and the public policy maker. Beliefs describe the knowledge a person has about objects, attributes, and benefits. An object, such as a particular brand, possesses various attributes and provides various benefits. Beliefs about the extent to which a brand possesses specific attributes and benefits may be formed from the exposure to and the processing of information obtained from advertising, from friends, or from experience with the product. Product attributes are the characteristics that a product may or may not have. Product benefits are the positive and negative outcomes provided by the attributes.

Particularly in high-involvement purchase situations, consumers may evaluate how highly they value various attributes of a product. Managers should perform research to identify the attributes that their target market considers to be important. Such considerations can influence both product design and promotional strategy. Consumer attitudes represent the amount of affect or feeling that a person holds for or against a stimulus object, such as a brand, person, company, or idea. In high-involvement situations, attitudes may be formed because the consumer holds a number of beliefs about an object that are positive or negative in nature. Attitudes may also be formed through principles of classical and operant conditioning. The mere exposure phenomenon suggests that positive feelings may result from repeated exposures to a previously neutral stimulus.

Consumption behaviors have been discussed in two different ways. The first is through "intentions to behave." Intentions to behave are the statements that consumers give when asked about their likelihood to engage in some behavior, such as buying a product, supporting a political candidate, or visiting a retail store. Actual consumer behavior involves an overt consumer action to purchase a product or service, visit a retail store, vote for a particular political candidate, and so forth.

Consumption behavior can result from a number of different processes that appear to be governed in part by the type of buying process in which the consumer is engaged. When the consumer is in a high-involvement situation, the standard learning hierarchy operates—in which behavior occurs after beliefs are formed and attitudes are created. In the low-involvement hierarchy, behavior appears to occur after a limited number of beliefs are formed. In such a situation, attitudes appear to play a minor role in influencing behavior and are formed only after the consumer purchases and uses the product. In the experiential hierarchy, affect occurs first, followed by behavior. Impulse purchases exemplify an experiential purchase. The behavioral influence hierarchy may be followed in situations where strong situational or environmental forces propel the consumer to engage in the behavior.

Multiattribute models attempt to predict consumer attitudes in high-involvement circumstances. In the attitude-toward-the-object model, information on the likelihood that an object possesses an attribute and on the evaluation of the goodness/badness of the attribute are combined to predict an attitude. In the behavioral intentions model, intentions to behave are predicted by obtaining information on the attitude toward performing the behavior and on the subjective norm, which assesses what the consumer believes other people think that he or she should do.

KEY TERMS

attitude
attitude-toward-the-object model
attribute importance
attributes
behavioral influence hierarchy
behavioral intention
benefit segmentation
benefits
consumer beliefs
consumer behaviors
demarketing
experiential hierarchy
global attitude measure
halo effect
hierarchies of effects
high-involvement hierarchy
impulse purchases
low-involvement hierarchy
mere exposure phenomenon
multiattribute model
objects
salient beliefs
standard learning hierarchy
subjective norm
theory of reasoned action

REVIEW QUESTIONS

1. Define the concepts of belief, attitude, and behavior.
2. Distinguish attribute–object, attribute–benefit, and object–benefit beliefs from each other.
3. Why should researchers attempt to identify the importance of product attributes to consumers? What are the factors that tend to influence attribute importance?
4. What is meant by the idea that beliefs, attitudes, and behaviors may form into hierarchies of effects?
5. What processes account for how beliefs are directly formed?
6. What processes account for the direct formation of attitudes?
7. Identify three ways in which behaviors may be induced without the formation of strong attitudes or beliefs.
8. How do the hierarchies of effects differ in high- and low-involvement circumstances?
9. How do the hierarchies of effects differ in experiential versus behavioral influence processes?
10. What conditions limit the ability of attitudes to predict behavior accurately?
11. What is meant by a multiattribute attitude model?
12. Differentiate the attitude-toward-the-object model from the behavioral intentions model.
13. What are the four functions of attitudes identified by Katz?
14. Why would a market researcher want to assess consumer global attitudes?

DISCUSSION QUESTIONS

1. List as many attributes as you can that consumers may seek in an automobile. You should be able to identify at least ten attributes. Select five of these attributes and identify the benefits consumers may receive if the characteristics are present in an automobile.
2. Consider the sports car segment versus the family car segment of the car market. Rank in order the five attributes that you think are most important for each of the segments.
3. An industry that has had problems in identifying the benefits of its product to consumers is the home computer industry. Identify the attributes of home computers. What are the tangible benefits consumers can receive from these attributes? How can these benefits be communicated to consumers?
4. Rough out a print advertisement that seeks to influence consumer beliefs about two attributes of a new soft drink. (You must create the new drink and identify its benefits.)
5. Describe the most recent commercial you have seen for a soft drink maker or a beer company. Which of the hierarchies of effects does the company seem to be assuming that consumers are using? Why?
6. Go through magazines and identify a print advertisement that appears to view consumers as in a high-involvement state and for which a multiattribute model might describe attitude formation. Discuss how the advertisement attempts to influence your attitude by giving information on multiple attributes.
7. Consider your own attitudes. Try to identify examples of attitudes you hold that represent each of the four functions of attitudes postulated by Katz.
8. Interview five of your friends. Using the attitude-toward-the-object model, assess their attitudes regarding a local fast-food restaurant. What are the managerial implications of the exercise for the restaurant?
9. Go through the multiattribute model computed for the High Fliers and the Charlie Conservatives. Why would both the belief ratings and evaluations be different for many of the attributes? Write a description of the two market segments based upon the information found in Table 8-4.

1. Kate Fitzgerald, "It's Green, It's Friendly, It's

ENDNOTES

1. Kate Fitzgerald, "It's Green, It's Friendly, It's Wal-Mart 'Eco-Store,'" *Advertising Age*, June 7, 1993, pp. 1, 44.
2. Melinda Guiles, "Fuel Economy Takes a Back Seat as Cars Get Faster and More Fun," *The Wall Street Journal*, October 1, 1985, p. 33.
3. Joseph White, "U.S. Auto Makers Decide Safety Sells," *The Wall Street Journal*, August 24, 1988, p. 17.
4. Raymond Serafin, "That's NO Dummy in Chrysler Ad," *Advertising Age*, April 16, 1990, p. 21.
5. Otis Port, "When It Comes to Cuddles, This Dog Is Best in Breed," *Newsweek*, April 1, 1991, p. 82.
6. James Helgeson, Alan Kluge, John Mager, and Cheri Taylor, "Trends in Consumer Behavior Literature: A Content Analysis," *Journal of Consumer Research*, Vol. 10 (March 1984), pp. 449–454.
7. M. Fishbein and I. Ajzen, *Belief, Attitude, Intention, and Behavior: An Introduction to Theory and Research* (Reading, MA: Addison-Wesley, 1975).
8. Durairaj Maheswaran and Brian Sternthal, "The Effects of Knowledge, Motivation, and Type of Message on Ad Processing and Product Judgments," *Journal of Consumer Research*, Vol. 17 (June 1990), pp. 66–73.
9. Scott Mackenzie, "The Role of Attention in Mediating the Effect of Advertising on Attribute Importance," *Journal of Consumer Research*, Vol. 13 (September 1986), pp. 174–195.
10. Donald R. Lichtenstein, Nancy M. Ridgway, and Richard G. Netemeyer, "Price Perceptions and Consumer Shopping Behavior: A Field Study," *Journal of Marketing Research*, Vol. 30 (May 1993), pp. 234–245.
11. This brief history of attitudes was adapted from Richard Petty, Thomas Ostrom, and Timothy Brock, *Cognitive Responses in Persuasion* (Hillsdale, NJ: Lawrence Erlbaum, 1981).
12. The definition was found in Petty et al., *Cognitive Responses in Persuasion*, p. 31.
13. Chris T. Allen, Karen A. Machleit, and Susan Schultz Kleine, "A Comparison of Attitudes and Emotions as Predictors of Behavior at Diverse Levels of Behavioral Experience," *Journal of Consumer Research*, Vol. 18 (March 1992), pp. 493–504. For a similar definition, see Darrel J. Bem, *Beliefs, Attitudes, and Human Affairs* (Belmont, CA: Brooks/Cole, 1970).
14. Fishbein and Ajzen, *Belief, Attitude, Intention, and Behavior*.
15. Phillip Zimbardo, E. Ebbesen, and C. Maslach, *Influencing Attitudes and Changing Behavior* (Reading, MA: Addison-Wesley, 1977). It should be noted that some researchers have defined attitudes in terms of three separate components—cognitions (beliefs), affect (feelings), and conation (behavioral intentions). However, such a conceptualization fails to distinguish these concepts such that each has its own set of determinants. Indeed, some evidence indicates that beliefs and feelings reside in completely different physiological systems. Thus beliefs may reside in a cognitive system influenced by cognitive-learning principles. In contrast, feelings and affect may reside in the autonomic nervous system, which is affected more by classical-conditioning principles. As a result, the author has chosen to separate the definitions of beliefs and of attitudes. For more information on this issue, see W. A. Scott, "Attitude Measurement," in *The Handbook of Social Psychology*, 2nd ed., Vol. 2, G. Lindzey and E. Aronson, eds. (Reading, MA: Addison-Wesley, 1968); T. M. Ostrom, "The Relationship Between the Affective, Behavioral, and Cognitive Components of Attitudes," *Journal of Experimental Social Psychology*, Vol. 5 (1969), pp. 12–30; and Robert A. Zajonc and Hazel Markus, "Affective and Cognitive Factors in Preferences," *Journal of Consumer Research*, Vol. 9 (September 1982), pp. 123–131.
16. The discussion of the functions of attitudes is based upon Charles Kiesler, Barry Collins, and Norman Miller, *Attitude Change: A Critical Analysis of Theoretical Approaches* (New York: John Wiley, 1969).

17. Daniel Katz, "The Functional Approach to Attitudes," *Public Opinion Quarterly*, Vol. 24 (1960), pp. 163–204. Also, see Sharon Shavitt, "Products, Personalities and Situations in Attitude Functions: Implications for Consumer Behavior," in *Advances in Consumer Research*, Vol. 16, Thomas Srull, ed. (Provo, UT: Association for Consumer Research, 1989), pp. 300–305.
18. For an excellent discussion on the functions of attitudes and on the role of attitudes in consumer behavior, see Richard J. Lutz, "The Role of Attitude Theory in Marketing," in *Perspectives in Consumer Behavior*, Harold Kassarjian and Thomas Robertson, eds. (Englewood Cliffs, NJ: Prentice-Hall, 1991), pp. 317–339.
19. Elnora Stuart, Terence Shimp, and Randall Engle, "Classical Conditioning of Consumer Attitudes: Four Experiments in an Advertising Context," *Journal of Consumer Research*, Vol. 14 (December 1987), pp. 334–349.
20. Kiesler et al., *Attitude Change*.
21. Robert Zajonc, "The Attitudinal Effects of Mere Exposure," *Journal of Personality and Social Psychology* monograph, Vol. 9 (1968), 2, pt 2.
22. Mackenzie, "The Role of Attention in Mediating the Effect of Advertising on Attribute Importance."
23. William Wilson, "Feeling More Than We Know: Exposure Effects Without Learning," *Journal of Personality and Social Psychology*, Vol. 37 (June 1979), pp. 811–821.
24. Walter Nord and J. Paul Peter, "A Behavior Modification Perspective on Marketing," *Journal of Marketing*, Vol. 44 (Spring 1980), pp. 36–47.
25. Michael Ray, "Marketing Communications and the Hierarchy-of-Effects," in *New Models for Mass Communications*, P. Clarke, ed. (Beverly Hills, CA: Sage Publications, 1973), pp. 147–176.
26. Robert Lavidge and Gary Steiner, "A Model for Predictive Measurements of Advertising Effectiveness," *Journal of Marketing*, Vol. 25 (October 1961), pp. 59–62.
27. Richard W. Olshavsky and Donald H. Granbois, "Consumer Decision Making—Fact or Fiction?" *Journal of Consumer Research*, Vol. 6 (September 1979), pp. 93–100.
28. Herbert Krugman, "The Impact of Television Advertising: Learning Without Involvement," *Public Opinion Quarterly*, Vol. 29 (October 1961), pp. 59–62. A variety of definitions of involvement have been proposed. For a good review, see John H. Antil, "Conceptualization and Operationalization of Involvement," in *Advances in Consumer Research*, Vol. 11, Thomas C. Kinnear, ed. (Provo, UT: Association for Consumer Research, 1984), pp. 203–209.
29. For an excellent discussion of low-involvement decision making, see F. Stewart De Bruicker, "An Appraisal of Low-Involvement Consumer Information Processing," in *Attitude Research Plays for High Stakes*, John Maloney and Bernard Silverman, eds. (Chicago: American Marketing Association, 1979), pp. 112–130.
30. Such justifications would work through a self-perception process. See Bem, *Beliefs, Attitudes, and Human Affairs*.
31. Dennis W. Rook and Stephen J. Hoch, "Consuming Impulses," in *Advances in Consumer Behavior*, Vol. 12, E. Hirschman and M. Holbrook, eds. (Provo, UT: Association for Consumer Research, 1985), pp. 23–27.
32. Chris T. Allen, Karen A. Machleit, and Susan Schultz Kleine, "A Comparison of Attitudes and Emotions as Predictors of Behavior at Diverse Levels of Behavioral Experience," *Journal of Consumer Research*, Vol. 18 (March 1992), pp. 493–504.
33. These ideas were expressed to me by Professor Russell Belk.
34. Numerous approaches to the study of attitudes exist. For a discussion of several of these, please see Richard J. Lutz, "The Role of Attitude Theory in Marketing," in *Perspectives in Consumer Behavior*, 4th ed., Harold H. Kassarjian and Thomas S. Robertson, eds. (Englewood Cliffs, NJ: Prentice-Hall, 1991), pp. 317–339.

35. For a full discussion of the Fishbein model, please see Martin Fishbein and Icek Ajzen, *Belief, Attitude, Intention and Behavior: An Introduction to Theory and Research* (Reading, MA: Addison-Wesley, 1975).

36. For a recent discussion of this issue, see Mackenzie, "The Role of Attention in Mediating the Effect of Advertising on Attribute Importance."

37. Allan Wicker, "Attitudes Versus Actions: The Relationship of Verbal and Overt Behavioral Responses to Attitude Objects," *Journal of Social Issues*, Vol. 25 (Autumn 1969), p. 65.

38. Robert Cialdini, Richard Petty, and John Caccioppo, "Attitude and Attitude Change," *Annual Review of Psychology*, Vol. 32 (1981), p. 366.

39. Linda F. Alwitt and Ida E. Berger, "Understanding the Link Between Environmental Attitudes and Consumer Product Usage: Measuring the Moderating Role of Attitude Strength," in *Advances in Consumer Research*, Vol. 20, Leigh McAlister and Michael Rothschild, eds. (Provo, UT: Association for Consumer Research, 1992), pp. 189–194.

40. Russell H. Fazio, Martha C. Powell, and Carol J. Williams, "The Role of Attitude Accessibility in the Attitude-to-Behavior Process," *Journal of Consumer Research*, Vol. 16 (December 1989), pp. 280–288.

41. Timothy D. Wilson, Douglas J. Lisle, and Dolores Kraft, "Effects of Self-Reflection on Attitudes and Consumer Behavior," in *Advances in Consumer Research*, Vol. 17, Marvin Goldberg, Gerald Gorn, and Richard Pollay, eds. (Provo, UT: Association for Consumer Research, 1990), pp. 79–85.

42. Icek Ajzen and Martin Fishbein, "Attitude-Behavior Relations: A Theoretical Analysis and Review of Empirical Research," *Psychological Bulletin* (September 1977), pp. 888–918. Readers should note that the behavioral intentions model is now called the "theory of reasoned action." I have retained the older name to emphasize its focus on predicting behavioral intentions.

43. Martin Fishbein, Susan E. Middlestadt, and David Trafimow, "Social Norms for Condom Use: Implications for HIV Prevention Interventions of a KABP Survey with Heterosexuals in the Eastern Caribbean," in *Advances in Consumer Research*, Vol. 20, Leigh McAlister and Michael Rothschild, eds. (Provo, UT: Association for Consumer Research, 1992), pp. 292–296.

44. Example of articles finding the behavioral intentions model superior to the attitude-toward-the-object model include Michael J. Ryan and E. H. Bonfield, "Fishbein's Intentions Model: A Test of External and Pragmatic Validity," *Journal of Marketing*, Vol. 44 (Spring 1980), pp. 82–95.

Readers should note that work continues on behavioral intentions models. For a recent comparison of three models of behavioral intentions, see Richard Netemeyer, J. Craig Andrews, and Scrinvas Durvasula, "A Comparison of Three Behavioral Intentions Models: The Case of Valentine's Day Gift-Giving," in *Advances in Consumer Research*, Vol. 20, Leigh McAlister and Michael Rothschild, eds. (Provo, UT: Association for Consumer Research, 1992), pp. 135–141.

45. R. J. Pomazal and J. J. Jaccard, "An Informational Approach to Altruistic Behavior," *Journal of Personality and Social Psychology*, Vol. 33 (1976), pp. 317–326. Also, see M. J. Ryan and E. H. Bonfield, "The Fishbein Extended Model and Consumer Behavior," *Journal of Consumer Research*, Vol. 2 (September 1975), pp. 118–136. Another problem with the Fishbein attitude models is that researchers have argued that placing the evaluation of the consequences on unidimensional scales anchored by "good" and "bad" is inappropriate. As discussed in Chapter 6, on motivation and affect, people tend to evaluate the goodness and badness of an object on separate dimensions. The same phenomenon appears to apply to attitudes as well. Thus two scales should be used to evaluate the goodness/badness of each attribute. For example, suppose that consumers were evaluating attitudes toward the attribute of "strength of the cleaning power" of a dishwashing detergent. Consumers would be asked to rate the attribute on two evaluative scales: "neutral" to "good" and "neutral" to "bad." In a study

investigating coupon usage, the researchers found that the positive consequences from coupon usage (e.g., monetary savings and approval from a spouse) are relatively independent of the negative consequences (e.g., time spent collecting coupons and shopping at nonpreferred stores). See Terence Shimp and Alican Kavas, "The Theory of Reasoned Action Applied to Coupon Usage," *Journal of Consumer Research*, Vol. 11 (December 1984), pp. 795–809.

46. The IBM PS/2 personal computer case was based upon an article by Paul Carroll, "IBM Seeks to Show Benefits of PS/2 Line at Trade Show," *The Wall Street Journal*, November 15, 1988, pp. B1, B11.

A Foul Taste at Perrier

Perrier Group of America, Inc., the U.S. unit of France's Source Perrier S.A., announced the product recall February 9, 1990. North Carolina regulators had released a report stating that Perrier was contaminated with benzene, a poisonous liquid shown to cause cancer in laboratory animals. Perrier requested the removal of the brand from supermarkets and restaurants throughout the United States and Canada, although the Food and Drug Administration said that the benzene levels did not pose "a significant short-term health risk" [1].

A Source Perrier official stated that the company believed the contamination occurred because an employee mistakenly used cleaning fluid containing benzene to clean machinery used on the bottling line that fills bottles for North America. Initially the recall affected only the United States and Canada—an inventory of some 70 million bottles. The recall was soon expanded worldwide, however, after Dutch and Danish officials also found benzene in some Perrier bottles. Unfortunately, Perrier's explanation for the recall kept changing. After traces of benzene were found in other parts of the world, company officials offered a different explanation: that benzene is naturally present in carbon dioxide, the gas that makes Perrier bubbly. A manager said that the substance is normally filtered out, but workers had failed to change the filters and the benzene had seeped into the water. Perrier insisted, however, that its famous spring in Vergeze, France, was unpolluted [2]. These inconsistent statements acted to raise more questions than they answered.

The question, however, was what long-term effects the incident would have on Perrier, which had positioned itself as naturally pure. An underpinning of the success of bottled waters is their perceived safety compared with ordinary tap water. Tom Pirko, a beverage consultant, described the incident as "the worst possible thing that could happen to a bottled water company. Purity is the franchise. The last possible thing that Perrier can afford to have happen is for the American public to think there is benzene in their spring, whether it gets filtered out or not" [3].

Another problem is that the product disappeared from the marketplace for three to five months—a period that severely tested the loyalty of many Perrier consumers. One marketing expert said "When a brand is consumed daily, out of sight is out of mind." The prospect of a Perrier-free market seemed to pose only minor difficulties for supermarkets and restaurants. During the recall, one analyst said, "Typically, bars and restaurants carry just one sparkling brand. Until now that has been Perrier. Now other sparkling waters will have a chance to get into Perrier's stronghold." Tom Kaplan, general manager of a restaurant in Los Angeles, added: "Now consumers have decided that other brands are better or at least as good, so Perrier no longer holds the monopoly on water" [4].

The recall came at a tough time for Perrier. Intense competition from other bottled water brands followed Perrier into the 1990s. In 1989 Perrier was the leading imported water, holding about 6% of the U.S. bottled water market. But while the total category was growing at about 10% annually, Perrier's growth slowed to about 5% a year. In an effort to regain lost market share during the recall period, the Perrier Group spent $25 million on a U.S. advertising campaign that said: "Perrier. Worth waiting for." (In 1989 Perrier Group spent just $6 million on U.S. advertising.) Some marketing experts said that the increase in advertising was a good start, but the ads themselves did little to treat the problem. Many of the ads were criticized for their lack of sincerity and credibility [5]. Perhaps more dangerous to Perrier was that some consumers made the discovery that any bottled water would do. Exacerbating the problem, the FDA required Perrier to drop the words "Naturally sparkling" from its label. The investigation had revealed that Perrier artificially carbonates its water after taking it out of the ground.

QUESTIONS

1. Define the problems facing Perrier.
2. Identify the consumer concepts related to beliefs, attitudes, and behaviors most relevant to the case. What does each concept say about the case?
3. Develop the managerial applications table for the Perrier case based upon the applicable consumer concepts. What managerial actions should Perrier have taken to minimize the crisis?

REFERENCES

1. E. S. Browning, Alix M. Freedman, and Thomas R. King "Perrier Expands North American Recall to Rest of Globe," *The Wall Street Journal*, February 15, 1990, pp. B1, B4.
2. Alix M. Freedman and Thomas R. King, "Perrier's Strategy in the Wake of Recall: Will It Leave the Brand in Rough Waters?" *The Wall Street Journal*, February, 12, 1990, pp. B1, B4.
3. "Perrier Finds Mystique Hard to Restore," *The Wall Street Journal*, December 12, 1990, pp. B1, B3.
4. G. Prince, "Best Sellers—Ranking the Top Soft Drink, Beer and Bottled Water Brands and Companies," *Beverage World*, March 1991, pp. 24–33.
5. "Perrier's Back—Whimsical Campaign to Support Its Return," *Advertising Age*, April 23, 1990, pp. 1, 84.

Chapter 9

Attitude, Belief, and Behavior Change: The Persuasion Process

CONSUMER VIGNETTE

Changing Attitudes About Drugs: A Marketing Challenge

One of the major problems facing the United States is the $110 billion illegal drug industry. To assist in combating the problem, a partnership between the media and advertising agencies was initiated in the late 1980s. The collaboration has resulted in a major campaign called "Drug-Free America," whose goal is to fight the threat by treating it as a marketing problem. As stated by Executive Director Tom Hedrick, the campaign "is competing with drug pushers for market share of non-users." Hedrick went on to say, "Everything we've been doing goes back to the belief in advertising's power to communicate messages strong enough to change attitudes and affect behavior over time."[1] Between March 1987 and November 1988, media support for the campaign totaled $150 million. In 1988 TV networks aired 2,000 free spots.

The campaign was based on solid market research foundations. The first study involved conducting over 7,000 interviews in malls across the United States. The goal was to obtain information on the attitudinal basis of drug use. Four target groups were identified for separate analysis: 9- to 12-year-olds, 13- to 17-year-olds, college students, and adults. As the director of the study stated, it "was designed to reveal the matrix of attitudes that form the basis of drug abuse—rather than focus on the phenomenon of drug abuse itself—and to track attitudinal change over time."

Information gleaned from the research formed the basis for the advertising campaign. One finding was that, among 9- to 12-year-olds, contact with older siblings had the greatest influence on attitudes and behavior. Further, older siblings feared they would influence their younger brothers and sisters. Similarly, among the 13- to 17-year-olds, an important factor was whether their friends were involved. Researchers also found that teenagers frequently wanted to help their friends. As a result of the research, Leo Burnett USA created an ad called "Catching Up to Her." The spot features a teenage girl who is forced to make a life-or-death decision regarding her drug-abusing girlfriend.

A year after the first study, a second study was conducted to assess changes in attitudes. The results indicated that across the United States attitudes toward drug use were becoming more negative. Furthermore, in the geographic areas chosen for high media exposure, attitude change was greater on most variables than in low-exposure areas. Several of the ads seemed to have a particularly strong impact. For example, one ad (called "Fried Brains") achieved a 95% recognition rate among college students. Seventy-five percent gave it positive ratings. Many of the ads were extremely powerful. A print ad called "Gun" shows in the top frame a close-up of the expressionless eyes of a woman. In the frame below one sees the eyes and nose with a gun barrel stuck up one nostril. The third frame shows the hand holding the gun with the word "COCAINE" written in bold letters. The final frame shows the entire face, pistol, and word. The ad vividly portrayed the idea that using cocaine is tantamount to committing suicide. Another print ad, using the same format as "Gun," shows a mother gently breastfeeding a new infant in the top frame. Other frames show different views of the touching scene. The idyllic vision is interrupted by the bottom frame that contains the copy "You're looking at a cocaine user giving her baby a fix."

INTRODUCTION

In the last chapter the discussion of beliefs, attitudes, and behavior focused on how they are formed and how they may be predicted. In many instances, however, the goal is to persuade someone else by changing preexisting attitudes and beliefs to influence consumer behavior. Indeed, one might argue that consumers rarely enter a situation with absolutely no preexisting attitudes and beliefs about an object. Even when a new product or service is introduced, consumers may have an initial positive or negative feeling toward it based upon previous experiences with other new introductions. For example, one of the problems faced by General Motors in the late 1980s was initial unfavorable reactions of some consumers to its new product offerings, such as the Chevrolet Beretta. Previous consumer experiences with new GM models, such as the Pontiac Fiero, had been poor, and publications (e.g., *Consumer Reports*) had warned consumers against buying new GM models in their first year out. Thus, even though the Beretta was a completely new model, GM needed to change the negative attitudes that already existed among many consumers to persuade them to purchase it.

The chapter-opening vignette illustrates a number of key points about attitude, belief, and behavior change. One of the first actions in creating a strategy for the campaign against drugs was to conduct a large-scale market research study. Managers cannot expect to influence consumer beliefs and attitudes without first obtaining information on the target market and the initial attitudes of its members. In addition, it is important to obtain initial belief and attitude readings for use as a baseline to determine if marketing communications effect any changes. The study conducted for the antidrug campaign helped identify the extent of attitude commitment among consumers. As discussed later in the chapter, extreme attitudes are difficult to change. The initial attitude study in the campaign also provided information on the involvement level of the target market in the topic area. Strategies to cause attitude change require different approaches depending on the consumer's level of involvement.

It is evident in the vignette that the campaign used ideas from multiattribute attitude models as a means of changing behavioral intentions. The behavioral intentions model, which was discussed in Chapter 8, has implications for changing consumer actions. The model suggests that one approach to swaying intentions and behavior involves influencing perceptions of how key reference persons, such as older siblings or friends in a peer group, view the behavior. Some of the ads were developed to suggest that teenagers help their friends to avoid drugs through peer influence. By influencing teenagers to believe that important others view drug use negatively, behavioral intentions may be changed.

Another factor found to influence the extent of attitude change involves the consumer's attitude toward the advertisement. Researchers involved in the "Drug-Free America" campaign recognized the importance of whether consumers reacted positively to their ads. The high recall rate and high positivity received regarding "Fried Brains" indicated its positive impact on college students. Figure 9-1 presents the ad; as you can see, its message is clear and powerful.

Figure 9-2 presents a model of belief, attitude, and behavior change. In the model, the change process begins with a message/communication with persuasive intent. Information processing of the message then occurs. At this point the change process can occur through three different paths: the decision-making path, the experiential path, and the behavioral influence path.

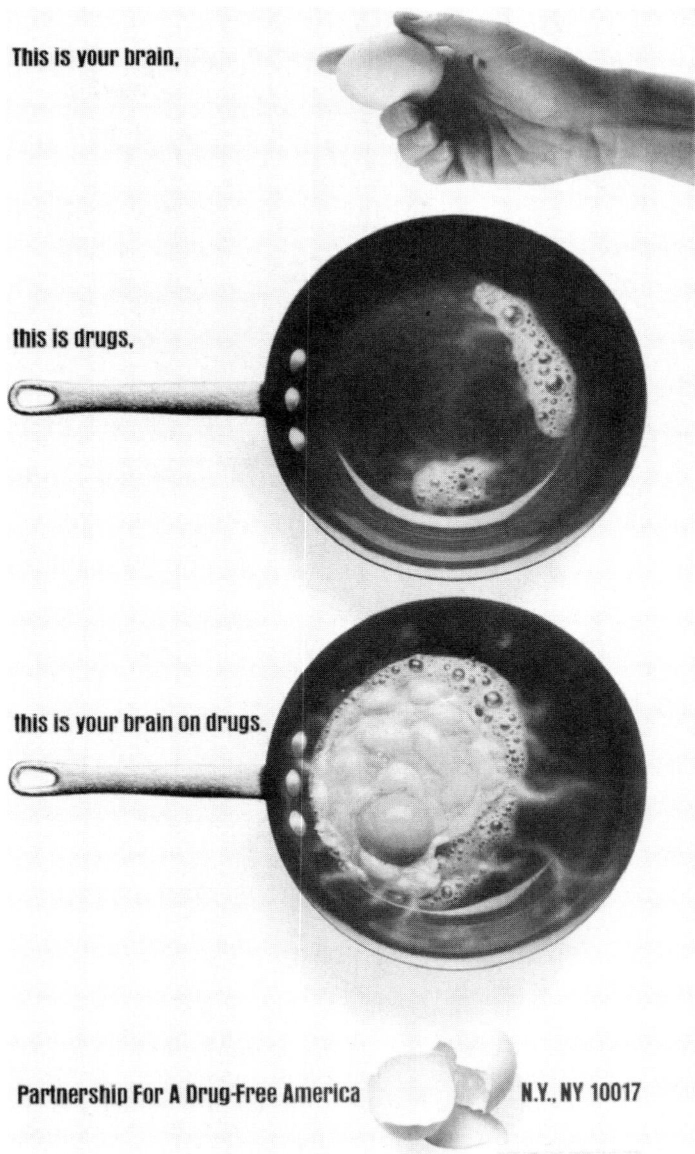

Figure 9-1 This ad received positive ratings on attitude-toward-the-ad measurements. (Courtesy of Partnership for a Drug-Free America.)

From the decision-making perspective, the path through which behavior is influenced begins with changes in the beliefs of the consumer. The study of belief change is closely related to the study of persuasion. **Persuasion** is defined as the explicit attempt to influence beliefs and attitudes. The psychological processes through which persuasion occurs have been categorized as to whether they take place under high- or low-involvement conditions. The first section of this chapter discusses the

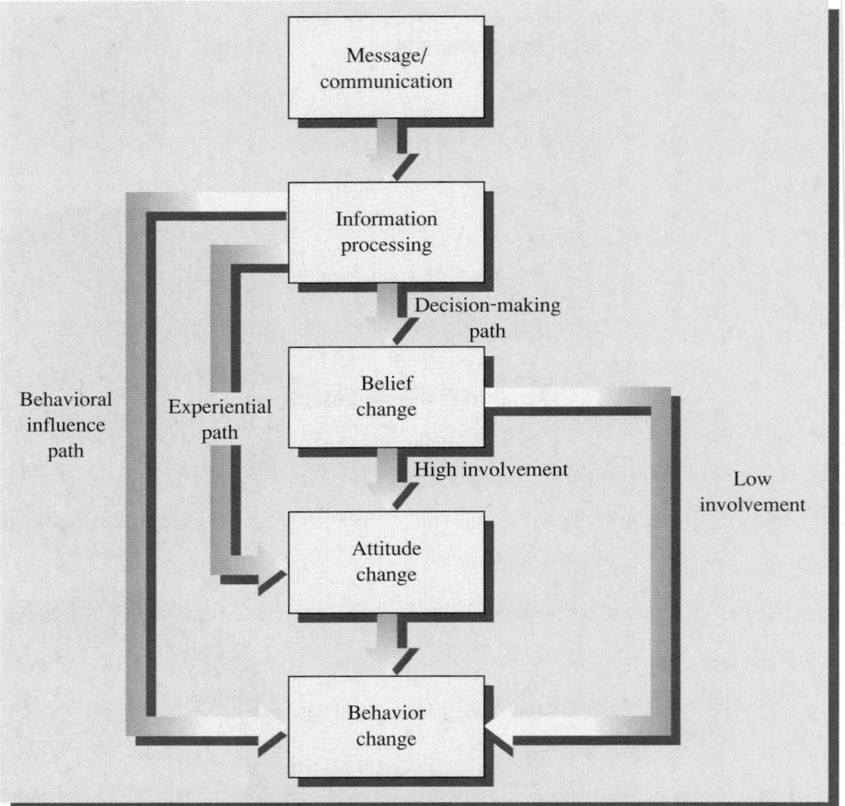

Figure 9-2 Paths to belief, attitude, and behavior change.

decision-making path and presents a model of persuasion, called the elaboration likelihood model.[2] This model of persuasion specifically discusses two routes to behavior change, depending upon whether the consumer is in a high- or low-involvement state. After presenting the elaboration likelihood model, the section reveals how the multiattribute models of attitude formation can be used to understand attitude, belief, and behavior change.

The second section of this chapter discusses the experiential path to persuasion. According to the experiential path, attitudes are changed directly without necessarily influencing beliefs first. In this section, three theoretical approaches to the experiential path to persuasion are presented: balance theory, the impact of reactance and dissonance upon attitudes, and the consumer's attitude toward the advertisement.

The third section of this chapter presents several strategies for behavioral change that follow the behavioral influence path. These strategies involve using techniques that induce consumers to comply with requests, without them necessarily forming beliefs or attitudes about the object of the behavior. This chapter concludes with a short case that illustrates how its concepts can influence managerial strategy.

THE DECISION-MAKING PATH TO PERSUASION

The Elaboration Likelihood Model

An approach to understanding the persuasion process, called the **elaboration likelihood model (ELM),** well illustrates the decision-making path to belief, attitude, and behavior change. In the ELM (depicted in Figure 9-3), the persuasion process begins when the consumer receives a communication. The term *communication* is defined broadly to include all aspects of the message, including the source of the message, the type of message given, and through what channel it moved (e.g., television, radio, or print media). Upon receiving the message, the consumer begins to process it. Depending upon such factors as the message content, the nature of the consumer, and the consumer's situation, the person processes a communication with higher or lower amounts of involvement. Involvement refers to the perceived personal relevance of the information. Depending upon the amount of involvement, belief and attitude change may take one of two routes.[3] When high-involvement information processing occurs, the person is said to take the **central route to persuasion**. In contrast, when in low-involvement circumstances, the consumer is said to be using the **peripheral route to persuasion**.

The Central Route to Persuasion

When attitude and belief change occur via the central route, the consumer attends more carefully to the message being received. The person more diligently considers the communication and compares it to his or her own attitudinal position. If the

Figure 9-3 Elaboration likelihood mode of persuasion.

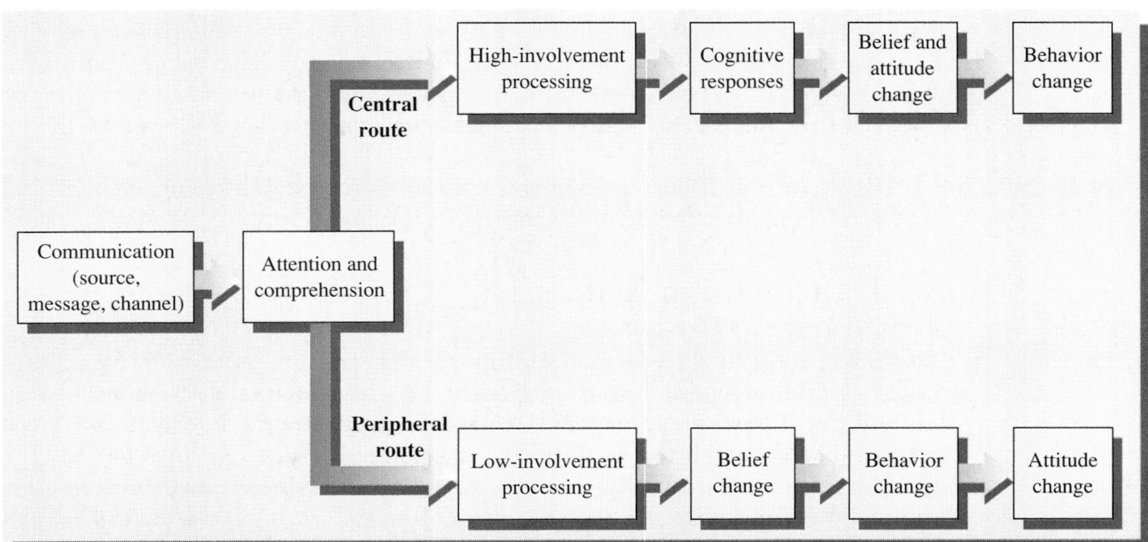

consumer has the ability to process the information, he or she is likely to generate a number of cognitive responses to the communication.[4] Based in part upon the extent to which the cognitive responses are supportive or nonsupportive of the message, the consumer may then have belief change. Following the changes in beliefs, the consumer may then experience attitude change. Evidence suggests that belief and attitude change, which occur through the central route, are relatively enduring and predictive of behavior.[5] Further, in the central route to persuasion, the quality of the arguments in the message should be the major factor influencing attitude change.

The Peripheral Route to Persuasion

When consumers engage in low-involvement information processing, they are said to be moving through the peripheral route to persuasion. In such instances, cognitive responses are much less likely to occur, because the consumer is not carefully considering the pros and cons of the issue. Instead, the consumer tends to use peripheral cues to determine whether to accept or reject the message. Peripheral cues include such factors as the attractiveness and expertise of the source, the mere number of arguments presented, and the positive or negative stimuli that form the context within which the message was presented (e.g., pleasant music). Beliefs may change in such circumstances, but it is unlikely that attitudes or feelings are then influenced. Thus measures of attitudes are likely to show them to be relatively temporary and unpredictive of behavior in such low-involvement circumstances.[6]

The elaboration likelihood model is directly related to the decision-making perspective on consumer behavior. As discussed in the last chapter, the decision-making perspective focuses on the idea that changes in beliefs lead to attitude and behavior change. In addition, within the decision-making perspective the involvement level has important consequences. The ELM makes a similar point. That is, the route to persuasion depends on the involvement of the consumer. In high-involvement circumstances a central route may be taken in which greater amounts of information processing occur. In low-involvement circumstances, on the other hand, a more peripheral route may be taken in which little information processing occurs.

The ELM is also consistent with the decision-making perspective in its proposal that the hierarchy of effects is different depending upon the route to persuasion. In the central route the standard hierarchy of effects occurs (i.e., beliefs lead to attitudes, which lead to behaviors). In the peripheral route the low-involvement hierarchy occurs (i.e., beliefs are followed by behavior, which is then followed by the formation of attitudes).

Highlight 9-1 discusses a possible ethical issue that can occur when attitude change is taking place in low-involvement circumstances.

Are There Individual Differences in the Route to Persuasion?

The elaboration likelihood model proposes that consumers may chronically use either a central or a peripheral route. Researchers have found that consumers consistently differ in the extent to which they diligently process information. A construct, called the **need for cognition**, was identified, which measures the extent to which consumers chronically exhibit high- versus low-involvement processing of information. Consumers who have a need to engage in high amounts of effortful cognitive activities are said to have a high need for cognition. Such people may tend

HIGHLIGHT 9-1

Ethical Issues in Changing Attitudes: The "Truth Effect"

You have probably heard the old aphorism "If you say something often enough, people will come to believe you." A phenomenon called the truth effect has direct bearing on the proverb. The truth effect states that if something is repeated often enough, people will begin to believe it. It occurs regardless of the actual truth value of the statement. The key issue appears to be whether or not clear feedback is obtained on the veracity of the statements. The phenomenon occurs because people use their familiarity with a statement to help them infer its truthfulness.

Recently, researchers tested whether the truth effect occurs in a consumer setting. Respondents were shown a series of statements of which half were true and half were false. For example, four of the statements and their truthfulness are

1. Consumers are more satisfied with State Farm homeowner's insurance than with Allstate. (true)
2. Red Lobster is the largest full-service dinner restaurant in the United States. (true)
3. All nondietetic margarines contain the same amount of fat. (false)
4. Stone-ground flour retains more nutrients than conventional flour. (false)

In the study respondents answered two lists of 104 questions in two separate sessions. Familiarity with the statements was varied by repeating half of the items found in the first session in the second session. Thus, in the second session, half of the items were new and half had been seen previously. In addition, the involvement level with each item was varied. To create high involvement, in the first session half of the subjects rated the items on a seven-point truth-evaluation scale. (The scale ranged from 1 = definitely false to 7 = definitely true.) To create low involvement, in the first session, the other half of the subjects rated the items on a seven-point comprehension scale. (The scale ranged from 1 = difficult to understand to 7 = easy to understand.) The idea was that if you asked people to assess the truthfulness of an item, it would make them think harder about its veracity. In the second session, all respondents rated the truthfulness of all 104 statements.

The results revealed a strong truth effect when respondents were working under low-involvement conditions. That is, for respondents who first considered whether or not they had seen a statement before, the mere repetition of an item caused them to rate it as more truthful in the second session. In contrast, those who had first considered the truthfulness of a statement did not show the effect. In sum, the study supported the idea that merely repeating a statement to people who do not actively consider its truthfulness will later inflate their perception of its truthfulness.

Is the truth effect important. The answer is a definite "yes." Consumers are exposed to hundreds of advertising messages a day. In most instances, they pay insufficient attention to them to consider their truthfulness. The net result is a situation that maximizes the possibility that for frequently repeated messages beliefs in their truthfulness will be enhanced. From a public policy perspective, the findings suggest the importance of monitoring the marketplace to ensure that the statements made by companies are *in fact true*.

Based on Scott A. Hawkins and Stephen J. Hoch, "Low-Involvement Learning: Memory Without Evaluation," *Journal of Consumer Research*, Vol. 19 (September 1992), pp. 212–224.

to habitually evaluate argument quality and require a central route to persuasion. Other consumers may have a low need for cognition and require a peripheral route to persuasion. Information on a target market's need for cognition has importance for advertisers.[8] More complex messages may be developed for consumers with a high need for cognition than for consumers with a low need for cognition. Table 9-1 presents the need for cognition scale.

TABLE 9-1

The Need for Cognition Scale

1. I really enjoy a task that involves coming up with new solutions to problems.
4. I would prefer a task that is intellectual, difficult, and important to one that is somewhat important but does not require much thought.
10. Learning new ways to think doesn't excite me very much.[a]
12. I usually end up deliberating about issues even when they do not affect me personally.
13. I prefer just to let things happen rather than try to understand why they turned out that way.[a]
15. The idea of relying on thought to make my way to the top does not appeal to me.[a]
16. The notion of thinking abstractly is not appealing to me.[a]
18. I find it especially satisfying to complete an important task that required a lot of thinking and mental effort.
19. I only think as hard as I have to.[a]
21. I like tasks that require little thought once I've learned them.[a]
22. I prefer to think about small, daily projects to long-term ones.[a]
23. I would rather do something that requires little thought than something that is sure to challenge my thinking abilities.[a]
24. I find little satisfaction in deliberating hard and for long hours.[a]
29. I don't like to have the responsibilities of handling a situation that requires a lot of thinking.[a]
31. I feel relief rather than satisfaction after completing a task that required a lot of mental effort.[a]
32. Thinking is not my idea of fun.[a]
33. I try to anticipate and avoid situations where there is a likely chance that I will have to think in depth about something.[a]
37. I think best when those around me are very intelligent.
39. I prefer my life to be filled with puzzles that I must solve.
40. I would prefer complex to simple problems.
41. Simply knowing the answer rather than understanding the reasons for the answer to a problem is fine with me.
43. It's enough for me that something gets the job done, I don't care how or why it works.[a]

Note: Only the 22 items found to be most highly related to the construct are shown. Items marked *a* are reverse scored.

SOURCE: John T. Cacioppo and Richard E. Petty, "The Need for Cognition," *Journal of Personality and Social Psychology*, Vol. 42 (1982), pp. 116–131.

The need for cognition acts to influence how consumers respond to central and peripheral cues given in advertisements. For example, in a recent series of studies researchers investigated how advertisements influenced high versus low need for cognition consumers.[7] In one study the researchers employed a peripheral cue—the physical attractiveness of a model in the ad who was endorsing a typewriter, a product that should have no relevance to physical attractiveness. The results revealed that for high need for cognition respondents, the attractiveness of the model had little impact on brand attitudes. In contrast, for the low need for cognition respondents, the brand was liked *much* more when the physically attractive model endorsed it. Thus, as predicted by the theory, the low need for cognition respondents were influenced by a peripheral cue (i.e., the physical attractiveness of the model), while the high need for cognition subjects were *not* influenced by the cue.

The same researchers conducted a second study in which they manipulated a "central cue"—the quality of the arguments presented for why consumers should buy a particular brand of typewriter. The strong arguments were

- four-year unconditional warranty,
- different type sizes available,
- adjustable spacing for pica or elite, and
- 30,000-word automatic spelling checker.

The weak arguments were

- thirty-day conditional warranty,
- manual operation for simplicity and convenience,
- availability only in standard elite font and type size,
- designed with the college student in mind.

The results of the study are depicted in Figure 9-4. They show that the quality of the arguments for a typewriter had virtually no impact on the low need for cognition respondents. Indeed, in the weak argument condition, the ratings of brand attitude toward the brand were slightly higher for the low need for cognition respondents. In contrast, for the high need for cognition respondents, the ratings strongly impacted their evaluations. That is, high need for cognition people rated the typewriter in the strong arguments condition much more positively.

These results reveal the extreme importance of marketing research being conducted to identify a target market's need for cognition. If a target market has a high need for cognition, it will tend to focus on central cues, such as argument quality. In contrast, if a target market has a low need for cognition, it will tend to emphasize peripheral cues, such as physical attractiveness and the number of (rather than the quality of) arguments.

Comprehension and the ELM

Research on consumers' ability to comprehend messages is relevant to the ELM. Historically, consumer researchers have argued that comprehension of a message is a prerequisite for persuasion to occur. That is, potential buyers must have an understanding of what is said to be influenced by the message. Recently, however, researchers have found that the relationship between comprehension and persuasion is more complex.

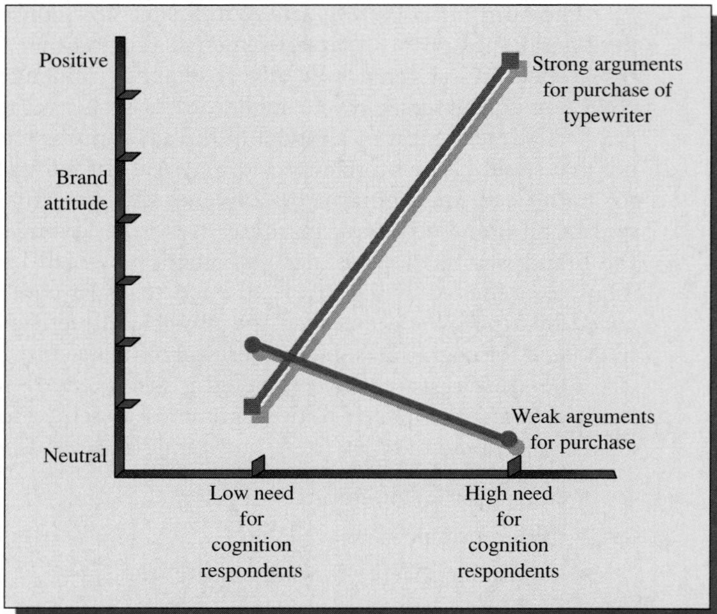

Figure 9-4 The need for cognition moderates the impact of argument quality on brand attitudes. (Source: Curtis P. Haugtvedt, Richard E. Petty, and John T, Cacioppo, "Need for Cognition and Advertising: Understanding the Role of Personality Variables in Consumer Behavior," *Journal of Consumer Psychology*, Vol. 1, no. 3, 1992, p. 250.)

In one series of studies the researchers presented respondents with messages that were easy or hard to comprehend about a new invention—a replacement eraser for ordinary lead pencils. In addition, the expertise of the inventor was varied. Some respondents learned that the inventor was an expert—an engineer at Stanford University with numerous patents. Others learned that the inventor was a novice in the area—a realtor who held no other patents. The results revealed that when the message was difficult to comprehend, the subjects relied on the expertise of the source to evaluate the product. However, when the message was easily comprehended, the expertise of the inventor had no impact on attitudes.[9]

The results of the study are consistent with the ELM. When the message is easily comprehended, high levels of processing can occur. As a result, respondents attend to the factual material contained in the message and source expertise has little or no impact on attitudes. In contrast, when messages are difficult to comprehend, consumers have little ability to process the information and resort to peripheral cues, such as source expertise, to form brand attitudes.

The managerial implications of the work on comprehension and persuasion are direct. Because consumers differ in their level of knowledge about a product category, advertisers must take care in creating messages that are complex and potentially difficult to comprehend. If consumers possessing low levels of knowledge receive a complex message, they are likely to form brand attitudes based to a large extent on the perceived expertise of the source of information. As a result, a general rule for firms to follow is to use experts in advertisements that may be difficult for consumers to comprehend. For example, when describing a complex new product, a computer company should ensure that an individual presents the information whom the target market would perceive to be an expert.

Multiattribute Models and the Decision-Making Path to Persuasion

The various multiattribute model of attitude formation can be applied to help change the beliefs, attitudes, and behaviors of a target.

Persuasion and the Attitude-Toward-the-Object Model

In the last chapter the attitude-toward-the-object model was discussed. It proposes that an attitude results from (1) the salient attributes on which a person evaluates an object, (2) a rating of the evaluation of the "goodness" or "badness" of the various attributes of an object, and (3) a rating of the person's belief of the extent to which the object possesses each of the attributes.

Based upon the attitude-toward-the-object model, communicators have several options for changing an existing attitude. First, they can attempt to change the perceived evaluation of an attribute. As noted earlier, this was one goal of the "Drug-Free America" campaign—that is, to show how negative the outcomes of using drugs can be. In the mid-1980s the "Where's the beef" advertisements initiated by Wendy's Inc. utilized such a strategy. The goal of the ads was to make highly salient the size of the hamburger patty that consumers were getting from competing fast-food chains. If consumers could be induced to evaluate small hamburger patties more negatively, a good chance existed that consumers' attitudes toward Wendy's larger burgers would improve.

Another strategy involves introducing a new attribute, rather than attempting to change the evaluation of an existing attribute. For example, in the 1980s the automobiles produced by GM began to receive excellent safety ratings from various automotive testing agencies. The company began to incorporate such information in its advertising as another reason why people should buy cars from GM. The goal was to add the attribute of safety and create the salient belief that GM cars protect their passengers. As discussed later in the chapter, it is generally easier to influence weakly held beliefs and attitudes than ones that are strongly held. Thus, if a person essentially has no belief about a particular attribute, it may be possible to create such a belief.

A third way of influencing attitudes through a multiattribute model approach is to change the belief that an object has a particular attribute. This is probably the easiest of the three approaches, because a company can use a variety of methods to show that the particular characteristic of the product has changed. For example, the company could use demonstrations or trustworthy endorsers to show and explain the change. Again, GM provides an example. The Chevrolet Division of GM developed a print advertisement designed in part to change beliefs about the "nimbleness" of the Corvette. The Corvette had previously been known as a fast car that possessed poor handling characteristics. In the ad, shown in Figure 9-5, the company sought to persuade consumers that the Corvette handles well by

Figure 9-5 This ad attempts to change consumers' belief about one attribute of the Corvette—its handling characteristics. (Reproduced with the permission of the Chevrolet Division of General Motors Corporation.)

comparing its ability to steer and handle under wet conditions to that of four other prestige sports cars. The ad effectively acts as a persuasion agent to change consumer beliefs about the handling of the sports car.

Persuasion and the Behavioral Intentions Model

The behavioral intentions model suggests that additional approaches to attitude change may be taken. One approach is to influence consumer perceptions of the consequences of a behavior. As noted earlier, among women and men the "Drug-Free America" campaign identified at least one new consequence of taking drugs. Many people may not have realized that taking a drug such as cocaine can addict a child who is nursing. By making salient this additional negative outcome of using cocaine, the campaign may have persuaded consumers not to engage in such behavior.

A second implication of the behavioral intentions model for attitude change involves the subjective norm component. The model explicitly considers the impact of other people on a consumer's intentions to behave. In the "Drug-Free America" campaign researchers recognized the importance of the teenager's peer groups in developing questions for the market research study. The results of the study confirmed the importance of reference groups, and advertisements were developed that attempted to show one peer helping another.

Researchers have recently found that different people react divergently to what others may think about them. A scale was developed to assess this tendency to pay attention to what others think. Called "The Attention to Social Comparison Information Measure," this scale is presented in Table 9-2. The behavioral intentions of those who score higher on the scale tend to be influenced to a greater degree by the opinions of others.

TABLE 9-2

The "Attention to Social Comparison Information Measure" (the ASTCI scale)

1. It is my feeling that if everyone else in a group is behaving in a certain manner, this must be the proper way to behave.
2. I actively avoid wearing clothes that are not in style.
3. At parties I usually try to behave in a manner that makes me fit in.
4. When I am uncertain how to act in a social situation, I look to the behavior of others for cues.
5. I try to pay attention to the reactions of others to my behavior in order to avoid being out of place.
6. I find that I tend to pick up slang expressions from others and use them as part of my own vocabulary.
7. I tend to pay attention to what others are wearing.
8. The slightest look of disapproval in the eyes of a person with whom I am interacting is enough to make me change my approach.
9. It's important to me to fit into the group I'm with.
10. My behavior often depends on how I feel others wish me to behave.
11. If I am the least bit uncertain as to how to act in a social situation, I look to the behavior of others for cues.
12. I usually keep up with clothing style changes by watching what others wear.
13. When in a social situation, I tend not to follow the crowd, but instead behave in a manner that suits my particular mood at the time.

Note: Item scoring: Respondents rated the items on a scale with endpoint marked 0 (always false) and 5 (always true). Item 13 requires reverse scoring.

SOURCE: William O. Bearden and Randall L. Rose, "Attention to Social Comparison Information: An Individual Difference Factor Affecting Consumer Conformity," *Journal of Consumer Research*, Vol. 16 (March 1990), pp. 461–471.

The social comparison scale was assessed in a study in which college students had to choose their preferred color in a sweatshirt. The students were first given the scale in a disguised form in which it was embedded in a series of life-style questions. A week later, the students were given the opportunity to choose which of two colors they liked better in a sweatshirt. Prior to making a recommendation, however, they received information that most people who supported a hated rival institution liked one color better than the other. Supporters of their own school liked the other color better. Thus one color was liked by a negative referent group and the other was preferred by a positive referent group. The results revealed that the normative influence of others did influence color choice to a greater extent among students who revealed by their answers to the scale that they were sensitive to social comparison information. Such results suggest that consumers may be segmented based upon their tendency to be influenced by others. Those with a low need to conform may require a different type of message than those with a strong tendency to conform to the opinions of others.[10]

Table 9-3 summarizes the implications of multiattribute models for attitude change and behavior.

TABLE 9-3

Five Methods of Changing Attitudes: A Multiattribute Perspective

Method 1

Change the perceived evaluation of the attributes.

Advantage: Can increase the attitude rating of a product or service without changing the product or service in any way.

Disadvantage: Very difficult to do because evaluation ratings are often tied to the consumer's self-concept.

Method 2

Change the product-attribute beliefs.

Advantage: Easier to do because the company can use demonstrations or trustworthy sources to present the message. Beliefs about the extent to which products contain attributes are not usually connected to a consumer's self-concept.

Disadvantage: May involve changing the product.

Method 3

Add a new attribute for consideration.

Advantage: Beliefs and attitudes are easier to change when they are weakly held.

Disadvantage: May involve changing the product or service. Requires extensive promotional efforts to get new information to target market.

Method 4

Influence perceptions of consequences of behavior.

Advantage: Can identify consequences not previously recognized.

Disadvantage: Target may not evaluate consequences as desired or may not perceive them to be likely.

Method 5

Influence perceptions of reference group reactions to behavior.

Advantage: Reference groups have a large impact on intentions to behave.

Disadvantage: Motivation to comply may be very low.

THE EXPERIENTIAL PATH TO ATTITUDE CHANGE

The persuasion process can also occur along an experiential path. When the consumer follows the experiential path, attitudes are influenced directly—the consumer's beliefs about the object or behavior do not necessarily change beforehand. Four theoretical approaches can be used to understand the experiential path to persuasion: balance theory, social judgment theory, the impact of reactance and dissonance on attitudes, and attitudes toward the advertisement.

Balance Theory

Researchers have found that attitudes may be changed by creating cognitive imbalance within the target of persuasion. The objective is to make use of people's tendency to maintain cognitive consistency among the various ideas and concepts about which they think. **Cognitive consistency** is the name applied to the human inclination to maintain a logical and consistent set of interconnected attitudes. Thus, by deliberately creating cognitive inconsistency, the skillful communicator can induce consumers to change their attitudes to bring their cognitive system back into balance. To explain the mechanisms behind the operation of cognitive consistency, it is first necessary to explain balance theory.

Balance theory was originated by one of the founders of social psychology, Fritz Heider.[11] As originally conceived, the theory dealt with the cognitive relationships between an observer (*o*), another person (*p*), and an impersonal object (*x*). In a consumer behavior setting, the observer represents the consumer, the other person might be a product endorser, and the impersonal object could be a brand. The idea of the theory is that cognitive elements may form a unit in which each is linked to the other. Cognitive elements are the entities about which consumers form attitudes and beliefs. They are similar to the nodes found in a semantic memory network, as discussed in Chapter 4.

Figure 9-6 shows an example of a triad of elements forming a cognitive unit. Two types of connections exist that join the cognitive elements within a unit—sentiment connections and unit relations. Sentiment connections are identical in definition to the term attitude used in this text. Thus sentiment connections are the observer's evaluation of other people and of other attitudinal objects. They are the positive or negative feelings that the observer may have toward the other person and the object. **Sentiment connections** are given a positive or negative algebraic sign depending upon whether the feeling toward *p* or *x* is positive or negative.

The second type of connection is called a **unit relation**, which occurs when the observer perceives that the person and object are somehow connected to each other. The factors that govern whether a person perceives a connection are the same principles of perceptual organization discussed in Chapter 3. Thus *p* and *x* would be perceived as having a unit relation through such principles as proximity, similarity, continuation, and common fate. As in the case of sentiment connections, the relationship between *p* and *x* may be either positive or negative. A positive unit relation indicates that *p* and *x* are perceived as related and as forming a unit. A negative sign indicates that an inverse relation exists between *p* and *x*. In addition, a null unit relation may exist. In such cases, no cognitive consistency forces operate to change attitudes.

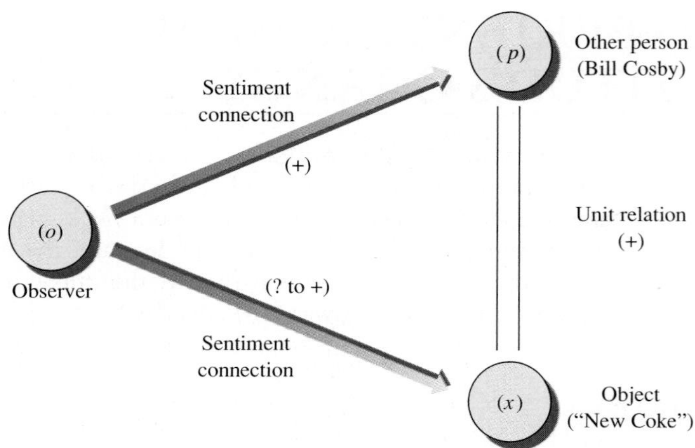

Figure 9-6 An example of cognitive elements in a balance theory framework.

The basic premise of **balance theory** is that people have a preference to maintain a balanced state among the cognitive elements of *p*, *o*, and *x*, if they are perceived as forming a unit. A balanced state was defined by Heider as a situation in which the cognitive elements fit together harmoniously with no stress for change. Such "harmony" occurred when the multiplication of the signs of the connections between the elements resulted in a positive value. As shown in Figure 9-7, a balanced state would result from three positive signs or from two negative signs and one positive sign. An imbalanced state would occur if two signs were positive and one sign was negative.

The key point made by Heider is that balanced states are preferred to imbalanced states. Further, if an imbalanced state is experienced, the person is motivated to change the signs of one or more of the cognitive relations. Through a type of unconscious, mental rationalization the person comes to view one or more of the sentiment connections and unit relations differently.

Although companies may not realize that they are using cognitive consistency procedures to change attitudes, one can identify numerous cases where their strategies employ principles of balance theory. Indeed, the use of celebrity endorsers to sponsor products fits balance model principles quite well. Companies strive to select endorsers who are viewed as positively as possible by consumers. From the perspective of balance theory, they are attempting to maximize the strength of the sentiment connection between the observer (*o*) and the person (*p*). In addition, successful companies attempt to create a unit relation between the endorser and the brand (*x*).

Various ways of establishing this unit relation include

1. Hiring endorsers who are known experts in using the product. For example, a tennis star, such as Steffi Graf, would endorse a company's tennis racket or tennis shoe.
2. Signing the endorser to long-term, exclusive contracts, so that the celebrity is associated only with the company's brand and no others. Manufacturers of

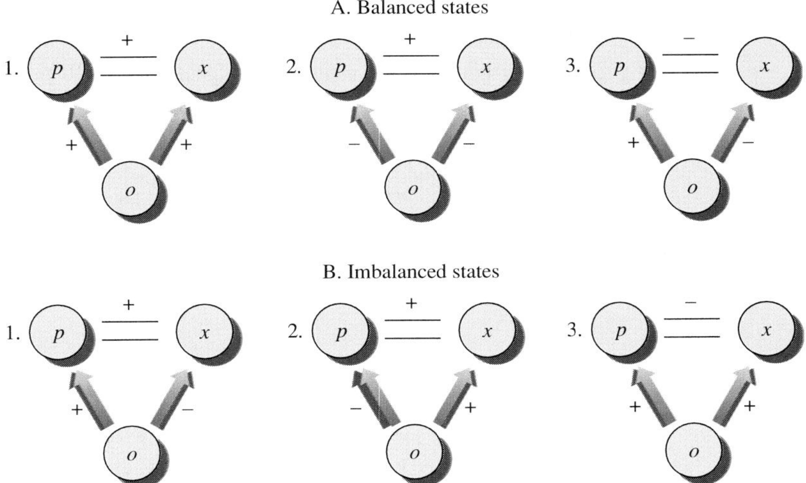

Figure 9-7 Examples of balanced and imbalanced states.

perfumes and cosmetics have long used such a strategy. For example, Elizabeth Taylor was signed to endorse exclusively White Diamonds perfume.

3. Having the endorser consistently wear or use the product when in public view, so that he or she is strongly associated with the product. Texaco Corporation long used Bob Hope as a celebrity endorser. Mr. Hope apparently took his duties with Texaco seriously and would occasionally mention Texaco in a positive way in his noncommercial appearances, such as golf tournaments.

A classic example of a company using a celebrity endorser was Coca-Cola's hiring of Bill Cosby to endorse New Coke. When the new Coca-Cola came out in early 1985, the immediate public reaction was quite mixed, and the company hired Bill Cosby to tout the taste of the product. The goal was to link Cosby (who was extremely popular) with the new product. With these strong positive connections, consumers may have felt a tendency to change their attitudes toward the product in a more favorable direction. The goal was to create cognitive imbalance. The hope was that consumers would achieve balance by changing their attitude toward the new Coca-Cola.

However, consumers do not always change attitudes as marketing managers plan. In general, one finds that consumers change the sign of the weakest connection in an imbalanced cognitive system.[12] Thus people who were strongly against the new cola formulation may have changed their impression of Bill Cosby in an unfavorable direction or decided that Cosby really did not believe what he was saying about the New Coke. Indeed, Coca-Cola quickly dropped Cosby as a spokesperson for the new brand.

An interesting prediction from balance theory is that one can create more favorable sentiment toward a brand (i.e., a positive sentiment connection) if someone that consumers dislike (i.e., the sentiment connection is minus) indicates that he or she dislikes the brand (i.e., unit relation is negative). Thus balance is achieved because two negative relations and one positive relation are created. (That is, a minus times a minus times a plus equals a plus.) An example of such an approach is found in commercials from Wendy's. In these commercials, unlikable characters were interviewed by a marketing researcher. They were shown two hamburgers and asked if they liked the succulent Wendy's burger or the competitor's dried-up piece of meat. The "nerdy" individuals responded that they preferred the dried-up meat. The ads were humorous and created an instance in which consumers have to reason as follows: "If that turkey dislikes the Wendy's burger, it must be really good." Figure 9-8 shows a storyboard for one of the ads in the campaign.

Social Judgment Theory and Influencing Attitudes

Thus far, the section has discussed the experiential path to persuasion from the perspective of balance theory. A second theoretical approach relevant to the experiential path is **social judgment theory**. According to this theory, the same factors that influence psychophysical judgments also influence attitude expression.

From a social judgment perspective, when individuals form an attitude about an object, they compare the incoming message to their initial attitude, which acts as a frame of reference for the judgment. As such, judgment requires a discrimination or choice between the frame of reference and the alternative. The frame of reference or initial attitude is formed through experience and represents an individual's prior experience, feelings, and beliefs on the issue in question. It acts as a type of anchor to which the issue in question is compared on the judgmental scale.[13] For example, a student may receive a communication from the university he or she is attending that tuition costs will be raised. The student already has developed an attitude about the level of tuition at the university, which acts as the frame of reference to which new communications are compared. The question addressed by social judgment theory concerns how the student perceives the communication and how it influences the student's attitude toward the idea of a tuition increase.

Latitudes of Acceptance and Rejection

One of the findings of social judgment theory is that people form **latitudes of acceptance** and **latitudes of rejection** around attitudinal frames of reference. Immediately surrounding this initial attitude is an area of acceptance. Communications falling within this range on the judgmental scale will tend to be assimilated. The **assimilation effect** refers to the idea that the communication will be viewed as more congruent with the position of the receiver than it really is because it falls within the latitude of acceptance. In such instances the receiver is likely to indicate that he or she agrees with the attitude statement. In effect, the initial attitude of the person is pulled toward the message leading to persuasion.

Contrast effects tend to occur when the attitude statement falls into the latitude of rejection. The latitude of rejection represents positions on the scale of judgment that are well outside of the latitude of acceptance. When an attitudinal statement is perceived as falling into the latitude of rejection, a contrast effect tends to occur, where the attitude statement is rejected and may be viewed as more opposed to the position of the receiver than it really is. The net result is that attitude change occurs

Figure 9-8 This ad illustrates principles from the balance theory. How is it that attitudes can become more positive when an unlikable person indicates that he or she doesn't like the product? (Courtesy of Wendy's International, Inc.)

in the direction opposite to that intended. Figure 9-9 diagrams the latitudes of acceptance and rejection.

The underlying judgment scale on which assimilation and contrast effects occur is the receiver's favorability or feeling toward the communication. For example, assume that a consumer receives the communication "GM sweats the details." This message was part of a campaign to persuade consumers that GM was attending to the "fit and finish" of its automobiles. If the statement falls within the receiver's latitude of acceptance, the statement may be assimilated such that the individual perceives it as closer to his or her initial attitude position than it really is. On the other hand, if the message falls within the latitude of rejection, a contrast effect may occur so that it is perceived as further from his or her initial attitude position than it really is.

The Effects of Commitment to a Position and Involvement

One of the findings of social judgment theory researchers is that people differ in their ability to accept or tolerate positions different from their own. The results of a number of studies have indicated that strong commitment to a position results in a widening of the latitude of rejection and a narrowing of the latitude of acceptance.[14] The level of commitment to an issue is associated with the extremity of the position held by the receiver—that is, if the receiver's initial position is either very positive or very negative, he or she tends to be more committed to the position.

A second factor associated with the size of the latitudes of acceptance and rejection appears to be the level of involvement of the receiver. To the extent that the receiver is highly involved in the issue, latitudes of acceptance and noncommitment will be smaller and the latitude of rejection larger.

The managerial implication of commitment and involvement is that persuasion becomes more difficult as levels of commitment and involvement increase. Consumers who are highly involved in a purchase tend to exert greater energy in searching for information and in examining the information obtained. Consequently, they are better able to reject communications that contain information not matching their initial attitudes. Such a conclusion meshes well with the elaboration likelihood model. That is, consumers who are highly involved tend to generate more counterarguments to messages. The result is that communications that do not seem to fit the

Figure 9-9 Latitudes of acceptance and rejection.

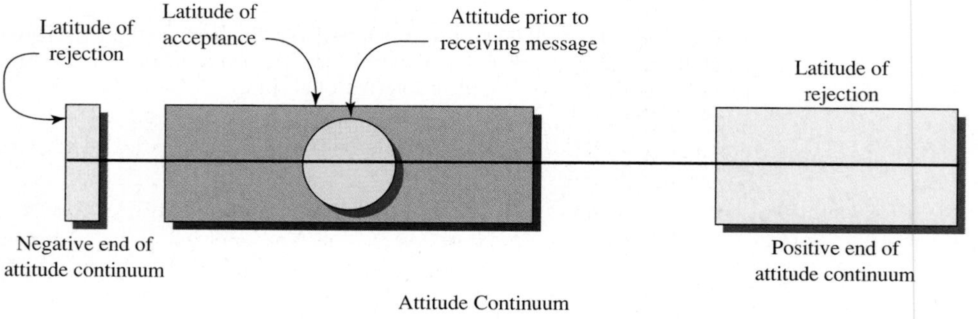

frame of reference may be simply rejected, without much thought being given to the ideas they contain. True believers in causes tend to show such tendencies. Thus ardent antibusiness crusaders may reject any positive statements about American corporations simply because the communication is positive—that is, it falls into their latitude of rejection.

Social Judgment Theory and Inducing Attitude Change

From a social judgment perspective, the relation of the communication to the individual's initial frame of reference is crucial in determining whether the persuasive message will change that person's attitude. The results of a number of studies indicate that to have the best chance of creating attitude change, communications should fall just within the boundaries of the latitude of acceptance.[15] Messages that fall into the latitude of rejection may actually result in a **boomerang effect**. A boomerang effect may occur when a message is perceived to fall into the latitude of rejection. In such instances, the communication attitude of the communication recipient may shift in the direction of that intended. In such an instance the message would be rejected, and the persuasion attempt would have be a failure.

The findings of social judgment theorists have managerial implications. Perhaps most important is the idea that, prior to developing persuasive communications, market research studies should be performed to identify the initial attitude of the target group on the communication issue. Furthermore, pretests of potential messages should be performed to determine the reaction of the target audience to them. Although identifying the exact locations of the regions of acceptance and rejection is difficult (because they vary from person to person), it is possible to create messages that will not boomerang. The problem, however, is that the natural tendency of firms is to create messages that are as strong as possible. Extreme messages are just the type that may cause the boomerang effect to occur. Rather than trying to induce large changes in the target audience with a single communication, a better goal is to attempt to change attitudes in small increments by creating messages just within the boundaries of the latitude of acceptance. Over time the audience may be moved slowly in the desired attitudinal direction.

Reactance, Dissonance, and the Experiential Path to Attitude Change

When a consumer is making a brand choice, he or she may have feelings of anxiety about making the purchase. Immediately before making the choice, a person may feel a great deal of conflict about whether or not to make a purchase or about which brand to buy. Similarly, shortly after making an important purchase, the consumer may experience severe feelings of anxiety and doubt about whether the correct purchase was made. As noted in Highlight 9-2, real estate professionals call such an experience buyer's regret. The negative feelings, which can occur both before and after a purchase, are caused by the psychological processes of reactance and dissonance. Because they tend to operate in high-involvement circumstances where salespeople are frequently involved, it is important that sales personnel and companies have a good understanding of them.

HIGHLIGHT 9-2

The Dissonance After Buying a New House

A number of years ago, my wife and I decided to take jobs at another university. Knowing that we would buy a house in the new town, we began an extensive search process to identify the characteristics of the "perfect home." For financial and time reasons, it was decided that only one of us could go to the new city to search for the home, and I got this important task. After arriving and going through about ten possible homes, the choice was quickly narrowed to two houses. The houses were priced the same and were about the same size, but here the similarities ended.

House A was in a great location next to the country club. It was immaculate. The furniture was beautiful; the yard was cut; the floors shined; I felt really good in the house.

House B was a pit. It was in an industrial part of town. The furniture was twentieth-century garage-sale fare; the yard was a mess; the curtains were torn; even the toilets were filthy. I felt bad. The problem was that House B had nicer features. The floor plan was better. The house was on a small lake. It had built-in furniture. Furthermore, according to the multiattribute model that we had developed, we should have had a more favorable attitude toward House B.

I called my wife and described the houses. After hearing that House B had a bay window, she said, "There's no choice, buy House B!" I then calmly explained that I felt much better in House A. Always logical, my wife responded that once we cleaned up the house and moved in our furniture, everything would be fine. Agreeing with my wife, I made an offer on House B. It was accepted, and the papers were signed.

The next day I was in agony. I knew I had blown it. As the real estate agent drove me to the airport, I told him how awful I felt. The real estate agent patted me on the back and told me that I had made a great purchase. He said that I was merely having a case of buyer's regret and that most people went through it.

Suddenly, a flash hit me: I was experiencing cognitive dissonance. I proceeded to explain to the realtor all about cognitive dissonance and how this buying situation would certainly create it. I noted that it was a highly important purchase, that we were committed to the decision, and that the two options were rated about the same, but that they excelled on different attributes. He listened patiently and then responded by saying that it still sounded like buyer's regret to him.

Well, what happened? We eventually arrived in the new town, moved in our furniture, and repainted the house. Further, as cognitive dissonance theory suggests, we grew to like the house. We lived in the house for six years. But after starting a family, we built a larger home in a more prestigious location. Looking back on the whole affair, I now realize that the original choice had been a poor one. We should have weighed the location of the house much more heavily in our decision process. The old real estate maxim is correct: "the three most important things in buying a house are location, location, location." The fact that my wife and I managed to persuade ourselves that we really liked the house, even when the lake dried up every summer and the industrial traffic passed by, is testimony to the powerful effects of cognitive dissonance.

Predecisional Reactance

When a consumer compares brands, a negative affective reaction may occur if the individual perceives that his or her behavioral freedom is being threatened. As discussed in Chapter 6, such threats to behavioral freedom can result in reactance. But how can the prospect of making a choice cause a person to believe that behavioral freedom is being lost? When a consumer must make a choice between two or more brands, one of the choices must be given up. Particularly if the choice is important and involves a high degree of financial and social risk, the threat of giving up one of the choices may create a reactance state. The feeling of reactance, in turn, leads the person to reevaluate positively the alternative that the person was about to give up.

A classic study was performed on how people evaluate alternatives prior to making a choice among decision alternatives.[16] In the study, individuals had to choose which of two people would give them a highly confidential interview concerning personal matters. Ratings of preferences for the two interviewers were taken at various time intervals prior to the time when the decision had to be made. The results showed that as the time prior to the decision decreased, the ratings of the two interviewers converged. **Reactance theory** explains such a convergence of feelings for two alternatives. Basically, each time the decision maker begins to commit himself or herself to an alternative, reactance is created because the freedom to choose the other alternative is lost. As a result, high degrees of decision conflict occur, and the feelings toward the two alternatives converge.

If the feelings about two important alternatives tend to converge prior to the decision, what happens to these feelings immediately after the decision? Some evidence suggests that shortly after an important decision an individual may experience reactance in the form of buyer's regret. One study investigated the postdecisional feelings of Army recruits who had just chosen their occupational specialties—an extremely important decision with potential life-and-death consequences.[17] The recruits were asked to rate their feelings about their decision at various times after the choice. Shortly after the decision the ratings of their choice decreased, indicating that the recruits had second thoughts about it. Although research on the predecisional and postdecisional effects of reactance have not been performed in the consumer area, it is likely that a similar effect would be found. Thus, after an important purchase, consumers may reevaluate the unchosen alternative so that it is actually viewed as superior to the chosen alternative.

Postpurchase Cognitive Dissonance

In Highlight 9-2, I discussed my own experience of buying a house. My feelings the day after purchasing the house were similar to those of the recruits soon after they selected their occupational specialties. In circumstances in which reactance occurs and the unchosen alternative is viewed more favorably than the alternative selected, the consumer becomes psychologically uncomfortable. I experienced it as an awful feeling making me almost sick to my stomach.

This state of psychological discomfort is called cognitive dissonance. **Cognitive dissonance** occurs when a logical inconsistency exists among cognitive elements. Leon Festinger, the originator of dissonance theory, stated that "two elements are in a dissonant relation if, considering these two alone, the obverse of one element would follow from the other."[18] In Highlight 9-2, the cognitive elements were the knowledge that I bought a house I didn't like and that I am a careful, prudent decision maker. These two ideas were in conflict and created a dissonant state. According to Festinger, the experience of dissonance is an aversive state, and people act to reduce it. After purchasing a product, three different means exist for reducing dissonance.

1. Break the link between the person's self-concept and the product by returning it or complaining about it.[19]
2. Add new information by reading material relevant to the purchase.
3. Psychologically reevaluate the desirability of the chosen alternative in a positive direction and the desirability of the unchosen alternative in a negative direction.

The first alternative has quite negative implications for the brand. If a person seeks to lower dissonance by returning the product or by engaging in negative word-of-mouth communications, the company loses one or more sales of the product. In the second alternative the consumer seeks to resolve the cognitive imbalance by obtaining greater amounts of information. The third approach to handling dissonance is reevaluating the desirability of the chosen alternative. In this case the consumer lowers the psychological imbalance by gradually changing the perception of the brand purchased and the brand(s) not purchased. Thus feelings toward the brand chosen become more favorable, and feelings toward the brands not chosen become less favorable.

A number of consumer researchers have investigated the predictions of dissonance theory. In one study consumers had to choose between a number of different record albums.[20] In the high-dissonance condition the albums were all rated relatively highly. In the low-dissonance condition one of the albums was clearly preferred by most of the participants. In the high-dissonance conditions preference for the chosen album increased after the purchase, while preference for the album not chosen decreased after the purchase. In the low-dissonance situation preferences remained essentially unchanged after the purchase. This finding supports the third means of dissonance reduction mentioned previously. In fact, the reevaluation of the chosen alternative in a favorable direction is a common means of reducing dissonance.

The record album experiment illustrates one of the necessary conditions for a person to experience cognitive dissonance after a purchase. Table 9-4 presents six factors that influence the degree of dissonance experienced.[21] The first two factors are interrelated. To experience dissonance the person must have favorable feelings about two or more of the alternatives. If one of the brands is clearly superior to the others, no dissonance will be felt. However, a second condition also exists. The brands that are perceived to be similar must also be rated differently on different attributes. In other words,o if the brands are perceived to be similar in every way, it would not make any difference which was chosen. However, if one is good in some areas and not so good in others, and if the other brand is good in the areas in which the first is poor, a great deal of conflict will be felt.

The remaining conditions necessary for dissonance are quite logical. The consumer must be able to choose freely among the alternatives. If he or she is forced to choose one brand, say, because of price or availability, dissonance will not be

TABLE 9-4

Factors Associated with the Creation of Cognitive Dissonance

1. Two or more alternatives are rated similarly in overall favorability.
2. Two or more alternatives, although rated similarly, are perceived to differ on specific attributes.
3. The person has free choice.
4. The person is committed to the decision.
5. The person is highly involved in the purchase.
6. The tendency of the person is to experience dissonance.

experienced. Further, the person must be committed to the decision. If it is possible to back out of it at any time, dissonance will not be felt. Another important factor is that the purchase must be a highly involving one that involves substantial perceived risk.[22] (The risk could be financial, social, time, performance, etc.) In such instances it becomes important to make the best choice, and people are more likely to feel conflict in their decision. Individual differences have been found to exist in experiencing dissonance—that is, some consumers feel greater conflict and doubt about their purchases than others.

Figure 9-10 diagrams the potential effects of reactance and dissonance on purchases in high-involvement, free-choice circumstances. Note that prior to the purchase, predecision reactance may cause a convergence of preference for the alternatives. Immediately after purchase a phase of buyer's regret may occur. Over a period of time, however, the effects of dissonance may act to influence preferences so that the favorability toward the purchased product increases and the favorability toward the forgone product decreases.

From a managerial perspective, the recognition of the effects of dissonance and reactance is important. When consumers have difficulty choosing between brands, the possibility exists that they will also experience severe cases of buyer's regret. Sales personnel should be aware of the effects of reactance and dissonance and take steps to minimize their negative impact. For example, the real estate agent mentioned in Highlight 9-2 helped me to overcome my buyer's regret over the purchase of a house. His approach involved pointing out to me that people frequently have second thoughts after buying a house and patting me on the back for having bought such a beautiful house and getting it for such a good price.

One thing that consumers may do when experiencing dissonance is search for additional information. The information sought may be either positive or negative toward their purchase.[23] One strategy that companies may implement is to try to contact consumers after their purchase. Researchers have investigated the effectiveness of following up purchases with favorable information about the product. In one study, consumer researchers investigated the effects of either sending letters, calling customers, or doing nothing after a purchase of a refrigerator.[24] The letters and phone calls thanked the customers for making the purchase and reassured them that they had made a wise purchase. The results revealed that sending a letter reduced doubt or dissonance in comparison to those who received no information. However,

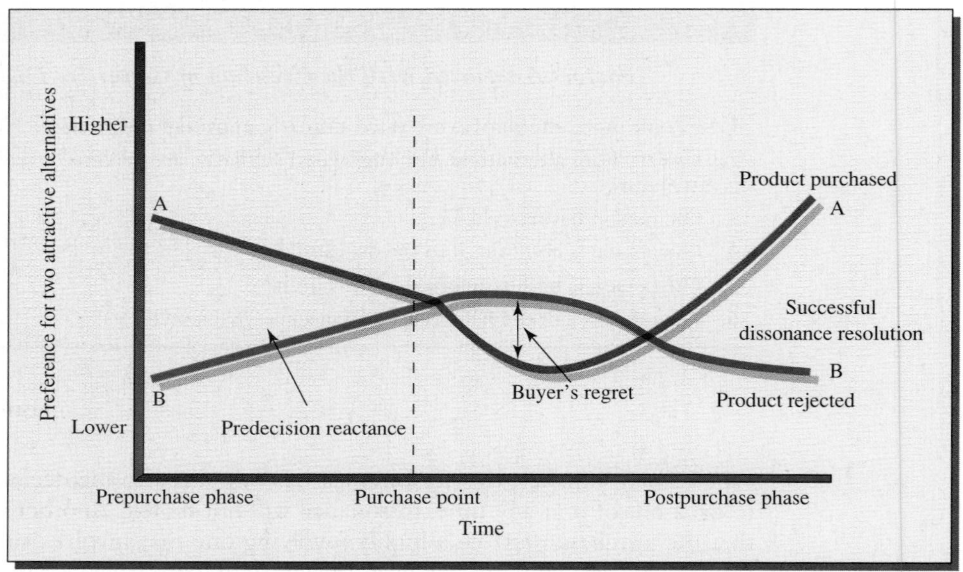

Figure 9-10 The effects of reactance and dissonance before and after purchase. In the example, product A was purchased. Dissonance was reduced satisfactorily such that the buyer preferred product A some time after making the purchase. (In the predecision reactance phase, attitudes toward alternatives A and B tend to converge. In the buyer's regret phase, the effects of reactance are fully felt and the buyer may like the unchosen alternative, option B, more than the chosen alternative, option A. In the dissonance resolution phase, the discomfort of liking the unchosen alternative more than the chosen alternative is reduced through a psychological reevaluation process.)

people who received a phone call actually had higher levels of doubt. The telephone call may have been so unusual that it actually frightened the buyers. These results show that care must be taken in developing strategies to reduce cognitive dissonance. Managers should employ market research to ensure that the strategy is having the desired impact.

Attitude Toward the Advertisement

A third approach to directly influencing attitudes without necessarily changing beliefs involves influencing consumer attitudes toward the advertisement. To persuade consumers to purchase their brands, firms employ various forms of advertising. Researchers have found that consumers develop attitudes toward advertisements, just as they do toward brands.[25] In turn, these attitudes toward ads may influence attitudes toward the brand. An **attitude toward the ad** is a consumer's general liking or disliking for a particular advertising stimulus during a particular advertising exposure.[26] Attitudes toward advertisements can result from a number of factors, including the content and imagery vividness of the ad, the mood of the consumer, and the consumer's emotions elicited by the advertisement. Evidence indicates that these factors can influence attitude toward the brand under both high- and low-involvement conditions, whether or not the consumer is familiar with the brand.[27]

A number of researchers have investigated the relationships between attitude toward the ad, emotions, the degree of ad imagery, attitude toward the brand, and brand cognitions (i.e., product-attribute beliefs). The following statements summarize some of the major findings of the research.[28]

1. The formation of attitudes toward the ad can influence attitudes toward the brand.
2. Emotions elicited by the ad (e.g., positive and negative affect as well as feelings of dominance and arousal) may influence the attitude toward the ad.[29]
3. The content of the advertisement may influence the emotions felt by the consumer.
4. The visual and verbal components of an ad may independently influence the attitude toward the advertisement, the formation of product-attribute beliefs, and time spent viewing the ad.
5. The degree of ad imagery influences feelings and emotions.
6. Attitude toward the ad can influence brand cognitions as well as attitude toward the brand.

A diagram of these relationships is found in Figure 9-11. Although the connections shown in the figure require further research and testing, they are plausible and have empirical support. They show that advertising content can be divided into both verbal and pictorial components. Each component may influence the formation of brand cognitions as well as feelings and emotions. The feelings and emotions that are elicited may influence the attitude toward the ad, which may then influence the attitude toward the brand. Brand cognitions may also influence the attitude toward the brand.

Researchers have also found that ads containing high levels of imagery more strongly impact attitudes toward the ad.[30] The term *imagery* refers to the extent to which an ad causes consumers to imagine their use of the product and to connect the ad to their own feelings and beliefs. Ads that employ concrete words, vivid verbal or pictorial images, instructions for consumers to imagine the use of the brand, and high levels of plausibility have been found to strongly impact consumers' attitudes toward the ad.

Recently, a meta-analysis of the research on attitude toward the ad was conducted in which all the previous work on the construct was analyzed quantitatively.[31] The results revealed that, as expected, ad attitude did directly impact brand attitude. Somewhat surprisingly, the researchers also found that ad attitude impacted brand cognitions. That is, the attitude toward the ad influenced consumers' beliefs about the product's attributes and benefits. This finding has potential managerial importance. Recently, researchers have found evidence that effects of attitudes toward the ad may only temporarily impact brand attitudes.[32] That is, because ad attitudes are composed of feelings and emotions, they may be more temporary. As a result, their persuasive impact may be short-lived. If ad attitudes also impact brand cognitions, however, their effects may have long-term impact.

Another beneficial impact of creating strong positive attitudes toward ads has been found. Positive attitudes toward an ad increase the time spent watching the

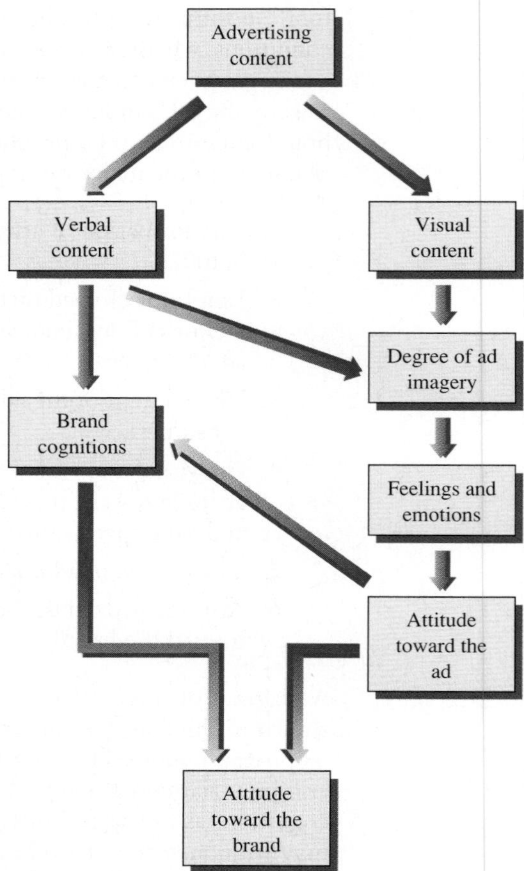

Figure 9-11
Attitude toward the ad and the persuasion process.

commercial. Although we know from our own actions that we spend more time watching some ads than others, the idea of investigating the factors that influence time viewing ads is a recent one. In the realm of television, consumers have two direct means of controlling the time spent watching an ad. First, they can "zap" the ad by switching to a new channel. Second, they can "zip" the ad by fast-forwarding through programs already recorded. In a recent study, 150 ads appearing in prime-time TV shows were recorded.[33] MBA students then were given the opportunity to watch 146 of the ads for 75 minutes. The students were given the ability to zip and zap the ads as they chose. The time they spent watching each ad was then recorded. In addition, the ads were independently rated for their content and emotional appeal. The results revealed that both zipping and zapping were reduced as the pleasure and arousal caused by the ad increased. Similarly, zipping and zapping decreased when its content was considered to be pleasing (i.e., the facts in the ad and its unique qualities were viewed positively). The managerial implication of these findings is that a firm should attempt to create ads that have positive emotional and factual qualities in order to reduce zipping and zapping.

The work on the effects of the attitude toward the ad nicely meshes with the experiential perspective on consumer behavior. This research shows the importance of feelings and emotions in influencing how attitudes toward the brand are changed. Indeed, research indicates that attitude change may be moderated by the emotions and feelings created by advertising as well as by how the advertising influences consumers' product-attribute beliefs.

Of course, the work on the attitudes toward the ad has major importance for advertisers, who must be concerned with both the pictorial and verbal content of advertisements and how these influence the formation of product-attribute beliefs and the creation of feelings and emotions. In fact, a new term has been developed for advertisements that effectively influence the feelings and emotions of consumers; these are called **transformational ads**. Such ads transform the experience of using a product or service by attaching feelings and emotions to its use. Transformational ads are discussed more fully in Chapter 10.

Perhaps the campaign that best represents the positive impact of creating positive attitude toward the ad is the California Raisin promotional efforts. Figure 9-12 presents a storyboard from the campaign. The great music ("Heard It Through the Grapevine") and the concrete imagery of the animated raisins resulted in highly positive feelings among consumers. Most important, it increased the sales of raisins by transforming the experience of eating them.

THE BEHAVIORAL INFLUENCE ROUTE TO BEHAVIOR CHANGE

So far, this chapter has discussed the processes through which beliefs and attitudes are changed. As noted in Chapter 8, through behavioral influence techniques our actions can be affected without necessarily influencing either beliefs or attitudes about the behavior. For example, the ecological design of buildings and spaces can strongly affect the behavior of people without their being aware of the influence. Similarly, strong reinforcers or punishers in the environment can induce people to take actions that they would prefer to avoid. At the extreme, the effects of behavioral influence techniques are illustrated by the armed robber who says, "Give me your money or your life." Most of us would comply with the request, even though we would rather not.

Sticking a gun in someone's ribs gets results because it changes the reward–cost matrix for outcomes. In such cases, the victim complies with a request out of necessity. The cost–benefit ratio for actions, however, can be influenced through much more subtle means than the use of a weapon. Indeed, a field of study exists that investigates the techniques one person can use to cause another to comply with requests. The techniques have been implemented by charities, by honest salespersons, and by everyday people. Unfortunately, the techniques also can be used by unscrupulous individuals to gain their own illicit ends. In the following sections four of these techniques are discussed—the ingratiation technique, the foot-in-the-door technique, the door-in-the-face technique, and the even-a-penny-will-help technique.

"WHAT'D HE HAVE FOR BREAKFAST?" :30

COMM'L NO.: QCCI 2300

RADIO ANNCR: Yep, it's a dull, boring morning.

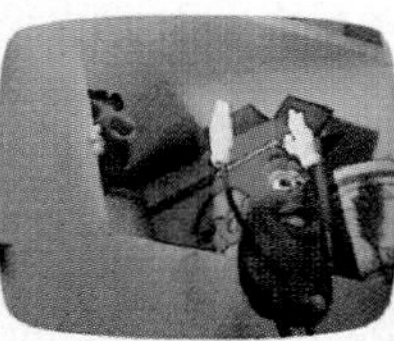

(SFX: SQUEAKY DOOR) Sixty five degrees...

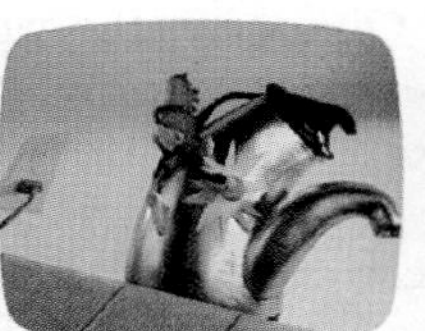

no wind...

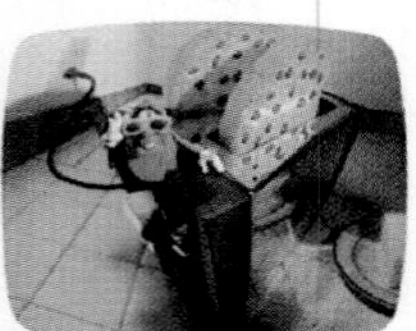

low clouds.

Dull.
(RAISIN CHANGES STATION; MUSIC UP)
SINGERS: YEAH...

I HEARD IT THROUGH THE GRAPEVINE.

SINGERS: WHOO, HOO.

SINGER: RAISED IN THE CALIFORNIA SUNSHINE...

SINGERS: WHOO, HOO.

SINGER: WHOA MY.

SINGERS: DON'T YA KNOW I HEARD IT,

YEAH, I HEARD IT—YEAH 'CAUSE I HEARD IT...

THROUGH THE GRAPE VINE, YEAH!

SINGER: I HEARD...

SINGERS: HEARD, HEARD, HEARD IT.
(MAN WHISTLES)

PAPER BOY: Wow! What'd he have for breakfast?
(MUSIC & SINGERS OUT)

Figure 9-12 The ads for California Raisins successfully transformed the experience of eating the dried fruit by creating strong feelings and emotions. (Courtesy of the California Raisin Advisory Board.)

Ingratiation Tactics

The term **ingratiation** refers to self-serving tactics engaged in by one person to make himself or herself more attractive to another.[34] In this case attractiveness refers to the overall positivity or negativity with which one person views another. An ingratiator builds on the knowledge that as the attractiveness of one person increases, the likelihood of another complying with his or her wishes increases. It is a subtle way of obtaining increased power over another person. Of course, everyone attempts to make herself or himself more attractive to favored others. With ingratiation, however, the efforts are manipulative and calculating. A number of different ingratiation techniques are available for use, but the common denominator among all the tactics is that the ingratiator subtly rewards the target in each case.

- *Appearing to be similar to the target.* One of the strongest findings in the social sciences is that people like others who are similar to them. Thus a skillful ingratiator attempts to assess the target and identify rapidly the person's attitudes, opinions, and interests. The ingratiator then modifies his or her own statements to match the perceived beliefs of the other. If successful, the target perceives the ingratiator to be similar and consequently like him or her more.
- *Conforming to the target's wishes.* One way of building the ego of another is to agree with him and conform to his wishes. In this manner the target is made to feel important by the ingratiator. The conformity subtly rewards the target and consequently builds the importance of the ingratiator to the target.
- *Offering compliments and gifts.* The ingratiator can build power by directly rewarding the target through compliments (e.g., "you solved that problem brilliantly") or through gifts (e.g., picking up a lunch tab). Figure 9-13 illustrates the use of a gift as an ingratiation technique. The ad by DeBeers, the huge diamond company, shows a younger woman responding positively to the gift of a diamond by an older man. Implied in the copy is the thought that if this man wants to keep this "young thing," he had better shower her with expensive gifts.
- *Expressing liking.* People tend to like others who like them. If the ingratiator can persuade the other that he or she is viewed with genuine affection, the target is likely to return the liking.
- *Asking advice.* By asking for advice, the ingratiator makes the other feel as though he or she is respected. This is a more indirect method of telling the other that he or she is liked.

Ingratiation tactics are effective methods of achieving increased power in a short-term relationship, such as a personal-selling situation. Indeed, one of the primary tactics of the skilled salesperson is to create a "close relationship" with the client. A major problem can occur, however, if the ingratiator is caught in the attempt to manipulate the target. If the target recognizes that he or she is being deliberately manipulated, the influence attempt is likely to boomerang, resulting in a loss rather than a gain of power. An ingratiator's dilemma, therefore, exists. The ingratiator cannot be too obvious in his or her attempts to reward the target. On the other hand, for the approach to be successful, the target must be rewarded in some way.[35]

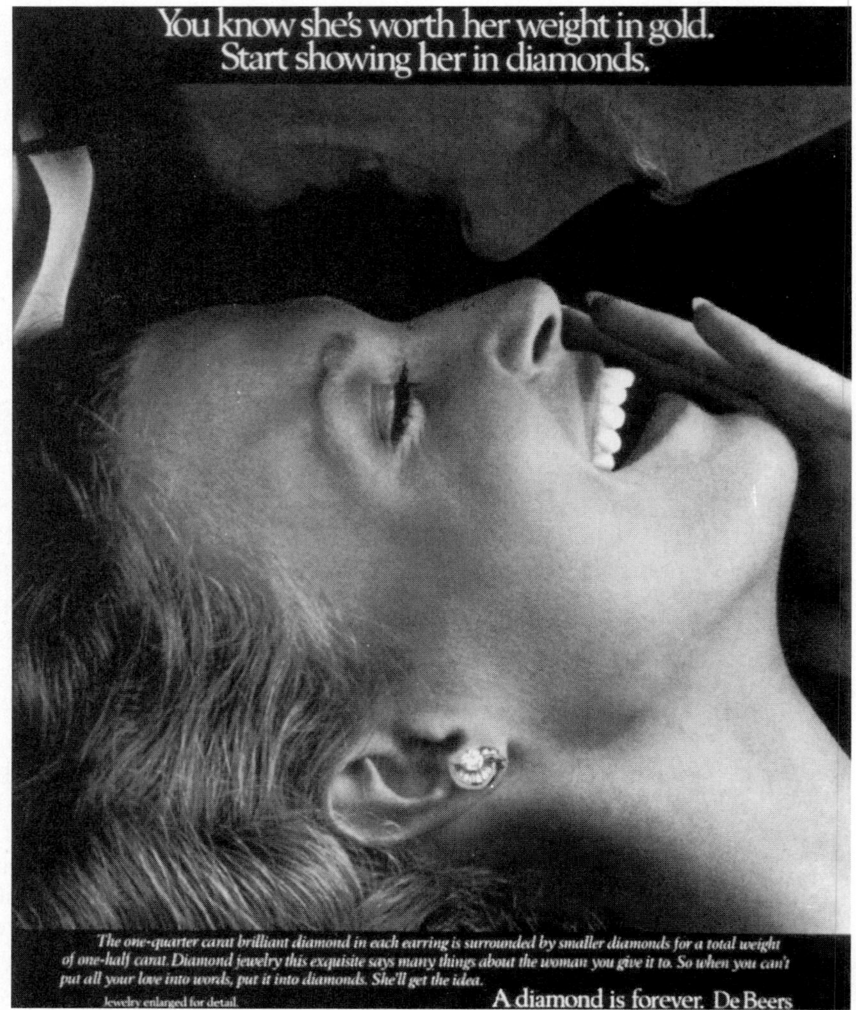

Figure 9-13 An ingratiation technique operates in this ad promoting the giving of diamonds as gifts. (Courtesy of DeBeers Consolidated Mines, Inc., and N. W. Ayer, Inc.)

The likelihood of the ingratiator being caught is quite high in a sales situation. A natural power difference exists between the prospect and the salesperson. The prospect knows that the salesperson wants to make a sale and is wary of his or her influence attempts. Thus the salesperson must come across as sincere and nonmanipulative.

The Foot-in-the-Door Technique

An old saying exists that if a successful salesman can merely get his foot in the door, he can make the sale. The foot-in-the-door technique shows that the adage has scientific support. A requester can increase the likelihood that a prospect will say yes to a moderate request if the person can be persuaded first to say yes to a smaller request. Thus, by getting a prospect to let him in the door, the skilled salesman has persuaded him or her to capitulate to a small request. The task of selling the person the product then becomes that much easier.

The **foot-in-the-door technique** operates through a self-perception mechanism—that is, by complying to the first, small request, the prospect forms an impression that he or she is the type of person who does such a thing. Later, when the second request is made, the person is more likely to agree to the request out of the need to be consistent with that self-perception.[36] The foot-in-the-door technique has been shown to influence people in a wide variety of settings. For example, in comparison to control groups, those who were first asked to do something very small more frequently agreed to a larger request when asked; examples included giving blood, counting traffic for a fictitious safety committee, and completing market research surveys. Similarly, one study found that people who were first contacted over the phone and asked a few short questions were later more likely to complete a long written questionnaire than were people who had not been contacted first on the phone.[37]

The foot-in-the-door technique can be applied to a number of areas in marketing. Thus far it has most frequently been used as an approach to increase the response rate to market research surveys. A more important area of use, however, is likely to be personal selling. The task of selling a product consists of a series of steps. For example, if a stockbroker can persuade a potential client to visit her office, the task of selling that person stock should be substantially easier, because the buying of the stock is consistent with the previous behavior of going to visit the broker.

The Door-in-the-Face Technique

In the foot-in-the-door technique a small initial request is followed by a larger request. The **door-in-the-face technique** again involves making an initial request. However, instead of being very small, the request is extremely large. In fact, it is so large that no one would be expected to comply to it. Again, in comparison to control groups that do not receive an initial request, the two-step approach results in a greater degree of compliance to the second request. Areas for which the door-in-the-face technique have been found to increase the rate of compliance include asking people to complete marketing surveys, to take juvenile delinquents to the zoo, and to count automobiles for a traffic-safety committee.

The self-perception mechanism that accounts for the effectiveness of the foot-in-the-door technique would suggest that the door-in-the-face technique should be ineffective in increasing compliance rates. After all, if a person first says no to a request, he or she should also say no to a second request. A completely different factor accounts for the success of the door-in-the-face strategy—the norm of reciprocity.[38] The **norm of reciprocity** states that if a person does something for you, you should do something in return for that person. The norm helps to grease the wheels of society by ensuring that efforts to help someone else will not go unrewarded. When the door-in-the-face strategy is implemented, the norm is illicitly invoked—that is, the requester makes the large request and never expects the person to comply with it. He or she then makes the smaller, more moderate request. The requester attempts to make it appear that he or she has given up something when the smaller request is made. The target then feels as though he or she must return the favor. The only possible way of reciprocating the imaginary gift is to say yes to the second request.

The door-in-the-face technique has more limited applications than does the foot-in-the-door strategy. Because it is based on the operation of the norm of reciprocity, the second request must be a smaller portion of the first request. Thus, if the large request is to complete a long survey, the second request should involve completing a shorter version of the survey. A second limitation of the door-in-the-face approach is that the same person must make both requests. The target must be made to feel that the requester is actually giving up something in the second request. If a different requester makes the request, nothing is perceived to be given up. A final difference is that the second request must immediately follow the first in the door-in-the-face procedure. The two requests can be made even a week or two apart with the foot-in-the-door approach. However, to create the impression that a concession is being made, the two requests must be made close in time (certainly within an hour or so) when the door-in-the-face strategy is implemented.

The Even-a-Penny-Will-Help Technique

The foot-in-the-door and the door-in-the-face techniques are based upon the norms of a consistent self-perception and of reciprocity, respectively. The **even-a-penny-will-help** technique is based upon the universal tendency for people to want to make themselves "look good." Most often used in charity contexts, the approach operates by asking the target to give money and by tacking on the phrase "even a penny will help" at the end of the request. Because everyone has a penny, the person would look foolish in saying no to the request. Thus the person must say yes. The problem is that the target cannot simply give a penny, because he or she would look completely foolish. Thus the person tends to give whatever is normatively appropriate for the situation and the charity.

Research investigating the technique has found that the total amount given to charities increases when the technique is used. Although individuals give slightly less money, on average, in comparison to those who did not receive the request, the larger number of people giving something more than compensates for the slightly smaller individual contributions.[39] It is important to recognize that the compliance tactic can be implemented in many ways in addition to merely saying "even a penny will help." A market researcher could ask the respondent to complete a survey and add the phrase "even answering a question or two would help." A salesperson making a "cold call" could state "even two minutes of your time would be appreciated." The adaptations of the technique are limitless.[40]

Managerial and Ethical Implications of the Techniques of Personal Influence

The four techniques of personal influence identified in this section are directly relevant to the personal-selling strategy of a firm. Meanwhile, it is the function of marketing research to evaluate the successfulness of their use. An important note should be added concerning the ethics of using the techniques of personal influence. Each of the four techniques has a Machiavellian element. In each case the influencer attempts to manipulate another individual by engaging in a subtle subterfuge. In the case of the door-in-the-face technique, for example, the influencer lies to the respondent, because the first request is a sham. This tactic is then in conflict with the critical principle that marketers and researchers should never lie to consumers. Fortunately, the ability to abuse the compliance techniques is self-limiting—that is, if overused, the employment of the tactics will be discovered by consumers and high levels of dissatisfaction will result.

A MANAGERIAL APPLICATIONS EXAMPLE

An example of a problem involving attitude change issues was faced by Procter & Gamble in the late 1980s concerning its brands in the $3.2 billion disposable diaper market. In 1975 P&G dominated the market for disposable diapers with a 75% market share. By 1987, however, market share was down to 54%. Kimberly-Clark was largely responsible for the decline. The company introduced Huggies in 1977, and by 1987 its market share had climbed to 34%. Due to its decreasing market share, P&G initiated a $500 million overhaul of its diaper operations in 1985.

Management shake-ups occurred, and additional technology was "thrown at" the product. Despite the shake-up, market share continued to decline. As one analyst stated, "consumers don't seem to appreciate subtle differences in diapers, such as five strands of elastic on a legband as opposed to three."[41] In 1987, however, P&G began testing a new product strategy. The company came out with Luvs Deluxe brand of disposable diapers. The premium-priced diapers incorporated many of the features of the previous deluxe line, including tearproof design, refastenable taping systems, fit guides, and optional Muppet Babies design. However, the attribute that really set the brand apart was the introduction of different diapers for boy and girl babies. In addition to having different colors on the box (i.e., pink for girls and blue for boys), changes were made in the placement of the superabsorbent material in the diapers themselves to account for the different patterns of urination exhibited by boy and girl babies. Advertisements said, "Boys and girls won't change, so we did." A P&G spokesperson explained, "Offering distinct colors helped parents pick out the boy and girl product. It adds a touch of fun."

Some analysts were unimpressed by the product innovation. Many considered the move to be a marketing gimmick and didn't anticipate that it would turn the company's market share problems around. However, in test markets in the Midwest the new diapers sold well, and in late 1988 the company began the rollout, supported by a $15 million national multimedia campaign.

The Consumer Behavior Analysis

The P&G example illustrates a number of applications of attitude change concepts to managerial strategy areas. The product innovation of creating different diapers for boys and girls can be analyzed from the perspective of the elaboration likelihood model. To the extent that consumers engage in extensive cognitive elaboration, they are likely to focus on their beliefs about the attributes of the products. In such an instance it would be crucial to develop excellent arguments concerning the benefits of the product.

If the choice of a diaper is a high-involvement decision for consumers who are willing to pay extra for a diaper, multiattribute models and particularly the attitude-toward-the-object model are applicable to the problem. Procter & Gamble attempted to influence attitudes by adding an attribute in the form of the different patterns of the placement of the absorbent material in the boy and girl diapers. Thus the strategy represents a case in which a new product was created to provide the benefit of a less leaky diaper. The attitude-toward-the-object model forces the researcher and manager to ask two questions: (1) To what extent do consumers positively evaluate the attribute? (2) To what extent do consumers believe that the diapers actually provide the benefits claimed?

An important element in the attitude-toward-the-object model concerns the salience of the attribute. If the attribute is not salient, it is not perceived as important and has little chance of influencing an attitude. Thus one role of advertising is to make the attribute vivid and salient to consumers. Focusing on the concept that boys and girls are different helps to achieve such salience. Even more important, however, was the decision to use different colors for the boxes. In addition to helping consumers to select the right box, this strategy also helps consumers to differentiate the product from competitors' offerings. Thus the focus on attributes could also have an impact on the approach used by management to differentiate the product from competitors.

Balance theory could also have implications for managerial action in this example. Balance theory suggests that attitudes may be influenced by the stimuli with which the new brand is associated. Thus, when developing promotional strategy, managers should consider identifying positive individuals or scenes and establishing a unit relation between the stimulus and the brand. For example, one strategy might involve using a well-known female celebrity endorser who recently had a new baby. The positive feelings associated with the celebrity could be attached to the brand because of the unit relation established between the product (diapers) and the endorser (celebrity with infant).

Of course, the work on attitudes toward the ad also has relevance to the problem. This work suggests that market research should be conducted on newly developed ads to ensure that the target market perceives them positively. After analyzing the problem and applying attitude change concepts to the marketing strategy, P&G could likely develop a profitable brand. The salience of the attribute and the importance of gender typing children for many parents makes it likely that the attribute would have an impact on attitudes and behavior. However, the key issue is whether the product lives up to the claims made. If consumers find that it does not provide the benefit claimed (i.e., less leakage), they are unlikely to repurchase it. Indeed, if such an outcome occurred, consumer attitudes would likely become negative, because the belief that the brand possesses the attribute would be extremely low.

The Managerial Applications Analysis

Table 9-5 presents the managerial applications analysis for the diaper case. Four consumer behavior concepts have particular relevance to the case—the elaboration likelihood model, the attitude-toward-the-object model, balance theory, and attitudes toward the ad.

The elaboration likelihood model suggests that managers should be highly concerned with the involvement level of the target market. Deciding which brand of diapers to purchase may well be a high-involvement process. (At least it was in this author's household.) Market research should be conducted to verify the involvement level of customers. In addition, the ELM suggests that managers should be highly concerned about the messages communicated to consumers through advertising and packaging. If they were in a high-involvement state, customers would scrutinize the messages and develop counterarguments to them. Care must be taken in the development of promotional strategy to ensure that communications are believable.

The attitude-toward-the-object model suggests that managers should conduct market research to examine the extent to which the target market positively evaluates

TABLE 9-5

Managerial Applications Analysis for P&G Diaper Case

Consumer Concepts	*Managerial Implications*
Elaboration likelihood model	*Market research*—Employ to identify the involvement level of the target market.
	Promotional strategy—Carefully analyze messages and packaging to ensure that they mesh with the processing requirements of low- versus high-involvement consumers.
Attitude-toward-the-object model	*Market research*—Employ to identify the beliefs and evaluations of the target market on the attributes of the brand.
	Segmentation—Identify market segments based upon the benefits sought in diapers.
	Positioning—Position brand based upon the key attributes of the product chosen for emphasis.
	Environmental analysis—Evaluate competitors' brand based on the attitude toward the object and compare to your brand.
	Marketing mix—Based upon identification of consumer beliefs and benefits sought, make appropriate product modifications.
Balance theory	*Promotional strategy*—Consider identifying highly positive endorsers or other entities (perhaps cartoon characters) to which the brand can be connected.
	Market research—Employ to identify the object to which the brand is connected.
Attitude toward the ad	*Promotional strategy*—Attempt to create ads to which consumers have positive affective reactions.
	Market research—Employ market research to assess the affective reactions of consumers to ads.

the attribute of superabsorbant material in different locations for boys and girls. Another central issue suggested by the attitude-toward-the object model concerns whether consumers believe the claims made about the diapers. That is, do the diapers really provide different protection for boys and girls? Clearly, the strategy of having different attributes in diapers for boys and girls influences the marketing mix (i.e., the product and the promotional strategy). In addition, the different attributes of the diapers act as a tool for segmenting the market based upon whether the user is a girl or boy baby. The basic approach of creating different diapers for boys and girls assumes that two distinct market segments exist. One can assume that P&G conducted market research to determine if parents of girls and boys evaluated positively the new attribute. To the extent that each group felt a need for something different in the diaper for their baby, based upon its sex, an opportunity exists for segmentation. One interesting question concerns whether parents of boys or girls are more likely to purchase the product.

Ideas from the attitude-toward-the-object model also have relevance to environmental analysis. In this case it is extremely important for P&G to conduct market research to identify consumers' beliefs, attitudes, and intentions regarding the new brand in relation to competitors' offerings. Such attitude studies should be conducted on an ongoing basis. The initial impressions of consumers may change after they have had experience with the brand.

Similarly, the consumer concept of balance theory applies to market research and the marketing mix. Balance theory ideas suggest that P&G should consider how to connect the brand to highly positive endorsers or scenes to influence attitudes. Market research should be conducted to identify potential endorsers or domestic situations to which consumers react positively. Through advertising, the endorsers or scenes can be successfully connected to the brand.

Likewise, the work on attitude toward the ad suggests that managers should use market research to assess consumer reactions to the advertisements developed to influence consumers. A goal should be to develop ads that create strong positive feelings in consumers because this affect is likely to be transferred to the brand.

SUMMARY

This chapter discussed belief, attitude, and behavior change as taking any one of three different paths—the decision-making path, the experiential path, and the behavioral influence path. The study of belief, attitude, and behavior change is closely related to the study of persuasion, which is the explicit attempt to influence beliefs and attitudes. In the decision-making path, beliefs are influenced first. The elaboration likelihood model explains the persuasion process from within the decision-making perspective. The ELM suggests that the mode through which persuasion occurs changes depending upon whether the consumer is in a high- or low-involvement state. In high-involvement conditions the consumer is said to move through the central route to persuasion, focusing on the nature of the arguments presented in a message. In low-involvement conditions, on the other hand, the consumer is said to move through the peripheral route to persuasion, focusing on a different set of cues—such as the attractiveness of the source of information or the context within which the information is presented.

From the perspective of the elaboration likelihood model, in high-involvement conditions the multiattribute models would be predictive of attitude change. The attitude-toward-the-object model suggests that three means exist to change attitudes: (1) change the belief that the object possesses an attribute, (2) change the evaluation of the positivity of an attribute, or (3) add a new attribute. The application of the behavioral intentions model brings up several additional points concerning how to change the intentions of consumers. First, intentions can be influenced by the person's perception of the desires of important reference individuals. Thus, to influence an intention, beliefs about the preferences of important reference individuals need to be changed. Another approach would involve influencing the person's motivation to comply with the referent. The behavioral intentions model also suggests that influencers may want to influence the person's attitude toward the behavior of engaging in some action. This approach requires either changing the belief about what consequences occur as a result of a behavior or changing the evaluation of those consequences.

The experiential approach suggests that attitudes can be changed directly without beliefs first being influenced. From a balance theory perspective, attitudes can be changed directly by creating cognitive imbalance. Cognitive imbalance is present if multiplying the signs of the cognitive elements results in a negative value. Because consumers have a need to maintain cognitive consistency, they tend to change one of the signs (usually the weakest in intensity) to create balance. According to balance theory, two types of connections exist between the cognitive elements. Sentiment connections resemble attitudes and involve the person's feeling about an object. Unit relations are established when the person perceives that two objects are connected to each other. Balance theory principles are readily applied to understanding the impact of product endorsers.

The processes of reactance and dissonance also influence attitudes. Reactance may cause consumers to view a product that was just purchased somewhat negatively. In some instances this may be combined with an elevation of feelings toward an unchosen alternative. These feelings result from the fact that, by making a choice, the consumer's behavioral freedom to choose is restricted. These feelings resulting from reactance can then lead to cognitive dissonance. The dissonance occurs when the consumer perceives that he or she has chosen an inferior alternative. The result is psychological discomfort. To assist consumers in reevaluating the chosen alternative in a more favorable direction, some companies have begun to communicate with consumers after the purchase to positively reinforce them for their choice.

Social judgment theory is the third theory that applies to the experiential approach to attitude change. It uses principles from psychophysics to explain how attitudes may be influenced. It assumes that attitudes may be placed on a scale anchored by highly positive or negative feelings. Around an attitude exists a latitude of acceptance. If information falls within the latitude of acceptance, it tends to be accepted. In such instances an assimilation effect is said to occur, and the original attitude is moved toward the position of the new information on the scale. Outside of the latitude of acceptance, however, exists a latitude of rejection. If a message is perceived to fall into the latitude of rejection, it is likely to be rejected. In such instances a boomerang effect may occur, such that the attitude actually moves in the opposite direction. Commitment to a position tends to make the attitude more extreme on the scale and the latitude of acceptance smaller. The net effect of commitment is that consumer attitudes are made more difficult to change. To cause attitude change, messages should be perceived by the consumer as falling just within the latitude of acceptance.

The final approach to the experiential path to attitude change is found in the work on attitudes toward the advertisement. Researchers have found that consumers may form feelings about the advertisements that they watch. These attitudes toward the ad are held independently of beliefs about the attributes possessed by the product. Thus the attitude toward the ad may influence the attitude toward the brand, regardless of beliefs about the product's attributes. The research in this area indicates that managers should be extremely careful in testing consumer attitudes toward the ads created.

KEY TERMS

assimilation effect
attitude toward the ad
balance theory
boomerang effect
central route to persuasion
cognitive consistency
cognitive dissonance
contrast effects
door-in-the-face technique
elaboration likelihood model (ELM)
even-a-penny-will-help technique
foot-in-the-door technique
ingratiation
latitude of acceptance
latitude of rejection
need for cognition
norm of reciprocity
peripheral route to persuasion
persuasion
reactance theory
sentiment connections
social judgment theory
transformational ads
unit relation

REVIEW QUESTIONS

1. According to the elaboration likelihood model, what are the two routes to persuasion? What factors cause a consumer to move through one route rather than another?
2. Through which of the routes of persuasion does attitude change tend to be more long-lasting? Why?
3. According to the attitude-toward-the-object model, what are the three ways in which attitudes may be changed?
4. According to the behavioral intentions model, what are the means through which intentions may be changed?
5. What are the sentiment connections and unit relations of balance theory?
6. What are the three ways of forming a unit relation between an endorser and a product?
7. What is meant by the terms *latitude of acceptance* and *latitude of rejection?*
8. What factors influence the width of the latitude of rejection?
9. From a social judgment perspective, how should one go about attempting to change an attitude?
10. How does reactance influence consumer attitudes?
11. What causes postpurchase dissonance to occur?
12. What are the means through which consumers can resolve dissonance?
13. What is a boomerang effect?
14. What factors may influence the formation of an attitude toward an ad?
15. How may the attitude toward the ad influence attitudes toward the brand?
16. What is meant by ingratiation? What are the means of ingratiation?

17. How does the foot-in-the-door compliance technique work?
18. How does the door-in-the-face compliance technique work?
19. How does the even-a-penny-will-help technique work?

DISCUSSION QUESTIONS

1. Consider the advertising for the following companies: Pepsi-Cola, Volvo, McDonald's, and IBM. Which of the ad campaigns would you consider to involve central routes to persuasion and which involve peripheral routes to persuasion? Why?
2. Over the past 15 years American auto manufacturers have faced the problem that consumers perceive their autos to be of poorer quality than Japanese autos. Assuming that U.S. manufacturers have overcome the quality problems, how might they persuade consumers of this fact?
   a. Sketch out an advertising campaign for the Ford Mustang to change consumers' perceptions of its quality using the attitude-toward-the-object model.
   b. Sketch out the campaign for the Mustang using balance theory principles.
   c. What are the implications of social judgment theory for the two advertising campaigns?
3. Multiattribute models have a great deal to say about changing attitudes. Develop three concrete ideas for using multiattribute models to persuade teenagers not to smoke.
4. Identify two advertisements that you have a positive attitude toward and two ads that you have a negative attitude toward. Do your attitudes toward the ads influence your perception of the products? Discuss the ads and their impact in relation to the model presented in Figure 9-11.
5. Some analysts have argued that Wendy's restaurants are having problems in the marketplace because of a lack of cleanliness. Discuss what your recommendations to management would be for changing consumer attitudes about Wendy's. In doing so, make sure you refer to the consumer concepts discussed in the chapter.
6. Think back upon one or two major decisions you have made in the past, such as buying a car or selecting which college or university to attend. Did you experience reactance prior to and immediately after the decision? How much dissonance did you feel after making the decision? How was the dissonance resolved? Please explain your answers.
7. According to reactance theory, the preference between two closely evaluated alternatives tends to converge as the time to make a decision nears. From a personal-selling perspective, what are some actions that a salesperson might take to keep this convergence of preferences from occurring?
8. Ingratiation is a device frequently used to influence others. Describe the various ingratiation tactics an automobile salesperson could use and their possible impact on customers.
9. You are working in the marketing department for a firm that does market surveys. Your boss tells you that she wants to use the foot-in-the-door technique to increase the response rate to telephone interviewers. She asks you to develop the specific wording for telephone surveyors to use, which would incorporate the foot-in-the-door technique. The research in question involves a ten-minute survey on the use of dishwashing detergent. Write out the specific words that the interviewers should use.
10. Complete the exercise in question 9, but write the words that would be used to implement the door-in-the-face technique.

ENDNOTES

1. The introductory vignette was based on an article by Cecelia Reed, "Partners for Life," *Advertising Age*, November 9, 1988, pp. 122, 126.
2. Richard Petty, John Cacioppo, and David Schumann, "Central and Peripheral Routes to Advertising Effectiveness: The Moderating Role of Involvement," *Journal of Consumer Research*, Vol. 10 (September 1983), pp. 135–146. For a recent article that investigates the relationship between motivation and the route to persuasion, see Scott B. Mackenzie and Richard A. Spreng, "How Does Motivation Moderate the Impact of Central and Peripheral Processing on Brand Attitudes and Intentions?" *Journal of Consumer Research*, Vol. 19 (March 1992), pp. 519–529.
3. Petty et al., "Central and Peripheral Routes to Advertising Effectiveness."
4. Richard Petty and John Cacioppo, "The Elaboration Likelihood Model of Persuasion," in *Advances in Experiential Social Psychology*, Vol. 19, Leonard Berkowitz, ed. (New York: Academic Press, 1986), pp. 123–205.
5. Robert B. Cialdini, Richard Petty, and John Cacioppo, "Attitude and Attitude Change," *Annual Review of Psychology*, Vol. 32 (1981), pp. 357–404.
6. John Cacioppo, Stephen Harkins, and Richard Petty, "The Nature of Attitudes and Cognitive Responses and Their Relations to Behavior," in *Cognitive Responses in Persuasion*, Richard Petty, Thomas Ostrom, and Timothy C. Brock, eds. (Hillsdale, NJ: Lawrence Erlbaum, 1981), pp. 31–54. Also, see Richard Petty, John Cacioppo, and D. Schumann, "Central and Peripheral Routes to Advertising Effectiveness." A number of studies have found evidence supportive of predictions made by the elaboration likelihood model. The work on the elaboration likelihood model is still relatively new, however, and several authors have noted that it has weaknesses. See Charles Areni and Richard Lutz, "The Role of Argument Quality in the Elaboration Likelihood Model," in *Advances in Consumer Research*, Vol. XV, Michael Houston, ed. (Provo, UT: Association for Consumer Research, 1988), pp. 197–203. Also, see Paul Miniard, Peter Dickson, and Kenneth Lord, "Some Central and Peripheral Thoughts on the Routes to Persuasion," in *Advances in Consumer Research*, Vol. 15, Michael Houston, ed. (Provo, UT: Association for Consumer Research, 1988), pp. 204–208. Another recent article is Paul W. Miniard, Deepak Sirdeshmukh, and Daniel E. Innis, "Peripheral Persuasion and Brand Choice," *Journal of Consumer Research*, Vol. 19 (September 1992), pp. 226–239.
7. Curtis P. Haugtvedt, Richard E. Petty, and John T. Cacioppo, "Need for Cognition and Advertising: Understanding the Role of Personality Variables in Consumer Research," *Journal of Consumer Psychology*, Vol. 1, no. 3 (1992), pp. 239–260.
8. Curt Haugtvedt, Richard Petty, John Cacioppo, and Theresa Steidley, "Personality and Ad Effectiveness: Exploring the Utility of Need for Cognition," in *Advances in Consumer Research*, Vol. 15, Michael Houston, ed. (Provo, UT: Association for Consumer Research, 1988), pp. 209–212.
9. S. Ratneshwar and Shelly Chaiken, "Comprehension's Role in Persuasion: The Case of Its Moderating Effect on the Persuasive Impact of Source Cues," *Journal of Consumer Research*, Vol. 18 (June 1991), pp. 52–62. It should be noted that the authors of the study interpreted their results from the perspective of another theoretical model called the heuristic–systematic model. Although their model does make predictions that diverge from the elaboration likelihood model, the results of their study can be interpreted from within that perspective as well.
10. William O. Bearden and Randall L. Rose, "Attention to Social Comparison Information: An Individual Difference Factor Affecting Consumer Conformity," *Journal of Consumer Research*, Vol. 16 (March 1990), pp. 461–471.
11. Fritz Heider, *The Psychology of Interpersonal Relations* (New York: John Wiley, 1958).
12. M. J. Rosenberg, "An Analysis of Affective-Cognitive Consistency," in *Attitude Organization and Change*, M. J. Rosenberg, C.

I. Hovland, W. J. McGuire, R. P. Abelson, and J. W. Brehm, eds. (New Haven, CT: Yale University Press, 1960), pp. 15–64.

13. Marvin Shaw and Philip Costanzo, *Theories of Social Psychology* (New York: McGraw-Hill, 1970).

14. For example, see M. Sherif and C. Hovland, "Judgmental Phenomena and Scales of Attitude Measurement," *Journal of Abnormal Psychology*, Vol. 48 (1953), pp. 135–141; and M. Sherif and C. Hovland, *Social Judgment: Assimilation and Contrast Effects in Communication and Attitude Change* (New Haven, CT: Yale University Press, 1961).

15. See, for instance, C. W. Sherif, M. Sherif, and R. Nebergall, *Attitude and Attitude Change: The Social Judgment-Involvement Approach* (Philadelphia: W. B. Saunders, 1956). For recent research on assimilation and contrast effects, see Norbert Schwarz and Herbert Bless, "Assimilation and Contrast Effects in Attitude Measurement: An Inclusion/Exclusion Model," in *Advances in Consumer Research*, Vol. 19, John Sherry, Jr., and Brian Sternthal, eds. (Provo, UT: Association for Consumer Research, 1992), pp. 72–77.

16. D. Linder and K. Crane, "A Reactance Theory Analysis of Predecisional Cognitive Processes," *Journal of Personality and Social Psychology*, Vol. 15 (1970), pp. 258–264.

17. E. Walster, "The Temporal Sequence of Post-Decisional Processes," in *Conflict, Choice, and Dissonance*, L. Festinger, ed. (Stanford, CA: Stanford University Press, 1964), pp. 112–127.

18. L. Festinger, *A Theory of Cognitive Dissonance* (Stanford, CA: Stanford University Press, 1957), p. 13.

19. E. Aronson, "Dissonance Theory: Progress and Problems," in *Theories of Cognitive Consistency: A Source Book*, R. Abelson, E. Aronson, W. McGuire, M. Rosenburg, and P. Tannenbaum, eds. (Chicago: Rand McNally, 1968), pp. 5–27.

20. L. LoSciuto and R. Perloff, "Influence of Product Performance on Dissonance Reduction," *Journal of Marketing Research*, Vol. 6 (August 1967), pp. 186–190.

21. For an excellent discussion on the factors required to experience dissonance, see C. A. Insko and J. Scholpler, *Experimental Social Psychology* (New York: Academic Press, 1972).

22. David Mazursky, Priscilla LaParbera, and Al Aiello, "When Consumers Switch Brands," *Psychology and Marketing*, Vol. 4 (Spring 1987), pp. 17–30.

23. R. Lowe and I. Steiner, "Some Effects of the Reversibility and Consequences of Decisions on Post Decision Information Preferences," *Journal of Personality and Social Psychology*, Vol. 8 (April 1968), pp. 172–179.

24. S. Hunt, "Post-Transactional Communication and Dissonance Reduction," *Journal of Marketing*, Vol. 34 (January 1970), pp. 46–51.

25. Andrew A. Mitchell and Jerry Olson, "Are Product Attribute Beliefs the Only Mediator of Advertising Effects of Brand Attitude?" *Journal of Marketing Research*, Vol. 18 (1981), pp. 318–332.

26. Richard Lutz, "Affective and Cognitive Antecedents of Attitude Toward the Ad: A Conceptual Framework," in *Psychological Processes and Advertising Effects: Theory, Research and Application*, L. F. Alwitt and A. A. Mitchell, eds. (Hillsdale, NJ: Lawrence Erlbaum, 1985), pp. 45–63.

27. Joseph Phelps and Esther Thorson, "Brand Familiarity and Product Involvement Effects on the Attitude Toward an Ad-Brand Attitude Relationship," in *Advances in Consumer Research*, Vol. 18, Rebecca H. Holman and Michael R. Solomon, eds. (Provo, UT: Association for Consumer Research, 1991), pp. 202–209.

28. These conclusions are based upon research by the following authors: Morris Holbrook and Rajeev Batra, "Assessing the Role of Emotions as Mediators of Consumer Responses to Advertising," *Journal of Consumer Research*, Vol. 14 (December 1987), pp. 404–420; Julie Edell and Marian Burke, "The Power of Feelings in Understanding Advertising Effects," *Journal of Consumer Research*, Vol. 14 (December 1987), pp. 421–433; and Mitchell and Olson, "Are Product Attribute Beliefs the Only Mediator of Advertising Effects of Brand Attitude?"

29. James Boles and Scot Burton, "An Examination of Free Elicitation and Response Scale Measures of Feelings and Judgments Evoked by Television Advertisements," *Journal of Academy of Marketing Science*, Vol. 20 (Summer 1992), pp. 225–233.

30. Paula Fitzgerald Bone and Pam Scholder Ellen, "The Generation and Consequences of Communication-Evoked Imagery," *Journal of Consumer Research*, Vol. 19 (June 1992), pp. 93–104. For more information on the effects of pictures on information processing and brand preferences, see Carolyn L. Costley and Merrie Brucks, "Selective Recall and Information use in Consumer Preferences," *Journal of Consumer Research*, Vol. 18 (March 1992), 464–474.

31. Steven P. Brown and Douglas M. Stayman, "Antecedents and Consequences of Attitude Toward the Ad: A Meta-analysis," *Journal of Consumer Research*, Vol. 19 (June 1992), pp. 34–51.

32. Amitava Chattopadhyay and Prakash Nedundadi, "Does Attitude Toward the Ad Endure? The Moderating Effects of Attention and Delay," *Journal of Consumer Research*, Vol. 19 (June 1992) pp. 26–33.

33. Thomas J. Olney, Morris B. Holbrook, and Rajeev Batra, "Consumer Responses to Advertising; The Effects of Ad Content, Emotions, and Attitude Toward the Ad on Viewing Time," *Journal of Consumer Research*, Vol. 17 (March 1991), pp. 440–453.

34. Edward E. Jones, *Ingratiation: A Social Psychological Analysis* (New York: Appleton-Century-Crofts, 1964).

35. Edward E. Jones and Harold B. Gerard, *Foundations of Social Psychology* (New York: John Wiley, 1967).

36. Peter H. Reingen and J. B. Kernan, "Compliance with an Interview Request: A Foot-in-the-Door, Self-Perception Interpretation," *Journal of Marketing Research*, Vol. 14 (August 1977), pp. 365–369.

37. Robert A. Hansen and Larry M. Robinson, "Testing the Effectiveness of Alternative Foot-in-the-Door Manipulations," *Journal of Marketing Research*, Vol. 17 (August 1980), pp. 359–364.

38. John C. Mowen and Robert Cialdini, "On Implementing the Door-in-the-Face Compliance Strategy in a Marketing Context," *Journal of Marketing Research*, Vol. 17 (May 1980), pp. 253–258.

39. Robert Cialdini and David Schroeder, "Increasing Compliance by Legitimizing Paltry Contributions: When Even a Penny Helps," *Journal of Personality and Social Psychology*, Vol. 34 (October 1976), pp. 599–604.

40. For a single theoretical explanation of the four compliance techniques based on the availability–valence hypothesis, see Alice Tybout, Brian Sternthal, and Bobby Calder, "Information Availability as a Determinant of Multiple Request Effectiveness," *Journal of Marketing Research*, Vol. 20 (August 1983), pp. 279–290. Also, see Edward Fern, Kent Monroe, and Ramon Avila, "Effectiveness of Multiple Request Strategies: A Synthesis of Research Results," *Journal of Marketing Research*, Vol. 23 (May 1986), pp. 144–152.

41. The Procter & Gamble disposable diaper example is based upon an article by Laurie Freeman, "P&G Rolls Diapers Aimed at Boys, Girls," *Advertising Age*, July 25, 1988, p. 6.

The NBA's Great Turnaround

In 1981 the National Basketball Association (NBA) was in trouble. During the 1980–81 season, 16 of the league's 23 teams lost money. Attendance was declining. That season CBS television refused to show live the sixth game of the NBA Championship series. Advertisers had begun to shun the league. To sell advertising to firms, representatives had to first persuade them that the players weren't all on drugs. The nadir was reached in 1982 when the *Los Angeles Times* reported that 75% of the league's players were on drugs.

By 1992, however, a metamorphosis had occurred. The NBA was the hottest sports enterprise going. Beginning in the 1983–84 season, the league broke attendance records for seven straight years. Stadiums were filled to 89% capacity. The average value of an NBA franchise tripled. Several teams, such as the Chicago Bulls, the New York Knicks, and the LA Lakers, were worth over $100 million. While the television ratings of every other sport fell, the NBA's increased by 21%. From 1983 to 1991, revenues increased from $44 million to over $1 billion.

What caused the dramatic change in the fortunes of the NBA? According to analysts, it began with the hiring of a new NBA commissioner, named David Stern, in early 1984. A lawyer with a flair for marketing, Stern brought an entirely new approach to the league. The president of the Players Association, Isiah Thomas (star guard of the Detroit Pistons), described it this way: "David came in and looked at the NBA and saw it as something more than just sports. It's really entertainment. It's a Michael Jackson tour, a Rolling Stones tour. He saw it as an NBA tour." David Stern compared the NBA to Disney Corporation. "They have theme parks, and we have theme parks. Only we call them arenas. They have characters: Mickey Mouse, Goofy. Our characters are named Magic and Michael [Jordan]. Disney sells apparel; we have apparel. They make home videos; we make home videos." Even advertisers are now beating down the league's doors. As one Madison Avenue executive said, "The NBA is clearly ahead of all the other leagues in terms of the warm and fuzzy feeling that fans and advertisers get as a result of association with the sport."

Thus the NBA was transformed from a narrowly defined sports enterprise to a broadly conceived entertainment organization. From selling videos, to clothing, to basketballs, to cologne in Europe, the NBA has become a money machine. Indeed, the biggest growth potential is in Europe, Japan, and China, where the NBA already sells the rights to broadcast its games. Basketball is played in 176 countries, and the NBA wants to become a part of the culture of all of them.

Perhaps the best example of the marketing emphasis that Stern brought to the league was the changes in the NBA All-Star game. Prior to his arrival it was a nonevent. Under Stern's guidance, it was transformed into an extravaganza—an All-Star Weekend with media parties and a series of competitions (e.g., the slam-dunk, the three-point shot, and the legends' contests) to go with the All-Star game itself.

But all these marketing actions would not have been possible without a basic change in the product. Just prior to the time Stern became commissioner, new rules were installed to control the drug problem. The Players Association created a highly effective drug screening program. A rookie orientation program was created that gave courses on how to deal with the press and to adjust to the life and pressures of the

NBA. A lottery was created to determine who would get the first pick in the college draft to discourage bad teams from losing intentionally at the end of the season. Coaches were sweet-talked and bullied, if necessary, to clean up their act. For example, when the coach of the Utah Jazz continued to complain publicly about the referees, Stern went ballistic. The coach's negative publicity hurt the league's image. He called the coach and was reported to have said, "If you can't control your players and coaches to get them to understand how we do business in this league, I'm going to fine you more money than you make selling tickets." As a marketing executive at Spalding Sports Worldwide said, "A good marketing guy knows that he has to get the product right before marketing it. That's what Stern did with basketball. He cleaned up the product first. Only then did he start marketing."

QUESTIONS

1. Define the problem faced by the NBA in the early 1980s.
2. Discuss the consumer behavior concepts that relate to the problems faced.
3. Develop the managerial applications analysis that matches the consumer behavior concepts with their managerial implications. Discuss the actions taken by David Stern and how the illustrate the relationship between the consumer concepts and managerial strategy.

Source: The case was based on an article by E. M. Swift and John Steinbreder, "From Corned Beef to Caviar," *Sports Illustrated*, June 3, 1991, pp. 74–90.

Chapter

10

Persuasive Communications

CONSUMER VIGNETTE

Unplugged Ads, Flat Oscilloscopes, and Bleeding Samurai

The gigantic, rough-and-tumble basketball player Charles Barkley glowered into the camera. He snarled:

> "I am not a role model.
>
> I'm not paid to be a role model.
>
> Parents should be role models.
>
> I'm paid to wreak havoc on the basketball court."

The "Just Do It" unique selling proposition of Nike shoes then flashed across the screen. The unusual ad broke new ground in the use of famous sports personalities to endorse athletic equipment. Called "unplugged" ads, their goal is to focus on athletic performance and depict athletes as real people with real problems.

Indeed, tying a celebrity to a brand name has become a major gamble for companies. Because celebrities are human, they are unpredictable. Consider companies like Nike, Gatorade, and McDonald's. Each employed Michael Jordan to endorse their products. How could they have anticipated that on October 5, 1993, he would suddenly, and without warning, end his basketball career. Collectively paying him over $28 million, they had to figure out how to refashion their entire ad campaigns.

Pepsi Cola, in particular, has had its share of problems. In 1993 Michael Jackson's world tour was interrupted during its Asian segment when charges of child molestation were filed in the United States. A few months later the company severed relations with the embattled superstar. This embarrassing situation followed on the heels of the sordid Mike Tyson affair. After signing a lucrative endorsement contract with Pepsi, the then world heavyweight boxing champion drove his Mercedes into a tree, was charged with wife beating, and was then convicted of raping a beauty queen.[1]

Have such horror stories caused ad executives to reconsider using celebrity endorsers? Maybe! One manager of an agency that markets celebrities to corporations said, "There's a real bad association between the players and their profiles as citizens, and advertisers are attracted to squeaky-clean images."[2] For example, in the summer of 1993 Burt Reynolds announced that he was divorcing Loni Anderson. Abruptly thereafter, the Florida Citrus Commission and Quaker State Motor Oil stopped employing him as an endorser.

Indeed, in the late 1980s, seven of the top ten television commercials used either fictional characters or fictional people, such as California Raisins, Spuds MacKenzie, and Ronald McDonald. Why is the use of fictional characters so rampant? Consider Garfield the Cat, who advertises for Embassy Suites Hotels. Although Garfield may overeat, he won't be charged with child molestation. In addition to the fact that he is unlikely to be charged with a crime, Garfield is humorous, and humor can be a highly effective communications tactic.

In addition to using humor in ads, advertisers have also mastered the art of frightening the audience. For example, one ad showed a man dying on an operating table. He whispered as the oscilloscope went flat, "I remember hearing somebody say I was . . . dead . . . I thought about Janice and Bobby. . . .Who'd take care of them now?" After quick work by the medical personnel, the man survived. The insurance company's campaign featured three other commercials—a woman drowning, a volunteer fireman overcome by smoke, and a man rushed to a hospital in an ambulance. The creation of fear can increase the perception of risk and influence consumer beliefs and attitudes.

While the characteristics of the source (e.g., an athlete or Garfield the Cat) and the message (e.g., fear or humor) influence consumers, the nature of the media vehicle may also impact the audience. In May 1988 *Consumer Reports* rated the Suzuki Samurai four-wheel-drive vehicle unacceptable because of its tendency to roll over. In one month sales dropped by two-thirds, and the existence of the brand was threatened.[3] Somehow, one cannot imagine the same sales outcome if the story had been broken by the *National Enquirer*. The nature of the media vehicle, along with the source and the content of the message, influence consumer reactions to persuasive communications—the topic of this chapter.

INTRODUCTION

Communications are omnipresent in our lives. Radio and television commercials, print advertisements, and messages from sales personnel all seek to communicate with us and ultimately to influence us. In our encounters with friends and acquaintances, persuasive communications are commonplace. A friend who says, "Hey, there's a great new movie showing at the Bijou—do you want to go?" is engaging in a persuasion attempt.

A **communication** involves the use of a sign to convey meaning. A **sign** may be a verbalization, an utterance, a body movement, a written word, a picture, an odor, a touch, or even stones on the ground to denote a property boundary. Thus, when one speaks of a communication, the referent may be the specific words spoken, a subtle change in voice quality, a gesture, the written word, or a pictorial representation.

Communications are received through all the senses. Extremely unambiguous messages can be communicated through smell and touch. Perfumes are worn to communicate sensual thoughts and feelings. A touch can communicate feelings of tenderness, sadness, and anger. The visual signs used to communicate information range from the obvious to the subtle. The clothing of a prostitute walking the street communicates certain clear-cut messages. In contrast, corporations spend millions of dollars to design logos that subtly communicate an image to the public.

This chapter analyzes in detail two specific factors that influence the effectiveness of the communication process: the characteristics of the source of information and the characteristics of the message that is communicated. Three other factors important to the communications process are not discussed in the chapter. They are (1) the context within which the message is delivered, (2) the nature of the channel/vehicle through which the message is communicated, and (3) the receiver. The receiver of the communication is an individual. Because individual differences in consumer behavior were discussed in Chapter 7, Personality and Psychographics, space limitations prohibit further analysis of this important topic. In a similar manner, the topics of media and context effects are covered in detail in advertising and promotional strategy texts. Again, other than noting their impact on communications, space limitations prevent their further discussion.

The chapter-opening vignette illustrated aspects of both source and message effects. A wide variety of sources exists to communicate a message. Celebrities such as Mike Tyson represent one type of source. The problem with celebrities, however, is that they can quickly become liabilities. The CEO of the ad agency that handles the Anheuser-Busch account stated, "It is better for a pitchman to die than to be caught alive in a scandal. When the person personifying your brand gets in trouble, the brand indirectly gets into trouble."[4] One means to avoid the problems of using real people is to create fictitious characters. Thus Metropolitan Life Insurance Company knows with certainty that the Peanuts characters are not going to die from a drug overdose or become involved in a sex scandal.

Not only do animated characters avoid embarrassments, they also effectively add humor to messages. Humor is just one type of message characteristic. Creating fear is another approach to persuasion, and it was used effectively in the "death bed" advertisements of the insurance company. Karl Malden effectively uses a financial fear appeal in his ads for American Express traveler's checks. Deodorant and dandruff shampoo ads deftly exploit the social fears of the audience.

As the advertisement shown in Figure 10-1 illustrates, fear appeals are also used as tools of public policy makers to influence consumers to avoid drinking and driving.

In addition to the source and the message, the channel and the vehicle through which a message is transmitted may also influence the effectiveness of the communication. Although not discussed here, these factors do have an impact on consumers. **Channels** are the media through which messages flow. A variety of channels exist, such as face-to-face interactions (e.g., a sales call), television, radio, billboards, newspapers, and magazines. **Vehicles** are the specific means within a channel through which a message is communicated. For example, *Consumer Reports* is a media vehicle. Because of the magazine's credibility with audiences, the article rating the Suzuki Samurai as unacceptable for safety reasons had a major impact on audiences.

In the sections that follow, a model of the communication process is presented. Next, the chapter discusses how source and message characteristics affect consumers. Finally, a managerial applications example is analyzed.

A MODEL OF THE COMMUNICATIONS PROCESS

Researchers have developed a **communications model** that depicts the relationships among the various factors that influence the effectiveness and impact of persuasive communications.[5] Figure 10-2 presents one version of this model. The model proposes that five separate categories of factors control the effectiveness of communications: source characteristics, message content, medium characteristics, contextual factors, and audience characteristics.

Figure 10-1 This advertisement was created to influence consumers to avoid drinking and driving. (Courtesy of Chuck Ruhr Advertising, Inc.)

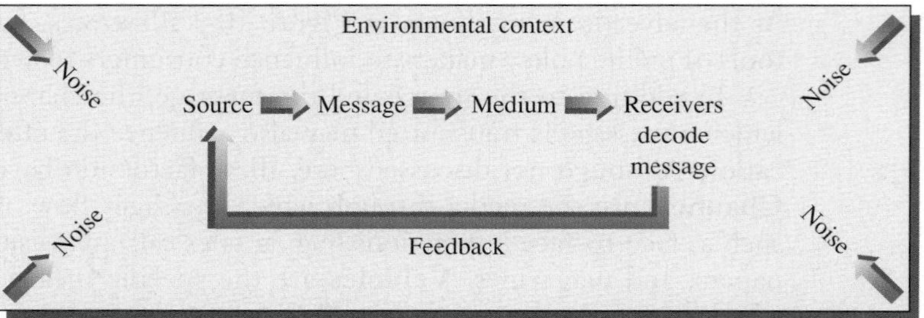

Figure 10-2 A communications model.

As shown in Figure 10-2, persuasive communications begin with a source of information who encodes and delivers a message. Numerous strategies exist for encoding messages. A communicator must think through such issues as whether a fear appeal should be used, whether a conclusion should be drawn at the end of the communication, and whether the message should be one-sided or two-sided.

The message is delivered through some medium of transmission. The medium could be face to face or via print, radio, or television. The characteristics of the medium influence the interpretation of the message as well as how its information is processed. The message is then received by members of an audience who decode and interpret the communication.

Various characteristics of the audience can moderate the effects of persuasive communications. Such factors as personality, sex, intelligence, and involvement in the issue mediate how receivers decode the information and react to the communication. Finally, the entire communications process takes place within a general environmental context. Various environmental stimuli may inhibit the communications process by distracting consumers, influencing their mood, or acting to create "noise" in the transmission of the message.

Because a communication begins with a source of information, this element of the communications model is discussed first.

SOURCE CHARACTERISTICS

Understanding the factors that influence the effectiveness of sources of information is extremely important to marketing managers and public policy makers. For example, in personal-selling situations the salesperson acts as a source of information. His or her effectiveness depends in part upon how he or she "comes across" to the client. Similarly, a frequent approach used by advertisers is to hire endorsers to advocate a product or service. In one study that investigated 243 commercials, over 38% used some type of endorser.[6]

Just what is a source of information? Many researchers view the term "source" very broadly. Thus a source can be a person (e.g., Bill Cosby), a company (e.g., Coca-Cola), or almost any other entity. For the purposes of this chapter, however, the concept of **source** is defined as an individual or character who is presenting information about some topic. Over the past 30 years researchers have identified a number of **source characteristics** that affect the ability of one person to influence another. These characteristics include the source's credibility, physical attractiveness, and likability.

Credibility of the Source

The concept of source credibility has long been recognized as an important element in determining the effectiveness of a source. The term **source credibility** refers to the extent to which a source is perceived to have expertise and trustworthiness. As such, source credibility is defined in terms of two major dimensions—source expertise and trustworthiness. Thus the greater the expertise and trustworthiness of a source of information, the more likely an observer will perceive the source as credible.

Source expertise refers to the extent of knowledge the source is perceived to have about the subject on which he or she is communicating. Recently, researchers reviewed over 150 articles investigating source effects.[7] The authors found that across all of the studies that found significant effects, differences in the characteristics of the source had on average about a 9% impact on respondents' ratings. Among the various types of source variables, source expertise was found to have the greatest impact on respondents' reactions to communications. When expertise was examined by researchers, it was found to have about a 16% impact on respondents' ratings. (That is, 16% of the variance in respondents' ratings was accounted for by changes in the level of expertise of the source.)

As noted, source expertise was found to have a 16% impact on the ratings of communications. Is a 16% change large enough to have any significant managerial implications? The answer is "yes"! For consumer goods firms, a one or two percentage-point change in market share can mean tens or hundreds of millions of dollars in sales. Because consumer responses to marketing communications, such as advertisements, directly impact sales, maximizing the positive impact of a marketing communication takes on extreme importance.

Source trustworthiness refers to the extent to which the source is perceived to provide information in an unbiased, honest manner.[8] Research has found that expertise and trustworthiness make an independent contribution to source effectiveness. The implication of this work is that if someone is perceived to be trustworthy, he or she can influence an audience, even if perceived to have relatively little expertise. Similarly, even though someone may be perceived to be untrustworthy, if perceived to be an expert, he or she will tend to have some persuasive ability.[9] Highlight 10-1 discusses the important role that trust plays in performing market research.

In general, highly credible sources are more effective than less credible sources.[10] Highly credible sources have been found to

1. Produce more positive attitude change toward the position advocated than less credible sources.
2. Induce more behavioral change than less credible sources.
3. Enhance the ability to use fear appeals, which involve physical or social threats.
4. Inhibit the creation of counterarguments to the message.

One important positive effect of using credible endorsers is that they tend to reduce counterargumentation. Advertisers realize that consumers often develop their own

HIGHLIGHT 10-1

Trust in Market Research

A key application area of consumer behavior concepts is **market research**. The market researcher can be viewed as both a source and receiver of information in two different types of exchange relationships. First, when gathering information from consumers, market researchers act as a source of information when a request is made for respondents to provide data about their perceptions of products, advertising, and other marketing communications. Second, market researchers act as a source of information when they pass on their analyses and conclusions to managers who use their information within the fi rm.

In each of the two exchange relationships, trust is an important factors. If market researchers are not trusted by consumers, the data received will be flawed. Similarly, if managers distrust their own market researchers, their recommendations and analyses will be ignored!

Recently, a study was conducted to identify the factors that influenced managers' trust in the recommendations and data provided by market researchers. The results showed that trust increased when managers believed that the researcher:

1. Had the following personal characteristics: personal integrity, expertise, tactfulness, sincerity, and congeniality.
2. Reduced the uncertainty of the findings.
3. Customized the results.
4. Kept the results confidential.
5. Produced the results in a timely manner.

Based upon Christine Moorman, Rohit Deshpande, and Gerald Zaltman, "Factors Affecting Trust in Market Research Relationships," *Journal of Marketing*, Vol. 57 (January 1993), pp. 81–101.

thoughts in response to a message. These thoughts, called **cognitive responses**, may be positive regarding the message (i.e., support arguments), may be negative toward the message (i.e., counterarguments), or may concern the characteristics of the source (source derogations).[11] When a highly trustworthy and expert endorser is used, however, people tend to lower their defenses and not think of as many cognitive responses. Because highly credible sources tend to inhibit the development of counterarguments, they may be more persuasive than less credible sources.

Researchers have found, however, that highly credible sources are not always more effective than less credible sources. In certain circumstances moderately credible sources may cause more attitude change than highly credible sources. In particular, in cases in which the audience is already favorably predisposed to the message, a less credible source can induce greater persuasion than a highly credible source.[12]

In sum, a credible spokesperson can change beliefs, attitudes, and behaviors in a favorable direction. Advertisers recognized this finding and began to emphasize the use of highly expert endorsers. In particular, it has become popular to use the chief executive officers (CEOs) of companies to endorse their products. The trend was initiated in large part by Lee Iacocca, the now-retired CEO of Chrysler Corporation, who almost single-handedly brought the company back from bankruptcy. Figure

10-3 shows one print ad featuring the tough-talking CEO. Other CEOs who have endorsed their products include Frank Perdue for his Perdue chickens, Victor Kiam for Remington razors ("I liked the razor so much, I bought the company"), Bill Marriott for Marriott Hotels, and David Mahoney trying harder for Avis.

Physical Attractiveness of the Source

To determine the importance of **source physical attractiveness**, one has only to watch television or examine print advertisements. Most television and print ads use physically attractive people. Indeed, physical attractiveness seems to be a requirement for television personalities and reporters.

Figure 10-3 Corporate CEOs such as Lee Iacocca, when he was CEO of Chrysler, are increasingly used to promote their companies in ads. (Courtesy of Chrysler Corporation.)

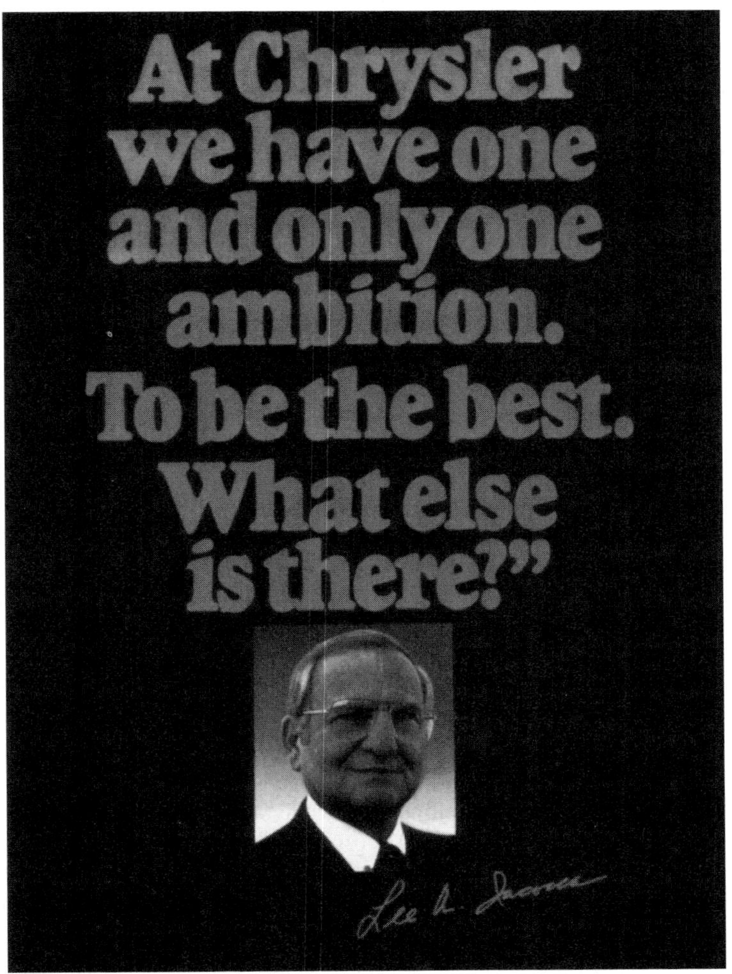

The research on the impact of physical attractiveness generally supports what we see around us every day. In general, the findings reveal that physically attractive communicators are more successful than unattractive ones in changing beliefs.[13] In addition, people tend to form positive stereotypes about physically attractive people. For example, one study found that college men and women expected physically attractive people to be more sensitive, warm, modest, happy, and so forth. Indeed, the results of the study were summarized as "What is beautiful is good."[14]

In the advertising area, researchers have investigated the impact of physical attractiveness of endorsers on consumers. The findings generally indicate that attractive individuals are perceived more positively and reflect more favorably on the brand endorsed. For example, in one study respondents were shown slides of either an attractive or an average-looking model engaging in various activities at the Cincinnati Zoo.[15] After seeing the slide show, respondents were asked to give their impressions of the presentation and of the model. In addition, they were asked if they would be willing to volunteer to assist the zoo. The results revealed that impressions of the slide show were significantly more favorable when an attractive model was used. The effect was particularly strong for males who observed an attractive female model. Males exposed to the attractive female were significantly more interested in attending a meeting and in passing a levy to finance the zoo.

Much of the work on physical attractiveness and product endorsers has investigated the effects of "sexually suggestive" advertisements. The research has shown that sexy advertisements do attract attention and facilitate recognition of the advertisements. However, consumer responses to sexually explicit ads are mixed. For example, one study found that the presence of physically attractive, partially clad models influenced an automobile's image in a favorable manner.[16] The same study also suggested that if the erotic nature of the ad was too high, it actually harmed recall of the ad when recall was measured a week after exposure to the ad.

Researchers have also found that physical attractiveness may interact with other variables.[17] In one study highly attractive and less attractive people endorsed either a coffee product or a perfume/cologne. The results showed that the sexy model produced greater intentions to buy the product when the product had a sexual appeal (i.e., when the product was the perfume). In contrast, if the product had nothing to do with attracting the opposite sex (i.e., the product was coffee), the unattractive source had more impact. Respondents in the study may have inferred that physically attractive endorsers would know something about perfume but have little knowledge of coffee. Although other explanations are possible for these results, they clearly indicate that using physically attractive and sexy models may not be appropriate for some types of products, such as coffee.

Recently, a researcher investigated the impact of the perceived physical attractiveness of models on ratings of advertisements for clothing.[18] It was hypothesized that respondents would make inferences about the personality of the models based upon their perceived physical attractiveness. The results revealed that changes in physical attractiveness did impact subject perceptions of the models' sociability, expertise, poise, and friendliness. In turn, these impressions influenced the respondents' attitude toward the ad. These ideas help to explain why in some instances highly physically attractive people are *not* the most effective sources. For example, when endorsing a perfume, if high physical attractiveness leads to inferences that the model has the personality characteristics of sociableness and sexual interest, positive reactions are likely to result. In contrast, in an ad for coffee, high physical attractiveness may lead to inferences of personality characteristics of low expertise and inability to make coffee. Negative reactions are likely to result.

In sum, consumers can derive numerous meanings from the physical attractiveness of the source. These meanings will be affected by the sex of the consumer and by the type of product being endorsed. As a result, managers should employ market research to ensure that an optimum match exists between endorser and product.

Likability of the Source

Source likability refers to the positive or negative feelings that consumers have toward a source of information. The volatile tennis player John McEnroe has been used as an example of someone who is considered physically attractive but unlikable. Developing a definition of the concept of likability is a difficult task because what is likable probably varies from person to person. In general, however, source likability appears to be related to the extent to which another person is viewed as behaving in a way that matches the desires of those who observe him or her. In addition, likability tends to increase when a source of information says pleasant things.[19] Thus a person may be likable because he or she acts on or espouses beliefs that are similar to those of the audience. In addition, likability may result from a source's ability to create a positive mood state among receivers of information.

The concept of likability has been studied by consumer researchers. In one study, likable celebrity endorsers (i.e., Robert Redford, Jaclyn Smith, Woody Allen, and Jean Stapleton) were compared in effectiveness to unlikable endorsers (i.e., Bo Derek, John Travolta, Howard Cosell, and Billy Jean King).[20] Interestingly, the unlikable celebrities were more effective endorsers in this study. Intentions to purchase a fictitious razor were higher when the product was endorsed by the unlikable endorsers. In addition, recognition measures of the ad were higher for the unlikable endorsers.

A potential explanation for the unexpected findings is the **match-up hypothesis**. Endorsers who match up with the product on relevant attributes may be more effective. For example, John McEnroe may have effectively endorsed Bic Razors because this frequently angry and outspoken individual may well match a product used to sever hair from the human body. In a similar manner, Carl Malden may be effective for American Express because his background as a TV cop matches the image of someone giving warnings about carrying around large amounts of cash.

These ideas suggest that likability is an important source quality. For example, the phenomenal success of Bill Cosby as an endorser appears to be based upon his extreme likability. Similarly, the use of some athletes as spokespersons is based upon their likability. Mike Tyson, the infamous boxer, cannot be used as an endorser because of his thorough disagreeableness. In contrast, Bo Jackson continues to be used by Nike to endorse its products because he is highly likable. Although injuries have dramatically reduced his athletic abilities, he still remains highly popular with consumers. An ad in which Bo Jackson endorses Nike sports equipment is shown in Figure 10-4.

Figure 10-4 Despite his injuries, Bo Jackson continues to be used as an endorser by Nike, in part because of his personal likability. (Courtesy of Nike, Inc. Photo by Richard Noble.)

Source Meaningfulness

In addition to having qualities such as credibility, physical attractiveness, and likability, sources of information also provide meanings. As a result of the connection between the source and a brand, such meanings can then be transferred. For example, by hiring Michael Jordan and connecting him with its salty-sweet beverage in advertisements, Gatorade hopes to transfer to its product the message that consuming the drink can enhance athletic potential. In this case, Jordan acts as a symbol representing a number of qualities, which may be transferred to the beverage.

Frequently, companies hire celebrities to endorse their brands. Examples are numerous: Michael Jackson for Pepsi, Michael Jordan for Nike, Jay Leno for

Doritos, and Elizabeth Taylor for Passion Perfume represent just a few of these associations. These well-known endorsers bring to the product an entire show business career, and with it an elaborate set of meanings represented by the stage persona that is known to consumers. In discussing the use of James Garner (a long-time endorser of Mazda autos) as an endorser, one analyst commented:

> Garner does not play himself the person nor does he play a particular fictive character (in advertisements). Instead, he plays what I would call the generalized James Garner role, the type for which James Garner is always cast—handsome, gentle, bumbling, endearing, a combination of Bret Maverick from "Maverick" and Jim Rockford from "The Rockford Files."[21]

The transfer of meaning from celebrity to product to consumer is diagrammed in Figure 10-5. The figure presents a flowchart in which a celebrity plays a number of roles over his or her career.[22] (Please note that although celebrities frequently come from show business, they may also gain their fame from politics, sports, business, or another area that places them in the public eye.) Based upon these roles, meanings become attached to the celebrity that are shared within a culture.

In sum, the celebrity becomes a cultural symbol. When the celebrity endorses a product in an advertisement, associations are formed so that the culturally derived meanings may be transferred to the product. Finally, in the consumption phase, the meaning may be transferred from the product to the consumer. Thus, when consumers drink Gatorade, some of the qualities of Michael Jordan may become symbolically attached to them.

A study was conducted to identify the meanings that are transferred from the celebrity Cher to Scandinavian Health Spas—a company that she has endorsed in the past.[23] Respondents were asked to describe the associations that they made between Cher and the spas based upon her advertisements for the company. Table 10-1 presents the results, in which six categories of responses were obtained. The most frequently mentioned association was becoming attractive and having a "great body" like Cher's. Most of the associations were quite positive, except for one category of "lacks credibility." In this case, respondents would occasionally mention that Cher obtained her body as much through plastic surgery as hard work. Also note that males and females diverged on some categories. For example, males viewed a spa

Figure 10-5 The transfer of meaning from celebrity to product to consumer.

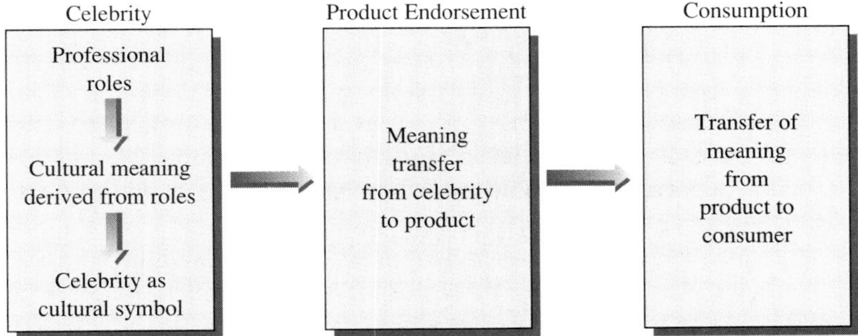

much more frequently as a place to meet the opposite sex, more frequently felt that Cher lacked credibility, and more often associated the word "sexy" with Cher and Scandinavian Health Spas. In contrast, females more frequently associated the words "hard work" with the advertisements.

In sum, advertisers can transfer meanings from celebrity spokespersons to the products they endorse. One can understand the phenomenon from a cultural perspective—in which consumers are viewed as having shared cultural perceptions of the symbolic characteristics of celebrities. On the other hand, one could approach the problem from an information processing perspective. In this case, segments of consumers are viewed as having similar schemas, or sets of associations, for a celebrity. When a brand is connected to the celebrity, the set of associations then becomes identified with the brand in a semantic memory network. From whichever approach the analyst chooses to understand the process, the managerial implication is the same. Endorsers should be well matched to the product for the appropriate transfer of meaning to occur.

Managerial Implications of Source Effects

A crucial decision for managers concerns what kind of source to use when developing advertising communications. The source of information is a vital component in delivering a message to an audience. The specific source used can also help a company to position a product. (For example, consumers would perceive a brand promoted by Bill Cosby quite differently from a brand promoted by Sylvester Stallone.) Careful market research studies should be performed to investigate audience reactions to the source and to track changes in reactions over time.

Finding a celebrity who is willing to make the endorsement and who is not already overexposed is difficult. In fact, one major advertising firm (Ogilvy &

TABLE 10-1

Associations Between Cher and Scandinavian Health Spas

	Number of Responses Made	
Association	*Males*	*Females*
Attractive/great body like Cher's	15	17
Health/fitness	12	6
Hard work	5	11
Sexy	11	5
Lacks credibility	10	4
Place to meet opposite sex	6	0

Based upon Lynn Langmeyer and Mary Walker, "A First Step to Identify Meaning in Celebrity Endorsers," in *Advances in Consumer Research*, Vol. 18, Rebecca Holman and Michael Solomon, eds. (Provo, UT: Association for Consumer Research, 1991), pp. 364–371.

Mather) has stopped using celebrities because of research showing that the audience assumes that the celebrity has been bought off.[24] Because of the problem of overexposure and the likelihood that consumers discount the endorsement of celebrities, a premium is paid for the services of "virgin" endorsers. Most U.S. companies would jump at the opportunity to hire such virgin endorsers as Woody Allen, Robert Redford, Paul Newman, or Sylvester Stallone to endorse their brand. Interestingly, celebrities who refuse to endorse products in the United States sometimes endorse products in Japan. Stallone is shown in one ad for Kirin Beer striding Rambo-like through water. Newman is shown talking with a little girl in an ad for a credit card.[25] Of course, the stars' justification for doing ads in Japan and not in the United States is to avoid tarnishing their image among their American fans. However, one study that investigated the effects of commercials on perceptions of celebrities found little evidence of such negative effects.[26] Possibly, the practice is so commonplace that the images of the celebrities are not tarnished.

Table 10-2 summarizes the major findings on source effects.

When selecting a source of information that is used advertisements, ethical and public policy issues may also arise. Highlight 10-2 discusses a current controversy in the advertising of cigarettes.

MESSAGE CHARACTERISTICS

The effects of message content and construction on receivers has been intensively studied by researchers. **Message content** refers to the strategies that may be used to communicate an idea to an audience. Examples of such strategies include decisions of whether to use emotional versus factual advertisements and whether to develop complex or simple messages. In contrast, **message construction** refers to

TABLE 10-2

Summary of Key Findings on Impact of Source Effects

1. Important source effect variables include credibility, expertise, trust, physical attractiveness, likability, meaning, and match-up with the product.
2. Source expertise has been found to have the greatest impact on consumer responses in comparison to other source effect variables.
3. Sources with high levels of credibility are more effective, enhance the ability to use fear appeals, and inhibit the formation of counterarguments.
4. In general, physically attractive people are more effective than less physically attractive people as sources.
5. To maximize source effectiveness, match up the source to the product.
6. Meanings derived from the characteristics of the source can be transferred to the product through their close association.
7. The perceived characteristics and personality of the source can interact with the nature of the product. Thus, in some circumstances, highly physically attractive or highly likable sources may not be the most effective.

HIGHLIGHT 10-2

Ethics and Public Policy Issues: Source Effects in Cigarette Advertising

Regulators and the public are rightly concerned about the impact of advertising on certain susceptible groups, such as children. In particular, cigarette companies have been criticized for marketing their brands to American youth. The campaign of Camel cigarettes that employs the suave cartoon character "Old Joe" the camel has been singled out for its effectiveness. As of 1993, the campaign increased the number of Camel smokers under 25 years of age by 5.1%. In addition, the percentage of women smoking Camels increased by nearly 10%.

The publication of these data resulted in the Federal Trade Commission launching an investigation into the campaign. Tobacco company representatives and some advertising executives argued that any bans on the advertising would violate the Constitution's First Amendment on freedom of speech. In contrast, a public advocate stated, "There are a thousand ways to advertise tobacco without using as your identifying image a cartoon character that primarily appeals to teenagers" [1].

In addition to being criticized for using a cartoon character, tobacco companies have been reproached for using models in ads that appear to be very young. In response, the companies voluntarily developed a provision stating that "Natural persons depicted as smokers in cigarette advertising shall be at least 25 years of age. . . ."

A recent study investigated whether tobacco companies were living up to their doctrine. In a carefully controlled study, the authors asked a broad spectrum of consumers (561 people) to estimate the age of the models in a series of print ads for cigarettes placed in magazines. The results revealed that 17% of the models were perceived to be significantly younger than 25 years of age. Furthermore, the ads with models perceived as more youthful were found predominantly in magazines targeted to younger audiences. Finally, the results revealed that regardless of the respondent's age, younger-looking models were perceived as more attractive than older-looking models [2].

The issues raised in the debate over tobacco advertising are tough. They pit two equally important values against each other—the right to freedom of speech and the right to protect the health of the nation's youth. The data provided by marketing researchers are critical to help to define the extent of the problem. In the end, however, it will be through a political process that the issues are finally resolved. If you are a student of consumer behavior with strong feelings about the issue, contact one of the members of Congress from your state to voice your views.

References

1. Ira Teinowitz and Steven W. Colford, "Old Joe a Winner Even with an Ad Ban," *Advertising Age*, August 16, 1993, pp. 1, 37.
2. Michael B. Mazis, Debra Jones Ringold, Elgin S. Perry, and Daniel W. Denman, "Perceived Age and Attractiveness of Models in Cigarette Advertisements," *Journal of Marketing* (January 1992), pp. 22–37.

the problem of how to physically construct a message. Examples of such a question include "Where should information be placed in a message to get maximum impact?" and "How often should information be repeated in a message?" Various considerations in constructing a message and in developing its content are discussed in the sections that follow.

Developing Message Content

The logical first step in creating a message is to decide on its content—that is, the communicator must identify the strategy that will be used to influence receivers in the desired manner. A variety of questions exist for communicators to consider in developing message content, including

- How simple or complex should the message be?
- Should a conclusion be drawn?
- Should comparisons be made to competitors?
- Should the message be one-sided or two-sided?
- Is it appropriate to use a fear appeal?
- Is it appropriate to use humor?
- To what extent should statistics be used versus more vivid and concrete descriptions?
- Should lectures or dramas be used to communicate the message?
- What life themes should be used to create meaning?

Message Complexity

From an information-processing perspective, a receiver must first be exposed to a message for the message to have any effect on a receiver. In addition, the receiver must attend to the information and comprehend it. A factor that strongly influences the ability of receivers to comprehend the information is **message complexity**. If the information is too complex or, worse yet, presented in a garbled, confusing manner, receivers are less likely to comprehend and be persuaded by the information. For example, in one study people received messages that argued for the desirability of sleeping less each night. Some received a comprehensible message, whereas others received a garbled, difficult-to-follow message. The results revealed that those who received the comprehensible message had more attitude change, regardless of the amount of sleep recommended and the credibility of the source.[27]

Excessively high message complexity may also result from attempts to place too much information in a communication. As noted in Chapter 4 on memory processes, consumers have a limited ability to process information. If too much information is given, they may become overloaded and react negatively. In the context of television commercials, the general rule is that no more than four major copy points can be communicated. If celebrity endorsers are used, even fewer bits of information can be processed by consumers because part of their cognitive capacity will be allocated to the endorser rather than to the message.

Drawing Conclusions

Another question involving the development of message content is whether the communicator should draw a conclusion for the audience. In a message the communicator may generate a number of arguments that support a particular position. These arguments may logically build on one another and lead to an inference that the audience should buy the product. Thus an advertiser might state: "Our brand is built better, will last longer, and is priced lower than other brands." The conclusion that could be drawn is that the consumer should go out and buy it. However, the question is: "Should the communication expressly draw the conclusion and tell the audience to go out and buy the product or let the audience draw the conclusion itself?"

Research on the effects of **drawing conclusions** indicates that whether or not to leave advertisements open-ended depends upon the complexity of the message and the involvement of the audience.[28] If the message is relatively complex or if the audience is not involved in the topic, it appears that a conclusion should be drawn in the message. In contrast, if the audience is highly involved and the message is not particularly complex for that audience, it may be better to let the audience make the inference. A recent study specifically investigated the role of audience involvement and conclusion drawing. The researchers found that for highly involved respondents, it was better not to draw conclusions. A key point was that the advertisement must be strong enough for the highly involved consumer to clearly draw the conclusion that the product advertised was actually better.[29]

Comparative Messages

A **comparative message** is one in which the communicator compares the positive and negative aspects of his or her position to the positive and negative aspects of a competitor's position. The approach is frequently used by advertisers who may explicitly identify one or more competitors for the purpose of claiming superiority over them.[30] Since the early 1970s the Federal Trade Commission has encouraged the use of comparative advertising out of the belief that naming a competitor would assist consumers in evaluating a claim of superiority.[31] Comparative advertising has been argued to be useful for small companies that are trying to enter a market, particularly if their claims are based on research done by independent third parties.[32] The opinion of many marketing managers was expressed by a Coca-Cola executive who said, "Comparative ads are good when you're new, but when you're the standard, it just gives a lot of free publicity to your competitors."[33]

Recent research studies have found evidence of the effectiveness of comparative advertisements. In most instances comparative advertising is initiated by a nonbrand leader or challenger in a product category. The goal of the challenger is for consumers to consider its brand as similar to the leader and to be a part of consumers' consideration sets. One study found that comparative advertising was successful in reducing the perceived difference between the challenger and the market leader across the three product categories investigated—toothpastes, cigarettes, and golf balls.[34]

Comparative ads can also be used to position and differentiate a brand. By directly comparing a low-market-share product to the dominant brand, managers can anchor it close to the position of the dominant brand in the consumer's mind.[35] Using the product category of toothpaste, researchers found that comparative advertisements showed evidence of superiority over noncomparative ads in anchoring a new brand closer to a dominant brand and in creating a clearer brand image. Thus direct comparisons between an unfamiliar brand and a market leader act to reposition the unfamiliar brand so that consumers perceive it to be more similar to the market leader.

What happens if comparative advertising occurs between well-known brands? The evidence indicates that if the attribute compared is typical of the brand category (e.g., a powdered cleanser that bleaches out tough stains), it is possible to differentiate the advertised brand from the comparison brand. That is, by making the claim that Cleanser A gets out stains better than Cleanser B, the firm can persuade consumers that the brands really are different. In contrast, if the comparison attribute is atypical and not highly salient (e.g., the cleanser is safe on delicate surfaces), consumers perceive the two brands to be highly similar. Consumers seem to assume that if the comparison is made on an attribute so unimportant, then there must be little difference between the brands.[36]

Recently, two different types of comparative advertisements have been identified. In **direct comparative advertisements**, one brand is compared specifically with another brand. In **indirect comparative advertisements**, the comparison brand is not specifically mentioned. Rather, the ad compares the brand indirectly to "competitors." Deciding which type of comparative to use depends upon the market share of the brand. One recent study found that low-market-share brands should directly compare themselves to the market leader. In contrast, moderate-market-share brands should use indirect comparative ads to avoid mentioning the name of the competitor and confusing consumers. Finally, the results revealed that market-share leaders should generally avoid comparative ads entirely.[37]

In sum, several conclusions can be drawn from the research on comparative advertising.

1. Comparative ads can be effective for low-market-share or new brands.
2. Moderate-market-share brands should use only indirect comparative advertising when comparisons are made to other moderate-share brands.
3. To differentiate its brand from another, a company should compare it to the competitor on typical/important attributes.
4. As a general statement, market leaders should avoid comparative advertising.

One- Versus Two-Sided Messages

Somewhat related to the use of comparative messages are communications in which both sides of an issue are mentioned. Figure 10-6 shows an advertisement that uses a two-sided message. The communication is from R. J. Reynolds Tobacco Company, and it addresses the difficult issue of smokers' rights. In one column is information from the nonsmokers' side, and in the other column is information from the smokers' side of the issue. The result is a **two-sided message** that communicates the idea that alternative viewpoints on the topic exist.

Research on the effectiveness of two-sided messages has shown that in some cases it can be an effective persuasion technique. Presenting both sides of an argument gives the appearance of fairness and may lower the tendency of consumers to argue against the message and the source. Particularly in cases when the audience is unfriendly, when it knows that opposition arguments exist, or when it is likely to hear arguments from the opposition, two-sided communications may be effective.[38]

Two-sided messages, however, are not always the most effective. In some instances giving only one side of an issue may result in the greatest attitude change. When the audience is friendly, when it is not likely to hear the other side's arguments, when it is not involved in the issue, or when it is not highly educated, **one-sided messages** may be more effective. In such instances presenting the other side to a message may simply confuse the audience and weaken the effects of the arguments for the issue.[39] Because many of the purchases that consumers make occur in low-involvement circumstances, marketers should probably have good evidence from marketing research studies that a two-sided message is effective before using it.

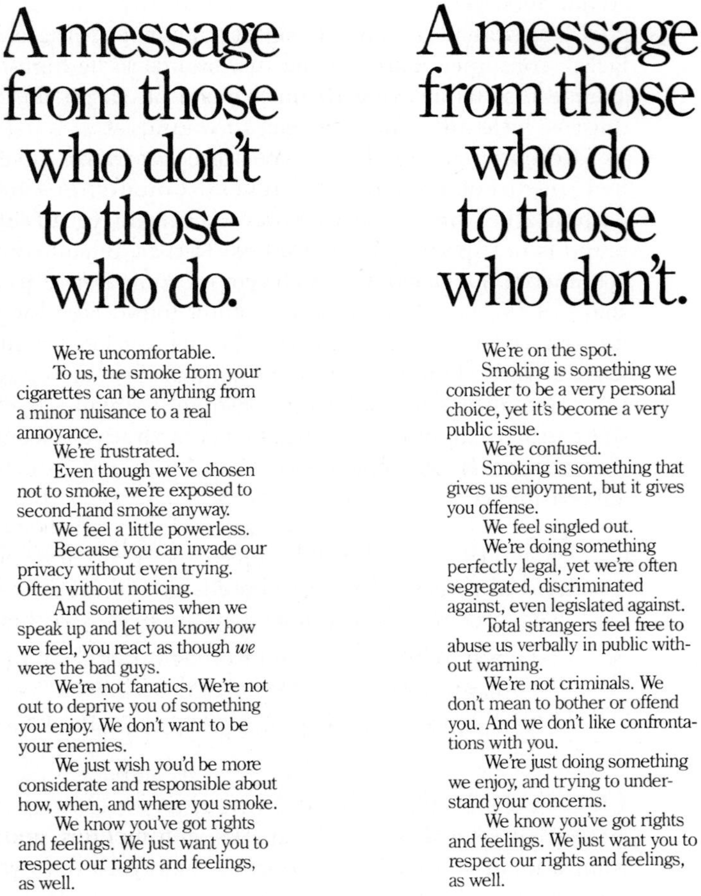

A message from those who don't to those who do.

We're uncomfortable.
To us, the smoke from your cigarettes can be anything from a minor nuisance to a real annoyance.
We're frustrated.
Even though we've chosen not to smoke, we're exposed to second-hand smoke anyway.
We feel a little powerless.
Because you can invade our privacy without even trying. Often without noticing.
And sometimes when we speak up and let you know how we feel, you react as though *we* were the bad guys.
We're not fanatics. We're not out to deprive you of something you enjoy. We don't want to be your enemies.
We just wish you'd be more considerate and responsible about how, when, and where you smoke.
We know you've got rights and feelings. We just want you to respect our rights and feelings, as well.

A message from those who do to those who don't.

We're on the spot.
Smoking is something we consider to be a very personal choice, yet it's become a very public issue.
We're confused.
Smoking is something that gives us enjoyment, but it gives you offense.
We feel singled out.
We're doing something perfectly legal, yet we're often segregated, discriminated against, even legislated against.
Total strangers feel free to abuse us verbally in public without warning.
We're not criminals. We don't mean to bother or offend you. And we don't like confrontations with you.
We're just doing something we enjoy, and trying to understand your concerns.
We know you've got rights and feelings. We just want you to respect our rights and feelings, as well.

Figure 10-6 This ad uses a two-sided message. (Courtesy of R. J. Reynolds Tobacco Company.)

In sum, two-sided messages must be used with care. The good news is that they do increase the perception of trustworthiness of the source—particularly when consumers perceive the marketer to have no ulterior motives or reasons for identifying an unfavorable characteristic of a brand.[40] (For example, the warning labels on cigarette packages result in a two-sided message. Cigarette companies are not seen as more trustworthy, however, because they are required by law to place the Surgeon General's warning on the package.) The bad news is that giving unfavorable information about a brand in a two-sided message lowers the strength of the message. If the message comes across as too weak, consumers will not be persuaded.[41] The managerial implication is that market research should be conducted to pretest consumer reactions to two-sided messages prior to their use.

Fear Appeals

In a **fear appeal**, a source communicates the message that unfortunate circumstances will result if the consumer fails to use a particular product or service. Many different types of fear appeals exist, and they are directly related to the various risks that consumers perceive. Thus the risk of bodily harm has been used to generate fear by companies that sell the safety of burglar alarms and by auto manufacturers that advertise the crash protection of their cars. Fear of financial risk is used by insurance companies. Social risk is also used effectively to generate fears by a variety of companies. Various companies selling deodorants, dandruff shampoo, and laundry detergents have successfully used fear appeals. By buying their products, consumers can avoid such "awful" maladies as "ring around the collar," they can "raise their hand if they're Sure," and they can scratch their heads without people snickering over their dandruff.

The view of the effectiveness of fear-arousing communications has changed considerably over the past 30 years. The first reported study on the use of fear appeals attempted to persuade consumers to brush their teeth more often. In the study one group of high school students was shown gory slides of diseased gums and given messages that tooth infections can lead to heart damage, kidney damage, and other disorders. Other groups were given less gruesome messages. The results revealed that the more fear the messages created, the less behavior change was observed. These early results caused many researchers to conclude that fear appeals were ineffective in persuasion.[42]

More recently, however, fear appeals have been shown to be effective in producing attitude change when used under certain conditions. Indeed, by 1970 over 20 studies had been performed revealing the effectiveness of fear-producing messages. The frequent use of fear by advertisers supports such research evidence. Companies that frequently use fear appeals are in such industries as life insurance, health insurance, burglar alarms, smoke alarms, automobiles, and even computers. Figure 10-7 shows an advertisement from Volvo that extols the virtues of the car in protecting its occupants in the event of a crash.

For fear appeals to be effective, researchers have found that the message should contain one or more of the following types of information. It should

1. Give specific instructions on how to cope with and reduce the fear.
2. Provide an indication that following the instructions will solve the problem.
3. Avoid giving high-fear messages to audiences that feel highly threatened and vulnerable to the threat.
4. Avoid giving high-fear messages to audiences that feel inferior or low in self-esteem.
5. Solve the problem quickly.

As noted by one set of authors, if these precautions are satisfied, "very frightening messages are almost always more persuasive than more factual appeals to reason."[43] A key reason why fear appeals can be successful is that they create emotional responses. These emotions then focus a person's attention on how to cope with the problem. The increased attention on coping responses makes it more likely that the person will learn how to respond to the threat.[44]

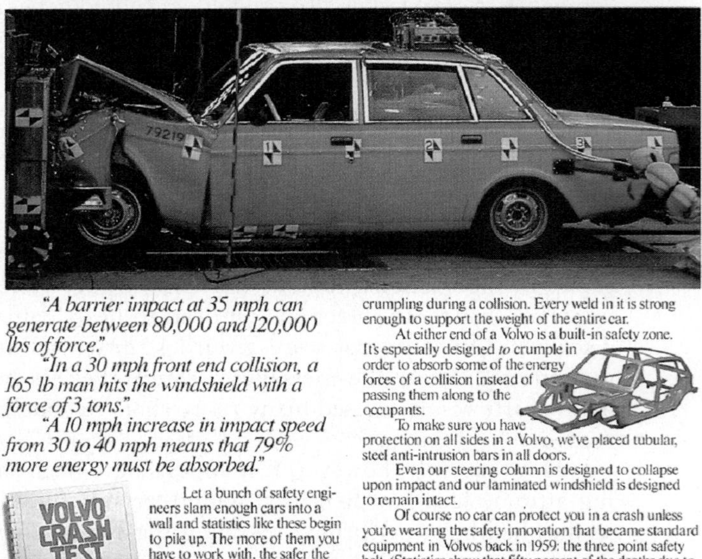

Figure 10-7 Volvo uses a not-so-subtle fear appeal in this ad. (Courtesy of Volvo Cars of North America Corporation.)

Humor in Messages

Like the use of fear appeals, the effectiveness of inserting **humor in messages** has been debated among marketing researchers. The use of humor in advertisements has varied over the years. A recent study found that 16% of the television commercials played in the United States used humor.[45] Research evidence on the impact of using humor has been mixed. Three negative effects can result from using humor. Most disturbing is the finding that using humor can reduce the comprehension of the message. For example, one study compared the recall of ad content in humorous ads to that in serious ads. The results showed that recall was significantly better in the serious version of the ad.[46] Second, using humor may shorten the life span of the ads.

Particularly if the humor is of a "gag" type, it may quickly fade and lose its positive effects. Third, humorous ads can also have unanticipated negative effects on various audiences. For example, shortly after Wendy's came out with its celebrated "Where's the beef?" ads, the Michigan Commission on Aging sent a letter of complaint. The letter suggested that the commercial gave the impression "that elderly people, in particular women, are senile, deaf and have difficulty seeing. We are sure it was not your intent to insult older people. We hope, however, in the future you will avoid stereotyping the elderly."[47]

Humor's unanticipated negative effects are in part explained by findings that different audiences may react in diverse ways to the same humor message. One study found that females may react more negatively to the injection of humor in ads than males.[48] Another study found that a variety of audience characteristics mediate the effects of humor, including sex, race, national origin, personality, and social attitudes.[49]

Recent studies are increasingly finding evidence that humor can have a positive persuasive impact. For example, in one field study, flyers were sent out to announce various types of social gatherings, including a neighborhood picnic, a clambake, and a fireman's muster. One set of announcements employed a humorous cartoon that captured a funny element of the event. Control flyers that employed no humor, but the same information, were also sent out to residents. The results revealed that in each instance, over 20% more people actually attended the social gatherings when the humorous flyers were used.[50] Thus, although using humor may have some liabilities, it clearly can provide benefits if used properly.

While humor can attract attention to an ad, it can also act to distract the audience from the message.[51] As noted earlier, such distraction can have the negative effect of lowering comprehension. Distraction, though, may have a positive effect as well: it may act to lower the counterarguments of the audience.[52] Indeed, one recent study found that a humorous ad improved attitudes toward the brand and recall of information in the advertisement.[53] A final positive effect of the use of humor has been found. Evidence exists that humor can enhance the credibility of a source of information. In particular, research has shown that when commercials are perceived to be dull, adding humor may enhance the audience's perception of the source's credibility.[54]

Like many other consumer behavior concepts, however, other variables moderate the effect of humor in advertisements. A recent study found that the prior brand evaluation of consumers influences reactions to humorous ads.[55] The authors created either humorous or nonhumorous ads for a pen. In addition, they varied prior evaluations by giving fictitious *Consumer Reports* ratings of the pen as part of another study. For some of the subjects, the pen was rated very positively. For others, the pen was rated negatively. Thus, when the respondents saw the advertisement, they already had formed an attitude regarding the pen. After seeing the ads, respondents then rated their attitudes toward the ad, their brand attitudes, and their purchase intentions. The results revealed a consistent pattern. When the ad was humorous and their prior evaluations were positive, their attitudes and purchase intentions increased substantially. However, when the ad was humorous and their prior evaluations were negative, their attitudes and purchase intentions plummeted. In contrast, the opposite pattern emerged for the serious ads. When prior evaluations were negative, attitudes and purchase intentions increased when a serious ad was used and decreased when a humorous ad was used. Figure 10-8 diagrams the effect for the

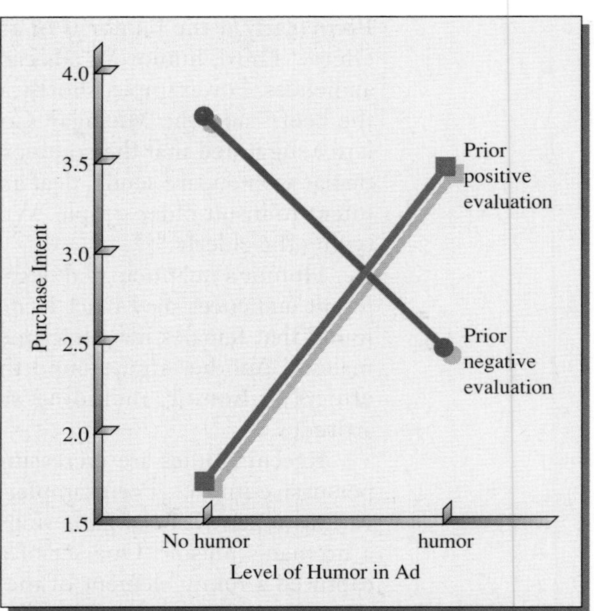

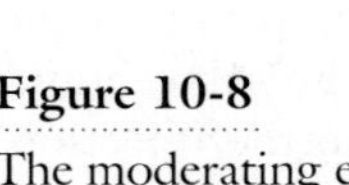

Figure 10-8

The moderating effect of prior brand evaluations of consumer responses to humorous ads. (Based upon Amitava Chattopadhyay and Kunal Basu, "Humor in Advertising: The Moderating Role of Prior Brand Evaluation," *Journal of Marketing Research*, Vol. 27, November 1990, pp. 466–476.)

measure of purchase intention. From a managerial perspective, then, humorous ads are best employed in order to reinforce positive attitudes.

Table 10-3 presents some "do's" and "don'ts" advocated by one advertising professional on the use of humor. Clearly, many companies perceive the benefits of using humor to outweigh its costs. The clever ads developed by Nike, Inc., which teamed Michael Jordan with Spike Lee, illustrate the effective use of comedy. Figure 10-9 presents a print ad from the Nike campaign.

An important issue in developing marketing strategy in the international marketing arena is whether or not humor can be used across international boundaries. Highlight 10-3 discusses recent research on whether humor can be used in an international marketing campaign.

Vivid Versus Abstract Information

A well-established finding in psychology is that messages using vivid, concrete words tend to have greater impact on receivers than messages containing more abstract information.[56] **Vivid messages** tends to attract and hold attention, as well as prompt the receiver to use his or her imagination. As such, vivid messages are more likely to be placed into long-term memory and later recalled than more pallid information.

What makes information vivid? Three factors have been found to increase the vividness of messages. First, to the extent that the message has personal relevance, it will tend to have a greater impact. As the involvement level of the message increases, so too should its impact. A second factor that increases the vividness of a message is concreteness. A concrete message gives a high degree of detailed, specific information about people, actions, and situations. For example, which of the following statements has more impact?

TABLE 10-3

Humor Can Sell

A variety of advertising executives have proposed various rules for using humor in advertising. Here is a list of do's and don'ts from one adman:

The Don'ts

1. Don't tell jokes because they wear out fast.
2. Never make fun of the product.
3. Don't use surprise endings; they surprise only once.
4. Don't make it hard for the viewer to figure out the humor.
5. Don't let the humor overwhelm the product.
6. Don't use humor when you can't figure out what else to do.

The Do's

1. Make the humor relevant.
2. Involve the audience in the humor early in the commercial.
3. Use the humor to sell the product's strong points.
4. Be charming, not funny.
5. Make humor simple and clear.
6. Integrate the humor with the message of the ad.

A number of highly successful advertising campaigns have been built around the use of humor. Below I have listed either a key phrase, a headline, or a key character from a well-known humorous ad campaign. See if you can recall the company doing the campaign. (The companies are listed under the list in reverse order.)

Alex, you better be drinking your water.
Less filling/Tastes great.
I can't believe I ate the whole thing.
Lemon (headline on print advertisement).
Hey, Vern, know what I mean?
Are you surprised?
A Charlie Chaplin impersonator is the key character in the ad.
Where's the beef?

(From bottom to top the companies were: Wendy's, IBM, NCR, Braum's Stores, Volkswagen, Alka-Seltzer, Miller Brewing Company, Stroh Brewery Company.)

SOURCE: Based in part on Anthony C. Chevins, "A Little Humor Carefully Used Can Work Wonders," *Journal of Broadcasting*, May 18, 1981, p. 22.

1. Jack sustained fatal injuries in a car wreck.
2. Jack was killed by a semitrailer that rolled over on his car and crushed his skull.[57]

Clearly, the second statement uses more concrete words and has much greater impact. Note the concreteness of the words, and feel the emotional impact that they carry. Good promotional messages should attempt to have such an impact, although in a more emotionally positive way. It has been argued that the high impact of certain books results from their ability to use highly concrete, emotional information. For

Figure 10-9 Nike employs humor to communicate a message in this ad featuring Michael Jordan and Spike Lee. (Courtesy of Nike, Inc.)

example, in the early 1900s Upton Sinclair's book *The Jungle* (R. Bentley, 1946) had a major impact on the public and was responsible in part for legislation that formed the Food and Drug Administration. Sinclair's graphic descriptions of the working conditions inside the meat-packing plants created an emotional stir that compelled congressional action. Here is a brief description of the "lard men" whose job it was to render the fat from the animals into lard for cooking and soap. Sinclair said that the men:

> . . .worked in tank-rooms full of steam, and in some which there were open vats near the level of the floor, their peculiar trouble was that they fell into the vats; and when they were fished out, there was never enough of them left to be worth exhibiting—sometimes they would be overlooked for days till all but the bones of them had gone out to the world as Durham's Pure Leaf Lard. (p. 117)

A final way in which to create more vivid, impact-laden messages is to make the information as close as possible to the receiver in terms of time, spatial proximity, and sensory proximity. Time proximity simply refers to using information that is as fresh and new as possible. For example, when a new product breakthrough occurs, managers should announce it as quickly as possible. Spatial proximity refers to the idea of placing information in a context that is linked as closely as possible to that experienced by the audience. Thus, if a product is targeted to one region of the country, television ads should be filmed in recognizable parts of the region. Sensory proximity refers to the concept of having the ideas in the message experienced firsthand by the audience or by someone else, such as an endorser, who can tell the audience what he or she experienced. One reason why automobile salespeople are so anxious to get you to drive a car is to have you obtain firsthand sensory experiences of the car.

HIGHLIGHT 10-3

Humor Across Cultures

Say, did you hear this joke? "It was spring 1993, and during a lull in the siege of Sarajevo, Yugoslavia, a line formed as thin, hungry people waited to get water from a tanker truck. A young, single woman stood, close behind a single young man in the line. Suddenly and unexpectedly, the young man broke wind, making quite a loud sound. The young woman excitedly tapped him on the shoulder and said, "Say, can you tell me where you found beans?"

This joke was one of many told by Bosnians during the hellish days of siege by Serbian forces. Bosnians thought that the joke was hilariously funny even though it involved the horrible experience that they faced. Interestingly, people in the United States also thought it to be funny as well. Anthropologists have argued that humor is universal. Is it possible that certain types of humor span cultural boundaries?

The question is important to advertisers because of their desire to standardize their marketing message across cultures. Humor can lower counterargumentation and improve attitudes toward the ad and brand. If it could be employed cross-culturally, it would substantially increase the cost effectiveness of advertising campaigns.

Recently, researchers tested the theory that humor results from incongruity or deviations from expectations. Thus a joke first creates incongruity. Then, the tension of the incongruity is broken in a playful way by a punchline that resolves the incongruity. For example, in the "water line" joke, breaking wind in a situation that could have romantic overtones is incongruous. Indeed, the normal reaction of people to someone else passing gas is disgust. However, in the punchline, the young woman's sudden interest in where the young man found the beans, which must have been responsible for his flatulence, is unexpected, but logical, given her situation. It resolves the incongruity in a playful way, and it makes us laugh.

In their study, the researchers rated over 1,000 television advertisements played in four countries—the United States, Germany, Thailand, and South Korea. Each of the ads was rated on whether or not the advertiser intended to create humor in the commercial. Overall, 15% of the ads employed humor, ranging from a high of 20% in Germany to a low of 10% in Korea. Among the ads intending humor, about 60% contained elements of incongruity.

The authors interpreted the results to indicate that the use of incongruity to create humor appears to be virtually universal. As such, ads that employ incongruity may have universal appeal. The authors also suggested, however, that it will also probably be necessary to adapt the ad in its creative presentation so as to conform to the norms and values of the culture. The goal of using humor cross-culturally, then, would be to design advertising that employs an underlying message that appeals worldwide while allowing for modification in each market.

Based upon Dana L. Alden, Wayne D. Hoyer, and Chol Lee, "Identifying Global and Culture-Specific Dimensions of Humor in Advertising: A Multinational Analysis," *Journal of Marketing*, Vol. 57 (April 1993), pp. 64–75.

Highly vivid information, however, does not always create more favorable impressions among consumers. Under some circumstances, vivid information may actually cause attitudes to become negative. The **availability–valence hypothesis**, which was developed to explain this phenomenon, states that judgments depend on the favorableness of the information available in memory.[58] If the available information is positive, judgments tend to be positive. In contrast, if the information is negative, judgments tend to be negative. Information that is vivid tends to be placed into memory in a more elaborate manner. It develops more connections to other concepts in semantic memory and as a result can be more available for retrieval. The impact of the information on attitudes depends on the valence, or direction, of its affect. Thus, if the information is positively valenced, it tends to lead to a series of positive thoughts. Conversely, if the information is negatively valenced, it tends to lead to a series of negative thoughts.

Lectures and Dramas

An interesting distinction has been made between lectures and dramas in communications.[59] A **lecture** occurs when a source speaks directly to the audience in an attempt to inform and persuade. Basically, a lecture is like an oration in which evidence is presented and arguments are made. We often see lectures in television commercials. Here a source talks to the audience, giving them information about the product. In contrast to a lecture, a **drama** occurs through indirect address in which the characters speak to each other and not to the audience. A drama is like a movie or play. In a television commercial a drama could be a comic sketch, a cartoon, or two or more characters interacting with each other about a product. The viewer is an eavesdropper who observes an imaginary setting that concerns a product or service.

When a person receives a lecture, facts are given, and the consumer recognizes that a persuasion attempt is unfolding. In such cases, characteristics of the source become extremely important, and the advertiser must be concerned with the types of cognitive responses developed by the audience. Dramas may work through a different mechanism. Because dramas are stories about the world, observational learning may occur. Viewers learn from the lessons revealed by the models in the communication. When a commercial drama rings true, the consumer is drawn into it and develops conclusions that may be applied to everyday life. As a result, less opportunity may exist for the consumer to develop counterarguments.

An example of a lecture in a print advertisement is found in messages by Mobil Corporation that appeared in major news magazines in 1988. Entitled "Something's Fishy Offshore," the corporate advertisement noted that for many years environmentalists had opposed drilling for oil offshore. The company noted that each time an application was made to drill, environmentalists would oppose the efforts because the rigs are "unsightly, messy, and will foul the seas and destroy the fish that dwell therein." The advertisement then pointed out that some environmental groups oppose the removal of offshore rigs because they provide a sanctuary for sea life. One entrepreneur even harvested mussels from rigs and sold them at premium prices. The ad concluded with the following paragraph:

> Seriously folks, here are the questions we'd like to pose. If rigs are the bane of the environmental movement, by what logic can environmentalists mourn their demise? Or could it be that rigs—and offshore drilling—aren't so bad after all?

Lectures can present information in a highly condensed form. However, they can frequently be dry and boring. In contrast, dramas have the potential to increase audience interest by creating emotional responses and by potentially transforming the meaning of using a product. **Transformational advertising** succeeds when a consumer associates the experience of using a product with a set of psychological characteristics not typically associated with the use of a product.[60] For example, an advertisement in which a woman is swept off her feet by an impassioned lover after getting the dishes "squeaky clean" is attempting to transform the experience of washing dishes. Normally, one does not associate sex with dishwashing. Such a commercial attempts to transform the experience by giving it a new psychological meaning.

When successful, such transformational ads are highly experiential. They involve the audience emotionally in the advertisement. They change how the audience thinks and feels about the product or service advertised. The marketing of perfume and colognes is based largely on attempts to transform the dabbing of something on one's skin into a romantic, sensual experience. In fact, one goal of such ads seems to be to transform a woman (man) into a gorgeous (handsome) creature having tremendous allure to the opposite sex.

Researchers have begun the process of investigating the effects of dramas and lectures on consumer information processing. In one study, respondents were shown one of four advertisements for Subaru automobiles.[61] The ads ranged in style from a strict lecture format to a straight drama. In the lecture format, a spokesperson made a series of claims about the quality of the car, including the statement that "in a recent consumer survey, consumers rated Subaru second only to Mercedes-Benz in terms of consumer satisfaction." In the straight drama ad, a college-age male asks his dad what kind of new car he should get. The father says, "Get another Subaru—it's been good to us." In the next scene the young man is seen speeding around the countryside in a new sports car. He gets home and his father is totally dismayed that his son would go against his advice, saying, "I thought we agreed you'd buy a Subaru." Acting as though he were astonished that his dad would doubt him, the son says, "But dad, I did."

When respondents were shown the ads, they reacted quite differently to the drama ad in contrast to the lecture ad. The lecture format ad resulted in more counterarguments. In addition, respondents seeing the lecture ad revealed much less empathy and self-participation with the events in the ad.

Similar results were found in a much larger study in which over 1,000 participants each rated 1 of 40 television ads that ranged in format from straight lecture to straight drama. Overall, researchers found no difference in the effectiveness of drama and lecture ads. What they did find, however, was that consumers reacted differently to them. The researchers found that the good drama ads were associated with the expression of greater amounts of feeling and less counterargumentation. In addition, the drama ads increased the respondents' perception of the authenticity of the commercial as well as their empathy toward the ad. In sum, they found that lectures were processed evaluatively, whereas dramas were processed empathically. Thus effective lectures depended upon the quality of the arguments overcoming the counterargumentation that resulted. In contrast, effective dramas worked to the extent that they involved consumers emotionally and to the extent that they seemed authentic and created empathy.[62]

Consumer responses to transformational versus informational ads also change depending upon the length of a television commercial. A recent study found that attitudes toward the ad and purchase intentions were higher when a 30-second, rather than a 15-second, version of a transformational ad was employed. In contrast, attitudes and purchase intentions actually decreased when respondents viewed the longer versions of informational ads.[63]

Table 10-4 summarizes the thoughts of one noted researcher/practitioner on what makes lectures and dramas effective.

TABLE 10-4

Effective Lectures and Dramas

I. Effective lectures
- **A.** Lecturer must have *credibility.*
- **B.** Lecture should attract attention via relevant means.
- **C.** Lecturer must appreciate the audience and not talk down.
- **D.** Lecturer should use illustrations relevant to the lecture.
- **E.** Lecturer should use illustrations that do not overwhelm the message.

II. Effective dramas
- **A.** Dramas must pass the *realism test.* (They must live up to the viewer's standards of what seems realistic.)
- **B.** Dramas can use fantasy. (However, characters must follow the rules of the fantasy.)
- **C.** In dramas the characters do *not* lecture each other. (This is not realistic.)
- **D.** The drama must be about the brand.
- **E.** The drama must be rich enough to engage the viewer.

SOURCE: William Wells, "Lectures and Dramas," in *Cognitive and Affective Responses to Advertising,* P. Cafferata and A. Tybout, eds. (Boston: D. C. Heath, 1987).

Life Themes and Message Construction

Researchers who approach the study of consumer behavior from an experiential perspective and who employ naturalistic research methodologies tend to focus on understanding the meanings derived by receivers of communications. They ask such questions as: "What meanings do the Pillsbury Doughboy and 'Old Joe' the Camel cigarette animal communicate to consumers?" One important finding of the research is that consumers interpret communications from the perspective of their own lives. Consider the copy presented here that was contained in an advertisement for Georgia-Pacific that appeared in *Newsweek* magazine in October 1993:

> You've remade yourself a hundred times, searching for what would fit, and last. College kid, philosopher, James Dean wannabe. Now you're looking at an ad for vinyl siding and it is stirring you to imagine ways of remaking your living space. Would you say your interests have evolved?

The ad then continues by identifying one of vinyl siding's key attributes—it is trouble free because it does not need to be repainted. Targeted to long-time homeowners (middle-class people 50 plus years old), the ad connects vinyl siding to their current life theme (that is, wanting to minimize hassle and future costs when they live on a fixed retirement income).

While the life theme of avoiding hassle and minimizing future costs appeals to older consumers, it is completely inappropriate for younger people. One researcher did in-depth case studies of three brothers (in their mid-thirties) who lived in Copenhagen, Denmark.[64] The researcher carefully probed the meanings that they extracted from advertisements and how these meanings fit into their life themes. For example, the life themes of one brother (code-named Anders) appeared to revolve around obtaining freedom and status. Such themes were exhibited in his interpretation of an advertisement for an expensive suit of clothes made by Lezard. For Anders, the Lezard suit was desirable because it symbolized economic achievement and the idea that only a few successful people, such as himself, could afford it. He obtained status by linking himself to the upper-class images portrayed in the print ad. He felt freedom because his wealth gave him new purchase options and opportunities.

From a managerial perspective, it is important to identify the life themes that dominate the thinking of important market segments. By linking an advertisement to life themes (e.g., freedom, achievement, and the avoidance of hassle mentioned above), it is more likely that consumers' level of attention and involvement will go higher. In addition, more positive attitudes toward the ad are likely to be created. Much more research, however, is required on the concept of life themes. Work is needed to further clarify the types of life themes used by consumers and how to measure them.

Message Structure

Although communicators must worry about message content, they must also be concerned with how the messages are structured. **Message structure** refers to how the source organizes the content of the message. For example, one major issue concerns where in the message important information should be placed. Another structural problem concerns how many times key pieces of information should be repeated in a message. For example, how many times in an advertisement should the brand name be mentioned?

Primacy and Recency Effects

Primacy and recency effects refer to the relative impact of information placed either at the beginning or the end of a message. A **primacy effect** occurs when material early in the message has the most influence; a **recency effect** occurs when material at the end of the message has the most influence. The question is not trivial. Either in a television commercial or in a formal presentation by a salesperson, the communicator wants to ensure that each piece of information has the maximum impact on the receiver. In addition, primacy and recency effects can occur when a series of messages is received. For example, when a number of commercials appear in succession on television, do those at the beginning, middle, or end of the sequence have the most impact?

Like research on other aspects of the message, the findings on primacy and recency effects have been somewhat mixed. One study found some evidence that, over time, primacy effects have more impact than recency effects. The researchers argued that the material heard early in the message tends to be persuasive for the simple reason that it is heard first. However, this material also tends to be forgotten quickly. Consequently, material heard at the end of the message may be remembered relatively better if the message is long and the response is assessed soon after the message is given. In contrast, if a delay occurs between the message and when the measure of persuasion is taken, a primacy effect will tend to be found. This occurs because both parts of the message will have had time to decay substantially, and the intrinsically more persuasive early parts of the message will then predominate.[65] This study suggests that the primacy effect may predominate over the long haul.

One finding can be stated unequivocally, however. Material presented in the middle of a message is relatively poorly remembered and has the least impact. Research on serial learning presented in Chapter 4 demonstrates the greater difficulty in retaining information placed in the middle of lists of material to be learned. Therefore, communicators should try to avoid placing the important parts of a message in the middle of a communication.

Repetition Effects

In Chapter 5, Behavioral Learning, the importance of repetition for learning was discussed. Whether for classical conditioning, operant conditioning, or cognitive learning, repetition of information must take place. With this knowledge in mind, the major question becomes one of how often the information should be repeated. Herbert Krugman has suggested that as few as three exposures to an advertisement may be sufficient.[66] In organizing an advertising strategy, marketers must consider **repetition effects**. Indeed, evidence suggests that too much repetition may result in consumers becoming increasingly negative toward the message. Such increased negativity has been called **advertising wear-out**.

Advertising wear-out was found in one study where members of church groups received either one, three, or five exposures to an advertisement for a fictitious toothpaste during a one-hour television show. The results of the study revealed that the number of counterarguments to the commercials increased as the number of repetitions increased.[67] Other researchers have likewise found that too much repetition can cause attitudes toward the ad to become more negative.[68]

Sophisticated advertisers, however, rarely present the same commercial over and over again. Instead, they create a series of different ads that carry the same basic message. In one study researchers tested such an approach by varying the content of each ad slightly. In this study the number of positive cognitive responses increased and the number of negative cognitive responses decreased as the message was repeated.[69]

Two-factor theory is a theoretical explanation of the overall effects of message repetition proposing that two different psychological processes are operating as people receive repetitive messages. In one process the repetition of a message causes a reduction in uncertainty and increased learning about the stimulus, resulting in a positive response.[70] However, in the other process tedium or boredom begins to occur with each repetition. At some point the tedium overtakes the positive effects, and the receiver begins to react negatively to the ad. Two-factor theory suggests that, to avoid the negative effects of boredom, the communicator should vary the ad with each repetition. Figure 10-10 diagrams the proposed relationships.[71]

In general, then, good evidence exists that advertising wear-out is a potential problem for corporations. The problem may be particularly acute for advertisements that use an informational approach, a hard-sell approach, or an irritating approach. A strategy that minimizes the effects of wear-out is to vary the execution of the ads so that the same message is conveyed via different ads. The advertising campaign for Miller Lite Beer illustrates this advertising concept. A storyboard from the series is shown in Figure 10-11. Such a strategy should be particularly effective when the purchase decision is low involvement in nature.[72]

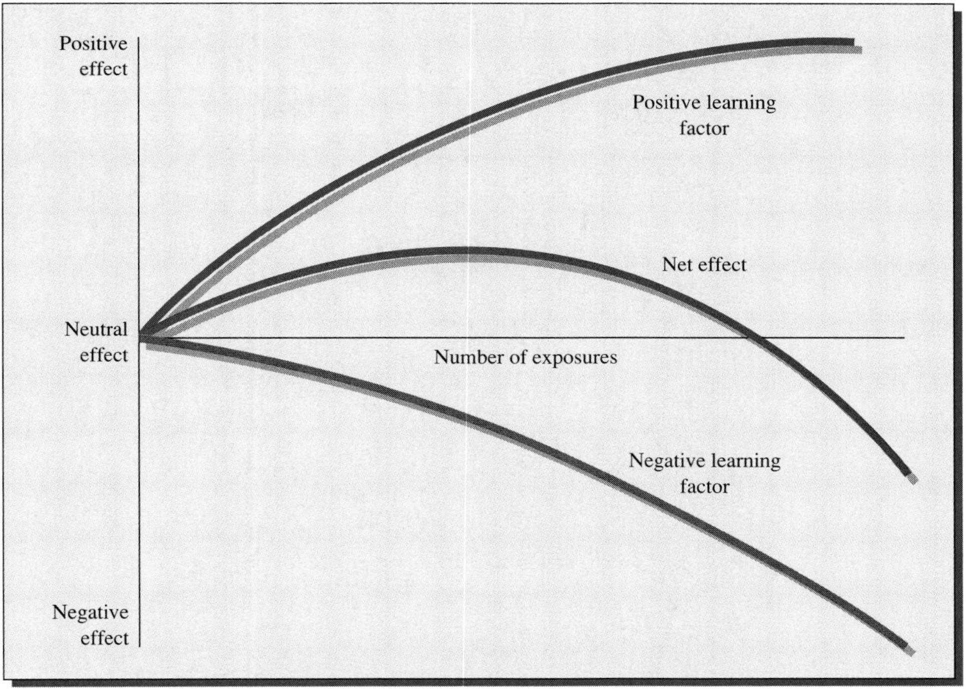

Figure 10-10 Two-factor theory and advertising wear-out. (Source: Amo Rethans, John Swasy, and Lawrence Marks, "Effects of Television Commercial Repetition, Receiver Knowledge, and Commercial Length: A Test of the Two-Factor Model," *Journal of Marketing Research*, Vol. 23, February 1986, pp. 59–61, published by the American Marketing Association.)

A MANAGERIAL APPLICATIONS EXAMPLE

In April 1986 E. F. Hutton, the large brokerage company, pleaded guilty to federal fraud charges. Partly in response to the public relations nightmare, the company hired Bill Cosby to act as a spokesperson. Some advertising professionals praised the choice of Cosby. One individual said, "They need to do something to repair the damage. It certainly won't rub off on Mr. Cosby, but he just might rub off on the company and it could be a stroke of genius." Another person said, "A lot of Bill Cosby's appeal for consumers is his easy and natural association with an important part of our lives: the goods and services we consume." The president of an ad agency on the West Coast described Cosby as "so nice and warm that it will have to rub off on the company in a positive way. His friendly, offhanded humor will make the company seem human, which is important in that type of business."[73]

Many advertising professionals, however, had severe misgivings about using Bill Cosby. One critic said, "Everybody loves Bill Cosby. To put it succinctly, I don't buy stocks from my grocer and I don't buy Jell-O from my stockbroker. The

Figure 10-11 The Miller Lite campaign avoided the effects of advertising wear-out by varying the content of the ads in the long-running campaign. (Courtesy of Miller Brewing Company.)

audience buying stocks is more sophisticated than the audience buying Jell-O, and if they feel they're being talked down to, it could have a backlash effect." Another observer noted, "Unless Cosby is recognized as a shrewd investor, I don't know what the fit is. The connection between an investment house and a Jell-O huckster and a Coke huckster is not immediately evident." Cosby's potential overexposure was also mentioned by some. "My problem with the whole thing is that I think he is borderline overexposed already. If I were Jell-O and Coke, I would be concerned that his appeal would be diluted."

Another perspective on the issue concerned what Cosby would say. One analyst said, "It all depends on how he will be used—will he stand up and stare, à la John Houseman, or will he be in the slice-of-life vignettes, or will they use him as an investor?" A New York City adman believed that the whole thing "depends on the idea and what he says."

The Consumer Behavior Analysis

A number of consumer concepts from the chapter apply to the problem of predicting how effective Bill Cosby would be as a spokesperson for E. F. Hutton. A careful reading of the comments by the advertising professionals revealed that they were particularly concerned with the effectiveness of Cosby as a source. They recognized his personal appeal and likability. However, several questioned his expertise in the brokerage business. If he failed to be perceived as having expertise in investing, the target market's perception of his credibility would be lowered. In addition, analysts were also concerned with his overexposure in numerous advertisements. If customers attributed his endorsement of E. F. Hutton to Cosby's desire to make money rather than to his belief in the company, their trust would be lowered. A combination of the perceptions of low trust and low expertise would lead to an ineffective endorsement.

The importance of the message was also emphasized by several of the analysts. A critical issue was what Cosby would say. With Cosby known for his humor, would a humorous appeal be appropriate? It seems likely that a humorous appeal would fail to match up with the type of message that would have to be delivered in a situation where a company was attempting to recover from criminal charges. Perhaps a lecture format would be most effective in such circumstances.

The importance of understanding the receiver of the communication was also mentioned by the advertising professionals. They noted that investors are sophisticated individuals. Would they respond favorably to a likable person who was known for a comedy show and for having previously endorsed such products as a gelatin dessert, a soft drink, a car, and a computer?

The Managerial Applications Analysis

Table 10-5 presents the managerial applications analysis for the E. F. Hutton case. Four consumer concepts from the chapter have specific managerial implications: source effects, message effects, match-up effects, and receiver effects. In each case, the concepts apply to market research and to the promotional strategy of the firm.

A major issue concerns whether Bill Cosby was an appropriate source to employ in the circumstances that E. F. Hutton faced. The investigation of source effects can be applied to market research, promotional strategy, and company positioning. Clearly, market research was required to analyze potential consumer reactions to his endorsement. Would consumers perceive him to have the expertise to endorse an investment firm? Would his many other endorsements cause consumers to distrust him? On the other hand, perhaps a likable personality might be effective in such circumstances. Only through market research could information relevant to these questions be obtained. Managers should also recognize that using Bill Cosby would influence the entire promotional strategy of the firm. Would he become a permanent spokesperson, or would he merely be used in this particular circumstance? In addition, if Cosby were used any length of time, he would have a strong impact on how

TABLE 10-5

A Managerial Applications Analysis of the Bill Cosby Case

Consumer Concepts	*Managerial Concepts*
Source effects	*Market research*—Analyze consumer reactions to the endorsement by Bill Cosby.
	Promotional strategy—Decide if you would employ Cosby as permanent endorser.
	Positioning strategy—Determine the effects that using Cosby will have on the positioning of the company. Will he cause the company to be viewed as being less serious?
Message effects	*Market research*—Conduct focus groups in which consumers are exposed to different versions of the message and obtain reactions.
	Promotional strategy—Suggest the type of message that would be most effective for Cosby to use. (In the end, a lecture format was chosen.)
Match-up effects	*Market research*—Perform analyses to determine the extent to which the target market perceives that Cosby matches a brokerage firm.
	Promotional strategy—Carefully consider the meanings that Cosby brings which will be associated with the firm. Analyze how the message can be constructed that links the positive aspects of Cosby's meanings to the firm.
Receiver effects	*Market research*—Conduct analyses to determine if there are different groups of consumers that will respond divergently to Cosby as the spokesperson.
	Segmentation—Consider developing different messages for the different groups or reaching the groups via different media.

the firm was positioned in consumers' minds. Hutton would have to recognize that the use of Bill Cosby could position the company as less serious, and perhaps more human, than other brokerage companies. E. F. Hutton managers would have to analyze their positioning strategy when they employed Cosby.

The type of message used by Cosby would be crucial for the success of the campaign. As it turned out, he used a lecture format in which he spoke directly to the audience in a warm and reassuring manner. In such circumstances, it is important for firms to carefully analyze reactions of the target market to the endorser and the message communicated.

Of particular concern in the case was whether Cosby matched up with the company and the message. Again market research had to be performed in which members of the target market viewed Cosby giving different messages. The goal was to find the message that linked Cosby to the company and to the message in a believable manner.

Finally, the company had to be vitally concerned with receiver effects. E. F. Hutton was attempting to reach a number of different market segments. The company had to determine if these different groups reacted differentially to Cosby and his message.

As it turns out, E. F. Hutton employed Bill Cosby for only a short time. Although no public information is available regarding the success of the campaign, little evidence exists that the use of the likable comedian was beneficial to E. F.

Hutton. Indeed, such an outcome would be expected from the consumer behavior analysis. Cosby's lack of credibility in the financial area, his overexposure, and the inability to match up his personal qualities with an investment company would make success unlikely.

SUMMARY

The general model of communications consists of a number of components, including source, message, medium, receiver, feedback, noise, and environmental context. In this chapter three major source characteristics were identified. The first characteristic, source credibility, is the extent to which the audience perceives the sender to have expertise and trustworthiness. Highly credible sources have been found to produce greater attitude and behavioral change in response to a communication. They may enhance the effectiveness of fear appeals and lower the counterarguments of audiences. However, for audiences already favorable to a topic, moderately credible sources show some evidence of being more effective.

The second source characteristic is physical attractiveness. In general, research shows that physically attractive communicators are more successful than unattractive sources. However, managers should be careful not to mistake a sexually suggestive communicator for a physically attractive source. In some instances the use of sexually suggestive ads can be counterproductive.

Likability, the third major characteristic, is the extent to which the source creates positive or negative feelings in the audience. Research evidence on the persuasive impact of likable and unlikable sources is mixed, and additional work is necessary before firm conclusions can be drawn on its impact.

Characteristics of the message are another important dimension of the communications process. Messages may have differential impacts depending upon their content and their structure. One content factor is the complexity of the message. Other content factors include whether conclusions are drawn, whether comparative messages are provided, whether the messages are one-sided or two-sided, whether fear appeals or humorous appeals are used, whether concrete or abstract information is included in the message, and whether a drama or lecture format is used. When studying message structure, the consumer researcher should focus on whether consumers may be influenced by primacy or recency effects. Another structural factor to consider is the amount of repetition required to influence the consumer.

KEY TERMS

advertising wear-out
availability–valence hypothesis
channels
cognitive responses
communication
communications model
comparative messages
direct comparative advertisements
dramas
drawing conclusions
fear appeal
humor in messages
indirect comparative advertisements
lectures
market research
match-up hypothesis
message characteristics
message complexity
message construction
message content
message structure
one-sided messages
primacy and recency effects
repetition effects
sign
source
source characteristics
source credibility
source expertise
source likability

source physical attractiveness
source trustworthiness
transformational advertising
two-factor theory
two-sided messages
vehicles
vivid messages

REVIEW QUESTIONS

1. Draw the communications model presented in the text. Briefly discuss each of the components of the model.
2. Identify six different methods for varying message content presented in the text.
3. What are the reasons for and against using comparative advertisements?
4. When should a communicator consider using a two-sided message? A one-sided message?
5. What are the elements a message should have to be an effective fear appeal?
6. Identify the advantages and disadvantages of using humor in messages.
7. What are three factors that tend to make messages more vivid?
8. Identify a potential theoretical explanation for why advertising wear-out occurs.
9. What are the basic source characteristics identified in the text?
10. What are the components of source credibility?
11. What are the benefits of using highly credible sources?
12. What are the benefits and liabilities of using sexually explicit ads?
13. What are the differential communications effects of lectures and dramas?
14. What is transformational advertising?

DISCUSSION QUESTIONS

1. Briefly describe a television, a print, and a billboard advertisement. Using the communications model, discuss each of the advertisements. (What source characteristics and message techniques are being used?)
2. Identify one excellent and one poor example of television ads that use celebrity endorsers. Discuss the factors that influence the effectiveness of the ads.
3. Write a television ad for your university. Create two versions—a lecture approach and a drama approach.
4. You are the account executive for an advertising firm working on developing a comparative advertising campaign for the Chrysler Fifth Avenue. The Fifth Avenue's major competitors are the midsize and larger cars produced by General Motors and Ford—such as the Ford Grand Marquis, the Buick LeSabre, and the Oldsmobile Delta 88. Try to sketch out a print advertisement that uses a comparative ad format. What things should you consider when developing the ad?
5. Identify three brands or types of products or services that you believe should use one-sided messages and three brands or types of products or services that you believe should use two-sided messages in their advertising. Explain your answers.
6. Go through magazines and find a print ad that uses a fear appeal. Criticize the ad based upon the criteria that have been identified as necessary for the creation of good fear appeals.
7. While you are watching television, identify a commercial that uses humor. Discuss the effectiveness of the advertisement. What do you think were the advertising goals of the sponsors of the ad?
8. Write the copy of a print ad for the Porsche 944 directed to high-involvement consumers. In the ad use highly concrete words and imagery.

ENDNOTES

1. Patrick McGeehan, "Endorsement KO? Marketers Grow Wary of Tyson," *Advertising Age*, July 4, 1988, p. 3.
2. Gary Levin, "Baseball's Endorsement Shutout," *Advertising Age*, February 15, 1993, p. 16.
3. Janice Steinberg, "Suzuki Acts to Right Slipping Samurai Sales," *Advertising Age*, July 25, 1988, p. S–10.
4. Alix Freedman, "Marriages Between Celebrity Spokesmen and Their Firms Can Be Risky Ventures," *The Wall Street Journal*, January 22, 1988, p. 17.
5. C. I. Hovland and I. L. Janis, *Personality and Persuasibility* (New Haven, CT: Yale University Press, 1959).
6. Terrence Shimp, "Methods of Commercial Presentation Employed by National Television Advertisers," *Journal of Advertising*, Vol. 5 (Fall 1976), pp. 30–36.
7. Elizabeth J. Wilson and Daniel L. Sherrell, "Source Effects in Communication and Persuasion Research: A Meta-Analysis of Effect Size," *Journal of the Academy of Marketing Science*, Vol. 21, no. 2 (Spring 1993), pp. 101–112.
8. Readers should note that not all researchers define trust in the manner described here. In some cases, trust has been defined as including expertise within its bounds. That is, trust is defined in the same manner as I have defined credibility in the chapter. For an example, see Christine Moorman, Rohit Deshpande, and Gerald Zaltman, "Factors Affecting Trust in Market Research Relationships," *Journal of Marketing*, Vol. 57 (January 1993), pp. 81–101.
9. Josh Wiener and John C. Mowen, "The Impact of Product Recalls on Consumer Perceptions," *Mobius: The Journal of the Society of Consumer Affairs Professionals in Business* (Spring 1985), pp. 18–21.
10. For an excellent review of the material on source credibility, see Brian Sternthal, Lynn Phillips, and Ruby Dholakia, "The Persuasive Effect of Source Credibility: A Situational Analysis," *Public Opinion Quarterly*, Vol. 42 (Fall 1978), pp. 285–314.
11. Peter Wright, "Cognitive Processes Mediating Acceptance of Advertising," *Journal of Marketing Research*, Vol. 10 (February 1973), pp. 53–62.
12. Brian Sternthal, Ruby Dholakia, and Clark Leavitt, "The Persuasive Effect of Source Credibility: Tests of Cognitive Response," *Journal of Consumer Research*, Vol. 4 (March 1978), pp. 252–260. The reason for the surprising finding lies in the nature of the cognitive responses elicited by highly credible and moderately credible endorsers. See the following article for a study on the topic: Ruby Roy Dholakia, "Source Credibility: A Test of Behavioral Persistence," in *Advances in Consumer Research*, Vol. 15, Melanie Wallendorf and Paul Anderson, eds. (Provo, UT: Association for Consumer Research, 1987), pp. 426–430.
13. Shelley Chaiken, "Communicator Physical Attractiveness and Persuasion," *Journal of Personality and Social Psychology*, Vol. 37 (August 1979), pp. 1387–1397.
14. Karen Dion, E. Berscheid, and E. Walster, "What Is Beautiful Is Good," *Journal of Personality and Social Psychology*, Vol. 24 (December 1972), pp. 285–290.
15. Kathleen Debevec and Jerome Kernan, "More Evidence on the Effects of Presenter's Physical Attractiveness: Some Cognitive, Affective, and Behavioral Consequences," in *Advances in Consumer Research*, Vol. 11, Thomas Kinnear, ed. (Provo, UT: Association for Consumer Research, 1984), pp. 127–132. For additional information on the impact of attractiveness, see also Paul Speck, David Schumann, and Craig Thompson, "Celebrity Endorsements—Scripts, Schema and Roles: Theoretical Framework and Preliminary Tests," in *Advances in Consumer Research*, Vol. 15, Michael Houston, ed. (Provo, UT: Association for Consumer Research, 1988), pp. 69–76.
16. M. Steadman, "How Sexy Illustrations Affect Brand Recall," *Journal of Advertising Research*,

Vol. 9 (March 1969), pp. 15–19. Also see Robert Chestnut, Charles LaChance, and Amy Lubitz, "The Decorative Female Model: Sexual Stimuli and the Recognition of Advertisements," *Journal of Advertising*, Vol. 6 (Fall 1977), pp. 11–14.

17. Michael Baker and Gilbert Churchill, "The Impact of Physically Attractive Models on Advertising Evaluations," *Journal of Marketing Research*, Vol. 14 (November 1977), pp. 538–555.

18. Anne M. Brumbaugh, "Physical Attractiveness and Personality in Advertising: More Than Just a Pretty Face?" in *Advances in Consumer Research*, Vol. 20, Leigh McAlister and Michael L. Rothschild, eds. (Provo, UT: Association for Consumer Research, 1993), pp. 159–164.

19. Jean-Charles Chebat, Michael Laroche, Daisy Baddoura, and Pierre Filiatrault, "Effects of Source Likability on Attitude Change Through Message Repetition," in *Advances in Consumer Research*, Vol. 20, Leigh McAlister and Michael L. Rothschild, eds. (Provo, UT: Association for Consumer Research, 1993), pp. 353–358.

20. Kahle and Homer, "Physical Attractiveness of the Celebrity Endorser."

21. Michael Schudson, *Advertising, the Uneasy Persuasion* (New York: Basic Books, 1984), p. 212.

22. Grant McCracken, "Who Is the Celebrity Endorser? Cultural Foundations of the Endorsement Process," *Journal of Consumer Research*, Vol. 16 (December 1989), pp. 310–321.

23. Lynn Langmeyer and Mary Walker, "A First Step to Identify the Meaning in Celebrity Endorsers," in *Advances in Consumer Research*, Vol. 18, Rebecca Holman and Michael Solomon, eds. (Provo, UT: Association for Consumer Research, 1991), pp. 364–371.

24. David Ogilvy, *Ogilvy on Advertising* (New York: Vintage Books, 1983).

25. Joanne Lipman, "Name Two U.S. Stars Reluctant to Appear in TV Ads in Japan: Finding Even One Isn't Easy as Money Defeats Pride; They Still Say 'No' in the States," *The Wall Street Journal*, November 4, 1987, pp. 1, 18.

26. Tina Kiesler, "The Flip Side of the Persuasion Equation: Does a Product Influence a Spokesperson's Public Image?" in *Advances in Consumer Research*, Vol. 15, Michael Houston, ed. (Provo, UT: Association for Consumer Research, 1988), pp. 62–68.

27. Alice Eagly, "The Comprehensibility of Persuasive Arguments as a Determinant of Opinion Change," *Journal of Personality and Social Psychology*, Vol. 29 (1974), pp. 758–773.

28. Bertram Raven and Jeffrey Rubin, *Social Psychology* (New York: John Wiley, 1983).

29. Alan G. Sawyer and Daniel J. Howard, "Effects of Omitting Conclusions in Advertisements to Involved and Uninvolved Audiences," *Journal of Marketing Research*, Vol. 28 (November 1991), pp. 467–474.

30. Kanti V. Prasad, "Communications Effectiveness of Comparative Advertising: A Laboratory Analysis," *Journal of Marketing Research*, Vol. 13 (May 1976), pp. 128–137.

31. Gerald Gorn and Charles Weinberg, "The Impact of Comparative Advertising on Perception and Attitude: Some Positive Findings," *Journal of Consumer Research*, Vol. 11 (September 1984), pp. 719–727.

32. William Wilkie and Paul Farris, "Comparison Advertising: Problems and Potential," *Journal of Marketing*, Vol. 39 (November 1975), pp. 7–15.

33. "Creating a Mass Market for Wine," *Business Week*, March 15, 1982, pp. 108–118.

34. Gorn and Weinberg, "Comparative Advertising."

35. Cornelia Broge and Rene Darmon, "Associative Positioning Strategies Through Comparative Advertising: Attribute Versus Overall Similarity Approaches," *Journal of Marketing Research*, Vol. 24 (November 1987), pp. 377–388.

36. Cornelia Pechmann and S. Ratneshwar, "The Use of Comparative Advertising for Brand Positioning: Association Versus

Differentiation," *Journal of Consumer Research*, Vol. 18 (September 1991), pp. 145–160.

37. Cornelia Pechmann and David W. Stewart, "The Effects of Comparative Advertising on Attention, Memory, and Purchase Intentions," *Journal of Consumer Research*, Vol. 17 (September 1990), pp. 180–191.

38. See, for example, studies by Russell Jones and Jack Brehm, "Persuasiveness of One- and Two-Sided Communications as a Function of Awareness: There Are Two Sides," *Journal of Experimental Social Psychology*, Vol. 6 (1970), pp. 47–56; Alan G. Sawyer, "The Effects of Repetition of Refutational and Supportive Advertising Appeals," *Journal of Marketing Research*, Vol. 10 (February 1973), pp. 23–33; and Michael Kamins and Henry Assael, "Two-Sided Versus One-Sided Appeals: A Cognitive Perspective on Argumentation, Source Derogation on Argumentation, Source Derogation, and the Effect of Disconfirming Trial on Belief Change," *Journal of Marketing Research*, Vol. 24 (February 1987), pp. 29–39.

39. G. C. Chu, "Prior Familiarity, Perceived Bias, and One-Sided Versus Two-Sided Communications," *Journal of Experimental Social Psychology*, Vol. 3 (1967), pp. 243–254.

40. Raven and Rubin, *Social Psychology*.

41. Ibid.

42. Cornelia (Connie) Pechmann, "How Do Consumer Inferences Moderate the Effectiveness of Two-Sided Messages?" *Advances in Consumer Research*, Vol. 17, Marvin E. Goldberg, Gerald Gorn, and Richard Pollay, eds. (Provo, UT: Association for Consumer Research, 1990), pp. 337–341.

43. The failure of two-sided messages to produce attitude change was illustrated in a study by Manoj Hastak and Jong-Won Park, "Mediators of Message Sidedness Effects on Cognitive Structure for Involved and Uninvolved Audiences," in *Advances in Consumer Research*, Vol. 17, Marvin E. Goldberg, Gerald Gorn, and Richard Pollay, eds. (Provo, UT: Association for Consumer Research, 1990), pp. 337–341.

44. John F. Tanner, Jr., James B. Hunt, and David R. Eppright, "The Protection Motivation Model: A Normative Model of Fear Appeals," *Journal of Marketing* (July 1991), pp. 329–336.

45. Dana L. Alden, Wayne D. Hoyer, and Chol Lee, "Identifying Global and Culture-Specific Dimensions of Humor in Advertising: A Multinational Analysis," *Journal of Marketing*, Vol. 57 (April 1993), pp. 64–75. Also, see Brian Sternthal and C. Samuel Craig, "Humor in Advertising," *Journal of Marketing*, Vol. 37 (October 1973), pp. 12–18.

One critical issue concerns the question, "What makes something humorous?" This topic is beyond the scope of this textbook. However, for a related discussion, see the Alden, Hoyer, and Lee article cited in this reference. Also, see "Edward F. McQuarrie and David Glen Mick, "On Resonance: A Critical Pluralistic Inquiry into Advertising Rhetoric," *Journal of Consumer Research*, Vol. 19 (September 1992), pp. 180–197.

46. Joan Cantor and Pat Venus, "The Effects of Humor on the Recall of a Radio Advertisement," *Journal of Broadcasting* (Winter 1980), p. 14.

47. Michael Norman, "'Where's the Beef?' All Over Town," *The New York Times*, February 11, 1984, Sec. L, p. 32.

48. H. Bruce Lammers, "Humor and Cognitive Responses to Advertising Stimuli: A Trade Consolidation Approach," *Journal of Business Research*, Vol. 11 (June 1983), p. 182.

49. Sternthal and Craig, "Humor in Advertising." Also, see Thomas J. Madden and Marc Weinberger, "The Effects of Humor on Attention in Magazine Advertising," *Journal of Advertising*, Vol. 11 (March 1982), p. 1.

50. Cliff Scott, David M. Klein, and Jennings Bryant, "Consumer Responses to Humor in Advertising: A Series of Field Studies Using Behavioral Observation," *Journal of Consumer Research*, Vol. 16 (March 1990), pp. 498–501.

51. John H. Murphy, Isabella Cunningham, and Gary Wilcox, "The Impact of Program Environment on Recall of Humorous Television Commercials," *Journal of Advertising*, Vol. 8 (Spring 1979), pp. 17–21.

52. P. Kelly and Paul J. Solomon, "Humor in Television Advertising," *Journal of Advertising*, Vol. 4 (Summer 1975), pp. 33–35.

53. Young Zhang and George M. Zinkhan, "Humor in Advertising: The Effects of Repetition and Social Setting," in *Advances in Consumer Research*, Vol. 18, Rebecca Holman and Michael Solomon, eds. (Provo, UT: Association for Consumer Research, 1991), pp. 813–818.

54. Lammers, "Humor and Cognitive Responses."

55. Amitava Chattopadhyay and Kunal Basu, "Humor in Advertising: The Moderating Role of Prior Brand Evaluation," *Journal of Marketing Research*, Vol. 27 (November 1990), pp. 466–476. For another recent study on humor in advertising, see Stephen M. Smith, "Does Humor in Advertising Enhance Systematic Processing?" in *Advances in Consumer Research*, Vol. 20, Leigh McAlister and Michael L. Rothschild, eds. (Provo, UT: Association for Consumer Research, 1993), pp. 155–158. This author found evidence that humor in an ad tends to lead to more peripheral processing so that the strength of ad claims is not evaluated as closely as when more serious ads are employed. Thus a more humorous ad positively impacted ratings only when weak claims were employed.

56. This section relies heavily on material found in Richard Nisbett and Lee Ross, *Human Inference: Strategies and Shortcomings of Social Judgment* (Englewood Cliffs, NJ: Prentice-Hall, 1980).

57. Ibid.

58. Jolita Kisielius and Brian Sternthal, "Examining the Vividness Controversy: An Availability-Valence Interpretation," *Journal of Consumer Research*, Vol. 12 (March 1986), pp. 418–431.

59. William Wells, "Lectures and Dramas," presentation at Association of Consumer Research meeting, fall 1987.

60. Christopher Puto and William Wells, "Informational and Transformational Advertising: The Differential Effects of Time," in *Advances in Consumer Research*, Vol. 11, Thomas Kinnear, ed. (Provo, UT: Association for Consumer Research, 1984), pp. 638–643.

61. Gregory W. Boller, "The Vicissitudes of Product Experience: 'Songs of Our Consuming Selves' in Drama Ads," in *Advances in Consumer Research*, Vol. 17, Marvin E. Goldberg, Gerald Gorn, and Richard Pollay, eds. (Provo, UT: Association for Consumer Research, 1990), pp. 321–326.

62. John Deighton, Daniel Romer, and Josh McQueen, "Using Drama to Persuade," *Journal of Consumer Research*, Vol. 16 (December 1989), pp. 335–343.

63. Surendra N. Singh and Catherine A. Cole, "The Effects of Length, Content, and Repetition on Television Commercial Effectiveness," *Journal of Marketing Research*, Vol. 30 (February 1993), pp. 91–104.

64. Norman Miller and Donald Campbell, "Recency and Primacy in Persuasion as a Function of the Timing of Speeches and Measurement," *Journal of Abnormal and Social Psychology*, Vol. 59 (1959), pp. 1–9.

65. David Glen Mick and Claus Buhl, "A Meaning-Based Model of Advertising Experiences," *Journal of Consumer Research*, Vol. 19 (December 1992), pp. 317–338.

66. Herbert Krugman, "Why Three Exposures May Be Enough," *Journal of Advertising Research*, Vol. 12 (December 1972), pp. 11–14.

67. George E. Belch, "The Effects of Television Commercial Repetition on Cognitive Response and Message Acceptance," *Journal of Consumer Research*, Vol. 9 (June 1982), pp. 56–65.

68. Marian Burke and Julie Edell, "Ad Reactions over Time: Capturing Changes in the Real World," *Journal of Consumer Research*, Vol. 13 (June 1986), pp. 114–118.

69. See the following study for research that supports this conclusion: Dena Cox and Anthony Cox, "What Does Familiarity Breed? Complexity as a Moderator of Repetition Effects in Advertising Evaluation," *Journal of Consumer Research*, Vol. 15 (June 1988), pp. 111–116. Also, see Arno Rethans, John Swasy, and Lawrence Marks, "Effects of Television Commercial Repetition, Receiver Knowledge, and Commercial Length: A Test of the Two-Factor Model," *Journal of Marketing Research*, Vol. 23 (February 1986), pp. 50–61.

70. L. McCullough and Thomas Ostrom, "Repetition of Highly Similar Messages and Attitude Change," *Journal of Applied Psychology*, Vol. 59 (June 1974), pp. 395–397.

71. D. E. Berlyne, "Novelty, Complexity, and Hedonic Value," *Perception and Psychophysics*, Vol. 8 (November 1970), pp. 279–286.

72. The encoding variability hypothesis also applies to the effects of repetition. See H. Rao Unnava and Robert E. Burnkrant, "Effects of Repeating Varied Ad Executions on Brand Name Memory," *Journal of Marketing Research*, Vol. 28 (November 1991), pp. 406–416. Also, see Robert Burnkrant and Hanumantha Unnava, "Effect of Variation in Message Execution on the Learning of Repeated Brand Information," in *Advances in Consumer Research*, Vol. 14, Mellanie Wallendorf and Paul Anderson, eds. (Provo, UT: Association for Consumer Research, 1987), pp. 173–176.

73. David Schumann, Richard Petty, and D. Scott Clemons, "Predicting the Effectiveness of Different Strategies of Advertising Variation: A Test of the Repetition-Variation Hypotheses," *Journal of Consumer Research*, Vol. 17 (September 1990), pp. 192–202.

74. Information for the managerial example was taken from "E. F. Hutton's Spokesman Idea a 'Cos' Celebre," *Advertising Age*, April 21, 1986, pp. 1, 124.

CHAPTER 10 CASE STUDY

HIV Strikes "Magic"

The unexpected announcement shocked the world—"Magic" Johnson is HIV positive. Earlier in 1991, *The Wall Street Journal* had called him the "perfect advertising spokesman." As a celebrity spokesperson, Johnson ranked behind only Bo Jackson, Michael Jordan, and Tommy Lasorda as the most persuasive sports figure. He endorsed products for such firms as Nestlé, Converse, Nintendo, Pepsi-Cola, Spalding Sports, and Kentucky Fried Chicken. How would these companies, who paid Magic about $12 million a year for his endorsements, react to his condition?

Initially, the companies, like the world at large, were stunned. A spokesperson for Pepsi said, "There's no road map to tell us where to go. This is all very new and happened very suddenly. No decisions have been made, nor should they be." A manager at Spalding said that, although the company was shocked and dismayed, "Magic Johnson has been a member of the Spalding team since he came into the NBA. He's a very important part of our family, and we will support him and his commitment to HIV research" [1].

Although the companies with which he had contracts reacted cautiously and supported Johnson, industry analysts were not as sanguine about the situation. One analyst suggested that he would be used in public relations capacities to make him and the companies look good. Most observers noted that a serious danger exists of associating a brand with AIDS. One analyst said, "Magic deserved every bit of the tribute he's getting, but the initial coverage is going to be upbeat and positive, and then the reality is going to set in. This is not the kind of thing people want to see in advertising. Advertising is not about grim realities. Advertising is fantasy, and AIDS is not fantasy" [2].

One advertising executive said of the situation, "It's not so cut-and-dried with him. It's not like when Bruce Willis announced he would be going in for alcohol rehab, and they pulled all of the [Seagram's] ads immediately." Another analyst said, "There is a potential risk, and with anyone else they might not be sure, but Johnson has a unique status. If suddenly Converse or KFC yanked his contract, there would be a backlash against the brand. But companies will have to use 'soft sell' on the brand side because the public is going to be sensitive to a brand exploiting this" [3].

When attention shifts from Magic Johnson's endorsement of products to his efforts to educate the public on AIDS, the view of his effectiveness takes a 180-degree turn. One leader in the movement to fight AIDS among African-Americans said, "Even though this is a personal tragedy, there is an opportunity to turn this into something positive. I think it will change the way people not only perceive the disease and AIDS, but how they relate to people with HIV because they view him as everyman. They think that if he can get it, maybe I can too. Things will definitely change now that Magic Johnson has spoken out" [4].

QUESTIONS

1. Define the problem faced by firms having contracts with Magic Johnson to endorse their products. Define the problem faced by AIDS activists.

2. What consumer behavior concepts from the chapter apply to the case?
3. Develop and discuss two managerial applications analyses—one from the perspective of firms for which Magic endorses products and one from the perspective of the campaign to educate the public on AIDS.

NOTES

1. Gary Levin, "Johnson Plans for Future Ads," *Advertising Age*, November 18, 1991, p. 47.
2. "HIV Revelation Tests Magic's Ad Appeal," *Advertising Age*, November 11, 1991, p. 2.
3. Ibid.
4. Cyndee Miller, "Advertisers Forced to Rethink 'Magic' as Their Spokesman," *Marketing News*, December 9, 1991, pp. 1, 2.

Chapter

11

Consumer Decision Processes I: Problem Recognition and Search

CONSUMER VIGNETTE

Compact Disc Problems and Searching for Information About Cars

After listening to his friend's compact disc player, the stereo buff knew that his expensive phonograph produced inferior sound and that vinyl records were becoming relics of the past. As a result, he purchased a new Kenwood compact disc player. While feeding the beast new $14 discs, he realized that his speakers didn't sound quite right. After consultations with salespeople at a local stereo outlet, two models were brought to his home for a trial run. During the demonstrations, he learned that the tweeter had quit working in one of his old speakers. This difficulty was quickly remedied by the sweet-sounding Infinity Kappa 7 speakers that he purchased. However, another difficulty surfaced. His current amplifier had insufficient wattage to properly drive the new speakers. To remedy this problem, he replaced his perfectly working 35-watt Sherwood receiver with a new 95-watt Yamaha receiver. Though he initially intended to spend only $300, the total stereo investment came to over $2,400.[1]

In the "Buying Guide" issue of *Consumer Reports*, a consumer can find repair record ratings for nearly every car sold in the United States. For the preceding six model years, the cars are rated on a 5-point scale on 17 different components—from the air conditioning to the transmission. In addition, an overall trouble index and a cost index are computed. For each automobile as many as 2,600 separate bits of information may be transmitted to the reader. Across the 80 or so models of cars evaluated in the "Buying Guide," consumers can encounter over 200,000 bits of information to process. Only a person highly involved in the decision process to buy a car would attempt to engage in the lengthy and complex process of systematically analyzing the wealth of information contained in this informative publication.

Recognizing the existence of a problem in a stereo system and searching for information about autos represent the first two stages of the consumer decision process. This chapter analyzes these stages, whereas Chapters 12 and 13 cover the remaining stages of consumer decision making—alternative evaluation, choice, and postacquisition evaluation.

INTRODUCTION

One of the important and traditional areas of study in consumer behavior has been the consumer decision-making process. The study of consumer decision making involves the analysis of how people choose between two or more alternative acquisitions and of the processes that take place before and after the choice. Textbook authors and researchers have extensively written on the stages through which consumers move when deciding which product or service to purchase.[2] However, consumers engage in a wide range of behaviors in addition to purchasing products and services. Indeed, instead of talking about a purchase process, it may be more appropriate to talk about an acquisition process.[3]

Two basic types of acquisitions exist. First, **monetary acquisitions** involve the purchase of a good or service with currency, personal checks, or credit. Thus consumers use money in any of its various forms to purchase products (e.g., clothing), services (e.g., banking services), and even ideas (e.g., hiring consultants, such as an interior decorator). **Nonmonetary acquisitions**, on the other hand, are processes whereby goods and services are obtained without the use of monetary resources. Examples of nonmonetary acquisitions include anything acquired through borrowing, trading, handmaking, finding, inheriting, or stealing.

Chapters 11, 12, and 13 discuss the decision-making processes that occur during the acquisition of products, services, and ideas. Five stages of the acquisition process have been identified: problem recognition, search, alternative evaluation, choice, and postacquisition evaluation. The consumer vignette illustrates the two components of the consumer decision process discussed in this chapter—problem recognition and search for information. The purchase of the stereo system illustrates how the recognition of one problem can lead to the recognition of additional consumer problems. Compact disc players, speakers, and receivers are complementary products. When one component of the system is upgraded, it may result in dissatisfaction with the other components as well. In the vignette, the consumer first recognized a problem in the sound quality of the turntable. This dissatisfaction in turn led to dissatisfaction with the speakers and the amplifier.

A strategy that retailers frequently use is to place complementary products together to assist consumers in the problem recognition process. Thus managers in men's and women's clothing stores frequently display together slacks, a shirt, and a coat to take advantage of the tendency for the solution of one problem to cause consumers to recognize other problems. A consumer may enter the retail store with the intention of purchasing a pair of slacks. Once the slacks are purchased, however, other problems are recognized, such as finding the right shirt to wear with the slacks. The net result is that the consumer walks out with an entire outfit.

The example from *Consumer Reports* depicts concepts related to the second decision-making stage—the search for information. An extensive search for information tends to take place in high-involvement purchases. When searching for information about autos, consumers seek to obtain inputs for the formation of beliefs about the attributes of various brands. The goal of such an extended search process is to make the most informed and logical decision possible.

In the process of acquiring products, services, and ideas, consumers engage in a host of everyday activities. Many companies are interested in learning as much as possible about the daily life patterns of consumers because daily activities influence the acquisition process. For example, paper products companies seek out such

TABLE 11-1

A Consumer Action Quiz

Here is a consumer quiz. Please answer each of the questions below.

1. On average how many ice cubes do consumers put in a glass?

   a. 2.2 **b.** 3.2 **c.** 4.2 **d.** 5.2

2. What percentage of Americans would rather have a tooth extracted than take a car to a dealership for repairs?

   a. 8% **b.** 38% **c.** 58% **d.** 88%

3. How much does each adult spend a year on flowers?

   a. $15 **b.** $20 **c.** $40 **d.** $60

4. If you send a husband and wife to a store separately to purchase beer, how likely is it that they will return with the same brand?

   a. 5% **b.** 10% **c.** 15% **d.** 40%

5. How many minutes a week do people spend vacuuming their houses?

   a. 15 **b.** 35 **c.** 55 **d.** 95

6. What percentage of consumers wet their toothbrush prior to placing toothpaste on it?

   a. 37% **b.** 47% **c.** 57% **d.** 67%

7. How many times does the average consumer blow his or her nose in a year?

   a. 156 **b.** 256 **c.** 456 **d.** 656

Each question concerns a consumer action that a company has investigated. Coca-Cola wants to know how much ice is put in a glass to help make decisions about the strength of the formulation of its product. Toothpaste manufacturers want to know how we brush our teeth to decide how watery to make their product. Companies that produce facial tissue count nose blows to know how many tissues to put in a box. Consumer actions take place prior to product purchase during the use of the product and after the use of a product. Companies can be interested in even the most intimate details. For example, toilet tissue manufacturers want to know what percentage of people neatly fold the tissue or merely ball it all up. By the way, the correct answer to each question is *b*.

mundane facts as how many times people blow their nose when they have a cold. This information can be used as an input into the decision of how many tissues to place in a box. Table 11-1 presents a consumer action quiz. Take it to find out what you know about some basic consumer activities.

This chapter has three major purposes. First, it develops a generic flowchart of the consumer decision process and briefly describes each of the stages of decision making. Second, the chapter discusses several alternative perspectives on decision making. The goal of this section is to present students with traditional views as well as more recent and controversial views on decision making. The final goal is to discuss in detail the first two components of the decision-making process—problem recognition and search for information.

A GENERIC FLOWCHART OF THE CONSUMER DECISION PROCESS

At the most complex level, **consumer decision making** consists of a series of five stages: problem recognition, search, alternative evaluation, choice, and postacquisition evaluation. (The stages are diagrammed in Figure 11-1.) In the problem

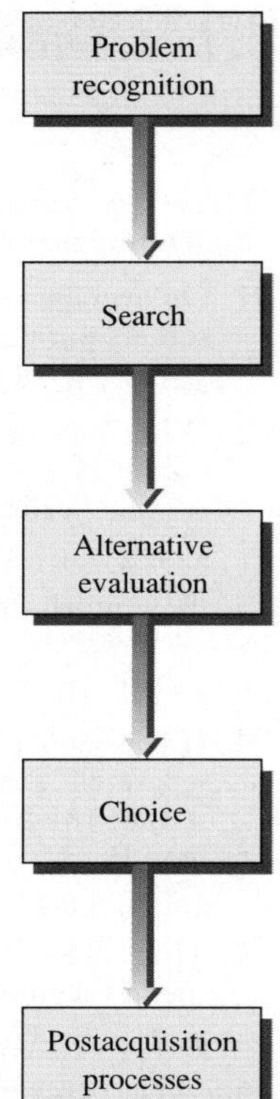

Figure 11-1
A generic flowchart of the consumer decision process.

recognition stage, consumers recognize that a need exists. If sufficiently strong, the need may motivate the person to enter the second stage, the search for information. The search for information may be either extensive or limited, depending upon the involvement level of the consumer. In the third stage consumers evaluate the alternatives that are identified for solving the problem. Alternative evaluation is synonymous with the formation of attitudes regarding the alternatives. Thus material from Chapter 8, Consumer Beliefs, Attitudes, and Behaviors, is particularly applicable to the evaluation stage.

Choice is the fourth stage, and it involves deciding which alternative action to select (e.g., which brand to choose, whether to spend or save, or from which store to purchase the product). Finally, in the postacquisition stage, the person consumes and uses the acquisition. In addition, he or she evaluates the outcomes of the consequences of the behavior and engages in acquisition disposal.

The generic decision-making process describes the steps in the decision-making process employed by businesses and organizations, as well as by consumers. Highlight 11-1 further discusses decision making in business-to-business marketing situations.

HIGHLIGHT 11-1

Decision Making in Business-to-Business Marketing

In a 1993 article published in the *Journal of Marketing* Michele Bunn stated that "A key to success in business-to-business markets is understanding customer buying behavior." To assist in achieving such understanding, she developed a taxonomy of buying decision approaches by sending questionnaires to over 2,000 purchasing managers of firms of varying sizes. She asked the managers to describe their last purchase for their firm on a series of dimensions: search for information, use of analysis techniques, relation to firm long-run strategy, and degree subject to written control procedures within the firm. Readers should note that these dimensions generally correspond to the generic decision process. Thus the search for information stage is common to both. The use of analysis techniques and the relation to long-run strategy dimensions correspond to the evaluation of alternatives stage. Finally, the degree of use of written control procedures is similar to the choice stage.

The results revealed six general buying approaches employed by the purchasing managers.

1. *Casual.* A purchase of low importance, wide set of options, little analysis, and no procedures implemented so that an order is simply transmitted, with no attention to strategic thinking. Example: Buying an inexpensive tool.
2. *Routine, low priority.* A purchase of moderate importance, wide choice of options, little search, some level of analysis, follow standard procedures, and superficial level of strategic thinking. Example: Reordering paper.
3. *Simple modified rebuy.* A purchase that is quite important, has narrow set of options, moderate level of search, moderate level of analysis, follows standard procedures, and high level of strategic thinking. Example: Reordering standard grease for machinery.
4. *Judgmental new task.* A purchase that is quite important, has narrow set of options, moderate amount of search, moderate level of analysis, little relevance to established procedures, and moderate level of strategic thinking. Example: Ordering a software system for billing, which was previously done by hand.
5. *Complex modified rebuy.* A purchase that is quite important, wide choice of options, high level of search, great deal of analysis, follow standard procedures, and high level of strategic thinking. Example: Purchase of new computer system for offices.
6. *Strategic new task.* A purchase of extreme importance, narrow set of options, high level of search, great deal of analysis, little reliance on established procedures, and very high level of strategic thinking. Example: Ordering machinery for new production line of a new product.

While the six types of decisions were developed for business-to-business purchase behavior, they also have application to consumer buying. Can you give examples, of each type of decision for purchases that you or your family have made?

Based upon Michele D. Bunn, "Taxonomy of Buying Decision Approaches," *Journal of Marketing*, Vol. 57 (January 1993), pp. 38–56.

ALTERNATIVE PERSPECTIVES ON CONSUMER DECISION MAKING

From the late eighteenth century through much of the 1970s, researchers viewed people as moving linearly through a decision-making process like that outlined in Figure 11-1. In the late 1970s, however, authors began to question the concept that all consumer purchases result from a careful, analytical process. Some authors suggested that in many instances consumers may not engage in any decision making at all prior to making a purchase. As stated in one article, "We conclude that for many purchases a decision process never occurs, not even on the first purchase."[4] In addition, authors began to recognize that many consumer behaviors do not merely involve the purchase of a good, such as an automobile. People also purchase experiences in the form of services such as vacation excursions, rock concerts, theater tickets, and so on.

The recognition that not all purchases result from extensive problem solving caused researchers to identify additional problems with the approach. Researchers also realized that the traditional decision-making view of consumer behavior tended to focus too much on the purchase of goods. As noted in the introduction to the chapter, many consumer actions do not directly involve the purchase of anything. Consumers borrow products, make budget allocation decisions, launch lawsuits, pass on rumors, and make store choice decisions. Due to the limitations of the traditional consumer decision process, researchers have gradually moved in the direction of proposing alternative decision-making models that place different levels of emphasis on each of the stages identified in the generic flowchart. For these reasons, this textbook identifies three perspectives on consumer behavior—the traditional decision-making perspective, the experiential perspective, and the behavioral influence perspective.

The Traditional Decision-Making Perspective

The traditional **decision-making perspective** emphasizes the rational, information-processing approach to consumer purchase behavior. It is closely related to the high-involvement hierarchy of effects approach to attitude formation discussed in Chapter 8. According to this approach, consumers move through each of the stages of the decision process in a linear fashion. The steps begin with a conscious recognition that a problem exists. The consumer then moves through an extensive search process for information. In the alternative evaluation stage, attitudes are formed about the various brands based upon the beliefs about the attributes of purchase alternatives. Thus attitudes result from the standard learning hierarchy discussed in Chapter 8. Choice is viewed as a complex process resulting from a detailed comparison of the alternatives.

In the 1970s, however, researchers began to recognize that in many situations consumers do not go through an extended decision process. Some authors suggested that the process diverges sufficiently in high- and low-involvement circumstances to talk about two categories of decision making.

Herbert Krugman was perhaps the first author to suggest that the decision process differs in high- and low-involvement cases.[5] He suggested that, under high-involvement conditions, extended decision making occurs. In contrast, under low-involvement conditions, limited decision making takes place and relatively less search behavior occurs. Further, because the low-involvement hierarchy of effects is operative when limited decision making occurs, the alternative evaluation stage is largely absent from the decision process. In limited decision making, the choice among alternative brands is made in a relatively simple manner. Thus simplified decision rules are used in the choice process.[6] Table 11-2 summarizes the acquisition process from the viewpoint of the extended and limited decision-making perspectives, as well as from the experiential and behavioral influence perspectives.

The Experiential Perspective

As noted previously in the text, the **experiential perspective** argues that many actions result from the human need to experience feelings and emotions. As a result, the decision-making process revolves around the consumer's goal of provoking feelings and emotions. As such, people may go through each of the decision-making stages; however, the focus is on the affective nature of the process. In contrast to the decision-making perspective, the experiential perspective recognizes consumers as "feelers" as well as thinkers—that is, they consume many types of products for the sensations, feelings, images, and emotions that the products generate.[7]

From an experiential perspective, problem recognition results from the realization that a difference exists between actual and desired affective states. Similarly, the

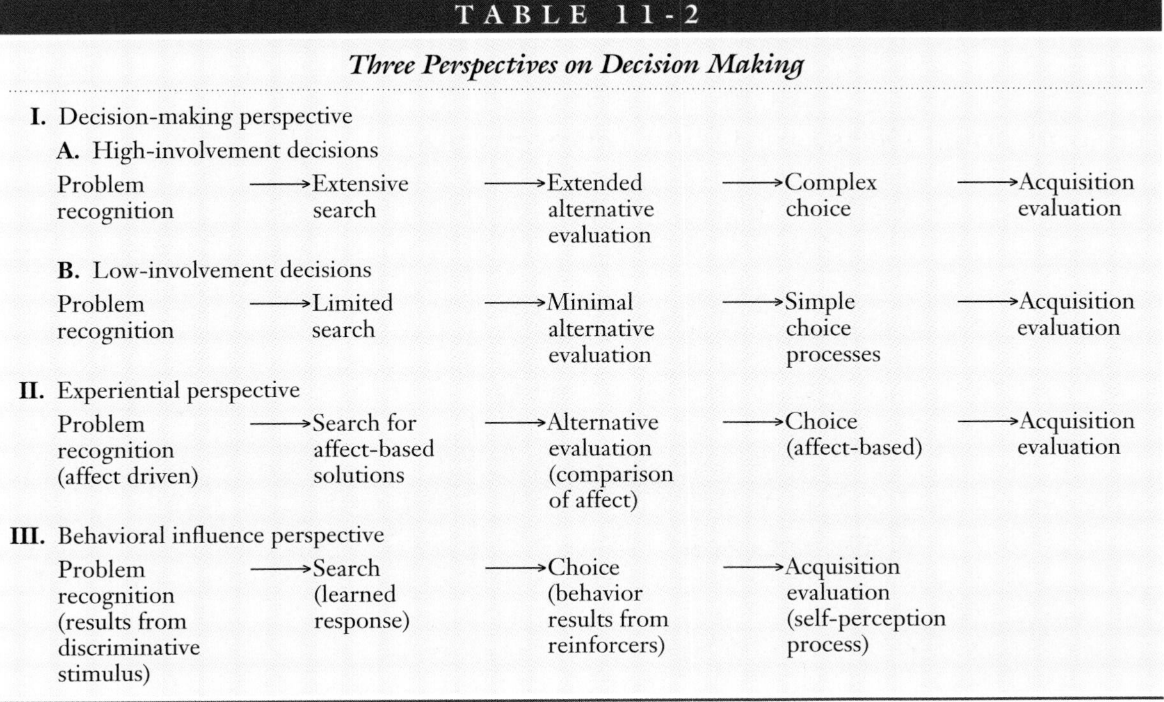

TABLE 11-2

Three Perspectives on Decision Making

I. Decision-making perspective				
A. High-involvement decisions				
Problem recognition	⟶ Extensive search	⟶ Extended alternative evaluation	⟶ Complex choice	⟶ Acquisition evaluation
B. Low-involvement decisions				
Problem recognition	⟶ Limited search	⟶ Minimal alternative evaluation	⟶ Simple choice processes	⟶ Acquisition evaluation
II. Experiential perspective				
Problem recognition (affect driven)	⟶ Search for affect-based solutions	⟶ Alternative evaluation (comparison of affect)	⟶ Choice (affect-based)	⟶ Acquisition evaluation
III. Behavioral influence perspective				
Problem recognition (results from discriminative stimulus)	⟶ Search (learned response)	⟶ Choice (behavior results from reinforcers)	⟶ Acquisition evaluation (self-perception process)	

search process involves seeking information concerning the likely affective impact of various alternatives. In the alternative evaluation stage, the various options are evaluated based upon their affective quality. Choice is based upon affective criteria (such as "Which product will make me feel better?"). Finally, postacquisition evaluation is based upon whether the outcome meets the emotional expectations of the consumer.

When approaching consumer behavior from a decision-making perspective, researchers tended to focus on functional goods, such as packaged goods and durables used by consumers to solve consumption problems. Thus consumer researchers analyzed the buying process for goods such as automobiles, toothpaste, laundry detergent, and homes. In contrast, when researchers began to investigate buying processes based upon an experiential perspective, the types of products considered changed. Examples of goods and services investigated from an experiential perspective included river rafting, parachuting, movies, art, novels, opera, casinos, and houses of ill repute.[8] When investigating these experiential purchases, researchers move away from studying problem solving to assessing the emotions and feelings that accompany consumer behavior.

American Express has employed advertisements that focus on experiential decision-making processes. Figure 11-2 reveals an American Express advertisement that focuses on feelings and emotions. Although the ad attempts to influence various

Figure 11-2 American Express subtly encourages experiential credit card spending with this ad. (Courtesy of American Express, Inc.)

beliefs (e.g., "no more interest charge 'surprises'"), it concludes with a statement of feelings—"You're happy." Obviously, if you are happy and have your finances under control, you can make impulse purchases and feel good about it.

Impulse Purchases

One type of purchase that may be categorized within the experiential domain is impulse buying. **Impulse purchases** may be defined as occurring when a consumer experiences a sudden, often powerful and persistent, urge to buy something immediately. The impulse to buy is hedonically complex and may stimulate emotional conflict. Also, impulse buying is prone to occur with diminished regard for its consequences.

Some authors have described impulse buying as a "buying action undertaken without a problem previously having been consciously recognized or a buying intention formed prior to entering the store."[9] Although little research has been done on the mechanism responsible for impulse purchases, it is likely that such purchases result from the consumer seeing a product and reacting with an extremely strong positive affect toward it. The positive feelings lead to a desire to experience the product or service, which results in a purchase. Impulse purchases occur frequently; various studies have found that as many as 39% of department store purchases and 67% of grocery store purchases may be unplanned.[10]

Closely related to impulse purchases are purchases and actions of consumers described as compulsive. **Compulsive consumption** is defined as ". . . a response to an uncontrollable drive or desire to obtain, use, or experience a feeling, substance, or activity that leads an individual to repetitively engage in a behavior that will ultimately cause harm to the individual and/or others."[11] One important societal problem emerging from compulsive consumption is addiction by consumers to drugs. Similarly, the behaviors of persons suffering from anorexia and bulimia are categorized as compulsive in nature. In the view of the author of this text, a decision-making or a behavioral influence approach will not provide satisfactory explanations for understanding compulsive behavior. To begin to understand the actions of consumers with compulsive disorders, the experiential approach to consumer behavior appears to be more useful. The relationship between compulsions and consumer affect and emotions was well described by one consumer researcher, who had experienced a compulsive disorder herself. She said:

> Addicted consumers appear to have in common an emotional vacancy that they are compelled to fill with *something*. If one substance or behavior is denied to them, they will simply seek out another. What addicts seek most is to escape themselves, their own minds, and their consciousness. They find it very painful to inhibit their own consciousness. Thus virtually any substance or activity that will alter, numb, or erase that consciousness becomes acceptable, if their preferred drug of choice is unavailable. Viewed in this way, it becomes apparent that all possible drugs cannot be removed from the addicted consumer. . . . What must be done, instead, is to repair the emotional hole in the addict's psyche.[12]

Variety-Seeking Purchases

Variety-seeking purchases may also be categorized in the experiential domain. Variety seeking refers to the tendency of consumers to spontaneously buy a new brand of product even though they continue to express satisfaction with the previously purchased brand. One explanation of variety seeking is that consumers attempt to reduce boredom by purchasing a new brand.[13] The theory of optimum stimulation has been proposed to explain this tendency to avoid boredom. Discussed more fully in Chapter 6, optimum stimulation theory posits that people have a need to maintain an appropriate level of activation.[14] If their activation falls too low or moves too high, they will take steps to change it. The switching of brands may be a method of increasing stimulation by bringing something new into a consumer's life.

Variety-seeking behavior is classified within the experiential perspective because the consumer buys the product to influence feelings. In other words, when consumers are bored, they are feeling suboptimal. By purchasing a new brand they attempt to make themselves feel better.

The Behavioral Influence Perspective

When approaching problems from the **behavioral influence perspective**, researchers focus on the behaviors of consumers and the contingencies of the environment that influence the behaviors. In general, behavioral-learning theorists wish to avoid discussions of internal states, and many would argue that a discussion of decision making is inappropriate. However, if some liberties are taken, the generic decision-making process can be interpreted from within the behavioral influence perspective.

From the behavioral influence perspective, problem recognition occurs when consumers are exposed to discriminative stimuli, which indicate that emitting a behavior may result in reinforcement. For example, when driving a car down a highway, the needle of the gas gauge pointing at "empty" acts as a discriminative stimulus. It tells consumers that if they stop to get gas, they will not be marooned on the highway.

From the behavioral influence perspective, the search process represents a learned behavior that, if elicited, may lead to reinforcement. Thus, from their past learning history, the reinforcement structure of the environment reinforces consumers so that when they identify and seek information about options, they obtain more positive outcomes.

The alternative evaluation stage is the one stage of the decision process that would *not* be considered from within the behavioral influence perspective. Alternative evaluation occurs within the consumer and cannot be linked directly to behavior; as such, behavioral influence researchers would not view it as amenable to investigation.

From the behavioral influence perspective, choice represents a behavior that results from the discriminative stimuli encountered during the search process. That is, information relating to price, quality, warranties, and so forth acts as a cue. From previous shopping experiences, these discriminative stimuli have become associated with obtaining outcomes with varying degrees of reinforcing and punishing properties. Based upon this learning history, choice is simply the behavior resulting from the relative influence of such discriminative stimuli and past experience with the reinforcers and punishers that result from the purchase.

In a similar manner, postacquisition processes represent the outcomes received by the consumer as a result of the purchase. If the result is positive, the consumer is reinforced and the buying behavior is more likely to occur again. In contrast, if the result is negative, punishment occurs, and the likelihood of making the purchase again declines.

Overview of the Three Perspectives

Table 11-3 summarizes the three perspectives on consumer decision making. It identifies how the perspectives diverge concerning three issues in decision making: (1) What are the environmental inputs? (2) What is the nature of the intervening response system? and (3) What is the type of behavior studied?

Each perspective tends to focus on a different environmental input. For example, the decision-making perspective tends to emphasize information inputs that involve tangible benefits. In contrast, the experiential perspective emphasizes the emotion-laden inputs, particularly those symbols that influence consumer feelings. The experiential perspective focuses more on the impact of sensual information, such as that transmitted by music, textures, and odors. The environmental inputs on which the behavioral influence perspective focuses involve the reinforcement structure of information. Also emphasized is the physical layout of the environment and the impact of situational factors on behavior.

TABLE 11-3

The Three Perspectives on Consumer Behavior

Perspective	*Environmental Inputs*	*Intervening Response System*	*Behavior*
Decision making	Information inputs to decision Verbal and written information Tangible benefits Economic benefits	Cognitive focus Belief formation Memory processes Cognitive responses Information processing High- and low-involvement processes	Purchase of utilitarian products or services
Experiential	Emotional inputs Symbols Visual information Affective themes (e.g., fear, sexual, patriotic) Music, textures, odors	Affective focus Affect formation Emotional responses Imagery/exploratory processes Need for optimal stimulation Opponent processes Reactance	Purchase of affective/experiential products or services Impulse purchases Variety seeking
Behavioral	Reinforcement structure of environment Physical layout of environment Unconditioned stimuli (e.g., music, money) Cultural values and norms Situational factors	Disavows need to discuss an intervening response system Will admit that different consumers may respond divergently to reinforcers	Argues that many purchases occur without strong beliefs or feelings Movement of consumers through environment Primitive consumption behaviors

SOURCE: John C. Mowen, "Beyond Consumer Decision Making," *Journal of Consumer Marketing*, Vol. 5 (Winter 1988), pp. 15–25.

Perhaps the area that differentiates these three perspectives the most is the intervening response system. The decision-making perspective focuses on belief formation, memory processes, information processing, and high- and low-involvement processes. In contrast, the experiential perspective emphasizes affect formation, emotional responses, imagery, and affective processes—such as classical conditioning, mere exposure effects, reactance, and opponent-process theory. In direct contradiction to the first two perspectives, the behavioral influence perspective disavows the need to discuss an intervening response system.

The third way to distinguish the three approaches is in terms of the type of behavior analyzed. The decision-making approach focuses on the purchase of utilitarian goods and services. On the other hand, those who emphasize experiential processes investigate the purchase of affect-laden goods and services and are more interested in analyzing impulse purchases and variety-seeking behavior. The behavioral influence perspective argues that all behavior is appropriate for behavioral analysis. However, proponents show more interest in the behaviors that clearly result from the effects of reinforcers in the environment, such as sales promotions and aspects of the physical environment.

Managerial Applications of the Three Perspectives

Each of the three perspectives on the consumer decision process has divergent managerial implications. As a general rule, the manager should analyze marketing problems from each of the three perspectives. For example, the owner of a restaurant named "Playmakers" commissioned a consumer behavior analysis of his business because profits were much lower than anticipated.

The consultant first approached the problem from the decision-making perspective. Here, she examined such factors as the quality of the food, the pricing structure, and the hours of operation. Next, she analyzed the restaurant from an experiential perspective. In this case, she examined how the decor of the restaurant influenced the feelings and emotions of customers. Finally, she employed the behavioral influence perspective and analyzed the reinforcers and punishers that consumer encountered in the restaurant. In particular, she surveyed patrons on the service and friendliness of employees, two factors that can be strong positive reinforcers or punishers. Based upon the consultant's analysis, the owner made a series of changes. He improved the quality of the food, dramatically improved the atmospherics of the restaurant, and increased the training of the waiters and waitresses. Only by analyzing the restaurant from each of the three perspectives on consumer decision making could such a well-rounded set of recommendations have been developed.

Approaching Problems from the Decision-Making Perspective

As noted earlier in the section, consumers can be seen as moving through either an extended or limited action process when viewed from the decision-making perspective. The type of decision process used depends in large part upon whether the consumer is in a high-involvement or a low-involvement state. Table 11-4 summarizes how the marketing mix of a firm could be influenced if the product or service tends to be purchased via a high-involvement or low-involvement decision process.

TABLE 11-4

Some Marketing Mix Strategies for Products Bought via High- and Low-Involvement Decision Processes

I. High-involvement decision processes
  A. Promotional strategy
    1. Sell product via skilled sales force
    2. Utilize strong peruasive arguments in messages
  B. Distribution strategy
    1. Utilize a more limited distribution system
    2. Ensure that distributors are trained to provide outstanding service
  C. Pricing strategy
    1. Consider charging premium prices
    2. Avoid use of frequent sales
    3. Consider policy of price bargaining with customers
II. Low-involvement decision processes
  A. Promotional strategy
    1. Place greater weight on mass advertising to create sales awareness
    2. Use heavy amounts of message repetition
    3. Utilize likable/attractive endorsers
    4. Keep arguments in advertisements simple
  B. Distribution strategy
    1. Utilize an extensive distribution strategy
  C. Pricing
    1. Attempt to be a low-cost producer
    2. Consider use of coupons and other price incentives to reach more price-conscious groups

When assessing a managerial problem from the decision-making perspective, researchers will ask whether consumers move through a high- or low-involvement decision process. The answer to this question will have a major impact on both advertising and sales management strategy. When consumers engage in high-involvement decision making, advertisers can create more complex messages. For example, Figure 11-3 shows an ad by Toshiba for a new medical scanner. Although the ad makes use of the name and skeleton of a famous celebrity (Kareem Abdul Jabbar), the message is complex. In addition, the ad nicely ties the use of Jabbar to a major attribute of the new product—that is, the ability to take a full-body X ray.

In the personal-selling area, when the target segment uses an extended decision process, the firm should consider employing a sales force to sell the product. Most products purchased under high-involvement circumstances have significant amounts of risk attached to them. In addition, the product or service is likely to be quite complex and difficult to understand. To reduce the perceived risk on the part of the consumer, a salesperson is frequently required to thoroughly explain the characteristics of the product or service and to reduce the various types of risk that the consumer may perceive.

Figure 11-3 The ad illustrates a message targeted to an audience likely to be engaged in high-involvement decision making. (Courtesy of Toshiba, Inc.)

The promotional strategy used to sell products purchased after limited decision making is quite different. Rather than relying on personal selling, mass advertising is more frequently employed. Products bought under low-involvement conditions tend to have less risk attached to them. They are frequently low-cost goods that can be distributed extensively and, therefore, require large amounts of advertising to support them.

Determining whether customers engage in limited or extended decision making should also influence pricing strategy. For products and services purchased via a limited decision-making process, price may be the single most important consideration for consumers. One research study found that among consumers who indicated that a purchase was unimportant, 52% said that price was the determining factor in making the purchase.[15] In many instances the competition among brands purchased via limited decision processes is fierce, and becoming the low-cost producer may be the key to success in the marketplace.

Approaching Problems from the Experiential Perspective

When problems are examined from the experiential perspective, managers focus on a different set of issues. The focus is more likely to be on entertainment, arts, and leisure products, rather than on more functional consumer goods. However, products can be purchased for experiential purposes as well. For example, an automobile may be bought for the thrill of having one's head snapped back as the driver attacks the road. The Pontiac Grand Am GT advertisement shown in Figure 11-4 acts to influence consumer beliefs about performance and price. In addition, it depicts the exciting experience obtained from driving the car.

Figure 11-4 Pontiac hopes to influence feeling, as well as beliefs, about driving a Grand Am GT. (Courtesy of the Pontiac Division of General Motors Corporation.)

The experiential perspective also recognizes that products and services carry subjective symbolic meanings for consumers.[16] In particular, products such as flowers, jewelry, perfume, after-shave lotion, and so forth are bought largely for the meanings they provide. Thus advertisements for the product should emphasize these symbolic elements. For example, in the long-running advertising campaign for diamonds, DeBeers uses such verbal statements as "This anniversary ask for her other hand" and "Give her the ultimate token of your love." In each case a diamond is symbolic of a man's love for a woman.

When problems are approached from the experiential perspective, one important managerial implication is that the methods employed to perform marketing research change. Highlight 11-2 discusses the use of ethnographic research methods employed by researchers in analyzing the high-risk leisure consumption of skydiving.

Approaching Problems from the Behavioral Influence Perspective

When managers approach a problem from the behavioral influence perspective, they focus on identifying the environmental forces that influence consumers. For example, the physical environment can be used to induce behaviors from consumers. Arranging aisles in a retail store to funnel consumers by desired products illustrates how the physical environment can impact behavior without changing either beliefs or feelings about the action.

The use of textures, smells, and lighting can also create an atmosphere that elicits desired responses among consumers. For example, in one field study researchers investigated the effects of lighting on where people sat in a restaurant. They found that the patrons tended to sit in the darker areas facing the light. Other researchers have found that lighting affects how close people sit to each other. If the goal is to have people sit close together, low levels of lighting should be maintained.[17]

The mere arrangement of the containers of food products on shelves in a grocery store can impact consumer buying decisions independently of their beliefs and attitudes about the product alternatives. For example, it is well known that brands placed at eye level will sell better than brands placed near the floor on grocery shelves.

More interesting are recent findings on how arranging containers on shelves impacted buying decisions.[18] In most grocery stores, managers arrange the cartons by brand. In the study, the researcher placed respondents in a simulated buying situation in which yogurt containers were arranged either by brands or by flavors. When the containers were arranged by brands, the shelf contained a brand (e.g., Dannon) and the flavors that Dannon offered were placed together. In contrast, when containers were arranged by flavor, there was a section for, say, vanilla, another section for strawberry, and so on. Within each flavor section, different brands were available. The results revealed that when respondents were asked to buy enough yogurt for six weeks, the shelf arrangement strongly affected their purchase intentions. When containers were arranged by brand, the subjects bought more different flavors of yogurt, but almost exclusively from one brand. When the shelf was arranged by flavor, however, the subjects bought more different types of brands but fewer different flavors. Thus the behavior of the respondents changed due to the mere arrangement of the cartons of yogurt even though beliefs and feelings about the flavors and brands did not change.

HIGHLIGHT 11-2

Ethnographic Research in the Experiential Domain of Skydiving

"She lives for this. . . . Ready! Set! Go! She dives through the door. Like a body surfer, she rides the wave of the wind down and away from the plane. She descends head first, at vertical speeds approaching 200 miles per hour, toward the tiny cluster of skydivers below her. Tacitly judging distance and speed, she decelerates to perfectly match their slower fall rate. . . . Gently, she settles into her assigned slot, taking a grip on the skydiver next to her. She smiles and calmly anticipates the next sequence in the dive; after all, the skydivers still have 30 seconds before impact." Over 2.5 million parachute jumps occur a year. About 1 in every 700 participants dies each year (or about 49 per year). Many additional participants are injured seriously, such as Richard Celsi, a co-author of the research paper on which this highlight is based. Given these poor odds of survival and the highly experiential nature of the sport, traditional research methods using questionnaires and/or experiments are inadequate for investigating the decision-making processes that take place in choosing to skydive. Instead, researchers have turned to the use of ethnographic methods borrowed from anthropologists.

In their study of skydivers, the researchers used a participant observation approach. One author, Richard Celsi, became an active member of a skydiving club and made over 650 jumps. The second and third authors of the paper went to meetings and observed the jumps from both inside the plane and on the ground. During the 30 months of investigation, the researchers conducted 135-plus formal interviews, took over 500 photographs, videotaped 50 skydives, and mourned the death of one club member who died parachuting during the time period. In addition, copious field notes were taken by each of the researchers. Triangulation procedures were employed in which each researcher compared and contrasted his interpretations of the experiences being analyzed.

From their ethnographic analysis, the authors identified three fundamental motives for why participants decided to begin skydiving. Foremost, were "normative motives." That is, to become part of a group and fulfill social expectations, people take the first plunge in skydiving. A second motive was hedonic in nature. The authors suggested that the hedonic motive evolves from thrill seeking, to pleasure seeking, to having the experience of flow. Experiencing self-efficacy was identified as the third motive for skydiving. That is, as concerns for safety and survival lessen, participants begin to focus on the self-confidence and achievement that result from learning how to manage risk and exert self-control when on the edge.

From the perspective of the generic model of decision making, each of these motives (i.e., group acceptance, thrill seeking, and self-acceptance) can lead directly to problem recognition. That is, when the actual levels of group acceptance, thrill seeking, or self-acceptance diverge from desired levels, becoming involved in skydiving may act to solve the problem.

Based upon Richard L. Celsi, Randall L. Rose, and Thomas W. Leigh, "An Exploration of High-Risk Leisure Consumption Through Skydiving," *Journal of Consumer Research*, Vol. 20 (June 1993), pp. 1–23.

Additional ways in which the physical environment may influence consumers will be discussed in Chapter 14.

A Caveat

As noted earlier in this chapter, the discussion of the experiential and behavioral influence perspectives is controversial to some researchers. Indeed, arguments can be made that decision making occurs whenever consumers engage in a behavior. The experiential and behavioral influence perspectives are discussed, however, to emphasize the role of affect/feelings and environmental factors in causing certain types of consumer actions. A single-minded focus on belief formation and rational information processing fails to capture adequately the richness of consumer behavior. Although each of the perspectives has a different focus on the importance and content of the stages of the decision process, it is still possible to discuss each stage from a generic perspective. The next two sections discuss problem recognition and search.

PROBLEM RECOGNITION

Problem recognition occurs when a discrepancy develops between an actual and a desired state of being. Note that the definition of problem recognition is identical to that of a need state. In essence, problem recognition occurs when a need state is felt. Thus the discussion in Chapter 6 on consumer need states applies to problem recognition. Typically, researchers seek to identify consumer problems by analyzing the factors that act to widen the gap between the actual state and the desired state. If the satisfaction with the **actual state** decreases, or if the level of the **desired state** increases, a problem may be recognized that propels a consumer to action. Figure 11-5 diagrams how such a process may work.[19]

Factors Influencing the Actual State

A variety of factors may cause the actual state to decrease below acceptable levels. A person could run out of a product, such as gasoline or toothpaste; a product could wear out; or a product may simply go out of style. Similarly, the person could use the product and find that it simply fails to meet expectations. Another set of factors that influence the actual state concern the internal state of consumers. People sometimes experience strong negative affective states, which are uncomfortable. The negative affective state could be caused by an internal change in the person, resulting in perceptions of hunger or thirst. Similarly, consumers may experience a need for

Figure 11-5 The problem recognition process.

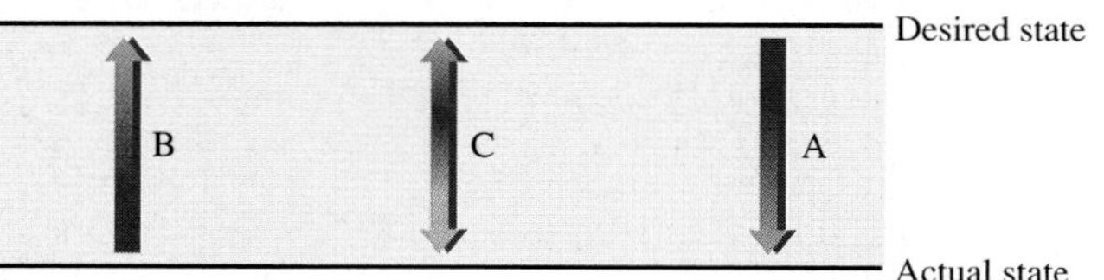

stimulation, because their activation level has fallen below acceptable levels. The negative affective state could also result from outside stimulation. The person could receive bad news, or a general situation could make the person uncomfortable (e.g., a consumer could be placed in a new social situation).

Factors Influencing the Desired State

Desired states tend to be influenced by factors that affect the aspirations and circumstances of the consumer. Thus such influences as culture, subculture, reference groups, and life-style trends can cause a person to change his or her desired state. For example, if a person joins an organization, such as a fraternity, sorority, or corporation, the pressures of the social group may change the person's perception of the appropriateness of wearing certain types of clothing. When a student graduates from college, a whole new set of dress requirements may be imposed. Thus the desired state changes, and needs develop for nice suits, briefcases, and shoes that would be considered inappropriate in a college environment.

Because consumers have a capacity to think, plan, and dream, they can create new desires. By being able to imagine themselves in new situations or owning new possessions, consumers may influence their own desired state. Of course, advertisers seek to encourage such "autistic thinking" by showing off products and services in highly inviting ways.

The ability of consumers to think ahead and imagine negative outcomes can also be used by advertisers. Figure 11-6 shows an ad from Black & Decker for a

Figure 11-6 Black & Decker seeks to create problem recognition by illustrating what can happen if a fire extinguisher is not readily available. (Courtesy of Black & Decker, Inc.)

household fire extinguisher. The ad vividly illustrates what can happen if a fire occurs in a kitchen. The ad does a good job of creating problem recognition because of the desire to avoid such a negative outcome.

Factors Influencing Both the Desired and Actual States

The promotional activities of marketers can create dissatisfaction by influencing either the desired or actual state. For example, suppose that a consumer currently uses Brand A. A company may attempt to create dissatisfaction with this brand by identifying areas in which the brand has problems, such as its high price or a high failure rate. Such information would probably influence the level of aspiration as well as the actual state. Other factors that can influence both the desired and actual states include aging, physical or psychological changes, or changes in a person's financial situation. For example, increases in salary levels can make a person dissatisfied with his or her current house while simultaneously increasing the desire for a larger home in a neighborhood with a higher social status.

Previous decisions of the person can also affect both the actual and the desired states. For example, if someone buys a house, a whole set of desires are created for new furniture, draperies, lawn products, and so forth. Similarly, the person may become highly dissatisfied with current furniture, because it is the wrong color or simply not in good enough condition to be placed in a new home. One of the major purposes of promotional campaigns is to influence the desired and actual states of consumers to create problem recognition.

Marketers hope to influence the desired and actual states of consumers by developing promotional campaigns that tie their product or service to popular life-style trends or that show their product or service being used by highly attractive individuals. The actual or desired state may also be influenced through the use of fear appeals. As discussed in Chapter 10, fear appeals involve developing messages that seek to scare consumers by showing what would happen if a product or service were not used. In an industrial-buying context, AT&T has made highly effective use of fear appeals. For example, in one highly effective campaign, the company employed a fear appeal in which a person was shown as in danger of losing his job because he failed to purchase an AT&T system. The fear of losing one's job illustrates a problem with the actual state.

The storyboard shown in Figure 11-7 reveals another advertisement developed by AT&T. It depicts a woman having a nostalgic long-distance conversation with her mother in France. This ad influences the desired state by showing the wonderful feelings that can result from calling loved ones overseas. It influences the actual state by focusing attention on how little it costs to make the call.

One final issue concerning problem recognition must be raised. Because consumers can plan and anticipate future needs, products and services may be purchased on a preneed basis. In fact, an entire range of products have been identified as **preneed goods**. Growth areas in preneed marketing include liability insurance, self-diagnostic health kits, prepaid legal services, and prepaid tuition plans for colleges. In some respects the ultimate in preneed problem recognition is the purchase of funeral services and burial plots long before the consumer's demise.[20]

Figure 11-7 AT&T attempts to create problem recognition. (Courtesy of AT&T.)

Managerial Applications of the Problem Recognition Stage

The analysis of the problem recognition stage applies to several managerial areas. One of the primary goals of promotional strategy is to cause consumers to recognize that an existing problem can be remedied by a product or service. To promote problem recognition, an advertisement or salesperson may attempt to create dissatisfaction with the actual state by identifying problems with an existing product or service. Another approach would be to attempt to use advertisements to influence consumers' goals and aspirations concerning the desired state.

Although such proactive attempts to create problem recognition sound good, this author suspects that in practice they may not be extremely successful. Efforts to create dissatisfaction with existing products and services are likely to come off as self-serving. Similarly, attempts to create consumer needs by changing aspirations have been heavily criticized as causing a materialistic society. A more reasonable strategy to follow probably involves working hard to identify existing consumer need states. As will be discussed in Chapter 13, consumers are frequently dissatisfied with the products and services they purchase. Effectively using marketing research to identify the causes of dissatisfaction may be the most effective route to finding new product opportunities.

CONSUMER SEARCH BEHAVIOR

After a consumer identifies a problem of sufficient magnitude to propel him or her to action, a search process is begun to acquire information about products or services that may eliminate the problem. The investigation of the consumer search process is highly important to marketers. In particular, it influences a company's promotion and distribution strategies. For example, suppose that a company learns through marketing research that consumers buy its brand of product based on a low-involvement decision process. This means that consumers are likely to engage in limited amounts of external search prior to making a purchase. In such an instance it is crucial that consumers immediately think of the company's brand when a problem is recognized. To create such top-of-the-mind awareness, high amounts of advertising are required so that the brand is recalled from long-term memory when the need arises. Such a strategy is used by fast-food companies, soft drink manufacturers, and beer producers. When consumers recognize hunger or thirst, in most instances they are not going to engage in extensive search for a product to fulfill the need. Instead, they are likely to choose the brand that immediately comes to mind. As a result, such companies spend huge amounts of money on advertising to ensure that their brands come to mind first when a problem is identified.

Researchers have found that two types of consumer **search processes** exist—internal search and external search.[21] **Internal search** involves the consumer attempting to retrieve from long-term memory information on products or services that may help to solve a problem. In contrast, **external search** involves the acquisition of information from outside sources, such as friends, advertisements, packaging, *Consumer Reports*, sales personnel, and so forth. In addition to distinguishing internal and external search, researchers have also made the distinction between prepurchase search and ongoing search. **Prepurchase search** involves the information-seeking activities that consumers engage in to facilitate decision making concerning a specific purchase in the marketplace. In contrast, **ongoing search** involves the search activities that are independent of specific purchase needs or decisions.[22]

Figure 11-8 presents a framework that helps distinguish between ongoing and prepurchase search. As shown in the figure, ongoing search tends to occur because a person is heavily involved in the product class, because the person seeks to build a bank of information for future use, or because the person finds that engaging in such activities results in fun and pleasure. One recent study investigated ongoing search in two product classes—clothing and personal computers. The authors found that heavy and light ongoing searchers could be identified. Heavy searchers had greater amounts of product knowledge and tended to engage in ongoing search because it was fun. Important to marketers was the finding that they also were heavy spenders within the product class.[23]

Although the distinction between prepurchase and ongoing search is clearly an important one, little research has been done on the topic. As a result, the discussion will now turn to issues involving internal search.

Figure 11-8 A framework for consumer information search. (Source: Peter Block, Daniel Sherrell, and Nancy Ridgway, "Consumer Search: An Extended Framework," *Journal of Consumer Research*, Vol. 13, June 1986, pp. 119–126. Reproduced with permission.)

	Prepurchase Search	Ongoing Search	
Determinants	• Involvement in the purchase • Market environment • Situational factors	• Involvement with the product class • Market environment • Situational factors	
Motives	• To make better purchase decisions	Build a bank of information for future use	Experience fun and pleasure
Outcomes	• Increased product and market knowledge • Better purchase decisions • Increased satisfaction with the purchase outcome	• Increased product and market knowledge leading to —future buying efficiencies —personal influence • Increased impulse buying • Increased satisfaction from search, and other outcomes	

Internal Search

Internal search occurs when consumers search through memory for information about alternatives for solving a problem. After a problem is recognized, consumers engage in internal search prior to external search. Depending upon the type of problem encountered, the degree of internal search may vary. If the purchase process involves extensive problem solving, the consumer may actively search long-term memory for information on brand alternatives. If the consumer is in a low-involvement purchase process, internal search tends to be highly limited. When the purchase process involves an experiential or behavioral influence purchase, it is likely that little or no internal search occurs. Rather than engaging in an information-processing task of searching through long-term memory for ideas, the consumer refers to his or her feelings or follows the contingencies of the environment.

When the purchase involves extensive problem solving or limited problem solving, consumers engage in an internal search for information by attempting to retrieve from long-term memory information relevant to the problem. One type of information that may be retrieved involves the brands that the consumer may or may not consider for purchase.

Figure 11-9 identifies five different categories, into one of which a brand must fall.[24] In this figure, internal search is viewed as proceeding via a two-stage process. First, the consumer retrieves from long-term memory those products and brands of

Figure 11-9 Categories of brands that consumers may retrieve from memory during internal search.

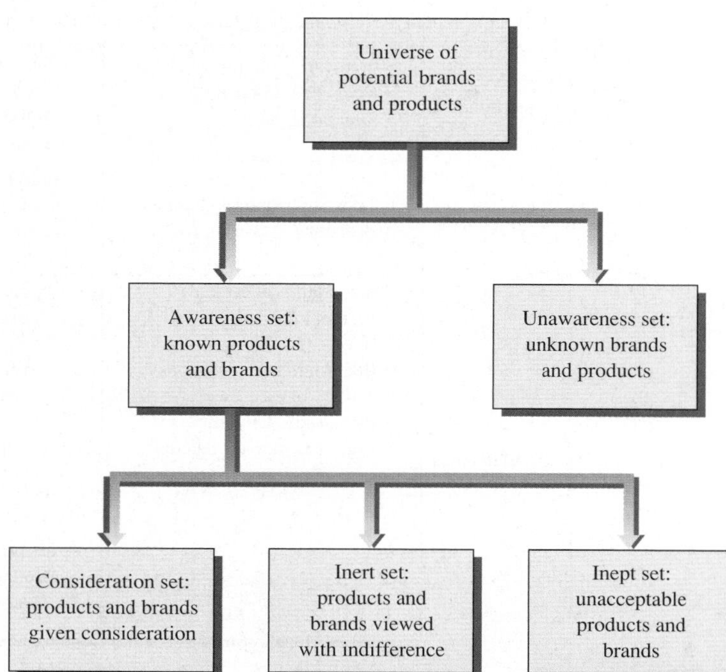

which he or she is aware. This **awareness set** is a subset of the total universe of potential brands and products available. At minimum a company wants its brand to be a part of the awareness set. If consumers are unaware of a brand, they are unlikely to ever consider it, unless they discover it in the external search process.

The importance of getting your brand into the awareness set is illustrated by a company called Avia. What does Avia International make? Market research indicated that in late 1990, only 4% of consumers knew that it made sneakers and sports apparel. As the marketing vice-president for the company said, "There's a whole segment of people who are not buying our shoes because they don't know who we are." As a result, the company undertook a major advertising campaign to create brand awareness. After noting that 90% of new products are pulled within three years of their introduction, one expert said that the major reason is that "In most cases, failures were the result of a lack of product recognition."[25]

After identifying the awareness set, the consumer separates the awareness group into three additional categories—the consideration set, the inert set, and the inept set. The **consideration set** (also called the evoked set) consists of those brands and products that are acceptable for further consideration. The **inert set** consists of the brands and products to which the consumer is essentially indifferent. The **inept set** consists of the brands and products that are considered unacceptable. Of course, the goal of a company is to have its brand placed in the evoked set and not placed in the inept set.

One critical issue concerning consideration set formation concerns whether it changes during the consumer acquisition process. Early researchers viewed the consideration set for a given product category as essentially fixed.[26] More recently, however, researchers have begun to question this view.[27] From an information-processing perspective, the consideration set may be viewed as the contents of working memory elicited when a person is asked to consider acceptable brands within a product class. From such a perspective, the consideration set is dynamic and may change as more information is added through external search.

Recent work on the consideration set has identified a number of factors that influence its size. For example, evidence suggests that the size of the consideration set decreases as the brand loyalty of consumers increases. Factors associated with an increase in the size of the consideration set include the education level of consumers, the size of consumers' families, the size of the awareness set, and the extent to which consumers recognize that different brands can be used in different situations.[28]

But just how large are the awareness and consideration sets for consumers? In one review of the research, the authors found that awareness set sizes ranged from a low of 3.5 for mouthwash to a high of 19.3 brands for laundry detergent. In general, consideration set size paralleled the size of the awareness set. Thus for mouthwash 1.3 brands were in the consideration set, whereas for laundry detergent 5.0 brands were in the consideration set.[29]

The authors of the study also suggested that consideration set size is a constant proportion of the size of the awareness set. Based upon a psychological phenomenon called the golden section proportion, they proposed that the consideration set should be either 63% or 37% of the size of the awareness set. In the study, the awareness and consideration set sizes were obtained for automobiles and television sets. Because the awareness set for televisions was expected to be small, the authors predicted that the consideration set would be 63% of the awareness set. The results revealed that the average awareness set size for televisions was 6.5, and the number of brands in the consideration set was 3.9, giving a proportion of 60%, which was extremely close to that predicted. For automobiles, the researchers hypothesized that the evoked set size would be 37% of the consideration set. The results revealed that the average awareness set size was 15.2 brands, and the number of brands in the consideration set was 5.8 for automobiles. This ratio was 38%, very close to that predicted. Although much research remains to be performed on the golden section proportion, the results of the study are provocative.

External Search

During external search, consumers solicit information from outside sources. Formally, external search is defined as the "degree of attention, perception, and effort directed toward obtaining environmental data or information related to the specific purchase under consideration."[30] Table 11-5 identifies the basic types of information sought in external search. These include information on the alternative brands available, the evaluative criteria on which to compare brands, the importance of the criteria, and the performance of the brands on the attributes.[31]

The amount and types of information sought in external search can be derived directly from the concepts involved in attitude formation and change discussed in Chapters 8 and 9. A consumer engages in external information search to gain information so that attitudes may be formed and changed. As such, the consumer searches to identify what alternative brands are available. In addition, a consumer may seek to identify the various evaluative criteria on which the brands may be compared. Information may also be sought to help the consumer decide how important the various evaluative criteria should be in the decision. The consumer engaging in extensive external search also seeks to form beliefs about the various alternatives. In particular, information is sought to form beliefs about the extent to which alternatives possess the attributes considered to be important. In addition, beliefs are formed about the benefits that the various attributes provide.

Measuring External Search Behavior

Traditionally, researchers have employed a number of indicators to assess the degree of external search engaged in by consumers. Some of these indicators include

TABLE 11-5

The Types of Information Sought via External Search

1. Alternative brands available
2. Evaluative criteria on which to compare brands
3. Importance of various evaluative criteria
4. Information on which to form beliefs
   - Attributes that brands possess
   - Benefits that various attributes provide

1. The number of stores visited.
2. The number of friends with whom the person discusses the product.
3. The number of buying guides consulted.
4. The number of salespeople or other store employees with whom the consumer talks.
5. The number of advertisements that the consumer sees, hears, or reads.

Some authors have noted that simply measuring the number of retailers visited, the number of buying guides consulted, and so forth is a poor measure of external information search. Another approach to assessing the external search process is to measure the extent to which a person relies on any particular source.[32] Also called the **instrumentality of search**, the approach involves assessing the extent to which the person relies on or finds useful the various sources of information. An example of a question used to assess the instrumentality of search might be: "To what extent did you rely on the advice of your friends, relatives, or neighbors, etc., in making this purchase decision?"

One study investigated the search behavior for major durable products (such as VCRs, stereo equipment, and televisions) and included a measure of instrumentality.[33] Researchers investigated the following categories of search: stores visited, interpersonal contacts with acquaintances, salespersons, neutral sources (e.g., reading *Consumer Reports*), and media advertising. The results revealed that the greatest amount of search occurred within the "stores visited" category. Similarly, visiting stores was rated as having the highest degree of instrumentality in making the purchase. This result does seem to make sense—that is, a rational shopper would search to a greater extent within the category that was perceived as the best place to get information.

The researchers also correlated the instrumentality ratings with the amount of search within each of the categories. An interesting finding was that the highest association occurred within the neutral sources category. Although relatively few people reported using neutral publications, such as *Consumer Reports*, those who did relied most heavily on them.

Factors Influencing the Degree of External Search

Consumers may be viewed as engaging in external search for the purpose of obtaining sufficient information to identify and compare alternatives. One issue concerns the question of what factors influence the degree of external search. Two divergent approaches can be identified for analyzing the factors that influence external search—an economic perspective and a decision-making perspective.

The Economic Perspective on Search

Economists who have tackled this question argue that consumers search as long as the marginal gains from search exceed the marginal costs of such a search.[34] From this viewpoint, consumers will continue searching only for as long as each incremental gain that results from the search is greater than the cost incurred to make the additional search. For example, suppose that you were searching for a used car. You live in a community of 50,000 people. You start looking in your city. You spend a week or so visiting the local used car dealers and scanning the "for sale" ads in newspapers. As a result of the search, you identify a couple of vehicles that are satisfactory. The next question is: Should you go to the big city that is 60 miles away to continue your search? In answering this question, you will compare the likely gain that could be obtained from going there (perhaps in terms of a better car for a lower price) against the costs of going there (more time spent, as well as travel and the psychic costs of dealing with more car salespersons). If you have found something satisfactory in your own community, the marginal benefits of going to the big city will probably be fewer than the marginal costs, and you will stop your search.

The problem with the economic approach is that it is difficult to quantify precisely marginal gains and costs. Despite the difficulty, however, these concepts should be considered by marketers. In general, the more costly it is for consumers to engage in external search, the less they will engage in the activity. A variety of factors can influence the cost of search, such as the physical proximity of stores, the cost of gasoline, and the value of the consumer's time.

In a like manner, one can predict that the greater the benefits of search, the greater the external search will be. Factors influencing the benefits obtained from search include the number of product alternatives available, the amount of product differentiation that occurs in the marketplace, and the amount of experience that the consumer has with the product category. If a number of different types of products are available in the marketplace and if they are highly differentiated, large benefits may be gained from external search behavior. In contrast, as the consumer gains experience with a product class, the benefits of additional search—and, as a consequence, the search process—will decrease. Thus at some point the costs of additional search exceed the benefits gained from it, and the search process stops.

Ideas from the economics of search have clear managerial implication. Firms marketing brands that are not leaders in the product category should attempt to lower the costs and increase the benefits of the consumer search process. In contrast, firms that do possess leading brands would like to convince consumers that additional search is a waste of time and money.

The Decision-Making Approach to the Search Process

Another approach to predicting the amount of external search conducted by consumers is to identify the type of purchase process in which they are engaged. In general, consumers engage in heavy amounts of external search only in a purchase process that involves extensive problem solving. Such extensive problem solving occurs under high-involvement conditions. Table 11-6 identifies a number of factors that are associated with consumers engaging in extensive problem solving. As seen in the table, three primary categories of factors influence the extent of problem solving and external search that a consumer pursues—factors associated with the risk of the product, factors associated with the characteristics of the consumer, and factors associated with the buying situation.

PRODUCT RISK FACTORS Evidence shows that as the perceived risk of a product increases, consumers tend to engage in more extensive problem solving and search.[35] The types of risk associated with the characteristics of a product are financial,

TABLE 11-6

Factors Associated with Consumers Engaging in Extensive Problem Solving

A. Factors associated with product risk
  1. Financial risk
  2. Performance risk
  3. Psychological risk
  4. Time risk
  5. Social risk
  6. Physical risk

B. Factors associated with consumer characteristics
  1. Consumer knowledge and experience
  2. Personality characteristics
  3. Demographic characteristics

C. Factors associated with the situation
  1. Amount of time available for purchase
  2. Number of product alternatives available
  3. Store locations
  4. Information availability
  5. Antecedent states of the consumer
  6. Social risk of the situation
  7. Task definition

performance, psychological, time, social, and physical. Thus, if a consumer recognizes a problem that can be solved only by purchasing a product or service that involves high perceived risk, it is more likely that the consumer will engage in extensive problem solving.

Some evidence exists that consumers may engage in greater amounts of search for services than for goods.[36] In a recent experimental study, researchers found that consumers less frequently purchased services outright than they did goods. In addition, the consumers tended to use the experiences of others as a source of information when they purchased services as compared to goods. The authors argued that these findings were obtained because services are more intangible and less standardized than goods, and as a result, they are inherently riskier.

Closely related to the concept of perceived risk is buyer uncertainty. That is, the greater the uncertainty of the consumer about the purchase, the greater the perceived risk. Interestingly, two different kinds of buyer uncertainty have been identified—knowledge uncertainty and choice uncertainty.[37] **Knowledge uncertainty** refers to the consumer's uncertainty concerning available features, their importance, and the performance of different brands on the various features. In contrast, **choice uncertainty** deals with the consumer's uncertainty about which of several brands to choose. Buyers can have knowledge uncertainty but low choice uncertainty, and vice versa. That is, an expert could have a great deal of information about the brands and still have difficulty in making a selection. Conversely, a novice could have little knowledge, and yet have no problem choosing among alternatives.

How do knowledge and choice uncertainty influence search behavior? The findings are somewhat surprising.[38] As one would expect, the greater the choice uncertainty, the greater the search behavior. In contrast, however, the greater the knowledge uncertainty, the less the search behavior. The most likely explanation for this finding is that knowledge uncertainty increases search costs. When people lack information, they feel uncomfortable interacting with salespeople and have difficulty interpreting marketing communications. As a result, they search less. From a managerial perspective, these results indicate that firms may have trouble communicating with consumers who have high knowledge uncertainty. If the cost structure allows, it may be best to reach such people with a well-trained sales force.

CONSUMER FACTORS The personality, demographic, and knowledge characteristics of the consumer also influence the extent of problem solving and external search behavior. For example, one researcher identified a group of consumers who perceived themselves as information seekers. This group was found to engage in more extensive external search prior to making a purchase.[39] Such personality characteristics as open-mindedness and self-confidence have been associated with greater amounts of external search.[40]

Other researchers have found that the less experience consumers have had with a product category, the greater is their information search behavior.[41] A number of studies have found that as consumers gain experience with a product category, their information search behavior decreases. This relationship between experience and external search, however, occurs only for those who have minimal experience levels. Some evidence exists that if the consumer has had little or no experience with a product class, he or she may feel threatened by the experience and engage in less search.[42] Such consumers probably have high knowledge uncertainty and, therefore, engage in less search.

A number of demographic characteristics have been found to be associated with higher levels of consumer search behavior. Higher levels of external search have been found for people having increased amounts of education and income. Similarly, individuals in higher-status occupations tend to engage in greater amounts of external search behavior.[43] Other researchers have found that search behavior tends to decrease as people grow older.[44]

SITUATIONAL FACTORS The characteristics of the consumer situation may also influence the amount of external search in which consumers engage. Thus the amount of time available to make a purchase may influence the amount of possible external search. Such antecedent states as fatigue, boredom, and sickness are also likely to negatively influence the ability of consumers to engage in external search. If the social risk of the purchase is perceived to be high, consumers are more likely to engage in greater amounts of external search. Similarly, how the person defines the purchase task is also likely to influence external search. If the purchase is to be made for some important occasion, such as the wedding of a close friend or an important party for business clients, it will be made with care and with greater amounts of external search.

Another situational factor deals with the nature of the market situation faced by the consumer. Researchers have found that as the number of product alternatives available increases, a tendency to engage in greater amounts of search results.[45] Similarly, the number of stores available and their proximity may also influence the amount of external search. When stores are numerous and in close physical proximity, consumers tend to engage in larger amounts of external search.[46] As one would expect, consumers tend to engage in large amounts of external search when shopping in large malls where a number of stores exist in close proximity to each other. These factors probably increase search because they reduce its costs.

One study investigated the search process for three product classes—televisions of various prices, videocassette recorders, and home computers.[47] External search effort was assessed by obtaining information on consumers' search efforts across media, retailers, people (e.g., friends, relatives, and neighbors), and neutral sources (e.g., reading *Consumer Reports*). The following findings were reported:

1. Product class knowledge was inversely related to total search effort.
2. As time availability increased, search effort increased.
3. As purchase involvement increased, total search effort increased.
4. As attitudes toward shopping increased, total search effort increased.

The results of the study supported a number of the relationships previously found for factors that influenced external search behavior.

How Much Search by Consumers?

Research has shown that consumers engage in surprisingly little external search, even when in extended problem-solving situations. For example, one study investigated the external search behavior for refrigerators.[48] The author found that 42% of the respondents visited only one store. Furthermore, 41% considered only one brand. Another study found that in 77% of the cases, consumers visited only one store when purchasing a small appliance.[49] Other researchers investigated the external search behavior for major appliances and automobiles. They concluded that "the amount of information sought by many buyers is small, even though information is accessible."[50]

Although consumers may visit few stores prior to purchasing appliances, one would expect them to engage in greater external search when all the options are in front of them. Such a situation is encountered when shopping in a grocery store. Here, all the options are arrayed on the shelves directly in front of the customer. The question then becomes: "In a grocery store, how much time do consumers spend before selecting a particular brand?" In addition, "How much can consumers remember about the price of the brand chosen?"

A recent study investigated these issues.[51] The authors found that shoppers on average spent only 12 seconds in their selection process for each good purchased. Immediately after they made a selection, they were asked to give the price of the brand selected. The researchers found that only 59% of the shoppers claimed to have checked the price. Less than half were actually able to state the correct price, and 32% gave a price that was off by an average of 15%. In fact, when a product was selling for a reduced price, less than half were even aware of the sale. The authors reported that executives of leading packaged goods firms were surprised and concerned with these results. Consumers tend not to engage in much external search, even in a grocery store. As a result, it is difficult to communicate with them via promotional strategy.

Although evidence shows that consumers engage in what appears to be low amounts of external search, one should not necessarily conclude that they are making purchases in an uninformed manner. Some evidence exists that the consumer self-report surveys used to gather such information may understate the actual amount of search by consumers—that is, when asked to describe their search process, many consumers forget all the steps they used.[52] In addition, consumers may frequently be quite experienced in the purchase of the product and simply may not need to engage in large amounts of external search to make a purchase.

Finally, consumers may engage in relatively little external search because they have engaged in extensive amounts of prepurchase search. Research indicates that a majority of consumers exhibit high levels of presearch decision activities.[53] Such presearch activities may result from the passive, low-involvement reception of information from marketing communications. On the other hand, they may result from consumers who have an enduring involvement with a product class and who consistently engage in high-involvement prepurchase search activities.[54]

Managerial Implications of the Search Stage

Analyzing the consumer search process is particularly important for promotional strategy and physical distribution. As noted previously, market researchers need to identify whether the target market engages in limited or extended decision making when purchasing the product. The entire promotion and distribution strategy will be influenced by the type of decision process used by consumers.

If consumers are likely to move through a high-involvement decision process, promotional efforts should focus on providing customers with information about the product or service so that informed decisions can be made. Distribution of the product or service does not have to be extremely extensive when high-involvement decision making is occurring because consumers are likely to travel farther to obtain the acquisition. However, the quality of the service provided is likely to be important to such customers. In contrast, if the decision process is of a low-involvement nature, then promotion should be highly extensive but relatively simple to create brand awareness. In addition, distribution needs to be extensive to have the product or service readily available.

A MANAGERIAL APPLICATIONS EXAMPLE

Between 1982 and 1989 the sales of draft beer sold in kegs and on tap declined steadily. As one marketing expert explained, "Americans had forgotten to drink draft." Then, in 1990 and again in 1991, sales of draft beer suddenly turned around. They grew by 2.7% in 1990. In 1991 they were holding their own, while sales of canned and bottled beers dropped by over 4%. What caused the sudden turnaround in sales when the consumption of alcoholic beverages in general was falling?[55]

A number of explanations were offered by marketing pundits. Among beer tasting experts, it is well known that draft beer simply tastes better than canned or bottled beer. Draft beer tends to be fresher, and because it is not pasteurized, it lacks the slightly cooked taste. As one expert said, "Americans are drinking less, but they're drinking better. Keg beer is in every instance better than bottled beer." The differences in taste may also have been accentuated by the advertising campaign for Miller Genuine Draft beer. By nationally advertising a bottled beer as draft, Miller Brewing may have alerted consumers to the differences in the taste of the various sudsy beverages.

A number of other factors may also have played a role. Keg beer usually costs less for taverns and bars to serve per serving. As a result, they frequently give customers discounts on draft beer. When the recession of the 1990s kicked in, consumers may have grown more price conscious. As a result, they have shifted their buying patterns. In addition, the 1990s brought a new attitude: showing off by buying products for their expensive labels became less socially acceptable. Sipping draft beer from a glass became the appropriate behavior. In addition, the burgeoning "green revolution" increased ecological consciousness. Thus drinking draft beer from a glass became viewed as a more ecologically sound act than gulping a brew from a can or bottle and then having to throw it away.

In the early 1990s, the rewards for offering draft beer were great. The trend was well illustrated at the Pearl Street Grill in Denver, Colorado. Its owner was having trouble selling a microbrand called "Pete's Wicked Ale." Then, the owner changed to a draft version of the brand and sales took off. Understating the situation, he said, "I would think those beers not available on tap would be at a disadvantage at this point."

The problem statement in the case can be framed in the following way. Given the various reasons for draft beer's surge in popularity, what are the implications for the managers of taverns, based upon the information contained in this chapter?

The Consumer Behavior Analysis

Just as with any other good or service, consumers go through a decision process when purchasing a beer in a tavern. Problem recognition occurs, followed by a search process, an evaluation of alternatives, choice, and postacquisition evaluation. A number of concepts from the chapter apply to the question of why consumers started buying more draft beer in the early 1990s. Such concepts include the decision-making perspective, the experiential perspective, problem recognition, and external search.

From the decision-making perspective, the analyst seeks to determine whether consumers are engaged in extended versus limited decision making. When buying a beer in a tavern, a consumer probably uses a limited decision process. In such an instance, the search process is quite brief and only a few attributes are used to evaluate the alternatives.

From the experiential perspective, the researcher seeks to identify the feelings and emotions that influence the purchase process. In the case of the purchase of beer, the consumer is probably looking for a brand that will provide the taste sensations desired. The analyst also attempts to determine the symbolic aspects of the consumption experience. The researcher would want to know what image various brands symbolize and what messages drinking a draft versus a bottled beer communicates to others.

From the perspective of the problem recognition stage, the analyst would want to identify the desired and actual states that influence customers in taverns. Do consumers go to bars because they are thirsty (i.e., the actual state has moved lower) or because they seek to interact socially with someone (i.e., the desired state has changed)? What is the desired state for the customer when purchasing a beer?

The search stage of the decision-making process also has implications for the consumer behavior analysis. Once in the tavern, consumers can rely totally on external search because they merely have to ask the bartender or waitress to list the brands available. This list can then be compared to the consideration set of beer brands already held by the customer. It may be the case that the positive publicity received by draft beers automatically places them in the consideration set.

The Managerial Applications Analysis

Table 11-7 presents the managerial applications analysis for the draft beer example, illustrating the four consumer concepts that relate to the case: the decision-making perspective, the experiential perspective, problem recognition, and search. When the case is viewed from the decision-making perspective, it has implications for marketing research, positioning, segmentation, and the marketing mix. Marketing research should be conducted to determine the key attributes used by patrons to select beers. (Note that the marketing research could be quite informal and involve conversations with a large number of customers.) To what extent do price, a concern for ecology or image, and superior taste influence choice? Depending upon the answer to this question, the manager could consider using the information to assist in positioning the tavern appropriately for the market segment that is being targeted.

For example, if it were found that consumers really purchased draft beer for taste and ecological reasons, these themes could be used to position the tavern. The positioning strategy would then be carried out via the marketing mix. In particular, the manager would have to carry appropriate products (i.e., brands of draft beer) and develop a promotional campaign that communicated these themes to customers. In the case of tap beer, it appears that a wide range of factors may influence consumers—such as price, taste, and ecology.

The experiential perspective applies to market research and the marketing mix. Again, market research should be conducted to determine the feelings and emotions sought by customers in the tavern. In addition, the manager should attempt to identify the symbolic meanings attached to various brands of draft and bottled beer. Such information would be useful in determining the mix of brands of beers to have in stock for the market segment that the manager is attempting to reach. Likewise, consumer attitudes toward various brands could influence the promotional strategy of the manager, as well as decisions regarding the type of atmosphere to create within the tavern. From an experiential perspective, the symbolism of purchasing a tap beer may have played a major role in shifting demand.

TABLE 11-7

Managerial Applications Analysis of the Draft Beer Case

Consumer Concepts	*Managerial Applications*
Decision-making perspective	*Market research*—Identify key attributes used by patrons to select beer and taverns.
	Product—Carry beers that possess key attributes desired by consumers.
	Positioning—Develop strategy to position tavern based upon beers sought.
	Segmentation—Target customers who desire the particular attributes and types/brands of beer.
	Promotional strategy—Develop ads, point-of-purchase displays, etc., to implement positioning and segmentation strategies.
Experiential perspective	*Market research*—Employ studies to identify the feelings and emotions sought by consumers in taverns. Identify symbols that impact customers.
	Promotional strategy—Employ advertising and point-of-purchase displays that use appropriate symbols to elicit feelings and emotions.
Problem recognition	*Market research*—Identify problems that going to a tavern can solve for consumers.
	Positioning—Position the tavern in a way that depicts how it can solve this problem.
	Promotional strategy—Employ advertising to portray the appropriate image of the tavern to customers.
Search	*Market research*—Identify the beers in the target market's consideration set and carry those beers.
	Positioning—Develop positioning strategy that involves carrying the brands in customers' consideration set.
	Promotional strategy—Communicate through advertising to customers information that will place the tavern in their consideration set.

Problem recognition applies to market research, positioning, and the marketing mix. The manager should conduct market research to identify the problems that customers seek to solve when they enter the tavern. Are they entering the tavern to drink heavily, to interact in a romantic, quiet atmosphere, or to have a great time with a crowd?

Finding the problem that drives the consumption process could then be used to position the tavern (e.g., as a bar for having a great noisy time). Advertising can then be used to communicate the desired image to consumers. In addition, the manager should build the physical facilities of the bar so as to create the desired atmosphere. In the case of tap beer sales, problem recognition may have influenced sales by a process in which customers sought a particular desired state of drinking a less expensive, good-tasting beer that lacked a prestigious name.

The search process applies to market research, to positioning, and to marketing mix. The tavern owner must identify the beers in the target market's consideration set. To be successful, the bar needs to carry a number of brands from this set of beers. Because of positive publicity surrounding tap beers, this category of brands may well be placed automatically into the consideration set. Thus positioning the tavern as carrying distinctive, low-priced, great-tasting draft beer could be a major plus. Of course, the positioning strategy would be implemented by advertising appropriately and by carrying an interesting product selection (i.e., brands of draft beer).

SUMMARY

Consumer decision making involves the analysis of how people choose between two or more alternative acquisitions and of the processes that take place before and after the choice. Acquisitions can occur when traditional purchases are made with money, personal checks, or credit. In addition, nonpurchase acquisitions also exist. Such acquisitions include borrowing a product, trading products or services, making a product, receiving an inheritance, and stealing. A generic consumer decision process can be identified that consists of five stages: problem recognition, search, alternative evaluation, choice, and postacquisition evaluation.

Three divergent perspectives can be used to examine the consumer decision process. The dominant approach in consumer behavior has been the decision-making perspective. From this perspective, consumers are viewed as decision makers who make rational decisions regarding the products and services they buy. Researchers have identified two different buying processes within the decision-making perspective. When consumers are highly involved in the purchase, they tend to engage in an extended decision-making process. In such high-involvement purchases consumers are described as moving through each of the five stages of the action process in a sequential manner.

On the other hand, when consumers perceive little personal importance in the purchase, they move through a limited decision process. The search stage is minimized and the alternative evaluation stage may be largely skipped. In limited decision making the choice process is much simpler than in high-involvement conditions.

From the experiential perspective, consumers are viewed as searching for products and services that elicit sensations, feelings, images, emotions, and fun. Some industries, such as the leisure industry, are based on creating experiences for people. The phenomenon of impulse buying also seems to result in large part from consumers attempting to gain new and different experiences.

The third approach to consumer buying is labeled the behavioral influence perspective. From this perspective, certain types of consumer behaviors are viewed as resulting from the effects of environmental forces rather than from the beliefs or feelings of consumers. In effect, behavior is induced directly. A variety of behaviors, such as store choice and even product choice, may result from the effects of such phenomena as cultures, small groups, other people, and situations.

The stages of problem recognition and search were discussed in this chapter as well. Problem recognition occurs when a sufficiently large discrepancy develops between an actual and a desired state of being. A variety of factors can raise and lower the level of both the desired and actual states.

The consumer search process consists of those steps taken to acquire information about the products and services that may eliminate the problem identified in the first decision stage. Two types of search have been identified. Internal search consists of the consumer's searching through long-term memory for information on brands that may eliminate the problem. External search involves the consumer in seeking outside sources of information on what products may eliminate a problem.

KEY TERMS

actual state
awareness set
behavioral influence perspective
choice uncertainty
compulsive consumption
compulsive purchases
consideration set
consumer acquisitions
consumer decision making
decision-making perspective
desired state
experiential perspective
external search
impulse purchases
inept set
inert set
instrumentality of search
internal search
knowledge uncertainty
monetary acquisitions
nonmonetary acquisitions
ongoing search
preneed goods
prepurchase search
problem recognition
search processes
variety-seeking purchases

REVIEW QUESTIONS

1. Explain what is meant by the term consumer decision making.
2. Define the term consumer acquisitions. What are the types of acquisitions that consumers may make?
3. Identify the stages of the generic consumer decision process.
4. Identify the three alternative perspectives on consumer acquisitions. How do these perspectives differ from each other in explaining the factors that influence the consumer decision process?
5. How does the movement of consumers through the stages of the decision process differ in high- and low-involvement conditions?
6. Contrast the experiential perspective with the decision-making view of consumer buying behavior.
7. Contrast the behavioral influence perspective with the decision-making view of consumer buying behavior.
8. Discuss the concept of consumer problem recognition. What are the factors that tend to influence the consumer's actual state and the consumer's desired state?
9. Discuss the factors that cause consumers to engage in extensive problem solving and high amounts of external search.
10. From the perspective of an economist, what are the factors that influence the amount of external search in which a consumer will engage?
11. Give three examples of how marketing mix strategies should differ in extended versus limited decision making.
12. Identify three implications each for the experiential and behavioral influence perspectives on managerial strategy.
13. Identify the categories of brands that consumers may retrieve from memory during internal search.

DISCUSSION QUESTIONS

1. Identify a consumer purchase you have made in which you engaged in an extensive decision process. What were the steps you went through in selecting the brand to purchase? To what extent did this series of steps match the high-involvement decision process discussion in the chapter?
2. Identify a consumer purchase you have made that was based largely upon an experiential buying process. What were the steps you went through in selecting the product or service in this case? What were the types of feelings and experiences you were seeking from the purchase?
3. Attempt to identify a recent purchase or activity that resulted largely from behavioral influence. To what extent did you have any feelings about the action? To what extent did you engage in any extensive amounts of search for the product or service purchased? What environmental factor was most responsible for the purchase or action?
4. Try to identify a consumer purchase or action in which more than one of the purchase processes was involved. Which of the processes were operating simultaneously? Which of the processes tended to dominate the decision?
5. List as many as you can of the purchases of over five dollars that you have made over the past several weeks. Categorize these as to whether they best fit into the high-involvement decision perspective, the low-involvement decision perspective, the experiential perspective, or the behavioral influence perspective. From which category did most of your purchases come?
6. To what extent do consumers characteristically use one of the purchase approaches more than others? To what extent do consumers show individual differences in their tendency to use one of the perspectives? For example, do some consumers tend to use a decision-making approach, whereas others tend to use an experiential approach in making their purchases?
7. How might advertising differ for products that are typically purchased under high-involvement conditions as opposed to products bought under low-involvement conditions?
8. Consider the product category of toothpaste. Identify your awareness set, consideration set, and inert set for the various brands of toothpaste that you can recall. What could a company do to move its toothpaste from the inert set to the consideration set?
9. Why would a company that markets razor blades be interested in encouraging consumers to engage in problem recognition? How might a company that markets razor blades encourage consumers to engage in problem recognition?
10. Under what circumstances would a company want consumers to engage in large amounts of search behavior? Under what circumstances would a company want consumers to minimize their search behavior?

ENDNOTES

1. From the diary of John C. Mowen, July 14, 1988.
2. The consumer decision process has been discussed in consumer behavior textbooks for over 20 years. Important contributors to its formulation were John Howard and Jagdish Sheth, *The Theory of Buyer Behavior* (New York: John Wiley 1969); James Engel, David Kollat, and Roger Blackwell, *Consumer Behavior*, 2nd ed. (New York: Holt, Rinehart and Winston, 1973); and Francesco Nicosia, *Consumer Decision Processes: Marketing and Advertising Implications* (Englewood Cliffs, NJ: Prentice-Hall, 1966).
3. Russell Belk, "ACR Presidential Address: Happy Thought," in *Advances in Consumer*

Research, Vol. 14, Melanie Wallendorf and Paul Anderson, eds. (Provo, UT: Association for Consumer Research, 1987), pp. 1–4.

4. Richard Olshavsky and Donald Granbois, "Consumer Decision Making—Fact or Fiction?" *Journal of Consumer Research*, Vol. 6 (September 1979), p. 98.
5. Herbert Krugman, "The Impact of Television on Advertising: Learning Without Involvement," *Public Opinion Quarterly*, Vol. 30 (Fall 1965), pp. 349–356.
6. For an excellent discussion of low-involvement decision making, see Stewart De Bruicker, "An Appraisal of Low-Involvement Consumer Information Processing," in *Attitude Research Plays for High Stakes*, John Maloney and Bernard Silverman, eds. (Chicago: American Marketing Association, 1979), pp. 112–130.
7. Meera P. Venkatraman and Deborah J. MacInnis, "The Epistemic and Sensory Exploratory Behaviors of Hedonic and Cognitive Consumers," in *Advances in Consumer Research*, Vol. 12, Elizabeth Hirschman and Morris Holbrook, eds. (Provo, UT: Association for Consumer Research, 1985), pp. 102–107.
8. Morris Holbrook and Elizabeth Hirschman, "The Experiential Aspects of Consumption: Consumer Fantasies, Feelings, and Fun," *Journal of Consumer Research*, Vol. 9 (September 1982), pp. 132–140.
9. Dennis Rook, "The Buying Impulse," *Journal of Consumer Research*, Vol. 14 (September 1987), pp. 189–199.
10. "Industrial Retail Selling Strategies Designed to Induce Impulse Sales," *Beverage Industry*, June 3, 1977, pp. 6ff.
11. Thomas C. O'Guinn and Ronald J. Faber, "Compulsive Buying: A Phenomenological Exploration," *Journal of Consumer Research*, Vol. 16 (September 1989), pp. 147–157.
12. Elizabeth C. Hirschman, "The Consciousness of Addiction: Toward a General Theory of Compulsive Consumption," *Journal of Consumer Research*, Vol. 19 (September 1992), pp. 155–179.
13. M. Venkatesan, "Cognitive Consistency and Novelty Seeking," in *Consumer Behavior: Theoretical Sources*, Scott Ward and Thomas Robertson, eds. (Englewood Cliffs, NJ: Prentice-Hall, 1973), pp. 354–384.
14. P. S. Raju, "Optimum Stimulation Level: Its Relationship to Personality, Demographics, and Exploratory Behavior," *Journal of Consumer Research*, Vol. 7 (December 1980), pp. 272–282. For a review of variety seeking, see Leigh McAlister and Edgar Pessemier, "Variety Seeking Behavior: An Interdisciplinary Review," *Journal of Consumer Research*, Vol. 9 (December 1982), pp. 311–322.
15. John L. Lastovicka, "The Low Involvement Point-of-Purchase: A Case Study of Margarine Buyers," paper presented at the First Consumer Involvement Conference, New York University, New York City, June 1982.
16. Sidney J. Levy, "Symbols for Sales," *Harvard Business Review*, Vol. 37 (July–August 1959), pp. 117–124.
17. Jeff Meer, "The Light Touch," *Psychology Today*, September 1985, pp. 60–67.
18. Itamar Simonson and Russell S. Winer, "The Influence of Purchase Quantity and Display Format on Consumer Preference for Variety," *The Journal of Consumer Research*, Vol. 19 (June 1992), pp. 133–138.
19. Gordon C. Bruner and Richard J. Pomazal, "Problem Recognition: The Crucial First Stage of the Consumer Decision Process," *Journal of Consumer Marketing* (Winter 1988), pp. 53–63.
20. C. Jayachandran and Nyroslaw Kyj, "Pre-Need Purchasing Behavior: An Overlooked Dimension in Consumer Marketing," *Journal of Consumer Marketing* (Summer 1987), pp. 59–66.
21. James R. Bettman, *An Information Processing Theory of Consumer Choice* (Reading, MA: Addison-Wesley, 1979).
22. Peter Bloch, Daniel Sherrell, and Nancy Ridgway, "Consumer Search: An Extended Framework," *Journal of Consumer Research*, Vol. 13 (June 1986), pp. 119–126.
23. Ibid.

24. For information on the categories of brands that consumers may retrieve from long-term memory, see F. May and R. Homans, "Evoked Set Size and the Level of Information Processing in Product Comprehension and Choice Criteria," in *Advances in Consumer Research*, Vol. 4, W. D. Perreault, ed. (Chicago: Association for Consumer Research, 1977), pp. 172–175. Also, see Naeim Abougomaah, John Schlacter, and William Gaidis, "Elimination and Choice Phases in Evoked Set Formation," *Journal of Consumer Marketing* (Fall 1987), pp. 67–73.

25. Joseph Pereira, "Name of the Game: Brand Awareness," *The Wall Street Journal*, February 14, 1991, p. B1.

26. John Howard and Jagdish Sheth, *The Theory of Buyer Behavior* (New York: John Wiley, 1969).

27. Michael Reilly and Thomas Parkinson, "Individual and Product Correlates of Evoked Set Size for Consumer Package Goods," in *Advances in Consumer Research*, Vol. 12, Elizabeth Hirschman and Morris Holbrook, eds. (Provo, UT: Association of Consumer Research, 1985), pp. 492–497.

28. Ibid.

29. Ayn E. Crowley and John H. Williams, "An Information Theoretic Approach to Understanding the Consideration Set/Awareness Set Proportion," in *Advances in Consumer Research*, Vol. 18, Rebecca Holman and Michael Solomon, eds. (Provo, UT: Association for Consumer Research, 1991), pp. 780–787.

30. Sharon Beatty and Scott Smith, "External Search Effort: An Investigation Across Several Product Categories," *Journal of Consumer Research*, Vol. 14 (June 1987), p. 84.

31. For an excellent current review of the factors associated with the extent of external search, see Beatty and Smith, "External Search Effort."

32. Jeff Blodgett and Donna Hill, "An Exploratory Study Comparing Amount-of-Search Measures to Consumers' Reliance on Each Source of Information," in *Advances in Consumer Research*, Vol. 18, Rebecca Holman and Michael Solomon, eds. (Provo, UT: Association for Consumer Research, 1991), pp. 773–779.

33. Ibid.

34. Arieh Goldman and J. K. Johansson, "Determinants of Search for Lower Prices: An Empirical Assessment of the Economics of Information Theory," *Journal of Consumer Research*, Vol. 5 (December 1978), pp. 176–186.

35. Konrad Dedler, I. Gottschalk, and K. G. Grunert, "Perceived Risk as a Hint for Better Information and Better Products," in *Advances in Consumer Research*, Vol. 8, Kent Monroe, ed. (Ann Arbor, MI: Association for Consumer Research, 1981), pp. 391–397.

36. Keith B. Murray, "A Test of Services Marketing Theory: Consumer Information Acquisition Activities," *Journal of Marketing*, Vol. 55 (January 1991), pp. 10–25.

37. Joel E. Urbany, Peter R. Dickson, and William L. Wilkie, "Buyer Uncertainty and Information Search," *The Journal of Consumer Research*, Vol. 16 (September 1989), pp. 208–215.

38. Ibid.

39. R. Kelly, "The Search Component of the Consumer Decision-Making Process—A Theoretic Examination," in *Marketing and the New Sciences of Planning*, C. King, ed. (Chicago: American Marketing Association, 1968), p. 273.

40. W. B. Locander and P. W. Hermann, "The Effect of Self-Confidence and Anxiety on Information Seeking in Consumer Risk Reduction," *Journal of Marketing Research*, Vol. 16 (May 1979), pp. 268–274.

41. See, for example, John Swan, "Experimental Analysis of Predecision Information Seeking," *Journal of Marketing Research* (May 1969), pp. 192–197.

42. J. R. Bettman and C. W. Park, "Effects of Prior Knowledge and Experience and Phase of the Choice Process on Consumer Decision Processes: A Protocol Analysis," *Journal of Consumer Research*, Vol. 7 (December 1980), pp. 234–247.

43. N. Capon and M. Burke, "Individual, Product Class, and Task Related Factors in Consumer

Information Processing," *Journal of Consumer Research*, Vol. 7 (August 1972), pp. 249–257.

44. J. Newman and R. Staelin, "Prepurchase Information Seeking for New Cars and Major Household Appliances," *Journal of Marketing Research*, Vol. 9 (August 1972), pp. 249–257.

45. D. R. Lehmann and W. L. Moore, "Validity of Information Display Boards: An Assessment Using Longitudinal Data," *Journal of Marketing Research*, Vol. 17 (November 1980), pp. 450–459.

46. G. S. Cort and L. V. Dominquez, "Cross Shopping and Retail Growth," *Journal of Marketing*, Vol. 14 (May 1977), pp. 187–192.

47. Beatty and Smith, "External Search Effort."

48. W. Dommermuth, "The Shopping Matrix and Marketing Strategy," *Journal of Marketing Research*, Vol. 2 (May 1965), pp. 128–132.

49. J. Udell, "Prepurchase Behavior of Buyers of Small Appliances," *Journal of Marketing*, Vol. 30 (October 1966), pp. 50–52.

50. Newman and Staelin, "Prepurchase Information Seeking."

51. Peter R. Dickson and Alan G. Sawyer, "The Price Knowledge and Search of Supermarket Shoppers," *Journal of Marketing*, Vol. 54 (July 1990), pp. 42–53.

52. J. Newman and B. Lockeman, "Measuring Prepurchase Information Seeking," *Journal of Consumer Research*, Vol. 2 (December 1975), pp. 216–222.

53. Girish Punj, "Presearch Decision Making in Consumer Durable Purchases," *Journal of Consumer Marketing*, Vol. 4 (Winter 1987), pp. 71–82.

54. Peter Bloch and Marsha Richins, "Shopping Without Purchase: An Investigation of Consumer Browsing Behavior," in *Advances in Consumer Research*, Vol. 10, Richard Bagozzi and Alice Tybout, eds. (Ann Arbor, MI: Association for Consumer Research, 1983), pp. 389–393.

55. Example based upon Marj Charlier, "Bars Cheer as More Patrons Order Drafts," *The Wall Street Journal*, September 27, 1991, pp. B1, B4.

CHAPTER 11 CASE STUDY

KFC Flounders with Fried Fowl

In 1991 Kentucky Fried Chicken Corporation changed its strategy. First, it changed the name of its restaurants from "Kentucky Fried Chicken" to "KFC" in an attempt to downplay the word "fried." Next, it streamlined its corporate logo, brightened the decor of its restaurants, and added skinless chicken to its menu to appeal to more health-conscious consumers. But the efforts showed little signs of success. In 1991 the amount of chicken consumed in fast-food restaurants increased by over 10%. A change in consumer tastes and preferences was occurring, and customers began switching from hamburgers to chicken. At KFC, however, store sales were flat, and executives at KFC's corporate parent, PepsiCo, Inc., were impatient [1].

Meanwhile, other fast-food restaurants launched a host of new non–fried chicken products. Wendy's developed a grilled chicken sandwich. Burger King created its BK Broiler. McDonald's offered nonfried chicken fajitas. However, in 1991, 90% of all fast-food chicken sales were of the fried variety. As one consultant said, "People talk much healthier than they buy." He argued that the jury is still out on whether consumers really buy healthy dishes at fast-food restaurants.

Some analysts suggested that KFC's problems stemmed from a wider range of problems than the word "fried" in its name. Its stores tend to be located in middle- or lower-income neighborhoods. In these locations, consumers are less health conscious. In addition, its franchises are owned by independently minded individuals, many of whom have resisted its new product offerings. Finally, the chain is so closely associated with chicken that a strategy to branch out to other types of entrees (e.g., hamburgers) would be extremely difficult. As one analyst said, "The marketing challenge is a matter of attracting new users without losing their current loyal following."

Then, there is the problem of "cannibalization." When the company brought out its Lite 'n' Crispy skinless chicken, consumers in some stores jumped at it. Although it is fried, the chicken does not have any skin, where most of the fat is contained. The problem was that, instead of attracting new customers, it merely took sales from other higher-margin chicken entrees served in the restaurants.

The company has also tried out baked and broiled chicken entrees. Both efforts failed, though. One spokesman for the company said, "It's not a no-brainer. We've learned a product has got to be unbelievably indulgent, special and unique and not eminently substitutable at home. Just another roast chicken is not what they're clamoring for."

The company has been more successful in its modernization efforts, however. By the end of 1991, 85% of its stores had been remodeled and had the new logo installed. It plans to build 5,000 more stores in the United States by the year 2000, one-third of which will offer delivery. But in 1991, the franchisees were becoming impatient. One store owner in Oklahoma said, "We hear a lot is in test, but haven't seen anything out there that's been a home run."

QUESTIONS

1. Identify the problems faced by KFC.
2. What consumer behavior concepts from Chapter 11 apply to the problem?

3. Develop a managerial applications analysis. Discuss the managerial implications of each of the consumer concepts identified.

REFERENCE

1. Laurie M. Grossman, "'Healthful' Approach Is Failing to Bring Sizzle to Kentucky Fried Chicken Sales," *The Wall Street Journal*, September 13, 1991, pp. B1, B8.

Chapter

12

Consumer Decision Processes II: Evaluation and Choice

CONSUMER VIGNETTE

On the Personal Dignity of Bathing Suits

More than one-third of the women who make the purchase call it "traumatic." Cathy Guisewite, author of the comic strip "Cathy," is a tiny size five, yet she barely escapes with "some shred of dignity." Karen Wapner, who sells these things, is putting off her purchase. She pines, "Maybe I'll get sick and lose weight in the next month, or maybe something exciting will happen and I'll be too busy to eat." After finding an unwanted bulge, a 30-year-old advertising coordinator groans, "Too small—I hate buying these. It's humiliating."[1]

What causes such distress among successful women? What is it that causes them to hope to get sick and to spend thousands of dollars on health club memberships? Quite simply, it's the fear of purchasing and being seen in a bathing suit. Men don't seem to have the problem. European women allegedly avoid the trauma. The answer lies in the nature of the evaluation process that takes place during consumer decision making. The cause of the distress results from the failure of American women's bodies to measure up to expectations of what they should look like. Formed by observing the perfect figures of beauty contestants and fashion models, for most women the expectations are impossible to meet and lead to feelings of inferiority and fear.

Whereas most women dread buying bathing suits, the revealing garments are a boon to *Sports Illustrated*. In February of each year, the magazine displays most of the perfect bodies of comely models in its famous swimsuit issue. During normal months, the magazine sells about 3 million copies; however, in February, sales jump to at least 5.5 million.[2] In addition, advertisers pay about 28% more than normal for their ads to appear in the issue. Newsstand buyers pay $3.95 instead of the regular $1.70

price. In 1989, *SI* also sold a videocassette version of the swimsuit issue along with the usual spate of calendars. Total revenues from the extravaganza were expected to run about $29 million. The profits from the one swimsuit issue are higher than the full-year profits of many other magazines, such as *Golf* or *Tennis* magazines.

How do you explain the phenomenon of the *Sports Illustrated* swimsuit issue? The answer lies in part in the nature of the choice process used to purchase products such as magazines. The problem of trying on swimsuits for women and the impact of swimsuits on *SI*'s sales illustrate the two major topics of this chapter—evaluation and choice processes.

INTRODUCTION

In the last chapter, the first two stages of the consumer decision process were discussed—problem recognition and search. This chapter focuses on the next two stages—evaluation and choice. During **alternative evaluation**, consumers form beliefs and attitudes regarding the decision alternatives. Because of this close connection, the material in Chapter 8, Consumer Attitudes, Beliefs, and Behaviors, is directly relevant to the discussion of alternative evaluation. **Choice** involves the actual selection of one acquisition option from two or more alternatives. This chapter will discuss a number of approaches that describe how consumers may make such choices.

The swimsuit vignette illustrates one of the factors that influences the alternative evaluation process. As the multiattribute model of attitude formation suggests, consumers may evaluate the extent to which they believe an object possesses a particular attribute and provides a particular benefit. When trying on swimsuits, women may be forming a belief of the likelihood that a particular swimsuit will make them look good. In forming the belief, however, some frame of reference is needed. The frame of reference is used as an anchor for the comparison. In many instances women use images of models and beauty queens as their anchor for comparison. Unfortunately, in comparison to this anchor, most women are likely to be highly disappointed.

A recent study found evidence of a negative impact of advertisements that employ highly attractive models.[3] In the study, college women were exposed to magazine ads that used either highly attractive models or no models. Ratings were later taken of the young women's self-perceived attractiveness. The results revealed that those who had seen the attractive models rated their own physical appearance significantly more negatively than those who did not see the models. In comparison to the highly attractive anchor created by the models, their own personal appearance failed to measure up satisfactorily. The concept of anchoring and adjustment and its impact on the evaluation process will be discussed later in the chapter.

The *Sports Illustrated* example reflects one of the approaches to understanding the choice process. When discussing how people make choices, the three perspectives on consumer behavior should be considered. It is possible to argue that the decision to purchase the swimsuit issue occurs after forming a series of dispassionate beliefs about the magazine, as the traditional multiattribute models of attitude formation would suggest. However, perhaps a more realistic way of viewing the choice process in this instance is to analyze it from the experiential perspective—that is, men may purchase the issue to obtain certain feelings and emotions. Thus choice could be based upon experiential processes in the *Sports Illustrated* example. Let us, then, analyze the processes through which alternative evaluation and choice occur.

ALTERNATIVE EVALUATION

In the alternative evaluation stage of the acquisition process, the consumer compares the options identified as potentially capable of solving the problem that initiated the decision process. When the options are compared, the consumer may form beliefs, attitudes, and intentions about the alternatives under consideration. Thus alternative evaluation and the development of beliefs, attitudes, and intentions are closely related.

Alternative evaluation can be analyzed from the viewpoint of the three perspectives on consumer behavior—the decision-making perspective, the experiential perspective, and the behavioral influence perspective. As suggested by the material on attitude formation, the nature of the alternative evaluation process is influenced by the type of hierarchy of effects occurring. From a high-involvement decision-making perspective, alternative evaluation follows the standard learning model in which the hierarchy of effects flows from belief formation to affect formation to behavioral intentions. In such instances the multiattribute models of attitude may be used to describe the evaluation process. Thus the result of alternative evaluation under high-involvement conditions is likely to be the development of global attitudes toward each of the acquisition options.

Figure 12-1 presents a print advertisement targeted at the high-involvement consumer. On the first page of the two-page ad, one sees a photo of the golfing superstar Jack Nicklaus and the headline "Try our new RPMs. We developed them to give the perimeter-weighted iron what it was missing. . . . feel!" Copy on the second page of the advertisement provides information on no fewer than seven different attributes. The goal of the ad is to provide information so that the golfing enthusiast may integrate it into a positive overall attitude toward the brand.

In low-involvement situations, alternative evaluation consists of the formation of a few rudimentary beliefs about the options under consideration. Indeed, relatively little alternative evaluation tends to occur under low-involvement conditions. Strong affective reactions (i.e., attitudes) are viewed as developing only after behavior occurs.

From the experiential perspective, the evaluation process is viewed as affect driven. The focus is not on belief formation but rather on affect creation. Thus the researcher investigates what feelings and emotions are elicited by the acquisition that is about to be made. Finally, from the behavioral influence perspective, consumers are conceptualized as never consciously comparing alternatives. Table 12-1 summarizes the alternative evaluation process from the decision-making, experiential, and behavioral influence perspectives.

TABLE 12-1

Alternative Evaluation and the Hierarchies of Effects

Hierarchy of Effect	*How Alternatives Compared*
High-involvement hierarchy	Beliefs about attributes are compared. Affective reactions are compared.
Low-involvement hierarchy	Limited number of beliefs about attributes are compared.
Experiential hierarchy	Affective reactions are compared.
Behavioral influence hierarchy	No internal comparison processes are recognized as occurring prior to behavior.

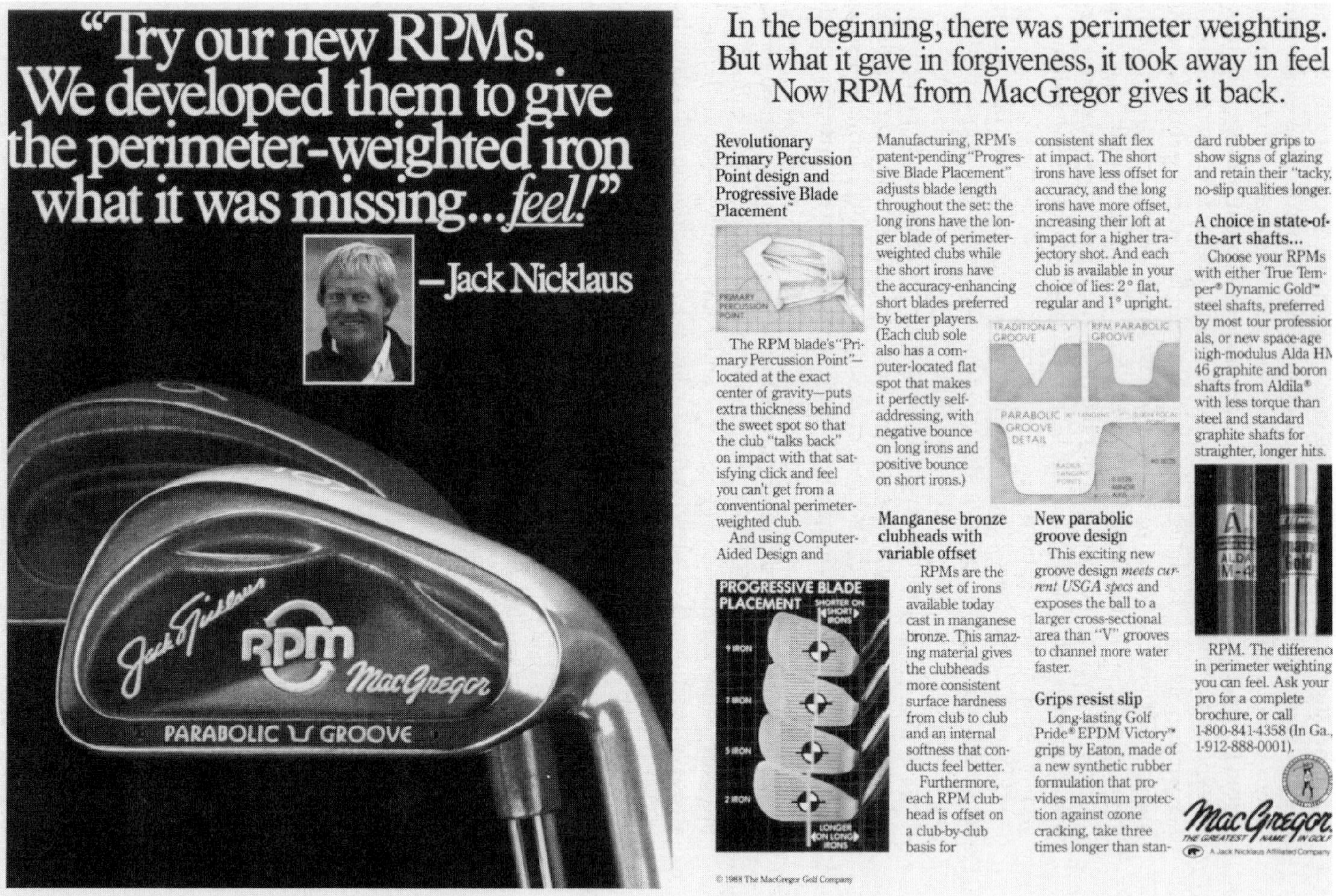

Figure 12-1 MacGregor attempts to influence the alternative evaluation process by providing the high-involvement golfing enthusiast with detailed information on the brand. (Courtesy of MacGregor Golf Company.)

Consumer Judgments and Alternative Evaluation

As noted, alternative evaluation occurs when consumers make overall assessments to compare and contrast options. When evaluating alternatives, consumers make two types of judgments. A **judgment** consists of a person (1) estimating the likelihood that something will occur and/or (2) valuing the goodness or badness of something. Judging probabilities and judging value are central to the alternative evaluation process. For example, suppose that a high school senior living in the southern part of Florida is comparing three schools—the University of South Florida, the University of Central Florida, and the University of Miami. When comparing these options, the student will make two types of judgments. First, she will act as though she estimates the likelihood that each option will perform as expected on each of the attributes on which it is being evaluated. Second, she will act as though she values the goodness or badness of each of the attributes.

Of course, readers will recognize that the judgment of probabilities and values closely resembles the processes described in the Fishbein attitude-toward-the-object model, which was discussed in Chapter 8. First, consumers judge the likelihood that an object possesses an attribute. The scale on which the judgment is made is a probability scale in which the person is asked to rate the likelihood that the object possesses the attribute. This process is equivalent to judging the likelihood that something will occur. Second, Fishbein's model proposes that people act as if they make a judgment of the value of an attribute in terms of its goodness or badness. Thus respondents are asked how good or bad various attributes are. In sum, the Fishbein model proposes that consumers make judgments about both probabilities and values.

In addition to forming attitudes, consumers also assess risk during the alternative evaluation stage. As noted in Chapter 6, **risk perception** is based upon consumers' judgments of the likelihood that negative outcomes will occur and of the degree of negativity of those outcomes. Thus, in addition to influencing consumer attitudes, judgments of likelihood and goodness/badness may also influence risk perception.

Because judging probability and value is central to the alternative process, a key question becomes: How do consumers make judgments of probability and of value? Good evidence exists that people employ judgmental heuristics to make such estimates. **Judgmental heuristics** are defined as the simple rules of thumb used by people to make estimates of probabilities and values. The next two sections discuss some of the factors that influence judgments of probabilities and values.

Judging Likelihood

An entire area of research has developed that focuses on describing how people judge likelihood. Thus, when people say, "I think that," or "chances are that," or "I believe that," they are implicitly making a judgment of the likelihood that something will occur.[4] In a consumer setting, probability judgments are made frequently. For example, when people estimate the quality of a product, they are attempting to determine the likelihood that the product contains the attribute of quality. Similarly, when people attempt to estimate the preferences of another person, they are evaluating the likelihood that the other will have certain likes and dislikes.

Researchers have identified a number of judgmental heuristics that consumers use to estimate probabilities. Three of the judgmental heuristics have particular relevance to consumer decision making. They are anchoring and adjustment, availability, and representativeness.

ANCHORING AND ADJUSTMENT When judging probability, people frequently make their estimates by starting from an initial value and then adjusting upward or downward to obtain the final answer. This process is called **anchoring and adjustment**. The problem is that the adjustments from the initial starting point often tend to be insufficient. Thus the starting point acts to distort the estimate. The result is that different starting points may result in different answers.

One recent study found that anchoring influenced probability estimates in predicting the preferences of spouses.[5] Husbands and wives must frequently estimate the preferences of their spouse when making purchases. In this study, husbands and wives predicted the preferences of their spouses for 20 new product concepts. The results revealed that both husbands and wives anchored heavily on their own preferences. Thus they tended to ask what they would like and then use that as the starting point, or anchor, for the decision.

An interesting finding in the spouse preference study was that using one's own preference was the best strategy for estimating the spouse's judgment. When the respondents attempted to adjust from their own preference, they tended to use criteria that were poor predictors of the spouse's preference. Thus attempting to guess what the spouse preferred tended to result in worse decisions. In many instances using one's own reactions may be the best strategy in judging the likes and dislikes of others.

Another study found evidence that anchoring on one's own reactions can improve judgment accuracy.[6] In this study MBA students, marketing managers, researchers, and everyday consumers made predictions about the activities, interests, and opinions of the American consumer. The preferences of American consumers were obtained through appropriate survey research techniques that used a national sample. Overall, the results revealed that all groups were relatively poor in their predictions. The everyday consumers and the experts (i.e., line managers and market researchers) were no different in their ability to predict preferences of American consumers. However, MBA students were significantly worse in the accuracy of their predictions. The results also revealed that because the "typical consumers" were so similar to those in the sample, they could anchor on their own opinions, which gave them a major advantage over MBA students and line managers. The specialized knowledge of the line managers enabled them to make more accurate adjustments than the typical consumer or MBA student. Finally, because the MBA students were so different from the average consumer and had little specialized knowledge, they were least accurate in their judgments. Table 12-2 presents the quiz used in the study. (Answers to the quiz are found in endnote 4.)

The importance of prior beliefs forming anchors was found by other authors who investigated how marketing research studies influenced the beliefs of simulated market researchers.[7] In the study, MBA students assumed the role of assistant product managers at Campbell Soup Company. They were given information about consumer reactions to two commercials. This information was either consistent or inconsistent with prior beliefs about which of the two commercials was superior. The results revealed that when the market research information confirmed prior beliefs, it tended to be rated higher and used in the decision making. However, when it was inconsistent, it was evaluated as poorly done and as less likely to be used.

Each of the studies presented here found that anchors caused consumers or managers to bias their estimates of probabilities in the direction of the anchor—that is, the judgments were assimilated toward the anchor. In some instances, however,

TABLE 12-2

***The Average American Consumer Quiz*[a]**

The following is a series of statements that have been used in attitude surveys of American consumers. Only *married* U.S. men and women participated in these surveys. The people were selected because they were representative of a broad cross-section of all American consumers. The survey respondents were selected through a quota sample, balanced on age, income, geographical area, and population density.

Consumers were asked whether they agreed or disagreed with each statement. For each statement, please estimate what percent of *married* American men and women agreed with each statement in 1986. Write a number between 0% to 100% in the columns to the right to indicate the percentage agreement.

	Percentage of Consumers Agreeing	
	Men	*Women*
1. A nationally advertised brand is usually a better buy than a generic brand.	______	______
2. I went fishing at least once in the past year.	______	______
3. I am a homebody.	______	______
4. Communism is the greatest peril in the world today.	______	______
5. The government should exercise more control over what is shown on television.	______	______
6. Information from advertising helps me make better buying decisions.	______	______
7. I like to pay cash for everything I buy.	______	______
8. The working world is no place for a woman.	______	______
9. I am interested in spices and seasonings.	______	______
10. The father should be the boss in the house.	______	______
11. You have to use disinfectants to get things really clean.	______	______

[a]Answers to the quiz are found in endnote 4.

SOURCE: Stephen Hoch, "Who Do We Know: Predicting the Interests and Opinions of the American Consumer," *Journal of Consumer Research*, Vol. 15 (December 1988), pp. 315–324. Reproduced with permission.

anchors can cause contrast effects to occur. The swimsuit example given in the chapter-opening vignette illustrates such a contrast effect. The bodies of the models shown in the media are so perfect that it is difficult for the average woman to perceive that her shape falls within a latitude of acceptance. As a result, a contrast effect occurs, and the woman feels inferior.

Research on anchoring and adjustment in consumer behavior literature reveals that many consumers use this heuristic device. Further, the research shows that in some instances it may actually improve judgment accuracy. This is the case when the evaluators making the judgment are highly similar to those whom they are assessing. However, if the evaluator is dissimilar to the target person, anchoring can lead to poor estimates.

THE AVAILABILITY HEURISTIC The **availability heuristic** states that people may assess the probability of an event by the ease with which the event can be brought to mind. Thus, the more easily an outcome can be recalled, the more likely people think that it will occur. In one classic demonstration of this effect, respondents were given lists that contained the names of men and women. In half the lists the men were more famous (hence more available in memory and easily recalled), and in the other half the women were more famous. The respondents were asked to judge which of the lists contained more names of men or more names of women. In reality both lists contained the same number of male and female names. The only factor that differed was how famous the males or females were. The results showed that even though the lists contained equal numbers of men and women, when one contained names of famous males, respondents estimated that it contained more names of males. Conversely, when the list contained the names of famous females, respondents estimated that it contained the names of more females. Because the names of famous males (or females) were more easily recalled, subjects' estimates were influenced by the availability heuristic.[8]

Of course, one of the major goals of advertising is to make information about a product highly available in memory. Thus, if one company is more successful than its competitors in associating a brand with a positive attribute, it may have a strong competitive advantage. Even though competing brands may rate just as highly on the attribute, if consumers cannot bring to mind the association, they will rate the likelihood of the competing brand possessing the attribute as low.

Researchers have found that one method of making an action or outcome available in memory is to induce consumers to imagine its occurrence. In one study, homeowners in a middle-class suburb were approached by a person selling cable television services.[9] In the information condition, the respondents were simply given factual information on the benefits of subscribing to the service, such as the costs and the programming received. In the imagination condition, respondents were given the same information, but additional words were inserted into the sales message that encouraged respondents to imagine and think about the various benefits. Thus the participants were asked to imagine how it would feel to be able to watch movies on the system. The results revealed that in the imagination condition, the respondents rated the service as more likely to provide the benefits suggested. Further, more homeowners actually subscribed to the cable TV service in the imagination condition than in the information condition.

Closely related to the availability heuristic is the **hindsight bias**. The hindsight bias states that people consistently exaggerate what could have been anticipated in foresight. Indeed, the problem is so pervasive that people even misremember their own predictions, resulting in the exaggeration in hindsight of what they knew in foresight. Thus, because information on what has happened in the past is so available in memory, people assume that it must have been highly likely to occur.

Hindsight is responsible for the Monday morning quarterback phenomenon in which armchair coaches second-guess the decisions made in the "heat of battle," during Sunday's game. In the consumer arena, hindsight may be responsible for people so highly criticizing companies and their management after blunders have been made. For example, how easy was it for managers to predict consumer reactions to the launch of "New Coke"? In hindsight, it is perfectly obvious that the product would have major problems. However, without the advantage of hindsight, the ability to forecast such an outcome was extremely unlikely.

THE REPRESENTATIVENESS HEURISTIC The **representativeness heuristic** is a rule of thumb in which a person determines the probability that "object A" belongs to "class B" by assessing the degree to which object A is similar to or stereotypical of class B.[10] Marketers frequently attempt to use the heuristic. For example, companies will bring out "knock-off" brands that have names and packaging similar to leading brands. The goal is to make consumers believe that the knock-off brand also performs in a manner similar to the national brand. To the extent that consumers use the representativeness heuristic, the ploy may be successful. An interesting question is, "Do you consider such practices to be ethical?"

One offshoot of the representativeness heuristic is the **law of small numbers**. People have a strong tendency to believe that a sample is a true representation of a population even when the sample is extremely small. This problem is frequently found among marketing managers who observe focus groups. Because the opinions expressed in focus groups are so vivid and salient, the manager may assume that they represent the views of the entire target market. However, as anyone familiar with survey research knows, one simply cannot use a small sample of people to make predictions about a population. What happens is that the people in the focus group appear to represent the target group and, therefore, to depict all relevant aspects of the target group. Of course, this is an erroneous perception. Some companies have recognized this problem and do not allow managers to observe focus groups directly.[11]

Similarly, the law of small numbers may account in part for the great impact of word-of-mouth communications on people. The reported experiences of others have a great impact on consumers, even though the experience of one person is an extremely poor predictor of the experiences of millions of other consumers. From the perspective of a multiattribute model, representativeness can be seen as a factor that influences estimates of the probability that an object has a particular attribute. Suppose that a friend describes to you an occasion at a restaurant in which he or she found a long piece of hair in the lasagna that was ordered. If the description was believable and representative of what can happen at a restaurant, it is likely to influence you strongly—that is, you are likely to form the belief that the restaurant has major problems with the attribute of cleanliness. Of course, your friend's experience represents only one observation; it could have simply been a highly rare event in an otherwise spotless kitchen. However, because of the representativeness bias, your evaluation of the restaurant may be highly negative.

The representativeness heuristic may explain why consumers may sometimes misbehave. Highlight 12-1 discusses the relation of the representativeness heuristic to the dark side of consumer behavior.

Judging Goodness or Badness

In addition to judging the probability that something will occur, consumers also evaluate the goodness or badness of the potential outcomes of decisions. As noted earlier, the perception of the goodness/badness of the attributes of an object will influence a consumer's attitude toward an object. Two general classes of factors influence the judgment of the goodness/badness of potential outcomes. The first is based upon how consumers value the alternatives. The second is based upon how the outcomes are related to the goodness/badness of the associations made between the outcome and a person's memories. Each of these classes of factors is discussed in the paragraphs that follow.

HIGHLIGHT 12-1

Punching Out Cartoon Characters Illustrates the Representativeness Heuristic

Here is a piece of trivia. What is a "walkaround"? A walkaround is a person who strolls through Disney World (or another theme park) dressed as a cartoon character. Therein lies the problem. Customers at theme parks sometimes treat them as though they were indestructible "toons" and punch them, taunt them, and even try to set them on fire.

Consider Betina Becker. One day, dressed as Daffy Duck, she was walking around Six Flags Magic Mountain theme, which lies just north of Los Angeles. Suddenly, a large man decided to show off for his wife and grandchildren by slugging Daffy in the ribs. However, unlike Daffy, who can come back from anything, Betina's ribs were broken.

The problem is particularly bad if you are a cartoon villain and encounter teenagers. Robb Englin noted that the situation became especially tense when he walked around as Sylvester the Cat or the Tasmanian Devil. He noted that sometimes guests would say something pleasant, then "They'd slap me in the face." Worst, however, are customers who yell in his face, saying things like, "You're not real, you're fake." As Mr. Englin said, "Sometimes they just keep following you. You really get to see how messed up some people are."

These misbehaviors illustrate how some consumers can carry the representativeness heuristic to ridiculous extremes. That is, these people see the walkaround cartoon character, place it in the "toon" category, and then treat the person inside the hot, sweaty suit as though he or she were an indestructible cartoon character.

Based upon Christine Gonzalez, "This Daffy Duck Has Ribs, and They Can Really Be Broken," *The Wall Street Journal*, August 3, 1993, pp. 1, 4.

VALUING GAINS AND LOSSES The **valuation of gains and losses** refers to an individual's psychological assessment of the goodness/badness of an outcome based on the level of the outcome in relation to a reference point or adaptation level. One approach to understanding how people value the goodness or badness of an object is through prospect theory.[12]

According to **prospect theory**, how people psychologically interpret the goodness or badness of an option (i.e., a prospect) does not necessarily match an "objective" measure of its value. This difference between "actual" and "psychological" valuations is captured in a graph called the hypothetical valuation function, which is displayed in Figure 12-2. The **hypothetical value function** is defined as the relationship between the psychological valuation of gains and losses in relation to the actual valuation of losses and gains that may result from a course of action.

In Figure 12-2, the horizontal axis represents the actual value of something. Thus $1,000 would be represented at the $1,000 point on the horizontal axis. The vertical axis represents the psychological value of the bet. The basic idea behind the hypothetical value function is that psychological values do not necessarily match actual values. The curve shows how the psychological values are predicted to deviate from actual values. (Note: If psychological values precisely followed actual values, a straight line running diagonally through the origin of the curve would result.) In the

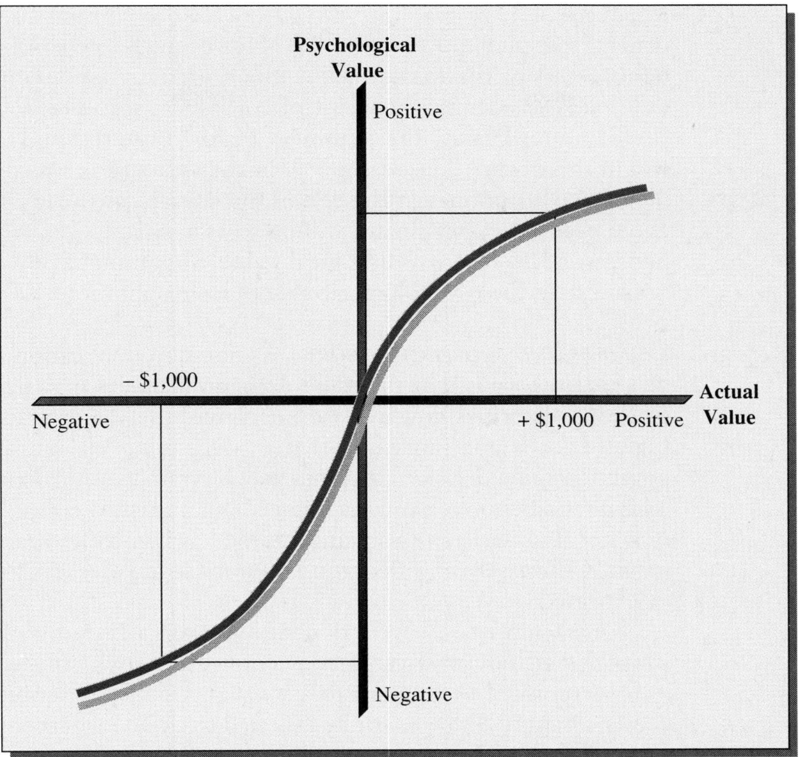

Figure 12-2 Prospect theory's hypothetical value function.

figure, the curve in the gain quadrant (i.e., the upper right-hand part of the diagram) starts out steep and then flattens as it moves away from the origin. This shows that increasing gains have decreasing psychological value. It is consistent with the economic concept of decreasing marginal utility, which states that each additional unit of something obtained brings proportionally less utility or satisfaction.

The hypothetical valuation function curve is steeper in the domain of losses (i.e., the bottom left quadrant) than in the domain of gains. Thus all else equal, losses are weighted more heavily than gains. The curve also flattens out in the domain of losses so that each additional loss means less to the person.

Four important ideas about how consumers value gains and losses can be deduced from the shape of the hypothetical value function.

Implication 1. Losses are given more weight than gains. Because the curve is steeper in the loss domain than in the gain domain, a loss of $1,000 will have more psychological impact than a gain of $1,000.

Implication 2. If people perceive that they are in the gain domain, they will tend to act conservatively.

Implication 3. If people perceive that they are in the loss domain, they will tend to take more risks.

Implication 4. The same decision can be framed from either a gain position or a loss position.

Implications 1, 2, and 3 are directly related to consumers' risk-taking tendencies. In general, people tend to avoid risk. However, if a person perceives that he is already behind and in the loss domain, much greater risk taking will tend to occur. For example, consider the behavior of consumers who bet at horse races. As the end of the day approaches, the gamblers begin to increasingly bet on long shots. Why would this occur? The reason is that they are in the loss domain because most gamblers have lost money at the end of the day. Because each additional loss has *less* psychological value, people are willing to take risks to get even. As a result, if a person had lost $100, the psychological value of gaining $100 and getting even is much greater than the psychological value of losing another $100.

FRAMING AND PROSPECT THEORY As noted in implication 4, one of the key points of prospect theory is that the same decision problem may be framed in different ways. **Framing** describes how a person perceives the value of a stimulus in relation to the hypothetical value function—that is, depending upon a decision maker's reference point, the same decision dilemma may be framed as involving either gains or losses.[14] The phenomenon is similar to describing a glass as either "half empty" or "half full" of water. If a decision problem is framed as involving a gain, risk aversion is likely to result. Conversely, if a decision is framed as involving a loss, greater risk taking can be expected.

One team of researchers demonstrated a framing effect in the risk-handling strategies of industrial vendor selection decisions.[15] In the experimental study, subjects were asked to respond to a written scenario describing a modified rebuy–purchase situation. Subjects in the task had to decide whether to award the contract to a vendor offering a guarantee or a vendor offering a 50–50 chance of either being better than or worse than the guaranteed offer. In addition, subjects were given a series of descriptions of various frames of reference that they could use to make the decision. The results revealed that decision makers who framed the decision in terms of the worst case outcome (focusing on losses) or who calculated expected values tended to choose the risky option. In contrast, those decision makers who framed the decision in terms of factors that caused them to focus on gains (e.g., historical performance and guaranteed performance) tended to choose the conservative option.

Another study used an experimental approach and found strong evidence of a framing effect among consumers. In the study, respondents were asked to give their impressions of ground beef. In the description of the product, it was framed as being either 75% lean or 25% fat. Thus, even though identical information was given to the consumers, the product was framed either positively or negatively. Ratings were taken on four scales: (1) good tasting/bad tasting, (2) greasy/greaseless, (3) high quality/low quality, and (4) fat/lean. In each instance, ratings differed significantly as a result of the framing manipulation. Thus, when framed as 75% lean, subjects rated the ground beef as significantly leaner, better tasting, less greasy, and higher quality.[16] The ground beef study indicates that how information is framed in promotional messages may have a strong impact on how consumers value the goodness or badness of the information.

The work on framing and prospect theory also has application to how consumers respond to changes in the price of a product. In particular, if a price change is framed as a change from the base price of the product, its impact will not be as great as if it were framed from the zero point on the prospect theory curve. Suppose that the price of a $1,000 product were reduced by $90. If framed as a change in the base price of the product, the impact on the typical consumer would be small because of the shape of the value function curve. That is, in relation to $1,000, a $90 rebate is a small change in the overall valuation of the price. However, if the price change were framed as a gain of $90—which was independent of the base price of the product—it would have a much larger psychological impact on the consumer. This occurs because the curve is much steeper as it passes through the origin of the hypothetical value function. Thus the $90 is like "found money" and can be used to buy something else.

How can companies cause consumers to perceive a reduction in price as a gain of *x* amount, rather than merely as a change in the base price of the product? Many of the sales promotion devices used by corporations may act in such a manner. In particular, rebates may cause a change in frame. Thus, if a consumer is sent a $500 check after the purchase of a $15,000 car, the consumer may perceive the money as a gain of $500. If the price were merely reduced by $500 at the time of purchase, the consumer would interpret the sales promotion quite differently. That is, psychologically $14,500 is not very different from $15,000. In contrast, $500 seems like a large sum of money in comparison to having nothing.

Other sales promotion devices, such as providing gifts, may operate similarly to rebates. For example, if a customer buys an expensive suit from a clothing store, the owner may frequently give him one or two silk ties. Such gifts are valued independently of the cost of the suit. Thus the ties' $50 to $60 value is perceived as a gain rather than as a reduction in the price of the $600 suit. As a result, it has much greater psychological value. In general, sales promotion devices such as rebates, gifts, and sweepstakes may be more effective than a mere reduction in price because of the effects of framing.[17]

TIME FRAMING AND VALUING GAINS AND LOSSES The distance in time between when a decision is made and when gains or losses occur will also influence their valuation. Researchers have found that people act quite rationally and psychologically discount gains and losses that occur in the future. Thus people would rather receive $1,000 today than wait a year to receive it. Conversely, people would rather pay $1,000 a year from now than pay it today.

It is crucial to recognize that most consumer purchases have both gains and losses attached to them. For example, when a person purchases a stereo system, the person gives up money (a loss) in return for gaining the stereo system. Because people want to have their gains in the present and postpone their losses, marketers can develop sales promotion devices that take advantage of this tendency. Thus consumers prefer to delay payments. A **delay-payment effect** occurs when customers are encouraged to receive a good or service in the present and are allowed to wait to pay for it at a later date. Because people tend to discount the psychological value of the future loss and because having the good *now* is so important, many consumers will pay a much higher price in the future so as to have it in the present. Of course, credit cards, "buy-now-pay-later-plans," and loans of all types are highly appealing to consumers because of the delay-payment effect.[18]

The temporal distance between what actually happens and what could have been has also been found to influence consumers. For example, consider how you would feel if the transmission on your car burned out the day after its warranty expired as compared to six months after the warranty expired. When a positive outcome is "just missed," people respond with a much stronger affective reaction. This idea has been used by advertisers. For example, ads soliciting organ donations (e.g., hearts and kidneys) have told stories of a child who died because a liver became available one week too late.[19]

The temporal distance between when a gain or loss occurs and "what could have been" occurs through the same discounting process as the delay-payment effect. That is, the farther away in time that a loss is experienced from when it is considered, the less psychological impact it has. Problems with consumer "self-control" also may be explained through this phenomenon. **Consumer self-control** refers to the ability of people to delay gratification and avoid making purchases that provide pleasure in the present but pain in the future.

Why is it that some consumers have great difficulty controlling their impulses? For example, people with food or drug addictions cannot resist the impulse to consume if a cookie or cocaine is available. For these unfortunate individuals, the pleasure of obtaining the cookie or drug in the present is overwhelming. In addition, the potential loss that could occur from ingesting the substance is remote in time. As a result, the addict consumes it, only to regret it later. This lack of consumer self-control results because for some people the pleasure of the moment is so extreme and the discounting of losses in the future is so great.[20]

MEMORIES AND JUDGING GOODNESS/BADNESS When people consider the possible outcomes of a consumer decision, they will recall semantic memories of similar events in the past. As discussed in Chapter 4 on memory processes, evaluative reactions (i.e., affective responses) are stored in semantic memory networks. Thus, when possible outcomes are considered, associations will result that may be positive or negative. For example, suppose that a woman is going to an important cocktail party and wants to buy a new dress. As she shops and compares alternatives, memories from past experiences with cocktail dresses will be elicited. For example, a particular dress may remind her of the one that she wore at the senior prom. Whether the experience was positive or negative will have a strong impact on her feelings about the dress that she is considering.

In sum, the associations that one makes with the alternatives to be evaluated will have a strong impact on the evaluation of their goodness/badness. One particular form of association, nostalgia, has received increased attention recently by consumer researchers.

Nostalgia ". . . refers to a longing for the past, a yearning for yesterday, or a fondness for possessions and activities associated with days of yore."[21] The research evidence suggests that for consumers, the targets of nostalgia are generally those experienced in the late teens and early twenties. For example, nostalgia for music appears to center on those songs that were popular when the person was about 23 years old.[22] In the mid-1990s, we are seeing a resurgence of advertisements that employ symbols and images from the 1960s. Thus a midwestern chain of fast-food restaurants, called "Sonic," is rapidly growing in part because of the use of television commercials featuring Frankie Avalon, known for his "beach blanket" movies from the 1960s. Why are symbols from the 1960s so "hot" in the mid-1990s? It was during the 1960s that the baby-boom generation was in its late teens and early twenties. Hoping to appeal to this huge group of consumers, advertisers are resorting to nostalgic appeals employing icons of that time period.

Recent research on nostalgia suggests that it is an individual difference variable.[23] Table 12-3 presents the items that make up a scale to measure "nostalgia

TABLE 12-3

A Nostalgia Scale

1. They don't make 'em like they used to.
2. Things used to be better in the good old days.
3. Products are getting shoddier and shoddier.
4. Technological change will ensure a brighter future. (reversed)
5. History involves a steady improvement in human welfare. (reversed)
6. We are experiencing a decline in the quality of life.
7. Steady growth in GNP has brought increased human happiness. (reversed)
8. Modern business constantly builds a better tomorrow. (reversed)

Note: Nine-point, agree–disagree scales were used.

SOURCE: Morris B. Holbrook, "Nostalgia and Consumption Preferences: Some Emerging Patterns of Consumer Tastes," *Journal of Consumer Research*, Vol. 20 (September 1993), pp. 245–256.

proneness." In the study, preferences for Academy Award–winning movies, which were released at varying points in time, were assessed. The results of the study revealed that women showed more nostalgic tendencies than men. In addition, those who were more nostalgic tended to like musicals rather than more violent films. Finally, as one might expect from differences in cultural tastes, men tended to prefer more violent movies than women.

How does nostalgia influence the determination of the goodness or badness of an option? Nostalgia is the name given to the experience of recalling from memory a past experience that is evaluated positively. It influences judgments of goodness/badness through the transference of affect to the alternative currently being evaluated. However, remember that not all memories are positive. In some instances, an alternative may elicit memories that are quite negative.

Highlight 12-2 discusses a problem faced by market researchers in a variety of industries. How can they predict how consumers will react to a product over time?

THE CONSUMER CHOICE PROCESS

After engaging in an evaluation of the alternatives, the consumer's next step in the decision process is to make a choice among alternatives. Consumers make different types of choices. They choose among alternative brands or services, and they make choices among stores. However, choices also are made at a more general level, with a person choosing between **noncomparable alternatives**. For example, people may choose between going on an expensive vacation, purchasing a car, or building a swimming pool. How consumers go about making choices is strongly influenced by the type of decision process in which they are engaged. Good evidence exists that the choice process differs if consumers use a high-involvement approach as compared to a low-involvement approach. Similarly, if the consumer is using an experiential orientation, the choice process may be altered. (Of course, when behavioral influence is taking place, the consumer is considered not to be making any type of conscious,

HIGHLIGHT 12-2

Marketing Research and Predicting Judgments of Goodness/Badness

Will consumers positively evaluate the taste of a new food product? Will a new design for the cabinet of a computer stand the test of time? Such questions are difficult to answer because they belong in the experiential domain of consumer behavior, where hedonic and aesthetic judgments are made.

Managers have great difficulty estimating consumer preferences because they tend to diverge from their target market in socioeconomic status. One option is for managers to hire "experts" to evaluate the new product offering. Such experts may be able to provide superior predictions of how consumers will respond to a new product offering over time. The idea of considering how consumers will react "over time" to a product is important. Through a process of adaptation, consumer valuations of the goodness/badness of a product can change as the number of exposures to the product increases.

In an interesting study, researchers had art experts rate 20 artworks of widely varying quality. In addition, a sample of undergraduate students also rated the same works once a week for four weeks. The results revealed that the experts' ratings were highly correlated with the *changes* in the ratings of the novices over the four rating periods. That is, the novices' ratings of the high-quality prints tended to improve with each repetition, while the ratings of the poor-quality prints tended to get worse with each rating. In sum, the research suggests that experts can be highly useful in predicting how consumers will respond over time to marketing offerings having a strong aesthetic–hedonic component.

Based upon Robert M. Schindler, Morris B. Holbrook, and Eric A. Greenleaf, "Using Connoisseurs to Predict Mass Tastes," *Marketing Letters*, Vol. 1 (1989), pp. 47–54.

mentalistic choice.) The next three sections discuss the choice process from the high-involvement, low-involvement, and experiential perspectives. Table 12-4 summarizes these approaches to the choice process.

Choice Under High- and Low-Involvement Conditions

The study of consumer choice under high- and low-involvement conditions has generally focused upon identifying the types of rules that people use to decide which alternative brand to purchase. Two broad categories of models—compensatory and noncompensatory—have been used to explain how consumers make choices among brands. The terms *compensatory* and *noncompensatory* refer to whether high ratings on one attribute can compensate for low ratings on another attribute. In high-involvement conditions, evidence exists that consumers use compensatory models. In contrast, consumers tend to use noncompensatory models of choice in low-involvement conditions.

An example is provided to illustrate the differences between the various models of choice. Shown in Table 12-5, the example involves a decision faced by the author

TABLE 12-4

Alternative Approaches to Predicting Choice

- **I.** High-involvement choice
  - **A.** Compensatory models (e.g., Fishbein model)
  - **B.** Phased models
- **II.** Low-involvement models
  - **A.** Conjunctive rule
  - **B.** Disjunctive rule
  - **C.** Elimination by aspects
  - **D.** Lexicographic rule
  - **E.** Frequency heuristic
- **III.** Experiential choice processes
  - **A.** Brand-loyal purchases
  - **B.** Affect–referral heuristic
  - **C.** Impulse purchases
- **IV.** Noncomparable choice processes
- **V.** Store choice

concerning which brand of power lawn mower to purchase. My consideration set consisted of four brands of self-propelled, gasoline-powered, 21-inch lawn mowers: a Toro recycler, a Toro bagger, a Lawnboy bagger, and a John Deere bagger. The Toro recycler was especially designed so that it would grind up the clippings into a fine mulch and deposit them back on the lawn so that they would be undetectable. The other models were standard rear-bagging lawn mowers with mulching attachments. The table identifies the attributes on which the lawn mowers were evaluated, the evaluations of the goodness/badness of the ratings, the estimates of the likelihood that the models possessed the attributes (i.e., both concepts derived from the Fishbein attitude-toward-the-object model), and the importance ratings of each of the attributes.

High-Involvement Choice

Under conditions of high involvement, consumers have been found to act as though they are using a compensatory model. In **compensatory models of choice**, consumers are viewed as analyzing each alternative in a broad evaluative fashion so that high ratings on one attribute may compensate for low ratings on other attributes.[24] In such a process, all the information on the attributes of a brand is combined into an overall judgment of the preference for the brand. Such an evaluation is made for each of the brand alternatives. According to the compensatory model, the brand that has the highest overall preference is then chosen. The Fishbein attitude-toward-the-object model discussed in Chapter 8 illustrates a compensatory model.

One aspect of compensatory models should be noted: an alternative is not necessarily rejected because it has low ratings on any particular attribute. Thus a consumer may rate a particular brand of automobile as poor in acceleration. However, because

TABLE 12-5

Which Lawn Mower to Choose? An Example of the Use of Alternative Choice Models

			Belief Rating and Consideration Set [a,b]			
Attribute	*Evaluation Rating*	*Importance Rating*	*Toro Recycler*	*Toro Bagger*	*Lawnboy Bagger*	*John Deere Bagger*
Low cost	+1	4	7(7)	2(2)	2(2)	6(6)
Blade brake clutch[c]	+2	8	1(2)	9(18)	10(20)	8(16)
Ease of operation	+2	7	9(18)	5(10)	4(8)	5(10)
Mulching[d]	+3	9	9(27)	5(15)	6(18)	5(15)
Consumer Reports rating	+2	5	8(16)	7(14)	6(12)	5(10)
			$\Sigma b_i e_i = 70$	$\Sigma b_i e_i = 59$	$\Sigma b_i e_i = 60$	$\Sigma b_i e_i = 57$

[a]Assume that a 5 or better on the belief ratings is required to surpass cutoff points on conjunctive and elimination by aspects models. Assume that 10 is required as a cutoff for the disjunctive model.

[b]$\Sigma b_i e_i$ is the formula for the Fishbein attitude model discussed in Chapter 8. Numbers in parentheses represent the multiplication of the evaluations times the belief ratings.

[c]The blade brake clutch allows the engine to run without the blade turning. This is important when bagging grass.

[d]The mower cuts grass into fine bits, which then are deposited back on the lawn. If this works well, no grass clippings are detectable after mowing.

the car is rated highly on other attributes and because judgment is based upon a global evaluation, the brand could still be chosen. The quality of having high ratings on some attributes compensate for low ratings on other attributes is the basis for calling these models *compensatory*.

In the lawn mower selection problem, if one assumes that the author employed a high-involvement decision process, a Fishbein attitude-toward-the-object model should predict the purchase selection. As seen in Table 12-5, the lawn mower with the highest rating was the Toro recycler, with an overall attitude score of 70. The closest competitor was the Lawnboy, with a rating of 60. The major reasons for the selection of the Toro recycler were its mulching feature and its ease of operation. High scores on these attributes were able to compensate for the very low rating on the blade brake clutch attribute, which this model lacked entirely.

Low-Involvement Choice

In low-involvement circumstances, consumers have been found to act as though they use **noncompensatory models of choice**. In these models, high ratings on some attributes may not compensate for low ratings on other attributes. These noncompensatory models are also called **hierarchical models of choice**. They are hierarchical because the consumer is viewed as comparing alternatives on attributes one at a time. Thus one attribute is chosen and all alternatives are compared on it. The person then moves to the next attribute and alternatives are compared on it. The process then continues in a hierarchical manner. For the decision maker, one advantage of the noncompensatory choice models is that they are relatively simple to implement. When consumers are in a low-involvement situation, they are not willing to engage in the large amounts of information processing required by a compensatory choice model. The noncompensatory models are essentially shortcuts to reach satisfactory decisions rather than optimal ones. Such a process has been called **satisficing**.[25] The noncompensatory models have also been called heuristic models of choice. As noted earlier in the chapter, heuristics are simple rules of thumb that people use to make satisfactory decisions rather than perfect ones. The use of heuristic choice models in low-involvement circumstances makes sense. In such cases, consumers are unconcerned with reaching optimal decisions; they merely want to make a decision that is "good enough."

Several noncompensatory choice models have been identified, using the conjunctive rule, the disjunctive rule, the elimination-by-aspects heuristic, and the lexicographic heuristic.[26]

THE CONJUNCTIVE RULE In many instances, consumers are faced with a decision where a large number of brand alternatives are available. Clearly, it would be impossible to investigate each brand in detail, so a shortcut is needed to simplify the process. One such shortcut involves the use of the **conjunctive rule**, in which the consumer sets minimum cutoffs on each attribute that he or she wishes to investigate. If the product fails to surpass the minimum cutoff level, the alternative is rejected. If the cutoff levels are set very stringently, it is possible that only one alternative is left after all others are eliminated. More frequently, cutoff points are set lower so that a number of alternatives remain. As such, the conjunctive rule is often used as an initial screening device to eliminate enough brands so that a more complex decision approach, such as a compensatory model, can be applied to select from the remaining alternatives.

In the lawn mower example, belief ratings had to equal or surpass a cutoff of 5 or more to be considered. Using this rule, only the John Deere bagger had belief ratings that reached the cutoff on each attribute. Each of the remaining alternatives had at least one belief rating below the cutoff point. Therefore, based upon the conjunctive model, the John Deere would be selected.

THE DISJUNCTIVE RULE The **disjunctive rule** is similar to the conjunctive rule in that minimum standards are set for each attribute considered. Alternatives are then evaluated on the attributes. The disjunctive rule differs in that any alternative that surpasses the minimum cutoff on any attribute is accepted. Usually the cutoff point is set very stringently. The alternative chosen by the disjunctive rule is the one that is rated extremely high on some attribute. It is as though the person is saying that he or she wants an alternative that is "great" on some attribute.

In the lawn mower example, belief ratings had to reach the extremely high cutoff score of 10 for the alternative to be considered under a disjunctive model. The only brand to have a 10 on any attribute was the Lawnboy bagger, which had a 10 on the blade brake clutch feature. Thus, if a disjunctive model were employed, the analysis would predict that the consumer would select the Lawnboy.

Note the key difference in the conjunctive and disjunctive models. Both set minimum standards for each attribute. However, in the conjunctive model, if a rating falls below the standard on any attribute, it is rejected. In the disjunctive model, if a rating is above the cutoff level on any attribute, the alternative is accepted. Therefore, as one might expect, cutoffs for the disjunctive model are typically set higher than for the conjunctive model.

Figure 12-3 shows an ad for a restaurant that focuses on making one point—the food is hot. The ad will be effective if consumers are using a disjunctive model and selecting a restaurant based upon whether it has one outstanding feature.

ELIMINATION BY ASPECTS According to the **elimination-by-aspects heuristic**, each alternative is thought of as a collection of aspects or attributes. Choice occurs via a hierarchical process in which the alternatives are compared on the most important attribute. Alternatives not surpassing the cutoff on the attribute are eliminated. The decision maker then moves on to the next most important attribute and eliminates alternatives not surpassing the cutoff point. The process continues until only one alternative remains. The likelihood of choosing any one attribute on which to compare alternatives is based upon its importance to the decision maker.

When the elimination-by-aspects heuristic is applied to the lawn mower example, one predicts that the John Deere bagger will be chosen. On the most important attribute of mulching, all brands surpassed the cutoff point of 5. On the second most important attribute, blade brake clutch, the Toro recycler was eliminated. On the third most important attribute, ease of operation, the Lawnboy bagger was eliminated. This left the Toro bagger and the John Deere bagger as the two remaining options. Both surpassed the cutoff on the *Consumer Reports* ratings. Because the Toro

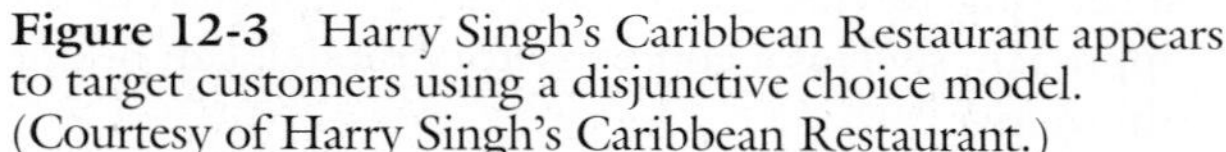

Figure 12-3 Harry Singh's Caribbean Restaurant appears to target customers using a disjunctive choice model. (Courtesy of Harry Singh's Caribbean Restaurant.)

bagger was below the cutoff on the final attribute of price, the model would predict that John Deere bagger would be chosen if an elimination-by-aspects heuristic were used. Note that the conjunctive and the elimination-by-aspects models make the same choice prediction if the same cutoff level is used. In this case, both heuristics used a cutoff of 5. If a cutoff of 6 had been employed, however, the results would have been different. In this case, on the first attribute of mulching, both the Toro bagger and the John Deere bagger would have been eliminated. On the second most important attribute of blade brake clutch, the Toro recycler would have been eliminated, leaving the Lawnboy bagger as the predicted choice.

THE LEXICOGRAPHIC HEURISTIC The **lexicographic heuristic** has strong similarities to the elimination-by-aspects approach. Both start with the consumer ranking the attributes in their order of importance. After determining the order of importance of attributes, the consumer then rates all alternatives on the most important attribute. At this point, however, the two approaches diverge. If a lexicographic model is used, the consumer then selects the alternative that is best on the most important attribute. If a tie occurs, the consumer moves to the next attribute and selects the alternative rated best on that attribute, and so forth. Thus the lexicographic model uses a harsher standard of choice than the elimination-by-aspects model. It eliminates alternatives only if they fail to possess an attribute by not surpassing the cutoff point. In contrast, in the lexicographic model an alternative is eliminated if it does not have the highest rating on the most important attribute. Only in cases of ties does one move on to the next most important attribute.

Looking again at the lawn mower example, consider which lawn mower the consumer would be predicted to select. If consumers employed the lexicographic heuristic, the analysis would predict the choice of the Toro recycler. On the most important attribute of mulching, it received the highest rating.

One can readily see why the lexicographic model is noncompensatory. That is, if a lexicographic model is employed, an alternative could be eliminated merely because it did not at least achieve a tie in the rating of the most important attribute.

Figure 12-4 presents an advertisement for Johnson's Baby Lotion that would be highly effective for consumers who use either a conjunctive or a lexicographic model. The ad provides four reasons for adults to use the product: (1) it is thicker and richer, (2) it absorbs fast, (3) it has ten skin softeners, and (4) it leaves a soft feeling all over. It is quite likely that marketing research was performed to identify the rank order of the most important product characteristics. The advertisement then was developed to show that the product possessed these attributes. For consumers using a conjunctive model, the ad would be effective because it shows that the product possesses each of the four attributes. It would also be effective for consumers using a lexicographic choice process. Note that the photo in the top left of the ad contains the statement "Thicker and richer than other lotions." Because consumers begin scanning the ad at the top left, they would encounter this persuasive message first. If a lexicographic model were used and the qualities of "thick and rich" were most important to consumers, then the brand should be chosen, provided that consumers believe the persuasive message.

Additional Choice Models

Two additional choice models have been identified—the frequency heuristic and phased choice strategies.

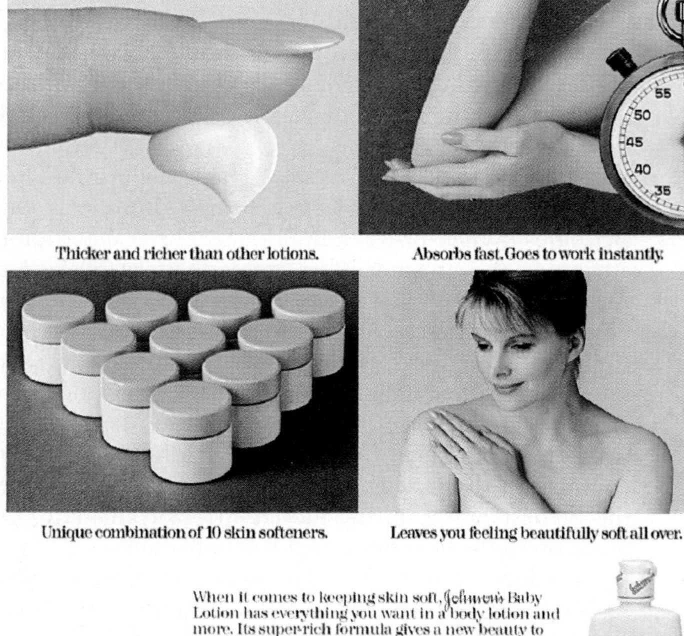

Figure 12-4 This Johnson & Johnson ad could appeal to consumers who use lexicographic or conjunctive heuristics to evaluate baby lotion. (Courtesy of Johnson & Johnson Baby Products Company.)

THE FREQUENCY HEURISTIC The **frequency heuristic** states that when consumers are in a low-involvement state, choice may be influenced by the "mere number of positive and negative attributes associated with a brand or by the mere number of dimensions on which one brand outperforms another."[27] When a frequency heuristic is used, consumers act as though they simply count the number of features on which one brand surpasses another. Little or no attention is allocated to the relative importance of the features.

An experiment demonstrated the operation of the frequency heuristic.[28] In the study, the low-involvement group was created by asking select respondents merely to rate the comprehensibility of information about three brands of automobiles. This would create low involvement because the task was extremely easy and required little cognitive effort. In contrast, respondents in the high-involvement group were told that they would be asked to make a choice among the three cars. The information that respondents received on the brands was then varied. In pretests, 12 features of cars were identified. Three were found to be extremely important—maneuverability, gas mileage, and warranty. The others were unimportant, such as tinted glass, chrome trim, and so on. Car A was then described as having nine unimportant attributes. Car B was described as having the three important attributes. Car C was described as having three randomly selected, unimportant attributes. All respondents were asked to make a choice among the three cars. The results revealed that when respondents were in the high-involvement condition in which they knew they would be making a choice, they chose Car A 52% of the time. In contrast, when they were in the low-involvement condition, they chose Car A 78% of the time. (In no cases did subjects select Car C.) These results strongly support the existence of a frequency heuristic. In the low-involvement conditions, significantly more respondents made their choice based upon the frequency of positive features of a brand recalled from memory rather than upon the importance of the features.

Advertisers frequently air commercials that appear to make use of the frequency heuristic when they employ a *piecemeal report strategy*. For example, auto companies have used comparative advertising in which their brand is selectively compared to a series of competitors on a number of different attributes. The ad might state that the vehicle has a trunk larger than a Mercedes, goes from 0 to 60 miles per hour faster than an Audi, and has more leg room than a BMW. In fact, the car might be a very poor brand and be exceeded by its competitors on every other dimension. However, because the attributes on which it surpasses the competition are systematically selected, the illusion is created that it has a high frequency of positive attributes. In a similar manner, advertisers who provide buyers with a series of extra gifts when a brand is purchased may be using the frequency heuristic. For example, sales promotions of perfumes sometimes provide a number of extra trinkets, such as "sample sizes" of makeup, that increase the perceived number of benefits obtained from the purchase.

PHASED STRATEGIES In a **phased strategy**, consumers sequentially use two noncompensatory models or use a noncompensatory model and then a compensatory approach. For example, a consumer first may use a conjunctive model to reduce the alternatives considered to three or four. The consumer could then use a lexicographic approach or even a Fishbein model to make the final choice. Such phased models are most likely used under high-involvement conditions.

Which Choice Models Do Consumers Use?

One study asked respondents to make choices among various automobile alternatives after being given seven attributes on which to rate the cars.[29] Table 12-6 presents the results. The study found that almost 61% of the respondents used a lexicographic model. Next most frequently used was a compensatory model (32.1%). A phased strategy of using a conjunctive model to screen alternatives, followed by a compensatory approach, was used 5.4% of the time. These three strategies accounted for 98.2% of the choices. Although the researchers did use a simulated buying situation and used students as respondents, it does indicate that consumers are likely to use noncompensatory models frequently in their decision making. It should be added, however, that the study did not analyze the extent to which respondents used all the types of choice models. For example, it did not analyze whether respondents used an elimination-by-aspects model or the frequency heuristic. More research is needed on this important issue.

TABLE 12-6

Frequency of Use of Choice Models in Brand Choice

Model/Choice	*Verbal Description*	*Percentage Using Approach*
Conjunctive (noncompensatory)	I chose the car that had a really good rating on at least one characteristic.	0.6
Lexicographic (noncompensatory)	I looked at the characteristic that was most important to me and chose the car that was best in that feature. If two or more cars were equal on that feature, I then looked at my second most important feature to break the tie.	60.7
Multiattribute (compensatory)	I chose the car that had a really good rating when you balance the good ratings with the bad ratings.	32.1
Phased (conjunctive-compensatory)	I first eliminated the cars with a really bad rating on any feature and then chose from the rest the one that seemed the best overall when you balance the good ratings with the bad ratings.	5.4
Other	(Category composed of several other types of heuristic models.)	1.8

SOURCE: Adapted from M. Reily and R. Holman, "Does Task Complexity or Cue Intercorrelation Affect Choice of an Information Processing Strategy? An Empirical Investigation," in *Advances in Consumer Research*, Vol. 4, W. D. Perrault, Jr., ed. (Atlanta, GA: Association for Consumer Research, 1977), p. 189.

Experiential Choice Processes

From the decision-making perspective, choice is viewed as involving the evaluation of alternatives based upon considerations of beliefs about the attributes possessed. The decision-making approach takes a cognitive, information-processing approach to choice. As a result, the involvement level of the consumer is critical in determining whether an extended choice process or a more limited choice process is used. In contrast, from the experiential perspective, choice is viewed as resulting from consumers considering their feelings about alternatives; little emphasis is placed on the development of beliefs about attributes. Several types of consumer choice can be categorized as experiential processes. These include choices based upon affect-referral, choices influenced by the effects of brand awareness, and choices based upon impulse.

The Affect–Referral Heuristic

One choice heuristic identified by researchers captures aspects of the experiential approach to choice. Called the **affect–referral heuristic**, the approach suggests that consumers sometimes elicit from memory the overall recollection of their evaluation of an alternative. Thus, rather than examining attributes or beliefs about attributes, a holistic approach is used in which consumers choose the alternative toward which they have the most positive feelings.

Affect–referral may be used to explain how consumers make brand-loyal purchases. Purchases made through brand loyalty have a strong affective component attached. Indeed, consumers who express strong brand loyalty also reveal highly positive attitudes toward the brand. Thus, when making a purchase, they do not go through an extended or even a limited decision process. Rather, they simply refer to their feelings when making a choice. For example, suppose that after many years, a consumer's Maytag washing machine finally broke down. She would be revealing brand loyalty if she merely called the local Maytag dealer and asked him to deliver the newest model available. When explaining her choice, she would say something like: "I love my Maytag. It works great. I would never dream of changing."

For example, one study found that consumers shopping for laundry detergent spent a median time of only 8.5 seconds making their selection.[30] Clearly, very little information processing occurred during that brief time period. The study found that over 90% of the respondents had something positive to say about the brand purchased. Brand loyalty occurs when a person repetitively purchases an alternative because of a strong positive affect toward it. Thus, when a person makes a purchase because of brand loyalty, one can argue that an affect–referral heuristic is being utilized.

The Effects of Brand Awareness

Brand awareness may also influence consumer choice through such an affect–referral process. In particular, new brands face an extremely difficult problem in capturing market share because national brands are purchased in large part based upon the positive affect associated with them. In a recent study, researchers asked respondents to choose among three alternative brands of peanut butter. In the *awareness condition*, one of the brands was a well-known national brand. In the *unawareness condition*, all three brands were unknown regional brands. As might be expected, when the national brand was known, 93.5% subjects chose it.[31]

What was interesting in the study, however, was what happened after subjects were given a chance to taste the brands. In pilot tests, the experimenters had respondents rate various brands of peanut butter on taste, and high- and low-taste-quality brands were identified. In the study, the good-tasting peanut butter was sometimes placed in the national brand's container and sometimes in the unknown brand's container. (In all cases, only one of the three jars contained the good-tasting peanut butter.) When the good-tasting peanut butter was placed in the unknown brand's jar, only 20% selected it—even after they had tasted the alternatives. In contrast, when the good-tasting peanut butter was placed in the national brand's jar, 77% chose it. These percentages must be compared to choices when all brands were unknown. In this case, the high-quality peanut butter was chosen 59% of the time. In sum, the positive feelings associated with the national brand overwhelmed the effects of actually tasting the peanut butter and, thereby, strongly influenced the choice process.

Impulse Purchases

When consumers utilize an experiential choice process, the purchase is made with little cognitive control and seems to happen in a largely automatic manner.[32] This description applies to brand-loyal purchases and impulse purchases as well. An **impulse purchase** has been defined as a "buying action undertaken without a problem having been previously recognized or a buying intention formed prior to entering the store."[33] An impulse purchase may be described as a choice made on the spur of the moment based upon the development of a strong positive feeling regarding an object. Impulse purchases occur frequently. Various studies have found that as many as 39% of department store purchases and 67% of grocery store purchases may be unplanned.[34] Impulse purchases have been described as "mindless reactive behavior."[35] Other researchers have noted that impulse purchases involve strong affective states. The behavior becomes somewhat automatic, has little intellectual control, and reveals a strong emotional content. As such, it is the antithesis of the rational consumption that one finds in high-involvement purchases and to a certain extent in low-involvement purchases.[36]

In one study of impulse purchases, researchers conducted depth interviews asking respondents to report on their feelings when they made impulse purchases.[37] One subject reported:

> I was in Beverly Hills just walking around, not intending to buy, when I saw some shoes on sale. So I went inside and tried them on and they fit fine. At that time I thought about buying one pair, then I got the feeling I had to try everything. They were just calling to me. You suddenly feel compelled to buy something. It feels like getting an idea. It's a fast feeling, and if I don't get it right away, I'll think of reasons why I don't need it.

In each case, the purchase seems to have been preceded by the consumer's strong feeling that a product should be purchased. The affective state led directly to a behavior without the person forming beliefs or thinking very hard about the purchase. It seems that in some cases consumers may act to repress thinking, which might dampen the feelings experienced.

Effects of Mood States on Choice

Impulse purchases, as well as those made as a result of brand loyalty, can be categorized as experientially oriented. In addition, mood appears to influence whether a person uses a decision-making or an experiential approach to choice. One research team found that people in a positive mood state responded more favorably to emotional appeals than to informational appeals. In contrast, people in negative mood states responded more favorably to informational appeals than emotional appeals. These findings were extended by the researchers to the choice process. They found that when people were in negative moods, they tended to rely on an informational approach to product selection. When in positive moods, choice was more closely related to a focus on their feelings and fantasies about using particular brands.[38]

Choices Among Noncomparable Alternatives

As noted earlier in the chapter, choices are not always made among comparable alternatives. Rather than merely deciding which brand of 35mm camera to purchase, a consumer must sometimes decide how to allocate resources among the general alternatives. Should the consumer spend $600 to purchase a high-quality camera, new stereo speakers, or a new business suit? The traditional noncompensatory models are of little assistance here because they require the decision maker to form beliefs about alternatives on common attributes. What do consumers do when the alternatives have no attributes in common other than price?

In a study where subjects had to choose among noncomparable alternatives, researchers noticed two trends.[39] First, subjects tended to focus on using more abstract attributes for their comparison of alternatives. Thus, when comparing cameras to speakers to business suits, they would compare the alternatives on such attributes as necessity, stylishness, cost, and innovativeness. Second, the respondents tended to shift to a more holistic strategy in which overall attitudes toward the alternatives were compared. In addition to comparing each alternative on abstract attributes, the respondents tended to evaluate each alternative separately to form and compare overall impressions of the various products.

Although these results are informative, much more research must be conducted on how people select among noncomparable alternatives. The area is important because some of consumers' most important decisions are made at this level. The question of which brand of auto to purchase is probably much less important than are issues such as whether a young adult should go to college or go to work and whether a married woman should start a family, concentrate on a career, or try to do both.

Choices Among Stores

Another area of research on choice concerns the store selection process. A critical issue for retailers involves developing an understanding of the factors that consumers use when selecting a store from which to purchase a product. The approaches to choice identified in the preceding sections are directly relevant to the issue. Using a decision-making perspective, retailers can identify the attributes that people use to evaluate alternative stores, determine whether consumers are in high- or low-involvement states, and identify the appropriate choice model. Researchers have found that consumers consider such attributes as the store's distance from the consumer's home, the overall prices of brands carried, and service.[40] Another factor that influences store choice is the **decision context**. Context refers to those situational or extrinsic factors that dictate the options available to the decision maker.[41] Thus the types of stores available, how many stores are available, and the presence of mail-order alternatives may strongly influence the nature of the choice process.

Other recent research on store choice has focused on the type of choice set used by consumers.[42] These researchers suggest that consumers evaluate retailers based upon the same types of sets discussed in the last chapter (i.e., awareness, unawareness, inert, inept, and consideration sets). However, they also suggest that several new types of sets exist. For example, the **interaction set** consists of those stores where a consumer allows himself or herself to be exposed to personal selling. Such stores have an opportunity to sell that is not shared by those in the **quiet set**. Consumers may enter stores belonging to the quiet set, but they tend not to interact with any sales personnel.

Consumers have been viewed as choosing stores based upon a logical decision-making process, and even upon feelings and emotions. It is less obvious that consumers may sometimes use superstitions to select a store. Superstitious behavior may be analyzed from the behavioral influence perspective. A consumer may repeat a certain behavior if a reinforcer happens to randomly follow that behavior. A contingency is created purely by accident, which may result in bizarre behavior. Such superstitious behavior is readily seen in some athletes, who may wear the same unwashed clothing for game after game after starting a winning streak.

Managerial Implications of Choice Processes

Knowledge of consumer choice processes may be used in designing the marketing mix, segmentation, environmental analysis, and marketing research. Conducting carefully developed market research studies is particularly important to identify the nature of the choice process used by consumers to purchase a product or service. Researchers need to identify whether the target market engages in high- or low-involvement purchasing. Further, the researchers need to assess the extent to which the target market uses an experiential approach to purchasing.

Identifying the choice process used by consumers to purchase a product or service may directly affect the development of the marketing mix. For example, suppose that the research revealed that consumers purchase via a low-involvement process and that the target market acts as though it uses a lexicographic approach to choice. In such instances, consumers identify the most important attribute and select the brand rated highest on this attribute. If two or more alternatives tie on the first attribute, consumers move to the second attribute, and so forth. In such cases, the product or service must be designed so that it performs well on the dominant attributes. Similarly, promotional strategy should focus on emphasizing product or service competence on the dominant attribute. In such cases, knowledge of the consumer choice process should directly influence product development and promotional strategy. Further, if price happens to be a dominant attribute, as it so often is, then the knowledge could influence pricing strategy as well.

An excellent example of a company developing its marketing mix around knowledge of consumer choice processes is Procter & Gamble's Charmin tissue. The dominant attributes in the purchase of a bathroom tissue are softness and price. P&G has developed a product, promotion, and pricing strategy that capitalizes on this fact. By pricing the product competitively and by creating a product that is indeed soft, the company has established the desired attributes. The noxious, but unforgettable, Mr. Whipple commercials drive home these points.

Knowledge of the choice process used by consumers also has implications for segmentation and positioning strategies. In some cases it may be possible to segment the market based upon the choice process used. The type of information given in advertisements to high-involvement, low-involvement, and experiential purchasers may have to be very different because of their diverse choice processes. Closely related is the positioning of a product or service. If market researchers identify segments of consumers who desire different attributes, a strategy must be developed to create and position products to fulfill the diverse desires.

A MANAGERIAL APPLICATIONS EXAMPLE

The Wall Street Journal stated in a lead article that "A sea change is roiling the personal computer industry, especially the market leaders, International Business Machines and Compaq Computer." Both companies had reported that sales of their PCs had fallen almost 20%. The price of Compaq's stock plummeted on the news.

While the market leaders in the personal computer industry were faltering, sales of clones were accelerating. For example, the products of AST Research and Dell

Computer were extremely strong. In addition, sales of Apple Computer's Macintosh increased by 85%. The company had announced major price reductions that quarter, and consumers were also enamored of the company's outstanding software and graphics capabilities.

The Wall Street Journal article identified a number of potential reasons for the dramatic change of fortune among companies in the volatile personal computer industry. First, PCs had become highly standardized around Intel Corporation's microprocessors, which give the computers their brain power. Second, user surveys indicated that on performance and quality many of the clones rated higher than either IBM or Compaq. Third, except for Apple's Macintosh, all the computers used the same software. Finally, the clones were priced much lower than either IBM or Compaq. These factors influenced corporate buyers as well as individuals. As an executive at a Fortune 500 firm said, "clones use essentially the same inner workings as more expensive brethren do and some have PCs that outperform IBM."[43]

In analyzing the problems of IBM and Compaq, consider what consumer concepts from this chapter apply in each case and, based upon these concepts, what managerial steps should be taken to react to the severe reduction in sales resulting from the impact of the clones and of Apple Computer.

The Consumer Behavior Analysis

A number of concepts from evaluation and choice apply to a consumer's decision to purchase a personal computer. First, buying a PC is normally a high-involvement purchase that results in extended decision making. Thus the *evaluation of alternatives* consists of buyers comparing beliefs about the attributes of competing brands. During the evaluation stage, buyers should also make judgments about the probability that the brands possess the attributes and about the goodness/badness of the attributes. In such instances, *judgmental heuristics* may influence the decision process. In particular, the *representativeness heuristic* could operate to the advantage of the clones. By selling clones through established retailers and by employing designs that look attractive and professional, manufacturers can create clones that appear representative or stereotypical of high-quality machines.

Because buyers would employ an extended decision-making process, they would tend to use either a *compensatory* or a *phased choice* model. If a phased choice model is used, buyers would most likely begin by eliminating unacceptable alternatives by first applying the *conjunctive* model. Thus key attributes can be identified, such as price, performance, reliability, and service. Minimum standards then are set for each attribute. Only the brands that meet minimum cutoff standards on each attribute are considered. Because many clones now have a low price, possess high quality, exhibit good reliability, and are sold by national retailers that provide good service, they would probably survive the initial screening process.

In the second stage of a phased model, buyers frequently use a compensatory approach. (In other cases, buyers may go directly to a compensatory model and skip the first stage of a phased model.) If a compensatory model is used, the positive features of a brand may compensate for its negative features. The problem for Compaq and IBM is that, despite their brand names, they are simply rated lower overall by buyers who compare them objectively to clones.

If buyers should use a *lexicographic model* as the second stage of a phased strategy, IBM and Compaq would have even more serious problems. In the lexicographic model, the attributes are ranked in importance, and the brand rated highest on the most important attribute is chosen. If price is rated as the most important attribute, a clone would be chosen instead of the more costly IBM or Compaq brands. The use of a lexicographic model does make sense as the second stage of a phased strategy. In the first stage of a phased strategy, all unacceptable brands are eliminated. Thus, when the lexicographic model is employed, decision makers know that they have obtained an acceptable alternative that performs best on the most important attribute.

The Managerial Applications Analysis

Table 12-7 presents the managerial applications analysis for the personal computer case. Three concepts introduced in this chapter have particular relevance: the evaluation of alternatives, the representativeness heuristic, and consumer choice processes.

The evaluation of alternatives stage has application to market research, positioning/differentiation, and the marketing mix. Market research should be conducted to determine the key attributes on which buyers evaluate personal computer brands, and to determine if buyers differentiate IBM and Compaq from the clones and from Apple Computer. In all likelihood, the results would reveal that IBM, Compaq, and the clones are viewed highly similarly and that only Apple's Macintosh is positioned divergently. This fact would have important implications for the marketing mix. In

TABLE 12-7

The Managerial Applications Analysis of the Computer Industry Case

Consumer Concepts	*Managerial Applications*
Evaluation of alternatives	*Market research*—Identify key attributes on which customers evaluate brands.
	Positioning—Position brand on attributes on which computer has competitive advantage.
	Marketing mix—Develop product that has superior performance on key attributes. Promote brand in manner that positions product strategically.
Representativeness heuristic	*Market research*—Identify the stereotypes that customers have regarding clones.
	Positioning/differentiation—Develop strategy that differentiates IBM and Compaq from any negative stereotypes.
	Promotional strategy—Consider using fear appeals that link clones to negative stereotypes.
Choice processes	*Market research*—Employ market research to determine the type of choice process used by the target market to select among options.
	Marketing mix—Price and promote product based in part upon the type of choice process used.

particular, IBM and Compaq must look carefully at their PCs to determine if they have any competitive advantage. They must then communicate what competitive advantage they have to customers via promotional strategy. Of course, they must also look carefully at product development to create innovative new products that surpass the clones on key attributes.

The representativeness heuristic also applies to market research, differentiation, and the marketing mix. Market research should be conducted to determine the positive and negative stereotypes that consumers may form toward clones. Communications should then be developed that differentiate IBM and Compaq from these negative stereotypes. Potentially, then, fear appeals could be developed that would link the clones to the negative images that consumers have of them.

Three concepts regarding choice process apply to this case—the compensatory choice model, the lexicographic model, and the conjunctive model. The basic goal of the manager should be to employ market research to identify the type of choice process used most frequently by the targeted market segments. In addition, the researchers should identify the relative importance of each of the attributes and the ratings of various competitive brands on each attribute. If the target market uses a lexicographic model and price is rated as the most important attribute, managers at Compaq and IBM may have to slash the price charged on their PCs to remain competitive. In contrast, if a compensatory model is used, a higher price may be offset by high ratings on other attributes, such as service and reliability. In this case, prices may not have to be reduced quite so much. However, increased promotional emphasis on the other positive attributes of PCs would be required.

In all likelihood, many customers employ some type of a phased strategy in the acquisition process. In this case, selection begins with the employment of a conjunctive model. The market researchers should seek to identify what cutoff value consumers use for the price attribute. The goal should be to ensure that their brand is not eliminated from consideration by decision makers in their target market because the price of the PC is higher than the cutoff. As a result of these findings, the price element of the marketing mix may have to be severely adjusted by IBM and Compaq.

To this point, the analysis has considered IBM's and Compaq's reactions only to the clones. However, Apple Computer presented a more difficult problem, because it was already highly differentiated from the market leaders and from the clones. Interestingly, IBM reacted to the situation by forming an alliance with Apple. In mid-1991 the companies announced a joint venture in which they would share technology and bring out new products together. Perhaps an old aphorism applies to the case—"If you can't beat them, join them."

SUMMARY

In the consumer decision process, the alternative evaluation and choice stages follow the problem recognition and search stages. Alternative evaluation, which concerns how consumers form overall evaluations regarding each of the alternatives under consideration, can be analyzed from the decision-making perspective. Here the researcher focuses on whether a high-involvement or a low-involvement process is taking place. Alternative evaluation can also be analyzed from the experiential perspective. Here the consumer researcher analyzes the extent to which evaluations are based on feelings and emotions.

When approaching alternative evaluation from the decision-making perspective, the researcher must be concerned with the judgment process. A judgment consists of estimating the likelihood that an event will occur or the goodness or badness of something. When judging the likelihood of an event occurring, people may use judgmental heuristics—or rules of thumb—such as anchoring and adjustment, availability, and representativeness.

When evaluating the goodness or badness of something, people's judgments may follow the predictions of prospect theory. Prospect theory suggests that the psychological value of a stimulus is different from the actual value of the stimulus. This results in people responding differently to losses and gains. Prospect theory has important implications for understanding how consumers respond to various types of sales promotion devices as well as changes in the prices of products. In addition, it has relevance to issues concerning the risk-taking tendencies of consumers.

Consumers must frequently choose among alternative courses of action. Such choices could involve deciding how much search to engage in, which product or service to purchase, and from which store to make a purchase. When analyzing the choice process, researchers should investigate whether choice is made under high- or low-involvement circumstances. Evidence indicates that in high-involvement choice, consumers tend to act as though they use compensatory choice models. In addition, they may use a phased model in which a noncompensatory model is employed first, such as the conjunctive rule, followed by a compensatory approach. In contrast, under low-involvement conditions consumers act as though they use a noncompensatory model. Examples of noncompensatory models include the conjunctive, disjunctive, lexicographic, and elimination-by-aspect rules.

Another perspective on choice is to view it as an experiential process. Here consumers are viewed as using affect and feelings as the basis for making their choices. Impulse purchases and choices based upon brand loyalty appear to work in part through such experiential motivations.

KEY TERMS

affect–referral heuristic
alternative evaluation
anchoring and adjustment
availability heuristic
choice
compensatory models of choice
conjunctive rule
consumer self-control
decision context
delay-payment effect
disjunctive rule
elimination-by-aspects heuristic
framing
frequency heuristic
hierarchical models of choice
hindsight bias
hypothetical value function
impulse purchase
interaction set
judgment
judgmental heuristics
law of small numbers
lexicographic heuristic
noncomparable alternatives
noncompensatory models of choice
nostalgia
phased strategy
prospect theory
quiet set
representativeness heuristic
risk perception
satisficing
valuation of gains and losses

REVIEW QUESTIONS

1. What occurs during the alternative evaluation process? How does involvement influence the alternative evaluation process?
2. Define consumer judgment. How do consumer judgments relate to the attitude-toward-the-object model?
3. What is a judgmental heuristic? State briefly the three types of judgmental heuristics used for estimating probabilities.
4. Define nostalgia and provide an example.
5. Draw a diagram of the prospect theory's hypothetical value function. What does prospect theory say about how people judge the value of something?
6. What is meant by the term "framing"? How can framing influence the risk-taking tendency of a consumer?
7. What is meant by noncomparable alternatives of choice?
8. How does the choice process differ under high- and low-involvement conditions?
9. How do the heuristic models of choice lead to satisfying behavior?
10. What is a conjunctive model of choice?
11. What is a disjunctive model of choice?
12. What is an elimination-by-aspects model?
13. How does a lexicographic choice model work?
14. How does a phased choice model work?
15. What would the attitude-toward-the-object model suggest about choice?
16. From the experiential perspective, how does choice occur?
17. What is the impact of mood on choice behavior?
18. How are choices among noncomparable alternatives likely to be made?
19. What are the factors that influence store choice?

DISCUSSION QUESTIONS

1. Consider how you evaluated alternatives when choosing which college to attend. Describe the process. Does it conform more closely to what would be expected from a high-involvement, low-involvement, experiential, or behavioral influence perspective?
2. Now recall exactly how you made the final choice. Which type of choice model most closely matches what you did? Please describe the choice process that you used.
3. Go to a large grocery store or a large mall and identify the various means through which retailers attempt to influence your feelings. Describe as precisely as you can what is being done to manipulate consumer emotions and moods.
4. Consider how you go about choosing gifts for other people. As part of the process, you probably attempt to make a probability judgment as to the likelihood that the receivers will like the various gifts you are considering. How do you estimate the probability that they will like the gifts? Provide an example of an instance when anchoring and adjustment, the representativeness heuristic, or the availability heuristic would be used to help make the judgment.
5. Think back to the various catastrophes that have occurred over the past few years. For example, in 1989 a terrorist bombing caused a Pan Am plane's crash over Scotland, and earthquakes in Armenia killed thousands of people. In these examples, the passengers on the flight were consumers of airline services and the residents of Armenia were consumers of architects' and contractors' buildings. Analyze how the news media and consumers of products and services reacted to the tragedy. To what extent was the outcome bias revealed?
6. Conduct an experiment on ten of your friends. Ask five of them to imagine that it is ten years in the future and that things have gone extremely well financially for them. In fact,

they have managed to build up savings of over $50,000. Tell them that they have a chance to get involved in a business deal. A two-in-three chance exists that the deal will be successful. If so, they will make $50,000. However, a one-in-three chance exists that the deal will fail, and they will lose $50,000. Ask them if they would invest in the deal. For the other five friends, tell them that things have not gone well. In fact, they are $50,000 in debt. Now, give them the same opportunity on the deal. Ask both groups to explain their decision. What does prospect theory predict that people in the two groups will do? Do your results support prospect theory?

7. Conduct an interview with five of your friends. Ask them to list their last two impulsive actions. Ask them to analyze why they engaged in the impulsive behavior. Considering the models of choice described in the text, which one seems to best describe what happened?
8. Consider how you make budget allocations among different activities and purchases. What kinds of trade-offs do you make in your purchases? How do you decide whether to spend your money on clothing, trips, school supplies (e.g., computers), or stereos? To what extent do your actions follow the process of making choices among noncomparable alternatives?
9. Describe the factors that most markedly influence which grocery store and department store you patronize. Do these correspond to the factors discussed in the text that influence store choice?

ENDNOTES

1. Francine Schwadel, "The Bare Facts Show a Suitable Swimsuit Is Difficult to Find," *The Wall Street Journal*, July 6, 1988, pp. 1, 6.
2. David Lieberman, "SI's Swimsuit Issue: More Than Meets the Eye," *Business Week*, January 16, 1989, p. 52.
3. Harry Davis, Stephen Hoch, and E. K. Ragsdale, "An Anchoring and Adjustment Model of Spousal Predictions," *Journal of Consumer Research*, Vol. 13 (June 1986), pp. 25–37.
4. Stephen Hoch, "Who Do We Know: Predicting the Interests and Opinions of the American Consumer," *Journal of Consumer Research*, Vol. 15 (December 1988), pp. 315–324. Answers to the consumer attitude quiz are
   (1) Men = 36, Women = 35;
   (2) Men = 52, Women = 34;
   (3) Men = 75, Women = 71;
   (4) Men = 63, Women = 61;
   (5) Men = 29, Women = 33;
   (6) Men = 66, Women = 74;
   (7) Men = 72, Women = 70;
   (8) Men = 17, Women = 11;
   (9) Men = 57, Women = 79;
   (10) Men = 68, Women = 50;
   (11) Men = 48, Women = 54.
5. Hanjoon Lee, Acito Acito, and Ralph Day, "Evaluation and Use of Marketing Research by Decision Makers: A Behavioral Simulation," *Journal of Marketing Research*, Vol. 24 (May 1987), pp. 187–196.
6. Amos Tversky and Daniel Kahneman, "Availability: A Heuristic for Judging Frequency and Probability," *Cognitive Psychology*, Vol. 5 (1973), pp. 107–232.
7. W. Larry Gregory, Robert Cialdini, and Kathleen Carpenter, "Self-Relevant Scenarios as Mediators of Likelihood Estimates and Compliance: Does Imagining Make It So?" *Journal of Personality and Social Psychology*, Vol. 43 (1982), pp. 89–99.
8. Daniel Kahneman and Amos Tversky, "Subjective Probability: A Judgment of Representativeness," *Cognitive Psychology*, Vol. 3 (1972), pp. 430–454.
9. Lee et al., "Evaluation and Use of Marketing Research by Decision Makers."
10. Daniel Kahneman and Amos Tversky, "Prospect Theory: An Analysis of Decisions Under Risk," *Econometrica*, Vol. 47 (March 1979), pp. 263–291.
11. Daniel Kahneman and Amos Tversky, "Choices, Values, and Frames," *American Psychologist*, Vol. 39 (1984), pp. 341–350.

12. For recent review articles on framing, see Alice A. Wright and Richard J. Lutz, "Effects of Advertising and Experience on Brand Judgments: A Rose by Any Other Frame," in *Advances in Consumer Research*, Vol. 20, Leigh McAlister and Michael L. Rothschild, eds. (Provo, UT: Association for Consumer Research, 1992), pp. 165–169. Also, see Donald J. Hempel and Harold Z. Daniel, "Framing Dynamics: Measurement Issues and Perspectives," in *Advances in Consumer Research*, Vol. 20, Leigh McAlister and Michael L. Rothschild, eds. (Provo, UT: Association for Consumer Research, 1992), pp. 273–279.

13. Christopher Puto, Wesley Patton, and Ronald King, "Risk Handling Strategies in Industrial Vendor Selection Decisions," *Journal of Marketing*, Vol. 49 (Winter 1985), pp. 89–98.

14. Irwin Levin, "Associative Effects of Information Framing," *Bulletin of the Psychonomic Society*, Vol. 25 (1987), pp. 85–86.

15. William D. Diamond and Abhijit Sanyal, "The Effects of Framing on the Choice of Supermarket Coupons," in *Advances in Consumer Research*, Vol. 17, Marvin E. Goldberg and Gerald Gorn, eds. (Provo, UT: Association for Consumer Research, 1990), pp. 488–493. Also, see John Mowen, Alan Gordon, and Clifford Young, "The Impact of Sales Taxes on Store Choice: Public Policy and Theoretical Implications," Proceedings of Summer Educators' Conference (Chicago: American Marketing Association, 1988).

16. John C. Mowen and Maryanne M. Mowen, "Time and Outcome Valuation: Implications for Marketing Decision Making," *Journal of Marketing* (October 1991), pp. 54–62.

17. Joan Meyers-Levy and Durairaj Maheswaran, "When Timing Matters: The Influence of Temporal Distance on Consumers' Affective and Persuasive Responses," *Journal of Consumer Research*, Vol. 19 (December 1992), pp. 424–433.

18. For another view of how problems of consumer self-control occur, see Stephen J. Hock and George F. Lowenstein, "Time-Inconsistent Preferences and Consumer Self-Control," *Journal of Consumer Research*, Vol. 17 (March 1991), pp. 492–507.

19. Morris B. Holbrook, "Nostalgia and Consumption Preferences: Some Emerging Patterns of Consumer Tastes," *Journal of Consumer Research*, Vol. 20 (September 1993), pp. 245–256. For other research on nostalgia, see William Havelna and Susan Holak, "The Good Old Days: Observations on Nostalgia and Its Role in Consumer Behavior," in *Advances in Consumer Research*, Vol. 18, Rebecca Holman and Michael Solomon, eds. (Provo, UT: Association for Consumer Research), pp. 323–329.

20. Morris B. Holbrook and Robert M. Schindler, "Some Exploratory Findings on the Development of Musical Tastes," *Journal of Consumer Research*, Vol. 16 (June 1989), pp. 119–124.

21. Holbrook, "Nostalgia and Consumption Preferences."

22. Dennis Gensch and Rajshekhar Javalgi, "The Influence of Involvement on Disaggregate Attribute Choice Models," *Journal of Consumer Research*, Vol. 14 (June 1987), pp. 71–82. This section on noncompensatory models relies heavily on work by Peter Wright, "Consumer Choice Strategies: Simplifying Versus Optimizing," *Journal of Marketing Research*, Vol. 11 (February 1976), pp. 60–67.

23. E. J. Johnson and J. E. Russo, "Product Familiarity and Learning New Information," *Journal of Consumer Research*, Vol. 11 (June 1984), pp. 542–550.

24. Alan Newell and Herbert Simon, *Human Problem Solving* (Englewood Cliffs, NJ: Prentice-Hall, 1972).

25. Joseph W. Alba and Howard Marmorstein, "The Effects of Frequency Knowledge on Consumer Decision Making," *Journal of Consumer Research*, Vol. 14 (June 1987), pp. 14–25.

26. Ibid.

27. M. Reilly and R. Holman, "Does Task Complexity or Cue Intercorrelation Affect Choice of an Information-Processing Strategy?: An Empirical Investigation," in *Advances in Consumer Research*, Vol. 4, W. D. Perrault, Jr., ed. (Atlanta, GA: Association for Consumer Research, 1977), pp. 185–190.

28. Wayne Hoyer, "An Examination of Consumer Decision Making for a Common Repeat Purchase Product," *Journal of Consumer Research*, Vol. 11 (December 1984), pp. 822–829.

29. Wayne D. Hoyer and Steven P. Brown, "Effects of Brand Awareness on Choice for a Common, Repeat-Purchase Product," *Journal of Consumer Research*, Vol. 17 (September 1990), pp. 141–148.

30. P. Weinberg and W. Gottwald, "Impulsive Consumer Buying as a Result of Emotions," *Journal of Business Research*, Vol. 10 (March 1982), pp. 43–87.

31. James Engel and Roger Blackwell, *Consumer Behavior* (Chicago: Holt, Rinehart and Winston, 1982).

32. "Industrial Retail Selling Strategies Designed to Induce Impulse Sales," *Beverage Industry*, June 3, 1977, pp. 6.

33. E. Langer and L. Imba, "The Role of Mindlessness in the Perception of Deviance," *Journal of Personality and Social Psychology*, Vol. 38 (September 1980), pp. 360–367.

34. Weinberg and Gottwald, "Impulsive Consumer Buying as a Result of Emotions," pp. 43–57.

35. Dennis Rook and Stephen Hoch, "Consuming Impulses," in *Advances in Consumer Research*, Vol. 12, E. Hirschman and M. Holbrook, eds. (Ann Arbor, MI: Association for Consumer Research, 1985), pp. 23–27.

36. Meryl Gardner and Ronald Hill, "Consumers' Mood States: Antecedents and Consequences of Experiential vs. Information Strategies for Brand Choice," *Psychology and Marketing*, Vol. 5, no. 2 (1988), pp. 169–182.

37. Michael Johnson, "Consumer Choice Strategies for Comparing Noncomparable Alternatives," *Journal of Consumer Research*, Vol. 11 (December 1984), pp. 741–753.

38. James Bruner and John Mason, "The Influence of Driving Time upon Shopping Center Preference," *Journal of Marketing*, Vol. 32 (April 1968), pp. 57–61.

39. Barbara Kahn, William Moore, and Rashi Glazer, "Experiments in Constrained Choice," *Journal of Consumer Research*, Vol. 14 (June 1987), pp. 96–113.

40. Susan Spiggle and Murphy Sewall, "A Choice Sets Model of Retail Selection," *Journal of Marketing*, Vol. 51 (April 1987), pp. 97–111.

41. Case based upon Stephen Kreider Yoder and G. Pascal Zachary, "PC Firms Are Roiled by Change as Clones Gain on Brand Names," *The Wall Street Journal*, May 16, 1991, pp. A1, A6.

42. Susan Spiggle and Murphy Sewall, "A Choice Sets Model of Retail Selection," *Journal of Marketing*, Vol. 51 (April 1987), pp. 97–111.

43. Case based upon Stephen Kreider Yoder and G. Pascal Zachary, "PC Firms Are Roiled by Change as Clones Gain on Brand Names."

CHAPTER 12 CASE STUDY

Buick Reclaims Customers

During the 1980s, consumer perceptions of American automobiles reached an all-time low. Despite incentives—such as rebates, below-market interest rates, and creative advertising—market shares plummeted. In large part customers shifted their buying from American to Japanese brands. The trend continued into the 1990s. For example, in 1991 General Motors lost another one-half-point market share (to 35.6%). The huge automaker had begun the 1980s with roughly a 55% share of the U.S. auto market. Despite the falling market share of U.S. automakers, the Buick Division of General Motors bucked the trend in the early 1990s. In 1990 Buick's sales increased by 6.6%, and in 1991 the division gained a full 1% increase in share to over 6% of the market. Perhaps most important, the company increased its market share without having to use profit-eroding rebates and sales incentives. What happened at Buick to cause this incredible turnaround in its fortunes?

In part, Buick's recent success represents a "bounce-back" from its problems of the early 1980s. Then management made a decision to reposition the division in an effort to appeal to younger customers. Sporty Skyhawks, cheapie Skylarks, turbocharged Gran Sports, and boring Rivieras were produced. The promising two-seat Reatta was created in a configuration that was underpowered and uncompetitive with the import challengers against which it was targeted. Similarly, quality was sacrificed as cars came off the production line with bad paint jobs, poorly fitting body panels, and windows that wouldn't stay up. Consumer satisfaction surveys ranked Buick near the bottom of the list. As a result of this confluence of problems, Buick's traditional buyers (white-collar professionals aged 45 and older) abandoned the venerable brand.

Buick's turnaround actually began in 1986 when a general manager, Edward Mertz, was hired. He quickly recognized that the company sold a supermarket of brands with greatly varying images. Mertz said, "People didn't know exactly what to expect from Buick." Seeing the trouble with such chaos, he decided to take the company back to its roots of building big substantial vehicles for professionals. Mertz saw Buick as the "Premium American Motorcar"—distinctive, substantial, powerful, and mature. Perhaps most important, Mertz reoriented the division to focus on quality. By 1989, the J. D. Powers market research firm rated the Buick LeSabre second in quality only to the Nissan Maxima. During 1990 and 1991, Buick was ranked first among American cars in quality.

Inspired by the favorable reviews, Buick initiated a series of changes. Mertz discontinued the smallest cars and the smallest engines and focused on building compact to full-size luxury models with V-6 and V-8 engines. Although still conservative, Buick styling became distinctive. Priced between $15,000 and $26,000, its vehicles were targeted to traditional Buick buyers—60-year-olds with a median income of $42,700 and 35% with college education. Roomy, easy to drive, with good power and good gas mileage, the "new" Buick's qualities matched those desired by the target market. (A full-size top-of-the-line Park Avenue gets better highway mileage than a similarly equipped Toyota Camry that is 560 pounds lighter.)

Mertz's attention to providing the car desired by Buick's target market can be seen in the last-minute design changes made in the new Regal only a year prior to its introduction in

1990. A dull gray vinyl dashboard was covered with wood-grain "appliques." Chrome accents were added to the exterior, and a choppy ride was smoothed by fine-tuning the suspension. As a result, the Regal went on to outsell its major competitor, the Ford Thunderbird, and become the most popular car in its class.

* * *

Thanks to Carol Hisey for developing the case.

QUESTIONS

1. Define the problem faced by Buick in the 1980s.
2. Discuss the consumer concepts from the chapter that apply to the case.
3. Develop the managerial applications analysis for the case. Discuss the managerial strategies that Buick developed and how they relate to the consumer concepts identified.

Chapter

13

Postacquisition Processes, Consumer Satisfaction, and Brand Loyalty

CONSUMER VIGNETTE

On Flow Experience, Litterers, and Bootmakers

ON FLOW EXPERIENCE The following quotes come from skydivers describing their "freefall" experience.

> Person 1: "When I'm in freefall, I don't think about anything else in the world. I'm not thinking of any problems. It's just kind of an escape that's free. You're just flying."
>
> Person 2. "You're thinking in split seconds. Everything seems to be in a time warp. Everything slows down. It's total concentration. To me it's completely relaxed because everything else is off my mind."[1]

These words describe the experience of flow—a transcendental state in which time stops and self-awareness ceases. The feeling of flow may well represent the ultimate consumption experience.

ON LITTERERS Daniel Syrek loves his job, saying, "These last 16 years have been the best of my life." Mr. Syrek is an expert on roadside litter. He spends his time peering into roadside culverts, eating the dust of semitrailer trucks, and dodging Coke bottles and beer cans tossed from passing vehicles. He casually throws out statistics on litter. When it rains, littering decreases by 50%, but when the temperature rises from 50 to 70 degrees, it doubles in volume. Seventeen percent of all litter blows out of the back of pickup trucks. Deliberate litter accounts for 55% of roadside trash.

He describes litterers as thoughtless slobs. He says, "They're bubbas. You have to hit them between the eyes with a 2 × 4." The state of Texas agreed with him and started its hard-hitting "Don't mess with Texas" advertising campaign. By Mr. Syrek's estimates, the campaign reduced littering by 60% and, as a result, saved millions of dollars in cleanup costs. But then he added that such belligerence will not work in all states. "People in other states just don't think the same way," he said. "Don't mess with Rhode Island? Get outta here; it won't work."[2] (The "Don't mess with Texas" bumper sticker is shown in Figure 13-1.)

ON BOOTMAKERS Now, consider Richard Barber's story. He wanted to get new rubber chain-link bottoms on his 30-year-old lounger boots. The boots had a "G. H. Bass" label, but when he called Bass, the service rep said that the boots were actually made by L. L. Bean. Richard then called the Maine bootmaker and reached Maggie. She explained that Bean could fix them and gave Richard instructions on how to send the boots with $24 to the company. After six weeks, though, the boots had not been returned. Richard called L. L. Bean again. Ann apologized for the delay, stating that today was a holiday, and asked if Richard could call back the next day. Richard called the next day, and Ann's boss, Steve, answered and apologized again for the delay. He said that they would track down the problem. The next day Ann called back and told Richard that the problem was that the Bass uppers would only fit on a size eight, which was too small for him. L. L. Bean would return his check and the old boots. Richard hung up, but then 20 minutes later, Steve was on the line again. Steve explained that they had figured out how to put size ten bottoms on the Bass uppers. He said: "They'll send them out this afternoon. Have a happy New Year. Sorry it took so long to get this solved."

Richard Barber was amazed at the service he had received. As a completely satisfied customer, he said, "Thirty years from now I hope I'm speaking with Maggie and Steve and Ann. They gave me a wonderful lift."[3]

Figure 13-1 Littering is one unfortunate result of product consumption. This "Don't mess with Texas" bumper sticker helped to reduce the state's littering by 60%. (Courtesy Texas Department of Transportation.)

INTRODUCTION

In the last two chapters, the first four stages of the consumer decision process were discussed: problem recognition, search, alternative evaluation, and choice. This chapter focuses on the last stage of consumer decision making: postacquisition processes. **Postacquisition processes** refer to the consumption, disposition, and postchoice evaluation of goods, services, and ideas. The stories in the introductory vignette identify three important areas in the study of postacquisition processes: product consumption, product disposition, and consumer satisfaction/dissatisfaction.

The first anecdote describes the reactions of two skydivers to the experience of consuming the sport of parachuting. The reactions of these skydivers aptly describe what has been called a "flow experience." Flow occurs during the time period in which a person is totally participating in the experience of consuming or using a good or service. During the "flow experience" self-awareness ceases, and the consumption experience, the self, and the context blend together so that all time awareness is lost.

While the "flow" experience is relatively rare, it well depicts an ultimate consumption experience. The feeling of flow could also occur in situations in which services are being received, such as at a rock concert or on a white-water river rafting excursion. At the other end of the continuum of consumption experiences are cases in which the consumer feels highly self-conscious and frustrated. For example, recall how you felt when you were attempting to put together or make something when you had been supplied with very poor directions for assembly. Understanding the feelings and cognitions that occur during the consumption of goods and services is increasingly becoming an important area of study for consumer researchers.

The second vignette introduces us to Daniel Syrek, who makes his living analyzing the litter thrown on highways. Approaching the problem from a scientific perspective, Dan has developed regression equations that can predict amounts of litter based upon such factors as season, air temperature, and traffic count. Why is his job important? After we purchase products, we must dispose of them in some manner. Unfortunately, the disposal of refuse is rapidly becoming an environmental nightmare. Dan Syrek's work is valuable because he is seeking to understand one of its components—highway litter. Finding solutions to the dilemma of how to deal with the trash that results from our consumer society is one of the major problems of the 1990s. As a result, the study of product disposition is an important area of postacquisition processes.

It should be noted that the study of product disposition lacks glamour, and some of the jobs associated with the field are even worse than Daniel Syrek's. Consider the job of the knacker. "Cy Osmer is an absolute godsend"—so says Stephen Taylor, who runs a dairy farm in New Hampshire. "I don't know what we'll do when Cy isn't around." Indeed, Mr. Taylor has good reason to worry, because when he spoke those words, Cy was 84 years old. Why is Cy so important to the agricultural community in New Hampshire and Vermont? Cy Osmer is a knacker—a person who picks up and disposes of dead animals, such as cows, horses, pigs, and other livestock. He takes the farm animals, who die from natural causes, and turns them into usable products, such as leather, dog food, bone meal, and tallow. Not a pretty job, but one that is absolutely mandatory in our society.[4]

The story of Richard Barber's experience with L. L. Bean illustrates the vital area of **consumer satisfaction/dissatisfaction (CS/D)**. After making a purchase, consumers continue to examine the outcomes of the exchange with the firm. If the product performs poorly or the company provides lousy service, consumers become dissatisfied. As a result, the company loses any chance of creating brand loyalty, and the likelihood that the consumer will make additional purchases from the company is dramatically lowered. L. L. Bean is consistently rated as the top mail-order retailer for service quality. Richard Barber's account of how the company treated him explains in part the company's phenomenal success. Figure 13-2 shows a page from a recent L. L. Bean catalog that describes the handmade quality of its boots.

Figure 13-3 presents a model of the consumer **postacquisition process**, which begins after a choice has been made and the consumer begins to consume or use the

Figure 13-2 A corporate strategy of L. L. Bean is to ensure consumer satisfaction by providing outstanding service after the purchase. The 81-year history of the firm is briefly described in this page from a recent catalog. (Courtesy of L. L. Bean, Inc.)

The Christmas Present with an 81 Year Past

Bean Boots by L.L. Bean

The best choice for all-round wear from spring to fall (worn with ragg wool socks, your feet will stay comfortable through most winter conditions). Full-grain leather tops are triple-needle stitched to waterproof rubber soles.

Please state size and width of your usual shoe size. Boot heights are measured from floor. Due to the natural give and stretch of leather, a short break-in period is required for the most comfortable fit. Designed for wear with heavy weight sock. Comfort rated to 32° and up. Made by us in Maine.

Colors: Tan uppers. Brown uppers (Original model only).

Men's Whole sizes only: 6", 8" and 10" heights offered in sizes 6 to 14 Narrow(B), 5 to 14 Medium(C/D) and 6 to 14 Wide(E/EE). 12" height offered in sizes 6 to 14 Narrow(B), Medium(C/D) and Wide(E/EE). Wt. approximately 2 lb. 14 oz. a pair.

GG11017 Men's

6"	$59.50	10"	$69.50
8"	$64.50	12"	$79.50

Women's The same features and construction as our men's—proportioned for a better women's fit. Wt. approximately 2 lb. 7 oz. a pair. Whole sizes only: 5 to 11 Medium(B).

GG11092 Women's

7" Tan or Brown upper/brown bottom	$65.00
7" Tan upper/navy bottom	$65.00
9" Tan or brown upper/brown bottom	$69.50

Handmade Quality

After eight decades, our Bean Boots are still one of the most practical gifts you can give.

Generations of customers have enjoyed the dry, comfortable performance of their Bean Boots and made them their first choice for all types of weather—from the spring thaw to the fall rains. Made by us in Maine since 1912.

Thinsulate Insulated L.L. Bean Boots

Cool-weather versions of our L.L. Bean Boot. Feature 200 gram Thinsulate™ Thermal Insulation in the rubber bottoms. Comfort rated to 10° and up (warmth varies with type of sock worn, level of activity and personal response to cold). Color: Tan.

GG10667 Men's

6"	$69.50
8"	$74.50
10"	$79.50

Men's whole sizes: 7 to 13 Narrow(B), Medium(C/D) and 8 to 13 Wide(E/EE).

GG10671 Women's

7"	$74.50

Women's whole sizes: 5 to 11 Medium(B).

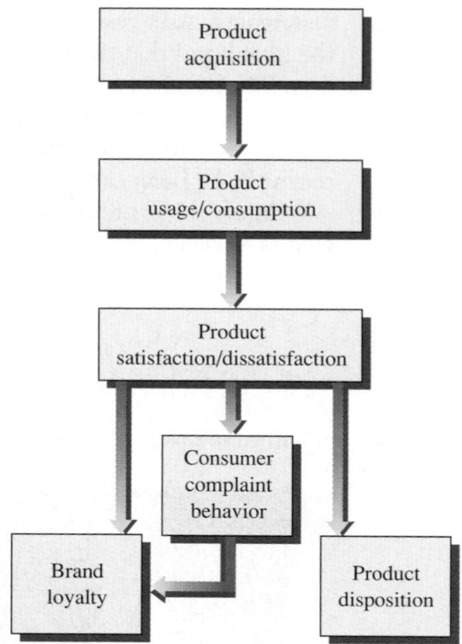

Figure 13-3
A model of the consumer post-acquisition process.

good or service. Postacquisition processes involve five major topics: (1) product usage/consumption, (2) consumer satisfaction/dissatisfaction, (3) consumer complaint behavior, (4) the disposition of goods, and (5) the formation of brand loyalty. During the consumption stage, consumers use and experience the product. This stage is then followed by the development of consumer satisfaction/dissatisfaction. If consumers are dissatisfied with the product's performance, complaint behavior may occur. The final two stages of the postacquisition process involve (6) how consumers dispose of the goods that they purchase and (7) how brand loyalty and future buying intentions are formed.

THE CONSUMPTION OF GOODS AND SERVICES

The **consumption** of a product involves its use and ultimate depletion. (Here, the term *product* refers to both goods and services.) For a good, such as an automobile, consumption involves how the car is used and the experiences that the driver obtains from it. Gradually, the car will undergo depletion as it wears out. In a similar manner, people also consume services. For example, the consumption of a restaurant meal results in its depletion. Thinking back to the chapter-opening vignette and the experience of "flow," consumption involves the experiences felt by the skydivers as they plummet toward the earth.

An understanding of how consumers use goods and services is important to managers. Indeed, managers must carefully analyze the impact of the product attributes on the consumption experience. For example, the attributes of a hospital include the competence of its physicians and nursing staff, the appearance of the physical facilities, the quality of the food, and the consideration and treatment of patients. Each of these attributes will impact the use experience of a patient.

The study of usage impacts marketers of goods, as well as services. For example, it has long been assumed that people do the dishes by putting dishwashing detergent in the sink, filling the sink with water, and then washing the dishes. Procter & Gamble hired a firm to observe consumers and their dishwashing habits.[5] The company placed television cameras in homes and recorded the daily activities of the families. One of the findings was that most people no longer fill their sink with sudsy water. Instead, they squirt the dishwashing liquid directly onto the dishes, pots, and pans. This behavior probably results from the fact that, with the prevalence of dishwashing machines, the number of dishes done by hand is small. Knowledge of such information could assist the company in new product development. For example, a less concentrated detergent works best if it is squirted directly onto the dishes.

The observation of how consumers use products can lead to the development of new market offerings. For example, a general manager at Kodak observed a tourist in Japan attempting to pry open a Kodak film container while holding his camera. The feat was impossible with one hand, and the man had to use his teeth to tear off the lid. The manager returned to headquarters, reported the problem, and now the lids can be pulled off with one hand.[6]

Another area in which information on product usage can be important is in avoiding product liability problems. Consumers have a nasty habit of finding unintended uses for products. Examples include using doors of ovens as stepping stools, using lawn mowers as hedge trimmers, and pouring perfume over candles to make them scented. In each of these cases, consumers were injured while misusing the products and then sued the companies under product liability laws. Although the way these products were used may seem rather bizarre, the plaintiff won the lawsuit in each case.

Companies must design a product so that it is safe in the use for which it was designed. In addition, companies should take steps to anticipate unintended uses of their products, and either design them for safe use or provide warnings that they should not be used in certain applications.[7] Aluminum stepladders carry a warning to consumers not to stand on the top of the ladder and to avoid use near electrical lines.

Measuring Product Usage

Marketers have identified four factors that are particularly important when assessing product usage.[8] First, the consumption frequency should be analyzed. Some products are used continuously (e.g., refrigerators and hot water heaters); most products, however, are used discontinuously (e.g., dishwashers, medical services, toothpaste, and autos). In general, companies want consumers to use their product or service as frequently as possible. (There are exceptions to this, such as efforts made to reduce or eliminate the abuse of drugs.)

Second, consumption amount is important for marketers to analyze. In many cases firms may develop strategies to increase the average amount of a product consumed. Dishwasher detergent manufacturers are guilty of this tactic. In fact, using the recommended amount of dishwashing powder may result in glasses becoming cloudy from the pitting caused by the undissolved powder. Such marketing strategies have inherent limitations, however. For example, marketers of alcoholic products would create a public outcry if campaigns blatantly urged consumers to drink more.

General Foods Corporation recognized a "consumption amount" problem in its sales of Grape-Nuts cereal.[9] Market research discovered that 18% of the families in Denver had purchased Grape-Nuts during a six-month period. This was the fourth best performance among all cereals. However, when purchase volume was examined, the researchers found that it was significantly less than average. As a result of the research, a strategy was developed to increase the amount of Grape-Nuts purchased. One element of the strategy involved suggesting to consumers that Grape-Nuts could be heated and eaten as a warm cereal. Other ads suggested that Grape-Nuts could be sprinkled on oatmeal, which was becoming popular in 1988 as a healthy breakfast food.

The consumption interval is the third factor to consider. With most products and services used discontinuously, an important goal is to lessen the interval between product usage. The auto industry is currently dealing with this problem. As quality and durability have improved, cars are lasting longer, and consumers are purchasing new cars less frequently. In response to the problem, auto companies are now making the terms of two- and three-year leases highly attractive. The short-term leases help to ensure that the interval between acquiring a new car is shortened considerably.

The consumption purpose is the fourth category that researchers consider. A classic example of a company that has attempted to increase the number of purposes for which a product may be used is Arm & Hammer, Inc. A few of the alternative uses suggested for its baking soda include baking, brushing teeth, freshening a carpet, and serving as an antacid. Consumption purpose is closely related to what is called *usage occasion*. Much more will be said about usage occasions in Chapter 14, Situational Influences.

The Consumption of Performance

Recently, researchers have begun to empirically investigate the nature of the consumption experience. Employing a dramatic framework, they suggest that in Western society people frame the consumption experience as though they were participating in a performance. Using naturalistic research methods borrowed from the fields of anthropology and sociology, their research studies have tended to investigate high-risk performances, such as skydiving[10] and white-water river rafting.[11]

What does it mean to say that consumers are participating in a performance? From a dramaturgical perspective, consumers and marketers act as though they are in a theatrical performance.[12] For example, when white-water rafting down the Colorado River, the participants and their guide are actors. The boat, life vests, food, mosquito repellents, and so on are the props for the play. The Colorado River and the canyon form the stage. Within this backdrop, a story is told. In the first stage of the story, conflicting forces are introduced. For example, participants ask themselves if they really want to participate in a white-water experience. During the second stage, tensions and emotions build as they experience fear, hunger, and cold. In the conclusion, the conflict is resolved and emotions are released.

Marketers seek to script the performance that occurs as they engage in the exchange process with consumers. Indeed, consumers and marketers can be viewed as in an "exchange play" in which each performs to a greater or lesser degree. For the purpose of this text, a **consumer performance** can be defined as an event in which a consumer and marketer act as performers and/or audience in a situation in which obligations and standards exist.[13] It is important to distinguish a performance from an occurrence. An occurrence happens as the result of an accident or "act of nature." It is unplanned and does not arise from any obligation. A recent example of an occurrence would be the events surrounding Hurricane Andrew, which devastated South Florida in 1992.

Table 13-1 distinguishes occurrences from three different types of performances. First, *contracted performance* happens when the consumer and marketer play a minimal role in the performance. Contracted performances most frequently involve the purchase and use of low-involvement products, such as detergent, toothpaste, and motor oil. A second type of performance occurs when the consumer and/or the marketer are clearly involved in the success of the exchange. Called *enacted performance*, the exchange occurs in a manner in which either the consumer or the marketer has latitude to blame or to give credit to the other for the outcome of the transaction. Enacted performance occurs most frequently in service exchanges or with high-involvement goods. For example, the performance of filling a tooth involves both the dentist and the patient. Similarly, the purchase of a car involves both the consumer and the salesperson in a complex exchange in which blame or credit can be assessed by either party.

The third type of performance is called *dramatistic performance*. Dramatistic performance occurs when both the consumer and marketer know that a show is occurring and each is alert to the other's role. The distinction between enacted and dramatistic performance can be blurry. However, dramatistic performance will tend to occur when the stakes are high and the consumer's and marketer's involvement level is quite high. In such instances, each actor is an audience to the other, and each becomes alert to the motives of the other in the performance. Each actor recognizes that the actions of the other could be contrived. An example would be the consumer who is purchasing a used car and who is extremely doubtful about the honesty and reliability of the seller. Similarly, the performances that occur on a white-water rafting expedition or during skydiving also have a dramatistic flare. It is during

TABLE 13-1

Types of Performances Occurring in Marketing Exchanges

1. *Contracted performance.* Both the consumer and the marketer have minimal interactions. Occurs with low-involvement goods.
2. *Enacted performance.* Both the consumer and the marketer have sufficient latitude to place blame for the outcome of the transaction. Occurs most frequently with high-involvement products.
3. *Dramatistic performance.* Both the consumer and the marketer know that a show is occurring. Each party becomes concerned with the motives of the other. Occurs most frequently in the highest-involvement situations, such as skydiving or buying an automobile.

dramatistic performances that stories unfold, consumer emotions run their highest, and flow is most likely experienced.

The concept that the consumption process is a type of performance is an important one. Particularly when purchasing services, the metaphor of a drama is appropriate. For example, a medical patient suffering from a life-threatening disease becomes a consumer wrapped up in a high-stakes drama. Thus the unfortunate person is involved as a participant in a theatrical performance with members of the medical profession.

The dramaturgy metaphor may hold for the purchase and use of goods as well. Indeed, a good can be described as having a "frozen potential for performance."[14] Thus consumers not only choose goods, but they also consume performances when they use the good. As noted previously, the purchase and use of an automobile has dramatistic elements. At the extreme, building a house in which tens or hundreds of thousands of dollars are invested can take on the characteristics of Greek tragedy.

Mood States and the Consumption Experience

Moods are temporary positive or negative affective states. An important issue concerns the impact of the consumption experience on mood states. As discussed in the chapters on information processing (Chapter 4) and choice (Chapter 12), consumer mood states may have a strong impact on what is remembered and on which brand is chosen. Moods may be influenced by what happens during the consumption of a product. The mood state that is created during the consumption process may, in turn, impact the overall evaluation of the product.

Little research has been done to determine what factors may influence mood during the consumption experience. Research in operant conditioning suggests that when organisms experience a positive reinforcer, they reveal positive affective states. For example, when given a bone, a dog wags its tail—a sign that the dog is experiencing a positive internal state. Similarly, when opening presents at Christmas, young children, and even many adults, smile and laugh during the experience. All these behaviors indicate that a positive mood state is being felt while in the presence of the positive reinforcer. Of course, punishers create the opposite set of reactions. For example, when customers purchase a restaurant meal and the food is poorly prepared, one can observe frowns and unhappy facial expressions. In the presence of the punisher, people are placed in a negative mood state. In sum, during the consumption experience consumers encounter reinforcers and/or punishers. One can expect that these will influence their mood state.

Many different stimuli may act to reward or punish consumers during the consumption experience. For example, smiles from clerks, salespeople, and waiters are highly reinforcing to consumers. As a result, they are likely to improve the mood states of consumers. A pleasing physical environment is also likely to create positive affective states. Similarly, the physical attractiveness of the people encountered may impact mood states. However, it should be emphasized that research supporting these speculations has not been performed.

A recent study, however, did investigate the impact of music on consumer mood states and on subsequent product evaluations.[15] In the study respondents either heard music that they rated very positively or music that they rated very negatively.

While listening to the music, they rated the taste of peanut butter. Premeasures indicated that the positively rated music caused the respondents to be placed in a more positive mood than those exposed to the negatively rated music. Different groups of subjects rated one of three different types of peanut butter, which in pretests were determined to taste very good, neutral, or very bad. The results revealed that the type of music did *not* impact brand evaluations for the good- or the bad-tasting peanut butter. However, for the neutral-tasting peanut butter, brand evaluations were significantly higher when the music was liked as compared to when it was disliked.

These results suggest that consumer affective reactions to the consumption experience will impact their evaluations of the product independently of the actual quality of the product. Postpurchase evaluations of products are closely related to the development of feelings of satisfaction or dissatisfaction with the exchange process, which is the topic of the next section in the chapter.

THE DEVELOPMENT OF POSTACQUISITION SATISFACTION/DISSATISFACTION

During and after the consumption and use of a product or service, consumers develop feelings of satisfaction or dissatisfaction. **Consumer satisfaction** is defined as the overall attitude regarding a good or service after its acquisition and use. It is a postchoice evaluative judgment resulting from a specific purchase selection.[16]

What are the factors that contribute to feelings of satisfaction or dissatisfaction (CS/D)? Figure 13-4 presents a model of CS/D. In the model, consumers are shown as first consuming/using the good or service. Based upon this experience, they evaluate its overall performance. This assessment of performance has been found to be closely related to the ratings of the quality of the product.[17] These perceptions of product quality are compared to the consumer's expectations of the product's performance. An evaluation process then takes place in which consumers act as though they compare actual performance to expected performance. Based upon the comparison of expected quality to performance quality, consumers will experience positive, negative, or neutral emotions depending upon whether expectations were confirmed. These emotional responses then act as inputs into the overall satisfaction/dissatisfaction perception. In addition, the level of satisfaction/dissatisfaction will also be impacted by the consumer's evaluation of the equity of the exchange. Finally, attributions of the cause of the product's performance will also impact the satisfaction/dissatisfaction attitude. The following sections discuss each of these ideas in some detail.

The Evaluation of Product Performance/Quality

Over the past 15 years, companies throughout the world have embraced the concept of total quality management. **Total quality management (TQM)** is a management philosophy based upon the idea that successful companies should continuously improve the quality of their products and that quality is defined by the customer.[18] A

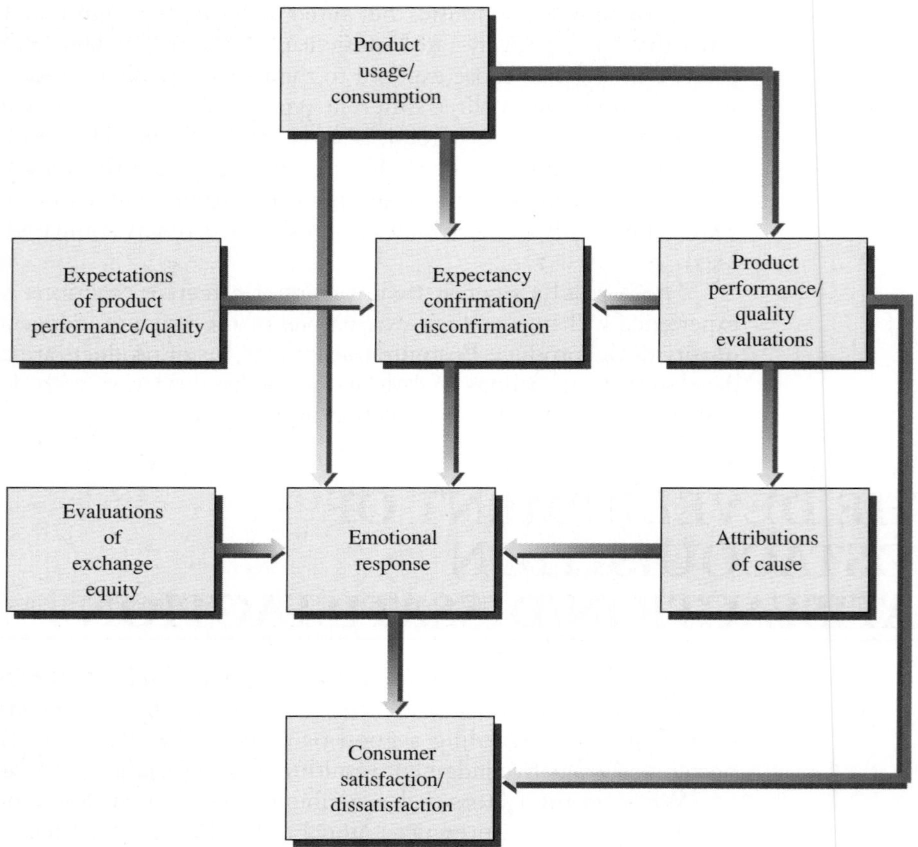

Figure 13-4 A model of consumer satisfaction/dissatisfaction.

critical element in the implementation of TQM programs is the concept that quality is consumer driven and that companies must assess consumer perceptions of quality.

Somewhat surprisingly, research on quality assessment in the consumer behavior and marketing literature has almost exclusively focused on measuring consumer evaluations of service quality. Little work has been done on the evaluation of perceptions of the quality of goods. Service quality has been defined as the customers' assessment of the overall excellence or superiority of the service.[19] Because this definition is quite broad, it can easily be expanded to include goods as well. Thus **product quality** is defined as the customers' overall evaluation of the excellence of the performance of the product.

A key issue in assessing perceived product performance concerns what dimensions consumers use to make the assessment. Researchers in the services area have identified five dimensions on which consumers evaluate service quality. These dimensions are found in Part A of Table 13-2.[20]

The five dimensions of service quality identified in Part A of Table 13-2 can be viewed as attributes on which consumers evaluate the overall performance of services. However, as applied to goods, this set of dimensions suffers from a major

TABLE 13-2

The Dimensions of Quality

A. Dimensions of Service Quality

1. *Tangibles.* Include physical facilities, equipment, and appearance of personnel.
2. *Reliability.* The ability of personnel to perform dependably and accurately.
3. *Responsiveness.* Providing customers with prompt service.
4. *Assurance.* The knowledge and courtesy of employees, as well as their ability to inspire trust and confidence.
5. *Empathy.* The ability of employees to care and to provide individualized attention.

SOURCE: A. Parasuraman, Valarie A. Zeithaml, and Leonard L. Berry, "SERVQUAL: A Multiple-Item Scale for Measuring Consumer Perceptions of Service Quality," *Journal of Retailing,* Vol. 64 (Spring 1988), pp. 12–36.

B. Dimensions of Product Quality

1. *Performance.* Performance on primary operating characteristics.
2. *Features.* The number of bells and whistles that supplement primary characteristics.
3. *Reliability.* Probability of failing or malfunctioning.
4. *Durability.* The life of the product.
5. *Serviceability.* Ease of repair, and the speed, courtesy, and timeliness of personnel.
6. *Aesthetics.* How the product looks, feels, and sounds.
7. *Conformance to specifications.* Degree to which the product meets production benchmarks.
8. *Perceived quality.* A catch-all category that includes the effects of brand image and other intangible factors that influence customers' perceptions of quality.

SOURCE: David A. Garvin, *Managing Quality: The Strategic and Competitive Edge* (New York: The Free Press, 1988).

problem. The dimensions focus to a large extent on the interaction between employees and customers. Thus other than the "tangibles" category, the dimensions fail to include attributes of a more concrete nature that would be associated with goods.

Another view of product quality proposes that it consists of eight dimensions. The eight categories are found in Part B of Table 13-2. Notice that only one dimension within the product quality categories overlaps with the service quality dimensions—reliability. Clearly, researchers need to perform research that identifies the fundamental dimensions of product quality that apply to both goods and services.

If one carefully analyzes Table 13-2, however, the 13 categories (i.e., 5 in Part A and 8 in Part B) can be reduced to 8. As developed by the author of this text, eight basic dimensions of product quality exist. They are

1. *Performance.* The absolute level of performance of the good or service on the key attributes identified by customers.
2. *Number of attributes.* The number of features/attributes offered.
3. *Courtesy.* The friendliness and empathy shown by people delivering the service or good.
4. *Reliability.* The consistency of the performance of the good or service.

5. *Durability.* The product's life span and general sturdiness.
6. *Timeliness.* The speed with which the product is received or repaired; the speed with which the desired information is provided or service is received.
7. *Aesthetics.* The physical appearance of the good; the attractiveness of the presentation of the service; the pleasantness of the atmosphere in which the service or product is received.
8. *Brand equity.* The additional positive or negative impact on perceived quality that knowing the brand name has on the evaluation of perceived quality.[21]

As noted, research will be required to confirm whether these eight categories fully represent the dimensions on which product quality is evaluated. In particular, the category of product aesthetics deserves additional research. One recent exploratory study of product design found aesthetic responses to be Gestalt (i.e., holistic) in nature and to be formed unconsciously. Two factors found to be related to aesthetic preferences were proportion (the ratio between the length and height of an object) and unity (the extent to which design elements appear "to go together").[22]

Table 13-3 provides examples of how each of the eight categories can be applied to a good (e.g., an automobile) or a service (e.g., an elegant restaurant).

A key question, however, concerns how each of the dimensions of product quality is combined to form an overall impression of quality. This text views the formation of overall product quality as a type of overall consumer belief. That is, beliefs are formed about each of the product's quality dimensions. These beliefs are then summed to create an overall belief regarding the quality of the product. Thus people act as though their perception of the overall performance quality of a product is formed via a type of multiattribute model.

The Development of Satisfaction/Dissatisfaction

A number of theoretical models have been proposed to explain the development of consumer satisfaction/dissatisfaction (CS/D). One approach is called the expectancy disconfirmation model. Developed in the 1970s, the expectancy disconfirmation model defines CS/D as the "evaluation rendered that the experience was at least as good as it was supposed to be."[23] However, a variety of additional theoretical approaches have been used to explain the formation of CS/D. These include equity theory, attribution theory, and experientially based affective feelings. In addition, the actual performance of a product has been suggested as a possibility.[24]

Expectancy Disconfirmation Model

The **expectancy disconfirmation model** is shown in Figure 13-5. Based upon the use of a particular product, as well as upon the use of other brands in the product class, consumers develop expectations of how the brand *should* perform. These performance expectations are compared to **actual product performance** (i.e., the perception of the product's quality). If quality falls below expectations, **emotional dissatisfaction** results. If performance is above expectations, **emotional satisfaction** occurs.[25] If performance is not perceived as different from expectancies, **expectancy confirmation** occurs.[26] Evidence indicates that when expectations and actual performance coincide, the consumer may simply not consciously consider his or her level of satisfaction with the product. Although expectancy confirmation is a positive state

TABLE 13-3

A Revised Set of Categories of Product Quality Applied to a Good and to a Service

Product Quality Dimensions	*Automobile Quality*
1. Performance	Level of horsepower, handling, fit and finish, resale value, and so on.
2. Number of attributes	Features such as air bags, ABS braking system, premium sound system, cup holders, and other extras not necessarily expected.
3. Courtesy	Friendliness and helpfulness of service personnel.
4. Reliability	Freedom from breakdown of vehicle, consistency of personnel in providing expected levels of service.
5. Durability	How long the car lasts before it wears out from use or before it becomes technologically out of date.
6. Timeliness	The ability of the company to provide the vehicle and its service in a timely way.
7. Aesthetics	The attractiveness and functionality of the layout and style of the car.
8. Brand equity	The extent to which the vehicle's brand name results in customers believing that it has high or low quality.
Product Quality Dimensions	***Restaurant Meal Quality***
1. Performance	The degree to which the food is prepared according to standards of taste and temperature. The degree to which wait staff know their jobs.
2. Number of attributes	The number of extra features provided with the meal, such as fresh flowers at the table, special breads provided as an appetizer, and free deserts.
3. Courtesy	The friendliness and helpfulness of the wait staff.
4. Reliability	The consistency with which the restaurant provides a high-quality dining experience.
5. Durability	The length of time that the effects of the service last.
6. Timeliness	The ability of the wait staff to provide service in a timely way.
7. Aesthetics	The atmosphere of the restaurant, the degree to which the food is pleasing to the eye, the physical attractiveness of the wait staff.
8. Brand equity	The extent to which the restaurant's brand name results in customers believing that it has high or low quality.

for the consumer, it may not result in strong feelings of satisfaction. Such strong feelings result only when actual performance deviates markedly from expected performance.

Product expectations act as a standard against which the actual performance of the product is assessed.[27] The level of performance expected of a product is influenced by the nature of the product itself, by promotional factors, by the effects of

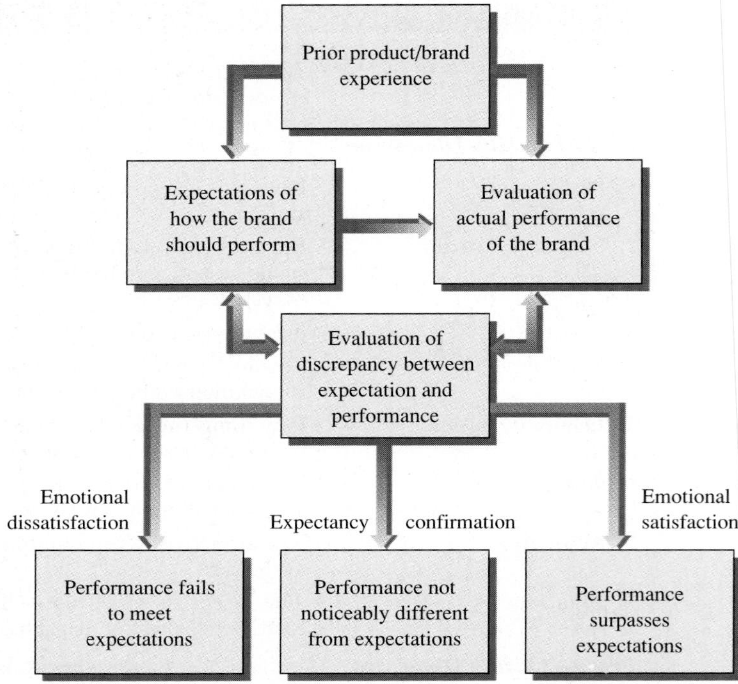

Figure 13-5 The formation of consumer satisfaction/dissatisfaction. (Adapted from a discussion in R. B. Woodruff, E. R. Cadotte, and R. L. Jenkins, "Modeling Consumer Satisfaction Processes Using Experience-Based Norms," *Journal of Marketing Research*, Vol. 20, August 1983, pp. 296–304, published by the American Marketing Association.)

other products, and by the characteristics of the consumer himself or herself. Concerning the product itself, a consumer's prior experiences with the product, its price, and its physical characteristics all influence how consumers expect it to perform. Thus, if the product has a high price, or if it has performed extremely well in the past, consumers may expect it to meet high performance standards.

How the company promotes the product through its advertising and through the communications of sales personnel may also influence the performance expectations of consumers. A consultant with a market research firm noted that advertising hype can create expectations that are greater than can possibly be satisfied. He cited Holiday Inn's abortive "No excuses" campaign. The company promised that problems would not occur for travelers; if they did occur, excuses would not be given, but a free night's lodging would. The program failed because of the difficulty of fulfilling such a promise, and because it unleashed an avalanche of grumblers and complainers.[28] The advertisement shown in Figure 13-6 illustrates how a company can create expectations. The ad from American Express provokes the expectation that, if billing problems occur, someone will be able to use their "judgment and initiative" to solve the problem.

Another set of factors influencing expectations of performance involves

Figure 13-6 American Express attempts to create service expectations. (Courtesy of American Express, Inc.)

consumers' experience with other products of a similar nature. These experiences with the product class may result in the formation of norms or standards about the level of performance that a particular brand should be able to achieve. For example, one key factor influencing consumer perceptions of the quality of medical services is the timeliness with which the medical care is delivered. Physicians and hospitals have been slow to recognize that consumers form their expectations of timeliness as much from their experiences with banks and restaurants as from their experience with other medical facilities.

A fourth set of factors influencing expectations of performance concerns the characteristics of the consumer. Some consumers simply expect more of products than others and, consequently, set higher standards. Likewise, some consumers may have wider latitudes of acceptance around the adaptation level than others. Consumers with very narrow regions of acceptance could be expected to be more easily dissatisfied than those with broad regions of acceptance. A study examined the effects of characteristics of the consumer on performance expectancy.[29]

Respondents ate meals at fast-food, family, and atmosphere/specialty restaurants and rated their experiences. The results revealed that consumers formed comparison standards based on total experience with the restaurant as well as on experience with the competing restaurants. Thus information about all the restaurants was used to develop expectancies. The authors also found that the type of standard set depended upon the type of restaurant. Different standards were set for fast-food, family, and specialty restaurants.

Highlight 13-1 discusses a number of factors that influence satisfaction in business-to-business marketing contexts. As readers will note, the violation of expectations plays a major role in creating dissatisfaction in business-to-business marketing, as well as in consumer marketing.

Equity Theory and Consumer Satisfaction

Another approach to predicting the CS/D that a consumer obtains from a product purchase is through equity theory. A number of researchers have argued that people analyze the exchange between themselves and other parties to determine the extent to which it is equitable or fair.[30] **Equity theory** holds that people analyze the ratio of their **inputs** and **outcomes** to the ratio of the inputs and outcomes of the partner in an exchange. If the person perceives that his or her ratio is unfavorable in relation to the other member of the exchange, the individual tends to have feelings of inequity. The following equation shows these ratios:[31]

$$\frac{\text{Outcomes of A}}{\text{Inputs of A}} \approx \frac{\text{Outcomes of B}}{\text{Inputs of B}}$$

Thus the outcomes that person A receives from an exchange divided by the inputs of person A to the exchange should equal the outcomes of person B from the exchange divided by the inputs of person B to the exchange. To the extent that the ratios are perceived as unequal, particularly when unfavorable to the consumer doing the evaluation, dissatisfaction is proposed to result.

From the perspective of equity theory, feelings of dissatisfaction result from the belief that a social norm has been violated. According to equity theory, a norm exists stating that each party to an exchange should be treated fairly or equitably. Thus satisfaction occurs when the ratios of outcomes and inputs for each party to the exchange are approximately equal. In contrast, inequity occurs when the buyer believes that his ratio of inputs to outcomes is worse than the seller's.

Just what are some examples of outcomes and inputs to a consumer exchange? Inputs are the information, effort, money, or time exerted to make an exchange

HIGHLIGHT 13-1

Maintain Business Relationships by Satisfying Customers

In 1983, David McDonough was one of the first dealers to sell Compaq Computer's IBM clones. His business prospered as Compaq grew rapidly for a decade. Then, in the spring of 1993, he began urging his customers not to buy from Compaq. What happened? It developed a new distribution strategy by selling through the mail and through superstores. Full-service dealers were left out in the cold with unfilled orders. Mr. McDonough had over 300 machines on back order. He said, "All these years, Compaq has been so loyal and we've been so loyal. Basically, they've destroyed a 10-year relationship" [1].

Grace Nichols is the CEO of Victoria's Secret—maker of sexy women's lingerie. When she became CEO in 1986, she developed a marketing strategy of selling her own private-label bras and panties rather than only the brand-name labels of others, such as Hanes and Vanity Fair. Her problem, however, was how to persuade these suppliers to make products for Victoria's Secret. After all, the suppliers had already built brand loyalty for their name.

After much negotiation, Ms. Nichols persuaded Vanity Fair to let her replace their labels with Victoria's Secret labels on bras carried in a few stores. Much to Vanity Fair's surprise, the bras sold just as well. By 1993, Victoria's Secret was Vanity Fair's biggest customer, with a $70 million account. To maintain quality, the pantyhose that come from Hanes must be produced in the same factory that makes its upscale DKNY stockings.

The success of Ms. Nichols' strategy is revealed in the opening of 50 new Victoria's Secret stores a year. One of the reasons for the success is the ability to build relationships with suppliers by maintaining extremely high-quality standards. As she described it, "Quality is not a place that you get to, because the goal always gets higher" [2].

Since diesel engines replaced steam engines in the 1950s, General Motors has held roughly 70% of the U.S. market for locomotives. The nearest competitor was General Electric. However, G.E.'s products suffered from serious quality problems. The chief mechanical officer of the Santa Fe Railroad said G.E.'s engines were ". . . too complex, with too many fittings, too many leaks, and too prone to break down." Some called the diesel engines U-boats—meaning that "they should be at the bottom of the sea." A CEO of one railroad actually flew to G.E.'s locomotive works, lectured the workers on the importance of maintaining quality, and threatened management with buying from the Japanese.

Then G.E. hired a new head for the locomotive division. First, he talked to his customers and got an earful of complaints. More important, he listened to the customers. Next, he began fixing problems quickly. The company then brought out a new model with impressive reliability. He then began a marketing campaign to get orders.

G.E. almost lost its locomotive business because of rampant customer dissatisfaction. However, a new CEO brought out more reliable products, shored up service, developed good relationships with customers, and launched an aggressive marketing campaign. The result was that by 1993 G.E. shipped over twice as many diesel locomotives as General Motors [3].

REFERENCES

1. Kyle Pope, "Dealers Accuse Compaq of Jilting Them," *The Wall Street Journal*, April 7, 1993, p. B1.
2. Stephanie Strom, "When Victoria's Secret Faltered, She Was Quick to Fix It," *The New York Times*, November 21, 1993, p. 10.
3. William M. Carley, "GE Locomotive Unit, Long an Also-Ran, Overtakes Rival GM," *The Wall Street Journal*, September 3, 1993, pp. 1, 4.

possible. Outcomes are the benefits and liabilities received from the exchange. Outcomes could consist of savings in time, of having a product or service perform in some desired way, or of receiving some level of compensation.

A number of authors have investigated equity theory in consumer behavior. For example, one study looked at the exchange process between the consumer and an airline.[32] For the consumer, his or her inputs to the exchange consist primarily of the money paid for the ticket. The consumer's outcomes consist of the quality of the service receives on the trip and the speed with which the airline gets the consumer to the destination. The results of the study revealed that if consumers perceived their inputs to be large because they paid higher than average fares, they tended to be dissatisfied with the service. Similarly, if they perceived that outcomes were poor because flights had been delayed for two hours, they also revealed a higher level of dissatisfaction.[33]

Other researchers have found that people may consider the outcomes of other consumers in determining their satisfaction with a transaction.[34] In the study, respondents assumed the role of having purchased an automobile. After the purchase, they found that another person had obtained either a better or worse deal on the auto. The results revealed that when the comparison consumer had received a better deal on the same car, the respondents were less satisfied with the transaction and with the auto dealer than when they had obtained the better buy. This study shows that factors other than the performance of the product may strongly influence feelings of satisfaction. Specifically, the evaluation of the overall equity of the purchase transaction appears to influence purchase satisfaction.

Readers should note that equity theory proposes a different process to explain CS/D than does the expectancy disconfirmation model presented in Figure 13-5. In the expectancy disconfirmation model, CS/D results from the comparison of actual performance to expected performance. As noted by one researcher, CS/D can result from either process. It remains for future research to examine how consumers combine feelings of equity or inequity with feelings of expectancy disconfirmation to obtain global feelings of satisfaction or dissatisfaction.[35]

Some researchers have already obtained information on the role of equity versus expectancy disconfirmation in influencing satisfaction.[36] In a study of over 400 new car buyers, researchers obtained measures of satisfaction with the salesperson, of the degree of equity or fairness in the transaction, and of the inputs and outcomes of the salesperson and of the buyer. The results revealed an interesting pattern of results. For buyers, fairness or equity was highly self-centered. That is, a fair deal was perceived when the buyer's outcome was high and the seller's inputs were high. Further, perceptions of fairness/equity had a greater impact on overall satisfaction than perceptions of expectation disconfirmation.

The managerial implications of the study are important. First, as the authors stated, "equitable exchange from the point of view of the buyer may be seen as inequitable exchange by the salesperson."[37] Second, consumers do form judgments of equity, and in this study these judgments had a greater impact on satisfaction than expectancy disconfirmation. This combination of findings makes the salesperson's job extremely difficult. It forces the salesperson to manage impressions such that buyers believe they are getting a great buy and the salesperson is giving up a great deal to make the sale. Unfortunately, such patterns of reactions may lead to an increasing tendency among salespeople to use hype and false statements to make sales.

On the Relation of Attribution Theory, Product Failure, and Consumer Satisfaction

As discussed in Chapter 6, **attribution theory** is concerned with how people identify the causes for action. The attributions that people make may strongly influence their postpurchase satisfaction with a product or service because they moderate feelings of CS/D. In particular, if a product fails (i.e., performance is below expectations), consumers will attempt to determine the cause of the failure. If the cause for failure is attributed to the product or service itself, feelings of dissatisfaction are likely to occur. Conversely, if the cause for failure is attributed to chance factors or to the consumer's own actions, feelings of dissatisfaction are less likely to occur.[38]

One study investigated consumer satisfaction with airlines that were experiencing problems of delayed flights. The study found evidence that consumer satisfaction is contingent upon the types of attributions made.[39] When the attribution was made to uncontrollable situational factors, such as fog or ice, anger tended *not* to result. However, if the cause for the delay was associated with stable factors, such as the actions of airline personnel over whom the airline had control, anger and dissatisfaction tended to occur. In general, attributional processes are most likely to impact CS/D when consumer involvement in and experience with (i.e., knowledge of) the good or service are high.[40]

Actual Product Performance

Researchers have found strong evidence that actual product performance influences satisfaction independent of the expectations held, matters of equity, and attributions made. Thus, even if the person fully expected a product to perform poorly, dissatisfaction would still result if it in fact performed poorly. A study investigated the effects of performance as well as the impact of attribution, expectations, and equity on satisfaction with a stock market selection.[41] The results revealed that performance, independent of expectations, influenced satisfaction. In addition, perceived product performance/quality appears to directly influence customer CS/D particularly when the product is unambiguous and easy to evaluate.[42]

AFFECT AND CS/D

CS/D may also be analyzed from an experiential perspective. The phrase **affect and CS/D** refers to the concept that the level of consumer satisfaction may be influenced by the positive and negative feelings that consumers associate with the product or service after its purchase. In one study, a researcher investigated the level of satisfaction with automobiles and cable television services after their purchase.[43] The researcher found that two dimensions of affective responses existed—a set of positive feelings and a set of negative feelings. These feelings were found to be independent of each other: consumers could simultaneously feel both positive and negative about a purchase. One can experience joy, interest, and excitement while also feeling anger, disgust, and contempt. For example, after purchasing an auto, a consumer may feel excited and proud while simultaneously being irritated and unhappy with the sales personnel.

The study also found that measures of CS/D were directly influenced by the affective feelings of the consumers. Researchers discovered a relationship whereby purchase led to affective reactions, which in turn led to feelings of CS/D. Thus, in addition to the cognitive knowledge that expectancies were disconfirmed, the feelings that surrounded the postacquisition process also appeared to affect the satisfaction with a product. A similar pattern of results has been found in CS/D with restaurants. Affective responses predicted satisfaction independent of the cognitive thoughts (beliefs about the server's attentiveness, friendliness, etc.) of the customers.[44]

In high-involvement situations, such as the purchase of an automobile, consumer satisfaction may have a strong emotional component. A recent study investigated the emotional responses of 125 new car buyers.[45] The authors found that the buyers could be classified into five satisfaction categories—happy/content, pleasant surprise, unemotional, unpleasant surprise, and angry/upset. Table 13-4 summarizes the results of the study. It reveals that those classified in the happy/content and pleasant surprise groups revealed high levels of satisfaction. Those identified as unemotional revealed moderate levels of satisfaction. In contrast, those falling in the unpleasant surprise group revealed some dissatisfaction. As might be expected, the most dissatisfied were those classified as angry/upset.

Table 13-5 summarizes the factors that influence the CS/D with a purchase, the same factors diagrammed in Figure 13-4. As can be seen in the figure, after a purchase and the use/consumption of the product, a series of cognitive and emotional reactions take place in the consumer, including expectancy confirmation/disconfirmation evaluations, evaluations of the equity of the exchange, evaluations of actual

TABLE 13-4

Emotions and Consumer Satisfaction

Satisfaction Classification	*Type of Emotion Experienced*	*Overall Satisfaction Level*[a]	*Level of Satisfaction*[b]	*Level of Dissatisfaction*[c]
Happy/content	Interested joy	54.0	9.1	1.3
Pleasant surprise	Joy and surprise	54.0	9.1	1.2
Unemotional	No emotions shown	45.6	8.0	2.3
Unpleasant surprise	Moderate levels of guilt, sadness, contempt, shame, anger	40.1	6.7	3.6
Angry/upset	High levels of fear, anger, disgust, and contempt	36.7	5.6	5.4
	Overall mean =	47.5	6.25	2.38

[a]Overall satisfaction measured by 12-item satisfaction inventory. Scores range from 12 to 60.

[b]Level of satisfaction measured by unipolar scale ranging from 0 to 10.

[c]Level of dissatisfaction measured by unipolar scale ranging from 0 to 10.

SOURCE: Robert A. Westbrook and Richard Oliver, "The Dimensionality of Consumption Emotion Patterns and Consumer Satisfaction," *Journal of Consumer Research*, Vol. 18 (June 1991), pp. 84–91.

TABLE 13-5

Summary of Factors Influencing Consumer Satisfaction/Dissatisfaction

- **I.** Expectancy disconfirmation
  - **A.** Factors influencing expectations
    - **1.** Characteristics of the product
    - **2.** Promotional factors
    - **3.** Other factors
    - **4.** Characteristics of the consumer
  - **B.** Factors influencing perception of actual performance
- **II.** Equity perceptions
- **III.** Attributions of causality
- **IV.** Actual product performance
- **V.** Consumer's affective state

product performance, and attributions of the cause of the outcomes. Take a second to look at Figure 13-4, and note that the figure depicts emotions and attributions as interacting together to influence consumer satisfaction/dissatisfaction. For example, if a product important to the consumer fails, the consumer is likely to have the immediate emotional response of anger. However, the anger is influenced by the attribution of cause made by the customer. If the person attributes the cause of the failure to factors beyond the control of the company, the dissatisfaction and anger felt are likely to be very mild. The extent of satisfaction/dissatisfaction, then, results from the manner in which the attribution of the cause interacts with the emotional response to the product performance evaluations.[46]

Managerial Implications of CS/D

Perhaps managers' most important goal relevant to postacquisition processes is to attempt to ensure the satisfaction of consumers. The factor most important to satisfaction is the level of performance of the product. If the level of product quality is high, consumers tend to be satisfied, even if they expected such high levels of performance. If the expectations of the consumer regarding product performance are not fulfilled, however, it is likely that dissatisfaction will result. Conversely, if the product meets or surpasses expectations, the consumer is rewarded for his or her purchase.

To ensure that product performance meets or exceeds expectations, managers should carefully analyze quality control and the promotion of the brand. In this regard, implementing total quality management programs can be critical for a company. A product may perform below expectations because it is produced or designed poorly or because promotional materials have promised more than it can deliver. Performance of competitive products, characteristics of the target market segment, and price of the product can also influence performance expectations.

A second means of maintaining postacquisition satisfaction is by providing outstanding levels of service after the sale. Indeed, many purchase decisions are based upon expectations that the company will provide excellent service after the sale. IBM has been successful in part because of the high levels of service that the company has traditionally offered. To provide outstanding service, managers should carefully monitor all five dimensions of service quality: tangibles, reliability, responsiveness, assurance, and empathy.

Managers should also consider consumer perceptions of equity and ask the question, "Do my customers feel as though they are being treated fairly?" In answering this question, the manager should identify how consumers view the inputs and outcomes of the two parties in the exchange process. Of particular concern to the manager is whether consumers recognize all the inputs the company has to the transaction. Certain service industries have problems with consumers not recognizing the quantity of inputs made by service providers to the transaction. For example, in the real estate industry, many home sellers complain that real estate commissions are too high. In a seller's market, their home, which they sell for $100,000, may only be on the market for a month or so. Because they see relatively little of the real estate agent, they perceive his or her inputs to be very small in relation to the outcomes (i.e., the commission received by the agent). The managerial implication is that the real estate agents should educate and inform their customers of all their inputs to the exchange.

Because of the managerial importance of maintaining and improving consumer satisfaction, it is critical that market research be conducted on the reactions of customers to their buying experience. Highlight 13-2 discusses some key issues in assessing consumer CS/D.

CONSUMER COMPLAINT BEHAVIOR

Once a consumer perceives that he or she is dissatisfied with a product or service, the problem becomes what to do about it. **Consumer complaint behavior** consists of any one of a number of different actions that are triggered by perceived dissatisfaction with a purchase episode.[47] Researchers have identified five dimensions of complaint behavior, which are listed in Table 13-6 with their associated actions. The five dimensions of behavior are

1. Do nothing or deal with the retailer in some manner.
2. Avoid using the retailer again and persuade friends and family to do the same.
3. Take overt action with third parties (e.g., launch legal action to obtain redress).[48]
4. Boycott the firm or organization.
5. Create an alternative organization to provide the good or service.[49]

The actions of not patronizing the brand or store, of telling friends about the problem, and of complaining are straightforward responses to product or service problems. When consumers seek redress to their dissatisfaction, they take steps to obtain some type of refund. The refund could be provided in the form of money or a new product. In addition, however, consumers can launch boycotts of firms as a means to change marketing practices and/or to promote social change. Finally, consumers have the

HIGHLIGHT 13-2

Some Problems in Measuring Consumer Satisfaction

When measuring satisfaction, researchers have traditionally assessed consumers' overall evaluation of the product, as well as satisfaction with specific attributes. Frequently, Likert scales are used. For example, to assess overall satisfaction with this consumer behavior course, the instructor might ask you to indicate your level of agreement with the following statement: "Overall, I was highly satisfied with the course in consumer behavior." A five-point scale might be used (Agree 1 2 3 4 5 Disagree). Other questions might be asked about satisfaction with the various characteristics of the course, such as lectures, the textbook, course handouts, testing, and the like. Frequently, regression equations are developed in which the attribute questions are used to predict an overall satisfaction rating. This general approach can be used to evaluate satisfaction with virtually any good or service.

Recently, researchers have identified some problems with this traditional approach to measurement. Perhaps the most difficult problem in measuring satisfaction is a strong positivity bias. In an article on this topic the researchers stated: "Virtually all self-reports of customer satisfaction possess a distribution in which a majority of the respondents indicate that customers are satisfied . . ." [1]. For example, across hundreds of different studies, the authors reported that on average, 65% of customers reported "high levels of satisfaction."

The implications of these findings are important for researchers. Foremost, to merely report a finding, such as "the majority of customers revealed high levels of satisfaction," is virtually meaningless. Almost always, this result is obtained.

One approach recommended by the authors is to ask about dissatisfaction rather than satisfaction. That is, ask respondents to agree or disagree with the statement "I was highly dissatisfied with the product." The authors' results indicated that such an approach lessens the extent of the positivity bias. A manager can then focus on taking steps to reduce the number of customers who are dissatisfied with the product.

Another critical issue in measuring satisfaction (or any other important marketing variable for that matter) concerns whether to employ multiple measures. From a measurement theory perspective, measuring the same variable several times with slightly different wording of the question increases the reliability and validity of the results. For example, when assessing overall satisfaction, researchers could ask respondents about their satisfaction levels, their overall evaluation of the product, and their overall experience with the product. Recently, however, researchers found that employing multiple measures can have an unexpected problem [2]. If consumers are asked to make an attitude rating several times, it will actually influence the attitude. (Remember, satisfaction judgments are like attitudes.) In particular, taking multiple measures of satisfaction is likely to crystallize consumers' evaluation of the product. This is particularly true for individuals with the *least* experience with the brand! In the final analysis, it is recommended that researchers use the minimum number of questions necessary to measure each construct. An added benefit is that it shortens the questionnaire.

REFERENCES

1. Robert A. Peterson and William R. Wilson, "Measuring Customer Satisfaction: Fact and Artifact," *Journal of Academy of Marketing Science*, Vol. 20 (Winter 1992), pp. 61–72.
2. Frank Kardes, Chris T. Allen, and Manuel Pontes, "Effects of Multiple Measurement Operations on Consumer Judgment: Measurement Reliability or Reactivity?" in *Advances in Consumer Research*, Vol. 20, Leigh McAlister and Michael Rothschild, eds. (Provo, UT: Association for Consumer Research, 1993), pp. 280–282.

TABLE 13-6

Types of Complaint Actions

1. Do nothing or deal with the retailer.
   a. Forget about the incident and do nothing.
   b. Definitely complain to the store manager.
   c. Go back or call retailer immediately and ask manager to take care of the problem.
2. Avoid using the retailer again and persuade friends to do the same.
   d. Decide not to use the retailer again.
   e. Speak to friends and relatives about your bad experience.
   f. Convince friends and relatives not to use the retailer.
3. Take overt action with third parties.
   g. Complain to a consumer agency.
   h. Write a letter to a local newspaper.
   i. Take some legal action against the retailer.
4. Boycott the organization.
5. Create an alternative organization to provide the good or service.

option of creating entirely new organizations to solve complaint problems. Examples of such organizations include Consumers Union, food-buying co-ops (which run IGA grocery stores), credit unions, and the American Association of Retired Persons.

Studies of consumer complaint behavior, however, have shown that a minority of dissatisfied customers actually takes overt action to complain to the company. For example, one study found that among a sample of 2,400 households, about one in five purchases resulted in some degree of dissatisfaction. In less than 50% of these instances of dissatisfaction did the buyer take action. The type of action taken by consumers depended in part on the type of product or service purchased. For low-cost, frequently purchased products, fewer than 15% of consumers took some action. In contrast, for household durables and automobiles, over 50% of consumers took some action if they were dissatisfied. The type of product that results in the most frequent action in reacting to dissatisfaction is clothing. As many as 75% of those experiencing dissatisfaction with clothing took some form of complaint action.[50]

In general, the models of consumer complaint behavior have identified two major purposes for complaining.[51] First, consumers complain to recover an economic loss. They may seek to make an exchange of the problem product for another product. They may seek to get their money back either directly from the company or store or indirectly through legal means. A second reason for engaging in some type of complaint behavior is to rebuild the self-image. Particularly when the self-image of a consumer is tied to the purchase of a product, dissatisfaction with the product may lower the person's self-image. To raise his or her self-image, the consumer may use negative word-of-mouth communications, may stop buying the brand, may complain to the company or Better Business Bureau, or may take legal action. In general, the self-image maintenance aspects of consumer complaint behavior have been insufficiently studied by researchers and companies.

Factors Influencing Complaint Behavior

A number of factors have been found to influence whether or not consumers complain. As noted, the type of product or service involved influences the tendency to complain. As the cost and social importance of the product rise, the tendency to complain tends to increase. Some authors have suggested that complaint behavior is related to the following variables:

1. The level of dissatisfaction of the consumer
2. The attitude of the consumer toward complaining
3. The amount of benefit to be gained from complaining
4. The personality of the consumer
5. To whom the blame for the problem is attributed
6. The importance of the product to the consumer
7. The resources available to the consumer for complaining[52]

The first two variables are particularly important to understanding complaint behavior. As one would expect, the greater the dissatisfaction of the consumer, the greater the tendency to complain. Similarly, consumers with a positive attitude toward complaining and with experience in complaining tend to complain more. Indeed, the results of a recent study indicate that factors 3 through 7, identified earlier, also influence a consumer's attitude toward complaining, which in turn influences the likelihood of actually complaining.[53] Thus, as the product increases in importance to the consumer, the attitude toward complaining improves and complaint behavior increases. Previous experience may be associated with increased complaint behavior because people with higher levels of experience know how to go about contacting appropriate authorities and, therefore, are less bothered by such a task.[54] Complaining requires certain resources, such as time, the ability to write letters, and the personal power to confront an employee of a firm and make him or her listen to a problem.

Similarly, attributions made by consumers have been found to relate to complaint behavior. Researchers have found that when consumers attribute product problems to the company rather than to themselves, complaint behavior increases. Furthermore, if the problem is viewed as being under the control of the company, complaining increases.[55] For example, if consumers attribute a problem in an auto to decisions purposely made by the company, complaint behavior is likely to be high. Such a situation occurred at General Motors in the early 1980s. For cost reasons the company made a decision to modify an existing gasoline engine to create a diesel engine for passenger cars. The modified engine suffered severe reliability problems because it was unable to withstand the extreme internal pressures that exist in a diesel engine. Consumer reaction was extremely harsh, and a class-action suit was successfully launched that cost GM millions of dollars.

In general, researchers have been only partly successful in relating demographic factors to consumer complaining behavior.[56] One study examined education, income, age, and experience with the product to determine how such factors related to complaining behavior. The results revealed that experience was by far the factor most closely related to the tendency to complain.[57] More recently, researchers found a modest relationship among age, income, and complaining behavior.[58] Consumers found to engage in complaining behavior after experiencing dissatisfaction tended to be younger and to have higher incomes. In another study, researchers found that consumers who possessed higher incomes and more education tended to complain more often.[59] Other investigators have examined a number of personality variables and their relationship to complaining behavior. Some evidence exists that individuals higher in dogmatism (close-mindedness) and self-confidence are more likely to complain.[60] Other researchers found that consumers who value individuality, uniqueness, and a sense of independence tended to complain more often. Perhaps to these people, complaining is one way to make themselves feel different from others.[61]

Corporate Reactions to Consumer Complaining

Surprisingly, evidence exists that many companies do not make systematic efforts to investigate the extent of CS/D with their products or services. For example, one survey of food marketers found that 60% had little or no idea of consumers' satisfaction with their products.[62] However, consumer-oriented firms do make special efforts to track CS/D with their products and services. The use of consumer hotline numbers is becoming increasingly popular for this purpose. Companies such as Procter & Gamble, Whirlpool, and 3M have used such toll-free numbers effectively. Because of the automobile's expense and personal importance, problems with cars are likely to result in complaints. Auto companies have responded by establishing regional service representatives whom consumers can call if satisfaction cannot be gained from the auto dealer.

Public policy makers have a major interest in consumer complaint behavior. If they find that consumer complaints are too frequent, they may become interested in developing regulations to ameliorate the problem. Of course, managers prefer to avoid the encroachment of government; the mere possibility of government intervention can be a strong impetus for companies to establish industry standards. The Council of Better Business Bureaus, Inc., has compiled information on the types of industries that receive the most complaints. Table 13-7 presents the top ten complaint categories by type of business. The table shows that mail-order companies received the largest numbers of complaints, followed by auto dealers.

When complaints do occur, managers should have mechanisms in place to handle them. The presence of toll-free numbers is one highly effective means of handling complaints. The presence of warranties is another way for consumers to have their complaints handled. Another approach has been developed that can diminish the ill feelings that may result from product problems—the service contract. Buying a service contract is somewhat like buying insurance. The customer pays a premium to guarantee that over some period of time certain problems that occur with a product will be fixed by the manufacturer or retailer. Service contracts have been adopted strongly by auto manufacturers. Some of the automobile companies have developed a fourth way of dealing with consumer complaints. They have put into place third-party arbitration programs. For example, General Motors, Ford, Chrysler, and Audi have developed programs in which consumers can present their automobile problem to an unbiased third person, who then decides exactly how the problem should be remedied.

One way of avoiding consumer complaints is for companies to act ethically in the exchange process with consumers. Highlight 13-3 discusses several ethical and public policy issues that directly relate to maintaining consumer satisfaction and avoiding complaints.

HIGHLIGHT 13-3

Unethical Selling Causes Multiple Forms of Dissatisfaction

Alan Andreasen, recent president of the Association for Consumer Research, suggested that unethical seller practices have major implications for research on consumer satisfaction/dissatisfaction: in particular, the way CS/D is measured may lower the chances of discovering ethical problems [1]. First, researchers tend to measure satisfaction with the outcomes of a purchase rather than with the process of buying. Second, satisfaction ratings tend to be taken on the initial evaluations of a product rather than on the longer-term experience with the brand. Third, the harm that occurs from unethical seller actions tends to be measured only in terms of economic loss rather than in terms of their psychological and emotion toll.

Examples of unethical selling practices are numerous. Consider the case in which a door-to-door salesperson sells hearing aids to elderly people by mumbling or speaking so softly that he is difficult to understand. Such a person may be able to trick the unsuspecting and susceptible older person into believing that she really does need a hearing aid.

Traditional measures of satisfaction are unlikely to record the dissatisfaction that will result from this purchase. If satisfaction measures are taken shortly after the purchase, the elderly individual will very likely have very positive things to say about the experience. After all, she can now hear the salesperson very well because he is no longer mumbling. What the measurement procedure fails to address is the process by which the hearing aid was sold, the long-term negative impact of the unethical practice, and the psychological as well as the monetary loss that the elderly person may suffer. That is, when the person learns at a later date that she has been tricked, she will be angry. In addition, her self-esteem may be damaged.

Unethical selling practices will have a long-term negative effect on consumer satisfaction with the marketplace. From this perspective, the study of how to measure consumer satisfaction and the effects of unethical selling practices becomes a public policy issue. As noted in Chapter 2, consumers also have ethical responsibilities. If the consuming public begins to believe that it is being consistently ripped off, one can anticipate that it will respond by getting even with retailers through its own set of unethical and possibly illegal behaviors.

On the other hand, when companies show unusually pro-consumer behavior, the public will respond positively. For example, in 1993 General Motors launched a massive recall of its highly successful Saturn automobiles. Responding quickly and proactively to reports that the wiring in the cars could short-circuit and cause fires, the company voluntarily recalled 350,000 cars. The response of customers was overwhelmingly positive, and the recall became a public relations bonanza. General Motors went out of its way to act responsibly and ethically. While the short-term cost was high (from $8 to $35 million), from a long-term perspective it will create enormous goodwill and loyalty among consumers [2].

REFERENCES

1. Alan R. Andreasen, "Unethical Seller Practices: A Neglected Issue in Consumer Satisfaction and Dissatisfaction," in *Advances in Consumer Research*, Vol. 20, Leigh McAlister and Michael Rothschild, eds. (Provo, UT: Association for Consumer Research, 1993), pp. 109–112.

2. Ray Serafin, "Saturn Recall a Plus—for Saturn!" *Advertising Age*, August 16, 1993, p. 4.

TABLE 13-7

The Top Ten Complaint Categories by Type of Business

Type of Business	*Percentage of Total Complaints*
1. General mail-order companies	23.4
2. Franchised auto dealers	5.9
3. Magazines ordered by mail	2.9
4. Miscellaneous home maintenance companies	2.9
5. Home furnishing stores	2.9
6. Auto repair shops	2.6
7. Department stores	2.3
8. Miscellaneous automotive	2.2
9. Television service companies	1.8
10. Dry cleaning/laundry companies	1.8

SOURCE: Adapted from data in Kevin Higgins, "Mail Order Industry Is Fighting the Old, Sleazy Image on Several Fronts," *Marketing News*, Vol. 17 (July 8, 1983), pp. 1, 12.

PRODUCT DISPOSITION

Although the study of how consumers dispose of acquisitions is fundamental, little research has been performed in the area. Figure 13-7 presents a taxonomy of **product disposition.**[63] Basically, a consumer has three alternative dispositional strategies after a product has been used for some period of time—keep it, get rid of it permanently, or get rid of it temporarily. Each of these alternatives has suboptions. For example, if the product is kept, it can continue to be used, converted to a new use, or stored. (Conversion to a new use could include such measures as using an old toothbrush as a cleaning device.) Similarly, if the product is to be removed permanently, a number of options exist: the product can be thrown away, given away, traded, or sold.

Table 13-8 presents the results of a study that investigated consumers' disposition decisions regarding six different products.[64] One clear pattern in the results is that, as the value of the product increased, consumers tended to dispose of the product through means that maximized the value returned. Thus refrigerators and stereo amplifiers were less frequently thrown away and more frequently sold.

The disposition of products should greatly concern marketing managers. For some types of products there exists a thriving aftermarket that can cut into sales of new products. For example, sales of used textbooks can severely lower the overall sales for a publisher. Although students benefit in the short term by having to pay less for used books, in the long run the cost of new textbooks is increased because fewer new books are sold and because new editions must be brought out sooner. Another enterprise based on product disposition is the used car market. The used car market is extremely large, and hundreds of thousands of people make their living

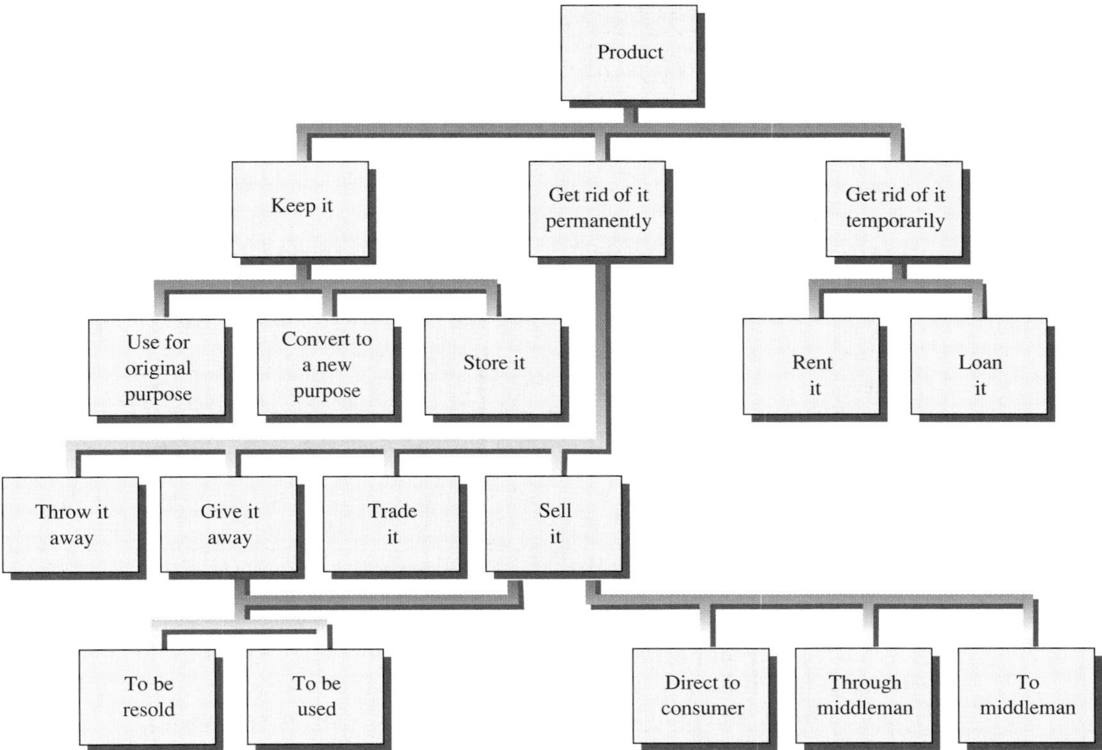

Figure 13-7 A taxonomy of product disposition. (Adapted by permission from J. Jacoby, C. Berning, and T. Dietvorsat, "What About Disposition?" *Journal of Marketing*, Vol. 41, April 1997, p. 23, published by the American Marketing Association.)

buying and selling used cars. With publications such as *Consumer Reports* now rating which used cars are best, new car buyers are beginning to consider the possible resale value of new cars. Figure 13-8 presents an ad for a retail store that specializes in the sale of used golf equipment.

BRAND LOYALTY

Closely related to consumer satisfaction and consumer complaining behavior is the area of brand loyalty. **Brand loyalty** is defined as the degree to which a customer holds a positive attitude toward a brand, has a commitment to it, and intends to continue purchasing it in the future. As such, brand loyalty is directly influenced by the consumer's satisfaction/dissatisfaction with the brand that has accumulated over time. In addition, evidence also indicates that it is influenced by perceptions of the product's quality.[65] Because it is as much as four to six times less costly to retain customers as it is to find new buyers, managers must develop strategies that seek to build and maintain brand loyalty.[66]

TABLE 13-8

Disposition Decisions of Six Test Products

	All Products	*Stereo Amplifier*	*Wrist-watch*	*Tooth-brush*	*Phono Record*	*Bicycle*	*Refrigerator*
Converted	7.9%	1.6%	1.8%	17.2%	9.6%	1.5%	7.5%
Stored	12.7	—	28.7	—	32.8	3.1	—
Thrown away	39.7	11.5	30.6	79.7	43.2	17.3	22.6
Given away	17.1	31.1	23.1	—	9.6	40.2	19.3
Sold	11.5	42.6	5.6	—	—	17.3	25.8
Rented	0.7	—	0.9	—	—	—	3.2
Loaned	0.3	—	—	—	—	1.5	1.0
Traded	5.3	4.9	5.6	—	0.8	3.2	20.4
Other	4.8	8.3	3.7	3.1	4.0	15.9	—

SOURCE: J. Jacoby, C. Berning, and T. Dietvorst, "What About Disposition?" *Journal of Marketing*, Vol. 4 (April 1977), p. 26, published by the American Marketing Association. Used by permission.

An illustration of the importance of brand loyalty is found in the actions of Air France. The airline targets "jet setters" who ride the supersonic Concorde on a once-a-month basis. These individuals are given interesting and unusual gifts, rather than coupons for $50 off their next $6,000 round trip. An example would be giving the videocassette of Jean Cocteau's *Beauty and the Beast* to the frequent flyers. As one

Figure 13-8 This ad illustrates one means of disposing of used golf equipment—selling it. (Courtesy of Play It Again Sports.)

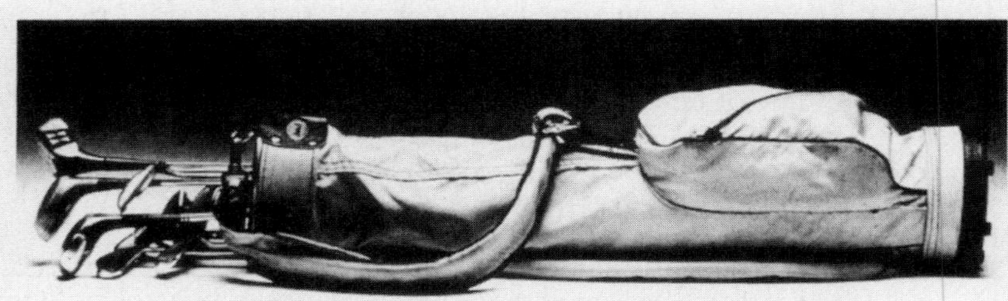

well-known marketing consultant said, brand loyalty needs to "... bond a customer to a marketer."[67] Having a large number of consumers "adopt" a brand, as though it were a pet or an important possession, is the goal of every brand manager.

Some Previous Definitions of Brand Loyalty

The definition of brand loyalty given at the beginning of the section is based in part on two general definitions of brand loyalty previously developed. The first was based upon a consumer's actual purchase behavior regarding the product. One such measure of actual purchase behavior is the **proportion of purchases method**, which is the most frequently used measure of brand loyalty in empirical research. In the proportion of purchases approach, all the brands purchased within a particular product category are determined for each consumer. The proportion of purchases going to each brand is identified. Brand loyalty is then measured in terms of some arbitrary proportion of purchases going to a particular brand. For example, if more than 50% of the purchases went to a particular brand during some time period, the consumer might be said to be loyal to the brand.

The problem with the behavioral measures of brand loyalty is that the real reasons for the purchase of a product cannot be identified. A particular product could be purchased because of convenience, availability, or price. If any of these factors changed, consumers might rapidly switch to other brands. In such instances consumers cannot be said to exhibit loyalty, because implicit in the idea of loyalty is that the consumer has more than a passing infatuation with the brand.

The problems seen in the behavioral measures of brand loyalty illustrate why it is important to distinguish the concepts of brand loyalty and repeat purchase behavior. With **repeat purchase behavior**, the consumer is merely buying a product repeatedly without any particular feeling for it. In contrast, the concept of brand loyalty implies that a consumer has some real preference for the brand. As a consequence, another approach to assessing brand loyalty was developed, based on the consumer's attitude toward the product, as well as his or her purchase behavior. Thus, for a consumer to exhibit brand loyalty, as opposed to simple repeat purchase behavior, the consumer must actively prefer and like the product.[68] An important earlier definition of brand loyalty follows:

> Brand loyalty is (1) the biased (i.e., nonrandom), (2) behavioral response (i.e., purchase), (3) expressed over time, (4) by some decision-making unit, (5) with respect to one or more alternative brands out of a set of such brands, and (6) includes a strong positive attitude toward the brand.[69]

This definition of brand loyalty has a number of implications for marketers. First, brand loyalty is not a random event. Whether or not a consumer becomes loyal to a particular brand can be controlled to some extent by the actions of a marketer. Second, mere verbal reports that someone is loyal to a product are insufficient to show brand loyalty. Verbal reports taken on consumer surveys should be backed up with records of the actual purchases made by the consumer. Third, to reveal brand loyalty, the repeat purchase behavior must be found over some lengthy period of time. Fourth, brand loyalty can be exhibited by decision-making units in addition to individual consumers. For example, decisions may be made jointly by husbands and wives such that they reveal brand loyalty in combination. Fifth, consumers may be loyal to more than one brand at a time. Out of a set of seven to ten competing brands, a consumer may be loyal to two or three while actively eliminating the others. Finally, brand loyalty results from some type of evaluative process that follows from the outcomes of previous purchases of the product. When a consumer has brand loyalty, he or she actively prefers the brand, is committed to the brand to some extent, and has developed positive feelings toward the brand.

With brand loyalty comes a commitment to a brand. **Brand commitment** has been defined as an emotional–psychological attachment to a brand within a product class.[70] Thus, whereas brand loyalty has both a behavioral and an attitudinal component, brand commitment tends to focus more on the emotional–feeling component. In a study of the brand commitment of consumers to soft drinks, the researchers found that brand commitment results from purchase involvement, which in turn results from ego involvement with the brand category.[71] According to the authors, such ego involvement results when a product is closely related to a consumer's important values, needs, and self-concept. The diagram below portrays the relationship among the factors.

Ego involvement → Purchase involvement → Brand commitment

In sum, brand commitment tends to occur most frequently with high-involvement products that symbolize consumers' self-concepts, values, and needs. Also, high-commitment products more frequently tend to be higher-priced consumer durables that possess greater perceived risk.[72]

Identifying Brand-Loyal Consumers

One important question asked by market researchers regards whether a group of consumers exists that is brand loyal across various types of products. Some evidence indicates that brand preferences are formed during childhood and adolescence.[73] If such preferences turn into loyalty among consumer segments, it would suggest that managers should begin targeting their customers early in their life cycles.

Research evidence also indicates that brand loyalty is a product-specific phenomenon. Very little evidence suggests that consumers have a general tendency to be loyal. Thus consumers who are loyal in one product category may or may not be loyal in any other product category. Efforts to identify demographic, socioeconomic, or psychological characteristics related to brand-loyal behavior have generally been unsuccessful.[74] One variable that has been found to be predictive of brand loyalty is store loyalty. Consumers who are loyal to particular stores also tend to be loyal to certain brands.[75] It is possible that by repeatedly shopping at the same stores, consumers find a limited number of brands available for each product category. Thus store-loyal consumers may be forced to buy certain brands because they are the only ones available in the stores where these consumers shop.

Managerial Implications of Brand Loyalty

Brand loyalty is important in the managerial areas of the marketing mix and market research. Managers should attempt to develop, price, and promote products in a manner that optimizes the chances of creating brand loyalty among its users. In addition, market research should be used to track consumer loyalty to the brand.

Importantly, the market research should include attitudinal as well as behavioral measures of brand loyalty. The monitoring of brand loyalty should be a constant, ongoing process. As one research article noted, "Things are happening in the marketplace on a week-to-week basis that have long-run implications for profitability and long-term survival."[76]

As noted previously in the text, marketing strategies involving sales promotion devices may inhibit the formation of brand loyalty. That is, consumers may attribute the purchase of a brand to the sales promotion rather than to the product's intrinsically positive qualities. As a result, consumers may react to promotions rather than buy products because of positive attitudes toward specific brands. One recent study found that sales promotion devices may cause even brand-loyal customers to switch brands. However, the researchers also found that the likelihood that the consumers would repurchase the new brand was low.[77] The evidence points to the conclusion that the quality of the product and of the advertising of the brand are the key factors in creating long-term brand loyalty.

Another managerial issue concerns researchers' findings that brands with smaller market shares tend to receive less brand loyalty among customers.[78] This phenomenon, labeled **double jeopardy**, occurs when the less popular brand, as defined by market share, also has lower brand loyalty among its customers. Explaining this finding is somewhat difficult. Certainly, in some instances, niche brands, such as Mercedes-Benz cars, can obtain high levels of brand loyalty from customers, despite their small market shares. But the overall pattern of double jeopardy is clear. One explanation of the phenomenon is that the high-market-share brands receive more advertising, and consumers are simply exposed to them more frequently. Another possibility, however, is that the direction of causality is reversed. That is, because consumers have lower satisfaction with certain brands, they also have lower brand loyalty. As a consequence, the market share of the brand is low. Whatever the reason for the double jeopardy effect, it illustrates the importance of brand loyalty for managers.

A final point is that brand loyalty is not an all-or-nothing phenomenon. It should be viewed as a continuum from complete loyalty to complete brand indifference. A number of distinctions can be made concerning types of brand loyalty. In some cases, consumers may have a divided loyalty between two brands. In other cases, they may be loyal to one brand but occasionally switch to other brands, perhaps to break the monotony and influence levels of arousal. In other instances, customers may be completely indifferent to distinctions between brands.[79] A number of buying patterns are listed here with their purchase sequence in which A, B, C, and D are different brands:

1. *Undivided loyalty*: A A A A A A A A
2. *Occasional switch*: A A B A A A C A A D A
3. *Switch loyalty*: A A A A B B B B
4. *Divided loyalty*: A A A B B A A B B B
5. *Brand indifference*: A B D C B A C D

An important managerial goal should be to identify where in these categories a firm's brand fits. Based upon this knowledge, appropriate managerial strategies should be taken to move customers up the scale from indifference, to divided loyalty, to occasional switch, and finally to undivided loyalty.

A MANAGERIAL APPLICATIONS EXAMPLE

The businessman boarded the Pan Am shuttle flight from New York City to Boston at 9:30 A.M. He planned on getting to Boston in plenty of time for his afternoon appointments. The plane took off and circled Logan Airport in Boston for two hours because of fog. It finally landed in Hartford, Connecticut, to refuel. The pilot announced that no one would be allowed to leave the plane, which frustrated the businessman and other passengers who wanted to exit the plane and rent a car for the short drive to Boston. The pilot then announced that the plane was returning to New York. The passengers rebelled, and the plane finally landed in Boston at 4 P.M. Having missed his meetings, the man simply caught a flight back home to New York.[80]

At the conclusion of his ordeal, the businessman decided to complain, and the Pan Am representative at the airport told him to complain to the customer service department in New York City. As instructed, the businessman went to the company's headquarters in midtown New York, only to be told that complaints were handled at LaGuardia Airport. At LaGuardia the first person contacted failed to return the call. When he finally did talk to someone, he was told that the "airline is not responsible for delays caused by the weather." By this time the businessman was highly frustrated. Partly in retaliation he wrote a column that appeared in *The New York Times*, titled "Hijacked to Hartford." The newspaper received numerous calls and letters in support of the column. Seeing a chance for some publicity, a vice president of Eastern's New York–to–Boston shuttle wrote the businessman a sympathy letter and offered him a free New York–to–Boston flight. The businessman declined, saying, "I would have been happy with an apology from Pan Am." Months after the incident, the businessman says that he still has not heard from Pan Am and that he will now only fly the Pan Am shuttle as a last resort. Interestingly, neither Pan Am nor Eastern airlines no longer own their East Coast shuttles. Could a lack of service quality partially account for their demise?

The Consumer Behavior Analysis

This case is an excellent example of how a company turned a manageable problem into one that caused it enormous amounts of negative publicity. A number of concepts from this chapter apply to the case, such as the *expectation disconfirmation model*. Most travelers expect that from time to time weather problems will force delays. Thus the mere fact that a delay occurred was not the problem. The difficulty occurred when Pan Am refused to let passengers off the plane in Hartford. This seemingly reasonable request was denied. Thus outcomes did not match expectations, and dissatisfaction resulted.

At this point the problem was still manageable if Pan Am's *complaint management program* had been sound. However, the series of snafus increasingly angered the passengers. The *Fortune* magazine article from which the example was taken noted that a strong correlation exists in the airline industry between customer contentment and profitability.[81] The companies that have the most complaints reach the U.S. Department of Transportation are not handling their complaints properly. As stated by one consultant on complaint behavior, "Turning away a complainer by telling him 'It's our policy' enrages him" The appropriate corporate attitude is exemplified by the director of customer satisfaction at Neiman-Marcus, who said, "We're not just looking for today's sale. We want a long-term relationship with our customers." Brand loyalty cannot be built by creating dissatisfied customers.[82]

The consumer concept of *service quality* also applies to the case. Managers must analyze how they deal with their customers along the five dimensions of service quality. Pan Am completely failed to match customer expectations on the dimensions of responsiveness and empathy.

A fourth consumer concept relevant to the Pan Am case concerns *attributions* for the cause of the product problem. When the problem was encountered, the businessman made attributions as to its cause. Although the weather was the precipitating event for his being late, it was the decision by Pan Am not to let the passengers out in Hartford that enraged him. Then, when the complaint was filed, the airline continued to hide behind the weather excuse. In the end, the businessman attributed the cause to Pan Am, which acted to increase the negativity of his emotions.

An important point to recognize is that consumer decision making is a circular process; it feeds back on itself. Thus postacquisition reactions to a purchase have implications for problem recognition, search, alternative evaluation, and choice for future purchases. For example, if dissatisfaction with a particular brand is high, consumers may exclude it from consideration in the future. It will not be included in the search process and, therefore, will not be evaluated. Such a phenomenon makes it difficult for a company to recover from dissatisfaction problems.

Many companies recognize the difficulty of recovering from problems and view the issue as one of controlling and improving quality. The director of customer affairs at Citicorp noted, "Our philosophy is that we never recover." Thus the company attempts to avoid mistakes.[83] At Citicorp managers must compose a list of the five worst things that can happen to customers. The goal is to make sure that none of these ever happen.

The Managerial Applications Analysis

Table 13-9 presents the managerial applications analysis for the Pan Am case. The first consumer concept related to the case, the expectancy disconfirmation model, applies to market research and to the marketing mix. Market researchers need to do the appropriate research to identify expectations customers possess when they enter an exchange relationship. This information is used to develop the marketing mix. Because Pan Am provides a service, managers should have developed plans for handling the various situations that could arise, including having to land in a different airport. Such contingency plans then become part of the general strategy for handling service problems.

The analysis of complaining behavior also influences the development of the marketing mix—specifically the public relations component of promotional strategy. Employees must be well trained in how to deal with the various types of complaints that consumers have against the company. They should be trained in techniques that minimize customer anger and qualified to take appropriate action.

Pan Am also needed to attend closely to product quality issues. Market research should be performed to determine how the company performs on each of the eight

TABLE 13-9

The Managerial Applications Analysis of the Pan American Case

Consumer Concepts	*Managerial Applications*
Expectancy disconfirmation	*Market research*—Identify service expectations held by consumers. Identify level of performance (i.e., service quality) perceived by consumers.
	Product development—Develop plans for providing service that minimizes chances of problems. Develop plans for handling service problems.
Complaining behavior	*Marketing mix*—Develop public relations strategy for handling customer complaints.
Product quality	*Market research*—Determine performance levels on the dimensions of product quality.
	Product development—Develop systems and procedures that provide service at levels that meets and/or exceeds customer expectations.
Consumer attributions	*Promotional strategy*—Train employees to be able to identify the attributions that customers may make for product failure. Train employees in how to communicate so that customers do not attribute product failure to the intentions of the airline.

dimensions of product quality. Then, procedures should be put in place to ensure that the service product meets, and preferably exceeds, customer expectations on each dimension. In the Pan Am case, ineptness caused the company to fail to respond appropriately to the businessman's complaints. In addition, company representatives failed to have any empathy for his feelings or needs.

The businessman's attributions of the cause of the problem strongly influenced his emotions in the situation. Employees need to be trained to understand the various types of attributions that customers may make for product problems. Because the way employees deal with customers is part of the service product, knowledge of attributional processes could influence the design of the marketing mix.

SUMMARY

Chapter 13 focused on the postacquisition stage of the decision process and brand loyalty. The postacquisition phase of the consumer buying process consists of four stages—acquisition consumption/usage, the formation of postacquisition purchase satisfaction or dissatisfaction, consumer complaint behavior, and product disposition. The postacquisition phase has a major impact on whether consumers will repurchase the product or service. In addition, consumers' expectations of how they will be treated in the postacquisition phase can influence brand loyalty.

Despite its importance, the acquisition consumption/usage stage of the postacquisition process has received relatively little attention from consumer researchers. Four areas of importance to managers in investigating consumption/usage are the frequency, amount, interval, and purpose of product or service consumption. One problem in consumption/usage is that consumers do not always use products in the ways expected by manufacturers. In particular, product misuse is a major cause of consumer injuries. However, the study of product usage can give ideas for changes in current products or for new products.

The satisfaction or dissatisfaction that consumers feel during and after product use influences the postacquisition attitudes of buyers. Feelings of satisfaction may be viewed as resulting from any one of several processes. One process is expectancy disconfirmation. When the performance of the acquisition fails to meet expectations, emotional dissatisfaction may result. When performance meets expectations, a consumer may be said to have expectancy confirmation. Although the consumer is satisfied with the purchase, he or she probably does not think much about it. It is when performance surpasses expectations that emotional satisfaction is likely to result from the purchase. The performance expected of a product or purchase is influenced by the nature of the product, by promotional factors, by the effects of other products, and by the characteristics of the consumer.

Satisfaction with a purchase may also be influenced by the actual performance of the product, by feelings of inequity, and by attributions. Feelings of inequity may occur when consumers perceive that the ratio of their outcomes to inputs is inferior to another's ratio of outcomes to inputs. The other person could be a retailer, a service agent of some type (e.g., a real estate agent or stockbroker), or even another consumer. Attributions occur when consumers identify the cause for actions. If a negative outcome occurs and consumers make an internal attribution to the firm, dissatisfaction tends to result.

If a consumer feels dissatisfied with a purchase, he or she may engage in consumer complaint behavior. Complaints can take many different forms, from simply not buying the product or service again to telling friends about the problem, to making verbal or written complaints, to seeking redress from the business or from the legal system. Consumers complain for two reasons: (1) to recover economic loss or (2) as a means of restoring their self-concept, which may be injured to some extent as a result of the product or service problem. Research into consumer complaining reveals that most consumers are satisfied with their purchases. Of those who are dissatisfied, the percentage who take some action to resolve their problem depends upon the type of product purchased. For low-cost household items as few as 15% of consumers appear to take some action. However, for socially visible products, such as clothing, the figure rises to about 75% of consumers taking some action. Corporations need to monitor consumer complaint behavior and have programs installed to deal with complaints. Some approaches to deal with complaints include the use of warranties, service contracts, consumer hotlines, and regional service representatives.

The final phase of the postacquisition process is product disposition. Consumers can dispose of products in three general ways. They can keep the product for later use, they can get rid of it permanently, or they can get rid of it temporarily by renting it or loaning it out. Managers should be aware of the various means of disposition used by consumers. For certain consumer durables, such as automobiles, how much a consumer can get for a product when he or she finishes using it is an important factor in selecting a brand. Some auto manufacturers, such as BMW, stress in their advertising the high resale value of the cars. In other instances regulations may exist regarding how products are to be disposed of. Particularly in the industrial area, a variety of hazardous chemicals must be disposed of in highly specific and often expensive ways.

Another important issue concerning postacquisition processes is that of brand loyalty. Brand loyalty is a nonrandom behavioral response that occurs over time and involves a strong positive attitudinal component. It is similar to the concept of brand commitment, which focuses largely on the extent to which consumers have positive feelings about a specific brand. Brand loyalty must be differentiated from repeat purchase behavior in which a consumer merely buys a brand because no others are available. Brand loyalty may also result from store loyalty because consumers select from the limited products that a given store carries.

KEY TERMS

actual product performance
affect and CS/D
attribution theory
brand commitment
brand loyalty
consumer complaint behavior
consumer performance
consumer satisfaction
consumer satisfaction/dissatisfaction (CS/D)
consumption
double jeopardy
emotional dissatisfaction
emotional satisfaction
equity theory
expectancy confirmation
expectancy disconfirmation
inputs/outcomes
postacquisition process
product disposition
product expectations
product quality
proportion of purchases method
repeat purchase behavior
total quality management (TQM)

REVIEW QUESTIONS

1. What factors influence the formation of postacquisition satisfaction and dissatisfaction?
2. Identify the factors that influence the formation of brand expectations.
3. How do feelings of equity influence satisfaction/dissatisfaction with an exchange?
4. How does the equity approach to understanding postacquisition satisfaction differ from the expectation confirmation approach?
5. What are the actions a consumer may take when he or she is dissatisfied with a product or service?
6. What are the two major reasons why consumers complain?
7. To what extent do consumers take overt action to complain when they are dissatisfied?
8. Eight factors have been identified that influence consumer complaining. Identify six of the eight factors.
9. Discuss the various ways in which consumers may dispose of a product.
10. Identify four actions companies can take to help ensure postacquisition satisfaction.
11. What is the definition of brand loyalty?

DISCUSSION QUESTIONS

1. Although you have probably never tried to use a lawn mower to trim a hedge, you probably have used products in unintended ways. Think back upon your own behavior and identify instances in which you have misused products. (For example, did you ever stick a knife into a toaster without unplugging it first?) Did your consumer misbehavior result in any problems? Could the manufacturer have done anything to prevent your actions?
2. Look through a magazine at the print advertisements. What kinds of expectations did the ads create, such as beliefs regarding product performance, postacquisition satisfaction, or the social benefits of owning the product? To what extent do you believe that the products will fulfill these expectations?
3. What are some of the actions the real estate industry might take as part of an effort to create consumer beliefs that an equitable relationship exists between the sellers of homes and the real estate agent?
4. Equity theory proposes that consumers analyze their purchases in relation to similar purchases made by other consumers. Identify one or two instances in which you compared the outcomes of a purchase you made to the outcomes of a similar purchase made by another consumer. What were the bases for comparison that you used? Did any feelings of inequity/dissatisfaction result from the comparison?
5. List several occasions when you expressed some type of consumer dissatisfaction. On the occasions when the retailers could do something about it, was the outcome satisfactory? What could the retailers have done to improve the outcome?
6. To what extent have you or would you consider the resale value of a car prior to purchasing it? Go to a bookstore and find one of the magazines that lists resale values of automobiles. Based upon resale value, which of the following sports cars would you purchase—Nissan 300ZX, Mazda RX7, Porsche 944, or Chevrolet Corvette?
7. Consider the sports car that you found in question 6 to have the highest resale value. How might its manufacturer emphasize this point when promoting the car? Please describe any advertising you have seen mentioning the resale value of an automobile or other product.
8. Identify a good or service to which you have brand loyalty. Identify the reasons for your loyalty. Next, identify a good or service for which you reveal repeat purchase behavior but lack brand loyalty. What could the firm do to move you from simple repeat purchase behavior to brand loyalty?
9. Consider the occasion on which you have been most angry with a firm as a result of a purchase of a good or service. What did they do to cause your emotions? What was the role of your own attributions in increasing or decreasing your anger? What specific actions could the firm have taken that would have helped to resolve your complaint?

ENDNOTES

1. Richard L. Celsi, Randall L. Rose, and Thomas W. Leigh, "An Exploration of High-Risk Leisure Consumption Through Skydiving," *Journal of Consumer Research*, Vol. 20 (June 1993), p. 8.
2. Marj Charlier, "Like Much in Life, Roadside Refuse Is Seasonally Adjusted," *The Wall Street Journal*, August 3, 1989, pp. A1–A12.
3. Richard Barber, "How L. L. Bean Restored My Soles—And Warmed My Soul," *The Wall Street Journal*, December 18, 1990, p. A12.
4. John Pierson, "Dead-Animal Trade Is Still the Lifeblood of One Hardy Soul," *The Wall Street Journal*, March 12, 1991, pp. A1, A5.
5. "Meanwhile, P&G Is Losing One of Its Best Customers," *The Wall Street Journal*, May 1, 1985, p. 31.

6. Leslie Helm, "Why Kodak Is Starting to Click Again," *Business Week*, February 23, 1987, pp. 134–138.

7. For a review of many of these problems, see John C. Mowen and Hal Ellis, "The Product Defect: Managerial Implications and Consumer Implications," in *The Annual Review of Marketing*, Ben Enis and Kenneth Roering, eds. (Chicago: American Marketing Association, 1981), pp. 158–172.

8. Philip Hendrix, "Product/Service Consumption: Key Dimensions and Implications for Marketing," Working Paper, Emory University, Atlanta, GA, August 1984.

9. Joanne Lipman, "Learning About Grape-Nuts in Denver," *The Wall Street Journal*, February 16, 1988, p. 33.

10. Celsi, Rose, and Leigh, "An Exploration of High-Risk Leisure Consumption Through Skydiving."

11. Eric J. Arnould and Linda L. Price, "River Magic: Extraordinary Experience and the Extended Service Encounter," *Journal of Consumer Research*, Vol. 2 (June 1993), pp. 24–45.

12. Erving Goffman, *The Presentation of Self in Everyday Life* (New York: Basic Books, 1959).

13. This definition of performance was developed for the textbook and specifically designed to incorporate the notion that an exchange process is taking place. It borrows ideas from the work of John Deighton, "The Consumption of Performance," *Journal of Consumer Research*, Vol. 19 (December 1992), pp. 362–372.

14. Ibid., p. 362.

15. Paul W. Miniard, Sunil Bhatla, and Deepak Sirdeshmukh, "Mood as a Determinant of Postconsumption Product Evaluations: Mood Effects and Their Dependency on the Affective Intensity of the Consumption Experience," *Journal of Consumer Psychology*, Vol. 1, no. 2 (1992), pp. 173–195.

16. Richard Oliver has distinguished satisfaction from attitude toward the object in his work. He argues that attitude toward the product or brand represents a more generalized evaluation of a class of purchase objects. The approach taken in this text is that attitudes occur at different levels of specificity. They can be highly abstract, such as one's attitude to his or her country, or highly specific, such as satisfaction with a specific purchase. All are affective reactions that range on a hedonic continuum from unfavorable to favorable. For a recent article on Richard Oliver's approach, see Robert A. Westbrook and Richard L. Oliver, "The Dimensionality of Consumption Emotion Patterns and Consumer Satisfaction," *The Journal of Consumer Research*, Vol. 18 (June 1991), pp. 84–91.

17. J. Joseph Cronin and Steven A. Taylor, "Measuring Service Quality: A Reexamination and Extension," *Journal of Marketing*, Vol. 56 (July 1992), pp. 55–68. Also, see R. Kenneth Teas, "Expectations, Performance Evaluation, and Consumers' Perceptions of Quality," *Journal of Marketing*, Vol. 57 (October 1993), pp. 18–34.

18. For example, see Deming W. Edwards, *Quality, Productivity, and Competitive Position* (Cambridge, MA: M.I.T., Center for Advanced Engineering Study, 1982). Also, see Joseph M. Juran, *Juran on Planning for Quality* (New York: The Free Press, 1988).

19. Valarie A. Zeithaml, "Consumer Perceptions of Price, Quality and Value: A Means–End Model and Synthesis of Evidence," *Journal of Marketing*, Vol. 52 (July 1988), pp. 2–22.

20. A. Parasuraman, Valarie A. Zeithaml, and Leonard L. Berry, "SERVQUAL: A Multiple-Item Scale for Measuring Consumer Perceptions of Service Quality," *Journal of Retailing*, Vol. 64 (Spring 1988), pp. 12–36.

21. Kevin Lane Keller, "Conceptualizing, Measuring, and Managing Customer-Based Brand Equity," *Journal of Marketing*, Vol. 57 (January 1993), pp. 1–22.

22. Robert W. Veryzer, "Aesthetic Response and the Influence of Design Principles on Product Preferences," in *Advances in Consumer Research*, Vol. 20, Leigh McAlister and Michael Houston, eds. (Provo, UT: Association for Consumer Research, 1993), pp. 224–228.

23. H. Keith Hunt, "CS/D: Overview and Future Research Directions," in *Conceptualization and Measurement of Consumer Satisfaction and Dissatisfaction*, H. Keith Hunt, ed.

(Cambridge, MA: Marketing Science Institute, 1977), pp. 455–488.

24. Richard Oliver and Wayne DeSarbo, "Response Determinants in Satisfaction Judgments," *Journal of Consumer Research*, Vol. 15 (March 1988), pp. 495–507.

25. R. B. Woodruff, E. R. Cadotte, and R. L. Jenkins, "Modeling Consumer Satisfaction Processes Using Experience-Based Norms," *Journal of Marketing Research*, Vol. 20 (August 1983), pp. 296–304.

26. R. L. Oliver, "A Cognitive Model of the Antecedents and Consequences of Satisfaction Decisions," *Journal of Marketing Research*, Vol. 17 (November 1980), pp. 460–469.

27. Woodruff et al., "Modeling Consumer Satisfaction."

28. Patricia Sellers, "How to Handle Customers' Gripes," *Fortune*, October 24, 1988, pp. 87–100.

29. Ernest Cadotte, Robert Woodruff, and Roger Jenkins, "Expectations and Norms in Models of Consumer Satisfaction," *Journal of Marketing Research*, Vol. 24 (August 1987), pp. 305–314.

30. J. S. Adams, "Toward an Understanding of Inequity," *Journal of Abnormal and Social Psychology*, Vol. 67 (1963), pp. 422–436.

31. The equity ratio shown has been criticized and is given primarily for pedagogical purposes. See John C. Alessio, "Another Folly for Equity Theory," *Social Psychological Quarterly*, Vol. 43 (September 1980), pp. 336–340.

32. R. P. Fisk and C. E. Young, "Disconfirmation of Equity Expectation: Effects on Consumer Satisfaction with Services," in *Advances in Consumer Research*, Vol. 12, E. C. Hirschman and M. B. Holbrook, eds. (Ann Arbor, MI: Association for Consumer Research, 1985), pp. 340–345.

33. For other studies of equity in consumer behavior, see J. W. Huppertz, S. J. Arenson, and R. H. Evans, "An Application of Equity Theory to Buyer-Seller Exchange Situations," *Journal of Marketing Research*, Vol. 15 (May 1978), pp. 250–260.

34. John C. Mowen and Stephen L. Grove, "Search Behavior, Price Paid, and the Comparison Other: An Equity Theory Analysis of Post-Purchase Satisfaction," in *International Fare in Consumer Satisfaction and Complaint Behavior*, Ralph Day and H. Keith Hunt, eds. (Bloomington: Indiana University School of Business, 1983), pp. 57–63.

35. J. E. Swan and Alice Mercer, "Consumer Satisfaction as a Function of Equity and Disconfirmation," in *Conceptual and Empirical Contributions to Consumer Satisfaction and Complaining Behavior*, Sixth Annual Conference, H. Hunt and R. Day, eds. (Bloomington: Indiana University Press, 1982), pp. 2–8.

36. Richard L. Oliver and John E. Swan, "Consumer Perceptions of Interpersonal Equity and Satisfaction in Transactions: A Field Survey Approach," *Journal of Marketing*, Vol. 53 (April 1989), pp. 21–35.

37. Ibid., p. 33.

38. Valerie Folkes, "Consumer Reactions to Product Failure: An Attributional Approach," *Journal of Consumer Research*, Vol. 10 (March 1984), pp. 398–409.

39. Valerie Folkes, Susan Koletsky, and John Graham, "A Field Study of Causal Inferences and Consumer Reaction: The View from the Airport," *Journal of Consumer Research*, Vol. 13 (March 1987), pp. 534–539.

40. T. N. Somasundaram, "Consumers' Reaction to Product Failure: Impact of Product Involvement and Knowledge," in *Advances in Consumer Research*, Vol. 20, Leigh McAlister and Michael Houston, eds. (Provo, UT: Association for Consumer Research, 1993), pp. 215–218.

41. Oliver and DeSarbo, "Response Determinants in Satisfaction Judgments." Also, see David Tse and Peter Wilton, "Models of Consumer Satisfaction Formation: An Extension," *Journal of Marketing Research*, Vol. 25 (May 1988), pp. 204–212.

42. Youjae Yi, "The Determinants of Consumer Satisfaction: The Moderating Role of Ambiguity," in *Advances in Consumer Research*, Vol. 20, Leigh McAlister and Michael Houston, eds. (Provo, UT: Association for Consumer Research, 1993), pp. 502–506.

43. Robert Westbrook, "Product/Consumption-Based Affective Responses and Postpurchase Processes," *Journal of Marketing Research*, Vol. 24 (August 1987), pp. 258–270.

44. Laurette Dube-Rioux, "The Power of Affective Reports in Predicting Satisfaction Judgments," in *Advances in Consumer Research*, Vol. 17, Marvin E. Goldberg, Gerald Gorn, and Richard W. Pollay, eds. (Provo, UT: Association for Consumer Research, 1990), pp. 571–576.

45. Robert Westbrook and Richard L. Oliver, "Dimensionality of Consumption Emotion Patterns and Consumer Satisfaction," *The Journal of Consumer Research*, Vol. 18 (June 1991), pp. 84–91.

46. This model is based in part on Lalita A. Manrai and Meryl P. Gardner, "The Influence of Affect on Attributions for Product Failure," in *Advances in Consumer Research*, Vol. 18 (Rebecca Holman and Michael Solomon, eds. (Provo, UT: Association for Consumer Research, 1991), pp. 249–254.

47. This definition is highly similar to one developed by Jagdip Singh, "Consumer Complaint Intentions and Behavior: Definitional and Taxonomical Issues," *Journal of Marketing*, Vol. 52 (January 1988), pp. 93–107.

48. The first three types of complaint actions were identified by William Bearden and Jesse Teel, "Selected Determinants of Consumer Satisfaction and Complaint Reports," *Journal of Marketing Research*, Vol. 20 (February 1983), pp. 21–28.

49. The last two means of complaint behavior were identified by Robert O. Herrmann, "The Tactics of Consumer Resistance: Group Action and Marketplace Exit," in *Advances in Consumer Research*, Vol. 20, Leigh McAlister and Michael Houston, eds. (Provo, UT: Association for Consumer Research, 1993), pp. 130–134.

50. A. Andreason and A. Best, "Consumers Complain—Does Business Respond?" *Harvard Business Review*, Vol. 55 (July–August 1977), pp. 93–101.

51. R. E. Krapfel, "A Consumer Complaint Strategy Model: Antecedents and Outcomes," in *Advances in Consumer Research*, Vol. 12, E. Hirschman and M. Holbrook, eds. (Ann Arbor, MI: Association for Consumer Research, 1985), pp. 346–350.

52. E. L. Landon, "A Model of Consumer Complaint Behavior," in *Consumer Satisfaction, Dissatisfaction, and Complaining Behavior*, Ralph Day, ed. (Bloomington: Symposium Proceedings, School of Business, University of Indiana, 1977), pp. 20–22.

53. Diane Halstead and Cornelia Droge, "Consumer Attitudes Toward Complaining and the Prediction of Multiple Complaint Responses," in *Advances in Consumer Research*, Vol. 18, Rebecca Holman and Michael Solomon, eds. (Provo, UT: Association for Consumer Research, 1991), pp. 210–216.

54. See K. Gronhaug and G. Zaltman, "Complainers and Noncomplainers Revisited: Another Look at the Data," in *Advances in Consumer Research*, Vol. 8, K. Monroe, ed. (Ann Arbor, MI: Association for Consumer Research, 1981), pp. 83–87.

55. Folkes et al., "A Field Study of Causal Inferences and Consumer Reaction."

56. Gronhaug and Zaltman, "Complainers and Non-Complainers Revisited."

57. Ibid.

58. W. O. Bearden and J. B. Mason, "An Investigation of Influences on Consumer Complaint Reports," in *Advances in Consumer Research*, Vol. 11, Thomas Kinnear, ed. (Ann Arbor, MI: Association for Consumer Research, 1987), pp. 223–226.

59. Michelle Morganosky and Hilda Buckley, "Complaint Behavior: Analysis by Demographics, Lifestyle, and Consumer Values," in *Advances in Consumer Research*, Vol. 14, Melanie Wallendorf and Paul Anderson, eds. (Provo, UT: Association for Consumer Research, 1987), pp. 223–226.

60. See J. Faricy and M. Maxio, "Personality and Consumer Dissatisfaction: A Multi-Dimensional Approach," in *Marketing in Turbulent Times*, E. M. Mazze, ed. (Chicago: American Marketing Association, 1975), pp. 202–208; and W. O. Bearden and J. E. Teel, "An Investigation of Personal Influences on Consumer Complaining," *Journal of Retailing*, Vol. 57 (Fall 1981), pp. 3–20.

61. Morganosky and Buckley, "Complaint Behavior."

62. R. C. Stokes, "Consumer Complaints and Dissatisfaction," speech before Food Update Conference, The Food and Drug Law Institute, Phoenix, AZ, April 1974.

63. J. Jacoby, C. K. Berning, and T. F. Dietvorst, "What About Disposition?" *Journal of Marketing*, Vol. 41 (April 1977), p. 23.

64. Ibid.

65. William Boulding, Ajay Kalra, Richard Staelin, and Valarie A. Zeithaml, "A Dynamic Process Model of Service Quality: From Expectations to Behavioral Intentions," *Journal of Marketing Research*, Vol. 30 (February 1993), pp. 7–27.

66. Melanie Wells, "Brand Ads Should Target Existing Customers," *Advertising Age*, April 26, 1993, p. 47.

67. Cyndee Miller, "Rewards for the Best Customers," *Marketing News*, July 5, 1993, pp. 1, 6.

68. Jacob Jacoby and Robert Chestnut, *Brand Loyalty, Measurement, and Management* (New York: John Wiley, 1978).

69. Ibid.

70. Sharon E. Beatty, Lynn R. Kahle, and Pamela Homer, "The Involvement-Commitment Model: Theory and Implications," *Journal of Business Research*, Vol. 16, no. 2 (March 1988), pp. 149–167.

71. Ibid.

72. Charles L. Martin and Phillips W. Goodell, "Historical, Descriptive, and Strategic Perspectives on the Construct of Product Commitment," *European Journal of Marketing*, Vol. 25, no. 1 (1991), pp. 53–60.

73. Lester Guest, "Brand Loyalty Revisited: A Twenty Year Report," *Journal of Applied Psychology*, Vol. 48 (April 1964), pp. 93–97.

74. See, for instance, Ronald Frank, William Massy, and Thomas Lodahl, "Purchasing Behavior and Personal Attributes," *Journal of Advertising Research*, Vol. 9 (December 1969), pp. 15–24.

75. James Carmen, "Correlates of Brand Loyalty: Some Positive Results," *Journal of Marketing Research*, Vol. 7 (February 1970), pp. 67–76.

76. Richard E. DuWors, Jr., and George H. Haines, Jr., "Event History Analysis Measures of Brand Loyalty," *Journal of Marketing Research*, Vol. 17 (November 1990), pp. 492.

77. Michael Rothschild, "A Behavioral View of Promotions Effects on Brand Loyalty," in *Advances in Consumer Research*, Vol. 14, Melanie Wallendorf and Paul Anderson, eds. (Provo, UT: Association for Consumer Research, 1987), pp. 119–120.

78. Andrew S. C. Ehrenbeg, Gerald J. Goodhardt, and T. Patrick Barwise, "Double Jeopardy Revisited," *Journal of Marketing*, Vol. 54 (July 1990), pp. 82–91.

79. A similar point was made by J. Paul Peter and Jerry C. Olson, *Consumer Behavior and Marketing Strategy* (Homewood, IL: Richard D. Irwin, 1990), p. 435.

80. The Pan Am case is based upon an article by Patricia Sellers, "How to Handle Customers' Gripes," *Fortune*, October 24, 1988, pp. 87–100.

81. Ibid.

82. Ibid.

83. Charles Riley, "Why Is Airline Food So Terrible?" *Fortune*, December 19, 1988, pp. 169, 172.

CHAPTER 13 CASE STUDY

The Medical Examination

Cal is a highly educated, upper-middle-income male, over 40, who is conscious of the need for a healthy life-style. Because he has a family history of heart disease, he has regular checkups to make sure all is well. In September 1991 he went in for his standard physical. Cal's expectations were that he would have a normal checkup and that he would be told to watch his cholesterol intake more closely, lose a little weight, continue his healthy life-style, and come back in a year.

One component of the physical is an exercise stress test. A bundle of electrodes are attached to the chest, and the patient then begins walking briskly on a treadmill. As Cal was walking comfortably along, his physician and the nurse suddenly began to have worried looks on their faces as they looked at the computer screen. Quickly, Cal was taken off the treadmill and placed on the examining table. The physician then explained that the EKG indicated a blockage in the heart. On the spot, the physician ordered more tests for Cal, which were to take place in five days. Cal was told to go home and not exert himself.

Five days passed and Cal arrived at the hospital for another examination. A busy professional, he rearranged his schedule for the two and one-half hours required for the tests. He was told not to eat for four hours prior to the test and to show up promptly at his appointment time at 10 A.M. in jogging clothes. He was told that the test would last about one and a half hours, and that he would then have to come back again two hours later to have a second picture taken of his heart, which would take only 30 minutes or so.

Understandably, Cal's anxiety level was elevated by the time of his designated appointment. He arrived on time and then waited 20 minutes to be seen by a nurse. Another 15 minutes went by as the staff hooked him up to the electrodes. An IV was inserted into his arm so that radioactive thallium could be injected into his vein during the exercise. (The amount of radioactivity in his heart would later be measured to determine if an adequate blood supply was reaching it.) After the "hook-up" was completed, he was told to sit on the examining table and wait for the doctor.

So, Cal sat and waited—alone. Clad only in running shorts, jogging shoes, and the wires, he quickly noticed that it was cold in the room—particularly as a circulating fan blew air across his bare torso every seven seconds. His only diversion during his wait was watching his heart rhythms on the monitoring machine to which he was attached. After he had sat on the table for 45 minutes, the cardiologist arrived and began with six attendants to work on Cal. After a huge Geiger counter read the level of radioactivity in his heart, he was told to return in two hours for a second measurement. The cardiologist added that the results would be available the next morning from his own physician. What was expected to have taken about two hours in total actually took about four hours.

The next morning Cal called his physician to inquire about the results of the tests. The nurse said that the physician was not available and that he would return the phone call. However, with no return call arriving from his physician by early afternoon, Cal called again. He learned that the primary care physician had gone on vacation. In addition, the physician's key nurse was off, and no one in the office knew of him or the tests he had taken the day before. He then asked if someone in the office could call the cardiologist to find out if the results were ready. A substitute attendant called the cardiologist. She returned the call to Cal and told him that the results were not ready. Perhaps they would be ready the next day.

The next day Cal waited impatiently throughout the morning for a phone call. When the call was not received by 11:30 A.M., he contacted the head nurse at the clinic. She said that nothing had arrived from the cardiologist. Perhaps they would hear something by the following Monday. Cal asked for the cardiologist's phone number to call him directly, but the head nurse said she was unable to give out that information.

At this point Cal's anxiety and frustration levels were greatly elevated. He took matters into his own hands and called a friend at the hospital who knew the cardiologist in question. The friend quickly returned the call and gave Cal the number. Cal then called the cardiologist directly and received the results of his tests. Fortunately, they revealed that the original diagnosis had been a false alarm. No blockage existed and his heart was perfectly normal. In all, the false alarm cost Cal a week of anxiety, $2,000 in medical bills, and intense unhappiness with the way he was treated.

* * *

Thanks to Jane Licata for developing the case.

QUESTIONS

1. Define the problem faced by the health care workers who treated Cal.
2. What consumer concepts from Chapter 13 explain Cal's feelings about his experience?
3. For which managerial strategy elements do the consumer concepts have implications? Develop the managerial applications analysis and discuss the managerial strategies that should be employed to improve the quality of the service offered by the medical staff.

Part 2 Case One

BEEF: REAL FOOD FOR REAL PEOPLE

In 1988 the National Beef Board management became concerned with the declining trend in beef sales as more and more consumers purchased chicken and fish. The market share of beef decreased as other meats' shares increased. Between 1976 and 1989, annual per capita consumption of beef decreased by 20.5% (from 94 pounds to 74.7 pounds). In contrast, annual per capita consumption of chicken increased by 46.5% (from 43 pounds to 63 pounds). During the time period, total meat consumption remained stable at around 230 pounds per person. Based upon this information, the board decided to investigate the matter to determine why sales were down for red beef and up for poultry and fish. What could be done about reshifting meat purchases back to beef?

HISTORY

For over 100 years cattlemen have been producing beef as a product and selling it to packers. What the packer and retailer did with the product and what consumers wanted was not the cattlemen's focus. Similarly, retailers had been offering consumers the same cuts of red meat in the same displays for almost as many years and saw no real need for change.

In contrast, the chicken industry was changing. In the past, chickens were raised for eggs. They were scrawny and provided little or no competition for the beef producers. Until 1964, 80% of the chickens sold for meat were sold whole. By 1988 whole chickens accounted for only 20% of those sold. The remaining 80% were sold precut and packaged to meet the changing needs of consumers.

While the poultry processors reacted to the market, cattlemen did nothing. They continued to concentrate on producing a more efficient animal, with little concern for what was happening around them. Beef sales continued to increase each year, and cattlemen and retailers thought everything was fine. In the late 1970s several trends began to emerge in the marketplace that were devastating to beef sales. The number of women working outside the home steadily increased. The number of one- and two-member households also increased. Americans became very health conscious and time oriented. All these things changed the products consumers wanted and their attitudes toward what they were receiving. By the early 1980s cattle producers and processors realized there was a problem with the sale of their product and that something needed to be done about it.

THE PROBLEMS

In the late 1970s and early 1980s consumers were flooded with information about cutting back on fatty foods and cholesterol. Much of the information consumers were receiving about the effects of fat in their diet was incorrect, as leaders of the beef industry knew. For example, research by the National Cattlemen's Association revealed that meat cuts were trimmed to an average of one-eighth of an inch of external fat at the retail level. The information the U.S.D.A. used in their nutrition composition charts assumed one-half inch of external fat, all of which was consumed.

Assuming a one-half-inch trim, researchers found that 8 ounces of uncooked "choice" top loin contained 142 grams of lean, 68 grams of fat, and 190 milligrams of cholesterol. The same cut of meat trimmed to only one-eighth-inch external fat contained 142 grams of lean, 28 grams of fat, and 120 milligrams of cholesterol. When this 8-ounce choice sirloin was cooked and separable fat was removed, it contained 110 grams of lean, 8.5 grams of fat, and 85 milligrams of cholesterol. These findings have been accepted by the U.S.D.A., and their charts were changed.

Working by itself, the industry could not do much to change the perception of red meat, so the beef board decided to try reaching consumers through the American Cancer Society. While working with the society, industry leaders discovered more nutritional misinformation. The figures concerning daily red meat consumption referred to meat containing all the fat, bones, and connective tissue. By removing these items from consumption measurements, it was found that consumers were only receiving 215 calories a day from red meat fat. This caloric intake accounts for 11% of a 2,000-calorie diet. Because health authorities recommended that 30% of calories come from fat, the analysis indicated that consumers were not getting too much fat from beef, as had been reported.

ACTIONS TAKEN BY THE BEEF PRODUCERS

In the fall of 1986 cattlemen across the United States voted on and passed the beef checkoff program. Under this program, producers (including importers) pay one dollar for each cow sold into the program. The money is used to promote beef. Before kicking off the campaign on February 1, 1987, extensive research was done to determine what consumers thought about beef and which consumers were buying beef. Results of the research led to a breakdown of beef buyers into five categories:

1. *Meat lovers*—Consider meat to be the best-tasting part of the meal and feel it is not too expensive. They have moderate concerns about meal preparation time and low concerns about health issues.
2. *Creative cooks*—Generally feel that meal preparation is exciting. This group is positive toward beef and has low concern about price.
3. *Price drivens*—Let economizing at the grocery store affect their purchases. They also have positive attitudes toward beef but think that it is expensive.
4. *Active life-styles*—Concerned with meal preparation time due to their time constraints. This group has a negative attitude toward beef.
5. *Health oriented*—Concerned with cutting back on fat, cholesterol, salt, preservatives/additives, and calories. They also have a negative attitude toward beef and have cut back on consumption of beef for health reasons.

These last two segments are the only ones with negative attitudes toward meat. They are, however, two of the largest segments. Exhibit 1 breaks the segments out in percentages. Exhibit 2 shows the changes in these segments from 1983 to 1987.

Further research helped the beef council to identify what consumers found important about beef. Exhibit 3, from a 1987 survey, shows the attributes considered most important by consumers. Many of these attributes, such as package size, cost, and fat content, must be addressed at the retail outlet rather than by the producer. The beef council began educating retail store personnel on the importance of appearance, lay-

EXHIBIT 1

Market Segments for Meat

Group	*% of Market*
Meat lovers	7.1
Creative cooks	21.2
Price drivens	22.2
Active lifestyles	22.2
Health oriented	27.3
Total	100.0

Based on attitudes–Total sample size is 1,514
SOURCE: "Executive Summary," *Consumer Climate for Meat*, National Livestock and Meat Board, 1987, p. 24.

EXHIBIT 2

Changes in Attitude Over Time

	Year		
Group	*1983*[a]	*1985*	*1987*
Meat lovers	22%	10%	7%
Creative cooks	20%	17%	21%
Price drivens	25%	23%	22%
Active lifestyles	16%	26%	22%
Health oriented	17%	24%	27%

Base–Total sample for each year
[a] Percentages represent percent of market held by group.
SOURCE: "Executive Summary," *Consumer Climate for Meat*, National Livestock and Meat Board, 1987, p. 25.

out, and availability of information to consumers. Videos and pamphlets for in-store display were sent to retailers by the National Livestock and Beef Board. They included information on beef in general, recipes, and how to purchase cuts of beef. Retailers were encouraged to be positive toward consumers, to help with purchase decisions and recipe ideas, and to provide smaller packages of beef.

Further education efforts by the council have attempted to reach consumers, nutritionists, health care professionals, and media personnel. Advertising in health care journals and nationwide health care seminars began in 1987. Over 600,000 copies of a book on feeding a child in its first five years were distributed to pediatricians, and 5,000 copies of a teaching kit on beef were distributed to health care practitioners to help answer clients' questions on the benefits of eating beef and veal. To supply the news media with correct information on beef, the beef industry held the National Beef Cook-Off in 1987. Schools received 16,000 packets providing facts about beef to sixth through eighth graders. An exercise and diet guide with quick preparation recipes was made available to those in the active life-styles and health-oriented groups.

According to a video put out by the beef checkoff program, the beef industry as a whole spent $1.07 billion on advertising in 1986 and around $1.68 billion in 1987 and $1.7 billion in 1988 [1]. The ads were run in magazines and newspapers and on television. The 1987–1988 beef council spokespersons were James Garner and Cybill Shepherd, both of whom were selected for their appeal to groups of light beef users between 15 and 54 years of age who are generally well educated. Both spokespersons left the campaign in mid-1988 and were replaced by basketball players Larry Bird and Michael Cooper. Informational print ads by the checkoff program have featured Houston Astros pitcher Nolan Ryan, ABC Olympic announcer Jim McKay, and Robert Mitchum, who appeals to the over-50 age group. The beef checkoff program was also a sponsor of the 1988 Calgary Olympics.

Beef producers also began to tinker with the beef product itself. Ranchers began experimenting with different breeds of cattle and various types of feed to produce beef with less fat. Some ranchers have begun raising longhorn cattle because of their lower fat content. Interestingly, this breed was the first one used commercially in

EXHIBIT 3

Attributes Considered Most Important by Consumers[a]

1. Easy preparation
2. Taste
3. Package sizes
4. Appeal to children
5. Value
6. Cost
7. Serving variety
8. Wholesomeness
9. Nutritional value
10. Salt content
11. Cholesterol content
12. Fat content
13. Calorie content
14. Fattening

[a] Bases on consumption frequency/attribute rating correlations ranked in order from most important to least important.
SOURCE: "Executive Summary," *Consumer Climate for Meat*, National Livestock and Meat Board, 1987, p. 25.

the United States because it could withstand the extended cattle drives to distant markets.

Using another approach, producers have begun to add value to the beef product by partially cooking it and/or packaging it in a more convenient form. Examples include prepackaged roast beef sandwiches, boil-in-the-bag products, and sliced dried beef. Of course, the goal of this strategy was to make the product more convenient for time-starved consumers. In another strategy, beef producers have begun to target Japan as a market. However, gaining the approval of Japan's Ministry of Health and Welfare has proven difficult for American producers.

THE RESULTS

Grocery stores reported as much as a 25% increase in beef sales when the in-store video displays were used. This appears to indicate that at least part of the promotional campaign has been effective. To determine what changes in beef sales had occurred, Burke Marketing Research interviewed 1,514 grocery shoppers by telephone between May 7 and May 21, 1987, concerning their consumption of and attitudes toward meat. The research found that the consumption of virtually all fresh meats remained stable between 1983 and 1987. Ground beef consumption increased steadily between 1983 and 1987. During the same time, fresh beef consumption increased slightly and then decreased to the original level.

The five groups referred to earlier reacted differently to beef during the 1983–1987 period. The meat lovers had increased the frequency of serving beef and continued to be the biggest consumers of beef. The price-driven segment had a steady decrease in beef consumption during the time period. Disappointingly, so did the creative cooks. However, it was discovered that the ads produced by the checkoff program helped many of those consumers who felt guilty about eating beef to feel less guilty.

CONCLUSION

The beef industry sat stagnant in the marketplace for so long that other meats, such as poultry and fish, passed by them. By 1991, however, the beef industry had been alerted and was beginning to take some positive action to get back in the running. Their checkoff campaign and other advertising seems to have paid off. Although results on the television ads featuring actors and athletes were not yet available in late 1988, other results indicate that the Beef Board has made progress. The big question facing the Beef Board today is where to head in the future.

* * *

Thanks go to Pamela Ann Gill for helping to develop the case.

QUESTIONS

1. Define the problems faced by beef producers. Which concepts from Part 2 of the text are most relevant for solving these problems? Please justify your answers.
2. What factors may affect the consumer decision-making process for purchasing beef?
3. When the beef industry first started stating that beef was healthy and that people really did not need to cut back on red meat consumption, people ignored the messages. From an attitude change perspective, why did this occur?
4. How could the multiattribute attitude models help the beef industry in planning its promotional campaign?
5. Some stores had substantial beef sales increases when the in-store video displays were used. From a decision-making viewpoint, what may have caused this?
6. Based on the results of the survey, have the Beef Board's efforts been successful? How could they improve their strategy in the future?
7. Classify each market segment of beef buyers into VALS I life-style classifications. In your opinion, would using VALS improve managerial decision making regarding beef? How? Would the LOV inventory potentially be useful in describing different segments of beef consumers?
8. What managerial implications might con-

cepts from the areas of cognitive and behavioral learning have for beef marketers?

9. Develop a managerial applications table that depicts five key individual consumer concepts that apply to the question of how to persuade consumers to consume more beef. What are the managerial implications of these concepts?

10. Develop a list of ten AIO statements that you believe would be important in identifying divergent segments of beef consumers. Briefly justify your inclusion of each statement.

SOURCES

1. "Beef Producer's Investment in Beef Producer's Profits— This Is the Story of the Beef Checkoff," *Beef Council*, June 1987.
2. Andrew Kupfer, "Where's the Beef? Check This Out," *Fortune*, July 29, 1991, pp 163–164.
3. Susan Moffat, "Japan, U.S. Suds, 'Yes.' Steaks, 'Maybe,'" *Fortune*, June 18, 1990, p. 9.

DELTA AIR LINES, INC., INCIDENTS AND ACCIDENTS

Delta Air Lines used to be the pride of America's skies. The Atlanta-based carrier had a record for safety and reliability second to none, and a Department of Transportation survey gave Delta the highest customer satisfaction rating in the industry. But a rash of incidents in the late 1980s severely tarnished that image and created high anxiety among some of the airline's most loyal customers. "This is like the Tylenol crisis," said John B. Galipault, president of the Ohio-based Aviation Safety Institute. "How is Delta's management going to deal with this? Are they going to fire all the pilots?" [1]

Delta's new chairman and chief executive officer, Ronald W. Allen, was pondering just that question. What should Delta's reaction be to its recent rash of incidents? Having been CEO for just four days when this statement was released, Mr. Allen was on the hot seat. Delta's market share (12%) and operating income ($237 million) ranked it fourth in the industry's "Big Five" listed in Exhibit 1 [2]. However, Delta's reaction to the recent negative publicity it had received would be crucial to the company's future.

HISTORY

Delta Air Lines, Inc., is a major carrier providing services to 132 domestic cities in 42 states and to 23 international destinations. Incorporated in 1967, Delta's primary hub is Atlanta, Georgia. The company also operates major hubs in Cincinnati, Dallas/Ft. Worth, and Salt Lake City. On December 18, 1986, Delta merged with Western Air Lines, Inc., and integrated Western's hub of Salt Lake City into its own route system. Today Delta accounts for about 75% of the commercial flights in Salt Lake City and over 50% of the commercial flights in Atlanta.

DELTA'S SAFETY PROBLEMS

The following is a brief summary of Delta's safety problems that occurred in July 1987.

- A Delta jet bound for Lexington, Kentucky, mistakenly landed in Frankfort, some 20 miles away.
- In Canadian airspace and over the Atlantic Ocean, a Delta jumbo jet wandered some 60 miles off course. A midair collision with a Continental jet was avoided by less than 100 feet. After the incident, an investigation uncovered the fact that the two pilots involved had discussed not reporting the incident.
- A plane bound for Salt Lake City had to return to Los Angeles International Airport

EXHIBIT 1

Ranking the Big Five

Name	*Market Share*	*Operating Income*	*Available Seat Miles*
Texas Air	20%	$237M	109,300
American	14	392	75,100
United	16	407	91,400
Delta	12	237	55,100
Northwest	10	167	48,400

SOURCE: "Winners in the Air Wars," *Fortune Magazine*, May 11, 1987.

because it could not be pressurized once it was off the ground.

- Two incidents involving Delta took place at Boston's Logan International Airport. First, a Delta plane that had received proper clearance for landing set down on the wrong runway. Later in the month, a Delta pilot was accused of taking off without proper authorization. A near collision was avoided when a USAir jet stopped just before entering the runway from which the Delta jet was taking off illegally. Delta claims that the air traffic controller who was on duty at the time was responsible for this incident. The pilot of the Delta jet claims he had received clearance for takeoff from the tower.

In addition, two years earlier Delta was involved in one of the worst air disasters in aviation history. On August 12, 1985, Delta Flight 191 attempted a landing during a violent thunderstorm. All but one of the passengers and crew were killed instantly when the plane crashed to the ground. The pilot involved was cleared of any charges of taking improper actions in the accident. The accident was blamed on wind sheer, a naturally occurring phenomenon that happens in violent storms.

More negative publicity hit Delta when it was rumored that they were comforting families of passengers in any way possible in an attempt to avoid costly lawsuits [3]. It was also rumored that Delta had investigated and was ready to disclose the undesirable past of a man whose family had threatened a lawsuit. The undesirable past of the passenger would decrease the dollar amount of any subsequent lawsuit. Although Delta was never charged with any type of blackmail or harassment complaints, the issue received a great deal of attention from the press.

SERVICE

Quality of service has always been an important ingredient to a successful marketing strategy in the airlines industry. As stated previously, Delta has developed a long-standing reputation for customer satisfaction. Exhibit 2 shows the results of a poll conducted independently of Delta [4].

EXHIBIT 2

Favorite/Least Favorite Airlines

Rank	*Favorite*	*Poll Points*
1	American	430
2	Delta	377
3	United	210
6	Northwest	38
7	Eastern (Texas Air)	36
9	Continental (Texas Air)	32
Rank	***Least Favorite***	***Poll Points***
1	Eastern	68
2	Continental	44
3	Northwest	38
4	United	22
N/R	American	—
N/R	Delta	—

SOURCE: "American Wins Its Wings," *Advertising Age*, July 27, 1987.

This poll was conducted prior to the rash of incidents that plagued the company. Business travelers and frequent fliers were asked to choose their favorite/least favorite airline based on a number of service characteristics, including the convenience of schedules, on-time performance, overbooking, baggage handling, and the attitudes of personnel. Delta finished second behind American. It is also interesting to note that Texas Air, United, and Northwest were all mentioned among the least favorite U.S. airlines. Reasons given for choosing American were its on-time performance and convenience of schedules. Delta was mentioned as being a "warm and friendly" airline. The poll went on to suggest a high level of discontent with the industry as a whole among consumers. Lateness/delays, employee attitudes, and overall poor service were the areas about which most consumers complained.

Consumers appear to be deeply frustrated.

Many business travelers feel trapped, with no alternative means of travel. Even so, travelers frustrated by service problems do not regularly change airlines. Studies conducted by Continental suggest that consumers use a "hierarchy of benefits based primarily on schedules and price to choose who they patronize," according to James V. O'Donnell, vice president of marketing. "Their hierarchies rarely involve whether they like or don't like the airline" [5].

Exhibit 3 shows data on customer complaints concerning the airlines. Quite often consumers feel helpless against the airlines. Deregulation has caused all airlines to tighten controls over costs. As a result, customer complaints across the industry are on the rise. However, Delta's complaint rate has stayed consistently low.

PAST ADVERTISING STRATEGIES

For many years Delta used the successful theme "Delta is ready when you are." In 1985 the slogan was changed to "Delta gets you there." Both ad campaigns were meant for radio and television broadcasts. In both cases the ads featured Delta employees smiling and singing together in a closely bunched choir. These ads effectively passed along the intended message of Delta being a close-knit, teamwork-oriented organization. The broadcasts featured 500 actual Delta employees lip-synching the words to the theme song, which is sung by 50 actual employees. All employees interested were asked to go through auditions for the parts [6].

In 1986 Delta began a new ad campaign featuring individual employees delivering "pep talks" on job satisfaction and pride. They attempted to explain why they enjoyed working for Delta. These ads also used actual employees and focused on presenting down-to-earth personalities. The ads attempted to articulate the reasons for Delta's success in customer satisfaction. According to Wayne Soph, Delta advertising manager, "We're in a mass transportation business, but we want to try and personalize the job as much as possible." The revised slogan for 1986 was "Delta gets you there with care" [7].

Delta's 1986 print media campaign focused on fare advertising and its expansion of capacity in Cincinnati. However, in June 1987 Delta launched a new tough-line campaign based on service superiority. The newspapers ads asked, "Want the truth about airline service? Ask the people who live on planes." The ads used Department of Transportation data on complaints and proclaimed Delta's service as superior [8].

* * *

Thanks go to Scott Williams for helping to develop the case.

EXHIBIT 3

Complaints per 100,000 Passengers (April 1987)

Continental	25.40
Eastern	6.98
Northwest	6.32
United	3.07
American	2.13
Delta	0.74

SOURCE: *The Wall Street Journal*, June 1, 1987.

QUESTIONS

1. What are the problems faced by Delta? Which concepts from Part 2 of the text are most relevant for solving these problems?
2. What factors influence whether the incidents and associated publicity will have a significant long-term adverse effect on Delta? Focus your answer to this question on concepts from the material on attitude formation and change.
3. What motivational concepts may influence consumers' perceptions of Delta? What are the managerial implications of these motivational concepts?
4. Develop an attitude-toward-the-object model that identifies the beliefs and evaluations on which airlines might be evaluated. Interview ten acquaintances and compare

their attitudes regarding Delta and one or more airlines of your choice.

5. Using the applicable consumer behavior concepts as a foundation for your answer, what managerial steps should Delta take to keep its market share from slipping? Construct a managerial applications table when answering this question.
6. Describe the decision-making process used by consumers when selecting an airline. Does the decision process differ for various segments of consumers?
7. What concepts from the chapters on information processing apply to Delta's problems or any airline that has recently experienced a disaster? What are some managerial implications of these strategies?

REFERENCES

1. Terry Johnson and Vern Smith, "What's Wrong with Delta?" *Newsweek*, July 27, 1987, p. 25.
2. Kenneth Labich, "Winners in the Air Wars," *Fortune*, May 11, 1987, pp. 68–69.
3. Cynthia Miller, "Damage Control," *The Wall Street Journal*, November 7, 1985, p. 33.
4. Robert Goldsborough, "American Wins Its Wings," *Advertising Age*, July 27, 1987, p. 41.
5. Judith Valente, "Gluttons for Punishment? Fliers Continue Using Airlines They Hate," *The Wall Street Journal*, July 27, 1987, p. 41.
6. Brian Moran, "Jingle Flies Again—for Delta," *Advertising Age*, April 11, 1985, p. 4.
7. Brian Moran, "Delta Employees Star in TV Spots," *Advertising Age*, November 10, 1986, p. 40.
8. Janet Meyers and Jennifer Lawrence, "Airlines Mull Service Claims," *Advertising Age*, June 15, 1987, p. 3.

When 6-year-old Joshua Bradosky opened the garage door for his mother's Audi 5000S in February 1986, the car suddenly accelerated forward, dragging Joshua through the family garage and fatally crushing him against the back wall. Joshua was alleged to be a victim of sudden acceleration syndrome (SAS), or the unintended surging forward or backward of a car when shifting the transmission from the park position to drive or reverse. Although sudden acceleration was reported to occur in many other reputable autos (e.g., Mercedes-Benz), Audi bore the claim of the "killer car." Through the end of 1988, the Audi 5000 series had been involved in 1,400 accidents and 320 injuries, and five to seven deaths were attributed to SAS. Although the SAS charges against Audi were eventually proven to be groundless, the negative publicity severely damaged the company.

HISTORY

Audi is and has been a reputable auto manufacturer, with Volkswagen of America as its corporate parent. Many attributes typically associated with German automobiles are also evident in Audi cars. Audi is well known for its advanced design, reliability, and luxury features. Audi asks a premium price for its autos and targets families who are willing to pay for the precision and performance expected from Audi's products.

The company can be traced back to 1900 when August Horch manufactured the twin-cylinder engine. Horch, a blacksmith by trade, engineered a "nonjerking" engine that outperformed any known single-cylinder model of the time. His later achievements included the production of the first eight-cylinder automobile.

The invention of front-wheel drive was introduced in 1931 by DKW, a founding company of Audi. In 1932 a group of automotive engineering companies, DKW, Horch, Audi, and Wanderer, formed Auto Union AG. The company chose a logo of four linked rings, each symbolizing the Auto Union's heritage.

The Auto Union continued producing innovative automobiles earning several honors, such as "car of the year" in 1964. In 1969 Audi NSU Union AG was formed. This union was formed primarily to maintain a competitive advantage in Germany and expand worldwide.

In 1976 Audi began manufacturing the 5000 model. The concept of the five-cylinder engine made the car a unique alternative offering both power and economy. In 1983 Audi introduced aerodynamic styling in its 5000 model. This design won numerous car-of-the year awards in both America and Europe.

THE SUDDEN ACCELERATION PROBLEM

From 1976 to 1982 the Audi 5000 experienced 13 complaints of sudden acceleration. The National Highway Traffic and Safety Administration (NHTSA) had already begun an investigation of automakers such as Mercedes, Datsun, Volvo, and others and had found no conclusive evidence of any mechanical defect. The NHTSA also investigated Audi at this time and approved a voluntary recall for possible floormat interference with the accelerator.

In September 1983 Audi began another voluntary recall to install a spacer on top of the brake pedal. This spacer would help reduce confusion between the brake pedal and the accelerator. In the Audi 5000 these pedals were an equal distance from the floor board, whereas in most American cars the brake pedal is farther from the floor board, causing drivers to lift their foot off the accelerator and pull their leg up to be able to place their foot on the brake pedal.

On February 23, 1986, *The New York Times* featured an article concerning unintended acceleration in GM, Ford, Toyota, and other vehicles, including Audi [1]. This article caused Alice Weinstein to get in touch with the New York Public Interest Groups. She alleged that two accidents occurring in her Audi 5000 were caused by SAS. This in turn led to an investigation by the New York attorney general [2].

On March 19, 1986, a petition by the Center for Auto Safety and the New York attorney general asked the National Highway and Safety Administration to investigate and recall all 1978–1986 Audi 5000 models equipped with automatic transmissions [3]. This petition was the beginning of an investigation that turned out to be a public relations nightmare for Audi.

Alice Weinstein continued her allegations and founded the Audi Victims Network. The network consisted of approximately 40 members who had all claimed to be victims of unintended acceleration in their 5000s. On May 28, 1986, representatives from Audi met with the network. The result of this meeting and increased media attention on the SAS problem was a third voluntary recall by Audi to further increase the vertical distance between the brake pedal and accelerator. Audi, whose name means "to listen," wanted to communicate that the company was doing all it could to solve the problem [4]. Unfortunately for Audi, network members interpreted this recall as placing the blame for alleged incidents solely on the driver and, as a result, were determined that Audi should take full responsibility.

In response to the public relations crisis, in June 1986 Audi began the "automatic shift lock" recall. This locking mechanism ensured that the brake pedal would be depressed when shifting out of park and into a gear. Audi spent $25 million installing the shift lock device on recalled cars. But the turmoil continued as consumer awareness increased.

"60 MINUTES" AND SAS

On November 23, 1986, "60 Minutes" broadcast a segment reporting on the unintended acceleration problem in Audi 5000 automobiles. Audi had agreed to assist "60 Minutes" in the broadcast, because Audi was genuinely interested in the problem. But the broadcast left viewers with the false impression that Audi was unconcerned, as CBS gave Audi no equal time for rebuttal or explanations.

The heart-rending segment featured distraught victims such as Mrs. Bradosky, who had seemingly been tagged by Audi as an inexperienced driver. Mrs. Bradosky said, "I got back into the car and put my foot on the brake to put it in drive and the car surged forward and I saw that I was going to hit him. So I put my foot on the brake, but it didn't stop the car." "60 Minutes" failed to report that after the accident the police report stated that Mrs. Bradosky's foot slipped off the brake and onto the accelerator. Also, the brake system was found to be in working condition after the accident.

The broadcast also featured an expert who caused a car to accelerate by simulating a transmission failure. What "60 Minutes" failed to report was that the experiment was conducted with a modified vehicle. In reality, the expert's experiment was not valid, and his theories were factually incorrect.

The broadcast spawned complaints from Audi owners of all model years. By the end of 1987 the number of complaints had skyrocketed from the number prior to the airing of the segment, as shown in Exhibit 1. Audi's sales, which had been about 75,000 in 1985, began a downward trend. In 1986 total sales were 60,0000 vehicles. By 1988 sales had fallen to just 22,943 [5]. Sales reached their nadir in 1990, when they fell below 20,000 units. Exhibit 2 shows sales information for 1980–1988.

AUDI'S RESPONSE

Audi made four recalls: one prior to 1983 to check for possible floormat interference, one in September 1983 to install the first spacer, one in May 1986 for the second spacer, and the fourth in June 1986 to install the automatic shift lock.

EXHIBIT 1

Accelerating Complaints (Complaints about Sudden Acceleration Reported to the National Highway Traffic Safety Administration–Numbers Are Approximate)

	1985	*1986*	*1987*
First 6 months	390	600	800
Second 6 months	375	400	1,800

SOURCE: National Highway Traffic Safety Administration.

Audi also did extensive testing to determine if there was indeed some mechanical or technical error causing the SAS problem in the Audi 5000 models. The testing found no fault in the engineering and performance of the cars. Therefore, Audi concluded that driver error must have caused the accidents.

After the "60 Minutes" program in late 1986, Audi kept fairly quiet concerning the issue. Audi did not try to refute the television broadcast. It pulled back its national advertising to reformulate its strategy and let time lapse after the alleged problem of SAS. It began offering a $5,000 rebate to owners of 1987 Audi 5000s in 1987. Owners of the models were having to sell or trade their cars for thousands of dollars less than their true worth. (Interestingly, consumers who understood the real story behind the SAS problem were finding terrific buys on quality vehicles.) Audi also produced a videotape explaining sudden acceleration to consumers who were interested.

With sales still declining dramatically in the spring of 1988, Audi began an aggressive $80 million, one-year effort to rebuild its image and sales [6]. The print ads were entitled "It's Time We Talked." The ad admitted that the lack of vocal response by Audi was perceived as a sign of weakness and an admission of guilt. It went on to state that Audi was waiting for the facts to speak for themselves. Ads appearing in the summer of 1988 featured titles such as "Audi Today: Designed for Safety." These ads gave toll-free numbers to assist consumers with any problems they encountered.

EXHIBIT 2

Audi's Troubled Sales (U.S. Sales– Numbers Are Approximate)

Year	*Sales*
1980	40,000
1981	50,000
1982	45,000
1983	47,000
1984	70,000
1985	74,061
1986	60,000
1987	40,000
1988	22,943

SOURCE: *Ward's Automotive Reports* and *The Wall Street Journal*, February 2, 1989, p. B1.

AUDI'S FUTURE

In January 1988 Richard L. Mugg became the chief executive officer of Audi. Mr. Mugg said that he was counting on the introduction of two new models in the 1989 model year, as well as some customer coddling, to restore the Audi image. The two new models were the Audi 100 and 200. They replaced the Audi 5000 and 5000CS [7]. These cars have been tagged "make-or-break" cars for Audi. Some experts felt that these cars may never reach their peak, due to the fact that exchange-rate-induced price increases were trimming sales of most European-made cars in the American market. In addition, Japanese automakers were beginning to crowd the sporty, luxury car market segment. Honda had the successful introduction of the Acura line, while Toyota and Nissan were preparing to introduce two new models in 1989.

CONCLUSION

The Audi 5000 models have been implicated in 1,400 accidents. These accidents have resulted in approximately 320 injuries and from five to seven fatalities [8]. Although SAS occurs in many other reputable autos, Audi has been tagged the "killer car." The reputation of Audi as a distinguished company known for its engineering expertise has been damaged by allegations resulting from these SAS incidents. After 1986 Audi's sales plummeted, and its North American operations were plunged into "red ink" because of the same SAS allegations. In 1985 Audi sold a record 74,061 cars in the United States. In 1988 sales fell to 22,943. Audi hoped that the unveiling of its two new models in 1989 might dispel the negative connotations of the Audi 5000. In addition, the company was becoming heavily involved in sports car races and racking up numerous wins.

In March 1989 Audi at last received some good news when the results of a study performed by the National Highway Traffic Safety Administration were released. The study supported conclusions of research performed in Japan and Canada. Driver fault, not mechanical problems, caused sudden acceleration. While not ending the controversy, the findings may help limit the damage of numerous liability claims. In fact, the company began to consider filing a lawsuit against "60 Minutes" [9].

* * *

Thanks go to Amy C. James for developing this case.

QUESTIONS

1. What implications for managerial strategy at Audi can be drawn from an understanding of the communications model?
2. For a manager at Audi, what factors would be important to increase customer postacquisition satisfaction?
3. What do concepts from the study of exchange processes say about Audi's SAS problems?
4. What could Audi have done in early 1986 to stem the negative publicity?
5. What factors motivated consumers to respond so negatively to Audi? Why didn't other auto companies experiencing SAS have such negative publicity?
6. Construct a managerial applications table and discuss its implications for Audi.

REFERENCES

1. J. Tomerlin, "Solved: The Riddle of Unintended Acceleration," *Road and Track*, February 1988, pp. 52–59.
2. Ibid.
3. Geoff Sundstrom, "NHTSA Steps Up Probe of Audi Sudden Acceleration," *Automotive News*, August 18, 1986, p. 4.
4. Tomerlin, "Solved."
5. Bradley Stertz, "U.S. Study Blames Drivers for Sudden Acceleration," *The Wall Street Journal*, February 2, 1989, p. B1.
6. Leslie Spencer, "Salem 1692, Revised," *Forbes*, November 12, 1990.
7. Jim Treece and John Templeman, "Can Audi Start Winning Races in the Showroom, Too?" *Business Week*, May 29, 1989, p. 47.
8. "Is Half a Recall Better Than None?" *Consumer Reports*, April 1987, p. 193.
9. Raymond Serafin, "Audi Mulls Suit vs. '60 Minutes,'" *Advertising Age*, April 3, 1989, p. 6.

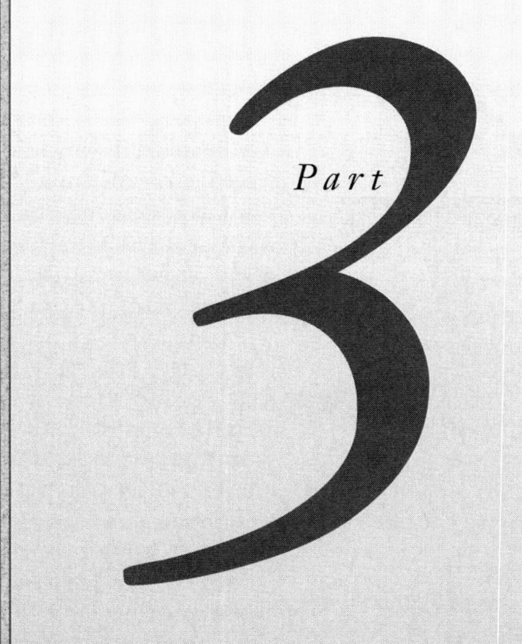

Part 3

THE CONSUMER ENVIRONMENT

Chapter

14

Introduction to the Consumer Environment and the Impact of Situational Influencers

CONSUMER VIGNETTE

Baseball, Eelpoints, and the Consumer Environment

October 1991. The Atlanta Braves played the Minnesota Twins in one of the greatest World Series of all time. The preceding year both teams had been last in their league; yet in 1991, they battled each other for baseball supremacy. The series went the full seven games—four of which ran into extra innings, including the final tension-filled game. Indeed, the World Series became a spectacle. When played in Atlanta, tens of thousands of fans chanted in unison the Braves war song, which reverberated eerily throughout the stadium. As they chanted, the fans swung plastic tomahawks together in chopping motions. Even Jane Fonda and Ted Turner joined in the action. The behavior, however, created a maelstrom of controversy as Native American Indians protested that the actions trivialized their cultural heritage.

Baseball can be seen as a metaphor for American society. Indeed, baseball, hot dogs, and apple pie symbolize the United States for many. Baseball is a focal point where diverse social classes and ethnic groups come together. Some athletes emerge from the lower classes and use the sport to climb the social class ladder. On the other hand, the upper classes strive to become part of the action. For example, A. Bartlett Giamatti was a world-renowned scholar of the Italian Renaissance and a past president of Yale University. Baseball was his real passion, though. In early 1989 he achieved his dream of becoming commissioner of major league baseball. When he took the job, his friends asked him what would happen to his intellectual life? He replied, "That presupposes that a university president has an intellectual life, which of course is nonsense."

What was Giamatti's major goal as the new commissioner of baseball? As he said it, the long-term issue was "to maintain an environment of sufficient agreeableness so that people will still want to come out and not just consume their leisure visually at home." The rowdiness and drunkenness at many baseball parks especially concerned Giamatti. He said, "The responsibility lies squarely with management to remember that without fans who enjoy being there, live, the whole enterprise does not exist."[1] Baseball lost a great man when in September 1989, a massive heart attack killed Bart Giamatti.

An important aspect of the consumer environment is the weather. Baseball commissioners worry each fall that cold weather will ruin a World Series. Similarly, each winter the people of Leech Lake, Minnesota, were concerned with retaining enough townspeople during their long cold winters even to field a baseball team. It seems that prior to 1979 the town shriveled during the winter when people moved to warmer climates. Then, an ex-Vietnam helicopter pilot had the idea of creating an Eelpoint Ice Fishing Festival in the middle of the winter.

Eelpoints are disgusting fish that are members of the cod family. Slimy and ugly, they tend to wrap themselves around the hand when a person attempts to take the hook out. Locals say that the standard way to prepare one is to "drive a nail through its head into a board and peel the skin off with pliers. Then throw the fish away and eat the board."[2]

Despite its unlikely focus on a disgusting fish, the festival quickly took off in popularity. During the annual festival, the town of 970 people grows to more than eightfold its normal size. Over 8,000 partiers arrive for the social event and begin erecting houses on the ice-locked lake. Once a team built a town on the ice, complete with working parking meters. The local fire department also actively participates. One year, on the second day of the festival, the chief burst into the eelpoint headquarters carrying his one-foot fishing rod and dangling a large minnow, which he claimed was an eelpoint. When the judges scoffed at him, he offered them some of his fireman's punch, a popular drink of brandy, rum, vodka, 190-proof grain alcohol, and orange juice. "The chief dips his lure into the mug, lets it steep awhile, then takes a sip. 'Gives it flavor, see?' he says."

ENVIRONMENTAL INFLUENCERS AND CONSUMER BEHAVIOR

Chapter 14 discusses the impact of situational influences on consumer behavior and begins Part 3, The Consumer Environment. The **consumer environment** is composed of those factors existing independently of individual consumers and firms that influence the exchange process. Figure 14-1 diagrams the consumer environment and its impact on the exchange process.

In Figure 14-1 the components of the consumer environment are placed within the set of dashed lines. At the most macro level of analysis, one finds the economic and the cultural/cross-cultural environments. They influence both the subcultural and the regulatory environments, each of which influence group and family

Figure 14-1 The consumer environment and the exchange process.

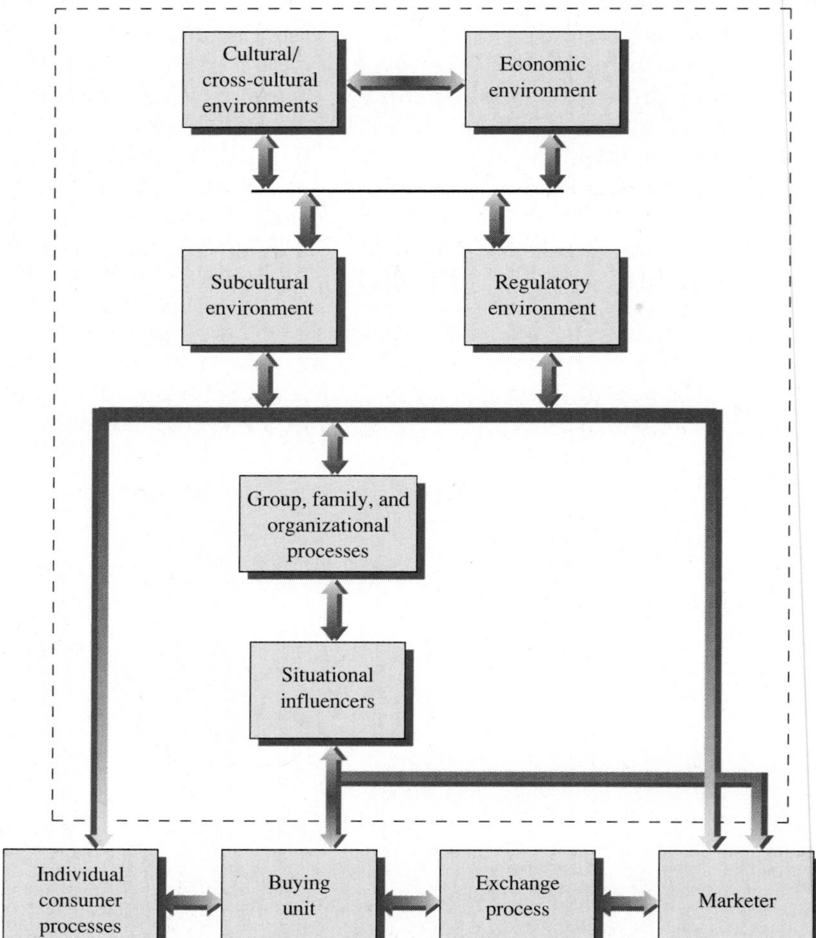

processes. In particular, the regulatory environment has a major impact on what the firm can or cannot do. In turn, group and family processes affect the situational influencers, as well as individual consumer processes and the marketer.

At the most micro level of analysis within the consumer environment, one finds the situational influencers—the topic of this chapter. Situational influencers affect the buying unit, the marketer, and the exchange process itself. Indeed, a marketing exchange can be conceptualized as resulting from the interaction of the buying unit, the marketer, and the situation at a particular time and place. This important interaction, called the **marketing triad**, is diagrammed in Figure 14-2. All the other factors identified in the text, from the individual consumer processes to the environmental influencers, come together to influence the situation, the buying unit, and the marketer.

Part 3 of the text is generally organized from the micro to the macro analysis of the consumer environment. As such, Part 3 begins with the analysis of situational influencers—the environmental factors that operate at the most micro level. Parts 1 and 2 of the text discussed the exchange process and the individual consumer processes that influence the buying unit. The natural next step is then to investigate the situational factors that form the element of the exchange triad that ties directly into the rest of the factors that compose the consumer environment.

The chapter-opening vignette illustrates a number of the influencers that compose the consumer environment. Baseball is a significant part of the culture of the United States, as well as of Canada. It is used as a cultural symbol of America in foreign countries. Its ritual actions, from playing the national anthem, to eating hot dogs, to the seventh-inning stretch, illustrate a cultural institution. Its focus on competition, achievement, informality, and opportunity illustrates some of the core values of the American culture. Within baseball one also finds a variety of subcultures. On the field one finds ethnic subcultures—particularly African-American, Hispanic, and Anglo ethnic groups. In the stands, one finds variations in social class, as well as ethnic subcultures. The upper classes sit in glass-enclosed, air-conditioned rooms; the professional classes array themselves in the box seats; and the middle classes huddle in the bleachers. With the heterogeneous set of subcultures participating in the sport, one invariably finds conflict arising. The controversy surrounding the

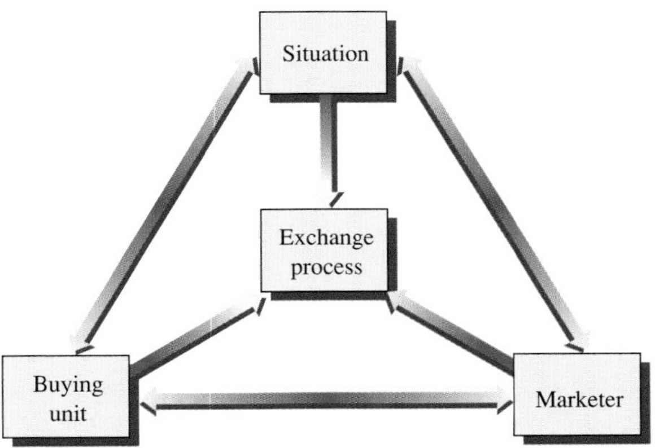

Figure 14-2
The marketing triad: situation, buying unit, marketer.

"tomahawk chop" in the 1991 World Series illustrates one of the many types of problems that may occur.

Baseball even illustrates elements of the regulatory environment. The game itself is controlled by rules and regulations. It is controlled by the regulators (i.e., the umpires), whose human foibles can dramatically influence the outcome of games. The economic environment certainly influences the game—as players are bought and sold and owners seek to maximize profits. These factors merged to cause the 1994 baseball strike.

Group and family processes are also seen in our national pastime. First, going to a baseball game for many fans is a part of family recreation. Second, those in the ballpark become part of a large, informal group. Within this group, the fans exhibit classic crowd behavior symptoms—from cheering, to fighting, to doing the wave, to making tomahawk chops.

Baseball also illustrates a number of features of consumer situations, which are discussed in the paragraphs that follow.

INTRODUCTION TO SITUATIONAL INFLUENCES

Consumer situations consist of those temporary environmental factors that form the context within which a consumer activity occurs at a particular time and place. Thus a consumer situation is composed of those factors that (1) involve the time and place in which a consumer activity takes place, (2) explain why the action takes place, and (3) influence consumer behavior. Consumer situations are relatively short-term events or happenings—they should be distinguished from more long-term environmental factors, such as the effects of culture, as well as personal factors that have a more long-lasting quality, such as an individual's personality. Examples of situations include the physical surroundings, social surroundings, time, the task definition, and antecedent states—all of which are described in Table 14-1.[3]

TABLE 14-1

Five Types of Consumer Situations

1. *Physical surroundings*—The concrete physical and spatial aspects of the environment encompassing a consumer activity.
2. *Social surroundings*—The effects of other people on a consumer in a consumer activity.
3. *Task definition*—The reasons that occasion the need for consumers to buy or consume a product or service.
4. *Time*—The effects of the presence or absence of time on consumer activities.
5. *Antecedent states*—The temporary physiological states and moods that a consumer brings to a consumption activity.

SOURCE: Russel Belk, "Situational Variables and Consumer Behavior," *Journal of Consumer Research*, Vol. 2 (December 1975), pp. 157–163.

The chapter-opening vignette illustrated a number of aspects of consumer situations. Giamatti's concern about retaining baseball fans focused on the impact of the physical and social surroundings on consumers. Physical surroundings can have a major impact on the experiences obtained by consumers. In a baseball stadium, designers attempt to create an atmosphere conducive to the overall enjoyment of the game. If the physical surroundings are unpleasant, due to a lack of sanitation or poor maintenance, fans will simply not come. Similarly, a major attraction of baseball is the social interactions that occur among fans in the stands. Baseball is a social sport with lots of time for talking, bantering, baiting of umpires and players, and casual conversation. If rowdy fans detract from the positive social aspects of the game, attendance will fall.

Another situational element is time. The pace of a baseball game is slow, allowing for a great deal of time for doing other things, such as socializing. The great comedian George Carlin has compared baseball to other sports on how they use time. Baseball simply moves slower than basketball or football. Baseball has the seventh-inning stretch. If the game is tied, they play extra innings. In baseball, no clock exists to compete against. Theoretically, a game could last forever. In contrast, in football and basketball, everyone is in a hurry. Pro basketball has a 24-second clock. Football likewise has a clock to compete against, most noticeably in the 2-minute warning. In sum, baseball seems to represent a throwback to an earlier era in which life was less rushed.

A fourth situational element is **task definition**, which is the reason or occasion for engaging in a consumer action. A baseball game or an eelpoint festival defines a task: these are occasions in which certain activities are expected. If consumers have knowledge that they are about to engage in a particular task, a series of activities are frequently expected. For example, when going to a baseball game, buying activities include purchasing tickets, finding parking or transportation, buying souvenirs, and purchasing food and liquid refreshment.

The eelpoint festival also illustrates several of the situational factors. The festival itself is an occasion that defines a whole series of tasks. To participate in the festival requires the purchase of warm winter clothing, appropriate gear for ice fishing, and the materials necessary to construct a house for fishing. Social surroundings are also important to the festival—one of the major attractions is the camaraderie that exists among the participants. Even the physical surroundings have a role in the festival. The harsh cold of the Minnesota winter strongly influences the general character of the festival, including its emphasis on ice fishing and the creation of ice houses. Finally, time plays a role in defining the nature of the festival. It is held in mid-February to mark the passing of the worst of the winter. The festival lasts for a specific time period—three days. During its duration, work stops and play time begins.

The study of situations has important implications for managers; after all, each managerial application area is influenced by situational factors. Products may be defined by the situations in which they are used. For example, wristwatches are positioned and consumers segmented in part based on usage situations. One can find formal watches, sports watches, everyday watches, and specialty watches (e.g., a diving watch). Thus groups of people (i.e., segments) may be identified with an unfulfilled situational need, such as a desire to have a watch with a timing function for jogging. A product is then developed to fit the needs of that situation, in this case a durable timepiece with a stopwatch capacity. Similarly, promotional materials may be created that clearly position the product in reference to its situational use and to its competitors.

In addition to product design, segmentation, and positioning, the study of situations has a variety of other managerial uses. People may obtain information on products only in specific situations (e.g., via the car radio while commuting). Thus how products are promoted may be influenced by the situational variations in information reception. Similarly, certain products may be bought only in certain situations (e.g., as a gift). Such information has an impact on pricing, promoting, and distributing the product.

This chapter discusses each of the situational factors that may influence consumers. Special attention is paid to the effects of the physical environment on consumers. In addition, the effects of time and the task definition are given extensive treatment. Less attention is given to the impact of the social surroundings, because this topic is discussed in Chapter 15, Group Processes I: Group, Dyadic, and Diffusion Processes. Similarly, antecedent states are discussed only briefly because of their close relationship to mood, which has been addressed in a number of earlier chapters. After analyzing the various types of situations, this chapter presents the important topic of "situation" by "buying unit" by "market offering" interactions. The last section presents a managerial applications example.

THE PHYSICAL SURROUNDINGS: WITH A FOCUS ON THE STORE ENVIRONMENT

Physical surroundings are the concrete physical and spatial aspects of the environment encompassing a consumer activity. Researchers have found that such stimuli as color, noise, lighting, weather, and the spatial arrangements of people or objects can influence consumer behavior. In the chapter-opening vignette the physical surroundings of a baseball park were discussed in terms of how they shape the behavior and actions of fans. Similarly, the physical environment of Minnesota shapes the leisure activities in which consumers engage, such as ice fishing.

Physical surroundings influence consumer perceptions through the sensory mechanisms of vision, hearing, smell, and even touch. Surroundings have particular importance to retailers; perhaps their most important task is to manage the physical environment to influence behaviors, attitudes, and beliefs of consumers in a desired manner. For example, physical surroundings have important implications for building a store image. If a retailer wants to present an upscale image, it is crucial that the surroundings match such an image. Thus uncomfortably hot temperatures, unpleasant smells, and loud colors and noises would not be appropriate for a hairstyling salon attempting to cater to wealthy customers.

The perception of bodily safety is another factor controlled in part by the physical surroundings. Ample nearby parking, adequate outdoor lighting, and open spaces enhance the feeling of security for shoppers. The presence of such physical attributes could increase nighttime shopping, particularly among the elderly, who are highly conscious of their vulnerability to crime.

Researchers have investigated the impact of the physical environment on consumer perceptions and behavior in several retailing areas. These studies, discussed shortly, have analyzed how music, crowding, store layout, store location, and store atmosphere affect buyers.

The Effects of Music on Shoppers

One component of the physical environment in retail stores that has been shown to influence consumers is the background music played in stores. In one study investigating the impact of music on the purchase process, two types of music were tested to see how they would affect supermarket shoppers.[4] Over a period of nine weeks no music, slow-tempo music, or fast-tempo music was played. The results showed that people walked slower or faster depending on whether fast or slow music was played. Sales on a daily basis increased by 38% when slower-cadenced music was played. Interestingly, when customers were asked questions about their awareness of the music, no differences were found among the groups. The effects of the music, therefore, seemed to operate at a level below consciousness. Because of the positive effects of music on customers and employees, companies have developed products, such as Muzak®, to provide music in the working and shopping environment. Indeed, in one ad, Muzak® claims that using environmental music by Muzak® results in employees working faster and making fewer mistakes.

A second study also looked at the impact of fast-paced versus slow-paced music on sales. Fast- or slow-paced background music was randomly assigned to be played on Friday and Saturday nights over eight consecutive weekends in a medium-sized restaurant in the Dallas/Ft. Worth area.[5] The results revealed that the pace of the music influenced consumers to spend more time in the restaurant. In slow-tempo conditions patrons took on average 56 minutes to complete their dinner. In contrast, it took 45 minutes to complete dinner in the fast-tempo conditions. As a result, the time spent waiting for food significantly increased. The increased time in the restaurant had no statistically significant impact on food sales; however, liquor sales went up significantly. Overall, the average gross margin per group was $55.82 in the slow-tempo condition and $48.62 in the fast-tempo condition.

The supermarket and restaurant studies are interesting because they demonstrated that the physical environment can influence buyer behavior. However, one should not immediately generalize and say that all retail stores should play slow-paced music. There may be consumption situations in which fast music would be more appropriate. For example, restaurants that have low margins and depend on high volume must have a high occupant turnover rate. In this case playing fast-paced music may speed up customers, thereby making seats available for other customers more quickly.[6]

The presence of music in the consumer environment is pervasive. For example, when consumers are placed on hold, firms will frequently play music to fill the silence and help make the wait seem less negative. Surprisingly, however, recent research found that music rated as more pleasant does *not* make time seem to pass more quickly. Thus "time does not necessarily fly" when people are having fun.[7] These results suggest that playing appealing, peppy music while people wait on "musical hold" or in waiting lines may prove counterproductive.

Research evidence also indicates that music is more effective if it matches the general situational context of the purchase. Thus, just as the source should match the message (as discussed in the chapter on communications processes), the type of music should match the purchase context. For example, one study found that when classical music, as opposed to the top forty, was played in a wine store, shoppers selected more expensive wines. As a result, they spent more money.[8] Clearly, the type of music should "fit" the situation.

The Effects of Crowding on Consumers

Crowding occurs when a person perceives that his or her movements are restricted because of limited space. The experience can result from an overabundance of people, from a limited physical area, or from a combination of the two.[9] The concept has particular relevance to retailers who must decide how to arrange floor space. When consumers experience the effects of crowding, a number of different outcomes may occur.[10] They may react by reducing their shopping time, by altering their use of in-store information, and by decreasing their communication with store employees. Potentially, crowding may increase shopper anxiety, lower shopping satisfaction, and negatively affect store image.

Researchers have distinguished between the terms density and crowding. **Density** refers to how closely packed people are. It is a term that refers to the physical arrangements of people in a space. **Crowding** refers to the unpleasant feelings that may result from a person perceiving that the density is too high and that perceived control of the situation has been reduced below acceptable levels.

A recent study investigated the relationships among density, crowding, and perceived control in a service encounter setting. A **service encounter** involves the interactions that occur between a consumer and representatives of an organization.[11] In the study, slides were taken of patrons in a bank and in a bar at various points in time. From among the 50 slides taken in the bar and the bank, those best representing high-, moderate-, and low-density situations in each setting were selected. Respondents then read descriptions of banking and bar situations, saw the photos, and were asked to estimate the reactions of a hypothetical customer to the situation faced. In the experiment, half of the respondents learned that the customer had little choice and the other half learned that the customer had choice about being in the buying situation (e.g., in the bank case, the person had to make a deposit immediately or could make it at another time).

The pattern of results supported a model of behavior shown in Figure 14-3. That is, the level of choice and the density of customers influenced the level of

Figure 14-3 The effects of density and crowding on consumer behavior in a retailing setting. (Figure based upon Michael K. Hui and John E. G. Bateson, "Perceived Control and the Effects of Crowding and Consumer Choice on the Service Experience," *Journal of Consumer Research*, Vol. 18, September 1991, pp. 174–184.)

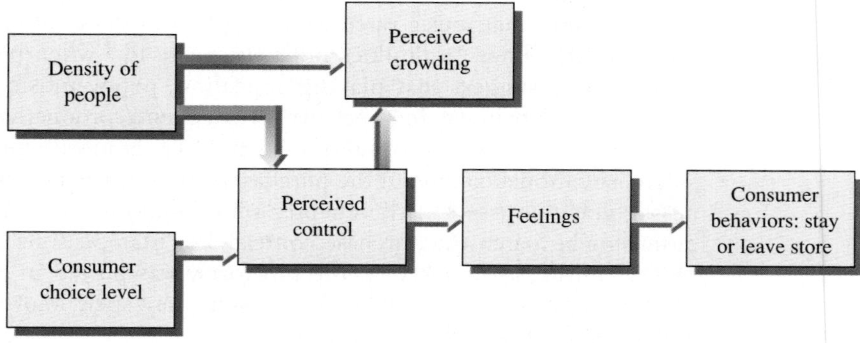

perceived control. In turn, perceived control and density influenced the experience of crowding. These factors then influenced the feelings of the consumer and his or her tendency to stay or leave the situation. The researchers found that when the hypothetical consumer had no choice, the raters actually perceived levels of density to be higher than when the consumer had a choice. Also, when little control was felt, the crowding was perceived as higher, feelings were more negative, and the hypothetical consumer was seen as wanting to leave the situation.

As with the case of music, though, in some circumstances high density levels may be perceived as beneficial. In the study just mentioned, higher density levels were associated with more perceived control in the bar setting but lower perceived control in the bank setting. Thus, when consumers are seeking an "experience," such as a being in a bar or attending a sporting event or rock concert, the high levels of density may enhance the overall impact. In any context there is probably some optimum level of density. For example, when dining out, one has an uncomfortable feeling if the restaurant is nearly empty. Conversely, if the restaurant is so full that you are jostled and receive poor service, the experience is equally negative. The optimum level of density is somewhere between the two extremes. Figure 14-4 depicts the excitement that can be generated by a crowd at a sporting event.

Consumer Crowd Behavior

In a number of circumstances consumers show the same kinds of behavior as found in the actions of hysterical crowds. In such instances consumers become irrational and do things as part of a crowd that they would never do alone. During the Christmas of 1983, consumers exhibited such crowd behavior. Cabbage Patch dolls became so important to shoppers that mobs literally formed outside of department stores when news spread that the store carried the dolls. In a number of instances people were injured, and police had to be called in to control the unruly shoppers.

In European and South American countries, spectators at important soccer events have been known to turn into mobs. For example, in April 1989, 93 people were killed at a soccer match in Sheffield, England. Most were killed as fans without tickets surged into the crowded stadium, crushing spectators against an 8-foot-high steel fence.

The factors that cause normal consumers to evolve into crowds are still not understood completely. In 1896 Gustav Le Bon, a Frenchman, suggested that people go into hypnotic trances when they are part of a mob, such that a collective mind is formed. A more likely explanation is that such a large grouping causes a high degree of physiological arousal among each of the members. The high arousal results in the tendency of each member of the crowd to act on his or her dominant idea or tendency. Because a similar idea brought the group together, the individuals within the crowd are likely to share the common tendency to action. Unfortunately, in many instances the dominant tendency involves aggressiveness, although it could also be the urge to buy, as in the case of the Cabbage Patch dolls. When combined with the fact that each person in a crowd becomes inconspicuous, individual responsibility is lost. Thus the usual norms that control behavior do not apply. The result is an unruly, highly aroused group of people who are not acting as individuals and are not subject to the standard norms that control behavior. The results can be riots, runs on banks, or panic buying of a product in short supply.

Figure 14-4 Crowds form a part of the situational context at sporting events and can increase excitement levels dramatically. (Reproduced courtesy of the Oklahoma State University Public Information Office.)

The Effects of Store Location

Those in real estate sales have a rule of thumb, which states that the primary factors influencing the value of a piece of property are *location, location, and location*. Those who study retailing echo this point, and location's contribution to store choice has received a large amount of research.

Store location influences consumers from several perspectives. The size of a trading area in which a store is located affects the overall number of people who are likely to be drawn to it. The analogy of a planet's gravitational effects has been used to predict how many people will go outside their town's boundaries to shop in other cities. Called the **gravitational model**, the formulation proposes that trading areas act like planets and attract outside shoppers in proportion to the relative populations of the towns in question and to the square of the inverse of the distance between the towns.[12]

Other research has found that the selection of which shopping center a consumer patronizes is influenced by the distance to the shopping center from the person's residence. A number of factors have been found to influence shopping center choice, such as price and variety. Nonetheless, one general rule is that the farther away a shopping center is, the less likely a person is to patronize it.[13]

In addition to actual distance, perceived distance may also influence store selection. Research has shown that consumers have "cognitive maps" of the geography of a city. Interestingly, the perceptual maps of the locations of retail stores may not match the actual relationships. Such factors as ease of parking, merchandise quality, and ease of driving to the shopping center can make the distance seem shorter or longer than it actually is.[14]

The Effects of Store Layout

Stores are designed to facilitate customer movement, to assist in the presentation of merchandise, and to help create a particular atmosphere. The overall goal is to maximize profits by increasing sales through a cost-effective store design. **Store layout** can influence consumer reactions and buying behavior. For example, the placement of aisles influences traffic flow. The location of items and departments relative to traffic flow can dramatically influence sales. In one case an appetizer-deli section was moved from the rear of a grocery store to a high-traffic area near the store's front. Sales in the department increased over 300%. This was significant because the profit margins were substantially higher in the deli than in other departments in the store.[15]

How seating arrangements are designed can dramatically influence communication patterns. It has been argued that airport terminals are designed to discourage people from talking comfortably to each other. Chairs are bolted down and placed so that people cannot face each other and converse from a comfortable distance. The reason for the antisocial arrangement of furniture in airports is presumably to drive people into airport bars and cafeterias, where space is arranged more comfortably—and where customers spend money.[16]

The Effects of Atmospherics

A store's atmosphere delivers a message to consumers, such as "this store has high-quality merchandise." **Atmospherics** is a more general term than store layout; it deals with how managers can manipulate the design of the building, the interior space, the layout of the aisles, the texture of the carpets and walls, the scents, colors, shapes, and sounds experienced by customers. Even the arrangement of merchandise, the types of displays, and the poses of mannequins can influence consumers' perceptions of store atmosphere. These elements are pulled together well in the definition developed by Philip Kotler, which describes atmospherics as "the effort to design buying environments to produce specific emotional effects in the buyer that enhance his probability of purchase."[17]

Atmosphere can be viewed as one component of store image. A variety of factors combine to create a store image, such as

1. The merchandise.
2. The store's service.
3. The clientele.

4. The store's convenience.
5. The store's promotional activities.
6. The store's atmosphere.[18]

Atmosphere, then, is that component of the store image resulting from the physical characteristics of the store.

Researchers have argued that store atmosphere influences the extent to which consumers spend beyond their planned levels in a store.[19] The store's atmosphere influences a shopper's emotional state, which then leads to increased or decreased shopping. Emotional state is made up of two dominant feelings—pleasure and arousal.[20] The combination of these elements results in the consumer spending either more or less time in the store.

Figure 14-5 diagrams these relationships. When the atmosphere arouses the consumer (say, from bright colors and a strong scent) and positive emotions already exist, the buyer tends to spend more time in the store and has an increased tendency to affiliate with people.[21] Such a situation is likely to result in increased buying. In contrast, if the environment is not pleasurable, increased arousal could result in decreased buying. Research by psychologists has shown that dominant tendencies are more likely to be activated when people become aroused. If the dominant tendency is to leave the store, increased arousal tends to increase the desire to leave.

Philip Kotler, among others, has emphasized the effects of atmospherics on emotions. His approach links the study of atmospherics directly to the experiential perspective on consumer behavior. However, atmospherics can also be understood from the behavioral influence perspective on consumer behavior. In particular, the layout of buildings and the design of traffic corridors in cities, malls, and stores directly influences the movements of consumers in many cases without their behavior first being influenced by either beliefs or feelings. As Winston Churchill was quoted as saying, "First we shape our buildings and then they shape us."[22]

Figure 14-5 Atmospherics and shopping behavior. (Adapted from a discussion in Robert Donovan and John Rossiter, "Store Atmosphere: An Environmental Psychology Approach," *Journal of Retailing*, Vol. 58, Spring 1982, pp. 34–57.)

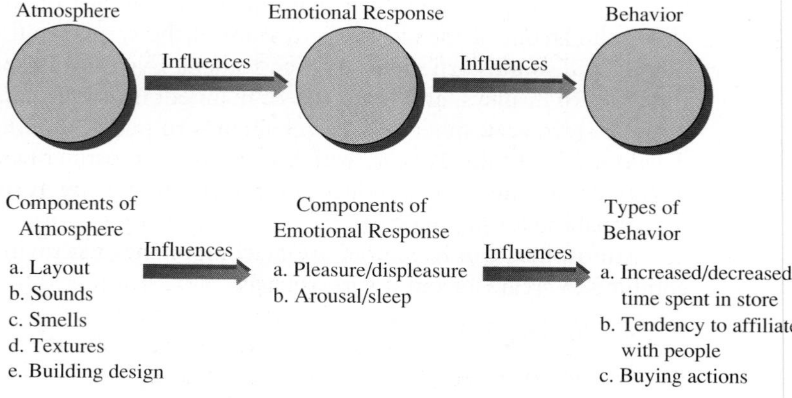

A variety of other studies have found that a building's atmosphere influences its inhabitants. Psychologists have found that surroundings can influence the mental outlook of people.[23] Some have suggested that increasing the number of windows and the sunlight admitted to rooms can actually improve people's mood. Observers have found that as illumination in a tavern increases, the noise level rises. Lowering the noise level and illumination increases the length of time customers will spend in a bar.[24] Even something as simple as carpeting can influence people. Administrators have reported that students are more restrained in carpeted hallways and classrooms, presumably because the atmosphere has been altered.[25]

The spatial arrangements found in a retail store have important consumer behavior effects, which can be summarized in four statements:

1. Space modifies and shapes consumer behavior.
2. Retail store space affects consumers through the stimulation of the senses.
3. Retail stores are like other aesthetic surroundings—they affect perceptions, attitudes, and images.
4. Stores can be programmed through space utilization to create desired customer reactions.[26]

In addition, researchers have proposed that atmosphere becomes increasingly important as the number of competitors increases, as the differences in product and price decrease among the competitors, and as the market becomes segmented on life-style and social class differences.[27] A retail store's atmosphere can be used as a tool to differentiate one retailer from another and to attract specific groups of consumers who seek the feelings derived from the atmosphere. Highlight 14-1 discusses some examples of how the physical environment can be used to influence consumers.

In general, the nature of retail stores shapes the experience of acquiring a product or service. In a service setting the physical and social surroundings may become a part of the service itself. For example, the nature of a concert or a play is shaped in large part by lighting, the characteristics of the set, the way sound is produced, and the characteristics of the other people who are sharing the experience. As a result, the investigation of the physical surroundings is a key element of market research.

SOCIAL SURROUNDINGS

The area of **social surroundings** deals with the effects of other people on a consumer in a consumption situation. The information provided in Chapter 15, Group Processes I: Group, Dyadic, and Diffusion Processes, applies directly to this topic. For example, the presence of a group can result in conformity pressures on a consumer. If a college student belongs to a fraternity or sorority, certain pressures may exist to purchase particular brands of beverages, clothing, and even automobiles. Similarly, knowledge that a consumption situation involves the presence of other people can dramatically influence a consumer's actions. The type of snack foods that someone buys may be affected by the knowledge that others will be present when the snacks are consumed. One author found that light/salty snacks tended to be bought in part as something to have around the house if friends should drop by.[28]

HIGHLIGHT 14-1

Managing the Physical Environment

Peter Drucker, the management guru, suggests that by looking at what is happening to retailing in Europe, we can see its future in North America. While for the last 30 years the mall and shopping centers have dominated retailing, a different trend is occurring in Europe. Instead, freestanding stores and mini-malls are where the action is. The reason, as stated by one successful discount European retailer, is that malls "... submerge the personality of the individual store into the anonymity of the parking lot." In addition, shopping is being redefined. Retailers are developing methods in which consumers "do not have to ask, do not have to wait. It means that customers know where goods are the moment they enter the store, in which colors and sizes, and at what price. It means providing *information*." In sum, people want "painless" shopping [1].

The threats of crime, rowdy crowds, traffic, and even homeless people are making consumers think twice about going to large urban malls. American firms, however, are beginning to respond to the environmental factors that are causing consumers to avoid malls and department stores. For example, in 1993 a huge mall, called CityWalk, opened near Los Angeles. The goal is to make the mall feel like a city. Combining entertainment and shopping, the mall reminds people of Venice Beach. Men lift barbells, with bikini-clad women watching them on a make-believe beach. The goal is to re-create the look and feel of L.A. without the crime. A public policy issue arises here, however. Rather than flee urban areas, wouldn't society be better off if companies cleaned up the very city blocks that they are imitating?

Other more traditional retailers are taking steps to spiff up their stores. For example, a

Similarly, other people can influence the impact of the communications situation on the consumer. For example, the presence of others in a room is likely to lessen the degree to which a television viewer pays attention to the advertisements that cross the screen. In a personal-selling situation, the presence of a friend could lower the impact of the sales presentation. Research on conformity found that subjects conformed to the views of a group even when they knew objectively that the group was wrong. However, if at least one other member of the group concurred with the subject in the experiments, the group conformity effect was lost.[29] Thus, in a sales encounter, it is likely that if a friend were brought along, he or she would lessen the impact of the sales presentation. That person could act to buttress the views of the buyer against the sales message of the seller.

Social motives sometimes explain why people go out and shop.[30] Shopping can be an important social experience for consumers. While on a shopping excursion, one can meet new people and possibly make friends with them. In one study researchers recorded the social interactions of 100 randomly selected individuals who entered a large mall alone.[31] In 51% of the cases the interactions between these subjects and others were informational, such as the person asking someone where to find an item. Twenty-three percent of the interactions were perfunctory, where the person acknowledged a person's presence. Interestingly, though, in 26% of the cases social interactions occurred. In these instances a conversation took place between the

Sears gutted one of its stores in Mexico City and put in new colors, lighting, and signage. The result was an overall increase in sales of 175%. Express has developed the strategy of designing its stores to resemble Parisian boutiques, including an Arc de Triomphe replica and mock Magritte murals. As one analyst said, "Even in tough economic times, retailers might cut back on staff or inventory, but they know it's not the time to skimp on store design" [2].

One key function of the design of stores and the physical environment is to create a desired mood state in customers. In malls, managers seek to create a friendly, happy mood that leads to increased buying. Movie and stage producers, on the other hand, sometimes seek to create a fearful, anxious mood. In early 1988 a Broadway play, *The Phantom of the Opera*, was launched. The play's director sought to place the audience in a creepy, jumpy mood prior to even going into the theater. To create this mood, the entire facade of the theater was painted black. On the marquee four large copper gas lights emitted an eerie blue glow. When the physical layout was combined with an excellent production, tickets for the show were the hardest to get in New York. Figure 14-6 shows a photo of the front of the theater.

REFERENCES

1. Peter Drucker, "The Retail Revolution," *The Wall Street Journal*, July 15, 1993, p. A14.
2. Cyndee Miller, "Glitzy Interiors Transform Stores into 'Destinations,' Boost Sales," *Marketing News*, August 30, 1993, p. 1.

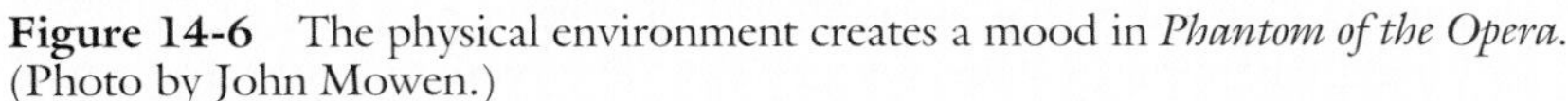

Figure 14-6 The physical environment creates a mood in *Phantom of the Opera*. (Photo by John Mowen.)

person and someone else. The authors interpreted these results as indicative of the importance of social interaction in the shopping experience. They even suggest that the rebirth of central business districts and older malls lies in the rejuvenation of their social significance.[32]

From a retailer's perspective, it is usually beneficial to encourage the social aspects of shopping. One study found that when a shopper is with others, he or she visits more stores and makes more unplanned purchases.[33] In fact, many products would not exist unless people gathered into social groupings. A small industry exists to supply party needs; there are companies that make noise makers, party napkins, specialized mixers, and so on. Even a basic beverage such as beer is consumed in contexts that are often social in nature. In an inventory of beer-drinking situations, half the contexts deal with social situations, such as

Entertaining close friends at home.

Giving a party.

Attending a social event for which you bring your own beverages.

Going to a tavern after work.

Going to a restaurant or lounge on Friday or Saturday night.

Taking a camping trip or beach trip or going on an extended picnic.[34]

Markets can be segmented and products positioned based upon social surroundings. People who anticipate being either alone or with others when using a product may become distinct target markets. For example, Chivas Regal Scotch began an advertising campaign that attempted to persuade people that the product could be consumed when guests were not present. The company was concerned that its market potential was being limited by positioning it as a liquor that was consumed only on special occasions with other people.

THE TASK DEFINITION

The reasons why people buy and consume a product or service are varied. These buying purposes form what is called the consumer's task definition, or the situational reasons for buying or consuming a product or service at a particular time and place. Examples of such buying purposes are plentiful. A purchase could be occasioned by some type of gift situation, such as Christmas, a birthday, graduation, or wedding. The reason for buying a beverage could be to satisfy thirst, to get "high," or to stay awake. In fact, the number of ways for consumers to define the task situation is probably infinite. It is up to the skilled marketing manager to identify such buying reasons that are not adequately met by existing products.

Closely related to the task definition is the usage situation. **Usage situations** form the context in which a product is used and influence the product characteristics sought by a consumer. For example, the usage situation of camping places a set of requirements on the preparation of eating utensils, food packaging, bedding, and shelter. These requirements center around the need for light weight, portability, and durability. The task definition of "going camping," therefore, is a situational factor that may influence the design of products. Those who choose the situation of living outdoors for short periods of time can become a heavy-spending market segment, as Coleman Company, Inc., has discovered.

Occasion-Based Marketing Opportunities

One problem for marketers is that a product can become locked into one usage situation, thereby severely limiting its market potential. Through habit consumers may come to use a product in a particular situation and not consider it appropriate for other situations. Orange juice is a perfect example. By convention, orange juice has become associated with breakfast. Although nutritious and tasty, the beverage has not been adopted by consumers as a thirst-quenching beverage in a way that rivals the soft drinks. The orange juice trade association has spent millions trying to redefine the task definition of the beverage. The campaign based on the theme "Orange juice isn't just for breakfast anymore" has brought national attention to the thirst-quenching aspects of the beverage, and only time will tell whether or not consumers will change their dietary habits.

Other examples of companies or trade associations attempting to change the usage situations of products are numerous. Turkey manufacturers have attempted to persuade Americans to eat the big birds on occasions other than Thanksgiving and Christmas. The uneven pattern of demand for the bird causes major production problems for turkey growers. Another example is the beef industry. In an attempt to broaden the situational usage of the product, the beef trade association has sponsored commercials suggesting that beef makes a good breakfast meat.

The ability of companies to recognize new or overlooked usage situations can result in the discovery of profitable market segments. In the mid-1980s the personal computer boom struck the United States. However, because of extreme competition, profit margins for the manufacturers were extremely thin. Many small companies flourished, however, not by making personal computers, but by tailoring the computer and accompanying software to specific businesses with unique needs. These small companies developed a vertical marketing approach in which they attempted to fulfill all the computer needs of the small business. By using a computer made by a large manufacturer, such as IBM, Digital, Apple, or Tandy, and by developing their own software, these companies could carve out marketing niches by computerizing churches, lumberyards, and medical offices. Such companies had a specific task definition for the computer, and the small entrepreneurial computer companies stepped in to fill this need.

Gift Giving

An important ritual in most societies is the giving and receiving of gifts. By engaging in the ritual pattern of giving, receiving, and giving back, people build reciprocal relations. Bonds of trust and dependence are formed that assist the parties in their everyday lives.[35] It has been suggested that gifts reflect various status hierarchies, denote rights of passage, such as graduations, and influence the socialization of children through the formation of gender roles (e.g., little boys receive toy soldiers and little girls receive Barbie dolls). Gift giving has strong symbolic qualities. Similar to advertisers, gift givers manage meanings conveyed about who the giver is, who the receiver is, and the nature of their relationship. For example, the failure to remove a price tag from a gift is a gross faux pas because it violates the symbolic notion that gifts are nonmonetary expressions of affection.[36]

In Western countries, such as the United States and Canada, gift giving has important economic benefits. In retail stores 30% of sales occur during the Christmas season. More important, Christmas buying has been estimated to account for 50% of annual retail profits. Conservative estimates are that 10% of all retail sales in North American are for gifts. So powerful is the effect of the Christmas season that consumers will even purchase gifts for those whom they consider to be "difficult." Difficult people include those who do not want or need gifts, are likely to be unappreciative of a gift, or are very different from the purchaser.[37]

Retailers recognize how important gift giving is to their profits and take full advantage of the many gift-giving occasions that have been prescribed by society. Table 14-2 provides a partial listing of the occasions when some type of gift is expected by children, husbands, wives, and acquaintances.

The type of gift situation may influence a consumer's involvement in the purchase. For example, the wedding of a close friend may involve the consumer in greater search and lead to more expensive, higher-quality presents than an occasion such as a thank-you for someone who watched his house for a couple of days.[38] Researchers have found that people were more conservative (i.e., purchased "safe" traditional goods) when buying gifts for their spouses than for themselves.[39] One possible reason is that they perceived much greater risk in buying for their spouses than for themselves. Research on what people give as gifts has found that clothing is the most popular item, followed by jewelry, sporting goods, homemade items, and phonograph records and tapes.[40]

TABLE 14-2

Some Gift-Giving Occasions

A. Various religious days	**D.** Legislated days
1. Christmas	**14.** Thanksgiving
2. Easter	**15.** Halloween
3. Hanukkah	**16.** Mother's Day
4. Confirmations	**17.** Father's Day
5. Christenings	**18.** Grandparent's Day
B. Birth-related days	**19.** Children's Day
6. Birthday	**20.** Valentine's Day
7. A child's birth	**E.** Leaving and coming
8. Baby shower	**21.** Going on trip—bon voyage
9. Expectant Mother's Day	**22.** Return from trip
C. Wedding-related days	**23.** Retirement
10. Weddings	**24.** Graduation
11. Wedding shower	**F.** Miscellaneous
12. Wedding anniversay	**27.** Sympathy
13. Wedding engagement	**28.** Hostess gifts
	29. Congratulations

An important question concerns why people give gifts. Gift giving can be analyzed from the perspective of the 2 × 2 matrix shown in Figure 14-7. On the vertical axis, one finds two gift types—voluntary gifts and obligatory gifts.[41] Voluntary gifts are those made with a minimum of outside pressures forcing the action. In contrast, obligatory gifts are those made as a result of strong social norms pressuring the person into the action. On the horizontal axis is the degree to which self-interest influences the gift. In cases of low self-interest, the giver has few ulterior motives for the action. In contrast, on occasions when high self-interest exists, ulterior motives play a predominant role in the gift giving.

Gift-giving motives are found in the four cells of the matrix found in Figure 14-7. When the gift is voluntary and low self-interest is present, an altruistic motive exists for the action. An example of an altruistic gift would be giving a friend a small present completely out of the blue to cheer him up. In contrast, when the gift is voluntary but high self-interest exists, the motive is frequently one of creating an obligation. Giving a woman an expensive present in the hopes of creating an obligation that she may reciprocate with sexual favors is an example. On the other hand, low-involvement ritual gifts occur when an obligation exists but the giver has low self-interest in the exchange. Giving presents to acquaintances at Christmas, birthdays, and graduations fits this category. Finally, when an obligation exists but the person has a high self-interest in the exchange, high-involvement reciprocity occurs. In such instances, there are strong pressures to give. The exchange relationship may be highly important to the person, and love or friendship may be involved. (An example would be purchasing an anniversary present for one's wife because forgetting the event would lead to extremely dire consequences.)

A recent study investigated differences in the gift giving of 299 men and women at Christmas in a large Canadian city. The results revealed that women were much more involved in the task than men. Women started shopping earlier (October rather than November), spent more hours shopping per gift (2.4 versus 2.1 hours), and had fewer of their gifts exchanged (10% versus 16%). The only area in which

Figure 14-7 Gift-giving motivations result from degree of self-interest and gift type.

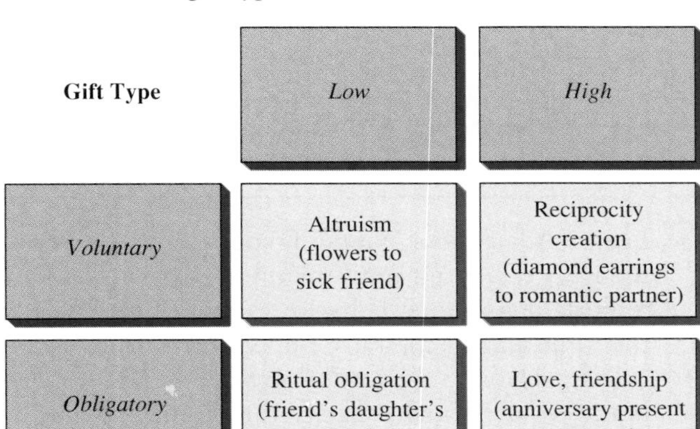

men surpassed women was in the amount spent per gift: $91.25 versus $62.13 (Canadian dollars).[42]

It should also be noted that consumers not only give gifts to others, they also purchase gifts for themselves. Indeed, many of the same situational variables that influence purchasing gifts for others also motivate consumers to buy for themselves. As noted by one researcher, **self-gifts** are premeditated, indulgent, relevant to the self, and are context bound.[43] They may be given as a reward for an accomplishment (e.g., making a high grade on a consumer behavior test), as therapy for a disappointment (e.g., failing to get a job that was wanted), or as part of a holiday or life transition (e.g., a birthday, graduation, or divorce).[44] Self-gifts may range in size from purchasing a donut to reward early-morning exercise to buying a new car to reward a recent promotion. Recent research has found that consumers higher in the personality trait of materialism tend to purchase self-gifts more frequently, particularly as a means to manage their moods. Such individuals appear to associate buying with happiness.[45] A quote from one of the respondents in the study illustrates how a self-gift can be purchased to buy happiness.

> I bought a diamond ring for myself. It made me feel worthwhile, loved, secure. My husband doesn't believe in giving diamond rings, so I had to accept the fact that I had to buy one for myself if I wanted to get all those good feelings.

In summary, the consumer's reason for making a purchase strongly influences his or her buying behavior. For example, when a consumer is buying clothing, the task definition specifies the attributes the article should possess. The female consumer must consider the qualities of women's clothing designed for a specific context, such as swimming, sunbathing, interviewing for a job, going to class, and going to a formal party. For the product manager, identifying the tasks in which consumers are involved can result in opportunities to design new products or to reposition established brands.

Prior to leaving gift giving, readers should keep in mind one recent research finding. In a series of four studies, the author found strong evidence that those who give gifts should take great pains to wrap them nicely.[46] Wrapping a gift results in more positive attitudes toward owning the product. Nicely wrapped gifts appear to place the recipients in a better mood state, which causes them to enjoy the entire process to a greater degree. So, for you gift givers out there—WRAP THOSE PRESENTS!

TIME AS AN ENVIRONMENTAL INFLUENCER

In his "Advice to a Young Tradesman," Ben Franklin said, "Remember that time is money." It was not until the mid-1970s, however, that time was recognized to be an important consumer behavior variable. Since then, some authors have even suggested that time may be the most important variable in consumer behavior because it plays a role in so many theoretical areas.[47] As discussed earlier in the text, definitions of brand loyalty should specify the period of time over which the buying behavior is considered. Similarly, studies of the diffusion of innovations require the consideration of how rapidly in time a new product or service is adopted. In behavioral learning theory (see Chapter 5) an important concept is that rewards must be given in close temporal proximity to a behavior to be effective. These examples represent only a few of the cases in which time is an important consumer behavior variable.

Time can be analyzed from three different perspectives: (1) individual differences in the conception of time, (2) time as a product, and (3) time as a situational variable.

Individuals and Time

At the individual level, various consumers may use time differently. People use their time in four different ways—work, necessities, housework, and leisure.[48] These groupings are arranged on a continuum of obligatory to discretionary uses of time. People have little control over when and how long they work. Somewhat more control exists concerning necessities, such as how long one sleeps and when one eats. The amount of effort spent on maintaining a clean, attractive place to live (i.e., housework) is much more variable. In fact, families in which both spouses work tend to spend less time on "household production." Finally, people have the most discretion in how they use their leisure time. Research has shown that leisure time is strongly affected by outside situational variables, such as the weather.[49]

Time can be viewed as a resource, and how people choose to spend their time says a great deal about them. The activities in which consumers engage can be categorized as to whether they are substitutable or complementary based upon their relationship to time.[50] **Substitute activities** are separate activities that satisfy the same need for the consumer; furthermore, the two activities are mutually exclusive in the sense that they cannot take place together. For example, participation in handball and racquetball would be considered by many as substitutes. Similarly, working in the garden versus playing golf are probably substitutes for most people. **Complementary activities** are those that naturally take place together. Thus a person may jointly engage in gardening and mowing the grass to fulfill the need of having a beautifully landscaped home. Complementary activities do not have to occur simultaneously. They can be defined over a period of time, such as a week or a month.[51] How consumers make choices in the way they use their time says a great deal about their life-styles.

Various constraining factors influence the substitutability and complementarity of activities. For example, it has been proposed that the employment status of the wife and the presence or absence of children may strongly influence how time is spent by husbands and wives. (These issues will be discussed in more detail in Chapter 16, which discusses family processes.) In fact, evidence exists that a husband's and wife's satisfaction with their marriage is influenced by the extent to which they share views on the complementarity and substitutability of activities. The evidence indicates that couples that jointly participate in activities have greater amounts of marital satisfaction.[52]

How individuals view time is even influenced by their culture.[53] Highlight 14-2 discusses how different cultures may view time in diverse ways.

Time as a Product

Of course, time can also be a type of product. Many purchases are made to buy time. Appliances such as microwave ovens, garbage disposals, and trash compactors exist in part for the purpose of saving time. Fast-food restaurants have flourished because

HIGHLIGHT 14-2

My Time Is Not Your Time

The amount of time available to consumers is an important situational variable. However, the discussion of time assumes a particular cultural perspective. Not everyone views time in the same way. Three separate ways of viewing time have been identified.

LINEAR SEPARABLE TIME The type of time on which most Americans and Western Europeans run is "linear separable." People on "Anglo" time have a set of perceptions not shared by much of the rest of the world. Time is viewed as divided into a past, present, and future. It can be divided up and allocated for specific tasks. Anglos speak of time as being spent, saved, wasted, and bought. For them, time is like a ribbon that stretches into the future. The objective is to spend time appropriately in the present so that the future will be better. A heavy future orientation exists. Activities are enjoyed not as ends in themselves but as means to an end.

CIRCULAR TRADITIONAL TIME People on circular time tend to be regulated by the natural cycles of the seasons, sun, and moon. For them time does not stretch into the future. Rather, it is circular, such that the future offers neither joy nor fear because it will be much like the present. People operating on circular time tend to do today only things that have to be done today. In the Spanish culture this is called *mañana*: people put off what can be put off and do what has to be done. Anglos who are engaged in international marketing often have trouble dealing with people who run on circular time. They may not see a relation between time and money and may have a habit of not appearing on time for meetings or of trying to accomplish several tasks at one time.

PROCEDURAL TRADITIONAL TIME People on procedure time tend to have little written history and are governed by the task rather than by the time. If asked when a meeting will occur, the response may be, "When the time is right." When asked how long the meeting will take, the response might be, "When the meeting is over." Because Native American culture follows such a pattern, the phenomenon has been called "Indian" time. This view of the world results in extremely loose time schedules. Such individuals see no connection between time and money, and the idea of wasting time is irrelevant. The task is the key.

Based on these divergent approaches to time, it is clear that when time is categorized as a situation, we are referring to "Anglo" time. Factors that might influence the buying behavior of Anglos would likely have much less influence on people running on "Indian" time.

Based on Robert Graham, "The Role of Perception of Time in Consumer Research," *Journal of Consumer Research*, Vol. 7 (March 1981), pp. 335–342.

consumers have a need to obtain nourishment while on the go. A name has been given to the individual who engages in such behavior—the time-buying consumer.

Corporations frequently use the time-saving qualities of their products as a key promotional idea. For example, the advertisement from Perception Technology shown in Figure 14-8 illustrates this concept. Using the bold headline "If you manage a call center, it's time we had a talk," the company effectively makes the point that their computerized voice response system can reduce costs by providing service continuously, that is, all the *time*.

Figure 14-8 The time-saving qualities of the product are a key promotional idea in the ad. (Courtesy of Perception Technology.)

If time acts as a product attribute, then one might expect advertisers to use time-oriented appeals in their promotional materials. A study investigated the changing usage of time-oriented appeals between 1890 and 1988. The researchers analyzed print ads in one magazine (*The Ladies' Home Journal*) over the 100-year period. The authors found that the proportion of ads that used time as the primary appeal in the ad increased in a linear fashion over the years. In 1890 less than 5% of the ads appealed predominantly to time. By the late 1980s nearly 50% of the ads included a time-oriented appeal as a major component of the print ad. An example can be found in an ad for Hunt's Manwich (from 1986) headlined "When it's dinner time and time is tight."[54] These results vividly depict the dramatic change in the importance of timeliness as a product attribute over the past 100 years.

Time as a Situational Variable

In addition to recognizing time as a product, it is important to understand **time as a situational variable**. Time is a factor that may influence a consumer's conduct in a given situation. In such cases, time is an independent variable or a factor that affects the actions of consumers.

Generally, the situational characteristic of time that influences consumers is its availability. How much time a consumer has available to do a task, such as buying a product, will influence the strategy used to select and purchase it. Information search is particularly influenced by the availability of time. Researchers have found that as time pressure increases, consumers spend progressively less time searching for information. Similarly, the utilization of available information decreases, and negative or unfavorable information is given more weight in a decision when time pressures are severe.[55]

Recently, an experiment was conducted to directly assess the impact of time pressure on grocery shopping. Actual grocery shoppers participated in the study as part of a consumer panel. They were assigned either to a control group that had no time pressure or to the experimental group, which was asked to complete their shopping in one-half the participants' expected shopping time. The results revealed that the time-pressured group more frequently failed to purchase intended products and made fewer unplanned purchases. Indeed, the results indicated that time pressure caused a decrease in the total number of products purchased. The results also indicated that time pressures caused greater problems when the respondents were shopping in unfamiliar stores.[56] The managerial implication of the study is that to facilitate shopping by time-pressed consumers, retailers should create a shopping environment that makes it easy to locate desired products.

Many products and services have been developed to save consumers time. Such products range from fast-food restaurants to jet aircraft to dental services. Figure 14-9 shows a humorous ad for dentures that uses speed of service as an important attribute.

Time may also interact with other variables to influence purchase behavior. For example, the length of time elapsed since a shopper's last meal has been shown to influence how much he buys at a grocery store.[57] Impulse purchases occur when people are hungry and the aisles seem to be lined with temptations. As noted by the researchers, a person who shops while hungry may find that his or her "imagination readily places potatoes and onions around roasts and transforms pancake mix into a steaming, buttered snack."[58]

Interestingly, a situation–consumer interaction was found in the research on hunger and grocery shopping. The food buying of shoppers classified as overweight was not affected by how long they had gone since their last meal. The effect of buying more when hungry occurred mainly for people of average weight. The authors interpreted the results as indicating that overweight consumers fail to use internal cues to determine their hunger. Rather, they use the presence of food to determine how much to buy and consume.[59] Situation–consumer interactions will be discussed in more detail later in the chapter.

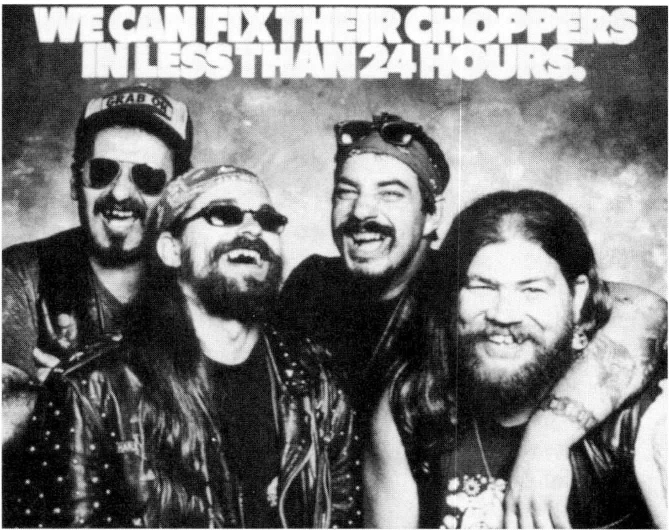

Figure 14-9 This humorous ad markets the firm's denture services as time-saving. (Courtesy of Drs Dental Lab.)

Time of day is an important situational variable that can be used as a means of segmenting products. For example, food products may be marketed for use in the morning (e.g., breakfast foods) or the evening. Michelob Lite beer created an entire advertising campaign whose theme was "The night belongs to Michelob Lite."

In one study a researcher found that time of day actually influenced information processing.[60] In the study respondents were exposed to six new 30-second television commercials over an hour-long period. The respondents saw the commercials in the morning, afternoon, or early evening. They were then given recall and recognition tests either immediately after viewing the commercials or after two hours had passed. The results revealed that immediate recall and recognition were best in the morning and worst in the evening. In contrast, recall and recognition after a two-hour delay were best in the evening and worst in the morning. The authors interpreted the findings as indications of differences in the diurnal rhythms in arousal. In the morning, when arousal is low, consumers may process information differently than in the early evening, when arousal may be higher. An alternative explanation, however, is that the effects of retroactive and proactive interference may operate differently in the morning and evening. Thus immediate recall is better in the morning because of a lack of proactive interference. In contrast, immediate recall is poorer in the evening because of high amounts of proactive interference. (Chapter 4 discusses retroactive and proactive interference.) Regardless of the explanation, these are provocative findings that indicate that advertisers may have to consider the time of day when consumers are exposed to ads when developing strategy.

The situational element of time can influence distribution strategy. Consumers experiencing a shortage of time may want to obtain products quickly and with minimal effort. The drive-through windows at fast-food restaurants exemplify a distribution system that allows customers to obtain burgers, fried chicken, and other foods rapidly. Mail-order, telephone-order, and computer-ordering systems for products have been developed over the years so that consumers do not have to take the time to go to a retail store to make a purchase.

ANTECEDENT STATES

Antecedent states are the temporary physiological and mood states that a consumer brings to a consumption situation. This situational factor relates closely to concepts of the individual consumer discussed in Part 2. Examples of antecedent states include such temporary states as hunger, thirst, lack of sleep, and mood. Mood states are temporary variations on how people feel, which range from happy feelings to neutral mood states to very negative feelings. (The effect of mood on the information processing of consumers was discussed in some detail in Chapter 4, Information Processing II: Memory.)

An example of how temporary physiological states may influence buying behavior was given in the last section. Consumers who shop for groceries while hungry are in danger of making unnecessary impulse purchases.[61] Burger King Corporation has tried to take advantage of hunger urges in its advertising. Using a musical theme in which a chorus sings, "Aren't you hungry, aren't you hungry for a Burger King now?" these television ads show a delicious-looking hamburger and suggest that the audience hurry down to buy one. The goal of such ads is to activate consumers' hunger pangs and tie the name Burger King directly to these urges. Gatorade has pursued a similar strategy by focusing on the temporary state of thirst. In the ads athletes dripping with sweat are shown gulping down Gatorade directly from the bottle. Again, the goal is to tie the beverage graphically to the physiological state it is designed to remedy.

These temporary physiological states may influence buying through two means. First, they may lead to problem recognition. For example, the gnawing hunger pangs in a person's stomach may cause the person to recognize a problem that needs to be solved.

The second way that physiological states may influence consumers is by changing the "feeling" component of the hierarchy of effects. (The various hierarchy of effects models were discussed in Chapter 8.) For example, when a person is hungry, the presence of food is likely to create highly positive feelings concerning consumption. Thus, when hungry, someone who enjoys red meat will have very positive feelings created when he or she sees a porterhouse steak. These unusually positive feelings may then lead to an increased likelihood of purchasing the food product. Similarly, if a shopper happens to be thirsty while in the store, the physiological state is likely to create positive feelings about assorted thirst-quenching beverages.

The Effects of Temporary Mood States on Consumers

Mood states have also been found to influence consumer behavior. In one survey people were asked why they shopped. Two of the reasons given were that they wanted to alleviate either depression or loneliness.[62] In such instances consumers expressed the idea that they used the shopping and purchasing experience to influence their temporary mood state.

Psychologists have conducted studies that investigate the effects of mood on gifts to charities, to others, and to themselves. In these studies, though, the researchers actually influenced the mood of subjects. After creating either positive or negative moods in the subjects, the researchers then took measures of how the changes in mood state affected behavior. In one mood change study, a group of second- and third-grade children were asked to think of something that made them very happy. Another group was asked to think of something that made them feel very sad. A third group was asked not to think of anything in particular. This process of having people think of happy or sad things has been shown to influence effectively a person's mood state. After having their mood influenced, the children were given a chance to help themselves to candy from a treasure chest. The results revealed that in comparison to the control group, those with either a positive or a negative mood took more candy for themselves.[63] Figure 14-10 shows the results of the study.

What the results of the mood study show is that people tend to reward themselves when they feel either good or bad. The mediator of the phenomenon appears to be the affective component of attitudes—the same concept suggested as the explanation for why hungry people buy more in a supermarket. As the authors of the mood study explained, "When one is feeling good, one tends to be more generous to oneself."[64] However, the phenomenon extends beyond self-generosity: a positive mood state likewise results in people being more generous to others.[65]

Why did the children in sad moods also indulge themselves more? The reason seems to be that they took more candy to make themselves feel better. Importantly, the impact of negative moods seems to extend to how much one person will help another. In general, the research evidence shows that people over the age of 6 will help others more when they are feeling bad than when they are in a neutral mood state. Again, the motivation seems to be that people derive good feelings from helping others. When a person feels bad, he or she may seek out ways to feel better and consequently help others more.

One study assessed the mood states and buying behavior of 89 shoppers in specialty stores. The results revealed positive correlations between the mood states of

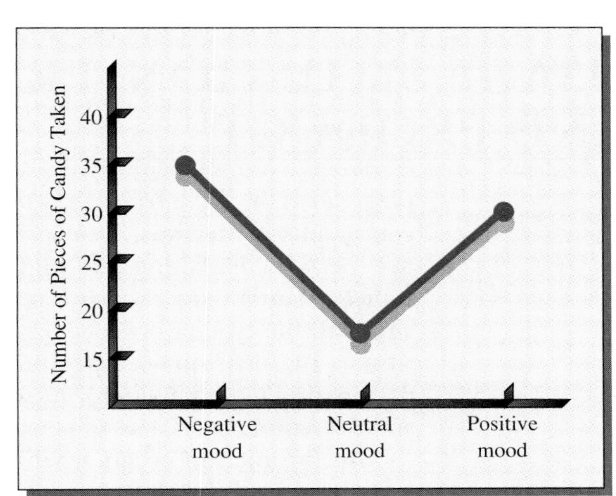

Figure 14-10

Effects of moods on self-reward. (Data from D. Rosenham, B. Underwood, and B. Moore, "Affect Moderates Self-gratification and Altruism," *Journal of Personality and Social Psychology*, Vol. 30, October 1974, pp. 546–552.)

the shoppers and (1) the number of items bought, (2) the amount of money spent, and (3) the actual time spent in the store.[66] Of course, in such correlational studies the cause–effect relationship is difficult to determine. Thus one question involves whether the positive mood state influenced buying or the buying influenced the mood state.

Some researchers have argued that factors within a retail store environment may influence mood. Factors such as a salesperson's smile, background music, lighting, and colors may all influence mood.[67] Researchers have found that evaluations of others made in a "beautiful" room were better than those made in an "average" or "ugly" room.[68] Other evidence indicates that the moods induced by retail environments may affect purchase intentions. For example, shopping intentions increased for stores rated as pleasant.[69]

Recent evidence suggests that temporary mood states may influence consumer reactions to advertisements. In the experiment, one-half of the subjects read an uplifting story that placed them in highly positive moods. All respondents then evaluated a print advertisement. The results revealed that those placed in a positive mood state had more favorable brand attitudes and fewer counterarguments to the ad. The authors suggested that those in positive mood states revealed less cognitive processing, which would cause fewer counterarguments to occur. In addition, positive mood state tended to cause subjects to process information peripherally. (See the elaboration likelihood model in Chapter 10.) Thus those in good moods were less affected by central cues, such as argument quality, and more influenced by peripheral cues, such as source attractiveness.[70]

Research on the effects of mood on consumer behavior is still in its infancy. Thus one cannot be sure that mood influences the buying of products in the same way that it affects the taking of candy or the distribution of coupons that can be used to obtain a prize.[71] As one important consumer researcher has observed, a lack of information exists on the impact of mood states on consumers. Such mood states may be particularly effective in influencing consumer buying behavior in retail settings—particularly at the point of purchase. Further, they may be even more important in the buying and selling of services than in the buying and selling of goods.

INTERACTIONS AMONG USAGE SITUATION, PERSON, AND PRODUCT

One can view the buying act as resulting from the interactions that occur among consumption situations, the characteristics of the buying unit/person, and the product (i.e., the marketing offering). Two-way interactions may occur in which consumer situations interact with personal factors (i.e., a situation–person interaction) and with the type of product/service being offered (i.e., a situation–product interactions). In addition, the product and the type of person may interact (i.e., a person–product interaction). In addition, three-way interactions may occur in which an interaction occurs among person, product, and situation variables.[72]

An **interaction** occurs when two or more factors combine to cause a consumer to behave in a different manner than if the two factors were not combined. A situation–product interaction occurs when two products are viewed as useful in different situations. For example, the product Gatorade would be seen by most consumers as appropriate in situations where a consumer has worked up a great thirst, such as after a competitive tennis match. On the other hand, drinking a quart of Canada Dry ginger ale after a hard workout sounds perfectly awful. In contrast, Gatorade would be an inappropriate mixer at a fashionable party, whereas Canada Dry ginger ale would be quite appropriate. Thus the factors of type of product and type of situation interact so that the type of product favored is determined by a situational context. Figure 14-11 diagrams the interactions.

Situation–product interactions form the basis for benefit segmentation. That is, different products are created to offer divergent benefits that may be used in different situations. For example, consider the various types of watches that are marketed. Diving watches were developed to allow someone to tell time while underwater. The benefit provided is the ability to know when one's air is about to run out. In contrast, formal watches were created as ornaments to be worn to decorate the wrist. Their benefit is that they look pretty.

An example of a situation–product interaction is illustrated by a research study developed to probe how purchase agents react to lunches in fancy versus ordinary restaurants. In the study the fanciness of the restaurant represents the type of product, and the reason for the lunch represents the situational factor. (Specifically, the reason for the lunch exemplifies a task definition factor.) The researchers found that the buyers had more favorable evaluations of the suppliers' position in the ordinary restaurant meetings as compared to fancy restaurant meetings. However, if the reason for the lunch had been a celebration within the firm for just having closed a contract, the fancy restaurant may have been more appropriate than the ordinary restaurant. The authors interpreted the results as indicating that sales representatives should be extremely careful in staging business lunches in fancy restaurants. They argued that the restaurant context should fit the business context.[73]

Researchers have investigated the relative contributions of situation, person, and product variables to consumer buying behavior.[74] Table 14-3 summarizes the findings

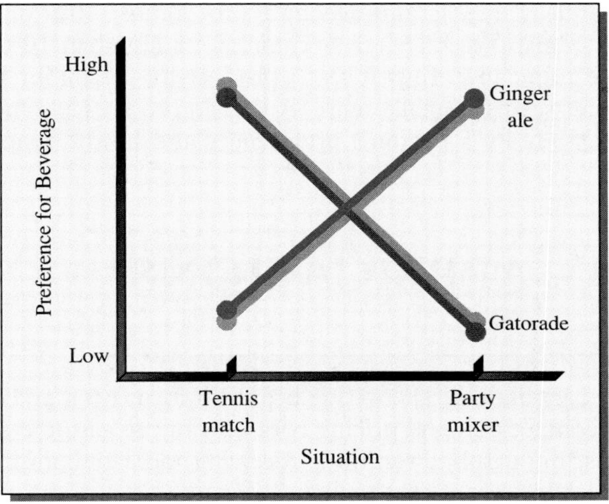

Figure 14-11

Situation-by-product interaction.

TABLE 14-3

Relative Effects of the Situation, Person, and Product on Consumer Buying

	Type of Product					
Source of Influence	*Beverages*	*Meals*	*Snacks*	*Fast Foods*	*Leisure Activities*	*Motion Pictures*
Person	0.5%	4.6%	6.7%	8.1%	4.5%	0.9%
Situation	2.7	5.2	0.4	2.2	2.0	0.5
Product	14.6	15.0	6.7	13.4	8.8	16.6
Product × situation	39.8	26.2	18.7	15.3	13.4	7.0
Person × situation	2.7	2.9	6.1	2.2	4.0	1.9
Product × person	11.8	9.7	22.4	20.1	21.2	33.7
Product × situation × person	[a]	[a]	3.4	[a]	[a]	[a]
Unexplained variance	27.8	36.4	35.6	38.7	46.1	39.4

[a]The percentages are how much variance each of the sources of influence accounted for.

SOURCE: Adapted from R. W. Belk, "Situational Variables and Consumer Behavior," *Journal of Consumer Research*, Vol. 2 (December 1975), p. 160.

of a number of studies. As can be seen, situation explains very little purchase behavior across the various products. It is the interaction of the situation with the product and the person that accounts for the largest fraction of consumer buying behavior. For beverage products, the interaction of the product and the situation accounted for almost 40% of the change in consumer purchases. It should be noted, however, that some authors have argued that the situation itself probably accounts for much more variance in behavior than these results indicate.[75]

An important point to observe in Table 14-3 is that the impact of the situation on consumer buying varied substantially across the types of product. For beverages, the situation and its interactions accounted for almost 40% of the change in consumer buying. Situations, however, accounted for less than 10% of the variation in motion picture attendance. In that case a product-by-person interaction predominated. Such a result seems to make sense. A decision to go see a motion picture would be governed largely by a person's preferences and by the type of movies that are playing.

A MANAGERIAL APPLICATIONS EXAMPLE

In recent years, gasoline retailers have begun to focus on marketing to a far greater extent due to competition and pricing pressures in the gasoline market.[76] Neglected for many years, the gasoline station is receiving increased attention from major oil companies. Several factors account for the increased focus on marketing. First, gasoline consumption has changed little in the last 15 years. Between 1978 and 1991 the number of gallons sold in the United States has actually decreased slightly. Gasoline retailers have found themselves competing for shares in a market that has not grown. Meanwhile, the high cost of real estate and stricter environmental regulations have caused a price squeeze.

The focus on marketing has resulted in a number of changes in how gasoline is sold. First, gasoline stations have moved toward selling a diversified array of products. More and more frequently, the stations are convenience stores that sell food as well as basic household supplies. For example, Ashland Oil Co. focuses on selling high-margin products, such as soda, cigarettes, and diapers. At the same time, store layouts have been redesigned to increase the likelihood that customers will purchase more high-margin, impulse items. One Ashland executive says that the company no longer thinks of itself as operating gasoline stations. The company is now a retailing firm. Amoco is even experimenting with placing Dunkin' Donuts, Burger King, and Dairy Queen stores at some stations.

A study conducted by Phillips Petroleum Co. found that speed of service has replaced price as the most important attribute in purchasing gasoline. As a result the company now builds its stations with side lanes. Cars can easily pass by each other to empty pumps. Mobil has installed pumps that fill up tanks in half the time. Companies are also experimenting with ways to allow customers to pay at the pump—a system that consumer studies show is favored by motorists.

Research has also shown that the lighting around a filling station strongly influences patronage at night. Woman customers are much more likely to purchase gasoline from a brightly lighted station. Shell Oil Co. claims that its lights, which are recessed in yellow canopies, provide a competitive edge because of their warm yellow glow.

Another recent trend in gasoline sales is toward providing a wider range of octane levels for customers. Higher margins on the expensive high-octane gasolines means increased profits. Interestingly, automakers say that the vast majority of cars need only regular unleaded to run properly. One Mobil executive said, "People buy a premium gasoline because they perceive a need."

The Consumer Behavior Analysis

The changing approach to marketing gasoline illustrates a number of aspects of the situational environment. For example, gasoline marketers are beginning to place particular emphasis on designing the physical environment. In considering where to locate the stations, how to arrange lighting and pump location, and how to design the interior of the retail stores, marketers attempt to influence consumer feelings, beliefs, and buying behavior.

The importance of time to consumers also affects managerial strategy. Efforts are being made to increase the speed with which a customer can fill up a car and pay for the gas. Task definition has relevance to what consumers purchase at a filling station. A need to fill up a car acts as the basic reason/occasion for going to a filling station; however, by effectively stocking high-margin impulse items, a retailer may be able to increase the total amount spent by a customer. Gasoline stations situated next to interstate highways are particularly appropriate for building a larger retail store.

People traveling long distances frequently have the simultaneous need for gasoline, food, bathroom facilities, and other miscellaneous products, such as games for kids, audio tapes for the cassette player, and medicines to combat motion sickness.

The Managerial Applications Analysis

Table 14-4 presents the managerial applications analysis for the gasoline marketing case. As can be seen in the table, three concepts pertaining to the situational environment have particular implications for managerial strategy—the physical environment of the gasoline station, the task definition, and time. When making decisions about how to build filling stations, managers must first understand how the physical environment affects consumers. The design of the store and the arrangement of the gasoline pumps are part of the overall product being offered to customers. Market research should be employed to develop an understanding of how consumers react to changes in lighting, the arrangement of pumps, and traffic flow. By creating a physical environment that is safe, clean, and pleasing to the eye, a gasoline marketer follows a positioning strategy that helps to differentiate his station from competitors'.

By recognizing that the task definition of filling up a car may include satisfying other needs as well, a manager may be better prepared for attempting to position a

TABLE 14-4

The Managerial Applications Analysis of the Gasoline Retailer Case

Consumer Concepts	*Managerial Applications*
Physical environment	*Product*—Design station so that arrangement of gasoline pumps is convenient and they are easy to use.
	Market research—Conduct studies to determine how consumers react to changes in lighting, arrangement of pumps, and traffic flow.
Task definition	*Market research*—Identify task definition of what customers do when they gas up their car.
	Positioning—Based upon the market research, design a positioning strategy that fulfills customers needs.
	Product—Design station so as to provide services that match positioning description.
Time	*Market research*—Determine to what extent consumers are pressed for time when using service station.
	Segmentation—Identify different target groups of customers that may have divergent time pressures.
	Product—Design service station so as to meet the time needs of diverse segments of customers.
	Promotional strategy—Promote service station in a manner that communicates overall positioning strategy of management.

filling station. As the Ashland executive commented, the company no longer positions its stores as filling stations. Rather, they are positioned as retail stores. Thus understanding the task definition has implications for market research, positioning, and the marketing mix. That is, managers should perform marketing research to determine what leads consumers to stop at gasoline stations. Based upon this information, it is possible to develop a product and service assortment that fulfills these needs. In turn, the store can be positioned through its various promotional activities in a manner that highlights its ability to fulfill these needs.

The situational variable of time also has implications for the development of managerial strategy. Again, marketing research should be conducted to determine the extent to which consumers are time pressed when they patronize a service station. It may be that different segments exist. For example, perhaps two groups exist—a time-pressed group and a more leisurely paced group. Product and service assortments can be developed for the two groups. In addition, promotional strategy can be employed to position the service station appropriately.

SUMMARY

Consumer situations are those temporary environmental circumstances that form the context within which a consumer activity occurs. Examples of situational factors that influence consumers are physical surroundings, social surroundings, the occasion for which a product is bought (task definition), time, and the consumer's temporary physiological and mood states (antecedent states). These situations may influence consumers when they receive communications about a product or service, when they make a purchase, and when they use the product or service.

The impact of the physical surroundings on consumers is particularly important for retailers. Store layout, atmospherics, crowding, music, and store location are all factors in the physical environment that can affect consumers. Social motives influence why people shop, their involvement in the purchase, and their conformity to the tastes and preferences of others. The task definition deals with the reasons why a product or service is bought. One can think of the task definition in terms of the occasion that spurs a purchase, such as a gift occasion, a party, or even a type of meal (e.g., breakfast and orange juice). Usage occasions can be utilized as a potent segmentation tool. For example, Sony's Walkman radios are positioned to be used while running.

Time is also an important situational variable. Consumers may be segmented based upon their perception and use of time. From this perspective time is viewed as a resource. How consumers choose to spend time reveals much about their lifestyles. Time can also be viewed as a product characteristic. Thousands of products have been created and positioned on the basis of their ability to save time. Time may be conceptualized as a situational variable. In this case the availability of time influences consumer actions. In addition, time of day may influence consumer actions, such as product choice and information processing.

Finally, antecedent states concern the temporary physical and mood states that influence consumer buying behavior. Whether people are happy or sad, hungry or thirsty, can influence their attitude about the purchase and how much they buy.

The type of situation can directly influence consumers' buying behavior. Frequently, however, the situation interacts with the product and the individual characteristics of consumers to influence buying behavior. For example, situations interact strongly with the type of product for beverages. The type of beverage bought for a party (choice from task definition) may be quite different from that bought for quenching thirst (choice from antecedent state).

KEY TERMS

antecedent states
atmospherics
complementary activities
consumer environment
consumer situations
crowding
density
gravitational model
interaction
marketing triad
mood states
physical surroundings
self-gifts
service encounter
social surroundings
store layout
substitute activities
task definition
time as a situational variable
usage situation

REVIEW QUESTIONS

1. Define the concept of a consumer situation. What are the five types of situations that have been identified?
2. Give an example of a situation–person interaction. Give an example of a situation–product interaction.
3. For which types of products does one find most of the variance in buying accounted for by situation–product interactions? For which types of products does one find most of the variance in buying accounted for by person–product interactions? (*Hint*: Look at Table 14-3.)
4. The effect of music on shoppers is one example of how physical surroundings can influence buying. Identify five other means through which the physical surroundings can influence buying.
5. What are the effects of a store's location on consumer store choice?
6. What are five factors that influence consumers' perceptions of a store's image?
7. Draw the model of how atmospherics influences shopping behavior presented in Figure 14-5. What are the components of store atmosphere?
8. How can the presence of other people influence the consumption situation, the purchase situation, and the communications situation?
9. Define the term task definition. Indicate five categories of gift-giving situations.
10. Identify four of the six reasons why people give gifts, as mentioned in the chapter.
11. Identify and give examples of three ways in which time may influence consumption activities.
12. Different cultures may view time divergently. Discuss the three views of time held in various cultures.
13. Define the concept of the antecedent state. What are two types of antecedent states and how might each influence consumption?

DISCUSSION QUESTIONS

1. The shoe industry is segmented to a large extent upon the usage situation of the product. Identify as many different usage situations as you can for which manufacturers have created different types of shoes.
2. The situation can interact with the type of person and with the type of product. Give an example of each. (*Hint:* Think about your own characteristics and preferences and about those of someone else who is quite different. Compare how each of you responds to various types of situations and products.)
3. Draw a diagram of the grocery store with which you are most familiar. Identify the specific physical features of the store that are designed to move customers in specific patterns and to encourage customers to purchase specific products.
4. From your own experience, think of two consumer behavior settings where large numbers of people were present. To what extent did you find that the presence of people enhanced the overall consumption experience? What are the circumstances in which large numbers of people detract from the consumption experience?
5. Draw a map of your community. Place on the map the location of where you live and where you attend college. Now draw in the locations of the retailers you most frequently patronize. Do you find any relationship between the location of the retailers and the location of your residence and college?
6. Considering all the components that help to create a store atmosphere, describe in one or two paragraphs the atmosphere of two popular eating or drinking establishments in your community. To what extent do you think the atmosphere of these establishments was consciously created?
7. List all the gifts you have given to people over the past year. What was the occasion that prompted the giving of each of these gifts? In which instances did you purchase a product that was designed specifically to be given as a gift?
8. Identify five products or services that differentiate themselves from competition based upon whether they save or use up time. How do these products communicate this benefit to consumers? Try to identify a new product or service that could be marketed as saving time for college students. To what extent is there a market for products and services that help you use up time?
9. Suppose you were an advertising executive assigned the task of developing a campaign for a company that sells exotic coffees. Your task is to design an advertising campaign based upon the idea that people drink coffee because of their good or bad moods. Develop a print ad carrying out this task.
10. Examine the ethical implications of oil companies selling high-octane gasoline to consumers who own cars that do not need the more expensive product.

ENDNOTES

1. Brenton Welling, "Of Spenser, the Red Sox, and Drinking in the Stands," *Business Week*, August 17, 1988, p. 66.
2. Erik Larson, "It Seems Every Fish Has Its Day—Even the Hated Eelpoint," *The Wall Street Journal*, February 20, 1987, pp. 1, 12.
3. Russell Belk, "An Exploratory Assessment of Situational Effects in Buyer Behavior," *Journal of Marketing Research*, Vol. 11 (May 1974), p. 160. For a view of situations from a more cognitive perspective, see Luk Warlop and S. Ratneshwar, "The Role of Usage Context in Consumer Choice: A Problem Solving Perspective," in *Advances in Consumer Research*, Vol. 20, Leigh McAlister and Michael L. Rothschild, eds. (Provo, UT: Association for Consumer Research, 1993), pp. 377–382.
4. Ronald E. Milliman, "Using Background Music to Affect the Behavior of Supermarket

Shoppers," *Journal of Marketing*, Vol. 46 (Summer 1982), pp. 86–91.

5. Ronald Milliman, "The Influence of Background Music on the Behavior of Restaurant Patrons," *Journal of Consumer Research*, Vol. 13 (September 1986), pp. 286–289.
6. For an excellent summary of the effects of music on consumers, see Gordon C. Bruner II, "Music, Mood, and Marketing," *Journal of Marketing*, Vol. 54 (October 1990), pp. 94–104. Also, see Judy I. Alpert and Mark I. Alpert, "Contributions from a Musical Perspective on Advertising in Consumer Behavior," in *Advances in Consumer Research*, Vol. 18, Rebecca H. Holman and Michael R. Solomon, eds. (Provo, UT: Association for Consumer Research, 1991), pp. 232–238. Readers should also note that a growing literature exists on the impact of music on consumer responses to advertising. For example, see Deborah J. Macinnis, "The Differential Role of Characteristics of Music on High- and Low-Involvement Consumers' Processing of Ads," *Journal of Consumer Research*, Vol. 18 (September 1991), pp. 161–173.
7. James J. Kellaris and Robert J. Kent, "The Influence of Music on Consumers' Temporal Perceptions: Does Time Fly When You're Having Fun?" *Journal of Consumer Psychology*, Vol. 1, no. 4 (1992), pp. 365–376.
8. Charles S. Areni and David Kim, "The Influence of Background Music on Shopping Behavior: Classical Versus Top-Forty," in *Advances in Consumer Research*, Vol. 20, Leigh McAlister and Michael L. Rothschild, eds. (Provo, UT: Association for Consumer Research, 1993), pp. 336–340.
9. Daniel Stokols, "On the Distinction Between Density and Crowding: Some Implications for Future Research," *Psychological Review*, Vol. 79 (May 1972), pp. 275–277.
10. G. Harrell, M. Hutt, and J. Anderson, "Path Analysis of Buyer Behavior Under Conditions of Crowding," *Journal of Marketing Research*, Vol. 17 (February 1980), pp. 45–51.
11. Michael K. Hui and John E. G. Bateson, "Perceived Control and the Effects of Crowding and Consumer Choice on the Service Encounter," *Journal of Marketing Research*, Vol. 18 (September 1991), pp. 174–184
12. William J. Reilly, *Methods for the Study of Retail Relationships* (Austin: Bureau of Business Research, University of Texas, 1929), p. 16.
13. James Bruner and John Mason, "The Influence of Driving Time upon Shopping Center Preference," *Journal of Marketing*, Vol. 32 (April 1968), pp. 57–61.
14. R. Mittelstaedt et al., "Psychophysical and Evaluative Dimensions of Cognized Distance in an Urban Shopping Environment," in *Combined Proceedings*, R. C. Curhan, ed. (Chicago: American Marketing Association, 1974), pp. 190–193.
15. "Store of the Month," *Progressive Grocer*, October 1976, pp. 104–110.
16. Robert Sommer, *Personal Space: The Behavioral Basis of Design* (Englewood Cliffs, NJ: Prentice- Hall, 1969).
17. Philip Kotler, "Atmospherics as a Marketing Tool," *Journal of Retailing*, Vol. 49 (Winter 1973–74), pp. 48–64
18. Jay Lindquist, "Meaning of Image," *Journal of Retailing*, Vol. 80 (Winter 1974–75), pp. 29–38.
19. Robert Donovan and John Rossiter, "Store Atmosphere: An Environmental Psychology Approach," *Journal of Retailing*, Vol. 58 (Spring 1982), pp. 34–57.
20. Albert Mehrabian and J. Russell, *An Approach to Environmental Psychology* (Cambridge, MA: M.I.T. Press, 1974).
21. Donovan and Rossiter, "Store Atmosphere."
22. Cited by Mary Jo Bitner, "Consumer Responses to the Physical Environment in Service Settings," in *Creativity in Services Marketing: What's New, What Works, What's Developing*, M. Venkatesan, Diane Schmalensee, and Claudia Marshall, eds. (Chicago: American Marketing Association, 1986), pp. 89–93.
23. Abraham Maslow and N. Mintz, "Effects of Aesthetic Surroundings," *Journal of Psychology*, Vol. 41 (1956), pp. 247–254.

24. Sommer, *Personal Space*.

25. Ibid.

26. Ron Markin, Charles Lillis, and Chem Narayana, "Social-Psychological Significance of Store Space," *Journal of Retailing*, Vol. 52 (Spring 1976), pp. 43–54.

27. Kotler, "Atmospherics as a Marketing Tool."

28. Russell Belk, "An Exploratory Assessment of Situational Effects in Buyer Behavior," *Journal of Marketing Research*, Vol. 11 (May 1974), p. 160.

29. Solomon E. Asch, *Social Psychology* (Englewood Cliffs, NJ: Prentice-Hall, 1952).

30. E. M. Tauber, "Why Do People Shop?" *Journal of Marketing*, Vol. 36 (October 1972), p. 47.

31. Richard Feinberg, Brent Scheffler, and Jennifer Meoli, "Social Ecological Insights into Consumer Behavior in the Retail Mall," *Proceedings of the Division of Consumer Psychology*, Linda Alwitt, ed. (New York: American Psychological Association, Division 23, 1987), pp. 17–19.

32. Ibid.

33. Donald H. Granbois, "Improving the Study of Customer In-Store Behavior," *Journal of Marketing*, Vol. 32 (October 1968), pp. 28–33.

34. William Bearden and Arch Woodside, "Consumption Occasion Influence on Consumer Brand Choice," *Decision Sciences*, Vol. 9 (April 1978), p. 275.

35. C. Levi-Strauss, *Structure Elementaires de la Parento* (Paris: Presser Universitaires de France, 1954).

36. Mary Finlay, "Motivations and Symbolism in Gift-Giving Behavior," in *Advances in Consumer Research*, Vol. 17, Marvin E. Goldberg, Gerald Gorn, and Richard W. Pollay, eds. (Provo, UT: Association for Consumer Research, 1990), pp. 699–706

37. Cele Otnes, Young Chan Kim, and Tina M. Lowrey, "Ho, Ho, Woe: Christmas Shopping for 'Difficult' People," in *Advances in Consumer Research*, Vol. 19, John Sherry, Jr., and Brian Sternthal, eds. (Provo, UT: Association for Consumer Research, 1992), pp. 482–487.

38. Keith Clarke and Russell Belk, "The Effects of Product Involvement and Task Definition on Anticipated Consumer Effort," in *Advances in Consumer Research*, Vol. 6, William Wilkie, ed. (Ann Arbor, MI: Association for Consumer Research, 1979), pp. 313–317.

39. E. W. Hart, "Consumer Risk Taking for Self and Spouse," unpublished doctoral dissertation, Purdue University, 1974.

40. Sharon Banks, "Gift-Giving: A Review and an Interactive Paradigm," in *Advances in Consumer Research*, Vol. 6, William Wilkie, ed. (Ann Arbor, MI: Association for Consumer Research, 1979), pp. 319–324.

41. The distinction between voluntary and obligatory gifts was pointed out by Cathy Goodwin, Kelly L. Smith, and Susan Spiggle, "Gift Giving: Consumer Motivation and the Gift Purchase Process," in *Advances in Consumer Research*, Vol. 17, Marvin E. Goldberg, Gerald Gorn, and Richard W. Pollay, eds. (Provo, UT: Association for Consumer Research, 1990), pp. 690–698. For another perspective on why consumers give gifts, see Mary Finley Wolfinbarger and Laura J. Yale, "Three Motivations for Interpersonal Gift Giving: Experiential, Obligated, and Practical Motivations," in *Advances in Consumer Research*, Vol. 20, Leigh McAlister and Michael Rothschild, eds. (Provo, UT: Association for Consumer Research, 1993), pp. 520–526.

42. Eileen Fischer and Stephen J. Arnold, "More Than a Labor of Love: Gender Roles and Christmas Gift Shopping," *Journal of Consumer Research*, Vol. 17 (December 1990), pp. 333–343.

43. David Glen Mick and Michelle DeMoss, "Self-Gifts: Phenomenological Insights from Four Contexts," *Journal of Consumer Research*, Vol. 17 (December 1990), pp. 322–332.

44. David Glen Mick and Michelle DeMoss, "Further Findings on Self-Gifts: Products,

Qualities, and Socioeconomic Correlates," in *Advances in Consumer Research*, Vol. 19, John Sherry, Jr., and Brian Sternthal, eds. (Provo, UT: Association for Consumer Research, 1992), pp. 140–1146.

45. Kim K. R. McKeage, Marsha L. Richins, and Kathleen Debevec, "Self-Gifts and the Manifestation of Material Values," in *Advances in Consumer Research*, Vol. 20, Leigh McAlister and Michael L. Rothschild, eds. (Provo, UT: Association for Consumer Research, 1993), pp. 359–364.

46. Daniel J. Howard, "Gift-Wrapping Effects on Product Attitudes: A Mood-Biasing Explanation," *Journal of Consumer Psychology*, Vol. 1, no. 3 (1992), pp. 197–223.

47. F. M. Nicosia and R. Mayer, "Toward a Sociology of Consumption," *Journal of Consumer Research*, Vol. 3 (September 1976), pp. 65–76.

48. Laurence Feldman and Jacob Hornik, "The Use of Time: An Integrated Conceptual Model," *Journal of Consumer Research*, Vol. 7 (March 1981), pp. 407–419.

49. Jacob Hornik, "Situational Effects on the Consumption of Time," *Journal of Marketing*, Vol. 46 (Fall 1982), pp. 44–55.

50. Morris Holbrook and Donald Lehmann, "Allocating Discretionary Time: Complementarity Among Activities," *Journal of Consumer Research*, Vol. 7 (March 1981), pp. 395–406.

51. U. N. Umesh, William Weeks, and Linda Golden, "Individual and Dyadic Consumption of Time: Propositions on the Perception of Complementarity and Substitutability of Activities," in *Advances in Consumer Research*, Vol. 14 (Provo, UT: Association for Consumer Research, 1987), pp. 548–552.

52. Ibid.

53. Robert Graham, "The Role of Perception of Time in Consumer Research," *Journal of Consumer Research*, Vol. 7 (March 1981), pp. 335–342.

54. Barbara L. Gross and Jagdish N. Sheth, "Time-Oriented Advertising: A Content Analysis of United States Magazine Advertising, 1890–1988," *Journal of Marketing*, Vol. 53 (October 1989), pp. 76–83.

55. Anthony D. Miyazaki, "How Many Shopping Days Until Christmas? A Preliminary Investigation of Time Pressures, Deadlines, and Planning levels on Holiday Gift Purchases," in *Advances in Consumer Research*, Vol. 20, Leigh McAlister and Michael L. Rothschild, eds. (Provo, UT: Association for Consumer Research, 1993), pp. 331–335. Also, see Peter Wright, "The Harassed Decision Maker: Time Pressures, Distractions, and the Use of Evidence," *Journal of Applied Psychology*, Vol. 59 (October 1974), pp. 555–561.

56. C. Whan Park, Easwar S. Iyer, and Daniel C. Smith, "The Effects of Situational Factors on In-Store Grocery Shopping Behavior: The Role of Store Environment and Time Available for Shopping," *Journal of Consumer Research*, Vol. 15 (March 1989), pp. 422–433.

57. R. E. Nisbet and D. E. Kanouse, "Obesity, Food Deprivation, and Supermarket Shopping Behavior," *Journal of Personality and Social Psychology*, Vol. 12 (August 1969) pp. 289–294.

58. Ibid.

59. Ibid.

60. Jacob Hornik, "Diurnal Variation in Consumer Response," *Journal of Consumer Research*, Vol. 14 (March 1988), pp. 588–591.

61. Nisbett and Kanouse, "Obesity, Food Deprivation."

62. Tauber, "Why Do People Shop?", p. 47.

63. D. L. Rosenhan, B. Underwood, and B. Moore, "Affect Moderates Self-Gratification and Altruism," *Journal of Personality and Social Psychology*, Vol. 30 (October 1974), pp. 546–552.

64. Ibid.

65. B. Moore, B. Underwood, and D. Rosenhan, "Affect and Altruism," *Developmental Psychology*, Vol. 8 (January 1973), pp. 99–104.

66. Elaine Sherman and Ruth Belk Smith, "Mood States of Shoppers and Store Image: Promising Interactions and Possible Behavioral Effects," in *Advances in Consumer Research*, Vol. 14, Paul Anderson and Melanie

Wallendorf, eds. (Provo, UT: Association for Consumer Research, 1987), pp. 251–254.

67. Meryl Gardner, "Mood States and Consumer Behavior: A Critical Review," *Journal of Consumer Research*, Vol. 12, no. 3 (1985), pp. 281–300

68. A. H. Maslow and N. L. Mintz, "Effects of Esthetic Surroundings: I. Initial Effects of Three Esthetic Conditions Upon Perceived Energy and Well-Being in Faces," *Journal of Psychology*, Vol. 41 (January 1956), pp. 247–254.

69. Robert Donovan and John Rossiter, "Store Atmosphere: An Environmental Psychology Approach," *Journal of Retailing*, Vol. 58 (Spring 1982), pp. 34–57.

70. Rajeev Batra, "The Role of Mood in Advertising Effectiveness," *Journal of Consumer Research*, Vol. 17 (September 1990), pp. 203–214

71. D. Kenrick, D. Baumann, and R. Cialdini, "A Step in the Socialization of Altruism as Hedonism," *Journal of Personality and Social Psychology*, Vol. 37 (May 1979), pp. 747–755.

72. S. Ratneswar and Alan G. Sawyer, "The Use of Multiple Methods to Explore Three-Way Person, Brand, and Usage Context Interactions," in *Advances in Consumer Research*, Vol. 19, John Sherry, Jr., and Brian Sternthal, eds. (Provo, UT: Association for Consumer Research, 1992), pp. 116–122.

73. Paul Schurr and Bobby Calder, "Psychological Effects of Restaurant Meetings on Industrial Buyers," *Journal of Marketing*, Vol. 50 (January 1986), pp. 87–97.

74. R. W. Belk, "An Exploratory Assessment of Situational Effects in Buyer Behavior," *Journal of Marketing Research*, Vol. 11 (May 1974), pp. 156–163.

75. Joseph Cote, "The Person by Situation Interaction Myth: Implications for the Definition of Situations," in *Advances in Consumer Research*, Vol. 13, Richard Lutz, ed. (Provo, UT: Association for Consumer Research, 1986), pp. 37–41.

76. Caleb Solomon, "The Latest Gasoline Additive? Marketing," *The Wall Street Journal*, December 15, 1988, p. B1.

CHAPTER 14 CASE STUDY

Eskimo Joe's: Stillwater's Jumpin' Little Juke Joint

Stan Clark graduated from Oklahoma State University in 1975. He put himself through college by selling pizzas, flowers, and hats. After graduation, he took his earnings from selling OSU "Cowboys" hats and leased an old stone building with a partner. Their goal was to open a bar. They tore down an unwanted barn and decorated the building with aged timbers. Clark and his partner did all the carpentry themselves and created a rustic, homey interior.

The next question concerned what to name the joint. The partner suggested "Eskimo Joe's" because they would sell the coldest beer in town. Clark was aghast—whoever heard of Eskimos in Oklahoma? But the partner wouldn't let go of the name. So they commissioned a freshman graphic arts major to design a logo. On his first draft, he came up with a design featuring an Eskimo staring with a big, toothy grin and a huge dog with a long, drooling tongue hanging out. The partners loved it, and the logo became the symbol of Eskimo Joe's. When the bar opened in July 1975, Stan and his partner greeted the new patrons and sold T-shirts bearing the bar's logo. Their first employee was hired from the crowd that arrived that night. From the unglamorous opening, the bar slowly grew in popularity.

After buying out his partner in 1978, Clark began to accelerate the marketing of Joe's. He understood the importance of creating events to attract customers. The characters in the logo (Eskimo Joe and his dog Buffy) were used to advertise the joint. "T-shirt nights" were created, and patrons who wore Eskimo Joe T-shirts received 10-cent draws of beer. Each summer, the bar celebrated its anniversary with "Joe's Weekend." Alumni of the university would return for a party at Joe's. Slowly, the weekend grew in importance. Then, in the mid-1980s, the mayor of the city condemned the weekend, charging that the crowds it attracted were urinating on her flowers. The media attention only served to attract more people. Clark used the occasion to ask local merchants and service clubs to sponsor booths. By the summer of 1991 Joe's Weekend had become an event. Streets were closed and dozens of portable potties were brought in to handle the 48,000 people who arrived for the party.

One of the turning points for Eskimo Joe's came in 1984 when the state of Oklahoma raised the drinking age for liquor to 21. In order to survive, the bar had to generate 50% of its sales in food. Clark persuaded a reluctant bank to loan him the money to put in a kitchen and buy an atrium for extra room. What looked like a major risk turned out to be a bonanza, however. The target market was suddenly expanded dramatically. As Stan Clark said, "I learned that a lot more people eat every day than drink every day."

By 1991 Eskimo Joe's had become a phenomenon. Eskimo Joe's T-shirts became the second best-selling T-shirt in the world—after Hard Rock Cafe shirts. (As of February 1992 more than 3 million had been sold. Indeed, you can purchase an Eskimo Joe sweatshirt by calling Joe's Clothes Worldwide at 1-800-256-JOES.) The banker who originally lent Stan Clark and his partner the money to start the business says that now Mr. Clark can buy and sell his bank.

When asked what factors are responsible for the remarkable success of Eskimo Joe's, Stan Clark says, "Our goal is to exceed customer expectations. You must treat customers right so that they have a great time." Clark believes that you do this by creating an environment where the employees love their job—their enthusiasm is then transferred to the customers. As Clark said, "Every time an employee interacts with a guest, that's a moment of truth. Guests must be made to feel welcome and wanted." Clark believes that how management treats its employees dictates how they treat customers. In turn, the interactions of the staff with the customers influences how the customers mingle with each other. Management shares little trade secrets with the staff (e.g., the hamburger is ground fresh every day). They pass this information on to customers, who in turn tell their friends.

A second reason for the success of Eskimo Joe's is its image and atmosphere. The old stone building makes people feel comfortable. The logo creates an offbeat, fun-loving image that carries over to the staff and to the customers. The building is filled with music played over an outstanding stereo system. The only guidelines for the music played are "no pop" and "no hard rock." When these factors are combined with a menu that features excellent food at low prices, people want to come to Eskimo Joe's to be seen by others and to meet others (see Figure C-1). As my own students tell me, "Eskimo Joe's is HOT."

Figure C-1 Nearly 50,000 people crowd the streets of Stillwater to be part of Joe's Weekend. (Courtesy of Stan Clark Worldwide.)

QUESTIONS

1. Define the problem faced by Stan Clark and his partner when they opened the bar.
2. Discuss the consumer concepts from the chapter that are illustrated in the case.
3. Develop the managerial applications table for the case. Discuss the managerial strategies that emerge from the consumer concepts identified in question 2.

* * *

Case prepared by John Mowen.

Chapter

15

Group Processes I: Group, Dyadic, and Diffusion Processes

CONSUMER VIGNETTE

Celebrities, Green Cards, Urban Legends, and Consumer Behavior

The effects of group, word-of-mouth, and diffusion processes are omnipresent in the consumer environment. Three examples are presented in the paragraphs that follow.

CASE 1 The commercial begins with a man sitting down looking at an imaginary reference book. He asks, "How 'bout Kellogg's Corn Flakes?" and begins to page through the book reading the names of the famous people who eat the breakfast cereal: "George Brett, Jamie Lee Curtis, Beach Boys, Diane Carol, Charles Bronson, Christie Brinkley, the list goes on and on." Amazed at the number of celebrities who eat the cereal, he digs into a heaping bowl of corn flakes.

CASE 2 Inside Walt Disney Productions, they called the movie "*Pretty Woman* for people who think." The problem was how to persuade consumers to go see a romantic comedy called *Green Card*, about a couple who get married, meet, and then fall in love. (Actually, the story is about a slobbish Frenchman who marries an American horticulturist to get his residency status. She marries him to get the husband she needs so that she can rent an apartment that she covets.) Marketers knew that the movie would be a hard sell. Although the French actor Gerard Depardieu is considered a legend and sex symbol in Europe, most Americans have never heard of him. Many of those who have perceive him as a shaggy, beefy, big-nosed bumpkin. The female lead in the movie, Andie McDowell, was also virtually unknown to American audiences.

The strategy employed by Disney executives was to criss-cross the United States, hosting upscale screenings of the movie at such places as New York's "21 Club" and the Los Angeles Museum of Art. Disney's director of marketing described the strategy as one of reaching opinion leaders. He hoped that favorable word-of-mouth information would gradually build so that as other movies faltered, *Green Card* would be shown in increasing numbers of theaters. In the end, the movie was a success in large part because of the word-of-mouth communications.[1]

CASE 3 The urban legend had been going around Utah for months. It finally reached national proportions when Ann Landers reported it in her newspaper column. The legend, as it was frequently told, is paraphrased as follows:

Wanting to have a nice tan for a trip, the young coed went to a tanning parlor. Not knowing much about tanning machines, she asked how long she could stay inside. After learning that she could only stay in for a half hour at a time and wanting to get a tan quickly for her trip, she proceeded to go to seven places and spend a half hour in each. As a result, she went totally blind and is in a hospital with 26 days to live. Basically, she microwaved herself, so that she cooked from the inside out. There's not a thing anyone can do for her but ease the pain.

Ann Landers called the hospital in which the coed was reputed to be staying. They had no record of such a patient but indicated that the story was circulating in the region.

INTRODUCTION

The three cases presented in the chapter-opening vignette illustrate the three main topics of this chapter: the effects of groups on exchange processes, dyadic exchange, and diffusion processes on consumer buying behavior. The Kellogg's Corn Flakes commercial illustrates an attempt to use an aspirational group to influence consumer behavior. Christie Brinkley, Charles Bronson, and the other celebrities are members of a group to which many of us aspire. If these "beautiful people" eat Kellogg's Corn Flakes, it ought to be okay—right?

The strategy behind the marketing of *Green Card* depicts the importance of dyadic exchanges and the role of opinion leaders in product adoption. With two stars virtually unknown to American audiences and a plot to which few could directly relate, Disney executives recognized that the movie would be difficult to advertise through traditional means. The director of the movie also realized that standard marketing practices had tainted audiences. He said that the movie industry releases "all these dumb movies, and then when they have one they like—one everybody likes, that's simple and honest—it turns out to be difficult to sell."[2] In the end what saved the movie was favorable word-of-mouth communication that attracted audiences to see it. Word-of-mouth communication is one of two basic types of dyadic exchanges that will be discussed in the chapter.

The baked coed urban legend illustrates how rumors and legends may diffuse through the population. The story is passed from person to person in a highly detailed manner. In fact, even the name of the hospital where the mythical coed was taken was given in the story. The themes of such urban legends consistently deal with the evils of modern technology, such as tanning booths. The study of diffusion processes, or how information is spread through consumer groups, is an important topic of this chapter.

As the chapter-opening cases illustrate, group, word-of-mouth, and diffusion processes are important elements of the consumer environment. A major reason for studying groups is that when people enter a group, they frequently act differently from when they are alone. As a result, groups are more than the sum of their parts. For example, why is it that restaurants usually add a 15% tip to the bill when more than four or five people eat together? The reason is that each member of a group of patrons gives a lower percentage tip than if he or she were eating alone. Being a part of a group causes each member to feel less responsible for providing a fair share of the tip.[3]

A study on shopping behavior also reveals the impact of groups on consumers. In the study the purchases of consumers were examined based upon the size of the shopping group in which they were located.[4] The results showed that when the consumers shopped alone, they tended to make their purchases as planned. However, as the size of the group increased, group members tended to move away from making their planned purchases. In groups of three or more, the number of shoppers who made more, purchases than planned increased by almost 100%. Similarly, the number of shoppers who purchased less than they planned increased by almost 100%. Table 15-1 shows these percentages.

This chapter is divided into four major sections, the first of which discusses how groups influence consumption. The second section discusses dyadic exchanges. The information that passes from one individual to another within groups may have an

TABLE 15-1

Effects of Group Size on Shopping Purchases

Purchases	*Person Alone*	*Three or More*
No items planned or purchased	3.7%	0.0%
Fewer purchases than planned	15.1	31.3
Purchases as planned	58.9	26.6
More purchases than planned	22.8	42.1

SOURCE: Data from Donald H. Granbois, "Improving the Study of Consumer In-Store Behavior," *Journal of Marketing*, Vol. 32 (October 1968), pp. 28–32, published by the American Marketing Association.

important impact on such consumer decisions as which product to purchase and which store or service provider to use (e.g., which doctor, dentist, or hair stylist to patronize). The third section analyzes the processes through which information and innovations diffuse through the environment. The last section presents the managerial implications of group processes on consumer behavior.

GROUP PROCESSES

A **group** is defined as a set of individuals who interact with one another over some period of time and who share some common need or goal. An entire series of exchange processes take place among the individuals within a group. Indeed, people will choose to remain in a group only if they can profit from it. That is, the rewards received from being in the group must equal or exceed the costs of remaining in the group. (Recall from Chapter 2 that the basic exchange equation is Profit = Rewards - Costs.) Consumers belong to numerous groups, each of which has some impact on buying behavior. For example, college students are likely to be members of a series of groups, such as families, sororities or fraternities, dorms, student organizations, and clubs. The family group, which is discussed in detail in Chapter 16, is particularly important because it is an important buying unit within the economy. In addition, friends make group decisions on where to shop and go to restaurants.

Groups influence buying in two general ways. First, they may influence the purchases made by individual consumers, such as a man purchasing a fraternity jacket. Second, members of a group must sometimes make decisions as a group. For example, a student club may have to decide where to hold a party and what refreshments to purchase.[5]

The study of group processes is also relevant to decision making within firms. The buying center within a firm is usually composed of several individuals who jointly make purchase decisions. In addition, employees within a firm frequently join into groups to decide where to have parties, which restaurant to go to for a celebration, and which radio station to listen to for background music.

Types of Groups

Sociologists have developed a variety of terms to describe the various types of groups a person may belong to, aspire to join, or avoid.[6] Table 15-2 provides a brief definition of the various groups. These include reference groups, primary and secondary groups, and formal and informal groups. The most important of these groups is the reference group.

Reference Groups

The term **reference group** is a broad one that encompasses a number of more specific types of groups. The common factor among the various types of reference groups is that each is used by the consumer as a point of reference to evaluate the correctness of his or her actions, beliefs, and attitudes.

One type of reference group is the aspiration group. **Aspiration groups** are those sets of people to whom a consumer hopes to belong. Therefore, an aspiration group can become a reference group for a consumer. One can see the effects of aspiration groups on college students in the spring of their senior year. At this point in time they are interviewing for jobs. Their aspiration group has suddenly changed and along with it their clothing—from jeans and cutoffs to business suits.

A **dissociative group** is another type of reference group. In this case, though, the consumer wishes to separate himself or herself from the group. The dissociative group still acts to form a point of reference; however, it is a point of reference with which the consumer wants to avoid being associated. Such separation from a group can occur when individuals are striving to move into higher social classes. They may attempt to avoid buying the products and services used by the dissociative reference groups (i.e., the social class that the consumer is attempting to leave). Figure 15-1 is a photo of a dissociative group for some people—smokers forced outside to puff.

TABLE 15-2

Types of Groups

Reference group—A group whose values, norms, attitudes, or beliefs are used as a guide for behavior by an individual.

Aspiration group—A group to which an individual would like to belong. If it is impossible for the individual to belong to the group, it becomes a symbolic group for the person.

Dissociative group—A group with which the person does not wish to be associated.

Primary group—A group of which a person is a member and with which that person interacts on a face-to-face basis. Primary groups are marked by intimacy among their members and by a lack of boundaries for the discussion of various topics.

Formal group—A group whose organization and structure are defined in writing. Examples include labor unions, universities, and classroom groups.

Informal group—A group that has no written organizational structure. Informal groups are often socially based, such as a group of friends who meet frequently to play golf, play bridge, or party together.

Figure 15-1 An example of a dissociative group for some consumers—smokers forced to move outside to puff.
(Photo by John Mowen.)

How Do Groups Influence Consumers?

Groups affect consumers through five basic means. Groups affect consumers through

1. Group influence processes.
2. The creation of roles within the group.
3. The development of conformity pressures.
4. The impact of social comparison processes.
5. The development of group polarization.

These are discussed in the paragraphis that follow.

Normative, Value-Expressive, and Informational Influence

The type of group having the most impact on consumers is the reference group. Reference groups affect people through norms, through information, and through the value-expressive needs of consumers. **Norms** are behavioral rules of conduct agreed upon by over one-half of the group to establish behavioral consistency within the group. Norms are rarely written down but are nonetheless generally recognized as standards for behavior by members of a group. They represent shared value judgments about how things should be done by members of the group.[7] **Normative influence** occurs when norms act to influence behavior. For example, the effects of unwritten corporate dress codes illustrate the impact of normative influence on the clothing purchased by employees. Similarly, norms can influence what and how much a person eats or drinks at a party and even the type of car a consumer purchases.

Groups can also influence consumers by providing them with information and encouraging the expression of certain types of values. **Informational influence** affects individuals when the group provides highly credible information that influences the consumer's purchase decisions. **Value-expressive influence** affects consumers when they sense that a reference group has certain values and attitudes pertaining to the consumption process. Because the person wishes to be a part of the group and to be liked by the members, he or she may act in ways that express these values and attitudes.

An additional important point about reference group influence should be made. Evidence exists that reference group influence may vary depending upon the type of product purchased. In particular, it has been suggested that reference group influence is higher for "public" products, such as wristwatches and automobiles, than for "private" products, such as refrigerators and mattresses.[8]

Roles

A **role** consist of the specific behaviors expected of a person in a position. Thus, when a person takes on a role, normative pressures exert influence on the person to act in a particular way.[9] An important role in consumer behavior is that of the *decider*. This person makes the final decision concerning which brand to choose. In industrial buying settings, identifying the decider is crucial. Often it is an individual outside of the purchasing department who must take responsibility for the outcome of the buying decision. Reaching this individual with the promotional message can make the difference in whether or not a sale is made.

The term **role-related product cluster** has been given to the set of products necessary for the playing of a particular role. For marketing managers the task of identifying those products that match the roles of consumers can be a profitable endeavor. For example, the role-related product cluster of a successful executive's office might include a secretary, a personal computer, a window on an upper floor, and an exercising device in the corner. An advertising campaign for the exercise equipment could tie its product symbolically to the rest of the product cluster as necessities for the upward-moving businessperson.

A classic study relevant to the role-related product cluster idea was performed in the 1950s. In the study, groups of housewives were given shopping lists that a "homemaker" had prepared. The two shopping lists were identical except for whether each contained the entry of drip-grind coffee or of instant coffee. The homemaker who bought the ground coffee was described by the respondents as "practical and frugal." In contrast, the homemaker who bought the instant coffee was seen as lazy, short-sighted, as an "office girl who is living from one day to the next in a haphazard sort of life."[10] The study indicates that in 1950 instant coffee was not a part of the role-related product cluster of someone who was a good homemaker. Interestingly, the 1950 study was repeated in the 1970s, and the results were dramatically different. The user of instant coffee was then described favorably, whereas the user of ground coffee was viewed as "old-fashioned."[11]

Conformity Pressures

Conformity may be defined as a "change in behavior or belief toward a group as a result of real or imagined group pressure."[12] Two types of conformity can be identified. The first is simple **compliance**, in which the person merely conforms to the wishes of the group without really accepting the group's dictates. The second is **private acceptance**, in which the person actually changes his or her beliefs in the direction of the group. A number of factors may increase the conformity pressures of a group; these are summarized in Table 15-3.

FACTORS WITHIN THE GROUP LEADING TO CONFORMITY Three aspects of groups may act to increase the conformity pressures felt by its members. One aspect is cohesiveness, which refers to how closely knit a group is. A group whose members have a high degree of loyalty and identification can exert greater influence on its members. The expertise of the group also affects conformity pressures. Because consumers are members of many groups, several different groups may have input into a particular purchase decision. The group whose members have more expertise relevant to the decision will have greater influence on the purchase.

The size of the group has also been found to influence decisions, particularly when the group is of a transient nature. In a classic series of experiments the psychologist Solomon Asch had people view a series of lines and judge which of the lines on one card matched the length of a line on another card. The task was quite simple, and when done alone the subjects made almost no errors. However, in the experimental conditions the researcher had confederates estimate the relative length of the lines prior to the subjects' doing so. These confederates, who actually worked for the experimenter, systematically gave a wrong answer. To the experimenter's surprise the subjects agreed with the confederates' judgments in 37% of the cases. The impact of the group was found to vary with the number of confederates. The likelihood of the subjects agreeing with the confederates increased until the size of the

TABLE 15-3

Factors Influencing the Conformity Pressures of a Group

I. Properties of the group
- **A.** Cohesiveness
- **B.** Size
- **C.** Expertise
- **D.** Group's view of product's salience

II. Properties of the person
- **A.** Information available to person
- **B.** Attractiveness of the group to person
- **C.** Person's need to be liked
- **D.** Type of decision the person faces

group reached about four people. After the group size got to four people, the impact of adding more individuals to the group was minimal.[13]

FACTORS WITHIN THE PERSON LEADING TO CONFORMITY The ability of a group to make a person conform depends upon the nature and needs of the person as well as the properties of the group. One such personal factor is the amount of information that the person has available for a decision. When little information is available for the decision or when the information is ambiguous, the group has more impact on the consumer's decision.

The attractiveness of the group and the person's need to be liked by the group often work together to create conformity pressures. In most cases the more the person wants to be a part of the group, the more he or she also wishes to be liked by its members. In such circumstances the individual tends to conform to group norms and pressures to fit in as well as possible.

TYPE OF DECISION The type of decision is a final factor that may influence the amount of conformity pressure felt by the person. Several studies have suggested that when a product is highly salient and conspicuous to others, conformity pressures increase.[14]

Perhaps the buying situation that best illustrates the impact of group conformity pressures on consumers involves home shopping parties. As said by one set of researchers, who analyzed a number of such parties through participant observation, "Generally, the parties had much of the flavor of a bridal shower, a sorority meeting, or even an adolescent girl's pajama party: the sense of being in a private ritual being performed away from men was marked."[15] In their study, they noted that nearly everyone who attended purchased something. A norm of purchasing existed to which the women felt pressured to conform. In effect, strong bonds of friendship ties created a type of "moral economy" in which buying was expected.

The term **market embeddedness** has been used to describe situations in which the social ties between buyer and seller supplement product value to enhance overall exchange utility. For example, at a Tupperware party, the guests purchase in part for the plastic containers and in part for the social benefits gained from going to the party. Those who attend home parties form a group, which for many plays the role of a reference group in their lives. Because of the close personal ties of the women in the group, conformity pressures are created to make purchases. For many of the women, the pressures enhance the overall experience and add utility to the purchase. In other words, they attend the parties as much (or possibly more than) for the friendships there as for the products that they can buy.

A recent study investigated market embeddedness in home buying parties. The authors surveyed over 500 invitees of such parties. They found that conformity pressures to make purchases increased to the extent that social relations within the group increased—particularly the tie between the hostess and the guest.[16]

Social Comparison Processes

Another way in which groups influence consumers involves people's need to assess their opinions and abilities by comparing themselves to others. The process through which people evaluate the "correctness" of their opinions, the extent of their abilities, and the appropriateness of their possessions has been called **social comparison**.[17] Thus, in addition to using groups to obtain factual information, consumers use groups to determine where they stand in reference to their opinions, abilities, and possessions.

Two approaches are used by consumers to obtain ability and opinion information. The first is through **reflected appraisal**. In this process the consumer examines the manner in which others in a reference group interact with him. Thus, if another person responds fondly to the person, compliments the person, and generally treats the person well, the individual will conclude that he is acting correctly. In contrast, if the other person responds negatively, the person will conclude that he is doing something wrong.

The second method of obtaining social comparison information is through **comparative appraisal**. Whereas a person must interact with others when reflected appraisal occurs, interaction is unnecessary in comparative appraisal. The consumer evaluates his own relative standing with respect to an attitude, belief, ability, or emotion by observing the behavior of appropriate reference others.[18]

An important point regarding social comparison processes is how a consumer selects an appropriate group for comparison. Evidence indicates that people compare themselves to others who are at about the same level on the given attributes rather than to others who show great differences.[19]

Social comparison, however, is not limited to contrasting oneself with peers. The idealized images of how one should look that are obtained from advertising can also influence one's self-image. A recent study reported a series of experiments on the topic. In one of the experiments, college women saw magazine ads that used either highly attractive models or no models. After exposure to the ads, they then rated photographs of female college students for attractiveness. They also rated their satisfaction with their own physical attractiveness. The results revealed that when exposed to the highly attractive models in the ads, the women were less satisfied with their own physical appearance and rated the photos of the other college women lower. Based upon the overall findings in the studies, the authors argued that advertising does cause social comparison to occur and that such comparisons can negatively affect feelings about the self.[20]

The potentially negative effect of young women engaging in social comparison is readily illustrated by looking through many women's magazines. For example, one advertisement for Body Drama lingerie features a young woman pensively looking away from the camera. Draped in a filmy nightgown, she reveals a highly attractive body—one to which women could compare their own. Because this woman makes her living as a fashion model and because the photographer spent hours creating the "perfect" photo, the ad creates an unrealistic image. Women are bombarded with such visual images. As a result, the social comparison process may cause them to feel dissatisfaction with their own bodies.

Group Polarization

Over 20 years ago psychologists began studying a highly perplexing group phenomenon—the **group shift**. In the early studies researchers provided groups and individuals with decision dilemmas and compared their choices. These early results revealed that groups tended to select the riskier alternative. For example, in one situation a man of moderate means was described as receiving a small inheritance. Groups and individuals had to decide how he should invest the money. The groups recommended more often than individuals that he invest the money in risky securities, which might produce large gains, than in conservative blue-chip stocks.

Later research found that conservative as well as risky shifts could occur. For example, one study investigated an interesting type of consumer behavior—racetrack betting. These researchers found that groups were more cautious in placing bets than individuals at the track.[21] Such findings caused researchers to change their views on group shifts. As a result, the name of the tendency of groups to cause people to shift their decisions, either in a more cautious or a more risky decision direction, was changed to the **group polarization phenomenon**.

Various explanations have been offered for the group polarization phenomenon. One factor accounting for group shifts is the information transmitted during group discussion of the problem. During the course of discussion, arguments are made for various decisions. The decision alternative receiving the greatest number of arguments typically is chosen.[22]

Another explanation for the group polarization phenomenon is called the *cultural value hypothesis*. Researchers have found that the shifts are almost always in the direction to which the individuals are already leaning. Thus the interaction of the members tends to emphasize this initial predisposition of the individual members. The social interaction then reinforces such predispositions and moves the group decision to a more extreme position than the average of the individual decisions.[23]

Group polarization effects have been shown to influence consumer decisions. For example, researchers found that shifts occurred among groups of housewives for decisions involving financial and sociopsychological risk.[24] In another study consumer scenarios were developed to assess group shifts for six different types of risk—financial, physical, social, time, functional, and psychological.[25] The results showed that group polarization effects occurred for some types of risk and that men and women differed in the types of shifts that occurred. For example, groups of women revealed risky shifts for social decisions, and groups of men revealed cautious shifts for functional decisions.

The study of group shifts is particularly relevant to industrial sales. If a group decision to purchase an industrial product or service is made, the salesperson needs to recognize that risky or conservative shifts are likely to occur. Because the dominant culture of most companies is toward financial conservatism, industrial sellers should tailor the marketing mix based upon this dominant value. The mix of pricing, quality control, performance, and delivery guarantees should be developed so as to emphasize the values likely to be predominant in the buying center. Performing marketing research to identify the dominant values of the buyers corporate culture would be appropriate in such cases.[26]

Managerial Implications of Group Influence

Group influence applies to each of the managerial areas. Managers can segment the market based upon group membership. Naturally existing groups of consumers make outstanding target markets for firms, because they are readily identifiable and reachable. For example, numerous companies target military veterans, public teachers, government workers, church groups, the National Rifle Association, and so on. Product and service offerings can be developed specifically for the members of the group. Promotional strategy can be built around the concept that the product/service is positioned as being offered specifically to the members of the group. Environmental analysis should be performed to determine the extent to which new membership groups are establishing themselves. Finally, marketing research should be performed to assess the attitudes and psychographic characteristics of the individuals who make up these groups.

Market researchers should also be aware that group processes may have a large impact on the results of focus groups.[27] In **focus groups** small numbers of consumers (usually 6 to 10) interact in an open-ended fashion with the assistance of a moderator to provide information on their beliefs and attitudes about specific topics. Because group polarization and social comparison phenomena will be operating, managers should be highly cautious in interpreting the results of focus groups. The group interaction itself may change consumer attitudes and beliefs. As a result, the results may not represent the beliefs and attitudes of the individuals prior to their arrival for the focus group session.

An excellent example of a company that targets a specific group is Campbell's Soup Company. Campbell's targets the parents of grade school children. In the program, school playground equipment can be obtained in return for the submission of labels from products produced by the company. In many schools children are mobilized to bring the labels of soup cans, V8 juice, and other products to the school. Campbell's then gives the school assorted types of playground equipment. In return, the company receives the goodwill of parents as well as increased sales.

DYADIC EXCHANGES

Dyadic exchange takes place when two individuals transfer resources between each other. Because the concept of exchange plays a central role in understanding consumer behavior, Chapter 2 was devoted to this critical topic. In this section, I will focus on two important types of dyadic exchange. The first type is word-of-mouth communications that take place between two consumers. The second type is the service encounter in which a consumer and a marketer engage in a dyadic interaction. These topics are discussed in the next two subsections of the chapter.

Word-of-Mouth Communications

Word-of-mouth communications refer to exchanges of comments, thoughts, or ideas (i.e., information) between two or more consumers, none of whom represent a marketing source.[28] Word-of-mouth communications have an extremely strong impact on consumer purchase behavior. One survey of consumers asked what factors influenced their purchases of 60 different products. The results revealed that referrals from others accounted for three times as many purchases as did advertising.[29] Another study done after World War II found that word-of-mouth influence was twice as effective as radio advertising, four times more effective than personal selling, and seven times as effective as newspapers and magazines.[30] Other research found that two-thirds of new residents in a community found their doctor through discussions with others.[31]

One general finding is that a **negativity bias** operates in word-of-mouth communications. Negative information is given more weight than positive information by consumers when they make decisions to buy a product or service. One piece of negative information about a product or service influences a consumer more than one, two, or even three pieces of positive information. For example, one study of a new coffee product found that after receiving positive information, 54% tried the product. However, after receiving negative information, only 18% tried it.[32] A number of reasons have been offered for the disproportionate influence of negative information. A likely explanation is that, because most products are pretty good, negative information is a rather rare occurrence. When it does occur, it then takes on greater importance because of its high saliency. One reason why word-of-mouth information has so much impact on consumers is that it is highly vivid and salient. As discussed in Chapter 10, vivid information has greater impact than more pallid information. Because word-of-mouth information comes directly from another person, who describes personally his or her own experiences, information tends to be more vivid than a medium such as printed communication. The net result is that word-of-mouth information is more accessible in memory and has a relatively greater impact on consumers.[33]

Why Does Word-of-Mouth Communication Occur?

The omnipresence of word-of-mouth communication results from the needs of both the sender and receiver of the information. The receiver may desire information because he or she fails to believe the advertisements and sales messages received in the marketplace. In addition, the receiver may be seeking additional information to lower anxiety about a seemingly risky purchase. When receivers are highly involved in a purchase decision, they tend to go through a longer search process for a product or service. A part of this search process may include asking friends and "experts" about various alternatives. In these high-involvement situations personal influence occurs with increased frequency.

Consumers may be motivated to seek the input of others in three additional purchase situations.[34] Consumers tend to be more involved in the purchase and seek the advice of others (1) when the product is highly visible to others, (2) when the product is highly complex, and (3) when the product cannot be easily tested against some objective criterion. In each case the consumer is in a high-involvement buying situation.

The process of influencing others also fulfills the needs of senders of information. The ability to provide information and to sway others in their decisions provides a person with feelings of power and prestige. Influencing others can also help the influencer erase doubts about his or her own purchase. By persuading another to buy a product that the influencer just purchased, the sender can ease his or her own anxieties about the purchase. In addition, by providing information to others, a sender can increase his or her involvement with a group. Thus, providing information serves to increase social interaction and the general cohesion of the group.[35] Finally, a person can engage in word-of-mouth communications to derive some benefit. That is, by giving someone else information, based upon the norm of reciprocity, the recipient should at some point in time return the favor. Table 15-4 summarizes the factors that promote word-of-mouth communications.

Word-of-Mouth Network Models

An important question for marketers concerns the issue of how certain service providers, such as doctors and attorneys, can have such thriving businesses without engaging in any formal promotional activities. One explanation is in word-of-mouth networks that form among consumers of these services.[36]

TABLE 15-4

Factors That Promote Word-of-Mouth Communications

I. The needs of the sender of information
- **A.** Gain feelings of power and prestige.
- **B.** Erase doubts about his or her own purchase.
- **C.** Increase involvement with a desirable person or group.
- **D.** Obtain a tangible benefit.

II. The needs of the receiver of information
- **A.** Seek information from sources more trustworthy than those who endorse products.
- **B.** Lower anxiety about a possibly risky purchase.
  1. Risk can result from the product because of its complexity or cost.
  2. Risk can result from the buyer's concern about what others will think.
  3. Risk can result from the lack of an objective criterion on which to evaluate the product.
- **C.** Less time spent in search of information.

Figure 15-2 diagrams a simple word-of-mouth network that exists among students at a university. The information being passed among the students concerns the recommendation of a hair stylist. In the diagram one can identify two types of connections. The lines with arrows represent referral relations. Referral relations consist of "who-told-whom-about-the-service" paths. Thus referral relations depict the word-of-mouth connections along which information on the service was spread. The lines without arrows represent social relations. Social relations refer to the extent of the tie between two individuals. Ties may be strong, weak, or nonexistent. An example of a strong tie would be two friends who frequently visit each other.

An example of a weak tie would be two acquaintances who happen to encounter each other and talk about the service while visiting.[37] In Figure 15-2 one can identify how information about the hair styling salon is passed. The information begins with person *A*, who appears to act as an opinion leader. She has strong ties with persons *B* and *I*. However, she passes information about the hair stylist to persons *B* and *F*. *B* then passes the information on to persons *C* and *D*. Person *I* receives information about the salon from an acquaintance *H*, who obtained it from friend *G*. Person *G* obtained the information from friend *F*, who obtained it from acquaintance *A*. Person *E* is connected only to acquaintance *A* via a referral linkage.

A number of learning points are contained in Figure 15-2. First, the fact that two people have strong ties (i.e., are friends) does not mean that information will be transmitted. For example, even though person *A* has a strong tie with person *I*, information about the salon is not communicated. Second, one can identify small interconnected groups of consumers that share strong ties. Thus individuals *B*, *C*, and *D* form one group, and individuals *F*, *G*, and *H* form a second group. One can also identify the network length by counting the number of referral lines that connect continuously. The longest network length in the figure is composed of four referrals—*A* to *F*, *F* to *G*, *G* to *H*, and *H* to *I*.

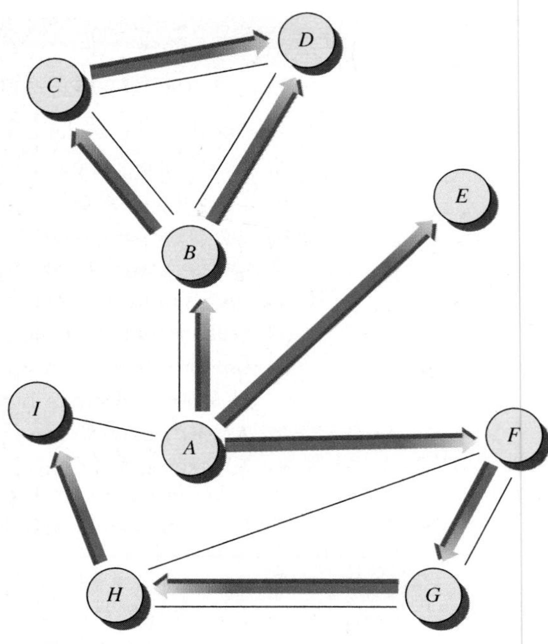

Figure 15-2
A word-of-mouth network.

A recent study investigated the information flow about three piano teachers in a southwestern city.[38] A complex set of referral and social relations was found among the individuals, and several interesting findings emerged from the study. One finding was that weak ties are particularly important for passing information across groups. Indeed, the results revealed that weak ties had a disproportionately greater tendency to act as bridges that allowed information to pass from one distinct group to another. Similarly, in Figure 15-2 one finds that person *A* is connected to group *F-H-G* only via the weak tie of the referral relation.

A second major finding of the research was that, within groups, strong ties were more likely than weak ties to activate flows of information. The reason for the relation between strong ties and information transmission is that social contact occurred with much greater frequency among friends. A third finding was that persuasion was greater when information came from strongly tied individuals. Weak ties seem to act as bridges across groups along which information is passed. Within the groups, however, strong ties are crucial to the flow of influence.

The analysis of referral networks highlights the point that both relational and informational ties exist among consumers. It emphasizes the concept that interpersonal communication is a social phenomenon and that people are embedded in larger social systems.[39]

Opinion Leadership

In studying word-of-mouth communication, one finds that some people more frequently provide information than others. Such individuals may become **opinion leaders**, who are defined as those consumers who influence the purchase decisions of others.

Opinion leadership does *not* appear to be a general trait held by specific individuals in which they influence others across a broad range of categories. Rather, evidence indicates that opinion leadership is specific to the product category and situation. Within a single product category, such as appliances, packaged goods, or household furnishings, an opinion leader may influence others across a number of different products. For example, one study found that people who were opinion leaders for small appliances were also opinion leaders for large appliances.[40] However, opinion leadership does not seem to occur across product categories. Another study found that no overlap of opinion leadership occurred across unrelated product categories, such as fashion and public affairs.[41]

Strong evidence exists that opinion leadership is influenced by the situation. Research has shown that opinion leadership tends to occur in situations that somehow involve the product category about which opinion leadership occurs. For example, one study found that word-of-mouth communications about Maxim coffee tended to occur in situations that involved food, such as talking about the brand during a coffee break.[42]

CHARACTERISTICS OF OPINION LEADERS Marketers have attempted to identify the characteristics of opinion leaders. However, these efforts have met with limited success. The most clear-cut finding is that opinion leaders tend to be involved with the product category. They are interested in the product category, tend to read special interest magazines about it, and are more knowledgeable about the category. Some evidence exists that opinion leaders may be more self-confident and socially active than followers. Opinion leaders may also have a somewhat greater social status than followers; however, they do belong to the same peer group as followers. Finally, they tend to be more innovative in their purchases than followers, but they are not the consumers who are "product innovators."[43] Attempts to find demographic and personality characteristics that pinpoint opinion leaders have in general not been successful.[44]

COMPARING OPINION LEADERS AND PRODUCT INNOVATORS In a variety of respects opinion leaders and product innovators are similar. Product innovators are the small set of people who are the first to buy new products. In a study of physicians, innovators and opinion leaders were found to be similar in a number of ways.[45] As compared to followers or noninnovators, they were more highly socially integrated into the medical community, they were more oriented to their professional goals than to their patients, they shared offices with other physicians, and they attended more medical conferences. Both innovators and opinion leaders showed a pattern of being highly active in their profession, of communicating with other doctors frequently, and of keeping up with new happenings in the medical literature.

Although innovators and opinion leaders share a variety of similarities, the evidence is that on some key characteristics, they are different people. The innovator may be described as an adventurer who strikes off on his or her own to buy new products. In contrast, the opinion leader is like an editor who can influence others but who can never be too far away from the goals, values, and attitudes of those whose opinions are being influenced. Innovators are individuals who are less integrated into social groups and feel freer to break group norms by adopting new products very early in their life cycle. In contrast, opinion leaders are more socially integrated and exert their influence in part because they do not espouse beliefs that are widely divergent from those of the group.[46]

MAVENS AND SURROGATES AS SOURCES OF PERSONAL INFLUENCE Researchers have found that in addition to opinion leaders and product innovators, two other sources of personal influence can be identified—the market maven and the surrogate consumer. **Market mavens** are defined as "individuals who have information about many kinds of products, places to shop, and other facets of markets and initiate discussions with consumers and respond to requests from consumers for market information."[47] As this definition suggests, these individuals play a broader personal influence role than do opinion leaders. The expertise of market mavens is not product specific; rather, it is based on more general market expertise. Market mavens may seek to obtain marketplace information to be useful to others in social exchanges and to provide a basis for conversations. In a sense, "market maven" is a role that consumers can adopt.

The market maven appears to be different from an opinion leader or a product innovator. Market mavens are aware of new products earlier, provide information to other consumers across categories, seek general market information, and are in general interested and attentive to the marketplace. In addition, market mavens are generally more aware of products in the marketplace. Thus their awareness set and consideration set of brands will be larger than average consumer's.[48]

The second new type of influencer that has been identified in the marketplace is the surrogate consumer. A **surrogate consumer** is a person who acts "as an agent retained by a consumer to guide, direct, and/or transact marketplace activities."[49] They can play a wide variety of roles, such as tax consultant, wine steward, interior decorator, stockbroker, or car buyer. Basically, the surrogate consumer is an additional layer in the channel of distribution between manufacturer and consumer. They tend to be used in very-high-involvement purchases in which the consumer desires to surrender some control to a more capable external agent. In sum, the consumer abdicates to the surrogate many of the information search, evaluation, and choice functions that take place in the consumer decision process. As such, the surrogate consumer plays an important role in the consumer purchase process for certain types of complex products and services, such as expensive furniture and investment securities.

Marketing managers should investigate the extent to which surrogates influence consumers in their purchase of a firm's products or services and seek to target these individuals with promotional materials. Table 15-5 summarizes the characteristics of the four types of influencers in the marketplace—opinion leaders, product innovators, market mavens, and surrogate consumers.

Service Encounters

The **service encounter** happens when a personal interaction occurs between a consumer and a marketer. A service encounter can occur in "pure service contexts," such as a physician's examination, cashing a check, or ordering a meal at a restaurant. In addition, service encounters occur in "mixed service contexts." For example, consider your involvement with your car. Certainly, the auto is a good (or a bad, depending upon your satisfaction with it). However, a number of service encounters occurred during and after your purchase. That is, when you bought it, you interacted with the seller. When having it serviced or repaired, you encountered additional firm representatives. In sum, during the service encounter, a consumption experience is occur-

TABLE 15-5

Characteristics of Four Types of Consumer Influencers

Influencer Type	*Basis for Expertise*	*Characteristics*
Opinion leader	Enduring involvement in product category	Enduring involvement, higher status, integrated into social group
Product innovator	Purchase of innovative product	Less integrated into social groups than opinion leaders
Market maven	General market knowledge	Demographic characteristics unknown; enjoys having general knowledge about the marketplace
Surrogate consumer	Knowledge specific to product category	Frequently a paid professional

ring. Just as discussed in the Chapter 13, the consumption experience will have a strong impact on the consumer's satisfaction/dissatisfaction with a product.

During the service encounter, the consumer and the marketer take on discrete roles.[50] These roles can be understood by using the dramaturgical metaphor discussed in Chapter 13. Thus the employee and the consumer act as though they are on a stage reading from a common "service script." This script creates expectations on both actors' parts. To the extent that either violates the script in a negative manner, dissatisfaction may result. Thus, if the service provider violates expectations (perhaps by being too pushy), the consumer will be dissatisfied. Conversely, if the consumer violates expectations (perhaps by ridiculing the employee), the employee will be dissatisfied with the encounter. Because an exchange is occurring, dissatisfaction can occur in both the service provider and the consumer.

The use of theater as a metaphor to describe the service encounter provides a vocabulary for understanding the exchange process. Figure 15-3 provides a diagram that depicts the service encounter as theater.[51] Like any production, one finds a stage where the play takes place. In addition, one has front and back regions for both consumer and firm. In the front region, both parties reveal impression management and protective practices. A backstage area also exists for both parties where rehearsal/practice occurs, secondary support exists (e.g., other people help the production), and management functions reside.

As noted earlier, both the consumer and the employee follow scripted roles during the service encounter. Recent research has identified three themes that may occur for each party in the encounter.[52] The three themes identified for consumers were autonomy, mutuality, and dependence. They depict the nature of the relationship that the consumer desires to form with the service provider. Consumers desire autonomy when they believe they have the information that they need and seek to engage in self-service. Those who purchase relatively low-involvement goods from retail stores frequently desire autonomy. In some cases, consumers may have a high degree of expertise and, as a result, seek autonomy. The sophisticated investor who purchases stocks from discount brokerage houses exemplifies this case.

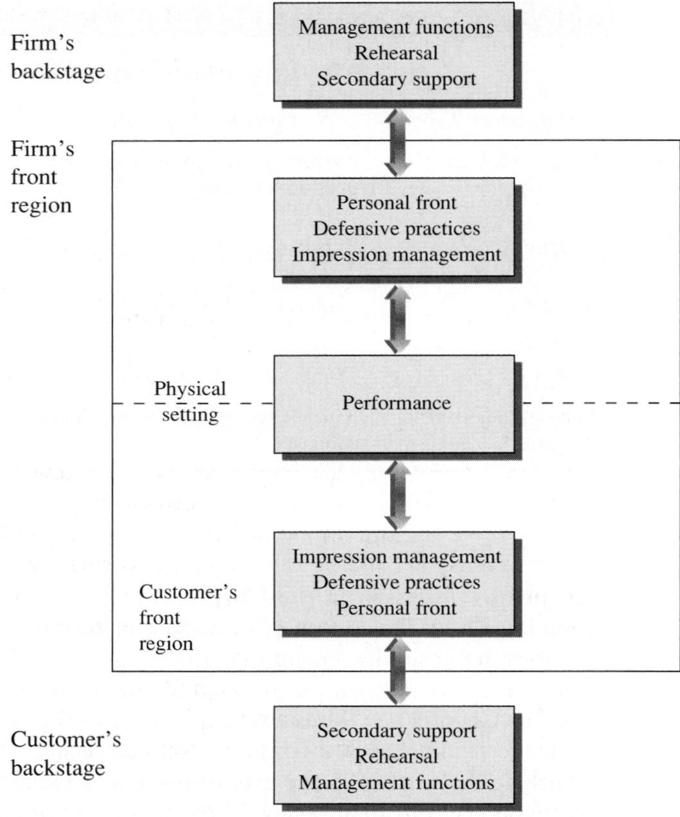

Figure 15-3 The service encounter as theatrical performance. (Adapted from Stephen Grove and Raymond Fisk, "The Service Encounter as Theater," in *Advances in Consumer Research*, Vol. 19, John F. Sherry, Jr., and Brian Sternthal, eds., Provo, UT: Association for Consumer Research, 1992, pp. 455–461.)

As product involvement increases and as consumer expertise decreases, consumers may seek either mutual cooperation or dependence in the relationship with the employee. When mutual cooperation occurs, a feeling of mutual synergy between employee and consumer results. Examples might include purchasing expensive clothing, original art, or stocks and bonds by a consumer with some knowledge about the risks and benefits involved. In contrast, if the consumer has limited knowledge or expertise, total dependence may be placed on the employee. In such cases the consumer wants the employee to take an active role and participate fully in the service encounter. At the extreme, the employee becomes a surrogate consumer.

Employee themes are symmetrical with the consumer themes. The three employee themes are indifference, cooperation, and dominance. For the manager, it is critical that employees match their actions to those desired by consumers. If the customer wants mutual cooperation, the employee should provide it without attempting to become dominant. The indifference theme, however, is a tricky one.

Generally, consumers who want autonomy do *not* want indifferent service providers. Rather, the consumer desires providers who leaves him or her alone until the consumer needs attention to complete the transaction.

Managerial Implications of Dyadic Exchange Processes

A company should have a clear understanding of the types of dyadic exchanges that occur in relation to their product. In particular, they must train their employees to take on the appropriate role when dealing with customers in service exchanges. Employees should strive to match the role to expectations of each customer. Thus, if a customer desires to make a purchase decision autonomously, the service provider should respect that wish. Failure to match customer service desires is likely to result in dissatisfaction.

In addition, the firm should identify the extent to which purchases of its products or services are influenced by word-of-mouth communication and by opinion leadership. It is a function of market research to find and identify opinion leaders, market mavens, and surrogate consumers. If such people exist, they should become a segment to which the company targets its promotional messages. As such, the study of opinion leadership is important to the managerial areas of market research, segmentation, and promotional strategy.

One industry that has identified and targeted an influential set of opinion leaders is the food industry. The industry has recognized that medical doctors have tremendous influence over what brands of food consumers eat. Medical doctors have traditionally been recognized as opinion leaders for such products as over-the-counter drugs. However, with the recent emphasis on health and nutrition, physicians have also become sources of information on the best foods to eat. Procter & Gamble has recognized this trend and is promoting its Citrus Hill Plus Calcium orange juice and low-saturated-fat Puritan Oil to doctors. Similarly, Nabisco advertises its Fleischmann's margarine and Egg Beaters to physicians. NutraSweet is also marketed to doctors. The Quaker Oats Company even sends out a quarterly newsletter called "Fiber Report" to doctors.[53]

DIFFUSION PROCESSES

The term *diffusion* refers to the idea that substances or even ideas can gradually spread through a medium of some type and reach a state of equilibrium. For example, if a drop of colored water is placed into a fish tank, it will gradually diffuse until it is evenly dispersed throughout the entire tank. Similarly, contagious diseases may be viewed as diffusing through the population. In a consumer behavior setting, **diffusion** refers to the process through which innovative ideas, products, and services spread through the consumer population.

In this section three different types of diffusion processes are discussed. The first concerns how information is transmitted through the consumer environment and introduces alternative models of information transmission. The second involves the diffusion of innovations. This discussion identifies the factors that influence how innovative products become accepted and adopted by consumers. The third deals with the problems caused by the spreading of rumors. Corporations are plagued by rumors about their products, and understanding the process of rumor spread and control is important for large companies.

Transmission Processes

A question of importance to marketers and sociologists concerns how communications flow within groups and the larger consumer environment. Several models of how information is transmitted from the mass media to the general population have been proposed. The **trickle-down theory** holds that trends, and particularly fashion trends, begin with the wealthy. To distinguish themselves from lower classes, the wealthy adopt styles of clothing and attitudes that separate them from the lower classes. The lower classes then attempt to emulate the wealthy by copying their actions. In this way the fashions and behaviors of the wealthy "trickle down" to the lower classes. The problem with the trickle-down theory is that in actuality, relatively little communication occurs between the classes. Most communications occur between people in the same social class. In addition, in today's mass-communication culture, information on fashion is transmitted almost instantaneously. Thus information exchange is much more like a flood than a trickle.

A second approach to the transmission of personal influence is the two-step flow model. The two-step flow model posits that mass communications first influence opinion leaders, who then influence followers. Rather than viewing influence as occurring between the social classes, the approach regards influence as horizontal within a class. The model hypothesizes that there are opinion leaders in each class who influence a large group of passive followers. The two-step flow model, however, has been shown to be overly simplistic. No passive group of followers has been identified. Similarly, opinion leaders have been found to be different for different products.

The approach that appears to represent the flow of personal influence best is the multistep flow model. Figure 15-4 diagrams the model. In this approach information is transmitted by the mass media to three distinct sets of people—opinion leaders, gatekeepers, and followers.[54] Each type of person is viewed as having the capability of giving information to the other categories of people. The opinion leader is the person who influences others about the particular piece of information transmitted by the mass media. The gatekeeper is an individual who has the capability of deciding whether or not others in a group will receive information. That person's opinions may or may not influence the others, however. The followers are those who are influenced by the opinion leader or by the information provided by the gatekeeper.

The multistep flow model recognizes a number of important pieces of information.

1. Mass communications can directly reach nearly everyone in the population.
2. For some products certain individuals, the opinion leaders, are able to influence a group of followers. However, for different products the roles of opinion leader and follower may be reversed.
3. Another group of individuals, the gatekeepers, can choose whether or not to provide information to opinion leaders and followers.
4. Communications can be transmitted back and forth between the three groups.

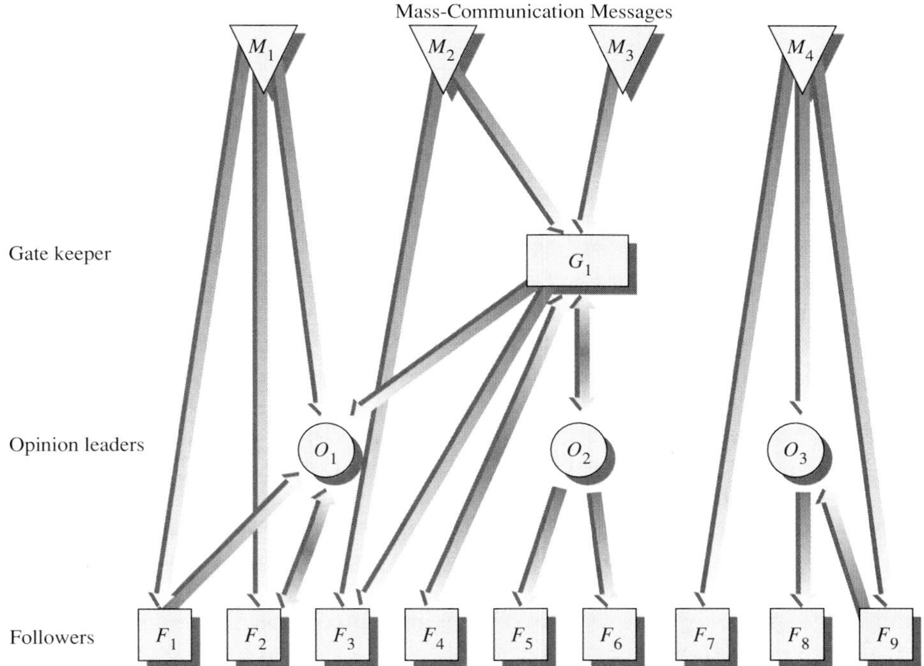

Figure 15-4 The multistep flow model

The Diffusion of Innovations

The study of the adoption of new products is an important one for marketers. To grow, a company must continually improve existing products and periodically develop new products for the changing marketplace. The study of product adoption is also important because of the relatively low success rate of new products. The overall cost of introducing a new consumer product has been estimated to be about $6 million. The chance of a new product being successful is estimated at about 20% for consumer goods.[55] Product innovations come in many varieties, from goods that have a positive impact on society (e.g., antibiotic medicines) to those that harm. Highlight 15-1 discusses one product innovation from the dark side of consumer behavior—cocaine—that has major public policy implications.

A **product innovation** is defined as a product that has been recently introduced and is perceived by consumers to be new in relation to existing products or services. Indeed, to be advertised as new, according to a proposal once made by the Federal Trade Commission, a product would have had to be in distribution for less than six months. Other factors also are relevant to whether a product is perceived as new in the marketplace. Perhaps most important is the extent to which it changes the behavior of consumers. A product that fails to alter the behavior or life-style of consumers cannot be described as new or innovative. In contrast, a product that causes consumers to engage in entirely new life-style patterns, such as those resulting from the introduction of television, are certainly highly innovative.

HIGHLIGHT 15-1

Cocaine as a Product Innovation

Cocaine, and particularly crack cocaine, creates major problems for American society. Over 3,000 deaths a year occur from it—many of which occur to people below the age of 40. The use of crack is strongly associated with crime, gangs, and violence. Increasingly, babies are born addicted, at an inestimable future social and monetary cost. Journalists and public policy makers have variously called the exploding use of crack cocaine a "disease," a "plague," and an "epidemic."

Recently, Elizabeth Hirschman wrote a thoughtful article on cocaine in which she questioned the disease metaphor. When cocaine use is described as a disease, a series of implications result. For example, the disease metaphor suggests that users are victims, rather than individuals who have made a choice of whether or not to take the drug. The metaphor also implies that the sellers are evil people, rather than individuals engaged in a very profitable business. Describing cocaine as a disease that strikes immoral people also ignores the social context of its use and the fact that, within some contexts, it may actually have positive effects. In sum, Dr. Hirschman suggests that rather than treating cocaine use as an addiction, perhaps a more effective approach would be to analyze it as a product innovation that is diffused through the consumer environment.

Like any other product, cocaine has moved through a life cycle. Indeed, in the roughly 100 years of use in the United States, its life cycle has been extended on three occasions with product adaptations. Originally, cocaine was discovered and used by South American Indians living in the Andes. These people chewed a wad of fresh coca leaves together with potash to give them energy. The practice continues today as *el coqueo* and is used as a mild stimulant, much as Americans consume tea, coffee, or tobacco.

When discovered by Europeans in the nineteenth century, it was quickly recognized that cocaine lost its potency on the long ocean voyages back to Europe. Soon thereafter, chemists succeeded in chemically isolating the active ingredient, which was called cocaine. This discontinuous innovation, marketed in the form of a powder, began to be mixed with wine in a drink called Vin Mariani. Billed as a medical tonic, it became very popular. Such famous people as Sigmund Freud, Thomas Edison, Pope Leo XIII, Ulysses S. Grant, and Sarah Bernhardt enjoyed the beverage. New concoctions were quickly spun off, including in 1885 the popular drink named Coca-Cola. By 1906, Americans consumed as much cocaine as they would in 1976. However, by the early 1900s, the addictive qualities of cocaine became recognized, and it became associated with deviance. By 1914, laws were changed, and usage plummeted.

For the next 50 years or so, use of cocaine in the United State remained low. Then another product innovation occurred. A new form of the substance was introduced, which could be snorted rather than drunk. Producing a much higher high, by the 1970s the product became known as the "champagne of drugs" and was associated with status, power, and glamour. Famous people (e.g., Richard Dreyfus, John Belushi, Chevy Chase, Mick Jagger, and Daryl Strawberry) were reputed to use it. Between 1977 and 1979, its use doubled. Again, however, the drug's addictive properties became readily apparent, and public opinion turned against it. Its use plummeted.

By the 1970s, however, the Colombian cocaine cartel had been formed. Unwilling to see its investment lost, the cartel engaged in product innovation. Freebasing was developed in which ether (a highly flammable substance) was employed to release the cocaine alkaloid from the base. The "high" obtained was even more intense. As a result, consumers demanded even more of the product. Again, however, a problem occurred. Frequently, accidents resulted in which the mixture caught fire. After the Richard Pryor accident, use again dropped dramatically.

During the late 1970s and early 1980s, product adaptation occurred rapidly. Suppliers quickly switched their product from one based on snorting to freebasing, to the ultimate—crack. "Crack" or "rock" was much safer and could be sold in small packages for a reasonable price ($5 to $20). This product could be mass marketed. Now, rather than being associated with status and glamour, crack reached into every nook and cranny of society. Even the distribution channel changed. Crack houses were created where dealers sold their product. To attract customers, the dealers would initially discount the product by, say, 50%. After brand loyalty was obtained (i.e., in the form of addiction), prices would be raised to retail levels. By the late 1980s, crack addiction was rampant, and the problem continues unabated into the 1990s.

Dr. Hirschman argues that to deal with the cocaine problem, public policy makers must treat it as a consumer good rather than as a disease. As such, one must look at the demand side, as well as the supply side. Perhaps by understanding the psychographic characteristics of users and the needs that the drug fulfills, policies can be developed that will demarket this product of the dark side of consumer behavior.

Based upon Elizabeth C. Hirschman, "Cocaine as Innovation," in *Advances in Consumer Research*, Vol. 19, John Sherry, Jr., and Brian Sternthal, eds. (Provo, UT: Association for Consumer Research, 1992), pp. 129–139.

Figure 15-5 presents a simple model of the diffusion process, identifying six key factors that influence the nature and extent of the diffusion of an innovation.[56] First, diffusion occurs within a social system or market. Second, diffusion depends upon the individual adoption decisions of thousands or even millions of consumers. The individual adoption process is synonymous with individual consumer decision making, discussed in the Chapters 11 through 13. The decisions of individuals are influenced by three factors—the characteristics of the innovation, the characteristics of innovators, and the personal influence process. These three factors make up the third, fourth, and fifth elements of the diffusion process. The final element is the nature of the diffusion process, which results from the influence of the five preceding elements. The sections that follow discuss in greater detail the elements of the diffusion process.[57]

The Social System

The study of the social system in which products are diffused is closely related to the analysis of the impact of cultural and subcultural processes on consumers. (See Chapters 17 and 18.) Thus only a few comments will be made here about the topic. Evidence indicates that the speed of diffusion is influenced by several aspects of the social system. First, the greater the compatibility between the innovation and the values of the members of the social system, the quicker is the rate of diffusion. Second, the more homogeneous (i.e., nonsegmented) the social system, the faster is the diffu-

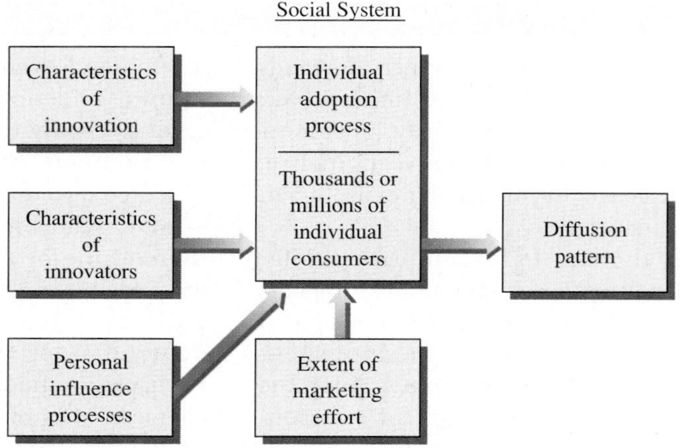

Figure 15-5 A model of the consumer diffusion process. (Based in part on ideas from Hubert Gatignon and Thomas Robertson, "A Propositional Inventory for New Diffusion Research," *Journal of Consumer Research*, Vol. 11, March 1988, pp. 849–867.)

sion process. The diffusion of innovations across cultures is dependent upon the distance between the countries and the social similarity of the cultures.[58]

Characteristics of the Innovation

Innovations have been described in terms of the extent to which the behavior of consumers is influenced by the new product, service, or idea. Three categories of innovations have been identified: continuous, dynamic continuous, and discontinuous. These categories are based upon just how "new" the innovation is. What one finds is that, as the novelty of the innovation increases, the amount of behavior change required by the consumer increases. In addition, one finds that many more continuous innovations enter the marketplace each year than either dynamic continuous or discontinuous inventions. Figure 15-6 diagrams the relationships between the amount of behavior change, the percentage of innovations in each category, and the type of innovation.

Continuous innovations have the least impact on consumers. They are usually modifications of existing products to improve performance, taste, reliability, and so forth. An example would be the changeover of General Motors from round automobile headlights to square headlights in the 1970s. The new product had no real impact on the behavior of consumers, but it was important in the marketplace to the auto company. Changing the headlights was one way that the company could differentiate its models from those of other companies.

Dynamic continuous innovation influence the life-styles of consumers to some degree. The dynamic continuous innovation generally involves some major change in an existing product. An example would be the building of diesel engine automobiles. Diesel engines require a new set of maintenance requirements and fuel-filling procedures for consumers. Other examples of dynamic continuous innovations

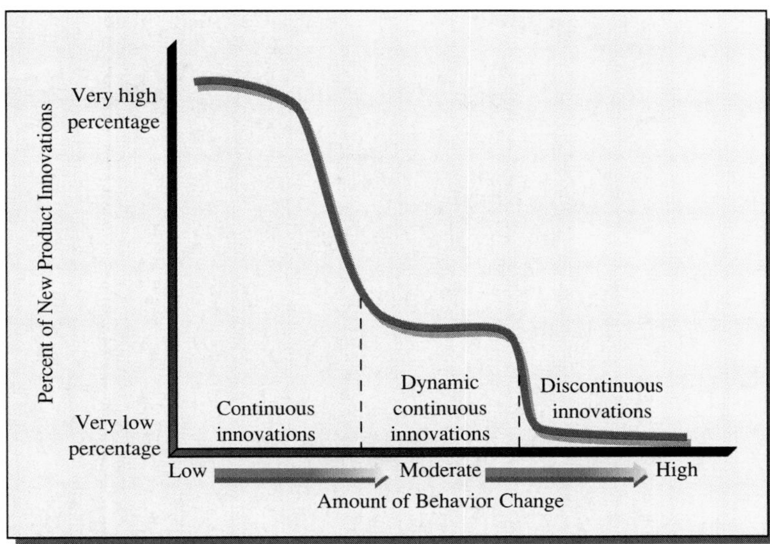

Figure 15-6 A continuum of product innovations and their behavioral impact.

include the introduction of the first compact cars, of microwave ovens, and of heat pumps for residential housing.

Discontinuous innovations are those that produce major changes in the life-styles of consumers. They come along much less frequently than the dynamic or continuous innovations. Examples include computers, televisions, radios, air conditioning, and airplanes. In each of these cases, the innovation changed how people lived. For example, radio and television have changed dramatically how people spend their leisure hours. One might anticipate that future products from the biotechnology revolution will likely have discontinuous properties.

One of the primary problems in developing new products and services is the fact that over 80% fail within the first couple of years. A number of principles have been suggested as necessary for the success of new products:

1. *Relative advantage*. The product must do something better, more cheaply, or more reliably than other products on the market.
2. *Compatibility*. The innovation needs to be consistent with the life-style, social system, and norms of the target market.
3. *Complexity*. Generally, the less complex a product, the faster it will be adopted and the greater the chances of its success.
4. *Trialability*. The easier it is for consumers to use the product and experience its benefits firsthand, the greater are its chances for success.
5. *Observability*. If consumers can see others successfully using the product, its adoption will be more rapid and its success more likely.[59]

Figure 15-7 presents an ad for the Panasonic KX-F90 communications center, which nicely illustrates a continuous innovation. Panasonic has taken the basic tele-

Figure 15-7 The Panasonic communications center is an example of a continuous innovation created by adding new attributes to an existing product. (Courtesy of Panasonic Company.)

phone and added a series of new product attributes—a fax, answering machine, and privacy ring. When the ad appeared in 1992, none of the attributes were new. However, combining them all into one system was innovative. The system should succeed in the marketplace because it had the qualities most associated with the success of innovations (relative advantage, trialability, observability, etc.).

Above all else, a new product must fulfill the needs of a target market. If the product does fulfill needs, the five qualities of observability, trialability, complexity, compatibility, and relative advantage should be thoroughly investigated prior to bringing a new product to market.

Another approach to distinguishing the innovation characteristics of products and services concerns the technological versus symbolic aspects of the innovation. One researcher has proposed that innovations can be categorized as to whether they are technological or symbolic.[60] A *symbolic innovation* is one that communicates a different social meaning than it did previously because of the acquisition of new intangible attributes. A *technological innovation* results from a change in the characteristics of a product or service through the introduction of a technological change. An example of a technological innovation would be a compact disc player. An example of a symbolic innovation would be the diffusion of new hairstyles or fashion styles through the population.

The concept that innovations can be either symbolic or technological adds an important dimension to their understanding. Indeed, the adoption of new symbols may play an important role in describing fashion trends. In addition, a key to understanding the diffusion of new political, religious, and life-style ideas may be to view them as involving the diffusion of symbols.

Characteristics of Innovators

One of the important problems faced by marketers of innovative products is identifying the characteristics of people who buy the product early in its life cycle. Names have been given to groups of individuals who adopt new products at various stages of the product life cycle; these are shown in Figure 15-8. Five different categories of

Figure 15-8 Categories of adopters.

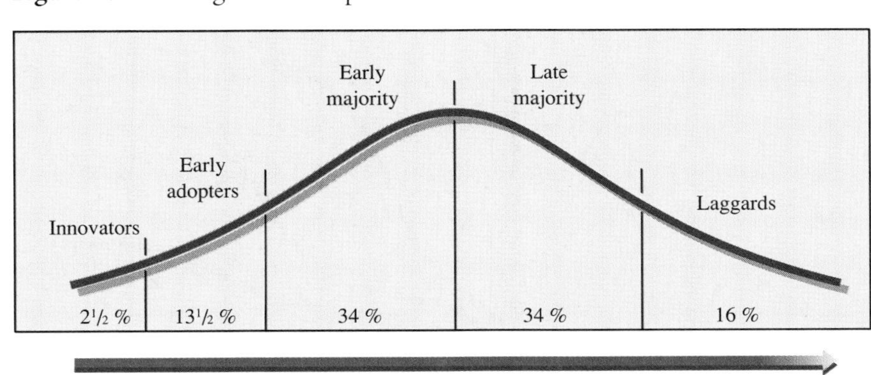

adopters have been identified. Innovators are those who make up the first 2.5% of the buyers of a new product. Early adopters make up the next 13.5% of buyers, followed by the early majority (the next 34%), the late majority (the next 34%), and finally the laggards (the last 16%).

Research conducted to identify a profile of innovators has suggested that people who are innovative tend to have higher incomes and higher levels of education, possess greater social mobility, have higher opinion leadership in the product category, and have more favorable attitudes toward risk.[61] A recent study investigated the characteristics of early adopters of new long-distance services. The results revealed that the early adopters tended to be younger, better educated, and heavy telephone users. In this study income was not related to early adoption.

The Individual Adoption Process

As noted earlier in the section, the individual adoption process is identical to the consumer decision-making process discussed in Chapters 11, 12, and 13. Thus the decision of an individual to adopt an innovation may result from extended decision making, limited decision making, an experiential process, or behavioral influence. The adoption of new symbols may be best understood as occurring through an experiential process. From the experiential perspective, consumers are viewed as adopting a symbolic product, service, or idea based upon their overall affective reactions to it, rather than by going through some type of lengthy decision process.

Factors Influencing the Diffusion Pattern

Figure 15-9 identifies the normal pattern of how innovative products diffuse through the population. Note that the curve describing the diffusion process in Figure 15-8 is S-shaped. During the introductory phase, the percentage of consumers adopting

Figure 15-9 The shape of the diffusion process.

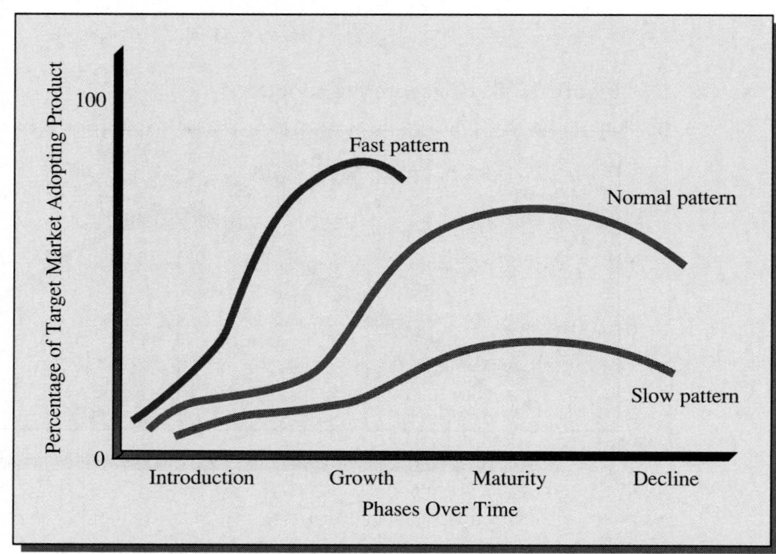

the product is small and slowly accelerating. As the product moves into the growth stage, the percentage accelerates and the curve bends upward rapidly. During maturity, the growth slows until it turns negative, marking the beginning of decline.

The exact shape of the curve depends upon a number of factors. If the innovation is adopted very quickly, the fast pattern found in Figure 15-8 results. If the adoption rate is slow, the pattern becomes much flatter and more drawn out. A number of factors affect the rapidity with which an innovation is adopted and, as a consequence, the shape of the curve. These include the characteristics of the product, the characteristics of the target market, and the amount of marketing effort exerted by the company.

1. *Characteristics of the product.* The same factors that influence the likely success of an innovation also influence the rapidity with which it is adopted. Thus, to the extent that it fulfills a need, is compatible, has a relative advantage, has low complexity, has observable positive features, and is easily tried, the product will be adopted more quickly.[62]
2. *Characteristics of the target market.* Products targeted to different target groups will exhibit divergent adoption patterns. For example, products that appeal to younger, more highly educated, change-oriented individuals are often quickly adopted, but these also run the risk of rapidly moving into decline.[63]
3. *Extent of marketing effort.* Companies can influence the growth curve of a product by the quality and extent of their marketing effort.

Readers should recognize that the shape of the diffusion pattern is not always S-shaped. In some instances it may show an exponential pattern—where the curve starts out slow and then increases at a rapid rate. Exponential patterns tend to result when the innovation is adopted via low-involvement decision making, when low switching costs exist, and when a relative lack of personal influence occurs. In contrast, the S-shaped curve tends to be found when personal influence is operating, when high switching costs exist, and when a high-involvement decision process is taking place.[64]

Various researchers have attempted to predict the shape of the diffusion curve by using mathematical models. One well-known model for predicting the adoption of durable goods stated that the adoption curve was based on the number of innovators who would initially try the product and on the number of imitators who bought the product because the innovators had bought it. By combining information on innovation and imitation propensities with knowledge of the total market potential of the product and of how many people had previously bought the product at various times, a good prediction of sales of various home appliances could be made.[65]

The Diffusion of Rumors

Rumors periodically plague firms both large and small. They are a kind of group contagion that result from the fears and anxieties of people. For example, national hysteria over the AIDS epidemic has spawned rumors. In at least two instances rumors were spread that an employee of a restaurant had AIDS and was infecting food. As soon as such a rumor begins to spread, business falls dramatically. Over the past 15 years, rumors have created major problems for such corporate giants as Xerox, Procter & Gamble, and McDonald's.

In 1978 the rumor began to spread that the dry toner used by Xerox in its copiers caused cancer. In 1979 Procter & Gambler began to be plagued by the rumor that the firm embraces satanism. Flyers addressed to conservative Protestant congregations noted that the P&G symbol contained a sorcerer's head and 13 stars—a sign of Satan. McDonald's Corporation has also been hit by rumors alleging satanism. However, even more disturbing has been the fiction that the company adds ground worms to its hamburger meat.

Between 1985 and 1986 sales of Corona Extra Imported Beer had increased by 170%. In 1987, however, after the company was plagued by rumors that the product was contaminated with urine, some markets experienced an 80% dropoff in sales.[66] The company sued distributors of Heineken beer for starting the rumor. (Heineken's sales had been severely harmed by the growth in Corona's sales.) The rumor alleged that the urine contamination was reported on the "Donahue" show and "60 Minutes."

Types and Causes of Rumors

Sociologists and psychologists have identified a number of different types of rumors.[67] **Pipe-dream rumors** represent wishful thinking on the part of the circulators. They are positive hopes concerning something that might happen, such as how much the Christmas bonus will be in a corporation. "Hot tips" in the stock market exemplify pipe-dream rumors. In this case, unscrupulous company employees circulate grandiose information about the prospects for a stock—in the hope that the public will begin to buy the company's shares, believing that a fortune can be made.

Another type of rumor, a **bogie**, is a fear rumor that spooks the marketplace. These are the type that have plagued Xerox, McDonald's, and Procter & Gamble. A bogie demolished the first king-sized menthol cigarette, Spud, in the 1940s.[68] A rumor spread that a leper worked in the plant where the brand was packaged. In six months the cigarette had disappeared from the marketplace.

Rumors can also be *self-fulfilling*. In this case the rumor is based on a perception of what could happen in the future if something else were to occur. "Bank runs" are examples of self-fulfilling rumors. It is true that if all the depositors in a bank suddenly withdraw their money, any bank would fail. In bad times this knowledge can "spook" people and result in the very behavior that the people were afraid would occur. Indeed, runs on banks occurred in the 1980s, forcing the closing of a number of banks across the United States.

In *premeditated* rumors, individuals with something to gain set out to spread rumors that may help them financially or otherwise. Such premeditated rumors can spread through the stock market and cause short-term shifts in the value of companies, which unscrupulous individuals can use to make money. Procter & Gamble believed that its Satan rumors resulted in part from the salespeople of a competing firm distributing the flyers describing the firm's supposed satanic activities. Procter & Gamble took the unprecedented step of filing lawsuits against five individuals.[69]

Finally, rumors can be *spontaneous* when people seek explanations for unusual events. One author suggested that the ground worm rumors striking McDonald's may have begun when a consumer found "tubular" matter in some hamburger.[70] Such matter could easily result from a small blood vessel not being ground up very well. To explain the material, the consumer leaps to the conclusion that the tube must have been a worm.

The right environment is required for rumors to be nourished to the point where they can move through the population. The two factors that seem to be required are uncertainty and anxiety. Rumors generally occur and spread most rapidly when times are bad, and people are down, uncertain about their future, and anxious about what will happen to their dreams. Thus it is not surprising that the rumors that struck McDonald's and Procter & Gamble were at their worst during the severe recession that struck the United States between 1980 and 1983.

In addition to uncertainty and anxiety, researchers have found that the importance and the ambiguity of a rumor influences its spread. A formula was developed to express the relationship:[71]

$$\text{Rumor} = \text{Ambiguity} \times \text{Importance}$$

During World War II, when meat shortages were experienced in the United States, rumors spread that whole sides of beef were being thrown away at Army camps. This was a very disturbing rumor stateside, considering that the meat shortage was important to people and most had no idea what was going on in the Army camps.

Urban legends, a phenomenon related to rumors, are considered in Highlight 15-2.

Managerial Implications of Diffusion Processes

Knowledge of diffusion processes is important to managers, particularly those involved in marketing new products and services. Product managers need to identify whether the innovation is continuous, dynamic continuous, or discontinuous. They need to investigate the extent to which an innovation has a relative advantage over competitors and is compatible with the values and life-style of their target market. Furthermore, the manager needs to assess the product's complexity, trialability, and observability. Through such analysis the marketing manager can get a feel for the likely growth curve of the product. Will the product be a slow starter that must be nurtured for a substantial length of time, or will a strong marketing effort allow it to start fast?

New products that are of a continuous nature and that break into a growing market have the potential to be fast starters. An example is the phenomenal growth of Compaq Computer Corporation in its first couple of years of existence. The Compaq computer was a continuous innovation—the first competitor to be compatible with the IBM personal computer and also to be portable. With a market already established and a product that possessed all the attributes necessary for success (i.e., observability, trialability, and so forth), it became in its first year the most successful company in the history of American business. In 1991, however, the company began to experience major marketing problems, its growth flattened, its CEO was fired, and its stock price plummeted. Compaq illustrates the problems that can occur when early growth rates are extremely high. Figure 15-10 presents a recent advertisement from this now mature company.

Monitoring information transmission processes is also important for marketing managers. Marketing research should be employed to identify exactly what a company's customers are communicating to others about its products or services. Studies at Ford Motor Company have found that satisfied customers tell 8 other

HIGHLIGHT 15-2

Urban Legends: Modern Folklore That Can Hurt Sales

"Say, did you hear the story about the little old lady who had just washed her pet poodle? Well, the dog had a cold; and because she wanted to dry it quickly she put it in her microwave oven. Ten minutes later she found the poor thing, cooked from the inside out."

The "microwaved" pet anecdote is one example of a number of urban legends that float around the country, often for years. Urban legends are realistic stories about incidents that are reputed to have occurred recently. Similar to folktales and old legends, they usually have some type of twist or moral to them. For example, the microwaved-poodle tales warns us of the problems of having too much technology.

Urban legends are diffused through the population much like rumors. However; they are longer and more specific and often are related to local happenings. They may even incorporate local rumors. Even the mass media will help to circulate the legends as something that really occurred. For example, the following story was carried in an Ann Landers column and is called the "Nude Housewife." A woman was doing her laundry in her basement when she impulsively decided to take off her soiled housedress and put it in the machine. Her hair was in rollers, and the pipes overhead were leaking. She spotted her son's football helmet and put it on her head. There she was, stark naked (except for the football helmet) when she heard a cough. The woman turned around and found herself staring into the face of the meter reader: As he headed for the door his comment was, "I hope your team wins, lady."

Unfortunately, urban legends can affect corporations. One such story involved a Kmart store in Dallas, Texas. A woman was described as looking for some fur coats that had been imported from Mexico. When she put her hand in one of the pockets, she felt a sharp pain. After a few minutes, her arm was turning black and blue. Later that day her arm had to be amputated because of a snake bite. One of the local newspapers tried to investigate the legend to see if it was true. They checked hospitals, insurance people, and even a person to whom it was supposed to have occurred. The woman had heard the legend but understood that the snake was in a basket of fruit.

This legend, which warns of the dangers of falling for terrific bargains, should be examined in light of American xenophobia.

Based on Jan Harold Brunvand, "Urban Legends Folklore for Today," *Psychology Today*, June 1980, pp. 50–62.

people about their cars. In contrast, dissatisfied customers tell 22 people about their complaints.[72] These results illustrate that it is crucially important for firms to track customer satisfaction and then take quick steps to remedy problems that may occur.

Managers should also monitor the environment for the spread of rumors. One expert suggested that companies should go through a series of actions if a rumor strikes them.[73]

Step 1: Ride out the rumor.
Step 2: Trace its origins.
Step 3: Treat it locally.
Step 4: Rebut it with facts, but don't deny the rumor before the public hears about it.

Figure 15-10 In the late 1980s, Compaq was in its growth stage. Now in its maturity, Compaq is using ads such as this one to maintain its market share. (Reprinted with permission of Compaq Computer Corporation. All rights reserved.)

Rumors, however, are rarely eradicated completely. Procter & Gamble's Satan rumor was still resurfacing in the mid-1980s, some six or seven years after it began. One executive with P&G stated, "Rumors are like matter. They can't be destroyed."[74] In fact, they can move from company to company. The worms-in-hamburger rumor illustrates such mobility—it struck Wendy's prior to jumping on McDonald's, the industry leader.

A possible problem, however, should be noted with the use of refutational strategies to eliminate rumor problems. A study was done to investigate the worm rumor and McDonald's hamburgers.[75] The authors found that when the rumor was refuted with facts (e.g., red worms cost five dollars per pound and could not possibly be used), the negative impression of McDonald's remained. Because a refutational strategy mentions the rumor, the consumer is reminded of the negative information in the rumor. One way around the problem may be to give the facts without mentioning the rumor. McDonald's has in fact done this with a major promotional campaign that advertises the fact that the hamburgers are made with 100% pure beef. No mention of the rumor is made in the advertising campaign.

A MANAGERIAL APPLICATIONS EXAMPLE

After 25 years of intensive work and over $700 million in capital expenditures, DuPont Co. chemists finally succeeded in producing the new fiber called Kevlar®. When efforts to develop the product began in the early 1960s, the goal was to create a fiber that would duplicate the phenomenal success of nylon and Dacron®. The result was a fiber that was lighter, yet five times stronger than steel. Only one problem existed, however. In what products could it be used?[76]

DuPont managers believed that Kevlar® would replace steel as the material of choice for use in automobile tires. In comparison to steel it was lighter, stronger, more heat resistant, and more easily capable of being woven into rubber compounds for making tires. After building a $500 million plant to produce the fiber, the company learned that tire makers had decided to use steel anyway. Steel was cheaper, and consumers liked the phrase "steel-belted radials." In the early 1980s the only demand for Kevlar® was for use in racing tires. As the marketing manager for the fiber said, "Kevlar® was the answer, but we didn't know for what."

To its credit DuPont recognized the problems in the early 1980s and overhauled the entire marketing effort of the product. It put together a team that swelled to over 1,000 people. Most focused on marketing research and developing new applications for the material. One manager described the turnaround in attitude: "We used to sell what we made. Now we make what we can sell." The company learned the hard way that a technological breakthrough does not necessarily mean financial success. As one consultant said, "If you have a new material, you have to beat the world's door down before it's accepted. You need a strong stomach to be able to withstand the valleys. But when the peak comes, you make obnoxious amounts of money."

By the late 1980s, DuPont's tenacity and patience began to pay off as new uses for the fiber began to be discovered. The breakthrough came when the U.S. Army adopted it for use in helmets and flak jackets. Police departments began to purchase bulletproof vests made of Kevlar®. Newer uses include trawling nets, golf clubs, racing sails, protective gloves, oceanic cables, and protective curtains for embassies. Most recently, Kevlar® is being used as one of the materials in the exotic composites out of which jet aircraft like the stealth bomber are made. By the late 1980s profits on the fiber were described as fair to reasonable as sales reached the $300 million per year mark. With annual growth of 10% expected, it looks as though the product is finally a success.

The Consumer Behavior Analysis

The problems of Kevlar® are readily analyzed by having knowledge of group, word-of-mouth, and diffusion processes. Ideas regarding the diffusion of innovations are especially important in this example. In considering Kevlar®, one must recognize that it is primarily an industrial product. Companies or agencies of the federal government would be the first to adopt the product. They might then fashion it into something else, such as flak jackets or auto tires. For these buyers, Kevlar® was probably viewed as a dynamic continuous innovation. Its properties were quite different from those of the materials it replaced, such as steel. Thus whole new processes would have to be developed to use it. In such circumstances, encouraging adoptions of the product can be quite difficult.

Marketers at DuPont had to go to extraordinary lengths to show Kevlar®'s relative advantage. Further, they had to demonstrate its compatibility with existing procedures and with the materials with which it would be used. As a result, DuPont was forced to use readily observed and understood demonstrations. For example, to obtain an order from the U.S. Army, Kevlar® flak jackets were hung over 100 goats and .38-caliber pistol bullets were fired into the animals. The goats escaped with only minor bruises. Under such circumstances one can readily see why the growth curve of Kevlar® was so slow. Indeed, it was only because DuPont put together a major marketing and new product development effort that the fiber began to turn a profit. It was this marketing team that identified the products into which Kevlar® could be made, how the products would be positioned, the market segments to which the products would be targeted, and how the product would be promoted.

Ideas from group influence suggest that conformity pressures might make it difficult for purchasing agents to specify the purchase of Kevlar®. Sales personnel should make special efforts to identify the "real" decision makers to whom purchasing agents conform. Similarly, because of the risk involved in adopting the new material, one could anticipate that if purchase decisions were made by members of a purchase group, conservative shifts could occur. Possibly, sales presentations could be developed that attempt to lower the perceived risk and the group polarization working against the sale.

DuPont management should also be aware of the possibility of rumors starting about the fiber. Because of its artificial nature, there is always the potential that cancer rumors might surface. Rumors could become a distinct possibility when the fiber begins to find uses in products destined for the general population, such as gloves. Environmental analysis should take place in order to quickly identify such a possibility.

The Managerial Applications Analysis

Table 15-6 presents the managerial applications analysis for the Kevlar® case. Four consumer concepts have particular relevance to the case—the diffusion of innovations, group polarization effects, conformity, and rumor transmission. Information on the diffusion of innovations applies to market research, segmentation, positioning, product development, and promotional strategy. Clearly, market research was required to identify potential uses for the product, as well as segments of consumers with needs matching the properties of the product (e.g., military requirements for a tough fabric from which to produce bulletproof vests). Using the analysis of the needs of the segments, new products made from Kevlar® could be developed and promotional strategies designed to increase the rapidity with which the product would diffuse through the environment. Positioning strategies could also be identified that would take advantage of the product's unique capabilities.

Group polarization and conformity effects have implications for market research and promotional strategy. Market research should be used to identify cultural norms within the targeted companies that may influence the decision process. Sales personnel could then develop persuasive arguments that could be used to minimize the chances of having a group shift occur that would harm the adoption process of Kevlar®. Similarly, market research should be undertaken to identify what pressures may exist within targeted firms that would push purchasing agents not to consider the product.

DuPont managers should also perform environmental analyses and be alert for the possible development of rumors. Because Kevlar® is a synthetic material, a possibility exists, as noted earlier, that rumors may emerge concerning its possible health-damaging effects. By closely monitoring newspaper, radio, and television communications, the company would be prepared to adopt appropriate public relations strategies to combat developing rumors.

TABLE 15-6

Managerial Applications Analysis of the Kevlar® Case

Consumer Concepts	*Managerial Implications*
Diffusion of innovations	*Market research*—Identify potential uses of product and characteristics of potential early adopters.
	Segmentation—Based upon market research, identify segments of early adopters who have specific needs potentially filled by Kevlar® products.
	Product development—Develop new products that fulfill the needs of these segments.
	Positioning—Develop positioning strategies that employ Kevlar®'s unique characteristics.
Group polarization	*Market research*—Identify cultural norms within targeted companies/industries that may influence decisions.
	Promotional strategy—Inform sales personnel of the potential effects of group polarization.
Conformity	*Market research*—Employ research to identify potential conformity pressures within companies that would impact the buying processes.
	Promotional strategy—Inform sales personnel of the potential effects of conformity pressures. Develop strategies to overcome such pressures.
Rumors	*Environmental analysis*—Perform research to analyze the environment for potential rumors that could surface regarding the use of Kevlar®.
	Promotional strategy—Employ appropriate public relations efforts to minimize the chances of rumor transmission.

SUMMARY

A group is a set of individuals who interact with one another over some period of time and who share some common need or goal. Groups are important to study because they are more than simply the sum of their parts. A variety of different types of groups exist that may have an impact on consumption. These include reference groups, aspiration groups, dissociative groups, formal and informal groups, membership groups, and primary groups. Such groups influence the behavior of consumers directly through informational influence, normative influence, and value-expressive influence. In addition, groups develop roles that may be adopted by consumers and that may, in turn, influence buying behavior. Finally, groups exert conformity pressures on their members, and when decisions are made, group discussion may polarize the choice process so that more extreme decisions are made.

Several models have been developed to explain how personal influence is transmitted. The trickle-down model holds that information moves from the upper classes to the lower classes. The two-step flow model holds that mass communications first influence opinion leaders, who in turn influence followers. In the multistep flow model, information is viewed as moving from the mass media to gatekeepers, opinion leaders, and followers. The approach holds that communications can pass back and forth between the three groups of people and that in different situations the members of the groups may interchange.

Within groups, consumers frequently engage in dyadic exchanges. Two types of dyadic exchanges exist. The first is the service encounter, in which the customer interacts with the product provider. The second is word-of-mouth communications. Word-of-mouth communications can have much greater persuasive impact than impersonal communications. In word-of-mouth network models, one consumer is viewed as communicating directly with another and passing on information about a product, service, or idea. Word-of-mouth network models seek to identify the patterns of how information flows among people.

It is often possible to identify opinion leaders in word-of-mouth communication. These individuals are important to companies because they control in part the positivity or negativity of the information that others receive. Although different people tend to be opinion leaders for different product categories, some common factors do characterize opinion leaders. In general, opinion leaders tend to be heavily involved in and knowledgeable about the product category. Similar to opinion leaders, market mavens are consumers who have information about many kinds of products and services and who pass on such information to others. They seem to take on roles as generalists who assist other consumers in the marketplace. Surrogate consumers are people who act as agents retained by consumers to guide, direct, and transact marketplace activities. They are frequently paid for the service provided. Examples of surrogates include wine stewards, tax consultants, and interior decorators.

Diffusion processes illustrate cases in which ideas, products, or emotions spread through a large number of people. Consumer researchers are particularly interested in the factors that influence how innovations are adopted by consumers. Factors that influence the rate of adoption include the type of innovation, the characteristics of the target market, and the extent of the marketing effort. Rumors represent another type of diffusion phenomenon. Rumors can be major threats to companies—they have sometimes resulted in the demise of products.

KEY TERMS

aspiration group
bogies
comparative appraisal
compliance
conformity
continuous innovations
diffusion
discontinuous innovations
dissociative group
dyadic exchange
dynamic continuous innovations
focus groups
formal group
group
group polarization phenomenon
group shift
informal group
informational influence
market embeddedness
market mavens
negativity bias
normative influence
norms
opinion leaders
pipe-dream rumors
private acceptance
product innovation
reference group
reflected appraisal
role
role-related product cluster
rumors
service encounter
social comparison
surrogate consumer
trickle-down theory
urban legends
value-expressive influence
word-of-mouth communications

REVIEW QUESTIONS

1. Define the concept of the group and identify the various types of groups.
2. Why is it that "groups are more than the sum of their parts"? Cite a specific example of how the buying patterns or actions of people differ when they engage in an activity as part of a group rather than as individuals.
3. Indicate how groups influence people through normative, value-expressive, and informational influence.
4. Define the concept of role. What are some examples of "role-related product clusters"?
5. Identify the various characteristics of the product and the properties of the person that can bring about conformity to group pressures.
6. How can social comparison processes influence consumers?
7. What is a group shift? What is a likely explanation for why group shifts occur? What types of consumer decisions might be influenced by group shifts?
8. Why is it that groups often give very poor tips in restaurants?
9. What is meant by the term diffusion? In a consumer behavior context, what is it that is diffused?
10. What are the various types of product innovations that have been identified?
11. What are the factors that can influence new product success by affecting the rate of diffusion?
12. What is meant by the term diffusion pattern? What are the factors that influence the type of diffusion pattern displayed by a product?
13. Identify the five categories of adopters and the relative size of each category.
14. What are the various approaches to dealing with corporate rumors? Identify four different types of rumors.
15. What is the negativity bias in word-of-mouth communications?
16. Identify the three models that describe how personal influence is transmitted through the population. Which of the models appears to be the most accurate?
17. What is the difference between an opinion leader and a product innovator?
18. What are market mavens and surrogate consumers?

DISCUSSION QUESTIONS

1. List the various reference groups that have an influence on you and categorize them into aspiration, dissociative, primary, and informal groups. Try to rank them as to their importance in influencing your consumption behavior. On what types of products, if any, do these groups influence your consumption?
2. Groups develop norms to help them function more smoothly. Consider the classroom situation at your university or college. What are the norms that guide the behavior of instructors as well as students in the classroom?
3. Groups can affect consumption through both value-expressive and informational influence. What are some examples of value-expressive and informational influence that could affect fraternity or sorority members in their purchase of an automobile and of a stereo?
4. What products would be considered part of a role-related product cluster for a college student and for a young mother and father with a new baby?
5. Consider the various groups of which you are a member. In which of these groups are conformity pressures the greatest? Why is this the case?
6. Suppose that you are a member of a buying center for a large, highly conservative corporation. Most major purchase decisions are reached through a consensus process among

five members of the group. In the current instance your group must decide whether to purchase a complex and expensive computer system from an established firm that charges high prices or from a smaller but competently run firm that charges lower prices. What would the group polarization phenomenon say about the likely decision?

7. Consider the following three products: compact disc players, pump toothpaste dispensers, and computers. Classify each of these as to their type of innovation. What type of diffusion pattern would you describe each as having? Please justify your answers.
8. Identify a recent rumor that involves corporations or their products. What should the company be doing to squash the rumor?
9. Diagram a word-of-mouth network for a service that you have recently obtained, such as where to get a haircut or which dentist to use. Go out and conduct brief interviews and attempt to track down the people who formed the linkages in the network.
10. Among the acquaintances that you have, identify people who act as opinion leaders, product innovators, market mavens, and surrogate consumers. Describe what each person does.
11. Think about the goods and services that you purchase. To what extent do word-of-mouth communications influence your purchases?
12. Suppose that you are a marketing manager for a regional brewery. How successful do you think a strategy would be of attempting to reach opinion leaders with communications so that they will pass these messages on to followers and, thereby, influence their behavior?

ENDNOTES

1. Richard Turner, "Disney's Star Is Foreign to U.S. Audiences," *The Wall Street Journal*, December 21, 1990, pp. B1, B5.
2. Ibid.
3. Michael Lynn and Bib Latane, "The Psychology of Restaurant Tipping," *Journal of Applied Social Psychology*, Vol. 14 (November–December 1984), pp. 549–561. For more information on tipping, please see John A. McCarty, L. Shrum, Tracey Conrad-Katz, and Zacho Kanne, "Tipping as Consumer Behavior: A Qualitative Investigation," in *Advances in Consumer Research*, Vol. 17, Marvin Goldberg, Gerald Gorn, and Richard Pollay, eds. (Provo, UT: Association for Consumer Research, 1990), pp. 723–727.
4. Donald H. Granbois, "Improving the Study of Consumer In-Store Behavior," *Journal of Marketing*, Vol. 32 (October 1968), pp. 28–32; "Eatery Ad Hits Gossip," *Advertising Age*, August 3, 1987, p. 6.
5. James C. Ward and Peter H. Reingen, "Sociocognitive Analysis of Group Decision Making Among Consumers," *Journal of Consumer Research*, Vol. 17 (December 1990), pp. 245–262.
6. Michael S. Olmstead, *The Small Group* (New York: Holt, Rinehart and Winston, 1962). For more on group processes, please see C. H. Cooley, *Social Organization* (New York: Schocken Books, 1962).
7. Marvin E. Shaw, *Group Dynamics* (New York: McGraw-Hill, 1971).
8. Francis Bourne, "Group Influence in Marketing and Public Relations," in *Some Applications of Behavioral Research*, R. Likert and S. P. Hayes, eds. (Basel, Switzerland: UNESCO, 1957). For a study that tested these ideas, see William Bearden and Michael Etzel, "Reference Group Influence on Product and Brand Purchase Decisions," *Journal of Consumer Research*, Vol. 9 (September 1982), pp. 183–194.
9. Shaw, *Group Dynamics*.
10. H. Haire, "Projective Techniques in Marketing Research," *Journal of Marketing*, Vol. 14 (April 1950), pp. 649–656.
11. F. E. Webster and F. von Pechman, "A Replication of the Shopping List Study,"

Journal of Marketing, Vol. 34 (April 1970), pp. 61–63.

12. Charles A. Kiesler and Sara B. Kiesler, *Conformity* (Reading, MA: Addison-Wesley, 1969), p. 7.
13. Solomon E. Asch, *Social Psychology* (Englewood Cliffs, NJ: Prentice-Hall, 1952).
14. V. Parker Lessig and C. Whan Park, "Promotional Perspectives of Reference Group Influence, Advertising Implications," *Journal of Advertising*, Vol. 7 (Spring 1978), pp. 41–47.
15. Brenda Gainer and Eileen Fischer, "To Buy or Not to Buy? That Is Not the Question: Female Ritual in Home Shopping Parties," in *Advances in Consumer Research*, Vol. 18, Rebecca Holman and Michael Solomon, eds. (Provo, UT: Association for Consumer Research, 1991), pp. 597–602.
16. Jonathan K. Frenzen and Harry L. Davis, "Purchasing Behavior in Embedded Markets," *Journal of Consumer Research*, Vol. 17 (June 1990), pp. 1–12.
17. Leon Festinger, "A Theory of Social Comparison Processes," *Human Relations*, Vol. 7 (May 1954), pp. 117–140.
18. Edward Jones and Harold Gerard, *Social Psychology* (New York: John Wiley, 1967).
19. Festinger, "A Theory of Social Comparison Processes." For a consumer study that supports these findings, see George P. Moschis, "Social Comparison and Information Group Influence," *Journal of Marketing Research*, Vol. 13 (August 1976), pp. 237–244.
20. Marsha L. Richins, "Social Comparison and the Idealized Images of Advertising," *Journal of Consumer Research*, Vol. 18 (June 1991), pp. 71–83.
21. R. E. Knox and R. K. Safford, "Group Caution at the Race Track," *Journal of Experimental Social Psychology*, Vol. 12 (May 1976), pp. 317–324
22. Helmet Lamm and David G. Myers, "Group-Induced Polarization of Attitudes and Behavior," in *Advances in Experimental Social Psychology*, Vol. 11, Leonard Berkowitz, ed. (New York: Academic Press, 1978), pp. 145–195.
23. Lamm and Myers, "Group-Induced Polarization."
24. Peter Reingen, "The Risky Shift in Ad Hoc and Natural Consumer Groups: A Test of the Polarization Hypothesis and a Majority Rule Explanation," in *Advances in Consumer Research*, Vol. 4, W. D. Perrault, ed. (Ann Arbor, MI: Association of Consumer Research, 1977), pp. 87–92.
25. Maureen Coughlin and P. J. O'Connor, "Risk Shifting in Joint Consumer Decision Making," in *Advances in Consumer Research*, Vol. 11, Thomas Kinnear, ed. (Ann Arbor, MI: Association for Consumer Research, 1984), pp. 165–169.
26. A recent study found evidence that group polarization could also occur when groups were asked to select a restaurant at which to eat. The article also tested three different mathematical models of group polarization. See Vithala R. Rao and Joel H. Steckel, "A Polarization Model for Describing Group Preferences," *Journal of Consumer Research*, Vol. 18 (June 1991), pp. 108–118.
27. Terry Bristol and Edward F. Fern, "Using Qualitative Techniques to Explore Consumer Attitudes: Insights from Group Process Theories," in *Advances in Consumer Research*, Vol. 20, Leigh McAlister and Michael Rothschild, eds. (Provo, UT: Association for Consumer Research, 1993), pp. 444–448.
28. This definition is based in part on one developed by Paula Fitzgerald Bone, "Determinants of Word-of-Mouth Communications During Product Consumption," in *Advances in Consumer Research*, Vol. 19, John F. Sherry, Jr., and Brian Sternthal, eds. (Provo, UT: Association for Consumer Research, 1992), pp. 579–583.
29. Stephen P. Morin, "Influentials Advising Their Friends to Sell Lots of High-Tech Gadgetry," *The Wall Street Journal*, February 28, 1983, p. 30.

30. Elihu Katz and Paul Lazarsfeld, *Personal Influence* (Glencoe, IL: Free Press, 1955).

31. Sidney Feldman and Merlin Spencer, "The Effect of Personal Influence in the Selection of Consumer Services," in *Proceedings of the Fall Conference of the American Marketing Association*, Peter Bennett, ed. (Chicago: American Marketing Association, 1965), pp. 440–452.

32. Johan Arndt, "Role of Product-Related Conversations in the Diffusion of a New Product," *Journal of Marketing Research*, Vol. 4 (August 1967), p. 292.

33. Paul M. Herr, Frank R. Kardes, and John Kim, "Effects of Word-of-Mouth and Product-Attribute Information on Persuasion: An Accessibility-Diagnosticity Perspective," *Journal of Consumer Research*, Vol. 17 (March 1991), pp. 454–462.

34. Thomas Robertson, Joan Zielinski, and Scott Ward, *Consumer Behavior* (Glenview, IL: Scott, Foresman, 1984).

35. Ernst Dichter, "How Word-of-Mouth Advertising Works," *Harvard Business Review*, Vol. 44 (November–December 1966), p. 148.

36. Peter Reingen and Jerome Kernan, "Analysis of Referral Networks in Marketing: Methods and Illustration," *Journal of Marketing Research*, Vol. 23 (November 1986), pp. 370–378.

37. Definitions are taken from Jacqueline Johnson Brown, "Social Ties and Word-of-Mouth Referral Behavior," *Journal of Consumer Research*, Vol. 14 (December 1987), pp. 350–362.

38. Ibid.

39. Reingen and Kernan, "Analysis of Referral Networks in Marketing."

40. Charles W. King and John O. Summers, "Overlap of Opinion Leadership Across Product Categories," *Journal of Marketing Research*, Vol. 7 (February 1970), pp. 43–50.

41. Katz and Lazarsfeld, *Personal Influence*, pp. 332–334.

42. Russell Belk, "Occurrence of Word-of-Mouth Buyer Behavior as a Function of Situation and Advertising Stimuli," in *Combined Proceedings of the American Marketing Association*, Series No. 33, Fred C. Allvine, ed. (Chicago: American Marketing Association, 1971), pp. 419–422.

43. Everett M. Rogers, *Diffusion of Innovations*, 3rd ed. (New York: Free Press, 1983), pp. 281–284.

44. Thomas Robertson and James Myers, "Personality Correlates of Opinion Leadership and Innovative Buying Behavior," *Journal of Marketing Research*, Vol. 6 (May 1969), p. 168.

45. James Coleman, Elihu Katz, and Herbert Menzel, *Medical Innovation: A Diffusion Study* (Indianapolis, IN: Bobbs-Merrill, 1966).

46. Ibid.

47. Lawrence Feick and Linda Price, "The Market Maven: A Diffuser of Marketplace Information," *Journal of Marketing*, Vol. 51 (January 1987), pp. 83–87.

48. Michael T. Elliott and Anne E. Warfield, "Do Market Mavens Categorize Brands Differently?" in *Advances in Consumer Research*, Vol. 20, Leigh McAlister and Michael Rothschild, eds. (Provo, UT: Association for Consumer Research, 1993), pp. 202–208.

49. Michael Solomon, "The Missing Link: Surrogate Consumers in the Marketing Chain," *Journal of Marketing*, Vol. 50 (October 1986), pp. 208–218.

50. Michael R. Solomon, Carol Surprenant, John A. Czepiel, and Evelyn G. Gutman, "A Role Theory Perspective on Dyadic Interactions: The Service Encounter," *Journal of Marketing*, Vol. 49 (Winter 1985), pp. 99-111.

51. Stephen J. Grove and Raymond P. Fisk, "The Service Experience as Theater," in *Advances in Consumer Research*, Vol. 19, John F. Sherry, Jr., and Brian Sternthal, eds. (Provo, UT: Association for Consumer Research, 1992), pp. 455–461.

52. Michael Guiry, "Consumer and Employee Roles in Service Encounters," in *Advances in Consumer Research*, Vol. 19, John F. Sherry, Jr., and Brian Sternthal, eds. (Provo, UT: Association for Consumer Research, 1992), pp. 666–672.

53. Laurie Freeman and Julie Erickson,

"Doctored Strategy, Good Marketers Push Products Through Physicians," *Advertising Age*, March 28, 1988, p. 12.

54. Henry Assael, *Consumer Behavior and Marketing Action* (Boston: Kent, 1983).

55. Derived from Glen L. Urban and John Hauser, *Design and Marketing of New Products* (Englewood Cliffs, NJ: Prentice-Hall, 1980).

56. Hubert Gatignon and Thomas Robertson, "A Propositional Inventory for New Diffusion Research," *Journal of Consumer Research*, Vol. 11 (March 1985), pp. 849–867. This article provides an excellent review of the diffusion literature and develops a comprehensive set of propositions concerning the factors influencing the diffusion process.

57. Other diffusion models also exist. A model based upon naturalistic observation of diffusion processes in Third World countries was developed by Eric J. Arnould, "Toward a Broadened Theory of Preference Formation and the Diffusion of Innovations: Cases from Zinder Province, Niger Republic," *Journal of Consumer Research*, Vol. 16 (September 1989), pp. 239–267.

58. Gatignon and Robertson, "A Propositional Inventory for New Diffusion Research." A recent article also noted that perceived consumption visibility and superordinate group influence would also impact new product adoption. See Robert Fisher and Linda Price, "An Investigation into the Social Context of Early Adopter Behavior," *Journal of Consumer Research*, Vol. 19 (December 1992), pp. 477–486.

59. Rogers, *Diffusion of Innovations*.

60. Elizabeth Hirschman, "Symbolism and Technology as Sources of the Generation of Innovations," in *Advances in Consumer Research*, Vol. 9, Andrew Mitchell, ed. (Provo, UT: Association for Consumer Research, 1981), pp. 537–541.

61. Gatignon and Robertson, "A Propositional Inventory for New Diffusion Research." A recent study employed cluster analysis techniques to identify a typology of product innovators. Three categories were identified—innovative communicators, less involved, and status maintainers. See David Midgley and Grahame Dowling, "A Longitudinal Study of Product Form Innovation: The Interaction Between Predispositions and Social Messages," *Journal of Consumer Research*, Vol. 19 (March 1993), pp. 611–625.

62. E. M. Rogers and F. F. Shoemaker, *Communication of Innovations: A Cross-Cultural Approach* (New York: Holt, Rinehart and Winston, 1971).

63. Coleman, Katz, and Menzel, *Medical Innovation: A Diffusion Study*.

64. Gatignon and Robertson, "A Propositional Inventory for New Diffusion Research."

65. Frank M. Bass, "A New Product Growth Model of Consumer Durables," *Management Science*, Vol. 15 (January 1969), p. 217. For more information on diffusion, please see David Midgley, "A Meta-Analysis of the Diffusion of Innovations Literature," in *Advances in Consumer Research*, Vol. 14, Melanie Wallendorf and Paul Anderson, eds. (Provo, UT: Association for Consumer Research, 1987), pp. 204–207.

66. Scott Hume, "Corona Fights Bad-Beer Rumors," *Advertising Age*, August 3, 1987, p. 6.

67. Excellent articles about rumors and their impact on business may be found in Robert Levy, "Tilting at the Rumor Mill," *Dun's Review*, July 1981, pp. 52–54; and James Esposito and Ralph Rosnow, "Corporate Rumors: How They Start and How to Stop Them," *Management Review*, April 1983, pp. 44–49.

68. Levy, "Tilting at the Rumor Mill."

69. "Procter & Gamble Rumor Blitz Looks Like a Bomb," *Advertising Age*, August 9, 1982, pp. 1, 68.

70. Esposito and Rosnow, "Corporate Rumors: How They Start and How to Stop Them."

71. G. W. Allport and L. Postman, *The Psychology of Rumor* (New York: Holt, 1947).

72. Damon Darlin, "Although U.S. Cars Are Improved, Imports Still Win Quality Survey," *The Wall Street Journal*, December 16, 1985, p. 27.

73. Levy, "Tilting at the Rumor Mill."

74. Ibid.

75. Alice Tybout, Bobby Calder, and Brian Sternthal, "Using Information Processing Theory to Design Marketing Strategies," *Journal of Marketing Research*, Vol. 18 (February 1981), pp. 73–79.

76. Laurie Hays, "Du Pont's Difficulties in Selling Kevlar Show Hurdles of Innovation," *The Wall Street Journal*, September 29, 1987, pp. A1, A20.

CHAPTER 15 CASE STUDY

Shriners Come Under Fire

Participating in secret initiation rituals endured by such notables as John Wayne, Clark Gable, and Gerald Ford before him, prospective Shriner Michael Vaughn began to question his decision to join the organization when the festivities began to turn kinky. In an organization known for its fun-loving public antics (such as riding around in parades on miniature bicycles and elaborate go-carts), mischievous initiation ceremonies could be expected. When they included branding irons, electrical shock, and strawberry sundaes in his underwear, however, Vaughn found the experience anything but humorous. So much so, in fact, that he filed a lawsuit for damages against the fraternity's Olekia Temple in Lexington, Kentucky, over what he says happened to him during bizarre initiation rites.

The first Shrine temple, known as Mecca, was founded in New York in 1872. Shriners' elaborate rituals and costumes, including the distinctive fez hat, exhibit Arabian themes inspired by actor William J. Florence, a founding father of the organization, who was fascinated with Middle Eastern culture. The Ancient Arabic Order of the Nobles of the Mystic Shrine is a hierarchical organization headquartered in Tampa, Florida. An Imperial Potentate reigns over the fraternity's 725,000 members, who make up 190 temples internationally. Shriners are well known for their philanthropic deeds. They support 22 children's hospitals, which provide free care for the needy.

In June 1989 Michael Vaughn was among nearly three dozen initiates at the Olekia Temple in Lexington, Kentucky. Prior to the initiation several doctors, who were present at the initiation, excused men with bad backs and heart problems, but they told Vaughn he could "take it," despite the fact that he had recently been treated by a chiropractor. As the initiation ensued, the men were asked to strip to their undershorts, blindfolded, and then led into a room where a red hot branding iron was waved in their faces. Initiates were then instructed to lie face down on a table. One by one, their undershorts were pulled down and, as described by Mr. Vaughn, "an unbelievably painful electric shock was applied to the buttocks." Red dye was then painted on the area. Next the men were made to sit on a bench that had been electrified, causing a jolt that sent the men "at least two feet in the air."

The delight of the onlooking Shriners continued as they watched the initiates perform their next ritual—marching around hand in hand on an electrified floor mat, which supposedly signified the blazing sands of the Sahara Desert. This final jolt caused a cramp in Mr. Vaughn's back, at which point he was allowed to rest briefly.

In the final task, a Shriner taped Vaughn's boxer shorts to his legs. Vaughn said afterward, "I figured they were going to put something down my shorts that they did not want to fall through." He assumed the "something" was in a nearby sink, where he spied strawberries, whipped cream, and ice cream. When Vaughn sat on a table, as the Shriners instructed him to do, the table collapsed. Crashing to the floor, he struck his head on the floor and was knocked unconscious. When he regained consciousness, Mr. Vaughn was administered an icepack and an apology. The table was not supposed to collapse, and the Shriners said that they regretted the accident. Vaughn left within a few minutes.

A few days later he consulted a neurologist who recommended a CAT scan and some physical therapy. Almost a year later, Michael Vaughn filed his suit in Fayette County Circuit Court, including charges of fraud, negligence, assault, and a "loss of hedonic pleasure." He also contends that he "wakes up at night with numbness in his arms and feels that he will never fully recover" from the odd rites, an event he describes as "shameful."

Differing viewpoints continue to surface from both sides. In an effort to ensure that impartial jurors will be available to hear the case, Judge George Barker has ordered court records sealed and both parties in the case silenced. Parker fears that, given the allegations, some people would laugh the plaintiff out of court, whereas "others would sock it to the Shrine for being a bunch of idiots." The Shriners are not commenting on the case; however, they have acknowledged in court documents that taping boxer shorts and administering electrical shocks can be included in initiation rituals. The Shriners' filing reads, "The defendant cannot confirm that anyone did such an activity" to Mr. Vaughn and "there is no duct tape used in such a procedure, but rather, two-inch masking tape." The Shriners also admit that a table tipped over on Vaughn but insist that he sustained no injuries as a result of the mishap. John Grant, a Florida state senator and 20-year member of the Shrine says, "Maybe somebody got into some whipped cream or electrical shocks. What's wrong with having a little bit of fun?" According to Cincinnati attorney Robert E. Manley, who specializes in fraternity law, "The event sounds like hazing, and that's generally looked upon as unlawful."

While the Shriners are standing their ground and defending their traditional rites of initiation, this controversy undeniably must be dealt with, as the Shriners are now forced to view their organization in a contemporary light. The Shriners are facing declining membership, and fewer young men these days seem to feel that the Shriners have something to offer them.

QUESTIONS

1. Define the problems faced by the Shriners.
2. What consumer concepts from the chapter help to explain these problems?
3. Construct a managerial applications table. Discuss the managerial implications of the consumer behavior concepts for the Shriners.

The case was based upon Alecia Swasy, "In the Hot Seat: Joining the Shriners Can Be Electrifying," *The Wall Street Journal*, November 4, 1991, pp. A1, A6.

Chapter

16

Group Processes II: Household and Organizational Processes

CONSUMER VIGNETTE

A "Shadow" Shocks the Family System

On December 4, 1993, a new member was added to the family of Bill and Barbara O'Connor—a 14-year-old horse named Shadow. For four years, the O'Connors' 10-year-old daughter Heather had been pleading for a horse. You see, horses meant everything to this child. She collected $14-plus model horses, eventually accumulating nearly 100. She read books about horses. She dreamed about horses. At times, she pretended to be a horse.

The O'Connor household is composed of four people: Bill and Barbara O'Connor (late forties, college professors) and two girls (Heather, aged 10, and Anna, aged 13). Major decisions in the family are made jointly. Whenever possible, the opinions of Anna and Heather are solicited. In Shadow's case, the decision to make the purchase was made by Barbara after consultations with Bill. Anna was informed that the purchase would take place. Her reaction to the $3,000-plus expenditure was to walk off in a huff and state emphatically, "Well, I had better get my own car when I'm 16 if you are going to spend that much money on Heather!" It was agreed that Heather would be the primary user and caretaker of the horse, with backup from Barbara.

The O'Connors next spent weeks of intensive information gathering. Professionals were contacted, and trips were taken to evaluate possible horses. Then, some friends, who were recognized experts on horse confirmation, helped the O'Connors purchase Shadow from a horse trader named Sam. None of the O'Connors had ever cared for horses before.

While Heather had taken horseback riding lessons for a number of years, she had not been trained in the intricacies of grooming. Candidly, the O'Connors did not realize that keeping a horse meant roughly one to two hours a day spent on exercising, feeding, and grooming the animal—not to mention mucking out its stall.

As novice equestrians, the O'Connors also had little understanding of how to handle a horse. They did not realize that horses continually test their owners. If the owner loses in these tests of will, the horse gradually begins to own the owner. The O'Connors lost each little contest with Shadow. He gradually began to pick up bad habits, such as moving around when groomed, failing to lift his hooves for picking, and periodically refusing to obey commands when being walked and ridden. As his behavior became more stubborn, the mood state of Heather and Barbara plummeted. Gradually, they began to be afraid of his 1,000-plus pound body. A horse trainer was hired to help. She pointed out that the O'Connors were giving a good horse bad habits.

Meanwhile, Bill and Anna were beginning to feel slighted. After work each day, Barbara would take Heather to the stable for the nightly ritual of feeding, riding, and grooming. They would then return home feeling highly frustrated, smelling like horses, and wondering where dinner was. The entire family became depressed. Bickering increased. Finally, a month to the day after the purchase, Shadow stepped on Heather for the second time. It was his final step. That night Bill called Sam, the horse trader. The following morning Shadow was gone, and Barbara and Heather cried.[1]

But the next day a "blue norther" raced through Oklahoma. As the family sat in front of a roaring fire and watched a gale lash snow at the pecan trees, Heather said, "I'm sure glad we're not mucking out the stable right now."

[1]The story of Shadow is true. The names of the people have been changed.

Figure 16-A Heather rides her horse, Shadow. Purchasing and disposing of the beast involved family decision making.

INTRODUCTION

The last chapter analyzed the factors that influence group processes, such as the impact of roles, normative influence, conformity pressures, and word-of-mouth communications. In this chapter, the two most fundamental types of groups are discussed—families and organizational groups. For many people the family is the most important primary group. The family not only shapes an individual's personality and general view of others, but also influences his or her values and attitudes about consumption. In addition, the family is an important consumption unit in and of itself. Most high-involvement consumer decisions involve input from more than one person. To some extent the entire family gets involved in such decisions as which car to buy, where to go on vacation, and whether or not to purchase a horse. Family members may even express preferences in low-involvement decisions, such as the brand of toothpaste or the kind of toilet tissue to buy. Some researchers have argued that the family should be the primary focus of study in consumer behavior.[1]

A second important type of group that engages in purchase behavior is the buying center within an organization. Buying centers make the purchases of the goods and services necessary for organizations to function. Organizations, such as businesses, governmental agencies, and nonprofit organizations, either formally or informally possess a buying center. While they vary in their degree of formalization, buying centers share the common characteristic of being composed of two or more people who make the procurement decisions for the group.

Families and buying centers have a number of similarities as well as a number of differences. Table 16-1 compares the family with other types of groups. One important difference is that family members share a high degree of intimacy and affection that does not exist in buying centers. The high degree of affection results in more permanent relationships, closer personal ties, and more cooperation within the family group.[2] Perhaps the most important similarity is that both families and other groups have a corresponding set of roles.

TABLE 16-1

Similarities and Differences Between Families and Buying Centers

A. *Similarities*

1. *Role structure*—Each type of group will have certain roles, such as deciders and buyers, that someone will have to fill.
2. *Conformity pressures*—Each will experience pressures to conform to the norms developed within the group.
3. *Group polarization*—When making decisions, each type of group may experience either risky or conservative shifts.
4. *Group conflict*—Within families and buying centers, conflict will inevitably arise as members disagree on the appropriate option to select.

B. *Differences*

1. Families are formed by marriage or birth, whereas other groups are formed by job or task.
2. Families have permanent relations, whereas other groups have relationships based on contracts.
3. Families are oriented toward interpersonal relationships whereas other groups are more goal oriented.
4. Families have more emotional ties, whereas other groups have more rational ties.
5. Families are more oriented toward intrinsic values, whereas other groups seek more extrinsic (i.e., material) rewards.
6. Families seek cooperative relationships, whereas other groups are more competitive and self-oriented.

SOURCE: The differences between families and other organizations are based upon work done by Jongdtee Park, Patriya S. Tansuhaj, and Richard H. Kolbe, "The Role of Love, Affection, and Intimacy in Family Decision Research," in *Advances in Consumer Research*, vol. 18, Rebecca Holman and Michal R. Solomon, eds. (Provo, UT: Association for Consumer Research, 1991), pp. 651–656.

Table 16-2 defines the types of roles that exist in most groups, including users, gatekeepers, influencers, deciders, buyers, and maintainers. In addition, as discussed in the last chapter, one also finds in all types of groups conformity pressures, group polarization, and group conflict. Highlight 16-1 discusses how both families and companies can have conflicts with suppliers.

In the vignette about the horse, Shadow, one can identify a number of **purchase roles**. Heather had the role of influencer, user, and maintainer. She wanted the horse badly and mustered all her arguments to persuade Barbara and Bill to make the purchase. In addition, she had strong input as to which horse to purchase. She would then be the primary user of the animal. It was expected that she would also be the person to maintain the horse (i.e., groom and care for it). Barbara took on the roles of decider and maintainer. She had ultimate authority as to whether a horse would be purchased. It was also expected that she would play an active role in caring for the horse and keeping Heather from getting hurt. Bill took on the role of buyer. He identified alternative horses to purchase and did the final negotiations with Sam, the horse trader. Both Bill and Barbara played the role of gatekeeper as they attempted to funnel the appropriate information to Heather.

TABLE 16-2

Types of Roles Found in Families and Buying Centers

Role	*Description*
Users	The persons who use the product that has been purchased. Users may or may not be consulted in the purchase process. They may initiate the decision process and then have no decision-making authority. They may also develop product specifications.
Gatekeepers	The persons who control the information employed by other members of the buying center. They may have influence over who talks to whom in the organization. They may have influence over what kind of information is obtained within the organization. They screen the types of information that deciders and influences possess.
Influencers	The persons who help in the evaluation of alternatives process. In business firms they are frequently engineers and other technicians. Consultants from outside the organization frequently become influencers.
Deciders	The persons who actually make the purchase decision, whether or not they have formal authority to do so. Frequently, deciders are hard to identify. They could be the company CEO or somebody behind the scenes who wields power.
Buyers	The persons who have the formal authority to make the purchase. In a business, the buyer may be the purchasing agent. In a family, it is frequently the person entrusted with the task of negotiating prices.
Maintainers	The persons who are responsible for the maintenance and upkeep of the product that has been purchased.

SOURCE: Based upon Frederick E. Webster, Jr., and Yoram Wind, *Organizational Buying Behavior* (Englewood Cliffs, NJ.: Prentice-Hall, 1972), pp. 77–80.

HIGHLIGHT 16-1

Conflict in Families and Organizations

A key similarity between family and organizational processes is that in both conflicts can occur. Within the American family, an important source of conflict in dual-career families involves the impact of the nanny. Called the ". . . domestic battle of the 1990s," the clash pits the working mother against the woman hired to care for her children (i.e., the nanny). The nanny's side of the story can be found in a quote from one woman: "I know mothers resent me because their kids take to me." After quitting a job in which the mother would call her at 4:00 A.M. because the baby was crying, she began to clean houses instead. She said, "I can deal with the kids. It's the mothers."

But there is another side to the story. Some nannies fall into the trap of thinking that they are the mothers. The president of the National Association of Nannies said, "A mother senses those kinds of feelings. There's a very fine line between loving a child and caring about a child and stepping over the line and invading a parent's territory." Thus the natural conflict between the maternal instincts of mother and nanny can create difficulties. In addition, however, clashes can also result from the inevitable differences in the cultural background and socioeconomic status of the nanny and the career woman (or, increasingly, the dad). Disagreements can occur over what television shows to let the children watch and what food to let the children eat. The net result is a precarious relationship in which either nanny or mother may fire the other.

A similar situation also occurs in the business world—particularly in the advertising business. Indeed, advertising agencies call them "the clients from hell." These are clients, such as Burger King, Ernest & Julio Gallo, and TWA, that place so many demands on ad agencies that many refuse to even compete for their business. For example, the problem with Burger King is that the corporate parent and its 1,200 franchises cannot agree on anything. The feud makes it almost impossible for an agency to please the two parties. In the case of E & G Gallo Winery, an 84-year-old chairman (Ernest Gallo) micromanages to such an extent that he personally requests dozens of storyboards that lay out advertising themes. When combined with his propensity to change ad agencies on what appear to be mere whims, he becomes a client that some firms avoid.

The relationship between nannies and mothers and between ad agencies and clients is much like a marriage. As one advertising executive said after declining to compete for an account with the automaker BMW, "As in a marriage, all agencies and all clients don't work well together."

Based upon Clare Ansberry, "Nannies and Mothers Struggle Over Roles in Raising Children," *The Wall Street Journal*, May 21, 1993, pp. 1, 6. Also, see Laura Bird, "The Clients That Exasperate Madison Avenue," *The Wall Street Journal*, November 22, 1993, pp. B1, B5.

This chapter discusses the processes that impact both families and organizational buying centers in the purchase process. Divided into three major sections, it begins with an analysis of the family and its relationship to household formation. Within this section the important topic of childhood socialization is also discussed. The chapter then moves to a discussion of the organizational buying center. It concludes with the managerial applications analysis.

FAMILIES AND HOUSEHOLDS

The term *family* is actually a subset of a more general classification—the household. **Households** are composed of all those people who occupy a living unit. Examples of households include

Roommates living in an apartment.

An unmarried couple living together.

A husband and wife with children.

Husband, wife, children, and grandparents living under one roof.

Two couples sharing the same house to save money.

The key similarity among all the examples is that the group must live in the same residence. Based upon the foregoing definition, a husband, wife, and children who live together are a household as well as a family.

A number of different types of families exist. The **nuclear family** consists of a husband, a wife, and their offspring. The **extended family** consists of the nuclear family plus other relatives, such as the parents of the husband or wife. Because of the high divorce rate in the United States, a growing number of single-parent families constitute households.

In many societies a husband and wife are expected to reside with one or the other of their parents. In the United States and Canada children from middle-class families tend to strike off on their own to form families away from their parents. Such a trend has been called the **detached nuclear family** structure. As noted by some researchers, the detached nuclear family is associated with the following characteristics:

1. Free choice of mates
2. Higher levels of divorce
3. Increased residential mobility
4. Entry of large numbers of women into the labor force
5. Lower responsibility of children to care for their parents in their old age.[3]

Over the past two decades major changes have occurred in the United States and Canada in the nature of households and families. New living arrangements have begun to be established that profoundly affect the number and size of households and families. Many of these changes are discussed in the next section on the demographics of households.

The Demographics of Households

Two general types of households of households can be identified—families and nonfamilies. As shown in Table 16-3, each of these categories can be further subdivided. In total, nine different household types can be identified, each of which may become a separate market segment for marketers. The table identifies the relative size of each of the household segments and projections for how the size will change between 1990 and 2000.

TABLE 16-3

Household Changes, 1990–2000

	1990		2000		1990–2000
	Households	*% of Total*	*Households*	*% of Total*	*Percentage Change*
All Households	93,347	100.0	110,140	100.0	18.0
Families	66,091	70.8	77,705	70.6	17.6
1. Married couples	52,317	56.0	60,969	55.4	16.5
2. With children at home	24,537	26.3	24,286	22.1	−1.0
3. With no children at home	21,522	23.1	31,365	28.5	45.7
4. Single fathers	1,153	1.2	1,523	1.4	9.0
5. Single mothers	6,599	7.1	7,473	6.8	4.1
6. Other families	6,022	6.5	7,741	7.0	28.5
Nonfamilies	27,257	29.2	32,434	29.4	15.6
7. Men living alone	9,049	9.7	10,898	9.9	20.4
8. Women living alone	13,950	14.9	16,278	14.8	14.1
9. Other nonfamilies	4,258	4.6	5,258	4.8	23.5

SOURCE: Based upon "The Big Picture," *American Demographics*, December 1993, p. 29.

As can be seen, for every seven families there are about three nonfamilies. Among families, married couples outnumber nonmarried couples (nonmarried couples include single fathers, single mothers, and a catch-all category that includes such families as children living with aunts and uncles). The nonfamily segment includes men and women living alone, as well other nonfamilies, composed mostly of cohabiting adults. Between 1990 and 2000, the household segment projected to grow fastest is "married couples with no children at home." This demographic trend will result from the aging of the baby boom generation born between 1946 and 1964. Of course, the data in Table 16-3 for the year 2000 are merely estimates. They were derived by editors at *American Demographics* magazine, and as the editors said, "small differences in assumptions can make a big difference in the final numbers."[4]

When targeting market segments, however, managers also must be concerned with their buying power. The household segment with the greatest buying power is childless couples aged 45 to 64. These individuals are in their peak earnings years. The household types with the least buying power are childless singles aged 45 and older and single parents.[5]

Data from the U.S. Census indicate that household growth has outpaced population growth. Consequently, since 1970, the average household size has fallen from 3.14 to 2.63 persons, and average family size has fallen from 3.58 to 3.17 persons. Reasons for the trend toward smaller households lie in an increasing divorce rate, the decision of young people to leave home prior to marriage, and the tendency of older people to maintain their own homes after other family members are gone.[6]

A trend toward later marriage is another factor linked to the decreasing size of households. In 1966 the average male was 22.8 years old and the female 20.5 years old at the time of first marriage. By the late 1980s the ages had moved to 25.8 years for men and 23.6 years for women. The number of women aged 25 to 29 who have never been married has doubled since 1970. In fact, by the late 1980s, 60.8% of women aged 20 to 24 had never married—a 50% increase from the 1980 figure.[7]

The trend toward later marriage has a number of implications. First, it suggests that more people will remain single. Second, it implies that fertility rates will decrease. Older couples simply have more trouble conceiving than do younger couples. Later marriages also increase the chances for premarital pregnancies because women are "at risk" longer prior to marriage. Finally, by remaining single longer, young people have more time to "invest" in themselves. They have time to pursue educational and work goals. Divorce is a growing fact of life for couples in the 1990s. In the late 1970s it was estimated that 35% of new marriages would end in divorce. That estimate has since been raised to 50%. The average length of marriage prior to a divorce was 6.9 years in 1986. One result of the higher divorce rate is a large increase in the number of single men and women caring for children under 18 years of age. Between 1970 and 1987, this number increased by over 100% for men and 90% for women.[8] A more positive sign, however, is that since the mid-1980s, divorce rates have declined slightly.[9]

Another major trend in family composition over the past 15 years is the increased frequency of two-career families. By the late 1980s, dual-career couples represented over 46% of all married couples. A study compared the overall expenditure patterns of one-earner and dual-earner households.[10] The results revealed a high level of consistency of expenditures between the two groups. Even on factors such as amount spent on food at home and food away from home, the expenditures were virtually identical. Interestingly, one area where the largest differences were found was "apparel and services." Here, nonworking-wife families had higher expenditures. Overall, the results indicated that family income had by far the largest impact on expenditure patterns.

Changes in family demographics can influence the design of the marketing mix in a variety of ways. For example, the rapid increase in the number of working women has dramatically changed the way marketers attempt to reach this group. The time demands on working women mean that the distribution system has had to be adjusted so that retail stores are open weekends and at night. Mail-order purchasing has increased in popularity due in part to the desire of working couples not to have to leave home for extended shopping trips after a day at the office. Companies in the clothing industry have introduced suits and shirts for working women that last and do not go out of style every year. The Victory Company has its president, Mary Sprague, featured in its ads. Wearing one of her shirts and ties, she states in the ad that her shirts work for the working woman. The ad copy states, "When you buy a Victory shirt, you know that the president of the company does more than stand behind her product. She stands in it."[11]

The Family Life Cycle

The **family life cycle** refers to the idea that families may move through a series of stages in a developmental fashion. Thus a family may begin as a married couple and then move through phases. Young children are born, the children grow older and eventually move out, and finally, the couple grows old. The concept of the family life cycle has been criticized because in many instances individuals may have more than one type of cycle. Some people are never married and move through a different set of stages. Divorce can cause people to move through the cycle a second time or result in the individual moving through the same type of cycle as a single person. Most consumer researchers, however, have retained the term family life cycle as best representing the idea that people go through identifiable stages in their lives and that a cycle recurs as grown children later marry and procreate.

Table 16-4 presents a 11-stage model of the family life cycle that is based upon the results of recent research.[12] This model, developed by Mary Gilly and Ben Enis, proved to be superior to three other family life-cycle models. The Gilly–Enis model has the advantage of focusing on the life-style of the stage, whether or not other adults or children are in a stage, and the age of the members of the household. The ages 35 and 65 are employed as cutoffs to distinguish stages of the life cycle. For example, there are three bachelor stages, based upon whether the person is less than 35, between 35 and 65, or over 65 years old. In most other life-cycle models, whether or not a person has been married or divorced plays a major role in distinguishing the stages. In the Gilly–Enis model, bachelor life-style is based upon age rather than whether or not the person has ever been married. Similarly, the "married" categories include cohabiting adults with any sexual orientation.

A number of studies have investigated the changing consumption patterns of specific products or services throughout the family life cycle. Spending on such items

TABLE 16-4

The Gilly–Enis Family Life-Cycle Model

Life-Cycle Stage	*Percentage of Total*	*Description*
Bachelor I	7.9%	Unmarried, under age 35
Bachelor II	13.3	Unmarried, under age 65
Newlywed	17.4	Married without children, under age 35
Single parent	5.9	Single parents, under age 65
Full nest I, children <6	9.9	Couple with female under age 35, with children under age 6
Delayed full nest, children <6	3.8	Couple with female over age 35, with children under age 6
Full nest II and III, with children >6 at home	22.2	Couple with children under or over age 6 at home
Childless couple	16.0	Couple under age 65, with no children at home
Older couple	5.9	Couple age 65 or over with no children at home
Bachelor III	7.4	Unmarried, over age 65
Other	0.5	Miscellaneous other groupings, such as children staying with other kin

SOURCE: Based upon Mary C. Gilly and Ben M. Enis, "Recycling the Family Life Cycle: A Proposal for Redefinition," in *Advances in Consumer Research*, vol. 9, Andrew A. Mitchell, ed. (Ann Arbor, MI: Association for Consumer Research, 1982), pp. 271–276. Note: the original scale had 14 categories, which were reduced to 11 in this depiction.

as restaurant meals, telephone service, and energy for home and car diverge dramatically across family life-cycle stages. Corporations have recognized that the family life cycle influences purchase patterns. Figure 16-1 shows an ad by Volvo, which points out that preferences in autos may change with the family life cycle.

A problem area for the family life-cycle concept involves the issue of whether life-cycle stage or income best accounts for spending differences among households. In one study the authors investigated the clothing expenditures of families.[13] In addition to collecting information on the stage of the family life cycle, they collected a variety of socioeconomic and demographic information. Their results revealed that income was the best predictor of clothing expenditures. Although stage of family life cycle did increase the predictive ability, its contribution was extremely small. From a managerial perspective, the results strongly suggest that marketers should collect information on the income level of family life segments before targeting them to ensure that they have the required buying power to be a viable market segment.

Family Role Structure

As noted in the introduction to the chapter, a group's role structure will influence its buying patterns. The chapter-opening vignette revealed that the buyers and users of a product may be different. In that case Bill and Barbara purchased the horse, but their daughter Heather was the user. In a similar manner, most men's underwear is bought by women. Also similarly, wives and girlfriends purchase 70% of the fragrances and colognes used by men.[14] Crayola, maker of children's writing instruments, had advertised mostly on children's television on Saturday mornings. After examining who really bought their products and the buyers' media habits, Crayola shifted its advertising to women's magazines. It was the mothers who were initiating and making the purchases, not the children. Cases where buyers and users of products differ illustrate the point that, within any small group, individuals may take on different roles to help the group function more smoothly.

Figure 16-2 presents an ad for Gatorade targeted to mothers. Although the beverage would be consumed by kids, the target of the ad is the mother, who is the decider and the purchaser of the product.

Role Overload

With the increase in the number of dual-career couples, the possibility exists that one or both spouses may have to take on a variety of different roles within the household. **Role overload** has been defined as a conflict "that occurs when the sheer volume of behavior demanded by the positions in the position set exceeds available time and energy."[16] Table 16-5 presents a scale that was developed to assess the extent of perceived role overload experienced by an individual. The experience of role overload has been found to be related to the wife's work involvement. In addition, a positive correlation has been found between role overload and the purchase of convenience goods and time-saving durable appliances.

Evidence indicates, however, that both husbands and wives can experience role overload.[17] Figure 16-3 diagrams the four possible combinations, which are (1) wife overloaded/husband underloaded, (2) husband overloaded/wife underloaded, (3) husband and wife overloaded, and (4) husband and wife underloaded. The particular

Figure 16-1 In this ad Volvo suggests that it still has a car appropriate for a more mature new life-cycle stage. (Courtesy of Volvo Cars of North America Corporation.)

Figure 16-2 Gatorade targets mothers in this ad, recognizing that moms are the buyers of these types of beverages. (Courtesy of Gatorade® Thirst Quencher.)

combination of role overload was proposed by the author to influence information acquisition and decision making within the household. The author argued that when one spouse is underloaded and one is overloaded, information acquisition activities are carried out by the underloaded spouse. In contrast, when both spouses

TABLE 16-5

A Scale to Measure Role Overload[a]

1. I have to do things I don't really have the time and energy for.
2. There are too many demands on my time.
3. I need more hours in the day to do all the things that are expected of me.
4. I can't ever seem to get caught up.
5. I don't ever seem to have time for myself.
6. There are times when I cannot meet everyone's expectations.
7. Sometimes I feel as if there are not enough hours in the day.
8. Many times I have to cancel appointments.
9. I seem to have to overextend myself in order to be able to finish everything I have to do.
10. I seem to have more commitments than some of the other wives (husbands) I know.
11. I find myself having to prepare priority lists (lists that tell me which things I should do first) to get done all the things I have to do. Otherwise I forget because I have so much to do.
12. I feel I have to do things hastily and maybe less carefully in order to get everything done.
13. I just can't find the energy in me to do all the things expected of me.

[a]Items assessed questions on five-point Likert scales anchored by "strongly agree-strongly disagree."

SOURCE: Michael Reilly, "Working Wives and Convenience Consumption," *Journal of Consumer Research*, vol. 8 (March 1982), pp. 407–418.

experience role overload, information acquisition activities are shortened and joint decision making is minimal. In addition, the couple tends to use convenience items extensively.

When a family consists of two working spouses, major time problems exist and role overload is likely. In such instances insufficient time exists to perform many household tasks, such as cleaning, cooking, paying bills, bathing children, and transporting children to doctors, dance lessons, and baseball practice. Traditionally, these tasks have fallen upon the wife as the keeper of the household. However, when the wife works for eight or more hours per day, the ability to perform all these tasks is almost nonexistent. Researchers have investigated how families with working wives adjust to the time crunch. In one study the authors found that working wives did not substitute capital equipment for their efforts any more than did nonworking wives. They did not use more outside cleaning services than nonworking wives to decrease their time commitments to the home. They did not spend less time in volunteer activities. Employed women also did not substitute the efforts of other family members for their own work. The employed wives did not sleep less than nonworking wives.[18]

How did the working wives handle the time crunch? The main means was through engaging in fewer leisure activities than nonworking wives. Families with working wives also tended to purchase more meals away from home, to use more disposable diapers, to engage in less housework, and to reduce the amount of time taken

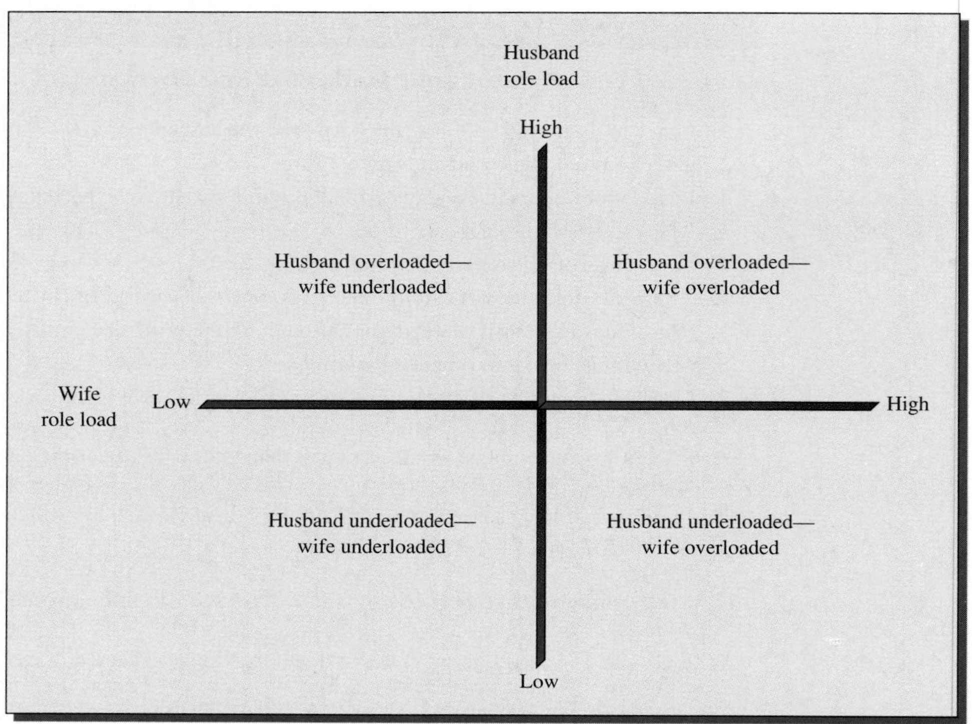

Figure 16-3 Comparison of husband and wife role loads. (Source: Ellen Burns, "Role Load in the Household," in *Advances in Consumer Research*, Vol. 14, Melanie Wallendorf and Paul Anderson, eds. Provo, UT: Association for Consumer Research, 1987, pp. 458–462.)

to care for family members. The one labor-saving device that has been associated with working wives is the microwave oven.[19]

Other than the use of microwave ovens, researchers have found that durables are *not* substituted for the time wives spend in household activities as they become more involved in outside jobs. Rather, they found that durables and wives' time were complements—that is, the more time a wife had to spend at home, the greater was the use of durable products. Thus, when wives had less time to spend at home, they had less need for durable products, such as home appliances, lawn and garden equipment, sports equipment, and furniture. These authors found that working women tended to solve the time problem by substituting one-use goods (e.g., frozen dinners) and purchased services (e.g., meals away from home and child day care).[20]

Family Decision Making

During the course of everyday living, thousands of decisions are made by family members. Some of the decisions are highly important, such as selecting which car to buy, where to move, and where to go on vacation. Other decisions are more mundane, like what to have for dinner or what should be planted in the garden. For two reasons the study of family decision making is quite difficult. First, in a similar manner to organizational buying units, the decision maker may not be the user or maintainer of the product. Second, families come in many different configurations. As a result, a family with a working mother, stay-at-home dad, and two small children will employ widely divergent decision-making processes than a single mother with two teenage sons living on welfare.[21]

A number of key issues in family decision making will be discussed in this section, including (1) determining which family members have the most influence on various household decisions, (2) identifying the stages in the decision process through which a family moves when making purchases, (3) identifying the role of children in family decision making, and (4) discussing power and conflict in the family.

Relative Influence of Decision Makers

A key question in studying family decision making concerns who in the family has the most influence on various types of decisions. An important early study in identifying the relative influence of family members on household decisions was conducted in Belgium.[22] The classic study identified four role specialization dimensions in the buying of products. The four dimensions are

1. *Wife-dominated decisions.* The wife plays a largely independent role in deciding what to buy.
2. *Husband-dominated decisions.* The husband plays a largely independent role in deciding what to buy.
3. *Autonomic decisions.* Decisions of lesser importance that either the husband or wife may make independently of the other are termed **autonomic decisions**.
4. *Syncratic decisions.* Decisions in which the husband and wife participate jointly are termed **syncratic decisions**.

The Belgian study was conducted in the early 1970s. Because of the changes that have occurred in society since that time and because the study was conducted in Europe, the conclusions must be interpreted with caution. However, research conducted in the United States has also found decisions that were wife dominated, husband dominated, and syncratic. One study investigated the decision patterns of financially secure, middle-aged couples.[23] The results revealed that husband-dominated decisions tended to focus on the details of automobile purchases (e.g., where to purchase the car). Wife-dominated decisions tended to involve the detailed aspects of kitchen and laundry purchases, such as what brand the new washer and dryer should be. Syncratic decisions appeared to predominate in the study. Areas in which syncratic decisions were found included vacations, home electronic appliances, home selection, when to purchase the next auto, and when to purchase new furniture.

One problem in doing research on husband–wife decision influence concerns the reliability and validity of the information obtained. A general tendency exists among some couples for the husband to systematically overestimate his influence, participation, and authority in household decisions. In other couples a tendency exists for the wife to underestimate her impact.[24] In general, researchers have found that for 10% to 50% of couples, significant disagreements existed in the reported relative influence of the spouses.[25]

A recent study investigated the effects of conflict on investment decision making among couples. The results suggested that the couples sought balanced and equitable outcomes in their bargaining over the type of investments to make. The couples sought to avoid conflict and showed empathy for each other's position. The authors suggested that couples sought fair outcomes to avoid a conflict of "making themselves or their negotiating partner unhappy."[26] While couples may seek to avoid conflict in decision making, disagreements are inevitable. A number of methods have been identified for resolving such conflicts, including (1) making a concession in return for the other reciprocating at a later date, (2) bargaining, (3) withdrawing, (4) overtly capitulating, and (5) compromising.[27]

Family Decision Stages

Just as there are different purchase roles, there are also different **family decision stages** in a decision to buy a product or service. The amount of influence exerted by the husband, wife, and children may vary depending on the stage of the decision process. In the Belgian study three such family decision stages were identified—problem recognition, search for information, and final decision.[28] These authors found that as the family decision stage moved closer to the final choice, the role specialization in general became more syncratic. Another study investigated who had the most influence in the buying process of automobiles and furniture.[29] The buying process for automobiles was divided into six steps:

1. When to buy.
2. How much money to spend.
3. What make to buy.
4. What model to buy.
5. What color to buy.
6. Where to buy.

Similarly, the furniture buying process had six steps:

1. What pieces to buy.
2. How much money to spend.
3. Where to buy.
4. When to buy.
5. What style to buy.
6. What color and fabric to choose.

For the automobile purchase most of the decision stages tended to be dominated by the husband. The wife consistently shared in or dominated the decision about what color to buy. The results for the furniture purchase were quite different. Here the wife tended to dominate all phases of the decision except for the issue of how much money to spend. An interesting aspect of the study was that each spouse stated an impression of his or her own influence. In most cases close agreement existed in the perceptions of the spouses. The only exception was a tendency for wives to indicate less often that they dominated the furniture purchase.

Influence in the Family

Researchers have looked specifically at the ability of members of the family to influence decisions. Three factors have been identified that strongly influence a member's family influence: financial resources of the family member, the importance of the decision to the family member, and the gender role orientations of the family members.[30] Researchers have found that, as financial contribution to the family unit increases, influence in the family also increases. Similarly, the importance of the decision to a family member also increases that person's influence on a particular decision. Influence on a decision is higher for a family member who is highly involved in the purchase and desires that it reflect his or her individual interests and preferences. How does a person increase his or her influence in such decisions? A likely explanation is that in the exchange process that takes place within a family, trades are made. A person may give up a degree of influence in one area to have greater amounts of influence in other areas.

A third factor affecting the amount of influence is the sex role orientation of the spouses. Gender role relates to the extent to which a family member follows traditional normative conceptions of how males and females should behave. One approach to studying gender roles is through the Bem Sex Role Inventory.[31] According to this approach, three roles can be identified. A masculine role consists of a person taking on the characteristics typically ascribed to males, such as strength, forcefulness, aggression, and decision making. A feminine role consists of a person taking on traditionally female characteristics, such as passivity, nurturance, kindness, and expressiveness. A psychologically androgynous person is able to take on the appropriate characteristics depending upon the circumstances. Thus such a person can be either nurturing or aggressive depending upon the situation.

The research on the effects of gender role suggests that families that are less traditional and more modern in their gender role orientation have a greater tendency to use a joint decision-making style. In general, gender role orientation is instrumental in defining the decision role responsibilities of husbands and wives.[32]

One cross-cultural study indirectly supports these views. In the study the perceptions of Mexican-American and Anglo wives were compared on the extent to which husbands dominated purchase decisions. The authors found that Mexican-American families tended to be more husband dominant in the purchase of durables.[33] Since Mexican-American families have more traditional gender role orientations, the results are compatible with previous research using middle-class Anglo families. As gender roles in a family become more modern and less traditional, the influence of female members is likely to increase.[34]

The Role of Children in Family Decision Making

The studies just discussed tended to ignore the role of children as influencers, decision makers, and users of products and services. Clearly, though, children do make a difference in family decisions.[35] For example, one recent study found that when children are present, couples more frequently create budgets for their households.[36] Children also influence decisions regarding the types of foods to buy, vacations, eating out, and so on. One study investigated the vacation decision process for couples and families.[37] The results revealed that families with children tended to establish less consensus on where to vacation and to have more husband-dominated decisions than did childless couples. Although children did not dominate the decision process, they had the potential to form alliances with either the husband or wife to produce a "majority" decision.

The influence of children on the purchase of breakfast cereals has been extensively investigated. Researchers have found that children make requests for breakfast cereals more frequently than for other product categories.[38] Other researchers have found that almost one-half of mothers interviewed at grocery checkout counters mentioned that their child had asked for a particular breakfast cereal. A relation between Saturday morning television viewing and cereal requests has been found such that the greater the amount of television viewing the greater the tendency to make requests for specific cereals.[39] In other research it was found that mothers exert little influence over cereal brand preferences among children less than 10 years of age. As the researcher noted, "Children appear to develop their own criteria for preferring brands of cereals and beverages that do not correspond with their mother's criteria."[40]

Figure 16-4 outlines the flow of parent–child interaction in breakfast cereal selection based upon the findings of a large-scale study in 20 supermarkets.[41] The results are quite interesting and show a number of surprising results. For example, parents tended to yield more often when the child demanded a cereal than when the child merely requested a particular cereal.

However, when the parent invited a cereal selection, he or she tended to agree with the child's selection much more frequently (about 90% of the time as compared to 71% when the child demanded the cereal). The age of the child was also found to influence the yielding of mothers to requests for cereals.[42] The results of the supermarket study also showed that the parent tended to initiate the choice of cereal more often for older children. Furthermore, the percentage of occasions when conflict occurred tended to be at a maximum when the children were between the ages of 6 and 8. Data were also analyzed to determine if the sex of the child or the social class

Figure 16-4 Flow of parent–child interaction in breakfast cereal selection. (Adapted by permission from Charles P. Atkin, "Observation of Parent-Child Interaction in Supermarket Decision Making," *Journal of Marketing*, Vol. 42, October 1978, p. 43, published by the American Marketing Association.)

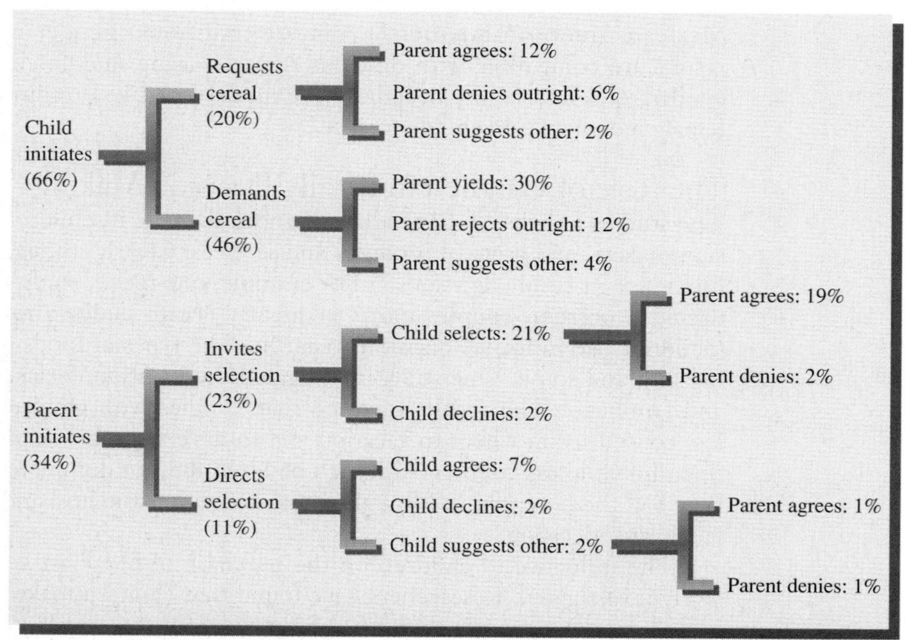

of the parent affected the trends. The results showed that the sex of the child had little effect. However, the social class of the family was related to the occasions of child unhappiness. Working-class families tended to have more frequent occasions when child unhappiness occurred.

The influence of children on household decisions increases as they grow older. One study of 161 adolescents and their parents found that as the adolescent's age increased, his or her influence on the various decision stages also increased. Another major finding was that peer communication was related to mentioning and discussing purchases with parents. These results demonstrate the large impact that peer groups have on adolescents' product preferences. The study also found that because adolescents increasingly earned money outside of the home, they had more input into purchase decisions.[43] These results are consistent with the concept that financial resources are related to power and influence within the family.

In other research, adolescents' and mothers' perceptions of their influence on family purchase decisions were compared. As one would expect, the adolescents believed their influence was greater than the mothers rated it. Similarly, the mothers rated their own influence as greater than the adolescents believed. The study did show that adolescents are active participants in family purchase decisions, even for products not for their own use. For example, even in the purchase of the family car both adolescents and mothers indicated that the young person had some impact on the decision.[44] In another study of adolescent influence on family decisions, the researchers found similar results. In addition, the researchers found that the perception of influence was more consistent between husbands and wives than between adolescents and parents—a finding that should not be surprising to either adolescents or their parents.[45]

Childhood Consumer Socialization

As noted earlier in the chapter, one reason for the family's importance is its role as a **socialization agent**.[46] Socialization may be defined as the process by which individuals acquire knowledge, skills, and dispositions that enable them to participate as members of society.[47] The general concept of socialization can be narrowed to that of childhood consumer socialization. **Childhood consumer socialization** refers to the "processes by which young people acquire skills, knowledge, and attitudes relevant to their functioning as consumers in the marketplace."[48]

Understanding how individuals are socialized into consumers is important for several reasons. First, knowledge of the factors influencing consumer socialization can provide information to marketers that may be useful in designing marketing communications. In American society children are potent consumers. It is estimated that children under 13 years of age directly spend $6.5 billion a year.[49] Second, public policy decisions concerning the rules and regulations of the marketing of products to children should in part be based on an understanding of the consumer socialization process. For example, one key question concerns how advertising affects children. For example, in 1993 the Federal Trade Commission seriously investigated taking legal action to prohibit the advertising campaign for Camel Cigarettes using "Joe Camel." The reason was that the fictional animal character is so popular among teenagers under 18. Children like cartoon characters, and the Joe Camel campaign either intentionally or unintentionally appeals to this attraction.

A Model of Consumer Socialization

Figure 16-5 presents a simple model of consumer socialization.[50] It suggests that consumer socialization is based upon three components—background factors, socialization agents, and learning mechanisms such as cognitive learning, operant conditioning, and modeling. Researchers have found that even young children (i.e., those under 5 years old) can learn how to make purchases and can be influenced by marketers. Key factors for such learning include presenting the information at the child's level and repeating it a number of times.[51]

Socialization background factors include such variables as the consumer's socioeconomic status, sex, age, social class, and religious background. Socialization agents are those individuals directly involved with the consumer who have influence because of their frequency of contact with the consumer, importance to the consumer, or control over rewards and punishments given to the consumer. Examples of socialization agents include parents, brothers and sisters, peers, teachers, the media, and media personalities, such as athletes, movie stars, and rock stars.

Researchers have investigated the impact of socialization agents and background factors on consumer socialization. In an important early study, the factors of family, mass media, newspaper readership, school, peers, age, social class, and sex were analyzed.[52] The study found that the family was important in teaching the "rational" aspects of consumption. The amount of communication in the family about consumption was also related to how often the adolescents performed socially desirable acts, such as giving to charities. The amount of television viewing was found to have a major impact on socialization in the study. Greater television viewing was associated with the learning of the "expressive" aspects of consumption. Thus high television viewing seemed to encourage consumption for emotional reasons, rather than for more rational reasons. In contrast, adolescents who read newspapers were found to possess a number of consumer skills. However, the newspaper readership could have resulted from the presence of these skills, rather than causing them.

Peers were found to be important socialization agents. They contributed particularly to the expressive element in which one buys for materialistic or social reasons (e.g., buying to "keep up with the Joneses"). For teenagers, buying to impress or be like others was clearly important. However, interaction among peers also was related to an increased awareness of goods and services in the marketplace. The school, though, was found to have very little influence on the socialization process. For whatever reasons, formal consumer education in school was unrelated to measures of consumer socialization.

Figure 16-5 A model of consumer socialization.

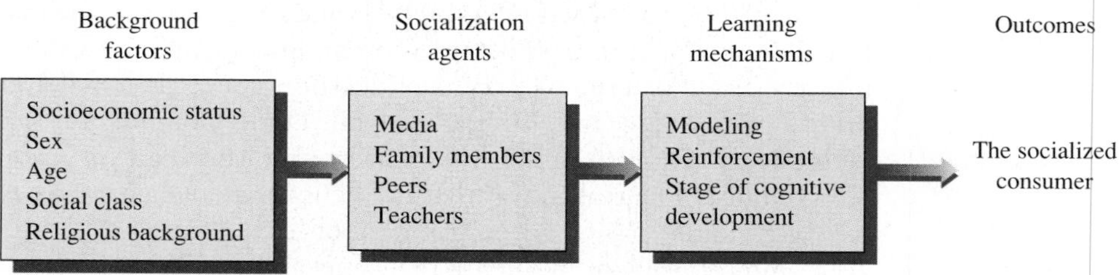

A current problem influencing childhood socialization in the United States is teenage pregnancy. In an attempt to influence young women and their peer group, public policy agencies have begun to use advertisements warning of the dangers of pregnancy. Figure 16-6 shows one of the ads. Social scientists have argued that what is learned early in life has an important and lasting effect on people. In areas such as criminology and psychiatry, theorists have noted that behaviors shown early in life tend to persist into adulthood. Some evidence exists that consumption behaviors learned early in life also persist. Studies have found that brand loyalty may be transmitted from parents to offspring and that favored brands may persist for periods of 12 years or longer.[53]

Both parents and peers have an impact on product preferences. A recent research study found that the impact of the nuclear family varies for products that are publicly or privately consumed.[54] Publicly consumed products are those that are visible in use, such as clothing, jewelry, and automobiles. Privately consumed products are those that others do not see, such as a refrigerator, mattress, or toothpaste. The results showed that peers strongly influenced preferences for public goods. In contrast, the nuclear family more strongly influenced preferences for private goods. Good evidence was found for the intergenerational transfer of brand loyalty from parents to children for privately consumed products.

In one summary of the findings on childhood socialization, the author noted that parents play an important role in childhood socialization, especially in providing information on the rational aspects of consumption.[55] However, the influence of parents is situation specific. Their impact varies across the stages of the decision process, across various types of products, and across various personal characteristics, such as age, socioeconomic class, and sex of the child.

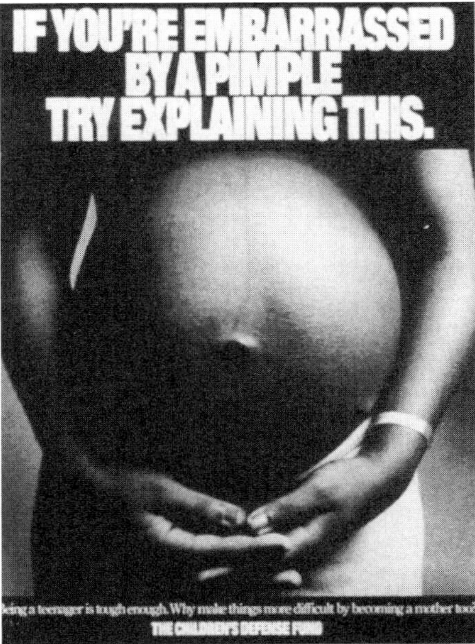

Figure 16-6
Unwanted teenage pregnancies create havoc in the lives of young women. This ad warns of the possibilities and problems of teenage pregnancy. (Courtesy of the Children's Defense Fund.)

A critical area of study concerns investigating the impact of divorce and single parenthood on childhood consumer socialization.[56] Authors have suggested that when major life changes occur to consumers, such as when parents divorce, a "teachable moment" occurs. At such teachable moments perceptions, attitudes, and behaviors may undergo dramatic change.[57] The impact may have positive or negative implications for the long-term ability of children to be effective consumers. In addition, one must ask: "What impact does high divorce rates and the dissolution of families have on the long-term health of a society?"

Socializing Parents

Authors have observed that socialization is a reciprocal process.[58] Just as parents socialize children, children may also socialize their parents. Within a family a series of exchange relations exist between the parents, as well as between the parents and the children. Within the interactions that occur between parents and children, information is transmitted in both directions. The information received by parents from their children about the marketplace may to some degree influence the beliefs and feelings of the adults. Thus a kind of reciprocal socialization takes place. Although the children are undoubtedly influenced to a greater extent, adults may also learn from the interactions. Researchers have recognized that cognitive and social development never ceases—it continues throughout a person's life. As such, one source of information that influences parents is their children.[59]

One question addressed by researchers concerns the factors that affect when children have the most influence on their parents.[60] One factor that researchers consider is the type of family communication pattern. In socio-oriented homes, where controversies are not allowed to surface and children are not allowed to argue with parents, less parental socialization occurs. In contrast, in concept-driven homes, children are encouraged to develop their own ideas and communicate these to parents. In such concept-driven homes more socialization by the parents is likely to occur. Other factors proposed to influence parental socialization by children include family structure (more occurs in single-parent homes), family socioeconomic status (more occurs in families of higher status), and extent of children's resources (more occurs when children earn income outside the home).

ORGANIZATIONAL BUYING BEHAVIOR

Just as individual consumers and families make purchases, so do organizations. Businesses, government agencies, and nonprofit organizations all make purchases to produce goods and/or services. At the heart of the purchase process in such organizations is the buying center. An **organizational buying center** is defined as those people in an organization who participate in the buying decision and who share the risks and goals of the decision.[61] Individuals within a business firm who frequently participate in a decision include managers, engineers, marketing personnel, accountants/finance personnel, and purchasing agents.

Because buying centers are composed of people, the same behavioral factors (i.e., psychological, sociological, and anthropological) that impact consumers will also impact the individuals within a organization. However, because an organization differs from a family in terms of its mission and its situational environment, one can expect that divergent factors impact the two types of groups. Table 16-6 compares and contrasts organizational buying and consumer buying across six dimensions. Readers should note, however, that in many circumstances the buying processes will be remarkably similar. For example, on the dimension of price, competitive bidding is used much more frequently in organizational buying than in consumer buying. If a family needs to purchase cooking oil, they will go to a local grocery store and buy a brand at list price. When McDonald's buys cooking oil, the company will take competitive bids, provide detailed specifications for the good, develop long-term relationships with suppliers, and involve management, research and development, and nutritionists in the decision. Exceptions do exist, however. For example, when purchasing automobiles, homes, and stereo components, consumers will frequently require competitive bids in the bargaining process.

Like consumers, when making decisions, organizational buyers move through a decision process that closely resembles the generic decision process described in Chapter 11. Thus organizational buyers will recognize problems, search for information, evaluate alternatives, make a choice, and then engage in postacquisition processes. Also, depending upon the risk level of the purchase, the involvement level of organizational buyers will change. Because of the high complexity of many organizational buying decisions, researchers have developed a more elaborate set of decision

TABLE 16-6

Organizational Versus Consumer Buying

Dimension	*Business Purchasing*	*Consumer Purchasing*
Product	More technical; greater quantities purchased; focus on services offered with product.	Less technical and more standardized; smaller quantities purchased.
Price	Frequent competitive bidding; list prices on standard items.	Generally buy on basis of list prices.
Promotion	Rely on information from sales personnel and trade magazines.	Relatively greater emphasis on advertising.
Distribution	Short channels; often purchased directly from manufacturers.	Longer distribution channels; most frequently purchase from retail stores or mail-order companies.
Customer relations	More enduring; complex focus on establishing relationships.	Often transaction specific and quite simple; frequently no long-term relationship formed.
Buying decision process	Involvement of more people in organization with diverse sets of needs; use more structured decision-making process.	Fewer people involved in process; buying process frequently unstructured.

stages through which organizations are proposed to move. These buying stages are found in Table 16-7. Note that in comparison to consumer decision making, a greater focus is placed on (1) anticipating problems, (2) determining and describing the characteristics of the product needed, (3) qualifying potential suppliers, (4) obtaining and analyzing proposals, and (5) deciding how to make the order (i.e., how many and over what time period).

When evaluating alternatives, organizational buyers will compare the options based upon the attributes of the product. Such factors as price, quality, service, the continuity of service, and the relationship with the seller have been identified as key attributes on which buying centers evaluate alternatives.[62]

Organizational Buying Situations

Researchers have identified three fundamental task definitions for **organizational buying situations**—new task, modified rebuy, and straight rebuy.[63] In a "new task" situation, the organization is faced with a purchase that has not been previously experienced. Frequently, new task situations involve major, high-risk purchases that send the organization into extensive problem solving. An example would be a window shutter manufacturer purchasing large machines to sand the louvers to replace workers who previously did the sanding by hand.

The "straight rebuy" occurs when a company has had long experience with a particular product. As a result, little new information is needed. As a result, the buying process becomes routinized. Frequently, extensive procedures have been developed in the company for making such purchases. In such cases purchasing agents simply follow these procedures.

The "modified rebuy" falls between the new task and the straight rebuy situations. In this instance the organizational buyer recognizes that benefits could be derived from reevaluating alternatives. In such instances, suppliers will engage in extensive personal selling efforts to influence purchasing agents.[64]

TABLE 16-7

Buying Stages of Organizations

Stage 1. Anticipation of a problem and/or recognition of a problem.
Stage 2. Identification of the characteristics and quantity of the needed product.
Stage 3. Development of a description of the characteristics and quantity of the product.
Stage 4. Search for and qualification of possible suppliers.
Stage 5. Acquisition of and the evaluation of alternate proposals.
Stage 6. Selection of suppliers based upon careful use of choice rules.
Stage 7. Selection and negotiation of how the order will be made.
Stage 8. Evaluation of the performance of the supplier.

SOURCE: Based upon Michael D. Hutt and Thomas W. Speh, *Business Marketing Management* (Fort Worth, TX: The Dryden Press, 1992), p. 70.

Another important situational variable that heavily impacts organizational buying is the factor of time. Increasingly, companies throughout the world are employing just-in-time purchasing practices. **Just-in-time**, or **JIT**, **purchasing** occurs when the organization attempts to have parts and materials delivered to the production process just at the moment they are needed. Developed by Toyota Motor Company, the JIT system has a number of goals, including reducing waste, lowering the costs of maintaining inventory, improving product quality, and responding very quickly to changes in consumers' needs.[65] The JIT approach to purchasing is closely related to the efforts of organizations to implement the *total quality management* programs discussed in Chapter 13. The three goals of reducing inventory to the minimal amount possible, of getting close to customers, and of continuously improving the quality of products require that companies develop extremely good relationships with their suppliers.

Building Relationships in Organizational Buying

Perhaps the most talked-about concept in the field of marketing in the mid-1990s is relationship marketing. **Relationship marketing** can be defined as the overt attempt of exchange partners to build a long-term association in which purposeful cooperation occurs, mutual dependence occurs, and social, as well as structural, bonds are developed. In sum, when relationships are formed, the parties join together (either formally or informally) so that they share to some degree the gains and/or losses that occur in their business operations.[66] Marketing relationships exist along a continuum from simple, one-time transactions to fully integrated hierarchical firms.[67] Table 16-8 defines the seven types of marketing relationships that can be identified.

The move to relationship marketing by companies in the United States and Canada was spurred by the success of Japanese corporations with just-in-time (i.e., *kanban*) systems and their dramatic improvements in product quality. Without strong mutual cooperation with suppliers, American firms could not implement JIT systems or achieve the quality levels required to compete against the Japanese. Importantly, the total quality management systems adopted by manufacturers are now being applied to service organizations, such as hospitals, banks, and even universities.

The most recent form of relationship marketing, which is just now beginning to be adopted by American corporations, is the network structure.[68] Called *keiretsu* by the Japanese, these complex groupings of firms have interlinked ownership and exchange relations. While they possess no formal organization, they have mutual interdependence and long-term stability. Such networks of firms create a situation in which high levels of mutual trust can be formed, which is necessary for the implementation of JIT systems.

Given this important trend in marketing to form relationships, the buyer center of an organization must respond appropriately. In many respects, the relationships that result resemble marriages. As in marriages, organizational relationships move through a series of stages: (1) awareness of the other, (2) exploration, (3) expansion, (4) commitment, and (5) dissolution.[69] As in marriages, managers in the organizational buying center must recognize that a give-and-take will exist with suppliers. Similarly, the sales force must be willing to adjust rapidly to the changing needs of its customers. Managers must recognize that, as in marriages, the dissolution phase will be much more difficult than in traditional contractual exchanges.[70] Finally, managers

TABLE 16-8

The Continuum of Marketing Relationships

Pure Transaction End of Continuum

Relationship Continuum		
↑	**1.** Transaction	One-time exchange.
	2. Repeated transactions	Frequently a contractual arrangement, transactions that are characterized as being quite formal and done at "arm's length."
	3. Long-term relationship	The engaging in repetitive transactions over time, though adversarial relationships still dominate. However, goals of firms are interrelated and interdependence is recognized. Competitive bidding is used on prices.
	4. Buyer–seller partnership	The recognition of mutual dependence. Each partner approaches total dependence upon the other. Mutual trust is strong. Prices are determined by negotiation rather than competitive bidding.
	5. Strategic alliance	A relationship that emerges when one or more functions between organizations are combined (such as R&D or manufacturing) so that both firms commit resources to reach a joint goal. A joint venture to produce a new product illustrates the strategic alliance.
	6. Network organizations	An organization that has developed multiple relationships (including partnerships, strategic alliances, and long-term relationships) with several other firm).
↓	**7.** Vertical integration	A number of organizations formally combined to create a new, larger company.

Fully Integrated Hierarchical Organization End of Continuum

SOURCE: Based upon Frederick E. Webster, Jr., "The Changing Role of Marketing in the Corporation," *Journal of Marketing*, vol. 56 (October 1992), pp. 1–17.

should understand that the development of buyer–seller partnerships and strategic alliances can create antitrust and ethical problems. This is an area in which the law is evolving, and managers must be concerned with potential legal difficulties.[71] Highlight 16-2 discusses some of these legal and ethical problems.

Another critical element in building long-term relationships is trust. **Relationship trust** is ". . . a willingness to rely on an exchange partner in whom one has confidence."[72] Thus, to reveal trust in a relationship, the members must reveal vulnerability to each other. In such cases, control of important resources is left with the other member of the exchange. As a result, the exchange members must rely on each other to fulfill their obligations in the exchange. When high levels of trust exist, the exchange process becomes more flexible and less bureaucratic, and legal entanglements are minimized.

The purchasing of market research information is one arena in which trust between organizational buyers and sellers is critical. Because market research information is used to develop new products and evaluate market strategies, a high level of relationship trust is necessary between the market research firm and the buying firm. Recently, investigators examined a series of factors that were predictive of high

HIGHLIGHT 16-2

Ethical Issues in Marketing Relationships

Corporations throughout the world are rushing to develop relationships with their suppliers and/or their customers. For example, Toyota is teaming up with a few small American parts suppliers to increase quality, efficiency, and design advances. Such an approach can lower costs, raise levels of trust, and increase overall levels of product quality. Indeed, with the adoption of total quality management and just-in-time manufacturing, the importance of forming close relationships with suppliers and customers has become critical.

As networks of relationships are formed among suppliers and customers, a number of interesting ethical problems may occur. Recently, two marketing scholars (Gregory Gundlach and Patrick Murphy) proposed that as one moves from discrete exchanges to relationship exchanges, the role of ethics increases while the role of contract law decreases. Because the partners are working together to achieve their mutual goals, principles of ethics and morality take on increased importance. As said by the authors, "The moral foundations of exchange transcend differing circumstances, parties, and occasions."

Four dimensions of ethical exchange were identified by Gundlach and Murphy—trust, equity, responsibility, and commitment. *Trust* refers to the exchange partners having confidence that each party will fulfill promises and obligations mutually agreed upon. *Equity* refers to the extent to which each party perceives that the ratio of its inputs and outcomes are roughly equal to the inputs and outcomes of the exchange partner. Equity is rooted in the principle that exchanges should be fair for each partner. *Responsibility* is also required in the exchange relationship. That is, both the purchaser and the seller must take responsibility for their actions and the impact of their actions on the other. Finally, *commitment* between the exchange partners is required. In other words, stability, sacrifice, and loyalty are expected to be demonstrated.

By following principles of trust, equity, responsibility, and commitment, the exchange partners are demonstrating an "enlightened self-interest." Thus it is a rational and prudent course of action to act in an ethical manner with exchange partners because in the long run each organization will be better off.

Based upon Gregory T. Gundlach and Patrick E. Murphy, "Ethical and Legal Foundations of Relational Marketing Exchanges," *Journal of Marketing*, Vol. 57 (October 1993), pp. 35–46.

---

levels of trust in market research relationships.[73] The results revealed that research integrity was the single most important factor in predicting the level of the purchasing firm's trust. Here, integrity refers to setting high standards and to maintaining objectivity throughout the research process. Other important predictors of trust were (1) willingness to explain the results, (2) maintaining the confidentiality of the results, (3) expertise, (4) tactfulness, (5) sincerity, (6) congeniality, and (7) timeliness.

Readers should compare and contrast the view of trust developed within the context of organizational buying and that developed within the communications literature. In Chapter 10, Communications Processes, source credibility was discussed. From the perspective of communications researchers, source credibility is composed of two factors—expertise and trust. In contrast, those studying organizational buying view trust as composed of integrity and expertise (as well as a series of other variables). Future research is required to untangle this unfortunately inconsistent use of terminology. One explanation is that the organizational buying researchers have simply replaced the word "credibility" with the word "trust." In like manner, they are using the word "integrity" in the same manner as the communication researchers used the word "trust."

The Role of Organizational Culture

Organizational culture refers to the shared values and beliefs that enable members to understand their roles and the norms of the organization.[74] An organization's culture influences interorganizational communications, relationships, and decision-making patterns.

A recent review of the literature identified six dimensions on which organizational cultures can be distinguished.[75] Shown and defined in Table 16-9, the six dimensions are (1) market driven versus customer driven, (2) task versus social focus, (3) conformity versus individuality, (4) safety versus risk focus, (5) intuitive versus planning focus, and (6) flexible versus inflexible to change. When two firms develop relational buying exchanges, such as those found in a JIT or a *keiretsu* structure, it is important that some degree of match exist across these six dimensions. Numerous examples exist of partnerships and alliances between firms collapsing because of culture clashes. A recent example occurred between Combustion Engineering Corporation and the Soviet Oil Ministry. Combustion Engineering's market-driven culture focused on pleasing customers, maintaining careful cost controls, and managing by consensus. These values conflicted with those of the Soviet Ministry, which focused on pleasing members of the hierarchy, ignoring costs, and managing by fiat.

TABLE 16-9

Six Dimensions of Organizational Cultures

1. *External versus internal emphasis*—Focus on satisfying customers/clients (market driven) in contrast to an accent on internal organization activities and product-driven orientation.
2. *Task versus social focus*—Focus on efficiency in reaching organizational activities as compared to fulfilling social needs of members of groups.
3. *Conformity versus individuality*—Focus on maintaining similarity in work habits, dress, and personal life versus tolerance for individual differences and idiosyncrasies.
4. *Safety versus risk*—Focus on conservative decision making and slow adoption of new practices versus desire to pioneer new products and give executives autonomy.
5. *Ad hockery versus planning*—Tendency to employ ad hoc solutions and intuition and to place low reliance on numbers and forecasts versus use of mathematical modeling, economic analysis, and elaborate planning.
6. *Adaptable versus rigid*—Focus on innovation, change, and cultural flexibility versus maintaining the status quo.

SOURCE: Based upon James W. Barnes and Edwin R. Stafford, "Strategic Alliance Partner Selection: When Organizational Cultures Clash," in *Enhancing Knowledge Development in Marketing*, vol. 4, David W. Cravens and Peter R. Dickson, eds. (Chicago: American Marketing Association, 1993), pp. 424–433.

A MANAGERIAL APPLICATIONS EXAMPLE

Conrad Lung was having trouble at work after his daughter was born. His wife also worked, and his 1-year-old daughter spent 11 hours per day in child care. "I had this image of my girl crying, and the image wouldn't leave me," he said. As his performance lagged, he became depressed and considered quitting his job as a vice president in a sporting goods firm. His mind went back to his work only after his parents moved next door and assumed child care responsibilities.[76] Mr. Lung's feelings are shared by millions of working parents. The author of a survey on working couples for *Fortune* magazine said, "Our major finding is that problems with child care are the most significant predictors of absenteeism and unproductive time at work." Indeed, finding satisfactory, much less outstanding, child care is the major problem for two-income families. As noted by one researcher, "A parking lot attendant is paid the same as a child care worker. If we assign the same importance to someone who parks our cars as to those who take care of our children, we have a serious social problem."

In response to the problem, some companies are beginning to actively assist employees with child care. A few companies actually provide facilities, others give financial assistance, and many give child care referral services. According to some analysts, child care may become the fringe benefit of the 1990s. *Fortune* sees the problem of adequate child care as not just the parents'; it is also the employers' problem and, ultimately, society's problem. As the author of the survey said, "Couples seem to feel that child care is their problem alone. It's not. It's an institutional problem. Families have changed much faster than the institutions that the family relies on."

The Consumer Behavior Analysis

Analyzing the problems of parental stress among two-career couples requires the use of many of the concepts identified in the chapter. The demographics of households suggest that the problem is potentially quite large. Women are increasingly pursuing careers, and males will inevitably begin to perform additional household duties. An *American Demographics* article noted that in 1985 women spent 7.5 fewer hours per week doing housework than in 1965. In contrast, during the same time period, males spent 5.2 more hours per week doing housework.[77] These trends will have a major impact on how companies promote services and products. In addition, it creates an increased need for child care services.

Obtaining high-quality child care is perhaps the greatest single problem for two-career families. Corporations such as Kinder-Care recognize the importance to parents of providing their children with an excellent child care environment. In particular, parents want their children to come home feeling good. Shown in Figure 16-7, the ad by Kinder-Care effectively communicates to parents the idea that their child will have positive experiences while in the company's care.

Family role structures also have implications for studying the changing family. As more women move into the work force, they increasingly take on external roles. Further, role overload is likely to occur for both spouses, which could cause major time pressures on the family.

Figure 16-7 Kinder-Care effectively communicates the promise that its facilities provide a positive child care environment. (Copyright© Kinder-Care Learning Centers, Inc. Reprinted with permission.)

Dual-income families with kids should expect significant changes in family decision making. Certainly, an increased tendency toward the sharing of decisions has emerged. In turn, many companies' marketing strategies have begun to target women in decision-making modes within the family. For example, insurance companies are increasingly targeting working wives with their products.

The Managerial Applications Analysis

Table 16-10 presents the managerial applications analysis for the case on child care issues. A particularly important consumer concept relevant to the case concerns the demographics of households. As a part of environmental analysis, managers should be alert to changes in the number of consumers with children, the number of working women, and the number of men who may become househusbands. These trends have implications for identifying segments of consumers that have particular child care needs. If the segments are large enough and have sufficient buying power, and if they can be reached, they can be targeted via the development of new products. In addition, promotional strategy can be geared to reaching these individuals. Finally, goods and services can be positioned specifically for these segments.

Family role structure is a second consumer concept that is important in the case. Because of the increase in the numbers of working wives, role overload is increasing. These ideas suggest the possibility that companies may position products and services for the family experiencing a role-overload situation. Of course, environmental analysis would be used to identify societal changes that influence the extent to which family role structures are changing.

TABLE 16-10

Managerial Applications Analysis of the Child Care Case

Consumer Concepts	*Managerial Applications*
Household demographics	*Environmental analysis*—Perform demographic analyses to predict future changes in household size and composition.
	Segmentation—If important demographic changes in household composition or size are identified, identify segments for targeting (e.g., single-parent households headed by a male).
Family role structure	*Environmental analysis*—Perform analyses to determine the characteristics of households experiencing role overload.
	Positioning—Position products and services for families experiencing role overload (e.g., dual-career families with children).
Family decision making	*Market research*—Perform research to determine the family decision-making process for the good or service offered by your firm.
	Promotional strategy—Based upon market research, adjust promotional strategy appropriately so as to target the appropriate individual (e.g., decider, influencer, user).

A third consumer concept, of particular relevance in this case, concerns family decision making. Market research should be conducted to determine the family decision-making process for a firm's goods/services. Because of changes in role structure and demographic patterns, one can expect that women increasingly will be making decisions for their families—or at least increasingly participating in syncratic decisions. Such women represent a market segment to which existing products can be positioned. Likewise, new products might be developed and promoted specifically for such women.

SUMMARY

Households and organizations are two of the basic types of consumption units. Households consist of all those living under one roof. They may or may not be related persons. Two important types of families are the nuclear family—consisting of husband, wife, and offspring—and the extended family—consisting of the nuclear family plus grandparents and other kinfolk. The tracking of the demographics of families and households is important for marketers. Such factors as family size, age at marriage, the divorce rate, and the number of employed women and men all have an influence on family purchase patterns.

Within organizations buying centers also make purchase decisions. A buying center is composed of two or more people who make the procurement decisions of a group. One of the most important similarities between household buying and organizational buying is that both groups have a similar set of roles. These include such roles as influencers, gatekeepers, deciders, buyers, and users. Family buying differs from organizational buying along several dimensions, including having more permanent relationships, closer personal ties, and more cooperation.

The family life cycle is an idea important to marketers. Families can be viewed as moving through a series of stages in a developmental fashion. As the parents grow older and the children, if any, age and leave, the family's purchase patterns change. Single individuals and couples without children have very different spending habits as compared to a family with two teenage children. Marketers should track the number of households in various stages of the family life cycle and analyze projections of how the distribution may change in the future. For example, as the number of young, single individuals decreases between 1990 and 1995, the manufacturers of motorcycles may experience problems. Not only will total demand probably decrease, but also the features desired on a bike will change. It should be noted, however, that income differences change along with the family life cycle. Many of the changes in consumption patterns may be explained by income differences that occur between the life-cycle stages.

Decisions within the family can be classified into four different categories: wife dominated, husband dominated, autonomic, and syncratic. These categories refer to the extent to which the husband and wife act independently versus together in making purchases. Research has shown that decision making tends to become increasingly shared as the decision stage moves from problem recognition to search to purchase. Children, though, should not be left out of family decision making. For certain types of products and services, the presence of children as well as their requests can influence the purchase decision.

Another factor that influences family decision making is how power is shared within a family and how conflicts are resolved. Power can be obtained from a variety of sources including economic means, cultural definitions, and degree of interpersonal dependence. Different people may use various techniques to resolve conflicts to achieve desired outcomes, such as using emotional appeals, rewards, or bargaining. One important function of the family that should not be overlooked is the consumer socialization of children. Consumer socialization is the process of learning the skills, knowledge, and attitudes that enable a person to function as a consumer. This learning takes place within the context of background factors, such as the individual's social class, religious background, and socioeconomic status. In addition, the process is influenced by socialization agents such as the media, family members, peers, and teachers.

An understanding of the aspects of the family discussed so far can assist managers in several ways. Tracking demographic and life-cycle changes can pay off through finding marketing opportunities and avoiding marketing mistakes. Understanding the family decision process can be important to marketers in designing the marketing mix. Markets may be segmented and products differentiated based upon the family life cycle. Marketing research must be continuously performed by consumer goods companies to provide information that can be used for segmentation, positioning/differentiation, and promotional strategy. Finally, knowledge of consumer socialization may help managers anticipate changes in the consumer regulatory environment.

Organizations make purchase decisions through organizational buying centers, which are composed of those people in an organization who participate in the buying decision and who share the risks and goals of the decision. Organizational and consumer decision making share many similarities. However, organizations will show greater emphasis on anticipating problems qualifying suppliers and analyzing proposals. Three basic organizational buying situations have been identified—the new task, the modified rebuy, and the straight rebuy.

A focus on total quality management has led organizations to place high levels of emphasis on just-in-time purchasing, in which supplies are obtained just prior to when they are needed in production. To implement JIT systems, it is crucial to build close relations with suppliers. Relationship marketing can be defined as the overt attempt of exchange partners to build long-term associations in which purposeful cooperation, mutual dependence, and close structural bonds occur. In many respects building successful marketing relationships is analogous to building a successful marriage. Particularly important is the building of relationship trust, or a willingness to rely on an exchange partner in whom one has confidence. Organizational culture refers to the shared values and beliefs that enable members to understand their roles and the norms of the organization. If the cultures of two organizations clash, it will be difficult for them to develop trust and lasting relationships.

KEY TERMS

autonomic decision
childhood consumer socialization
detached nuclear family
extended family
family decision stage
family life cycle
household
just-in-time (JIT) purchasing
nuclear family
organizational buying center
organizational buying situations
organizational culture
purchase roles
relationship marketing
relationship trust
role overload
socialization agent
socialization background factors
syncratic decision

REVIEW QUESTIONS

1. How do families differ from other types of groups?
2. What are the types of purchase roles found in most groups?
3. Differentiate the terms household and family. Identify three different types of families.
4. Identify three key demographic changes in households expected to occur between 1990 and 2000.
5. Identify three major trends in household demographics that have occurred over the past 20 years.
6. Identify the 11 stages of the family life cycle presented in this chapter.
7. How do consumption patterns change as people move through the stages of the family life cycle?
8. Identify and briefly discuss four types of purchase roles that exist within families.
9. Four role specialization dimensions have been described regarding family decision making. Identify these dimensions and indicate possible purchases that would fall within each dimension.
10. Researchers have investigated the purchase steps for both furniture and automobiles. What decision steps are common to both types of purchases?
11. What factors affect the extent of influence in a family?
12. Children have an important influence on family decision making. What are the major types of decisions on which children influence their parents?

13. Draw the diagram of consumer socialization presented in the text.
14. What factors influence the socialization of parents?
15. Give a definition of an organizational buying center.
16. What are the dimensions on which organizational buying differs from consumer buying?
17. What are the three types of organizational buying situations?
18. Identify the seven stages of the continuum of marketing relationships.

DISCUSSION QUESTIONS

1. Consider the changes in household size over the past 25 years. How have these changes probably influenced the automobile industry and the housing industry?
2. Ask two female friends and two male friends what they think is the proper age for marriage. How do these ages match the average age at which couples were married in the 1960s and the 1990s? What do you think will be the trend in the age of marriage over the next ten years?
3. Consider the various life-cycle stages discussed in the chapter. How is the size of the various stages likely to change over the next ten years? What industries are likely to reap positive effects from these changes? What industries are likely to experience problems?
4. Think about your own family. Which individuals in your family have the roles of gatekeeper, influencer, decider, buyer, and preparer? To what extent do these roles change across different product categories? Now think about a nonhousehold organization to which you belong (e.g., a fraternity, sorority, or dorm group). Which individuals have these same buying roles in this organization?
5. Identify what you see as husband-dominated, wife-dominated, autonomic, and syncratic purchases for middle-class Americans today.
6. It is interesting to study how mothers and fathers react to the requests of children in grocery stores. Go to a grocery store and eavesdrop on two parent–child interactions. What type of requests does the child make? How do the parents handle the requests? To what extent do the requests seem to result from the influence of advertising?
7. Consider who influences whom for buying decisions in your own family. Who tends to hold the most influence? To what extent does the influence change across situations? Why are the influence relationships arranged as they are?
8. In several criminal court cases, the defense has argued that the defendant should be found innocent of a crime because he was influenced to commit the crime by viewing it on television. To what extent do you think that television is a socialization agent of children? To what extent do you believe that television can cause people to commit antisocial actions without recognizing the gravity of their actions?
9. Compare the brands of products that you prefer to those your parents prefer. To what extent do they coincide? To what extent do you attribute these similar preferences to the socialization process?
10. The decision of how many children to have is an important one. What are the factors that you think you will consider or that you are now considering relevant to having children? To what extent do you personally believe that consumer researchers can view children as a "consumption item"?
11. Consider the relationships that you have formed with various exchange partners (whether involving buying relationships or other types of relationships (friendships, dating, etc.). Provide examples of relationships that match each of the seven types of marketing relationships found in Table 16-8.

ENDNOTES

1. Harry L. Davis, "Decision Making Within the Household," in *Selected Aspects of Consumer Behavior: A Summary from the Perspective of Different Disciplines* (Washington, DC: National Science Foundation, 1977), pp. 73–97.
2. Jong Hee Park, Patriya S. Tansuhaj, and Richard H. Kolbe, "The Role of Love, Affection, and Intimacy in Family Decision Research," in *Advances in Consumer Research*, Vol. 18, Rebecca H. Holman and Michael R. Solomon, eds. (Provo, UT: Association for Consumer Research, 1991), pp. 651–656.
3. Gerald Zaltman and Melanie Wallendorf, *Consumer Behavior: Basic Findings and Managerial Implications* (New York: John Wiley, 1983), p. 168.
4. The Editors, "The Future of Households," *American Demographics*, December 1993, pp. 27-40.
5. U.S. Bureau of the Census, *Statistical Abstracts*, from various years.
6. U.S. Census Bureau, *Current Population Surveys*, 1991.
7. James Wetzel, "American Families: 75 Years of Change," *Monthly Labor Review*, March 1990, pp. 4–13.
8. *Statistical Abstracts of the United States*, Item 150, Social Data, Section 1, 1988.
9. Wetzel, "American Families."
10. Rose M. Rubin, Bobye J. Riney, and David J. Molina, "Expenditure Pattern Differentials Between One-Earner and Dual-Earner Households: 1972–1973 and 1984," *Journal of Consumer Research*, Vol. 17 (June 1990), pp. 43–52.
11. Susan Roy, "Victory Seamlessly Slits the Three-Piece Suit," *Advertising Age*, April 2, 1984, p. 33.
12. Charles M. Schaninger and William D. Danko, "A Conceptual and Empirical Comparison of Alternative Life Cycle Models," *Journal of Consumer Research*, Vol. 19 (March 1993), pp. 580–594.
13. Janet Wagner and Sherman Hanna, "The Effectiveness of Family Life Cycle Variables in Consumer Expenditure Research," *Journal of Consumer Research*, Vol. 10 (December 1983), pp. 281–291.
14. P. Sloan, "Matchabelli Name Readied for Men's Fragrance Line," *Advertising Age*, September 18, 1978, p. 3.
15. "Research, High TV Costs Push Crayola into Print," *Advertising Age*, September 18, 1978, p. 3.
16. Michael Reilly, "Working Wives and Convenience Consumption," *Journal of Consumer Research*, Vol. 8 (March 1982), pp. 407–418.
17. Ellen Foxman and Alvin Burns, "Role Load in the Household," in *Advances in Consumer Research*, Vol. 14, Melanie Wallendorf and Paul Anderson, eds. (Provo, UT: Association for Consumer Research, 1987), pp. 458–462.
18. Sharon Nickols and Karen Fox, "Buying Time and Saving Time: Strategies for Managing Household Production," *Journal of Consumer Research*, Vol. 10 (September 1983), pp. 197–208.
19. R. S. Oropesa, "Female Labor Force Participation and Time-saving Household Technology: A Case Study of the Microwave Oven from 1978 to 1989," *Journal of Consumer Research*, Vol. 19 (March 1993), pp. 567–579.
20. W. Keith Bryant, "Durables and Wives' Employment Yet Again," *Journal of Consumer Research*, Vol. 15 (June 1988), pp. 37–47.
21. Robert Boutilier, "Pulling the Family's Strings," *American Demographics*, August 1993, pp. 44–48.
22. Harry L. Davis and Benny P. Rigaux, "Perception of Marital Roles in Decision Processes," *Journal of Consumer Research*, Vol. 1 (June 1974), pp. 51–62.
23. Alvin Burns, "Husband and Wife Purchase Decision-Making Roles: Agreed, Presumed, Conceded, and Disputed," in *Advances in Consumer Research*, Vol. 4, William Perreault, ed. (Atlanta, GA: Association for Consumer Research, 1977), pp. 50–55.
24. Ibid.

25. Elizabeth Moore-Shay and William Wilkie, "Recent Developments in Research on Family Decisions," in *Advances in Consumer Research*, Vol. 15, Michael Houston, ed. (Provo, UT: Association for Consumer Research, 1988), pp. 454–460. Also, see Alvin Burns and Jo Anne Hopper, "An Analysis of the Presence, Stability, and Antecedents of Husband and Wife Purchase Decision Making Influence Assessment Agreement and Disagreement," in *Advances in Consumer Research*, Vol. 13, Richard Lutz, ed. (Provo, UT: Association for Consumer Research, 1986), pp. 175–180.

26. Michael B. Menasco and David J. Curry, "Utility and Choice: An Empirical Study of Wife/Husband Decision Making," *Journal of Consumer Research*, Vol. 16 (June 1989), pp. 87–97.

27. William J. Qualls and Francoise Jaffe, "Measuring Conflict in Household Decision Behavior: Read My Lips and Read My Mind," in *Advances in Consumer Research*, Vol. 20, John Sherry, Jr., and Brian Sternthal, eds. (Provo, UT: Association for Consumer Research, 1993), pp. 522–531.

28. Davis and Rigaux, "Perception of Marital Roles."

29. A. Shuptrine and G. Samuelson, "Dimensions of Marital Roles in Consumer Decision Making: Revisited," *Journal of Marketing Research*, Vol. 13 (February 1976), pp. 87–91.

30. William Qualls, "Household Decision Behavior: The Impact of Husbands' and Wives' Sex Role Orientation," *Journal of Consumer Research*, Vol. 14 (September 1987), pp. 264–279.

31. Sandra Bem, "The Measurement of Psychological Androgyny," *Journal of Consulting and Clinical Psychology*, Vol. 42 (1974), pp. 155–162.

32. Qualls, "Household Decision Behavior."

33. Giovanna Imperia, Thomas O'Guinn, and Elizabeth MacAdams, "Family Decision Making Role Perceptions Among Mexican-American and Anglo Wives: A Cross Cultural Comparison," in *Advances in Consumer Research*, Vol. 12, Elizabeth Hirschman and Morris Holbrook, eds. (Provo, UT: Association for Consumer Research, 1985), pp. 71–74.

34. For information on conflict in the family, see William Qualls, "Toward Understanding the Dynamics of Household Decision Conflict Behavior," in *Advances in Consumer Research*, Vol. 15, Michael Houston, ed. (Provo, UT: Association for Consumer Research, 1988), pp. 442–448; Margaret Nelson, "The Resolution of Conflict in Joint Purchase Decisions by Husbands and Wives: A Review and Empirical Test," in *Advances in Consumer Research*, Vol. 15, Michael Houston, ed. (Provo, UT: Association for Consumer Research, 1988), pp. 436–444; and Rosann L. Spiro, "Persuasion in Family Decision Making," *Journal of Consumer Research*, Vol. 9 (March 1983), pp. 393–402.

35. For a general review and critique of the literature on children's influence on purchase decisions, see Tamara F. Mangleburg, "Children's Influence in Purchase Decisions: A Review and Critique," in *Advances in Consumer Research*, Vol. 17, Marvin E. Goldberg, Gerald Gorn, and Richard W. Pollay, eds. (Provo, UT: Association for Consumer Research, 1990), pp. 813–825.

36. Amardeep Assar and George S. Bobinski, Jr., "Financial Decision Making of Baby-boomer Couples," in *Advances in Consumer Research*, Vol. 18, Rebecca H. Holman and Michael R. Solomon, eds. (Provo, UT: Association for Consumer Research, 1991), pp. 657–665.

37. Pierre Filiatrault and J. R. Brent Richie, "Joint Purchasing Decisions: A Comparison of Influence Structure in Family and Couple Decision-Making Units," *Journal of Consumer Research*, Vol. 7 (September 1980), pp. 131–140.

38. Scott Ward and Daniel Wackman, "Children's Purchase Influence Attempts and Parental Yielding," *Journal of Marketing Research*, Vol. 9 (August 1972), pp. 316–319.

39. For a review of this literature, see Charles K. Atkin, "Observations of Parent-Child Interaction in Supermarket Decision Making," *Journal of Marketing*, Vol. 42 (October 1978), pp. 42–45.

40. Kenneth Bahn, "Do Mothers and Children Share Cereal and Beverage Preferences and Evaluative Criteria?" in *Advances in Consumer Research*, Vol. 14, Melanie Wallendorf and Paul Anderson, eds. (Provo, UT: Association for Consumer Research, 1987), p. 281.

41. Atkin, "Observations of Parent-Child Interaction."

42. Ibid.

43. George Moschis and Linda Mitchell, "Television Advertising and Interpersonal Participation in Family Consumer Decisions," in *Advances in Consumer Research*, Vol. 13, Richard Lutz, ed. (Provo, UT: Association for Consumer Research, 1986), pp. 181–185.

44. Ellen Foxman and Patriya Tansuhaj, "Adolescents' and Mothers' Perceptions of Relative Influence in Family Purchase Decisions: Patterns of Agreement and Disagreement," in *Advances in Consumer Research*, Vol. 15, Michael Houston, ed. (Provo, UT: Association for Consumer Research, 1988), pp. 449–453.

45. Ellen R. Foxman, Patriya S. Tansuhaj, and Karin M. Ekstrom, "Family Members' Perceptions of Adolescents' Influence in Family Decision Making," *Journal of Consumer Research*, Vol. 15 (March 1989), pp. 482–491.

46. For an overview of current research on consumer socialization, see Scott Ward, Donna M. Klees, and Daniel B. Wackman, "Consumer Socialization Research: Content Analysis of Post-1980 Studies, and Some Implications for Future Work," in *Advances in Consumer Research*, Vol. 18, Rebecca H. Holman and Michael R. Solomon, eds. (Provo, UT: Association for Consumer Research, 1991), pp. 798–803.

47. David A. Goslin, "The Nature of Socialization," in *Handbook of Socialization Theory and Research*, D. A. Goslin, ed. (Chicago: Rand McNally, 1969.)

48. Scott Ward, "Consumer Socialization," *Journal of Consumer Research*, Vol. 1 (September 1974), pp. 1–14.

49. Horst Stipp, "New Ways to Reach Children," *American Demographics*, August 1993, pp. 50–54.

50. Various authors have developed models of the socialization process; see Gilbert A. Churchill and George Moschis, "Television and Interpersonal Influences on Adolescent Consumer Learning," *Journal of Consumer Research*, Vol. 6 (June 1979), pp. 23–35.

51. Laura A. Peracchio, "How Do Young Children Learn to Be Consumers? A Script-processing Approach," *Journal of Consumer Research*, Vol. 18 (March 1992), pp. 425–440.

52. George Moschis and Roy Moore, "Decision Making Among the Young: A Socialization Perspective," *Journal of Consumer Research*, Vol. 6 (September 1979), pp. 101–112.

53. L. Guest, "Brand Loyalty—Twelve Years Later," *Journal of Applied Psychology*, Vol. 39 (December 1955), pp. 405–408.

54. Terry Childers and Akshay R. Rao, "The Influence of Familial and Peer-Based Reference Groups on Consumer Decisions," *Journal of Consumer Research*, Vol. 19 (September 1992), pp. 198–211.

55. George P. Moschis, "The Role of Family Communication in Consumer Socialization of Children and Adolescents," *Journal of Consumer Research*, Vol. 11 (March 1985), 898–913.

56. Ritha Fellerman and Kathleen Debevec, "Till Death Do We Part: Family Dissolution, Transition, and Consumer Behavior," in *Advances in Consumer Research*, Vol. 19, John F. Sherry, Jr., and Brian Sternthal, eds. (Provo, UT: Advances in Consumer Research, 1992), pp. 514–521.

57. Alan R. Andreasen, "Life Status Changes and Changes in Consumer Preferences and Satisfaction," *Journal of Consumer Research*, Vol. 11 (December 1984), pp. 784–794.

58. Karin Ekstrom, Patriya Tansuhaj, and Ellen Foxmann, "Children's Influence in Family Decisions and Consumer Socialization: A Reciprocal View," in *Advances in Consumer Research*, Vol. 16, Melanie Wallendorf and Paul Anderson, eds. (Provo, UT: Association for Consumer Research, 1987), pp. 283–287.

59. Orville Brim, "Adult Socialization," in *Socialization and Society*, J. Clausen, ed. (Boston: Little, Brown, 1968).

60. This material is based upon work by Ekstrom et al., "Children's Influence in Family Decisions and Consumer Socialization."

61. Michael D. Hutt and Thomas W. Speh, *Business Marketing Management* (Fort Worth, TX: The Dryden Press, 1992), p. 66.

62. Hutt and Speh, *Business Marketing Management.*

63. Erin Anderson, Wujin Chu, and Barton Weitz, "Industrial Purchasing: An Empirical Exploration of the Buyclass Framework," *Journal of Marketing*, Vol. 51 (July 1987), pp. 71–86.

64. For a more complex view of organizational buying situations, see Michele D. Bunn, "Taxonomy of Buying Decision Approaches," *Journal of Marketing*, Vol. 57 (January 1993), pp. 38–56.

65. Ernest Raia, "JIT in Purchasing: A Progress Report," *Purchasing*, February 23, 1989, p. 18. Also, see John Flanagan and James P. Morgan, *Just-in-Time for the '90s* (Washington, DC: DREF, 1989), pp. 19.

66. This definition of relationship marketing was developed by the author of the text. In particular, ideas for the definition were developed from Gregory T. Gundlach and Patrick E. Murphy, "Ethical and Legal Foundations of Relational Marketing Exchanges," *Journal of Marketing*, Vol. 57 (October 1993), pp. 35–46.

67. Frederick E. Webster, Jr., "The Changing Role of Marketing in the Corporation," *Journal of Marketing*, Vol. 58 (October 1992), pp. 1–17.

68. Ibid.

69. F. Robert Dwyer, Paul H. Schurr, and Sejo Oh, "Developing Buyer-Seller Relationships," *Journal of Marketing*, Vol. 51 (April 1987), pp. 11–27.

70. Jeffrey J. Stoltman, James W. Gentry, and Fred Morgan, "Marketing Relationships: Further Consideration of the Marriage Metaphor with Implications for Maintenance and Recovery," in *Enhancing Knowledge Development in Marketing*, David Cravens and Peter Dickson, eds., AMA Educators' Proceedings (Chicago: American Marketing Association, 1993), pp. 28–35.

71. Gundlach and Murphy, "Ethical and Legal Foundations of Relationship Marketing Exchanges."

72. Christine Moorman, Gerald Zaltman, and Rohit Deshpande, "Relationships Between Providers and Users of Market Research: The Dynamics of Trust Within and Between Organizations," *Journal of Marketing Research*, Vol. 29 (August 1992), pp. 314–329.

73. Christine Moorman, Rohit Deshpande, and Gerald Zaltman, "Factors Affecting Trust in Market Research Relationships," *Journal of Marketing*, Vol. 57 (January 1993), pp. 81–101.

74. Rohit Deshpande and Frederick E. Webster, Jr., "Organizational Culture and Marketing: Defining the Research Agenda," *Journal of Marketing*, Vol. 53 (January 1989), pp. 3–15.

75. John W. Barnes and Edwin R. Stafford, "Strategic Alliance Partner Selection: When Organizational Cultures Clash," in *Enhancing Knowledge Development in Marketing*, Vol. 4, David W. Cravens and Peter R. Dickson, eds. (Chicago: American Marketing Association, 1993), pp. 424–433.

76. The example was based on Fern Schumer Chapman, "Executive Guilt: Who's Taking Care of the Children?" *Fortune*, February 16, 1987, pp. 30–37.

77. John Robinson, "Who's Doing the Housework?" *American Demographics*, December 1988, pp. 24–28, 63.

CHAPTER 16 CASE STUDY

Targeting the Family in the 1990s

Companies are beginning to recognize that they must appeal to both children and adults—in large part because in the United States children control the spending of between $55 billion and $132 billion. As a result, companies have begun to consider how they can appeal to both children and adults. For example, H. J. Heinz discovered that children under 18 consume one-third more ketchup than adults. In addition, they frequently choose the family brand. The company then developed an ad in which a dark-haired, self-confident high school boy impresses a pretty girl when he performs the following feat. First, he places a Heinz ketchup bottle on its side on the edge of a roof. He then hurtles down several flights of stairs and buys a hot dog. He then casually holds it out to catch the first drop of ketchup that has finally oozed from the bottle. A Heinz product manager said, "Our research shows that kids like the commercials because they aspire to be teenagers, and adults like them because they bring back memories of their youth." Heinz believes the ads added 2% to its sales volume [1].

Similarly, executives at movie companies are asking themselves how they can create a product that will attract adults as well as children to their films. If a movie company can attract mom and dad, as well as the kids, the number of paid patrons has on average doubled. A master at this dual marketing strategy is Disney Studios.

Disney's first direct attempt to target adults, as well as children, occurred in 1989 with the release of the animated movie *The Little Mermaid*. Disdaining the syrupy-sweet, air-headed heroines of old (e.g., Snow White and Cinderella), animators turned Ariel into a feisty, independent, and impetuous young woman. In addition to having a body that would make Mattel's Barbie envious, Ariel possessed a talent (i.e., singing) that modern parents attempt to create in their children through endless lessons. In other words, Ariel appealed to fathers and mothers almost as much as she enthralled 6-year-old girls (and boys, for that matter).

Next, Disney brought out *Beauty and the Beast*—another animated masterpiece. Promoting the movie even more directly to parents, Disney played up the idea that some viewed it as worthy of an Academy Award. Indeed, it initially opened at Cinema I on New York's East Side rather than at the local neighborhood theater. At the evening shows, adults outnumbered children by a ratio of 10 to 1. The company even created different poster art for adults and children. For the kids, it developed cheery, vibrantly colorful posters that displayed the various animated characters in the movie. In the newspaper ads, Disney used romantic artwork showing muted images of Beauty and the Beast dancing. In the movie, Belle became the first Disney heroine to be extremely well read—in this case, appealing to parents' desire to have literate kids [2].

The copy of an advertisement in the Sunday edition of *The New York Times* transparently depicts Disney's strategy. Quoting liberally from a review by Gene Siskel and Roger Ebert, the ad copy stated: "One of the very finest films of all time. Two enthusiastic thumbs up, way up. It's a legitimate candidate for Oscar consideration for Best Picture. It's breathtaking. I liked it more than *The Little Mermaid*. Sophisticated and funny, romantic and scary, Disney's *Beauty and the Beast* is an instant classic. It's thrilling, and you don't have to bring a kid along to have fun."

* * *

Thanks to Carol Hisey for her assistance in developing the case.

QUESTIONS

1. Define the problem identified in the case. Why is the problem important to marketers?
2. Discuss the consumer concepts from the chapter that apply to the case.
3. Develop a managerial applications table for the marketing of *Beauty and the Beast*.

Discuss the marketing strategies employed by Disney that illustrate the managerial use of the consumer concepts.

NOTES

1. Janet Maslin, "Target: Boomers and Their Babies," *The New York Times*, Sunday, November 24, 1991, Section 2, pp. 1, 39.
2. Patricia Sellers, "The ABC's of Marketing to Kids," *Fortune*, May 8, pp. 114-120.

Chapter 17

Cultural Processes I: Culture and Popular Culture

CONSUMER VIGNETTE

Mixed Signals on Guns

Susan, a college freshman, swings the pistol around, squeezing off imaginary shots. Looking at the salesclerk, she asks, "Could I get a bigger grip?" Susan and her father are shopping for a handgun that she can take with her when she rides her horse on mountain trails. Her dad says, "A lot of strange characters are showing up on the trails, and I thought she could use a gun, maybe just something small to keep in her bag." She adds, "It's scary out there." They finally settle on a $322.25 Smith & Wesson .38, which the clerk describes as having plenty of stopping power, because "You want to be able to put him down with the first shot, not play around."[1]

Indeed, in 1993 and 1994 sales of guns skyrocketed in the United States. Between 1991 and 1993 sales of imported firearms increased by 345%. By January 1994, the demand for weapons was so strong that distributors and retailers were in near panic. At SHOT (the Shooting, Hunting, Outdoor Trade show), one retailer was begging importers of a Russian sniper rifle to sell him as many as they could. An Armenian importer said that he could sell as many guns as he could get to the United States. Indeed, on December 23, 1993, a huge Russian cargo jet landed in Columbus, Ohio, with enough semiautomatic SKS long guns to equip an entire infantry division.

What caused this incredible rush to purchase guns? Many suspect that it was the fear that the Clinton administration in the White House would succeed in placing curbs on imported weapons, which can cost one-third less than equivalent U.S.-made guns. As one rifle manufacturer put it, "To call for curbs on imports would be letting the government get its sticky fingers on the gun industry."[2]

Simultaneously with the consumer rush to buy guns, a countertrend was occurring in New York City. Reebok, Toys 'R' Us, and other retailers were offering to exchange "toys for guns." For example, Reebok and Dial-A-Mattress gave gun owners a $100 gift certificate when they turned in a weapon. The idea originated with the son of a carpet store owner named Fernando Mateo. After his teenage son said that he would gladly give up his Christmas toys to get guns off the streets, Mr. Mateo put up $5,000 of his own money to offer the $100 gift certificates from Toys 'R' Us. The money quickly ran out, and Toys 'R' Us chipped in $20,000. Later Foot Locker pledged another $25,000 for its own program. By January 6, 1994, over $70,000 in corporate and private donations had gone into the programs. A Reebok spokesperson said, "Toys 'R' Us can count on us. We want to stop the violence and make our cities a safe place."[3]

INTRODUCTION

Culture has been defined in a variety of ways. One classic definition states that **culture** is a set of socially acquired behavior patterns transmitted symbolically through language and other means to the members of a particular society.[4] Another definition states that culture is "the interactive aggregate of common characteristics that influence a group's response to its environment."[5] Cultures may be distinguished in terms of their regulation of behavior, the attitudes of the people, the values of the people, the life-style of the people, and the degree of tolerance of other cultures.[6] Another perspective comes from the symbolic interactionists, who view culture as composed of a set of competing images transmitted through media via important signs/symbols.[7]

Culture may be described as a way of life. It includes the material objects of a society, such as guns, footballs, autos, bibles, forks, and chopsticks. Culture is also made up of ideas and values; for example, most Americans endorse the belief that people have a right to choose between different brands of products. This value is not shared by people in some socialist countries. Culture consists of a mix of institutions that include legal, political, religious, and even business organizations. Some may even symbolically represent a society—for example, McDonald's or Anheuser-Busch. The ways we dress, think, eat, and spend our leisure time are all components of our culture.[8]

A number of additional ideas are necessary to gain an overall understanding of culture. A culture is *learned*—it is *not* present in our genes. Thus it is transmitted from generation to generation, influencing future members of the society. The process of learning one's own culture is called **enculturation**. The difficult task of learning a new culture is called **acculturation**. Recently, researchers have distinguished the level of acculturation from the level of cultural identification. **Cultural identifi-cation** refers to the society in which a person prefers to live. As such, it is attitudinal in nature. In contrast, the level of acculturation is behavioral in nature, referring to the extent that the actions of the immigrant conform to the norms and mores of a new culture.

A culture is also *adaptive*. It changes as a society faces new problems and opportunities. Just as organisms evolve, so do cultures. They take on new traits and discard old useless ones to form a new cultural base. The sexual revolution that occurred during the 1960s in the United States exemplifies such cultural adaptation. The development of the birth control pill set into motion forces that created an environment conducive to a change in the way society viewed women and sexual relations. More recently, the AIDS epidemic has influenced all sexually active people, whether American, Canadian, or Japanese, to return to more conservative sexual values.

Finally, culture satisfies needs. By providing **norms**, or rules of behavior, a culture gives an orderliness to society. By providing **values**, a culture delineates what is right, good, and important. People need to know what is expected of them, what is right and wrong, and what they should do in various situations. Culture is the element that fulfills such societal requirements. For example, currently in American culture, its members are feeling a strong need for physical safety from violence. As shown in the chapter-opening vignette, this cultural need resulted in two diametrically opposed movements—one to purchase weapons and one to encourage people to voluntarily turn in their guns.

The task of identifying the elements of one's own culture is difficult. In fact, it has been suggested that understanding one's own culture requires knowing something of another culture— to realize that other people really do things differently.[9] For example, by international standards Americans are fanatics concerning personal hygiene. In most other parts of the world, deodorants are rarely used, baths are much less frequently taken, and teeth are brushed rarely. Indeed, toilet paper is unheard of in some areas of the globe. The American preoccupation with fresh breath appears silly to some Mediterranean cultures whose cuisines are partially built around garlic. However, cultural discomfort is bidirectional. Visitors from mainland China are somewhat revolted when they learn that Americans actually sell food for animals in the same place where food is sold for people.

Components of Culture

A number of key concepts are used by scholars to describe cultures. As noted, each culture has a set of values that denote the end states for which to strive. As one compares and contrasts cultures, the relative importance of various values will differ. For example, in both the United States and Japan, the values of individualism and showing allegiance to the group are present. However, the importance of the group is much stronger in Japan. In the United States individualism is a more important value.

All societies have a distinctive set of norms. Norms are more specific than values and dictate acceptable and unacceptable behaviors. Two general types of norms exist. **Enacted norms** are those that are explicitly expressed, sometimes in the form of laws. An example would be on which side of the road you drive a car. In the United States people drive on the right side. In contrast, in England and Japan people drive on the left. This can create problems for international travelers. When I first traveled to Britain, I was almost run over by a car. I was attempting to walk across a busy traffic intersection. A car was turning left in front of me. The person in the right-hand seat was smiling at me—an action I took to indicate that I should go across the street. As I stepped off the curb, the car continued on, nearly knocking me over. Quickly jumping back, I realized that I was looking at the passenger rather than the driver.

The second type of norm is embedded in the culture and only learned through extensive interaction with the people of the culture. Called **cresive norms**, they are of three types:[10]

Customs. Handed down from generation to generation, **customs** apply to basic actions such what ceremonies are held and the roles played by the sexes.

Mores. **Mores** are customs that emphasize the moral aspects of behavior. Frequently, mores apply to forbidden behaviors, such as, in fundamentalist Moslem countries, the showing of skin by women.

Conventions. **Conventions** describe how to act in everyday life, and they frequently apply to consumer behavior. For example, the landscaping of yards varies widely from society to society. In the Unites States, yards are frequently very large and covered with grass. In Germany, yards frequently feature neat flower gardens. In Japan, yards are small, elaborately planted with bushes, and frequently feature the sound of bubbling water.

Another element of culture is the myths held by its people. **Myths** are stories that express key values and ideals of a society. For example, in the United States a popular mythological character is "Superman." A curious figure, Superman displays important values within the American culture, such as great strength and a mild-mannered exterior (recall Teddy Roosevelt's famous phrase, "Speak softly, but carry a big stick."). He fights crime and injustice. In addition, he reveals a strong puritanical streak by not being able to become romantically involved without serious negative consequences. As noted by one authority on the topic, myths help to (1) explain the origins of existence, (2) reveal a set of values for the society, and (3) provide models for personal conduct.[11]

The creation of myths is extremely important to marketers. For example, the Superman myth was created via a comic book. Some other consumer myths include fictional characters, such as Santa Claus, Indiana Jones, E.T., the Playboy Bunny, and the Easter Bunny. It is ironic that the bunny has been chosen by marketers to represent two very different sets of values and behavioral standards. In addition, cultural myths may also be based upon real people, such as George Washington cutting down the cherry tree. A more recent cultural myth is based upon Sam Walton building WalMart and becoming the richest man in the United States while maintaining a simple, frugal life-style.

Each culture also has its own set of symbols, rituals, and values to which marketers can tie their products and services. For example, in the United States the eagle is a symbol representative of strength, courage, and patriotism. Companies wanting to create such an image may use the eagle in their advertising or packaging. Whirlpool Corporation has undertaken such a strategy in promotions for its household appliances. In contrast, in Australia the koala is an important symbol that is used by companies to link themselves symbolically to the island country. Various rituals are also important to culture. For example, in late January of each year millions of people in the United States gather together in small groups, sit in front of a television set, and eat fattening food while watching the Superbowl. In 1994, corporations responded to this mass party atmosphere by spending $800,000 plus for 30 seconds of time to advertise their products.

Values also vary widely across cultures. In the United States, the freedom to own guns is deeply ingrained. As described in the chapter-opening vignette, even college women have become caught up in a buying frenzy when a threat was perceived to this freedom. The surge to purchase guns occurred at the same time that another movement to provide incentives for people to turn in their weapons was underway. This countermovement resulted in part from the operation of another value—the belief in the importance of maintaining social order. Shorter-term changes in the values on which people focus form the popular culture of a society. Figure 17-1 shows a photo of a young woman considering the purchase of a pistol for herself.

The Cultural Matrix

The cultural matrix shown in Figure 17-2 visually depicts three important sets of factors that compose a culture. It is the intertwining of distinctive sets of values, of the institutional–social environment, and of the material environment that creates the overall cultural fabric of a society. As shown in the figure, the material environment consists of such factors as the technical–scientific level of the society, the extent and type of natural resources present, the geographical landscape and placement of the society, and the degree of economic prosperity of the society. The institutional–social environment includes the legal, political, religious, business, and

Figure 17-1 This college-age woman is considering the purchase of a handgun. How does this act illustrate U.S. culture?" (Photo by John Mowen.)

subcultural groups that compose the society. Discussed at length in Chapter 18, subcultures are subdivisions of a national culture centered on some unifying characteristic, such as social class or ethnic group membership.

A culture is also influenced by the dominant values of the society. Values will be discussed in a separate section in the chapter. In the American culture, key values include individualism, freedom, and achievement.

It should also be noted that culture can be impacted by additional factors, such as natural disasters and wars. For example, when Europeans discovered the Americas, entire civilizations of native people were eliminated by the diseases carried by the invaders. In 1994, war gripped Sarajevo in what used to be Yugoslavia. Only ten years before, the Winter Olympic Games had been held in this beautiful city. The brutality and death of war completely changed the culture of the geographic region. Highlight 17-1 discusses the impact of the war on one consumer activity—smoking cigarettes.

As time passes, changes will occur in the external environment, the social institutions, and the values found within the cultural matrix. In addition, a constant interplay of movements and countermovements takes place within the matrix. As a result, new ideas and trends are constantly bubbling to the surface. These ideas and trends form what is called "popular culture."

Popular culture is constantly changing. Because of these changes, variations in fashion and life-styles occur. In turn, these may lead to corporate catastrophes or

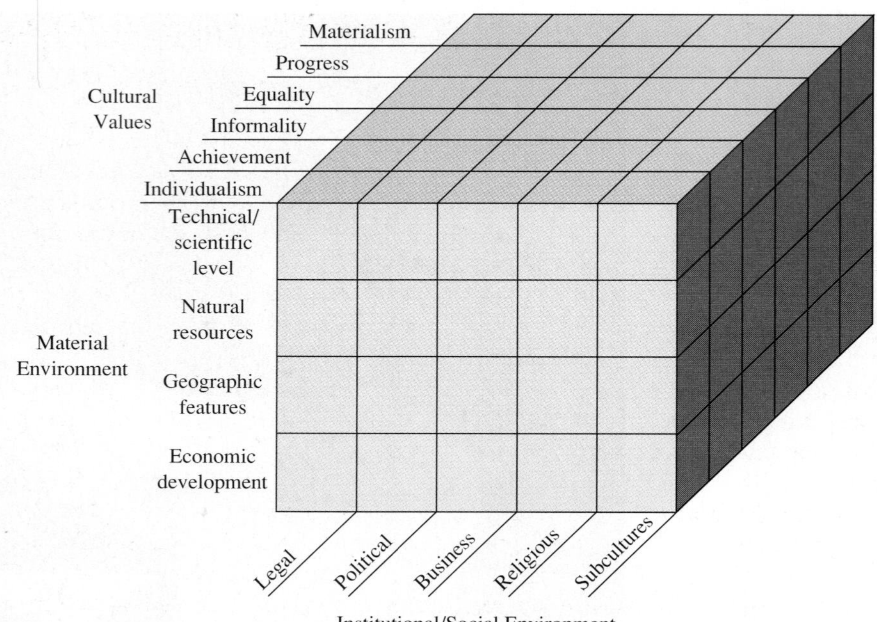

Figure 17-2 The cultural matrix.

marketing opportunities. For example, in the 1980s popular culture in the United States emphasized fitness and slimness. As a result, the marketers of running shoes, weight-lifting machines, and related athletic equipment experienced explosive growth. During this time period, the sales of a small company in Tulsa, Oklahoma, named Stair Master Corporation, exploded as part-time athletes purchased these expensive devices to simulate the exercise of climbing stairs. However, in the 1990s, popular culture changed. Between 1985 and 1990, participation in fitness programs declined by 10%.[12] The decline in physical activity occurred for all age groups—not just the aging baby boomers. Such changes created massive problems for companies selling fitness devices. Meanwhile, a shift from hard physical exercise to walking occurred. As a result, manufacturers of walking shoes experienced high growth levels. A section of the chapter is devoted to a detailed discussion of popular culture.

Chapter Overview

This chapter discusses culture and its impact on consumer behavior in the United States. It first analyzes the role of consumer goods within a culture. The next two sections present information on cultural rituals and symbols. The chapter then discusses popular culture, which represents the shorter trends that occur within the overall fabric. Finally, the chapter presents a managerial applications example.

INTERNATIONAL HIGHLIGHT 17-1

Cigarette Smoking Thrives in Sarajevo

While the number of cigarette smokers has plummeted in the United States over the past years, in war-torn Sarajevo cigarettes became a status symbol and even a means of exchange. Indeed, while other industries collapsed under the pressure of daily artillery and mortar shelling, government officials made sure that the one cigarette factory kept churning out its product. The going rate for a package of "real American Marlboros" in September 1993 was $15—enough to feed a family of three for ten days.

One soldier said, "Smoking is the one luxury we enjoy, but for most people it's more necessary than food." The 30-year-old Bosnian soldier continued, "Smokers will tell you they can survive on only one meal a day if they can smoke." Prior to the war, a 25-year-old lawyer disdained smoking. But once the war started, she quickly picked up the habit. She said, "I have nothing against cigarettes any more. When I hold a cigarette, my hands don't shake. You are afraid for your own life at almost every moment here, and cigarettes really help you not to think about it."

As stated in the text, culture is adaptive. In times of great stress, the change can occur very quickly. During the war in Bosnia and Herzegovina, the dire warnings of the long-term ill effects of smoking were laughed away. When people face the possibility of being blown away every day, the idea of worrying about developing cancer in 30 years is laughable. The extremes of war well illustrate how the types of consumer goods that are valued in a culture depend a great deal on the particular circumstances faced by the people of a society.

Based upon Chuck Sudetic, "Cigarettes a Thriving Industry in Bleak Sarajevo," *The New York Times*, September 5, 1993, p. 5.

THE ROLE OF CONSUMER GOODS IN A CULTURE

An important question for consumer researchers involves the issue of what role consumer goods play in a culture. Figure 17-3 diagrams the relationship between consumer goods, individual consumers, and the culturally constituted world. The significance of goods lies in their ability to carry and communicate cultural meaning. Goods may be viewed as "way stations of meanings."[13] **Cultural meanings** refer to the values, norms, and shared beliefs that are symbolically communicated. They are transferred from the culturally constituted world to consumer goods and from consumer goods to individuals.

The culturally constituted world may be viewed as a lens through which individuals interpret the world around them. The culturally constituted world is made up of the values, mores, and norms that make up a particular society. As such, it forms a kind of blueprint that designates how people should act and behave. As shown in Figure 17-3, the transfer of meaning from culture to object may take place through advertising and fashion systems. The transfer of meaning from consumer goods to individuals may take place through various rituals, including possession, exchange, grooming, and divestment rituals.

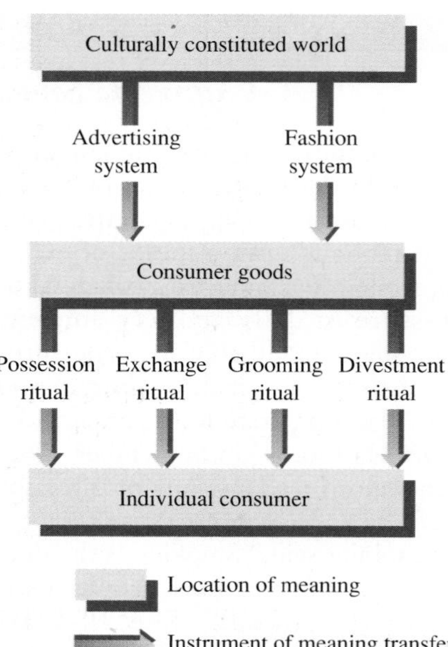

Figure 17-3
Communicating cultural meaning. (Reproduced with permission from Grant McCracken, "Culture and Consumption: A Theoretical Account of the Structure and Movement of the Cultural Meaning of Consumer Goods," *Journal of Consumer Research*, Vol. 13, June 1986, pp. 71–84.)

Advertising may be viewed as a kind of conduit through which meaning pours from the culturally constituted world to consumer goods. By positioning a product the advertiser imbues it with meaning. For example, Pontiac has used the theme "We build excitement" extensively in recent years. Their goal is to position the brand as an exciting, youthful automobile. Through this positioning process, meanings are drawn from the culturally constituted world and transferred to the automobile through the advertisements.

The fashion system is a broader, more diffuse set of agents of transfer. It includes magazines, newspapers, opinion leaders, and, at the margins of society, the hippies, punks, and gays. The fashion system appears to act somewhat like the multistep flow model in the diffusion of innovations. (See Chapter 15 for more on diffusion processes.) For example, the characters in television shows may act to give meaning to various products and services. Television programs such as "Dynasty" and "Dallas" have acted to transfer meaning to clothing and accessories that represent the nouveau riche in American society. More recently, "Roseanne" has done the same for products and services representative of the blue-collar, working class.

In Figure 17-3 consumer goods and services are depicted as transferring cultural meanings to individuals. In essence, then, people use goods to link cultural meanings to themselves. The clothing we wear, the cars we drive, the locations of our houses, and things we have in our houses represent ourselves to others. If the meaning that we attach to our material objects is understood by others, we successfully portray who and what we are to others. As one authority has stated, "What can be said of clothing can be said of virtually all other high-involvement product categories and several low-involvement ones. Clothing, transportation, food, housing exteriors and interiors, and adornment all serve as media for the expression of the cultural meaning that constitutes the world."[14]

It has been argued that, through various rituals, meanings of objects are transferred to the individual. A ritual is a kind of symbolic series of actions that link the person to the material good. For example, in exchange rituals material objects are given and received. The exchange of gifts at birthdays and Christmas illustrates such rituals. Gifts possess symbolic properties that act to transfer cultural meanings, such as love, from one person to another. Rituals will be discussed in more detail later in the chapter.

As discussed earlier, the transfer of cultural meaning to individuals through material goods is based upon the use of rituals. Through the advertising and fashion systems, cultural meanings are attached to goods and services. Rituals then act to attach symbolically the meaning of products and services to the person. Thus products and services can be used to define who and what a person is to others. The next three sections discuss these concepts in greater detail. The next section on core American values relates to the cultural meanings that people hope to attach to themselves. The section on rituals discusses in greater detail the nature and characteristics of this important transfer mechanism. Finally, the third section discusses a few of the important ways through which we are affected by cultural symbols.

CULTURAL VALUES IN THE UNITED STATES AND CANADA

Values are enduring beliefs about ideal end states and modes of conduct. In general, values tend to be few in number. They are more abstract than attitudes, and they serve as standards to guide actions, attitudes, and judgments. As such, specific attitudes about objects tend to reflect and support a person's values. Within a society, **cultural values** represent the shared meanings of ideal end states and modes of conduct. Thus cultural values depict a society's shared meaning of what is important and what end states of existence people should seek.[15]

The values that make up the culturally constituted world in the United States have a variety of sources. One important source of our culture is the European heritage of the early settlers of the United States and Canada. The flight from religious persecution and authoritarian monarchies indelibly etched into the American culture the values of individualism and freedom. Some have argued that the frontier created the values of rugged individualism, informality, equality, and diligence.[16] Certainly, the Judeo-Christian heritage of early Americans also influenced what were to become core American values.[17]

A number of authors have developed lists of core American values. Frequently mentioned values include beliefs in the importance of

1. Individualism.
2. Youthfulness.
3. Progress.
4. Materialism.
5. Activity.
6. Achievement.
7. Efficiency.
8. Informality.

9. Equality.
10. Distrust of government.

Other values sometimes mentioned include freedom, external conformity, humanitarianism, authority, respect for institutions, mastery of the environment, and religion. The "Protestant ethic" also flows deeply through the social fabric of the United States. Thus values relating to hard work and frugality are important to many Americans. Such themes are sometimes used by advertisers. For example, the ad developed by the Peace Corps, shown in Figure 17-4, illustrates an appeal to a work ethic to obtain volunteers. In addition, the ad holds forth the promise of learning about new cultures.

Figure 17-4 The Peace Corps employs an appeal to the cultural value of the work ethic. (Courtesy of the Peace Corps.)

We need someone with the ambition of an investment banker, the patience of a driving instructor and the optimism of a weatherman.

We have a unique opportunity for someone very special.

A chance to spend two years in another country. To live and work in another culture. To learn a new language and acquire new skills.

The person we're looking for might be a farmer, a forester, or a retired nurse. Or maybe a teacher, a mechanic, or a recent college graduate.

We need someone to join over 5,000 people already working in 60 developing countries around the world. To help people live better lives.

We need someone special. And we ask a lot. But only because so much is needed. If this sounds interesting to you, maybe you're the person we're looking for. A Peace Corps volunteer. Find out. Call us at **1-800-424-8580, Ext. 93.**

Peace Corps.
The toughest job you'll ever love.

Ad Council

PEACE CORPS CAMPAIGN
MAGAZINE AD NO. PC-2247-87—7" x 10"
Volunteer Agency: Ted Bates & Company, Volunteer Coordinator: Edward MacEwen, GTE.
CM-7-87

One must recognize, however, that countercurrents tend to exist regarding cultural values. For example, in the United States the respect for institutions has been steadily falling since the mid-1970s. Similarly, the ecology movement, with its emphasis on living in harmony with nature, clearly acts as a counterforce against the value of mastering the environment. As noted earlier, culture is adaptive, and one should expect to occasionally see movements that are inconsistent with the traditional values of a culture.

The values of a culture can be recognized by consumers in foreign countries who are considering making purchases. For example, Europeans associate the United States with rugged individualism. Highlight 17-2 discusses the impact of this perception on the sales of American products to European consumers.

A psychologist who has investigated values extensively is Milton Rokeach. Rokeach identified what he called terminal values and instrumental values.[18] Terminal values are desired end states—how people would like to eventually experience their lives. Instrumental values are the behaviors and actions required to achieve the terminal states. Table 17-1 presents a set of 24 terminal and instrumental values identified by consumer researchers as important to consumption.[19] The 24-item list of values is shorter than the original **Rokeach value scale**, because a number of his items, such as "world at peace" and "courageous," have limited applicability to consumer behavior.

INTERNATIONAL HIGHLIGHT 17-2

Some Europeans Appreciate American Values and Products

What do Jack Daniels, Jeep, Nordic Track, and Land's End have in common? All are marketing their products (whether whiskey, four-wheel vehicles, aerobic equipment, or clothing) in Europe by touting their American origins. After visiting the United States on a number of occasions, a retired carpet executive from England said that he became hooked on the "unusual quality of the goods." Liking the "rugged American look," when he discovered that you can buy Land's End merchandise from England, he began ordering from the company.

While the plight of EuroDisney indicates that caution is warranted (the French version of Disneyland has lost hundreds of millions of dollars), many American companies have begun to link their products directly to America. Thus, in Europe, Jeep calls itself "the American legend." Similarly, Jim Bean's print ad campaign in the United Kingdom reads, "The American Spirit Since 1795." When Budweiser switched to an ad campaign that featured scenes of fishing in Montana and a Nevada truck stop, strong sales gains resulted.

One young British civil servant said that he used to have a typical European attitude about U.S. products—that is, "rather tacky and lacking in taste." But, after seeing a Bose stereo system in Florida, he purchased one for himself. He said, "I'm much more prepared to accept American goods. I'm very fond of America."

While the new European attitude toward the United States is highly positive for exporters, remember that in the 1970s there was a backlash against American symbols. If American companies fail to maintain quality products, the love affair will be of short duration.

Based upon Dana Milbank, "Made in America Becomes a Boast in Europe," *The Wall Street Journal*, January 19, 1994, pp. B1, B5.

TABLE 17-1

Shortened Rokeach Value Scale

Terminal	*Instrumental*
1. A comfortable life	**14.** Ambitious
2. An exciting life	**15.** Broadminded
3. A sense of accomplishment	**16.** Capable
4. A world of beauty	**17.** Cheerful
5. Equality	**18.** Clean
6. Family security	**19.** Imaginative
7. Freedom	**20.** Independent
8. Happiness	**21.** Intellectual
9. Inner harmony	**22.** Logical
10. Pleasure	**23.** Responsible
11. Self-respect	**24.** Self-control
12. Social recognition	
13. Wisdom	

SOURCE: J. Michael Munson and Edward McQuarrie, "Shortening the Rokeach Value Survey for Use in Consumer Research," in *Advances in Consumer Research*, vol. 15, Michael Houston, ed. (Provo, UT: Association for Consumer Research, 1988), pp. 381–386.

Consumer Research on Cultural Values

One important research issue concerns how cultural values influence specific consumption decisions. Figure 17-5 shows the sequence of moving from global values to domain-specific values to evaluations of product attributes.[20] **Global values**, which correspond closely to Rokeach's terminal values, consist of people's enduring beliefs about desired states of existence. **Domain-specific values** are beliefs pertaining to more concrete consumption activities. Examples include beliefs that manufacturers should give prompt service, guarantee their products, help eliminate environmental pollution, be truthful, and so forth. Evaluations of product attributes are highly specific beliefs about individual products. For example, how well does a Corvette handle? Is it easy to repair? (A thorough discussion of product beliefs takes place in Chapter 8.)

The researchers found that people with different global values also exhibited divergent domain-specific values and product evaluations. Indeed, the differences in global values translated to markedly different product preferences. For example, those with global values emphasizing logic, an exciting life, and self-respect preferred compact cars and outdoor recreation. Those with global values emphasizing national security and salvation were more attracted to standard-sized cars and television.

Figure 17-5 exemplifies what are called means–end chain models. **Means–end chain** models identify the linkages between consumer desires for specific product

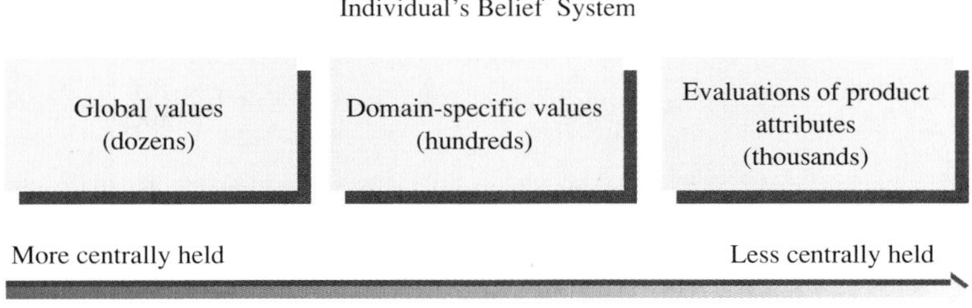

Figure 17-5 Organization of the value–attitude system. (Adapted by permission from Donald E. Vinson, Jerome Scott, and Lawrence Lamont, "The Role of Personal Values in Marketing and Consumer Behavior," *Journal of Marketing*, Vol. 41, April 1977, p. 46, published by the American Marketing Association.)

features with increasingly abstract concepts, such as benefits desired and values that are important to an individual. For example, consider a person who desires to purchase a car that has a small, fuel-efficient engine. Three major benefits result from this feature—good gas mileage, lower cost to buy and operate, and protection of the environment. In turn, these benefits lead to a frugal life-style. Finally, a frugal life-style leads to the terminal value of a clean environment. In sum, the purchase of a car with the attribute of a small engine acted as a means to reach the desired end state of a cleaner environment. The process of probing to identify the linkages between means (i.e., attributes) and terminal values (i.e., end states) is called **laddering**.[21]

As will be discussed later in the chapter, values are also closely connected to social change. As the culture of a society changes, so too do the values of the individuals that make up the society. Changes in values can directly influence managerial strategy. For example, Stouffer's Inc. recognized that the values of many female grocery shoppers were changing. Their values were shifting away from emphasizing their roles as "servants for the family." Values were moving toward self-fulfillment and working for the self. Based upon this recognition, the company successfully introduced a line of frozen entrees that were positioned as fulfillment oriented. In fact, the positioning phrase used in advertisements was "Set yourself free."

Cultural Value Orientations

Researchers have been interested in identifying the dimensions on which the value of various cultures differ. In a recent summary of the research, scholars identified six basic dimensions of cultural values.[22] These include

1. *Individual versus collective*—the extent to which a culture values the individual more than the group or the group more than the individual.
2. *Masculinity/femininity*—the extent to which the characteristics of one sex are valued over those of the other.
3. *Time orientation*—the extent to which the members of the society are oriented to the past, present, or future.

4. *Uncertainty avoidance*—the extent to which members of the society are willing to tolerate ambiguity and unusual behavior.
5. *Activity orientation*—the extent to which the society values action versus reflection.
6. *Relationship to nature*—the extent to which the society lives in harmony with nature or attempts to dominate nature.

One can compare the United States and Japan on these various dimensions. In comparison to the culture of the United States, the Japanese culture is more collective, more masculine, more past and future oriented, more uncertainty avoidant, lower in activity orientation, and more in harmony with nature.[23]

Research on the List of Values Scale

An index developed specifically for consumer research on values is called the *LOV scale*. (LOV stands for List of Values; this subject was discussed in Chapter 7.) One study using the scale investigated how values in the United States changed between 1976 and 1986.[24] In the study the researchers conducted a national survey of consumers in 1976 and again in 1986. Table 17-2 presents the results of the study. The results show which values the respondents identified as most important. Overall values were quite stable over the time span. Between the 1976 and 1986 figures, the correlation ratio was .91 for males and .77 for females. These high correlations indicate only small changes in values. Note, however, that the correlation of females was lower than that of males, indicating a greater change in women's values. An analysis assessing the change in values by age showed that the most change occurred among those less than 30 years old.

Research on the LOV scale has found that the values of a person may influence his or her attitudes, which in turn influence behavior. One study investigated the

TABLE 17-2

Value Changes in the United States

	Total		*Male*		*Female*	
	1976	*1986*	*1976*	*1986*	*1976*	*1986*
Self-respect	21.1	23.0	21.7	22.4	20.6	23.5
Security	20.6	16.5	20.5	17.1	20.7	15.9
Warm relationships	16.2	19.9	13.1	13.6	18.5	25.7
Sense of accomplishment	11.4	15.9	14.3	20.1	9.2	12.2
Self-fulfillment	9.6	6.5	9.5	7.2	9.6	5.8
Being well respected	8.8	5.9	8.5	5.7	9.0	6.1
Sense of belonging	7.9	5.1	5.6	3.8	9.6	6.3
Fun/enjoyment/excitement	4.5	7.2	6.9	10.0	2.7	4.6

SOURCE: Lynn Kahle, Basil Poulos, and Ajay Sukhdial, "Changes in Social Values in the United States During the Past Decade," *Journal of Advertising Research*, vol. 28 (February/March 1988), pp. 35–41. Reprinted with permission of the Advertising Research Foundation.

characteristics of those who shop for natural foods. The results revealed that people who emphasize internal values (i.e., self-fulfillment, excitement, sense of accomplishment, and self-respect) like and purchase natural foods more than people who emphasize external values (i.e., sense of belonging, being well respected, and having security).[25]

Through environmental analysis and marketing research, managers can gain an understanding of how cultural values change in a society. For example, changes in values—such as increased desires for pleasure, excitement, and fun—could influence how products are named, what their colors are, and how they are designed. In advertising, such values would influence the underlying tone of the message and the choice of models. Such a trend can be seen in advertising for Coca-Cola, whose many themes have included "The Pause That Refreshes," "Things Go Better with Coke," "Have a Coke and a Smile," "I'd Like to Give the World a Coke," "It's the Real Thing," and "Coke Is It." The theme of "giving the world a Coke" occurred in the 1960s, when international tensions were high and Americans were highly concerned with world peace. The advertisement showed people of different countries in a long line, holding hands, and passing a Coke. The advertisement had dramatic impact and spawned a popular song. Similarly, the theme "Coke Is It," which began in late 1982, seemed to capture the cultural spirit of the time with its emphasis on self in the so-called "me" generation. These themes seemed to catch the changes in cultural values that moved through the United States during the 1960s, 1970s, and 1980s. Figure 17-6 presents several of the print ads from these campaigns.

Research on the Value of Materialism

Perhaps the value having the greatest impact on consumer behavior is that of **materialism**. The text has already discussed materialism as an individual difference variable in Chapter 7, Personality, Semiotics, and Psychographics. A number of researchers have attempted to identify whether the emphasis on the cultural value of materialism has changed in the United States. They approached the question by content analyzing popular literature, such as comic books and popular novels. (Content analysis involves coding the themes of written material into various categories.) One recent study investigated the frequency with which materialistic themes appeared in several comic books, such as *Archie*, *Uncle Scrooge McDuck*, and *Richie Rich*. An example of a materialistic theme is found in a 1965 edition of *Archie*:

> Veronica tells Archie that having everything she wants bores her, and Betty convinces Archie to go out with her instead so that Veronica feels challenged. It works, but Veronica wins, thanks to her new outfits that catch Archie's eye.[26]

The author of the study examined the time period from the 1940s to the mid-1980s, finding little evidence of changes in materialistic themes over the 40-year period. Interestingly, he argued that the comic books may have a positive socializing influence on children. The values portrayed in the comic books were generally positive ones. The stories indicated that wealth can be either good or bad. When the role models acted poorly, bad fortune occurred to them. The wealthy in the stories were encouraged not to flaunt their riches. The deserving poor were portrayed as honest, intelligent, and clean. They lacked only the opportunity or circumstance to be wealthy.[27]

Considering sources other than comic books, however, one does find evidence of changes in materialism as a value. For example, one study investigated the frequency

Figure 17-6 Reading clockwise, these advertisements for Coca-Cola come from the 1930s, 1960s, 1970s, and 1980s. They portray subtle changes in U.S. culture over the time period. (Coca-Cola and Coke are trademarks of the Coca-Cola Company and are used with permission.)

with which brand names were mentioned in popular novels.[28] It found a more than fivefold increase in the usage of brand names between 1946 and 1975. Some critics charge that the manner in which companies name products is making the "sacred profane." For example, "True" cigarettes and "First Romance" towels can be viewed as taking sacred words and symbols and making them profane by connecting them with products. Indeed, the charge seems to have some merit. Some individuals might consider the nature of "truth" tainted by an affiliation with a cigarette name—which is, by extension, an affiliation with companies that have avoided telling consumers of the harmful effects of smoking.

When one investigates the themes found in advertisements, another perspective on materialism in American society is obtained. Some authors have distinguished two types of materialism—instrumental and terminal. **Instrumental materialism** involves obtaining a material good to perform some activity. As such, instrumental materialism is viewed as benign, because the good acts as an instrument for the accomplishment of something else. In contrast, **terminal materialism** is defined as occurring when possession is the end in itself. Terminal materialism is viewed as potentially destructive because it leads to such unbecoming traits as envy, possessiveness, selfishness, and greed.[29]

One study investigated 2,000 print advertisements having to do with the interior or the exterior of houses. The ads, which spanned the years 1901 through 1979, were content analyzed to determine the frequency with which material goods were cast in terms of their type of appeal or theme. Figure 17-7 diagrams the major findings. The results revealed that utilitarian themes, in which the product's benefits were described in terms of practicality and efficiency, decreased in frequency over the time span. In

Figure 17-7 Materialistic themes in print advertising. (Source: Russell Belk and Richard Pollay, "Materialism and Magazine Advertising During the Twentieth Century," in *Advances in Consumer Research*, Vol. 13, Elizabeth Hirschmand and Morris Holbrook, eds., Provo, UT: Association for Consumer Research, 1985, pp. 394–398.)

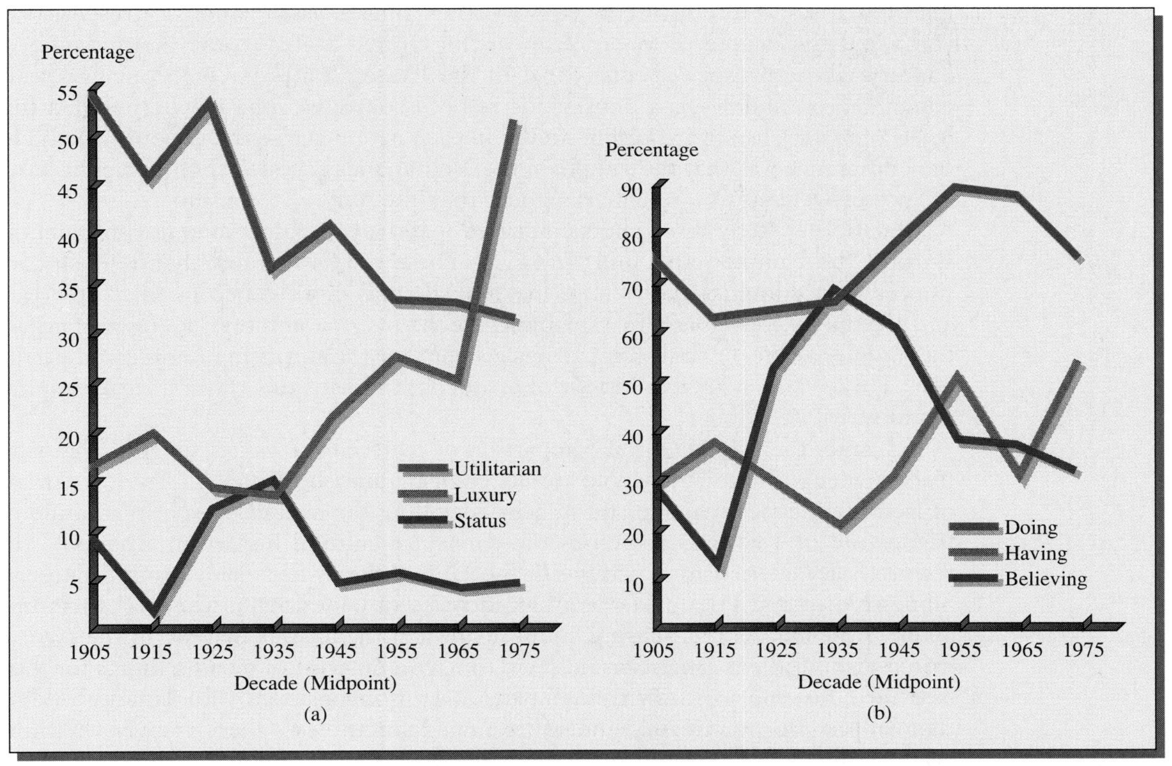

contrast, themes involving luxury appeals increased dramatically. Although themes of "having" revealed a tendency to increase over the time period, themes of "doing" tended to dominate. "Doing" themes involve showing consumers engaged in activities that are aided by the product or service. As such, these ads can be considered examples of instrumental materialism, as opposed to terminal materialism. The authors interpreted the results of the study as indications that advertising themes have come to emphasize materialism more frequently in the later half of the twentieth century. Although appeals to luxury have increased substantially over time, the underlying themes of such ads have more frequently been of an instrumental nature. As the authors explained,

> It is also evident that this materialistic emphasis has been more involved with instrumental themes of using the advertised items than with terminally materialistic themes of having the product for its own sake. If we have become a culture of consumption, it does not yet appear that this consumption is an end rather than a means to other ends.[30]

An interesting question concerns whether men or women reveal greater amounts of materialism. As long ago as the sixth century B.C., the philosopher Pythagoras suggested that women are more sharing and less materialistic than men. A recent study investigated the materialism and sharing behavior of men and women in Germany and Canada. Across both nationalities, women were found to be more sharing, generous, nurturant, and caring than men. One explanation suggested by the authors was that material goods mean different things to men than to women. For men, material goods help establish power and competitive relations. For women, though, material goods are a part of social relations.[31]

Although the evidence indicates that the United States is clearly materialistic, a question arises as to how it compares to other industrialized nations. A recent study compared the degree of materialism in the United States to the Netherlands—a country whose prosperity equals that of the United States.[32] Questionnaires were completed by middle-class households in both countries. The results revealed that levels of materialism were highly similar in each nation across the various scales. The only difference was that the sample in the Netherlands revealed slightly higher levels of "possessiveness" toward material goods than the American consumers.

In another study researchers compared materialistic values among consumers in Europe, the United States, and Turkey.[33] These results revealed that Turkish consumers were simultaneously more materialistic and more generous than American and European consumers. In explaining the results, the authors suggested that factors unique to the Turkish culture may account for the surprising findings. In particular, Turkey has an ancient history of prosperity; perhaps this cultural legacy continues to reveal itself today.

Overall, the cross-cultural comparison of materialistic values suggests that simple statements about why people are materialistic must be avoided. Clearly, a variety of factors influence materialistic values—including the overall prosperity and industrialization of a nation, as well as the particular cultural history of a nation. The research on materialism as a value in the United States has yielded mixed findings. Some studies find little evidence of an increase in materialism, whereas others find ample evidence. As the housing study suggested, the answer may lie in the type of materialism studied. Americans do seem to have a mistrust of owning things for their own sake. An emphasis on terminal materialism is inconsistent with American values that emphasize practicality and efficiency. Nonetheless, there is overwhelming evidence that the United States is a materialistic society. As one author said, "The findings indicate the pervasiveness of a consumer culture in the mid-twentieth century and suggest that the baby boom generation, reared in material abundance, may be unabashedly materialistic."[34]

When developing the marketing mix, firms should analyze core values of the culture to which the product is being marketed. The strategy works both for American firms marketing in foreign countries and for foreign firms marketing in the United States. For example, Novotrade, Inc., a Hungarian company, makes computer games. It had successfully exported the games to Europe but was having a difficult time entering the U.S. market successfully. The problem seemed to be that the themes of the games were too peaceful. According to one expert, "Americans want antisocial software where the main character is destroyed or maimed. The [Hungarian] games are simply too peaceful, too prosocial." Novotrade offers nonviolent games such as Pet's Clinic, where the goal is to diagnose the illness of a dog. A spokesman for the company said, "Maybe we won't be the best sellers in the world, but there are a lot of people who want to play peaceful games."[35]

CULTURAL RITUALS

Cultural rituals are socially standardized sequences of actions that are periodically repeated, provide meaning, and involve the use of cultural symbols. They have some purpose and generally have a beginning, middle, and end. Rituals can be public or private. They vary from large-scale civic rituals, such as the Super Bowl, to private and personal rituals involving prayer. The behaviors involved in a ritual are "scripted" so that they are formal and prescribed by convention. The behaviors tend to recur and follow a fixed pattern, and in many cases they involve the consumption and use of products.[36]

The characteristics of rituals just identified are embodied in its formal definition: The term *ritual* refers to a type of expressive, symbolic activity constructed of culturally sanctioned behaviors that occur in a fixed, episodic sequence and tend to be repeated over time. Ritual behavior is dramatically scripted and acted out and is performed with formality, seriousness, and inner intensity.[37]

Rituals should be distinguished from habits. Habits are repetitive, engaged in over time, and can have inner intensity. For example, each of us has a sequence of events in which we engage to drive a car from home to work or school. Such sequences of actions are considered to be habits rather than rituals. Rituals differ from habits on three criteria. First, rituals are prescribed by society rather than by the individual. Second, people are more consciously aware of what takes place in a ritual. Third, rituals have greater symbolic meaning and have more affect attached to them.[38]

Table 17-3 shows a typology of ritual experience. As is evident in the table, rituals exist at various levels of abstraction. At the most abstract levels, they have cosmological value. These include religious, magic, and aesthetic rituals. At the most concrete level rituals are biologically determined, such as in the grooming and mating rituals of animals. The types of rituals shown in the table also reveal that rituals have functional value. For example, the cultural rituals of graduation and marriage act as rites of passage that symbolically denote a change in a person's status. Similarly, rituals can play the role of passing on knowledge and creating bonds within groups. Thus holiday celebrations, the exchange of gifts, and office luncheons are enacted to fulfill specific goals within groups.[39]

TABLE 17-3

A Typology of Ritual Experience

Primary Behavior Source	Ritual Type	Examples
Cosmology	Religious	Baptism, meditation, mass
	Magic	"Healing," gambling
	Aesthetic	Performing arts
Cultural values	Rites of passage	Graduation, marriage
	Cultural	Festivals, Valentine's Day, Ground Hog Day, Super Bowl
Group learning	Civic	Memorial Day parade, elections, trials
	Small group	Pancake Day, fraternity initiation, business negotiations, office luncheons
	Family	Mealtime, bedtime, birthday and holiday celebrations
Individual aims and emotions	Personal	Grooming, household rituals
Biology	Animal	Greeting, mating

SOURCE: Dennis Rook, "The Ritual Dimension of Consumer Behavior," *Journal of Consumer Research*, vol. 12 (December 1985), pp. 251–264. Reprinted with permission.

Rituals commonly have four elements: artifacts, scripts, performance roles, and an audience. Consider, for example, the various aspects of a college basketball game. One can identify in the ritual the artifacts (i.e., basketball, pompons, beer), the script (i.e., the rules of the game), the performance roles (i.e., players, referees, coaches), and the audience. Of course, rituals vary in formality and in the extent to which each of the four elements is present. For example, the morning bathroom ritual is performed without an audience—unless one considers the person doing the ritual to be an audience to himself or herself while watching the transformation take place.

At the cultural level, researchers have identified four specific types of rituals.[40] *Exchange rituals* involve the exchange of gifts, information, goods, and money. *Possession rituals* involve acts in which a person engages to lay claim, display, and protect possessions. For example, housewarming parties and overzealous car waxing can be viewed as possession rituals. **Grooming rituals** act to ensure that the special, perishable properties resident in clothing, hairstyles, and looks are present. In some cases the grooming ritual is not performed on the consumer but on a product. An example is the constant grooming of lawns by middle-class homeowners. A fourth type of ritual is the **divestment ritual**, which may be performed to erase the meaning associated with the previous owner of the good. For example, after buying a used house, consumers will frequently engage in cleaning and redecorating behaviors to lay claim to the possession. Another type of divestment ritual may occur when a person disposes of a personalized item, such as a special coat, car, or house. In many of these cases consumers remove all vestiges of their ownership. Thus, prior to leaving a house, a consumer may empty it of all personal symbols.

The list of consumption-related rituals is long. They include rites of passage (e.g., weddings, baby showers, and funerals), religious ceremonies, holiday festivities (e.g., Christmas, Thanksgiving), family activities (e.g., television viewing at prescribed times, the summer vacation, and Sunday dinner), and large-scale public rituals (e.g., singing the national anthem, watching parades and sports events).[41] The television ritual has become extremely important to our society. As one author noted, "Television provides a series of common, shared experiences and images which have become part of the collective shared traditions of our society."[42] In fact, the three-hour "prime-time" entertainment block has had a long history in the United States, going back before the inception of television. In the nineteenth century popular theater performances lasted three hours. The three-hour block continued in vaudeville early in the twentieth century and later was used in double-bill movies. Currently, the prime-time television ritual begins at seven or eight o'clock in the evening and ends with the late news.

For manufacturers and retailers, success often lies in recognizing the importance of culturally prescribed consumer rituals and tying the company's products to these rituals. By identifying ritualistic patterns of behavior, marketers are equipped to design and promote products that might serve as artifacts in the activities. For example, the beauty ritual involves a long series of steps for many women. Some adroit marketers have attempted to lengthen the ritual by adding new steps and products/artifacts, such as using an astringent to close facial pores after washing one's face. Clinique has used such a tactic in developing its line of products. Similarly, Vidal Sassoon has developed a three-step process of cleansing hair—involving a shampoo, remoisturizer, and finishing rinse. Sassoon's successful ad campaign seeks to change a woman's hair-washing habits into rituals prescribed by the firm by promising to provide an important benefit to the consumer—prettier, healthier hair.

CULTURAL SYMBOLS

In addition to values and rituals, cultures have symbols. **Cultural symbols** are entities that represent ideas and concepts.[43] In Chapter 3 this text discussed the field called semiotics, which investigates the meaning of symbols. As the chapter noted, symbols are important because they communicate complex ideas rapidly with a minimum of effort. For example, if a company wants to communicate the concept of patriotism, a useful symbol is the American flag. By adroitly using symbols, companies and advertisers can tie cultural values to their products or services, thereby enhancing product attractiveness to consumers.

It can be argued that people "consume" symbols.[44] That is, products may be evaluated, purchased, and consumed based in part on their symbolic value. For a product to have symbolic value, it must have a shared reality among consumers. Thus large numbers of consumers must have a common conception of the symbolic meaning of the product. For example, for an automobile to have "prestige" value, others in the relevant social group must view it in the same manner as the buyer.[45]

Companies frequently symbolize the characteristics of their products via the names chosen for them. For example, auto manufacturers have been highly fond of naming their products after animals. The manufacturers have sought to translate the characteristics of the animal, such as swiftness, agility, and aggressiveness, to the automobile. Perhaps breeds of cats are most frequently used as names for cars. Examples include jaguars, cougars, lynxes, wildcats, bobcats, and pumas.

Numerous symbols exist in the American culture. The symbol of money—and occasionally power or greed—is the dollar sign ($). One symbol to denote Christian spiritual meanings is the cross. To denote contemplation, a smoking pipe might be used. Similarly, wearing glasses can indicate intelligence and possibly physical weakness—à la Clark Kent, Superman's alter ego. Planting a tree reveals permanence, and so forth. Figure 17-8 shows the use of the military uniform and of General Douglas MacArthur as symbols in the advertisement for Ray•Ban sunglasses.

Colors also have symbolic value. In the United States, depending upon the context, black can have a variety of symbolic meanings. When worn at funerals, it indicates mourning. In contrast, black bras, garter belts, and panties suggest high levels of sex appeal. When worn on special occasions, it takes on a highly formal tone. For example, Gloria Vanderbilt brought out a line of black, "formal" jeans for women. Blue indicates coolness, for example, "Ice Blue Aqua-Velva." White means purity, for example, wedding dresses and milk products. Pink is feminine, and for babies blue is masculine.

Clothing also has important symbolic meaning for consumers. Table 17-4 identifies a variety of functions that clothing may have for consumers, as well as the potential symbolic value of such clothing. For example, one of the functions of clothing is to act as an emblem of group membership. The popularity of tee-shirts and hats that possess a group emblem well illustrates the symbolic nature of clothing.

Although all cultures use symbols, they may be more important in some cultures than in others. For example, Japan has been called the empire of signs.[46] Indeed, this statement is true both literally and figuratively. Japan's urban landscape is cluttered with signs, some flashing incessantly and others meticulously lettered. Figuratively, the Japanese culture engages in a large number of symbolic activities. The practice of exchanging business cards (*meishi*) has a great symbolic function. The great care taken in wrapping and packaging plays a role in the spiritual and cultural life of the country. In addition, the Japanese have a great fondness for borrowing words from other cultures and using them in their promotional materials.

The use of foreign words in promotional materials may have several symbolic meanings for the Japanese. The foreign words may connote something new or modern, they may indicate a Western influence, and they may symbolize prestige. One researcher attempted to count the number of English loanwords in a Japanese dictionary but gave up after recording 7,000 instances. Fully 80% of loanwords in Japan are taken from English. Examples of such loanwords include *botsu* (boots), *tobako* (cigarette), and *kitchin* (kitchen). Interestingly, the infiltration of Japanese loanwords into English has been much less prevalent.

Two researchers spent a summer in Japan investigating the use of English loanwords by Japanese companies.[47] They observed that Japanese beverage companies frequently include several sentences of English prose in their advertising. For example, one ad for Kirin beer was written in English and said: "The legendary KIRIN is a symbol of good luck. Open up KIRIN today, and you'll see what it is all about." Japanese promotional messages frequently use similes and metaphors and sound very strange to Americans. One beverage, called Pokka White Sour, featured a promotional message in English: "Pokka White Sour is refreshing and white like Alpine snow. Its sour taste of yogurt will extend on your tongue softly and be a sweetheart."

Figure 17-8 Ray•Ban sunglasses use military symbols in this effective print advertisement. Indeed, Douglas MacArthur actually did wade ashore on the Philippines wearing Ray•Ban sunglasses, as portrayed in this ad. (Courtesy of Bausch and Lomb, Inc.)

TABLE 17-4

Clothing: Its Functional Uses and Symbolic Meanings

Function of Apparel	*Use of Apparel*	*Symbolic Meaning*	*Example of Apparel*
Camouflage	Hide the body	Sexually conservative	Robes
	Cover blemishes or injuries		Cosmetics, patches
Display	Reveal body parts	Sexually explicit	Tight or skimpy clothing
Utilitarian	Protect the body	"Down-to-earth," practical	Some jeans, raincoats
Aesthetic	Beautify or enhance the body	Love of beauty	Jewelry
Souvenir	Reminder of the past	Love of family or experience	Charm bracelet
Emblematic	Group membership	Show membership in a group	Fraternity jacket
	Connotative	Reveal social class or wealth	Expensive jewelry

SOURCE: Adapted in part from a table in Rebecca Holman, "Apparel as Communication," in *Symbolic Consumer Behavior*, Elizabeth Hirschman and Morris Hollbrook, eds., Proceedings of the Conference on Consumer Aesthetics and Symbolic Consumption (Ann Arbor, MI: Association for Consumer Research, May 1980), p. 8.

It will be interesting to see if we find U.S. advertisers using Japanese loanwords as Japan becomes fully established as a dominant world economic power.

Knowledge of the meaning of symbols is particularly important when a company begins to market its products or services internationally. Chapter 19 of the text discusses the highly important area of international marketing and cross-cultural processes.

POPULAR CULTURE

What were the two largest exports by U.S. firms in the early 1990s? Aircraft and related equipment were ranked number one, and popular culture was ranked number two. Just one component of the popular culture scene (popular culture software, which includes movies, music, television programming, and home video) provided a surplus of $8 billion to the balance of trade. Interestingly, Japanese and European firms have recognized the importance of popular culture and purchased many of the major U.S. popular culture software companies. The net result is that only one of the top five global record companies and four of the top eight global movie studios are American.[48]

So what is popular culture? Many definitions have been proposed. For the purposes of understanding its impact on consumer behavior, the following definition is most appropriate: ". . . **popular culture** is the culture of mass appeal." As such, popular culture has the following characteristics:[49]

1. It taps into the experiences and values of a significant portion of the population.
2. It does not require any special knowledge to understand it.

3. It is produced in such a way that large numbers of people have easy access to it.
4. It most frequently influences behavior that does not involve work or sleep.

To understand popular culture, one must distinguish it from "high" culture. **High culture** is exclusive in style, content, and appeal. It frequently harks back to the "old masters" of art, theater, music, and literature. To the advocates of high culture, popular culture frequently appears to be loud, brassy, and even immoral. The cult of the pop star Madonna is frequently used as an illustration.

As many scholars have noted, however, the distinction between "high" and "popular" culture can be blurry. For example, when Walt Disney produced *Fantasia*, he borrowed from high culture the music of great classical composers, such as Beethoven. A huge popular success, *Fantasia* has become part of popular culture. Yet it employs elements of high culture. Or consider Leonardo DeVinci's painting, the "Mona Lisa." A high-culture icon, her image has been used to advertise 9-Lives Cat Food, Lindsay Olives, Prince Spaghetti Sauce, and Minolta copiers. Indeed, Shakespeare's works originated as popular culture by appealing to mass audiences who sought entertainment in the working-class theaters of his day.

Examples of Popular Culture

Because popular culture involves anything that has mass appeal and is used in nonwork activities, the range of subject matter encompassed by the term is extremely large. For example, in the 1989 edition of the *Handbook of American Popular Culture*, 46 articles appeared on distinct subjects. In many instances, the topics were expected, such as advertising, fashion, music, and television as popular culture. In other instances, the topics were unexpected, such as death, pornography, propaganda, and even science.[50] Brief discussions of several areas of popular cultures follow.

Advertising

Advertising becomes popular culture when its images, themes, and icons are embraced by the mass public. Examples of figures from advertising that have achieved popular culture status include Ronald McDonald, Toni the Tiger, the Energizer Bunny, and the Pillsbury Doughboy. Supermodel Cindy Crawford's career began to take off when she appeared in a commercial for Diet Pepsi.

Television

As a medium, television acts to create popular culture. Indeed, one scholar said that television ". . . has become preeminently *the* popular culture and a primary purveyor of values and ideas."[51] In the mid-1990s, television shows such as "Beavis and Butt-Head" were being heavily criticized for promoting mindless gutter humor. Meanwhile, emerging from the throats of countless teenage boys was the familiar laugh, "Huh-huh. Huh-huh" of Beavis and Butt-Head. Television can even transform news events into popular culture. For example, in February 1994, CBS broadcast during prime time a television special called "Nancy Kerrigan and Friends." The corporation capitalized on the enormous popularity of the young figure skater as she made her comeback after being attacked by associates of her competitor, Tonya Harding. Meanwhile, television comedians reinterpreted the events to suit their own ends. With tongue-in-cheek, Jay Leno described two forthcoming prime-time specials—"Nancy Kerrigan and *Friends*" and "Tonya Harding and *Accomplices*."

Researchers have found that heavy television viewing can even impact consumers' views of the world. For example, heavy television viewers have been found to overestimate the amount of violence in the United States and to overestimate the degree of affluence in the country.[52]

Music

Of course, music can also shape popular culture. The phenomenon of rap music illustrates the enormous impact of music on the consumer behavior of a generation. Rap music can be traced back to 1968, the year in which it was invented in the Bronx, a borough of New York City. During the 1970s break dancing emerged, and in 1979 the first rap label was established. In 1981 Blondie's hit song "Rapture" rose to number one on the charts, and in 1985 MTV began a rap program; the first rap-based movie was produced in 1990. By 1993, rap moved into mainstream popular culture when Coca-Cola employed rap music in its advertising with performers dressed in the baggy, hip-hop fashions associated with the music phenomenon.[53]

The countercurrents of popular culture are well illustrated in the music industry. On the one hand, one finds near-pornographic rap groups like 2-Live-Crew providing one set of values, whereas in the country and western scene, performers like Garth Brooks are singing about fidelity to his wife and the joys of having children.

Fashion

The concept of fashion can be defined either narrowly or broadly. According to the narrow interpretation fashion is identified with clothing, costumes, and bodily adornment. For example, the hip-hop clothing of rap musicians and the practice of piercing the body to insert rings for the purpose of adornment exemplify fashion in popular culture.

The broader definition of fashion extends the concept to include any use of products to express self-image or role position. As such, **fashion** is a set of behaviors temporarily adopted by a people because the behaviors are perceived to be socially appropriate for the time and situation.[54] From this perspective fashion involves the adoption of symbols to provide an identity. The symbols may include clothing, jewelry, automobiles, housing, artwork, or any other socially visible object that communicates meaning within the popular culture.

Even the books that people read (or whether they read books at all) can act as symbols that communicate information to others. As such, the types of trade books published go in and out of fashion. In the mid-1990s, books by famous celebrities were in fashion. For example, on February 6, 1994, four of the top ten *New York Times* best-selling nonfiction books were written by celebrities—Rush Limbaugh, the ex-Secretary of Education William Bennet, Jerry Seinfeld, and Howard Stern. In the realm of fiction, sophisticated detective novels (by authors like Michael Crichton [*Rising Sun*] and John Grisham [*The Firm*]) had become popular.

A consumer researcher analyzed the consumption ideology found in another best-selling author of detective stories—Robert B. Parker, who writes the "Spenser for Hire" series. Noting that detective stories have displaced the cowboy novel in popular culture, the researcher stated that such novels express certain American values. In these novels the detective acts as a type of mythical hero who possesses special powers and who overcomes weaknesses often involving alcohol and problems with women. In the Spenser series an important theme is knowing how and what to consume. As the researcher Cathy Goodwin said, "Knowing how and what to consume, but sometimes consciously choosing to be inappropriate, is evidence of superiority, strength or originality."[55]

Fashion is inherently dynamic, as it constantly changes over time. One cannot overemphasize the importance of the symbolic value of fashion. Indeed, symbolic value frequently overwhelms any "utilitarian" value. One merely has to look at the pain endured by women who wear such pieces of clothing as corsets and high-heeled shoes to understand the relative weight given to symbolic versus utilitarian value of the consumer behavior. Of course, males have their own fashions and, like women, endure physical discomfort/pain to obtain hair transplants and tatoos.

Fashion trends have a number of characteristics. These are briefly discussed in the paragraphs that follow.[56]

1. *Type of trend.* Two basic types of fashion trends have been identified. In the **cyclical fashion trend** members of a society adopt styles that are progressively more extreme in one direction or another. Examples include skirt lengths and tie widths. In the **classic fashion trend** particular looks become a "classic," such as the blue pin-striped suit.
2. *Speed of trend.* The trend may be very fast or slow. For example, some trends are simply fads and come and go quickly: consider the trend of wearing sneakers with laces untied. An example of a long-lasting trend is shaving of facial hair by most men and of underarm hair by most women in the United States.
3. *Fashion turning points.* Within cyclical fashion trends, at some point in the cycle the progression becomes so severe that a turning point is reached because a technological barrier or a cultural barrier has been reached. For example, in the late eighteenth century the hoop skirt became progressively wider until women could no longer move through doors. Similarly, in the 1970s, miniskirts became progressively shorter until a cultural barrier was reached in the form of having some modesty.
4. *The degree of individual-level adherence to the trend.* While in the overall society fashion trends can be discerned, at the individual level each person appears to behave in an almost random manner regarding the trend. Indeed, some people will take delight in dressing or behaving in exactly the opposite manner prescribed by the trend. In turn, these countertrends may become the basis for new fads.

How Does Popular Culture Develop?

As discussed earlier in the chapter, within the overall cultural matrix of a society, one finds numerous trends and countertrends. These arise from the interplay of changes in the material environment, the institutional–social environment, and cultural values. These shorter-term trends that bubble up from the cultural matrix come and, in most cases, go. Given the name popular culture, while they last such mass trends may influence tens of millions of people in their everyday life. In some cases a popular culture trend becomes so ingrained in the overall cultural matrix that over time it becomes a part of "high" culture. Examples include the works of Shakespeare, jazz music, and certain ethnic cuisines, such as northern Italian food.

The impact of rap music and hip clothing on popular culture exemplifies how the cultural matrix acts as a cauldron within which the mixture of material environment, the institutional environment, and societal values combines to boil up trends. Originating in the youth of the black subculture of urban New York City, the movement expressed traditional American values of individualism, freedom from conformity, youthfulness, activity, equality, informality, and achievement. In the process, however, the carriers of the movement frequently behaved in ways that were highly threatening to the status quo. Other elements of the cultural matrix combining to impact the rap movement include economics (the movement was spawned in a culture of poverty), geography (the urban enclaves of New York City), and legal environment (reaction against the perceived harassment by police).

As the popular culture trends bubble up from the cultural matrix, however, important media and opinion leaders must begin to communicate the symbols that

SOCIAL MARKETING HIGHLIGHT 17-3

McDonald's Health Strategy Runs into Popular Culture

In the mid-1990s, McDonald's Corporation became caught between two conflicting trends in popular culture. In the early 1990s, critics accused McDonald's and other fast-food chains of contributing to rampant heart disease because of their high-fat menus. Responding quickly to the assault, McDonald's introduced lower-fat shakes and began frying its fries in vegetable oil rather than animal fat. In addition, the company introduced its much heralded McLean Deluxe low-fat hamburger.

While a public relations coup, the low-fat strategy did not fare so well on the bottom line. With popular culture beginning to downplay exercise and healthy eating, the McLean quickly became a McDud. Few patrons purchased the low-fat burger. While it does have less fat and calories than other burgers of the same size, it suffers from several problems, most notably regarding taste, price, and the seaweed factor. The McLean contains 1% seaweed, a factor that comedians took great delight in calling to everyone's attention.

But perhaps the most devastating force to work against the McLean was a revival of a countertrend in popular culture toward heavy eating. Consumers had grown tired of low-fat, tasteless meals that left them hungry. One indicant was that bacon sales increased in 1992 for the first time in years. As a result of the countertrend, fast-food restaurants responded to fill the needs (and stomachs) of consumers: Burger King brought out meat loaf, Pizza Hut produced double pizzas, Wendy's introduced the double bacon and cheeseburger. Not to be outdone, McDonald's brought out the Mega Mac—a half pound of beef on a three-piece bun that made the Big Mac look puny in comparison.

But perhaps in the end McDonald's did have the best of both worlds. By keeping the McLean, it cut short criticism that it was socially irresponsible. At the same time it was able to introduce the Mega Mac for the rest of us.

Based upon Richard Gibson, "Too Skinny a Burger Is a Might Hard Sell, McDonald's Learns," *The Wall Street Journal*, April 15, 1993, pp. A1, A6.

carry the meanings of the trend. The media include television, radio, print, movies, the theater, and so on. Important mass opinion leaders include performers, songwriters, journalists, advertisers, sports celebrities, and various editors. Other important people, such as presidents, can act as opinion leaders as well. For example, in 1961 John F. Kennedy walked down Pennsylvania Avenue for his inauguration without a hat. The sight of the youthful, bare-headed president resulted in a shift in fashion that devastated the hat industry of the day.

In sum, the diffusion of popular culture occurs through a process that mimics the spread of innovations. Thus the material covered in Chapter 15 on diffusion processes directly applies to popular culture. The spread of popular culture can be fast or slow. It diffuses through a process that most closely approximates the multistep diffusion model. It has a life cycle that can be short (i.e., a fad) or very long (e.g., the Beatles continue to be popular today). But its impact cannot be underestimated. Marketers who want to link their products to the fads and fashions that push the hot buttons of masses of people should develop an advanced understanding of popular culture.

As these ideas suggest, changes in popular culture may have important implications for managers. Highlight 17-3 discusses how changes in popular culture have created difficulty for McDonald's Corporation—an institution that itself is a part of popular culture.

A MANAGERIAL APPLICATIONS EXAMPLE

After soaring for years, sales of athletic shoes leveled off in 1993 and the earnings of companies such as Reebok and Nike fell well below analysts' estimates. As a result of the unpleasant surprises in earnings, the stock prices of the companies plunged. Because of the sudden and unexpected change in consumer demand, market researchers sought to identify the cause of the problem.

One culprit identified was the high cost of athletic shoes. With the United States and Europe still in recession in 1993, consumers appeared to be balking at the high prices. Indeed, price rollbacks began to occur. For example, Reebok's Shaq Attack shoe was reduced in price from $135 to $105. Similarly, Nike's Air Jordan shoe was reduced from $135 to $125 a pair.

A second and possibly more serious reason for the downturn, however, lurked on the horizon. A new fashion trend was beginning to emerge. Called the grunge look, the trend began with a group of Seattle musicians. Fitting this trend perfectly was a type of shoe developed by a German doctor just after World War II to help cure his foot problems. Made of stiff leather and "modernized" with an air-cushion sole, the product was increasingly drawing attention. Usually manufactured in black, the shoes/boots are large, ungainly, and ugly. They are the antithesis of the nimble, fleet athletic shoes that they seem to be replacing.[57]

The original shoe is called Dr. Martens or Docs. Now owned by London Underground International, sales in the United States doubled in 1993 to about $67 million. Meanwhile, dozens of knock-off brands were being hastily introduced into the marketplace. For example, Converse, Inc., introduced its own versions called the Lug Boot and the Lug Clog. In a commercial for the shoe, entitled "Ugly," a young male says, "There are a lot more what you call 'ugly' people in my world than beautiful people."

Why did the popularity of these shoes suddenly mushroom? According to *The Wall Street Journal*, the key turning point occurred when rhythm and blues performer Bobby Brown and rap superstar Hammer began performing in them in 1992. The shoes nicely matched the grunge look in clothing that began with Seattle musicians Nirvana, Alice in Chains, and Pearl Jam. As one Kmart executive said, "Kids are stepping out of sneakers and into these shoes for a night out on the town." Meanwhile, a stock analyst noted, "Not everyone these days is a Michael Jordan wannabe."

The Managerial Applications Analysis

The problem statement can be phrased in the following manner. If the Doc Martens case is approached from the perspective of Nike and Reebok, a key issue concerns whether these companies should begin marketing their own versions of the shoes and, if so, what marketing strategy these companies should use.

Table 17-5 presents the managerial applications of the case. As can be seen in the table, three key consumer behavior concepts from the chapter apply to the case: cultural values, cultural symbols, and popular culture.

A number of cultural values prevalent in U.S. society apply to the case. These include individualism, practicality, and informality. Doc Martens and its equivalents tap into these basic beliefs about what is good and proper. The shoes/boots are also linked to the color black, which is a cultural symbol in the United States. Just as Henry Ford's first cars came in black, most of the grunge boots sold are also in black. Unless linked expressly to highly formal occasions, black is associated with a lack of pretentiousness and practicality—hallmarks of the grunge look. Finally, Docs are rapidly becoming part of popular culture. When worn by important opinion leaders, such as Hammer, the shoes/boots become a fashion statement. Whether the fashion trend will merely become a short-lived fad or go on to have a lasting impact is a key managerial question for companies such as Nike and Reebok.

The three consumer concepts have application to each of the managerial application areas. Marketing research should be conducted to test the hypothesis that the shoes are linked to the cultural values of individualism, practicality, and informality. If the answer is found to be "yes," then companies can develop positioning strategies based upon these ideas. In addition, market segments can be identified, such as teenagers, for whom these values are particularly important. Finally, advertising strategies can be developed to communicate these values to the target markets.

Cultural symbols should also be linked directly to the product. In the promotional strategy for the shoes, decisions should be made concerning what symbols to link to the product. For example, should their black color be used extensively in advertisements and point-of-sale materials? Since the fashion trend originated with musicians, should the product be linked symbolically to these individuals in promotional efforts? Does this mean that the importance of athletes for endorsements is diminishing and that of performers increasing? Such questions must be answered by conducting carefully developed market research studies.

The impact of changes in popular culture must also be linked to managerial strategy. One critical question for the companies concerns whether the fashion cycle

TABLE 17-5

Managerial Applications Analysis of Doc Martens Shoes

Consumer Concepts	*Managerial Applications*
Cultural values	*Market research*—Perform research to test hypothesis that grunge shoes are linked to cultural values of individualism, practicality, and informality.
	Positioning strategies—Position shoes as being worn by individuals who are noncomformist, practical, and informal.
	Segmentation—Identify segments of consumers who respond well to the product and positioning strategy, e.g., teenage males.
	Promotional strategy—Develop advertising and point-of-purchase materials that communicate positioning strategy.
Cultural symbols	*Market research*—Determine what cultural symbols should be associated with product, such as the color black. Also, determine if, in popular culture, the influence of athletes is waning.
	Promotional strategy—Develop advertising messages, packaging, and point-of-purchase materials that employ the symbols identified.
Popular culture	*Market research*—Employ focus groups and depth interviews to probe the target markets perception of athletic shoes. Are there signs that the fashion trend is in the decline? Similarly probe to determine consumer reactions to the "grunge look" fashion trend.
	Product strategy—Based upon market research, estimate demand for the types of shoes, and manufacture appropriate numbers of shoes to meet the demand.
	Promotional strategy—Based upon market research, employ advertising as appropriate to lengthen the product life cycle of athletic shoes and/or speed up the adoption process of "grunge-style" shoes/boots.
	Market research—Employ market research to identify the values associated with current popular culture trends and whether these match up with the product.

is changing so that the wearing of athletic shoes for everyday and formal use is on the decline. To answer this question, managers should perform market research studies with attention paid to using depth interviews and focus groups. A similar question concerns whether the grunge shoes/boots will become a lasting trend or merely a fad. Again, carefully designed market research studies are required. The answer will directly influence product strategy (i.e., how much to invest in production of the shoes/boots). In addition, it will influence how the product is promoted. For example, if managers conclude that a significant chance exists that it is merely a fashion fad, they may alter their advertising to lengthen its life cycle.

In sum, given the notoriously short life cycle of fashions among teenagers, Nike and Reebok must look carefully at the impact of a move toward "grunge-style" shoes. They will have to develop strategies to lengthen the life cycle of the purchase of athletic shoes for nonathletic wear. In addition, they will have to hedge their bets by developing their own line of grunge shoes and boots.

SUMMARY

A culture is composed of the socially acquired behavior patterns transmitted symbolically through language and other means to the members of a particular society. Culture is a way of life. It consists of the learned values, norms, rituals, and symbols of a society, which are transmitted through both the language and the symbolic features of the society. Cultural values consist of the shared views of a society concerning the desired states of existence and the appropriate economic, social, religious, and other behaviors in which its members engage. Cultural norms represent the rules of behavior that people are expected to follow. Three types of norms are customs, mores, and conventions.

Cultural symbols are concrete objects that represent abstract concepts. Symbols can be utilized by managers in naming their products and in designing promotional materials. Cultural rituals are periodically repeated patterns of behavior. Tying products to the rituals can be a successful marketing strategy. Cultural myths are stories that express key values and ideals of a society.

A culture is learned through the process of enculturation. A new, foreign culture is learned through acculturation. Cultures are adaptive, and their customs, values, and norms fulfill needs of the society. Three important sets of factors compose culture, and they make up the cultural matrix. These factors are the institutional–social environment, the material environment, and the cultural values.

Consumer goods act to transfer meaning from the culturally constituted world to consumers. Goods may be said to be "way stations" of meaning. The culturally constituted world acts as a lens through which individuals interpret the world around them. Meaning is transferred from the culturally constituted world to goods through the advertising and fashion systems. Meaning is transferred from goods to people through various types of rituals.

A number of values have been identified that compose the culturally constituted world in the United States. These include individualism, youthfulness, progress, materialism, activity, achievement, efficiency, informality, and equality. Research has shown that the values a person holds can influence consumption decisions. Specifically, global values may influence domain-specific values, which in turn may influence the purchase decision. Values contained in the List of Values scale have been found to be predictive of the purchase of natural foods. Recent research on the value of materialism has indicated that the United States is a highly materialistic society. However, the focus seems to be on instrumental materialism, rather than on the more negative terminal materialism.

Cultural rituals are standardized sequences of actions that are periodically repeated. Rituals are dramatically scripted and acted out, and are performed with formality, seriousness, and intensity. From a consumer behavior perspective, they serve to symbolically link the meaning of a product to an individual. Rituals are composed of four elements: artifacts, scripts, performance roles, and audience. Four types of consumer rituals have been identified: exchange, possession, grooming, and divestment rituals. Examples of rituals having a strong impact on consumer behavior include Christmas, graduations, and weddings.

All cultures have symbols, which are entities that represent ideas and concepts. People can be said to consume symbols—that is, products and services are purchased in part because of their symbolic properties. An important point is that the same symbol may be used to represent divergent ideas in different cultures.

Popular culture is the culture of mass appeal. It taps into the experiences and values of the masses, does not require any special knowledge to understand it, and involves nonwork activities. In contrast, high culture is exclusive in content, style, and appeal. Examples of popular culture include advertising, television, music, and fashion. Popular culture develops from the overall cultural matrix of a society. The recent impact of rap music illustrates how popular culture can bubble up through the cultural matrix.

KEY TERMS

acculturation
classic fashion trend
conventions
cresive norms
cultural identification
cultural meaning
cultural rituals
cultural symbols
cultural value
culture
customs
cyclical fashion trend
divestment rituals
domain-specific values
enacted norms
enculturation
fashion
global values
grooming rituals
high culture
instrumental materialism
laddering
materialism
means–end chain
mores
myths
norms
popular culture
Rokeach value scale
terminal materialism
values

REVIEW QUESTIONS

1. Define the concept of culture. What are its basic characteristics?
2. What is the role of consumer goods in culture? What translates the meaning of culture to consumers?
3. What are seven core American values that have been identified?
4. Identify four examples each of the terminal values and instrumental values defined by Milton Rokeach. How do instrumental and terminal values differ?
5. Consumers may be regarded as having belief systems that include global values, domain-specific values, and evaluations of product attributes. Define these terms and indicate how they are related.
6. Define the concept of a cultural symbol. What are examples of clothing that act as symbols to consumers?
7. What is popular culture? What are its characteristics?
8. Identify four examples of popular culture.
9. How is popular culture formed?

DISCUSSION QUESTIONS

1. Some editorial writers have argued that movies and television shows produced in the United States are teaching children to be violent. Instances of 9- to 12-year-olds actually murdering other children were cited as examples. To what extent do you think that the media can influence such cultural values of people?
2. Two popular television shows in 1992 were “Roseanne” and “Fresh Prince of Bel Air.” Compare and contrast the cultural values that these two shows portray.
3. Global values, domain-specific values, and evaluations of product attributes are often related. Consider the attributes that you prefer in

automobiles. How do these preferred attributes reflect your domain-specific values and global values?

4. Describe a ritual that you go through consistently in your everyday life. It could be a religious ritual, some type of grooming ritual, or even one involving the preparation of food, among other things. To what extent is this ritual shared by others?
5. Go through a magazine and look at the advertisements. Identify as many cultural symbols as you can that are shown in the ads. In each case, what is the advertiser attempting to do by using the symbol?
6. Consider the popular singer Madonna. What is the symbolic function of the clothing she wears?
7. Identify a current popular cultural trend that is influencing the behavior of students at your college campus. Where did this trend emerge? What values are transmitted by this trend? How long do you think its life cycle will be?

ENDNOTES

1. Drummond Ayres, Jr., "For Aisles and Aisles, Buyers and Guns Galore," *The New York Times*, January 16, 1994, p. 10.
2. Carroll Bogert, "Comrades Do a Booming Business," *Newsweek*, January 24, 1994, p. 31.
3. Riccardo A. Davis, "Gun Exchange Strikes Nerve," *Advertising Age*, January 3, 1994, pp. 1, 3.
4. Melanie Wallendorf and M. Reilly, "Distinguishing Culture of Origin from Culture of Residence," in *Advances in Consumer Research*, Vol. 10, R. Bagozzi and A. Tybout, eds. (Ann Arbor, MI: Association for Consumer Research, 1983), pp. 699–701.
5. Geert Hofstede, *Culture's Consequences* (Beverly Hills, CA: Sage Publications, 1980).
6. David Tse, Kam-hon Lee, Ilan Vertinsky, and Donald Wehrung, "Does Culture Matter? A Cross-Cultural Study of Executives' Choice, Decisiveness, and Risk Adjustment in International Marketing," *Journal of Marketing*, Vol. 52 (October 1988), pp. 81–95.
7. This comment was made by the sociologist, and my friend, Chuck Edgley, who made numerous other helpful comments on this chapter.
8. Sunkyu Jun, A. Dwayne Ball, and James W. Gentry, "Modes of Consumer Acculturation," in *Advances in Consumer Research*, Vol. 20, Leigh McAlister and Michael L. Rothschild, eds. (Provo, UT: Association for Consumer Research, 1993), pp. 76-82.
9. Henry Fairchild, *Dictionary of Sociology* (Totawa, NJ: Littlefield, Adams, 1970).
10. George J. McCall and J. L. Simmons, *Social Psychology: A Sociological Approach* (New York: The Free Press, 1982).
11. Joseph Campbell, *Myths, Dreams, and Religion* (New York: E. P. Dutton, 1970).
12. John P. Robinson and Geoffrey Godbey, "Has Fitness Peaked?" *American Demographics*, September 1993, pp. 36–42.
13. Much of the discussion of the cultural meaning of goods is based upon Grant McCracken, "Culture and Consumption: A Theoretical Account of the Structure and Movement of the Cultural Meaning of Consumer Goods," *Journal of Consumer Research*, Vol. 13 (June 1986), pp. 71–84.
14. Ibid., p. 78.
15. For an interesting discussion of the definition of values, see L. J. Shrum, John McCarty, and Tamara Loeffler, "Individual Differences in Value Stability: Are We Really Tapping True Values?" in *Advances in Consumer Research*, Vol. 17, Marvin Goldberg and Gerald Gorn, eds. (Provo, UT: Association for Consumer Research, 1990), pp. 609–615.
16. Theodore Wallin, "The International Executives' Baggage: Cultural Values of the American Frontier," *MSU Business Topics*, Vol. 24 (Spring 1976), pp. 49–58.
17. Cora DuBois, "The Dominant Value Profile in American Culture," *American Anthropologist*,

Vol. 57 (December 1955), pp. 1232–1239. Also, see Janet T. Spence, "Achievement American Style," *American Psychologist*, December 1985, pp. 1285–1295.

18. Milton Rokeach, *Understanding Human Values* (New York: The Free Press, 1979).

19. J. Michael Munson and Edward McQuarrie, "Shortening the Rokeach Value Survey for Use in Consumer Research," in *Advances in Consumer Research*, Vol. 15, Michael J. Houston, ed. (Provo, UT: Association for Consumer Research, 1988), pp. 381–386.

20. D. E. Vinson, J. Scott, and L. Lamont, "The Role of Personal Values in Marketing and Consumer Behavior," *Journal of Marketing*, Vol. 41 (April 1977), pp. 44–50.

21. Thomas J. Reynolds and Jonathan Guttman, "Laddering Theory, Method, Analysis, and Interpretation," *Journal of Advertising Research*, Vol. 28 (February/March 1988), pp. 11–34.

22. John A. McCarty and Patricia M. Hattwick, "Cultural Value Orientations: A Comparison of Magazine Advertisements from the United States and Mexico," in *Advances in Consumer Research*, Vol. 19, John F. Sherry, Jr., and Brian Sternthal, eds. (Provo, UT: Association for Consumer Research, 1992), pp. 34–38.

23. These differences were developed by the author in conjunction with Michael Minor, an expert on the Japanese culture. It should be noted that both cultures are heterogeneous, and there will be many exceptions to the general trends identified.

24. Lynn Kahle, Basil Poulos, and Ajay Sukhdial, "Changes in Social Values in the United States During the Past Decade," *Journal of Advertising Research*, Vol. 28 (February/March 1988), pp. 35–41.

25. Pamela Homer and Lynn Kahle, "A Structural Equation Test of the Value-Attitude-Behavior Hierarchy," *Journal of Personality and Social Psychology*, Vol. 54, no. 4 (April 1988), pp. 638–646.

26. Russell W. Belk, "Material Values in the Comics: A Content Analysis of Comic Books Featuring Themes of Wealth," *Journal of Consumer Research*, Vol. 14 (June 1987), pp. 26–42.

27. Ibid. The somewhat surprising finding that material values reveal little evidence of growing in importance had been found previously. One study compared values in the late 1950s to values in the late 1970s. Values of wealth and accumulation of property and luxury goods actually decreased during the time period. Interestingly, the values of comfort and relaxed living increased in frequency slightly during the time span. See Harold Kassarjian, "Males and Females in the Funnies: A Content Analysis," in *Personal Values and Consumer Psychology*, Robert Pitts and Arch Woodside, eds. (Lexington, MA: Lexington Books, 1984), pp. 87–109. Another researcher compared the values portrayed in comic books to those found in underground "comix" between 1971 and 1972 and between 1981 and 1982. Comix books arose on college campuses as a means to provide artistic and journalistic freedom for young writers and authors who opposed the Vietnam War. In general, their messages were antiwar, pro-drugs, and pro-sexual freedom. Surprisingly, the results revealed that materialistic themes were more prevalent in the underground comix books than in comic books. Materialistic themes decreased in frequency in the ten-year period in comic books while increasing substantially in frequency in the underground comix. See Susan Spiggle, "Measuring Social Values: A Content Analysis of Sunday Comics and Underground Comix," *Journal of Consumer Research*, Vol. 13 (June 1986), pp. 100–113.

28. Monroe Friedman, "The Changing Language of a Consumer Society: Brand Name Usage in Popular American Novels in the Postwar Era," *Journal of Consumer Research*, Vol. 11 (March 1985), pp. 927–938.

29. Russell Belk and Richard Pollay, "Materialism and Magazine Advertising During the Twentieth Century," in *Advances in Consumer Research*, Vol. 12, Elizabeth Hirschman and Morris Holbrook, eds. (Provo, UT: Association for Consumer Research, 1985), pp. 394–398.

30. Ibid., p. 397.

31. Floyd W. Rudmin, "German and Canadian Data on Motivations for Ownership: Was

Pythagoras Right?" in *Advances in Consumer Research*, Vol. 17, Marvin Goldberg and Gerald Gorn eds. (Provo, UT: Association for Consumer Research, 1990), pp. 176–181.

32. Scott Dawson and Gary Bamossy, "Isolating the Effect of Non-Economic Factors on the Development of a Consumer Culture: A Comparison of Materialism in the Netherlands and the United States," in *Advances in Consumer Research*, Vol. 17, Marvin Goldberg and Gerald Gorn, eds. (Provo, UT: Association for Consumer Research, 1990), pp. 182–185.

33. Guliz Ger and Russell W. Belk, "Measuring and Comparing Materialism Cross-Culturally," in *Advances in Consumer Research*, Vol. 17, Marvin Goldberg and Gerald Gorn, eds. (Provo, UT: Association for Consumer Research, 1990), pp. 186–192.

34. Spiggle, "*Measuring Social Values*," p. 100.

35. Bob Davis, "These Hungarian Computer Games May Be Too Pacific for U.S. Tastes," *The Wall Street Journal*, September 21, 1984, p. 33.

36. Dennis Rook, "Ritual Behavior and Consumer Symbolism," in *Advances in Consumer Research*, Vol. 11, Thomas Kinnear, ed. (Ann Arbor, MI: Association for Consumer Research, 1984), pp. 279–284.

37. This definition was taken almost entirely from Dennis Rook, "The Ritual Dimension of Consumer Behavior," *Journal of Consumer Research*, Vol. 12 (December 1985), pp. 251–264. A small change was made to add the idea that rituals are culturally mandated to help distinguish the idea of a ritual from that of a habit.

38. These ideas were developed by Mary A. Stanfield Tetreault and Robert E. Kleine III, "Ritual, Ritualized Behavior, and Habit: Refinements and Extensions of the Consumption Ritual Construct," in *Advances in Consumer Research*, Vol. 17, Marvin Goldberg and Gerald Gorn, eds. (Provo, UT: Association for Consumer Research, 1990), pp. 31–38.

39. Rook, "The Cultural Dimension of Consumer Behavior."

40. McCracken, "Culture and Consumption."

41. Ray Brown, ed., *Rituals and Ceremonies in Popular Culture* (Bowling Green, OH: Popular Press, 1980).

42. Michael Marsden, "Television Viewing as Ritual," in *Rituals and Ceremonies in Popular Culture*, Ray Brown, ed. (Bowling Green, OH: Popular Press, 1980).

43. Charles Morris, *Signs, Language, and Behavior* (New York: George Braziller, 1946).

44. Elizabeth Hirschman, "Comprehending Symbolic Consumption: Three Theoretical Issues," in *Symbolic Consumption Behavior*, Elizabeth Hirschman and Morris Holbrook, eds., *Proceedings of the Conference on Consumer Aesthetics and Symbolic Consumption*, May 1980, pp. 4–6, 15.

45. Ibid.

46. This section was based on an article by John Sherry and Eduardo Camargo, "May Your Life Be Marvelous: English Language Labelling and the Semiotics of Japanese Promotion," *Journal of Consumer Research*, Vol. 14 (September 1987), pp. 174–188.

47. Ibid.

48. John Huey, "America's Hottest Export: Pop Culture," *Fortune*, December 31, 1990, pp. 50–60.

49. This definition, as well as the discussion of the characteristics of popular culture, was taken from Michael J. Bell, "The Study of Popular Culture," in *Concise Histories of American Popular Culture*, M. Thomas Inge, ed. (Westport, CT.: Greenwood Press, 1982), p. 443.

50. M. Thomas Inge, *Handbook of American Popular Culture*, 2nd ed. (Westport, CT: Greenwood Press, 1989).

51. Robert S. Alley, "Television," in *Handbook of American Popular Culture*, 2nd ed. (Westport, CT: Greenwood Press, 1989), p. 1368.

52. W. James Potter, "Three Strategies for Elaborating the Cultivation Hypothesis," *Journalism Quarterly*, Vol. 65 (Winter 1988), pp. 930–939.

53. For a recent discussion of rap music and its impact on children's advertising, see M.

Elizabeth Blair and Mark N. Hatala, "The Use of Rap Music in Children's Advertising," in *Advances in Consumer Research*, Vol. 19, John F. Sherry, Jr., and Brian Sternthal, eds. (Provo, UT: Association for Consumer Research, 1992), pp. 719–724.

54. George B. Sproles, *Fashion: Consumer Behavior Toward Dress* (Minneapolis, MN: Burgess, 1979).

55. Cathy Goodwin, "Good Guys Don't Wear Polyester: Consumption Ideology in a Detective Series," in *Advances in Consumer Research*, Vol. 19, John F. Sherry, Jr., and Brian Sternthal, eds. (Provo, Utah: Association for Consumer Research, 1992), pp. 739–745.

56. These characteristics were originally developed by Christopher M. Miller, Shelby H. McIntyre, and Murali K. Mantrala, "Toward Formalizing Fashion Theory," *Journal of Marketing Research*, Vol. 30 (May 1993), pp. 142–147.

57. The Doc Martens case is based upon Joseph Pereira, "Footwear Fad Makes Nike, Reebok Run for Their Money," *The Wall Street Journal*, June 24, 1993, pp. B1, B5.

CHAPTER 17 CASE STUDY

Will Fur Revive?

In 1987 sales of fur peaked in the United States at $1.8 billion. From there, however, things fell apart and sales plunged to just $1 billion in 1991. The impact on manufacturers and retailers was devastating. Bloated inventories and rampant discounting of prices led to losses and bankruptcies.

What caused the dramatic change in fortunes within the fur industry? Two factors clearly had an impact. Most publicized were efforts by animal rights groups to discourage affluent consumers from purchasing furs. Going so far as to throw red paint on people wearing fur, the animal rights groups received widespread publicity in the late 1980s and early 1990s. However, spokespersons for the fur industry claim that the impact of the antifur crusaders is vastly overblown. Indeed, as reported in *The Wall Street Journal*, the "Fur Council says its research shows that fur sales reflect the state of the economy and that animal rights activities are not a significant factor."

Thus, the second, and possibly more important, factor influencing fur sales was the state of the economy. As the United States went into recession in the early 1990s, sales plunged. A tax on expensive luxury goods implemented in 1991 severely hurt sales. When that was lifted, sales jumped. Then, in late 1993, when details of the Clinton administration's 1994 budget became public, sales turned down again because of increased taxes on the wealthy—the main target market for furriers.

Despite these problems, however, sales of furs did increase in 1992 by 10%. As a result, prices firmed, and the remaining furriers in the business began to make money. In addition, colder than usual winters in 1992 and 1993 helped fur sales.

Some argue that the improving economy and changes in consumer sentiment regarding wearing fur bode well for the industry. Others maintain, however, that antifur groups remain potent forces. Antifur parades were held during Thanksgiving in 1993. In addition, "speakouts" were held in which people wearing fur were confronted on the street by hostile individuals carrying signs saying, "There is no excuse for wearing fur."

The fur industry, however, continues to discount the impact of animal rights groups. The industry viewpoint is that fur must be tied to current fashion trends. As one industry spokesperson said, "Fur needs to look like fashion, instead of just looking like fur." Indeed, others take an even stronger position, saying, "Fur has become a fashion industry, which is better for the future of fur."

QUESTIONS

1. Define in your own words what problems are faced by the fur industry.
2. What consumer behavior concepts from the chapter apply to the case?
3. What are the managerial implications of the consumer behavior concepts?
4. Consider the cultural matrix identified in the chapter. Which of the consumer concepts identified in the matrix have application to the case?

Based upon Patrick M. Reilly, "Furriers Hustle to Keep Sales Warm," *The Wall Street Journal*, September 21, 1993, pp. B1, B8.

Chapter 18

The Subcultural Environment and Demographics

CONSUMER VIGNETTE

Changing Subcultural Patterns in the United States

The subcultural milieu of the United States is undergoing profound changes. Ranging from the "browning of America," to the increasing recognition of gays, to the aging of the population, these upheavals are transforming American society. Indeed, forecasters estimate that within 100 years, Anglo-Americans will compose less than 50% of the population of the United States.

What is the fastest-growing subcultural group in the United States? The answer is not African-Americans or Hispanics but Asian-Americans. In the 1980s over 40% of all immigrants to the United States came from Asia. Some estimate that by the year 2050, the number of Asian-Americans will nearly equal the number of Hispanics in the United States, who by then will be the largest minority. Asian-Americans are already becoming a potent economic and intellectual force. The percentage of Asian-Americans who graduate from college is twice the percentage of white Americans. In addition, incomes of Asian-Americans are significantly higher than are those of Anglo-Americans.[1]

If Asian-Americans are the fastest-growing minority, which group has become the hottest target market for companies? The answer is—Hispanics. Demographers estimate that by the year 2010, the number of Hispanics in the United States will double, and the group will become the largest minority.[2] Estimates are that throughout the 1990s, Hispanics will account for 40% of U.S. population growth.[3] The group already has tremendous buying power—over $150 billion. Marketing to Hispanics, however, is not an easy task. Filiberto Fernandez, the manager of Hispanic marketing for Polaroid, said, "We're not a melting pot, we're a salad bowl. We mix, but we don't blend."[4] As a result, marketing mistakes are common. For example, when chicken king Frank Perdue translated his slogan "It takes a tough man to make a tender chicken" into Spanish, it came out "It takes a sexually excited man to make a chick affectionate." Similarly, Budweiser once became the "queen of beers," and another beer company translated its slogan, "Let go!", into "Get diarrhea!"[5]

Perhaps just as profound as the changing ethnic population of the United States is its changing age composition and income distribution. Indeed, some forecasters are predicting the possibility of generational warfare. During the 1980s, the percentage of children under 17 years of age living below the poverty line increased from less than 15% to over 20%. However, the percentage of people over 65 below the poverty line decreased from 25% to 13%. Today, roughly 3.5 workers support each person on social security. By the year 2025, estimates are that fewer than two workers will exist to support each person on social security. The threat exists that young workers, who coincidentally have young children, will rebel at the inequity of a system that rewards the old and punishes the young.[6]

Another major subcultural change is recognition of the size of the gay and lesbian groups. While accurate statistics are difficult to obtain, the gay and lesbian subcultures represent from 5 to 15 million Americans and spend from $394 to $514 *billion* a year on consumer goods. As one manager in a clothing firm said, ". . . even if the figures are cut in half, they're still impressive. . . . Anecdotally, we know that gays and lesbians are urban, they spend money on clothes, and they're influential in fashion.[7]

With the dramatic increase in the number of gay and lesbian publications (at least seven magazines now exist), a business-to-business marketing problem has arisen. The magazines are finding it difficult to persuade mainstream advertisers to place ads within their covers. As one executive in a gay publication said, "What I have to sell is a comfort level to people who unfortunately have a preconceived notion of what this market is about. It's more difficult to overcome the prejudice than it is to sell the product."[8]

"The times, they are a-changin,'" and with them the dominant subcultural influences in the Unites States.

WHAT IS A SUBCULTURE?

The United States and Canada are composed largely of immigrants from throughout the world and their descendants. Although a "U.S." culture does exist, the melting pot has not created a homogeneous mass of people out of the hodgepodge of settlers. North America is "a mixture of subcultures reflecting the national heritage, language, religious, racial, and geographic diversity of a vast continent populated primarily by waves of immigrants from many diverse cultures and subcultures."[9]

A culture depicts the way of life of a society. However, within the overall culture of North America, subgroups exist that retain some of the values, beliefs, and symbols of their culture of origination. These groups form subcultures that can become important target markets for marketers. For example, the need of Jews to have kosher food makes them a tempting target for marketers willing to control adequately the preparation of food products. Meanwhile, mainstream marketers, such as ConAgra, have begun to market kosher foods because consumers are attracted to the wholesome image of the food products. For example, 60% of the sales of Hebrew National's frankfurters go to non-Jewish customers.[10]

In addition to originating from immigration, subcultures can also develop from naturally occurring subdivisions within a society. All societies contain such subgroups, which may be based on age, social class, and regional differences. In each case some factor causes differences in values and life-styles sufficient to create a subculture. Thus, in the United States a combination of retirement, common physical problems, and similar housing needs has resulted in the development of the elderly subculture.

A **subculture** may be defined as a subdivision of national culture, based on some unifying characteristic, such as social status or nationality, whose members share similar patterns of behavior that are distinct from those of the national culture.[11] Numerous demographic characteristics have been used to identify subcultures, including

Nationality (e.g., Hispanic, Italian, Polish)
Race (e.g., African-American, Native, Asian-American)
Region (e.g., New England, Southwest)
Age (e.g., elderly, teenager)
Religion (e.g., Catholic, Jewish)
Sex (i.e, male, female)
Social class (e.g., upper class, lower class)

Subcultures Versus Demographics

The concepts of subcultures and demographics are closely related. **Demographic variables** describe the characteristics of populations. Examples of demographic variables include

Nationality	Marital status
Age	Income
Religion	Region
Sex	Race
Occupation	Education

Of course, many of these demographic variables also describe subcultures. Thus, within the demographic category of religion, one can identify a number of distinct subcultural groups in the United States, including Jews, born-again Christians, and Moslems. However, when one speaks of cultures or subcultures, the focus is on the group's values, customs, symbols, and actions. People do not necessarily belong to a subculture because they are young or old, African-American or Chinese, rich or poor. Such demographic features merely describe the characteristics of a population of people. The reason why a marketer might speak of an African-American subculture is that a demographic characteristic conveniently describes a group of people who may have similar behavior patterns.

The focus of the present chapter is on subcultural processes. Through an understanding of subcultures one can gain a feeling for the values, customs, and life-styles of large groups of people. However, because demographic variables are used to describe subcultures, the chapter will inevitably also discuss demographics and demographic trends. In some respects this chapter could have been called "The Demographic Environment."

The chapter-opening-vignette identified several major subcultural changes occurring in the United States. Changes in the age distribution, the ethnic distribution, and attitudes toward gays and lesbians have had a major impact on marketing strategy. For example, with the changing nature of the social classes, retailers have either had to go upscale or go to the lower end. Companies such as Sears, which have traditionally focused on the middle class, have been losing market share to specialty stores on the upper end and discount department stores on the lower end. During the 1980s and early 1990s, the sales of specialty stores such as The Limited and The Gap grew by over 20% per year. In contrast, the sales for JCPenney and Sears stores grew by 6% or less per year.

Readers should also note that large groups of people may form subcultures based upon a shared interest in a particular type of product. For example, professional musicians and artists form distinct subcultures that many companies attempt to reach with a unique marketing mix. Similarly, in the 1960s a psychedelic subculture formed around a shared interest in hallucinogens. Highlight 18-1 discusses the possibility of the reemergence of a psychedelic subculture with some rather bizarre tastes and preferences.

The present chapter will discuss certain key subcultural groups that are more mainstream in nature than those who smoke toads. It begins with the important topic of age subcultures.

AGE SUBCULTURES

As consumers move through their life cycle, predictable changes in values, life-styles, and consumption patterns occur. A 5-year-old has a completely different set of needs from a 20-year-old, who in turn has different needs from a 65-year-old. Because various age groupings of consumers have similar values, needs, and behavioral patterns, and because people in the groupings tend to cluster together, they form subcultures that may constitute important market segments. Furthermore, as the numbers of people in age categories change because of variations in birthrates, new marketing opportunities may result.

SOCIAL MARKETING HIGHLIGHT 18-1

A New Psychedelic Subculture—The Toad Smokers?

In the 1960s, a drug culture flourished among middle-class hippies attempting to discover meaning in life through hallucinogens. Indeed, psychedelic drugs became part of popular culture with songs, such as the Beatles' "Lucy in the Sky with Diamonds," whose nouns were code words for LSD. However, when well-known celebrities (e.g., Jimmie Hendrix, John Belushi, Janice Joplin, and Jim Morrison) began dying from drug overdoses, the movement lost steam. More recently, celebrities like River Phoenix, Len Bias, and Kurt Cobain further tarnished the carefree, antiauthoritarian image of the drug culture. The misuse of illegal (and legal) drugs in ways that lead to death and the destruction of careers represents the dark side of consumer behavior.

Amazingly, however, against this backdrop of pain and anguish an old, old practice is finding acceptance within the drug subculture—smoking toads. The phenomenon appears to have been resurrected by a physician and drug culture researcher named Andrew T. Weil. In 1992 he published in an obscure anthropological journal an article about ancient practices of Native Americans involving the smoking of toads. As part of his research, Dr. Weil smoked dried venom from a Colorado River toad. He described the experience as producing "a sense of wonder and well-being." Weil said that he had ". . . seen people take one deep puff and fall over backward as they exhale."

Interestingly, the practice of getting high from toads had been described in the underground press for several years prior to the publication of Dr. Weil's article. However, the recommended approach was to "lick" the frogs rather than smoke them. According to the doctor, however, toad venom contains dozens of chemicals that frequently kill dogs that attempt to eat toads. Possibly the practice got an added boost from a rock band named the Toad Lickers. Its leader, Mojo Nixon, says that they have never really licked toads, however. Indeed, toad licking became a part of popular culture when it was portrayed on the popular TV shows "LA Law" and "Beavis and Butt-head."

Colorado River toads do produce a venom that contains the hallucinogenic agent 5-MeO-DMT. Dr. Weil described in his article how toad skins are found at Indian ceremonial sites that were used a thousand years ago. One unintended effect of the article, however, was to produce a stampede to capture the football-sized frog so that its parotid glands could be excised, dried, and smoked. As potential toad toasters fanned out across the Southwest to capture the animal, its very existence has become threatened. Indeed, the California legislature recently passed a law making it a misdemeanor to possess a Colorado River toad. One drug officer even predicted that eventually the penalty will be stronger for having a toad than for possessing the drug. According to the officer, "The environmentalists have more clout than the cops."

Bill Richards, "Toad-Smoking Gains on Toad-Licking Among Drug Users," *The Wall Street Journal*, March 7, 1994, pp. A1, A6.

An analysis of age trends is also important to marketers because highly accurate measures of the age composition of the population can be projected into the future more easily than most other demographic factors, such as income or occupation. Such projections allow marketers to recognize potential marketing opportunities years in advance, which greatly simplifies the planning process.

One factor that strongly influences the age distribution of the population is immigration. Immigrants, whether legal or illegal, tend to be younger, and recently more of them have been of Spanish and East Asian origin. Immigrant women tend to have high birthrates. It has been estimated that the Hispanic population grows at a rate of 1.8% a year in comparison to 0.6% a year for the entire United States population.[12] Because of the youth of the immigrants and their higher fertility rates, **immigration** is the single most important factor retarding the aging trend of the United States population.

Three age groupings that have critical importance to marketers are discussed in this section—the baby-boom generation, the so-called generation X, and the elderly.

The Baby Boomers

Although some debate may exist as to whether the **baby-boom generation** actually forms a subculture, sufficient life-style similarities exist among the huge group of Americans born between 1946 and 1964 that the group has a large impact on marketers and the economy as a whole. The United States is currently experiencing fundamental changes in the age characteristics of its population. The major reasons for the shifts in the average age of Americans over the next 40 years lie in the dramatic changes in birthrates over the last half century. During the Great Depression of the 1930s a "birth dearth," or **baby bust**, occurred. The number of children born to the average woman during her lifetime (i.e., the **fertility rate**) dropped to the replacement level of 2.1 births. Total births dropped 25%.[13]

The Depression birth dearth was followed by the post–World War II baby boom. Here the fertility rate shot past 3.8, and the total number of births increased by one-third over Depression levels. The baby boom lasted through 1964. It, however, was followed by another baby bust. Caused by changes in the technology of birth prevention (e.g., the "pill") and by the emergence of the working woman, this baby bust sent fertility rates plunging to as low as 1.8 in 1976—a rate far below the replacement level.[14] Lasting from 1965 to 1980, the latest baby bust group is now called "generation X" by marketers.

This series of changes in the birthrate created a huge bulge of 77 million people. As time passes and the boomers grow older, the bulge moves through the population like a melon being digested by a boa constrictor.[15] For example, in 1980 there were fewer than 25 million Americans in their forties; however, by the year 2000 the number will almost double. As the years pass the bulge moves, growing older and changing the nature of the marketplace. In 1970 the majority of the baby boomers were between 6 and 24 years of age. Marketers of soft drinks and fast foods were ecstatic over the hordes of teenyboppers clamoring for their products. By 1995, though, the baby boomers will be in their thirties and forties. Such consumers, who tend to be affluent, will have a new set of product needs and wants. For example, the market for first homes will decrease and demand for home furnishings will increase as baby boomers begin to purchase expensive furniture, draperies, and carpets.

Table 18-1 gives an overview of the U.S. population between 1992 and 2005. As can be seen, two age groups will have a sizable decrease in numbers between 1992 and 2005. Those 25 to 34 years old will decrease by 13.9%, and the number of children under 5 years old will decrease by 2.8%. A huge increase will occur among

TABLE 18-1

Projections of the U.S. Population, 1992–2005

	Population (1,000)		*Percentage Distribution*		*Percentage Change*	
Age Group	*1992*	*2005*	*1992*	*2005*	*1980–1992*	*1992–2005*
Under 5	19,497	18,959	7.6%	6.6%	11.8%	−2.8%
5–17	46,666	52,802	18.3	18.4	−3.4	13.1
18–24	25,941	28,111	10.2	9.8	−13.9	8.4
25–34	42,382	36,495	16.6	12.7	16.7	−13.9
35–44	39,867	42,284	15.6	14.8	46.5	6.1
45–54	27,404	41,610	10.7	14.5	12.0	51.8
55–64	20,924	29,647	8.2	10.4	−1.8	41.7
65–74	18,452	18,523	7.2	6.5	17.4	0.4
75 and over	13,789	17,892	5.4	6.2	31.2	29.8
Total	254,922	286,324				

SOURCE: U.S. Department of Commerce. *Statistical Abstract of the United States, 1993* (Washington, DC: U.S. Government Printing Office, 1993).

those between 45 and 54 years old. Of course, these represent the baby boomers. The second greatest increase in numbers will occur among those between 55 and 64 years of age.[16]

Implications for Marketing Strategy

One of the prime marketing requirements for consumer goods firms (clothing, food, entertainment, etc.) is the tracking of the baby-boom generation. Indeed, a marketing law might be phrased as "Those who live by the baby boom shall die by the baby boom."[17] As their tastes and preferences change with the passing years, the fortunes of manufacturers are dramatically affected. For example, with their traditional target market of 5- to 17-year-olds declining by more than one-half million during the 1980s, McDonald's Corporation was threatened not only with possible declines in revenues, but also with the loss of their primary work force—teenagers. To navigate the changing age demographics, the company hired retired people to work behind the counters. It also began to add breakfast menus to attract working people. In the process it identified another emerging trend—the two-career family that didn't have time for breakfast at home.[18]

Other companies have not fared as well. For example, in 1981 Levi Strauss, Inc., was the world's largest clothing manufacturer when jeans production peaked at 560 million pairs. However, by the mid-1980s profits began to turn down dramatically. The company closed plants and realigned management. As of 1988, sales were down 20% from their 1981 peak, and the company still had not been able to turn things around. In 1988 the company launched a $20 million ad campaign targeted to males in their thirties and forties. The ads show scenes like a father teaching his child to fish and a construction worker atop a steel girder at sunrise. The ads pitched the message: "Life is full of simple pleasures like the comfort of Levi's jeans. Or had you forgotten?"[19]

Not all is positive for the baby-boom generation, though. Because of their large numbers, the baby boomers have had major problems finding jobs in the marketplace. Many are chronically underemployed. One author has described baby boomers as a generation "caught in a squeeze between spiraling costs and stagnating salaries."[20]

Generation X

As a result of the financial problems of baby boomers, some marketers have begun to target **generation X** or the "baby busters." Born between 1965 and 1980, generation X is small, but it possesses $125 billion in discretionary income. Given a variety of names, such as "afterboomers" and "flyers" (i.e., fun-loving youth en route to success), the group is noted for valuing religion, formal rituals (e.g., proms), and materialism.[21] Because of the group's relatively small size, employers must compete for them in the job market. For example, the U.S. Army began its Army College Fund, which allows enlistees to save up to $25,200 during their term of service for college. One researcher at the Rand Corporation estimated that busters in service jobs will earn 15% more than boomers did at any given age.[22]

Despite a positive economic future, members of generation X have until recently been ignored by marketers. As one executive said, ". . . as baby boomers enter middle age, marketers are being forced to confront generation X. These people will fuel the growth for product categories from fast food to liquor to apparel to soft drinks." In the television arena, Fox Broadcasting (e.g., "The Simpsons") and MTV (e.g., "Beavis and Butt-head") are specifically targeting the group. In particular, advertising managers are concerned with how to reach this group. "If you've got a magazine that features photographs of yuppies, they [generation X] are not going to read that magazine," explained one media executive. Another manager described the group in the following way: "You've got to work hard to get in under the radar of these people. As soon as they think you're trying to sell them something, they turn off and walk away."[23]

Because of its youthfulness and its spending power, generation X is increasingly being taken seriously by marketers. In addition, the group is just moving into the time span when its members are beginning to purchase autos, houses, and other "big-ticket" items. The vice president-general manager of Nissan USA said that generation X now accounts for 25–30% of its auto sales. He added, "As they age and move up in income, they'll grow in importance. We want to make a good first impression."[24]

The Graying of America

A third major age trend in the United States is the "graying of America." The aging of the population will be one of the most dominant demographic factors for the foreseeable future. In 1990 the ratio of those over 30 to those under 30 jumped to 124 people over 30 for every 100 under 30.[25] By the year 2000 the ratio should move to 145 to 100, and by the year 2030 it should reach 176 over 30 to 100 under 30.

Barring global war or other disasters, the population of those under 30 will never again be as large as it was in 1983. By the year 2020 those over 65 will outnumber teenagers two to one.[26]

A number of factors influence the accuracy of age projections. The birthrates, mortality rates, and immigration rates all influence the projected population and its characteristics in the years ahead. Unfortunately, each is difficult to predict accurately. Birthrates are influenced by the technology available to prevent births, as well as by cultural values and life-style patterns. **Mortality rates** have been falling since the 1970s. Life expectancy increased by three years during the 1970s, and projections are that they increased another two to three years in the 1980s. Estimates are that by 1990 men will live on average 72 years and women 81 years. Because of the striking difference in the life expectancy of men and women, an aging population means more women. Elderly women will increasingly form an important segment for marketers to target. Indeed, of those over 85 years old, women outnumber men by almost two and one-half to one.

The Mature Consumer

Just who is the **mature consumer**? No specific age is associated with becoming "mature," elderly, a senior citizen, or reaching one's "golden years." Marketers find that attitude, more than age, defines the mature marketplace.[27] However, a series of events occur between the ages of 55 and 65 that set apart the aging consumer from younger people. During this time period, retirement has occurred or is being anticipated. In all likelihood income will be reduced and become relatively fixed after retirement, making inflation a threat. Health concerns become more important at about this age, and close friends begin to die. Most important for marketers is the projection that by the year 2020, it is likely that over 30% of the U.S. population will be 55 years old or older.

Another important point for marketers is that mature consumers are well off financially. While only 23% of American consumers are 55 years of age or older, they control 75% of the nation's wealth and about half of its discretionary income.[28] In 1961 a third of all those 65 years of age or over were classified as poor by the federal government. In the late 1980s fewer than 12% could be classified as poor, less than the national average figure of over 14%. Mature consumers also have a great deal of free time. In 1900, 60% of all men over 65 were still working. In 1940 the figure was 40%. In the late 1980s only 15% of men over 65 still worked.[29] This early retirement trend resulted in large part from the stronger financial position of mature consumers in the 1980s. Such early retirement gives mature consumers a large amount of discretionary time that can be used for leisure-time pursuits.

On two major dimensions mature consumers—here defined as age 55 or older—differ from younger people. First, in certain ways they process information differently. In particular, their visual, hearing, and taste senses decrease in acuity. The changes in information-processing abilities indicate that marketers should be concerned with how much time the elderly are given to make a decision. Providing additional time for information processing—for instance, by making an advertisement longer or by having a salesperson go slowly—may assist older consumers. In addition, marketers should pretest the way the information is organized.

A recent study found that information-processing differences influence the extent to which the elderly are able to search for nutritional information about cereals. Compared to younger consumers, the elderly were less able to search intensely for nutritional information on packages and select an appropriate cereal.[30] From a public policy perspective, the results suggest that as nutritional information becomes more readily available to consumers on packages, the elderly may not be able to make appropriate use of it.

A second way in which mature consumers differ from younger consumers is in the decrement that occurs in motor skills. As people become more elderly, their ability to walk, to write, to talk clearly, and to drive a car can gradually deteriorate. In many cities companies are now providing a variety of services to the elderly to help them accommodate these age-related handicaps. Examples of such services include in-home food delivery, yard and house cleaning, fix-up services, and nursing care.

Table 18-2 identifies how the elderly differ from younger consumers on a number of dimensions. In terms of shopping, those over 65 shop more frequently but spend less per shopping trip. They also shop less frequently at night. They use more coupons, pay with cash rather than credit cards, and shop less frequently at discount stores.

One major finding concerning the elderly is that they are cautious consumers. Older people have been found not to risk being wrong for the sake of acting fast.

TABLE 18-2

Consumption and Buying Habits of Mature Consumers Compared to Younger Consumers

1. Shopping behaviors
   - a. Shop more frequently
   - b. Spend less per shopping trip
   - c. Shop less often at night
   - d. Use coupons
   - e. Pay with cash—not credit cards
   - f. Shop less at discount stores
2. Media habits
   - a. Watch 60% more TV, particularly in the daytime
   - b. Read more newspapers
   - c. Listen to less radio, particularly FM
3. What they want from retailers
   - a. Courteous treatment
   - b. Personal assistance
   - c. Delivery service
   - d. Rest facilities (e.g., benches)

SOURCES: Adapted from K. L. Bernhardt and T. C. Kinnear, *Advances in Consumer Research*, vol. 3 (Ann Arbor, MI: Association for Consumer Research, 1976), pp. 449–452; and Zarrel Lambert, "An Investigation of Older Consumers' Unmet Needs and Wants at the Retail Level," *Journal of Retailing*, vol. 55 (Winter 1979), p. 43.

They do things at their own time and pace.[31] In addition, it has been found that the higher the perceived risk, the less likely the elderly are to try a product.[32] Another phenomenon that occurs as people grow older is an increase in the amount of time spent watching television. While all Americans spend more time watching television than any other activity except sleep and work, for the elderly TV is used for both entertainment and obtaining information. The importance of TV increases in part because of a general decrease among the elderly of social contact with other people.[33]

Of major interest to marketers is the finding that the elderly generally feel younger than they actually are.[34] One implication for managers is that promotional materials should focus on portraying the elderly at the age they feel rather than at their chronological age.

ETHNIC SUBCULTURES

Another demographic variable frequently used to describe subcultures is ethnicity. Although used in a variety of ways, **ethnicity** generally refers to a group bound together by ties of cultural homogeneity. Thus the group is linked by similar values, customs, dress, religion, and language. Ethnicity is frequently closely linked to nationality or region of origination. Thus one may speak of Mexican-Americans, African-Americans, Asian-Americans, and Anglo-Americans as ethnic groups, because each shares a common national or geographic ancestry along with a similar culture. Table 18-3 provides population projections for each of these groups from 1992 to 2020. This section of the chapter will discuss two ethnic subcultures in some detail—African-Americans and Hispanics.

TABLE 18-3

U.S. Population Projections for White, Black, Asian, and Hispanic Groups

	White	*Black*	*Asian*	*Hispanic**
% Distribution				
1992	83.4%	12.4%	3.3%	9.5%
2000	81.7	12.9	4.5	11.1
2010	79.6	13.6	5.9	13.2
2020	77.7	14.2	7.2	15.2
% Change				
1992–2000	5.6	12.2	45.4	26.8
2000–2010	5.7	13.8	42.4	28.5
2010–2020	5.5	13.1	32.0	24.5

*Persons of Hispanic origin may be of any race.

SOURCE: U.S. Department of Commerce, *Statistical Abstract of the United States, 1993*. (Washington, DC: U.S. Government Printing Office, 1993).

The African-American Subculture

A number of factors shape the **African-American subculture**, which represents 12% of the U.S. population. One major contributor is income deprivation. In the late 1980s, 36.2% of African-American households had incomes of under $10,000. In contrast, 26.7% of Hispanic households and 17% of white households had incomes below $10,000.[35] Other factors influencing the subculture are (1) educational deprivation, (2) a young, highly mobile family structure headed by a high proportion of females, and (3) a concentration of its population in central cities. Discrimination has also had a pervasive impact on the ability to obtain jobs, obtain an education, and move into the neighborhoods of choice.

Despite these historical disadvantages, the African-American subculture is a market segment that is growing in importance. As shown in Table 18-4, it has impressive buying power, it is increasing in size faster than the general population, and it is rising in socioeconomic status.

The African-American subculture is also marked by the importance of religious and social organizations. African-Americans disproportionately belong to fundamentalist Protestant groups and to specific political parties—particularly the Democratic party. To reach African-Americans some companies have recognized the need to sponsor activities for African-American groups and organizations. In one case Quaker Oats sponsored "The Quaker Gospel Salute." Consumers were asked to send a proof of purchase from the Quaker products they bought along with the name of their favorite gospel choir. For each proof received, Quaker sent 10 cents to the church or nonprofit organization of the sender's choice. The four choirs receiving the most recommendations were given a $1,000 contribution from Quaker.[36]

Even though the African-American consumer may be relatively easily recognized because of skin color, the subculture is not homogeneous.[37] Researchers have identified a variety of segments of African-Americans. For example, in one case three segments were identified—the affluent, mature shoppers; the less affluent; and African-American youth.[38] Recently, researchers found that different groups of African-American consumers have divergent views of rap music. While the sound is popular

TABLE 18-4

Factors Making African-Americans an Important Market Segment

1. *Spending power:* $213 plus billion in annual expenditures.
2. *Average family annual expenditures:* $19,130.
3. *Increasing size:* During the 1990s, will increase in size by 12.2% to represent 12.9% of the U.S. population.
4. *Youth:* Median age is 28 years as compared to 34 for whites.
5. *Geographic concentration:* 65% of African-Americans live in top 15 U.S. markets.
6. *Unique tastes and preferences:* For example, African-Americans spend far more than whites on boys' clothing, rental goods, radios, and cognac.

SOURCES: *Statistical Abstract of the United States, 1993,* and Eugene Morris, "The Difference in Black and White," *American Demographics,* January 1993, pp. 44–49.

with lower-class African-Americans and youths, older individuals in the middle class frequently respond negatively to the music. National advertisers who employ rap music to reach African-American audiences may in fact be turning off the very people they are attempting to reach, according to the authors. The researchers noted that perhaps national advertisers should follow the lead of an Atlanta radio station which plays "songs you grew up on, and no rap."[39]

Marketers face a number of critical issues in the promotion of products to African-American consumers. One concerns the use of African-American models in advertisements. Researchers have found that African-Americans are underrepresented in advertising. For example, a recent study of the portrayal of African-Americans in trade publications found that in the 1970s the use of African-Americans increased dramatically. However, during the 1980s, the use of African-American models leveled off. Interestingly, the researchers did find an increasing tendency to portray African-Americans in managerial roles during the 1980s.[40]

A second critical issue involves liquor and cigarette advertising. Because African-Americans spend relatively more of their income on liquor and cigarettes than whites, advertising that specifically targets the group frequently draws fire from public interest groups. For example, in 1991 Heileman Brewing Company attempted to launch a new brand with high alcohol, called PowerMaster, that was targeted to urban African-Americans. After a public outcry, it backed off the brand. The next year the company was again criticized when it sought to bring out Crazy Horse malt liquor—another high-octane brand. In 1993 Heileman began a repositioning effort for its Colt 45 malt liquor by using an ad in which a young African-American college graduate gives advice to a younger friend. One official with the Institute on Black Chemical Abuse said, ". . . it's in poor taste. It's inaccurate to portray someone like the gentleman, with this sense of mission, yet acting as a proponent of malt liquor right there on the street."[41]

A third critical issue concerns the understanding of the African-American family structure. A key quality of the African-American family structure is its derivation from its African origination. In Africa individuals live in broad extended families composed of those related by marriage and even adopted members. Thus in the United States what may appear to be a broken home may only be a part of an extended family. As said by one group of researchers, "Only by considering the extended family in its entirety can African-American family structure be understood."[42]

The Hispanic Subculture

Hispanics are the second-fastest-growing major minority group in the United States. (Asian-Americans are currently the fastest-growing subcultural group.) A combination of high fertility rates, high immigration rates, the close proximity of Puerto Rico, from which Hispanics can legally enter the United States, and continued problems of illegal immigration have led to a rapidly expanding population. Some researchers have forecast the possibility that if all Hispanics living in the United States were counted, the group would be identified as the largest minority in the United States sometime during the 1990s.[43]

The **Hispanic subculture** is based upon a number of factors that bind the group together. A common language unites most Hispanics. In fact, only 1% of Hispanics do not speak Spanish at all.[44] A common religion, Catholicism, also imparts a sense of commonality to Hispanics. (Over 85% of Hispanics are Catholic.) Hispanics also tend to live in urban areas. Eighty percent live in metropolitan areas compared to 75% of the African-American population.[45] Because Hispanics share a similar language and religion and because they are geographically concentrated, they make an outstanding target market for firms.

The Hispanic subculture is also marked by a constant influx of new members through legal and illegal immigration. A circular pattern exists such that Hispanics enter the United States, stay for a length of time, and then leave. It has been estimated that 30% of Mexican immigrants eventually return to Mexico, and it has been suggested that this is the reason why American products sell so well in our southern neighbor nation.[46]

Concerning their value structure, Hispanics reveal a highly conservative pattern. They are more likely than Anglos to express traditional American values concerning the importance of hard work; they are optimistic regarding their future standard of living; they are materialistic and seek the "good life."[47] Hispanics tend to be more family oriented than Anglos, to live more for the present, and to be somewhat less competitive.[48] The conservative nature of Hispanics was well illustrated in the 1988 presidential election. One pollster said, "Hispanics are too damn conservative. The more money they make, the more conservative they become and the more predisposed they are to Republicanism."[49]

Hispanic Segmentation

An important aspect of the study of Hispanics is recognizing that they are not one homogeneous group. Thus it is probably inappropriate to speak of a *single* Hispanic market segment.[50] Actually, at least four distinct groups, or Hispanic segments, exist—Mexican-American (60%), Cubans (5%), Puerto Ricans (14%), and Hispanos (21%). The Hispanos are people who have long lived in the United States. They are centered in New Mexico and consider themselves original Americans because their ancestors arrived hundreds of years ago with the Spanish conquistadors.[51] Among the four Hispanic groups, Spanish is spoken differently, differences in food preferences exist, and differences in political attitudes are present. Perhaps most important, these groups tend to live in different areas of the country. Estimates are that around the year 2000, Hispanics will outnumber Anglos in California. Florida's Dade County (the location of Miami) is already one-half Hispanic.

Each of the Hispanic groups can be reached easily because of their geographic concentration. Los Angeles, where 2.1 million Hispanics live, is considered to be the prime target area for reaching Mexican-Americans. Similarly, Miami contains the largest concentration of Cubans and New York City the greatest number of Puerto Ricans. Among the Hispanic groups, the Cubans have the highest income (average annual family income was $27,294 in 1988), whereas Puerto Ricans have the lowest (average annual family income was $15,185 in 1988).[52]

Problems in Marketing to Hispanics

A number of problems exist in trying to market to the Hispanic subculture. Perhaps the major difficulty is that four segments of the subculture exist. Marketing to Puerto Ricans is not the same as marketing to Cubans, to Hispanos or to Mexican-Americans. In fact, cultural differences may exist within each segment. One advertising executive noted that if the United States and Mexico went to war, the Hispanics in California would probably fight for Mexico, whereas those in Texas would fight for America.[53]

A second problem in marketing to Hispanics is the differences in the type of Spanish spoken. One company sold ink for fountain pens that was advertised as "not clogging the pen." The word *embarazo* was used for the word "clog." The problem was that in some Latin countries *embarazo* also means pregnancy. Many Hispanics interpreted the ad as making claims that the ink was a type of contraceptive device. Similarly, the word for "earring," *pantella*, can mean "television screen" or even "lampshade" to some Hispanics. Some companies have simply had trouble translating their standard messages into Spanish. Coca-Cola's slogan, "It's the real thing," had to be changed when officials learned that the translation had an off-color meaning in Spanish.[54]

Comparing Anglo, African-American, and Hispanic Consumption

One study surveyed Anglo, African-American, and Hispanic consumers to compare the groups on a variety of consumption characteristics.[55] The results were inconsistent with a number of stereotypes concerning the groups. First, no evidence was found for differences in brand loyalty among the groups. For brand loyalty only an age effect occurred—in which respondents over 55 reported being more brand loyal. Second, both African-Americans and Hispanics viewed trading stamps more positively than did Anglo consumers. A number of other interesting findings were obtained in the study. No differences were found among the groups on coupon use, impulse buying, shopping for generic products, and the tendency to shop for specials. Both African-Americans and Hispanics showed a greater tendency to shop for bargains. Overall, though, the results did not reveal large differences among the groups on any of the variables. In general the differences that were found were small.

In sum, marketers must avoid assuming that stereotypes of ethnic subcultures are accurate when marketing to them. Marketing strategy should be based upon sound marketing research and environmental analysis. Table 18-5 presents a number of important facts about the Hispanic market.

TABLE 18-5

Some Key Characteristics of the Hispanic Subculture

1. Mexicans make up two-thirds of U.S. Hispanic households.
2. Six in 10 Hispanics fall into the modest means or low-income clusters of consumers.
3. Fourteen percent of Hispanic households have incomes of over $50,000.
4. Approximately 7.2 million Hispanics live in the United States.
5. Nearly 70% of Hispanics speak Spanish as their dominant language at home—a percentage that was rising in the early 1990s.
6. Over 80% of Hispanics watch Spanish TV and listen to Spanish radio—a percentage that has been steadily rising.

SOURCE: Patricia Braus, "What Does Hispanic Mean?" *American Demographics*, June 1993, pp. 46–49.

REGIONAL SUBCULTURES

Another major subcultural variable of interest to marketers concerns how populations arrange themselves in the various regions of the United States. Measuring and predicting the demographic patterns of **regional subcultures** is important to marketers for two reasons. First, different regions have distinct life-styles resulting from variations in climate, culture, and the ethnic mix of people. Consequently, different product preferences exist. For example, regional preferences exist for foods and beverages. Some coffee manufacturers blend their coffee differently for the various regions—heavier in the East, lighter in the West, and with chicory in Louisiana. Highlight 18-2 discusses another way in which behavior may vary across regions and the cities within them—the degree to which people help each other.

A second reason for studying regional subcultures is that their growth rates and size may vary dramatically. For many types of goods it is important to shorten the distribution channel as much as possible. New production facilities should be built in areas experiencing the greatest population growth. In addition, companies looking for new growth opportunities may try to focus on regions expected to experience population increases.

Dramatic changes are occurring in the populations of the regions of the United States. In the past, the Northeast and North Central regions were the most heavily populated. However, by the 1980s, two of the five most populated states (California, New York, Texas, Pennsylvania, and Illinois) were in the lower half of the United States. Then, in 1986 Florida replaced Illinois on the list. In 1990 California and Texas became the top two states in population. As a result of the shifting demographics, corporations are changing their marketing emphasis, and in many cases their corporate headquarters, to better focus on emerging markets.[56]

Table 18-6 shows regional population winners and losers in the 1980s and early 1990s. Readers should note that while California, Florida, and Arizona had large percentage increases during the 1980s, they were replaced by Idaho, Washington, and Utah in the early 1990s. The likely explanation for the change is that the economic recession of the early 1990s hit these states particularly hard, and as a result, their population growth dramatically slowed.

Regional population shifts occur for several reasons. One factor that helps explain the shifts is the work force's search for jobs. During the severe recession of 1980–1982, many workers moved from the North Central states to the West and Southwest in search of employment. People also move for life-style reasons. Florida has grown rapidly because of the huge influx of retirees seeking the sun in their retirement years. Consequently, Florida is the nation's oldest state, with a median age of 36.6 years—nearly five years above the national average.[57]

A third reason for regional population shifts is differences in birthrates. Differences in birthrates take longer to manifest themselves, but over a 10- to 20-year period the variations become meaningful. In general, the West is younger than the Northeast and North Central states. The median age in the Northeast is over 30 years, whereas in the West it falls dramatically. For example, Alaska's median age is 28.3. Utah is the youngest state, with a median age of 25.5 years. In Utah's case a confluence of demographic factors accounts for the state's youthfulness. The Mormon population and influence in Utah is large. A central focus of the religion is the importance of the family and of childbearing, which, in turn, keeps the median age relatively low.

HIGHLIGHT 18-2

Consumer Helping Behavior—Regional Differences

Here is a quiz. Consider the following cities—Rochester, New York; Memphis, Tennessee; San Diego, California; Los Angeles, California; and New York, New York. How would these cities rank in terms of the degree to which their citizens would help other people? This question was asked, and answered, by a researcher named Robert Levine.

Over a two-year period, Dr. Levine's research group spent its summer vacations traveling across the United States to test for the degree to which people in 36 cities would help others. Six measures of helping were used. On five of the six measures, the researcher would do something that required the help of a nearby passerby.

1. Dropping a pen—Would people give a pen back to the researcher?
2. Hurting a leg—Would people help a person with a bandaged leg pick up magazines that were dropped?
3. Making change—Would a passerby make change for a quarter?
4. Returning a lost letter—Would strangers mail a lost letter that had been placed under the windshield of their car?
5. Helping a blind person—Would a stranger help a blind person cross a busy street?
6. United Way contributions—Would passersby make contributions to United Way in the city?

If you guessed that the order of the cities was inversely related to their helping behavior, you are right. Among the 36 cities, people in Rochester were the most helpful. Here are the rankings in order of helpfulness: Rochester = 1, Memphis = 4, San Diego = 19, Los Angeles = 34, and New York = 36.

What factors were responsible for the large differences in helpfulness found across the cities? Dr. Levine suggested that the degree of "cityness" explains the findings. The higher the density of an urban area, the less helping behavior one finds. Quoting frequently from Ralph Waldo Emerson, Levine said, "Cities give not the human senses room enough." As a result, one finds that the increasing density of people increasingly drives strangers apart.

Readers may also wish to ponder the following question: Is the study of helping behavior part of consumer behavior? Certainly, giving to United Way, making change, and sending back lost letters involve consumer activities. Perhaps consumer researchers should consider the study of consumer helping behavior.

Robert V. Levine, "Cities with Heart," *American Demographics*, October 1993, pp. 46–54.

The combination of a net inflow of migration and a youthful population portend future above-average population growth in the Western states. The youthful population there will tend to have higher birthrates than the older populations found in the Northeast and North Central states.

Figure 18-1 shows the Census Bureau's regional division of the United States. One study found that differences in values on the LOV scale (the List of Values scale) occurred across the divisions of the United States identified by the Bureau of the Census.[58] One possible reason for the effect is its political boundary basis. Political boundaries may take on significance beyond purely political issues. For

TABLE 18-6

Percentage Shifts in Populations by States

1990–1992		1980–1990	
Fastest Percentage Growth			
Nevada	10.4%	Nevada	50.1%
Alaska	6.7	Alaska	36.9
Idaho	6.0	Arizona	34.8
Washington	5.5	Florida	32.7
Utah	5.2	California	25.7
Slowest Percentage Growth			
North Dakota	−0.5	West Virginia	−8
Maine	−0.3	Iowa	−4.7
Connecticut	−0.2	North Dakota	−2.1
New Hampshire	0.1	Pennsylvania	0.1
Rhode Island	0.2	Louisiana	0.3

SOURCE: *Statistical Abstract of the United States, 1993.*

example, a certain pride in one's state exists that resembles rooting for the home team. Thus, all of Indiana feels pride when the Hoosiers win a national basketball championship or when Notre Dame is ranked number one in football. Table 18-7 presents the distribution of values across the census regions of the United States.

Geodemographics

An area of study having a major impact on marketing research is that of geodemographics. **Geodemographics** takes as its unit of analysis the neighborhood (i.e., census blocks) and obtains demographic information on consumers within such neighborhoods. Census blocks found to contain people with similar demographic characteristics are then clustered together to form potential target markets for firms. This process of identifying large groups of neighborhoods possessing households that are demographically similar is called **cluster analysis**. One basic concept of geodemographics is that individuals within a neighborhood have similar demographic characteristics, buying patterns, and values. A second important concept is that neighborhoods may be placed into similar categories, even when they are widely separated.[59] Thus geodemographic analysis can be an important managerial tool. In particular, geodemographics is a vital component of direct marketing. By directly contacting consumers with similar geodemographic profiles through direct mail or telephone calls, firms can precisely target a market segment. The result is a much more efficient use of a firm's resources. A number of national firms offer geodemographic analysis, such as ACORN, ClusterPlus, PRIZM, and Micro-Vision.

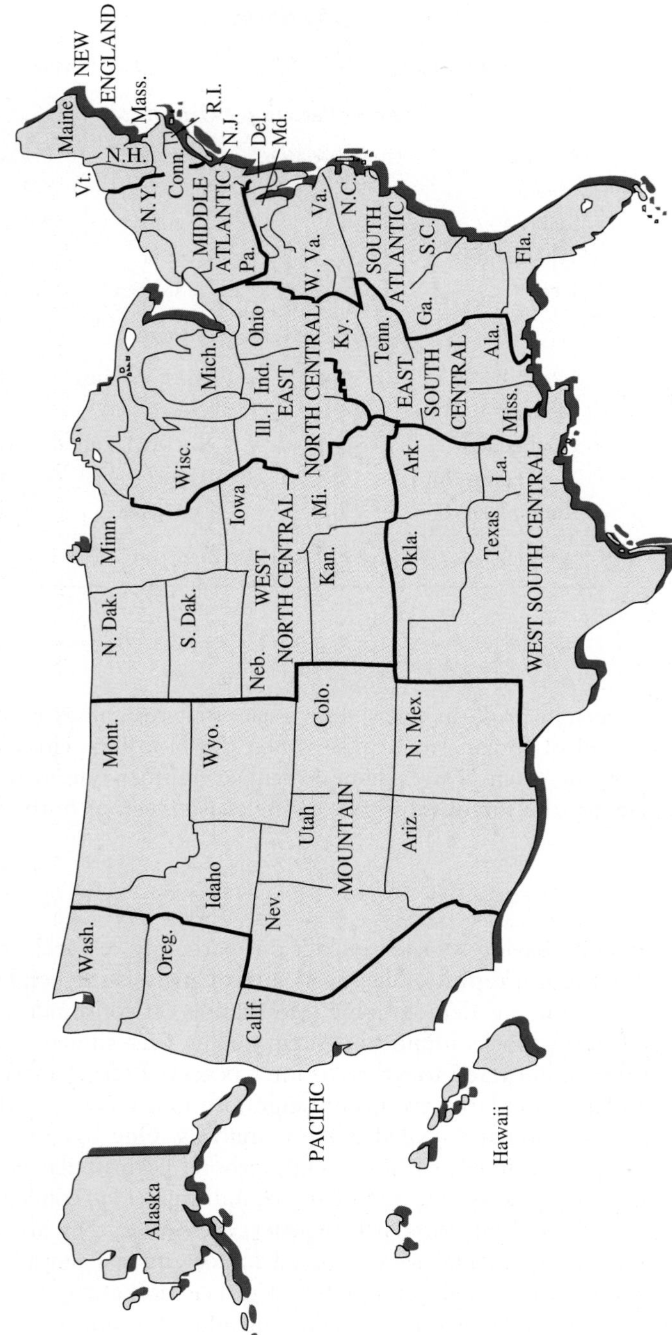

Figure 18-1 Nine Census Bureau regions. (Adapted by permission from *Marketing News*, May 13, 1983, Section 2, p. 8, published by the American Marketing Association.)

TABLE 18-7

Distribution of Values Across Census Regions of the United States

Values	*New England*	*Middle Atlantic*	*South Atlantic*	*East South Central*	*East North Central*	*West North Central*	*West South Central*	*Moun-tain*	*Pacific*	*N*
Self-respect	22.6%	18.6%	23.1%	23.4%	20.2%	16.7%	23.8%	29.2%	19.8%	471
Security	21.2	18.0	18.3	26.9	22.1	20.6	23.8	18.1	18.5	461
Warm relation-ships with others	13.9	16.8	15.7	11.4	16.0	21.6	14.9	15.3	17.6	362
Sense of accomplishment	13.9	13.0	10.7	9.6	11.4	14.7	6.8	8.3	12.1	254
Self-fulfillment	8.0	10.0	10.1	7.8	9.3	8.3	6.5	6.9	15.0	214
Being well respected	8.8	7.7	9.8	12.0	10.0	7.4	14.0	4.2	3.5	196
Sense of be-longing	7.3	8.8	9.2	7.8	7.4	6.9	6.4	13.9	7.0	177
Fun/enjoyment/ excitement	4.4	7.1	3.3	1.2	3.5	3.9	4.7	4.2	6.4	100
Total	100.0	100.0	100.0	100.0	100.0	100.0	100.0	100.0	100.0	2235
N	137	339	338	167	430	204	235	72	313	

N = the number of people in the column or row. Thus, for the "self-respect" value, 471 listed it as most important. Of the 137 New Englanders who answered the survey, 22.6 percent listed the self-respect value as most important.

SOURCE: Lynn Kahle, "The Nine Nations of North America and the Value Basis of Geographic Segmentation," *Journal of Marketing*, vol. 50 (April 1986), pp. 37–47. Published by the American Marketing Association. Reprinted with permission.

Geodemographic analysis is a marketing research technique that is used in segmenting the marketplace, repositioning brands, and designing the marketing mix. For example, neighborhoods identified as being in the same cluster become market segments. L. L. Bean was one of the early users of geodemographic analysis to segment the marketplace. As a company that mails expensive catalogs to potential customers, the company had to find a cost-effective way of identifying "L. L. Bean types." A company called PRIZM was hired to develop a geodemographic profile of the market segment that L. L. Bean should target. Catalogs were then sent to zip codes that possessed a high percentage of "L. L. Bean type" neighborhoods. The company then slowly built a data base that not only identified where their clients lived, but also the magazines they read, the television shows they watched, and even the products they owned.[60]

An example of the use of geodemographics to assist in a repositioning effort occurred when *Apartment Life* magazine changed its name to *Metropolitan Home*. The goal of management was to reposition the magazine to a more upscale audience. By tracking the zip codes of new subscribers, management could then determine whether the repositioning effort was having the desired effect of attracting more affluent readers.

Geodemographic analysis can assist managers in designing the marketing mix by providing a detailed profile of where customers live, what they buy, and what their demographic characteristics are. In particular, the location of stores and the selection of merchandise for stores can be guided by geodemographics. Recently, market researchers have used geodemographic analysis to identify where to locate new golf courses. By determining where golf courses are currently located and by identifying a demographic profile of golfers and where they live, researchers can pinpoint areas of the United States that have a surplus of golfers in relation to the number of courses available. Figure 18-2 presents a map that depicts the concentrations of golfers in the Michigan area, with darkly shaded areas representing high concentrations of golfers. The map was drawn to assist managers in deciding whether to build a new golf resort called Sugar Loaf. Based on the map, do you think that the resort would be successful?

Should Companies Segment by Geography?

This question is very similar to the question surrounding the issues of global marketing. Little doubt exists that a national marketing effort is less expensive than a regionally based strategy. As one consultant succinctly said, "Breadth of choice equals complexity; complexity equals increasing costs."[61] For example, when Campbell's Soup Co. divided the country into 22 regions, it had to promote 88 employees to brand sales managers, retrain its sales force, and make major changes in production—all costly moves. In addition, an effort to target a specific region frequently brings retaliation from local companies. Thus, when Campbell's introduced Spicy Ranchero Beans into the Southwest, the area's dominant marketer of beans, Ranch Style Beans, retaliated with heavy advertising and sales promotions. Similarly, when the president of Domino's Pizza, Inc., was asked about regional marketing, he said, "regional efforts would blow our whole advertising budget." As a result, the company only offers variations in toppings across regions, leaving national advertising to focus on speedy home delivery.[62]

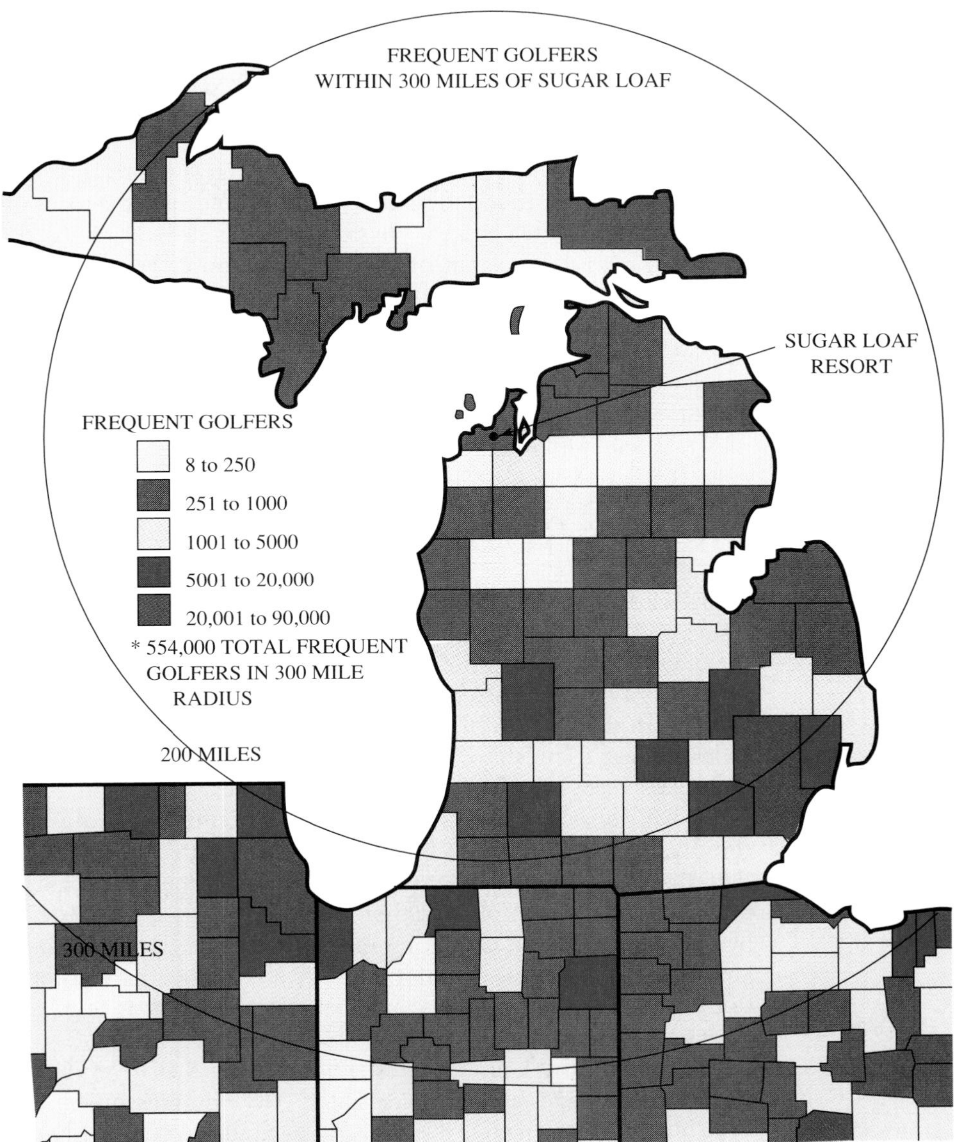

Figure 18-2 A geodemographic map that shows the concentration of golfers in Michigan near a new resort—Sugar Loaf.

Despite the problems of developing regional marketing strategies, many companies have begun to segment the market based upon regions. For example, the divisions of General Motors have begun regional marketing efforts. Chevrolet has broken its advertising group into five parts—a national group, plus four regional groups. As one executive stated, "Chevy is making a long-term commitment to bring marketing decisions closer to the market."[63] Chrysler has changed its strategy by dividing the United States into five regions. Indeed, all the U.S. auto manufacturers are targeting California. There only about 50% of the cars sold are made by U.S. manufacturers, compared to some 70% elsewhere in the country. Similarly, Frito-Lay, the nation's largest salty-snack marketer, has divided its effort into eight regional offices. These offices will control promotional budgets in their areas. The goal is to compete head to head with local and regional snack food vendors. The regionalization should give the company the ability to act flexibly and quickly to changes in the marketplace. As an executive stated, "Basically there's no such thing as a national program for promotion coming out of Frito-Lay anymore. We will tailor our marketing to our prime trading areas."[64]

The use of geodemographics is an extremely important segmentation tool. Indeed, without geodemographics, direct-marketing firms would have great difficulty competing against traditional retailers. The marriage of demographics with geographic analysis has created an extremely important segmentation device in the form of geodemographic analysis.

SOCIAL CLASS SUBCULTURES

Social classes may be defined as the relatively permanent and homogeneous strata in a society that differ in their status, wealth, education, possessions, and values. All societies possess a hierarchical structure in which the residents are stratified into "classes" of people layered on top of each other. Both actual and perceptual factors distinguish the groups. In concrete terms, the classes differ in their occupations, lifestyles, values, friendships, manner of speaking, and possessions. In perceptual terms, each class recognizes that status differences exist between classes. Individuals perceive that different classes have diverging amounts of prestige, power, and privilege. Finally, the persons with whom members of the social classes associate differ. Behavior is restricted so that members of a class tend to socialize, both formally and informally, with each other rather than with members of other classes. As observed by one theorist, social classes are multidimensional. Three primary factors differentiate the social classes—economic status (e.g., occupation, wealth, house type and location), educational credentials, and behavioral standards (e.g., community participation, aspirations, and recreational habits).[65]

Currently, the United States is undergoing a change in the composition of the social classes. One demographer stated: "By any measure, the share of households with middle-class incomes has steadily declined. A fractured economy has also fractured any sense of common progress."[66] The middle class is being split in part by well-educated two-income families moving into the upper-middle class. Unfortunately, however, at the other extreme are a group of single mothers and baby boomers stuck in low-paying jobs who have fallen to the lower-middle class. A Harvard University economist said that "the country has moved in the direction of becoming a nation of haves and have-nots, with less in between."[67]

In the egalitarian culture of the United States, however, discussions of social class may make people uncomfortable. For example, when answering an interviewer's question about social class, one woman said, "It's the dirtiest thing I've ever heard of."[68] Despite its unpleasant connotations, the study of social class has important managerial implications for marketers.

In comparison to the way it is used by sociologists, marketing managers interpret the social class concept more narrowly. Marketers are concerned with how the buying patterns of social classes differ rather than with the political, institutional, and cultural reasons for their existence. For marketers the social classes are seen as subcultures with distinct life-styles, buying patterns, and motivations.[69] Thus the social classes can be viewed as potential market segments that possess divergent needs, wants, and desires for products and services.

What Are the Social Classes?

A variety of different classification schemes have been developed to rank the social classes. Depending on the classification system, the number of categories of social class varies from as few as two to as many as nine. Regardless of the number of categories proposed, they are ordered in a manner that begins with some type of elite upper class and ends with a lower class.

A frequently used social class scheme is Warner's Index of Status Characteristics (ISC).[70] Warner's index uses four variables as indicators of social class: occupation, source of income, house type, and dwelling area. The indicators are weighted, with occupation most heavily emphasized and dwelling area least heavily emphasized in the composite index. Based on the total ISC score, an individual is classified into one of six categories:

1. **Upper-upper class**
2. **Lower-upper class**
3. **Upper-middle class**
4. **Lower-middle class**
5. **Upper-lower class**
6. **Lower-lower class**

A variety of other classification schemes have been developed. The U.S. Bureau of the Census uses three variables to form a socioeconomic status index—income, occupation, and education. The average of these scores results in an index with four classifications:

1. Lower class
2. Lower-middle class
3. Upper-middle class
4. Upper class

The most valid approach for measuring social class is through the use of multi-item indices. Table 18-8 lists four social class scales and the variables that each uses to rank the social classes.

Table 18-9 provides a recent **social class hierarchy** scheme and summarizes some of the characteristics of the social classes. The descriptions given in the table have proven quite accurate for at least the last 50 years in the United States. However, recent trends are creating some subtle changes. One trend is a new group of people who might be placed in the lower-upper class. These are upper-middle-class professionals who

TABLE 18-8

Measuring Social Class

	Social Class Index			
Variable	***Hollingshead***	***Warner***	***Census Bureau***	***Coleman***
Occupation	*	*	*	*
Source of income		*		
House type		*		*
Dwelling area		*		
Family income			*	
Education	*		*	*
Neighborhood housing				*
Wife's occupation				*
Wife's education				*
Religious affiliation				*
Associations				*

Names of indices:
Hollingshead: Index of Social Position (ISP).
Warner: Index of Status Characteristics (ISC).
Census: Census Bureau Index of Socioeconometric Status (SES).
Coleman: Index of Urban Status (IUS).
Note: The indices have various "weighting" schemes for the variables—that is, some variables are more important than others in calculating social status in the four indices.

marry and form high-powered two-income families. Earning from $60,000 to $140,000 a year, these families have substantially greater expendable incomes than do traditional upper-middle-class families with a single breadwinner.[71] Because of their high incomes and their need to juggle two careers, these families have become a separate target market.

Marketers do employ social class indices in their research. AT&T used the Census Bureau index to develop a profile of the telephone-style consciousness of consumers.[72] The results of the study revealed some surprising findings. Most notably, the lower-middle class was found to be very style conscious. For example, they felt that phones should come in patterns and designs as well as colors. Similarly, they agreed more often than other social classes with the statement "A telephone should improve the decorative style of a room." In contrast, the lower-middle class sought only phones that work and were unconcerned with style. The results of the study suggested that in addition to the obvious target markets of upper-class and upper-middle-class consumers, AT&T should *not* forget the lower-middle-class customer in promoting their decorator telephones.

Differences between social classes can be seen in their communication patterns. One study found that people can identify an individual's social class simply by hearing him or her read something.[73] Social classes differ in their speech cadence, voice modulation, and fluency of speech. The choice of words also varies among the social classes.[74] Lower classes describe the world in more concrete terms than do the

TABLE 18-9

The Social Class Hierarchy

A. *Upper Americans*

Upper-upper (0.3%): The world of inherited wealth and old family names. Work occurs as a matter of choice, and members often serve on the boards of directors of major corporations. Serves as a reference for lower classes. Not a major market segment because of its small size.

Lower-upper (1.2%): The newer social elite, drawn from current professionals, corporate leadership. May be extremely wealthy, but the money is relatively new. Is an achieving group and will spend money to show its wealth. Will guard its social class position because of insecurity. Is a major market for specialized luxury goods, such as Mercedes automobiles.

Upper-middle (12.5%): The rest of college graduate managers, intellectual elite, and professionals. Life-style centers on private clubs, causes, and the arts. Collegiate credentials expected. Housing is extremely important to this group—particularly where the house is located. The quality and appearance of the products are important to this group.

B. *Middle Americans*

Middle class (32%): White-collar workers and their blue-collar friends. Live on "the better side of town," try to "do the proper things." Have white-collar friends and acquaintances. Respectability is a key idea to this group. Home ownership, high moral standards, and focus on the family are important ideals. They tend to have high school educations or some college but do not reach high levels in their organizations.

Working class (38%): Blue-collar workers; lead "working class life-style" whatever the income, school background, and job. Jobs tend to be monotonous, although affluence is possible if they have a union job. Tend to stay close to their parents and relatives and live in older parts of town. Do have money for consumer products and, with the middle class, represent the market for mass consumer goods.

C. *Lower Americans*

Upper-lower (9%): Working, not on welfare. Living standard is just above the poverty level. Behavior judged "crude," "trashy." Tend to be unskilled workers.

Lower-lower (7%): On welfare, visibly poverty stricken, usually out of work (or have the "dirtiest jobs"). Some are bums, common criminals. Has become separated from the upper-lower group because it exists on government transfer payments. With the upper-lower class, accounts for only 6–7% of disposable income.

SOURCE: Data adapted from Richard P. Coleman, "The Continuing Significance of Social Class in Marketing," *Journal of Consumer Research*, vol. 10 (December 1983), pp. 265–280.

middle and upper classes. If asked where he or she obtained bubble gum, a lower-class child would likely state a person's name. An upper-class child would simply say "from the grocery store."

Although most marketers agree that social class is an important concept, published examples of its use in marketing are sparse. After all, a number of problems exist in the use of social class as a segmentation variable. Some of these problems are identified in Table 18-10.

One problem in measuring social class that should be highlighted is that the measures assume that an individual's social class is an average of his or her position on several dimensions of status. The consistency with which an individual reveals a

TABLE 18-10

Problems in the Use of Social Class by Marketers

1. *What is its definition?* Little agreement has been reached on how to measure the concept.
2. *The choice-behavior fallacy.* Social class by itself is a poor predictor of buying behavior. However, such a result should be expected when only a single indicator such as social class is used. Many factors influence product choice behavior in addition to social class.
3. *The husband-only fallacy.* The social class of the husband cannot be used as the sole criterion for determining a family's status. Because of the prevalence of working wives and because many pairings of husbands and wives are inconsistent regarding social class, this sexist practice is misleading.
4. *The present social class fallacy.* One cannot assume that a family's current social class is governing their life-style and buying behavior. A family's life-style, beliefs, and values are based not only on both partners' current status, but also on the status of their parents. The socialization process creates a tendency to maintain a certain life-style, even if one's social status has moved up or down.
5. *The effect of aspirations.* People differ in their desire to get ahead and move up in social class. In addition, a person's reference group may be of a different social class. Such an individual would tend not to share the consumption behaviors of members of his or her objectively measured social class.

particular social class across a number of dimensions is called **status crystallization**. Some have argued that those who have low crystallization are more prone to express liberal ideas and advocate changes in the social order.[75] An example of low crystallization would be a Hispanic attorney whose parents were laborers.

Social Class and Buying Behavior

Because of the problems of the social class concept, one must use caution in interpreting the findings of studies investigating its impact on buying behavior. One finding of importance is that the reasons for shopping differ among the social classes. The upper classes tend to shop not only out of necessity but also for pleasure.[76] Higher-class women tend to favor stores with a high-fashion image, such as department stores and specialty shops. Lower-class women favor mass merchandisers and stores with price appeal. The importance of maintaining a certain social image is revealed in the shopping patterns of the upper classes. Products that reflect differences in class, like furniture, are viewed as "socially risky." Upper-class consumers tend to purchase such products from specialty shops and department stores geared to providing more personal service in an upscale atmosphere. For low-risk products, such as toasters, the upper-class shopper is perfectly willing to buy a brand-name product from a discounter.

The social classes also differ in how much they search for information prior to and during shopping. Middle- and upper-class consumers tend to engage in more information search prior to making a purchase. For example, prior to buying appliances they may read newspapers, brochures, and test reports. In contrast, lower-class consumers are more apt to rely on in-store displays and salespeople.[77] In general, lower-class consumers have less product information. They are less informed about product prices and are no more likely to buy products "on sale" than upper-class consumers. Upper-class consumers are also less likely to use price as an indicator of quality. They tend to judge the quality of products on their merits rather than on their price.

Another study found that upper-class men are likely to play tennis or golf, jog, ski, attend social activities, read, and do political and community volunteer work. Men in the lower classes are more likely to play football, lift weights, ride motorcycles, or do nothing.[78] The research further revealed that the upper classes attend more concerts and college football games. Lower classes watch more television, do more fishing, and go to baseball games and drive-in movies more often.

Concerning exposure to the various media, the upper classes are more frequent readers of magazines and newspapers than lower classes.[79] In addition to watching less television, the upper classes tend to focus on current events, drama programs, and sports. Lower classes watch more soap operas, quiz shows, and situation comedies.[80]

Social Class and Income

One issue concerning social class is its relationship to household income. Some have argued that income is really a better predictor of buying behavior than social class. Early research on the issue was mixed. A study conducted in the mid-1970s found that income was a better predictor of the use or nonuse of entertainment services. However, social class better predicted the frequency of use of the services.[81]

More recently, research has shown that the better predictor depends on the type of product or service investigated.[82] Social class was found to be a better predictor of purchases that were not high cost but that symbolically represented life-styles and values. For example, usage of various food items, such as sweet beverages and wines, was predicted by social class. Income was a superior predictor of purchases of major appliances, as well as the frequency of usage of soft drinks, mixers, and distilled alcohol. A combination of social class and income was a good predictor of expensive status products such as autos and clothing.

Related to the income–social class debate is the **relative income hypothesis**. Research conducted in the early 1960s revealed that people within the same social class may have different consumption patterns based upon their relative incomes.[83] For example, individuals with high incomes in a social class were labeled **overprivileged**. Conversely, people with low incomes in the same class were labeled **underprivileged**. In their automobile purchases, overprivileged consumers were found to purchase higher-prestige autos.

What the relative income hypothesis reveals is that income cannot be ignored when one investigates consumers. One must remember, however, that income and social class are correlated. Those with higher incomes tend to have higher educations, more upscale occupations, nicer homes, better furniture, and so forth.

Just what is the correlation between income and social class? One eminent researcher estimated the correlation to be relatively low (around $r = 0.40$) in the 1980s.[84] Three reasons were cited for the relatively low correlation. First, social class has historically been based more on occupational differences than on income. Even in the 1990s, many blue-collar workers may earn more than white-collar workers, yet their social status is lower. Second, differences in age can lower the correlation. Young workers traditionally earn much less income than older workers. However, a young stockbroker making $40,000 is in the middle class, whereas a 50-year-old cabinet maker earning $40,000 is in the working class. Finally, family variation in the number of earners has affected the income–social class correlation. With increasing divorce rates it has become relatively common for a woman to head a family. Unfortunately, women traditionally earn less than men. Thus incomes of families headed by a female tend to be lower. In contrast, families where both spouses hold jobs will have relatively higher incomes. However, in most cases neither divorce nor two incomes will influence social class status—only the relative amounts of income available.

Spending Versus Saving

In general, the upper social classes are much more interested in saving than the lower social classes. In one study consumers were asked what they would do if their incomes were doubled for the next ten years.[85] Upper classes indicated that much of the money would be saved. Further, they specified how it would be saved. They frequently mentioned some type of investment vehicle for saving. In contrast, lower-class consumers more often indicated spending goals. When saving was mentioned, the vehicle was usually some type of low-interest-bearing savings account.

Psychological Differences Among the Classes

Many of the differences noted in the consumption behaviors of the social classes can be accounted for by certain differences in the way they psychologically view the world.[86] The middle classes tend to focus on the future. They are generally self-confident, are willing to take risks, believe that they can control their fate, and see their horizons as broad. The middle classes stress rationality, tend to have an urban identification, think abstractly, and see themselves tied to national happenings. In contrast, the lower classes focus on the present and past. They are concerned with security and limited in their horizons. They do not have a well-structured view of the world and are concerned with their family and themselves. Rationality is not emphasized in their buying processes.

Psychological differences in the social classes were demonstrated in a study that investigated how various groups of consumers differed in their perception of the symbolism of products.87 The results revealed that lower-class individuals tended to believe that those who owned big houses and nice cars obtained them because of "good luck." In contrast, consumers with higher social status attributed the ability to purchase status symbols to the self-motivation of the owner. Such results indicate more of a fatalistic view of life among the lower social classes. These psychological and life-style changes are summed up by the following quotation:

> For twenty years researchers have found that "working-class life styles have been almost impervious to change in their basic characteristics—i.e., the limited horizons, the centrality of family and clan. The chauvinistic devotion to nation and neighborhood have been little altered by the automobile, telephone, or television. The modernity—and change—that these people seek is in possessions, not in human relationships or "new ideas." For them, "keeping up with the times" focuses on the mechanical and recreational, and thus ease of labor and leisure is what they continue to pursue."[88]

Social Class and Life-styles

As a macroenvironmental force, social class standing strongly influences consumers' life-styles. Four generalizations can be made concerning the impact of social class on consumer life-styles. These generalizations are discussed in the paragraphs that follow and summarized in Table 18-11.

Social Class Influences Consumer Life-styles

Perhaps the most important contribution of social class to the understanding of consumer behavior is that it strongly influences a person's life-style. First discussed in Chapter 7, life-style refers to how one lives. Weber was perhaps the earliest researcher to link social class and life-style together, although he tended to view life-style as more closely linked to status than to class. Some consumer researchers have even argued that life-style is the "essence of social class."[89] The style of consumption (i.e., life-style) may be viewed as an expression of a particular social class. How consumers live is directly influenced by their education, household income, occupation, and type of house. Thus level of education tends to influence a person's activities, interests, opinions, values, and beliefs. Household income tends to influence the capacity to purchase consumer goods and to express interests. Occupation tends to influence the type of people with whom a person associates, as well as the types of products and services that are purchased to play the occupational role. Indeed, the products and services that a person must have to engage effectively in a particular role is called a *role-related product cluster*. Thus a stereotypic view of the role-related product cluster of a professor might be lots of books, an old Volvo, a slightly out-of-fashion sport coat with elbow patches, and a pair of poorly fitting spectacles.

Social Class Is Predictive of Resources Owned

Four resource dimensions have been identified that are influenced by social class—financial, social, cultural, and time. First, those in higher social classes tend to have greater financial resources because of their occupations or inherited wealth.

TABLE 18-11

Social Class and Consumer Life-styles

1. *Social class influences consumer life-styles.* Social classes are in part expressed through the life-style led by consumers. Similarly, to express a particular social class, a particular life-style should be led.
2. *Social class is predictive of resources owned.* The possession of financial, social, cultural, and time resources is predicted in part by an individual's social class.
3. *Goods and services may be purchased as status symbols.* Individuals may purchase goods and services to express their class membership. Goods and services that are owned by members of other classes are classified as fraudulent.
4. *The consumption of status symbols is a skill.* The ability to purchase appropriate material goods to represent one's current or aspired status is a learned skill. Surrogate consumers can be hired to assist the individual in making the correct status statement.

Second, as one moves higher in social class level, the ability to participate socially increases, and associations are made with those of higher social standing. In general, the level of social participation increases as social status increases. Social skill and social standing appear to be closely linked.[90] Third, those in higher social classes tend to have familiarity with cultural matters. In addition, higher education credentials provide "cultural capital" for individuals. Finally, those in higher social classes tend to have a broader time horizon than do those in lower social classes. Those with a restricted time horizon are at a competitive disadvantage in meeting the demands of the middle and upper classes. The higher social classes require people to have longer time horizons and to delay gratification while building personal skills through education. Those in higher social classes frequently have less "free time," but have a greater degree of flexibility in choosing the activities to spend their time on.

Goods and Services May Be Purchased as Status Symbols

An important concept is that products and services may be purchased as a means of showing membership in a particular social class. Goods and services may represent social class standing because of various restrictions that make it difficult for individuals not in the social class to own them. These restrictions tend to arise from the individuals in lower social classes not having the resources to purchase or effectively use the status symbols. For example, it takes a high level of income to purchase a Mercedes-Benz, a car that has come to represent membership in the lower-upper class for many individuals. Similarly, it takes a high level of educational resources to allow a person to read and enjoy magazines, such as *The New Yorker*, that are indicative of upper-middle-class standing.

It has long been recognized that to depict social status, people must display appropriate material items. The reason is that in today's modern world, we frequently encounter individuals who are strangers. The only way to ascertain the person's status is through visual cues. Thus one's social status is depicted visually through material goods. A problem exists, however, in portraying social class through material goods. If the ownership of a material symbol is diffused across levels of the class hierarchy, it becomes a **fraudulent symbol**.[91] That is, if members of different social classes display the same symbol of status, it will not accurately depict the meaning desired.

Indeed, for a material item to adequately symbolize social class standing, accuracy is required in both the encoding and decoding stages.[92] Ownership of the material item must be homogeneous within a single social class for accurate encoding to occur. Thus people within the class should consistently possess the material good. Examples of material symbols that are consistently owned by people within a social class (i.e., encoding accuracy) include furniture, clothing, and housing.[93] In addition, society as a whole must agree that possession of the material good symbolizes a particular social class standing. When a shared status meaning is attached to a material good by society at large, accuracy in decoding occurs. Examples of material symbols that society as a whole decodes in a consistent manner are clothing, health care, automobiles, and housing.

An example of a material symbol that is accurately encoded and decoded is the possession of hired household help. The presence of chauffeurs, cooks, and gardeners is indicative of an individual in the upper classes. A recent article reviewed the literature on status recognition in the 1980s.[94] It noted that during the 1960s and 1970s, a decline in the use of material goods as status symbols occurred. In part the trend may have resulted from a shift in the sentiments of Americans away from materialism to a more simple life-style. In addition, rising affluence during the time period may have made many material goods fraudulent. Only highly expensive items such as houses, yachts, stables, and private jet aircraft retained the ability to communicate status.[95] Indeed, the "radical chic" movement of the period involved higher social class individuals adopting the fashion styles of lower classes. Researchers who content analyzed advertisements also confirmed the trend toward a decrease in status-oriented themes during the 1960s in particular.[96]

Consumption of Status Symbols Is a Skill

The adroit purchase of goods and services can be used to solidify or help advance an individual's social class standing. Individuals who fail to represent their social class via the "correct" visible symbols risk scorn and the use of the disrespectful title "nouveau riche." For this reason, learning to make the correct purchases is a type of skill. In fact, a successful TV comedy series, "The Beverly Hillbillies," was built upon the problems of lower-class people suddenly thrust into the world of the lower-upper class.

An argument can be made that a great deal of status anxiety may currently exist in the United States. The number of consumption guides, fashion experts, interior decorators, and real estate professionals (all of whom emphasize location, location, location) suggest a great concern about making things look correct. People would not hire these surrogate consumers if the accurate display of symbolic material goods were unimportant. Indeed, the need to purchase the "correct" goods and services to support or help advance status has created an entire class of surrogate consumers.

Other Subcultures

Space limitations restrict a full discussion of all the various subcultures available for target marketing. As mentioned in the consumer vignette, Asian-Americans represent a fast-growing, highly educated, and high-income group of consumers. One company targeting Asian-Americans is Metropolitan Life Insurance Co. A senior vice president at the firm stated, "Asian Americans are our kind of market. They're family oriented and solidly educated, and they're looking for financial security.[97]

Subcultures are also formed based upon religious differences. In the United States religious groups specifically targeted by marketers include born-again Christians and Jews. Various pollsters have concluded that born-again Christians make up some 33% of the U.S. population—a tempting target for both religious and secular products.[98] Although it is much smaller, the Jewish subculture is also a tempting target because of their specific dietary needs and high incomes. Gender-based subcultures also exist. In a wide variety of products, ranging from disposable diapers to automobiles, marketers use different marketing mix strategies to reach male and female consumers.

A MANAGERIAL APPLICATIONS EXAMPLE

An excellent example of an industry heavily influenced by demographic and subcultural trends over the past 30 years is the toy industry. During the late 1950s and 1960s, the toy industry flourished. Members of the baby-boom generation were in their childhood. With their numbers expanding, the total market for toys grew rapidly. Although the growth of the industry slowed in the 1970s with the shrinking number of children born, sales were surprisingly strong. The reason was that the divorce rate increased and households became smaller. With each adult obligated to supply toys to the few children being born during the baby-bust years, sales of toys stayed strong. When births rose in the early 1980s as the baby boomers began to have children, toy manufacturers again got on the fast track. Companies like Toys 'R' Us did extremely well.

An executive at Coleco, another major toy manufacturer, identified how demographic and subcultural analyses have importance. He said that demographics are used in his company to develop profiles of customers for new product development (i.e., marketing mix strategy and segmentation), for research (i.e., market research), and for media planning (i.e., promotional strategy). As he said, "The idea is to know who we are selling to and how to reach them."[99]

The toy business, however, goes far beyond inexpensive presents for young children. Consider Cara, a precocious 8-year-old, who begins and ends each day thinking about horses. She collects Bryer model horses—which currently number more than 60 in her stable. She attends Bryer model horse shows and subscribes to a newsletter on model horses. At the model horse shows, collectors (mostly women in their thirties and forties and young girls from 6 to 12) buy and sell Man-of-War, Secretariat, and other famous models. In this female equivalent of baseball card collecting, exceptionally rare models can cost hundreds of dollars.

Men also collect toys. Indeed, if one subscribes to a magazine called *Toy Shop*, one finds hundreds of ads for old toys that are now collectibles. The serious collectors tend to be 35 to 54 years old. The readers of *Toy Shop* average over $50,000 in household income, and 70% have attended college. They spend on average over $2,000 on toy collections. What do they collect? Currently, toys that came out of the *Star Wars* movies are favored by many collectors. But the most valuable items tend to come from the 1950s and 1960s. One store owner who specializes in selling collectible toys uses the following rule of thumb to decide what collectors want: "If it screwed you up when you were growing up, I deal in it."[100]

The Consumer Behavior Analysis and the Managerial Implications

A number of concepts from this chapter apply to issues that face the toy industry. Of key importance is the role of the baby-boom generation. Currently, this group is in the middle of its years of child rearing. Because of the group's enormous size, the market for children's toys is flourishing. However, manufacturers must recognize that by the late 1990s, the number of new births will begin to decrease, causing potential problems for the industry. As shown in the managerial applications analysis in Table 18-12, the study of the baby-boom group should focus particularly upon the development of the marketing mix, segmentation, and environmental analysis. Environmental analysis should be conducted to track the changes in the size of the children's toy market. Segments of appropriate size and buying power can then be identified, and specific products can be developed and promoted for the target groups.

A second consumer concept of importance to toy manufacturers is the study of demographic changes in the population. Thus, in addition to carefully analyzing age trends, toy manufacturers should conduct broader-scale demographic analyses. Environmental analyses should be conducted to identify changes in the ethnic composition of the population, which may reveal new segments of consumers to be targeted. For example, the high growth rate of the Hispanic market (and the group's high fertility rate) may make Hispanic children a lucrative target market. Market research can be conducted to identify the unmet toy needs of Hispanic kids, and products can then be developed for them.

The specific needs and interests of various social classes should also be considered by toy manufacturers. In the managerial applications example, an adult segment of toy collectors was identified. When analyzing from the perspective of social class standing, one readily recognizes that, on the basis of education, income, and occupation, this segment is largely made up of middle-class consumers. This information can be used to segment the marketplace and to develop elements of the marketing mix. For example, by

TABLE 18-12

Managerial Applications Analysis of the Toy Industry

Consumer Concepts	*Managerial Applications*
Baby-boom generation	*Segmentation*—Target baby-boom parents and their children as customers.
	Environmental analysis—Track changes in the size, age, and buying power of the baby-boom generation.
	Marketing mix—Develop promotional strategy that is consistent with values of baby-boom parents. Develop toy products that are consistent with values, needs, and wants of the baby-boom generation.
Ethnic groups	*Environmental analysis*—Track changes in size of key ethnic groups.
	Segmentation—Target ethnic groups growing rapidly in size, such as Hispanics and Asians.
Social class	*Segmentation*—Identify key market segments based upon social class that may have divergent needs and wants for toys. Can combine with other subcultural variables, such as age and sex, to pinpoint specific target groups. For example, preteen, middle-class girls are a target for model horses. Similarly, middle-class males may be target for adult toys.
	Product—Develop toy products and promote them in a manner that meets the needs of the social class subcultures identified.

knowing that the collectors tend to come from the middle class, marketers can structure accordingly the pricing (i.e., moderate prices will work best) and promotional strategy (sellers will not be able to use hype tactics because of the sophistication of the buyers).

SUMMARY

A subculture is a group of people that represents a subdivision of a national culture. One or more unifying features distinguish the group, whose members share patterns of behavior distinct from that found in the national culture. Demographic characteristics are often used to identify subcultures, such as age, nationality, and religion.

Age groupings having particular importance for marketers in the 1990s are the baby-boom generation and the elderly. Although not a subculture in the strict sense of the word, the baby-boom generation does have extreme importance to marketers because of their size and buying power. With the baby-boom generation now in their thirties and forties, their influence is increasing rapidly as they move toward their peak earning years. The elderly represent a legitimate subculture because of their distinct life-styles and buying patterns.

Relatively little has been written about the African-American subculture over the past ten years, and marketers have downplayed somewhat the importance of this large market segment. Factors shaping the African-American subculture include a common racial background, a history of economic and educational deprivation, and a pattern of racial discrimination. The Hispanic subculture is the second-fastest-growing ethnic subculture in the United States. A high birthrate and massive inflows of immigrants contribute to the rapid increase in the number of Hispanics. The subculture is united by a common religion, a common language, and common nationalities of origin. Four important Hispanic groups exist in the United States—Cubans, Puerto Ricans, Mexicans, and Hispanos. Despite differences in when these groups arrived and in their previous homelands, they can all be considered as subsegments of the large Hispanic group.

Another basis for the classification of subcultures is the region of a country. A region may develop a distinct subculture for several reasons. Differences in the religion, ethnicity, and nationality of the people who settle in an area can be extremely important in developing a distinct set of values and behavior patterns. For example, Utah has a distinct subculture in large part because of the influence of the Mormon church, which dominates the state. Mormon doctrine teaches a conservative way of life with a heavy emphasis on the family and on helping others. Hispanic influence is pervasive throughout the Southwest.

The social classes also represent distinct subcultures. Social classes are the relatively permanent and homogeneous strata in a society. A variety of factors distinguish the social classes, including occupation, wealth, education, possessions, values, housing, and associations. For marketers the study of social class has implications for each of the marketing management areas. In particular, a market may be segmented along lines of social class. Products can be developed, promoted, and positioned to appeal to members of a particular class. Managers must ensure that environmental analysis and market research take place to identify potential changes in the composition of the social classes. Such changes can act as environmental threats or opportunities to the firm.

A number of social class scales have been developed. The most common variables used to measure social class are occupation, education, and house type. Family income is another important variable to consider when investigating social class. For marketers, four target groups based on social class exist—a broad upper class, a white-collar middle class, an affluent working class, and a poor lower class.

It may be argued that the most important contribution of social class to the understanding of consumer behavior is that it strongly influences consumers' life-styles. Some researchers have argued that life-style is the essence of social class. Social class membership is often predictive of the resources owned by consumers. In addition, products and services may be purchased for the symbolic value that they have in representing a particular social class. One can even view the consumption of status symbols as a skill that can be developed. If a consumer is uncomfortable with his or her skill level, surrogate consumers can be paid to assist in making purchases that represent the appropriate social status.

KEY TERMS

African-American subculture
baby-boom generation
baby bust
cluster analysis
demographic variables
ethnicity
fertility rate
fraudulent symbol
generation X
geodemographics
Hispanic subculture
immigration
lower-lower class
lower-upper class
mature consumer
middle class
mortality rate
overprivileged
regional subcultures
relative income hypothesis
social class
social class hierarchy
status crystallization
status groups
subculture
underprivileged
upper-lower class
upper-middle class
upper-upper class
working class

REVIEW QUESTIONS

1. Identify six different types of subcultures in the United States.
2. What is the definition of the term subculture? How are subcultures different from demographic variables?
3. Describe the age distribution of the baby-boom group of consumers. Describe the impact of the baby boom on two industries.
4. Table 18-1 presents projected U.S. population trends between 1992 and 2005. Based upon the table, identify the age groups that will increase and decrease during the time period.
5. What are the various factors that influence the accuracy of age projections of the population?
6. Identify three ways in which the elderly process information differently than the rest of the adult population.
7. Identify four factors that make the African-American subculture an important target market. What are the factors that companies should consider when deciding whether to market directly to African-Americans?
8. What factors make the Hispanic subculture the second-fastest-growing group in the United States?
9. Four segments of Hispanics have been identified, based upon their Spanish ancestry. Identify the four segments; indicate their relative sizes and where they are located.
10. What are the reasons for regional shifts in population?
11. Define the concept of social class. How do marketers tend to use this concept in comparison to sociologists?

12. Identify the social classes as defined by Coleman and found in Table 18-9. What is the relative size of each of the social classes?
13. Indicate the four variables most frequently used to assess social class.
14. Delineate four of the six problems identified in the use of the social class concept by marketers.
15. Provide two examples each of how upper and lower social classes differ in shopping patterns and in leisure activities.
16. What is the correlation between social class and income? For what types of products may social class be a better predictor of buying patterns than income?
17. Discuss the relative income hypothesis.
18. Identify the ways that social class may influence consumer life-styles.

DISCUSSION QUESTIONS

1. Subcultures can be found in most large collections of people. Consider the university or college you are now attending. Identify as many subcultures as you can within your school. Describe the norms, values, and behaviors of the subcultures that set them apart.
2. Because of the long lead times required for planning and bringing new products to market, managers must often look five to ten years into the future. What marketing opportunities and problems might the baby-boom group present to managers between the years 1995 and 2000?
3. Suppose that you were the marketing director for an investment group that decided to develop a shopping center specifically targeted to the elderly market. What types of services, stores, and amenities would you attempt to provide in the shopping center? What problems might be encountered in targeting a shopping center specifically for the elderly?
4. Compare and contrast how a company might attempt to market a product, such as blue jeans, to African-Americans, Hispanics, and Anglos. Specifically consider the selection of media and the development of advertising themes.
5. Suppose that you were marketing director for a company that planned to open a chain of new department stores targeted to consumers with incomes above $80,000. What geographic considerations would influence your decisions as to where to place the stores?
6. Identify a product for which the marketing mix must be varied across the geographic regions of the United States. State the reasons why the marketing mix should be varied for the product.
7. Consider what subcultural variables you would use to divide the United States geographically. Draw a map of the United States, show the boundaries of the regions that you identify, and justify your analysis.
8. Consider the types of department stores in your region of the country. Identify the social classes that each of these stores appears to target.
9. Just as one can assign people to social classes, one can also rank institutions of higher education into prestige categories. Identify two universities or colleges that can be placed into each of the following prestige classifications: highest prestige, moderately high prestige, middle prestige, moderately low prestige, and low prestige. What criteria delineate how the universities are classified?
10. Why is it that people in the United States (including instructors, students, and the author of this text) tend to be uncomfortable discussing the topic of social class?
11. Based upon the knowledge you have of your friends and acquaintances, do you think that social class mobility is increasing or decreasing in the United States? What are the primary means of gaining mobility today in the United States?
12. Conduct a quick survey among ten of your acquaintances. Attempt to identify the types of goods and services that they purchase as status symbols.

ENDNOTES

1. "America's Super Minority," *Fortune*, November 24, 1986, pp. 148–164.
2. Thomas Exter, "How Many Hispanics?" *American Demographics*, May 1987, pp. 36–39, 67.
3. Patricia Braus, "What Does Hispanic Mean?" *American Demographics*, June 1993, pp. 46–49, 58.
4. Julia Lieblich, "If You Want a Big, New Market," *Fortune*, November 21, 1988, pp. 181–188.
5. Carlos Garcia, "Hispanic Market Is Accessible, If Research Is Designed Correctly," *Marketing News*, January 4, 1988, p. 46.
6. Alan Otten, "Warning of Generational Fighting Draws Critics—Led by the Elderly," *The Wall Street Journal*, January 13, 1987, p. 31.
7. Bradly Johnson, "The Gay Quandary," *Advertising Age*, January 18, 1993, pp. 29, 35.
8. Gary Levin, "Mainstream Domino Effect," *Advertising Age*, January 16, 1993, p. 32.
9. Robert E. Pitts, Guest Editorial, "The Hispanic Subculture: Subcultural Complexity and Marketing Opportunity," *Psychology and Marketing*, Vol. 3, no. 4 (1986), pp 243–246.
10. Suein L. Hwang, "Kosher-Food Firms Dive into the Mainstream," *The Wall Street Journal*, April 1, 1993, pp. B1, B6.
11. D. O. Arnold, *The Sociology of Subcultures* (Berkeley, CA: Glendasary Press, 1970).
12. R. T. Reynolds, B. Robey, and C. Russell, "Demographics of the 1980s," *American Demographics*, Vol. 2 (January 1980), pp. 11–19.
13. Ibid.
14. "Americans Change," *Business Week*, February 20, 1978, pp. 64–80.
15. Campbell Gibson, "The Four Baby Booms," *American Demographics*, November 1993, pp. 37–40.
16. U.S. Department of Commerce, Bureau of the Census, *Statistical Abstract of the United States, 1988*, 108th ed. (Washington, DC: U.S. Government Printing Office, 1988), p. 15.
17. Landon Jones, "The Baby-Boom Consumer," *American Demographics*, Vol. 3 (February 1981), pp. 28–35.
18. Ibid.
19. Ronald Alsop, "Blue Jeans Falter as Main Market Ages," *The Wall Street Journal*, November 9, 1988, p. B1.
20. Betsy Morris, "Many Baby Boomers Find They Are Caught in a Financial Squeeze," *The Wall Street Journal*, December 17, 1985, pp. 1, 12.
21. Ronald Alsop, "Busters May Replace Boomers as the Darlings of Advertisers," *The Wall Street Journal*, November 12, 1987, p. 35.
22. Jan Bryant Quinn, "Investing in the Baby Bust," *Newsweek*, November 23, 1987, p. 57.
23. Scott Donation, "The Media Wakes Up to Generation-X," *Advertising Age*, February 1, 1993, pp. 16–17.
24. Raymond Serafin and Cleveland Horton, "X Marks the Spot for Car Marketing," *Advertising Age*, August 9, 1993, p. 8.
25. Gregory Spencer and John Long, "The Census Bureau Projections," *American Demographics*, Vol. 5 (April 1983), pp. 24–31.
26. Bryant Robey, "Age in America," *American Demographics*, Vol. 3 (July/August 1981), pp. 14–19.
27. Gabrielle Sandor, "Attitude (Not Age) Defines the Mature Market," *American Demographics*, January 1994, pp. 18–21.
28. Rick Christie, "Marketers Err by Treating Elderly as Uniform Group," *The Wall Street Journal*, October 31, 1988, pp. B1, B3.
29. Fabian Linden and Paul Ryscavage, "How We Live" (New York: The Conference Board and Washington, DC: U.S. Bureau of the Census, 1986).

30. Catherine A. Cole and Siva K. Balasubramanian, "Age Differences in Consumers' Search for Information: Public Policy Implications," *Journal of Consumer Research*, Vol. 20 (June 1993), pp. 157–169.

31. Jack Botwinick, *Aging and Behavior: A Comprehensive Integration of Research Findings*, 2nd ed. (New York: Springer Publishing, 1978).

32. L. G. Schiffman, "Perceived Risk in New Product Trial by Elderly Consumers," *Journal of Marketing Research*, Vol. 9 (February 1972), pp. 106–108.

33. Rose L. Johnson, "Age and Social Activity as Correlates of Television Orientation: A Replication and Extension," *Advances in Consumer Research*, Vol. 20, Leigh McAlister and Michael L. Rothschild, eds. (Provo, UT: Association for Consumer Research, 1993), pp. 257–261.

34. Lois Underhill and Franchellie Cadwell, "What Age Do You Feel?" *The Journal of Consumer Marketing*, Vol. 1 (Summer 1983), pp. 18–27. Also, see Benny Barak and Leon Schiffman, "Cognitive Age: A Nonchronological Age Variable," in *Advances in Consumer Research*, Vol. 8, Kent B. Monroe, ed. (Ann Arbor, MI: Association for Consumer Research, 1981), p. 604; and Barbara Stern and Stephen Gould, "Ideal Age Concepts: An Exploration," in *Advances in Consumer Research*, Vol. 15, Michael J. Houston, ed. (Provo, UT: Association for Consumer Research, 1988), pp. 146–152.

35. U.S. Department of Commerce, Bureau of the Census, *Statistical Abstract of the United States, 1986*, No. 690, "Income, Expenditures, and Wealth" (Washington, DC: U.S. Government Printing Office, 1986), p. 422.

36. Herbert Allen, "Grass-Roots Involvement Touches the Market's Heart," *Advertising Age*, November 29, 1982, pp. M10, M11.

37. Thomas Barry and Michael Harvey, "Marketing to Heterogeneous African-American Consumers," *California Management Review*, Vol. 17 (Winter 1974), pp. 50–57.

38. Lafayette Jones, "An Uncompromising Challenge," *Advertising Age*, November 29, 1982, pp. M12, M14.

39. Lydia A. McKinley-Floyd, J. R. Smith, and Hudson Nwakanma, "The Impact of Social Class on African American Consumer Behavior: An Interdisciplinary Perspective," in *Marketing Theory and Applications*, C. Whan Park and Daniel C. Smith, eds. (Chicago: American Marketing Association, 1994), pp. 384–389.

40. Thomas H. Stevenson, "A Content Analysis of the Portrayal of African-Americans in Trade Publication Advertising," *Journal of Current Issues and Research in Advertising*, Vol. 14 (Spring 1992), pp. 67–74.

41. Laura Bird, "Critics Shoot at New Colt 45 Campaign," *The Wall Street Journal*, February 17, 1993, p. B1.

42. Judy Cohen and Carol Kaufman, "Consumption Choice Within the African-American Extended Family," *Advances in Consumer Research*, Vol. 19, John Sherry, Jr., and Brian Sternthal, eds. (Provo, UT: Association for Consumer Research, 1992), pp. 338–345.

43. Maurice Ferre, "Decade of the Hispanic," *Advertising Age*, February 15, 1982, pp. M14, M16.

44. Jack Honomichl, "Never Lose Sight of Hispanic Pride," *Advertising Age*, February 15, 1982, pp. M38, M39.

45. Cheryl Russell, "The News About Hispanics," *American Demographics*, Vol. 5 (March 1983), pp. 15–25.

46. B. G. Yovovich, "Cultural Pride Galvanizes Heritages," *Advertising Age*, February 15, 1982, pp. M9, M44.

47. B. A. Brusco, "Hispanic Marketing: New Application of Old Methodologies," *Theme*, May/June 1981, pp. 8–9.

48. Danny Bellinger and Humbato Valencia, "Understanding the Hispanic Market," *Business Horizons*, May/June 1982, p. 49.

49. Ed Fitch, "How Bush Courted the Hispanic Vote," *Advertising Age*, November 7, 1988, p. 33.

50. Joel Saegert, Francis Piron, and Rosemary Jimenez, "Do Hispanics Constitute a Market Segment?" *Advances in Consumer Research*, Vol. 19, John Sherry, Jr., and Brian Sternthal, eds. (Provo, UT: Association for Consumer Research, 1992), pp. 28–33.

51. "Hispanics: Markets Within a Market," *Sales and Marketing Management*, July 27, 1981, p. A33.

52. Ibid.

53. John Sugg, "Miami's Latino Market Spans Two Continents," *Advertising Age*, February 15, 1982, pp. M9, M44.

54. Theodore Gage, "Beer Still Tops Wine Spirits," *Advertising Age*, February 15, 1982, pp. M10, M11, M22, M23.

55. Robert E. Wilkes and Humberto Valencia, "Shopping-Related Characteristics of Mexican Americans and African-Americans," *Psychology and Marketing*, Vol. 3 (1986), pp. 247–259.

56. Joe Schwartz, "Fourth to Florida," *American Demographics*, October 1987, p. 14.

57. Joel Garreau, *The Nine Nations of North America* (Boston: Houghton Mifflin, 1981).

58. Lynn Kahle, "The Nine Nations of North America and the Value Basis of Geographic Segmentation," *Journal of Marketing*, Vol. 50 (April 1986), pp. 37–47.

59. David J. Curry, *The New Marketing Research Systems: How to Use Strategic Database Information for Better Marketing Decisions* (New York: John Wiley and Sons, Inc., 1993).

60. Ibid.

61. Alix M. Freedman, "National Firms Find That Selling Local Tastes Is Costly, Complex," *The Wall Street Journal*, February 9, 1987, p. 17.

62. Ibid.

63. Raymond Serafin, "Chevy Spends Big in Texas," *Advertising Age*, February 3, 1986, p. 69.

64. Jennifer Lawrence, "Frito Play: New Basics Strategy Takes on Regional Rivals," *Advertising Age*, March 30, 1987, pp. 1, 70, 71.

65. Richard Coleman, "The Continuing Significance of Social Class in Marketing," *Journal of Consumer Research*, Vol. 10 (December 1983), pp. 265–280.

66. John Koten, "A Once Tightly Knit Middle Class Finds Itself Divided and Uncertain," *The Wall Street Journal*, March 9, 1987, p. 21.

67. David Wessel, "U.S. Rich and Poor Increase in Numbers; Middle Loses Ground," *The Wall Street Journal*, September 22, 1986, pp. 1, 14.

68. R. H. Tawney, *Equality* (London: Union Books), 1981.

69. James Carmen, *The Application of Social Class in Market Segmentation* (Berkeley, CA: Institute of Business and Economic Research, 1965).

70. W. J. Warner, M. Meeker, and K. Eels, *Social Class in America: Manual of Procedure for the Measurement of Social Status* (Chicago: Science Research Associates, 1949).

71. Joan Throckmorton, "Targeting the Fragmented Middle Class," *Direct Marketing*, August 1982, pp. 70–71.

72. Marvin Roscoe, A. Leclaire, and L. Schiffman, "Theory and Management Applications of Demographics in Buying Behavior," in *Foundations of Consumer and Industrial Buying Behavior*, Arch G. Woodside, J. Sheth, and P. Bennett, eds. (New York: American Elsevier, 1977), pp. 74–75.

73. Dean Ellis, "Speech and Social Status in America," *Social Forces*, Vol. 45 (March 1967), pp 431–437.

74. Leonard Schatzman and A. Strauss, "Social Class and Modes of Communication," *American Journal of Sociology*, Vol. 60 (January 1955), pp. 329–338.

75. Gerhard Lenski, "Status Crystallization: A Non-Vertical Dimension of Social Status," *American Sociological Review*, Vol. 21 (August 1956), pp. 458–464.

76. Stuart Rich and Subhash Jain, "Social Class and Life Cycle as Predictors of Shopping Behavior," *Journal of Marketing Research*, Vol. 5 (February 1968), pp. 43–44.

77. V. Kanti Prasad, "Socioeconomic Product Risk and Patronage Preferences of Retail Shoppers," *Journal of Marketing*, Vol. 39 (July 1975), pp. 42–47.

78. *The Playboy Report on American Men*, survey conducted by Louis Harris and Associates (New York: Playboy Enterprises, 1979), pp. 53–54, 57.

79. Leah Rozen, "Coveted Consumers Rate Magazines Over TV: MPA," *Advertising Age*, August 20, 1979, p. 64.

80. Sidney J. Levy, "Social Class and Consumer Behavior," in *On Knowing the Consumer*, Joseph W. Newman, ed. (New York: John Wiley, 1966), p. 155.

81. R. D. Hisrich and Michael Peters, "Selecting the Superior Segmentation Correlate," *Journal of Marketing*, Vol. 38 (July 1974), pp. 60–63.

82. Charles M. Schaninger, "Social Class Versus Income Revisited: An Empirical Investigation," *Journal of Marketing Research*, Vol. 18 (May 1981), pp. 192–208.

83. Richard P. Coleman, "The Significance of Social Stratification in Selling," in *Marketing: A Mature Discipline*, Martin L. Bell, ed. (Chicago: American Marketing Association, 1960), pp. 171–184.

84. Coleman, "Continuing Significance of Social Class."

85. Ibid.

86. Pierre Martineau, "Social Classes and Shopping Behavior," *Journal of Marketing*, Vol. 23 (October 1958), pp. 121–130.

87. Russell Belk, Robert Mayer, and Kenneth Bahn, "The Eye of the Beholder: Individual Differences in Perceptions of Consumption Symbolism," in *Advances in Consumer Research*, Vol. 9, Andrew Mitchell, ed. (Ann Arbor, MI: Association for Consumer Research, 1981), pp. 523–529.

88. Cited in Coleman, "Continuing Significance of Social Class."

89. J. H. Myers and Jonathan Guttman, "Life Style: The Essence of Social Class," in *Lifestyle and Psychographics*, William Wells, ed. (Chicago: American Marketing Association, 1974), pp. 235–256.

90. Much of this section is based upon ideas suggested by James Fisher, "Social Class and Consumer Behavior: The Relevance of Class and Status," in *Advances in Consumer Research*, Vol. 14, Melanie Wallendorf and Paul Anderson, eds. (Provo, UT: Association for Consumer Research, 1987), pp. 492–496.

91. Erving Goffman, "Symbols of Class Status," *British Journal of Sociology*, Vol. 2 (December 1951), pp. 294–304.

92. Russell Belk, "Developmental Recognition of Consumption Symbolism," *Journal of Consumer Research*, Vol. 9 (June 1982), pp. 887–897.

93. Scott Dawson and Jill Cavell, "Status Recognition in the 1980s: Invidious Distinction Revisited," in *Advances in Consumer Research*, Vol. 14, Melanie Wallendorf and Paul Anderson, eds. (Provo, UT: Association for Consumer Research, 1987), pp. 487–491.

94. Ibid.

95. Paul Blumberg, "The Decline and Fall of the Status Symbol: Some Thoughts on Status in Post-Industrial Society," *Social Problems*, Vol. 21 (April 1974), pp. 480–498.

96. Russell Belk and Richard Pollay, "Images of Ourselves: The Good Life in Twentieth Century Advertising," *Journal of Consumer Research*, Vol. 11 (March 1985), pp. 887–897.

97. Ronald Alsop, "Firms Translate Sales Pitches to Appeal to Asian-Americans," *The Wall Street Journal*, April 10, 1986, p. 27.

98. Brad Edmondson, "Bringing in the Sheaves," *American Demographics*, August 1988, pp. 28–32, 57.

99. David Finlay, "Demographics for Fun and Games," *American Demographics*, Vol. 3 (November 1981), pp. 38–39.

100. S. K. List, "More than Fun and Games," *American Demographics*, August 1991, pp. 44–47.

Marketing in the Ghetto

In May 1991 the Concourse Plaza Shopping Center opened in one of the worst sections of the Bronx. Its first day it sold over $250,000 of merchandise to 10,000 customers. The developer of the shopping center said, "Until recently, most retailers have been too scared to go into inner-city areas. The developers chased easy deals in the suburbs. But now that the suburbs are saturated, the greatest opportunities are in the inner cities." Indeed, a sort of retailing vacuum exists in the inner cities. As a result, savvy marketers are rediscovering profits in these areas. For example, Woolworth's has developed a corporate strategy of entering the ghetto areas under appropriate circumstances. An executive said, "If we see a need in the community, we're willing to take a risk and go in there."

As Woolworth's is discovering, marketing in the inner city is different from that in the suburbs. For example, different assortments in the sizes of shoes are required. Similarly, the customers prefer different colors to those liked by customers in the suburbs. Although security costs are higher, the price of land and buildings is lower. As a result, Woolworth's inner-city stores enjoy profit margins a full percentage point higher than those in the suburbs.

Some argue that the opportunities for grocery stores are even higher than for department stores. In the inner city, most food stores are bodegas—small convenience stores—that must charge high prices. As a result, larger grocery stores (e.g., Tops in the Bronx) have done well. One executive said, "Quality retailers will always do well here because their competition is shoddy, overpriced merchandisers."

Those with experience in managing retail stores in the ghetto say that inner cities should be viewed as Third World, undeveloped countries. Just as Americans tell the Poles, the Peruvians, and the Bangladeshis "to free your markets from government control and encourage private enterprise," the same advice holds for the inner city. Analysts argue that ghetto areas have become pockets of socialism in the United States, because federal, state, and local governments have become the dominant economic force. For example, in one area of East Harlem, called "El Barrio," the city government owns 62% of the land and two-thirds of the residents live in public housing.

One concept that clearly does not work in the inner cities are huge, politically inspired projects. Big efforts, such as the multimillion-dollar effort to restore the Apollo Theater in Harlem, have resulted in bankruptcy. Instead, what is needed, according to one Peruvian economist, is to "unleash the innate entrepreneurial energies of their people."

One of the biggest problems for such entrepreneurs is access to capital. Community banks have begun to help in some cities, such as Chicago. In some cases informal sources of credit are created. For example, Korean grocers can obtain credit from revolving credit associations. Similarly, West Indians can become members of "sousou" groups, whose members make periodic payments into a pot. Each can take a turn at receiving the whole pot. In another instance small businesses form into groups of five or so. Each receives credit, but if any fail, the entire group loses its credit. The resulting peer pressure forces the members to work extra hard.

Overall, great opportunities exist in the inner cities. For example, one analysis done of East Harlem concluded that its residents have a yearly buying potential of $374 million. But, because retailers have shied away, sales amount to only $192 million. The difference goes to suburban stores to which the residents must travel long distances.

QUESTIONS

1. Define the problems faced by a retailer considering entry into an inner-city area.
2. What consumer behavior concepts from the chapter apply to the case?
3. Take the perspective of a retailer considering the possibility of entering an inner city. Develop a managerial applications table for the retailer. Discuss the managerial issues that the retailer must face that result from the consumer analysis.

Based upon Mark Alpert, "The Ghetto's Hidden Wealth," *Fortune*, July 29, 1991, pp. 167–173.

Chapter

19

*Cross-cultural and International Issues in Consumer Behavior**

* This chapter was written by John C. Mowen and Michael S. Minor.

CONSUMER VIGNETTE

Marketing Across Cultures

As the importance of exports increases for U.S. corporations, the study of consumers from diverse cultures takes on increased importance. Consider the following quotation: "In Germany, everything is forbidden unless it's allowed. In Britain, everything is allowed unless it's forbidden. And in France, everything is allowed even if it's forbidden."[1]

The quotation says much about the differences in the culture of the three Western industrialized nations. Recognizing differences in the life-style patterns and customs of people in different cultures is a major managerial problem for those engaging in international marketing. For example, a medical doctor in India was trying to figure out why his patients who had leg amputations kept throwing away the artificial feet that he so painstakingly fitted. Patients were using crutches rather than the satch foot, which was well designed and completely accepted in Western societies. The doctor investigated the problem and realized that Indians tend to live on the ground. They sit on the ground with crossed legs—the stiff satch foot would not allow such a movement. The doctor then designed a new foot with a flexible rubber ankle. The jaipur foot, which allowed a person to sit on the ground, was an immediate success.[2]

Tastes and preferences for food may also differ widely across cultures. New England lobstermen hated the prickly sea urchins that drove tasty lobsters into deep water. Recently, however, attitudes toward the sea urchins have begun to change. It seems that the Japanese love the taste of uni, the orange-yellow reproductive organs of the sea urchin. Americans, however, have a difficult time swallowing the stuff. When the owner of a uni processing plant in Maine ate the delicacy in front of a *Wall Street Journal* reporter, the workers cringed. Heads turned, eyes rolled, and one worker screamed, "Oh my God! He's eating the stuff. You're gross."[3]

When marketing in foreign cultures, major mistakes can be made if differences in lifestyles are ignored. For example, Procter & Gamble's initial attempts to sell disposable diapers in Japan were largely unsuccessful. Assuming that the diaper-changing habits of American and Japanese mothers were the same, P&G marketed the same diapers in both countries. Extremely slow sales, however, caused P&G to rethink the assumption. It seems that Japanese moms change their babies' diapers more than twice as frequently as American moms. Thus they wanted thin diapers, which could be stored easily. A Japanese company caught on more quickly and brought out a thin disposable diaper, the Moony, that quickly gained a 23% market share. A P&G executive said, "It was clear that we were out of the ballgame."[4]

One class of American products that frequently succeeds abroad is the cinema export. American-made movies have strong appeal to many overseas audiences. Because of the high profit potential, a movie will be distributed overseas within about six months of its release in the United States. Despite their general popularity, it can be difficult to predict which American-made films will be popular overseas. For example, the "Rambo" movies were particularly well received in the Middle East. (In Lebanon the character was perceived by some to be a fellow terrorist.) Similarly, while Al Pacino is a well-known actor here, he is a bigger star abroad. Posters for *Scent of a Woman* displayed in the United States featured Pacino less prominently than did the posters used overseas.[5]

While pop culture is diffused in the United States via television and movies, in Japan another media vehicle is employed—comic books, called *manga*. As one scholar said, "Manga is the dominant force in Japanese pop culture, the way television is in the U.S." Thus in one story an ex-baseball slugger, Astigmia "Sam" Yagami, saves the voluptuous blonde Maki from American thugs. The action takes place inside a deserted baseball stadium, where Sam annihilates the American villains with a shower of machine-gun bullets and hand grenades. After Sam rushes Maki to safety, she stands naked in front of Sam and says, "This is your reward. Have your way with me."[6] (Clearly, as in American culture, Japanese pop culture also reveals sexism.)

Cultural differences are also reflected in religious preferences and symbols. For example, Japan's Yokohama Rubber Company pulled hundreds of off-road tires from the market in Brunei after complaints from the Muslim community. It seems that the tread leaves a design that resembles a verse in the Koran.[7]

INTRODUCTION

The importance of understanding culture is well illustrated when marketers unsuccessfully sell their products abroad. By recognizing the differences between their own culture and that of the targeted society, managers can avoid multimillion-dollar mistakes. On the other hand, diverse cultures often share certain interests. For example, enthusiasm for basketball is exploding throughout Europe, and Michael Jordan is an American symbol of the sport even though he has retired. The ad for Nike basketball shoes in Figure 19-1 promotes the Air Jordan shoe to French-speaking cultures by showing Jordan engaged in a slam dunk.

The chapter-opening vignette deals with a number of aspects of how consumer behavior concepts apply across diverse cultures. The problem with the satch foot in India illustrates the role of **cultural rituals** in consumer behavior. The Indian ritual of sitting on the ground and discussing politics, family affairs, and business with

Figure 19-1 Michael Jordan has become an American symbol and his popularity extends to the marketing of basketball shoes in French-speaking cultures. (Courtesy of Nike, Inc.)

others doomed the rigid satch foot. The vignette also indicates the importance of carefully analyzing the life-styles of the people in different cultures to assess whether a product will fit the "everyday" behavior patterns of a different culture. The difference in the interpretation of Rambo in the United States and Lebanon indicates how a character can symbolize completely different qualities in two cultures. The discussion of manga illustrates how cultural values can be communicated within a culture. The story of "Sam" Yagami saving the buxom blonde from American thugs says a great deal about certain cultural values in Japan. Just as the xenophobia of Americans is displayed when the Japanese are portrayed as villains in American movies (e.g., Odd Jobs in *Goldfinger* and many of the Japanese in *Rising Sun*), the Japanese display their own fear and dislike of foreigners by portraying Americans as thugs in their manga.

However one defines culture, it is important to remember that **cultures** and **nations** are not the same. A nation can be precisely identified, but cultures cannot.[8] For example, Japan is a country with definite borders, but the Japanese carry their culture with them when they visit as tourists or when they decide to emigrate to another country.

Cross-cultural Use of Symbols

Differences in customs are readily seen in the use of **cultural symbols**. Cultural symbols are signs that have meanings peculiar to a specific society or group. For example, the practice of exchanging business cards *(meishi)* has a great symbolic function. The great care taken in wrapping and packaging plays a role in the spiritual and cultural life of the country. In addition, the Japanese have a great fondness for borrowing words from other cultures and using them in their promotional materials. The use of foreign words in promotional materials may have several symbolic meanings for the Japanese audience. The foreign words may connote something new or modern, they may indicate a Western influence, and they may symbolize prestige.

The symbolic meaning of various holidays also varies across cultures. For example, in the Japanese culture Christmas has little to do with celebrating the birth of Jesus. Instead, Christmas Eve (which is considered more important than the day after) is to young people a night for lovers, so hotels are booked up to a year in advance. For everyone, it's a good day to eat fried chicken and strawberry shortcake. On Christmas Eve Kentucky Fried Chicken's Japan unit sells about five times that of an average day.[9]

The symbolic meaning of nonverbal communication can also create problems in the international arena. For example, in 1993 AT&T launched its "i Plan" around the world. In print advertisements that appeared in the United States, the dot above the "i" in "i Plan" was replaced by a thumbs-up sign. A problem occurred, however, when the symbol was considered for the Russian and Polish markets. In those countries, it makes a big difference whether the viewer sees the palm of the hand or the back of the hand. It seems that a "thumbs-up" sign in which the palm is seen conveys a highly negative meaning to Poles and Russians. As a result, a decision was made to portray the "thumbs-up" sign from a back-of-the-hand perspective.[10]

Knowledge of the meaning of symbols is particularly important when a company begins to market its products or services internationally. The next section discusses this important issue.

INTERNATIONAL MARKETING AND CONSUMER BEHAVIOR

For international marketing to succeed, managers must have an excellent understanding of foreign cultures. As such, **cross-cultural analysis** involves the study of the values, attitudes, language, and customs of other societies.

Is international marketing something that students in Iowa, Texas, New York, and California should be concerned about? Yes! So far in the 1990s, exports have accounted for more than 11% of the gross national product of the United States, almost doubling since 1970. If we count both imports and exports of merchandise, this figure amounts to more than 50% of the country's total output of goods. Even the farming-oriented states of the Great Plains depend upon exports of grains to foreign countries. A particularly important area of growth for U.S. firms is the export of services.

An international marketing scholar eloquently made the case that U.S. firms simply are not trying hard enough to trade internationally. For instance, the port city of Hong Kong has no legal barriers to entry, yet the United States is not represented by one trading company there. The cars driven are European and Japanese, and no American department stores or supermarkets can be found. Based upon our performance in Hong Kong, the researcher argued that American companies would be disinclined to significantly improve trade with Japan, even if Japan dropped all import duties. The United States must dispense with parochialism and do the hard work of traveling, of learning languages and customs, and of learning foreign markets, the researcher stated, in order to change the trade picture that threatens to make it a second-rate nation.[11]

Table 19-1 identifies seven categories of differences in foreign cultures that affect international business. Of these, perhaps the most important are differences in

TABLE 19-1

International Business Cultural Factors

1. *Language:* Spoken, written, mass media, linguistic pluralism
2. *Values:* As related to time, achievement, work, wealth, change, risk taking, science
3. *Politics:* Nationalism, sovereignty, power, imperialism, ideologies
4. *Technology and material culture:* Transportation, energy system, communications, urbanization, science
5. *Social organization:* Social mobility, status systems, authority structures, kinship
6. *Education:* Literacy, human resource planning, higher education
7. *Religion:* Philosophical systems, sacred objects, rituals

SOURCE: Adapted from Vern Terpstra and Kenneth David, *The Cultural Environment of International Business* (Cincinnati, OH: Southwestern Publishing, 1991).

languages and **cultural values**. Differences in language can severely impede the communication process. Value differences as to what is good and appropriate have a more subtle, but equally important, impact on marketing. For example, values related to the acceptability of body hair on women severely limit the ability of companies to market razors successfully in some countries. The Austrian marketing director for Gillette once said, "We don't have to advertise women's razors here. I can personally give razors to all four Austrian women who want them."[12]

Companies in the United States have begun to recognize that firms are increasingly sending their employees overseas. Figure 19-2 presents an ad for AT&T directed to U.S. personnel (and their family members) who may go overseas. The ad points out that in different cultures the language may be difficult, the food different, and the customs unfamiliar, but a phone call home will always be easy.

An understanding of foreign cultures will also lead to the realization that ethical assumptions are not necessarily identical across cultures. Highlight 19-1 discusses some dilemmas raised because of differences between our values and those of other countries.

Cultural Differences Between East Asia and the United States

Over the past couple of decades America's trade ties with Europe have decreased in importance. Foreign trade has increasingly been focused on Third World, or developing, countries as well as on countries around the Pacific Rim. The **Pacific Rim** includes North America, South America, Australia, Indonesia, East Asia, and Siberia. This region holds 50% of the world's population and will hold six of the world's ten "supercities" by the year 2000.[13]

East Asia in particular should become increasingly important to the United States. Composed of Japan, Korea, China, and Southeast Asia, the region has over 26% of the world's population and is the dominant exporter of automobiles, electronics, and computer chips. The culture, however, has marked dissimilarities to that found in the United States. East Asian countries follow the Confucian ethic, a moral philosophy that does not subscribe to a supreme being and emphasizes the virtues of work, frugality, and education.[14]

Within the region Japan is increasingly becoming a trading partner and economic competitor of the United States. In the 1980s the Japanese began using a phrase for this "joint economy" of both partnership and competition—*nichibei*—which is a combination of the Japanese characters for Japan (*nihon*) and American (*beikoku*, or rice country).[15] Table 19-2 compares and contrasts a number of the values found in the two societies. One of the major cultural differences between the countries is how the societies view the individual. In the United States the individual is seen as more important than the state, whereas in Japan the group, family, and state are relatively more important. As one international consultant put it, "The Japanese are a consensus-bonded, group-oriented culture. . . . Americans are individually motivated and independently oriented."[16]

The differences in the cultures can also be seen in how companies view employees and customers. Japanese companies tend to assume that their customers are correct and honest in all cases. The attitude of American companies tends to go in the other direction. Similarly, Japanese firms motivate their employees with job security and longevity. However, as one American executive noted about U.S. firms, "It is not

Figure 19-2 In this ad AT&T targets a market segment of Americans living abroad with the reminder that even in a different culture, a familiar voice is just a phone call away. (Courtesy of AT&T, 1990.)

HIGHLIGHT 19-1

Ethical Considerations in International Consumer Behavior Practices

Although we may assume that ethical conduct involves nothing more than obeying the law, this viewpoint may be simplistic. In fact, one author notes that ethical issues can arise in at least the following contexts:

1. The types of products we produce or sell overseas;
2. Our advertising or marketing practices;
3. Business conduct in countries where physical security is a consideration;
4. Hiring and promotion practices where discrimination and racism exist; and
5. Requests for payments to secure contracts or sales.

The following scenarios describe situations where ethical issues are involved. What would you do?

1. As soon as Hungary's communists fell from power, Marlboro signs went up, followed by Camel and Lucky Strike. Four Western cigarette companies bought the government tobacco monopoly and intended to advertise their products. However, the former communist regime had banned cigarette advertising in 1978. The cigarette companies fought back, putting up signs as quickly as the government tore them down. The cigarette companies presented themselves as principled defenders of free speech, opposed to a law left over from a decidedly odious and undemocratic regime.
2. Under the Foreign Corrupt Practices Act, American companies can make payments to "facilitate" government action (such as hastening the customs inspection of a shipment of goods) but cannot resort to bribery (securing entry of the same goods without an inspection). Of course, "speeding up" an inspection is hard to separate from asking the inspector to do an inspection with one eye closed.
3. A customer asks for a falsified invoice on imported goods for recordkeeping. She requests that you deposit the difference in a bank in a foreign country. The customer explains that her daughter will be going to school abroad next year, and due to currency restrictions in the customer's country this is the only way of moving funds abroad for her daughter's use.
4. In country X it is clear that women are discriminated against. In your position as CEO, you are considering whether to send your marketing vice president, a female, to this country to negotiate a contract.
   a. If you decide to do so because of your own beliefs, how do you justify the decision to impose your belief system on the citizens of country X?
   b. Sending your vice president may increase the odds that the negotiations will fail. Do you have an ethical responsibility to your own company to increase the chances of success by sending someone more acceptable to your foreign counterparts?

Based on Henry W. Lane and Joseph J. DiStephano, *International Management Behavior* (Boston: PWS-Kent, 1992); and Barry Newman, "The Marlboro Man Gets Bushwacked by an Old Red Foe," *The Wall Street Journal*, September 24, 1993, pp. A1, A8.

TABLE 19-2

Comparison of Values in United States and Japan

United States	*Japan*
Judeo-Christian theism	Confucianism
Individualism	Affiliation
Protestant ethic	Virtues of frugality, work, education
Democracy	Democracy
Liberty	Government over individual
Private property	Close-knit social structure
Merit differentiation	Mutuality of obligations
Equality	Vertical relationships
Self-fulfillment	Family/group orientation
Rationality	Emotion/intuition
Youthfulness	Maturity

SOURCE: Adapted from Robert Bartels "National Culture—Business Relations: United States and Japan Contrasted," in *International Marketing Management*, Erdener Kaynak ed. (New York: Praeger Publishers, 1984).

unusual for a management person to have one bad season and return from vacation and find his office locked and his name no longer on the door."[17] Table 19-3 compares the characteristics of typical U.S. and Japanese firms.

The Japanese are also a more conservative people than Americans. For example, *Playboy* magazine has been in Japan only since 1975, and *Penthouse* is finding it difficult to break into the Japanese market. A *Penthouse* executive called Japan the most conservative country in which the magazine publishes.[18] Although bare-breasted women are often shown on late-night television, by law no pubic hair is allowed to be shown in the print or television media in Japan. Conservatism is also revealed in the more formal communications style of the Japanese. For example, if a Japanese executive were to state that something is "difficult" to do, what he may actually mean is "no." He is simply being polite.[19] A backslapping, joking American executive or salesperson might have difficulty in successfully dealing with the more reserved Japanese.

While cultural values are rather difficult to change, the Japanese are beginning to adopt some values that are more Western in orientation. For example, after years of working longer hours than their counterparts in other rich countries, the Japanese are now learning to value their leisure time. The government has asked businesses to reduce the usual five-and-a-half-day week, and government employees began working only five days a week in May 1992.[20] Millions of Japanese are engaging in such leisure activities as foreign travel. Exposure to shopping in other countries helps to increase their demand for consumer goods.

Japan is East Asia's richest market, and Taiwan, South Korea, Singapore, and Hong Kong are also top markets for U.S. products. Many U.S. companies are even more intrigued by the 1.2 billion potential consumers in the People's Republic of

TABLE 19-3

Characteristics of Two Familiar Organizational Ideal Types: A and J

Type A (American)	*Type J (Japanese)*
Short-term employment	Lifetime employment[a]
Individual decision making	Consensual decision making
Individual responsibility	Collective responsibility
Rapid evaluation and promotion	Slow evaluation and promotion
Explicit, formalized control	Implicit, informal control
Specialized career path	Nonspecialized career path
Segmented concern	Holistic concern

[a]Japanese attitudes toward lifetime employment are changing in the 1990s, although there is still more reluctance to fire employees (and change jobs) than in the United States. See Jacob M. Schlesinger and Masayoshi Kanabayashi, "On the Street: Many Japanese Find Their 'Lifetime' Jobs Can Be Short-Lived," The *Wall Street Journal*, October 8, 1992, p. A10.

SOURCE: Wesley Johnson, "Industrial Buying Behavior: Japan Versus the U.S," in *Advances in Consumer Research*, vol. 14, Mellanie Wallendorf and Paul Anderson, eds. (Provo, UT: Association for Consumer Research, 1987), p. 329.

China. China has the world's fastest-growing economy, and consumer preferences are changing, as shown by the composition of the "three bigs," the most longed-for consumer items. Once a watch, bicycle, and a sewing machine, and in the 1980s a color TV, a washing machine, and a tape recorder, in the 1990s VCRs, air conditioners, and stereos top the list.[21]

Researchers have investigated differences in decision making among people in the United States, Japan, China, and Korea. In one study researchers investigated differences in the exchange process among executives from the People's Republic of China, Japan, Korea, and the United States.[22] In this study the executives were engaged in a simulated negotiation exercise in which they had to reach an agreement on the price of three products that would be sold. In all cases the negotiations occurred within the same culture. Thus Americans negotiated with Americans, Japanese negotiated with Japanese, and so on. A number of interesting results were found. First, Japanese buyers were found to have greater status than the sellers. As the authors expected, in each case the buyers received greater profits than did the sellers. (A similar effect was also found for Koreans.) Second, for Americans, the key to successful negotiations was the use of problem-solving strategies. These problem-solving strategies involved cooperation and information exchange. Third, for the Chinese, competitive strategies yielded higher economic rewards. Fourth, the Koreans' negotiation style incorporated aspects of the American negotiation model and the Japanese model. Finally, the authors argued that if a universal principle could be found in the research, it was that interpersonal attractiveness had strong influences on negotiation outcomes for all four cultural groups. The more interpersonally attractive the partners were to each other, the better the outcomes.

Cultural Differences Between Latin America and the United States

With the ratification of the North American Free Trade Agreement (NAFTA) in 1993, we can expect that trade with Mexico—already our third largest trading partner—will leap upward. Nor will the free trade agreements stop there. The United States has agreed to negotiate free trade agreements with all other Latin American countries, beginning with Chile.

American-made products are viewed positively in Latin America. In Mexico, approximately 90% of the movie videos rented are made in Hollywood and are usually adapted with subtitles rather than Spanish dubbing.[23] Other U.S. exports are also highly prized. The number of U.S. franchises with outlets in Mexico quadrupled in the early 1990s to more than 100. "Cristina," an imported Cuban-American TV talk show, patterns itself after "Oprah" and other American talk shows that dwell on psychological and sexual trends.[24]

As trade increases with Latin America, however, cultural differences will create difficulties. For example, a nonverbal activity that can lead to discomfort for North Americans is the *abrazo*, or embrace, a common mode of greeting in Latin America. It may take some practice for *norteamericanos* to learn how to turn their heads a bit so that they don't bump noses!

Like some Asian cultures (and unlike North Americans), Latin Americans don't seem to "be on the clock" when trying to do business. They like to let a personal relationship evolve, which then leads to doing business.

Language is a unifying force among the people of Latin America, but that unity isn't monolithic. We realize that the British, Americans, and Australians speak the same language, but with variations—what are "bangers and mash," anyway?—and the same variability is found in Spanish. For example, *café* (a place for snacks) can be variously called *un cabaré* in Colombia, *un cafetín* in Mexico, *un milonguero* in Argentina, *un boiti* in Central America, and *una tapesa* in Spain. In addition, a variant dialect of Spanish is beginning to appear in Los Angeles, and along the U.S.-Mexican border you hear a Spanish-English mix that one author calls "Spanglish."[25]

Cultural Differences Between Eastern Europe and the United States

The **Eastern Europe** landmass stretches from the eastern border of Germany to the shores of the Pacific Ocean, and is composed of people as diverse as the European Czechs and the Mongoloid people of far eastern Siberia. With a population of some 425 million (compared to 357 million in all of Western Europe), this area has enormous profit potential. Across this vast land, many cultures exist. The one commonality is that for over 40 years all the people were under the control of the Soviet Union, which has now disappeared.

Incomes in Eastern Europe are much lower than in Western Europe, and productivity declined in the early 1990s during the political turmoil and vast economic readjustments. The retail setting is austere: typically stores have few toilets, no air conditioning, little in the way of carpeting, and only the most rudimentary displays. Pricing frequently has little relation to production costs. On the other hand, demand for Western products is high: one Swedish furniture retailer had to drop catalog sales in Hungary and stop advertising in Hungary and Poland because both generated demand it couldn't satisfy. This combination of high demand and low purchasing power has created new shopping patterns, such as patrons accumulating silverware and tableware one spoon or cup at a time.[26]

Not all Eastern European countries are poor, however. Czechoslovakia boasted the sixth wealthiest people in the world before World War II. This background contributes to its rapid adaptation to market structures and Western tastes.[27]

The disintegration of the Soviet Union and its satellites threw open a huge market hungry for consumer goods, especially for imported goods banned under communism. Playboy has licensed overseas editions in Poland, Hungary, and the Czech Republic. It airs selected pay-per-view television offerings in Bulgaria and sells home videos in Slovenia and Croatia.[28] Not only are the people of Eastern Europe anxious for consumer goods, Western items are status symbols as well. For example, the Twix bar is a favorite for Russian teenage boys hoping to impress their girlfriends with American confections.[29]

Marketing to consumers in Eastern Europe, however, does take an understanding of the different cultures of the people and of their unfamiliarity with Western-style business practices. For example, when European and American products first began to arrive, Eastern Europeans felt that advertising tricked consumers. When Procter & Gamble introduced its shampoo and conditioner, "Wash and Go," customers had not heard of hair conditioner, nor did they want it. Polish bars began serving a drink derisively called "Wash and Go—a shot of vodka with a water chaser."[30] They greeted free samples with suspicion, reasoning that the product must be of low quality if the company was giving it away.[31]

Gradually, however, as these consumers acquire more experience, they should become more comfortable with marketing activities. For example, one research study found that 89% of a 500-person focus group assembled by Leo Burnett's Prague office believed ads provide useful information and nearly 60% said they use the information in deciding what to buy. According to Marek Janicki, managing director of ITI-McCann-Erickson in Warsaw, "In the past, producers were king. Now the customer is king. People are happy someone is trying to get their attention."[32]

Cultural Differences Between Western Europe and the United States

By comparison with other areas of the globe, Western Europe can appear to be a very attractive area for U.S. businesses seeking to expand abroad. First, Western Europe is large (there are 310 million people in the European Community and millions more in non-EC Western Europe) and relatively wealthy. Second, there is a feeling among many Americans that Western Europe is culturally accessible.

While the size and wealth of Western Europe are highly appealing, the region does contain remarkable cultural diversity. Cultural differences exist both between the United States and Western Europe and between the nations and cultures within Western Europe. For example, an important difference between U.S. and German citizens is their attitude toward debt and credit cards. Although we in the United States use debt relatively freely, the German word for debt—*schulden*—also means guilt.[33] For this reason Germans are more reluctant to make credit card purchases than we are.

Within Western Europe, the European Community (EC) has a common agricultural policy, a coordinated monetary system, and open borders, but there are cultural differences among countries within the EC. Also, a significant part of Western Europe does not belong to the EC. Countries within Western Europe have different preferences, even on such mundane matters as the appropriate size of paper napkins.[34] Unilever's food division sells a different tomato soup in Rotterdam than in Brussels, uses another recipe in France, and still another in Germany. Lever found that Germans want detergents that are environmentally safe and will pay a premium for them. Spaniards, however, want a cheaper product that will get shirts white and soft. Greeks want smaller detergent packages to hold down the cost of each store visit.[35] In short, the "Euroconsumer" does not yet exist.

Table 19-4 identifies some of the key dimensions on which cultures in the United States, Mexico, the Czech Republic, France, and Japan can be compared.

When dealing with individuals from a different culture, a number of difficult problems may arise. These are discussed in the next section.

Cross-cultural Problem Areas

Translations

In addition to dealing with the difficulties of everyday speech in foreign countries, marketers must be aware of the problem of accurately translating their product's brand name into new languages. Examples of mistranslations abound.[36] For example, Colgate-Palmolive introduced its Cue toothpaste into the French market without changing the name. They did not realize that, in French, "cue" is a pornographic word. A paper manufacturer accidentally had its name translated into Japanese. The name became "He who envelops himself in ten tons of rice paper." General Motors

TABLE 19-4

Comparing the United States, Mexico, the Czech Republic, France, and Japan: Key Dimensions

	United States	*Mexico*	*Czech Republic*	*France*	*Japan*
Attitudes toward uncertainty	Risk acceptant	Risk averse	Risk averse	Risk averse	Risk averse
Individualistic versus group oriented	Individualistic	Group oriented	Group oriented	Individualistic	Group oriented
Nurturing versus macho	Macho	Macho	Nurturing	Nurturing	Very macho
Attitudes toward authority[a]	Low	High	High	High	High

[a]The degree to which survey respondents felt that authority figures, such as their bosses, were to be deferred to. U.S. respondents were less inclined to defer to their supervisors than were those from the other countries listed.

SOURCE: Adapted from Geert Hofstede, *Culture's Consequences* (Beverly Hills, CA: Sage Publications, 1980).

had "body by Fisher" translated into "corpse by Fisher" in Flemish. When the American film *City Slickers* went to France, its title became *Life, Love and Cows*.[37]

The list of translation faux pas is long. The method of avoiding such problems is called **back translation**. The process involves successively translating the message back and forth between languages by different translators. In this way, subtle and not so subtle differences in meaning can be located.[38]

Although back translation will solve literal translation issues, there is a question of whether the context is the same, even if the words are translated accurately. Is leasing a car meaningful in a culture where leasing isn't prevalent? Even using a translator fluent in both languages won't necessarily solve this potential problem. For example, a Nigerian who has spent enough time in the West to speak English with great fluency has also to some degree internalized Western values. To that extent he no longer reflects the same values as his compatriots in Nigeria.[39]

One new technology with considerable promise is translation software, which offers the alluring possibility of foreign language translation at your fingertips (keyboard). Earlier attempts at computerized translation in the 1950s led to such miscues as "the spirit is willing but the flesh is weak" rendered via computer as "the vodka is strong but the meat is rotten." Even current software suffers errors such as "Hypothermia means low body temperature. It is caused by exposure to the cold" translated in Spanish as "Hypothermia means to say temperature gets off the body and is caused by the exposition to the cold." Nonetheless, progress is being made.[40]

National Languages and Dialects

Frequently the language question is more nuanced than simply using the national language. In roughly ascending order of the level of confusion, China, India, and Africa present great linguistic challenges to Westerners.

China, a huge country divided by high mountain ranges and peopled by several major ethnic groups, has a number of Chinese "languages" that are mutually unintelligible. One of the authors visited a village in Taiwan where neither the national nor the dominant regional language was spoken, but yet a third "Chinese." He could speak only with children, who had learned the national language in school. His companion, who spoke two Chinese dialects fluently and understood a third, was in the same position.

China is ever so slowly being tied together by a common language. Children are taught to speak a national language based on the dialect of the capital, Beijing. The written language is based on the same character set, but with local variations. Even more languages exist in India than in China. One official census of India gave a figure of 826 different languages and dialects. Although in fact there are only four major language families with more than 1 million speakers each (fewer than in Europe), there is great diversity.[41]

As a practical matter, coverage of India is less complicated. Each of the 26 states has three official languages: English, Hindi, and the predominant state language. To assure complete coverage, many advertisers place the same ad in an English paper, a Hindi newspaper, and a local language newspaper.

Language may even affect the location of foreign businesses in India. Hindi is a northern Indian language, and Indians in the south see little reason to speak it instead of English. Their English is therefore generally better than that of northerners, and foreign businesspeople find that southern India provides a better environment in which to work.

Although English, French, and to a lesser extent Portuguese are spoken in Africa as a legacy of the colonial past, there are over 1,000 mutually unintelligible languages. Some languages (such as Swahili, Hausa, and Mandingo) had become lingua francas (universal languages) in certain areas of Africa before the arrival of the Europeans. Nonetheless, the problem of linguistic appropriateness is a major challenge.[42]

Other language issues arise as a result of politics. In some countries certain foreign languages are taboo among specific groups of people. For example, many older Koreans speak Japanese because Japan occupied Korea before and during World War II. Many of these Koreans are also angry about the occupation and refuse to speak Japanese even though they can.

When the Soviet Union disintegrated, many of the former states declared linguistic as well as political independence from Moscow. For example, Kyrgyzstan, Kazakhstan, and Turkmenistan not only use their own languages in preference to Russian—they have also decided to use the Latin alphabet instead of the Russian Cyrillic alphabet![43]

Time Perception

Time (which is discussed in greater detail in Chapter 14) is an important situational factor influencing consumers. In international settings it can cause problems because different cultures may view time divergently. Time is a commodity in the United States. For example, Americans speak of "spending" and "wasting" time. As a consequence, Americans hate to be kept waiting. In many other cultures, time is much less important. A foreign executive may keep an American client waiting for 45 minutes or longer and think nothing of it. To the foreign businessperson 45 minutes is insignificant and the minimum length of time one should expect to wait.[44]

A U.S. professor described his experience of teaching classes in Brazil as traumatic at first, because students arrived late to class and then hung around after class for no apparent reason. Partway through the semester, he asked the students how many minutes before and after the agreed time would it be before someone was considered early or late. For Brazilian students the average was 54 and 34 minutes, respectively. For students in a comparable California university, it was 24 and 19 minutes. The Brazilian students were more casual in their approach to time.[45]

Some argue that an emphasis on time denotes a culture that maintains a very-fast-paced life-style. A study was performed that investigated the accuracy of bank clocks, the average walking speed of pedestrians on a city street, and how long it took postal clerks to sell a stamp in several cultures. On all three measures Japan had the most accurate/fastest times. The United States or England was either second or third on each. Finally, Indonesia tended to have the most relaxed pace. It would be interesting to determine where the slower-paced Hispanic cultures would place, given their emphasis on *mañana*, which means "tomorrow."[46]

Symbols

As already discussed, divergent cultures may have different symbols to communicate meaning. Thus what something means in one culture may not be the same in other cultures. For example, the number seven is unlucky in Ghana and Kenya but lucky in India and the Czech Republic. The number four is unlucky in Japan because the words for "four" and "death" are pronounced identically. The triangle is negative in Hong Kong and positive in Colombia. In some remote areas of the world, people believe that when their picture is taken their "spirit" has been captured. Purple is associated with death in many Latin American countries. In Mexico yellow flowers are a sign of death, whereas in France they denote infidelity. The expression "wearing a green hat" means that a man's wife is cheating on him in Taiwan. Similarly, gifts may represent different feelings in different cultures. One does not give cutlery in Russia, Germany, or Taiwan.[47] Never surprise your Japanese host with a gift. By accepting it (and refusal is impossible), he incurs an obligation to reciprocate immediately with a gift of exactly equivalent value. If the gift is not available in Japan, the price may be unknown, and your host will agonize over what to do.

Friendship

Americans tend to make friends easily, but they also drop them rapidly. In some countries, friendship replaces the legal or contractual system.[48] Therefore, friends are made very slowly and retained for great lengths of time. As a consequence, the Chinese, Japanese, and others view with skepticism Americans who come on strong; they tend to see such Americans as insincere and superficial.

Etiquette

Matters of etiquette can also create discomfort and misunderstandings. For example, Americans may not understand the Japanese exchange of business cards, or *meishi*, which is a necessary social ritual. With the exchanges Japanese individuals are able to gauge their respective levels of status.[49] There is a precise ritual to exchanging name cards in Japan. They must be given with both hands, rather than one (this is also true for China and Korea). In China, the exchange of name cards is a matter of both etiquette and practicality. Many people have the same last names, and many characters sound alike in spoken Chinese. So name cards are used to build personal "phone books": calling "information" might be an exercise in futility!

The exchange of hugs and a kiss on the cheek among males in Eastern Europe strikes many Americans as strange and inappropriate. However, the ritual is a basic part of the manner in which people are greeted in that part of the world. Another matter of etiquette that differs around the world is how food is eaten. For example, many Europeans consider eating food with your fingers (e.g., sandwiches or french fries) disgusting. The Japanese find the Western practice of blowing one's nose on a handkerchief, then putting this effluvia in a pocket or purse, rather than disposing of it, very disgusting. Instead of getting formal when embarrassed, Thais giggle. This causes them problems with Westerners, who assume they are being made fun of.[50]

Nonverbal Behavior

Nonverbal behaviors are those actions, movements, and utterances that people use to communicate in addition to language. These include movements of the hands, arms, head, and legs, as well as body orientation and the space maintained between people. Different cultures have divergent norms concerning such nonverbal behavior. Such differences can be seen in various cultures as forms of interpersonal spatial relations. Americans have four zones surrounding them—intimate, personal, social, and public.[51] The intimate zone is from 0 to 18 inches away. Public zones are from 12 feet or farther away. Business tends to be conducted in the social zone of 4 to 7 feet.

People in other cultures, however, may not space themselves in the same way as Americans. In Middle Eastern and Latin American cultures, people tend to interact at a much closer distance. Consequently, an American may become uncomfortable as a foreign businessman closes in on him. The result of such interaction has been described as a sort of waltz, with the American backtracking and the foreign client pursuing. The problem is that the foreigner sees the American as standoffish, whereas the American sees the foreigner as pushy.[52]

Another aspect of nonverbal behavior is the influence of context: that is, how one says something is as important as what one says.[53] The United States is a low-context country. Most of the information in a message is contained in explicit code—that is, language. In Japan, a high-context country, the Japanese look for meaning in what is not being said—silences, gestures, and so on. For example, in the United States the precise wording of agreements is very important, and in business transactions this means that contracts are critical. Since attorneys are specialists in writing contracts, legal input is important. In Japan, however, precise wording is less important than the intentions of the parties to an agreement. Divining intention requires an atmosphere of trust, so agreeing to do business takes a bit longer. Once someone has agreed to do something, words written on paper mean proportionately less. So, in Japan "a person's word is his bond," but in the United States, written contracts tend to be relied upon. For Americans a disconcerting result is that the Japanese often ask for contracts to be renegotiated based on the intention of the parties. That intention is interpreted from the context of the discussion and not from the precise words used.

Ethnocentricity

Ethnocentrism refers to the common tendency for people to view their own group as the center of the universe, to interpret other social units from the perspective of their own group, and to reject persons who are culturally dissimilar. This natural proclivity further leads to a tendency for people to blindly accept those people who are culturally similar. Thus the symbols and values of the person's ethnic or national group become objects of pride, whereas symbols of other groups may become objects of contempt.[54]

When marketing in new cultures, business executives must strenuously avoid the tendency to look down on others because they do things differently. Furthermore, they must inhibit the urge to try to change the behavior of foreign peoples because what they do is not as "good" as the American way. One can see this attitude in the actions of Simmons, Inc., a company that tried unsuccessfully to convert the Japanese to sleeping on beds. The problem of ethnocentricity, though, does not exist only in Americans. An American executive working for a Japanese firm noted that his Japanese bosses believed that American consumers should behave like Japanese consumers.[55] With high gas prices and interest rates, the Japanese could not understand why Americans did not use motorbikes as their main transportation mode.

Executives must recognize that consumption patterns can differ substantially across cultures. Recognizing differences, however, can be difficult. When no evidence is present to suggest otherwise, people tend to believe that what they like and dislike, others will also like and dislike. The following are examples of some culturally based differences in consumption found in other countries.

- Married men in France use more cosmetics and beauty aids than their wives.[56]
- Dutch women report more interest in high-fashion clothing than American women.[57]

- In some Middle Eastern countries "hot" and "cold" refer to the heaviness of a food rather than to the food's spiciness or temperature.[58]

Similarly, attitudes toward consumption activities differ markedly across cultures. When given the statement "A house should be dusted and polished three times a week," 86% of the Italians agreed, whereas only 25% of Americans did. To the statement, "Everyone should use a deodorant," 89% of Americans agreed, but only 53% of Australians agreed.[59]

When in a foreign country, even the most basic liberties that Americans enjoy may be unavailable. For example, the ability to move freely varies across cultures. In Moslem countries, the activities of women are greatly restricted. A Singer Company manager was jailed when he encouraged Sudanese women to leave their homes to attend demonstration classes for sewing machines. The manager's solution was to have men attend the classes. They became convinced of the value of the machines and ordered their wives to attend the classes.[60]

The tendency to exhibit ethnocentrism can be used as a segmentation variable. In fact, a consumer ethnocentrism scale has been developed. As shown in Table 19-5, the scale measures American consumers' tendency to prefer to purchase U.S.-made products. Research conducted on the scale indicates that those who were high in consumer ethnocentrism were more prone to accentuate the positive aspects of domestic products and to discount the virtues of foreign-made items. They reacted more positively to advertisements that used an "American-made" theme. In addition, a product's American origin and construction was rated higher as a purchase consideration by those with higher levels of ethnocentrism.[61] The consumer ethnocentrism scale has been shown to apply cross-nationally to French, Japanese, and German subjects as well.[62]

Several studies have been conducted to investigate the extent to which "made in America" themes have a positive impact on consumer attitudes and buying intentions. The use of such themes can potentially evoke feelings of patriotism and prove beneficial for companies. The overall results of the research are, however, quite mixed. For example, one study assessed consumer decision making before and after the introduction of the "Made in the USA" television campaign.[63] The $40 million campaign was run by a coalition of 245 U.S. textile and apparel companies. The campaign used nationally known celebrities, who touted American-made apparel as superior in quality and style. The researchers found that the respondents had positive attitudes toward domestically produced goods. However, when actual purchase preference was considered, the campaign had little effect when compared to other product attributes, such as style, quality, and fiber content.

Early research on the **country of origin** issue had found evidence that U.S. consumers did consider this factor when making a purchase. For example, in 1985 a *Wall Street Journal*/NBC nationwide telephone poll found that 53% claimed to look at the labels for the country of origin. Of those who looked at the labels, 76% claimed to generally choose domestically produced apparel.[64] Follow-up research in the United States and Canada, however, revealed that when 1,458 consumers were asked why they purchased a clothing product, only one person said "country of origin." The authors stated, "the percentage of those who searched for domestically produced goods because they cared about protection of the home industry was much lower than the percentage of those who expressed a concern for buying Canadian or U.S.-made clothing."[65]

TABLE 19-5

Consumer Ethnocentrism Scale

	Item
1.	American people should always buy American-made products instead of imports.
2.	Only those products that are unavailable in the United States should be imported.
3.	Buy American-made products. Keep America working.
4.	American products, first, last, and foremost.
5.	Purchasing foreign-made products is un-American.
6.	It is not right to purchase foreign products, because it puts Americans out of jobs.
7.	A real American should always buy American-made products.
8.	We should purchase products manufactured in America instead of letting other countries get rich off of us.
9.	It is always best to purchase American products.
10.	There should be very little trading or purchasing of goods from other countries unless out of necessity.
11.	Americans should not buy foreign products, because this hurts American businesses and causes unemployment.
12.	Curbs should be put on all imports.
13.	It may cost me in the long run, but I prefer to support American products.
14.	Foreigners should not be allowed to put their products on our markets.
15.	Foreign products should be taxed heavily to reduce their entry into the United States.
16.	We should buy from foreign countries only those products that we cannot obtain within our own country.
17.	American consumers who purchase products made in other countries are responsible for putting their fellow Americans out of work.

“Response format is a 7-point Likert-type scale: strongly agree = 7; strongly disagree = 1. Range of scores is from 17 to 119.

SOURCE: Reprinted with permission from Terence Shimp and Subhash Sharma, “Consumer Ethnocentrism Construction and Validation of CETSCALE,” *Journal of Marketing Research*, vol. 24 (August 1987), pp. 280–289, published by the American Marketing Association.

It seems that, while a “Made-in-the-U.S.A.” campaign will enhance the overall corporate image, better-made products or price are more important. Still, if quality and price are competitive, American-made goods have a strong appeal that may be growing.

One possible factor that may influence the tendency of consumers to reveal ethnocentric buying is the specific region in which they live. One study polled consumers in North Carolina about their views on textile imports and the “Made in the U.S.A.” campaign.[66] In Greenville, North Carolina, a city whose economy is significantly affected by foreign imports, 92% of those polled stated that they would pay more to limit imports of both cars and clothing. In a more urbanized city (e.g., Winston-Salem), less economically threatened by foreign imports, only 32% stated that they would pay more to limit clothing imports and only 23% stated that they would pay more to limit auto imports. The likely explanation for these dramatic differences is that consumer ethnocentrism increases when foreign competition directly affects one's job and economic viability.

Binational Products

The issue of consumer ethnocentrism is made more complicated by current manufacturing trends, where product components are often made in one country but the product is assembled in another, or where a product is designed in one country but made in another. Where are these **binational** products "from"? Generally speaking, it appears that consumers are influenced by their view of both countries. This means that manufacturers need to carefully consider the locations of all the steps in processing. For example, having a product designed in Japan can mitigate the effects of having the product made in a country with a poor reputation for quality.[67]

Other Ethnocentrism Effects

Another way ethnocentrism may be displayed is in the tendency for consumers in richer societies to assume that products from poorer countries are less preferable than those from richer countries. This effect may even extend to consumers from poorer countries, who may prefer richer-country products to their native products.[68] On the other hand, this tendency may not mean that consumers in richer countries do not want to buy any products from poorer countries. It appears that consumers display preferences for goods that match their notion of the country of origin. For example, while athletic footwear from China might not be attractive to U.S. consumers, sandals might be a good match.[69]

Cross-cultural Marketing Strategy

A major issue in international marketing concerns whether or not to standardize the marketing plan across national boundaries. The debate has focused on two well-known marketers. One is Philip Kotler, who argues against standardization across markets. The other is Theodore Levitt, who argues that a rapid homogenization of the world's wants and wishes is occurring for the "advanced" things that the world makes and sells.[70] Levitt gives as one example the image, which many retain, of the 1979 Iranian hostage crisis. During the worst of the period when the Iranians held the U.S. embassy hostage, one could see on television "inflamed young men in fashionable French-cut trousers and silky body shirts open to the waist, with raised modern weapons, thirsting for blood in the name of Islamic fundamentalism."[71]

No simple answer exists to the question of whether the marketing mix can be standardized. In some countries, like Japan and Russia, distribution systems are quite different from those found in the United States. Likewise, products must often be adapted to the tastes and preferences of different cultures. For example, a U.S. company found that its room deodorizer had to undergo reformulation prior to entering the British market. The fragrance was made stronger, and the packaging was changed in order to appeal to British consumers.[72] The issue of standardization strikes most strongly in the advertising area. Throughout the 1960s, Pepsi-Cola saved about $8 million annually by standardizing promotional films.[73] Other companies like Coca-Cola and Levi Strauss have adopted a strategy of attempting to standardize their world image.[74]

Impulse, a spray deodorant/perfume, followed a global advertising strategy by using a "boy meets girl" love story theme across the 31 countries in which it was marketed. To allow for cultural differences, the company permitted each of the local agencies to shoot its own version of the basic storyboard. Each of the commercials uses the same copyline: "If a complete stranger suddenly gives you flowers—that's impulse. Men just can't resist acting on Impulse." The romantic fantasy commercials involve a young man acting irrationally when a woman wearing the perfume walks by. Upon smelling the perfume, he searches for a flower seller, grabs a bunch of flowers, and chases after the woman. The successful brand was first developed in 1972 in South Africa, from where it moved to Brazil. The product did not reach the United States until 1982. Within two years of its debut in West Germany, it had garnered 36% of the country's total deodorant market.[75]

Although standardized marketing efforts across countries are cheaper to develop and put into practice, serious problems occur for many, if not most, products. The goal of a global marketer is to have what Coca-Cola calls "One sight, one sound, one sell."[76] In most cases, however, too many obstacles get in the way of this goal for it to be implemented. Differences in such variables as government regulations, electrical outlets and voltages for electrical products, and cultural customs make standardized marketing impractical in many instances. For example, government authorities in Britain did not allow Philip Morris to use commercials showing the Marlboro cowboy on the grounds that children worship cowboys and would take up smoking. The final commercials showed noncowboys driving around Marlboro country in jeeps.[77] In other cases the issue is "what works." In like manner, recent Pepsi ads in Israel feature a young man in army boots doing pushups. In Israel the military is held in high esteem by almost everyone, and teenagers idolize soldiers in elite combat units rather than rock stars or sports celebrities.[78] This campaign, while appropriate for Israel, might stimulate controversy elsewhere.

Even in the product category of athletic shoes, companies must exercise caution in employing a standardized marketing effort. For example, the athletic shoe makers Nike and Reebok now have 50% of the $4.5 billion market for athletic shoes in Europe, up from 5% just a decade ago. In this case European buyers want the shoes because they are American and are identified with such American icons as Charles Barkley and Michael Jordan. The popularity of the 1992 Olympic basketball dream team in Europe helped to increase the popular image of these American brands at the expense of their European rivals, Adidas and Puma. "America's image may be the last remaining export by U.S. firms," according to Michael Atmere, publisher of *Footwear Plus*.

European buyers of Nike and Reebok shoes are interested in an American experience, so the physical product isn't altered. In both print advertising and on TV tag liners in Italy, Germany, the Netherlands, or France all read the same way, in English: "Just do it" or "Planet Reebok." But subtle changes are necessary. Reebok deleted weight lifting and boxing from commercials in France because of French aversion to violence. Europeans don't play sports as much as Americans and don't visit sporting goods stores as often. So Reebok also sells its shoes in about 800 traditional shoe shops in France.[79]

Highlight 19-2 provides an unusual example of how the globalization of the marketplace and the disintegration of the Soviet Union have led to a curious problem for Budweiser, "The King of Beers."

HIGHLIGHT 19-2

A Tale of Two Budweisers

A curious case of adaptation has occurred in the case of beer. In 1531, King Ferdinand of Germany liked a South Bohemian beer so much that he ordered that it be the beer of his royal court, the "Beer of Kings." The Germans called the beer "Budweiser" after the German name of the town where it was made, Budweis.

In 1876 Adolphus Busch of St. Louis, Missouri, created a new beer, borrowed a name from the Old World, trademarked the name Budweiser, and added a new slogan, "The King of Beers." At the turn of the century, the two Buds clashed over rights to the name. In 1911 they agreed on a settlement. Busch got North America and Budvar got Europe. Budweiser (Europe) remained a robust beer brewed in small batches, while Budweiser (U.S.) became a leviathan, adapted to blander American preferences.

South Bohemia later became part of the country of Czechoslovakia and in 1993, when the country divided, part of the Czech Republic. Now the Czech Republic is selling off its state-owned enterprises—and Budweiser (U.S.) wants to buy Budweiser (Europe). The Czechs have been reluctant to sell to a firm whose beer, to Czech tastes, bears little resemblance to their own robust Budweiser.

Based on Shailagh Murray, "Privatization: Emotion Joins Economics as Factor in Czech Sell-offs," *The Wall Street Journal Europe*, June 21, 1993; Roger Thurow, "The King of Beers and the Beer of Kings Are at Lagerheads," *The Wall Street Journal*, April 2, 1992, pp. A1, A8; and Anonymous, "Czech Government Closer to Brewery Stake Auction," *The Wall Street Journal*, July 28, 1993, p. A10.

Examples of the problems of global marketing abound. While forms of clothing in North America and Western Europe are identical, storage isn't. In Europe walk-in or built-in closets barely exist, so closet wardrobes, almost a curiosity here, are big European sellers.[80] Kool-Aid sells well in Venezuela but cannot be sold in Europe. Nestlé, the huge Swiss company, sells coffee in every country in the free world. However, the advertising and the taste of the coffee vary from country to country. Philip Kotler argues that "There are only a very few products, if any, that you can safely standardize."[81] Indeed, a general disenchantment with global advertising appears to exist among American firms. For example, in 1987 *Advertising Age* ran a story entitled "Goodbye Global Ads."[82] The article stated:

> In the aggregate, these cases suggest that the much heralded age of global marketing is not yet at hand. To the contrary, there is evidence that a backlash against global marketing may be building.

The article goes on to cite instance after instance of global marketing failures. For example, Kodak attempted to take its "Kodak Is Color" campaign worldwide. After the campaign bombed in the Middle East, the international account director for the firm's ad agency stated, "You can't have one commercial worldwide."

The Wall Street Journal reached a similar conclusion in 1988 in an article entitled "Marketers Turn Sour on Global Sales Pitch Harvard Guru Makes."[83] The article stated:

> Not only are cultural differences very much still with us, but marketing a single product one way everywhere can scare off customers, alienate employees, and blind a company to its customers' needs.

The idea that companies can completely standardize their marketing plans around the world contradicts the marketing concept. The consumer should be at the center of the marketing plan. Because consumers differ in various degrees around the world, so too should marketing plans differ. One recent study found some evidence that companies are increasingly tailoring their efforts to the culture.[84] Indeed, in some countries resentment seems to exist concerning the sameness of McDonald's stores and of Coca-Cola campaigns found around the world.[85] These multinational companies have become symbols of the United States. In countries where Americans are viewed less favorably, a marketing mix tailored to the culture is crucial.

Nonetheless, the "Harvard guru" (Dr. Theodore Levitt) stands adamantly behind his notion that global advertising can succeed with a "homogenized audience all over the world." He tells advertisers to "achieve what MTV achieves. They communicate powerful fashion, design. and music messages around the world without using different music videos of the same songs for different countries."[86]

A number of companies have adopted a compromise strategy to the standardization question. In this strategy a firm develops a base product and customizes the accompanying elements of the offering (i.e., price, promotion, and distribution channels) for a region, such as Latin America, Europe, or Asia. While an overall promotional theme may be developed to be employed worldwide, the implementation of this theme (for example, deciding whether to translate a slogan directly or to paraphrase it) is done locally. Called **pattern advertising**, this approach is an example of what the Japanese call *dochakuka*: "think globally, act locally."[87]

Pattern advertising can even apply to packaging and brandmarks. When Coca-Cola expanded into the former Soviet Union, there was already a high level of awareness for their famous script logo. However, the word "Enjoy," which is part of the logo, when translated into Russian, connoted sensuality, which is not appropriate for a soft drink. The word "Enjoy" was changed to "Drink."[88] The pattern of the brandmark was retained but subtly changed for the specific environment. The Impulse perfume promotional campaign that was mentioned earlier is an example of a pattern advertising campaign.

Tangible Products Versus Services

The degree to which standardization is possible also depends upon the nature of the product. As Figure 19-3 illustrates, different types of products are more—or less—likely to be successful in a standardized format. Generally, services (as well as industrial products) are less likely than consumer products to need adaptation to local markets. Management consultants, lawyers, and accounting firms are able to practice in much the same ways in different countries, although specifics (such as laws and accounting practices) may differ. Similarly, industrial products are seldom country specific, since there are few cultural differences in how a screw works! On the other

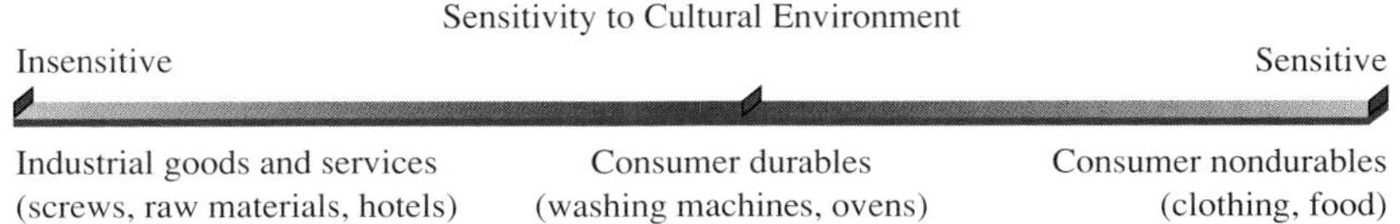

Figure 19-3 Different types of products tend to be more or less sensitive to foreign environment. The more sensitive a product is, the greater the need to adapt the product to the local environment.

hand, food products are more likely to be country specific. The Chinese may like hamburgers as a break in the usual routine, but they have a saying that if they go three days without eating rice, they're still hungry no matter what else they eat.

A Conclusion to the Standardization Debate?

In the long term, both Professors Kotler and Levitt are probably correct. As incomes increase, people do seem to want many of the same products. And the younger the customer, the more this seems to be true. London yuppies may be more like rich young Parisians than like their older countrymen. However, cultural influence remains strong, and it will be some time, if ever, before Professor Kotler's advice can be ignored. Highlight 19-3 discusses some research findings suggesting that the industrialized countries, contrary to Professor Levitt's assumptions, are less alike now than they were in years past.

In 1986 investigators from *Fortune* magazine interviewed executives from 12 large U.S. companies that obtain 20% or more of their sales from overseas. Based upon the interviews, three rules of international marketing were identified.[89]

1. Never rush into a new market. The company must develop an understanding of the culture, develop satisfactory suppliers, and hire foreign nationals to manage the operations.
2. Restructure operations to fit the conditions of the country. Schick controls over 70% of the stainless steel razor blade market in Japan because it restructured its operations there in order to fit into Japan's unusual distribution system.
3. Be flexible in marketing and product design. Basically, this rule says to avoid global marketing. Even Boeing must adapt its planes to local conditions. Thus it outfits its 737 jets with special braces to protect them against damage from bumpy Third World runways.

THE ROLE OF MARKETING RESEARCH IN INTERNATIONAL MARKETING

To identify differences in taste preferences and in the meaning of symbols across cultures, a firm must engage in marketing research. Major problems exist, however, in performing marketing research across cultures. One issue involves how to standard-

HIGHLIGHT 19-3

Are We Becoming Less, Rather than More, Alike?

There is actually some indication that as time passes the peoples of different nations are becoming less, rather than more, similar. In a recent study, researchers found that the industrialized countries seemed to be diverging on certain key dimensions, particularly in recent years. Professors Craig, Douglass, and Grien employed a large number of economic, demographic, market infrastructure, and quality of life variables to examine the 12 members of the European Community, the 6 members of the European Free Trade Association (EFTA), and the United States and Japan from 1960 to 1988. They found that despite increased interaction and communication during the period, the countries were actually growing less alike. For example, these countries enjoyed a roughly similar standard of living (measured by such indicators as per capita income and the number of passenger cars) in 1960, with the exception of the United States, where standards were markedly different. By 1988, however, there were much larger differences between the countries. Further, much of the change occurred in the 1980s.

Although the macroeconomic variables they researched were not designed to directly indicate consumer preferences, the study results are provocative. They suggest that the standardization–adaptation debate should remain on the mind of anyone interested in global trends in consumer behavior.

Based on C. Samuel Craig, Susan P. Douglas, and Andreas Grein, "Patterns of Convergence and Divergence Among Industrialized Nations: 1960–1988," *Journal of International Business Studies* (Fourth Quarter 1992), pp. 773–787.

ize measures of consumption values. Recently, it was suggested that researchers may be more successful by focusing on perceived attribute importance as a means of standardizing measures across cultures. Thus a large pool of attributes can be developed that are likely to be important to individuals in diverse cultures. Studies can be done in each culture to identify those attributes most important to individuals in that culture. A pilot study conducted with individuals in Japan, Singapore, Hong Kong, South Korea, and Taiwan supported the general approach.[90]

A MANAGERIAL APPLICATIONS EXAMPLE

In 1990 Amway Corporation's Japanese sales of nearly $600 million almost equaled those in the United States. Interestingly, the company had been in Japan only 11 years as compared to over 30 years in the United States. Why is the company so successful in Japan, a market where so many other American companies have faltered?[91]

One factor is that an American image still retains its popularity in Japan. The jars and bottles that contain Amway's household products have the Amway name and logo written in English on the label. Even the product description is written in English beside the Japanese translation.

A second factor is that many young Japanese workers in their twenties and thirties are moving into direct distribution because of the hierarchical and stultifying atmosphere of Japanese corporations. Whereas most American Amway distributors are retirees, in Japan they are much younger. As one Amway distributor explained: "People are starting to wonder what they could do as a single gear in a company. They want to have fun, they want to do something. When they join Amway, there's something that clicks."

Although the distributors may be fleeing the rigid corporate life to go on their own, they still make full use of the group mentality of Japan. In Japanese culture the importance of friendship and the group leads people to value the building of *jinmyaku*, or a network of human contacts. Because Amway distributors sell mostly to friends, the *jinmyaku* become indispensable. Similarly, the Amway culture emphasizes group meetings and pep rallies, which fit well into the Japanese value system. Like their Japanese corporate cousins, who go drinking at the end of the day, the distributors gather together for "after-Amway" dinners.

Japanese Amway distributors are well aware of opportunities to enhance their life-styles. Amway products can be sold part time, and with the 30% commissions, one's income can be increased substantially. Many have been able to buy American-style apartments for the first time. Indeed, the Japanese propensity toward hard work is readily seen in the distributors. Back from an American tour, one Japanese distributor said, "People in America separate their work from the days they take off. But in Japan, you'd never refuse someone who needs a hand on a particular day."

Finally, the success of Amway can also be partially ascribed to its distribution system. Because it moves its goods directly to its distributors, the company avoids the import-resistant Japanese middlemen.

As a result of all these factors, Amway is a smashing success in Japan. The company enjoys incredible group loyalty from its Japanese distributors. One employee noted that if polo shirts could be purchased with the Amway logo on them, "we'd line up to buy them."

The Consumer Behavior Analysis

Four consumer concepts from the chapter have particular relevance to the case. One of the reasons for Amway's success in Japan is the set of values that dominate the society. The Japanese focus on affiliation and the group fits in well with the corporate culture of Amway. It enhances the ability of the company to create a well-trained, highly motivated sales force. Similarly, the importance of the mutuality of obligations and of group membership also helps the distributors find a ready-made set of individuals who might buy products. However, although many of the traditional values of Japan remain strong, some are changing. For example, materialistic values appear to be increasing, and appeals to materialism must certainly play a role in the recruitment of distributors.

An example of cultural ritual can be seen in the habit of Japanese businesspersons to go out after the workday for dinner and drinks. Again, this ritual fits perfectly with the business culture of Amway. Thus the distributors maintain contacts by going to dinner with each other at the end of the business day.

Cultural symbols are used extensively by Amway in Japan. The use of English words and the Amway logo on the labels of their products have meaning to the

Japanese. The Japanese continue to look positively on the American culture overall, even though the relationship between the two nations occasionally shows signs of fraying.

Finally, cross-cultural analysis should be performed to compare and contrast the American and Japanese cultures. For example, a critical issue for companies wishing to enter the Japanese market concerns how to deal with the Japanese distribution system, which differs so dramatically from that found in the United States. Fortunately, Amway was able to circumvent this problem by selling directly to its distributors. In addition, they created a Japanese subsidiary that makes some of the products in Japan.

The Managerial Applications Analysis

Table 19-6 presents the managerial applications analysis for the Amway case. Cultural values have particular application to the distribution and promotion of Amway products. For example, the emphasis on the importance of the group in the society plays a critical role in finding potential buyers. Similarly, an understanding of cultural rituals helps Amway to motivate its Japanese sales force. Cultural symbols are used by Amway to link its products to the American culture. Indeed, the name Amway literally refers to the "American way." Symbols of the United States are placed on the labels of its products and act as promotional tools that help to position the company. Finally, cross-cultural analysis should be performed to monitor changes in both Japanese and American culture. In particular, the company needs to monitor the environment so that it can react if the economic friction between the countries develops into deeper cultural resentments.

TABLE 19-6

Managerial Applications Analysis of the Amway Case

Consumer Concepts	*Managerial Implications*
Cultural values	*Distribution*—Employ a distribution system that is consistent with values emphasizing the importance of affiliation, the group, and the extended family.
	Promotion—Train sales personnel so that they understand how to work with the strong social ties of the Japanese.
Cultural rituals	*Promotion*—Make sales contacts by engaging in Japanese cultural rituals, such as going out for drinks after work with potential clients.
Cultural symbols	*Promotion*—Employ symbols that are positively evaluated by the Japanese.
	Positioning—Use appropriate symbols of the United States to position the company.
Cross-cultural analysis	*Environmental analysis*—Monitor cultural trends in the United States and Japan for their possible impact on the Japanese. In particular, the potential impact of economic friction between the countries should be carefully monitored.

SUMMARY

Cross-cultural analysis involves the study of the values, attitudes, language, and customs of another society. Such analyses are highly important in the international marketing efforts that have become so important for the United States. Factors to consider in international marketing are differences in language, values, laws, politics, technology, education, and religion. Specific problem areas include translating product names and campaign themes, as well as accounting for cultural differences in time perception, symbols, etiquette, and nonverbal behavior. Another tendency to avoid is cultural ethnocentricity, or the tendency to believe that the values, beliefs, and ways of doing things as specified by one's own culture are right and correct.

Of particular importance to marketers in the United States are the East Asian countries on the Pacific Rim. The cultures of these societies differ in a number of important ways from the United States, such as in decision making, face saving, and the role of the individual versus the group. However, because of their growing economic importance, it is crucial for the United States to engage in vigorous trade with them. Other important areas include Latin America and Eastern and Western Europe.

A major debate in international marketing concerns the extent to which a marketing plan can be standardized across cultures. Although such standardization can bring about large economies of scale, in practice the approach is difficult to implement successfully. Although all consumers may have similar emotions, such as love, hate, greed, and envy, expression and symbolism can be dramatically different as one moves from culture to culture. As a result, a marketing plan in most cases must be tailored to some degree to match the consumer preferences of each culture. Because exporting is so economically significant to the United States, international marketing—and with it the study of foreign cultures—is becoming increasingly important for American companies. Three rules identified for those who engage in international marketing are (1) never rush into a new market, (2) restructure operations to fit the conditions of the country, and (3) be flexible in marketing and product design.

The study of culture and cross-cultural issues has importance to each of the components of the managerial schema—the marketing mix, segmentation, positioning, environmental analysis, and market research.

KEY TERMS

back translation
binational
country of origin
cross-cultural analysis
cultural rituals
cultural symbols
cultural values
culture versus nation
East Asia
Eastern Europe
ethnocentrism
nonverbal behaviors
Pacific Rim
pattern advertising

REVIEW QUESTIONS

1. Identify five of the seven categories of differences in foreign cultures that may affect international business.
2. Compare and contrast the cultural values of Japan and the United States.
3. Eight cross-cultural problem areas were identified in the text. Identify four of these pitfalls and discuss how they could influence the reactions of consumers to marketing offerings.
4. What is meant by cross-cultural ethnocentricity?
5. What problem is back translation meant to solve?
6. Argue for and against the merits of using a global marketing strategy.
7. Which strategy may be a good compromise between global and adaptive marketing strategies, and why?
8. What are the three rules of international marketing?

DISCUSSION QUESTIONS

1. A U.S. firm in Spain gave a picnic at which U.S. executives donned chef's hats and served food to the workers. The workers felt uneasy and wouldn't socialize with the bosses. Why?
2. In this chapter the statement was made that "The Japanese are a consensus-bonded, group-oriented culture; Americans are individually motivated and independently oriented." What are the advertising implications of this statement? To what extent do you agree with the statement that Americans are individually motivated and independently oriented?
3. Compare how easy it would be to standardize the advertising of a perfume versus the advertising of a soft drink around the world.
4. Suppose that you are marketing director for the firm that produces California Coolers, the citrus-based alcoholic product that is sold similarly to beer. You wish to sell the product internationally. What types of problems might you have in selling the product in such countries as Mexico, India, Japan, Saudi Arabia, France, and Britain?

ENDNOTES

1. Bob Hagerty, "Trainers Help Expatriate Employees Build Bridges to Different Cultures," *The Wall Street Journal*, June 14, 1993, pp. B1, B6.
2. "The Nature of Things," aired on the Public Broadcasting System, January 1, 1986.
3. Christopher Chipello, "A Miracle in Maine: Sea Urchin Is Turned into the Golden Uni," *The Wall Street Journal*, March 18, 1988, pp. 1, 9.
4. Alecia Swasy, "Don't Sell Thick Diapers in Tokyo," *The New York Times*, October 3, 1993, p. F9.
5. Thomas R. King, "Local Lures: For International Movie Marketers, Posters Are the Center of Attention," *Wall Street Journal Global Entertainment Supplement*, March 26, 1993, p. R13.
6. Damon Darlin, "Grown Men in Japan Still Read Comics and Have Fantasies," *The Wall Street Journal*, July 21, 1987, pp. 1, 10. See, also Nicholas Bornoff, *Pink Samurai: Love, Marriage, and Sex in Contemporary Japan* (New York: Pocket Books, 1991).
7. "Where the Koran Meets the Road," *Playboy*, March 1993, p. 15.
8. Terry Clark, "International Marketing and National Character: A Review and Proposal for an Integrative Theory," *Journal of Marketing*, Vol. 54 (October 1990), pp. 66–79.

9. Yumiko Ono, "Love and Chicken Fill Christmas Eve in Very Merry Japan," *The Wall Street Journal*, December 17, 1991, pp. A1, A9.

10. Riccardo A. Davis, "Many Languages—1 Ad Message," *Advertising Age*, September 20, 1993, p. 50.

11. Charles Steilen, "International Success Requires Full Marketing Commitment," *Marketing News*, December 4, 1987, p. 5.

12. Anne B. Fisher, "The Ad Biz Gloms onto Global," *Fortune*, November 12, 1984, p. 80.

13. Hank Koehn, "Scenario Calls for Pacific Rim to Flex Its Economic Muscle by the Year 2010," *Marketing News*, July 22, 1983, p. 16; and Donald A. Ball and Wendell H. McCulloch, Jr., *International Business: Introduction and Essentials* (Homewood, IL: Richard D. Irwin, 1993).

14. Gerson Goodman, "American Samurai," *Sales and Marketing Management*, October 12, 1981, pp. 45–48.

15. Robert Gilpin, *The Political Economy of International Relations* (Princeton, NJ: Princeton University Press, 1987).

16. Goodman, "American Samurai."

17. Ibid.

18. Jack Burton, "Penthouse Takes on Playboy in Japan," *Advertising Age*, June 27, 1983, p. 10.

19. Ibid.

20. "Changes in Japan's Workweek," *The Wall Street Journal*, May 4, 1992, p. A17.

21. Valarie Reitman, "Enticed by Visions of Enormous Numbers, More Western Marketers Move into China," *The Wall Street Journal*, July 12, 1993, pp. B1, B6.

22. John Graham, Dong Kim, Chi-Yuan Lin, and Michael Robinson, "Buyer-Seller Negotiations Around the Pacific Rim: Differences in Fundamental Exchange Processes," *Journal of Consumer Research*, Vol. 15 (June 1988), pp. 48–54.

23. Matt Moffett, "Mexico: JFK, Si! Madonna, No!" *Wall Street Journal Global Entertainment Supplement*, March 26, 1993, p. R15.

24. Matt Moffett, "Amigos for Now: Mexicans Anticipate Passage of Trade Pact Will Lift Economy," *The Wall Street Journal*, April 20, 1993, pp. A1, A13.

25. Frances de Talavera Berger, *¡Mierda!: The Real Spanish You Were Never Taught in School* (New York: Plume, 1990).

26. Stephen D. Moore, "Sweden's Ikea Forges into Eastern Europe," *The Wall Street Journal*, June 29, 1993, p. A6.

27. Frederick Kempe and Cacilie Rohwedder, "Top Executives Name Czech Republic Most Attractive for Future Investments," *The Wall Street Journal*, July 9, 1993, p. A6.

28. Susan Carey, "Playboy Looks Overseas as U.S. Climate Grows Hostile," *The Wall Street Journal*, September 29, 1993, p. B4.

29. Neela Banerjee, "Russia Snickers After Mars Invades," *The Wall Street Journal*, July 13, 1993, p. B1.

30. Dan Michaels and Shailagh Murray, "Advertising: Eastern Europe's Window of Opportunity Is Still Open," *The Wall Street Journal Europe*, July 7, 1993.

31. William R. Putsis, Jr., "Marketing in Eastern Europe: Lessons From Early Entrants," *Yale Management*, 1993, pp. 14–21.

32. Michaels and Murray, "Advertising: Eastern Europe's Window."

33. Robert Guenther, "Citicorp Pushes Its Bank Cards Overseas," *The Wall Street Journal*, August 20, 1990, p. B1.

34. Janet Guyon, "A Joint-Venture Papermaker Casts Net Across Europe," *The Wall Street Journal*, December 7, 1992, p. B6.

35. E. S. Browning, "In Pursuit of the Elusive Euroconsumer," *The Wall Street Journal*, April 23, 1992, p. B1.

36. For an excellent discussion of the problems of translation, see David A. Ricks, *Blunders in International Business* (Cambridge, MA: Blackwell, Grid, 1993).

37. "Did We Say That?" *Playboy*, September 1993, p. 15.

38. James Engel and Roger Blackwell, *Consumer Behavior* (New York: The Dryden Press, 1982).

39. Eric J. Arnould and Melanie Wallendorf, "On Identical Methods in Cross-Cultural Research, or the Non-Comparability of Data Obtained with Seemingly-Comparable Measures," presented at the 1993 American Marketing Association Educators' Meeting, February 20–23, 1993, Newport Beach, CA.

40. William M. Bulkeley, "Translation Software Falls Short of Fluency," *The Wall Street Journal*, February 1, 1993, p. B6.

41. *Encyclopedia Americana*, 1991, Vol. 14, pp. 881–882.

42. Ibid., Vol. 1, pp. 269–270.

43. Martha Brill Olcott, "Central Asia's Catapult to Independence," *Foreign Affairs*, Vol. 71 (Summer 1992), pp. 108–130.

44. Edward T. Hall, *The Hidden Dimension* (Garden City, NY: Doubleday, 1966).

45. Robert Levine and Ellen Wolff, "Social Time: The Heartbeat of Culture," *Psychology Today*, March 1985, pp. 28–35.

46. Ibid.

47. S. B. Hitchings, "Beware When Bearing Gifts in Foreign Lands," *Business Week*, December 6, 1976, pp. 91–92.

48. Hall, *The Hidden Dimension*.

49. S. Lohr, "Business Cards: A Japanese Ritual," *The New York Times*, September 13, 1981, pp. D1–D2.

50. Karen Swenson, "Roaches and Redheads: Touring a Small Thai Town," *The Wall Street Journal*, July 1, 1993, p. A12.

51. Edward T. Hall, *The Silent Language* (Garden City, NY: Doubleday, 1959).

52. H. W. Smith, "Territorial Spacing on a Beach Revisited, A Cross-National Explanation," *Social Psychology Quarterly*, Vol. 44 (June 1981), pp. 132–137.

53. Edward T. Hall, *Beyond Culture* (Garden City, NY: Anchor Books, Doubleday, 1976).

54. Terence Shimp and Subhash Sharma, "Consumer Ethnocentrism: Construction and Validation of the CETSCALE," *Journal of Marketing Research*, Vol. 24 (August 1987), pp. 280–289.

55. Goodman, "American Samurai."

56. P. Kotler, *Marketing Management: Analysis, Planning, Implementation and Control* (Englewood Cliffs, NJ: Prentice-Hall, 1988), p. 386.

57. D. J. Tigert, C. W. King, and L. Ring, "Fashion Involvement: A Cross Cultural Comparative Analysis," in *Advances in Consumer Research*, Vol. 7, J. C. Olson, ed. (Chicago: Association for Consumer Research, 1980), p. 17.

58. A. Mehrabian and J. Russell, *An Approach to Environmental Psychology* (Cambridge, MA: MIT Press, 1974), p. 10.

59. T. Plummer, "Consumer Focus in Cross-National Research," *Journal of Advertising*, Vol. 6 (Spring 1977), pp. 10–11.

60. J. Douglas McConnell, "The Economics of Behavioral Factors in Multi-National Corporations," in *Combined Proceedings of American Marketing Association*, Series No. 33, Fred C. Alvine, ed. (Chicago: American Marketing Association, 1971), p. 261.

61. Shimp and Sharma, "Consumer Ethnocentrism." See also Joel Herche, "A Note on the Predictive Validity of the CETSCALE," *Journal of the Academy of Marketing Science*, Vol. 20 (Summer 1992), pp. 261–264.

62. Richard G. Netemeyer, Srinivas Durvasula, and Donald R. Lichenstein, "A Cross-National Assessment of the Reliability and Validity of the CETSCALE," *Journal of Marketing Research*, Vol. 28 (August 1991), pp. 320–327.

63. Richard Ettenson, Janet Wagner, and Gary Gaeth, "Evaluating the Effect of Country of Origin and the 'Made in the USA' Campaign: A Conjoint Approach," *Journal of Retailing*, Vol. 64 (Spring 1988), pp. 85–100.

64. H. Gilman, "Clothing Shoppers Talk Domestic But Look First for Style, Savings," *The Wall Street Journal*, October 15, 1985, p. 31.

65. Susan Hester and Mary Yuen, "The Influence of Country of Origin on Consumer Attitude and Buying Behavior in the United States and Canada," in *Advances in Consumer Research*, Vol. 14, Melanie Wallendorf and Paul

Anderson, eds. (Provo, UT: Association for Consumer Research, 1987), pp. 538–542.

66. Sayeste Daser and Havva Meric, "Does Patriotism Have Any Marketing Value—Exploratory Findings for the 'Crafted with Pride in U.S.A.' Campaign," in *Advances in Consumer Research*, Vol. 14, Melanie Wallendorf and Paul Anderson, eds. (Provo, UT: Association for Consumer Research, 1987), pp. 536–537.

67. Paul Chao, "Partitioning Country of Origin Effects: Consumer Evaluations of a Hybrid Product," *Journal of International Business Studies*, Vol. 24 (Second Quarter 1993), pp. 291–306: and Richard Ettenson and Gary Gaeth, "Consumer Perceptions of Hybrid (Bi-National) Products," *Journal of Consumer Marketing*, Vol. 8 (Fall 1991), pp. 13–18.

68. Warren J. Bilkey and Eric Nes, "Country-of-Origin Effects on Product Evaluations," *Journal of International Business Studies* (Spring/Summer 1982), pp. 89–99; Paramesuar Krishnakumar, "An Exploratory Study of the Influence of Country of Origin on the Product Images of Persons from Selected Countries," unpublished Ph.D. dissertation, the University of Florida, Gainsville, 1974; and David K. Tse and Gerald J. Gorn, "An Experiment of the Salience of Country-of-Origin in the Era of Global Brands," *Journal of International Marketing*, Vol. 1, no. 2 (1993), pp. 57–76.

69. Myung-Kyoo Choi, John C. Mowen, and Michael S. Minor, "The Effect of Country of Origin on Product Evaluations: A Test of the Matchup Hypothesis," unpublished manuscript; and Martin S. Roth and Jean B. Romeo, "Matching Product Category and Country Image Perceptions: A Framework for Managing Country-of-Origin Effects," *Journal of International Business Studies*, Vol. 23 (Third Quarter 1992), pp. 477–497.

70. Theodore Levitt, *The Marketing Imagination* (New York: The Free Press, 1983).

71. Ibid.

72. "Europeans Insist on Pretesting," *Advertising Age*, August 24, 1981, p. 38.

73. R. Heller, "How Pepsi-Cola Does It in 110 Countries," in *New Ideas for Successful Marketing*, J. S. Wright and J. L. Goldstucker, eds. (Chicago: American Marketing Association, 1966), p. 700.

74. D. Chase and E. Bacot, "Levi Zipping Up World Image," *Advertising Age*, September 14, 1981, pp. 34, 36.

75. Brian Oliver, "A Little Romance Puts Impulse on Global Path," *Advertising Age*, June 24, 1985, pp. 39, 40.

76. Fisher, "The Ad Biz Gloms onto Global."

77. Ibid.

78. Amy Dockser Marcus, "Out of Step: The Poor Grow Poorer in Israel as the Army Rejects More Youths," *The Wall Street Journal*, August 13, 1993, pp. A1, A6.

79. Joseph Pereira, "Off and Running: Pushing U.S. Style, Nike and Reebok Sell Sneakers in Europe," *The Wall Street Journal*, July 22, 1993, pp. A1, A8.

80. Allyson L. Stewart, "U.S. Puts Pier Pressure on Europe's Retailers," *Marketing News*, August 2, 1993, pp. 6, 7.

81. Fisher, "The Ad Biz Glooms onto Global."

82. Julie Hill and Joseph Winski, "Goodbye Global Ads," *Advertising Age*, November 16, 1987, pp. 22, 36.

83. Joanne Lipman, "Marketers Turn Sour on Global Sales Pitch Harvard Guru Makes," *The Wall Street Journal*, May 12, 1988, pp. 1, 8.

84. Fisher, "The Ad Biz Gloms onto Global."

85. S. W. Dunn, "Effect of National Identity on Multi-National Promotional Strategy in Europe," *Journal of Marketing*, Vol. 40 (October 1976), p. 51.

86. Kevin Goldman, "Prof. Levitt Stands By Global-Ad Theory," *The Wall Street Journal*, October 13, 1992, p. B7.

87. An excellent discussion of "going local" can be found in Alan S. Parter, *Going Local: How Global Companies Become Market Insiders* (London: The Economist Intelligence Unit, 1993).

88. Murray I. Tubliner, "Brand Name Selection Is Critical Challenge for Global Marketers," *Marketing News*, August 2, 1993, pp. 7, 11.

89. Kenneth Labich, "America's International Winners," *Fortune*, April 14, 1986, pp. 34–46.

90. David Tse, John Wong, and Chin Tiong Tan, "Towards Some Standardized Cross-Cultural Consumption Values," in *Advances in Consumer Research*, Vol. 15, Michael Houston, ed. (Provo, UT: Association for Consumer Research, 1988), pp. 387–395. Other problems also exist in doing market research across cultures. For a discussion of problems in measurement, see Gaurav Bhalla and Lynn Lin, "Cross-Cultural Marketing Research: A Discussion of Equivalence Issues and Measurement Strategies," *Psychology and Marketing*, Winter 1987, pp. 275–285. For a discussion of the problems of doing group rather than individual analysis, please see Chin Tan, Jim McCullough, and Jeannie Teoh, "An Individual Analysis Approach to Cross-Cultural Research," in *Advances in Consumer Research*, Vol. 14, Mellanie Wallendorf and Paul Anderson, eds. (Provo, UT: Association for Consumer Research, 1987), pp. 394–397.

91. Case based upon Yumiko Ono, "Amway Translates with Ease into Japanese," *The Wall Street Journal*, September 21, 1990, pp. B1, B4.

CHAPTER 19 CASE STUDY

Coke Is It—All Over the World

Coca-Cola has a simple plan—dominate the world soft drink market. Amazingly, Coke is accomplishing this feat. It sells about 47% of all the soda consumed in the world—more than twice the amount of Pepsi. But the company is not resting on its laurels. It wants to expand market share by employing traditional American marketing tactics to accomplish this feat. One of its main targets is the new Europe. As the CEO of its major European competitor, Cadbury Schweppes, observed, "The way Coke is approaching the new Europe is extraordinary. Coke is more aggressive than any company I know" [1].

The company's aggressiveness can be seen in its European marketing. In the early 1980s soft drink sales were growing at about 4% a year in Europe, but profits were flat. Coke, however, viewed the European market as having great promise. Soft drinks were only the fourth favorite beverage of Europeans—behind coffee, milk, and beer—and per capita soft drink consumption was only 30% of U.S. levels. Based upon these data, the company poured $385 million into Western Europe, and by the late 1980s, volume was increasing by 10% a year. With this success under its belt, Coke feels confident about the 1990s. Coke's president, Donald Keough, said, "We think the Nineties is the decade of Europe" [2].

Coke's ventures overseas, however, have not been universally successful. Consider the company's experience in France, where it has sold soft drinks for over 70 years. In the 1980s Coke poured enormous sums of money into the French market in order to expand its market share. Despite these efforts, the drink never really caught on, due largely to cultural differences. As one Parisian said: "It's very chemical. In France, fine food is like religion, and Coke is like junk food. It's just not my culture" [3].

One of Coke's most profitable markets is Japan, where it has a 30% market share compared to Pepsi's minuscule 2% share. To increase its share, Pepsi-Cola began airing in Japan a version of its M. C. Hammer ad in which Hammer is able to perform his high-energy rap songs only while drinking a Pepsi. When he sips a Coke, however, he retreats to become a boring "crooner" as he sings the unhip old song, "Feelings." Although the Japanese like Hammer, mentioning the two brands together in a comparative advertisement was considered by some to be unnecessary, arrogant, and in poor taste. Toshio Uamaki, professor of advertising at a Japanese university, said, "As a Japanese, I wonder if it is necessary to take such hysterical action to promote a product. You would never see Nissan do such a thing against Toyota or vice versa" [4].

On the other hand, the goal of the ad was to break Japanese norms to appeal to a younger group of consumers. As a Japanese marketer at Pepsi explained, "We want this ad to be a trigger to start up our campaign." One of the problems faced by Pepsi is that it cannot use its phrase "the choice of a new generation," because Pepsi is not the choice in Japan. Instead, it uses the phrase "Pepsi loves you." Although Coke wants to have one clear worldwide image, it recognizes that it cannot sell just one product worldwide. For example, in Indonesia the company set out to change the tastes of consumers. As part of an effort to replace traditional beverages, such as tea and tropical drinks, the company began selling indigenous flavored drinks with carbonation. Favorites were strawberry-, pineapple-, and banana-flavored sodas. As the head of Coke's Pacific Group explained, "We're getting the Indonesian palate accustomed to carbonated beverages." He believes that eventually Coca-Cola will surpass the local flavors because, over time, palates "search for a less sweet taste." Such actions, however, have brought criticism. One United Nations report stated that Coke and Pepsi had "virtually wiped out from the market all traces of indigenous beverages in the Philippines" [5].

But perhaps most crucial to Coke's success is that it symbolizes the United States to the young people of the world. Subhash C. Jain, a marketing professor at the University of Connecticut, said, "Young people in developing countries drink Coca-Cola because they believe they are living like Americans." Jain said that in India poor people scrape together $1 per can for the product, which is smuggled in from Nepal. As one Coke executive said, "We always have to carry proudly the fact that Coca-Cola is the symbol of American free enterprise" [6].

QUESTIONS

1. What consumer concepts are illustrated by the case of Coca-Cola?
2. Develop a managerial applications table. For each of the consumer concepts identified, discuss one or more managerial strategy implications.
3. Do you perceive any ethical problems in Coca-Cola's attempt to replace traditional beverages with soft drinks in Third World countries?

NOTES

1. Patricia Sellers, "Coke Gets Off Its Can in Europe," *Fortune*, August 1990, pp. 68–72.
2. Michael J. McCarthy, "As a Global Marketer, Coke Excels by Being Tough and Consistent," *The Wall Street Journal*, December 19, 1989, p. A6.
3. Ibid.
4. Yukimo Ono, "Pepsi Challenges Japanese Taboo as It Ribs Coke," *The Wall Street Journal*, March 6, 1991, p. B1.
5. Douglas Shinsato, "Cola Wars in the Japanese Theater," *The Wall Street Journal*, July 8, 1991, A6.
6. Ibid.

* * *

Thanks go to Pat Gearhart for assisting in the development of the case.

Chapter 20

*The Regulatory Environment and Consumerism**

* This chapter was written by John C. Mowen and Michael S. Minor.

CONSUMER VIGNETTE

The Dark Side of Consumer Behavior

From 1980 through 1993, Abbott Laboratories raised the prices on its infant formula product, Similac, 18 times, far outpacing either inflation or the price increases in its primary ingredient, milk. During this period, Abbott had led an infant industry movement to discourage advertising, which made it more difficult for new competitors to enter the market and establish their products. A new competitor that entered the industry—the food giant Nestlé—gained only a small market share, despite selling a similar product that was cheaper. Promoting their products primarily through pediatricians, Abbott and its primary competitors—Bristol-Myers and American Home Products—had contributed about $1 million annually to the American Academy of Pediatrics and another $3 million toward the cost of building the Academy's headquarters in Illinois. As a result of these actions, federal antitrust cases were filed against the companies. To settle the cases, the three companies agreed to pay a total of over $230 million—but they denied any wrongdoing.[1]

For years Procter & Gamble called its Citrus Hill orange juice "fresh." The Federal Drug Administration (FDA), however, investigated the claim and found that the juice was made from frozen concentrate. As a result, the FDA ordered P&G to stop making the claim on product labels. Indeed, under new leadership the FDA began showing an increasing interest in food claims. In 1991 the agency began attacking claims that food products contained "no cholesterol." In many cases, the claims were made to make consumers perceive that the products were low in fat. Although a food may have no cholesterol because it is made from plants, it could still contain a great deal of saturated fat. As a result of the FDA's new-found interest in regulating business, companies such as P&G, Keebler, and Borden scrambled to change the labels on food products (especially potato chips) to meet the new guidelines.[2] P&G has since decided to discontinue Citrus Hill orange juice.

Consumers may also engage in behaviors that are personally destructive. An example of such self-destructive activities is the growing misuse of steroids. Publicity about steroids reached its zenith when Canadian sprinter Ben Johnson had his Olympic gold medal and world record in the 100-meter dash taken away after he tested positive for steroid use at the 1988 Olympic Games. Unfortunately, the publicity may have actually increased the use of steroids by teenagers to build muscles. Federal authorities estimate that $100 million a year is spent on the illicit use of steroids. As one FDA official said, "Guys want to look good at the beach. High-school kids think steroids may enhance their ability to get an athletic scholarship, play pro sports, or win the girl of their heart."[3]

The use of illegal drugs and steroids illustrates how consumers can harm themselves. However, consumers can also inflict harm when not acting in an illegal or even negligent manner. An example is the problem of how to dispose of trash. By the early 1990s the United States was producing over 200 million tons of household and commercial refuse annually.[4] Since then, the problem of where to put all the waste has grown even more acute. Indeed, only four states have suitable locations for future landfills needed to bury the debris. Through the consumption process, consumers interact with the natural environment by using resources and creating waste. How to resolve problems created by consumption may well be the key regulatory issue of the 1990s.

Finally, in some cases the actions of consumers may damage companies. In 1993 Pepsi and Diet Pepsi cans were reported to contain hypodermic needles. Originally confined to the Seattle, Washington, area, in less than a week additional claims were made in other parts of the United States. Pepsi's "crisis management" team briefly considered recalling all Pepsi (some retailers took supplies off the shelf temporarily), and Pepsi's CEO, Craig Weatherup, had discussions with the commissioner of the FDA in which a recall was considered. In the second week of the crisis, however, several people were arrested for filing false reports, and a Colorado customer was captured by a surveillance camera putting a needle into an opened can, then calling a salesclerk's attention to the "found" object. Shortly thereafter the FDA commissioner appeared on TV and explained that his agency couldn't identify even one case of tampering. The crisis was over in only two weeks.[5]

INTRODUCTION

As the chapter-opening vignette reveals, consumer behavior has a dark side. Companies can prey on consumers through unscrupulous behavior, such as in the case of Abbott Laboratories and its accomplices in their marketing of infant formula. Similarly, companies can make false product claims, as P&G did when it labeled its Citrus Hill Orange Juice as "fresh." On the other side of the coin, however, consumers may also engage in negligent behavior. Examples include actions that harm consumers themselves, such as the consumption of drugs like steroids and cocaine. In addition, consumers may actually harm companies. The case of the unscrupulous people who falsely accused Pepsi of placing hypodermic needles in cans illustrates how consumers can injure firms. To decrease the likelihood of such activities occurring, as well as the harm that results, the government develops laws and regulations that manage the buying and selling of goods and services. This backdrop of externally imposed rules is called the regulatory environment.

The **regulatory environment** consists of the laws and regulations that federal, state, and local governments develop to exert control over business practices. One goal of such laws and regulations is to protect consumers from the actions of unscrupulous firms. Thus in the United States the Federal Trade Commission (FTC) oversees the marketing practices of firms that sell over the telephone. The FTC prohibits "unfair or deceptive acts or practices" by merchants and attempts to monitor the consumer environment for evidence of such practices. Similarly, state attorney generals are charged with the responsibility of enforcing state statutes, which may include laws designed to protect consumers.

Regulatory agencies seek to protect consumers against outright scams. In addition, they attempt to control less obvious, but nonetheless illegal, activities of firms, such as when slightly used products are sold as new. In 1987 Chrysler Corporation was found to have been selling vehicles that had been driven as many as 400 miles by corporate managers as part of a quality improvement program. The odometers had been disconnected during the testing. Other examples include selling as new grand pianos or yachts that had been used as demonstrators.[6]

In addition to protecting consumers against unscrupulous companies, regulatory agencies also serve to protect consumers from themselves. Consumers can sometimes engage in negligent behavior that poses risks to themselves and to others. The FDA is charged with enforcing laws that forbid the use of various types of drugs. The growing use of steroids exemplifies one such misused product. In fact, advertising campaigns have been initiated to inform consumers of the problems of AIDS. Figure 20-1 shows one of the ads from the campaign.

Unfortunately, the list of how consumers may behave negligently is long. Drinking while driving is one particularly important area of concern. Nearly 17,700 alcohol-related traffic fatalities occur per year. Nearly 2 million people are arrested for drunk driving annually.[7] In attempting to control the carnage on the highways, many state legislatures have passed more stringent penalties for drunk driving. In addition, consumer groups such as Mothers Against Drunk Driving (MADD) have been formed. The laws and regulations, however, directly affect companies that market alcoholic beverages. For example, in 1991 the surgeon general of the United States attacked ads suggesting that drinking beer enables a person to have more fun and attract the opposite sex. As a result, beer companies began their own campaigns against drinking and driving.

Figure 20-1 Government and advertising organizations sometimes join forces to create messages to warn consumers about AIDS. (Courtesy of the Advertising Council.)

This chapter begins with an overview of the development of consumerism, a movement that heightened both government and corporate sensitivity to consumers' needs in the marketplace. Indeed, one can argue that many of the laws and regulations that pertain to consumers resulted from the consumers' movement. Next, the chapter discusses the creation and activities of several of the important federal agencies that regulate the consumer environment. The chapter then presents and analyzes several major public policy issues, such as deceptive advertising practices, marketing tactics aimed at children, and environmentalism. Several types of negligent consumer behavior are also detailed. The chapter then addresses the importance of corporate social responsibility. Indeed, some argue that there would be less need for regulatory agencies if companies consistently acted in a socially responsible manner. The chapter concludes with the presentation of a managerial applications example.

CONSUMERISM

Consumerism has traditionally been viewed as the "set of activities of government, business, independent organizations, and concerned consumers that are designed to protect the rights of consumers."[8] The development of the consumer movement spans approximately 80 years and can be roughly categorized into four eras.[9] Table 20-1 presents a chronology of the major events that occurred during consumerism's evolution. Four major eras of the consumerism movement have been identified.

The Muckraking Era

The first consumerism era was the muckraking era (1905–1920). In 1905 Upton Sinclair wrote *The Jungle*, which depicted the atrocious conditions existing in the Chicago meat-packing industry. The public furor that arose from the book's revelations sparked national awareness of the need for consumer protection. Subsequently, Congress passed the Pure Food and Drug Act (1906), the Federal Meat Inspection Act (1907), the Federal Trade Commission Act (1914), the Clayton Act (1914), and the Water Power Act (1920).

The Information Era

During the time period between 1927 and 1939, the writings of Stuart Chase and F. J. Schlink in their book, *Your Money's Worth*, once again stimulated interest in the consumer's plight in the marketplace. The primary focus of the book was on advertising and packaging techniques designed to enhance product sales rather than aid the consumer in the correct product selection. *Your Money's Worth* called for objective product-testing agencies that would not be influenced by any one manufacturer but would provide independent product evaluations to consumers. One such agency to arise at this time was the Consumers Union, publisher of *Consumer Reports*. A single unfavorable article by this nonprofit agency can doom a product.

Probably the most important legal development during the information era was the passage of the Wheeler–Lea Act, an amendment to the Federal Trade Commission Act of 1914. This act gave the FTC a more consumer-oriented perspective. Specifically, the Wheeler–Lea amendment gave the FTC additional responsibility concerning deceptive acts and practices. In addition, the FTC was given the power to issue cease-and-desist orders, fine companies for not complying with such orders, and investigate companies even without a formal complaint against them.[10]

TABLE 20-1

The Development of the Consumer Movement

Date	***Event***
	The Muckraking Era
1905	Upton Sinclair's *The Jungle*
1906	Pure Food and Drug Act
1907	Federal Meat Inspection Act
1914	Federal Trade Commission Act
1914	Clayton Act
1920	Water Power Act
	The Information Era
1927	Stuart Chase and F. J. Schlink's *Your Money's Worth*
1933	Kallet and Schlink's *10,000,000 Guinea Pigs*
1936	Robinson–Patman Act
1938	Food, Drug, and Cosmetics Act
1938	Wheeler–Lea Act
1939	Wool Products Labeling Act
	Continuing Consumer Concern
1951	Fur Products Labeling Act
1953	Flammable Products Act
1957	Poultry Products Inspection Act
1960	Hazardous Substances Labeling Act
	Modern Consumer Movement
1962	Kennedy's Enumeration of Consumer Rights
1965	Ralph Nader's *Unsafe at Any Speed*
1966	Cigarette Labeling and Advertising Act
1966	Fair Packaging and Labeling Act
1966	Child Protection Act
1966	National Traffic and Motor Vehicle Safety Act
1968	Consumer Credit Protection Act
1972	Consumer Product Safety Act
1975	Magnuson–Moss Warranty–Federal Trade Commission Improvement Act

SOURCE: Data adapted from Rogene Buchholz, *Business Environment and Public Policy* (Englewood Cliffs, NJ: Prentice Hall, 1982).

The Era of Continuing Concern

The era of continuing consumer concern (1951–1960) was the next major time period in the consumer movement. During World War II and the immediate postwar years, the focus shifted away from consumerism. The nation experienced a new prosperity and a hunger for products that had been denied during the war. Public energy was concentrated on rebuilding lives rather than fighting for consumer rights. As a consequence, fewer pieces of legislation were passed during the era. Among the regulations passed were the Fur Products Labeling Act, which provided mandatory specifications relating to labeling and advertising fur products; the Flammable Products Act, which prohibited the making of garments from flammable material; and the Hazardous Substances Labeling Act, which required warning labels on household products that contained toxic, flammable, or irritating substances.

The Modern Consumer Movement

The modern consumer movement lasted from 1962 until 1980, when President Ronald Reagan was inaugurated. The modern consumer movement began with the enumeration of the four consumer rights by President John F. Kennedy in 1962. These rights are the right to safety, the right to be informed, the right to redress or to be heard, and the right to choice. Many of the subsequent congressional acts were designed to aid in the protection of these rights.

Another critical event during this time was the publication of Ralph Nader's book *Unsafe at Any Speed*. This book criticized General Motors' attitude toward automobile safety, with particular emphasis on the Chevrolet Corvair. The attention Nader drew from his book incited interest in other consumer areas.

Several important acts were passed between 1962 and 1975. For example, the Cigarette Labeling and Advertising Act (1966) required the surgeon general's warning with regard to the health hazards of smoking on all cigarette packages. The Child Protection Act (1966) banned the sale of hazardous toys and goods intended for children. The Consumer Credit Protection Act (1968) required that consumers be informed of the full terms and finance charges for consumer loans and installment purchases. In addition, the Consumer Product Safety Act of 1972 established the Consumer Product Safety Commission.

With the inauguration of President Reagan in 1980, the vigor of the consumer movement clearly faded. One former government official described the consumer movement as going "from Nader to nadir after President Reagan took office."[11] A combination of factors appears to have been responsible for the decline. Perhaps foremost was the severe reduction in funding for government agencies. For example, the staff of the Environmental Protection Agency was cut by 50%.[12] In addition to the funding cuts, the basic philosophy of the Reagan administration certainly set back the consumer movement. Market regulation in the form of incentives (marketable air pollution permits) and disincentives (advance disposal fees on nonrecyclable products and packaging) were favored over "command-and-control" forms of nonmarket regulation.[13]

Back to Activism?

The question remains as to whether the change of environment found in the Reagan and Bush years will continue into the future. In an era of severe international competition, the costs of heavy-handed regulation can be severe.

The Clinton administration in its early years has attempted to be both reformer of government and advocate of government action at the same time. The presidency has also been encumbered by other public policy issues of great importance, such as health care, national service, and NAFTA passage. Vice President Gore—a staunch environmentalist—has seen his hopes for a strong antipollution policy deferred.

In general terms, however, Clinton is inclined to be active. As one example of Clinton's more activist approach, the prescription drug industry in early 1993 proposed self-regulation rather than government price controls as a remedy for rapidly escalating drug prices. Under the proposal by the Pharmaceutical Manufacturers Association, average annual drug price increases would be limited to the annual rate of inflation. In February 1993 Clinton blasted drug manufacturers when he introduced a program aiming to ensure that every American child is immunized.[14]

THE DEVELOPMENT OF MAJOR GOVERNMENTAL REGULATORY AGENCIES

One of the consequences of the consumer legislation was the establishment of government agencies whose purpose entailed guarding consumers against unfair business practices. This section examines some of the major agencies to evolve during the past 75 years.

The Federal Trade Commission

This commission was established in 1914 as a result of the Federal Trade Commission Act for the purpose of curtailing unfair trade practices and limiting monopolies. Some of the options available to the FTC when violations occur include the imposition of fines, the refund of money or return of property, the awarding of damages, and public notification of violations. For example, the FTC ordered ITT-Continental, the maker of Profile Bread, to correct its claim that consumption of the bread would aid in losing weight. In actuality, the bread contained seven fewer calories per slice than most other breads. As a result of FTC intervention, one-fourth of the company's advertising carried the corrective message for one year.[15] The FTC also issues guidelines regarding the use of the comparative price format in advertising, a practice that has been increasing.[16]

The Food and Drug Administration

The FDA traces its roots to the Food and Drug Act of 1906. This act has undergone several amendments to enlarge the FDA's responsibility. The goal of the FDA is to protect consumers from unsafe and impure food, drugs, cosmetics, and therapeutic devices. The dominant activities of this agency include guarding against the mislabeling of food, drugs, cosmetics, or therapeutic devices; identifying and eliminating improper food preparation or packaging; and establishing quality standards. Criminal prosecution and seizure of the product in violation are two remedies available to the FDA.[17] Recently, the FDA announced limitations on health claims for vitamin, herbal, and mineral dietary supplements. Under these limits, antioxidant vitamins can't be claimed to prevent cancer and heart disease, nor can zinc be linked with the prevention of immune deficiency in the elderly.[18] The FDA is also responsible for the approval of new drugs for the seriously ill (such as cystic fibrosis and the HIV virus). It must walk a thin line between ensuring that companies aren't allowed to provide consumers with drugs that are incompletely tested and therefore might do more harm than good, and denying potentially breakthrough treatments out of an abundance of caution. In recent years the FDA has tried to accelerate reviews for drugs for the seriously ill based on the theory that these patients don't have as much to lose from new treatments.

The National Highway Traffic Safety Administration

This agency was created in 1970 by the Highway Safety Act. Its responsibilities include regulating the safety performance of new and used motor vehicles and their equipment, investigating motor vehicle safety defects, and establishing required average fuel economy standards for new motor vehicles. This agency also has the power to order recalls for safety defects that are not covered by any of their mandatory standards.[19]

For example, the NHTSA was the agency responsible for the recall of 14.5 million Firestone "500" radial tires and 1.4 million Ford Pintos and Bobcats during the 1970s.[20]

The Consumer Product Safety Commission

The need for such an agency became apparent after a National Commission study found that product-related accidents resulted in 20 million injuries annually. In addition, 30,000 deaths and 110,000 permanently disabling injuries have been attributed to this type of accident. These product-related incidents cost the economy some $5.5 billion.[21] Consequently, the Consumer Product Safety Act (1972) established this agency to investigate the causes of product-related accidents and to develop appropriate responses.[22] The commission's primary responsibilities involve

1. Identifying products that may be unsafe.
2. Establishing labeling and product safety standards.
3. Recalling defective products.
4. Banning products that pose an unreasonable risk.[23]

The Federal Hazardous Substances Act, the Poison Packaging Prevention Act, the Flammable Fabrics Act, and the Refrigerator Safety Act also fall within the agency's realm. The CPSC has the authority to impose fines ranging from $50,000 to $500,000 with a possible one-year jail sentence, to initiate product recalls, to order refunds, and to disperse public earnings.[24]

Future Directions in Consumerism and Regulatory Agencies

What future orientation might consumerism take? For the consumer, changing times should find him or her (1) exercising a larger role in the marketplace and perhaps becoming more concerned about health and safety issues even as industrialized societies grow healthier and safer on average; (2) joining buying clubs or cooperatives and sharing ownership of expensive goods (e.g., time sharing of condominiums); and (3) participating in consumer organizations at the local level.[25] From the Federal Trade Commission's perspective, its areas of concern will likely focus on the "marketing" of professional services, the use of comparative disclosures (e.g., energy efficiency ratings on appliances), and the implications of the "new media" such as videodiscs and cable television for marketers.[26] Other marketing issues concern commercial use of the Internet and the proposed "information superhighway."

Another trend is activism on the part of state attorney generals. For example, New York State's attorney general vigorously prosecuted Sears, Inc., for false price advertising shortly after the company announced its "Everyday Low Price" campaign. Similarly, the attorney general of Texas energetically pursued the Volvo Corporation when it was discovered that certain advertisements were deceptive. The ads showed a "monster" truck rolling over a series of cars. All the roofs of the cars caved in, except for the Volvo. However, the Volvo's roof had been reinforced prior to the demonstration, a fact that the ad neglected to convey.[27]

The internationalization of our economy will increase our exposure to consumer-related practices in other countries. One of the major concerns during the negotiation of NAFTA (the North American Free Trade Agreement) was possible harm to U.S. citizens living along the border, who may be exposed to the effects of Mexico's environmental law enforcement, which is generally considered to be less stringent than in the United States.

Several countries have gone further than the United States in the passage of strong consumer legislation. Norway banned several forms of sales promotion—trading stamps, contests, premiums—as being "unfair" instruments for promoting products. Thailand requires food processors selling national brands to market low-price brands also so that low-income consumers can also find economy brands on the shelves. In India, food companies need special approval to launch brands that duplicate what already exists on the market, such as another cola drink.[28] Also in India, the 15th of the month is "Customer's Day" at all nationalized banks, and bank management attends to routine complaints on the part of customers.[29] In China, nationwide television has been used to encourage viewers to call special hotlines to expose substandard products.[30] These and other consumer-related developments have not surfaced in the United States, but they suggest how far regulations could be pushed to constrain marketing practice.

Some Major Public Policy Issues in the Consumer Domain

As discussed in the previous section, the most recent consumerism movement originated during the 1960s, with extensive interest and growth occurring in the 1970s. Some of the major consumer issues to evolve during this time period involved deceptive advertising, advertising aimed at children, and environmental protection.

Deceptive Advertising

Since 1984 the FTC has held that an advertisement may be deemed **deceptive advertising** if it has the "capacity to deceive a measurable segment of the public."[31] The commission usually considers a deception rate of 20 to 25% to be "measurable," although this percentage could be reduced if consumers stand to lose a large amount of money or could incur physical injury as a result of the deception.[32] Whether or not the advertiser actually intended to deceive consumers is considered irrelevant. Table 20-2 displays the different categories of deceptive claims that may be present in advertising considered misleading by the FTC.

Corrective Advertising

In response to the increased attention given to deceptive advertising tactics in the 1960s and early 1970s, the FTC began to order corrective measures from some of the guilty parties. The incident that sparked the idea of **corrective advertising**

TABLE 20-2

Categories of Deceptive Claims

Objective Claim—A standard for comparison exists against which the claim may be compared to determine if it is deceptive or not. Example: a Poly-Grip commercial that claimed denture wearers could eat foods such as corn on the cob or apples without fear of their dentures loosening. In reality, the front teeth of many dentures are for cosmetic purposes. Poly-Grip would not be effective for these types of dentures.

Subjective or Opinion Claim—This type of claim is difficult to prove false because trade "puffery" or evaluative claims are allowed. The FTC's position is that advertisements that claim that certain products are "the best" are not usually taken seriously by the average consumer.

Implied Claim—This claim involves the overall impression the consumer has concerning a product or service apart from the literal advertising text, or "deception by innuendo." Example: In 1962 a television commercial was shown whose purpose was to display the superiority of Libby plate glass over plain glass. In fact, plate glass does possess many attributes that ordinary glass does not. However, as a means of demonstrating this notion, the commercial showed an outdoor scene filmed from the inside of two car windows—the windows representing each of the two forms of glass. From the inside of the "ordinary glass," viewers saw a distorted scene. The view through the "plate glass" window pictured a perfect view. In actuality, the "ordinary glass" scene had been filmed through a window smeared with Vaseline and the "plate glass" scene has been filmed out of a rolled-down window.

Claim with Two Meanings—If an advertisement has two meanings, one of which is false, then the entire ad is considered deceptive. Example: In an advertisement from the National Commission on Egg Nutrition that encouraged individuals to eat eggs, the FTC issued a cease-and-desist order that prevented the commercial from containing the statement "There is no scientific evidence that eating eggs increases the risk of . . . heart disease." The commission decided that research in this area still provided mixed results such that the claim should not be made.

Unsubstantiated Claim—Affirmative claims for a product that are not reasonably supported. Examples: "Miracle" weight-loss products and cosmetics that claim to retard aging or remove wrinkles.

Evaluating the Sufficiency of Information—An advertisement can be deemed deceptive if it fails to disclose relevant facts or conditions. Example: Fresh Horizons, a bread that was positioned as having a high fiber content. However, packaging and advertising must disclose that the source of the fiber is tree pulp.

SOURCE: Based on Dorothy Cohen, "Protecting Consumers from Unfairness and Deception," in *Consumerism and Beyond: Research Perspectives on the Future Social Environment,* Paul N. Bloom, ed. (Cambridge, MA: Marketing Science Institute, 1982), pp. 68–74.

involved Campbell's soup advertisements in which clear marbles were placed in the bottom of a soup bowl, causing the vegetables to float on top. Consumers were left with the impression that the soup contained more vegetable pieces than it actually did. The FTC issued a cease-and-desist order that banned this practice.[33]

Perhaps the most famous of all corrective advertising cases involved Warner-Lambert's claim that Listerine mouthwash could prevent or lessen the severity of colds and sore throats. The company began manufacturing Listerine in 1879 and advertising the product in 1921. Thus for more than 50 years Warner-Lambert had been making this claim. In 1975 the FTC issued its order that Warner-Lambert must attempt to correct the misimpressions that their advertisements had created. From September 1978 to February 1980, Warner-Lambert spent more than $10 million on corrective advertising. Nearly 95% of this money was devoted to television commercials.[34]

Advertising Substantiation

In 1971 the FTC initiated its **advertising substantiation** program as a result of the siege of criticism against advertising. The objective of this program was twofold. First, consumers would be provided with information that might help them make rational choices. Second, competition would be encouraged as other companies challenged advertising claims.[35] Thus the FTC could require companies to provide tests, studies, or other data that supposedly support the advertisements' claims regarding the product's safety, performance, efficacy, quality, or comparative price.[36]

One example involved Bristol-Myers Company. Their advertisements for analgesics used phrases such as "here's proof," "medically proven," or "doctors recommend." In addition, the commercials used visual cues that implied these statements, such as having the spokesperson in a white coat or in a laboratory setting. Such tactics suggested the superiority of their products over those of their competition. The FTC held that in the category of over-the-counter drugs it would be easy for the advertiser to make misleading claims because many consumers are not able to evaluate these claims adequately for themselves. Thus the commission ordered that Bristol-Myers conduct two well-controlled clinical tests to substantiate its claims of superiority based on scientific evidence. In addition, Bristol-Myers was to stop claiming that any group recommends its products unless the company possessed a reasonable basis for its claim.[37]

The substantiation program was not designed, however, to apply to claims that were merely trade puffery. As a result, this program is often criticized for encouraging marketers to engage in evaluative advertising—vague, subjective claims such as "Our brand tastes the best"—which offers limited relevant information to the consumer.[38] Some researchers suggest that evaluative advertising may delude consumers into believing that the brand is somehow unique or superior to those of the competition. However, public policy makers are unlikely to challenge such advertising due to the abstract nature of the claims.[39]

Future Directions

Despite the attempts made during the past 15 years to monitor deception in advertising, studies show that consumers continue to express concern over potentially misleading advertising. Table 20-3 displays consumers' views of the proportion of advertising that they consider misleading across the various media. Although television advertising has had a greater quantity of misleading advertisements, the respondents in this study viewed telephone advertising as the form with the greatest proportion of

TABLE 20-3

Perceptions of Advertising as Misleading

	All	*Most*	*Some*	*Few*	*None*	*Uncertain*
Telephone	27.0%	40.2%	18.6%	3.7%	3.7%	6.8%
Mail	10.5	50.8	27.5	4.1	3.4	3.7
Television	5.4	33.1	47.8	10.0	1.7	2.0
Home distribution	6.0	27.0	39.3	15.8	4.6	7.4
Magazines	3.8	21.8	50.2	16.3	3.1	4.8
Radio	2.4	17.2	54.1	15.5	3.4	7.2
Classified ads	3.2	17.2	40.0	24.9	3.9	10.9
Newspapers	1.7	16.6	49.7	22.4	5.2	4.5

SOURCE: Adapted with permission from Howard G. Schultz and Marianne Casey, "Consumer Perceptions of Advertising as Misleading," *Journal of Consumer Affairs*, vol. 15 (1981), pp. 340–357.

misleading advertising. Direct mail placed a close second. These results suggest that greater emphasis might be placed on consumer education material that addresses the issues of mail fraud and telephone misuse.[40]

Children's Advertising

Both marketing managers and public policy makers have reacted to criticisms of advertising, particularly advertising directed at children. Children are a significant target market. In 1989 children between the ages of 4 and 12 spent $6.2 billion of their own money and at least $3.7 billion of their parents' money, not to mention the purchases they influenced. Advertisers spend $100 million on Saturday morning child-focused advertising alone.[41]

Also, children prefer nationally labeled brands (often more profitable than private-label brands). A study cited by *The Wall Street Journal* shows that while 70% of adults have become big buyers of private-label store brands, only 7% of children would even consider the stuff: they want brand-name gifts and designer clothes. Brands offer children a common commercial language, something identifying them as part of a group.[42]

The controversy surrounding children's advertising grew so intense in the late 1970s that the FTC considered banning all advertising aimed at young children.[43] Marketing managers and public policy makers have benefited from consumer behavior research and theory that examines children's responses to advertising.[44] Some key issues that researchers have investigated include:

- Can children tell the difference between commercials and programming?
- Do children understand the selling intent of commercials?
- Do commercials make children want products that are not good for them?

The need for continued concern regarding children's exposure to television is dependent on the influence television has on children. According to some researchers, the influence of TV has slipped in recent years as such techniques as children's membership clubs and catalog marketing programs have flourished.[45] One of the reasons the influence of TV may have declined is because children may be seeing fewer commercials. In 1990 the Children's Television Act limited the advertising children would see on children's television programs—no more than 10.5 minutes per hour on weekends and no more than 12 minutes per hour during the week.

Environmental Protection

The energy crisis during the mid-1970s prompted government officials to request that American consumers conserve many natural resources that had been taken for granted for many years.

Environmental "consciousness" has certainly increased. Studies report finding that 78% of consumers would switch to an environmentally friendly product container even it were priced as much as 5% higher than a less friendly product. An *Adweek* poll indicates that 96% of consumers say environmental concerns influence their purchase decisions. Surveys of international corporate executives have shown that over 90% of respondents report that changes are being made to existing products and new product offerings to reflect this demand.[46]

On the other hand, in most cases consumers seem to be willing to make only minor concessions in convenience, and few are willing to make major behavioral changes. For example, 70% of Canadians indicated that they would participate in household recycling programs, but only 50% would use returnable containers, and only 33% would pay more for environmentally safe products.[47]

One major obstacle appears to hinder the transition from consciousness of the environment to effective conservation programs. Most consumers do not personally accept responsibility to conserve resources, although most individuals would likely state that they favor conservation efforts.[48] Russell Belk and his associates stressed that the attribution of causality for the energy crisis is critical in determining whether or not an individual will conserve. When an individual attributes the cause of the energy shortage to a nonpersonal source (such as the government, foreign powers, or major oil companies), then she or he feels that a nonpersonal solution (such as government intervention) is the answer. However, if the individual perceives the general public as the source of blame, then the person is more likely to engage in conservation behavior.[49]

Conservation behavior can be divided into three basic categories: curtailment behavior, maintenance behavior, and efficiency behavior.[50] Curtailment behavior involves reducing consumption by modifying current behavior. Examples of this form of conservation behavior include adjusting the thermostat, washing clothes in cold water, and driving less. Maintenance behavior involves making sure that energy-consuming equipment and appliances are in good working order. Tuning up the car and getting the furnace cleaned are two examples of maintenance behavior. Efficiency behavior focuses on reduction in energy consumption via structural changes in the home or travel environment. Purchasing a more fuel-efficient car, installing solar panels, or insulating the attic are examples of efficiency behavior. The degree of information seeking, financial risk involved, and modification in life-style vary with the type of conservation behavior. Therefore, policy makers need to design their conservation programs to complement the form of conservation behavior they are trying to encourage.

Despite the obvious difficulties, there is some evidence that progress is being made. From 1988 to 1991 yard waste composting facilities more than doubled to about 1,400. In 1989 alone, about 550 landfills were shut down and the number of materials recovery facilities more than doubled over the previous year.[51] The Environmental Defense Fund reports that the national recycling rate increased from 10 percent in 1988 to 17 percent, and curbside recycling programs have grown from about 1,000 to over 5,400.[52]

NEGLIGENT CONSUMER BEHAVIOR

Most of us would agree with the statements "Seatbelts save lives," "Smoking is hazardous to your health," and "Drinking and driving don't mix." Yet many consumers, in some manner or other, exhibit what might be termed negligent behavior. **Negligent behavior** is composed of those actions and inactions that may negatively affect the long-term quality of life of individuals and society. This type of behavior can occur in two different contexts. The first form of negligent behavior occurs due to the consumption of a product that in and of itself presents a hazard of some sort. The consumption of cigarettes and certain drugs are two examples that fall into this category. A second type of negligent behavior occurs when the consumer uses a product in an unsafe manner or fails to use safety features and follow safety instructions. Failure to use seatbelts and not following dosage instructions for over-the-counter drugs are examples of this form of negligent behavior.[53]

Two approaches exist to induce people to act in a safer manner. One involves legislation that creates laws forcing consumers to wear seatbelts, bans the advertising and sale of cigarettes, and imposes stiffer penalties for drunk driving. An alternative approach involves the use of marketing techniques to encourage more appropriate consumer actions. Consumer behavior research and theory provide insight into how both marketers and public policy makers can influence consumers to behave in a safer manner.

Getting People to Buckle Up

Automobile accidents claim the lives of more than 30,000 individuals a year and result in 500,000 more injuries. Seatbelts could have prevented more than half of these deaths and injuries, yet only approximately 15% of American drivers and passengers wear their seatbelts.[54] Beliefs that they would never be in an accident, that seatbelts do not provide much benefit even if you do wear them, and that seatbelts are uncomfortable are just a few excuses offered by consumers.

Early attempts to persuade consumers to wear their seatbelts were dominated by a fear appeal approach depicting the grisly results of nonuse. A National Safety Council campaign in 1969 involving more than $50 million worth of public service media space and air time resulted in no change in the claimed use of seatbelts. A subsequent strategy in Michigan used the more emotionally charged theme of "Somebody needs you." At a cost of some $2.1 million, the observed increase in seatbelt usage was 4.4%, about 270,000 persons. Despite the expense of such projects, the results have been found to be short-lived. If the reminder to buckle up is not present, many individuals do not make the effort—simply because it is not ingrained in their routine or because they do not devote their attention to the situation. Figure 20-2 presents storyboards of ads run during 1986.

The theory of operant conditioning provides an additional perspective on this problem. As noted in Chapter 5, the positive reinforcement of a behavior increases the likelihood of that behavior's being repeated. The application is clear. To increase the likelihood that people will wear seatbelts, they need to be rewarded when they buckle up. Some studies have found that rewarding individuals when they are wearing their seatbelts can more than double usage.[55] Rewards need not be elaborate—perhaps discount coupons or bingo chips—and they can easily be administered at any drive-through location.

Another researcher suggested a different approach to encouraging people to buckle up: flash cards. Drivers or passengers who themselves are buckled up display a flash card that reads "Please buckle up—I care" to occupants of other vehicles. After the other individuals have buckled up, the "flasher" then shows a card that says "Thank you for buckling up." In one study, this method resulted in a 22% compliance rate.

Flash cards represent one example of how to reinforce seatbelt use. However, one author has stated that "there seems to be no form of educational campaign or message that will persuade more than a small percentage of American motorists to voluntarily wear seatbelts."[56] The author suggested that legislating seatbelt usage would most likely be the only effective means of getting consumers to buckle up.

An interesting adjunct to the discussion over seatbelt use is the question of compensating behavior.[57] As early as 1970, an argument was made that seatbelt use should not be mandatory—because seatbelt use provides the driver with an added sense of security which would translate into more reckless driving. A recent study finds, however, that this offsetting (or compensatory) behavior is likely to occur only among drivers who are "risk lovers."[58] (Attitudes toward risk are discussed in Chapter 6.)

To Puff or Not to Puff

Until the late 1960s, consumers were exposed to nearly 3,000 cigarette commercials per week representing 38 different brands. Concern over the health hazards that cigarette smoking presents had gained attention in the 1950s. However, it was not until the issuance of the surgeon general's report in 1964 that public policy makers began to exert considerable efforts to alter the public's smoking behavior. The Department of Health and Human Services (DHHS) spent more than $2 million in 1967 in an effort to inform consumers of the health hazards of smoking. DHHS used such tactics as bumper stickers that read "Smoke, Choke, Croak" and endorsements from athletic stars such as Peggy Fleming and Bart Starr claiming, "I don't smoke." In general, the approach was to depict smokers as distraught coughers, whereas nonsmokers were portrayed as happy and healthy.[59]

These promotional efforts had some limited impact. Between 1967 and 1968, cigarette sales fell by 1.3 billion, and the number of U.S. smokers dropped by 1.5 million to 70 million. However, rather than a steady decline in cigarette sales

THE ADVERTISING COUNCIL, INC.

SAFETY BELT EDUCATION CAMPAIGN

U.S. DEPARTMENT OF TRANSPORTATION

"DUMMY CAM" :30 CNTD-2130

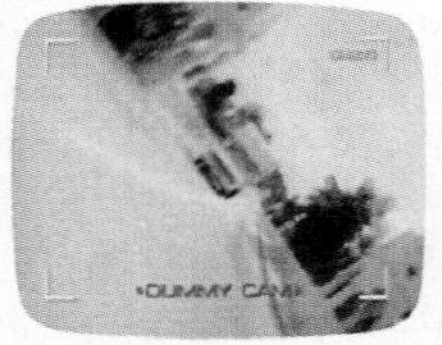

YOU COULD LEARN A LOT FROM A DUMMY. BUCKLE YOUR SAFETY BELT.

LARRY: Vince, that new dummy cam is great. VINCE: Yeah. It'll sure give people a whole new outlook on what it's like when you don't wear a safety belt. (SFX: VINCE & LARRY SCREAM & SHOUT; CRASH, RUMBLE, ETC.) LARRY: I think they'll get the picture. ANNCR VO: You could learn a lot from a dummy. Buckle your safety belt.

"DESERT JEANS" :30 CNTD-2230 (Also available in :20 length, CNTD-2120.)

(MUSIC, WIND)

(SFX: BRAKES)

GIRL: Excuse me. Do you wear your safety belt?

VINCE: Why no. I don't wear my safety belt.

GIRL: Thank you.

(SFX: WINDOW CLOSING)

(WIND)

ANNCR VO: You could learn a lot from a dummy. Buckle your safety belt.

"ANY QUESTIONS" :15 CNTD-2115

VINCE: Okay. For the last time, this is your head.

This is your head when you don't wear a safety belt.

(SFX: EXPLOSION) Any questions?

ANNCR VO: You could learn a lot from a dummy. Buckle your safety belt.

"AIRBAGS" :30 CNTD-7203

(SFX: CAR REVVING) VINCE: Hey, thanks to these airbags here, this job is now a piece o'cake, Lar. LARRY: But, Vince– VINCE: Yeah, I'll tell ya something, partner, I just might stick around a few more years. LARRY: But, Vince– VINCE: No more dashboard de jour or Vince under glass– LARRY: But, Vince– Look out! (SFX: BOTH SCREAM) Even with airbags, Vince, you still gotta remember to buckle your safety belt. VINCE: Now you tell me. ANNCR VO: You could learn a lot from a dummy. Buckle your safety belt.

Volunteer Agency: Leo Burnett U.S.A.
Volunteer Campaign Director: Harold J. Handley, McCormic & Co., Inc. 7/93

Figure 20-2 A persuasive appeal to encourage consumers to buckle up. (Courtesy of the Advertising Council.)

or the number of smokers, the major behavioral trend has been toward the purchase of low-tar and low-nicotine brands.

Despite a ban on television commercials promoting the product, the cigarette industry continues to survive. Some researchers state that poor communications strategies by antismoking groups are in part to blame, but the root causes are the strong social reward for smoking in some circles (such as among teenagers) and certain "deeply held cognitive positions." In fact, consumer awareness of the major health effects of smoking is now quite high. Indeed, researchers have found that smokers now overestimate, rather than underestimate, the risk of lung cancer from smoking.[60] These results suggest that many smokers simply tune out or develop counterarguments for antismoking messages.

During the mid-1990s, the negative publicity concerning smoking and the actions of cigarette manufacturers grew in intensity. In particular, the advertising campaign employing "Joe Camel" by R. J. R. Nabisco was attacked for targeting the youth of America. In 1994 *Advertising Age* and the Roper organization conducted a national poll, which found that 68% of Americans believe that cigarette ads influence children and teens to smoke. Further, the results revealed that two-thirds of Americans, including half of all smokers, wanted the U.S. government to place greater restrictions on cigarette advertising. Over 50% of those polled wanted all cigarette advertising banned.[61] With a staunch antismoking surgeon general (Jocelyn Elders) also attacking cigarette manufacturers, it is likely that antismoking legislation will be passed.

Drinking and Driving

Each year nearly 25,000 people are killed and 900,000 are injured as a result of drunk driving.[62] In the 1980s increased attention was given to the issue of drinking and driving, in part because of the efforts of the national organization Mothers Against Drunk Driving. Public policy makers could make greater use of consumer behavior research concerning this area. Following are some of the methods currently used, along with their strengths and weaknesses.[63]

Informing and Educating

This approach assumes that individuals act rationally in an effort to further their self-interest. Thus the public should be presented with objective information about the hazards of drunk driving.[64] When developing such information campaigns, advertisers have frequently used a fear-inducing message appeal. Highlight 20-1 discusses the use of fear in changing behavior. The Department of Transportation and the Ad Council initiated an advertising campaign against drinking and driving. One of the ads is shown in Figure 20-3. As can be seen, a strong fear appeal is used. The message in this appeal would be difficult to misperceive.

Social Controls

The majority of liquor advertisements portray the beverage as a drink consumed in the presence of others and as a means of heightening one's acceptability. The social controls strategy plays on the understanding that individuals are influenced by the actions and attitudes of those around them. The dominant theme employed in this tactic is to have social influencers disapproving of drunk driving. Examples of this

HIGHLIGHT 20-1

Researching Consumer Behavior

USAGE PATTERNS AND SAFETY As we can see from examples in the text, the same techniques used in consumer research to enhance product marketability may help illustrate usage patterns that will lead to enhanced safety features or safer usage practices.

For example, consumer research could shed light on the best method of presenting appeals to stop such practices as drug use and sexual behavior that may transmit diseases such as AIDS. As discussed in the text, the Advertising Council campaign against drunk driving primarily uses fear tactics, while NBC's campaign is more positively oriented.

A study by Tanner and his associates analyzed the effectiveness of using fear appeals vis-à-vis the transmission of sexually transmitted diseases among college students. They found that fear appeals do generate perceptions of threat and therefore greater attention (as well as greater learning). However, if the recipient of the fear appeal has experience or has learned coping responses (say, via word of mouth), the odds of making an inappropriate response are high. The best method seems to be a combination approach, with a fear appeal followed by illustrations of both poor responses and good responses. For example, a public service announcement should first illustrate the problems of sexually transmitted diseases, show why inappropriate responses (such as assuming that current sexual partners "aren't the type" to carry STDs) are inappropriate, and then suggest better responses (such as using condoms).

Another study has explored the well-known link between peer pressure, the desire for conformity, and drug use. This study of college and high school students suggested that the likelihood of refusing to go along with drug use by peer groups was increased if the subject was provided plausible reasons for the group's deviant behavior, such as the notion that group members were smoking marijuana because they just wanted to "fit in." The implication seems to be that advertisements designed to decrease drug use should include information on why members of peer groups behave as they do.

Based on Suzanne Benet, Robert E. Pitts, and Michael La Tour, "The Appropriateness of Fear Appeal Use for Health Care Marketing to the Elderly: Is It OK to Scare Granny?" *Journal of Business Ethics*, Vol. 12 (1993), pp. 45–55; Gregory W. Boller and Alan J. Bush, "Commentary on 'The Growing Threat of AIDS: How Marketers Must Respond,'" *Journal of Health Care Marketing*, Vol. 10 (September 1990), pp. 61–63; John F. Tanner, Jr., James B. Hunt, and David R. Eppright, "The Protection Motivation Model: A Normative Model of Fear Appeals," *Journal of Marketing*, Vol. 55 (July 1991), pp. 36–45; and Randall L. Rose, William O. Bearden, and Jesse E. Teel, "An Attributional Analysis of Resistance to Group Pressure Regarding Illicit Drug and Alcohol Consumption," *Journal of Consumer Research*, Vol. 19 (June 1992), pp. 1–13. The use of fear appeals is also discussed in Chapter 10.

strategy include campus meetings of the SADD (Students Against Drunk Driving) organization or commercials showing family and friends taking car keys away from the person who overindulged.

NBC has created a public service campaign using social controls. Rather than using scare tactics like the Advertising Council, the NBC spots feature popular stars describing what they find attractive in the opposite sex. The advertisements suggest that these stars find drinking too much and taking drugs to be unattractive practices.[65]

Figure 20-3 A strong fear appeal developed to reduce drunk driving. (Courtesy of the Advertising Council.)

Economic Incentives

Using concepts derived from behavior modification theory, one approach might be to reward individuals for demonstrating the desired behavior. Insurance companies currently use this approach by providing reduced rates to individuals who agree not to drink and drive. Some restaurants give a free meal to the person who agrees not to drink so that he or she can drive his or her friends who are drinking home. The limitation of this approach is that some individuals may refrain from drinking and driving only if they perceive the benefits as outweighing the costs.

Economic Disincentives

Rather than rewarding individuals for not drinking and driving, the use of economic disincentives punishes individuals who drink and drive. This punishment could occur directly—through fines, car repair costs, and high insurance premiums—or indirectly—through an excise tax on alcohol that would result in higher liquor prices. However, consumers may continue to drink and drive if they feel the benefits of their behavior still outweigh the costs. These campaigns appear to have paid dividends. Over the decade ending in 1992, alcohol-related traffic fatalities declined from 25,165 to 17,699. This decline is part of an overall decline in alcohol consumption. The National Institute on Alcohol Abuse and Alcoholism reports that in 1991 drinking per capita fell to its lowest mark since 1965, with hard liquor intake declining to near-1949 levels.[66]

Gambling

Gambling is a form of addictive consumption that affects an estimated 8 to 12 million people. While a compulsive gambler is most likely a member of a minority group who makes less than $25,000 a year, many addicts are high-income professionals. Like drug users, compulsive gamblers may exhibit a "high" while engaging in the activity, followed by depression when they stop.[67] Although we often think of gambling in connection with casinos, which have spread from Las Vegas and New Jersey to such locales as riverboat gambling (16 boats operate in five different states), 37 states now have state-run lotteries that make it easy to gamble with nothing more than a visit to the local convenience store.[68]

Gambling exists in many countries. In Japan, 17 billion yen a year, equal to one-fourth of the national government's budget, is spent on pachinko, a game that appears to be addictive for the Japanese. The game is played on an upright pinball-like machine, where steel balls drop through formations of nails. Pachinko is even easier to play than the state lotteries in the United States, since pachinko parlors can be found on virtually any busy street, with over 14,500 parlors in operation and 3.1 million machines. *Fortune* magazine estimates that an owner of a pachinko machine manufacturing company, Kenkichi Nakajima, is the fourth wealthiest individual in the world.[69]

Other countries with gambling include Taiwan, where a state-run lottery was declared reinstated in 1993,[70] and Russia, where McCracken Brooks Communications of Minneapolis created a lottery in 1993 to raise money for the Goodwill Games in St. Petersburg. A Greek telecommunications company, Intracom, is running Russia's largest lottery, which is using high-technology electronics and is the first in that country to be run by a foreign company.[71] Globally, state-run lottery winnings in 1992 totaled $71.6 billion, with the United States the biggest winner at $20.5 billion.[72]

Compulsive Consumption

Some shoppers "shop till they drop" because they consume compulsively. The activity is compulsive rather than pleasurable or functional. They turn to shopping the way other addicts use alcohol or drugs. Like other addicts, they seek the experience to protect their self-image, but when they end the experience they feel more self-loathing, are subject to the disapproval of others, and this produces guilt. They attempt to escape this self-loathing by engaging in the experience again. According to some psychologists, this type of experience isn't pleasurable even while the addict is engaged in the activity.[73] Other forms of **compulsive consumption** are shown in Table 20-4.

Product Misuse

Many of us would never think of using a blow dryer in the shower or a lawn mower to trim the hedges. Nor would we think that using a cellular phone in a car may lead to an accident, although it happens. Consumers' misuse of products in such a fashion has prompted marketers and public policy makers to exert special precautions in the design and testing of products. In fact, the majority of product-related injuries result not from a flaw in the product itself but from misuse of an otherwise safe product.[74] As one individual put it, "The most dangerous component is the consumer, and there's no way to recall him."[75] In addition to misusing products, consumers can abuse services. Figure 20-4 shows one example. The sign clearly warns

TABLE 20-4

Compulsive Consumption: Some Examples

Compulsive Consumption: Some Examples
Alcoholism
Drug abuse
Eating disorders (anorexia, bulimia)
Compulsive gambling
Compulsive buying
Compulsive sexuality
Kleptomania
Compulsive working
Compulsive exercising
Compulsive television watching

SOURCE: Based on Elizabeth C. Hirschman, "The Consciousness of Addiction: Toward a General Theory of Compulsive Consumption," *Journal of Consumer Research*, vol. 19 (September 1992), pp. 155–179.

against climbing in the stream bed of the mountain river: yet, these consumers ignore the warning. The action is negligent because rain many miles away can cause flash floods.

Given that even the most meticulously designed and packaged product is potentially hazardous through consumer misuse, what steps can marketers and public policy makers take to ensure maximum safety for consumers? Two primary means exist

Figure 20-4 An example of negligent consumer behavior. (Photo by John Mowen.)

for resolving this dilemma. The first approach involves setting government safety standards for almost every type of industry. If a company's products fail to meet such standards, then the products are subject to recall. However, it has been estimated that "no more than 20 percent of all consumer product related injuries can be addressed by feasible regulation of the production and distribution of consumer products."[76]

The other alternative lies in consumer education. The rationale behind a consumer education program is that "increased knowledge leads to safer behavior, since the consumer has a better understanding of how products work and is able to assess more accurately the hazards associated with these products."[77] One study examined the impact of a consumer education course on high school students' safety-related knowledge and resulting behavior. The author found that although the students were more aware of the hazards of certain products' misuse, that knowledge did not lead to proper use of the products. In other words, individuals do not always behave the way they know they should with respect to product safety.

Table 20-5 shows various possible explanations for consumer misuse of "safe" products.

CORPORATE SOCIAL RESPONSIBILITY

Prior to the 1960s most individuals generally accepted the idea that business's primary objective was to obtain economic profit. This thinking began to change, however, as America's social values changed. Today many companies use much energy, time,

TABLE 20-5

Consumer Misuse of "Safe" Products: Some Potential Explanations

1. *Action slips*—A performance error resulting from faulty cognitive processing. This is particularly likely when the consumer is focusing on the desired end results rather than the more mundane actions necessary to arrive at the desired state.
2. *Error proneness*—The tendency not to be vigilant, especially during routinely performed activities.
3. *Reinforcement*—The consumer takes a risk but doesn't suffer any consequences. Each successive trial that doesn't result in harm reinforces the action.
4. *Hedonic goals*—Consumers focused on fantasy, fun, and feelings are less likely to calculate the risks involved.
5. *Ritual/socially sanctioned misuse*—Campus beer bashes.
6. *Individual irrationality*—The actions of obsessive, compulsive, or addictive personalities.
7. *Advertising*—Advertising representations may be partially responsible for unsafe behavior because they encourage extreme forms of product use.

SOURCE: Adapted from Jeffrey Stoltman and Fred Morgan, "Psychological Dimensions of Unsafe Product Usage," in *Marketing Theory and Applications*, vol. 4, Rajan Varadarajan and Bernard Jaworski, eds. (Chicago: American Marketing Association, 1993).

and money to portray themselves as good corporate citizens who act in a socially responsible manner. **Corporate social responsibility** refers to the idea that business has an obligation to help society with its problems by offering some of business's resources.[78] In other words, apart from the traditional goal of making a profit, corporations should also be concerned with such needs as the environment, education, and consumer safety.[79] Several arguments exist to support the notion that having a positive corporate social responsibility image is important for companies.

Succeeding in the Long Run

One argument for being socially responsible involves a long-term rather than short-term perspective of time. A business's self-interest could be advanced if, rather than focusing on short-run profits, which would discourage certain expenditures devoted to societal problems, the business instead embraced a long-run view. This position would allow for the necessary expenditures to engage in socially responsible activities, yet would provide future benefits in the form of consumer approval and loyalty.[80] For example, the Adolph Coors Company, which has a reputation of being antiunion, was struck by the Brewery Workers on April 5, 1977. One week later the AFL-CIO approved a boycott of the company's beer. The AFL-CIO later claimed that this action resulted in a 70% decline in first-quarter profits that year. Although increased competition could also have accounted for the decline, the negative publicity undoubtedly harmed the image of the Coors brand.[81] In the late 1980s the company settled its labor disputes, and its market share among blue-collar workers began to improve.

Acquiring a Positive Public Image

By acting in socially responsible ways, companies can create a positive public image.[82] For example, one study revealed that customers are less likely to blame the company for accidents when the product has safety standards that exceed, rather than simply meet, government safety standards. Also, consumers are less likely to blame the manufacturer when products include safety warnings.[83]

Another way that companies may reveal socially responsible behavior is by making speedy product recalls. Some researchers have suggested that a product recall could be seen as a corporate opportunity, in that the situation allows the company to show its ability to act professionally in a consumer-oriented fashion.[84] A series of studies by the first author of this chapter examined the impact that product recalls could have on consumer impressions of a company. These studies found that consumers perceived a familiar company as significantly less responsible for a product defect than an unfamiliar company;[85] consumers viewed companies that reacted to product defects prior to intervention by the Consumer Product Safety Commission as less responsible for the defects;[86] and consumer impressions of the company were influenced by the speed with which the company initiated a product recall.[87] Table 20-6 gives an overview of the implications of these findings. One well-known recent case of a corporate response to a tragedy is discussed in Highlight 20-2.

HIGHLIGHT 20-2

The Tylenol Tragedy: An Example of Corporate Social Responsibility

In early October 1982 seven persons in the Chicago area died as a result of cyanide-laced Extra-Strength Tylenol capsules. Within 24 hours Johnson & Johnson, the makers of Tylenol, initiated a nationwide recall of the 93,400 bottles of lot MC2880, the first batch from which the poisoned capsules came. Subsequently, additional batches were recalled, bringing the total to 264,400 bottles. Johnson & Johnson also issued half a million mailgrams to physicians, hospitals, and wholesalers warning them of the danger. In addition, McNeil Consumer Products, the subsidiary of Johnson & Johnson that manufactures Tylenol, offered a $100,000 reward for information leading to a conviction in the case. The company also offered cash refunds or tablet exchanges for the 22 million bottles of capsule-form Tylenol.

According to the recommendations given in Table 20-6, the makers of Tylenol conducted a "by-the-book" recall. But did such action actually minimize the adverse effects, as the research suggested it would? In what was termed "a marketing miracle," Tylenol had regained most of its number one market share by the end of December—just three short months after the tragedy occurred.

Much of this success is attributed to Johnson & Johnson's courageous marketing efforts (millions of coupons for a free bottle of Tylenol were distributed) and to its direct action approach. In addition, many industry analysts credited Johnson & Johnson's reputation of concern for public health and well-being for tiding the company over during the first critical days and encouraging loyal customers to return to the product.

Unfortunately, the Tylenol tragedy was replayed in early 1986 when another poisoning occurred. Again, Johnson & Johnson acted responsibly by recalling the product. However, in this case the company went further and permanently withdrew Tylenol capsules from the market.

Based on "The Tylenol Scare," *Newsweek*, October 11, 1982, pp. 32–36; and Michael Waldholz, "Tylenol Regains Most of No. 1 Market Share, Amazing Doomsayers," *The Wall Street Journal*, December 24, 1982, pp. 1, 6.

Avoiding Government Regulation

A final reason for companies to act socially responsible is to avoid government regulation.[88] Given the values society holds today, if business does not respond to societal demands on its own, consumer groups may exert pressure on government to intervene. All business functions concern themselves to some degree with social responsibility. However, the burden falls mostly on the marketer. Indeed, when a company is perceived as acting unethically or in an irresponsible fashion, marketing is the function most likely to be blamed.[89] Marketers can best avoid this label by following the strategies suggested previously—namely, by maintaining a positive initial corporate image and by responding quickly when difficulties arise. In addition, companies can stress the benefits of their products. For example, in Figure 20-5 an advertisement for Dow Chemical is presented. In the ad the company shows a student graduating

TABLE 20-6

Overview of Product Recall Implications

- Companies should strive to maintain a highly visible, positive corporate image. Such a company is less subject to a negative consumer response when a recall is initiated.
- Companies should establish a recall plan that can be quickly implemented should disaster strike. Consumers have a more favorable impression of companies that react quickly in a product-safety situation.
- When a problem is first discovered, it may be best to overstate the problem to the public. Consumers will subsequently develop more favorable impressions of the company when they hear that the problem is not as severe as first expected. If the company displays the reverse behavior—that is, minimizes the problem, only to later discover that the difficulty is worse than first announced—the result can be negative consumer impressions.
- Companies should endeavor to manufacture the safest products possible. The safer the products, the less likelihood of severe injuries, negative consumer opinions, and product liability awards.
- Companies should not shy away from press coverage of product recalls. Information from independent sources such as the media, especially when the company is described as behaving in a socially responsible manner, can generate favorable consumer impressions.

SOURCE: Adapted from Joshua Wiener and John C. Mowen, "Product Recalls: Avoid Beheading the Messenger of Bad News," *Mobius*, vol. 4 (1985), pp. 18–21.

from college who is anxious to start work for a company that attempts to find ways to improve the food supply for starving kids. The ad effectively positions Dow as a company concerned with social responsibility.

Occasionally the desire to be socially responsible is made more difficult by economic realities. For example, Stride Rite Corp., a shoe manufacturer, has a history of being a corporate "good citizen." From 1990 to 1993 the company was honored with 14 public service awards, including ones from the National Women's Political Caucus, Northeastern University, the Northeast Human Resources Association, and Harvard University. However, while the corporation as a whole has also been quite profitable, the company in 1993 closed a plant in Tipton, Missouri, laying off 280 workers in a depressed area, and 14 other plant closings have already taken place. In most cases these jobs have gone overseas, where labor is cheaper. Some are wondering whether such gestures as foundation contributions, sending free sneakers to impoverished foreign countries, and the like are as socially responsible as simply providing jobs at home, even if overseas production would be a bit more profitable.[90]

A MANAGERIAL APPLICATIONS EXAMPLE

The managerial application of concepts from the regulatory environment can be seen in problems faced by Sears, Roebuck & Co. in New York City. In 1988 an ongoing battle between the company and the city began to spill over into the public

Figure 20-5 Dow emphasizes its commitment to social responsibility in this ad. (Courtesy of Dow Chemical U.S.A.)

arena as the city pressured Sears to stop engaging in various forms of misleading advertising. For example, the city wanted the company to stop the practice of promoting a discount price without also explaining whether the markdown was based upon the regular price of the merchandise (i.e., the merchandise could be marked up prior to announcing the sale). Another misleading practice charged against Sears involved advertising that a bargain was about to end when in fact the sale would go on indefinitely.

Executives at Sears believed that their advertising was not deceptive and that the company was being unfairly singled out by the Department of Consumer Affairs in New York City. In fact, the company issued a press release in June 1988 warning that, if it lost its fight, it would "virtually discontinue advertising in New York City, including national publications and network broadcasts in that market." When a Sears attorney was asked if the company's intransigence might harm its image, he was quoted as saying, "I don't care what the public thinks." Sears executives did not seem particularly concerned either. One manager stated, "Our reputation for dealing with the American public is 100 years old. Our policies haven't changed. The phrase 'Satisfaction Guaranteed or Your Money Back' is still over the door at every store."[91]

Four years later, Sears was in hot water again. The California Consumer Affairs Department charged that 33 Sears auto centers located in that state had overcharged customers by an average of $223 in nearly 90% of the cases investigated. The deception and overcharges were caused by a quota system that corporate headquarters had established. The quota system set minimum sales volumes for parts, services, and repairs for every eight-hour shift. Service advisors were instructed to sell a certain number of shock absorbers or struts per hour worked. Those who failed to meet the quotas were transferred.

In an open letter appearing as a full-page advertisement on June 18, 1992, Sears's chairman and CEO, while acknowledging that "mistakes may have occurred," maintained that the company would "never knowingly violate" their customers' trust. A week later, New Jersey officials also charged the company with similar violations.

On June 23, the chairman appeared at a press conference and accepted personal blame for the problem. Two days later, a second full-page advertisement appeared. The chairman acknowledged that "our incentive compensation and goal-setting program inadvertently created an environment in which mistakes have occurred" and concluded that Sears' incentive and quota programs were at fault. He stated that these programs had been done away with and been replaced by an incentive system that awarded service advisors for high levels of customer satisfaction. In addition, an outside firm had been retained to conduct unannounced "shopping audits" to ensure that the mistakes were not repeated.

The Consumer Behavior Analysis and Its Managerial Implications

What do you think of Sears's strategy in 1988? When concepts from the regulatory environment are used to analyze the problem, four categories of issues emerge. These are identified in Table 20-7, which portrays the managerial applications analysis. The first consumer concept to consider when analyzing the case is the nature of the regulations that pertain to sales promotions and the capabilities of the regulatory agencies to enforce their regulations. In the New York City case, Sears was being sued in civil court. Thus Sears had a chance of winning. However, if the case went to a civil trial, it would certainly result in massive negative publicity against the firm. In addition, the possibility existed of large fines being levied. Meanwhile, the attention being given to the case in New York was beginning to cause other states to look at Sears's practices.

The examination of regulatory agencies and applicable laws has implications for environmental analysis and promotional strategy. Sears should perform a careful environmental analysis of its situation to identify precisely the reactions of competitors, such as Kmart, as well as those of the various regulatory agencies. The company must ascertain whether or not it is failing to comply with appropriate regulations. It must stand ready to change its promotional strategy to respond appropriately to the charges filed by governmental/regulatory agencies.

Second, managers should analyze the problem from the perspective of how consumerist groups could react. Again, the outcome could be quite negative. One consumer advocate stated, "Sears has the strange idea that they should abide by the lowest common denominator of consumer protection behavior." An attorney for one consumer interest group stated that he would begin lobbying for tougher consumer advertising laws. The study of consumer groups is a market research function. Again, based upon the reactions of the consumer groups, Sears must stand ready to change its promotional strategy.

TABLE 20-7

Managerial Applications Analysis of the Sears Case

Consumer Concepts	***Managerial Applications***
Regulatory agencies	*Environmental analysis*—Do appropriate legal analysis to ensure that actions are in compliance with laws and regulations.
	Promotional strategy—Develop public relations and advertising strategies for coping with adverse publicity that could result from charges filed by legal/regulatory agencies.
Consumerist groups	*Market research*—Use market research to determine how consumerist groups view the company.
	Promotional strategy—Employ public relations and advertising to influence how the company is perceived by consumer groups.
	Positioning—Position the company as being pro-consumer in its activities.
	Marketing mix—Develop marketing mix strategy that implements the pro-consumer strategy.
Sensitive consumer issues	*Promotional strategy*—Evaluate advertising to ensure that it is not misleading and does not offend minority groups.
	Market research—Analyze marketing mix strategy to ensure that vulnerable segments (e.g., children and the elderly) in the marketplace are treated fairly.
Corporate social responsibility	*Marketing mix*—Analyze entire marketing mix strategy to ensure that it follows principles that represent socially responsible behavior.
	Market research—Do research to determine if consumers perceive the firm to be socially responsible.
	Positioning—Develop strategy to position the firm as being socially responsible.

Third, the question should be asked as to whether the issue involves a sensitive public policy issue. In general, misleading advertising is considered by regulators to be sensitive. If it were found that certain population groups, such as the elderly, were negatively affected, Sears's problem could become far worse. The sensitivity issue underscores the importance of segmenting the marketplace and identifying groups of consumers that may be particularly vulnerable. Market research must be employed to perform the analysis. If sensitive groups were identified, changes in promotional strategy would be warranted.

Finally, the problem can be analyzed from the viewpoint of corporate social responsibility. Here the answer seems fairly clear. Sears's actions were not those that one would expect from a socially responsible company. At minimum, the company should stop the practices while fighting New York City in court. Indeed, one New York City official stated that "Sears is the largest and most consistent consumer law breaker in New York City." Sears's tactics have even been criticized by securities analysts—a group known for its focus on profits rather than social responsibility. As one analyst said, "This is bureaucratic management rigidity, not good business sense. You'd think Sears would say, 'You're right. Let's get on the consumer side of this thing.' Instead, they seem to want to get dragged kicking and screaming into losing market share."

The consumer concept of corporate social responsibility has direct implications for the positioning of the firm and for the marketing mix. Companies should strive to create a "good citizen" image. Further, such corporate efforts should be real and not simply based upon public relations hype. Such efforts help to position a company as one that puts customers first. Of course, such actions are accomplished via the marketing mix. Thus pricing, promotion, product development, and distribution should be undertaken in a manner that is socially responsible. In addition, these actions should be communicated via public relations. In addition to developing a marketing mix that is consumer oriented, companies may show that they are good citizens by actively assisting in United Way campaigns, contributing to local charities and schools, and having executives serve on key community boards.

SUMMARY

The regulatory environment consists of the laws and regulations that governments develop to exert control over businesses and consumers. Such laws and regulations may be enforced by organizations at the federal, state, and local levels.

Closely related to the overall regulatory environment is the area of consumerism. Problems and issues addressed by consumer groups frequently foreshadow areas in which new laws and regulations will be created. Consumerism consists of the set of activities of government, business, independent organizations, and concerned consumers that are designed to protect the rights of consumers. The movement spans a time period of over 80 years. Four major eras of the consumer movement have been identified—the muckraking era (1905–1920), the information era (1927–1939), the era of continuing consumer concern (1951–1960), and the modern consumer movement (1962–1980).

A number of federal regulatory agencies have been created that attempt to protect consumers from unscrupulous business practices. The Federal Trade Commission was formed to curtail unfair trade practices and limit monopolies. The

Food and Drug Administration serves to protect consumers from unsafe and impure food, drugs, cosmetics, and therapeutic devices. The National Highway Traffic Safety Administration regulates the safety performance of new and used motor vehicles and their equipment, investigates motor vehicle safety defects, and establishes required average fuel economy standards for new motor vehicles. The Consumer Product Safety Commission investigates and responds appropriately to product-related accidents that harm consumers.

Certain issues and groups are of particular importance in our society and, as a result, receive increased regulatory attention. One such issue is that of deceptive advertising. Because of the potentially large impact of the media on consumers, lawmaking bodies have paid particular attention to creating laws that make it illegal to mislead consumers. A particularly important group of consumers that regulatory agencies seek to protect is children. Whenever companies market products to children, they must take special care to ensure that they are acting responsibly. A third sensitive area is that of environmental protection.

Another problem area that deals with public policy issues concerns negligent consumer behavior, which refers to those actions and inactions that negatively affect the long-term quality of life of individuals or society in general. Failure to wear seatbelts, smoking, drunk driving, and product misuse are a few examples of negligent behavior. One difficult public policy issue involves determining the extent to which regulatory agencies can create laws that restrict negligent actions of consumers.

Closely related to the regulatory environment are issues involving the importance of corporate social responsibility. In general, the more socially responsible corporations behave, the less need exists for consumeristic laws and regulations.

Acting in a socially responsible manner can help the company survive in the long run, improve its public image, and decrease the likelihood of government intervention in corporate affairs.

KEY TERMS

advertising substantiation
compulsive consumption
conservation behavior
consumerism
corporate social responsibility
corrective advertising
deceptive advertising
negligent behavior
regulatory environment

REVIEW QUESTIONS

1. Identify the four phases of the consumer movement presented in the text.
2. What is the current status of the consumer movement?
3. In 1982 one of the three most important consumer concerns was high prices. What do you think is the primary consumer concern today?
4. What are the consumer regulation roles of the FTC, the FDA, and the NHTSA?
5. What are the categories of deceptive advertising that the FTC has considered in the past?
6. To what extent can children tell the difference between commercials and programming?
7. To what extent do commercials tend to make children desire products that are not necessarily good for them?
8. What are the three basic types of conservation behavior?

9. What is the definition of negligent consumer behavior?
10. Identify four examples of negligent consumer behavior.
11. What are the primary methods now being used to attack the problem of drunk driving?
12. What is meant by the idea of corporate social responsibility? Give four examples of how companies can act in a socially responsible manner.
13. Identify the reasons for and against businesses actively attempting to portray themselves as socially responsible.
14. According to the text, what are the factors that influence consumer reactions to companies that issue product recalls?
15. What are three ways that companies might be able to make children's advertising more acceptable to parents?

DISCUSSION QUESTIONS

1. What are the consumer issues that you think are most important—deceptive advertising, waste disposal, drinking and driving, or some other problem area? Do you believe that corporate treatment of consumers has improved or worsened over the past five years?
2. Some have argued that the modern consumer movement ended with the beginning of the Reagan presidency in 1980. To what extent do you agree or disagree with this statement?
3. In 1986 the Federal Trade Commission began to consider whether or not it should take some action to force the large car rental corporations (e.g., Hertz and Avis) to comply more quickly with manufacturers' requests to recall automobiles to fix mechanical problems. In your view, to what extent should government agencies intervene to force such companies (or for that matter individuals) to comply with manufacturers' requests to bring cars in when product recalls occur? What kinds of actions could or should a government agency take?
4. From an attributional perspective, what may have been the effect of Listerine's corrective ad, which read, "While Listerine will not help prevent colds or sore throats or lessen their severity, breath tests prove Listerine fights onion breath better than Scope"? (Note: Attribution theory was discussed in Chapter 6, Consumer Motivation and Affect.)
5. Political commercials have been called the most deceptive in advertising. Discuss the types of deception that may occur in political advertisements. Try to give specific examples of each type of deception you have seen or heard.
6. Watch Saturday morning cartoons and observe the advertising directed toward children. What are the types of advertising appeals that are being used? To what extent are cartoon characters being used in the advertising? What are your views on what guidelines should be given to companies that advertise to children?
7. During the mid-1980s the emphasis on conservation of resources waned from levels found in the 1970s. What are some of the reasons for these changes? What types of programs do you feel are most effective in promoting the conservation of various natural resources?
8. A variety of approaches exist in controlling negligent consumer behavior. Within the context of controlling drunk driving, discuss the alternative means through which public policy makers can attempt to reduce this consumer problem behavior. Which approaches do you consider to be the most effective?
9. Two different viewpoints exist concerning the social responsibility of corporations. One states that the only responsibility of a company is to make a profit for its stockholders. The other viewpoint states that businesses have a responsibility to help improve society. Defend your viewpoint on this issue.
10. Compare the behavior of Sears's management in 1988 and 1992. Which response to the regulatory environment is likely to serve Sears best in the long run?

ENDNOTES

1. Thomas M. Burton, "Spilt Milk: Methods of Marketing Infant Formula Land Abbott in Hot Water," *The Wall Street Journal*, May 25, 1993, pp. A1, A6; and "The Sour Taste of Baby-Formula Pricing," *Consumer Reports*, October 1993, p. 626.
2. Lois Therrien, John Carey, and Joseph Weber, "The Cholesterol Is in the Fire Now," *Business Week*, June 10, 1991, pp. 34–35.
3. Stanley Penn, "As Ever More People Try Anabolic Steroids, Traffickers Take Over," *The Wall Street Journal*, October 4, 1988, pp. 1, 24.
4. Faye Rice, "Where Will We Put All That Garbage?" *Fortune*, April 11, 1988, pp. 96–100.
5. Marcy Magiera, "Pepsi Weathers Tampering Hoaxes," *Advertising Age*, June 21, 1993, pp. 1, 46; and Magiera, "The Pepsi Crisis: What Went Right," *Advertising Age*, July 19, 1993, pp. 14–15.
6. "Dear Chrysler: Outsiders' Advice on Handling the Odometer Charge," *The Wall Street Journal*, June 28, 1987, p. 19; and John Bussey, "Pretested or Used? Some Products Bought as New May Have History," *The Wall Street Journal*, July 27, 1987, p. 19.
7. Robert Tomsho, "One for the Road: How Hard It Is to Get Drinkers Off Highways Is Clear in New Mexico," *The Wall Street Journal*, December 31, 1993, pp. 1, 4; and George Hackett and Michael Lerner, "The Menace on the Roads," *Newsweek*, December 21, 1987, pp. 42–43.
8. Louis Harris et al., *Consumerism in the Eighties*, Study No. 822047 (Louis Harris and Associates, 1983), p. 12. Referenced in D. S. Smith and P. N. Bloom, "Is Consumerism Dead or Alive? Some New Evidence," in *Advances in Consumer Research*, Vol. 11, T. C. Kinnear, ed. (Ann Arbor, MI: Association for Consumer Research, 1984), pp. 369–373.
9. David A. Aaker and George S. Day, *Consumerism: Search for the Consumer Interest* (New York: The Free Press, 1974).
10. Rogene A. Buchholz, *Business Environment and Public Policy* (Englewood Cliffs, NJ: Prentice-Hall, 1982).
11. Joe L. Welch, *Marketing Law* (Tulsa, OK: Petroleum Publishing, 1980).
12. *The New York Times*, January 21, 1983, p. A16.
13. Thomas A. Hemphill, "Self-Regulating Industry Behavior: Antitrust Limitations and Trade Association Codes of Conduct," *Journal of Business Ethics*, Vol. 11 (December 1992), pp. 915–920.
14. Marc Reisch, "Drug Price Controls: Manufacturers Prescribe Self-Regulation," *Chemical and Engineering News*, March 22, 1993, p. 6; and "Drug Industry Tries PR Antidote for Attacks," *Tulsa World*, February 20, 1993, p. B7.
15. "U.S. Environmental Agency Making Deep Staffing Cuts," *The New York Times*, January 3, 1982, p. 20.
16. Dhruv Grewal and Larry D. Compeau, "Comparative Price Advertising: Informative or Deceptive?" *Journal of Public Policy and Marketing*, Vol. 11 (Spring 1992), pp. 52–62.
17. William L. Wilkie, Dennis L. McNeill, and Michael B. Mazis, "Marketing's 'Scarlet Letter': The Theory and Practice of Corrective Advertising," *Journal of Marketing*, Vol. 48 (Spring 1984), pp. 11–31.
18. Albert R. Karr, "FDA Bans Unproven Health Claims by Makers of Some Diet Supplements," *The Wall Street Journal*, December 30, 1993, p. B4.
19. Buchholz, *Business Environment*.
20. Ibid.
21. Walter Guzzardi, "The Mindless Pursuit of Safety," *Fortune*, April 9, 1979, pp. 54–64.
22. Buchholz, *Business Environment*.
23. Rachel Dardis, "Economic Analysis of Current Issues in Consumer Product Safety: Fabric Flammability," *Journal of Consumer Affairs*, Vol. 14 (Summer 1980), pp. 109–123.
24. Welch, *Marketing Law*.
25. Paul Slovic, "Public Perceptions of Risk," *Risk Management*, March 1992, pp. 54–58; and Buchholz, *Business Environment*.

26. Edward J. Metzen, "Consumerism in the Evolving Future," in *Consumerism and Beyond*, Paul N. Bloom, ed. (Cambridge, MA: Marketing Science Institute, 1982), pp. 16–20.

27. Kenneth L. Bernhardt and Ronald Stiff, "Public Policy Update: Perspectives on the Federal Trade Commission," in *Advances in Consumer Research*, Vol. 8, Kent B. Monroe, ed. (Ann Arbor, MI: Association for Consumer Research, 1981), pp. 452–454.

28. Philip Kotler, *Marketing Management: Analysis, Planning, Implementation and Control* (Englewood Cliffs, NJ: Prentice-Hall, 1991).

29. Gurjeet Singh, "Business Self-Regulation and Consumer Protection in India," *Journal of Consumer Policy*, Vol. 16 (1993), pp. 1–33.

30. Youngho Lee and Ann C. Brown, "Consumerism in China," in Salah S. Hassan and Roger D. Blackwell, *Global Marketing: Perspectives and Cases* (Fort Worth, TX: The Dryden Press, 1994.

31. Francine Schwadel, "Sears Calls It 'Low Prices,' New York Calls It Misleading," *The Wall Street Journal*, December 22, 1989, pp. B1, B4.

32. Lee D. Dahringer and Denise R. Johnson, "The Federal Trade Commission Redefinition of Deception and Public Policy Implications: Let the Buyer Beware," *Journal of Consumer Affairs*, Vol. 18 (1984), pp. 326–342.

33. "Legal Developments in Marketing," *Journal of Marketing*, Vol. 49 (Winter 1985), p. 155.

34. Wilkie et al., "Marketing's 'Scarlet Letter.'"

35. Armstrong et al., "A Longitudinal Evaluation."

36. John S. Healey and Harold H. Kassarjian, "Advertising Substantiation and Advertiser Response: A Content Analysis of Magazine Advertisements," *Journal of Marketing*, Vol. 47 (Winter 1983), pp. 107–117.

37. Dorothy Cohen, "The FTC's Advertising Substantiation Program," *Journal of Marketing*, Vol. 44 (Winter 1980), pp. 26–35.

38. "Legal Developments in Marketing," *Journal of Marketing*, Vol. 49 (Spring 1985), p. 149.

39. Terence A. Shimp and Ivan I. Preston, "Deceptive and Nondeceptive Consequences of Evaluative Advertising," *Journal of Marketing*, Vol. 45 (Winter 1981), pp. 22–32.

40. Ibid.

41. M. Suzanne Clinton and Ronald D. Taylor, "Advertising to Children: A Synthesis of the Literature," *Advances in Marketing*, Daryl O. McKee, Daniel L. Sherrell, and Faye W. Gilbert, eds. (New Orleans, LA: Southwestern Marketing Association, 1993).

42. Kyle Pope, "Better to Receive: How Children Decide on Gifts They Want and Plot to Get Them," *The Wall Street Journal*, December 24, 1993, pp. A1, A5.

43. Howard G. Schutz and Marianne Casey, "Consumer Perceptions of Advertising as Misleading," *Journal of Consumer Affairs*, Vol. 15 (Winter 1981), pp. 340–357.

44. *FTC Staff Report on Television Advertising to Children* (Washington, DC: Government Printing Office, 1978).

45. Pope, "Better to Receive."

46. Lisa Collins Troy, "Consumer Environmental Consciousness: A Conceptual Framework and Exploratory Investigation," in *Enhancing Knowledge Development in Marketing*, Vol. 4, David W. Cravens and Peter R. Dickson, eds. (Chicago: American Marketing Association, 1993).

47. Ida E. Berger, "A Framework for Understanding the Relationship Between Environmental Attitudes and Consumer Behaviors," in *Marketing Theory and Applications*, Vol. 4, Rajan Varadarajan and Bernard Jaworski, eds. (Chicago: American Marketing Association, 1993).

48. Theo M. M. Verhallen and W. Fred van Raaij, "Household Behavior and the Use of Natural Gas for Home Heating," *Journal of Consumer Research*, Vol. 8 (December 1981), pp. 253–257.

49. Russell Belk, John Painter, and Richard Semenik, "Preferred Solutions to the Energy Crisis as a Function of Causal Attributions," *Journal of Consumer Research*, Vol. 8 (December 1981), pp. 306–312.

50. J. R. Brent Ritchie and Gordon H. G. McDougall, "Designing and Marketing Consumer Energy Conservation Policies and

Programs: Implications from a Decade of Research," *Journal of Public Policy and Marketing*, Vol. 4 (1985), pp. 14–32.

51. Royce Anderson, "Consumer Response to Mandatory Recycling," in *Marketing Theory and Applications*, Vol. 4, Rajan Varadarajan and Bernard Jaworski, eds. (Chicago: American Marketing Association, 1993).

52. Eric Cato, "Bringing the Message Home," *KPMG World* (2), 1993, p. 5.

53. Thomas C. Kinnear and Cynthia J. Frey, "Demarketing of Potentially Hazardous Products: General Framework and Case Studies," *Journal of Contemporary Business*, Vol. 7 (1978), pp. 57–68.

54. E. Scott Geller, "Seat Belt Psychology," *Psychology Today*, May 1985, pp. 12–13.

55. Ibid.

56. Paul Slovic, "Only New Laws Will Spur Seat Belt Use," *The Wall Street Journal*, January 30, 1985, p. 26.

57. Michael Minor, "Accident Risks and Automotive Safety: Safety Belt Use in the U.S.," *Proceedings of the First U.S.–Japan Conference on Risk Management*, Saburo Ikeda and Kazuhiko Kawamura, eds. (Nashville, TN: Vanderbilt University, 1984).

58. Harinder Singh and Mark Thayer, "Impact of Seat Belt Use on Driving Behavior," *Economic Inquiry*, Vol. 30 (October 1992), pp. 649–658.

59. Kinnear and Frey, "Demarketing of Potentially Hazardous Products."

60. John E. Calfee and Debra Jones Ringold, "The Cigarette Advertising Controversy: Assumptions About Consumers, Regulations, and Scientific Debate," in *Advances in Consumer Research*, Vol. 19, John F. Sherry, Jr., and Brian Sternthal, eds. (Provo, UT: Association for Consumer Research, 1992), pp. 557–562.

61. Steven W. Colford and Ira Teinowitz, "Teen Smoking and Ads Linked," *Advertising Age*, February 21, 1994, pp. 1, 36.

62. *National Accident Sampling System* (Washington, DC: Government Printing Office, 1982), p. 14.

63. Laurel Hudson and Paul N. Bloom, "Potential Consumer Research Contributions to Combating Drinking and Driving Problems," in *Advances in Consumer Research*, Vol. 11, Thomas C. Kinnear, ed. (Provo, UT: Association for Consumer Research, 1984), pp. 676–681.

64. Janet R. Hankin, Ira J. Firestone, James J. Sloan, and Joel W. Ager, "The Impact of the Alcohol Warning Label on Drinking During Pregnancy," *Journal of Public Policy and Marketing*, Vol. 12 (Spring 1993), pp. 10–18.

65. Ibid.

66. Tim W. Ferguson, "Calm Down: Risk Is Not All Around," *The Wall Street Journal*, December 14, 1993, p. A17; and Judith Valente, "Scotch Makers Tell Youth It's Hip to Be Old-Fashioned," *The Wall Street Journal*, December 29, 1993, pp. B1, B5.

67. Bob Smith, "Compulsive Gamblers: In Over Their Heads," *HR Focus*, February 1992, p. 3.

68. R. S. Salomon, Jr., "Hooked," *Forbes*, May 10, 1993, p. 197.

69. Masayasu Goto, "Letters: Pleasures of Pachinko," *Japan Update*, December 1993, p. 1; and Isao Shinohara, "Pachinko Is Japan's Most Popular Leisure Game," *Tokyo Business Today*, March 1990, pp. 32, 33.

70. Lisa Gates, "Place Your Bets: Taiwan Plans to Reintroduce State Lotteries," *Far Eastern Economic Review*, March 1993, p. 51.

71. Scott Hume, "U.S. Agency Creates Lottery in Russia," *Advertising Age*, February 22, 1993, p. 12; and Joanne Levine, "Russia: Intracom Gambles on a Lottery Pay-Out," *International Management*, March 1993, p. 24.

72. Gates, "Place Your Bets."

73. Gerhard Scherhorn, "The Addictive Trait in Buying Behavior," *Journal of Consumer Policy*, Vol. 13 (1990), pp. 33–51; Elizabeth C. Hirschman, "The Consciousness of Addiction: Toward a General Theory of Compulsive Consumption," *Journal of Consumer Research*, Vol. 19 (September 1992), pp. 155–179; and Hirschman, "Cocaine as Innovation: A Social-Symbolic Account," in *Advances in Consumer Research*, Vol. 19, John F. Sherry, Jr., and Brian Sternthal, eds.

(Provo, UT: Association for Consumer Research, 1992), pp. 129–139.

74. Richard Staelin, "The Effects of Consumer Education on Consumer Product Safety Behavior," *Journal of Consumer Research*, Vol. 5 (June 1978), pp. 30–40.

75. Guzzardi, "The Mindless Pursuit."

76. Staelin, "The Effects of Consumer Education."

77. Ibid.

78. Buchholz, *Business Environment*.

79. Kenneth E. Miller and Frederick D. Sturdivant, "Consumer Responses to Socially Questionable Corporate Behavior: An Empirical Test," *Journal of Consumer Research*, Vol. 4 (June 1977), pp. 1–7.

80. Buchholz, *Business Environment*.

81. "Coors Undercuts Its Last Big Union," *Business Week*, July 24, 1978, pp. 47–48.

82. Buchholz, *Business Environment*.

83. Mitch Griffin, Barry J. Babin, and William R. Darden, "Consumer Assessments of Responsibility for Product-Related Injuries: The Impact of Regulations, Warnings, and Promotional Policies," in *Advances in Consumer Research*, Vol. 19, John F. Sherry, Jr., and Brian Sternthal, eds. (Provo, UT: Association for Consumer Research, 1992), pp. 870–878.

84. G. Fisk and R. Chandran, "How to Trace and Recall Products," *Harvard Business Review* (November/December 1975), pp. 90–96.

85. John C. Mowen, "Further Information on Consumer Perceptions of Product Recalls," in *Advances in Consumer Research*, Vol 7, Jerry Olson, ed. (Ann Arbor, MI: Association for Consumer Research, 1980), pp. 519–523.

86. Ibid.

87. John C. Mowen, David Jolly, and G. S. Nickell, "Factors Influencing Consumer Responses to Product Recalls: A Regression Analysis Approach," in *Advances in Consumer Research*, Vol. 8, Kent Monroe, ed. (Ann Arbor, MI: Association for Consumer Research, 1981), pp. 405–407.

88. Buchholz, *Business Environment*.

89. Patrick Murphy and Gene Laczniak, "Marketing Ethics: A Review with Implications for Managers, Educators, and Researchers," in *Review of Marketing*, Ben M. Enis and Kenneth J. Roering, eds. (Chicago: American Marketing Association, 1981), pp. 251–266.

90. Joseph Pereira, "Split Personality: Social Responsibility and Need for Low Cost Clash at Stride Rite," *The Wall Street Journal*, May 28, 1993, pp. A1, A4.

91. This section is based upon Robert Johnson and John Koten, "Sears Has Everything, Including Messy Fight Over Ads in New York," *The Wall Street Journal*, June 28, 1988, pp. 1, 14; Tung Yin, "Sears Is Accused of Billing Fraud at Auto Centers," *The Wall Street Journal*, June 12, 1992, pp. B1, B5; Gregory A. Patterson, "Sears' Brennan Accepts Blame for Auto Flap," *The Wall Street Journal*, June 23, 1992, pp. B1, B4; and "Open Letter to Sears Customers," advertisements, *The Wall Street Journal*, June 15, 1992, p. C15, and June 25, 1992, p. C11.

CHAPTER 20 CASE STUDY

The Diaper Dilemma

A "green revolution" is occurring in the production and marketing of products. Manufacturers are struggling to develop products that consumers perceive to be safe for the environment. One of the toughest environmental issues concerns trash. The average American family produces 6.73 bags of trash per week—about twice the level of Japanese families. Collectively, American consumers generate 160 million tons of garbage a year. Because of the gargantuan load of trash produced in the United States, landfills are now overflowing. One of the most difficult waste disposal issues concerns what to do with diapers. Babies go through approximately 7,800 diapers between birth and toilet training—at a cost of about $1,800 per child. The stakes are huge in this dilemma. For example, diaper sales account for 16% of Procter & Gamble's total sales and 23% at Kimberly-Clark. The problem, however, is that disposable diapers make up about 5% of the trash in landfills [1].

The newest competitors in the diaper market are cloth diaper delivery services. Although they almost disappeared with the introduction of disposable diapers, in the 1990s they are once again aggressively seeking customers by stressing environmental issues and their willingness to frequently deliver fresh cloth diapers. The diaper services and the cotton industry have begun a battle to convince consumers to return to these old-fashioned favorites by charging that disposable diapers are ecologically harmful. In 1993, some diaper services began offering disposable diapers as well for environmentally conscious customers who prefer to outfit their babies outside the home or who take their children to a day care center that has cloth diapers.

In response to environmental concerns, Procter & Gamble has undertaken a small pilot program to see if disposable diapers can be recycled. The goal is to redefine the concept of disposable by turning the material into a resource. Teaming up with a small Seattle recycling company, disposable diapers are picked up at curbside from as many as 1,000 families and delivered to a recycling center. There the plastic liner is separated from the paper pulp and sanitized. The reclaimed material from the recycled diapers is then used to produce products such as plastic flower pots, drywall backing, and computer paper.

Composting diapers is another option being considered by P&G. Composting is a natural recycling process for breaking down organic material. The corporation is working with a composting company in Minnesota to turn diaper parts into humus, an organic part of the soil. There are only ten such composting plants in the United States, but P&G hopes that it can eventually motivate local governments to build systems that would compost 30% to 60% of U.S. garbage. When P&G began to advertise its efforts, however, environmentalists turned red. They charged that the ads were misleading because composting facilities were nearly nonexistent for most consumers [2].

The issues are particularly tough because, according to the Natural Resources Defense Council, neither cloth nor disposable diapers are clearly better for the environment. Both use needed resources and cause pollution of some kind. The cotton used in cloth diapers is grown with large amounts of pesticides that can harm the environment. Energy and water are needed to both produce and wash cloth diapers. Estimates are that washing cloth diapers requires about 9,620 gallons of water per child per year. On the other hand, disposable diapers account for approximately 5% of the garbage found in landfills. Oil is utilized in the manufacturing of disposable diapers, and an estimated 1 billion trees per year are required for the pulp found in the inner absorbency layer [3].

The cross-currents of thinking among consumers and "experts" are creating severe marketing problems for companies. Claims must be monitored carefully. For example, seven states sued Mobil Corporation for claiming that its Hefty garbage bags are biodegradable. In addition, creating environmentally safe products often adds costs. In surveys, over 90% of consumers claim that they will make special efforts to buy from companies that are trying to protect the environment. When actual buying is observed, however, the effects appear to be minimal. For example, the senior research scientist at the Natural Resources Defense Council, an environmental group, put both of his babies into disposable diapers. In another case, Heinz developed a squeezable ketchup bottle made of plastic. Consumers flocked to it, but environmentalists hated it because it could not be recycled like glass. After three years and $8 million, Heinz developed a recyclable plastic bottle for the ketchup. The problem, however, is that because few recycling centers exist, almost none of the expensive new ketchup bottles will ever be reused [4].

* * *

Thanks to Jeri L. Jones for developing the case.

QUESTIONS

1. Define the problem faced by producers of disposable diapers.
2. Discuss the consumer behavior concepts from the chapter that apply to the case.
3. Construct a managerial applications table for the "diaper dilemma." Discuss the managerial implications of the consumer concepts identified.

NOTES

1. Laurie Freeman, "Diaper Services Unwrapping Market Potential," *Advertising Age*, February 14, 1988, p. 26; and Valarie Reitman, "Diaper Firms Fight to Stay on the Bottom," *The Wall Street Journal*, March 23, 1993, pp. B1, B10.
2. Mark Landler, "Suddenly, Green Marketers Are Seeing Red Flags," *Business Week*, February 25, 1991, pp. 74–75.
3. Jaclyn Fierman, "The Big Muddle in Green Marketing," *Fortune*, June 3, 1991, pp. 91–100.
4. Melinda Beck, "Buried Alive," *Newsweek*, November 27, 1989, pp. 66–76.

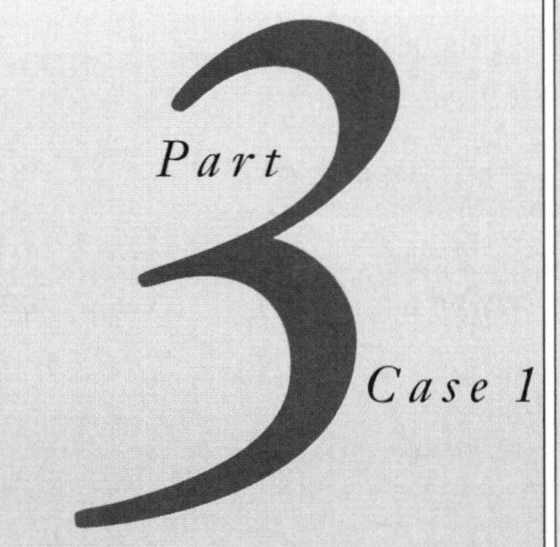

R.J. REYNOLDS TOBACCO COMPANY LAUNCHES "PREMIER"

Since 1981 America's cigarette industry has been contending with a drop in demand. Rising retail prices, increased publicity about the dangers of smoking, anti-smoking regulations, and liability lawsuits have brought about a steady decline in tobacco consumption. Annual per capita consumption of cigarettes was 4,287 in 1966. By 1987 the per capita consumption of cigarettes was 3,196. But cigarette companies have never been richer. In 1987 smokers—50 million of them—spent $33.3 billion on cigarettes in the United States. With the average pack of cigarettes costing about $1.17, up from $1.02 in 1985 and 47.3 cents in 1975, profits are at an all-time high.[1] Exhibit 1 shows the after-tax profits per dollar of sales. Will this trend of declining consumption persist and will the trend eventually harm profitability? R. J. Reynolds Tobacco Company hoped that its new product, Premier, would slow the trend.

EXHIBIT 1

After-Tax Profit per Dollar of Sales

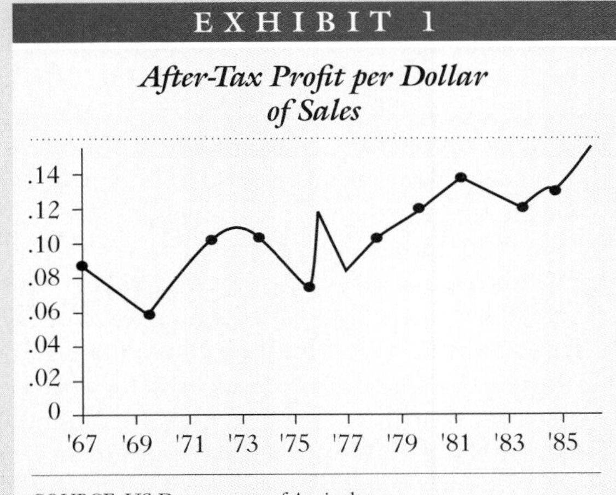

SOURCE: US Department of Agriculture.

HISTORY

In 1875 Richard Joshua Reynolds left a partnership with his father in tobacco farming and manufacturing in Virginia to move to Winston, North Carolina. There he invested $2,300 in a plot of ground, a factory, and equipment to set up his own tobacco production plant. By 1906 Reynolds was producing one-seventh of the nation's plug (chewing) tobacco, with that figure rising to one-fourth by 1912.

Camel was introduced as the company's first major cigarette brand in 1913. Four years after its introduction Camel was the nation's best-selling cigarette. Winston cigarettes went on the market in 1954. By 1966 Winston was the best-selling cigarette in the nation; it held that position for ten years. Winston is now number two. Salem, introduced in 1956, is the nation's best-selling menthol brand. In 1969 Doral, one of the first "low-tar" cigarettes, was introduced. Vantage, introduced in 1970, was the first nationally popular "low-tar" brand and continues to be a leader in that segment.

Now, introduced in 1976, was the company's first entry into the "ultra-low-tar" category. More 120s, introduced nationally in 1975, is the leader among 120mm cigarettes. Century, the first American brand to offer smokers twenty-five cigarettes per pack for the same price as a standard twenty-cigarettes pack, was introduced in June 1983. In July 1984 the company introduced a new formulation of Doral. The new Doral was the first brand-name cigarette to be

EXHIBIT 2

Some Tobacco Products of RJR

Camel
- Regular (nonfilter)
- Filters
- Filters 100s
- Filters Hard Pack
- Lights
- Lights Hard Pack
- Lights 100

Century
- 25s
- 25s Lights
- 25s Filters 100s
- 25s Lights 100s
- 25s Menthol 100s

Doral
- Filter
- (menthol)
- 100s Filter
- 100s (menthol)
- Full Flavor 85s
- Full Flavor 100s
- Ultra Lights 100s

More
- 120s Filter
- 120s (menthol)
- Lights 100s (box)
- Lights 100s (menthol; box)
- Lights 120s (menthol)
- Lights 120s

Now
- Filter (box)

Menthol
- 100s Filter
- 100s (box)
- 100s (menthol)

Ritz
- 100s (box)
- 100s (menthol; box)

Salem
- (menthol)
- 100s (menthol)
- Lights (menthol)
- Lights 100s (menthol)
- Lights 100s (menthol; box)
- Ultra (menthol)
- Ultra 100s (menthol)
- Slim Lights 100s (menthol; box)

Vantage
- (menthol)
- 100s
- 100s (menthol)
- Ultra Lights
- Ultra Lights 100s

Winston
- (box)
- 100s
- Lights 100s
- Lights 80s (box)
- Lights 100s (box)
- Ultra Lights
- Ultra Lights 100s

priced competitively with generics.[2] Ritz, a cigarette produced in association with world-famous fashion designer Yves Saint Laurent, was introduced in April 1986. Exhibit 2 lists all of R. J. Reynolds's U.S. tobacco products.

RJR'S "NEW" CIGARETTE

Beginning on September 1, 1988, consumers in Phoenix, Tucson, and St. Louis could sample a cigarette that represented the industry's highest promotion budget, newest technology, and biggest controversy. The cigarette was Premier, the only cigarette to date to come with instructions for use. Premier was a "smokeless" cigarette, which according to RJR reduced "controversial compounds," cut side-stream smoke and eliminated all ashes. "We believe this will prove to be a major alternative that expands more options for smokers," said Edward A. Horrigan, Jr., chairman and chief executive officer of the R. J. Reynolds Tobacco Company unit.[3] RJR selected the three cities as test markets to see if a product costing 25% more than king-sized cigarettes could capture U.S. smokers' loyalty.

An unlit Premier looked normal, but it was different from other cigarettes because it heated, rather than burned, tobacco. The end that was lighted was actually an insulated carbon tip fitted to a tobacco-wrapped aluminum cylinder. Inside the cylinder were hundreds of tiny, nicotine-laced "flavor beads." When the smoker inhaled, the warmed air was drawn across the flavor capsule. The air then passed through two filters. The first was made of a tobacco blend designed to cool the air, and the second was a standard synthetic fiber filter. According to R.J. Reynolds, the exhaled smoke dissipated quickly, like steam, with no tobacco smell. The smoker ignited the carbon end and drew smoke through the flavor capsules, tobacco, and two filter segments at the tip. Once the carbon tip was used up, the cigarette extinguished itself in roughly the same amount of time it takes a typical king-sized cigarette to burn down. Exhibit 3 shows the anatomy of a Premier cigarette.[4]

Extensive research and testing on Premier were conducted by RJR on its own, and several independent labs studied the chemical and toxicological characteristics of the cigarette. RJR's objectives in developing the cigarette were twofold. One objective was to provide the tobacco taste and smoking pleasure of regular cigarettes, while eliminating the mainstream and sidestream smoke.[5] The other objective was "to try to pull back into the marketplace cigarette smokers who recently left, and hold onto cigarette smokers who are thinking of leaving," according to Lawrence Adelman of Dean Witter Reynolds.[6] According to Paine-Webber analyst Emanuel Goldman, "the objective is to have an impact on cigarette demand just like previous technological breakthroughs—filters and low tar."[7] There was

EXHIBIT 3

The "Smokeless" Cigarette

THE "SMOKELESS CIGARETTE"

The carbon heats, but does not burn, the tobacco jacket and the flavor capsule to produce a "smoke" that is cooled by passing through a tobacco filter and then a conventional filter:

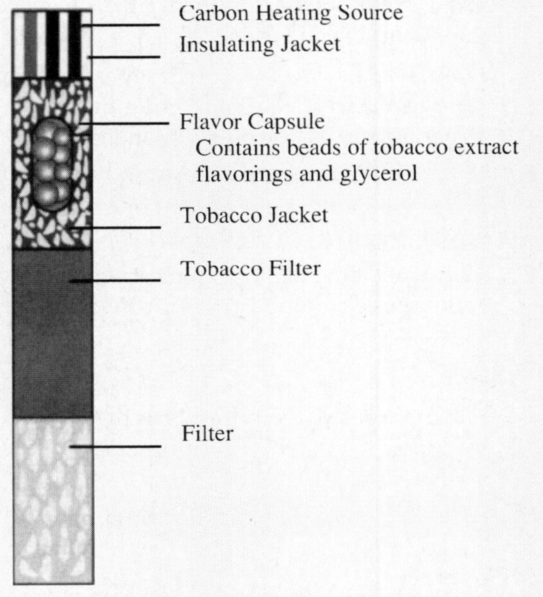

also interest in making the cigarette socially acceptable to nonsmokers, thereby skirting some of the new no-smoking rules.

The company spent $150 million on Premier in the first year for development costs, advertising, and other costs.[8] The three test market cities sent out mixed signals: early sales were a drag in one location and strong in the others. Curiosity about Premier led to initial sales, but not always to repeat sales. Many who tried Premier complained about the taste. Some claimed it was terrible, some that it had no flavor, and some that it was too potent. One smoker, Richard Adams, claimed, "the taste doesn't get it."[9] Patricia Silvia stated, "If you enjoy smoking, you wouldn't enjoy one of these."[10] By keeping tabs on the test markets, RJR could tell the age and sex of the buyer; the best locations to sell Premier, the frequency of repeat purchases, the brands Premier smokers abandoned, and the pattern of switching between Premier and other brands.[11]

As mentioned above, the price of Premier was about 25% higher than that of king-sized cigarettes. This was due to greater production costs, and it meant that a pack of Premier would sell for between $1.51 and $2.31, depending on the area and state and local taxes.[12] Ads for Premier took advantage of the cigarette's novelty value. The main theme was, "It's been called revolutionary. We call it cleaner." Ads were placed in such magazines as *Better Homes & Gardens*, *Family Circle*, *Field & Stream*, *Newsweek*, *People*, *Sports Illustrated*, and *Time* in an attempt to reach people over 25 who could afford the slightly higher price for the cigarette. To make the cigarette smoke more attractive to new users. RJR ran specials (e.g., buy two, get two free) and discounts on future purchases. The instructions on the pack told smokers that a good-quality butane lighter was best, matches would work, but a car cigarette lighter would not. The pack also displayed the surgeon general's warning about cigarette smoking damaging health.

CONTROVERSY OVER PREMIER

On November 3, 1988, the American Medical Association filed petitions with regulators in the two test states asking that the test marketing of Premier be blocked. The AMA also filed a petition with the Food and Drug Administration asking that Premier be regulated as a drug because the direct inhalation of the drug nicotine through the flavor beads allowed faster absorption, which would mean greater addiction. AMA Executive Vice-President James Sammons stated, "We are simply unwilling to accept on faith the new product of an industry that still denies that smoking is unhealthy."[13] Surgeon General C. Everett Koop stated, "I don't see how you cannot regulate that cigarette as a drug. They call it a cigarette, and they want to call it a cigarette because cigarettes are not regulated."[14] Many drug-addiction specialists refer to Premier as a drug-delivery system that could easily be modified to smoke "crack." If so declared, Premier would have to be withdrawn from the market, and RJR would have to provide detailed proof of the product's safety before it could be put back on the market. Further complicating the problem was that the brand could not be promoted based upon its health benefits and safety. Such a strategy would refute industry claims that smoking has not been proven to be unhealthy and would open the company to lawsuits.

Seth Moskowitz, senior public relations representative for RJR, remarked, "We're disappointed that people are trying to ban our cigarette. Our cigarette is not a drug. It is like other cigarettes and provides the same taste and enjoyment of other cigarettes."[15] Health groups also attacked Premier's slogan, "The Cleaner Smoke." The Coalition on Smoking and Health said, "The message is clear. It is not a message of making a cigarette less dirty; it is a message of making claims that the cigarette is less harmful."[16] RJR rejects this claim.

What happened to Premier? After five months of test marketing RJR pulled the brand. Analysts identified a number of possible reasons for the sudden decision. One was that RJR had recently been purchased by Kohlberg Kravis Roberts for $25 billion in borrowed money. The firm may simply have been attempting to cut its losses. Another possibility was that consumer response to the brand was disastrous. However, corporate officials had long argued that they expected the brand to take years to catch on. Another possibility was that the firm wanted to avoid the legal fights brewing over whether the brand was a drug delivery system.[17] The inability of RJR to make health claims about the product, the opposition from numerous consumer groups, the brand's poor taste, and its high cost may have doomed it to failure.

* * *

Thanks to Bobby Joe Walters for developing this case.

QUESTIONS

1. Discuss the consumer behavior concepts from Part 3 of the text that may have caused the failure of Premier.
2. What type of product innovation would Premier be considered? Identify specific concepts from the diffusion of innovations literature that might explain Premier's failure.
3. If you were responsible for an ad campaign for Premier, what type of reference group would you have used to achieve a favorable image?
4. How might personal influence have had an impact on Premier's success?
5. Do you feel a two-sided message would have been useful to RJR in marketing Premier? What information would you include?
6. What ethical issues, if any, should RJR's management have considered in the marketing of Premier?
7. Construct a managerial applications table and discuss its implications for Premier.

NOTES

1. Hillary Stout, "Cigarettes: Still Big Business," *New York Times,* June 12, 1988, p.F4.
2. RJR Tobacco Company, Information Packet, 1988.
3. Betty Morris, "Smokeless Cigarette Is Expected to Pose Big Marketing Challenge," *The Wall Street Journal,* September 18, 1987, p.35.
4. RJR Tobacco Company.
5. Joanne Silberner, "Less Smoke May Mean Less Ire," *U.S. News and World Report,* October 3, 1988, p.69.
6. Stuart Elliot, "RJR: High Stakes on Low Smokers," *USA Today,* October 2, 1988, p.1B.
7. Ibid.
8. Judann Dagholi, "Is Premier Blowing Smoke?" *Advertising Age,* September 26, 1988, p.24.
9. Ed Bean, "Anti-Smoking Forces Set Strategy to Fight Smokeless Cigarette," *The Wall Street Journal,* March 2, 1988, p.29.

10. Ibid.
11. Ibid.
12. Robert Steyer, "Smoke Screened," *St. Louis Post-Dispatch*, October 23, 1988, p.67; October 21, 1988, p.81.
13. "AMA Moves to Block Smokeless Cigarette," *Pittsburgh Post-Gazette*, November 3, 1988.
14. Elliot, "High Stakes on Low Smokes."
15. Dagholi, "Is Premier Blowing Smoke?"
16. Michael Waldholz, "FDA Feels Heat on Smokeless Cigarette," *The Wall Street Journal*, March 1, 1989, p.81.
17. Peter Waldman and Betsy Morris, "RJR Nabisco Abandons `Smokeless' Cigarette," *The Wall Street Journal*, March 1, pp.B1, B6.

Part 3 Case 2

THE PARKER PEN COMPANY GOES GLOBAL

In June 1984, the Parker Pen Company began its much-touted worldwide advertising campaign. The goal was to centralize packaging, pricing, promotion, and production under one umbrella so that Parker Pen would have "one look, one voice." But Parker's U.S. division reported an operating loss of $9.1 million in 1985, with the company as a whole losing $500,000. In 1987 Parker reported a $23.4 million pretax profit for the fiscal year. This U.S. division of Parker reported a $1.2 million profit that year. Worldwide sales were $210 million, up 22% from the 1986 figure of $172 million. What caused the sudden drop in profits for Parker between 1984 and 1986 and then the tremendous turnaround in 1987?

HISTORY

The Parker Pen Company began marketing its pens internationally in 1903. In 1984 it sold pens in 154 countries, from which 80% of its sales came. Historically, the company has produced "upscale" writing instruments. The founder, George Parker, believed that if you "make something better, people will buy it."

Parker is a medium-sized company. Sales of its writing instruments have never topped $225 million. Much of the profit of the writing instrument line of business comes from Great Britain, in part because of the legendary work of its advertising agency there—Lowe Howard-Spink Marschalk.

In 1984 the company was experiencing serious problems. It held only a 6% share of the world market for pens, and the company was receiving serious challenges from the Japanese, Paper Mate, Bic, Pentel, and other firms at the low end of the market. At the high end, A. T. Cross Co. was aggressively marketing its products. In addition, Parker's plant in Janesville, Wisconsin, was highly inefficient; there workers performed many of the assembly functions by hand. Finally, the product line had proliferated to over 500 writing instruments. Many of these were purchased by distributors and subsidiaries around the world from outside sources. A total of forty advertising agencies promoted Parker Pens around the world.

A variety of problems external to the firm also existed. In addition to the heavy competition already mentioned, fluctuations in the value of the American dollar were causing problems. During the 1970s and early 1980s, the weak dollar actually helped the company. However, as the dollar strengthened in 1983 and 1984, foreign currency transactions began to take their toll. The cheap foreign currencies were being translated into fewer and fewer dollars. The end results of all these problems were shrinking sales, a declining market share, and red ink.

THE GLOBAL MARKETING PLAN

Initiated in 1984, the goals of the worldwide marketing campaign were to develop a single image throughout the globe and to save time and money in doing so. As stated by one of the Parker Pen executives, "Our name can stand for something across many price points, regardless of the pen or the audience."

In order to implement the global marketing concept, a team was brought in with previous international marketing experience. The person developing many of the ideas had previous world brand experience with Marlboro cigarettes. He felt that products perceived similarly throughout the world could be marketed globally with similar themes. This followed closely the theory of Harvard professor Theodore Levitt, who in 1983 announced to consumer marketers that the "global village" had come. Citing Coca-Cola and Levi's blue jeans as examples, he stated that people everywhere wanted to buy the same products and live the same way. His conclusion was that "smart companies should sell standardized products the same way, everywhere."

In order to produce a world-class product the company needed a world-class ad agency. As a result, Ogilvy and Mather was given the account. Numerous agencies were dropped as part of the reorganization, including Lowe Howard-Spink Marschalk in London. The ads created by this agency had been almost legendary. For example, one print ad featured the resting body of a workman with a Parker Pen sticking out of his chest. The headline read, "Rediscover the Lost Art of the Insult."

The new advertising strategy involved producing the same ads across markets and even across products. For example, one ad created by Ogilvy and Mather was headlined "It's wrought from pure silver and writes like pure silk." Below the headline was a photo of the pen and then some text. The ad was translated verbatim into French, German, and Arabic, among others. The worldwide advertising them was to be "Make your mark with a Parker." The same graphic layout and approved Parker logo and graphic designs were to be centrally supplied and used. Indeed, at one point management suggested to the ad agency that the copy of ads be minimized so that they would not have to worry so much about translations.

Another aspect of the global strategy involved largely getting out of the high-priced end of the pens selling for under three dollars. This segment of the market accounted for over 65 percent of the business. The company decided to sell one upscale line, named Premier, but it would largely be a "positioning device." The overall strategy consisted of the active marketing of high-volume, low-priced pens produced in a new, fully automated plant.

THE OUTCOME

This experiment in global marketing was dead within nine months of its initiation. In fact, less than two years after it began the experiment, the writing instruments division of Parker Pen had been sold. Indeed, after only six months one manager said, "I think our ship is sinking." A number of factors were cited for the failure. Major problems existed in the start-up of the new, high-volume, computer-controlled plant that had been built. Internal struggles existed within the company as some factions fought the global strategy. The centralization was rigidly enforced, and people were pushed around. One manager, who was responsible for millions of dollars of business in one foreign country, was told, "There's your [advertising] book; get on with it." Moreover, the basic marketing strategy appeared to have also been flawed.

According to Carl Speilvogel, CEO of a worldwide ad agency, "Theodore Levitt's comment about the world becoming homogenized is bunk. There are about two products that lend themselves to global marketing—and one of them is Coca-Cola." In general, worldwide marketing is not successful because it is dull. Says Gary Stibel of the New England Consulting Group in Westport, Connecticut, "It's marketing to the lowest common denominator."

The new owners, former executives of the old Parker Pen Company, have reinstated the policy of each country doing its own advertising, as was the strategy prior to 1984. They have also downplayed the cheap pens in advertising. About 40% of the sales still come from pens priced under three dollars, but the more expensive pens carry the company on fatter margins and greater profits.

In the fall of 1987, Parker celebrated its one hundredth anniversary. To commemorate the occasion, Parker introduced the Duofold Centennial pen. The upscale pen retailed for about $200. Oddly enough, a global advertising campaign was used. The ads, created by Lowe

Howard-Spink Marschalk, were designed to convey a single statement about the company and its new product.

Parker plans to sell more pens to the same type of customer in the future. The idea behind this is that, unlike twenty years ago, people no longer own one fine pen. According to Mr. Jacques Margry, a Parker Pen executive, "Today a single consumer has one very good quality fountain pen, two good fountain pens, three good quality ball pens, and a jar of writing sticks."

QUESTIONS

1. Using concepts from Part 3, construct a managerial applications table for the Parker Pen case. Identify the consumer behavior concepts relevant to the case. What are the managerial implications of these concepts?
2. What were the flaws in the global marketing strategy that contributed to the experiment's failure? Did the global campaign have any good points? To what extent can the same advertising theme be used across prices, types of pens, and countries?
3. To what extent do you think the various managers in the countries in which Parker Pen sold its products would be motivated to follow the global strategy? What steps could be taken to gain the backing of managers around the world?
4. Parker Pen moved to a strategy of producing high-volume, low-priced pens. Evaluate this marketing strategy from a global marketing perspective.
5. What situational factors might influence the purchase of low-priced versus high-priced pens? How would such situational factors influence management strategy?
6. How successful do you feel the global strategy will be for the new Duofold pen? What cultural factors will influence its success?
7. Construct a managerial applications table pertaining to the globalization strategy used in 1984. Discuss the managerial implications of the matrix.

NOTES

1. Kevin Cote, "Parker Pen Finds Black Ink," *Advertising Age*, July 13, 1987, p.49.
2. Lori Kesler, "Parker Rebuilds a Quality Image," *Advertising Age*, March 21, 1988, pp.5–12.
3. Joanne Lipman, "Marketers Turn Sour on Global Sales Pitch Harvard Guru Makes," *The Wall Street Journal*, May 12, 1988, p.1.
4. "Parker Pen Pins Hopes on World-Brand Campaign," *Advertising Age*, June 25, 1984, p.74.
5. Joseph M. Winski and Laurel Wentz, "Parker Pen: What Went Wrong?" *Advertising Age*, June 2, 1986, pp.1, 60, 61, 71.

GLOSSARY

Abstract information: Pallid information, lacking concreteness and communication effectiveness.

Absolute threshold: The lowest level at which a stimulus can be detected 50% of the time.

Acceptable risk: The level of risk that a consumer will tolerate when purchasing a product or service.

Acculturation: The difficult task of learning a new culture.

Achievement motivation: The motivation identified by David McClelland to strive for success and to perform up to one's capabilities.

Acquisition phase: The first of three phases of consumer buying—acquisition, consumption, and disposition.

Actual product performance: A consumer's perception of the level of performance displayed by a product. Actual performance is compared to expected performance to determine product satisfaction.

Actual state: The state of being experienced by a consumer at any particular point in time. When the actual diverges sufficiently from the desired state, need recognition is said to occur.

Adaptation: A process in which an organism has repeated experience with a stimulus and habituates to it.

Adaptation level: The level of intensity of a stimulus to which a consumer has become accustomed or adapted.

Advertising substantiation: The concept, developed by the Federal Trade Commission, that companies must provide evidence for the truth of their advertising claims.

Advertising wear-out: Occurs when consumers are overexposed to an advertisement, resulting in decreased positivity.

Affect: A class of mental phenomena uniquely characterized by a consciously experienced, subjective feeling state, commonly accompanying emotions and moods.

Affect and CS/D: The concept that the level of consumer satisfaction is influenced by the positive and negative affective responses elicited by a product after its purchase.

Affect–referral heuristic: A rule of thumb in which a consumer chooses a product based upon an overall recollection of his or her evaluation of an alternative.

African-American subculture: The subculture in the United States composed of dark-skinned people whose ancestry can be traced to Africa.

AIO statements: Used in psychographic inventories to obtain information on consumers' activities, interests, and opinions.

Alternative evaluation: The formation of attitudes regarding the choice alternatives.

Anchoring and adjustment: A judgmental heuristic that is used to make an estimate of the level of a stimulus on a scale. The level is estimated by starting at some reference point and then adjusting away from it.

Antecedent states: The temporary physiological and mood states that a consumer brings to a consumption situation.

Applied behavior analysis: A process in which environmental variables are manipulated to alter behavior.

Articulation: A component of consumer knowledge that describes how finely a person can discriminate differences along a dimension.

Aspiration group: A group to which an individual would like to belong. If it is impossible for the individual to belong to the group, it becomes a symbolic group for the person.

Assimilation effect: The idea that a communication may be viewed as more congruent with the position of the receiver than it really is because it falls within the latitude of acceptance.

Associationist school: Eighteenth-century learning theorists who investigated such phenomena as the serial-position effect and paired-associate learning.

Atmospherics: The process through which consumer reactions may be influenced by the design of buildings and spaces, including the interior space; the layout of the aisles; the texture of the carpets and walls; and the scents, colors, shapes, and sounds experienced by customers.

Attention: The allocation of cognitive capacity to an object or task.

Attention stage: The stage of information processing in which a person allocates cognitive capacity to a stimulus.

Attitude: The amount of affect or feeling for or against a stimulus.

Attitude toward the ad: A consumer's positive and negative feelings held toward a particular advertisement.

Attitude toward the behavior: A consumer's positive and negative feelings held toward engaging in a particular behavior.

Attitude-toward-the-object model: A model of consumer choice based upon how consumers combine their beliefs about product attributes to form attitudes about various brand alternatives.

Attribute–benefit belief: A belief about the extent to which an attribute provides a specific benefit.

Attribute importance: The relative importance of a product or service characteristic to a consumer in relation to other characteristics.

Attribute–object belief: The belief that an object possesses a particular attribute.

Attributes: The characteristics or features that an object may or may not have.

Attribution theory: Identifies the various means through which people determine the causes of action of themselves, others, and objects.

Augmenting principle: A principle from one of the attribution theory models stating that the role of a given cause in producing a given effect is discounted if other plausible causes are also present.

Autonomic decisions: Decisions of lesser importance that either the husband or wife may make independently of the other.

Availability heuristic: The concept that people may assess the probability of an event based on the ease with which the event can be brought to mind.

Availability–valence hypothesis: The hypothesis that judgments depend on the favorableness of information available in memory.

Awareness set: A subset of the total universe of potential brands and products available of which a consumer is aware.

Baby-boom generation: The large post-World War II group of people born between 1946 and 1964

Baby bust: A period after 1964 when fertility rates plunged far below the replacement level, resulting in fewer children being born in the United States.

Back translation: A process involving successive translations of a message back and forth between languages by different translators. In this way, subtle and not-so-subtle differences in meaning can be located.

Balance theory: A type of cognitive consistency approach in which people are viewed as maintaining a logical and consistent set of interconnected beliefs.

Basic exchange equation: Profit = Rewards – Costs.

Behavioral economics: An approach to economics based upon the investigation of the behavior of individual consumers. An example is the use of survey research methods to assess the economic confidence of consumers.

Behavioral influence hierarchy: The proposal that, in some instances, the hierarchy of effects begins with a behavior, followed by the formation of beliefs and attitudes.

Behavioral influence perspective: The view that strong situational or environmental forces may propel a consumer to engage in buying behavior without having formed either feelings or affect about the object of the purchase.

Behavioral intentions: The determination of a consumer to engage in some act, such as purchasing a product or service.

Behavioral intentions model: A consumer choice model that states that behavior results from the formation of specific intentions to behave.

Behavioral learning: A process in which experience with the environment leads to a relatively permanent change in behavior or the potential for a change in behavior.

Beliefs: The cognitive knowledge people have of the relations among attributes, benefits, and objects.

Benefit segmentation: The division of the market into relatively homogeneous groups of consumers based upon similarities of needs.

Benefits: The outcomes that product or service attributes may provide.

Binationals: A situation in which product components are made in one country but the product is assembled in another, or in which a product is designed in one country but made in another.

Bogies: Fear rumors that may spook the marketplace.

Boomerang effect: Occurs when a message results in a change of attitude opposite in direction to that intended.

Brand commitment: The emotional–psychological attachment to a brand.

Brand expectations: The expectations that a consumer forms regarding the performance of a brand.

Brand knowledge: The amount of experience with and information that a person has about particular products or services. Consumers possessing greater amounts of knowledge can think about a product across a number of dimensions and make finer distinctions among brands.

Brand loyalty: The biased behavioral response, expressed over time by some decision-making unit, to one or more alternative brands out of a set of such brands that results from a psychological (decision-making) process.

Butterfly curve: The curve showing that the preference for a stimulus is at its greatest level at points just higher or lower than the adaptation level.

Buyer's regret: A postacquisition phenomenon in which the preference for a chosen alternative actually falls below that of a rejected alternative.

Buying unit: The individual, family, or group that makes a purchase decision.

CAD model: A personality scale developed to measure the interpersonal orientation of consumers. CAD stands for compliance, aggression, and detachment.

Central route to persuasion: In high-involvement information processing, a path to persuasion in which a person diligently processes the arguments of the source of information.

Channels: The media through information flows.

Childhood consumer socialization: Processes by which young people acquire skills, knowledge, and attitudes relevant to their functioning as consumers in the marketplace.

Choice: The process in which consumers make a choice between two or more alternative courses of action.

Choice uncertainty: The degree of uncertainty about which of several brands to select.

Classic fashion trend: A fashion trend in which particular looks become a classic, such as the blue pin-striped suit.

Classical conditioning: A type of learning in which a conditioned stimulus is paired with an unconditioned stimulus. Through repetition, the conditioned stimulus will eventually elicit a conditioned response.

Closure: A principle of perceptual organization that describes the tendency of people to fill in missing information to create a holistic image.

Cluster analysis: The use of demographic variables to identify where groups of similar consumers are located geographically.

Clutter: An overabundance of advertisements that decreases communications effectiveness.

Cognitive complexity: A personality characteristic that describes the degree of structural intricacy of the organizing schemas used by different groups of consumers to code and store information in memory.

Cognitive consistency: The tendency of people to maintain a logical and consistent set of interconnected attitudes.

Cognitive dissonance: A state that occurs when one cognition does not logically follow from another.

Cognitive learning: A field that focuses on understanding such mental processes as thinking, remembering, problem solving, and learning.

Cognitive responses: The thoughts that consumers may develop in response to messages.

Cognitive personality theories: Personality theories positing that individual differences result from variations in how people process information, think, and learn.

Commitment: The degree to which an attitude position can be changed. As the level of commitment to an attitude position increases, it becomes more difficult to change the attitude.

Communication: The use of a sign to convey meaning. A sign may be a verbalization, an utterance, a body movement, a written word, a picture, an odor, a touch, or even stones on the ground to denote a property boundary.

Communications model: A model stating that sources encode messages that travel through a channel and are processed by receivers, who then provide feedback to the source.

Comparative appraisal: The consumer's evaluation of his or her own relative standing with respect to an attitude, belief, ability, or emotion through observation of the behavior of appropriate reference others.

Comparative messages: Messages in which the communicator compares the positive and negative aspects of his or her position to the positive and negative aspects of a competitor's position.

Comparison level: The minimum level of positive outcome (profit) that an individual feels he or she deserves from an exchange.

Comparison level for alternatives: The lowest level of outcomes a person will accept in light of available alternative opportunities.

Comparison level for outcomes: The minimum level of positive outcomes a person believes he or she deserves from an exchange.

Compensatory models of choice: A class of choice models in which consumers are viewed as analyzing each alternative in a broad evaluative fashion. A choice is said to be compensatory when high ratings on some attributes may compensate for low ratings on other attributes.

Competitive positioning: The positioning of a product relative to key competitors on important attributes.

Complaint behavior: The overt actions taken by consumers to bring their product or service dissatisfaction to the attention of others.

Complementary activities: Activities that naturally take place together.

Complex exchange: An exchange that involves a set of three or more actors enmeshed in a set of mutual relations.

Compliance: The act of conforming to the wishes of another person or group without necessarily accepting the group's dictates.

Comprehension: The process of making sense of stimuli so that they may be understood.

Comprehension stage: The stage of information processing in which the person organizes and interprets information.

Compulsive consumption: Consumption marked by an impulse or urge to engage in behavior that may be harmful to the consumer while simultaneously denying its possible negative effects.

Compulsive purchases: Purchases marked by an impulse or urge to engage in behavior that may be harmful to the consumer while simultaneously denying its possible negative effects.

Conditioned response: The response elicited by the conditioned stimulus when classical conditioning occurs.

Conditioned stimulus: A previously neutral stimulus that, when paired with an unconditioned stimulus, may elicit a conditioned response.

Conformity: A change in behavior or belief as a result of real or imagined group or individual pressure.

Conjunctive rule: A type of choice heuristic in which the consumer sets minimum cutoffs on each product attribute. If the product rating falls below the minimum cutoff level on any attribute, the product is rejected from further consideration.

Conservation behavior: Action consumers take to conserve resources, including curtailment behaviors, maintenance behaviors, and efficiency behaviors.

Consideration set: The set of alternative brands that the consumer regards as acceptable for further consideration.

Consumer actions: Those behaviors in which consumers engage in the acquisition, consumption, and disposition of goods, services, and ideas.

Consumer acquisitions: The goods, services, and ideas that consumers obtain in the marketplace.

Consumer behavior: The study of the decision-making units and the processes involved in acquiring, consuming, and disposing of goods, services, experiences, and ideas.

Consumer beliefs: The cognitive knowledge people have of the relations among attributes, benefits, and objects.

Consumer complaint behavior: A multiple set of actions triggered by perceived dissatisfaction with a purchase episode.

Consumer decision making: The analysis made in choosing between two or more alternative acquisitions and the processes that take place before and after the choice.

Consumer environment: The environmental influencers that affect buying behavior, such as cultural, situational, and economic influencers.

Consumer ethnocentrism: A scale measuring the tendency of consumers to prefer to purchase U.S.-made products.

Consumer expectations: A person's prior beliefs about what should happen in a given situation.

Consumer incentives: The products, services, information, and even other people that are perceived to satisfy a need.

Consumer information processing: The process in which consumers are exposed to information, attend to it, comprehend it, place it in memory, and retrieve it for later use.

Consumer knowledge: The amount of experience and information that a person has about particular products or services.

Consumer marketing: The marketing of a good or service by one consumer to another.

Consumer performance: An event in which a consumer and

a marketer act as performers and/or as audience in a situation in which obligations and standards exist.

Consumer primacy: The concept that the consumer should be at the center of the marketing effort.

Consumer rights: The rights, identified by John F. Kennedy, of safety, information, redress, and choice. More recently some have suggested that the right to health care and the right to a home should be added to the list.

Consumer ritual: Standardized sequences of actions that are periodically repeated.

Consumer satisfaction/dissatisfaction: The general feelings that a consumer develops about a product or service after its purchase.

Consumer self-control: The extent to which a consumer can exert regulate his or her wants and needs.

Consumer situations: The temporary environmental and personal factors that form the context within which a consumer activity occurs.

Consumer well-being: The extent to which an individual's needs and wants are satisfied.

Consumerism: The movement made up of activities of government, business, independent organizations, and concerned consumers that are designed to protect the rights of consumers.

Consumption phase: A researcher's analysis of how consumers actually use a product or service and the experiences that the consumer obtains from such use.

Context: The background factors within which consumer behavior occurs.

Context effects: The concept that the background or context in which stimuli are embedded will influence the perception of the stimuli. Thus the background programming in which an advertisement is placed may influence the interpretation of the advertisement.

Contingencies of reinforcement: The temporal relationship between a behavior and its reinforcers or punishers that acts to shape consumer behavior.

Continuous innovations: A modification of an existing product to improve performance, taste, reliability, and so forth. Continuous innovations result in few, if any, consumer life-style changes.

Country of origin: The country from which a good or service originates.

Contrast effects: Occur when the attitude statement falls into the latitude of rejection, so that it is perceived as more opposed to the receiver's position than perhaps it really is.

Conventions: Norms that describe how to act in everyday life.

Corporate social responsibility: The idea that business has an obligation to help society with its problems by offering resources.

Corrective advertising: Advertising that is mandated by a federal agency to correct consumer impressions that were formed by previously misleading advertising.

Cresive norms: Norms embedded in the culture that include three types: conventions, mores, and customs.

Cross-cultural analysis: The study of foreign cultures and their values, languages, and customs.

Crowding: A psychological state that occurs when a person perceives that his or her movements are restricted because of limited space.

Cultural ethnocentricity: The feeling among some consumers that the values, beliefs, and ways of doing things as specified by one's own culture are "right," "correct," and generally better than those of other cultures.

Cultural identification: A feeling of attachment to the society in which a person prefers to live.

Cultural meanings: Cultural ideas transferred to consumers through material goods and rituals.

Cultural rituals: Standardized sequences of actions that are periodically repeated. They have some purpose and generally have a beginning, middle, and end.

Cultural symbols: Entities that represent the shared ideas and concepts of a culture.

Cultural values: What is considered to be right or wrong and important or unimportant in a culture.

Culture: A set of socially acquired behavior patterns transmitted symbolically through language and other means to the members of a particular society. It is a way of life.

Culture versus nation: A nation is a state that may contain a culture. A culture is a way of life that may extend far beyond national borders.

Customs: Handed down from generation to generation, customs refers to basic actions such as the ceremonies held and the roles played by the sexes.

Cyclical fashion trend: The adoption of styles that are progressively more extreme in one direction or another. Examples include skirt lengths and tie widths.

Deceptive advertising: An advertisement may be deemed deceptive if it has the "capacity to deceive a measurable segment of the public."

Decision context: Situational or extrinsic factors that dictate the options available to the decision maker.

Decision-making perspective: Occurs when consumers move through a series of rational steps when making a purchase. These steps include problem recognition, search, alternative evaluation, choice, and postacquisition evaluation.

Decision process: The steps through which consumers move when purchasing a product or service, including problem recognition, search, alternative evaluation, choice, and postacquisition evaluation.

Decreasing marginal utility: The concept that, as a consumer obtains more of something, each additional unit brings less utility or satisfaction.

Defense mechanisms: Psychological adjustments made by people to keep themselves from recognizing personality qualities or motives that might lower self-esteem or heighten anxiety.

Delay-payment effect: This effect occurs when a customers are encouraged to buy a good or service in the present and are allowed to pay for it at a later date.

Demand curve shift: The shift of the demand curve to the right or left.

Demand elasticity: The variation in quantity demanded of a good that is caused by changes in the price of that good. For example, an elastic demand curve results in small changes in price, causing large changes in quantity demanded.

Demarketing: A process of employing the marketing mix to decrease consumer demand for a product.

Demographic variables: Characteristics of various groups of people as assessed by such factors as age, sex, income, religion, marital status, nationality, education, family size, occupation, and ethnicity.

Density: How closely packed consumers are in a particular situational context.

Depth interviews: Long, probing, one-on-one interviews to identify hidden reasons for purchasing products and services.

Desired state: The preferred state that a consumer would like to achieve. When differences between the desired state and the actual state are sufficiently large, a need state is said to exist.

Detached nuclear family: Pattern in which children from middle-class families tend to strikeout on their own to form families away from their parents.

Difference threshold: The minimum amount of difference in the intensity of a stimulation that can be detected 50% of the time.

Diffusion: The idea that substances or even ideas can gradually spread through a medium of some type and reach a state of equilibrium.

Dimensionality: A type of consumer knowledge referring to the number of different ways that a person can think about something.

Direct comparative advertisements: Advertisements in which one brand is specifically compared to another.

Direct influence of attitudes, beliefs, and behaviors: The concept that attitudes, beliefs, and behaviors may be formed directly.

Discontinuous innovations: Innovations that produce major changes in the life-styles of consumers.

Discounting principle: The idea from attribution theory that people will examine the environmental pressures that impede or propel a particular action. When a person moves with the environmental pressures, little understanding of the person's true motivations can be gained; therefore, the information is discounted.

Discrete exchange: A one-time interaction in which money is paid for a commodity. Discrete exchanges are short, one-time purchases that do not involve the creation of a relationship.

Discretionary expenditures: Expenditures that can be postponed or eliminated.

Discriminative stimuli: Stimuli that occur in the presence of a reinforcer but that do not occur in its absence.

Disjunctive rule: A choice heuristic in which an option is judged acceptable if any of its attributes surpass a cutoff level.

Disposition phase: The phase of postacquisition in which the consumer determines what to do with an acquisition after it has been used.

Dissociative group: A reference group with whom the person does not wish to be associated.

Dissonance: An imbalanced state that results when a logical inconsistency exists among cognitive elements.

Divestment rituals: Rituals performed to erase the meaning associated with the previous owner of a good (e.g., thoroughly cleaning a new home prior to moving in).

Dogmatism: A personality characteristic marked by closed-mindedness and rigidity in the approach to the social environment.

Domain-specific values: Beliefs relevant to economic, social, religious, and other activities.

Door-in-the-face technique: A compliance technique that involves the requester first making a very large request, which is usually refused by the target. This request is then followed by a moderate request, which is more often complied with than if no large request were made.

Double jeopardy: Occurs when a less popular brand, as defined by market share, also has less brand loyalty among its customers.

Drama: An advertising technique of indirect address in which the characters speak to each other and not to the audience.

Drawing conclusions: A message strategy in which the presenter draws the conclusions of the message for the audience.

Drive: The physiological arousal that occurs when a need is felt.

Dyadic exchange: A exchange that takes place between two parties.

Dynamic continuous innovations: Innovations that involve some major change in an existing product and minor changes in the behavior of consumers.

East Asia: Composed of Japan, Korea, China, and Southeast Asia, the region has over 26% of the world's population and is the dominant exporter of automobiles, electronics, and computer chips.

Eastern Europe: The landmass stretching from the eastern border of Germany to the shores of the Pacific Ocean, composed of people as diverse as the European Czechs and the Mongoloid people of far eastern Siberia.

Economic cycle: The cycle that traces the flow of an economy. It has four phases—peak, recession, trough, and recovery.

Economic environment: The set of factors involving monetary, natural, and human resources that influence the behavior of individuals and groups.

Economic optimism-pessimism: The reactions of consumers to various economic and personal events that result in the presence or absence of feelings of economic confidence.

Ego: The component of the personality defined in psychoanalytic theory as standing for reason and good sense and as following the reality principle.

Elaboration likelihood model (ELM): A model proposing that the route to persuasion depends on the involvement of the consumer. The highly involved consumer engages in greater amounts of information processing than the less involved consumer.

Elimination-by-aspects heuristic: A choice heuristic in which consumers rank attributes in order. Alternatives are eliminated if they do not possess the first attribute. Those alternatives left are then evaluated on the next attribute, and so forth, until only one alternative remains.

Emotional dissatisfaction: A postacquisition state that occurs when the actual performance is perceived to be lower than the expected performance.

Emotional satisfaction: A post-acquisition state that occurs when the actual performance exceeds the expected performance.

Enacted norms: Norms that are explicitly expressed, sometimes in the form of laws. An example would be on which side of the road you drive a car.

Encoding: The process of transferring information from short-term to long-term memory for permanent storage.

Enculturation: The process of learning one's own culture.

Enduring involvement: Occurs when a product relates to a consumer's needs, values, or self-concept. Marked by a continuing interest in a product category.

Environmental analysis: The assessment of the forces and institutions external to the firm and of how these may influence the marketing effort.

Environmental influence factors: The components of the environment that influence behavior, including situational, group, family, cultural, subcultural, economic, and regulatory influencers.

Environmental level of analysis: Analysis of those factors outside of the person that influence consumer behavior, such as the effects of situations, groups, culture, subcultures, and the regulatory environment.

Equity: Occurs when the ratio of the outcomes and inputs is perceived by one party to an exchange to equal the ratio of the outcomes and inputs of the other party to the exchange.

Equity theory: Holds that people will analyze the ratio of their outcomes and inputs to the ratio of the outcomes and inputs of the partner in an exchange.

Ethical dilemma: A decision that involves the trade-off of lowering one's personal values in exchange for increased organizational and personal profits.

Ethical exchange characteristics: The things that must occur for an ethical exchange to take place, such as both parties knowing the full nature of an agreement before entering into it.

Ethics: The study of normative judgments concerned with what is morally right and wrong, good and bad.

Ethics matrix: A matrix that identifies when ethical problems may occur. Such a matrix is based upon exchanges of information between consumers and businesses.

Ethnicity: The national or racial background of a group of people.

Ethnocentrism: The universal tendency for people to view their own group as the center of the universe, to interpret other social units from the perspective of their own group, and to reject persons who are culturally dissimilar.

Euroconsumers: Consumers in Western Europe who supposedly share common desires for a broad range of goods and services. This assumption is incorrect.

Even-a-penny-will-help technique: A compliance technique in which a person makes a request and then states that any contribution, no matter how paltry, would help.

Evoked set: Consists of those brands and products recalled from long-term memory that are acceptable for further consideration.

Exchange: The process through which goods, services, and ideas are transferred between two or more social actors.

Exchange process: A transfer of something tangible or intangible, actual or symbolic, between two or more social actors.

Exchange rituals: Rituals in which products or services are exchanged among consumers.

Expectancy confirmation: Results when the performance of a product is perceived to meet a consumer's expectations.

Expectancy disconfirmation: Results when the performance of a product fails to meet a consumer's expectations.

Expectancy disconfirmation model: A model of consumer satisfaction/dissatisfaction based upon whether a brand meets or exceeds consumer expectations.

Expectations: A person's prior beliefs about what should happen in a given situation.

Expected product performance: The level of performance anticipated of a product or service by a consumer.

Experiential hierarchy: The hierarchy of effects in which affect occurs first, followed by behavior and then belief formation.

Experiential perspective: Occurs when consumers make purchases principally because of strong positive feelings, rather than because of lengthy rational decision making or strong environmental pressures.

Exposure: The initial information-processing stage, in which consumers receive information through their senses.

Expressive needs: Desires by consumers to fulfill social and/or aesthetic requirements.

Expressive role: A role found in many groups, in which a person helps maintain the group and provides emotional support for its members.

Extended family: Consists of the nuclear family plus the husband's or wife's mother and other kinfolk.

Extended self: The concept that possessions may become a part of the self-concept and, therefore, extend the self to include impersonal entities.

External attribution: An attribution of the cause of action to some factor outside of an individual, such as attributing the reason for an endorsement to the money paid to the endorser.

External exchange: An exchange between parties that are in separate groups, such as between two families or two firms.

External roles: Involves communications and involvement with people outside of the family.

External search: The consumer's soliciting information from outside sources rather than from his or her memory.

Extinction: A gradual reduction in the frequency of occurrence of an operant behavior that results from a lack of reinforcement of the response.

Fads: Temporary fashion or other trends followed by a group.

Family decision stages: The steps in the decision process used by a family to purchase products or services.

Family life cycle: The idea that families may move through a series of stages in a developmental fashion.

Fashion: A set of behaviors temporarily adopted by a people because they are perceived to be socially appropriate for the time and situation.

Fear appeals: A type of message in which the communication is designed to create some level of fear in the target audience.

Feelings: The affective responses and emotions that consumers have.

Fertility rate: The number of births per 1,000 women of childbearing age.

Figure–ground: A principle of perception whereby the figure is the object observed moving against the ground. The ground is the context or background within which the figure is observed.

Focus groups: Groups of five to ten consumers who are encouraged to talk freely about their feelings and thoughts concerning a product or service.

Foot-in-the-door technique: A compliance technique that operates through the influencer making two requests; the first, a small request, is followed by a moderately sized second request.

Forgetting: The inability to recall from memory some desired piece of information. Forgetting occurs when either the retrieval or the response generation process breaks down.

Formal exchange: An explicit written, or verbal contract. This will frequently occur in external exchanges.

Formal group: A group whose organization and structure are defined in writing.

Framing: A process in which a person evaluates a stimulus change as occurring from either a loss or a gain position. Framing has been found to influence risk-taking behavior.

Fraudulent symbol: A material good that is stripped of class symbolism when its ownership is diffused across levels of the class hierarchy.

Free riding: An act whereby a consumer obtains product information from sales personnel and then uses the information to make a purchase from a low-cost discount store that does not offer personal service.

Frequency heuristic: The rule of thumb used by consumers in some low-involvement settings, in which the liking for a brand is based merely on the number of positive attributes associated with it.

Functions of attitudes: The concept that attitudes exist for a reason, that is, to help people interact more effectively with the environment.

Fundamental attribution error: The tendency of people to attribute the cause of a person's actions to that person's disposition and personality.

Gatekeeper: An individual who has the ability to control information to a decision maker.

Generation X: The post babyboom group born between 1965 and 1980.

Geodemographics: The use of demographic variables to identify where consumers with similar buying patterns are geographically concentrated.

Gestalt psychologists: An influential group of psychologists prominent during the early twentieth century who believed that biological and psychological events do not influence behavior in isolation from each other.

Global attitude measures: Measures that assess consumers' overall like and dislike for an object by using semantic differential scales.

Global values: Enduring beliefs about desired states of existence or modes of behavior.

Goal-directed action: Behavior directed toward obtaining an incentive object, such as a product or service.

Goal-directed behavior: Actions directed toward obtaining goods, services, or ideas that will decrease the gap between a desired and an actual state.

Goods: Tangible products.

Gravitational model: The concept that trading areas act like planets, attracting outside shoppers in proportion to the relative populations of the towns in question and to the square of the inverse of the distance between the towns.

Grooming rituals: An individual's acts to ensure that special, perishable properties resident in clothing, hairstyles, and looks are maintained.

Group: A set of individuals who interact with one another over some period of time and who share some common need or goal.

Group polarization phenomenon: The tendency of groups to be either more risky or more cautious than individuals when making decisions.

Group shift: The tendency of group decisions to show either more or less risk-taking propensities than the average of the decisions of the individuals in the group.

Habitual purchases: Purchases that occur as a result of a habit.

Halo effect: The concept that positive or negative feelings about one characteristic will generalize to influence feelings about other, possibly unrelated, characteristics.

Hedonic consumption: The consumption of products and services based primarily on the desire to experience pleasure and happiness.

Hedonism: The desire to gain pleasure through the senses.

Heuristic models of choice: Models of choice in which consumers take shortcuts in information processing to make decision making less complex.

Heuristics: Simplified rules of thumb used to make decision making less complex.

Hierarchical models of choice: Models of choice in which the consumer is viewed as comparing alternatives on attributes one at a time.

Hierarchies of effects: Various models that explain the order in which beliefs, feelings, and behavior occur.

High culture: Culture that is exclusive in style, content, and appeal. It frequently harks back to the "old masters" of art, theater, music, and literature.

High-involvement decision making: The decision process that occurs when consumers perceive high personal importance in a decision. It is marked by extended decision making and high levels of information processing.

High-involvement hierarchy: The hierarchy of effects in which belief formation occurs first, followed by the creation of affect, followed by a behavior.

Higher-order conditioning: Occurs when a conditioned stimulus acts to classically condition another, previously neutral stimulus.

Hindsight bias: The tendency of people to consistently exaggerate what could have been anticipated in foresight.

Hispanic subculture: The subculture of the Hispanic population in the United States, in which four groups have been identified—Cubans, Puerto Ricans, Mexicans, and other Hispanics.

Hostselling: The use of a program character to promote a product.

Household: A group of people living under one roof.

Humor in messages: A type of message based upon using humor.

Hypothetical value function: In prospect theory the relationship between actual levels of the value of a stimulus and the psychological value of the stimulus.

Id: One of the three elements of the personality identified by Freud. The id is based upon the pleasure principle and immediate gratification.

Ideal self: How a person would ideally like to perceive himself or herself.

Identification: The normal process through which children ac-quire appropriate social roles by consciously and unconsciously copying the behavior of significant others.

Image congruence hypothesis: The hypothesis that a consumer selects products and stores that correspond to his or her self-concept.

Immigration: To come into a country of which one is not a native for permanent residence.

Impersonal threats: Threats to behavioral freedom that come from impersonal sources.

Impulse purchase: Buying action undertaken without a problem previously having been consciously recognized or without a buying intention formed prior to entering the store.

Incentives: The products, services, and people that are perceived as satisfying needs.

Income effect: An economic principle stating that, when prices are lowered, consumers can afford more of a product without giving up other alternatives.

Index of Consumer Sentiment: An index of consumer economic confidence developed at the University of Michigan Center for Survey Research.

Indirect comparative advertisement: A comparative ad in which the competing brand's name is never specifically mentioned.

Individual influence factors: The major concepts investigated when analyzing individual consumers: information processing; behavioral learning; motivation; personality and psychographics; attitudes, beliefs, and behaviors; communications; and decision making.

Individual level of analysis: An analysis that focuses on identifying the processes that influence a person in the acquisition, consumption, and disposition phases.

Industrial marketing: The marketing of a product by one firm to another firm.

Industrial purchase behavior: The process corporations use to purchase goods, services, and ideas.

Inept set: Consists of the brands and products that are considered unacceptable.

Inert set: Consists of the brands and products to which consumers are essentially indifferent.

Influence: The attempt of one person to impact the behaviors, attitudes, or beliefs of another person.

Informal exchange: Unwritten social contracts are created between parties. Occurring more frequently in internal exchanges, social norms and peer pressure replace formal contracts.

Informal group: A group that has no written organizational structure.

Information: The content of what is exchanged with the outer world as we adjust to it and make our adjustment felt upon it.

Information overload: A state experienced by a consumer resulting from receiving more information than can be comfortably processed during a period of time.

Information processing: The process through which consumers receive stimulation, transform it into meaningful information, store the information in memory for later use, and retrieve the information for decision making.

Information salience: The degree to which information is vivid and capable of attracting attention.

Informational influence: One method through which a group may influence an individual, in which the information that the group possesses is transferred to and has an effect on that individual.

Ingratiation: Self-serving tactics engaged in by one person to make himself or herself more attractive to another.

Ingratiator's dilemma: The problem that occurs when the ingratiator is caught manipulating the target person, the result being a loss rather than a gain of power.

Inner-directed persons: Within the VALS psychographic inventory, persons who seek intense involvement in whatever they do.

Innovativeness: The degree to which a consumer adopts new products, services, and ideas prior to others.

Inputs: In balance theory, the contributions to an exchange made by each of the parties to the exchange.

Instrumental materialism: Obtaining material goods to perform some activity or achieve some goal.

Instrumental response: The behaviors (operants) of an organism that have been operantly conditioned.

Instrumental role: Within a group, the role filled by the person who deals with the problem of getting the group to achieve certain goals and complete certain tasks.

Instrumental values: Behaviors and actions required to achieve various terminal states.

Instrumentality of search: An approach for measuring external search by assessing the extent to which a person relies on various types of outside information, such as the number of friends with whom a purchase is discussed.

Integrated group: A category within the VALS psychographic inventory that describes consumers who are mature and balanced and who have managed to "put together" the best characteristics of the inner and outer personalities.

Interaction: Occurs when two or more factors combine to cause a consumer to behave in a different manner than if the two factors were not combined.

Interaction set: Those stores where a consumers allows himself or herself to be exposed to personal selling.

Internal attribution: An attribution that the cause for an action was internal to the person or thing in question, rather than to some external factor.

Internal exchange: Exchanges that occur between parties within a group.

Internal roles: Duties inside the family.

Internal search: The first phase of the search process, in which the consumer attempts to retrieve from long-term memory information on products or services that will help to solve a problem.

Internalization: Occurs when an individual accepts influence because it is intrinsically rewarding.

Interpersonal processes: The communications that occur between two people at any particular point in time.

Interpretant: A person's reaction to and meaning derived from a sign.

Interpretation: A process whereby people draw upon their experience, memory, and expectations to interpret and attach meaning to a stimulus.

Interpretation process: The process in which people draw upon their experience, memory and expectations to attach meaning to a stimulus.

Interpretive research methods: Qualitative methods in which the researcher attempts to identify the meanings of the symbols and rituals employed by consumers.

Intrinsic satisfaction: Satisfaction that results from an internal interest in doing something, rather than from the external benefits of doing it.

Involuntary attention: An innate response that occurs when a consumer is exposed to something surprising, novel, threatening, or unexpected.

Involvement: The level of perceived personal importance or interest evoked by a stimulus (or stimuli) within a specific situation.

Involvement responses: The level of complexity of information processing and the extent of decision making by a consumer.

Judgment: Assessments of (1) the likelihood that something will occur or (2) the goodness or badness of something.

Judgmental heuristics: The simple rules of thumb used by people to make estimates of probabilities and values.

Just-in-time (JIT) purchasing: A corporate philosophy associated with total quality management in which a company seeks to purchase goods and services at the last possible minute prior to when they are required for the production process.

Just noticeable difference (JND): The difference in the amount of stimulation required for a person to recognize that a change has occurred 50% of the time.

Knowledge uncertainty: Consumers' uncertainty about the available features, their importance, and their performance for alternative brands.

Laddering: The process of probing to identify the linkages between means (i.e., attributes) and terminal values (i.e., end states).

Latitudes of acceptance and rejection: The areas surrounding a person's attitude about an issue. When messages fall within these areas, they are assimilated and, in turn, viewed as consistent with the attitude of the person.

Law of contiguity: States that things that are experienced together become associated.

Law of demand: States that there is an inverse relationship between the price of the product and the quantity demanded of the product.

Law of small numbers: A judgmental bias that occurs when a person assumes that the characteristics of a population can be estimated by a small number of data points.

Learning mechanisms: Processes through which a person retains information from the environment.

Learning through education: Obtaining information from companies in the form of advertising, sales personnel, and the consumer's own directed efforts to seek data.

Learning through experience: The process of gaining knowledge through actual contact with products. Overall, learning through experience is a more effective means to gain consumer knowledge.

Lecture: An advertising technique that occurs when a source speaks to the audience in an attempt to inform and persuade.

Lexicographic heuristic: A noncompensatory choice model in which the consumer first ranks the attributes and then selects the brand rated highest on the highest-ranked attribute. If a tie occurs, the next most important attribute is used.

Libido: A term in psychoanalytic theory that refers to sexual energy.

Life-style: How one lives.

Likert scale: An attitude scale that involves asking a consumer to indicate the amount of his or her agreement or disagreement with a statement.

Limited capacity: A characteristic of short-term memory.

List of Values (LOV) Scale: Assesses the dominant values of a person. Although not strictly a psychographic inventory, it has been applied to the same types of problems as VALS.

Logical empiricist research methods: Research methods that involve collecting and analyzing quantitative data.

Long-term memory: The type of memory that has unlimited capacity and that permanently stores information.

Low-involvement hierarchy: The hierarchy of effects that occurs in low-involvement decision making, in which beliefs are formed first, followed by behavior, and finally by attitude formation.

Lower Americans: A description of social class that refers to the combination of the upper-lower and lower-lower social classes.

Lower-lower class: The lowest of the social classes. Members are typically out of work (or have the dirtiest jobs) and include bums and common criminals.

Lower-upper class: The next to highest social class, composed of the newer social elite drawn from current professional and corporate leadership.

Managerial applications analysis: An analysis in which the consumer behavior concepts are identified that are pertinent to a problem and their managerial implications noted.

Market embeddedness: The term used to describe situations in which the social ties between buyer and seller supplement product value to enhance overall exchange utility.

Market mavens: Individuals who have information about many kinds of products, places to shop, and other facets of markets. They initiate discussion with consumers and respond to requests from consumers for market information.

Market research: An analysis of consumers and market carried out by market researchers to provide information to managers.

Market segmentation: The subdivision of a market into distinct subsets of customers, where any subset may conceivably be selected as a target market to be reached with a distinct marketing mix.

Marketer: The firm, nonprofit organization, government agency, political candidate, or other consumer who wishes to cause an exchange to occur.

Marketing: The human activity directed at satisfying needs and wants through human exchange processes.

Marketing environment: The totality of the forces and institutions that are external and potentially relevant to a firm.

Marketing mix: The elements of product promotion, distribution, and pricing over which marketing managers can implement analysis, planning, and control.

Marketing strategy: The use of environmental analysis and market research to plan and control the marketing mix in order to segment the market and position and differentiate products.

Marketing triad: The interaction of a buying unit, the marketer, and the consumer situation at a particular time and place to influence an exchange process.

Match-up hypothesis: The concept that endorsers who match up with the product on relevant attributes may be more effective.

Materialism: The importance a consumer attaches to worldly possessions, where at the highest levels possessions assume a central place in life and provide the greatest sources of satisfaction and dissatisfaction.

Mature consumer: A person 65 years old or older. Mature consumers differ from younger people in information-processing and consumption patterns.

Means–end chain: A model that depicts the relation of a level of abstractness of attributes to the consequences of a behavior and to the values expressed by the behavior.

Medium: The channel through which a message is passed.

Memory-control processes: Methods of handling information that people use to get information into and out of memory.

Mere exposure phenomenon: A psychological process in which positive feelings toward and evaluations of a stimulus may be formed simply through repeated exposures to the stimulus.

Message characteristics: Those aspects of a message that influence consumer reactions, such as the use of humor or fear appeals.

Message complexity: The complexity of information that a message contains.

Message construction: The problem of how to physically construct a message. Factors to be considered in message construction are message content and message structure.

Message content: The strategies that may be used to communicate an idea to an audience, such as the use of fear appeals or humor.

Message structure: How the source organizes the content of the message, such as where in the message to place the most important information.

Method of loci: A technique to aid the memorization of lists by creating a mental image of a house that has locations in which the items of the list may be placed. To recall the list, the person takes a "mental" stroll back through the house picking up the items.

Middle Americans: The name given to a combination of the social classes including the middle class, lower-middle class, and working class.

Middle class: Average-income white-collar workers and their blue-collar friends who live on "the better side of town" and try to "do the proper things."

Miller's law: The concept that people can process in short-term memory only seven, plus or minus two, chunks of information at a time.

Model: Someone whose behavior another person attempts to emulate.

Modeling: The process through which someone attempts to emulate the behavior of another.

Monetary acquisitions: Acquisitions made with currency, personal checks, or credit.

Money: Currency accepted for use as a medium of exchange.

Mood states: A temporary state characterized by positive or negative feelings.

Mores: Customs that emphasize the moral aspects of behavior. Frequently, mores apply to forbidden behaviors, such as, in fundamentalist Moslem countries, the showing of skin by women.

Mortality rate: The number of people per 1,000 who die per year.

Motivation: An activated state within a person that leads to goal-directed behavior.

Multiattribute models: Models that identify how consumers combine their beliefs about product attributes to form attitudes and make choices among various brand alternatives.

Multiple-store model: A model in which three different types of memory storage systems are identified—sensory memory, short-term memory, and long-term memory.

Multistep flow model: A model of personal influence that states that information is transmitted from the mass media to three distinct sets of people—gatekeepers, opinion leaders, and followers.

Myths: Stories that express key values and ideals of a society.

Need-driven person: A psychographic person identified in the VALS inventory who is characterized as striving simply to meet basic food and housing needs.

Need for affiliation: A basic social need identified by McClelland that is similar in nature to Maslow's belongingness need.

Need for cognition: A scale that assesses the extent to which people tend to engage in and enjoy greater amounts of effortful cognitive activities.

Need for power: A basic social need, identified by McClelland, to gain and exercise control over others.

Needs: Result from a discrepancy between an actual and a desired state of being.

Negative reinforcer: Reinforcers that increase the likelihood of a behavior occurring by removing an aversive stimulus.

Negativity bias: The finding that negative information is given more weight than positive information by consumers when they make decisions to buy a product or service.

Negligent behavior: The actions and inactions of consumers that may negatively affect the long-term quality of life of themselves and society. Examples include drunk driving, product misuse, and failing to use seatbelts.

Noncomparable alternatives: Two or more choice options in different product categories, such as deciding whether to purchase a new car or build a new addition to a house.

Noncompensatory models of choice: Models of choice that emphasize that high ratings on some attributes will not compensate for low ratings on other attributes.

Nonmonetary acquisitions: Acquisitions made when goods or services are traded, borrowed, made, inherited, found, or stolen.

Nonverbal behaviors: Actions, movements, and utterances that people use to communicate in addition to language. These include movements of the hands, arms, head, and legs, as well as body orientation and the space maintained between people.

Normative influence: Occurs when norms act to influence behavior.

Norm of reciprocity: A societal norm that states that, if a person does something for another, the second person should respond with appropriate reciprocal action.

Norms: Rules of behavior.

Nostalgia: A longing for the "good old days."

Nuclear family: Consists of a husband, wife, and offspring.

Object–attribute belief: The belief that an object possesses a specific attribute.

Object–benefit belief: The belief that an object will provide a specific benefit.

Objects: The products, people, companies, and things about which people hold beliefs and attitudes.

Observational learning: A process in which people learn by observing the actions of others.

Occupational demographics: The area that focuses on the jobs Americans hold and on the past and future changes in these jobs.

One- versus two-sided messages: The issue of whether persuasive messages should present only one side or both sides of an issue.

Ongoing search: Involves the search activities that are independent of specific purchase needs or decisions.

Operant conditioning: A process in which the frequency of occurrence of a behavior is modified by the consequences of the behavior.

Operants: The naturally occurring actions of an organism in the environment.

Opinion leader: Those people who influence the purchase decisions and opinions of others.

Opponent-process theory: The psychological process in which a person receives a stimulus that elicits an immediate positive or negative reaction. This reaction is followed by a second emotional reaction that is opposite in valence to the feeling initially experienced.

Opportunity cost: The concept that, when a person buys a product or engages in one task, he or she simultaneously forgoes buying another product or engaging in another task.

Optimum stimulation level: A person's preferred amount of physiological activation or arousal.

Organization: Deals with how people perceive the shapes, forms, figures, and lines in their visual world.

Organizational buying center: The group within a firm responsible for making purchases and for sharing the risks and goals of such decisions.

Organizational buying situations: Researchers have identified three fundamental task definitions for organizational buying situations—new task, modified rebuy, and straight rebuy.

Organizational culture: The shared values and beliefs that enable members to understand their roles and the norms of the organization.

Orientation reflex: The physiological response of a person to a novel or unexpected stimulus that involves an increase in arousal and the orientation of the person to the stimulus.

Outcomes: The results of an exchange that a person assesses in relation to the inputs to determine if the exchange was equitable.

Outer-directed persons: Psychographic persons identified by the VALS inventory who tend to focus on what people think of them and gears their lives to the "visible, tangible, and materialistic."

Overprivileged: Individuals with high incomes within a particular social class, in contrast to the underprivileged, who have lower incomes.

Pacific Rim: The countries that are situated on the Pacific Ocean.

Paired-associate learning: The learning of pairs of words or concepts by attempting to associate them with each other.

Pattern advertising: While an overall promotional theme may be employed worldwide, the implementation of this theme (e.g., deciding whether to translate a slogan directly or to paraphrase it) is done locally. This approach is an example of what the Japanese call *dochakuka*: "think globally, act locally."

Perceived freedom: A motivational need experienced by people to maintain their behavioral freedom.

Perceived risk: A consumer's perception of the overall favorability of a course of action based upon an assessment of the possible outcomes and on the likelihood that those outcomes will occur.

Perception: The ways in which people organize information received and interpret this information so that it has meaning.

Perceptual organization: How people perceive the shapes, forms, figures, and lines in their visual world.

Peripheral route to persuasion: Persuasion that occurs in low-involvement circumstances when little information elaboration is provided.

Personal influence: Refers to the idea that one individual may intentionally or unintentionally influence another in his or her beliefs, attitudes, or intentions about something.

Personal marketing: The marketing of one's own self to others.

Personal value: The meanings of ideal end states and modes of conduct possessed by an individual.

Personality: The distinctive patterns of behavior, including thoughts and emotions, that characterize each individual's adaptation to the situations of his or her life.

Persuasion: A process in which a communication is delivered to change beliefs or attitudes in a desired manner.

Phased strategy: A strategy of combining various decision heuristics to make a product or service choice (e.g., using a conjunctive model, followed by a lexicographic model).

Physical surroundings: The concrete physical and spatial aspects of the environment encompassing a consumer activity.

Pioneering advantage: The advantage held by a good or service that is the first to enter the marketplace.

Pipe-dream rumors: Wishful thinking or positive hopes concerning something that is going to happen.

Pleasure principle: A psychoanalytic concept upon which the id operates.

Popular culture: The culture of mass appeal that taps into the experiences and values of a significant portion of the population.

Popular delusion: A broad-based rumor, involving wishful thinking among large numbers of people, that a fortune can be made.

Positions: A person's place in a group or social system that possesses a specific status.

Positive reinforcer: A stimulus whose presence as a consequence of a behavior increases the probability of the behavior recurring.

Possession rituals: Acts that a person engages in to lay claim, display, and protect possessions, such as auto waxing.

Postacquisition processes: The consumer behaviors that occur after the purchase of a product.

Preneed goods: Goods or services that are purchased prior to the need is actually felt (e.g., funeral service arrangements and insurance).

Preneed problem recognition: Problem recognition that occurs in anticipation that a need will occur (e.g., prepaid tuition plans for college).

Prepurchase search: The information-seeking activities that consumers engage in to facilitate decision making concerning a specific purchase in the marketplace.

Price elasticity: Refers to the extent to which changes in price influence consumer buying. A price inelastic product would reveal little change in purchase patterns as a result of changes in price.

Price–quality relationship: The concept that consumers associate higher quality with higher prices and vice versa.

Primacy and recency effects: The relative impact of information placed either at the beginning or the end of the message. Primacy refers to earlier information having greater impact. Recency refers to the most recent information having the greater impact.

Primary group: A group of which a person is a member and with whom that person interacts on a face-to-face basis.

Priming: Occurs when a small amount of exposure to a stimulus leads to an increased drive to be in the presence of the stimulus.

Private acceptance: Occurs when a person changes his or her beliefs in the direction of the group.

Proactive interference: The type of forgetting that occurs when earlier information already received interferes with the recall of information received later.

Problem recognition: The first stage of decision making. It occurs when the actual state falls below the desired state. It is a type of need recognition.

Product–attribute association: The relationship between the brands held in a consumer's memory and the qualities or attributes of the brands.

Product consumption/usage: An element of the postacquisition stage of consumer decision making that involves the consumption and use of a product.

Product differentiation: The process of developing the marketing mix so that consumers can distinguish one brand from other brands.

Product disposition: What consumers do with a product after they have completed their use of it.

Product expectations: A person's prior beliefs about what attributes a product should possess.

Product innovation: A new type of product that could be either continuous, dynamic continuous, or discontinuous in nature.

Product innovators: A small set of people who are the first to buy new products.

Product positioning: The use of the marketing mix to cause consumers to perceive a product in a certain way relative to other brands. A brand's position is usually described in relation to the characteristics of other brands.

Product quality: The level of performance of a product on each of its key dimensions/attributes.

Proportion of purchases method: A measurement of brand loyalty based upon assessing the proportion of purchases that go to a particular brand.

Prospect theory: Plots how consumers psychologically value positive and negative outcomes in relation to their actual worth.

Psychoanalytic theory of personality: An approach to personality based upon the work of Sigmund Freud and his followers.

Psychographics: A general approach to measuring life-styles that frequently makes use of questions assessing activities, interests, and opinions.

Psychological reactance: A motivational state experienced when a person's need for freedom has been violated.

Psychophysical judgment: A judgment by a person of the physical properties of a stimulus, such as its weight.

Public policy: The investigation of the laws and regulations that affect consumers.

Punisher: Any stimulus whose presence after a behavior decreases the likelihood of the behavior occurring.

Purchase roles: The various roles in the buying and using of products filled by family members or industrial buying groups.

Quiet set: The set of stores that consumers will enter but without interaction with sales personnel.

Reactance: A motivational state that results when a person believes that his or her behavioral freedom is threatened.

Reactance theory: A motivational theory based upon the idea that if a person's need for freedom is violated, he or she will react to restore the freedom.

Reality principle: The principle of psychoanalytic theory that controls the functioning of the ego.

Recall task: A task in which the consumer must retrieve the information from long-term memory without the assistance of memory aids.

Recognition task: A task in which information is placed in front of a consumer and the consumer must indicate whether he or she has previously seen the information.

Reference group: A group whose values, norms, attitudes, or beliefs are used as a guide for behavior by an individual.

Referral relations: Consist of "who-told-whom-about-the-service" paths. Referral relations depict the word-of-mouth connections along which information about a service is spread.

Reflected appraisal: A process in which the consumer examines the manner in which others in a reference group interact with him or her.

Regional subcultures: The subculturally distinct groups that may develop according to location in various regions of the United States.

Regulatory environment: The laws and regulations that federal, state, and local governments develop to exert control over business practices.

Rehearsal: The process in which an individual may maintain information in short-term memory or transfer it to long-term memory by silent verbal repetition.

Reinforcements: Stimuli that occur after a behavior, affecting the likelihood that the behavior will be emitted again by an organism.

Relational exchange: The idea that transactions must be viewed in terms of their history and anticipated future.

Relationship marketing: A philosophy in which the marketer seeks to build long-term relations and mutual trust with clients.

Relationship quality: The extent to which consumers trust a salesperson and are satisfied with a salesperson's past performance.

Relationship trust: The degree to which members of an exchange relationship have confidence in each other and in their ethical practices.

Relative income hypothesis: A hypothesis derived from research conducted in the early 1960s that revealed that people within the same social class may have different consumption patterns based upon their relative incomes.

Repeat purchase behavior: Purchase behavior in which a consumer merely buys a product repeatedly without actually having brand loyalty toward it.

Repetition effects: The repetition of information given in advertisements to promote learning without creating advertising wearout.

Representativeness heuristic: A rule of thumb in which a person determines the probability that object A belongs to class B by assessing the degree to which object A is similar to or stereotypical of class B.

Resources, types: Assets that are exchanged between parties, including goods, services, information, feelings, status, and money.

Respondent conditioning: The process of classically conditioning an organism.

Response generation: The concept that the recall of a memory results from the person actively constructing a response, rather than simply pulling from memory, an accurate representation of the stored information.

Retrieval: The process in which an individual searches through long-term memory to identify within it the information to be recalled.

Retrieval cues: Verbal or visual information, originally contained in an advertisement, that is placed on the product or packaging to assist consumers' memories during decision making.

Retroactive interference: The concept that recently learned material interferes with the recollection of older material in memory.

Risk perception: The likelihood and degree of negativity which consumers perceive that outcomes may possess.

Rokeach value scale: A scale developed to assess the predominant values of people.

Role: The specific behaviors expected of a person in a position. Thus, when a person takes on a role, normative pressures exert influence on the person to act in a particular way.

Role conflict: A case in which individuals simultaneously occupy two roles that may entail conflicting demands, such as being both a mother and an executive.

Role overload: A state of conflict that occurs when the sheer volume of behavior demanded by the positions in a person's position set exceeds available time and energy.

Role-related product cluster: The set of products necessary for the playing of a particular role.

Roles: The specific behaviors expected of a person in a certain position.

Rumors: Information or stories in general circulation that lack factual certainty.

Salience effects: Occur when stimuli stand out from background information, so that attention is directed toward those stimuli.

Salient beliefs: Important attribute–object beliefs activated when a person evaluates an attitudinal object.

Satisficing: The concept that consumers will frequently attempt to make only satisfactory decisions rather than perfect decisions because of limitations in time, information-processing ability, or appropriate facts.

Schedule of reinforcement: A schedule, formed by the frequency and timing of reinforcers, that can dramatically influence the pattern of operant responses.

Schema: The total package of associations brought to mind when a memory node is activated.

Search process: A search for information that may be either extensive or limited, depending upon the involvement level of the consumer.

Secondary reinforcer: A previously neutral stimulus that acquires reinforcing properties through its association with a primary reinforcer.

Segmentation: The subdivision of the marketplace into relatively homogeneous subsets of consumers who can be reached with a distinct marketing mix.

Segmenting by demand elasticity: The process of segmenting consumers based upon the differential slopes of their demand curves (e.g., on airline flights, vacationers versus business travelers).

Selective attention: The concept that consumers selectively decide to which stimuli they should attend.

Selective exposure: The concept that consumers selectively decide to which stimuli they expose themselves.

Self-concept: The totality of the individual's thoughts, perceptions, and feelings having reference to himself or herself as an object.

Self-gifts: Gifts that are given by a person to himself or herself.

Self-perception: The concept that an individual may observe his or her own actions to infer attitudes and beliefs.

Semantic concepts: The meanings attached to words, events, objects, and symbols.

Semantic memory: How people store the meanings of verbal material in long-term memory.

Semiosis analysis: The process of identifying an object, a sign, and an interpretant to analyze the meaning of a symbol.

Semiotics: The analysis of how people obtain meaning from signs.

Sensation: The stimulation of a person's sensory receptors and the transmission of the sensory information to the brain and spinal cord via nerve fibers.

Sensory memory: The extremely brief memories that result from the firing of nerve fibers in a person's brain.

Sentiment connections: A term from balance theory used to denote an affective connection between two cognitive elements.

Serial learning: The process through which people learn lists of items.

Serial-position effect: The finding that items at the beginning and at the end of a list are learned more rapidly than items in the middle of a list.

Service encounter: The interaction that occurs between a consumer and a representative of an organization.

Service quality: A customer's overall assessment of the excellence of a service.

Services: Products exchanged that are intangible and that someone does for someone else.

Shaping: A process through which a new operant behavior is created by reinforcing successive approximations of the desired behavior.

Short-term memory: The function in which a person temporarily stores information while it is being processed. Short-term memory is noted for its limited capacity.

Sign tracking: The concept that organisms have a tendency to orient themselves toward and attend to unconditioned stimuli.

Signs: The words, gestures, pictures, products, and logos used to communicate information from one person to another.

Simple exchange: Characterized by two parties in a reciprocal relationship.

Situational involvement: Involvement that occurs over a short period of time and is associated with a specific situation, such as a purchase.

Slippage: The marketing term for the percentage of customers who purchase a product but fail to redeem a premium offer.

Social class: The relatively permanent and homogeneous strata in a society that tend to differ in their status, occupations, education, possessions, and values.

Social class hierarchy: The ordering of the social classes from lower to higher.

Social comparison: The process through which people evaluate the correctness of their opinions, the extent of their abilities, and the appropriateness of their possessions.

Social facilitation: The concept that a person become aroused when performing a task in front of other people. The arousal tends to enhance performance on easy tasks and hinder performance on difficult tasks.

Social fences: Occur when a short-term punisher causes large numbers of people to avoid engaging in a behavior that would have benefited the group of people.

Social judgment theory: A psychological theory that describes how an individual reacts to attitudinal statements depending upon the relationship of the statement to the person's own attitude.

Social learning: The theory proposing that people will observe the actions of others to develop patterns of behavior.

Social–psychological personality theories: Personality theories that are based upon individual differences in how people respond to social situations.

Social relations: The network of ties between individuals. Ties may be strong, weak, or nonexistent.

Social surroundings: The effects of other people on a consumer in a consumption situation.

Social threats: External pressure by other people to induce a consumer to do something.

Social traps: The psychological phenomenon related to the finding that individuals may respond to short-term reinforcers, which can lead to long-term negative outcomes for a group.

Socialization agents: Individuals directly involved with a consumer who have influence because of their frequency of contact with the consumer, who have importance to the consumer, or who have control over rewards and punishments given to the consumer.

Socialization background factors: Factors that influence the socialization process, which include such variables as the consumer's socioeconomic status, sex, age, social class, and religious background.

Source: An individual or character who is presenting information about some topic.

Source characteristics: Those aspects of a source, such as credibility and physical attractiveness, that influence consumers.

Source credibility: A construct used to describe sources of information. Source credibility is composed of the dimensions of expertise and trustworthiness.

Source expertise: The extent to which a source is perceived to have knowledge about the subject on which he or she is speaking.

Source likability: The positive or negative feelings that consumers have toward a source of information.

Source physical attractiveness: The extent to which a source is perceived to have physical beauty.

Source trustworthiness: The extent to which a source is perceived to provide information in an unbiased, honest manner.

Specific positioning: The attempt to create strong connections between the product, certain key attributes, and the product's benefits in consumers' minds.

Spontaneous brand switching: Consumers' tendency to periodically buy a new brand, even when nothing indicates that they are unhappy with the brand previously used.

Standard learning hierarchy: A high-involvement hierarchy of effects in which beliefs occur first, followed by the development of feelings or affect, followed by the occurrence of a behavior.

Standardization of the marketing plan: The proposal that marketing plans can be standardized in international marketing.

Status: A person's social standing in the class hierarchy.

Status crystallization: The extent to which a person's social status is consistent across various dimensions, such as education, occupation, and housing type.

Status groups: Groups based upon social distinctions and differences in social prestige and respect.

Stimulus discrimination: Occurs when an organism behaves differently in the presence of one stimulus than in the presence of another stimulus.

Stimulus generalization: Occurs when an organism's behavior in the presence of one stimulus generalizes so that it appears in the presence of another similar stimulus.

Store layout: The physical organization of a store that creates specific traffic patterns, assists in the presentation of merchandise, and helps to create a particular atmosphere.

Subculture: A subdivision of national culture based on unifying characteristics, such as social status or religion, whose members share similar patterns of behavior distinct from that of the national culture.

Subjective norm: A major component of the behavioral intentions attitude model. The subjective norm introduces into this model the powerful effects of reference groups on behavior.

Subliminal perception: The concept that stimuli presented below the level of conscious awareness may influence behavior and feelings.

Substitute activities: Activities that satisfy the same need for the consumer and are mutually exclusive (they cannot take place together).

Substitution effect: The economic principle that, when the price of a product falls, it may be substituted for similar goods that are now relatively more costly.

Superego: In psychoanalytic theory, the conscience or "voice within" a person that echoes the morals and values of parents and society.

Surrogate consumer: A person retained by a consumer to act as an agent to guide, direct, or transact marketplace activities.

Symbolic innovation: An innovation that, through the acquisition of new, intangible attributes, communicates a different social meaning than it did previously.

Symbols: Things that stand for or express something else.

Syncratic decision: Important decisions in which the husband and wife participate jointly.

Task definition: The occasion that spurs a purchase, such as a gift occasion, a party, or even a type of meal.

Tastes and preferences: Subjective inclinations that may change and act to shift the demand curve.

Technological innovation: A change in the characteristics of a product or service that results through the introduction of a technological change.

Terminal materialism: A type of materialism in which having possessions is seen as an end in itself. Terminal materialism is viewed as potentially destructive because it leads to such unbecoming traits as envy, possessiveness, nongenerosity, and greed.

Terminal values: Desired end states—how people would like to experience their lives.

Theory: A set of interrelated statements defining the causal relationships among a group of ideas.

Theory of reasoned action: A theory that describes the factors posited to influence the behavioral intentions of an individual.

Time as a situational variable: The concept that the amount of time available to consumers forms a situational context that acts to influence their acquisition, consumption, and disposition of products and services.

Time compression: The electronic process through which radio or television commercials may be compressed, such that they last a shorter length of time.

Tolerance for ambiguity: A personality construct that assesses how a person reacts to situations that have varying degrees of ambiguity or inconsistency.

Total quality management (TQM): A management philosophy based on the idea that successful companies should continuously improve the quality of their products and that quality is defined by the customer.

Trait: Any characteristic on which a person may differ from another in a relatively permanent and consistent way.

Transformational advertising: Advertising that causes a consumer to associate the experience of using a product with a set of psychological characteristics not typically associated with its use. This acts to transform the experience of purchasing and using the product.

Trickle-down theory: A model of mass communications that holds that information moves from the upper classes to the lower classes.

Two-factor theory: An explanation of advertising wear-out. In one process, the repetition of a message causes a reduction in uncertainty and increased learning about the stimulus, resulting in a positive response. In the other process, tedium or boredom begins to occur with each repetition.

Two-sided message: A message that presents both sides of an argument as a tactic to be more persuasive.

Two-step flow model: A model of mass communications that holds that mass communications first influence opinion leaders, who in turn influence followers.

Types of risk: Various risk factors that may influence consumers including financial risk, performance risk, physical risk, psychological risk, social risk, time risk, and opportunity loss risk.

Unawareness set: Consists of the unknown brands and products.

Unconditioned response: The reflexive, involuntary response elicited by an unconditioned stimulus.

Unconditioned stimulus: Any stimulus capable of eliciting autonomically an unconditioned response.

Underprivileged: The people within a given social class who have low incomes relative to other members of that social class.

Unique selling proposition: A quick, hard-hitting phrase that captures a major feature of a product or service.

Unit relation: As defined in balance theory, a relationship that is attributed when an observer perceives that two cognitive elements are somehow connected to each other.

Upper Americans: A description of a group of social classes including the upper-upper, lower-upper, and upper-middle class.

Upper-lower class: A social class described as working, not on welfare, whose living standard is just above poverty, whose behavior may be judged as crude and trashy, and that tends to consist of unskilled workers.

Upper-middle class: A social class composed of college graduates, managers, the intellectual elite, and professionals.

Upper-upper class: The highest status group, marked by its small size and "old" money.

Urban legends: A type of folklore that describes fictitious occurrences and happenings in urban life.

Usage situation: A type of situation based upon the task definition. The situation in which a product or service is expected to be used.

Utilitarian needs: Desires of consumers to correct basic instrumental problems, such as filling a car's gas tank or removing a spot from a rug.

VALS life-style classification scheme: A psychographic approach in which consumers are divided into four broad groups of individuals—the need-driven, the inner-directed, the outer-directed, and the integrated groups.

VALS 2: A new psychographic model developed by SRI International that identifies relationships between consumer attitudes and purchase behavior based upon three categories of self-identity orientations.

Valuation of gains and losses: A process described in prospect theory in which a person values the level of positive or negative outcomes.

Value–attitude system: The relation of global values to domain-specific values to evaluations of product attributes within a consumer's belief system.

Value-expressive influence: The concept that the values and attitudes of a reference group will influence a person who wishes to be part of and liked by that group.

Values: Beliefs of what is good, right, and appropriate in behavior.

Variety-seeking purchases: Buying a new brand spontaneously, even though no dissatisfaction is expressed with the previously purchased brand.

Vehicles: The specific means within a channel by which a message is communicated, such as Vogue magazine as a vehicle within the print medium.

Vicarious learning: A type of learning that occurs when a person observes the reinforcements received by others contingent on their actions.

Vivid messages: Messages using vivid, concrete words, which to have a greater impact on receivers than messages containing more abstract information.

Voluntary attention: A process in which the consumer actively searches out information to achieve some type of goal.

von Restorff effect: The effect by which a unique item in a series of relatively homogeneous items is recalled much more easily than those surrounding items.

Warner's index of social characteristics: Uses four variables as indicators of social class—occupation, source of income, house type, and dwelling area.

Weber's law: The concept that as the intensity of a stimulus increases, the ability to detect a difference between two levels of the stimulus decreases.

Word-of-mouth communications: Face-to-face communications among people.

Word-of-mouth network: The relations between individuals through which personal influence may occur.

Working class: The social class composed of individuals who engage in blue-collar trades, such as carpentry, plumbing, and assembly line work.

Working memory: A hypothetical memory component in which individuals actively process information.

Zapping: The process in which consumers avoid seeing commercials by switching channels on their television with a remote control device.

Zeigarnik effect: The tendency of people to continue to process information about a task until it is completed.

Name Index

Subject Index